Lecture Notes in Computer Science   9020

Commenced Publication in 1973
Founding and Former Series Editors:
Gerhard Goos, Juris Hartmanis, and Jan van Leeuwen

More information about this series at http://www.springer.com/series/7410

Jonathan Katz (Ed.)

Public-Key Cryptography – PKC 2015

18th IACR International Conference
on Practice and Theory in Public-Key Cryptography
Gaithersburg, MD, USA, March 30 – April 1, 2015
Proceedings

 Springer

Editor
Jonathan Katz
University of Maryland
College Park
Maryland
USA

ISSN 0302-9743   ISSN 1611-3349   (electronic)
Lecture Notes in Computer Science
ISBN 978-3-662-46446-5   ISBN 978-3-662-46447-2   (eBook)
DOI 10.1007/978-3-662-46447-2

Library of Congress Control Number: 2015933270

LNCS Sublibrary: SL4 – Security and Cryptology

Springer Heidelberg New York Dordrecht London
© International Association for Cryptologic Research

Printed on acid-free paper

Springer-Verlag GmbH Berlin Heidelberg is part of Springer Science+Business Media
(www.springer.com)

Preface

The 18th IACR International Conference on Practice and Theory of Public-Key Cryptography (PKC 2015) was held from March 30 to April 1, 2015 in Gaithersburg, MD (USA), on the campus of the National Institute of Standards and Technology (NIST). The conference, sponsored by the International Association for Cryptologic Research (IACR), focuses on all technical aspects of public-key cryptography.

These proceedings contain 36 papers selected by the Program Committee from 118 submissions. Each submission was reviewed by at least three experts. Submissions by Program Committee members received at least four reviews and were held to stricter standards by the program chair when decisions were made. Following the initial reviews, the committee discussed the papers and solicited further reviews over a 6-week period. This was a challenging task, and I thank the members of the Program Committee—along with the External Reviewers—for all their hard work.

The conference program also featured two invited talks: one by Antoine Joux on recent progress in computing discrete logarithms, and the other by Sanjam Garg on cryptographic program obfuscation. I thank the speakers for accepting the invitation to speak at the conference.

I would like to close by thanking Rene Peralta, the General Chair, for his help throughout this process. I would also like to thank Sara Caswell of NIST for helping both Rene and me with several administrative challenges that arose during the planning. It is now my second chance to thank Shai Halevi for his web submission and review software, which was used for the review process of this conference. Shai was also always available for questions as they came up. Finally, I would like to thank IACR for hosting the submission server, and Christian Cachin, Greg Rose, and Abhi Shelat (all acting on behalf of IACR) who helped at many points along the way.

January 2015   Jonathan Katz

Organization

PKC 2015

18th IACR International Conference on Practice and Theory of Public-Key Cryptography

Gaithersburg, MD, USA

March 30–April 1, 2015

Sponsored by the
International Association for Cryptologic Research

General Chair

Rene Peralta   NIST, USA

Program Chair

Jonathan Katz   University of Maryland, USA

Program Committee

Michel Abdalla	ENS and CNRS, France
Shweta Agrawal	IIT Delhi, India
Melissa Chase	Microsoft Research, USA
Sherman S.M. Chow	Chinese University of Hong Kong, Hong Kong
Jean-Sébastien Coron	University of Luxembourg, Luxembourg
Jean-Charles Faugère	Inria, France
Sebastian Faust	EPFL, Switzerland
Dario Fiore	IIMDEA Software Institute, Spain
Georg Fuchsbauer	IST Austria, Austria
Steven D. Galbraith	University of Auckland, New Zealand
Pierrick Gaudry	LORIA, France
Matthew D. Green	Johns Hopkins University, USA
Goichiro Hanaoka	AIST, Japan
Carmit Hazay	Bar-Ilan University, Israel
Eike Kiltz	Ruhr-Universität Bochum, Germany
Benoît Libert	ENS Lyon, France
Shengli Liu	Shanghai Jiao Tong University, China
Anna Lysyanskaya	Brown University, USA
Mark Manulis	University of Surrey, UK

Sarah Meiklejohn	University College London, UK
Dustin Moody	NIST, USA
Michael Naehrig	Microsoft Research, USA
Adam O'Neill	Georgetown University, USA
Chris Peikert	Georgia Institute of Technology, USA
Dominique Schröder	Saarland University, Germany
Peter Schwabe	Radboud University Nijmegen, The Netherlands
Jae Hong Seo	Myongji University, Korea
Damien Stehlé	ENS Lyon, France
Rainer Steinwandt	Florida Atlantic University, USA

External Reviewers

Scott Aaronson	Stefan Dziembowski
Shashank Agrawal	Edvard Fagerholm
Shweta Agrawal	Pooya Farshim
Jacob Alperin-Sheriff	Serge Fehr
Nuttapong Attrapadung	Rob Fitzpatrick
Saikrishna Badrinarayanan	Nils Fleischhacker
Shi Bai	Ryo Fujita
Marco Baldi	David Galindo
Foteini Baldimtsi	Essam Ghadafi
Abhishek Banerjee	Sergey Gorbunov
Lejla Batina	Divya Gupta
Aurelie Bauer	Francisco Rodriguez-Henriquez
Fabrice Benhamouda	Zhengan Huang
Sasha Berkoff	Andreas Hülsing
David Bernhard	Laurent Imbert
Olivier Blazy	Chen Jie
Florian Boehl	Bhavana Kanukurthi
Joppe Bos	Sriram Keelveedhi
Angelo De Caro	Dakshita Khurana
Dario Catalano	Franziskus Kiefer
Nishanth Chandran	Elena Kirshanova
Jie Chen	Anna Krasnova
Paul Christiano	Ranjit Kumaresan
Carlos Cid	Fabien Laguillaumie
Craig Costello	Russell W.F. Lai
Dana Dachman-Soled	Adeline Langlois
Gareth T. Davies	Hyung Tae Lee
Apoorvaa Deshpande	Kwangsu Lee
Julien Devigne	Tancrede Lepoint
Leo Ducas	Feng-Hao Liu
Sylvain Duquesne	Patrick Longa
Ratna Dutta	Adriana Lopez-Alt

Vadim Lyubashevsky
Giulio Malavolta
Alex Malozemoff
Joana Marim
Daniel Masny
Maike Massierer
Takahiro Matsuda
Alexander May
Andrew Miller
Pratyay Mukherjee
Khoa Nguyen
Phong Nguyen
Ryo Nishimaki
Luca Nizzardo
Jiaxin Pan
Anat Paskin-Cherniavsky
Alain Passelègue
Arpita Patra
Geovandro C.C.F. Pereira
Ray Perlner
Ludovic Perret
Thomas Peters
Duong Hieu Phan
Krzysztof Pietrzak
David Pointcheval
Antigoni Polychroniadou
Frederic de Portzamparc
Bertram Poettering
Baodong Qin
Carla Ràfols
Bobba Rakesh
Guenael Renault

Yusuke Sakai
Palash Sarkar
Jacob Schuldt
Nicolas Sendrier
Barak Shani
Dan Shumow
Mark Simkin
Benjamin Smith
Daniel Smith-Tone
Pierre-Jean Spaenlehauer
Ron Steinfeld
Mario Strefler
Henry Tan
Susan Thomson
Mehdi Tibouchi
Berkant Ustaoglu
Serge Vaudenay
Muthu Venkitasubramaniam
Daniele Venturi
Vanessa Vitse
Alexandre Wallet
Brent Waters
Shota Yamada
Bo-Yin Yang
Aaram Yun
Greg Zaverucha
Tao Zhang
Ye Zhang
Zongyang Zhang
Yongjun Zhao
Hong-Sheng Zhou

Contents

Efficient Constructions

Cryptography with Imperfect Keys

Interactive Proofs

Lattice-Based Cryptography

Identity-Based, Predicate, and Functional Encryption

Public-Key Encryption

Simulation-Based Selective Opening CCA Security for PKE from Key Encapsulation Mechanisms

Shengli Liu[1]([✉]) and Kenneth G. Paterson[2]

[1] Department of Computer Science and Engineering,
Shanghai Jiao Tong University, Shanghai 200240, China
`slliu@sjtu.edu.cn`
[2] Information Security Group, Royal Holloway,
University of London, Egham, London
`kenny.paterson@rhul.ac.uk`

Abstract. We study simulation-based, selective opening security against chosen-ciphertext attacks (SIM-SO-CCA security) for public key encryption (PKE). In a selective opening, chosen-ciphertext attack (SO-CCA), an adversary has access to a decryption oracle, sees a vector of ciphertexts, adaptively chooses to open some of them, and obtains the corresponding plaintexts and random coins used in the creation of the ciphertexts. The SIM-SO-CCA notion captures the security of unopened ciphertexts with respect to probabilistic polynomial-time (ppt) SO-CCA adversaries in a semantic way: what a ppt SO-CCA adversary can compute can also be simulated by a ppt simulator with access only to the opened messages. Building on techniques used to achieve weak deniable encryption and non-committing encryption, Fehr *et al.* (Eurocrypt 2010) presented an approach to constructing SIM-SO-CCA secure PKE from extended hash proof systems (EHPSs), collision-resistant hash functions and an information-theoretic primitive called Cross Authentication Codes (XACs). We generalize their approach by introducing a special type of Key Encapsulation Mechanism (KEM) and using it to build SIM-SO-CCA secure PKE. We investigate what properties are needed from the KEM to achieve SIM-SO-CCA security. We also give three instantiations of our construction. The first uses hash proof systems, the second relies on the n-Linear assumption, and the third uses indistinguishability obfuscation ($i\mathcal{O}$) in combination with extracting, puncturable Pseudo-Random Functions in a similar way to Sahai and Waters (STOC 2014). Our results establish the existence of SIM-SO-CCA secure PKE assuming only the existence of one-way functions and $i\mathcal{O}$. This result further highlights the simplicity and power of $i\mathcal{O}$ in constructing different cryptographic primitives.

© International Association for Cryptologic Research 2015
J. Katz (Ed.): PKC 2015, LNCS 9020, pp. 3–26, 2015.
DOI: 10.1007/978-3-662-46447-2_1

1   Introduction

Selective Opening Attacks (SOAs) concern a multi-user scenario, where an adversary adaptively corrupts a set of users to get their secret state information. In the case of public key encryption (PKE), we assume that several senders send ciphertexts encrypting possibly correlated messages to a receiver. The SOA adversary is able to (adaptively) corrupt some senders, exposing their messages and also the random coins used to generate their ciphertexts. Security against selective opening attacks (SOA security) considers whether the uncorrupted ciphertexts remain secure.

There are two ways of formalizing SOA security: indistinguishability-based (IND-SO) and simulation-based (SIM-SO). According to whether the adversary is able to access to a decryption oracle during its attack, SOA security is further classified into IND-SO-CPA, IND-SO-CCA, SIM-SO-CPA and SIM-SO-CCA. In the formalization of SOAs, we allow a probabilistic polynomial-time (ppt) adversary to get the public key, a vector of challenge ciphertexts, and to adaptively corrupt (open) some ciphertexts to obtain opened plaintexts and random coins (and also access to a decryption oracle in the case of SO-CCA). The IND-SO security notions require that the real messages (used to generate the challenge ciphertexts) and re-sampled messages conditioned on the opened messages are computationally indistinguishable to an SOA adversary. Here we have to assume that the joint message distributions are *efficiently conditionally re-samplable* after the opened messages are exposed. On the other hand, the SIM-SO security notions have no such limitations. They require that what a probabilistic polynomial-time (ppt) SOA adversary can compute from the information it has learned can be simulated by a ppt simulator only knowing the opened plaintexts. SIM-SO security seems to be stronger than IND-SO security and significantly harder to achieve. We note the existence of a stronger IND-SO security notion, namely full IND-SO security, which imposes no limitation on the joint message distributions. However, there is no PKE achieving full IND-SO-CPA security yet. The relations among SIM-SO security, IND-SO security, and traditional IND-CPA/CCA security were explored in [5,17].

Lossy encryption [3] has shown itself to be a very useful tool in achieving IND-SO-CPA security. Different approaches to achieving IND-SO-CCA security include the use of lossy trapdoor functions [23], All-But-N [14], and All-But-Many lossy trapdoor functions [15]. The basic idea is to make sure that only challenge ciphertexts are lossy encryptions, while ciphertexts queried by the adversary are normal encryptions. If there exists an efficient opener which can open a lossy encryption to an encryption of an arbitrary message, then an IND-SO-CCA secure PKE can also been shown to be SIM-SO-CCA secure. However, it seems that, to date, only a single, DCR-based PKE scheme [15] is known to have this property.

In [12], Fehr *et al.* proposed a black-box PKE construction to achieve SIM-SO-CCA security based on an Extended Hash Proof System (EHPS) associated with a subset membership problem, a collision-resistant hash function and a new information-theoretic primitive called Cross-Authentication Code (XAC). As pointed in [18,19], a stronger property of XACs is needed to make the security proof rigorous.

1.1 Our Contributions

We generalize the black-box PKE construction of Fehr *et al.* [12] by using a special kind of key encapsulation mechanism (KEM) in combination with a strengthened XAC. Essentially, the KEM replaces the EHPS component in [12], opening up a new set of construction possibilities. In more detail:

- We characterise the properties needed of a KEM for our PKE construction to be SIM-SO-CCA secure. At a high level, these properties are that the KEM should have efficiently samplable and explainable (ESE) ciphertext and key spaces; *tailored* decapsulation; and *tailored*, constrained chosen-ciphertext (tCCCA) security. Here tailored decapsulation roughly means that the valid ciphertexts output by the KEM are sparse in the ciphertext space, while tCCCA security is an extension of the CCCA security notion of [16]. If a KEM has all three properties, then we say that it is a *tailored KEM*.
- We show three constructions for tailored KEMs, including one based on hash proof systems (HPS) [8], a specific KEM from the n-Linear assumption [16] (but different from the HPS-based one) and one constructed from indistinguishability Obfuscation ($i\mathcal{O}$) in combination with an extracting puncturable Pseudo-Random Function (PRF) [24]. Consequently, we obtain PKEs of three different types, all enjoying SIM-SO-CCA security. Thus, by adopting the KEM viewpoint, we significantly enlarge the scope of Fehr *et al.*'s construction.
- Since our PKE construction does not rely on collision-resistant hash functions, we immediately obtain the following results:
  - PKE with SIM-SO-CCA security from HPS and strengthened XACs (as compared to the PKE construction of [12] using EPHS, a strong XAC, and a collision-resistant hash function).
  - PKE with SIM-SO-CCA security from the n-Linear assumption in a way that differs from our HPS-based construction.
  - PKE with SIM-SO-CCA security assuming only the existence of $i\mathcal{O}$ and one-way functions.

1.2 Ingredients of Our Main Construction

We follow the outline provided by the black-box PKE construction of Fehr *et al.* [12]. Observing that the EHPS used in [12] can actually be viewed as a KEM, our construction can be considered as a generalization of their result. We first outline the properties of KEMs and XACs needed for our result, before describing the construction and its security analysis at a high level.

The KEM component in our construction needs to be "tailored" with the following properties:

(1) **Efficiently samplable and explainable (ESE) domains.** The key space $\mathcal{K}$ and ciphertext space $\mathcal{C}$ of the KEM should both be ESE domains. (Meaning that, given a randomised sampling algorithm SampleD for $\mathcal{D}$, there exists an efficient algorithm, SampleD$^{-1}(\mathcal{D}, \cdot)$, with the property that, given element d from a domain $\mathcal{D}$ as input, SampleD$^{-1}(\mathcal{D}, \cdot)$ outputs value R such that d can be "explained" as having been sampled using R, i.e., $d = $ SampleD$(\mathcal{D}; R)$.)

(2) **Tailored decapsulation.** The valid ciphertexts output by the encapsulation algorithm constitute only a (small) subset of ciphertext space $\mathcal{C}$. When the input is a ciphertext randomly chosen from $\mathcal{C}$, the decapsulation will either output $\perp$ with overwhelming probability or output a key that is almost uniformly distributed over $\mathcal{K}$.

(3) **Tailored, constrained CCA (tCCCA) security.** The output of the encapsulation algorithm is computationally indistinguishable from (K^R, ψ^R), a pair of key and ciphertext randomly chosen from $\mathcal{K} \times \mathcal{C}$, for any ppt adversary, even if the adversary has access to a constrained decryption oracle. The adversary is allowed to make queries of the form $(\psi, P(\cdot))$ to the constrained decryption oracle, where ψ is an element of $\mathcal{C}$ and $P(\cdot)$ is a ppt predicate, such that $P(\cdot): \mathcal{K} \rightarrow \{0, 1\}$ evaluates to 1 only for a negligible fraction of keys. The constrained decryption oracle will provide the decapsulated K to the adversary if only if $P(K) = 1$.

We will also need a strengthened XAC definition. A strengthened ℓ-XAC is a collection of algorithms XAC = (XGen, XAuth, XVer) having the following properties:

Authentication and Verification. Algorithm XAuth computes a tag $T \leftarrow$ XAuth$(K_1, \ldots, K_\ell)$ from ℓ inputs (which will be random keys in our construction). Any K_i used in generating the tag T almost always satisfies XVer$(K_i, T) = 1$.

Security against Impersonation/Substitution Attacks. Security against impersonation attacks means that, given a tag T, a randomly chosen key K will almost always fail verification with this specific tag, i.e., XVer$(K, T) = 0$. A substitution attack considers an (all-powerful) adversary who obtains a tag $T = $ XAuth$(K_1, \ldots, K_\ell)$ and tries to forge a tag $T' \neq T$ such that XVer$(K_i, T') = 1$, where K_i is one of the keys used in computing T. Security against substitution attacks requires that, if K_i is randomly chosen, then any adversary succeeds in outputting T' with $T' \neq T$ and XVer$(K_i, T') = 1$ with negligible probability, even if it is given T and all keys except K_i as input.

Strongness and Semi-Uniqueness. Strongness says that when K_i is randomly chosen, then K_i, given $(K_j)_{j \in [\ell], j \neq i}$ and the tag $T = $ XAuth $(K_1, \ldots, K_\ell)$, is re-samplable with the correct probability distribution.

That is to say, there exists a ppt algorithm $\mathsf{ReSample}((K_j)_{j\in[\ell],j\neq i},T)$ such that $\mathsf{ReSample}$ outputs a key $\hat{K}_i$ that is statistically indistinguishable from K_i, even given $(K_j)_{j\in[\ell],j\neq i}$ and $T = \mathsf{XAuth}(K_1,\ldots,K_\ell)$. Semi-uniqueness says that it is possible to parse a key K as $(K_x, K_y) \in \mathcal{K}_x \times \mathcal{K}_y$ for some sets $\mathcal{K}_x, \mathcal{K}_y$, and for every $K_x \in \mathcal{K}_x$ and a tag T, there is at most one $K_y \in \mathcal{K}_y$ such that (K_x, K_y) satisfies $\mathsf{XVer}((K_x, K_y), T) = 1$.

1.3 Overview of Our Main Construction

Given a tailored KEM KEM and a strengthened $(\ell + s)$-XAC XAC, our construction of a PKE scheme PKE is as follows. (See Figure 4 for full details.)

- The public key of PKE is the public key pk_{kem} of KEM, an injective function F with domain $\mathcal{C}^\ell$ and range $(\mathcal{K}_y)^s$, and a vector of values $(K_{x_1},\ldots,K_{x_s}) \in (\mathcal{K}_x)^s$. The secret key of PKE is sk_{kem}, the secret key of KEM.
- The encryption operates in a bitwise mode. Let the ℓ-bit message be $m_1||\ldots||m_\ell$.
  - When $m_i = 1$, we set $(K_i, \psi_i) \leftarrow \mathsf{KEM.Encap}(pk_{kem})$.
  - When $m_i = 0$, we choose (K_i, ψ_i) randomly from $\mathcal{K} \times \mathcal{C}$.
  - After encrypting ℓ bits, we compute $F(\psi_1,\ldots,\psi_\ell)$ to get $(K_{y_1},\ldots,K_{y_s})$, and construct s extra keys $K_{\ell+j} = (K_{x_j}, K_{y_j})$ for $j = 1,\ldots,s$. All $\ell + s$ keys are then used to compute a tag $T = \mathsf{XAuth}(K_1,\ldots,K_{\ell+s})$.
  - Finally, the PKE ciphertext is $C = (\psi_1,\ldots,\psi_\ell,T)$.
- The decryption also operates in a bitwise fashion. Omitting some crucial details, we first recompute $(K_{y_1},\ldots,K_{y_s})$ using F and $(\psi_1,\ldots,\psi_\ell)$, reconstruct $K_{\ell+j}$ for $j = 1,\ldots,s$, and then verify the correctness of T using each $K_{\ell+j}$ in turn. Assuming this step passes, for each i, we compute $K_i \leftarrow \mathsf{KEM.Decap}(sk_{kem}, \psi_i)$, and set the recovered message bit as the output of $\mathsf{XVer}(K_i, T)$. (When $K_i = \bot$, we set $\mathsf{XVer}(K_i, T) = 0$).

Now, in the above decryption procedure, a KEM decapsulation error occurs whenever $m_i = 0$. However, ψ_i is random in this case, and the tailored decapsulation makes sure that the output of $\mathsf{KEM.Decap}(sk_{kem}, \psi_i)$ is either $\bot$ or a random key K; in either case, $\mathsf{XVer}(K_i, T)$ is 0 except with negligible probability because of the security of XAC against impersonation attacks.

1.4 SIM-SO-CCA Security of Our Main Construction

We follow the techniques of non-committing and deniable encryption [6,7,10,20] and try to create equivocable ciphertexts that not only can be opened arbitrarily but that are also computationally indistinguishable from real ciphertexts. In our construction, the equivocable ciphertexts are in fact encryptions of ones. Note that tCCCA security of KEM ensures that $(K, \psi) \approx_c (K^R, \psi^R)$, where (K, ψ) is the output of $\mathsf{KEM.Encap}(pk_{kem})$ and (K^R, ψ^R) is randomly chosen from $\mathcal{K} \times \mathcal{C}$. On the other hand, both $\mathcal{K}$ and $\mathcal{C}$ are ESE. Therefore, (K, ψ) encrypting 1 can always be explained as a random pair (K^R, ψ^R) encrypting 0 by exposing the randomness output from $\mathsf{SampleK}^{-1}(\mathcal{K}, K)$ and $\mathsf{SampleC}^{-1}(\mathcal{C}, \psi)$.

However, this is not sufficient in the SO-CCA setting since the adversary is able to query its decryption oracle and perform corruptions, and it might then be easy for the adversary to distinguish an encryption of ones and an encryption of a real message. For example, consider an adversary that is given a ciphertext $C = (\psi_1, \psi_2, \ldots, \psi_\ell, T)$, where C is either an encryption of ones but opened as zeros with re-explained randomness, or an encryption of zeros being opened honestly. In fact, opened randomness exposes all K_i's to the adversary. Then the adversary can generate a different ciphertext $C' = (\psi_1, \psi_2, \ldots, \psi_\ell, T')$ as follows. A new tag T' ($T' \neq T$) is computed as $T' := \mathsf{XAuth}(K_1', K_2, \ldots, K_{\ell+s})$, where K_1' is randomly chosen and all other K_i's ($2 \leq i \leq \ell + s$) are the same as in T. The decryption of C' will be $(0, 1, \ldots, 1)$ if C is an encryption of ones but $(0, 0, \ldots, 0)$ if C is an encryption of zeros! The problem is that the opened randomness discloses K_i and that gives too much information to the adversary, especially when (K_i, ψ_i) encodes 0. To solve this problem, we have to use a different method to open K_i so that the adversary obtains no extra information about K_i when (K_i, ψ_i) encodes 0: first, we use algorithm ReSample of XAC to resample K_i to obtain a statistically indistinguishable $\hat{K}_i$; then we call $\mathsf{SampleK}^{-1}(\mathcal{K}, \hat{K}_i)$ and $\mathsf{SampleC}^{-1}(\mathcal{C}, \psi_i)$ to open $(\hat{K}_i, \psi_i)$ to an encryption of 0. Now an encryption of ones, say $C = (\psi_1, \psi_2, \ldots, \psi_\ell, T)$, is able to play the role of an equivocable ciphertext, due to the tCCCA security of KEM and the security of XAC.

Consequently, we can build a simulator $\mathcal{S}$ with respect to an adversary $\mathcal{A}$ to prove SIM-SO-CCA security: $\mathcal{S}$ simulates the real environment for $\mathcal{A}$ by generating public and private keys, and uses the private key to answer $\mathcal{A}$'s decryption queries; $\mathcal{S}$ creates n challenge ciphertexts all of which are encryptions of ones; when $\mathcal{A}$ makes a corruption query concerning a challenge ciphertext C, $\mathcal{S}$ can open C bit-by-bit according to the real message. If the bit m_i is 1, it opens (K_i, ψ_i) honestly, otherwise it opens (K_i, ψ_i) to 0 by using ReSample, $\mathsf{SampleC}^{-1}$ and $\mathsf{SampleK}^{-1}$.

1.5   Related Work

The SOA security notion was first formally proposed by Dwork et al. [11]. SIM-SO-CPA and IND-SO-CPA notions were given by Bellare et al. [3]. The relations among SOA security notions and traditional IND-CPA security were investigated in [5,17]. Bellare et al. [4] proposed the first SIM-SO-CPA secure Identity-Based Encryption (IBE), while also adopting the non-committing technique and weak deniable encryption. Lai et al. [21] proposed the first construction for SIM-SO-CCA secure IBE from a so-called extractable IBE, a collision-resistant hash function, and a strengthened XAC. Recently, Sahai and Waters [24] introduced the puncturable programming technique and employed puncturable PRFs and Indistinguishability Obfuscation ($i\mathcal{O}$) to obtain a variety of cryptographic primitives including deniable encryption with IND-CPA security, PKE with IND-CPA and IND-CCA security, KEM with IND-CCA security, injective trapdoor functions, etc. It should be noted that any IND-CPA secure deniable encryption with ESE ciphertext space implies a PKE with SIM-SO-CPA security. Therefore, the deniable encryption scheme in [24] that is based on a puncturable PRF and $i\mathcal{O}$

implicitly already gives us a SIM-SO-CPA secure PKE. Our result establishes that SIM-SO-CCA security is achievable from puncturable PRFs and $i\mathcal{O}$ as well, albeit via the combination of an IND-CCA secure KEM and a strengthened XAC.

2 Preliminaries

We use $s_1, \ldots, s_t \leftarrow S$ to denote picking elements $s_1, \ldots, s_t$ uniformly from set S. Let $|S|$ denote the size of set S. Let $[n]$ denote the set $\{1, \ldots, n\}$. Let $s_1 \| s_2 \| \ldots$ denotes the concatenation of strings. For a probabilistic polynomial-time (ppt) algorithm A, we denote $y \leftarrow A(x; R)$ the process of running A on input x with randomness R, and assigning y as the result. Let $\mathcal{R}_A$ denote the randomness space of A, and $y \leftarrow A(x)$ denote $y \leftarrow A(x; R)$ with R chosen from $\mathcal{R}_A$ uniformly at random. Let U_n denote the uniform distribution over $\{0, 1\}^n$. A function $f(\kappa)$ is *negligible*, denoted by $neg(\kappa)$, if for every $c > 0$ there exists a κ_c such that $f(\kappa) < 1/\kappa^c$ for all $\kappa > \kappa_c$. Let $\approx_c$ (resp. $\approx_s$) denote computational (resp. statistical) indistinguishability between two ensembles of random variables.

We use boldface letters for vectors. For a vector $\mathbf{m}$ of finite dimension, let $|\mathbf{m}|$ denote the length of the vector. For a set $I = \{i_1, i_2, \ldots, i_{|I|}\} \subseteq [|\mathbf{m}|]$, we define $\mathbf{m}[I] := (\mathbf{m}[i_1], \mathbf{m}[i_2], \ldots, \mathbf{m}[i_{|I|}])$.

We refer to the full version of this paper [22] for the definition and an example of *Strengthened Cross Authentication Codes*.

2.1 Public Key Encryption

A public key encryption (PKE) scheme is made up of three ppt algorithms:

KeyGen(1^κ) takes as input the security parameter κ, and outputs a public key and a secret key (pk, sk).

Enc(pk, M) takes as input the public key pk and a message M and outputs a ciphertext C.

Dec(sk, C) takes as input the secret key sk and a ciphertext C and outputs either a message M or a failure symbol $\perp$.

The correctness of a PKE scheme is relaxed to allow a negligible decryption error $\epsilon(\kappa)$. That is, $\mathsf{Dec}(sk, \mathsf{Enc}(pk, M)) = M$ holds with probability at least $1 - \epsilon(\kappa)$ for all $(pk, sk) \leftarrow \mathsf{KeyGen}(1^\kappa)$, where the probability is taken over the coins used in encryption.

Let $\mathbf{m}$ and $\mathbf{r}$ be two vectors of dimension $n := n(\kappa)$. Define $\mathsf{Enc}(pk, \mathbf{m}; \mathbf{r}) := (\mathsf{Enc}(pk, \mathbf{m}[1]; \mathbf{r}[1]), \ldots, \mathsf{Enc}(pk, \mathbf{m}[n]; \mathbf{r}[n]))$. Here $\mathbf{r}[i]$ is the fresh randomness used for the encryption of $\mathbf{m}[i]$ for $i \in [n]$.

2.2 Simulation-Based, Selective Opening CCA Security of PKE

We review the simulation-based definition of security for PKE against selective opening, chosen-ciphertext adversaries from [12]. Let $\mathcal{M}$ denote an n-message sampler, which on input string $\alpha \in \{0, 1\}^*$ outputs an n-vector $\mathbf{m} = (\mathbf{m}[1], \ldots, \mathbf{m}[n])$ of messages. Let R be any ppt algorithm outputting a single bit.

Definition 1 (SIM-SO-CCA Security). *A PKE scheme* PKE=(KeyGen, Enc, Dec) *is simulation-based, selective opening, chosen-ciphertext secure (SIM-SO-CCA secure) if for every ppt n-message sampler* $\mathcal{M}$, *every ppt relation R, every restricted, stateful ppt adversary* $\mathcal{A} = (\mathcal{A}_1, \mathcal{A}_2, \mathcal{A}_3)$, *there is a stateful ppt simulator* $\mathcal{S} = (\mathcal{S}_1, \mathcal{S}_2, \mathcal{S}_3)$ *such that* $\mathsf{Adv}^{so\text{-}cca}_{\mathsf{PKE},\mathcal{A},\mathcal{S},n,\mathcal{M},R}(\kappa)$ *is negligible, where*

$$\mathsf{Adv}^{so\text{-}cca}_{\mathsf{PKE},\mathcal{A},\mathcal{S},n,\mathcal{M},R}(\kappa) = \left| Pr\left[\mathsf{Exp}^{so\text{-}cca\text{-}real}_{\mathsf{PKE},\mathcal{A},n,\mathcal{M},R}(\kappa) = 1 \right] \right.$$
$$\left. - Pr\left[\mathsf{Exp}^{so\text{-}cca\text{-}ideal}_{\mathsf{PKE},\mathcal{S},n,\mathcal{M},R}(\kappa) = 1 \right] \right|$$

and experiments $\mathsf{Exp}^{so\text{-}cca\text{-}real}_{\mathsf{PKE},\mathcal{A},n,\mathcal{M},R}(\kappa)$ *and* $\mathsf{Exp}^{so\text{-}cca\text{-}ideal}_{\mathsf{PKE},\mathcal{S},n,\mathcal{M},R}(\kappa)$ *are defined in Figure 1. Here the restriction on* $\mathcal{A}$ *is that* $\mathcal{A}_2, \mathcal{A}_3$ *are not allowed to query the decryption oracle* $\mathsf{Dec}(\cdot)$ *with any challenge ciphertext* $\mathbf{c}[i] \in \mathbf{c}$.

$\mathsf{Exp}^{so\text{-}cca\text{-}real}_{\mathsf{PKE},\mathcal{A},n,\mathcal{M},R}(\kappa)$:	$\mathsf{Exp}^{so\text{-}cca\text{-}ideal}_{\mathsf{PKE},\mathcal{S},n,\mathcal{M},R}(\kappa)$:
$(pk, sk) \leftarrow \mathsf{KeyGen}(1^\kappa)$	
$(\alpha, a_1) \leftarrow \mathcal{A}_1^{\mathsf{Dec}(\cdot)}(pk)$	$(\alpha, s_1) \leftarrow \mathcal{S}_1(1^\kappa)$
$\mathbf{m} \leftarrow \mathcal{M}(\alpha), \mathbf{r} \leftarrow \text{coins}$	$\mathbf{m} \leftarrow \mathcal{M}(\alpha)$
$\mathbf{c} \leftarrow \mathsf{Enc}(pk, \mathbf{m}; \mathbf{r})$	$(I, s_2) \leftarrow \mathcal{S}_2(s_1, (1^{|\mathbf{m}[i]|})_{i \in [n]})$
$(I, a_2) \leftarrow \mathcal{A}_2^{\mathsf{Dec}_{\notin \mathbf{c}}(\cdot)}(a_1, \mathbf{c})$	$out_\mathcal{S} \leftarrow \mathcal{S}_3(s_2, \mathbf{m}[I])$
$out_\mathcal{A} \leftarrow \mathcal{A}_3^{\mathsf{Dec}_{\notin \mathbf{c}}(\cdot)}(a_2, \mathbf{m}[I], \mathbf{r}[I])$	return $R(\mathbf{m}, I, out_\mathcal{S})$
return $R(\mathbf{m}, I, out_\mathcal{A})$	

Fig. 1. Experiments used in the definition of SIM-SO-CCA security of PKE

2.3   Key Encapsulation Mechanisms

A Key Encapsulation Mechanism (KEM) KEM consists of three ppt algorithms (KEM.Kg, KEM.Enc, KEM.Dec). Let $\mathcal{K}$ be the key space associated with KEM.

KEM.Kg(1^κ) takes as input a security parameter κ and outputs public/secret key pair (pk, sk).
KEM.Encap(pk) takes as input the public key pk and outputs a key K and a ciphertext (or encapsulation) ψ.
KEM.Decap(sk, ψ) takes as input the secret key sk and a ciphertext ψ, and outputs either a key K or a failure symbol $\perp$.

The correctness condition on a KEM KEM is that KEM.Decap(sk, ψ) = K holds for all $\kappa \in \mathbb{N}$, all $(pk, sk) \leftarrow$ KEM.Kg(1^κ), and all $(K, \psi) \leftarrow$ KEM.Encap(pk).

2.4   Efficiently Samplable and Explainable (ESE) Domain

A domain $\mathcal{D}$ is said to be *efficiently samplable and explainable* (ESE) [12] if associated with $\mathcal{D}$ are the following two ppt algorithms:

$\mathsf{Exp}_{\mathsf{KEM},\mathcal{A}}^{\mathrm{VCI}\text{-}b}(\kappa):$ 　　　　　　　　　　　　　$\widetilde{\mathsf{Decap}}_{\neq\psi^*}(P,\psi)$

　$(pk, sk) \leftarrow \mathsf{KEM.Kg}(1^\kappa)$ 　　　　　　If $\psi = \psi^*$ return $(\perp)$

　$\psi_0^* \leftarrow \mathcal{C},\ (K^*, \psi_1^*) \leftarrow \mathsf{KEM.Encap}(pk)$ 　　　$K \leftarrow \mathsf{KEM.Decap}(sk, \psi)$

　　　　　　　　　　　　　　　　　　　　If $P(K) = 0$ return $(\perp)$;

　$b' \leftarrow \mathcal{A}^{\widetilde{\mathsf{Decap}}_{\neq\psi_b^*}(\cdot)}(pk, \psi_b^*)$ 　　　　Else return (K)

　$\mathrm{Return}(b')$

Fig. 2. Experiment for defining Valid Ciphertext Indistinguishability of KEMs. Here $\widetilde{\mathsf{Decap}}_{\neq\psi^*}(P, \psi)$ denotes a constrained decryption oracle, taking as input predicate $P(\cdot)$ and encapsulation ψ.

$\mathsf{Sample}(\mathcal{D}; R)$: On input (a description of) domain $\mathcal{D}$ and random coins $R \leftarrow \mathcal{R}_{\mathsf{Sample}}$, this algorithm outputs an element that is uniformly distributed over $\mathcal{D}$.

$\mathsf{Sample}^{-1}(\mathcal{D}, x)$: On input (a description of) domain $\mathcal{D}$ and *any* $x \in \mathcal{D}$, this algorithm outputs R that is uniformly distributed over the set $\{R \in \mathcal{R}_{\mathsf{Sample}} \mid \mathsf{Sample}(\mathcal{D}; R) = x\}$.

Clearly $\mathcal{D} = \{0, 1\}^\kappa$ is ESE with $R = \mathsf{Sample}(\mathcal{D}; R) = \mathsf{Sample}^{-1}(\mathcal{D}, R)$. It was shown by Damgård and Nielsen in [10] that any dense subset of an efficiently samplable domain is ESE as long as the dense subset admits an efficient membership test. Hence, for example, $\mathbb{Z}_N^*$ for a RSA modulus N is ESE.

3   KEM Tailored for Construction of PKE with SIM-SO-CCA Security

We describe the properties that are required of a KEM to build SIM-SO-CCA secure PKE; the construction itself is given in the next section.

3.1   Valid Ciphertext Indistinguishability (VCI) of KEMs

Suppose $\mathsf{KEM} = (\mathsf{KEM.Kg}, \mathsf{KEM.Encap}, \mathsf{KEM.Decap})$ is associated with an efficiently recognizable ciphertext space $\mathcal{C}$. For fixed κ, let $\Psi \subset C$ denote the set of possible key encapsulations output by $\mathsf{KEM.Encap}$, so $\Psi = \{\psi : \psi \leftarrow \mathsf{KEM.Encap}(pk; r), (pk, sk) \leftarrow \mathsf{KEM.Kg}(1^\kappa), r \leftarrow \mathsf{Coins}\}$. The set Ψ is called the *valid ciphertext set* (for κ).

Definition 2 (Valid Ciphertext Indistinguishability) . *Let KEM be a KEM with valid ciphertext set Ψ and ciphertext space $\mathcal{C}$. Define the advantage of an adversary $\mathcal{A}$ in the experiment depicted in Figure 2 to be*

$$Adv_{\mathsf{KEM},\mathcal{A}}^{\mathrm{VCI}}(\kappa) := \left| \Pr\left[\mathsf{Exp}_{\mathsf{KEM},\mathcal{A}}^{\mathrm{VCI}\text{-}0}(\kappa) = 1 \right] - \Pr\left[\mathsf{Exp}_{\mathsf{KEM},\mathcal{A}}^{\mathrm{VCI}\text{-}1}(\kappa) = 1 \right] \right|.$$

Then KEM is said to be Valid Ciphertext Indistinguishable (VCI) *if for all ppt adversaries $\mathcal{A}$, $Adv_{\mathsf{KEM},\mathcal{A}}^{\mathrm{VCI}}(\kappa)$ is negligible.*

$\mathsf{Exp}_{\mathsf{KEM},\mathcal{A}}^{tccca-b}(\kappa):$

   $(pk, sk) \leftarrow \mathsf{KEM.Kg}(1^\kappa)$
   $K_0^* \leftarrow \mathcal{K},\ \psi_0^* \leftarrow \mathcal{C}$
   $(K_1^*, \psi_1^*) \leftarrow \mathsf{KEM.Encap}(pk)$
   $b' \leftarrow \mathcal{A}^{\widetilde{\mathsf{Decap}}_{\neq \psi^*}(\cdot)}(pk, K_b^*, \psi_b^*)$
   $\mathsf{Return}(b')$

$\widetilde{\mathsf{Decap}}_{\neq \psi^*}(P, \psi)$

   If $\psi = \psi^*$ return $(\perp)$
   $K \leftarrow \mathsf{KEM.Decap}(sk, \psi)$
   If $P(K) = 0$ return $(\perp)$;
   Else return (K)

Fig. 3. Experiment for defining IND-tCCCA security of KEMs. Here $\widetilde{\mathsf{Decap}}_{\neq \psi^*}(P, \psi)$ denotes a constrained decryption oracle, taking as input predicate $P(\cdot)$ and encapsulation ψ. Predicate $P(\cdot)$ may vary in different queries.

3.2 Tailored KEMs

To be of service in our construction of SIM-SO-CCA secure PKE, we need a KEM that is tailored to have the following three properties, as explained in the introduction: (1) the key space $\mathcal{K}$ and ciphertext space $\mathcal{C}$ of the KEM should both be ESE domains; (2) the valid ciphertexts output by the encapsulation algorithm constitute only a small subset of ciphertext space $\mathcal{C}$, and the decryption of a random ciphertext results in failure or a random key; (3) the KEM has tailored, constrained CCA security. We define the last of these three properties next.

Definition 3 (IND-tCCCA Security for KEMs). *Let KEM be a KEM with ciphertext space $\mathcal{C}$ and valid ciphertext set Ψ, let $\mathcal{A}$ be a ppt adversary, and consider the experiment $\mathsf{Exp}_{\mathsf{KEM},\mathcal{A}}^{tccca-b}(\kappa)$ defined in Figure 3. Define the advantage $\mathsf{Adv}_{\mathsf{KEM},\mathcal{A}}^{tccca}(\kappa)$ of $\mathcal{A}$ by:*

$$\mathsf{Adv}_{\mathsf{KEM},\mathcal{A}}^{tccca}(\kappa) := \left| \Pr\left[\mathsf{Exp}_{\mathsf{KEM},\mathcal{A}}^{tccca-0}(\kappa) = 1\right] - \Pr\left[\mathsf{Exp}_{\mathsf{KEM},\mathcal{A}}^{tccca-1}(\kappa) = 1\right] \right|.$$

Then KEM is said to be secure against tailored, constrained chosen ciphertext attacks (IND-tCCCA secure) if for all ppt adversaries $\mathcal{A}$ with negligible uncertainty $uncert_\mathcal{A}(\kappa)$ (in κ), the advantage $\mathsf{Adv}_{\mathsf{KEM},\mathcal{A}}^{tccca}(\kappa)$ is also negligible in κ. Here, the uncertainty of $\mathcal{A}$ is defined as $uncert_\mathcal{A}(\kappa) := \frac{1}{q_d}\sum_{i=1}^{q_d}\Pr[P_i(K) = 1]$, which measures the average fraction of keys for which the evaluation of predicate $P_i(\cdot)$ is equal to 1 in the tCCCA experiment, where P_i denotes the predicate used in the i-th query by $\mathcal{A}$, and q_d the number of decapsulation queries made by $\mathcal{A}$.

Constrained CCA (CCCA) security for PKE was introduced in [16] as a strictly weaker notion than IND-CCA security. The main difference between IND-CCCA security and our newly defined IND-tCCCA security is that, in the IND-CCCA definition, the adversary is given a pair (K_b^*, ψ^*) where ψ^* is always a correct encapsulation of K_1^*, while in the IND-tCCCA definition, the adversary is given a pair (K_b^*, ψ_b^*) where, when $b = 0$, ψ_b^* is just a random element of $\mathcal{C}$ and, when $b = 1$, ψ_b^* is a correct encapsulation of K_b^*. However, IND-CCCA security and VCI together imply IND-tCCCA security for KEMs:

Lemma 1. *Suppose that KEM is a KEM having an efficiently recognizable ciphertext space* $\mathcal{C}$. *If KEM is both IND-CCCA secure and VCI then it is also IND-tCCCA secure.*

Proof. Recall that the VCI and CCCA experiments are almost the same except for the construction of the adversary's challenge. Let $(K^{(R)}, \psi^{(R)})$ be chosen from $\mathcal{C} \times \mathcal{K}$ uniformly at random. Let (K, ψ) be the output of KEM.Encap in the CCCA experiment. IND-CCCA security implies $(K, \psi) \approx_c (K^{(R)}, \psi)$. The VCI property implies that $\psi \approx_c \psi^{(R)}$, hence $(K^{(R)}, \psi) \approx_c (K^{(R)}, \psi^{(R)})$ when $K^{(R)}$ is chosen uniformly and independently of everything else. Finally, $(K, \psi) \approx_c (K^{(R)}, \psi^{(R)})$ follows from transitivity. $\qquad\square$

Tailored Decapsulation. We also tailor the functionality of our KEMs' decapsulation algorithms to suit our PKE construction.

Definition 4 (Tailored Decapsulation) . *Suppose* KEM $=$ (KEM.Kg, KEM.Encap, KEM.Decap) *is a KEM. Then KEM is said to have* tailored decapsulation *if there exists a negligible function* $\eta(\kappa)$ *such that for all* (pk, sk) *output by KEM.Kg(1^κ), one or the other of the following two cases pertains:*

- KEM.Decap *rejects a random* $\psi' \in \mathcal{C}$, *except with negligible probability, i.e.,*

$$\Pr\left[\text{KEM.Decap}(sk_{kem}, \psi') \neq \perp \mid \psi' \leftarrow \mathcal{C} \right] \leq \eta(\kappa).$$

- KEM.Decap *outputs* $\eta(\kappa)$-*uniform keys on input a random element from* $\mathcal{C}$. *That is, the statistical distance between the output and a uniform distribution on* $\mathcal{K}$ *is bounded by* $\eta(\kappa)$:

$$\frac{1}{2} \sum_{k \in \mathcal{K}} \left| \Pr\left[\text{KEM.Decap}(sk_{kem}, \psi') = k \mid \psi' \leftarrow \mathcal{C} \right] - \frac{1}{|\mathcal{K}|} \right| \leq \eta(\kappa).$$

Remark. The former case implies that valid ciphertexts are sparse in the whole ciphertext space, i.e., $|\mathcal{V}|/|\mathcal{C}|$ is negligible. In the latter case, VCI (when VCI holds for all $(pk, sk) \leftarrow$ KEM.Kg(1^κ)) alone might imply IND-tCCCA security of KEM, since the decapsulated key is uniquely determined by the secret key and the ciphertext (be it valid or invalid).

4 Construction of PKE with SIM-SO-CCA Security from Tailored KEMs

Let KEM $=$ (KEM.Kg, KEM.Encap, KEM.Decap) be a KEM with valid ciphertext set Ψ, efficiently recognizable ciphertext space $\mathcal{C}$, and key space $\mathcal{K} = \mathcal{K}_x \times \mathcal{K}_y$. We further assume that:

(1) KEM.Decap has tailored functionality as per Definition 4 (this will be used for the correctness of our PKE construction);

KeyGen(1^κ) :
  $(pk_{kem}, sk_{kem}) \leftarrow$ KEM.Kg(1^κ)
  $K_{x_1}, \ldots, K_{x_s} \leftarrow \mathcal{K}_x$
  $pk = (pk_{kem}, (K_{x_j})_{j \in [s]}, F)$
  $sk = (sk_{kem}, pk)$.
  Return(pk, sk)

Enc($pk, m_1 \| \ldots \| m_\ell$) :
  Parse pk as $(pk_{kem}, (K_{x_j})_{j \in [s]}, F)$
  For $i = 1$ to ℓ
    If $m_i = 1$
      $(K_i, \psi_i) \leftarrow$ KEM.Encap(pk_{kem})
    Else $\psi_i \leftarrow \mathcal{C}; K_i \leftarrow \mathcal{K}$
  $(K_{y_1}, \ldots, K_{y_s}) \leftarrow F(\psi_1, \ldots, \psi_\ell)$
  For $j = 1$ to s
    $K_{\ell+j} \leftarrow (K_{x_j}, K_{y_j})$
  $T \leftarrow$ XAuth($K_1, \ldots, K_{\ell+s}$)
  Return $(\psi_1, \ldots, \psi_\ell, T)$

Dec(sk, C) :
  Parse C as $(\psi_1, \ldots, \psi_\ell, T)$
  For $i = 1$ to ℓ
    $m_i' \leftarrow 0$
  $(K_{y_1}', \ldots, K_{y_s}') \leftarrow F(\psi_1, \ldots, \psi_\ell)$
  For $j = 1$ to s
    $K_{\ell+j}' \leftarrow (K_{x_j}, K_{y_j}')$
  If $\bigwedge_{j=1}^{s}$ XVer($K_{\ell+j}', T$) $= 1$
    For $i = 1$ to ℓ
      $K_i' \leftarrow$ KEM.Decap(sk_{kem}, ψ_i)
      If $K_i' = \bot$, then $m_i' \leftarrow 0$
      Else $m_i' \leftarrow$ XVer(K_i', T)
  Return($m_1' \| m_2' \| \ldots, m_\ell'$)

Fig. 4. Construction of PKE scheme PKE from tailored KEM and $(\ell + s)$-XAC

(2) KEM is IND-tCCCA secure (this will be used in the SIM-SO-CCA security proof of the PKE construction).

(3) Both the key space $\mathcal{K}$ and the ciphertext space $\mathcal{C}$ of KEM are efficiently samplable and explainable domains, with algorithms (SampleK, SampleK^{-1}) and (SampleC, SampleC^{-1}) (these algorithms are also used in the security analysis).

We refer to a KEM possessing all three properties above as being a *tailored* KEM.

Let $F : \mathcal{C}^\ell \to (\mathcal{K}_y)^s$ be an injective function (such functions are easily constructed using, for example, encodings from $\mathcal{C}$ to bit-strings and from bit-strings to $\mathcal{K}_y$, provided s is sufficiently large). Let XAC = (XGen, XAuth, XVer) be a $\delta(\kappa)$-strong and semi-unique $(\ell+s)$-XAC with tag space $\mathcal{XT}$ and key space $\mathcal{XK}$; suppose also that $\mathcal{XK} = \mathcal{K} = \mathcal{K}_x \times \mathcal{K}_y$. Our main construction of PKE scheme PKE = (KeyGen, Enc, Dec) with message space $\{0, 1\}^\ell$ is shown in Figure 4.

Note that in the decryption, if XVer($K_{\ell+j}', T$) $= 1$ for all $j \in [s]$, then the recovered bit m_i' equals 0 if and only if the decapsulated key K_i' equals $\bot$ or XVer(K_i', T) $= 0$.

Correctness. Encryption and decryption are performed in bitwise fashion. Suppose $m_i = 1$. Then (K_i, ψ_i) are the encapsulated key and corresponding valid encapsulation; by the correctness of KEM and XAC, the decryption algorithm outputs $m_i' = 1$, except with negligible probability fail$_{\mathsf{XAC}}$. Suppose $m_i = 0$. Then K_i and ψ_i are chosen independently and uniformly at random from $\mathcal{K}$ and $\mathcal{C}$, respectively. It follows that the tag T is independent of ψ_i. Now, during the decryption of the i-th bit, according to the tailored property of KEM.Decap,

K_i' is either $\perp$ (and thus $m_i' = 0$) with probability at least $1 - \eta(\kappa)$, or K_i' is $\eta(\kappa)$-close to being uniformly distributed on $\mathcal{K}$. In the latter case, it holds that $m_i' = 0$ except with probability $\eta(\kappa) + \mathsf{Adv}_{\mathsf{XAC}}^{\mathsf{imp}}(\kappa)$ due to the $\eta(\kappa)$-uniformity of the key and the security of XAC against impersonation attack. Consequently, decryption correctly undoes encryption except with probability at most $\ell \cdot \max\{\mathsf{fail}_{\mathsf{XAC}}(\kappa), \mathsf{Adv}_{\mathsf{XAC}}^{\mathsf{imp}}(\kappa) + \eta(\kappa)\}$, which is negligible.

Lemma 2. *PKE scheme PKE in Figure 4 has the property that, if two distinct ciphertexts $C, \hat{C}$ both pass the verification step $\bigwedge_{j=1}^{s} \mathsf{XVer}(K_{\ell+j}, T) = 1$ during decryption, then they must have different tags $T \neq \hat{T}$.*

Proof. The proof is by contradiction and relies on the injectivity of F. Let $C = (\psi_1, \ldots, \psi_\ell, T)$ and $\hat{C} = (\hat{\psi}_1, \ldots, \hat{\psi}_\ell, \hat{T})$ be two different ciphertexts. Let $(K_{y_1}, \ldots, K_{y_s}) = F(\psi_1, \ldots, \psi_\ell)$ and $(\hat{K}_{y_1}, \ldots, \hat{K}_{y_s}) = F(\hat{\psi}_1, \ldots, \hat{\psi}_\ell)$. Suppose $\bigwedge_{j=1}^{s} \mathsf{XVer}((K_{x_j}, K_{y_j}), T) = \bigwedge_{j=1}^{s} \mathsf{XVer}((\hat{K}_{x_j}, \hat{K}_{y_j}), \hat{T}) = 1$. If $T = \hat{T}$, then $C \neq \hat{C}$ implies $(\psi_1, \ldots, \psi_\ell) \neq (\hat{\psi}_1, \ldots, \hat{\psi}_\ell)$, which further implies $K_{y_j} \neq \hat{K}_{y_j}$ for some $j \in [s]$, by the injectivity of F. On the other hand, we know that $\mathsf{XVer}((K_{x_j}, K_{y_j}), T) = 1$ and $\mathsf{XVer}((\hat{K}_{x_j}, \hat{K}_{y_j}), \hat{T} = T) = 1$; the semi-unique property of XAC now implies that $K_{y_j} = \hat{K}_{y_j}$, a contradiction. $\square$

The SIM-SO-CCA security of PKE will rely on Lemma 2, which in turn relies on the injectivity of F. The size of F's domain is closely related to parameter s: generally the parameter s will be linear in ℓ. Since we need a $(\ell + s)$-XAC in the construction, the size of public key will be linear in ℓ. The size of tag T in the ciphertext will also grow linearly in s and therefore in ℓ. To further decrease the size of public key and tags in our PKE construction, we can employ a collision-resistant (CR) hash function $\mathsf{H} = (\mathsf{HGen}, \mathsf{HEval})$ mapping $\mathcal{C}^\ell$ to $\mathcal{K}_y$ instead of the injective function F (see the full paper [22] for definitions). Then an $(\ell+1)$-XAC is sufficient for the construction, and this results in more compact public keys and tags, but requires an additional cryptographic assumption. The construction using CR hash functions is given in Figure 5.

Theorem 1. *Suppose KEM is a tailored KEM, and the $(\ell + s)$-cross-authentication code XAC is $\delta(\kappa)$-strong, semi-unique, and secure against impersonation and substitution attacks. Then the PKE scheme PKE constructed in Figure 4 is SIM-SO-CCA secure. More precisely, for every ppt adversary $\mathcal{A} = (\mathcal{A}_1, \mathcal{A}_2, \mathcal{A}_3)$ against PKE in the SIM-SO-CCA real experiment that makes at most q_d decryption queries, for every ppt n-message sampler $\mathcal{M}$, and every ppt relation R, we can construct a stateful ppt simulator $\mathcal{S} = (\mathcal{S}_1, \mathcal{S}_2, \mathcal{S}_3)$ for the ideal experiment, and a ppt adversary $\mathcal{B}$ against the IND-tCCCA security of KEM, such that:*

$$\mathsf{Adv}_{\mathsf{PKE}, \mathcal{A}, \mathcal{S}, n, \mathcal{M}, R}^{\mathsf{so\text{-}cca}}(\kappa) \leq n\ell \cdot \mathsf{Adv}_{\mathsf{KEM}, \mathcal{B}}^{\mathsf{tccca}}(\kappa)$$
$$+ n\ell^2 q_d \cdot \left(\mathsf{Adv}_{\mathsf{XAC}}^{\mathsf{sub}}(\kappa) + \mathsf{Adv}_{\mathsf{XAC}}^{\mathsf{imp}}(\kappa) + \eta(\kappa)\right) + n\ell \cdot \delta(\kappa).$$

$$
\begin{array}{ll}
\underline{\mathsf{KeyGen}'(1^\kappa):} & \underline{\mathsf{Dec}'(sk, C):} \\
\quad (pk_{kem}, sk_{kem}) \leftarrow \mathsf{KEM.Kg}(1^\kappa) & \quad C = (\psi_1, \ldots, \psi_\ell, T) \\
\quad K_x \leftarrow \mathcal{K}_x,\ H \leftarrow \mathsf{HGen}(1^\kappa). & \quad \text{For } i = 1 \text{ to } \ell \quad m_i' \leftarrow 0 \\
\quad pk = (pk_{kem}, K_x, H) & \quad K_y' \leftarrow H(\psi_1, \ldots, \psi_\ell) \\
\quad sk = (sk_{kem}, pk) & \quad K_{\ell+1}' \leftarrow (K_x, K_y') \\
\quad \text{Return}(pk, sk) & \quad \text{If } \mathsf{XVer}(K_{\ell+1}', T) = 1 \\
\underline{\mathsf{Enc}'(pk, m_1 \| \ldots \| m_\ell):} & \quad\quad \text{For } i = 1 \text{ to } \ell \\
\quad \text{For } i = 1 \text{ to } \ell & \quad\quad K_i' \leftarrow \mathsf{KEM.Decap}(sk_{kem}, \psi_i) \\
\quad\quad \text{If } m_i = 1 & \quad\quad \text{If } K_i' = \perp, \text{ then } m_i' \leftarrow 0 \\
\quad\quad\quad (K_i, \psi_i) \leftarrow \mathsf{KEM.Encap}(pk_{kem}) & \quad\quad \text{Else } m_i' \leftarrow \mathsf{XVer}(K_i', T)\} \\
\quad\quad \text{Else } \psi_i \leftarrow \mathcal{C}; K_i \leftarrow \mathcal{K} & \quad \text{Return}(m_1' \| m_2' \| \ldots, m_\ell') \\
\quad K_y \leftarrow H(\psi_1, \ldots, \psi_\ell) & \\
\quad K_{\ell+1} \leftarrow (K_x, K_y) & \\
\quad T = \mathsf{XAuth}(K_1, \ldots, K_{\ell+1}) & \\
\quad \text{Return } (\psi_1, \ldots, \psi_\ell, T) &
\end{array}
$$

Fig. 5. Construction of PKE scheme PKE' from tailored KEM, $(\ell + 1)$-XAC and CR hash function

The proof of this theorem, our main result, can be found in the full paper [22]. Here we only give a high level overview. We construct a ppt simulator $\mathcal{S}$ as follows.

- $\mathcal{S}$ generates a public/private key pair and provides the public key to $\mathcal{A}$.
- $\mathcal{S}$ answers $\mathcal{A}$'s decryption queries using the private key.
- $\mathcal{S}$ prepares for $\mathcal{A}$ a vector of n challenge ciphertexts, each ciphertext encrypting ℓ ones.
- When $\mathcal{A}$ decides to corrupt a subset of the challenge ciphertexts, $\mathcal{S}$ obtains the messages corresponding to the corrupted ciphertexts and opens the corrupted ciphertexts bit-by-bit according to the messages. If bit m_i should be opened to 1, $\mathcal{S}$ reveals to $\mathcal{A}$ the original randomness used by KEM.Encap to generate (K_i, ψ_i). If bit m_i should be opened to 0, $\mathcal{S}$ first explains ψ_i with randomness output by $\mathsf{SampleC}^{-1}(\mathcal{C}, \psi_i)$ (as if ψ_i were randomly chosen). Then $\mathcal{S}$ uses algorithm ReSample of XAC to resample K_i to get $\hat{K}_i$, and explains $\hat{K}_i$ with randomness output by $\mathsf{SampleC}^{-1}(\mathcal{K}, \hat{K}_i)$ (as if $\hat{K}_i$ was randomly chosen).
- $\mathcal{S}$ finally outputs whatever $\mathcal{A}$ outputs.

The essence of the SIM-SO-CCA security proof is then to show that encryptions of 1's are computationally indistinguishable from encryptions of real messages, even if the adversary can see the opened (real) messages and the randomness of a corrupted subset of the challenge ciphertexts of his/her choice, and have access to the decryption oracle. This is done with a hybrid argument running from Game 0 to Game $n\ell$. In Game k the first k bits of messages are 1's and are opened as $\mathcal{S}$ does while the last $n\ell - k$ bits come from the real messages and are opened honestly. The proof shows that Games k and $k - 1$ are indistinguishable using the tCCCA security of the tailored KEM and the security properties of the strengthened XAC.

If the k-th bit of the messages is 1, Games k and $k-1$ are identical. Otherwise, a tailored KEM adversary $\mathcal{B}$ can be constructed to simulate Game k or $k+1$ for adversary $\mathcal{A}$. $\mathcal{B}$ is provided with a public key pk_{kem}, a challenge (K^*, ψ^*) and a constrained decryption oracle, and is going to tell whether (K^*, ψ^*) is an output of KEM.Encap(pk_{kem}) or a random pair. $\mathcal{B}$ can generate a public key for $\mathcal{A}$. When preparing the vector of challenge ciphertexts, $\mathcal{B}$ will encrypt the first $k-1$ bits from the real messages, use (K^*, ψ^*) as the encryption of the k-th bit, and encrypt $n\ell - k$ ones for the remaining bits. If (K^*, ψ^*) is an output of KEM.Encap(pk_{kem}), the challenge vector of ciphertexts is just that in Game k, otherwise it is just that in Game $k-1$. Finally, to answer $\mathcal{A}$'s decryption query $C = (\psi_1, \ldots, \psi_\ell, T)$, $\mathcal{B}$ can query $(\psi_i, \mathsf{XVer}(\cdot, T))$ (note that $\mathsf{XVer}(\cdot, T)$ is a predicate) to his own constrained decryption oracle if $\psi^* \neq \psi_i$; $\mathcal{B}$ then replies to $\mathcal{A}$ with decrypted bit 0 iff $\mathcal{B}$ gets $\bot$ from its own oracle. The decryption is correct because $\mathcal{B}$'s oracle outputs $\bot$ iff the decapsulated key is $K_i = \bot$ or $\mathsf{XVer}(K_i, T) = 0$. If $\psi^* = \psi_i$, $\mathcal{B}$ is not allowed to query his own oracle, but can instead respond to $\mathcal{A}$ with the output of $\mathsf{XVer}(K^*, T)$ as the decrypted bit. This decryption is also correct with overwhelming probability for the following reasons: (1) If K^* is the encapsulated key of ψ^*, then $\mathsf{XVer}(K^*, T) = 1$ and decryption is correct. (2) If (K^*, ψ^*) is a random pair, then all the information leaked about K^* is just the very tag T^* that is computed by K^* during the generation of some challenge ciphertext. The semi-uniqueness of XAC guarantees that $T \neq T^*$, and the adversary's corruption only reveals information about a re-sampled $\hat{K}^*$. The security of XAC against substitution attacks shows that even if $\mathcal{A}$ knows T^* and all keys other than K^*, then $\mathcal{A}$ forges a different tag T such that $\mathsf{XVer}(K^*, T) = 1$ with negligible probability. Therefore, $\mathcal{B}$ will almost always respond to $\mathcal{A}$ with bit 0, which is the correct answer.

The security of our modified construction using CR hash functions is stated in the following theorem, whose proof is similar to that of Theorem 1.

Theorem 2. *Suppose KEM is a tailored KEM, the $(\ell + 1)$-cross-authentication code XAC is $\delta(\kappa)$-strong, semi-unique, and secure against impersonation and substitution attacks, and H is collision-resistant. Then the PKE scheme PKE' constructed in Figure 5 is SIM-SO-CCA secure. More precisely, for every ppt adversary $\mathcal{A} = (\mathcal{A}_1, \mathcal{A}_2, \mathcal{A}_3)$ against PKE' in the SIM-SO-CCA real experiment that makes at most q_d decryption queries, for every ppt n-message sampler $\mathcal{M}$, and every ppt relation R, we can construct a stateful ppt simulator $\mathcal{S} = (\mathcal{S}_1, \mathcal{S}_2, \mathcal{S}_3)$ for the ideal experiment, a ppt adversary $\mathcal{B}$ against the IND-tCCCA security of KEM, and a ppt algorithm $\mathcal{F}$ against the collision-resistance of H such that:*

$$\mathsf{Adv}^{so\text{-}cca}_{PKE',\mathcal{A},\mathcal{S},n,\mathcal{M},R}(\kappa) \leq n\ell \cdot \mathsf{Adv}^{tccca}_{KEM,\mathcal{B}}(\kappa)$$
$$+ n\ell^2 q_d \cdot \left(\mathsf{Adv}^{sub}_{XAC}(\kappa) + \mathsf{Adv}^{imp}_{XAC}(\kappa) + \eta(\kappa) \right)$$
$$+ n\ell \cdot \delta(\kappa) + \mathsf{Adv}^{cr}_{H,\mathcal{F}}(\kappa).$$

5 Instantiations

In this section, we explore three different constructions of tailored KEMs, each suitable for the application of Theorems 1 and 2. The first is based on any Strongly Universal$_2$ hash proof system, the second is a direct construction relying on the n-Linear Assumption and a target collision-resistant hash function, while the third uses indistinguishability obfuscation.

5.1 Strongly Universal$_2$ Hash Proof Systems

We use hash proof systems [8] to build tailored KEMs suitable for application in our main theorem.

Let $\Psi \subset \mathcal{C}$ be a language. The hardness of the *subset membership problem* for Ψ with respect to $\mathcal{C}$ requires that a random element from Ψ is indistinguishable from a random element from $\mathcal{C}$. Let $\mathcal{K}$ be a set and $\Lambda_{sk} : \mathcal{C} \to \mathcal{K}$ be a hash function indexed with $sk \in \mathcal{SK}$. Then Λ_{sk} is said to be *projective* if there exists a map $\mu : \mathcal{SK} \to \mathcal{PK}$ such that $\mu(sk) \in \mathcal{PK}$ defines the action of Λ_{sk} on the subset Ψ; μ is then said to be a *projection* on subset Ψ.

A hash proof system (HPS) HPS consists of three algorithms (HPS.param, HPS.pub, HPS.priv). The randomized algorithm HPS.param(1^κ) outputs params $= (\mathbb{G}, \mathcal{C}, \Psi, \mathcal{PK}, \mathcal{SK}, \Lambda, \mu)$, where $\mathbb{G}$ is a group. The secret key sk is randomly chosen from $\mathcal{SK}$, and the public key is computed as $pk = \mu(sk)$ where μ is a projection on Ψ. Algorithm HPS.Pub(pk, ψ, w) is given the public key pk, an element $\psi \in \Psi$ and its witness w, and outputs an encapsulated key $K =$ HPS.Pub(pk, ψ, w) such that $K = \Lambda_{sk}(\psi)$. Algorithm HPS.Priv(sk, ψ) recovers $K = \Lambda_{sk}(\psi)$ using sk.

The *Strongly Universal$_2$ (SU$_2$)* property of an HPS characterizes the unpredictability of $\Lambda_{sk}(\psi)$ for $\psi \in \mathcal{C} \setminus \Psi$.

Definition 5 . *Let* HPS $=$ (HPS.param, HPS.pub, HPS.priv) *be a hash proof system. Then* HPS *is said to be* SU$_2$ *if*

$$\Pr\left[\Lambda_{sk}(\psi) = K \mid pk = \mu(sk), \psi', K' = \Lambda_{sk}(\psi')\right] = 1/|\mathcal{K}|,$$

for all $pk \in \mathcal{PK}$, *all* $\psi, \psi' \in \mathcal{C} \setminus \Psi$ *with* $\psi' \neq \psi$ *and all* $K, K' \in \mathcal{K}$, *where the probability is taken over* $sk \leftarrow \mathcal{SK}$.

Given that HPS is an SU$_2$ HPS, a KEM KEM can be constructed as shown in Figure 6. The output params of HPS.param is used as a set of public parameters implicitly used as input in the algorithms of KEM. Notice that the valid ciphertext set for KEM is Ψ.

Theorem 3. *Let* HPS *be an* SU$_2$ *HPS with* params $= (\mathbb{G}, \mathcal{C}, \Psi, \mathcal{PK}, \mathcal{SK}, \Lambda, \mu)$. *Suppose the subset membership problem is hard for* Ψ *with respect to* $\mathcal{C}$. *Then the KEM* KEM *constructed from* HPS *as shown in Figure 6 is IND-tCCCA secure. Furthermore, if* Ψ *is sparse in* $\mathcal{C}$, *and both* $\mathcal{C}$ *and* $\mathcal{K}$ *are efficiently samplable and explainable, then* KEM *is a tailored KEM.*

KEM.Kg(1^κ):	KEM.Encap(pk):	KEM.Decap(sk, ψ):
$sk \leftarrow \mathcal{SK}$	$\psi \leftarrow \Psi$ with witness w	$K \leftarrow$ HPS.Priv(sk, ψ)
$pk = \mu(sk)$.	$K \leftarrow$ HPS.Pub(pk, ψ, w)	
Return (pk, sk)	Return(K, ψ)	Return(K)

Fig. 6. Construction of a KEM from an SU_2 hash proof system

Proof. It was already proved in [16] that the SU_2 property and the hardness of the subset membership problem for Ψ with respect to $\mathcal{C}$ implies the IND-CCCA security of KEM. On the other hand, public and secret key pairs can be generated independently from $\mathcal{C}$ and Ψ and the subset membership problem holds even if the secret key is known to the adversary. More precisely, when an adversary $\mathcal{B}$ is given ψ and tries to distinguish whether ψ is randomly chosen from Ψ or $\mathcal{C}$, it can establish a VCI experiment for a VCI adversary $\mathcal{A}$ as follows: first call $(pk, sk) \leftarrow$ KEM.Kg(1^κ) and use sk to answer decryption queries. $\mathcal{B}$ gives pk to $\mathcal{A}$ and gives ψ as the challenge ciphertext. Finally $\mathcal{B}$ outputs whatever $\mathcal{A}$ returns. It is clear that $\mathcal{B}$ has the same advantage as $\mathcal{A}$. This implies that the VCI property holds for KEM under the hardness of the subset membership problem. Then IND-tCCCA security follows from Lemma 1.

The SU_2 property of HPS implies that

$$\Pr\left[\text{KEM.Decap}(sk, \psi) = K\right] = \Pr\left[\text{HPS.Priv}(sk, \psi) = K\right] = \frac{1}{|\mathcal{K}|}$$

for all invalid ciphertexts $\psi \in \mathcal{C} \setminus \Psi$, all $K \in \mathcal{K}$, and all $pk = \mu(sk)$, where the probability is taken over $sk \leftarrow \mathcal{SK}$. Then

$$\Pr\left[\text{KEM.Decap}(sk, \psi) = K \mid \psi \leftarrow \mathcal{C}\right] = \Pr\left[\text{KEM.Decap}(sk, \psi)\right] = K \mid \psi \in \Psi \cdot \frac{|\Psi|}{|\mathcal{C}|}$$

$$+ \Pr\left[\text{KEM.Decap}(sk, \psi) = K \mid \psi \in \mathcal{C} \setminus \Psi\right] \cdot \left(1 - \frac{|\Psi|}{|\mathcal{C}|}\right)$$

$$= \Pr\left[\text{KEM.Decap}(sk, \psi) = K \mid \psi \in \Psi\right] \cdot \frac{|\Psi|}{|\mathcal{C}|} + \frac{1}{|\mathcal{K}|} \cdot \left(1 - \frac{|\Psi|}{|\mathcal{C}|}\right) \leq \frac{|\Psi|}{|\mathcal{C}|} + \frac{1}{|\mathcal{K}|}.$$

Noting that $\Pr\left[\text{KEM.Decap}(sk, \psi) = K \mid \psi \in \Psi\right]$ lies between 0 and 1, it follows that the statistical distance between KEM.Decap(sk, ψ) (when ψ is uniformly selected from $\mathcal{C}$) and the uniform distribution is at most $|\Psi|/|\mathcal{C}|$, which is negligible due to the sparseness of Ψ. This establishes that KEM.Decap has tailored functionality.

Finally, KEM is a tailored KEM because it has samplable and explainable domains $\mathcal{C}$ and $\mathcal{K}$, it has IND-tCCCA security, and KEM.Decap has tailored functionality. $\square$

Remark 1. As pointed out in [12], both DDH-based and DCR-based HPS could have samplable and explainable platform groups. For example, we can choose the subgroup of order q in $\mathbb{Z}_p^*$ (with $p = 2q + 1$) as the DDH group, and choose $\mathbb{Z}_{N^2}^*$ as the DCR group.

KEM.Kg(1^κ):	KEM.Encap(pk):	KEM.Decap(sk, ψ):
$b \leftarrow \mathbb{Z}_p; h \leftarrow g^b$	For $i = 1$ to n	For $i = 1$ to n
For $i = 1$ to n	$\quad r_i \leftarrow \mathbb{Z}_p; c_i \leftarrow g_i^{r_i}$	$\quad$ Check if $c_i \in \mathbb{G}$
$\quad a_i, \alpha_i, \beta_i \leftarrow \mathbb{Z}_p$	$t = \mathsf{TCR}(c_1, \ldots, c_n)$	$t = \mathsf{TCR}(c_1, \ldots, c_m)$
$\quad g_i \leftarrow g^{a_i}; \omega_i = a_i^{-1}b$	$\pi \leftarrow \prod_{i=1}^{n}(u_i^t v_i)^{r_i}$	If $\prod_{i=1}^{n} c_i^{\alpha_i t + \beta_i} \neq \pi$
$\quad u_i \leftarrow g_i^{\alpha_i}; v_i \leftarrow g_i^{\beta_i}$	$K \leftarrow h^{r_1 + \ldots + r_n}$	$\quad$ Return ($\bot$)
$pk = (h, (g_i, u_i, v_i)_{i \in [n]})$	$\psi \leftarrow (c_1, \ldots, c_n, \pi)$	$K \leftarrow \prod_{i=1}^{n} c_i^{\omega_i}$
$sk \leftarrow ((\alpha_i, \beta_i, \omega_i)_{i \in [n]}, pk)$	Return(K, ψ)	Return(K)
Return (pk, sk)		

Fig. 7. KEM from n-Linear Assumption [16]

5.2 Tailored KEM Based on n-Linear Assumption

Let $\mathcal{G}(1^\kappa)$ be a group generator, that is, a ppt algorithm which outputs $(\mathbb{G}, g, p)$ where $\mathbb{G}$ is a group of prime order p (having κ bits) and g a generator of $\mathbb{G}$.

Definition 6 . *The n-Linear Assumption for $\mathcal{G}(1^\kappa)$ states that for all ppt adversaries $\mathcal{B}$, the advantage of $\mathcal{B}$ defined below is negligible.*

$$Adv_{\mathcal{B}}^{n\text{-}lin}(\kappa) := \left| \Pr\left[\mathcal{B}(g_1, \ldots, g_n, g_1^{r_1}, \ldots, g_n^{r_n}, h, h^{\sum_{i=1}^{n} r_i}) = 1 \right] \right.$$

$$\left. - \Pr\left[\mathcal{B}(g_1, \ldots, g_n, g_1^{r_1}, \ldots, g_n^{r_n}, h, h^z) = 1 \right] \right|,$$

where $(\mathbb{G}, g, p) \leftarrow \mathcal{G}(1^\kappa)$, $(g_i)_{i \in [n]}, h \leftarrow \mathbb{G}$ and $(r_i)_{i \in [n]}, z \leftarrow \mathbb{Z}_p$.

In [16], Hofheiz and Kiltz presented a KEM based on the n-Linear Assumption for a group generator $\mathcal{G}(1^\kappa)$ and a target collision-resistant hash function, and proved its IND-CCCA security. We replicate the algorithms of this KEM in Figure 7. Note that this construction does not fall into the category of HPS-based KEMs.

Lemma 3. *If the n-Linear Assumption holds for $\mathcal{G}(1^\kappa)$, and TCR is target collision-resistant, then the Hofheinz-Kiltz KEM in Figure 7 is IND-tCCCA secure.*

Proof. In view of the results of [16] and Lemma 1, we need only prove that the KEM in Figure 7 has the VCI property.

Given an adversary $\mathcal{A}$ winning the VCI experiment with non-negligible probability, we can construct a ppt algorithm $\mathcal{B}$ solving the n-Linear problem with help of $\mathcal{A}$ with non-negligible probability. Let $(g_1, \ldots, g_n, g_1^{r_1}, \ldots, g_n^{r_n}, h, K^*)$ be a challenge instance from the n-Linear problem, where $K^* = h^{\sum_{i=1}^{n} r_i}$ or K^* is a random element from $\mathbb{G}$. Here, $\mathcal{B}$ simulates the VCI experiment for $\mathcal{A}$ using its input $(g_1^{r_1}, \ldots, g_n^{r_n}, h, K^*)$.

- $\mathcal{B}$ chooses $(x_i, y_i)_{i \in [n]}, z, z' \leftarrow \mathbb{Z}_p^*$, and computes $u_i = g_i^{x_i} h^z$ and $v_i = g_i^{y_i} h^{z'}$ for $i \in [n]$. $\mathcal{B}$ sets $pk = ((g_i, u_i, v_i)_{i \in [n]}, h)$. All the elements in pk is randomly distributed, as in the real VCI experiment. Here $\mathcal{B}$ implicitly sets $sk = ((\alpha_i, \beta_i, \omega_i)_{i \in [n]}, pk)$ with $\alpha_i = x_i + \omega_i z$, $\beta_i = y_i + \omega_i z'$ and $\omega_i = \log_{g_i} h$.

– $\mathcal{B}$ computes the challenge ciphertext $\psi^* = (c_1^*, \ldots, c_n^*, \pi^*)$ for $\mathcal{A}$, where $c_i^* := g_i^{r_i}$ for $i \in [n]$, $t^* = \mathsf{TCR}(c_1^*, \ldots, c_n^*)$ and $\pi^* = (K^*)^{zt^*+z'} \prod_{i=1}^{n} (c_i^*)^{x_i t^* + y_i}$.

  • If $K^* = h^{\sum_{i=1}^{n} r_i}$, we have $\pi^* = \prod_{i=1}^{n} \left(u_i^{t^*} v_i \right)^{r_i}$. Hence ψ^* is just a valid ciphertext output by the KEM's encapsulation algorithm with randomness $(r_i)_{i \in [n]}$.

  • If K^* is random, then π^* is also random, so that ψ^* is uniformly distributed in $\mathcal{C} = \mathbb{G}^n$.

– $\mathcal{B}$ uses $((x_i, y_i)_{i \in [n]}, z, z')$ to answer $\mathcal{A}$'s constrained decryption queries (P, ψ). Let $\psi = (c_1, \ldots, c_n, \pi)$. We have that $t = \mathsf{TCR}(c_1, \ldots, c_n) \neq t^*$ due to the target-collision resistance of TCR. $\mathcal{B}$ computes $K = \left(\frac{\pi}{\prod_{i=1}^{n} c_i^{x_i t + y_i}} \right)^{1/(zt+z')}$. If $P(K) = 1$ then $\mathcal{B}$ returns K; otherwise $\mathcal{B}$ returns $\perp$.

  • If ψ is consistent, i.e., ψ satisfies $\prod_{i=1}^{n} c_i^{\alpha_i t + \beta_i} = \pi$, then $\pi = h^{(zt+z') \sum_{i=1}^{n} r_i'} \cdot \prod_{i=1}^{n} c_i^{x_i t + y_i}$, where $t = \mathsf{TCR}(c_1, \ldots, c_n)$ and $r_i' = \log_{g_i} c_i$. Then $K = h^{\sum_{i=1}^{n} r_i'}$ is exactly the encapsulated key. Thus the correct K is returned to $\mathcal{A}$ when $P(K) = 1$.

  • If ψ is NOT consistent, then $\pi \neq \prod_{i=1}^{n} c_i^{\alpha_i t + \beta_i}$. Let $\beta = \log_g \pi$, $\omega = \log_g h$, $a_i = \log_g g_i$, and $r_i' = \log_{g_i} c_i$. Then $\gamma := \beta - \sum_{i=1}^{n} a_i r_i' (\alpha_i t + \beta_i) \neq 0$. Consequently, $\log_g K = \gamma/(zt + z') + \omega \sum_{i=1}^{n} r_i'$. The following $2n+2$ equations in $2n+2$ unknowns $((x_i, y_i)_{i \in [n]}, z, z')$ are linearly independent, as long as $t \neq t^*$, which is guaranteed by the target-collision resistance of TCR:

$$\log_g u_i = a_i x_i + \omega z \quad i = 1, 2, \ldots, n$$

$$\log_g v_i = a_i y_i + \omega z' \quad i = 1, 2, \ldots, n$$

$$\log_g \pi^* = \sum_{i=1}^{n} a_i r_i (t^* x_i + y_i) + (\log_g K^*) \cdot (t^* z + z')$$

$$\gamma \left(\log_g K - \omega \sum_{i=1}^{n} r_i' \right)^{-1} = zt + z'.$$

This establishes that $zt + z'$ is uniformly distributed over $\mathbb{Z}_p$. Therefore, $\log_g K$ is uniformly distributed over $\mathbb{Z}_p$ and the predicate P satisfies $P(K) = 0$ except with negligible probability. As a result, ψ will be correctly rejected (due to the failed predicate) except with negligible probability.

Hence, $\mathcal{B}$ provides an almost perfect decryption oracle to $\mathcal{A}$ as long as $t \neq t^*$, for all queried encapsulations $\psi \neq \psi^*$.

– Eventually, $\mathcal{B}$ returns what $\mathcal{A}$ returns.

Finally, $\mathcal{A}$'s non-negligible advantage in the VCI game is converted into $\mathcal{B}$'s non-negligible advantage in breaking the n-Linear Assumption.   □

KEM.Kg(1^κ):
 $k \leftarrow \mathsf{PGen}(1^\kappa)$
 $pk \leftarrow i\mathcal{O}(\mathsf{Encap}(k, \cdot))$
 $sk \leftarrow k$
 Return (pk, sk)

KEM.Encap(pk):
 $r \leftarrow \{0,1\}^\kappa$
 $(K, \psi) \leftarrow i\mathcal{O}(\mathsf{Encap}(k, r))$
 Return(K, ψ)
Encap(k, r):
 $\psi \leftarrow \mathsf{PRG}(r)$
 $K \leftarrow \mathsf{PEval}(k, \psi)$
 Return(K, ψ)

KEM.Decap(sk, ψ):
 $k \leftarrow sk$
 $K \leftarrow \mathsf{PEval}(k, \psi)$
 Return(K)

Fig. 8. Sahai-Waters KEM from $i\mathcal{O}$ and Puncturable PRF [24]

Theorem 4. *Suppose that the n-Linear Assumption holds for $\mathcal{G}(1^\kappa)$, and TCR is target collision-resistant. If groups $\mathbb{G}$ output by $\mathcal{G}(1^\kappa)$ are samplable and explainable, then the KEM in Figure 7 is a tailored KEM.*

Proof. We note that the ciphertext space $\mathcal{C}$ equals $\mathbb{G}^{n+1}$ and the encapsulated key space $\mathcal{K}$ equals $\mathbb{G}$. If group $\mathbb{G}$ is samplable and explainable, so are $\mathcal{C}$ and $\mathcal{K}$.

Next, we have $|\mathcal{C}| = p^{n+1}$. For a valid ciphertext $\psi = (c_1, \ldots, c_n, \pi)$, we note that π is uniquely determined by $c_1, \ldots, c_n$ and pk. Therefore, the valid ciphertext set $|\Psi|$ has size p^n. Consequently, a random ciphertext from $\mathbb{G}^{n+1}$ passes the verification test $\pi = \prod_{i=1}^{n} c_i^{\alpha_i t + \beta_i}$ in the decapsulation algorithm with negligible probability $1/p$. Therefore, the decapsulation algorithm has tailored functionality.

Together with Lemma 3, it follows that the KEM in Figure 7 is a tailored, and therefore suitable for the application of Theorem 1.

5.3 Tailored KEM Based on Indistinguishability Obfuscation and Puncturable PRF

Background definitions for this construction can be found in [24] and the full paper [22].

Sahai and Waters [24] gave a KEM construction from an indistinguishability obfuscator ($i\mathcal{O}$) and a puncturable PRF, as shown in Figure 8. Their construction makes use of a Pseudo-Random Generator (PRG) PRG : $\{0,1\}^\kappa \rightarrow \{0,1\}^{2\kappa}$ and a puncturable PRF family PRF = (PGen, PEval, Punc) whose functions map $\{0,1\}^{2\kappa}$ to $\{0,1\}^\kappa$. We assume that (descriptions of) PRG and PRF are implicitly part of the inputs to KEM.Kg, Encap, and KEM.Decap in Figure 8.

The ciphertext space of the KEM is $\mathcal{C} = \{0,1\}^{2\kappa}$, the valid ciphertext set is $\Psi = \{\psi \mid \psi = \mathsf{PRG}(r); r \in \{0,1\}^\kappa\}$, and the key space is $\mathcal{K} = \{0,1\}^\kappa$. Obviously, both of $\mathcal{C}$ and $\mathcal{K}$ are efficiently samplable and explainable with $\mathsf{SampleC}^{-1}(\mathcal{C}, \psi) := \psi$ and $\mathsf{SampleK}^{-1}(\mathcal{K}, K) := K$.

Lemma 5. *If $i\mathcal{O}(\cdot)$ is an indistinguishability obfuscator for P/poly, PRG is a secure PRG, and PRF is a puncturable PRF, then the Sahai-Waters KEM in Figure 8 is IND-tCCCA secure.*

Proof. In [24], the Sahai-Waters KEM was proved to be IND-CCA secure, so it is obviously IND-CCCA secure.

Next we prove the VCI property, based on the security of PRG. If there is a ppt adversary $\mathcal{A}$ that can distinguish a random ciphertext from a random valid ciphertext with non-negligible probability, then we can construct a ppt algorithm $\mathcal{B}$ that breaks the security of PRG. Suppose $\mathcal{B}$ is given an element ψ^* and tries to decide whether ψ^* is the output of PRG or a randomly chosen element from $\mathcal{C}$. $\mathcal{B}$ will simulate a VCI experiment for $\mathcal{A}$. It first chooses a puncturable PRF PRF and calls KEM.Kg(1^κ) to generate (pk, sk). The public key pk is given to $\mathcal{A}$. Then $\mathcal{B}$ gives ψ^* as the challenge encapsulation to $\mathcal{A}$. Using the secret key sk and algorithm PEval, $\mathcal{B}$ is able to provide a (constrained) decryption oracle for $\mathcal{A}$. Finally, $\mathcal{B}$ outputs whatever $\mathcal{A}$ outputs. Then it is easy to see that $\mathcal{A}$'s non-negligible advantage in the VCI security game results in a non-negligible advantage for $\mathcal{B}$ in breaking the security of PRG.

The IND-CCCA security and VCI property in combination with Lemma 1 establish that the Sahai-Waters KEM in Figure 8 has IND-tCCCA security. □

Extracting puncturable PRFs are a strengthening of puncturable PRFs introduced in [24]; essentially, an extracting puncturable PRF acts as a strong extractor on its inputs.

Definition 7 (Extracting puncturable PRF). *Let $\epsilon(\cdot)$ and $\mathsf{h}_{min}(\cdot)$ be functions. A puncturable PRF family PRF=(PGen, PEval, Punc) mapping $\{0,1\}^{\ell_1(\kappa)}$ to $\{0,1\}^{\ell_2(\kappa)}$ is said to be extracting with error $\epsilon(\kappa)$ for min-entropy function $\mathsf{h}_{min}(\kappa)$ if for all $\kappa \in \mathbb{N}$ and for all random variables X on $\{0,1\}^{\ell_1(\kappa)}$ with min-entropy greater than $\mathsf{h}_{min}(\kappa)$, the statistical distance between $(k, \mathsf{PEval}(k, X))$ and $(k, U_{\ell_2(\kappa)})$ is at most $\epsilon(\kappa)$, where $k \leftarrow \mathsf{PGen}(1^\kappa)$ and $U_{\ell_2(\kappa)}$ denotes the uniform distribution over $\{0,1\}^{\ell_2(\kappa)}$. The family PRF is said to be extracting puncturable if the error $\epsilon(\kappa)$ is negligible (for some choice of function h_{min}).*

The existence of extracting puncturable PRFs is implied by the existence of one-way functions, as was proved in [24]:

Lemma 4. *[24] Assume that one-way functions exist. Then for all efficiently computable functions $\ell_1(\kappa)$, $\ell_2(\kappa)$, $e(\kappa)$ and $\mathsf{h}_{min}(\kappa)$ such that $\ell_1(\kappa) \geq \mathsf{h}_{min}(\kappa) \geq \ell_2(\kappa) + 2e(\kappa) + 2$, there exists an extracting puncturable PRF family PRF = (PGen, PEval, Punc) mapping $\{0,1\}^{\ell_1(\kappa)}$ to $\{0,1\}^{\ell_2(\kappa)}$ with error function $\epsilon(\kappa) = 2^{-e(\kappa)}$ and min-entropy function $\mathsf{h}_{min}(\kappa)$.*

Lemma 6. *If PRF is an extracting puncturable PRF obtained from Lemma 4, then the decapsulation algorithm KEM.Decap of the Sahai-Waters KEM in Figure 8 has tailored functionality.*

Proof. We show that the output of PRF(sk, ψ) is statistically close to the uniform distribution on $\{0,1\}^\kappa$ so long as ψ is chosen from $\mathcal{C}$ uniformly at random, and the puncturable PRF satisfies the bounds in Lemma 4.

Recall that PRF maps 2κ bits to κ bits. When ψ is randomly chosen from $\{0,1\}^{2\kappa}$, the min-entropy of ψ is 2κ. According to Lemma 4, the statistical distance between $(k, \mathsf{PEval}(k, \psi))$ and (k, U_κ) is upper-bounded by $2^{-(\kappa/2-1)}$, where $k \leftarrow \mathsf{PGen}(1^\kappa)$ and U_κ is the uniform distribution over $\{0,1\}^\kappa$. Hence, KEM.Decap has $2^{-(\kappa/2-1)}$-tailored functionality. $\qquad\qquad\square$

Theorem 7. *If $i\mathcal{O}(\cdot)$ is an indistinguishability obfuscator for P/poly, PRG is a secure PRG, and PRF is an extracting puncturable PRF, then the Sahai-Waters KEM in Figure 8 is a tailored KEM.*

Proof. The fact that the KEM in Figure 8 is a tailored KEM follows immediately from Lemma 5, Lemma 6 and the fact that $\mathcal{C} = \{0,1\}^{2\kappa}$ and $\mathcal{K} = \{0,1\}^\kappa$ are efficiently samplable and explainable.

The existence of one-way functions implies the existence of PRGs and extracting puncturable PRFs. Hence the existence of one-way functions and $i\mathcal{O}$ implies the existence of a tailored KEM by the above theorem. Such a tailored KEM can further be used to build a PKE scheme encrypting ℓ bits at a time with the help of an information-theoretically secure $(\ell + s)$-XAC (for suitable parameter s), by following the construction in Figure 4; the SIM-SO-CCA security of the PKE scheme follows from Theorem 1. Thus we obtain the following corollary:

Corollary 8 . *Suppose one-way functions and indistinguishability obfuscation for P/poly exist. Then there exists a PKE scheme with SIM-SO-CCA security.*

Acknowledgments. This work was done while Shengli Liu visited Prof. Kenneth G. Paterson's research group at Royal Holloway, University of London. The first author was supported by the National Natural Science Foundation of China (NSFC Grant No. 61170229 and 61373153), the Specialized Research Fund for the Doctoral Program of Higher Education (Grant No. 20110073110016), and the Scientific innovation projects of Shanghai Education Committee (Grant No. 12ZZ021). The second author was supported by EPSRC Leadership Fellowship EP/H005455/1 and by EPSRC Grant EP/L018543/1.

References

1. Barak, B., Goldreich, O., Impagliazzo, R., Rudich, S., Sahai, A., Vadhan, S.P., Yang, K.: On the (im)possibility of obfuscating programs. In: Kilian, J. (ed.) CRYPTO 2001. LNCS, vol. 2139, pp. 1–18. Springer, Heidelberg (2001). http://dx.doi.org/10.1007/3-540-44647-8_1
2. Barak, B., Goldreich, O., Impagliazzo, R., Rudich, S., Sahai, A., Vadhan, S.P., Yang, K.: On the (im)possibility of obfuscating programs. J. ACM **59**(2), 6 (2012). http://doi.acm.org/10.1145/2160158.2160159
3. Bellare, M., Hofheinz, D., Yilek, S.: Possibility and impossibility results for encryption and commitment secure under selective opening. In: Joux, A. (ed.) EUROCRYPT 2009. LNCS, vol. 5479, pp. 1–35. Springer, Heidelberg (2009)
4. Bellare, M., Waters, B., Yilek, S.: Identity-Based encryption secure against selective opening attack. In: Ishai, Y. (ed.) TCC 2011. LNCS, vol. 6597, pp. 235–252. Springer, Heidelberg (2011). http://dx.doi.org/10.1007/978-3-642-19571-6_15

5. Böhl, F., Hofheinz, D., Kraschewski, D.: On definitions of selective opening security. In: Fischlin, M., Buchmann, J., Manulis, M. (eds.) PKC 2012. LNCS, vol. 7293, pp. 522–539. Springer, Heidelberg (2012). http://dx.doi.org/10.1007/978-3-642-30057-8_31

6. Canetti, R., Dwork, C., Naor, M., Ostrovsky, R.: Deniable encryption. In: Kaliski Jr., B.S. (ed.) CRYPTO 1997. LNCS, vol. 1294, pp. 90–104. Springer, Heidelberg (1997). http://dx.doi.org/10.1007/BFb0052229

7. Canetti, R., Feige, U., Goldreich, O., Naor, M.: Adaptively secure multi-party computation. In: Miller, G.L. (ed.) Proceedings of the Twenty-Eighth Annual ACM Symposium on the Theory of Computing, pp. 639–648. ACM, Philadelphia (1996). http://doi.acm.org/10.1145/237814.238015

8. Cramer, R., Shoup, V.: Universal hash proofs and a paradigm for adaptive chosen ciphertext secure public-key encryption. In: Knudsen, L.R. (ed.) EUROCRYPT 2002. LNCS, vol. 2332, pp. 45–64. Springer, Heidelberg (2002)

9. Cramer, R., Shoup, V.: Design and analysis of practical public-key encryption schemes secure against adaptive chosen ciphertext attack. SIAM J. Comput. 33(1), 167–226 (2004). http://dx.doi.org/10.1137/S0097539702403773

10. Damgård, I.B., Nielsen, J.B.: Improved non-committing encryption schemes based on a general complexity assumption. In: Bellare, M. (ed.) CRYPTO 2000. LNCS, vol. 1880, pp. 432–450. Springer, Heidelberg (2000). http://dx.doi.org/10.1007/3-540-44598-6_27

11. Dwork, C., Naor, M., Reingold, O., Stockmeyer, L.J.: Magic functions. J. ACM 50(6), 852–921 (2003). http://doi.acm.org/10.1145/950620.950623

12. Fehr, S., Hofheinz, D., Kiltz, E., Wee, H.: Encryption schemes secure against chosen-ciphertext selective opening attacks. In: Gilbert, H. (ed.) EUROCRYPT 2010. LNCS, vol. 6110, pp. 381–402. Springer, Heidelberg (2010). http://dx.doi.org/10.1007/978-3-642-13190-5_20

13. Garg, S., Gentry, C., Halevi, S., Raykova, M., Sahai, A., Waters, B.: Candidate indistinguishability obfuscation and functional encryption for all circuits. In: 54th Annual IEEE Symposium on Foundations of Computer Science, FOCS 2013, pp. 40–49. IEEE Computer Society, Berkeley (2013). http://doi.ieeecomputersociety.org/10.1109/FOCS.2013.13

14. Hemenway, B., Libert, B., Ostrovsky, R., Vergnaud, D.: Lossy encryption: constructions from general assumptions and efficient selective opening chosen ciphertext security. In: Lee, D.H., Wang, X. (eds.) ASIACRYPT 2011. LNCS, vol. 7073, pp. 70–88. Springer, Heidelberg (2011)

15. Hofheinz, D.: All-But-Many lossy trapdoor functions. In: Pointcheval, D., Johansson, T. (eds.) EUROCRYPT 2012. LNCS, vol. 7237, pp. 209–227. Springer, Heidelberg (2012)

16. Hofheinz, D., Kiltz, E.: Secure hybrid encryption from weakened key encapsulation. In: Menezes, A. (ed.) CRYPTO 2007. LNCS, vol. 4622, pp. 553–571. Springer, Heidelberg (2007)

17. Hofheinz, D., Rupp, A.: Standard versus selective opening security: separation and equivalence results. In: Lindell, Y. (ed.) TCC 2014. LNCS, vol. 8349, pp. 591–615. Springer, Heidelberg (2014). http://dx.doi.org/10.1007/978-3-642-54242-8_25

18. Huang, Z., Liu, S., Qin, B.: Sender-Equivocable encryption schemes secure against chosen-ciphertext attacks revisited. In: Kurosawa, K., Hanaoka, G. (eds.) PKC 2013. LNCS, vol. 7778, pp. 369–385. Springer, Heidelberg (2013). http://dx.doi.org/10.1007/978-3-642-36362-7_23

19. Huang, Z., Liu, S., Qin, B., Chen, K.: Fixing the sender-equivocable encryption scheme in eurocrypt 2010. In: 2013 5th International Conference on Intelligent Networking and Collaborative Systems, pp. 366–372. IEEE, Xi'an city (2013). http://dx.doi.org/10.1109/INCoS.2013.69

20. Katz, J., Ostrovsky, R.: Round-Optimal secure two-party computation. In: Franklin, M. (ed.) CRYPTO 2004. LNCS, vol. 3152, pp. 335–354. Springer, Heidelberg (2004). http://dx.doi.org/10.1007/978-3-540-28628-8_21

21. Lai, J., Deng, R.H., Liu, S., Weng, J., Zhao, Y.: Identity-Based encryption secure against selective opening chosen-ciphertext attack. In: Nguyen, P.Q., Oswald, E. (eds.) EUROCRYPT 2014. LNCS, vol. 8441, pp. 77–92. Springer, Heidelberg (2014). http://dx.doi.org/10.1007/978-3-642-55220-5_5

22. Liu, S., Paterson, K.G.: Simulation-based selective opening cca security for pke from key encapsulation mechanisms. Cryptology ePrint Archive, Report 2015/010 (2015). http://eprint.iacr.org/

23. Peikert, C., Waters, B.: Lossy trapdoor functions and their applications. In: Dwork, C. (ed.) STOC 2008, pp. 187–196. ACM (2008)

24. Sahai, A., Waters, B.: How to use indistinguishability obfuscation: deniable encryption, and more. In: Shmoys, D.B. (ed.) Symposium on Theory of Computing, STOC 2014, pp. 475–484. ACM, New York (2014). http://doi.acm.org/10.1145/2591796.2591825

On the Selective Opening Security of Practical Public-Key Encryption Schemes

Felix Heuer$^{(\boxtimes)}$, Tibor Jager, Eike Kiltz, and Sven Schäge

Horst Görtz Institute for IT-Security, Ruhr University Bochum, Bochum, Germany
{felix.heuer,tibor.jager,eike.kiltz,sven.schaege}@rub.de

Abstract. We show that two well-known and widely employed public-key encryption schemes – RSA Optimal Asymmetric Encryption Padding (RSA-OAEP) and Diffie-Hellman Integrated Encryption Standard (DHIES), the latter one instantiated with a one-time pad, – are secure under (the strong, simulation-based security notion of) selective opening security against chosen-ciphertext attacks in the random oracle model. Both schemes are obtained via known generic transformations that transform relatively weak primitives (with security in the sense of one-wayness) to INDCCA secure encryption schemes. We prove that selective opening security comes for free in these two transformations. Both DHIES and RSA-OAEP are important building blocks in several standards for public key encryption and key exchange protocols. They are the first practical cryptosystems that meet the strong notion of simulation-based selective opening (SIM-SO-CCA) security.

Keywords: Public key encryption · Selective opening security · OAEP · DHIES · SIM-SO-CCA

1 Introduction

Consider a set of clients $A_1, \ldots, A_n$ connecting to a server S. To encrypt a message m_i, each client A_i draws fresh randomness r_i and transmits ciphertext $c_i = \mathsf{Enc}_{pk_S}(m_i; r_i)$ to S. Assume an adversary observes these ciphertexts, and is then able to "corrupt" a subset of clients $\{A_i\}_{i \in \mathcal{I}}, \mathcal{I} \subseteq \{1, \ldots, n\}$, for instance by installing a malware on their computers. Then, for all $i \in \mathcal{I}$, the adversary learns not only the message m_i, but also the randomness r_i that A_i has used to encrypt m_i. Attacks of this type are called *selective-opening* (SO) attacks (under sender corruptions) and a central question in cryptography is whether the unopened ciphertexts remain secure.

At a first glance, one may be tempted to believe that security of the non-corrupted ciphertexts follows immediately, if the encryption scheme meets some standard security notion, like indistinguishability under chosen-plaintext (IND-CPA) or chosen-ciphertext (INDCCA) attacks, due to the fact that each user A_i samples the randomness r_i independently from the other users. However, it has been observed [3,4,14–16] that this is not true in general, see e.g. [26] for an overview.

© International Association for Cryptologic Research 2015
J. Katz (Ed.): PKC 2015, LNCS 9020, pp. 27–51, 2015.
DOI: 10.1007/978-3-662-46447-2_2

RESULTS ON SO SECURITY. Defining the right notion of security against selective opening attacks has proven highly non-trivial. There are three notions of security that are not polynomial-time equivalent to each other, two indistinguishability-based notions usually denoted as weak IND-SO and (full) IND-SO security, and a simulation-based notion of selective opening security referred to as SIM-SO security. Previous results showed that SIM-SO-CCA and full IND-SO-CCA security are the strongest notions of security [5,11,26]. However, only SIM-SO-CCA has been realized so far [20,24,25]. Unfortunately, the existing constructions are very inefficient and rather constitute theoretical contributions. Intuitively, SIM-SO security says that for every adversary in the above scenario there exists a simulator which can produce the same output as the adversary without ever seeing any ciphertext, randomness, or the public key. It is noteworthy that unlike weak IND-SO security, which requires message distributions that support "efficient conditional re-sampling" (cf. [6]), SIM-SO is independent of the concrete distribution of the messages.

1.1   Our Contributions

In this paper we show that two important public key encryption systems are secure under the strong notion of SIM-SO-CCA security. Previous results only established INDCCAsecurity of the resulting schemes. Most notably, our results cover the well-known DHIESscheme, instantiated with a one-time pad, and RSA-OAEP. Our results show that SIM-SO security essentially comes for free in the random oracle model. This yields the first practical public key encryption schemes that meet the strong notion of SIM-SO-CCA security.

FIRST CONSTRUCTION: DHIES. The first construction we consider is a generalization of the well-known "Diffie-Hellman integrated encryption scheme" (DHIES) [1]. (DHIESor "Hashed ElGamal Encryption" uses a MAC to make plain ElGamal encryption INDCCA secure.) This generic idea behind DHIESwas formalized by Steinfeld, Baek, and Zheng [44] who showed how to build an IND-CCAsecure public key encryption system from a key encapsulation mechanism (KEM) that is one-way under plaintext checking attacks (OW-PCA). OW-PCA is a comparatively weak notion of security in which the adversary's main task is to decapsulate a given encapsulation of some symmetric key. In addition to the public key, the adversary has only access to an oracle which checks, given a KEM key and a ciphertext, whether the ciphertext indeed constitutes an encapsulation of the KEM key under the public key. This construction is INDCCAsecure in the random oracle model [44]. We show that it is furthermore SIM-SO-CCA secure in the random oracle model. We stress that our result generically holds for the entire construction and therefore for any concrete instantiation that employs the one-time pad as symmetric encryption. Most importantly, it covers the well-known DHIESscheme (when instantiated with a one-time pad) that is contained in several public-key encryption standards like IEEE P1363a, SECG, and ISO 18033-2. DHIESis the de-facto standard for elliptic-curve encryption.

SECOND CONSTRUCTION: OAEP. The second construction of public key encryption schemes that we consider is the well-known Optimal Asymmetric Encryption Padding (OAEP) transformation [8]. OAEPis a generic transformation for constructing public-key encryption schemes from trapdoor permutations that was proposed by Bellare and Rogaway. Since then, it has become an important ingredient in many security protocols and security standards like TLS [19,40], SSH [23], S/MIME [27,39], EAP [17], and Kerberos [34,38].

We show that OAEPis SIM-SO-CCA secure when instantiated with a *partial-domain trapdoor permutation* (cf. Section 4.1). Since it is known [22] that the RSA permutation is partial-domain one-way under the RSA assumption, this implies that RSA-OAEPis SIM-SO-CCA secure under the RSA assumption. In fact, our result holds not only for trapdoor permutations, but for *injective* trapdoor functions as well.

Since SIM-SO-CCA security implies INDCCAsecurity, our proof also provides an alternative to the INDCCAsecurity proof of [22]. Interestingly, despite that we are analyzing security in a stronger security model, our proof seems to be somewhat simpler than the proof of [22], giving a more direct insight into which properties of the OAEPconstruction and the underlying trapdoor permutation make OAEPsecure. This might be due to the fact that our proof is organized as a *sequence of games* [9].

Complementing the work of [2,12,22], our result gives new evidence towards the belief that the OAEPconstruction is sound, and that OAEP-type encryption schemes can be used securely in various practical scenarios.

1.2 Related Work

The problem of selective-opening attacks is well-known, and has already been observed twenty years ago [3,4,14–16]. The problem of constructing encryption schemes that are provably secure against this class of adversaries without random oracles has only been solved recently by Bellare, Hofheinz, and Yilek [6]. In [6], the authors show that *lossy* encryption [36] implies security against selective openings under chosen-plaintext attacks (SO-CPA). This line of research is continued in [24] by Hemenway *et al.*, who show that re-randomizable encryption and statistically hiding two-round oblivious transfer imply lossy encryption. From a cryptographic point of view, the above works solve the problem of finding SO-CPA secure encryption schemes, as there are several constructions of efficient lossy or re-randomizable encryption schemes, e.g. [6,24,36]. When it comes to selective openings under chosen-ciphertext attacks, the situation is somewhat different. Hemenway *et al.* [24], Fehr *et al.* [20], Hofheinz [25], and Fujisaki [21] describe SIM-SO-CCA secure encryption schemes which are all too inefficient for practical applications. More recently, an identity-based encryption scheme with selective-opening security was proposed [10]. It is noteworthy, that the most efficient public key encryption systems proven to be weak IND-SO secure do not meet the stronger notion of SIM-SO security. Lately, SIM-SO-CCA security for IBE has been achieved [32].

STATE-OF-THE-ART OF THE PROVABLE SECURITY OF OAEP. The OAEP construction was proved INDCCAsecure if the underlying trapdoor permutation is partial-domain one-way [8,22,41]. Since the RSA trapdoor permutation is a partial-domain one-way function, this yields the INDCCAsecurity of RSA-OAEPas well. Fischlin and Boldyreva [12] studied the security of OAEPwhen only one of the two hash functions is modelled as a random oracle, and furthermore showed that OAEPis non-malleable under chosen plaintext attacks for random messages without random oracles. The latter result was strengthened by Kiltz *et al.* [30], who proved the IND-CPA security of OAEPwithout random oracles, when the underlying trapdoor permutation is *lossy* [36]. Since lossy encryption implies IND-SO-CPA security [6], this immediately shows that OAEP is IND-SO-CPA secure in the standard model. However, we stress that prior to our work it was not clear if OAEPmeets the stronger notion of SIM-SO security, neither in the standard model nor in the random oracle. Backes *et al.* [2] showed that OAEPis secure under so-called *key-dependent message* attacks in the random oracle model.

There also exist a number of negative results [13,31] showing the impossibility of instantiating OAEPwithout random oracles.

STATE-OF-THE-ART OF THE PROVABLE SECURITY OF DHIES. The INDCCAsecurity of DHIESin the random oracle model has been shown equivalent to the Strong Diffie-Hellman (sDH) assumption [1,44].

2   Preliminaries

For $n \in \mathbb{N}$ let $[n] := \{1, \ldots, n\}$. For two strings μ, ν, we denote with $\mu \| \nu$ the string obtained by concatenating μ with ν. If L is a set, then $|L|$ denotes the cardinality of L. We assume implicitly that any algorithm described in the sequel receives the unary representation 1^κ of the security parameter as input as its first argument. We say that an algorithm is a PPT algorithm, if it runs in probabilistic polynomial time (in κ). For a set A we denote the sampling of a uniform random element a by $a \xleftarrow{\$} A$, while we denote the sampling according to some distribution $\mathfrak{D}$ by $a \leftarrow \mathfrak{D}$.

2.1   Games

We present definitions of security and encryption schemes in terms of games and make use of sequences of games to proof our results. A game G is a collection of procedures/oracles {INITIALIZE, $P_1, P_2, \ldots, P_t$, FINALIZE} for $t \geq 0$, where P_1 to P_t and FINALIZE might require some input parameters, while INITIALIZE is run on the security parameter 1^κ. We implicitly assume that boolean flags are initialized to false, numerical types are initialized to 0, sets are initialized to $\emptyset$, while strings are initialized to the empty string ϵ. An adversary $\mathcal{A}$ is *run in game* G *(by challenger* $\mathcal{C}$*)*, if $\mathcal{A}$ calls INITIALIZE. During the game $\mathcal{A}$ may run the procedures P_i as often as allowed by the game. If a procedure P was called by $\mathcal{A}$, the output of P is returned to $\mathcal{A}$, except for the FINALIZE procedure. On $\mathcal{A}$'s call of FINALIZE the game ends and outputs whatever FINALIZE returns. The output *out* of a game G that runs $\mathcal{A}$ is denoted as $G^{\mathcal{A}} \Rightarrow out$. If a game's output is either 0 or 1, $\mathcal{A}$ *wins* G if $G^{\mathcal{A}} \Rightarrow 1$. Further, the *advantage* $\mathbf{Adv}(G^{\mathcal{A}}, H^{\mathcal{A}})$ of $\mathcal{A}$ in *distinguishing* games G and H is defined as $|\Pr[G^{\mathcal{A}} \Rightarrow 1] - \Pr[H^{\mathcal{A}} \Rightarrow 1]|$. For $\mathcal{A}$ run in G and $\mathcal{S}$ run in game H the *advantage* of $\mathcal{A}$ is defined as $|\Pr[G^{\mathcal{A}} \Rightarrow 1] - \Pr[H^{\mathcal{S}} \Rightarrow 1]|$. Setting a boolean flag "ABORT ..." to *true* implicitly aborts the adversary.

2.2 Public Key Encryption Schemes

Let $\mathfrak{M}$, $\mathfrak{R}$, $\mathfrak{C}$ be sets. We say that $\mathfrak{M}$ is the *message space*, $\mathfrak{R}$ is the *randomness space*, and $\mathfrak{C}$ is the *cipertext space*. A public key encryption scheme PKE = (PKEGen,Enc,Dec) consists of three polynomial-time algorithms.

- Gen generates, given the unary representation of the security parameter 1^{κ}, a key pair $(sk, pk) \leftarrow \mathsf{Gen}(1^{\kappa})$, where pk defines $\mathfrak{M}$, $\mathfrak{R}$, and $\mathfrak{C}$.
- Given pk, and a message $m \in \mathfrak{M}$ Enc outputs an encryption $c \leftarrow \mathsf{Enc}_{pk}(m) \in \mathfrak{C}$ of m under the public key pk.
- The decryption algorithm Dec takes a secret key sk and a ciphertext $c \in \mathfrak{C}$ as input, and outputs a message $m = \mathsf{Dec}_{sk}(c) \in \mathfrak{M}$, or a special symbol $\perp \notin \mathfrak{M}$ indicating that c is not a valid ciphertext.

Notice, that Enc is a probabilistic algorithm; we make the used randomness only explicit when needed. In that case we write $c = \mathsf{Enc}(m; r)$ for $r \xleftarrow{\$} \mathfrak{R}$. We require the PKE to be correct, that is for all security parameters 1^{κ}, for all $(pk, sk) \leftarrow \mathsf{PKEGen}(1^{\kappa})$, and for all $m \in \mathfrak{M}$ we have $\Pr[\mathsf{Dec}_{sk}(\mathsf{Enc}_{pk}(m)) = m] = 1$

2.3 SIM-SO-CCA Security Definition

Definition 1. Let PKE := (PKEGen, Enc, Dec) be a public-key encryption scheme, let $n = n(\kappa) > 0$ be a polynomially bounded function, $\mathfrak{D}$ a distribution over a message space, $\mathfrak{R}$ a randomness space and $\mathcal{R}$ a relation. We consider the following games, whereby an adversary $\mathcal{A}$ is run in the REAL-SIM-SO-CCA$_{\mathsf{PKE}}$ game (Figure 1), while a simulator $\mathcal{S} := \mathcal{S}(\mathcal{A})$ is run in the IDEAL-SIM-SO-CCA$_{\mathsf{PKE}}$ game (Figure 2) . We demand that $\mathcal{A}$ and $\mathcal{S}$ call ENC exactly one time before calling OPEN or FINALIZE. Further, $\mathcal{A}$ is not allowed to call DEC on any c_i. To an adversary $\mathcal{A}$, a simulator $\mathcal{S}$, a relation $\mathcal{R}$ and n we associate the advantage function

$$\mathbf{Adv}_{\mathsf{PKE}}^{\mathsf{SIM\text{-}SO\text{-}CCA}}(\mathcal{A}, \mathcal{S}, \mathcal{R}, n, \kappa) :=$$

$$|\Pr[\mathsf{REAL\text{-}SIM\text{-}SO\text{-}CCA}_{\mathsf{PKE}}^{\mathcal{A}} \Rightarrow 1] - \Pr[\mathsf{IDEAL\text{-}SIM\text{-}SO\text{-}CCA}_{\mathsf{PKE}}^{\mathcal{S}} \Rightarrow 1]|.$$

PKE is SIM-SO-CCA secure if for every PPT adversary $\mathcal{A}$ and every PPT relation $\mathcal{R}$ there exists a PPT simulator $\mathcal{S}$ such that $\mathbf{Adv}_{\mathsf{PKE}}^{\mathsf{SIM\text{-}SO\text{-}CCA}}(\mathcal{A}, \mathcal{S}, \mathcal{R}, n, \kappa) \leq \mathsf{negl}(\kappa)$.

Procedure INITIALIZE	Procedure ENC($\mathfrak{D}$)	Procedure DEC(c)
$(pk, sk) \xleftarrow{\$} \mathsf{PKEGen}(1^\kappa)$	$(m_i)_{i \in [n]} \leftarrow \mathfrak{D}$	Return $\mathsf{Dec}_{sk}(c)$
Return pk	$(r_i)_{i \in [n]} \xleftarrow{\$} \mathfrak{R}$	
	$(c_i)_{i \in [n]} := \mathsf{Enc}_{pk}(m_i; r_i)$	Procedure OPEN(i)
Procedure FINALIZE(out)	Return $(c_i)_{i \in [n]}$	$\mathcal{I} := \mathcal{I} \cup \{i\}$
Return $\mathcal{R}((m_i)_{i \in [n]}, \mathfrak{D}, \mathcal{I}, out)$		Return (m_i, r_i)

Fig. 1. REAL-SIM-SO-CCA$_{\mathsf{PKE}}$ game

Procedure INITIALIZE	Procedure ENC($\mathfrak{D}$)	Procedure OPEN(i)
Return ϵ	$(m_i)_{i \in [n]} \leftarrow \mathfrak{D}$	$\mathcal{I} := \mathcal{I} \cup \{i\}$
	Return ϵ	Return m_i
Procedure FINALIZE(out)		
Return $\mathcal{R}((m_i)_{i \in [n]}, \mathfrak{D}, \mathcal{I}, out)$		

Fig. 2. IDEAL-SIM-SO-CCA$_{\mathsf{PKE}}$ game

3 Transformation from Any OW-PCA Secure KEM

3.1 Key Encapsulation Mechanisms and Message Authentication Codes

Definition 2. Let $\mathfrak{K}$ a key space. $\mathfrak{R}$ a randomness space, and $\mathfrak{C}$ a ciphertext space.

A Key Encapsulation Mechanism (KEM) consists of three PPT algorithms $\mathsf{KEM} = (\mathsf{KEMGen}, \mathsf{Encap}, \mathsf{Decap})$ defined to have the following syntax.

- KEMGen generates a key pair (pk, sk) on input 1^κ: $(pk, sk) \leftarrow \mathsf{KEMGen}(1^\kappa)$, where pk specifies $\mathfrak{K}$, $\mathfrak{R}$ and $\mathfrak{C}$.
- Encap is given pk and outputs a key $k \in \mathfrak{K}$ and an *encapsulation* $c \in \mathfrak{C}$ of k: $(c, k) \leftarrow \mathsf{Encap}_{pk}$.
- Given sk, Decap decapsulates $c \in \mathfrak{C}$: $k \leftarrow \mathsf{Decap}_{sk}(c)$, where $k \in \mathfrak{K}$.

We require correctness: for all $\kappa \in \mathbb{N}$, for all (pk, sk) generated by $\mathsf{KEMGen}(1^\kappa)$, and for all (c, k) output by Encap_{pk} we have $\Pr[\mathsf{Decap}_{sk}(c) = k] = 1$. We make the randomness used in Encap only explicit when needed. Without loss of generality we assume Encap to sample $k \xleftarrow{\$} \mathfrak{K}$, and $\mathfrak{K}$, $\mathfrak{C}$ to be exponentially large in the security parameter: $|\mathfrak{K}| \geq 2^\kappa$, $|\mathfrak{C}| \geq 2^\kappa$.

A KEM has unique encapsulations if for every $\kappa \in \mathbb{N}$ and every (pk, sk) output by $\mathsf{KEMGen}(1^\kappa)$ it holds that $\mathsf{Decap}_{sk}(c) = \mathsf{Decap}_{sk}(c') \Rightarrow c = c'$ for all $c, c' \in \mathfrak{C}$.

We introduce a security notion for KEMs that appeared in [35], namely *one-way* security in the presence of a *plaintext-checking oracle* (OW-PCA) amounting an adversary to test if some c is a *valid* encapsulation of a key k. That is, on input (c, k) and given the sk the oracle returns $\mathsf{CHECK}_{sk}(c, k) := (\mathsf{Decap}_{sk}(c) \stackrel{?}{=} k) \in \{0, 1\}$. Since an indistinguishability based security notion is out of reach, once $\mathcal{A}$ is granted access to CHECK, we make use of a weaker security notion, given in the following definition.

Definition 3. Let KEM = (KEMGen, Encap, Decap) be a Key Encapsulation Mechanism and $\mathcal{A}$ an adversary run in the OW-PCA$_{KEM}$ game stated in Figure 3. We restrict the adversary to call CHALLENGE exactly one time and define $\mathcal{A}$'s advantage in winning the OW-PCA$_{KEM}$ game as

$$\mathbf{Adv}_{KEM}^{OW\text{-}PCA}(\mathcal{A}, \kappa) := \Pr[OW\text{-}PCA_{KEM}^{\mathcal{A}} \Rightarrow 1].$$

A KEM is OW-PCA secure, if $\mathbf{Adv}_{KEM}^{OW\text{-}PCA}(\mathcal{A}, \kappa)$ is negligible for all PPT $\mathcal{A}$.

Procedure INITIALIZE(1^κ)	**Procedure** CHALLENGE	**Procedure** Check(k, c)
$(pk, sk) \xleftarrow{\$} \text{KEMGen}(1^\kappa)$	$(k^*, c^*) \xleftarrow{\$} \text{Encap}_{pk}$	Return $(\text{Decap}(c) \overset{?}{=} k)$
Return pk	Return c^*	**Procedure** FINALIZE(k)
		Return $(k \overset{?}{=} k^*)$

Fig. 3. OW-PCA$_{KEM}$ game

Definition 4. Let $\mathfrak{M}$ be a message space and let $\mathcal{T}$ be a set (*tag space*). A Message Authentication Code MAC consists of the following three PPT algorithms MAC = (MACGen, Tag, Vrfy), whereby

- MACGen generates a key k on input 1^κ: $k \leftarrow \text{MACGen}(1^\kappa)$.
- Tag_k computes a tag $t \in \mathcal{T}$ for a given message $m \in \mathfrak{M}$: $t \leftarrow \text{Tag}_k(m)$.
- Given a message $m \in \mathfrak{M}$ and a tag $t \in \mathcal{T}$, Vrfy_k, outputs a bit: $\{0, 1\} \leftarrow \text{Vrfy}_k(m, t)$.

We require MAC to be correct: For all $\kappa \in \mathbb{N}$, all keys k generated by MACGen(1^κ), all $m \in \mathfrak{M}$ and all tags computed by $\text{Tag}_k(m)$ we have $\Pr[\text{Vrfy}_k(m, \text{Tag}_k(m)) = 1] = 1$. For a fixed MAC and k, given message m we call a tag t / the tuple (m, t) valid, if $\text{Vrfy}_k(m, t) = 1$.

Definition 5. For an adversary $\mathcal{A}$ and a MAC MAC := (MACGen, Tag, Vrfy) we consider the sUF-OT-CMA$_{MAC}$ (strongly unforgeable under one-time chosen message attacks) game, where $\mathcal{A}$ is allowed to call TAG at most once.

Procedure INITIALIZE(1^κ)	**Procedure** TAG(m)
$k \xleftarrow{\$} \text{MACGen}(1^\kappa)$	$t \leftarrow \text{Tag}_k(m)$
Return ϵ	Return t
Procedure Finalize(m^*, t^*)	**Procedure** Vrfy($\tilde{m}, \tilde{t}$)
Return $(\text{Vrfy}_k(m^*, t^*) \wedge (m^*, t^*) \neq (m, t))$	Return $\text{Vrfy}_k(\tilde{m}, \tilde{t})$

We define the advantage of $\mathcal{A}$ run in the sUF-OT-CMA$_{MAC}$ game as

$$\mathbf{Adv}_{MAC}^{sUF\text{-}OT\text{-}CMA}(\mathcal{A}, \kappa) := \Pr[sUF\text{-}OT\text{-}CMA_{MAC}^{\mathcal{A}} \Rightarrow 1].$$

MAC is sUF-OT-CMA secure, if $\mathbf{Adv}_{MAC}^{sUF\text{-}OT\text{-}CMA}(\mathcal{A}, \kappa) \leq \text{negl}(\kappa)$ holds for all PPT adversaries $\mathcal{A}$.

Note that we only require one-time security, so a sUF-OT-CMA secure MAC can be constructed information-theoretically.

3.2 The Transformation

Before we prove our results on the selective-opening security of schemes built from KEMs, we recall a well known transformation ([44]) to turn a given KEM into a PKE scheme. Notice, that we instantiated the symmetric encryption with a one-time-pad.

Let KEM = (KEMGen, Encap, Decap) be a KEM, $\mathcal{H}$ a family of hash functions, and let MAC = (MACGen, Tag, Vrfy) be a MAC. The public-key encryption scheme $\mathsf{PKE}_{\mathsf{KEM,MAC}}$ obtained by the transformation is given in Figure 4.

Procedure $\mathrm{PKEGEN}(1^\kappa)$	**Procedure** $\mathrm{ENC}(m)$	**Procedure** $\mathrm{DEC}(c^{(1)}, c^{(2)}, c^{(3)})$
$(pk_{\mathsf{KEM}}, sk_{\mathsf{KEM}}) \xleftarrow{\$} \mathsf{KEMGen}(1^\kappa)$	$(k, c^{(1)}) \xleftarrow{\$} \mathsf{Encap}_{pk_{\mathsf{KEM}}}$	$k \leftarrow \mathsf{Decap}_{sk_{\mathsf{KEM}}}(c^{(1)})$
$H \xleftarrow{\$} \mathcal{H}$	$(k^{sym}, k^{mac}) := H(k)$	$(k^{sym}, k^{mac}) := H(k)$
$pk := (pk_{\mathsf{KEM}}, H)$	$c^{(2)} := k^{sym} \oplus m$	if $\mathsf{Vrfy}_{k^{mac}}(c^{(2)}, c^{(3)}) = 1$
$sk := sk_{\mathsf{KEM}}$	$c^{(3)} := \mathsf{Tag}_{k^{mac}}(c^{(2)})$	Return $c^{(2)} \oplus k^{sym}$
Return pk	Return	else
	$(c^{(1)}, c^{(2)}, c^{(3)})$	Return $\bot$

Fig. 4. Transformation $\mathsf{PKE}_{\mathsf{KEM,MAC}}$ from KEM and MAC to PKE

It is well known, that the given construction turns a OW-PCA KEM into a INDCCA secure PKE scheme in the random oracle model [44]. Our next theorem strengthens this results by showing that $\mathsf{PKE}_{\mathsf{KEM,MAC}}$ is even SIM-SO-CCA secure.

Theorem 6. *Let* KEM *be a* OW-PCA *secure KEM with unique encapsulations and let* MAC *be a* sUF-OT-CMA *secure MAC. Then* $\mathsf{PKE}_{\mathsf{KEM,MAC}}$ *is* SIM-SO-CCA *secure in the random oracle model. In particular, for any adversary* $\mathcal{A}$ *run in the* REAL-SIM-SO-CCA$_{\mathsf{PKE}_{\mathsf{KEM,MAC}}}$ *game, that issues at most* $q_h \leq 2^{\kappa-1}$ *hash and* $q_d \leq 2^{\kappa-1}$ *decryption queries and obtains n ciphertexts, and every* PPT *relation* $\mathcal{R}$, *there exists a simulator* $\mathcal{S}$, *a forger* $\mathcal{F}$ *run in the* sUF-OT-CMA$_{\mathsf{MAC}}$ *game, and an adversary* $\mathcal{B}$ *run in the* OW-PCA$_{\mathsf{KEM}}$ *game with roughly the same running time as* $\mathcal{A}$ *such that*

$$\mathbf{Adv}^{\mathsf{SIM\text{-}SO\text{-}CCA}}_{\mathsf{PKE}_{\mathsf{KEM,MAC}}}(\mathcal{A}, \mathcal{S}, \mathcal{R}, n, \kappa) \leq$$

$$n \cdot \left(\frac{q_h + q_d}{2^{\kappa-1}} + \mathbf{Adv}^{\mathsf{sUF\text{-}OT\text{-}CMA}}_{\mathsf{MAC}}(\mathcal{F}, \kappa) + \mathbf{Adv}^{\mathsf{OW\text{-}PCA}}_{\mathsf{KEM}}(\mathcal{B}, \kappa) \right). \quad (1)$$

Let us have a high-level look at our proof. Up to some small syntactical changes G_0 constitutes of the REAL-SIM-SO-CCA$^{\mathcal{A}}_{\mathsf{PKE}_{\mathsf{KEM,MAC}}}$ game.

The later simulator $\mathcal{S}$ will provide $\mathcal{A}$ with message-independent dummy encryptions c_i. This allows $\mathcal{S}$ to claim that $c_i = \mathsf{Enc}_{k_i}(m_i, r_i)$ for some arbitrary m_i after sending c_i to $\mathcal{A}$, if $\mathcal{A}$ should decide to open c_i. Game G_2 introduces the dummy encryptions, while G_1 serves as a preparational step.

After calling $\mathrm{ENC}(\mathfrak{D})$, $\mathcal{A}$ is allowed to make OPEN, HASH and DEC queries in an arbitrary order. Assume, that $\mathcal{A}$ did not[1] query $\mathrm{OPEN}(i)$ before calling $\mathrm{HASH}(k_i)$ or issuing a valid decryption query $(c_i^{(1)}, \cdot, \cdot)$. Since the indexset of opened messages $\mathcal{I}$ is part of $\mathcal{A}$'s output $\mathcal{S}$ wants to simulate, $\mathcal{S}$ may not query $\mathrm{OPEN}(i)$ if $\mathcal{A}$ did not make the same call. Neither can $\mathcal{S}$ answer such a query, since it would fix k_i^{sym} and thereby m_i before $\mathcal{A}$ made a potential $\mathrm{OPEN}(i)$ query. Therefore, we need to block $\mathrm{HASH}(k_i)$ and valid $\mathsf{Dec}(c_i^{(1)}, \cdot, \cdot)$ queries, if $\mathcal{A}$ did not call $\mathrm{OPEN}(i)$ before. Considering valid decryption queries, these two cases can occur: 1) $H(k_i)$ is already defined, or 2) $H(k_i)$ not defined. Game G_3 takes care of case 2), while we block $\mathcal{A}$'s hash queries $\mathrm{HASH}(k_i)$ for unopened c_i in game G_4 - that is, ruling out case 1) as well.

Proof: Let q_h be the number of hash queries and let q_d be the number of decryption queries issued by $\mathcal{A}$, let $n = n(\kappa)$ be a polynomial in κ. For $i \in [n]$ let: m_i denote the ith message sampled by the challenger, r_i the ith randomness used by Encap: $(k_i, c_i^{(1)}) \leftarrow \mathsf{Encap}(r_i)$, $(k_i^{sym}, k_i^{mac}) \leftarrow H(k_i)$ the ith key-pair generated by hashing k_i and $c_i := (c_i^{(1)}, c_i^{(2)}, c_i^{(3)})$ the ith ciphertext. Without loss of generality, the games samples $(r_i)_{i \in [n]}$ as part of $\mathrm{INITIALIZE}$. We proceed with a sequence of games which is given in pseudocode in Figure 5.

Game 0. We model H as a random oracle. Challenger $\mathcal{C}_0$ keeps track of issued calls (either by the game or $\mathcal{A}$) of $\mathrm{HASH}(s)$ by maintaining a list L_H. For a query s, $\mathrm{HASH}(s)$ returns h_s if there is an entry $(s, h_s) \in L_H$, otherwise HASH samples h_s at random, adds (s, h_s) to L_H, and returns h_s; we write $H(s) := h_s$ only and implicitly assume an update operation $L_H := L_H \cup \{(s, h_s)\}$ to happen in the background.

We introduce small syntactical changes: Challenger $\mathcal{C}_0$ samples $(k_i^{sym}, k_i^{mac})_{i \in [n]}$ uniformly random and sets $(H(k_i))_{i \in [n]} := (k_i^{sym}, k_i^{mac})$ while $\mathrm{INITIALIZE}$ is run. Additionally, G_0 runs Encap_{pk} to generate $(k_i, c_i^{(1)})_{i \in [n]}$ during $\mathrm{INITIALIZE}$.

Claim 0. $\mathbf{Adv}(\mathrm{REAL\text{-}SIM\text{-}SO\text{-}CCA}^{\mathcal{A}}_{\mathsf{PKE}_{\mathsf{KEM},\mathsf{MAC}}}, \mathsf{G}_0^{\mathcal{A}}) = 0.$

Proof: Apparently, it makes no difference if the challenger samples $(r_i)_{i \in [n]}$ and runs $\mathsf{Encap}(r_i)$ on demand as part of ENC or in advance while $\mathrm{INITIALIZE}$ is run. Since H is modeled as a random oracle, $H(s)$ is sampled uniformly random for every fresh query $\mathrm{HASH}(s)$. Therefore $\mathcal{C}_0$ does not change the distribution by sampling (k_i^{sym}, k_i^{mac}) in the first place and setting $H(k_i) := (k_i^{sym}, k_i^{mac})$ afterwards. ∎

---

[1] Neither $\mathrm{HASH}(k_i)$ nor $\mathrm{DEC}(c_i^{(1)}, \cdot, \cdot)$ queries are a tripping hazard, once $\mathcal{A}$ called $\mathrm{OPEN}(i)$.

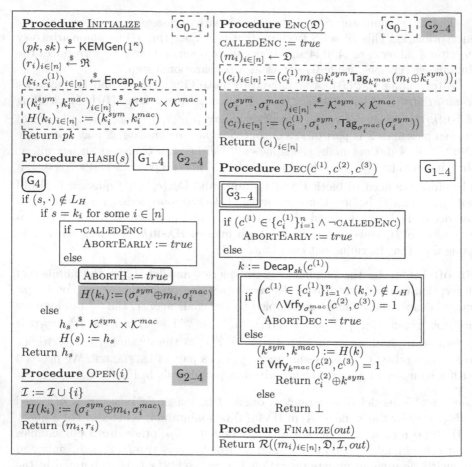

Fig. 5. Sequence of games G_0 to G_4. Boxed code is only executed in the games indicated by the game names given in the same box style at the top right of every procedure.

Game 1. We add an abort condition. Challenger $\mathcal{C}_1$ raises the event ABORTEARLY and aborts[2] $\mathcal{A}$, if $\mathcal{A}$ did not call ENC before calling either HASH(k_i) or DEC($c_i^{(1)}, \cdot, \cdot$) for some $i \in [n]$.

Claim 1. $\mathbf{Adv}(\mathsf{G}_0^{\mathcal{A}}, \mathsf{G}_1^{\mathcal{A}}) \leq n \cdot (q_h + q_d) \cdot 2^{-(\kappa-1)}$.

Proof: Since games G_0 and G_1 are identical until ABORTEARLY is raised, it follows that $\mathbf{Adv}(\mathsf{G}_0^{\mathcal{A}}, \mathsf{G}_1^{\mathcal{A}}) \leq \Pr[\text{ABORTEARLY}]$. Let VIAHASH and VIADEC be the events that ABORTEARLY was caused by either a hash or a decryption query

---

[2] Notice, that $\mathcal{C}_1$ aborts even if such a decryption query is invalid.

of $\mathcal{A}$. Let s_i denote the ith hash and $d_i = (d_i^{(1)}, d_i^{(2)}, d_i^{(3)})$ the ith decryption query of $\mathcal{A}$. It holds that

$$\Pr[\text{AbortEarly}] = \Pr[\text{viaHash}] + \Pr[\text{viaDec}]$$

$$\leq \Pr[s_1 \in \{k_i\}_{i=1}^n] + \sum_{i=2}^{q_h} \Pr[s_i \in \{k_i\}_{i=1}^n | \bigwedge_{j=1}^{i-1} s_j \notin \{k_i\}_{i=1}^n]$$

$$+ \Pr[d_i^{(1)} \in \{c_i^{(1)}\}_{i=1}^n] + \sum_{i=2}^{q_d} \Pr[d_i^{(1)} \in \{c_i^{(1)}\}_{i=1}^n | \bigwedge_{j=1}^{i-1} d_j^{(1)} \notin \{c_i^{(1)}\}_{i=1}^n]$$

$$= \sum_{i=1}^{q_h} \frac{n}{2^\kappa - (i-1)} + \sum_{i=1}^{q_d} \frac{n}{2^\kappa - (i-1)} \leq \sum_{i=1}^{q_h} \frac{n}{2^\kappa - q_h} + \sum_{i=1}^{q_d} \frac{n}{2^\kappa - q_d} \leq \frac{n(q_h + q_d)}{2^{\kappa-1}}.$$

Above holds since Encap samples $k \xleftarrow{\$} \mathfrak{K}$ and KEM has unique encapsulations. ∎

Game 2. We change the encryption procedure and answer hash queries in a different way. $\mathcal{C}_2$ does not program $H(k_i)$ for $i \in [n]$ anymore. Enc still samples m_i, and samples $\sigma_i^{sym} \xleftarrow{\$} \mathcal{K}^{sym}$, $\sigma_i^{mac} \xleftarrow{\$} \mathcal{K}^{mac}$, to compute $c_i = \text{Enc}_{k_i}(m_i) := (c_i^{(1)}, \sigma_i^{sym}, \text{Tag}_{\sigma_i^{mac}}(\sigma_i^{sym}))$. If $\mathcal{A}$ should call $\text{Hash}(k_i)$ for $i \in [n]$ or $\text{Open}(i)$, the challenger programs $H(k_i) := (\sigma_i^{sym} \oplus m_i, \sigma_i^{mac})$. Keep in mind that as from now $(k_i, \cdot) \notin L_H$ implies that $\text{Open}(i)$ was not called.

Claim 2. $\mathbf{Adv}(\mathsf{G}_1^{\mathcal{A}}, \mathsf{G}_2^{\mathcal{A}}) = 0$.

Proof: Assuming that AbortEarly does not happen in game G_2, the keys k_i^{sym} and k_i^{mac} are still uniformly random when $\mathcal{A}$ calls Enc. Therefore $(c_i^{(2)})_{i \in [n]} = m_i \oplus k_i^{sym}$ is uniform and $(c_i^{(3)})_{i \in [n]}$ is a valid tag of a uniformly random message under a key from the uniform distribution. Consequently, challenger $\mathcal{C}_2$ can sample $(c_i^{(2)})_{i \in [n]} := \sigma_i^{sym}$ uniformly and can compute the tags using a uniform key σ_i^{mac} without changing the distribution of the encryptions $(c_i)_{i \in [n]}$. $\mathcal{C}_2$ does not program $H(k_i)$ for $i \in [n]$ anymore, but has to keep H consistent. If $\mathcal{A}$ calls $\text{Hash}(k_i)$ or $\text{Open}(i)$, $\mathcal{C}_2$ sets $H(k_i) := (\sigma_i^{sym} \oplus m_i, \sigma_i^{mac})$. ∎

Game 3. We add another abort condition. If $\mathcal{A}$ already called Enc, issues a decryption query $(c_i^{(1)}, c^{(2)}, c^{(3)}) \notin \{c_i\}_{i=1}^n$, where $H(k_i)$ is not defined, and $\text{Vrfy}_{\sigma_i^{mac}}(c_i^{(1)}, c^{(2)}, c^{(3)})$ verifies, challenger $\mathcal{C}_3$ raises AbortDec and aborts $\mathcal{A}$.

Claim 3. $\mathbf{Adv}(\mathsf{G}_2^{\mathcal{A}}, \mathsf{G}_3^{\mathcal{A}}) \leq n \cdot \mathbf{Adv}_{\mathsf{MAC}}^{\mathsf{sUF\text{-}OT\text{-}CMA}}(\mathcal{F}, \kappa)$.

Proof: Games G_2 and G_3 are identical until AbortDec happens, it suffices to bound $\Pr[\text{AbortDec}]$.

Let $\mathsf{MAC} := (\mathsf{MACGen}, \mathsf{Tag}, \mathsf{Vrfy})$ be the MAC used by the sUF-OT-CMA challenger. We construct an adversary $\mathcal{F}$ against the sUF-OT-CMA security of MAC having success probability $\Pr[\text{AbortDec}]/n$. The reduction is straight forward: $\mathcal{F}$ runs adversary $\mathcal{A}$ as in game G_3, but picks $i^* \xleftarrow{\$} [n]$ during Initialize. Computing the i^{*th} ciphertext, $\mathcal{F}$ queries its sUF-OT-CMA challenger for $t^* := \text{Tag}(\sigma_{i^*}^{sym})$ instead of using its own Tag procedure and sends $(c_i)_{i \in [n]}$ to $\mathcal{A}$. If $\mathcal{A}$ should call Open(i^*), challenger C_3 apparently was unlucky in hiding its own challenge and aborts the adversary. Querying its $\text{Vrfy}_k(\cdot, \cdot)$ oracle, $\mathcal{F}$ can detect when $\mathcal{A}$ issues a valid query $\text{Dec}(c_i^{(1)}, c^{(2)}, c^{(3)})$ for some $i \in [n]$, returns $(c^{(2)}, c^{(3)})$ to its sUF-OT-CMA challenger and aborts $\mathcal{A}$.

Assume that AbortDec happens, i.e. $\mathcal{A}$ makes a valid decryption query $(c_i^{(1)}, c^{(2)}, c^{(3)}) \notin \{c_i\}_{i \in [n]}$, while $H(k_i)$ is still undetermined. Notice, that we must not allow $H(k_{i^*})$ to be fixed since $k_{i^*}^{mac}$ is only known to the sUF-OT-CMA challenger. Let $(c_i^{(1)}, \tilde{c}^{(2)}, \tilde{c}^{(3)}) \in \{c_i\}_{i \in [n]}$ be the ciphertext c_i, whose first component matches the first entry of $\mathcal{A}$'s valid decryption query. Hence, $c^{(3)}$ is either a new valid tag for $\tilde{c}^{(2)}$ or $c^{(3)}$ is a valid tag for a "new" message $c^{(2)}$, since $(c^{(2)}, c^{(3)}) \neq (\tilde{c}^{(2)}, \tilde{c}^{(3)})$. In both cases $\mathcal{F}$ wins its sUF-OT-CMA challenge by returning $(c^{(2)}, c^{(3)})$, if $\mathcal{F}$ picks the right challenge ciphertext to embed t^*. The claim follows by rearranging

$$\mathbf{Adv}_{\text{MAC}}^{\text{sUF-OT-CMA}}(\mathcal{F}, \kappa) \geq \Pr[\text{AbortDec}]/n. \qquad \blacksquare$$

Game 4. We add one more abort condition. Challenger C_4 raises the event AbortH if $\mathcal{A}$ already called Enc, issues a hash query $\text{Hash}(k_i)$ for $i \in [n]$ and did not call Open(i) before.

Claim 4. $\mathbf{Adv}(G_3^{\mathcal{A}}, G_4^{\mathcal{A}}) \leq n \cdot \mathbf{Adv}_{\text{KEM}}^{\text{OW-PCA}}(\mathcal{B}, \kappa)$.

Proof: Games G_3 and G_4 are identical until AbortH happens. Given adversary $\mathcal{A}$ run in the REAL-SIM-SO-CCA game, we construct an adversary $\mathcal{B}$ against the OW-PCA security of KEM having success probability $\Pr[\text{AbortH}]/n$ as depicted in Figure 6. Adversary $\mathcal{B}$ receives a pk and a challenge encapsulation $c^* \leftarrow$ Challenge of some key k^* and aims to output k, given access to an $\text{Check}(\cdot, \cdot)$ returning $\text{Check}_{sk}(k, c) := (\text{Decap}_{sk}(c) \stackrel{?}{=} k)$.

$\mathcal{B}$ runs $\mathcal{A}$ as $\mathcal{A}$ is run in game G_3 except for the following differences: After calling Initialize, $\mathcal{B}$ guesses an index $i^* \xleftarrow{\$} [n]$. $\mathcal{B}$ creates c_i as before, but hides its own challenge in the first component of the i^{*th} ciphertext. Let's assume that AbortH happens. Since $\mathcal{B}$ knows $\{c_i^{(1)}\}$ for $i \in [n] \setminus \{i^*\}$, it can detect if $\mathcal{A}$ queries $\text{Hash}(s)$ for $s \in \{k_i\}$ where $i \in [n] \setminus \{i^*\}$, while $\mathcal{B}$ can invoke its Check oracle to detect the query $\text{Hash}(k_{i^*})$ since $\text{Check}(k_{i^*}, c_{i^*}^{(1)}) = 1$. Therefore $\mathcal{B}$ does not have to guess when AbortH happens. If $\mathcal{A}$ should call Open(i^*), $\mathcal{B}$ apparently guessed i^* wrong[3] and aborts $\mathcal{A}$. Running the reduction, $\mathcal{B}$ has to maintain the conditions for AbortDec. Therefore it suffices to check if $c^{(1)} \in \{c_i^{(1)}\}_{i=1}^n$ and

---

[3] $\mathcal{A}$ cannot ask to open every single challenge ciphertext, since AbortH occurs.

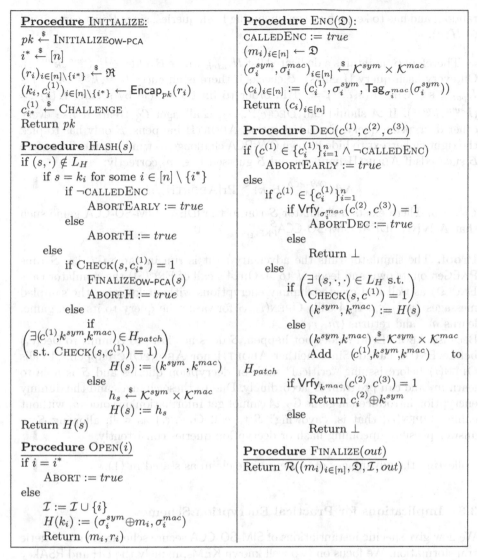

Fig. 6. Reduction to KEM's OW-PCA security given by the game interface for $\mathcal{A}$

$\mathsf{Vrfy}_{\sigma_i^{mac}}(c^{(2)}, c^{(3)})$ hold, because $H(k)$ cannot be defined, since neither ABORTH, nor ABORT via OPEN happened.

It remains to explain how $\mathcal{B}$ (unable to compute $k = \mathsf{Decap}_{sk}(c^{(1)})$) answers decryption queries without knowing sk. To answer these queries we make use of the nifty "oracle patching technique" from [18]. If $\mathcal{A}$ calls $\mathsf{DEC}(c^{(1)}, c^{(2)}, c^{(3)})$, $\mathcal{B}$ checks if $H(k)$ is already defined by querying $\mathsf{CHECK}(s, c^{(1)})$ for every $(s, \cdot) \in L_H$. If there is such a s, $\mathcal{B}$ uses $(k^{sym}, k^{mac}) := H(s)$. If not, $\mathcal{B}$ picks (k^{sym}, k^{mac}) at random and has to keep an eye on upcoming hash queries, since $\mathcal{B}$ just committed to $H(k)$.

Therefore $\mathcal{B}$ maintains a dedicated list H_{patch} where $\mathcal{B}$ adds $(c^{(1)}, (^{sym}, k^{mac}))$. On every hash query $\text{HASH}(s)$, $\mathcal{B}$ checks if there is an entry $(c^{(1)}, k^{sym}, k^{mac}) \in H_{patch}$ s.t. $\text{CHECK}(s, c^{(1)}) = 1$ in order to fix the oracle by setting $H(s) := (k^{sym}, k^{mac})$. If $\mathcal{A}$ should call $\text{DEC}(c_{i^*}^{(1)}, \cdot, \cdot)$, challenger $\mathcal{C}_3$ treats it like every other decryption query. Considering that ABORTH happens, $\mathcal{B}$ only has to pick the right ciphertext to hide its own OW-PCA challenge to win its game. Therefore $\mathcal{B}$ succeeds if ABORTH happens and $\mathcal{B}$ guessed $i^* \in [n]$ correctly:

$$\mathbf{Adv}_{\text{KEM}}^{\text{OW-PCA}}(\mathcal{B}, \kappa) \geq \Pr[\text{ABORTH}]/n. \qquad \blacksquare$$

Claim 5. There exists a simulator $\mathcal{S}$ run in the IDEAL-SIM-SO-CCA game such that $\mathbf{Adv}(\mathsf{G}_4^{\mathcal{A}}, \text{IDEAL-SIM-SO-CCA}_{\text{PKE}_{\text{KEM,MAC}}}^{\mathcal{S}}) = 0$.

Proof: The simulator runs the adversary as it is run in game G_4, i.e. $\mathcal{S}$ runs PKEGen on its own and feeds pk to $\mathcal{A}$. On $\mathcal{A}$'s call of $\text{ENC}(\mathfrak{D})$ the simulator calls $\text{ENC}(\mathfrak{D})$ as well and creates dummy encryptions without knowing the sampled messages $(m_i)_{i \in [n]}$. If $\mathcal{A}$ calls $\text{OPEN}(i)$, $\mathcal{S}$ forwards the query to its own game, learns m_i, and returns (m_i, r_i) to $\mathcal{A}$.

Because ABORTEARLY does not happen, $\mathcal{S}$ does not have to commit to $\text{Dec}(c_i)$ before ENC is called. Since neither ABORTH nor ABORTDEC happen, $\mathcal{A}$ calls $\text{OPEN}(i)$ before issuing "critical" hash or decryption queries and $\mathcal{S}$ is able to learn m_i and can program H accordingly. Due to these changes and the dummy encryption introduced in game G_2, $\mathcal{A}$ cannot get information on some m_i without calling $\text{OPEN}(i)$, that is, "avowing" $\mathcal{S}$ to call $\text{OPEN}(i)$ as well, allowing $\mathcal{S}$ to answer possibly upcoming hash or decryption queries consistently. $\blacksquare$

Collecting the advantages of $\mathcal{A}$ we get the claim as stated in (1). $\blacksquare$

3.3   Implications for Practical Encryption Schemes

We now give specific instantiations of SIM-SO-CCA secure scheme via our generic transformation. We focus on two well known KEMs, namely the DH and RSAkey encapsulation mechanism.

DHIES. Let $\mathbb{G}$ be a group of prime-order p, and let g be a generator. The Diffie-Hellman KEM DH-KEM $=$ (Gen, Enc, Dec) is defined as follows. The key-generation algorithm Gen picks $x \xleftarrow{\$} \mathbb{Z}_p$ and defines $pk = X := g^x$ and $sk = x$; the encapsulation algorithm Encap_{pk} picks $r \xleftarrow{\$} \mathbb{Z}_p$ and returns $(c = g^r, k = X^r)$; the decapsulation algorithm $\text{Decap}_{sk}(c)$ returns $k = c^x$. OW-PCA security of the DH-KEM is equivalent to the strong Diffie-Hellman (sDH) assumption [1]. The sDH assumption states that there is no PPT adversary $\mathcal{A}$ that, given two random group elements $U := g^u, V := g^v$ and a *restricted* DDH oracle $\mathcal{O}_v(\cdot, \cdot)$ where $\mathcal{O}_v(a, b) := (a^v \stackrel{?}{=} b)$ computes g^{uv} with non-negligible probability.

Procedure PKEGen(1^κ)	**Procedure** Enc(m)	**Procedure** Dec(c_1, c_2, c_3)
$H \xleftarrow{\$} \mathcal{H}$	$r \xleftarrow{\$} \mathbb{Z}_p$	$(k^{sym}, k^{mac}) \leftarrow H(c_1{}^x)$
$x \xleftarrow{\$} \mathbb{Z}_p$	$(k^{sym}, k^{mac}) \leftarrow H(X^r)$	if $\mathsf{Vrfy}_{k^{mac}}(c_2, c_3) = 1$
$X := g^x$	$c_1 := g^r$	$\quad$ Return $c_2 \oplus k^{sym}$
$pk := (\mathbb{G}, g, p, X)$	$c_2 := k^{sym} \oplus m$	else
$sk := x$	$c_3 := \mathsf{Tag}_{k^{mac}}(c_2)$	$\quad$ Return $\perp$
Return (pk, sk)	Return (c_1, c_2, c_3)	

Fig. 7. The Diffie-Hellman Integrated Encryption Scheme DHIESinstantiated with a one-time pad

Let MAC be a MAC with message-space and key-space $\{0,1\}^\ell$ and let $\mathcal{H} :$ $\mathbb{G} \mapsto \{0,1\}^{2\ell}$ be a family of hash functions. The security of DHIES $=$ PKE$_{\mathsf{DH\text{-}KEM,MAC}}$ (depicted in Figure 7)(instantiated with a one-time pad) is stated in the following corollary, whose proof is a direct consequence of Theorem 6.

Corollary 7. DHIES instantiated with a one-time pad is SIM-SO-CCA secure in the random oracle model, if MAC is sUF-OT-CMA and the sDH assumption holds.

RSA-KEM. We obtain another selective-opening secure encryption scheme, if we plug in the RSA-KEM in the generic transformation given in Figure 4. Thereby, OW-PCA security of the RSA-KEM holds under the RSA assumption [42]. Under the RSA assumption, PKE$_{\mathsf{RSA\text{-}KEM,MAC}}$ (as described in ISO18033-2 [42]) is SIM-SO-CCA secure in the random oracle model.

Both reductions for the OW-PCA security of the DH-KEM, RSA-KEM, respectively, are tight, while both KEMs have unique encapsulations.

4   The OAEP Transformation

In this section we show that OAEPis SIM-SO-CCA secure when instantiated with a *partial-domain one-way trapdoor permutation* (see Section 4.1). Since it is known [22] that the RSApermutation is partial-domain one way under the RSAassumption, this implies that RSA-OAEPis SIM-SO-CCA secure under the RSAassumption. In fact, our result works not only for trapdoor permutations, but for *injective* trapdoor functions as well. Since SIM-SO-CCA security implies INDCCAsecurity, our proof also provides an alternative to the INDCCAsecurity proof of [22].

4.1   Trapdoor Permutations and Partial-Domain Onewayness

Recall that a trapdoor permutation is a triple of algorithms $\mathcal{T} = (GK, F, F^{-1})$, where GK generates a key pair $(ek, td) \xleftarrow{\$} GK(1^\kappa)$, $F(ek, \cdot)$ implements a permutation

$$f_{ek} : \{0,1\}^k \to \{0,1\}^k \tag{2}$$

specified by ek, and $F^{-1}(td, \cdot)$ inverts f_{ek} using the trapdoor td. Let us write the function f_{ek} from (2) as a function

$$f_{ek} : \{0,1\}^{\ell+k_1} \times \{0,1\}^{k_0} \to \{0,1\}^k$$

with $k = \ell + k_1 + k_0$.

Definition 8. Let $\mathcal{T}$ be a trapdoor permutation as given above and $\mathcal{B}$ an adversary run in the PD-OW$_{\mathcal{T}}$ game given in Figure 8. We restrict $\mathcal{B}$ to call CHALLENGE exactly one time and define $\mathcal{B}$'s advantage in winning the PD-OW$_{\mathcal{T}}$ game as

$$\mathbf{Adv}_{\mathcal{T}}^{\text{PD-OW}}(\mathcal{B}, \kappa) := \Pr[\text{PD-OW}_{\mathcal{T}}^{\mathcal{B}} \Rightarrow 1].$$

Moreover, if $\mathbf{Adv}_{\mathcal{T}}^{\text{PD-OW}}(\mathcal{B}, \kappa) \leq \mathsf{negl}(\kappa)$ for all probabilistic polynomial-time (in κ) adversaries $\mathcal{B}$, we say that $\mathcal{T}$ is a *partial-domain secure* trapdoor permutation.

Procedure INITIALIZE(1^κ)	**Procedure** CHALLENGE	**Procedure** FINALIZE(s')
$(ek, td) \xleftarrow{\$} GK(1^\kappa)$	$(s,t) \xleftarrow{\$} \{0,1\}^{\ell+k_1} \times \{0,1\}^{k_0}$	Return $(s \overset{?}{=} s')$
Return ek	$y := F(ek, (s,t))$	
	Return y	

Fig. 8. PD-OW$_{\mathcal{T}}$ game

4.2 Optimal Asymmetric Encryption Padding (OAEP)

Let $\mathcal{T} = (GK, F, F^{-1})$ be a trapdoor permutation. The OAEP encryption scheme is defined as follows.

- The key generation $\mathsf{Gen}(1^\kappa)$ computes a key pair $(ek, td) \leftarrow GK(1^\kappa)$ for the trapdoor permutation. It defines two hash functions

$$G : \{0,1\}^{k_0} \to \{0,1\}^{\ell+k_1} \text{ and } H : \{0,1\}^{\ell+k_1} \to \{0,1\}^{k_0}$$

and outputs $sk = td$ and $pk = (ek, G, H)$.
- To encrypt a message $m \in \{0,1\}^\ell$, the sender draws a random value $r \xleftarrow{\$} \{0,1\}^{k_0}$. Then it computes

$$s = m\|0^{k_1} \oplus G(r) \qquad t = r \oplus H(s).$$

The ciphertext is $C = F(ek, (s,t)) = f_{ek}(s,t)$.
- To decrypt a ciphertext C, the decryption algorithm $\mathsf{Dec}_{sk}(c)$ uses $sk = td$ to apply the inverse permutation to c, and obtains $(s,t) = F^{-1}(td, c)$. Then it computes $r = t \oplus H(s)$ and $\mu = s \oplus G(r)$, and parses $\mu \in \{0,1\}^{\ell+k_1}$ as $\mu = m\|\rho$ with $m \in \{0,1\}^\ell$ and $\rho \in \{0,1\}^{k_1}$. If $\rho = 0^{k_1}$, then the decryption algorithm outputs m. Otherwise $\perp$ is returned.

The OAEP padding process is illustrated in Figure 9.

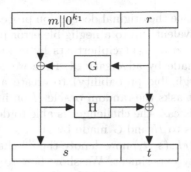

Fig. 9. The OAEP padding process

4.3 Security of OAEP against SO-CCA Attacks

In this section we will analyze the security of the OAEP scheme. We will prove that OAEP is SIM-SO-CCA-secure in the random oracle model [7], assuming the partial-domain onewayness of the trapdoor permutation $\mathcal{T}$. Note that a proof in the random oracle model is the strongest result we can hope for, since SIM-SO-CCA-security implies INDCCA security, and it is known [31] that OAEP can not be proven INDCCA secure without random oracles.

Theorem 9. *Let* OAEP *be the scheme described in Section 4.2 and* $\mathcal{T} = (GK, F, F^{-1})$ *be a trapdoor permutation. Then* OAEP *is* SIM-SO-CCA *secure in the random oracle model (where both hash functions* G *and* H *are modeled as random oracles). In particular, for every PPT relation* $\mathcal{R}$*, every adversary* $\mathcal{A}$ *run in the* REAL-SIM-SO-CCA$_{\mathrm{OAEP}}$ *game that issues at most* q_h *queries to* H*,* q_g *queries to* G*,* q_d *decryption queries, and obtains* n *ciphertexts, there exists a simulator* $\mathcal{S}$ *and an adversary* $\mathcal{B}$ *in the* PD-OW$_{\mathcal{T}}$ *experiment such that*

$$\mathbf{Adv}_{\mathrm{OAEP}}^{\mathrm{SIM\text{-}SO\text{-}CCA}}(\mathcal{A}, \mathcal{S}, \mathcal{R}, n, \kappa) \leq \delta$$

where

$$\delta = q_d \cdot \left(2^{-k_1} + q_g \cdot 2^{-k_0}\right) + n(q_g + n) \cdot 2^{-k_0} + nq_h \cdot \mathrm{Adv}_{\mathrm{pd}}^{\mathcal{T}}(\mathcal{B}, \kappa) + nq_g \cdot 2^{-\ell - k_1}.$$

Intuition for the proof of Theorem 9. We prove the theorem in a sequence of games, starting with the REAL-SIM-SO-CCA$_{\mathrm{OAEP}}$ experiment. From game to game we gradually modify the challenger, until we end up in a game where the challenger can act as a simulator in the IDEAL-SIM-SO-CCA$_{\mathrm{OAEP}}$ experiment. Our goal is to modify the challenger such that in the final game it does not need to know message m_i before the adversary asks OPEN(i). To this end, we have to describe how the challenger is able to create "non-committing" ciphertexts $c_1, \ldots, c_n$ in the ENC-procedure, which can then be opened to any message m_i when $\mathcal{A}$ issues an OPEN(i)-query.

In a first step, we replace the original decryption procedure that uses the real trapdoor td with an equivalent (up to a negligible error probability) decryption procedure, which is able to decrypt ciphertexts by examining the sequence of random oracle queries made by adversary $\mathcal{A}$. Here we use that $\mathcal{A}$ is not able (except for some non-negligible probability) to create a new valid ciphertext $c = F(ek, (s, t))$, unless it asks the random oracle H on input s and G on input $H(s) \oplus t$. However, in this case the challenger is able to decrypt c by exhaustive search through all queries to H and G made by $\mathcal{A}$.

For $i \in [n]$ let $c_i = F(ek, (s_i, t_i)$ now denote the ith challenge ciphertext that $\mathcal{A}$ receives in the security experiment. We show how to construct an attacker against the partial-domain one-wayness of $\mathcal{T}$, which is successful if the adversary $\mathcal{A}$ ever asks $H(s_i)$ before $\text{OPEN}(i)$ for any $i \in [n]$. Thus, assuming that $\mathcal{T}$ is secure in the sense of partial-domain one-wayness, it will never happen that $\mathcal{A}$ asks $H(s_i)$ before $\text{OPEN}(i)$, except for some negligible probability.

Finally, we conclude with the observation that from $\mathcal{A}$'s point of view all values of $H(s_i)$ remain equally likely until $\text{OPEN}(i)$ is asked, which implies also that it is very unlikely that $\mathcal{A}$ ever asks $G(t_i \oplus H(s_i))$ before $\text{OPEN}(i)$. This in turn means that the challenger does not have to commit to a particular value of $G(t_i \oplus H(s_i))$, and thus not to a particular message $m_i || 0^{k_1} = s_i \oplus G(t_i \oplus H(s_i))$, before $\text{OPEN}(i)$ is asked.

Proof of Theorem 9. The proof proceeds in a *sequence of games*, following [9,43], where Game 0 corresponds to the REAL-SIM-SO-CCA$_{\text{OAEP}}^{\mathcal{A}}$-experiment with adversary $\mathcal{A}$ and a challenger, called $\mathcal{C}_0$. From game to game, we gradually modify the challenger, until we obtain a challenger which is able to act as a simulator in the IDEAL-SIM-SO-CCA$_{\text{OAEP}}^{\mathcal{S}}$ experiment.

Let us first fix some notation. We denote with q_g the number of queries issued by $\mathcal{A}$ to random oracle G, with q_h the number of queries to H, and with q_d the number of decryption queries. For $i \in [n]$ we will denote with c_i the ith component of the challenge ciphertext vector $(c_i)_{i \in [n]}$, and we write c_i as $c_i = f_{ek}(s_i, t_i)$.

Game 0. Challenger $\mathcal{C}_0$ executes the REAL-SIM-SO-CCA experiment with attacker $\mathcal{A}$ by implementing the procedures described in Figure 10. Note that $\mathcal{C}_0$ also implements procedures to simulate the random oracles G and H. To this end, it maintains four lists

$$L_G \subseteq \{0,1\}^{k_0} \times \{0,1\}^{\ell + k_1} \qquad L_H \subseteq \{0,1\}^{\ell + k_1} \times \{0,1\}^{k_0}$$

$$L_G^{\mathcal{A}} \subseteq \{0,1\}^{k_0} \qquad\qquad L_H^{\mathcal{A}} \subseteq \{0,1\}^{\ell + k_1}$$

which are initialized to the empty set in the INITIALIZE procedure.

To simulate the random oracle G, the challenger uses the *internal* procedure G_{int}, which uses list L_G to ensure consistency of random oracle responses. The adversary does not have direct access to procedure G_{int}, but only via procedure G, which stores all values r queried by $\mathcal{A}$ in an additional list $L_G^{\mathcal{A}}$. This allows us to keep track of all values queried by $\mathcal{A}$. Random oracle H is implemented similarly, with procedures H_{int} and H, using list s L_H and $L_H^{\mathcal{A}}$.

Procedure INITIALIZE	**Internal procedure** $H_{int}(s)$	**Internal procedure** $G_{int}(r)$
$(ek, td) \xleftarrow{\$} GK(1^\kappa)$	If $(s, h_s) \notin L_H$	if $(r, h_r) \notin L_G$
Return ek	$\quad h_s \xleftarrow{\$} \{0,1\}^{k_0}$	$\quad h_r \xleftarrow{\$} \{0,1\}^{\ell+k_1}$
	$\quad L_H := L_H \cup (s, h_s)$	$\quad L_G := L_G \cup (r, h_r)$
Procedure ENC($\mathfrak{D}$)	Return h_s	Return h_r
$(m_i)_{i\in[n]} \leftarrow \mathfrak{D}$		
for $i \in [n]$:	**Procedure** $H(s)$	**Procedure** $G(r)$
$\quad r_i \xleftarrow{\$} \{0,1\}^{k_0}$	$L_H^A := L_H^A \cup \{s\}$	$L_G^A := L_G^A \cup \{r\}$
$\quad s_i := m \|0^{k_1} \oplus G_{int}(r_i)$	Return $H_{int}(s)$	Return $G_{int}(r)$
$\quad t_i := r_i \oplus H_{int}(s_i)$		
$\quad c_i := F(ek, (s_i, t_i))$	**Procedure** DEC(c)	**Procedure** FINALIZE(out)
Return $(c_i)_{i\in[n]}$	$(s, t) := F^{-1}(td, c)$	Return
	$r := t \oplus H_{int}(s)$	$\quad \mathcal{R}((m_i)_{i\in[n]}, \mathfrak{D}, \mathcal{I}, out)$
Procedure OPEN(i)	$m\|\rho := s \oplus G_{int}(r)$	
$\mathcal{I} := \mathcal{I} \cup \{i\}$	if $\rho = 0^{k_1}$	
Return (m_i, r_i)	$\quad$ Return m	
	else	
	$\quad$ Return $\perp$	

Fig. 10. Procedures of Game 0

By definition we have

$$\mathbf{Adv}(\text{REAL-SIM-SO-CCA}^A_{\text{OAEP}}, G_0^A) = 0.$$

In the following games we will replace C_0 with challenger C_i in Game i. In the last game, we replace the challenger with a simulator.

Procedure DEC$_1$(c)	**Procedure** ENC$_2$($\mathfrak{D}$)
for $(r, h_r, s, h_s) \in L_G \times L_H$:	$(m_i)_{i\in[n]} \leftarrow \mathfrak{D}$
$\quad$ if $\begin{pmatrix} c = F(ek, (s, r \oplus h_s)) \\ \wedge\ s \oplus h_r = m\|0^{k_1} \end{pmatrix}$	for $i \in [n]$:
	$\quad s_i \xleftarrow{\$} \{0,1\}^{\ell+k_1}, t_i \xleftarrow{\$} \{0,1\}^{k_0}$
$\quad\quad$ Return m	$\quad c_i := F(ek, (s_i, t_i))$
Return $\perp$	$\quad r_i := H(s_i) \oplus t_i$
	$\quad$ if $r_i \in L_G$
	$\quad\quad$ ABORTG $:= true$
	$\quad h_{r_i} := s_i \oplus m_i\|0^{k_1}$
	$\quad L_G := L_G \cup \{(r_i, h_{r_i})\}$
	Return $(c_i)_{i\in[n]}$

Fig. 11. Replacement procedures DEC$_1$ and ENC$_2$

Game 1. In this game, C_1 proceeds exactly as C_0, except that instead of implementing procedure DEC, it uses procedure DEC$_1$ from Figure 11 to respond to decryption-queries. Note that procedure DEC$_1$ does not require the trapdoor td to perform decryption.

Claim 1. It holds that $\mathbf{Adv}(G_0^A, G_1^A) \leq q_d \cdot \left(2^{-k_1} + q_g \cdot 2^{-k_0}\right)$.

Proof. Game 1 is perfectly indistinguishable from Game 0, unless $\mathcal{A}$ makes a decryption query with ciphertext c, such that $\mathrm{DEC}(c) \neq \mathrm{DEC}_1(c)$. Note that this can only hold if $\mathcal{A}$ queries a ciphertext c with $(s, t) = F^{-1}(td, c)$, such that

$$(s, \cdot) \notin L_H \quad \text{or} \quad (t \oplus H(s), \cdot) \notin L_G$$

where $\cdot$ is any value, but it holds that $G(t \oplus H(s)) \oplus s = m\|\rho$ with $\rho = 0^{k_1}$.

Consider a single chosen-ciphertext $c = F(ek, (s, t))$. Suppose that $(s, \cdot) \notin L_H$. In this case $H(s)$ is uniform and independent from $\mathcal{A}$'s view. The probability that there exists $(r, \cdot) \in L_G$ such that $r = H(s) \oplus t$ is therefore at most $q_g \cdot 2^{-k_0}$, since we assumed that the adversary issues at most q_g queries to G.

If $(r, \cdot) \notin L_G$ then $G(r)$ is uniform and independent from $\mathcal{A}$'s view, thus the probability that $G(r) \oplus s = m\|0^{k_1}$ has the correct syntax is at most 2^{-k_1}.

Since the adversary issues at most q_d chosen-ciphertext queries, we have $\mathbf{Adv}(\mathsf{G}_0^{\mathcal{A}}, \mathsf{G}_1^{\mathcal{A}}) \leq q_d \cdot \left(2^{-k_1} + q_g \cdot 2^{-k_0}\right)$.

Game 2. Challenger $\mathcal{C}_2$ proceeds exactly like $\mathcal{C}_1$, except that it implements procedure ENC_2 from Figure 11 instead of ENC. Note that this procedure first samples (s_i, t_i) uniformly random, then computes $c_i = F(ek, (s_i, t_i))$, and finally programs the random oracle G such that c_i decrypts to m_i.

Claim 2. It holds that $\mathbf{Adv}(\mathsf{G}_1^{\mathcal{A}}, \mathsf{G}_2^{\mathcal{A}}) \leq n(q_g + n) \cdot 2^{-k_0}$.

Proof. Note that procedure ENC_2 first defines $r_i := H(s_i) \oplus t_i$ for uniformly random $t_i \xleftarrow{\$} \{0, 1\}^{k_0}$. Thus, r_i is distributed uniformly over $\{0, 1\}^{k_0}$, exactly as in Game 1. Now suppose that $r_i \notin L_G$, thus ENC_2 does not terminate. In this case the hash function G is programmed such that $G(r_i) = h_{r_i} = s_i \oplus m_i\|0^{k_1}$. Since s_i is uniformly distributed, so is $G(r_i)$, exactly as in Game 1. Thus, ENC_2 simulates procedure ENC from Game 1 perfectly, provided that it does not terminate.

Note that the procedure terminates only if $r_i \in L_G$. Since all values $r_1, \ldots, r_n$ are distributed uniformly, because the s_i-values are uniformly random, this happens with probability at most $n(q_g + n) \cdot 2^{-k_0}$.

Procedure OPEN(i)	Procedure OPEN(i)
$\mathcal{I} := \mathcal{I} \cup \{i\}$	$\mathcal{I} := \mathcal{I} \cup \{i\}$
if $s_i \in L_H^{\mathcal{A}}$	if $s_i \in L_H^{\mathcal{A}}$
$\quad$ ABORTS $:= true$	$\quad$ ABORTS $:= true$
Return (m_i, r_i)	if $r_i \in L_G^{\mathcal{A}}$
	$\quad$ ABORTR $:= true$
	Return (m_i, r_i)

Fig. 12. Modified OPEN-procedures of Games 3 (left) and 4 (right)

Game 3. We add an abort condition to the OPEN-procedure (see the left-hand side of Figure 12). Challenger $\mathcal{C}_3$ proceeds exactly like $\mathcal{C}_2$, except that it raises event ABORTS and terminates, if $\mathcal{A}$ ever queried s_i to H for some $i \in [n]$ *before* querying OPEN(i).

Note that in Game 3, the attacker never evaluates H on input s_i for any $i \notin \mathcal{I}$, or the game is aborted.

Claim 3. It holds that $\mathbf{Adv}(\mathsf{G}_2^{\mathcal{A}}, \mathsf{G}_3^{\mathcal{A}}) \leq n \cdot q_h \cdot \mathsf{Adv}_{\mathsf{pd}}^{\mathcal{T}}(\mathcal{B}, \kappa)$.

Proof. Game 3 proceeds identically to Game 2, until event ABORTS is raised. Thus we have

$$\mathbf{Adv}(\mathsf{G}_2^{\mathcal{A}}, \mathsf{G}_3^{\mathcal{A}}) \leq \Pr[\text{ABORTS}]$$

We construct an adversary $\mathcal{B}$ against the partial-domain onewayness of $\mathcal{T}$. $\mathcal{B}$ receives as input ek and $y = f_{ek}(s, t)$ for uniformly random $(s, t) \xleftarrow{\$} \{0,1\}^{\ell + k_1} \times \{0,1\}^{k_0}$. It proceeds exactly like $\mathcal{C}_3$, except for the following. At the beginning of the game it sets $pk := ek$ and guesses two indices $j \xleftarrow{\$} [n]$ and $q \xleftarrow{\$} [q_h]$ uniformly random, and sets $c_j := y$. Note that c_j is correctly distributed (cf. the changes introduced in Game 2). When $\mathcal{A}$ makes its qth query s^* to H, then $\mathcal{B}$ returns s^* and terminates.

Assume that ABORTS happens. Then, at some point in the game, $\mathcal{A}$ makes the *first* query s' to H such that $s' = s_i$ is a partial-domain preimage of some c_i. With probability $1/q_h$ it holds that $s^* = s_i$. Moreover, with probability $1/n$ we have $i = j$. In this case $\mathcal{B}$ obtains the partial preimage $s = s_j$ of $y = c_j$. Thus, $\mathcal{B}$ succeeds, if ABORTS happens and if it has guessed $j \in [n]$ and $q \in [q_h]$ correctly. This happens with probability $\Pr[\text{ABORTS}]/(n \cdot q_h)$, which implies that

$$\Pr[\text{ABORTS}] \leq n \cdot q_h \cdot \mathsf{Adv}_{\mathsf{pd}}^{\mathcal{T}}(\mathcal{B}, \kappa).$$

Game 4. We add another abort condition to the Finalize-procedure (see the right-hand side of Figure 12). Challenger $\mathcal{C}_4$ raises event ABORTR and terminates, if $\mathcal{A}$ ever queries r_i to $G_{\mathcal{A}}$ for some $i \in [n]$, before querying OPEN(i). Otherwise it proceeds like $\mathcal{C}_3$.

Claim 4. It holds that $\mathbf{Adv}(\mathsf{G}_3^{\mathcal{A}}, \mathsf{G}_4^{\mathcal{A}}) \leq n \cdot q_g \cdot 2^{-\ell - k_1}$.

Proof. Note that $\mathcal{A}$ never queries s_i before querying OPEN(i) (or the game is aborted), due to the changes introduced in Game 3. Thus, for all $i \notin \mathcal{I}$, $H(s_i)$ is uniformly random and independent of $\mathcal{A}$'s view. Therefore, all $r_i = t_i \oplus H(s_i)$ are uniformly random and independent of $\mathcal{A}$'s view. Since $\mathcal{A}$ issues at most q_g queries to G, and we have $1 \leq i \leq n$, this implies $\mathbf{Adv}(\mathsf{G}_3^{\mathcal{A}}, \mathsf{G}_4^{\mathcal{A}}) \leq n \cdot q_g \cdot 2^{-\ell - k_1}$.

Game 5. Note that the attacker in Game 4 never issues a query $G(r_i)$ before asking OPEN(i), as otherwise the game is aborted. Thus, the challenger does not have to define the hash value $G(r_i)$ before OPEN(i) is asked. Therefore we can move the definition of $G(r_i)$ from the ENC$_2$-procedure to the OPEN-procedure.

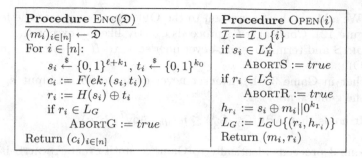

Fig. 13. New procedures for Game 5

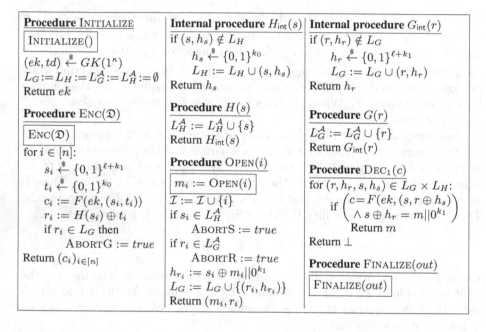

Fig. 14. Procedures used by the simulator to implement the REAL-SIM-SO-CCA$^A_{\text{OAEP}}$ experiment. Instructions in boxes correspond to calls to the IDEAL-SIM-SO-CCA$^S_{\text{OAEP}}$-experiment made by the simulator.

Therefore we replace the procedures ENC_2 and OPEN from Game 4 with procedures ENC and OPEN described in Figure 13. Note that the only difference is that for each $i \in [n]$ the hash value $G(r_i)$ is not defined in the ENC-procedure, but in the OPEN procedure. Moreover, this modification is completely oblivious to $\mathcal{A}$, which implies

$$\mathbf{Adv}(\mathsf{G}_4^A, \mathsf{G}_5^A) = 0.$$

Game 6. Note that in Game 5 the encryption procedure samples a message vector $(m_i)_{i \in [n]}$, but the messages are only used in the OPEN-procedure. This allows us to construct a simulator, whose procedures are described in Figure 14. Note that the view of $\mathcal{A}$ when interacting with the simulator is *identical* to its view when interacting with challenger $\mathcal{C}_5$, which implies

$$\mathbf{Adv}(\mathsf{G}_5^{\mathcal{A}}, \mathsf{G}_6^{\mathcal{A}}) = 0$$

Acknowledgments. We thank Zhengan Huang and Shengli Liu for their valuable comments. Felix Heuer and Eike Kiltz were (partially) funded by a Sofja Kovalevskaja Award of the Alexander von Humboldt Foundation and the German Federal Ministry for Education and Research. Felix Heuer was also partially funded by the German Israeli Foundation. Sven Schäge is supported by Ubicrypt, the research training group 1817/1 funded by the German Research Foundation (DFG). Part of this work was done while he was employed at University College London and supported by EPSRC grant EP/J009520/1.

References

1. Abdalla, M., Bellare, M., Rogaway, P.: The oracle Diffie-Hellman assumptions and an analysis of DHIES. In: Naccache [33], pp. 143–158
2. Backes, M., Dürmuth, M., Unruh, D.: OAEP is secure under key-dependent messages. In: Pieprzyk, J. (ed.) ASIACRYPT 2008. LNCS, vol. 5350, pp. 506–523. Springer, Heidelberg (2008)
3. Beaver, D.: Plug and play encryption. In: Kaliski Jr., [29], pp. 75–89
4. Beaver, D., Haber, S.: Cryptographic protocols provably secure against dynamic adversaries. In: Rueppel, R.A. (ed.) EUROCRYPT 1992. LNCS, vol. 658, pp. 307–323. Springer, Heidelberg (1993)
5. Bellare, M., Dowsley, R., Waters, B., Yilek, S.: Standard security does not imply security against selective-opening. In: Pointcheval, Johansson [37], pp. 645–662
6. Bellare, M., Hofheinz, D., Yilek, S.: Possibility and impossibility results for encryption and commitment secure under selective opening. In: Joux [28], pp. 1–35
7. Bellare, M., Rogaway, P.: Random oracles are practical: a paradigm for designing efficient protocols. In: Ashby, V. (ed.) ACM CCS 1993, pp. 62–73. ACM Press, Fairfax (1993)
8. Bellare, M., Rogaway, P.: Optimal asymmetric encryption. In: De Santis, A. (ed.) EUROCRYPT 1994. LNCS, vol. 950, pp. 92–111. Springer, Heidelberg (1995)
9. Bellare, M., Rogaway, P.: The security of triple encryption and a framework for code-based game-playing proofs. In: Vaudenay, S. (ed.) EUROCRYPT 2006. LNCS, vol. 4004, pp. 409–426. Springer, Heidelberg (2006)
10. Bellare, M., Waters, B., Yilek, S.: Identity-Based encryption secure against selective opening attack. In: Ishai, Y. (ed.) TCC 2011. LNCS, vol. 6597, pp. 235–252. Springer, Heidelberg (2011)
11. Böhl, F., Hofheinz, D., Kraschewski, D.: On definitions of selective opening security. In: Fischlin, M., Buchmann, J., Manulis, M. (eds.) PKC 2012. LNCS, vol. 7293, pp. 522–539. Springer, Heidelberg (2012)
12. Boldyreva, A., Fischlin, M.: On the security of OAEP. In: Lai, X., Chen, K. (eds.) ASIACRYPT 2006. LNCS, vol. 4284, pp. 210–225. Springer, Heidelberg (2006)
13. Brown, D.R.L.: What hashes make RSA-OAEP secure? Cryptology ePrint Archive, Report 2006/223 (2006). http://eprint.iacr.org/

14. Canetti, R., Dwork, C., Naor, M., Ostrovsky, R.: Deniable encryption. In: Kaliski Jr. [29], pp. 90–104
15. Canetti, R., Feige, U., Goldreich, O., Naor, M.: Adaptively secure multi-party computation. In: 28th ACM STOC, pp. 639–648. ACM Press, Philadephia (1996)
16. Canetti, R., Halevi, S., Katz, J.: Adaptively-Secure, non-interactive public-key encryption. In: Kilian, J. (ed.) TCC 2005. LNCS, vol. 3378, pp. 150–168. Springer, Heidelberg (2005)
17. Clancy, T., Arbaugh, W.: Extensible Authentication Protocol (EAP) Password Authenticated Exchange. RFC 4746 (Informational) (November 2006)
18. Cramer, R., Shoup, V.: Design and analysis of practical public-key encryption schemes secure against adaptive chosen ciphertext attack. SIAM J. Comput. **33**(1), 167–226 (2003)
19. Dierks, T., Rescorla, E.: The Transport Layer Security (TLS) Protocol Version 1.2. RFC 5246 (Proposed Standard). Updated by RFCs 5746, 5878, 6176 (August 2008)
20. Fehr, S., Hofheinz, D., Kiltz, E., Wee, H.: Encryption schemes secure against chosen-ciphertext selective opening attacks. In: Gilbert, H. (ed.) EUROCRYPT 2010. LNCS, vol. 6110, pp. 381–402. Springer, Heidelberg (2010)
21. Fujisaki, E.: All-but-many encryptions: A new framework for fully-equipped UC commitments. Cryptology ePrint Archive, Report 2012/379. http://eprint.iacr.org/ (2012)
22. Fujisaki, E., Okamoto, T., Pointcheval, D., Stern, J.: RSA-OAEP is secure under the RSA assumption. In: Kilian, J. (ed.) CRYPTO 2001. LNCS, vol. 2139, pp. 260–274. Springer, Heidelberg (2001)
23. Harris, B.: RSA Key Exchange for the Secure Shell (SSH) Transport Layer Protocol. RFC 4432 (Proposed Standard) (March 2006)
24. Hemenway, B., Libert, B., Ostrovsky, R., Vergnaud, D.: Lossy encryption: constructions from general assumptions and efficient selective opening chosen ciphertext security. In: Lee, D.H., Wang, X. (eds.) ASIACRYPT 2011. LNCS, vol. 7073, pp. 70–88. Springer, Heidelberg (2011)
25. Hofheinz, D.:. All-but-many lossy trapdoor functions. In: Pointcheval, Johansson [37], pp. 209–227
26. Hofheinz, D., Rupp, A.: Standard versus selective opening security: separation and equivalence results. In: Lindell, Y. (ed.) TCC 2014. LNCS, vol. 8349, pp. 591–615. Springer, Heidelberg (2014)
27. Housley, R.: Use of the RSAES-OAEP Key Transport Algorithm in Cryptographic Message Syntax (CMS). RFC 3560 (Proposed Standard) (July 2003)
28. Joux, A. (ed.): EUROCRYPT 2009. LNCS, vol. 5479. Springer, Heidelberg (2009)
29. Kaliski Jr., B.S. (ed.): CRYPTO 1997. LNCS, vol. 1294. Springer, Heidelberg (1997)
30. Kiltz, E., O'Neill, A., Smith, A.: Instantiability of RSA-OAEP under chosen-plaintext attack. In: Rabin, T. (ed.) CRYPTO 2010. LNCS, vol. 6223, pp. 295–313. Springer, Heidelberg (2010)
31. Kiltz, E., Pietrzak, K.: On the security of padding-based encryption schemes - or - why we cannot prove OAEP secure in the standard model. In: Joux [28], pp. 389–406
32. Lai, J., Deng, R.H., Liu, S., Weng, J., Zhao, Y.: Identity-Based encryption secure against selective opening chosen-ciphertext attack. In: Nguyen, P.Q., Oswald, E. (eds.) EUROCRYPT 2014. LNCS, vol. 8441, pp. 77–92. Springer, Heidelberg (2014)

33. Naccache, D. (ed.): CT-RSA 2001. LNCS, vol. 2020. Springer, Heidelberg (2001)
34. Nadeau, T., Srinivasan, C., Farrel, A.: Multiprotocol Label Switching (MPLS) Management Overview. RFC 4221 (Informational) (November 2005)
35. Okamoto, T., Pointcheval, D.: REACT: Rapid Enhanced-security Asymmetric Cryptosystem Transform. In: Naccache [33], pp. 159–175
36. Peikert, C., Waters, B.: Lossy trapdoor functions and their applications. In: Ladner, R.E., Dwork, C. (eds.) 40th ACM STOC, pp. 187–196. ACM Press, Victoria (2008)
37. Pointcheval, D., Johansson, T. (eds.): EUROCRYPT 2012. LNCS, vol. 7237. Springer, Heidelberg (2012)
38. Raeburn, K.: Encryption and Checksum Specifications for Kerberos 5. RFC 3961 (Proposed Standard)(February 2005)
39. Ramsdell, B., Turner, S.: Secure/Multipurpose Internet Mail Extensions (S/MIME) Version 3.2 Message Specification. RFC 5751 (Proposed Standard) (January 2010)
40. Rescorla, E.: Preventing the Million Message Attack on Cryptographic Message Syntax. RFC 3218 (Informational) (January 2002)
41. Shoup, V.: OAEP reconsidered. Journal of Cryptology 15(4), 223–249 (2002)
42. Shoup, V.: ISO 18033-2: An emerging standard for public-key encryption. Final Committee Draft (December 2004). http://shoup.net/iso/std6.pdf
43. Shoup, V.: Sequences of games: a tool for taming complexity in security proofs 13166 received (November 30, 2004). shoup@cs.nyu.edu (last revised January 18, 2006)
44. Steinfeld, R., Baek, J., Zheng, Y.: On the necessity of strong assumptions for the security of a class of asymmetric encryption schemes. In: Batten, L.M., Seberry, J. (eds.) ACISP 2002. LNCS, vol. 2384, pp. 241–256. Springer, Heidelberg (2002)

How Secure is Deterministic Encryption?

Mihir Bellare[1]([✉]), Rafael Dowsley[2], and Sriram Keelveedhi[1,2]

[1] Department of Computer Science and Engineering,
University of California San Diego, San Diego, USA
`mihir@eng.ucsd.edu`
[2] Institute of Theoretical Informatics, Karlsruhe Institute of Technology,
Karlsruhe, Germany

Abstract. This paper presents three curious findings about deterministic public-key encryption (D-PKE) that further our understanding of its security, in particular because of the contrast with standard, randomized public-key encryption (R-PKE):

- It would appear to be a triviality, for any primitive, that security in the standard model implies security in the random-oracle model, and it is certainly true, and easily proven, for R-PKE. For D-PKE it is not clear and depends on details of the definition. In particular we can show it in the non-uniform case but not in the uniform case.
- The power of selective-opening attacks (SOA) comes from an adversary's ability, upon corrupting a sender, to learn not just the message but also the coins used for encryption. For R-PKE, security is achievable. For D-PKE, where there are no coins, one's first impression may be that SOAs are vacuous and security should be easily achievable. We show instead that SOA-security is impossible, meaning no D-PKE scheme can achieve it.
- For R-PKE, single-user security implies multi-user security, but we show that there are D-PKE schemes secure for a single user and insecure with two users.

1 Introduction

Public-key encryption (PKE) schemes are usually randomized, in order to achieve goals like IND-CPA [29]. BBO [5] introduced deterministic PKE (D-PKE), arguing that it offers practical benefits over randomized PKE (R-PKE) in certain applications. These include efficient search on encrypted databases [5] and resilience in the face of the low-quality randomness that pervades systems [6,41].[1]

BBO [5] provide a definition PRIV of "best possible" security for D-PKE, and ROM constructions achieving it. Equivalent, IND-style formulations appear in [10]. These definitions are unusual, and achieving them in the standard model

---

[1] Weak randomness leads to catastrophic failures in R-PKE including the ability to recover the plaintext from the ciphertext in schemes including GM, El Gamal and Rabin-SAEP [36].

© International Association for Cryptologic Research 2015
J. Katz (Ed.): PKC 2015, LNCS 9020, pp. 52–73, 2015.
DOI: 10.1007/978-3-662-46447-2_3

(SM) is challenging. Emerging as a practically-motivated notion of theoretical depth and interest, D-PKE has attracted significant foundational work as researchers aim to understand the properties and achievability of the basic definitions and variants [10,11,19,20,28,33,39]. We continue this line of work.

OUR WORK. This paper shows that determinism impacts security in beyond-obvious ways. Specifically, we consider three questions. The first is whether security in the standard model implies security in the ROM. The second is whether D-PKE is secure under selective-opening attack. The last is whether single-user security implies multi-user security. Fig. 1 summarizes our findings, which are discussed in more depth below. On the practical side, our work indicates that care must be taken in the use of D-PKE. On the theoretical side it indicates further foundational subtleties for D-PKE, and, more broadly, for multi-stage security definitions, in the wake of those already indicated in [40,42].

BACKGROUND. In R-PKE, the encryption algorithm Enc takes the public (encryption) key pk, message m and coins r to return a ciphertext $c = \mathsf{Enc}(pk, m; r)$. The basic notion of security is IND-CPA [7,29]. An adversary is a pair (A_1, A_2) of PT algorithms. The game picks keys (pk, sk) and a challenge bit b. We run A_1 on input pk to get a pair (m_0, m_1) of messages and state information st. The game picks random coins r, computes challenge ciphertext $c = \mathsf{Enc}(pk, m_b; r)$ and runs A_2 on c, st to get a bit b'. Security requires that $2\Pr[b = b'] - 1$ is negligible.

In D-PKE [5], there are no coins, Enc taking pk, m to return $c = \mathsf{Enc}(pk, m)$. Such a scheme cannot achieve IND-CPA. The notion we use is IND [10], an indistinguishability variant of the PRIV notion of [5]. An adversary is a pair (A_1, A_2) of PT algorithms. The game picks keys (pk, sk) and a challenge bit b. We run A_1 (it does not get pk) to get a pair $(\mathbf{m}_0, \mathbf{m}_1)$ of vectors of messages (but no state information). The game computes challenge ciphertext vector $\mathbf{c} = \mathsf{Enc}(pk, \mathbf{m}_b)$, encryption being component-wise, and runs A_2 on $\mathbf{c}, pk$ to get a bit b'. Security requires that $2\Pr[b = b'] - 1$ is negligible. Important restrictions are that (1) A_1 does not get the public key (2) each individual message in the vectors $\mathbf{m}_0, \mathbf{m}_1$ has high min-entropy, meaning is statistically unpredictable, and (3) A_1, A_2 do not communicate directly, meaning no state information is passed from A_1 to A_2. These restrictions are necessary, for without them security is not achievable.

In the ROM [14], both stages of the adversary have access to the random oracle RO, whether for R-PKE or D-PKE. In the latter case, the min-entropy condition is required to hold even given (conditioned on) the RO.

DOES SM-SECURITY IMPLY ROM-SECURITY? That security in the standard model (SM) implies security in the ROM appears to be a triviality or tautology, true for any primitive. To be specific, suppose we have a standard-model R-PKE scheme, meaning the algorithms of the scheme make no calls to RO. Suppose it is IND-CPA in the SM. Then it is IND-CPA in the ROM. Intuitively this seems clear because if the scheme does not use the RO, then giving the adversary access to RO cannot violate security. If we want to prove the claim formally, we could do so by reduction. Given a ROM adversary (A_1, A_2), we build SM adversary

(B_1, B_2) with the same advantage by just having B_1 and B_2 simulate the RO. Thus, B_1 maintains a table H, and runs A_1. When the latter makes a query $RO(x)$, adversary B_1 checks if $H[x]$ is defined, and, if not, picks it at random, in either case returning $H[x]$ to A_1 as the answer. When A_1 halts with output (m_0, m_1) and state st_A, adversary B_1 halts with output (m_0, m_1) and state st_B, where the latter consists of st_A plus the populated (defined) part of table H, which has polynomial size. Now B_2, given c, st_B, runs $A_2(c, \mathsf{st}_A)$, continuing to respond to A_2's oracle queries via table H, suitably augmenting it as necessary for new queries. Eventually B_2 returns whatever A_2 returns. It is clear that SM adversary (B_1, B_2) simulates ROM adversary (A_1, A_2) perfectly and has the same advantage.

The claim that SM security implies ROM security, and the simulation argument above to establish it, hardly seem specific to R-PKE. It would appear to be true that SM security trivially implies ROM security for any primitive via such an argument.

But for D-PKE, the argument fails, and whether SM security implies ROM security is not clear. To see why, let us try to mimic the above argument for D-PKE. We can design B_1, simulating A_1, in the same way. The difficulty is that B_1 cannot pass its partial table H to B_2, for no state information is allowed to flow from B_1 to B_2. This leaves B_2 stuck. It could simulate a new RO for A_2, but in the real ROM game, A_1, A_2 see the same RO, not different ones. The question this raises is whether the difficulty is inherent, meaning SM security does not imply ROM security, or whether some alternative argument can show the implication.

We find that the answer depends on details of the definition. Let $\mathrm{IND_u}, \mathrm{IND_{nu}}$ denote, respectively, the uniform and non-uniform renditions of IND. That is, in the first case, the adversaries are TMs while in the second they are families of circuits. We show that SM security implies ROM security for $\mathrm{IND_{nu}}$. Our proof works by starting with ROM adversaries $\mathsf{A_1}, \mathsf{A_2}$, hardwiring a $q(\cdot)$-wise independent hash function h into the circuits of B_1, B_2, and having these circuits use h to simulate RO for A_1, A_2, with $q(\cdot)$ depending on the number of oracle queries of A_1 and A_2. We show that there exists a "good" choice of h under which the simulation is correct. However, in the case of $\mathrm{IND_u}$, we were not able to settle the question. That is, we see no way to prove that SM security implies ROM security (it is not clear how to perform a simulation, and it is not clear there is any other approach to the proof) but nor can we imagine a counterexample (it would need to exploit the fact that the scheme is secure for uniform adversaries but not for non-uniform ones, for otherwise the claim is true).

Intuitively, it is hard for us to imagine how a SM scheme can be insecure in the ROM, meaning how an adversary can exploit the RO when scheme algorithms do not even use it.[2] We found it curious that it was not obvious how to prove this and that it is not clear if it is even true in the uniform case.

---

[2] One might imagine the adversary gaining an advantage by having B_1 pick messages that depend on the RO in some clever way. The reason this does not appear to help the adversary is that each message is required to have high min-entropy even conditioned on the entire random oracle.

Primitive	SM $\Rightarrow$ ROM	SOA	SU $\Rightarrow$ MU
R-PKE	Yes	Yes	Yes
D-PKE	Sometimes	No	No

Fig. 1. Summary of our results: The first column indicates whether or not security in the standard model (SM) implies security in the ROM, the "sometimes" for D-PKE reflecting that we can show it in the non-uniform case but not in the uniform case. The second column indicates whether or not security against selective-opening attack (SOA) is achievable. The third column indicates whether or not single-user (SU) security implies multi-user (MU) security.

These findings show further subtleties for multi-stage security definitions following ones already discovered by [40, 42], making D-PKE a central test case in this subtle and surprising domain.

IS SOA-SECURE D-PKE ACHIEVABLE? In a selective opening attack (SOA) on a R-PKE scheme, a vector $\mathbf{m}$ of n messages is chosen from some distribution, a vector $\mathbf{r}$ of random and independent coins is chosen, and the adversary A is given the ciphertext vector $\mathbf{c} = \mathsf{Enc}(pk, \mathbf{m}; \mathbf{r})$. A responds with a subset I of $\{1, \ldots, n\}$. In the message-only version of the attack, it is returned $\langle \mathbf{m}[i] : i \in I \rangle$; in full SOA, it is returned both $\langle \mathbf{m}[i] : i \in I \rangle$ and $\langle \mathbf{r}[i] : i \in I \rangle$. In either case, to win, it has to compute some non-trivial information about $\langle \mathbf{m}[i] : i \notin I \rangle$. Security for the message-only version is implied by IND-CPA, as shown in [17], and is thus easily achievable. Security for full SOA is not implied by IND-CPA [9]. However, using lossy encryption [12,17,32,38], it is shown in [12,17] that there exist schemes that provide full SOA under standard assumptions, so full SOA security is achievable, under standard assumptions in the standard model. Subsequently, further schemes have been provided as well [27,30].

The question of security of D-PKE under SOA has not been considered before, and we initiate an investigation. A vector $\mathbf{m}$ of n messages is again chosen from some distribution, and the adversary A is given the ciphertext vector $\mathbf{c} = \mathsf{Enc}(pk, \mathbf{m})$. A responds with a subset I of $\{1, \ldots, n\}$, is returned $\langle \mathbf{m}[i] : i \in I \rangle$, and, to win, has to compute some non-trivial information about $\langle \mathbf{m}[i] : i \notin I \rangle$. We note that what we have defined is the message-only version. Naturally, there is no "full" SOA here, since there are no coins used, and thus none to expose.

The difficulty of achieving SOA-secure R-PKE lies in exposure of the coins. Since D-PKE has no coins, one's first impression may be that SOA-security for it would be like message-only SOA-security for R-PKE and thus easy to achieve. To the contrary, we show that SOA-secure D-PKE is impossible. That is, there is no D-PKE scheme that is SOA-secure. Given *any* D-PKE scheme, we give an attack violating SOA-security.

The contrast with R-PKE is two-fold. For the latter, SOA is easy in the message-only case, and, with exposure of coins, even if not easy, it is achievable. But for D-PKE, it is simply not achievable. The key element of our proof is to show that for any D-PKE scheme there is an algorithm that can impose and verify an association between a message and ciphertext that is unique with high probability, *even for dishonestly chosen public keys*. We combine this with the technique of BDWY [9] to obtain our impossibility result. We note that for R-PKE the BDWY technique did not show impossibility of (full) SOA for all R-PKE schemes, but for a subclass of them, while we are using the technique to rule out SOA-security for *all* D-PKE schemes.

The problem of SOA-security has been the subject of many works [2,3,12,16–18,21–24,26,27,30,31,34,37]. These have looked at R-PKE, commitment and IBE. We are the first to consider SOA for D-PKE.

DOES SU SECURITY IMPLY MU SECURITY? The basic IND-CPA notion for R-PKE [29] is a single-user (SU) setting, meaning there is only one public key in the game. In practice, many users, each with their own key pair, could encrypt messages, and these messages may be related. Security of R-PKE in the multi-user (MU) setting was defined in [1,4]. They showed that SU security implied MU security, meaning any R-PKE scheme that meets the usual SU IND-CPA notion is also MU secure.

It is natural to ask whether the same is true for D-PKE, namely whether SU security, in the form of IND, implies MU security. We define MU security for D-PKE and show that the answer to the question is "no." That is, we present a counter-example, namely a D-PKE scheme that we show meets the standard SU IND definition, but we give an attack showing that it fails to be MU-secure. Indeed, it is insecure even with just two users, meaning when there are two public keys in the picture.

BBO [5] had conjectured that indeed SU security did not in general imply MU security for D-PKE. Our results prove and confirm this conjecture. Brakerski and Segev [20] define MU security of D-PKE in the auxiliary input setting and give a scheme that achieves it for messages that are block sources, but they do not show a separation between the SU and MU settings. Dodis, Lee and Yum [25] give another example of a setting where SU security does not imply MU security, namely optimistic fair exchange.

2 Preliminaries

NOTATION AND CONVENTIONS. We let $\lambda \in \mathbb{N}$ denote the security parameter. If $n \in \mathbb{N}$ then we let 1^n denote the string of n ones and $[n]$ denote the set $\{1, \ldots, n\}$. If A is a finite set, then let $|A|$ denote its size, and $a \xleftarrow{\$} A$ denote sampling a uniformly at random from A. The empty string is denoted by ε. If a and b are two bit strings, we denote by $a \parallel b$ their concatenation. We use boldface letters for vectors. For any vector $\mathbf{x}$, we let $|\mathbf{x}|$ denote the number of its components. We say $\mathbf{x}$ is an n-vector if $|\mathbf{x}| = n$. For $i \in [|\mathbf{x}|]$ we let $\mathbf{x}[i]$ denote the i-th component of $\mathbf{x}$. We let $\mathrm{Maps}(D, R)$ denote the set of all functions $f\colon D \to R$.

Algorithms are randomized, unless otherwise specified as being deterministic. "PT" stands for "polynomial-time," whether for randomized algorithms or deterministic ones. If A is an algorithm, we let $y \leftarrow A(x_1, \ldots; r)$ denote running A with random coins r on inputs $x_1, \ldots$ and assigning the output to y. We let $y \xleftarrow{\$} A(x_1, \ldots)$ be the resulting of picking r at random and letting $y \leftarrow A(x_1, \ldots; r)$. We let $[A(x_1, \ldots)]$ denote the set of all y that have positive probability of being output by $A(x_1, \ldots)$. A function $\epsilon \colon \mathbb{N} \to \mathbb{R}$ is negligible if for every polynomial p, there exists $\lambda_p \in \mathbb{N}$ such that $\epsilon(\lambda) \leq 1/p(\lambda)$ for all $\lambda \geq \lambda_p$. An algorithm A is uniform if there exists a Turing machine T which halts with the output of A on all inputs. An algorithm A is non-uniform if there exists a sequence of circuits $\{C_\lambda\}_{\lambda \in \mathbb{N}}$ such that C_λ computes $A(1^\lambda, \ldots)$.

GAMES. Our definitions and proofs use the code-based game-playing framework of [15] with some of the syntax of [40]. A game $G(\lambda)$ (see Fig. 2 for an example) consists of a MAIN procedure, and possibly others, and begins by executing MAIN, which runs an adversary A after some initialization steps. A is given oracle access to certain game procedures. After A finishes executing, G performs steps with A's output to produce some output itself. We assume that boolean variables are initialized to false, that sets are initialized to $\emptyset$, strings are initialized to ϵ, and that integers are initialized to 0. We denote by $G^A \Rightarrow y$ the event that an execution of G with A outputs y. We abbreviate $G^A \Rightarrow$ true as G^A.

FUNCTIONS FAMILIES. A family of functions HF is a PT, deterministic algorithm that defines for each $\lambda \in \mathbb{N}$ a map $\mathsf{HF}(1^\lambda, \cdot, \cdot) \colon \{0,1\}^{\mathsf{HF.kl}(\lambda)} \times \{0,1\}^{\mathsf{HF.il}(\lambda)} \to \{0,1\}^{\mathsf{HF.ol}(\lambda)}$. Here $\mathsf{HF.kl}, \mathsf{HF.il}, \mathsf{HF.ol} \colon \mathbb{N} \to \mathbb{N}$ are the key, input and output lengths of HF, respectively. We extend HF to vectors (in a component-wise way) via

$$\mathsf{HF}(1^\lambda, k, \mathbf{x}) = (\mathsf{HF}(1^\lambda, k, \mathbf{x}[1]), \ldots, \mathsf{HF}(1^\lambda, k, \mathbf{x}[|\mathbf{x}|]))$$

for all $\lambda \in \mathbb{N}$, all $k \in \{0,1\}^{\mathsf{HF.kl}(\lambda)}$ and all vectors $\mathbf{x}$ over $\{0,1\}^{\mathsf{HF.il}(\lambda)}$.

3 Deterministic PKE

We provide definitions for D-PKE following [5,10]. We give a unified treatment of the ROM and the SM by regarding the latter as a special case of the former.

D-PKE. A deterministic public key encryption (D-PKE) scheme DE specifies four PT algorithms and related functions as follows. The parameter generator algorithm DE.Pg takes as input a unary representation 1^λ of the security parameter $\lambda \in \mathbb{N}$ and returns the system parameters $\pi \in \{0,1\}^{\mathsf{DE.pl}(\lambda)}$ which are common to all users. The key generation algorithm DE.Kg takes as input π and outputs a public encryption key $pk \in \{0,1\}^{\mathsf{DE.pkl}(\lambda)}$ and a secret decryption key sk. Given inputs $1^\lambda, \pi, pk$, a message $m \in \{0,1\}^{\mathsf{DE.ml}(\lambda)}$ and access to an oracle R: $\{0,1\}^{\mathsf{DE.ROil}(\lambda)} \to \{0,1\}^{\mathsf{DE.ROol}(\lambda)}$, the deterministic encryption algorithm DE.Enc outputs a ciphertext $c = \mathsf{DE.Enc}^{\mathrm{R}}(1^\lambda, \pi, pk, m)$. Given inputs $1^\lambda, \pi, sk$, a ciphertext c and oracle R, the deterministic decryption algorithm DE.Dec output either a message $m \in \{0,1\}^{\mathsf{DE.ml}(\lambda)}$, or $\bot$. Here DE.pl, DE.pkl, DE.ml: $\mathbb{N} \to \mathbb{N}$ are the parameter, public key and message length functions of DE, respectively, while DE.ROil, DE.ROol: $\mathbb{N} \to \mathbb{N}$ are the RO input and output length functions, respectively. Correctness requires that for all $\lambda \in \mathbb{N}$, all $\pi \in [\mathsf{DE.Pg}(1^\lambda)]$, all $[(pk, sk) \in$

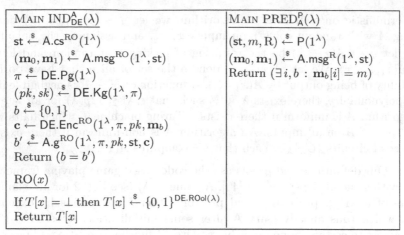

Fig. 2. The IND game used to define security of D-PKE scheme DE and the PRED game used to define unpredictability of adversary A

$[\mathsf{DE.Kg}(1^\lambda, \pi)]$, all $m \in \{0,1\}^{\mathsf{DE.ml}(\lambda)}$ and all $\mathrm{R} \in \mathrm{Maps}[\mathsf{DE.ROil}(\lambda), \mathsf{DE.ROol}(\lambda)]$ we have $\mathsf{DE.Dec}^{\mathrm{R}}(1^\lambda, \pi, sk, \mathsf{DE.Enc}^{\mathrm{R}}(1^\lambda, \pi, pk, m)) = m$. We extend $\mathsf{DE.Enc}$ to take input vectors of messages by defining $\mathsf{DE.Enc}^{\mathrm{R}}(1^\lambda, \pi, pk, \mathbf{m}) = (\mathsf{DE.Enc}^{\mathrm{R}}(1^\lambda, \pi, pk, \mathbf{m}[1]), \ldots, \mathsf{DE.Enc}^{\mathrm{R}}(1^\lambda, \pi, pk, \mathbf{m}[|\mathbf{m}|]))$, and similarly we let $\mathsf{DE.Dec}^{\mathrm{R}}(1^\lambda, \pi, sk, \mathbf{c}) = (\mathsf{DE.Dec}^{\mathrm{R}}(1^\lambda, \pi, sk, \mathbf{c}[1]), \ldots, \mathsf{DE.Dec}^{\mathrm{R}}(1^\lambda, \pi, sk, \mathbf{c}[|\mathbf{c}|]))$. We say that DE is a standard-model (SM) scheme if $\mathsf{DE.Enc}, \mathsf{DE.Dec}$ make no oracle queries, and in this case we will omit the superscript R to $\mathsf{DE.Enc}, \mathsf{DE.Dec}$.

IND SECURITY. We define IND security of a D-PKE scheme DE following BFOR [10]. An IND adversary A specifies a common-state generation algorithm A.cs, a message-generation algorithm A.msg and a guessing algorithm A.g, all PT. On input 1^λ, algorithm A.cs generates state information st that will be passed to both A.msg and A.g. Algorithm A.msg, on input 1^λ, st returns a pair $(\mathbf{m}_0, \mathbf{m}_1)$ of vectors of messages with $|\mathbf{m}_0| = |\mathbf{m}_1| = \mathsf{A.nm}(\lambda)$ and $\mathbf{m}_0[i], \mathbf{m}_1[i] \in \{0,1\}^{\mathsf{DE.ml}(\lambda)}$, where A.nm: $\mathbb{N} \to \mathbb{N}$ is the number-of-messages function associated to A. It is required that the strings (messages) $\mathbf{m}_0[1], \ldots, \mathbf{m}_0[|\mathbf{m}_0|]$ are distinct and the strings (messages) $\mathbf{m}_1[1], \ldots, \mathbf{m}_1[|\mathbf{m}_1|]$ are distinct. Also associated to DE are functions $\mathsf{DE.ROil}, \mathsf{DE.ROol}$, the input and output length of the RO that is used by the scheme. We say that A is a standard-model adversary if it makes no oracle queries, and in this case we may omit giving it an oracle.

The $\mathrm{IND}^{\mathsf{A}}_{\mathsf{DE}}(\lambda)$ game associated with DE and adversary A is described on the left of Fig. 2. We define the advantage of A via $\mathbf{Adv}^{\mathsf{ind}}_{\mathsf{DE,A}}(\lambda) = 2 \cdot \Pr[\mathrm{IND}^{\mathsf{A}}_{\mathsf{DE}}(\lambda)] - 1$ for all $\lambda \in \mathbb{N}$. If $\mathcal{A}$ is a class (set) of adversaries then we say that DE is $\mathrm{IND}[\mathcal{A}]$-secure if $\mathbf{Adv}^{\mathsf{ind}}_{\mathsf{DE,A}}(\cdot)$ is negligible for all $\mathsf{A} \in \mathcal{A}$. It is convenient to view $\mathrm{IND}[\mathcal{A}]$ as a set, so that $\mathsf{DE} \in \mathrm{IND}[\mathcal{A}]$ iff DE is $\mathrm{IND}[\mathcal{A}]$-secure. With this framework, we can now obtain various variants of the notion by varying and restricting the class $\mathcal{A}$.

First, we must impose the necessary condition that messages being encrypted have high min-entropy. In game PRED of Fig. 2, the predictor adversary P begins by specifying st and a guess m as to a message that A.msg will generate. It also specifies the function $R \in \mathsf{Maps}[\mathsf{DE.ROil}(\lambda), \mathsf{DE.ROol}(\lambda)]$ that will play the role of the RO. This captures the requirement that high min-entropy is required across all choices of the oracle. We let $\mathbf{Adv}^{\mathsf{pred}}_{\mathsf{A,P}}(\lambda) = \Pr[\mathrm{PRED}^{\mathsf{P}}_{\mathsf{A}}(\lambda)]$ for all $\lambda \in \mathbb{N}$. We say that A is unpredictable if $\mathbf{Adv}^{\mathsf{pred}}_{\mathsf{A,P}}(\cdot)$ is negligible for all P. We stress that here P is not restricted to PT but may be computationally unbounded. If A is a standard model adversary then we may omit R in the output of P.

Following [10], our adversaries A are three stage. If A.cs always returns ε then we say that A has trivial initial state and we may refer to A as a two-stage adversary. In BFOR [10], definitions of security are relative to two-stage adversaries, three-stage ones being introduced in order to facilitate proofs. Accordingly, our definitions of security will also be in terms of two-stage adversaries.

We are now ready to define adversary classes of interest. We consider two dimensions: the model (ROM or SM), and the type of computation (non-uniform or uniform). With two choices in each category, we get 4 classes of adversaries and 4 corresponding notions of security for D-PKE. Proceeding to the details, we let $\mathcal{A}_3$ be the class of all PT, 3-stage, unpredictable adversaries and $\mathcal{A}_2 \subseteq \mathcal{A}_3$ the class of all PT, 2-stage unpredictable adversaries. We let $\mathcal{A}^{\mathrm{rom}}$ denote the class of ROM adversaries, and $\mathcal{A}^{\mathrm{sm}} \subseteq \mathcal{A}^{\mathrm{rom}}$ the class of SM adversaries. We let $\mathcal{A}^{\mathrm{nu}}$ denote the class of non-uniform adversaries, and $\mathcal{A}^{\mathrm{u}} \subseteq \mathcal{A}^{\mathrm{nu}}$ the class of uniform adversaries. Then our 4 classes are $\mathcal{A}_2^{\mathrm{xm-xu}} = \mathcal{A}^{\mathrm{xm}} \cap \mathcal{A}^{\mathrm{xu}} \cap \mathcal{A}_2$ for $\mathrm{xm} \in \{\mathrm{rom, sm}\}$ and $\mathrm{xu} \in \{\mathrm{nu, u}\}$. The 4 corresponding notions of D-PKE security are $\mathrm{IND}[\mathcal{A}_2^{\mathrm{xm-xu}}]$ for $\mathrm{xm} \in \{\mathrm{rom, sm}\}$ and $\mathrm{xu} \in \{\mathrm{nu, u}\}$.

4 Does SM Security Imply ROM Security?

We now explore if a D-PKE scheme that is IND-secure in the standard model (SM) is IND-secure in the ROM.

PROBLEM AND APPROACH. It is easy to show that a SM R-PKE scheme retains its security in the ROM, where the adversary has access to the random oracle, because a SM adversary can simply simulate the random oracle for a ROM adversary. Indeed, that SM security implies ROM security seems to have been viewed as trivial and true for any primitive. We are about to see, however, that for D-PKE the answer is less clear.

We are given a SM D-PKE scheme DE that is secure in the SM, meaning its algorithms make no calls to RO and it is secure against adversaries that make no calls to RO. We ask if DE remains secure in the ROM, meaning when the adversary is allowed to query RO. The reason an adversary A may be able now to do more is that A.msg may create messages that depend in some clever way on RO and then A.g could exploit the fact that it has access to the same RO to figure out something about the messages from the ciphertexts. Intuitively, however, it is difficult to see how this could happen because messages are required to have high min-entropy even given RO. However, it is not clear how to prove it, which raises the question of whether it is even true. The difficulty is that no communication is allowed from the message-finding stage of the adversary to the guessing stage, and so a simulating SM adversary has no obvious way to ensure that these two stages have a common view of the random oracle it is simulating.

We will first present Lemma 1 showing the claim is true in the 3-stage adversary formulation of the IND games. Namely given a SM D-PKE scheme and given a 3-stage ROM adversary A, we show how to simulate A with a 3-stage SM adversary B so that the latter has the same advantage as A. The proof uses a $q(\cdot)$-wise independent hash function, with the polynomial q depending on A, as the common initial state created by B.cs. The lemma is true both in the uniform and the non-uniform settings. However, recall that IND security is defined with respect to adversaries that have trivial initial state, meaning are two stage. And in our reduction, B will have non-trivial initial state even if A has trivial initial state. So the lemma does not directly show that IND in the SM implies IND in the ROM. In the non-uniform case, however, we can flatten the constructed 3-stage adversary B into an equivalent one with trivial initial state, thereby concluding that if SM D-PKE scheme DE is in $\mathrm{IND}[\mathcal{A}_2^{\mathrm{sm-nu}}]$ then it is also in $\mathrm{IND}[\mathcal{A}_2^{\mathrm{rom-nu}}]$. In the uniform setting we have no obvious way to remove the non-trivial initial state of B, and thus are not able to conclude that DE being in $\mathrm{IND}[\mathcal{A}_2^{\mathrm{sm-u}}]$ implies it is in $\mathrm{IND}[\mathcal{A}_2^{\mathrm{rom-u}}]$. This very basic question (surprisingly) remains open.

q-WISE INDEPENDENT FUNCTION FAMILIES. We say that a family HF of functions is $q(\cdot)$-wise independent if for all $\lambda \in \mathbb{N}$, all $q(\lambda)$-vectors $\mathbf{x}$ over $\{0,1\}^{\mathsf{HF.il}(\lambda)}$ all of whose entries are distinct, and all $q(\lambda)$-vectors $\mathbf{y}$ over $\{0,1\}^{\mathsf{HF.ol}(\lambda)}$ we have $\Pr[\mathsf{HF}(1^\lambda, k, \mathbf{x}) = \mathbf{y}] = 2^{-q(\lambda)\cdot\mathsf{HF.ol}(\lambda)}$, where the probability is over k chosen at random from $\{0,1\}^{\mathsf{HF.kl}(\lambda)}$.

FROM SM SECURITY TO ROM SECURITY WITH 3 STAGES. The following lemma says that for any SM D-PKE scheme (meaning, the scheme algorithms do not call the RO), a 3-stage ROM adversary A may be simulated by a 3-stage SM adversary B who achieves the same advantage as A. It does not follow that a 2-stage ROM adversary can be simulated by a 2-stage SM adversary since our constructed adversary B will have non-trivial initial state even if the given adversary A had trivial initial state.

Lemma 1. Let DE be a standard-model D-PKE scheme. Let $A \in \mathcal{A}^{\mathrm{rom}} \cap \mathcal{A}_3$ be a 3-stage, PT ROM adversary. Then there is a 3-stage, PT standard-model adversary $B \in \mathcal{A}^{\mathrm{sm}} \cap \mathcal{A}_3$ such that

$$\mathbf{Adv}_{\mathsf{DE},\mathsf{B}}^{\mathrm{ind}}(\lambda) = \mathbf{Adv}_{\mathsf{DE},\mathsf{A}}^{\mathrm{ind}}(\lambda) \tag{1}$$

for all $\lambda \in \mathbb{N}$. Furthermore, if A is unpredictable then so is B and if A is uniform then so is B.

Proof (Lemma 1). Without loss of generality, we assume that there exists a polynomial $q : \mathbb{N} \to \mathbb{N}$ such that for all $\lambda \in \mathbb{N}$, adversary A always makes exactly $q(\lambda)$ RO queries in game $\mathrm{IND}_{\mathsf{DE}}^{\mathsf{A}}(\lambda)$. Let HF be a $q(\cdot)$-wise independent family of functions with $\mathsf{HF.il} = \mathsf{DE.ROil}$ and $\mathsf{HF.ol} = \mathsf{DE.ROol}$. We define SM adversary B as follows:

$\underline{B.cs(1^\lambda)}$

$k \xleftarrow{\$} \{0,1\}^{HF.kl(\lambda)}$

$st_A \xleftarrow{\$} A.cs^{ROSim}(1^\lambda)$

Return (k, st_A)

$\underline{ROSim(x)}$

Return $HF(1^\lambda, k, x)$

$\underline{B.msg(1^\lambda, st_B)}$

$(k, st_A) \leftarrow st_B$

$(\mathbf{m}_0, \mathbf{m}_1) \xleftarrow{\$} A.msg^{ROSim}(1^\lambda, st_A)$

Return $(\mathbf{m}_0, \mathbf{m}_1)$

$\underline{ROSim(x)}$

Return $HF(1^\lambda, k, x)$

$\underline{B.g(1^\lambda, \pi, pk, st_B, \mathbf{c})}$

$(k, st_A) \leftarrow st_B$

$b' \xleftarrow{\$} A.g^{ROSim}(1^\lambda, \pi, pk, st_A, \mathbf{c})$

Return b'

$\underline{ROSim(x)}$

Return $HF(1^\lambda, k, x)$

That is, B.cs picks at random a key defining a member of HF and passes it to B.msg, B.g. The latter use the function $HF(1^\lambda, k, \cdot)$ to simulate the RO of A, via the ROSim procedure. Since A makes at most $q(\lambda)$ queries to RO, the $q(\lambda)$-wise independence of the family should result in a perfect simulation of the RO. Also, since both B.msg and B.g use the same function, A.msg and A.g will see a consistent RO across their two stages. As a result we expect that (1) is true.

Formally proving that (1) is true, however, is not straightforward because the RO queries are adaptive and $q(\cdot)$-wise independence is a non-adaptive condition, so some care must be taken. In [8] we provide an analysis that handles this, and do not discuss it further here.

It is clear that if A is uniform then so is B. Assuming A is unpredictable we now have to show that B is unpredictable. Let P_B be a predictor adversary for B. We define a predictor adversary P_A for A as follows. On input 1^λ it runs $P_B(1^\lambda)$ to get back (st_B, m). (Since B is SM, P_B returns a pair, not a triple.) It parses st_B as (k, st_A) and returns $(st_A, m, HF(1^\lambda, k, \cdot))$. Then we have $\mathbf{Adv}_{A,P_A}^{pred}(\cdot) = \mathbf{Adv}_{B,P_B}^{pred}(\cdot)$. But the LHS is negligible by assumption, so the RHS is negligible as well. □

We note that alternatively, in place of a family of $q(\cdot)$-wise independent functions, we could have used a PRF, the key being chosen by B.cs and included in the state so that it is passed to B.msg, B.g. The latter would use the PRF under this key to simulate the RO for A.msg, A.g, respectively. O'Neill used this technique [35, Lemma 3.3.2] to partially remove the RO for a restricted class of D-PKE schemes.

SM SECURITY IMPLIES ROM SECURITY IN THE NON-UNIFORM SETTING. The following theorem uses Lemma 1 to show that if a D-PKE scheme DE is IND-secure in the standard model with respect to non-uniform adversaries, then it is IND-secure in the ROM with respect to non-uniform adversaries. The proof uses non-uniformity in a crucial way, and hence cannot be adapted to the uniform setting.

Theorem 1. *Let* DE *be a SM D-PKE scheme such that* DE $\in$ IND$[\mathcal{A}_2^{\text{sm−nu}}]$. *Then* DE $\in$ IND$[\mathcal{A}_2^{\text{rom−nu}}]$.

Proof. Let A $\in \mathcal{A}_2^{\text{rom−nu}}$ be an unpredictable, non-uniform PT ROM adversary with trivial initial state. By Lemma 1, we get an unpredictable, non-uniform PT SM adversary B $\in \mathcal{A}^{\text{sm}} \cap \mathcal{A}^{\text{nu}} \cap \mathcal{A}_3$ such that $\mathbf{Adv}_{\text{DE,B}}^{\text{ind}}(\cdot) = \mathbf{Adv}_{\text{DE,A}}^{\text{ind}}(\cdot)$. However, B.cs is *not* trivial, so the assumption that DE $\in$ IND$[\mathcal{A}_2^{\text{sm−nu}}]$ does not allow us to conclude that $\mathbf{Adv}_{\text{DE,B}}^{\text{ind}}(\cdot)$, and hence $\mathbf{Adv}_{\text{DE,A}}^{\text{ind}}(\cdot)$, is negligible. We modify B to an unpredictable, trivial initial state, non-uniform SM adversary C $\in \mathcal{A}_2^{\text{sm−nu}}$ with $\mathbf{Adv}_{\text{DE,C}}^{\text{ind}}(\cdot) = \mathbf{Adv}_{\text{DE,B}}^{\text{ind}}(\cdot)$. Now the assumption that DE $\in$ IND$[\mathcal{A}_2^{\text{sm−nu}}]$ means that $\mathbf{Adv}_{\text{DE,C}}^{\text{ind}}(\cdot)$ is negligible and hence so is $\mathbf{Adv}_{\text{DE,A}}^{\text{ind}}(\cdot)$, showing that DE $\in$ IND$[\mathcal{A}_2^{\text{rom−nu}}]$ as desired. To obtain C from B, we simply use coin fixing, namely we hardwire a best choice of the key k chosen randomly by B.cs(1^λ) into the circuits C.msg$(1^\lambda, \cdots)$ and C.g$(1^\lambda, \cdots)$ while letting C.cs always return ε. $\square$

We note that the issues and difficulties associated with showing that SM security implies ROM security could also be viewed as arising from definitional short-comings of existing formulations, and addressed definitionally, for example by making the three-stage definition the basic one with respect to which security is measured. Lemma 1 directly implies that if DE is a SM D-PKE scheme, then: (1) If DE $\in$ IND$[\mathcal{A}^{\text{sm}} \cap \mathcal{A}^{\text{u}} \cap \mathcal{A}_3]$ then DE $\in$ IND$[\mathcal{A}^{\text{rom}} \cap \mathcal{A}^{\text{u}} \cap \mathcal{A}_3]$ and (2) If DE $\in$ IND$[\mathcal{A}^{\text{sm}} \cap \mathcal{A}^{\text{nu}} \cap \mathcal{A}_3]$ then DE $\in$ IND$[\mathcal{A}^{\text{rom}} \cap \mathcal{A}^{\text{nu}} \cap \mathcal{A}_3]$. That is, for 3-stage adversaries, SM security implies ROM security both in the uniform and non-uniform settings. However the question of whether the implication holds for two-stage adversaries and the current definitions would still be interesting.

5   Is SOA Security Achievable?

We initiate an investigation of SOA security for D-PKE. We provide definitions and then show that the goal is impossible to achieve in the SM, meaning no SM D-PKE scheme achieves it.

What makes this interesting is that the difficulty of achieving SOA security in the R-PKE case arises from the fact that an attacker obtains not only messages but the coins underlying the opened ciphertexts. If it only obtained messages, security is easy to achieve [17]. Since in D-PKE there are no coins, one might think security would be also easy to achieve. But in fact this is not true.

PRELIMINARIES. We let $\perp_n$ denote the vector of length n all of whose entries are $\perp$. For a set $I \subseteq [|\mathbf{x}|]$ we let $\mathbf{x}[I]$ denote the $|\mathbf{x}|$-vector whose i-th component is $\mathbf{x}[i]$ if $i \in I$ and $\perp$ otherwise.

Collision resistance of a function family HF is defined via game $\text{CR}_{\text{HF}}^{\text{X}}(\lambda)$ associated to HF, adversary X and $\lambda \in \mathbb{N}$. The game starts by picking $k \xleftarrow{\$} \{0,1\}^{\text{HF.kl}(\lambda)}$. Then X is run with inputs $1^\lambda, k$ to return $x_0, x_1 \in \{0,1\}^{\text{HF.il}(\lambda)}$. The game returns true if $x_0 \neq x_1$ and $\text{HF}(1^\lambda, k, x_0) = \text{HF}(1^\lambda, k, x_1)$, and false

MAIN REAL$_{DE}^{A}(\lambda)$	MAIN IDEAL$_{DE}^{A,S}(\lambda)$	MAIN PRED$_{A}^{P}(\lambda)$
$k \xleftarrow{\$} \text{A.cs}(1^{\lambda})$	$k \xleftarrow{\$} \text{A.cs}(1^{\lambda})$	$(I, \text{st}) \xleftarrow{\$} \text{P}(1^{\lambda})$
$\mathbf{m} \xleftarrow{\$} \text{A.msg}(1^{\lambda})$	$\mathbf{m} \xleftarrow{\$} \text{A.msg}(1^{\lambda})$	$\mathbf{m} \xleftarrow{\$} \text{A.msg}(1^{\lambda})$
$\pi \xleftarrow{\$} \text{DE.Pg}(1^{\lambda})$	$\text{st} \xleftarrow{\$} \text{S}^{\text{COR}}(1^{\lambda}, k)$	$m \xleftarrow{\$} \text{P}(\text{st}, \mathbf{m}[I])$
$(pk, sk) \xleftarrow{\$} \text{DE.Kg}(1^{\lambda}, \pi)$	$w \xleftarrow{\$} \text{A.g}(1^{\lambda}, k, I, \text{st}, \mathbf{m}[I])$	Return $(\exists i \notin I : \mathbf{m}[i] = $
$\mathbf{c} \xleftarrow{\$} \text{DE.Enc}(1^{\lambda}, \pi, pk, \mathbf{m})$	Return $(w = \text{A.f}(1^{\lambda}, \mathbf{m}))$	$m)$
st	$\xleftarrow{\$} \text{COR}(I)$	
$\text{A.cor}^{\text{COR}}(1^{\lambda}, \pi, pk, k, \mathbf{c})$	Return $\mathbf{m}[I]$	
$w \xleftarrow{\$} \text{A.g}(1^{\lambda}, k, I, \text{st}, \mathbf{m}[I])$		
Return $(w = \text{A.f}(1^{\lambda}, \mathbf{m}))$		
$\text{COR}(I)$		
Return $\mathbf{m}[I]$		

MAIN CCR$_{DE,z}^{C}(\lambda)$
$(\pi, pk) \xleftarrow{\$} \text{C}(1^{\lambda})$
If (not $\text{DE.Vf}(1^{\lambda}, \pi, pk)$) then return false
$\mathbf{m}_0, \mathbf{m}_1 \xleftarrow{\$} (\{0,1\}^{\text{DE.ml}(\lambda)})^{z(\lambda)}$
$\mathbf{c}_0 \leftarrow \text{DE.Enc}(1^{\lambda}, \pi, pk, \mathbf{m}_0)$
$\mathbf{c}_1 \leftarrow \text{DE.Enc}(1^{\lambda}, \pi, pk, \mathbf{m}_1)$
For $i = 1, \ldots, z(\lambda)$ do
If $((\mathbf{c}_0[i] = \mathbf{c}_1[i])$ and $(\mathbf{m}_0[i] \neq \mathbf{m}_1[i]))$
then return true
Return false

Fig. 3. The REAL, IDEAL, PRED and CCR games

otherwise. The advantage of X is defined as $\mathbf{Adv}_{HF,X}^{cr}(\lambda) = \Pr[\text{CR}_{HF}^{X}(\lambda)]$ and we say that HF is collision resistant if $\mathbf{Adv}_{HF,X}^{cr}(\cdot)$ is negligible for all PT X.

DEFINING SOA SECURITY. Providing a meaningful definition of SOA-security for D-PKE takes some care. A definition based on semantic security for relations, as given for R-PKE in [9,12], is trivially unachievable for D-PKE because a ciphertext is already partial information about a plaintext. Thus we consider semantic security for functions, where the adversary, given ciphertexsts, aims to figure out a function of the message, this function not being given the public key and thus unable to encrypt. Additionally we must continue to require that messages do not depend on the public key and are unpredictable. Our definition is simulation-based and combines ideas from the basic (non-SOA) definitions of secure D-PKE [5,10] with ideas from the definitions of SOA-security for R-PKE from [9,12].

In Fig. 3 is the "real" game REAL$_{DE}^{A}$ associated to D-PKE scheme DE and adversary A. PT common state generation algorithm A.cs is executed on input 1^{λ} to get a common state k that will be passed to the A.cor stage of A. (Other stages can get it too, but since our results are negative, not giving it only makes the results stronger.) Then PT message generator A.msg is executed on input

1^λ to get a A.nm(λ)-vector of messages over $\{0,1\}^{\text{DE.ml}(\lambda)}$, where A.nm is the number-of-messages function associated to A. Then public parameters and keys are generated. (It is important that the messages do not depend on the public parameters or public key of DE for the same reason as with PRIV [5] and IND [10], namely that otherwise security is trivially unachievable.) Then the vector of messages is encrypted, component-wise, to get a vector **c** of ciphertexts. The PT corruption algorithm A.cor gets $1^\lambda, \pi, pk, k, \mathbf{c}$ and an oracle COR to which it is allowed exactly one query, this consisting of a subset I of $[\text{A.nm}(\lambda)]$, indicating positions at which it wants **m** opened. In response it gets $\mathbf{m}[I]$, meaning the values $\mathbf{m}[i]$ for $i \in I$, and returns state information st. The PT guessing algorithm A.g gets $1^\lambda, k, I, \text{st}, \mathbf{m}[I]$, where I is the COR-query previously made by A.cor and recorded by the game, and outputs a guess w as to the value of A.f$(1^\lambda, \mathbf{m})$. Here deterministic PT algorithm A.f, called the information function, represents the information about **m** that the adversary is trying to compute. The game returns true iff the guess is correct.

The "ideal" game $\text{IDEAL}_{\text{DE}}^{\text{A,S}}$ of Fig. 3 is associated to DE, adversary A and a simulator S. Here, the common state and message vector are chosen as before, but the game neither chooses parameters and public key, nor generates any ciphertexts. The simulator is given no information about **m**, but has access to oracle COR, to which it is allowed exactly one query, this consisting of a subset I of $[\text{A.nm}(\lambda)]$. In response S gets $\mathbf{m}[I]$ and must then return state information st that should resemble the output of A.cor. The rest is as in the real game.

We need to restrict A.msg to reflect the inherent weaknesses of D-PKE, analogous to the restrictions made in defining PRIV and IND. Namely we require a message-distinctness condition and a message unpredictability (high min-entropy) condition. Before detailing definitions, we note that the A.msg in Theorem 2 simply outputs uniform, independently distributed messages of superlogarithmic length, so both the conditions will be trivially met, and thus a reader can skip the rest of this paragraph if they wish. Proceeding, since ciphertext equality leaks plaintext equality in D-PKE, we require the following message-distinctness condition: there is a negligible function ν such that $\Pr[\exists i, j : (i \neq j) \wedge (\mathbf{m}[i] = \mathbf{m}[j])] \leq \nu(\lambda)$ where the probability is over $\mathbf{m} \xleftarrow{\$} \text{A.msg}(1^\lambda)$. Second, we require that A is unpredictable, which we define to mean that $\mathbf{Adv}_{\text{A,P}}^{\text{pred}}(\lambda) = \Pr[\text{PRED}_{\text{A}}^{\text{P}}(\lambda)]$ is negligible for all P (we emphasize that here P is not restricted to be PT), where game $\text{PRED}_{\text{A}}^{\text{P}}$ is shown on the middle, bottom of Fig. 3. The unpredictability condition we define here is very strong, requiring that each component message of **m** has high min-entropy even given the others, but this only strengthens our results since they are negative. We let $\mathcal{A}^{\text{soa}}$ denote the class of all PT A that satisfy the message distinctness and unpredictability conditions.

We define the soa-advantage of an adversary A with respect to DE and a simulator S via

$$\mathbf{Adv}_{\text{DE,A,S}}^{\text{soa}}(\lambda) = \Pr\left[\text{REAL}_{\text{DE}}^{\text{A}}(\lambda)\right] - \Pr\left[\text{IDEAL}_{\text{DE}}^{\text{A,S}}(\lambda)\right]$$

for all $\lambda \in \mathbb{N}$. We say that DE is SOA-secure if for all $A \in \mathcal{A}^{\text{soa}}$, there exists a PT simulator S such that $\mathbf{Adv}_{\text{DE,A,S}}^{\text{soa}}(\cdot)$ is negligible.

The definitions and results here are all in the standard model. Our impossibility result does not rule out achieving an appropriate (programmable) ROM version of our definition of SOA-security for D-PKE. In [8] we further discuss the definitional choices made here.

APPROACH. BDWY [9] show that if CR hash functions exist then any R-PKE scheme satisfying a certain binding property they define is not SOA-secure. Roughly, binding says that encryption remains injective even on dishonestly-chosen public keys. Not all R-PKE schemes satisfy this binding property, but many common ones do, and the BDWY result shows in particular that IND-CPA does not imply SOA for R-PKE. In the D-PKE case, rather than ask for schemes that are binding, we introduce a verification algorithm that, given a dishonestly-generated public key, tests the extent to which the encryption induced by this key is an injective function. If it is far from injective, verification will catch it, and otherwise we have some sort of binding. We then show that such a verification algorithm exists for *every* D-PKE scheme. Adapting the technique of BDWY we can then use this to show that no D-PKE scheme is SOA-secure.

INJECTIVITY VERIFICATION. Let DE be a D-PKE scheme. A *verification algorithm* DE.Vf for DE is a PT algorithm that takes as input $1^\lambda, \pi, pk$ and returns a boolean value. Here, π and pk play the role of parameters and a public key but are to be thought of as adversarially chosen and not necessarily ones that would actually arise in honest parameter and key generation. Informally, DE.Vf checks if the provided π, pk induce an almost injective function on valid DE messages. We impose a requirement we call completeness, which says that for all $\lambda \in \mathbb{N}$, all $\pi \in [\mathsf{DE.Pg}(1^\lambda)]$ and all $(pk, sk) \in [\mathsf{DE.Kg}(1^\lambda, \pi)]$ we have DE.Vf$(1^\lambda, \pi, pk) = \mathsf{true}$. That is, if the parameters and key are honestly chosen then the verifier accepts. To formalize the requirement for adversarially chosen π, pk, consider the game described in Fig. 3, and define the ciphertext collision resistance advantage of an adversary C via $\mathbf{Adv}^{\mathrm{ccr}}_{\mathsf{DE},z,\mathsf{C}}(\lambda) = \Pr\left[\mathrm{CCR}^{\mathsf{C}}_{\mathsf{DE},z}(\lambda)\right]$. Here adversary C picks π, pk, so the encryption function induced by them, unlike that induced by an honestly-generated π, pk, may not be injective. The advantage of the adversary is the probability that it can get some non-injectivity to surface via collisions. The following lemma says that it is possible to design a verification algorithm that makes it hard for any adversary to defeat CCR.

Lemma 2. *Let* DE *be a D-PKE scheme and* $z\colon \mathbb{N} \to \mathbb{N}$. *Define the verification algorithm* DE.Vf *as follows:*

DE.Vf$(1^\lambda, \pi, pk)$
If $(|\pi| \neq \mathsf{DE.pl}(\lambda)$ or $|pk| \neq \mathsf{DE.pkl}(\lambda))$ then return false
For $t = 1, \ldots, z(\lambda)$ do
  $\mathbf{m}'_0[t] \xleftarrow{\$} \{0,1\}^{\mathsf{DE.ml}(\lambda)}$; $\mathbf{m}'_1[t] \xleftarrow{\$} \{0,1\}^{\mathsf{DE.ml}(\lambda)}$
  If $((\mathsf{DE.Enc}(1^\lambda, \pi, pk, \mathbf{m}'_0[t]) = \mathsf{DE.Enc}(1^\lambda, \pi, pk, \mathbf{m}'_1[t])) \wedge (\mathbf{m}'_0[t] \neq \mathbf{m}'_1[t]))$
    then return false
Return true

Then DE.Vf *is PT and complete. Also for any (not necessarily PT) adversary* C *we have* $\mathbf{Adv}_{DE,z,C}^{ccr}(\lambda) \leq \frac{1}{4}$ *for all* $\lambda \in \mathbb{N}$.

Proof. Lemma 2] For any $\lambda \in \mathbb{N}$, any $\pi \in \{0,1\}^{DE.pl(\lambda)}$ and any $pk \in \{0,1\}^{DE.pkl(\lambda)}$ let $\mathbf{CP}_{DE}(1^\lambda, \pi, pk)$ equal the probability that there exists $t \in [z(\lambda)]$ such that

$$DE.Enc(1^\lambda, \pi, pk, \mathbf{m}_0[t]) = DE.Enc(1^\lambda, \pi, pk, \mathbf{m}_1[t]) \text{ and } \mathbf{m}_0[t] \neq \mathbf{m}_1[t]$$

where the probability is over $\mathbf{m}_0, \mathbf{m}_1 \xleftarrow{\$} (\{0,1\}^{DE.ml(\lambda)})^{z(\lambda)}$. In game CCR the probability that the test performed using DE.Vf is passed is $1 - \mathbf{CP}_{DE}(1^\lambda, \pi, pk)$. If such test is passed, the probability that some ciphertext collision appears (thus making the game CCR return true) is upper bounded by $\mathbf{CP}_{DE}(1^\lambda, \pi, pk)$. Since passing the verification algorithm's test and having some ciphertext collision is the only combination in which game CCR returns true, for any adversary C, we get

$$\mathbf{Adv}_{DE,z,C}^{ccr}(\lambda)$$
$$\leq \max_{\pi \in \{0,1\}^{DE.pl(\lambda)}} \max_{pk \in \{0,1\}^{DE.pkl(\lambda)}} \left((1 - \mathbf{CP}_{DE}(1^\lambda, \pi, pk)) \, \mathbf{CP}_{DE}(1^\lambda, \pi, pk) \right)$$
$$\leq \frac{1}{4}$$

where the last inequality is from the maximum of the quadratic function. □

IMPOSSIBILITY OF SOA SECURITY. In order to prove that a given D-PKE scheme DE is not SOA-secure we need to prove the existence of an adversary $A \in \mathcal{A}^{soa}$ such that for *every* PT simulator S, the function $\mathbf{Adv}_{DE,A,S}^{soa}(\cdot)$ is *not* negligible. We assume a collision-resistant hash function HF in the following.

Theorem 2. *Let* DE *be a D-PKE scheme such that* $2^{-DE.ml(\cdot)}$ *is negligible. Assume the existence of a collision-resistant family of functions. Then, there exists a PT adversary* $A \in \mathcal{A}^{soa}$ *such that, for all PT simulators* S *there exists a function* ν *that is not negligible and is such that* $\mathbf{Adv}_{DE,A,S}^{soa}(\lambda) \geq \nu(\lambda)$ *for all* $\lambda \in \mathbb{N}$. *Furthermore, message sampler* A.msg *returns a vector of uniformly and independently distributed messages.* □

The proof follows the template of the proof from [9] but makes crucial use of Lemma 2. We use a variant of the reset lemma of [13].

Proof (Theorem 2). Let HF be a collision-resistant family of functions. Let $z(\cdot) = HF.ol(\cdot) + DE.pkl(\cdot) + DE.pl(\cdot)$. Let $n(\cdot) = 2z(\cdot)$. Let A be the adversary defined in Fig. 4. We should emphasize that the hash function here is not being applied element-wise, but to the ciphertext vector as a whole. Here, DE.Vf is the verification algorithm provided by Lemma 2 for DE. We first note that $A \in \mathcal{A}^{soa}$. Indeed, A is unpredictable due to the assumption that $2^{-DE.ml(\cdot)}$ is negligible and the fact that messages in the message vector are independently and uniformly

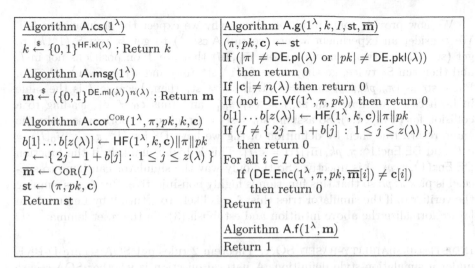

Fig. 4. Adversary A for the proof of Theorem 2

distributed. It also satisfies the distinctness condition since $2^{-\text{DE.ml}(\cdot)}$ is negligible and $n(\cdot)$ is a polynomial. Next we note that

$$\Pr\left[\text{REAL}_{\text{DE}}^{\text{A}}(\lambda)\right] = 1 \tag{2}$$

for all $\lambda \in \mathbb{N}$. This follows from the description of A and the completeness of the verifier. We will build adversaries X and C such that

$$\Pr\left[\text{IDEAL}_{\text{DE}}^{\text{A,S}}(\lambda)\right] \leq 2^{-\text{DE.ml}(\lambda)z(\lambda)} + \sqrt{\mathbf{Adv}_{\text{DE},z,\text{C}}^{\text{ccr}}(\lambda) + \mathbf{Adv}_{\text{HF,X}}^{\text{cr}}(\lambda)} \tag{3}$$

for all $\lambda \in \mathbb{N}$. But by the assumption that HF is CR and by Lemma 2, we have that the above probability is not negligibly close to 1 and hence

$$\mathbf{Adv}_{\text{DE,A,S}}^{\text{soa}}(\cdot) = 1 - \Pr\left[\text{IDEAL}_{\text{DE}}^{\text{A,S}}(\cdot)\right] \tag{4}$$

is a function that is not negligible.

It may seem strange that security fails for A.f that always returns 1, because this function does not leak anything about $\mathbf{m}$. What we are saying is that it is not possible to prove even this simple, intuitive claim, meaning to give a simulator for an adversary relative to this simple information function.

We proceed to prove (3). Given any S, we divide it in two parts, S_1 and S_2. S_1 is the execution until the point at which the subset that will be corrupted is chosen, and S_2 is the rest of the execution. We assume without loss of generality that S_1 forwards the coins to S_2, so S_2 is deterministic. This means we can view S as operating as follows:

Simulator $\text{S}^{\text{COR}}(1^\lambda, k)$

$(\text{st}^*, I) \xleftarrow{\$} \text{S}_1(1^\lambda, k)$; $\overline{\mathbf{m}} \leftarrow \text{COR}(I)$; $\text{st} \leftarrow \text{S}_2(1^\lambda, \text{st}^*, \overline{\mathbf{m}})$; Return st

We now provide some intuition about why we expect the simulator to fail. We consider an experiment where we run $A.cs(1^\lambda)$ to get k, run $S_1(1^\lambda, k)$ to get (st^*, I), pick two, random vectors $\overline{m}_0, \overline{m}_1$ that are $\perp$ on positions not in I, and then run S_2 twice, getting $st_0 \leftarrow S_2(1^\lambda, st^*, \overline{m}_0)$ and $st_1 \leftarrow S_2(1^\lambda, st^*, \overline{m}_1)$. Parse st_b as (π_b, pk_b, c_b) for $b = 0, 1$. If $st_0 \neq st_1$ then, because I is the same in both cases, we have $(\pi_0, pk_0) = (\pi_1, pk_1)$ and thus $c_0 \neq c_1$, leading to a collision for $HF(1^\lambda, k, \cdot)$. So assume $st_0 = st_1 = (\pi, pk, c)$. If both runs make the game return $true$ then by definition of $A.g$ we have $DE.Enc(1^\lambda, \pi, pk, \overline{m}_0[I]) = c[I]$ and $DE.Enc(1^\lambda, \pi, pk, \overline{m}_1[I]) = c[I]$. This is highly unlikely if the function $DE.Enc(1^\lambda, \pi, pk, \cdot)$ is injective. So the only way the simulator can hope to succeed is pick π, pk so that this function is highly non-injective. But $A.g$ is running the verifier so if the simulator tries this, $A.g$ is likely to return 0 by Lemma 2. In [8] we formalize the above intuition and establish (3) via the reset lemma.   □

INDISTINGUISHABILITY-BASED SOA. Theorem 2 rules out SOA-secure D-PKE under a simulation-style definition. A natural question is whether SOA-secure D-PKE may be achieved under a weaker definition, in particular an indistinguishability style one. Indeed, for R-PKE, SOA-security definitions in both styles have been made and investigated, and the indistinguishability style is easier to achieve [12,17,18,31]. The difficulty is that for D-PKE it is not clear how to give a meaningful indistinguishability style definition of SOA-security. For R-PKE, the indistinguishability definition involves conditional re-sampling of the un-opened messages. In the D-PKE case we cannot provide the un-opened messages in the distinguishing test, since the adversary could easily win by re-encrypting to check versus the ciphertexts. It is not clear to us what could be done instead. Additionally, even for R-PKE, re-sampling is rarely polynomial time so either we consider security for a very limited set of distributions or we have a non-polynomial time game, and both choices have problems. Defining some achievable notion of SOA-secure D-PKE is an interesting open problem.

6   Does SU Security Imply MU Security?

We now define mIND, the multi-key version of IND security, and show a separation between the two notions by showing the existence of a D-PKE scheme that is IND-secure but not mIND-secure.

mIND SECURITY. Let DE be a D-PKE scheme. An mIND adversary A specifies a common-state generation algorithm $A.cs$, a message-generation algorithm $A.msg$ and a guessing algorithm $A.g$, all PT. On input 1^λ, algorithm $A.cs$ generates state information st that will be passed to both $A.msg$ and $A.g$. Algorithm $A.msg$, on input $1^\lambda, st$ returns a pair (m_0, m_1) of $A.nu(\lambda)$ by $A.nm(\lambda)$ matrices over $\{0,1\}^{DE.ml(\lambda)}$, where $A.nu$ is the number-of-users function associated to A and $A.nm$ is the number-of-messages function associated to A. It is required that for each b, i the strings $m_b[i, 1], \ldots, m_b[i, A.nm(\lambda)]$, which are the messages encrypted under the public key $pk[i]$ of user i, be distinct. (However, messages

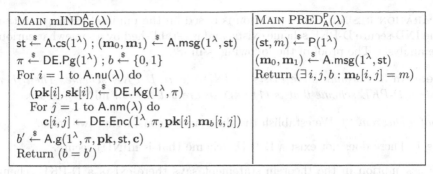

MAIN $\text{mIND}_{\text{DE}}^{\text{A}}(\lambda)$	MAIN $\text{PRED}_{\text{A}}^{\text{P}}(\lambda)$
$\text{st} \xleftarrow{\$} \text{A.cs}(1^\lambda)\ ;\ (\mathbf{m}_0, \mathbf{m}_1) \xleftarrow{\$} \text{A.msg}(1^\lambda, \text{st})$	$(\text{st}, m) \xleftarrow{\$} \text{P}(1^\lambda)$
$\pi \xleftarrow{\$} \text{DE.Pg}(1^\lambda)\ ;\ b \xleftarrow{\$} \{0, 1\}$	$(\mathbf{m}_0, \mathbf{m}_1) \xleftarrow{\$} \text{A.msg}(1^\lambda, \text{st})$
For $i = 1$ to $\text{A.nu}(\lambda)$ do	Return $(\exists\, i, j, b : \mathbf{m}_b[i, j] = m)$
$\quad (\mathbf{pk}[i], \mathbf{sk}[i]) \xleftarrow{\$} \text{DE.Kg}(1^\lambda, \pi)$	
$\quad$ For $j = 1$ to $\text{A.nm}(\lambda)$ do	
$\quad\quad c[i, j] \leftarrow \text{DE.Enc}(1^\lambda, \pi, \mathbf{pk}[i], \mathbf{m}_b[i, j])$	
$b' \xleftarrow{\$} \text{A.g}(1^\lambda, \pi, \mathbf{pk}, \text{st}, \mathbf{c})$	
Return $(b = b')$	

Fig. 5. The mIND game used to define multi-user security of D-PKE scheme DE and the PRED game used to define unpredictability of adversary A

$\overline{\text{DE}}.\text{Pg}(1^\lambda)$	$\overline{\text{DE}}.\text{Enc}(1^\lambda, (\pi, pk^*), pk, m)$
$\pi \xleftarrow{\$} \text{DE.Pg}(1^\lambda)$	$c \leftarrow \text{DE.Enc}(1^\lambda, \pi, pk, m)$
$(pk^*, sk^*) \xleftarrow{\$} \text{DE.Kg}(1^\lambda, \pi)$	$c^* \leftarrow \text{DE.Enc}(1^\lambda, \pi, pk^*, m)$
Return (π, pk^*)	Return (c, c^*)
$\overline{\text{DE}}.\text{Kg}(1^\lambda, (\pi, pk^*))$	$\overline{\text{DE}}.\text{Dec}(1^\lambda, (\pi, pk^*), sk, (c, c^*))$
$(pk, sk) \xleftarrow{\$} \text{DE.Kg}(1^\lambda, \pi)$	$m \leftarrow \text{DE.Dec}(1^\lambda, \pi, sk, c)\ ;\ \text{Return } m$
Return (pk, sk)	

Fig. 6. D-PKE scheme $\overline{\text{DE}}$ constructed from D-PKE scheme DE

may repeat across columns, meaning the same message may be encrypted under different public keys.)

The $\text{mIND}_{\text{DE}}^{\text{A}}(\lambda)$ game associated with DE and adversary A is described on the left of Fig. 5. We define the advantage of A via $\mathbf{Adv}_{\text{DE,A}}^{\text{mind}}(\lambda) = 2 \cdot \Pr[\text{mIND}_{\text{DE}}^{\text{A}}(1^\lambda)] - 1$ for all $\lambda \in \mathbb{N}$. We let $\mathbf{Adv}_{\text{A,P}}^{\text{pred}}(\lambda) = \Pr[\text{PRED}_{\text{A}}^{\text{P}}(\lambda)]$ for all $\lambda \in \mathbb{N}$, where game PRED is in the middle in Fig. 5. We say that A is unpredictable if $\mathbf{Adv}_{\text{A,P}}^{\text{pred}}(\cdot)$ is negligible for all P. If $\mathcal{A}$ is a class (set) of adversaries then we say that DE is mIND[$\mathcal{A}$]-secure if $\mathbf{Adv}_{\text{DE,A}}^{\text{mind}}(\cdot)$ is negligible for all $\text{A} \in \mathcal{A}$. It is convenient to view mIND[$\mathcal{A}$] as a set, so that $\text{DE} \in \text{mIND}[\mathcal{A}]$ iff DE is mIND[$\mathcal{A}$]-secure. If A.cs always returns ε then we say that A has trivial initial state and we may refer to A as a two-stage adversary. Let $\mathcal{A}_2^{\text{m}}$ be the class of all PT, 2-stage unpredictable uniform adversaries, and for any polynomial $n \colon \mathbb{N} \to \mathbb{N}$ let $\mathcal{A}_{2,n}^{\text{m}}$ be the class of all $\text{A} \in \mathcal{A}_2^{\text{m}}$ for which $\text{A.nu} = n$. Then security for n users is captured by mIND[$\mathcal{A}_{2,n}^{\text{m}}$] and security for any number of users is captured by mIND[$\mathcal{A}_2^{\text{m}}$].

In the case of IND we had four variants, depending on whether adversaries were uniform or non-uniform and whether we were in the SM or the ROM. For simplicity, we address mIND in the uniform, SM case. The separation extends to the other three cases. Thus, below, the understanding is that IND, mIND_n, mIND refer, respectively, to IND[$\mathcal{A}_2^{\text{sm-u}}$], mIND[$\mathcal{A}_{2,n}^{\text{m}}$] and mIND[$\mathcal{A}_2^{\text{m}}$].

SEPARATION RESULT. Our separation is based on the minimal assumption that some IND-secure D-PKE scheme exists, and is established by a somewhat curious case analysis. The proof of the following is in [8].

Theorem 3. *Assume there exists an IND-secure D-PKE scheme. Then there exists a D-PKE scheme that is (1) IND-secure but (2) not mIND$_2$-secure.*

Proof (Theorem 3). We establish the theorem by considering two cases.

Case 1: There does not exist a D-PKE scheme that is mIND$_2$-secure.

The assumption in the theorem statement says there exists a D-PKE scheme DE that is IND-secure. But the assumption made for Case 1 says that no D-PKE scheme is mIND$_2$-secure. So in particular DE is not mIND$_2$-secure. This establishes the theorem trivially in this case.

Case 2: There exists a D-PKE scheme that is mIND$_2$-secure.

Let DE be a D-PKE scheme that is mIND$_2$-secure. We construct from it a D-PKE scheme $\overline{\mathsf{DE}}$ that is (1) IND-secure but (2) not mIND$_2$-secure. This establishes the theorem in Case 2. Since either Case 1 or Case 2 must be true, we have established the theorem overall.

The D-PKE scheme $\overline{\mathsf{DE}}$ is shown in Fig. 6. The parameters of the new scheme include a public key pk^* for the old scheme. The new encryption of a message m under public key pk consists of two encryptions of m under the old scheme, one with pk and the other with pk^*. Intuitively, (2) is true because if users 1, 2 encrypt messages m_1, m_2 then the second components of their ciphertexts are equal iff $m_1 = m_2$, allowing an adversary to detect whether or not $m_1 = m_2$. On the other hand, (1) is true because pk^* can be viewed as a key of a dummy second user in the old scheme. Encryption in the new scheme is then tantamount to encryption of m under two independent keys of the old scheme, which is secure by the assumed mIND$_2$-security of the old scheme. We now proceed to the details.

We first establish (2), that $\overline{\mathsf{DE}}$ is not mIND$_2$-secure, via the following adversary $\mathsf{A} \in \mathcal{A}_{2,2}^{\mathrm{m}}$. Let $\mathsf{A.cs}(1^\lambda)$ return ε. Let $\mathsf{A.msg}(1^\lambda, \varepsilon)$ return 2 by 1 matrices $(\mathbf{m}_0, \mathbf{m}_1)$ defined via

$$\mathbf{m}_0[1,1], \mathbf{m}_0[2,1], \mathbf{m}_1[1,1] \xleftarrow{\$} \{0,1\}^{\mathsf{DE.ml}(\lambda)} \; ; \; \mathbf{m}_1[2,1] \leftarrow \mathbf{m}_1[1,1] \; .$$

Let $\mathsf{A.g}(1^\lambda, (\pi, pk^*), \mathbf{pk}, \varepsilon, \overline{\mathbf{c}})$ parse $(\mathbf{c}[i,1], \mathbf{c}^*[i,1]) \leftarrow \overline{\mathbf{c}}[i,1]$ for $i = 1, 2$. If $\mathbf{c}^*[1,1] = \mathbf{c}^*[2,1]$ then it returns 1 else it returns 0. Then $\mathbf{Adv}_{\overline{\mathsf{DE}},\mathsf{A}}^{\mathrm{mind}}(\lambda) \geq 1 - 2^{-\mathsf{DE.ml}(\lambda)}$.

To establish (1), that $\overline{\mathsf{DE}}$ is IND-secure, let $\overline{\mathsf{A}} \in \mathcal{A}_2$. We will provide $\mathsf{A} \in \mathcal{A}_{2,2}^{\mathrm{m}}$ such that

$$\mathbf{Adv}_{\overline{\mathsf{DE}},\overline{\mathsf{A}}}^{\mathrm{ind}}(\lambda) \leq \mathbf{Adv}_{\mathsf{DE},\mathsf{A}}^{\mathrm{mind}}(\lambda) \tag{5}$$

for all $\lambda \in \mathbb{N}$. Then (1) follows from the assumption that DE is mIND$_2$-secure. Let $\mathsf{A.cs} = \overline{\mathsf{A}}.\mathsf{cs}$ return ε. Let $\mathsf{A.nm} = \overline{\mathsf{A}}.\mathsf{nm}$. Let $\mathsf{A.nu} = 2$. Define $\mathsf{A.msg}$ and $\mathsf{A.g}$ as follows:

$\underline{\mathsf{A.msg}(1^\lambda, \varepsilon)}$

$(\overline{\mathbf{m}}_0, \overline{\mathbf{m}}_1) \overset{\$}{\leftarrow} \overline{\mathsf{A}}.\mathsf{msg}(1^\lambda, \varepsilon)$

For $j = 1, \ldots, \mathsf{A.nm}(\lambda)$ do

$\quad \mathbf{m}_0[1, j] \leftarrow \overline{\mathbf{m}}_0[j] \; ; \; \mathbf{m}_0[2, j] \leftarrow \overline{\mathbf{m}}_0[j]$

$\quad \mathbf{m}_1[1, j] \leftarrow \overline{\mathbf{m}}_1[j] \; ; \; \mathbf{m}_1[2, j] \leftarrow \overline{\mathbf{m}}_1[j]$

Return $(\mathbf{m}_0, \mathbf{m}_1)$

$\underline{\mathsf{A.g}(1^\lambda, \pi, \mathbf{pk}, \varepsilon, \mathbf{c})}$

For $j = 1, \ldots, \mathsf{A.nm}(\lambda)$ do

$\quad \overline{\mathbf{c}}[j] \leftarrow (\mathbf{c}[1, j], \mathbf{c}[2, j])$

$b' \overset{\$}{\leftarrow} \overline{\mathsf{A}}.\mathsf{g}(1^\lambda, (\pi, \mathbf{pk}[2]), \mathbf{pk}[1], \varepsilon, \overline{\mathbf{c}})$

Return b'

Then (5) follows.   □

We remark that the proof of Theorem 3 is non-constructive. It proves the existence of a scheme that is IND-secure but not mIND_2-secure but does not put in our hands a concrete, specific example of such a scheme. This is because, although either Case 1 or Case 2 in the proof must be true, we do not know which. We also remark that our proof makes crucial use of the system parameters. Whether or not single and multi-user security are equivalent for D-PKE in the absence of system parameters is an interesting open question.

Acknowledgments. We thank Bjorn Tackmann, Peter Gazi and Adam O'Neill for valuable discussions. We thank the PKC 2015 reviewers for their valuable comments. Bellare was supported in part by NSF grants CNS-1228890 and CNS-1116800. Work done while Keelveedhi was at UCSD, supported in part by NSF grants CNS-1228890 and CNS-1116800.

References

1. Baudron, O., Pointcheval, D., Stern, J.: Extended notions of security for multicast public key cryptosystems. In: Welzl, E., Montanari, U., Rolim, J.D.P. (eds.) ICALP 2000. LNCS, vol. 1853, pp. 499–511. Springer, Heidelberg (2000)
2. Beaver, D.: Plug and play encryption. In: Kaliski Jr., B.S. (ed.) CRYPTO 1997. LNCS, vol. 1294, pp. 75–89. Springer, Heidelberg (1997)
3. Beaver, D., Haber, S.: Cryptographic protocols provably secure against dynamic adversaries. In: Rueppel, R.A. (ed.) EUROCRYPT 1992. LNCS, vol. 658, pp. 307–323. Springer, Heidelberg (1993)
4. Bellare, M., Boldyreva, A., Micali, S.: Public-key encryption in a multi-user setting: security proofs and improvements. In: Preneel, B. (ed.) EUROCRYPT 2000. LNCS, vol. 1807, p. 259. Springer, Heidelberg (2000)
5. Bellare, M., Boldyreva, A., O'Neill, A.: Deterministic and efficiently searchable encryption. In: Menezes, A. (ed.) CRYPTO 2007. LNCS, vol. 4622, pp. 535–552. Springer, Heidelberg (2007)
6. Bellare, M., Brakerski, Z., Naor, M., Ristenpart, T., Segev, G., Shacham, H., Yilek, S.: Hedged public-key encryption: how to protect against bad randomness. In: Matsui, M. (ed.) ASIACRYPT 2009. LNCS, vol. 5912, pp. 232–249. Springer, Heidelberg (2009)
7. Bellare, M., Desai, A., Pointcheval, D., Rogaway, P.: Relations among notions of security for public-key encryption schemes. In: Krawczyk, H. (ed.) CRYPTO 1998. LNCS, vol. 1462, p. 26. Springer, Heidelberg (1998)

8. Bellare, M., Dowsley, R., Keelveedhi, S.: How secure is deterministic encryption? Cryptology ePrint Archive, Report 2014/376 (2014). http://eprint.iacr.org/2014/376

9. Bellare, M., Dowsley, R., Waters, B., Yilek, S.: Standard security does not imply security against selective-opening. In: Pointcheval, D., Johansson, T. (eds.) EUROCRYPT 2012. LNCS, vol. 7237, pp. 645–662. Springer, Heidelberg (2012)

10. Bellare, M., Fischlin, M., O'Neill, A., Ristenpart, T.: Deterministic encryption: definitional equivalences and constructions without random oracles. In: Wagner, D. (ed.) CRYPTO 2008. LNCS, vol. 5157, pp. 360–378. Springer, Heidelberg (2008)

11. Bellare, M., Hoang, V.T., Keelveedhi, S.: Instantiating random oracles via UCEs. In: Canetti, R., Garay, J.A. (eds.) CRYPTO 2013, Part II. LNCS, vol. 8043, pp. 398–415. Springer, Heidelberg (2013)

12. Bellare, M., Hofheinz, D., Yilek, S.: Possibility and impossibility results for encryption and commitment secure under selective opening. In: Joux, A. (ed.) EUROCRYPT 2009. LNCS, vol. 5479, pp. 1–35. Springer, Heidelberg (2009)

13. Bellare, M., Palacio, A.: GQ and schnorr identification schemes: proofs of security against impersonation under active and concurrent attacks. In: Yung, M. (ed.) CRYPTO 2002. LNCS, vol. 2442, p. 162. Springer, Heidelberg (2002)

14. Bellare, M., Rogaway, P.: Random oracles are practical: a paradigm for designing efficient protocols. In: Ashby, V. (ed.) ACM CCS 1993, pp. 62–73. ACM Press, November 1993

15. Bellare, M., Rogaway, P.: The security of triple encryption and a framework for code-based game-playing proofs. In: Vaudenay, S. (ed.) EUROCRYPT 2006. LNCS, vol. 4004, pp. 409–426. Springer, Heidelberg (2006)

16. Bellare, M., Waters, B., Yilek, S.: Identity-based encryption secure against selective opening attack. In: Ishai, Y. (ed.) TCC 2011. LNCS, vol. 6597, pp. 235–252. Springer, Heidelberg (2011)

17. Bellare, M., Yilek, S.: Encryption schemes secure under selective opening attack. Cryptology ePrint Archive, Report 2009/101 (2009). http://eprint.iacr.org/2009/101

18. Böhl, F., Hofheinz, D., Kraschewski, D.: On definitions of selective opening security. In: Fischlin, M., Buchmann, J., Manulis, M. (eds.) PKC 2012. LNCS, vol. 7293, pp. 522–539. Springer, Heidelberg (2012)

19. Boldyreva, A., Fehr, S., O'Neill, A.: On notions of security for deterministic encryption, and efficient constructions without random oracles. In: Wagner, D. (ed.) CRYPTO 2008. LNCS, vol. 5157, pp. 335–359. Springer, Heidelberg (2008)

20. Brakerski, Z., Segev, G.: Better security for deterministic public-key encryption: the auxiliary-input setting. In: Rogaway, P. (ed.) CRYPTO 2011. LNCS, vol. 6841, pp. 543–560. Springer, Heidelberg (2011)

21. Canetti, R., Dwork, C., Naor, M., Ostrovsky, R.: Deniable encryption. In: Kaliski Jr., B.S. (ed.) CRYPTO 1997. LNCS, vol. 1294, pp. 90–104. Springer, Heidelberg (1997)

22. Canetti, R., Feige, U., Goldreich, O., Naor, M.: Adaptively secure multi-party computation. In: 28th ACM STOC, pp. 639–648. ACM Press, May 1996

23. Canetti, R., Halevi, S., Katz, J.: Adaptively-secure, non-interactive public-key encryption. In: Kilian, J. (ed.) TCC 2005. LNCS, vol. 3378, pp. 150–168. Springer, Heidelberg (2005)

24. Damgård, I.B., Nielsen, J.B.: Improved non-committing encryption schemes based on a general complexity assumption. In: Bellare, M. (ed.) CRYPTO 2000. LNCS, vol. 1880, p. 432. Springer, Heidelberg (2000)

25. Dodis, Y., Lee, P.J., Yum, D.H.: Optimistic fair exchange in a multi-user setting. In: Okamoto, T., Wang, X. (eds.) PKC 2007. LNCS, vol. 4450, pp. 118–133. Springer, Heidelberg (2007)
26. Dwork, C., Naor, M., Reingold, O., Stockmeyer, L.J.: Magic functions. Journal of the ACM 50(6), 852–921 (2003)
27. Fehr, S., Hofheinz, D., Kiltz, E., Wee, H.: Encryption schemes secure against chosen-ciphertext selective opening attacks. In: Gilbert, H. (ed.) EUROCRYPT 2010. LNCS, vol. 6110, pp. 381–402. Springer, Heidelberg (2010)
28. Fuller, B., O'Neill, A., Reyzin, L.: A unified approach to deterministic encryption: new constructions and a connection to computational entropy. In: Cramer, R. (ed.) TCC 2012. LNCS, vol. 7194, pp. 582–599. Springer, Heidelberg (2012)
29. Goldwasser, S., Micali, S.: Probabilistic encryption. Journal of Computer and System Sciences 28(2), 270–299 (1984)
30. Hemenway, B., Libert, B., Ostrovsky, R., Vergnaud, D.: Lossy encryption: constructions from general assumptions and efficient selective opening chosen ciphertext security. In: Lee, D.H., Wang, X. (eds.) ASIACRYPT 2011. LNCS, vol. 7073, pp. 70–88. Springer, Heidelberg (2011)
31. Hofheinz, D., Rupp, A.: Standard versus selective opening security: separation and equivalence results. In: Lindell, Y. (ed.) TCC 2014. LNCS, vol. 8349, pp. 591–615. Springer, Heidelberg (2014)
32. Kol, G., Naor, M.: Cryptography and game theory: designing protocols for exchanging information. In: Canetti, R. (ed.) TCC 2008. LNCS, vol. 4948, pp. 320–339. Springer, Heidelberg (2008)
33. Mironov, I., Pandey, O., Reingold, O., Segev, G.: Incremental deterministic public-key encryption. In: Pointcheval, D., Johansson, T. (eds.) EUROCRYPT 2012. LNCS, vol. 7237, pp. 628–644. Springer, Heidelberg (2012)
34. Nielsen, J.B.: Separating random oracle proofs from complexity theoretic proofs: the non-committing encryption case. In: Yung, M. (ed.) CRYPTO 2002. LNCS, vol. 2442, p. 111. Springer, Heidelberg (2002)
35. O'Neill, A.: Stronger security notions for trapdoor functions and applications. Ph.D. Thesis, Georgia Institute of Technology (2012)
36. Ouafi, K., Vaudenay, S.: Smashing SQUASH-0. In: Joux, A. (ed.) EUROCRYPT 2009. LNCS, vol. 5479, pp. 300–312. Springer, Heidelberg (2009)
37. Panjwani, S.: Tackling adaptive corruptions in multicast encryption protocols. In: Vadhan, S.P. (ed.) TCC 2007. LNCS, vol. 4392, pp. 21–40. Springer, Heidelberg (2007)
38. Peikert, C., Vaikuntanathan, V., Waters, B.: A framework for efficient and composable oblivious transfer. In: Wagner, D. (ed.) CRYPTO 2008. LNCS, vol. 5157, pp. 554–571. Springer, Heidelberg (2008)
39. Raghunathan, A., Segev, G., Vadhan, S.: Deterministic public-key encryption for adaptively chosen plaintext distributions. In: Johansson, T., Nguyen, P.Q. (eds.) EUROCRYPT 2013. LNCS, vol. 7881, pp. 93–110. Springer, Heidelberg (2013)
40. Ristenpart, T., Shacham, H., Shrimpton, T.: Careful with composition: limitations of the indifferentiability framework. In: Paterson, K.G. (ed.) EUROCRYPT 2011. LNCS, vol. 6632, pp. 487–506. Springer, Heidelberg (2011)
41. Ristenpart, T., Yilek, S.: When good randomness goes bad: Virtual machine reset vulnerabilities and hedging deployed cryptography. In: NDSS 2010. The Internet Society, February / March 2010
42. Wichs, D.: Barriers in cryptography with weak, correlated and leaky sources. In: Kleinberg, R.D. (ed.) ITCS 2013, pp. 111–126. ACM, January 2013

E-Cash

Divisible E-Cash Made Practical

Sébastien Canard[1]([✉]), David Pointcheval[2], Olivier Sanders[1,2],
and Jacques Traoré[1]

[1] Orange Labs, Applied Crypto Group, Caen, France
{sebastien.canard,olivier.sanders,jacques.traore}@orange.com
[2] École normale supérieure, CNRS & INRIA, Paris, France
David.Pointcheval@ens.fr

Abstract. Divisible E-cash systems allow users to withdraw a unique coin of value 2^n from a bank, but then to spend it in several times to distinct merchants. In such a system, whereas users want anonymity of their transactions, the bank wants to prevent, or at least detect, double-spending, and trace the defrauders. While this primitive was introduced two decades ago, quite a few (really) anonymous constructions have been introduced. In addition, all but one were just proven secure in the random oracle model, but still with either weak security models or quite complex settings and thus costly constructions. The unique proposal, secure in the standard model, appeared recently and is unpractical. As evidence, the authors left the construction of an efficient scheme secure in this model as an open problem.

In this paper, we answer it with the first efficient divisible E-cash system secure in the standard model. It is based on a new way of building the coins, with a unique and public global tree structure for all the coins. Actually, we propose two constructions: a very efficient one in the random oracle model and a less efficient, but still practical, in the standard model. They both achieve constant time for withdrawing and spending coins, while allowing the bank to quickly detect double-spendings by a simple comparison of the serial numbers of deposited coins to the ones of previously spent coins.

1 Introduction

Electronic Cash (E-cash), introduced by Chaum [20,21], is the digital analogue of regular money. It allows users to withdraw coins from a bank and to spend them to merchants, in an anonymous way, thus perfectly emulating conventional cash transactions.

Unfortunately, with E-cash, as any digital data, coins can easily be duplicated, and thus spent several times. It is therefore essential to be able to detect double-spending and even to identify the defrauders. As for group signatures [4,6], one solution could be to give to a specific entity the ability of revoking anonymity for any transaction of his choice. However, such an approach (called *fair* E-cash [9,31]) weakens the anonymity of the scheme because, ideally, user's privacy should be guaranteed as long as the user is honest. Moreover, such an entity should

J. Katz (Ed.): PKC 2015, LNCS 9020, pp. 77–100, 2015.
DOI: 10.1007/978-3-662-46447-2_4

be trusted by all the users or distributed among a large group of authorities, which makes the tracing procedure, in case of fraud, quite costly.

E-cash systems achieve their ultimate goal when the user's side of the protocol is implemented on a mobile device (*e.g.* a smartphone). However, the limited power of such devices along with the strong time constraints of electronic transactions require very efficient withdrawal and spending procedures. Moreover, even if the bank is more powerful than the users, it has to centralize a huge number of transactions, and thus double-spending detection should be made as efficient as possible. Reconciling security requirements with efficiency is therefore the main challenge when designing E-cash systems.

1.1   Related Work

Compact E-Cash. Camenisch, Hohenberger and Lysyanskaya [10] described the first compact E-cash system (later extended to systems supporting additional features [12,14,16]), allowing users to withdraw wallets with 2^n coins at once. Each coin is associated with a unique serial number, allowing the bank to efficiently detect double-spending. Unfortunately, while the withdrawal of many coins can be done at once, the spending procedure is done coin by coin, which is a major drawback for concrete use. Indeed, in order to provide a good granularity, one must use coins of one cent, and thus transactions often involve thousands of coins. An alternative could be the use of coins with several denominations, but then one should use several systems in parallel for each value, and in addition anonymity would be more difficult to achieve since users would withdraw different kinds of coins. Then, the bank could classify the users according to their withdrawals and then infer where users spend their money from the coins the merchants deposit.

Divisible E-Cash Systems. The purpose of divisible E-cash systems is to address this problem of splitting coins of large values. As above, users withdraw a large coin of value 2^n (or withdraw 2^n coins at once), but can spend it in several times by dividing it (or spend several coins at once): more concretely, one can spend a coin of value 2^ℓ, for any $0 \leq \ell \leq n$, at once, instead of spending 2^ℓ unitary coins, which is clearly much more efficient.

Since their introduction, many schemes have been proposed [19,27–29] but they only achieved quite weak levels of anonymity. Indeed, transactions involving the same coin (from the same withdrawal) were all linkable, except with [27], which however still reveals which part of the coin is spent (which is not compatible with the highest security notion) and in addition requires a trusted authority to recover spenders' identities.

Canard and Gouget [13] introduced the first truly anonymous E-cash system. Unfortunately, it makes use of complex zero-knowledge proofs of knowledge (ZKPK) and of groups of different but related orders, whose generation requires a huge computational power. Despite its inefficiency (pointed out in [2,15]) this system was a proof of concept: a "truly" anonymous divisible E-cash system is possible. Au, Susilo, and Mu [2] proposed a more efficient scheme but at the cost of an unconventional security model where the bank is only ensured that it will not loose money on average (provided that it can legally impose fines on users, which is not necessarily the case). Canard and Gouget [15] later proposed another construction, but still with groups of different orders, leading to rather inefficient ZKPK. All these schemes were proven secure in the random oracle model (ROM) [5]. More recently, Izabachène and Libert [26] provided the first construction with security proven in the standard model. However their construction is rather inefficient, especially the deposit phase whose computational cost for the bank depends on the number of *previously* deposited coins with a pairing computation between every new coin and every past coin. Such a downside makes the scheme impractical, leading the authors to leave the construction of an efficient scheme secure in the standard model as an open problem.

1.2 Our Contribution

In this paper, we address this open problem, with the first *really* efficient divisible E-cash system. It can be designed either in the ROM or the standard model. Our main contribution is a new way for building the serial numbers. As noticed in [26], the use of serial numbers is indeed the best approach for the bank to quickly detect double-spending.

In previous solutions [2,13,15], every divisible coin is associated with a binary tree whose nodes correspond to expendable amounts. When a user withdraws a coin, he selects a random number k_ϵ associated with the root of the tree and then computes, for each internal node s, the corresponding number k_s, using k_ϵ and a one-way function. The user then obtains signatures on these numbers (or on elements accumulating them) from the bank and defines the coin to be the binary tree along with the signatures. However, to ensure that the user will not spend more than the amount he has withdrawn, he will have to prove (either during the spending or the withdrawal protocol) that the tree (and so the numbers k_s) is well-formed. Unfortunately, the construction from [2] is not compatible with any zero-knowledge proof construction because the numbers k_s are computed using a hash function, modeled as a random oracle. The authors therefore proposed a *cut-and-choose* method to detect cheaters which leads to the problem mentioned above. Canard and Gouget [13,15] used groups of different orders which are compatible with zero-knowledge proofs in the ROM (although they are rather inefficient) but not in the standard model since the Groth-Sahai [25] methodology does no longer work in this setting.

In our construction, we use a totally different approach: instead of using one tree by coin, we define, in the public parameters, one single tree which will be common to all the coins. The key point of this solution is obvious: users no longer have to prove that the tree is well-formed. Moreover, it considerably alleviates the withdrawal procedure since the bank no longer has to certify each tree.

We will use bilinear groups (*i.e.* a set of three cyclic groups $\mathbb{G}_1, \mathbb{G}_2$ and $\mathbb{G}_T$ of prime order p along with a bilinear map $e : \mathbb{G}_1 \times \mathbb{G}_2 \to \mathbb{G}_T$), which are compatible with Groth-Sahai proofs. In a nutshell, our system works as follows: it uses a unique tree T of depth n (for coins of value 2^n), where each leaf f is associated with an element $\chi_f \in \mathbb{G}_T$ and each internal node s is associated with an element $g_s \in \mathbb{G}_1$. In addition to these group elements, the public parameters also contain, for each leaf f and any node s on the path to f, an element $\widetilde{g}_{s \mapsto f} \in \mathbb{G}_2$ such that $e(g_s, \widetilde{g}_{s \mapsto f}) = \chi_f$ (a setup algorithm will efficiently generate these parameters). When a user withdraws a coin, he gets a certificate on some random scalar $x \in \mathbb{Z}_p$, which will implicitly define all the serial numbers associated with this coin as χ_f^x for each leaf f. To spend a node s of height ℓ in the tree, corresponding to a value of 2^ℓ, the user can compute $t_s \leftarrow g_s^x$ and prove that it is well-formed: such a proof can easily be done in either the ROM or the standard model. Informally, the unlinkability property follows from the fact that it is hard, given g_s^x and $g_{s'}^x$ for two nodes s and s', to decide whether they were computed using the same x (and thus belong to the same tree) under the XDH assumption. However, using the elements $\widetilde{g}_{s \mapsto f}$, the bank will be able to recover the 2^ℓ serial numbers by computing $e(t_s, \widetilde{g}_{s \mapsto f}) = \chi_f^x$ for each f in the subtree below s. A double-spending means that two transactions involve two nodes s and s' with non-disjoint subtrees: a common leaf f is in both subtrees issued from s and s', and so the bank will detect a collision between the serial numbers since $e(t_s, \widetilde{g}_{s \mapsto f}) = \chi_f^x = e(t_{s'}, \widetilde{g}_{s' \mapsto f})$.

Of course, several problems have to be addressed to fulfill all the security requirements, but the above key idea allows to design a system with constant cost for both the withdrawal and spending protocols, which can be proven secure in either the random oracle and the standard models.

1.3 Organization

In Section 2, we review some classical definitions and notations. Section 3 describes the security model for divisible E-cash. We provide a high level description of our construction in Section 4, and a more detailed presentation in Section 5. Eventually, security proofs are given in Section 6.

2 Preliminaries

Bilinear Groups. Bilinear groups are a set of three cyclic groups $\mathbb{G}_1$, $\mathbb{G}_2$, and $\mathbb{G}_T$ of prime order p along with a bilinear map $e : \mathbb{G}_1 \times \mathbb{G}_2 \to \mathbb{G}_T$ with the following properties:

1. for all $g \in \mathbb{G}_1, \widetilde{g} \in \mathbb{G}_2$ and $a, b \in \mathbb{Z}_p$, $e(g^a, \widetilde{g}^b) = e(g, \widetilde{g})^{a \cdot b}$;
2. for $g \neq 1_{\mathbb{G}_1}$ and $\widetilde{g} \neq 1_{\mathbb{G}_2}$, $e(g, \widetilde{g}) \neq 1_{\mathbb{G}_T}$;
3. e is efficiently computable.

Computational Assumptions. Our construction will rely on several computational assumptions that have been considered reasonable in well chosen groups:

- the DL assumption holds in the group $\mathbb{G}$ if it is hard, given $(g, g^x) \in \mathbb{G}^2$, to output x;

- the XDH **assumption** holds in bilinear groups $(\mathbb{G}_1, \mathbb{G}_2, \mathbb{G}_T)$ if it is hard, given $(g, g^x, g^y, g^z) \in \mathbb{G}_1^4$, to decide whether $z = x \cdot y$ or z is random;
- the q − SDH **assumption** [8] holds in a group $\mathbb{G}$ if it is hard, given a tuple $(g, g^x, g^{x^2}, \ldots, g^{x^q}) \in \mathbb{G}^{q+1}$, to output a pair $(m, g^{\frac{1}{m+x}})$.

Digital Signature Scheme. A digital signature scheme Σ is defined by three algorithms:

- the key generation algorithm $\Sigma.\mathtt{Keygen}$ which outputs a pair of signing and verification keys $(\mathsf{sk}, \mathsf{pk})$ – we assume that sk always contains pk;
- the signing algorithm $\Sigma.\mathtt{Sign}$ algorithm which, on input the signing key sk and a message m, outputs a signature σ;
- and the verification algorithm $\Sigma.\mathtt{Verify}$ which, on input m, σ and pk, outputs 1 if σ is a valid signature on m under pk and 0 otherwise.

The standard security notion for a signature scheme is *existential unforgeability under chosen message attacks* (EUF-CMA) [24] which means that it is hard, even given access to a signing oracle, to output a valid pair (m, σ) for a message m never asked to the oracle. In this paper we will also use two weaker different security notions for signature schemes. The former is the security against selective chosen message attacks, which limits the oracle queries to be asked before having seen the key pk. The latter is a *strong* one-time security notion where the adversary can ask only one query to the signing oracle, but *strong* means that an output with a new signature on an already signed message is also considered a forgery. In our instantiation in the full version [17], we use a deterministic one-time signature, and thus one-time security is equivalent to strong one-time security.

3   Divisible E-cash System

3.1   Syntax

As in [13,15], a divisible e-cash system is defined by the following algorithms, that involve at least three entities: the bank $\mathcal{B}$, a user $\mathcal{U}$ and a merchant $\mathcal{M}$. Although not necessary, it is often easier to assume that the $\mathtt{Setup}$ algorithm is run by a trusted entity (we refer to Remark 3 in Section 4 for more discussion).

- $\mathtt{Setup}(1^k, V)$: On inputs a security parameter k and an integer V, this probabilistic algorithm outputs the public parameters $p.p.$ for divisible coins of global value V. We assume that $p.p.$ are implicit to the other algorithms, and that they include k and V. They are also an implicit input to the adversary, we will then omit them.
- $\mathtt{BKeygen}()$: This probabilistic algorithm executed by the bank $\mathcal{B}$ outputs a key pair $(\mathsf{bsk}, \mathsf{bpk})$. It also sets L as an empty list, that will store all deposited coins. We assume that bsk contains bpk.

- Keygen(): This probabilistic algorithm executed by a user $\mathcal{U}$ (resp. a merchant $\mathcal{M}$) outputs a key pair (usk, upk) (resp. (msk, mpk)). We assume that usk (resp. msk) contains upk (resp. mpk).
- Withdraw($\mathcal{B}$(bsk, upk), $\mathcal{U}$(usk, bpk)): This is an interactive protocol between the bank $\mathcal{B}$ and a user $\mathcal{U}$. At the end of this protocol, the user gets a divisible coin C of value V or outputs $\perp$ (in case of failure) while the bank stores the transcript Tr of the protocol execution or outputs $\perp$.
- Spend($\mathcal{U}$(usk, C, bpk, mpk, v), $\mathcal{M}$(msk, bpk, v)): This is an interactive protocol between a user $\mathcal{U}$ and a merchant $\mathcal{M}$. At the end of the protocol the merchant gets a master serial number Z of value v (the amount of the transaction they previously agreed on) along with a proof of validity Π or outputs $\perp$. $\mathcal{U}$ either updates C or outputs $\perp$.
- Deposit($\mathcal{M}$(msk, bpk, (v, Z, Π)), $\mathcal{B}$(bsk, L, mpk)): This is an interactive protocol between a merchant $\mathcal{M}$ and the bank $\mathcal{B}$. $\mathcal{B}$ checks that Π is valid on v and Z and that (v, z, Π) has never been deposited (corresponding to the case of a cheating merchant). $\mathcal{B}$ then recovers the m (for some $m \geq v$) serial numbers $z_1, \ldots, z_m$ corresponding to this transaction and checks whether, for some $1 \leq i \leq m$, $z_i \in L$. If none of the serial numbers is in L, then the bank credits $\mathcal{M}$'s account of v, stores (v, Z, Π) and appends $\{z_1, \ldots, z_m\}$ to L. Else, there is at least an index $i \in \{1, \ldots, m\}$ and a serial number z' in L such that $z' = z_i$. The bank then recovers the tuple (v', Z', Π') corresponding to z' and publishes $[(v, Z, \Pi), (v', Z', \Pi')]$.
- Identify($(v_1, Z_1, \Pi_1), (v_2, Z_2, \Pi_2)$, bpk): On inputs two different valid transcripts (v_1, Z_1, Π_1) and (v_2, Z_2, Π_2), this deterministic algorithm outputs a user's public key upk if there is a collision between the serial numbers derived from Z_1 and from Z_2, and $\perp$ otherwise.

It is worthy to note that the Identify algorithm does not require knowledge of any secret element and can thus be run by anyone. So, there is no need for a VerifyGuilt algorithm (as provided in [13,15]) since any entity can be convinced of the culpability of a user by recovering his public key upk from the transcripts published by the bank.

3.2   Security Model

Besides the usual *correctness* property (informally meaning that an honest user running a Withdraw protocol with an honest bank will receive a divisible coin accepted by any honest merchant), a secure e-cash system must achieve several security properties, defined through games between an adversary $\mathcal{A}$ and a challenger $\mathcal{C}$. Our security model makes use of the following oracles.

- $\mathcal{O}$Add() is an oracle used by $\mathcal{A}$ to register a new honest user (resp. merchant). The challenger runs the Keygen algorithm, stores usk (resp. msk) and returns upk (resp. mpk) to $\mathcal{A}$. In this case, upk (resp. mpk) is said *honest*.
- $\mathcal{O}$Corrupt(upk/mpk) is an oracle used by $\mathcal{A}$ to corrupt an honest user (resp. merchant) whose public key is upk (resp. mpk). The challenger then returns

$\text{Exp}_{\mathcal{A}}^{anon-b}(1^k, V)$

1. $p.p. \leftarrow \text{Setup}(1^k, V)$
2. $\text{bpk} \leftarrow \mathcal{A}()$
3. $(v, \text{upk}_0, \text{upk}_1, \text{mpk}) \leftarrow \mathcal{A}^{\mathcal{O}\text{Add}, \mathcal{O}\text{Corrupt}, \mathcal{O}\text{AddCorrupt}, \mathcal{O}\text{Withdraw}_{\mathcal{U}}, \mathcal{O}\text{Spend}}()$
4. If upk_0 or upk_1 is not registered, then return 0
5. If $c_{\text{upk}_i} > m_{\text{upk}_i} \cdot V - v$ for $i \in \{0, 1\}$, then return 0
6. $(v, Z, \Pi) \leftarrow \text{Spend}(\mathcal{C}(\text{usk}_b, C, \text{mpk}, v), \mathcal{A}())$
7. $b^* \leftarrow \mathcal{A}^{\mathcal{O}\text{Add}, \mathcal{O}\text{Corrupt}, \mathcal{O}\text{AddCorrupt}, \mathcal{O}\text{Withdraw}_{\mathcal{U}}, \mathcal{O}\text{Spend}^*}()$
8. If upk_0 or upk_1 has been corrupted, then return 0
9. Return $(b = b^*)$

Fig. 1. Anonymity Security Game

the corresponding secret key usk (resp. msk) to $\mathcal{A}$ along with the secret values of every coin withdrawn by this user. From now on, upk (resp. mpk) is said *corrupted*.

- $\mathcal{O}\text{AddCorrupt}(\text{upk}/\text{mpk})$ is an oracle used by $\mathcal{A}$ to register a new corrupted user (resp. merchant) whose public key is upk (resp. mpk). In this case, upk (resp. mpk) is said *corrupted*. The adversary could use this oracle on a public key already registered (during a previous $\mathcal{O}\text{Add}$ query) but for simplicity, we reject such case as it will gain nothing more than using the $\mathcal{O}\text{Corrupt}$ oracle on the same public key.
- $\mathcal{O}\text{Withdraw}_{\mathcal{U}}(\text{upk})$ is an oracle that executes the user's side of the Withdraw protocol. This oracle will be used by $\mathcal{A}$ playing the role of the bank against the user with public key upk.
- $\mathcal{O}\text{Withdraw}_{\mathcal{B}}(\text{upk})$ is an oracle that executes the bank's side of the Withdraw protocol. This oracle will be used by $\mathcal{A}$ playing the role of a user whose public key is upk against the bank.
- $\mathcal{O}\text{Spend}(\text{upk}, v)$ is an oracle that executes the user's side of the Spend protocol for a value v. This oracle will be used by $\mathcal{A}$ playing the role of the merchant $\mathcal{M}$.

In our experiments, we denote users by their public keys upk, the value spent by user upk during $\mathcal{O}\text{Spend}$ queries by c_{upk}, and the number of divisible coins withdrawn by this user by m_{upk}. This means that the total amount available by a user upk is $m_{\text{upk}} \cdot V$.

Anonymity. Informally, anonymity requires that the bank, even helped by malicious users and merchants, cannot learn anything about a spending other than what is available from side information from the environment. We define the anonymity experiments $\text{Exp}_{\mathcal{A}}^{anon-b}(1^k, V)$ as described on Figure 1. After the challenge phase, the $\mathcal{O}\text{Spend}$ queries are restricted to avoid $\mathcal{A}$ trivially wins: $\mathcal{A}$ then has access to a $\mathcal{O}\text{Spend}^*$ oracle that is the same as the $\mathcal{O}\text{Spend}$ oracle except that it cannot be asked on upk_i if $c_{\text{upk}_i} > m_{\text{upk}_i} \cdot V - v$, for $i \in \{0, 1\}$. Otherwise one can easily deduce which user has spent v during the challenge phase.

$\text{Exp}_{\mathcal{A}}^{tra}(1^k, V)$

1. $p.p. \leftarrow \text{Setup}(1^k, V)$
2. $(\text{bsk}, \text{bpk}) \leftarrow \text{BKeygen}()$
3. $[(v_1, Z_1, \Pi_1), \ldots, (v_u, Z_u, \Pi_u)] \xleftarrow{\$} \mathcal{A}^{\mathcal{O}\text{Add}, \mathcal{O}\text{Corrupt}, \mathcal{O}\text{AddCorrupt}, \mathcal{O}\text{Withdraw}_\mathcal{B}, \mathcal{O}\text{Spend}}(\text{bpk})$
4. If $\sum_{i=1}^{u} v_i > m \cdot V$ and $\forall i \neq j, \text{Identify}((v_i, Z_i, \Pi_i), (v_j, Z_j, \Pi_j)) = \perp$,
   then return 1
5. Return 0

Fig. 2. Traceability Security Game

We define $\text{Adv}_{\mathcal{A}}^{anon}(1^k, V)$ as $\Pr[\text{Exp}_{\mathcal{A}}^{anon-1}(1^k, V)] - \Pr[\text{Exp}_{\mathcal{A}}^{anon-0}(1^k, V)]$. A divisible e-cash system is *anonymous* if, for any probabilistic polynomial adversary $\mathcal{A}$, this advantage is negligible. Of course, the adversary must choose the users involved in the challenge phase among the registered users, and never corrupted, and cannot ask them to spend more than withdrawn, hence restrictions in steps 4, 5, and 8 respectively.

Remark 1. The scheme from [27] achieves an *unlinkability* property, meaning that it is hard to link two spendings from the same coin. This protocol makes use of a tree for the global coin, and each transcript reveals which part of the tree (*i.e.* which node) is spent. In some cases, this property can be enough (we describe informally in Section 4.2 a protocol fulfilling this property) but we stress that a scheme revealing the spent nodes in a tree structure is not anonymous (according to our above model) even if it is unlinkable (and our main scheme given in Section 5 is anonymous in the sense of the above definition). Indeed, to break the anonymity of such a scheme, the adversary can make one $\mathcal{O}\text{Withdraw}_\mathcal{U}(\text{bsk}, \text{usk}_i)$ and then $(V-1)$ $\mathcal{O}\text{Spend}(\text{upk}_i, 1)$ queries, for each user $(i \in \{0, 1\})$. Therefore, it will only remain one unspent node s_{upk_i} for each user. If the nodes are randomly selected among the unspent nodes during a spending (which is even worse if this is deterministic or chosen by the adversary), with overwhelming probability, the two unspent nodes will not be the same for the two users upk_0 and upk_1: $s_{\text{upk}_0} \neq s_{\text{upk}_1}$. The node involved in the challenge phase will then reveal the user identity.

Traceability. Informally, traceability requires that no coalition of malicious users can spend more than they have withdrawn, without revealing their identity. We define the traceability experiment $\text{Exp}_{\mathcal{A}}^{tra}(1^k, V)$ as described on Figure 2. We denote by m the total number of coins withdrawn during the entire experiment. It is assumed that $\{(v_1, Z_1, \Pi_1), \ldots, (v_u, Z_u, \Pi_u)\}$ is a set of different and valid transcripts (else, we do not consider the invalid or duplicated ones when computing the sum $v = \sum v_i$). We define $\text{Adv}_{\mathcal{A}}^{tra}(1^k, V)$ as $\Pr[\text{Exp}_{\mathcal{A}}^{tra}(1^k, V) = 1]$. A divisible e-cash system ensures the *traceability* property if, for any probabilistic polynomial adversary $\mathcal{A}$, this advantage is negligible.

$\mathsf{Exp}_{\mathcal{A}}^{excu}(1^k, V)$

1. $p.p. \leftarrow \mathsf{Setup}(1^k, V)$
2. $\mathsf{bpk} \leftarrow \mathcal{A}()$
3. $[(v_1, Z_1, \Pi_1), (v_2, Z_2, \Pi_2)] \leftarrow \mathcal{A}^{\mathcal{O}\mathsf{Add}, \mathcal{O}\mathsf{Corrupt}, \mathcal{O}\mathsf{AddCorrupt}, \mathcal{O}\mathsf{Withdraw}_{\mathcal{U}}, \mathcal{O}\mathsf{Spend}}()$
4. If $\mathsf{Identify}((v_1, Z_1, \Pi_1), (v_2, Z_2, \Pi_2), \mathsf{bpk}) = \mathsf{upk}$ and upk not corrupted, then return 1
5. Return 0

Fig. 3. Exculpability Security Game

Remark 2. The E-cash systems from [2,13,15,26] considered the *balance* property, requiring that no coalition of users can spend (and then later accepted for deposit) more than they have withdrawn, and the *identification* property, requiring that no coalition of users can double-spend a coin without revealing their identity. We argue that traceability is enough. Indeed, an adversary against the *balance* property must produce $[(v_1, Z_1, \Pi_1), \ldots, (v_u, Z_u, \Pi_u)]$ (with $\sum_{i=1}^{u} v_i > m \cdot V$) that the bank accepts as valid, not duplicated and not double-spent. This adversary can therefore be easily converted into an adversary against our traceability experiment.

Similarly, an adversary against the *identification* property must produce two valid transcripts (v_1, Z_1, Π_1) and (v_2, Z_2, Π_2) which are detected as a double-spending but such that the $\mathsf{Identify}$ algorithm does not output one name from the collusion: either this is a name outside the collusion, we deal with this case below, with the exculpability, or $\mathsf{Identify}((v_1, Z_1, \Pi_1), (v_2, Z_2, \Pi_2)) = \bot$. By legally spending all the remaining parts of this coin, one breaks the traceability property too.

Exculpability. Informally, exculpability requires that the bank, even cooperating with malicious users and merchants, cannot falsely accuse honest users of having double-spent a coin. We define the exculpability experiment $\mathsf{Exp}_{\mathcal{A}}^{excu}(1^k, V)$ as described on Figure 3. We emphasize that any adversary able to spend a coin of a honest user can easily break the exculpability property, by simple making a double-spending in the name of this honest user. We define $\mathsf{Adv}_{\mathcal{A}}^{excu}(1^k, V)$ as $\Pr[\mathsf{Exp}_{\mathcal{A}}^{excu}(1^k, V) = 1]$. A divisible e-cash system is *exculpable* if, for any probabilistic polynomial adversary $\mathcal{A}$, this advantage is negligible.

4 Our Construction: Intuition

Our construction makes use of a binary tree, as in most previous works [2,13,15]. The main difference is the way the tree is built. In the previous systems, each user constructs his own tree by selecting elements $k_{i,j}$ associated with the nodes of the tree and then has to get certificates on all of them (during the $\mathsf{Withdraw}$ protocol) and more importantly, must prove (either during the $\mathsf{Withdraw}$ protocol or the

Spend one) that these elements are well-formed. This latter proof led to complex systems with either unconventional security properties [2] or costly operations in groups of different orders [13,15].

In our system, there is only one tree, which is part of the public parameters. It allows us to avoid proving its well-formedness and so to achieve a better efficiency while working with zero-knowledge proofs compatible with the Groth-Sahai methodology [25]. In the following we first describe our **Setup** algorithm and then give a high level description of our divisible e-cash system.

4.1   Setup

Notation. Let $\mathcal{S}_n$ be the set of bitstrings of size smaller than or equal to n and $\mathcal{F}_n$ be the set of bitstrings of size exactly n. We then define, $\forall s \in \mathcal{S}_n$, the set $\mathcal{F}_n(s)$ as $\{f \in \mathcal{F}_n : s$ is a prefix of $f\}$. For every $s \in \mathcal{S}_n$, $|s|$ denotes the length of s.

Intuitively, since we will make use of a tree of depth n for coins of value $V = 2^n$, as illustrated on Figure 4, each node of the tree (or its path from the root) will refer to an element $s \in \mathcal{S}_n$, the root to the empty string ϵ, and each leaf to an element of $\mathcal{F}_n$. For any node $x \in \mathcal{S}_n$, $\mathcal{F}_n(s)$ contains all the leaves in the subtree below s.

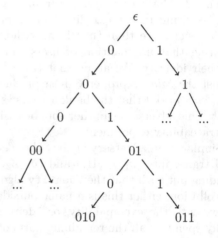

Fig. 4. Divisible coin

Public Parameters. Let $(\mathbb{G}_1, \mathbb{G}_2, \mathbb{G}_T, e)$ be the description of bilinear groups of prime order p, g, h, u_1, u_2, w (resp. $\tilde{g}$) be generators of $\mathbb{G}_1$ (resp. $\mathbb{G}_2$), $G = e(g, \tilde{g})$ is thus a generator of $\mathbb{G}_T$, and $H : \{0,1\}^* \to \mathbb{Z}_p$ be a collision-resistant hash function. In addition, a trusted authority generates

- for each $s \in \mathcal{S}_n$, $r_s \xleftarrow{\$} \mathbb{Z}_p$ and $(g_s, h_s) \leftarrow (g^{r_s}, h^{r_s})$;
- for each $f \in \mathcal{F}_n$, $l_f \xleftarrow{\$} \mathbb{Z}_p$;
- for each $s \in \mathcal{S}_n$, for each $f \in \mathcal{F}_n(s)$, $\tilde{g}_{s \mapsto f} \leftarrow \tilde{g}^{l_f/r_s}$.

The public parameters $p.p.$ are set as the bilinear groups $(\mathbb{G}_1, \mathbb{G}_2, \mathbb{G}_T, e)$, with the generators $g, h, u_1, u_2, w, \tilde{g}$, and $\mathbb{G}$, the hash function H, as well as all the above elements $\{(g_s, h_s), s \in \mathcal{S}_n\}$ and $\{\tilde{g}_{s \mapsto f}, s \in \mathcal{S}_n, f \in \mathcal{F}_n(s)\}$. In addition, according to the setting, either the random oracle model or the standard model, we also have

- another hash function $\mathcal{H} : \{0,1\}^* \to \mathbb{Z}_p$, that will be modeled by a random oracle;

– or a CRS for the Groth-Sahai [25] proofs and a one-time signature scheme Σ_{ots} (such as the one from [8]).

It is worthy to note that users and merchants need to know the groups and the generators, but then just $\{(g_s, h_s), s \in \mathcal{S}_n\}$ (along with $\mathcal{H}$, or CRS and Σ_{ots}). The set $\{\widetilde{g}_{s \mapsto f}, (s, f) \in \mathcal{S}_n \times \mathcal{F}_n\}$ is only used by the bank, while $\{l_f, f \in \mathcal{F}_n\}$ is not useful anymore in the system.

Remark 3. An entity knowing the random scalars (r_s, l_f) used to generate the public parameters will be able to break the anonymity of our scheme. This problem already appears when generating the CRS from Groth-Sahai proofs (whose construction is not specified in [26]). To avoid the need of a trusted entity (although this last one would intervene only during the Setup phase) the public parameters can be cooperatively generated by the bank and a set of users. For example,

– one party can first generate $a_s, c_f \xleftarrow{\$} \mathbb{Z}_p$ for all $s \in \mathcal{S}_n$ and $f \in \mathcal{F}_n$, compute $A_s \leftarrow g^{a_s}$ and $\widetilde{A}_{s \mapsto f} \leftarrow \widetilde{g}^{c_f/a_s}$, and prove knowledge of a_s and c_f;
– the second party will then select random $b_s, d_f \xleftarrow{\$} \mathbb{Z}_p$, compute $B_s \leftarrow A_s^{b_s}$ and $\widetilde{B}_{s \mapsto f} \leftarrow \widetilde{A}_s^{d_f/b_s}$, and prove knowledge of b_s and d_f.

If the proofs are valid then $g_s \leftarrow B_s$ and $\widetilde{g}_{s \mapsto f} \leftarrow \widetilde{B}_{s \mapsto f}$.

4.2   High Level Description

The main challenge when designing a divisible e-cash system is to describe an efficient way for the bank to recover all the serial numbers of the spent coins without endangering the anonymity of the honest users. For the sake of clarity, we describe our construction in three stages.

– In the first one, we describe a system fulfilling a weak anonymity property (called *unlinkability*, see Remark 1, in Section 3.2) meaning that no one can decide, given two transcripts of the Spend protocol, whether they were produce by using the same global coin but where the spent part (*i.e.* the node) of the coin can be revealed;
– In the second stage, we show how to increase the level of anonymity, reaching a stronger version of unlinkability (that we call *strong unlinkability*) meaning that it is now impossible to decide which node was spent. However, the level of the node is inevitably revealed since it corresponds to the amount paid by the user.
– Eventually, it remains to explain how to recover the identity of a double-spender without the help of a trusted entity. This is done in our third stage where we describe the construction of a security tag which, added to the scheme from the second stage, leads to an anonymous divisible e-cash system in the sense of the definition given in Section 3.2.

All our three stages use the same idea: each divisible coin is associated with a secret scalar $x \xleftarrow{\$} \mathbb{Z}_p$, known to the user only, and certified by the bank during the Withdraw protocol.

Unlinkability. To spend a value of $v = 2^\ell$, the user first selects an unspent node s at level $n - \ell$, computes $t_s \leftarrow g_s^x$ and proves in a zero-knowledge way that t_s is well formed and that x is certified. This can be efficiently performed in either model: the random oracle model or standard model.

Since we consider here the *unlinkability* property, the user can reveal the chosen s so that $\mathcal{B}$ can compute, for each $f \in \mathcal{F}_n(s)$, the 2^ℓ elements $S_f(x) \leftarrow e(t_s, \widetilde{g}_{s \mapsto f}) = e(g_s, \widetilde{g}_{s \mapsto f})^x = G^{x \cdot l_f}$ which actually are the 2^ℓ serial numbers. Indeed, these elements only depend on (i) the spent leaves and (ii) the secret of the coin, which makes the bank able to detect double-spending (*i.e.* two identical spent leaves, which equivalently means that two nodes s and s' are such that one of them is the prefix of the other): the bank simply checks whether for some f, there are s and s' such that $e(t_s, \widetilde{g}_{s \mapsto f}) = G^{x \cdot l_f} = e(t_{s'}, \widetilde{g}_{s' \mapsto f})$.

For honest users, the unlinkability property follows from the fact that it is hard, knowing g_s, $g_{s'}$ and g_s^x, to decide whether an element of $\mathbb{G}_1$ is random or equal to $g_{s'}^x$ under the XDH assumption.

Strong Unlinkability. We now want to leak less information about the node s: actually, just its level can be leaked, since it corresponds to the value of the transaction. To address this issue, the bank will now certify every element g_s, using a different key for each level of the tree (and so according to the value), and publish all certificates. To prove that t_s is well-formed, the user now has to prove that he used a certified value g_s of the appropriate level, which is still possible in either the random oracle model or the standard model, with a slight increase of the size of the proof. Since the bank does not know the exact node s, but only its level $n - \ell$, given t_s, it now needs to compute and stores all the elements $e(t_s, \widetilde{g}_{s' \mapsto f})$ for every leaf f and every node s' of the same level $n - \ell$. Of course, some of these elements (and maybe most of them) do not correspond to any valid serial number, but the point is that all the 2^ℓ valid serial numbers will be among them, making the bank able to detect double spendings.

Remark 4. One has to take care of additional false positive cases for a leaf f: for two distinct coins whose associated secrets are x_1 and x_2 respectively ($x_1 \neq x_2$), there exist four nodes $r_{s_1}, r_{s_1'}$ and $r_{s_2}, r_{s_2'}$ such that $e(g^{x_1 r_{s_1}}, \widetilde{g}^{y_f / r_{s_1'}}) = e(g^{x_2 r_{s_2}}, \widetilde{g}^{y_f / r_{s_2'}})$, and thus $x_1 r_{s_1} r_{s_2'} = x_2 r_{s_1'} r_{s_2}$. For randomly chosen x's, this happens with negligible probability.

Anonymity. Once a double-spending is detected, the procedure for recovering the user's identity depends on the kind of opening we want. In the case of fair e-cash systems, an opening authority uses, as for group signatures schemes, the knowledge of some trapdoor to recover the identity of the user from any valid transaction. Such system can be used in association with the above strongly unlinkable solution to provide identification of the double spender. However, to reach the true anonymity property we must avoid such a powerful authority and then allow anyone to recover this identity from any double-spent coins, and only in case of fraud.

Let $\mathsf{usk} \in \mathbb{Z}_p$ be the secret key of a user and $\mathsf{upk} \leftarrow g^{\mathsf{usk}}$ his public key. When spending a node s, each user will also compute and send a security tag $v_s \leftarrow \mathsf{upk}^r \cdot h_s^x$, where r is deterministically obtained by hashing some public information $info$ related to the transaction (amount, date, public key of the merchant, etc). Of course, it will also have to prove that this tag is well formed (x and upk are certified and h_s corresponds to the same node as g_s).

If the bank detects a double-spending, it means that there are two transcripts containing (t_s, v_s) and $(t_{s'}, v_{s'})$ such that there exists $f \in \mathcal{F}_n$ which is a descendant of both s and s'. Therefore, we have both $e(t_s, \widetilde{g}_{s \mapsto f}) = e(t_{s'}, \widetilde{g}_{s' \mapsto f}) = G^{x \cdot l_f}$ and $e(h_s, \widetilde{g}_{s \mapsto f}) = e(h_{s'}, \widetilde{g}_{s' \mapsto f}) = e(h, \widetilde{g})^{l_f}$. Anyone can then compute, from the involved transcripts and the public parameters, $T \leftarrow e(v_s, \widetilde{g}_{s \mapsto f})$ and $T' \leftarrow e(v_{s'}, \widetilde{g}_{s' \mapsto f})$. Using the bilinearity of the pairing we get:

$$
\begin{aligned}
T \cdot T'^{-1} &= e(\mathsf{upk}^r, \widetilde{g}_{s \mapsto f}) \cdot e(h_s^x, \widetilde{g}_{s \mapsto f}) \cdot e(\mathsf{upk}^{-r'}, \widetilde{g}_{s' \mapsto f}) \cdot e(h_{s'}^x, \widetilde{g}_{s' \mapsto f})^{-1} \\
&= e(\mathsf{upk}, \widetilde{g}_{s \mapsto f}^{r} \cdot \widetilde{g}_{s' \mapsto f}^{-r'}).
\end{aligned}
$$

It remains to check, for each registered upk_i, whether $T \cdot T'^{-1} = e(\mathsf{upk}_i, \widetilde{g}_{s \mapsto f}^{r} \cdot \widetilde{g}_{s' \mapsto f}^{-r'})$. We recall that r and r' are scalar deterministically computed from the transaction information $info$, and thus publicly computable.

The Identify algorithm thus has a linear cost in the number of registered users, but we can argue that this is not a major drawback because it will be run *offline* and double-spending should not occur too often: the possibility of tracing back defrauders is an incentive not to try to cheat. Note that this algorithm does not make use of any private information, it can thus be run in parallel by many users, as for the public traceability in broadcast encryption [18].

5 Our Divisible E-Cash System

5.1 The Protocol

In this section, we focus on the anonymous version of our solution. We then describe all the algorithms in more details, except the Setup one, already fully described above. Our Spend protocol will make use of non-interactive zero-knowledge (NIZK) proofs which can be provided either in the random oracle model (using the Fiat-Shamir heuristic [22]) or in the standard model (using the Groth-Sahai proof systems [25], since we are in a bilinear setting). Even if the frameworks are similar, some algorithms differ according to the model. We provide in the full version [17] some instantiations of our protocol.

- BKeygen(): Upon receiving the public parameters, the bank will select two different signatures schemes:
  - $\Sigma_0 = (\mathsf{Keygen}, \mathsf{Sign}, \mathsf{Verify})$, whose message space is $\mathbb{G}_1^2$, to sign some elements of the public parameters. We can use the structure preserving construction from [1]. But we stress that we do not need the EUF-CMA security. A signature scheme secure against selective chosen-message attacks would be enough.

- $\Sigma_1 = (\text{Keygen}, \text{Sign}, \text{Verify})$, whose message space depends on the security model.

  * **ROM:** The message space is $\mathbb{Z}_p^2$. But we additionally require that Σ_1 is compatible with a protocol $\Sigma_1.\text{SignCommit}$ which, given (u_1^x, u_2^y) for some $(x, y) \in \mathbb{Z}_p^2$ (and so a kind of commitment of (x, y)), outputs a valid signature σ on (x, y) (we can then use the scheme from [11] or a variant of [8]).

  * **Standard Model:** The message space is $\mathbb{G}_1^2$, and we can then use again the scheme from [1].

  The bank will then get $(\text{sk}_1, \text{pk}_1) \leftarrow \Sigma_1.\text{Keygen}(p.p.)$ and $(\text{sk}_0^{(i)}, \text{pk}_0^{(i)}) \leftarrow \Sigma_0.\text{Keygen}(p.p.)$ for each level of the tree, $0 \le i \le n$, and compute, for every $s \in \mathcal{S}_n$, $\tau_s \leftarrow \Sigma_0.\text{Sign}(\text{sk}_0^{(|s|)}, (g_s, h_s))$. Eventually, it will set bsk as sk_1 and bpk as $(\{\text{pk}_0^{(i)}\}_i, \text{pk}_1, \{\tau_s\}_{s \in \mathcal{S}_n})$.

- Keygen(): Each user (resp. merchant) selects a random $\text{usk} \leftarrow \mathbb{Z}_p$ (resp. msk) and gets $\text{upk} \leftarrow g^{\text{usk}}$ (resp. $\text{mpk} \leftarrow g^{\text{msk}}$). In the following we assume that upk (resp. mpk) is public, meaning that anyone can get an authentic copy of it.

- Withdraw($\mathcal{B}(\text{bsk}, \text{upk}), \mathcal{U}(\text{usk}, \text{bpk})$): To withdraw a divisible coin, the user first selects a random $x \in \mathbb{Z}_p$ and computes u_1^{usk} and u_2^x. He then sends $\text{upk}, u_1^{\text{usk}}, u_2^x$ and proves, using for example the Schnorr's interactive protocol [30], knowledge of x and usk. If the proof is valid and if u_2^x was not previously used, the bank

  * **ROM:** runs the $\Sigma_1.\text{SignCommit}$ on $(u_1^{\text{usk}}, u_2^x)$ and sends the resulting signature σ to the user who sets $C \leftarrow (x, \sigma)$.

  * **Standard Model:** computes $\sigma \leftarrow \Sigma_1.\text{Sign}(\text{sk}_1, (u_1^{\text{usk}}, u_2^x))$ and sends it to the user who sets $C \leftarrow (x, \sigma)$.

- Spend($\mathcal{U}(\text{usk}, C, \text{bpk}, \text{mpk}, 2^\ell), \mathcal{M}(\text{msk}, \text{bpk}, 2^\ell)$): To spend a value 2^ℓ, the user selects an unspent node s of level $n - \ell$ and computes $r \leftarrow H(\textit{info})$ and $(t_s, v_s) \leftarrow (g_s^x, \text{upk}^r \cdot h_s^x)$. He must then prove that t_s and v_s are well-formed, *i.e.* that he used values certified during a withdrawal, hence a proof of knowledge of σ, and that he used a valid pair (g_s, h_s), hence a proof of existence of τ_s. The protocol in the ROM differs from the one in the standard model.

  * **ROM:** The user provides a zero-knowledge proof of knowledge of usk, x, g_s, h_s, τ_s, and σ such that:

$$t_s = g_s^x \wedge v_s = (g^r)^{\text{usk}} \cdot h_s^x \quad \wedge \quad \Sigma_1.\text{Verify}(\text{pk}_1, (\text{usk}, x), \sigma) = 1$$

$$\wedge \quad \Sigma_0.\text{Verify}(\text{pk}_0^{(n-\ell)}, (g_s, h_s), \tau_s) = 1.$$

  Using appropriate signature schemes, as shown in the full version [17], such zero-knowledge proofs of knowledge 'à la Schnorr' can be done. The global proof is then converted into a signature of knowledge Π on the message r, using the Fiat-Shamir heuristic [22].

  * **Standard Model:** The user first generates a new key pair $(\text{sk}_{ots}, \text{pk}_{ots}) \leftarrow \Sigma_{ots}.\text{Keygen}(1^k)$ and computes $\mu \leftarrow w^{\frac{1}{\text{usk} + H(\text{pk}_{ots})}}$. He then computes

Groth-Sahai commitments to usk, x, g_s, h_s, τ_s, σ, μ, $U_1 = u_1^{\mathsf{usk}}$, $U_2 = u_2^x$ and provides a NIZK proof π that the committed values satisfy:

$$t_s = g_s^x \wedge v_s = (g^r)^{\mathsf{usk}} \cdot h_s^x \wedge U_2 = u_2^x \wedge U_1 = u_1^{\mathsf{usk}} \wedge \mu^{(\mathsf{usk}+H(\mathsf{pk}_{ots}))} = w$$

along with a NIWI proof π' that the committed values satisfy:

$$1 = \Sigma_0.\mathtt{Verify}(\mathsf{pk}_0^{(n-\ell)}, (g_s, h_s), \tau_s) \wedge 1 = \Sigma_1.\mathtt{Verify}(\mathsf{pk}_1, (U_1, U_2), \sigma)$$

Again, using appropriate signature schemes, as shown in the full version [17], the Groth-Sahai methodology [25] can be used. Finally, the user computes $\eta \leftarrow \Sigma_{ots}.\mathtt{Sign}(\mathsf{sk}_{ots}, H(t_s\|v_s\|\pi\|\pi'\|r))$ and sends it to $\mathcal{M}$ along with $t_s, v_s, \mathsf{pk}_{ots}, \pi, \pi'$.

In both cases, the merchant checks the validity of the proofs and of the signatures and accepts the transaction if everything is correct. In such a case, he stores $Z \leftarrow (t_s, v_s)$ and either the signature of knowledge Π in the ROM or $\Pi \leftarrow (\pi, \pi', \mathsf{pk}_{ots}, \eta)$ in the standard model.

- $\mathtt{Deposit}(\mathcal{M}(\mathsf{msk}, \mathsf{bpk}, (2^\ell, Z, \Pi)), \mathcal{B}(\mathsf{bsk}, L, \mathsf{mpk}))$: Upon receiving a transcript, the bank will check that it was not previously deposited and verify its validity. Then, for each s' of level $n - \ell$ and $f \in \mathcal{F}_n(s')$ it will compute $z_i \leftarrow e(t_s, \widetilde{g}_{s' \mapsto f})$ and check whether $z_i \in L$. If $\forall i, z_i \notin L$ then the bank will add these elements to this list (see Remark 5) and store the transcript $(2^\ell, Z, \Pi)$. Else, there is an element $z' \in L$ such that $z_i = z'$. The bank will recover the corresponding transcript $(2^{\ell'}, Z', \Pi')$ and output $[(2^\ell, Z, \Pi), (2^{\ell'}, Z', \Pi')]$.

- $\mathtt{Identify}((2^{\ell_1}, Z_1, \Pi_1), (2^{\ell_2}, Z_2, \Pi_2), \mathsf{bpk})$: To recover the identity of a double-spender, the entity running this algorithm will first check the validity of both transcripts and return $\perp$ if one of them is not correct. He then computes, for $i \in \{1, 2\}$ and for every leaf f, the lists $S_{i,f} \leftarrow \{e(t_{s_i}, \widetilde{g}_{s \mapsto f}),$ where $s \in \mathcal{S}_n$ is the prefix of length $|s_i|$ of $f\}$, and returns $\perp$ if there is no collision between $S_{1,f}$ and $S_{2,f}$ for any leaf f. Else, we can assume (see Remark 4) that we have $e(t_{s_1}, \widetilde{g}_{s_1 \mapsto f}) = e(t_{s_2}, \widetilde{g}_{s_2 \mapsto f})$ with $t_{s_1} = g_{s_1}^x$ and $t_{s_2} = g_{s_2}^x$ for some $s_1, s_2 \in \mathcal{S}_n$. As explained in section 4.2, $e(v_{s_1}, \widetilde{g}_{s_1 \mapsto f}) \cdot e(v_{s_2}, \widetilde{g}_{s_2 \mapsto f})^{-1} = e(\mathsf{upk}, \widetilde{g}_{s \mapsto f}^r \cdot \widetilde{g}_{s' \mapsto f}^{-r'})$ so it remains to compute $e(\mathsf{upk}_i, \widetilde{g}_{s \mapsto f}^r \cdot \widetilde{g}_{s' \mapsto f}^{-r'})$ for each public key upk_i until we get a match, in which case one outputs upk_i.

Remark 5. Since the node used to spend a coin C is not known, the bank has to store 2^n elements z_i each time a transcript is deposited by a merchant, even if the amount deposited is 2^ℓ with $\ell \le n$: one for each leaf f. In the worst case scenario (if the user only spends values of 1), a divisible coin of 2^n will require that the bank stores 2^{2n} elements. However, the bank does not need to store the elements $z_i \in \mathbb{G}_T$, it may only store $H'(z_i)$ (for some hash function H') and so compare the (smaller) hash values. If a collision is found, the bank will first recover and compare the elements z_i from the involved transcripts to ensure that this collision was not due to the function H' (which would anyway be quite unlikely). Hash tables or Bloom filters can be used to improve on the storage efficiency.

Even if the constructions in both models are quite similar, there are some necessary differences, especially in the Spend protocol. Our results concerning the security of our scheme will then also differ according to each model. The security proofs of the following theorems are provided in Section 6.

Theorem 6. *In the random oracle model, assuming that the hash function H is collision-resistant, our divisible e-cash system is anonymous under the* XDH *assumption, traceable if Σ_0 is secure against selective chosen-message attacks and Σ_1 is an EUF-CMA secure signature scheme, and achieves the exculpability property under the* DL *assumption.*

Theorem 7. *In the standard model, assuming that the hash function H is collision-resistant, our divisible e-cash system is anonymous under the* XDH *assumption, traceable if Σ_0 is secure against selective chosen-message attacks and Σ_1 is an EUF-CMA secure signature scheme, and achieves the exculpability property under the $q - $ SDH assumption if Σ_{ots} is a strong one-time signature scheme.*

5.2   Efficiency

We compare in Figure 5 the efficiency of our construction with the one of [15], which is the most efficient protocol in the ROM, and the one of [26], which is the only construction in the standard model.

The different settings of these constructions make this comparison difficult but this table can still be useful to compare the asymptotic complexity of the different algorithms. We refer to the full version [17] for instantiations of our construction. One may note some differences between our table and the one provided in [15]. They are due to the fact that the authors of [15] denote the computations of accumulators by Acc. Since these accumulators can store up to 2^{n+2} elements their computations actually involve up to 2^{n+2} exponentiations (during the creation of these accumulators inside the withdrawal protocol) while their definitions significantly increase the size of the public parameters (hence the 2^{n+3} elements).

The scheme from [15] uses subgroups of $\mathbb{Z}_{r_i}$ for some primes r_i and bilinear groups of similar orders for their accumulators. Assuming that the parameters of the accumulators (which are elliptic curve points) are provided in a compressed way (*i.e.* only one coordinate by point) and that q is an approximation of the orders of the different groups, we will consider that each element involved in their protocol has a $|q|$-bit representation. The scheme from [26] and the one described in this paper use bilinear groups of prime order p. For a 128-bits security level, we have $|p| = 256$, $|\mathbb{G}_1| = 256$ and $|\mathbb{G}_2| = 512$ by using Barreto-Naehrig curves [3] whereas $|q|$ must be greater than 3072 for [15] (see [23]).

Public Parameters. A downside of our protocol is the size of the public parameters. However, it is worthy to note that by using the curve parameters from [3] and the structure preserving signature scheme from [1], the storage space

Schemes	Canard-Gouget [15]	Izabachène-Libert [26]	Our work
Standard Model	no	yes	yes
Public Parameters	$2^{n+3}\|q\| + 1\ pk$	$2\ \mathbb{G}_1 + 1\ \mathbb{G}_2 + 1\ pk$	$(n+2)\ pk + 1\ \mathbb{G}_2$ $+ (2^{n+2}+3)\ \mathbb{G}_1$ $+ (2^{n+1}-1)\ \|\text{Sign}\|$
Withdraw Computations	$(2^{n+3} + 2^{n+2} - 5)\text{exp}$ $+ (n+2)\ \text{Sign}$	1 Sign	1 Sign
Coin Size	$(2^{n+2} + n + 1)\ \|q\|$ $+ (n+2)\ \|\text{Sign}\|$	$3\ \|p\| + \|\text{Sign}\|$	$2\ \|p\| + \|\text{Sign}\|$
Spend Computations	$NIZK\{\ 3\ \text{exp}^*$ $+ 2\ \text{Sign} + 2\ \text{Pair}\ \}$ $+ 1\ \text{exp}$	$NIZK\{\ (n-l)\ \text{exp}$ $+ (7(n-l)+6)\ \text{Pair}$ $+ 1\ \text{Sign}\ \}$ $+ (8(n-l)+4)\ \text{exp}$	$NIZK\{\ 2\ \text{exp}$ $+ 2\ \text{Sign}\ \} + 3\ \text{exp}$ $+ 1\ \text{Sign}$
Transfer size of Spend	$3\ \|q\| + \|NIZK\|$	$3(n-l)\ \mathbb{G}_2 +$ $3(n-l)\mathbb{G}_T + \|NIZK\|$	$3\ \mathbb{G}_1 + 1\ \|\text{Sign}\|$ $+\|NIZK\|$
Deposit Computations	2^{l+1}exp	unbounded	$2^n\ \text{Pair}$
Deposit size	$2^l\ \|q\| + \|\text{Spend}\|$	$\|\text{Spend}\|$	$2^n\ \mathbb{G}_T + \|\text{Spend}\|$

Fig. 5. Efficiency comparison between related works and our construction for coins of value 2^n and Spend and Deposit of value 2^l. The space and times complexities are given from the user's point of view. exp refers to an exponentiation, pair to a pairing computation, Sign to the cost of the signature issuing protocol, from the user point of view, whose public key is pk. $NIZK\{\text{exp}\}$ denotes the cost of a $NIZK$ proof of a multi-exponentiation equation, $NIZK\{\text{pair}\}$ the one of a pairing product equation and $NIZK\{\text{Sign}\}$ the one of a valid signature. $NIZK\{\text{exp}^*\}$ refers to the cost of a proof of equality of discrete logarithms in groups of different orders.

required by these parameters for $n = 10$ (enabling users to divide their coin in 1024 parts) is 330 KBytes which can easily be handled by any smartphone. Our parameters (see the full version [17]) require then less storage space than the ones of [15] (since $2^{10+3} \cdot \|q\| = 3.1$ MBytes). For the bank, the additional cost of storing the elements $\{\tilde{g}_{s \mapsto f}\}$ is only 721 KBytes.

Withdrawal and Spending. The strong time constraints of electronic transactions require very efficient withdrawal and spending protocols. Compared to any paper in the literature with similar security level (especially [15] and [26]), our protocol is the only one to achieve constant time for both the Withdraw and the Spend protocols. Moreover, even if the Spend protocol from [15] can be performed in constant time, it involves zero-knowledge proofs in groups of different orders which are rather complex, even in the ROM.

Deposit. Unfortunately, our Deposit protocol involves up to 2^n pairings and so is less efficient than the one from [15]. For $n = 10$ it means that the bank must compute 1024 pairings. Even if they can be computed in parallel and even if each of them can be performed on a computer in less than 1 ms [7], the computational cost is significant. However, since this protocol is run offline (without the strong time constraints of the previous protocols) and since the computational power of a bank can be assumed to be far more important than the one of a computer, we argue that the cost for the bank remains reasonable. Regarding the storage size, the bank must store 2^n serial numbers by transaction. As explained in Remark 5, the bank does not need to store the elements z_i but only their hash values $H'(z_i)$ for some hash function H' whose output space can be rather small since, in the event of a collision, the bank will first recompute the elements z_i before running the Identify algorithm. For example, considering that the output space of H' has a 80 bits size, the space required to store the serial numbers of one million transactions is about 10 GBytes, which is still practical for the bank.

Finally, we stress that our Deposit protocol is the first one in the standard model with a bounded computational cost, *i.e.* which does not depend on the number of previous transactions, as in [26] (excepted for the lookup in tables for double-spending detection).

6   Security Proofs

The proofs of anonymity and traceability are similar in the ROM and in the standard model so we only describe one proof for both models. This is no longer the case for the exculpability property which requires two different proofs.

6.1   Proof of Anonymity

Let $\mathcal{A}$ be an adversary against the anonymity with advantage ϵ. We construct a reduction $\mathcal{R}$ using $\mathcal{A}$ against XDH challenges in $\mathbb{G}_1$. Let (g, g^x, g^y, g^z) be a XDH-challenge in $\mathbb{G}_1$, $\mathcal{R}$ randomly selects $f^* \in \mathcal{F}_n$ and generates the public parameters as follows.

- $(h, u_1, u_2) \leftarrow (g^c, g^{d_1}, g^{d_2})$ for some $c, d_1, d_2 \xleftarrow{\$} \mathbb{Z}_p$
- For each $f \in \mathcal{F}_n$, $l_f \xleftarrow{\$} \mathbb{Z}_p$
- For each $s \in \mathcal{S}_n$, $r_s \xleftarrow{\$} \mathbb{Z}_p$
- For each $s \in \mathcal{S}_n$:
    - If s is a prefix of f^* then $g_s \leftarrow (g^y)^{r_s}$
    - Else $g_s \leftarrow g^{r_s}$
    - $h_s \leftarrow g_s^c$
- For each $s \in \mathcal{S}_n$, for each $f \in \mathcal{F}_n(s)$, output $\widetilde{g}_{s \mapsto f} \leftarrow \widetilde{g}^{\frac{l_f}{r_s}}$.

In this way, only the prefixes of f^* will involve challenge elements. In the standard model, $\mathcal{R}$ also generates a simulated common reference string. Let q_w be a bound on the number of $\mathcal{O}$Withdraw queries, $\mathcal{R}$ randomly selects i^* from $[0, q_w]$ and answers to the oracle queries as follows:

- $\mathcal{O}\mathrm{Add}()$ queries: $\mathcal{R}$ runs the Keygen algorithm and returns upk (or mpk).
- $\mathcal{O}\mathrm{Withdraw}_{\mathcal{U}}(\mathrm{bsk}, \mathrm{upk})$ queries: When the adversary makes the ith query to the $\mathcal{O}\mathrm{Withdraw}_{\mathcal{U}}$ oracle, the reduction acts normally if $i \neq i^*$ and as if the secret value of the coin is x otherwise (by sending $(g^x)^{d_2}$ and simulating the proof of knowledge, since x is not known by $\mathcal{R}$). The chosen public key corresponding to this last case will be denoted upk^*.
- $\mathcal{O}\mathrm{Corrupt}(\mathrm{upk}/\mathrm{mpk})$ queries: $\mathcal{R}$ acts normally if the query was not made on upk^*. Else, it aborts the experiment.
- $\mathcal{O}\mathrm{AddCorrupt}(\mathrm{upk}/\mathrm{mpk})$: $\mathcal{R}$ stores the public key which is now considered as registered.
- $\mathcal{O}\mathrm{Spend}(\mathrm{upk}, 2^\ell)$ queries: $\mathcal{R}$ is able to deal with any of these queries if $\mathrm{upk} \neq \mathrm{upk}^*$. Else, the reduction is able to answer as long as $c_{\mathrm{upk}} < m_{\mathrm{upk}} \cdot 2^n - 2^\ell$ (and aborts otherwise) since this condition means that there is at least one unspent node s which is not the prefix of f^*. The reduction can then compute a valid pair $(t_s, v_s) \leftarrow ((g^x)^{r_s}, \mathrm{upk}^r \cdot t_s^c)$ where $r \leftarrow H(info)$ and simulates the non-interactive proof (which is possible even in the standard model since we use a simulated CRS).

During the challenge phase, $\mathcal{A}$ outputs $\{\mathrm{upk}_0, \mathrm{upk}_1\}$ along with a value 2^ℓ. Of course, it is assumed that none of these users has spent more than $m_{\mathrm{upk}_b} \cdot 2^n - 2^\ell$. If $\mathrm{upk}^* \notin \{\mathrm{upk}_0, \mathrm{upk}_1\}$ then $\mathcal{R}$ aborts, else it selects the prefix s^* of length $n - \ell$ of f^*, which cannot have been spent, by the assumption made on the $\mathcal{O}\mathrm{Spend}$ queries. $\mathcal{R}$ also provides a simulated proof and then answers the oracle queries as previously. Since $g_{s^*} = (g^y)^{r_{s^*}}$, the reduction returns $(t_{s^*}, v_{s^*}) \leftarrow ((g^z)^{r_{s^*}}, (\mathrm{upk}^*)^r \cdot t_{s^*}^c)$, which is valid for upk^* iff $z = x \cdot y$. $\mathcal{R}$ returns a random element from $\mathbb{G}_1^2$ if $z \neq x \cdot y$. Then, $\mathcal{R}$ uses the bit returned by $\mathcal{A}$ to solve the XDH challenge.

When $\mathcal{A}$ selects the users involved in the challenge phase, it actually selects the two subsets S_0 and S_1 of the withdrawn coins belonging to these users. The condition on the challenge phase implies that there is at least one coin in each subset which has not been totally spent. If the coin withdrawn during the i^{*th} query is one of them, $\mathcal{R}$ will not abort. Its probability of success in breaking the XDH-assumption is then greater than $2\epsilon/q_w$.

6.2 Proof of Traceability

Let $\mathcal{A}$ be an adversary against the traceability. We construct a reduction $\mathcal{R}$ using $\mathcal{A}$ against the unforgeabiliy of Σ_0 or Σ_1. $\mathcal{R}$ generates the public parameters as in the Setup algorithm and selects $0 \leq i^* \leq n$. It then generates n keys pairs $(sk_0^{(i)}, pk_0^{(i)}) \leftarrow \Sigma_0.\mathrm{Keygen}(1^k)$ for $1 \leq i \neq i^* \leq n$ and uses $sk_0^{(i)}$ to sign (g_s, h_s) such that $|s| = i$. Finally, it sends (g_s, h_s) for every $s \in \mathcal{S}_n$ such that $|s| = i^*$ to the $\Sigma_0.\mathrm{Sign}$ oracle which returns the signatures τ_s along with the verification key $pk_0^{(i^*)}$. $\mathcal{R}$ also receives the public key pk_1 from the challenger of the experiment of the EUF-CMA security of Σ_1 and sets its public key as $(\{pk_0^{(j)}\}_j, pk_1, \{\tau_s\}_{s \in \mathcal{S}_n})$. The reduction will proceed as usual when it receives

$\mathcal{O}$Add, $\mathcal{O}$Corrupt, $\mathcal{O}$AddCorrupt and $\mathcal{O}$Spend queries and uses its Σ_1.Sign oracle to answer $\mathcal{O}$Withdraw$_\mathcal{B}$ queries.

Let q_w be the number of withdrawn queries. In order to succeed, $\mathcal{A}$ must output u valid transcripts $(2^{\ell_j}, Z_j, \Pi_j)$ such that $\sum 2^{\ell_j} > q_w \cdot 2^n$ and such that $\texttt{Identify}((2^{\ell_i}, Z_i, \Pi_i), (2^{\ell_j}, Z_j, \Pi_j)) = \perp$ for every $1 \leq i \neq j \leq n$. The perfect soundness of the proof implies that each transcript $(2^{\ell_j}, Z_j, \Pi_j)$ involves a pair (g_j, h_j) and a signature τ_j such that $\Sigma_0.\texttt{Verify}((g_j, h_j), \tau_j, pk_0^{(n-l_j)}) = 1$. We may then assume that $(g_j, h_j) = (g_{s_j}, h_{s_j})$ for some $s_j \in \mathcal{S}_n$ such that $|s_j| = n - l_j$. Else, $((g_j, h_j), \tau_j)$ is a valid forgery which breaks the security of Σ_0 with probability $\frac{1}{n+1}$ (i.e. if $i^* = n - l_j$).

Let $x_1, ..., x_{q_w}$ be the q_w secret values (one for each withdrawn coin). Since an amount of $\sum 2^{\ell_j} > q_w \cdot 2^n$ has been deposited, the bank has computed $\sum 2^{\ell_j}$ elements $z_i \leftarrow e(t_{s_j}, \widetilde{g}_{s_j \mapsto f})$. If $\{z_i\}_i \subset \{e(g, \widetilde{g})^{l_f \cdot x_i}\}_{f \in \mathcal{F}_n, 1 \leq i \leq q_w}$ then there is at least one couple (i, j) such that $i \neq j$ and $z_i = z_j$, because the size of the last set is $q_w \cdot 2^n$. Such a collision implies (see remark 4) that the security tags v_{s_i} and v_{s_j} have been produced with the same secret x and so with the same public key upk which would have been returned by the $\texttt{Identify}$ algorithm. We can therefore assume that $\{z_i\}_i \not\subset \{e(g, \widetilde{g})^{l_f \cdot x_i}\}_{f \in \mathcal{F}_n, 1 \leq i \leq q_w}$, implying that at least one of the element t_{s_j} is equal to $g_{s_j}^x$ for some $x \notin \{x_1, ..., x_{q_w}\}$. We can then extract, from the corresponding spending, a valid forgery σ on $(\texttt{usk}, x)$ in the ROM and on $(u_1^{\texttt{usk}}, u_2^x)$ in the standard model and so breaks the security of Σ_1.

6.3 Proof of Exculpability

We distinguish the proof in the ROM from the one in the standard model.

ROM: Let $\mathcal{A}$ be an adversary against the exculpability property. We construct a reduction $\mathcal{R}$ using $\mathcal{A}$ against the DL challenges in $\mathbb{G}_1$. Let (g, g^α) be a DL challenge, $\mathcal{R}$ generates the public parameters as in the $\texttt{Setup}$ algorithm and selects $1 \leq i^* \leq q_a$ where q_a is a bound on the number of $\mathcal{O}$Add queries. $\mathcal{R}$ will answer the oracle queries as follows.

- $\mathcal{O}$Add() queries: When the adversary makes the i-th $\mathcal{O}$Add query to register a user, $\mathcal{R}$ will run the $\texttt{Keygen}$ algorithm if $i \neq i^*$ and set $\texttt{upk}^* \leftarrow g^\alpha$ otherwise.
- $\mathcal{O}$Corrupt(upk/mpk) queries: $\mathcal{R}$ returns the secret key if $\texttt{upk} \neq \texttt{upk}^*$ and aborts otherwise.
- $\mathcal{O}$AddCorrupt(upk/mpk) queries: $\mathcal{R}$ stores the public key which is now considered as registered.
- $\mathcal{O}$Withdraw$_\mathcal{U}$(bsk, upk) queries: $\mathcal{R}$ acts normally if $\texttt{upk} \neq \texttt{upk}^*$ and simulates the interactive proof of knowledge of α otherwise.
- $\mathcal{O}$Spend(upk, 2^ℓ) queries: $\mathcal{R}$ acts normally if $\texttt{upk} \neq \texttt{upk}^*$ and simulates the non-interactive proof of knowledge of α otherwise.

The adversary then outputs two valid transcripts $(2^{\ell_1}, Z_1, \Pi_1)$ and $(2^{\ell_2}, Z_2, \Pi_2)$ which accuse upk of double-spending. If $\texttt{upk} \neq \texttt{upk}^*$ then $\mathcal{R}$ aborts. Else, at least one of this transcript was not produced by $\mathcal{R}$ (else it would have double-spent its own coins). The soundness of the signature of knowledge implies then that we can extract α from this forged transcript. $\mathcal{R}$ is then able to solve the discrete logarithm problem in $\mathbb{G}_1$ since it will not abort with probability $1/q_a$.

Standard Model: An adversary $\mathcal{A}$ against the exculpability property outputs two transcripts accusing an honest user upk of double-spending. As explained above, at least one of these transcripts was not produced by $\mathcal{R}$. Let pk'_{ots} be the one-time signature key used in this forged transcript, there are two kinds of attacks that can be mounted by $\mathcal{A}$:

- Type-1 Attack: pk'_{ots} is one of the key used by $\mathcal{R}$ to answer a $\mathcal{O}$Spend query.
- Type-2 Attack: pk'_{ots} was not used by $\mathcal{R}$ to answer $\mathcal{O}$Spend queries.

Clearly, an adversary succeeding in a Type-1 attack with non-negligible probability can be used to break the security of the one-time signature scheme Σ_{ots}. We therefore only consider Type-2 attacks in what follows.

Let $(g, g^\alpha, ..., g^{\alpha^{q_s}})$ be a SDH-challenge where q_s is a bound on the number of $\mathcal{O}$Spend queries, $\mathcal{R}$ generates the public parameters as in the **Setup** algorithm (except that it sets u_1 as g^t for some random $t \in \mathbb{Z}_p$) and selects $1 \le i^* \le q_a$ where q_a is a bound on the number of $\mathcal{O}$Add queries. $\mathcal{R}$ computes q_s key pairs $(sk_{ots}^{(i)}, pk_{ots}^{(i)}) \leftarrow \Sigma_{ots}.\mathsf{Keygen}(1^k)$ and sets w as $g^{\prod_{i=1}^{q_s}(\alpha + H(pk_{ots}^{(i)}))}$ (which is possible using the SDH challenge [8]). The reduction will answer the oracle queries as follows.

- $\mathcal{O}$Add() queries: When the adversary makes the i-th $\mathcal{O}$Add query to register a user, $\mathcal{R}$ will run the **Keygen** algorithm if $i \ne i^*$ and set $\mathsf{upk}^* \leftarrow g^\alpha$ otherwise.
- $\mathcal{O}$Corrupt(upk/mpk) queries: $\mathcal{R}$ returns the secret key if $\mathsf{upk} \ne \mathsf{upk}^*$ and aborts otherwise.
- $\mathcal{O}$AddCorrupt(upk/mpk) queries: $\mathcal{R}$ stores the public key which is now considered as registered.
- $\mathcal{O}$Withdraw$_\mathcal{U}$(bsk, upk) queries: $\mathcal{R}$ acts normally if $\mathsf{upk} \ne \mathsf{upk}^*$ and simulates the interactive proof of knowledge of α otherwise.
- $\mathcal{O}$Spend(upk, 2^ℓ) queries: $\mathcal{R}$ acts normally if $\mathsf{upk} \ne \mathsf{upk}^*$. Else, to answer the j-th query on upk^*, it will recover the pair $(sk_{ots}^{(j)}, pk_{ots}^{(j)})$ and computes $\mu \leftarrow g^{\prod_{i=1, i \ne j}^{q_s}(\alpha + H(pk_{ots}^{(i)}))}$ which verifies $\mu = w^{\frac{1}{\alpha + H(pk_{ots}^{(j)})}}$. It then uses $sk_{ots}^{(j)}$ as in the **Spend** protocol.

The adversary then outputs two valid transcripts $(2^{\ell_1}, Z_1, \Pi_1)$ and $(2^{\ell_2}, Z_2, \Pi_2)$ which accuse upk of double-spending. If $\mathsf{upk} \ne \mathsf{upk}^*$ then $\mathcal{R}$ aborts. The soundness of the proof implies that the forged transcript was signed using a key sk_{ots} and so that the proof involves an element $\mu = w^{\frac{1}{\alpha + H(pk_{ots})}}$. Since here we consider Type-2 attacks, $pk_{ots} \notin \{pk_{ots}^{(i)}\}_i$, so $\mathcal{R}$ extracts from the proof the element μ which can be used to break the q_s-SDH assumption in $\mathbb{G}_1$ (as in [8]).

$\mathcal{R}$ is then able to solve the SDH problem or to break the security of Σ_{ots} since it will not abort with probability $1/q_a$.

7   Conclusion

In this work, we have proposed the first practical construction of divisible E-cash which can be instantiated and proven secure in both the random oracle and standard models. Our Withdraw and Spend protocols are efficient and can be performed in constant times. Moreover, the bank can detect double-spendings by comparing the serial numbers of deposited coins to the ones of previously spent coins. Our protocol thus answers the problem left open by Izabachène and Libert. However, the computational cost and the storage space of our Deposit protocol remains important but we argue that it is reasonable to assume that the bank has enough storage capacity and computational power. Finally, the way we build our tree is also compatible with divisible E-cash systems achieving weaker notions of anonymity (such as unlinkability) leading to very efficient protocols without these downsides (see the full version [17]).

Acknowledgments. This work was supported in part by the French ANR Project ANR-12-INSE-0014 SIMPATIC and ANR-11-INS-0013 LYRICS, and in part by the European Research Council under the European Community's Seventh Framework Programme (FP7/2007-2013 Grant Agreement no. 339563 – CryptoCloud).

References

1. Abe, M., Groth, J., Haralambiev, K., Ohkubo, M.: Optimal structure-preserving signatures in asymmetric bilinear groups. In: Rogaway, P. (ed.) CRYPTO 2011. LNCS, vol. 6841, pp. 649–666. Springer, Heidelberg (2011)
2. Au, M.H., Susilo, W., Mu, Y.: Practical anonymous divisible e-cash from bounded accumulators. In: Tsudik, G. (ed.) FC 2008. LNCS, vol. 5143, pp. 287–301. Springer, Heidelberg (2008)
3. Barreto, P.S.L.M., Naehrig, M.: Pairing-Friendly elliptic curves of prime order. In: Preneel, B., Tavares, S. (eds.) SAC 2005. LNCS, vol. 3897, pp. 319–331. Springer, Heidelberg (2006)
4. Bellare, M., Micciancio, D., Warinschi, B.: Foundations of group signatures: Formal definitions, simplifiedrequirements, and a construction based on general assumptions. In: Biham, Eli (ed.) EUROCRYPT 2003. LNCS, vol. 2656, pp. 614–629. Springer, Heidelberg (2003)
5. Bellare, M., Rogaway, P.; Random oracles are practical: A paradigm for designing efficient protocols. In: Ashby, V. (ed.) ACM CCS 1993, pp. 62–73. ACM Press, Fairfax (1993)
6. Bellare, M., Shi, H., Zhang, C.: Foundations of group signatures: the case of dynamic groups. In: Menezes, A. (ed.) CT-RSA 2005. LNCS, vol. 3376, pp. 136–153. Springer, Heidelberg (2005)
7. Beuchat, J.-L., González-Díaz, J.E., Mitsunari, S., Okamoto, E., Rodríguez-Henríquez, F., Teruya, T.: High-Speed software implementation of the optimal ate pairing over barreto–naehrig curves. In: Joye, M., Miyaji, A., Otsuka, A. (eds.) Pairing 2010. LNCS, vol. 6487, pp. 21–39. Springer, Heidelberg (2010)
8. Boneh, D., Boyen, X.: Short signatures without random oracles and the SDH assumption in bilinear groups. Journal of Cryptology **21**(2), 149–177 (2008)

9. Brickell, E.F., Gemmell, P., Kravitz, D.W.: Trustee-based tracing extensions to anonymous cash and the making of anonymous change. In: Clarkson, K.L. (ed.) 6th SODA, pp. 457–466. ACM-SIAM, San Francisco (1995)

10. Camenisch, J.L., Hohenberger, S., Lysyanskaya, A.: Compact E-Cash. In: Cramer, R. (ed.) EUROCRYPT 2005. LNCS, vol. 3494, pp. 302–321. Springer, Heidelberg (2005)

11. Camenisch, J.L., Lysyanskaya, A.: Signature schemes and anonymous credentials from bilinear maps. In: Franklin, M. (ed.) CRYPTO 2004. LNCS, vol. 3152, pp. 56–72. Springer, Heidelberg (2004)

12. Camenisch, J., Lysyanskaya, A., Meyerovich, M.: Endorsed e-cash. In: 2007 IEEE Symposium on Security and Privacy, pp. 101–115. IEEE Computer Society Press, Oakland (2007)

13. Canard, S., Gouget, A.: Divisible E-Cash systems can be truly anonymous. In: Naor, M. (ed.) EUROCRYPT 2007. LNCS, vol. 4515, pp. 482–497. Springer, Heidelberg (2007)

14. Canard, S., Gouget, A.: Anonymity in transferable E-cash. In: Bellovin, S.M., Gennaro, R., Keromytis, A.D., Yung, M. (eds.) ACNS 2008. LNCS, vol. 5037, pp. 207–223. Springer, Heidelberg (2008)

15. Canard, S., Gouget, A.: Multiple denominations in E-cash with compact transaction data. In: Sion, R. (ed.) FC 2010. LNCS, vol. 6052, pp. 82–97. Springer, Heidelberg (2010)

16. Canard, S., Gouget, A., Traoré, J.: Improvement of efficiency in (unconditional) anonymous transferable E-Cash. In: Tsudik, G. (ed.) FC 2008. LNCS, vol. 5143, pp. 202–214. Springer, Heidelberg (2008)

17. Canard, S., Pointcheval, D., Sanders, O., Traoré, J.: Divisible e-cash made practical. Cryptology ePrint Archive, Report 2014/785 (2014). http://eprint.iacr.org/

18. Chabanne, H., Phan, D.H., Pointcheval, D.: Public traceability in traitor tracing schemes. In: Cramer, R. (ed.) EUROCRYPT 2005. LNCS, vol. 3494, pp. 542–558. Springer, Heidelberg (2005)

19. Chan, A.H., Frankel, Y., Tsiounis, Y.: Easy come - easy go divisible cash. In: Nyberg, K. (ed.) EUROCRYPT 1998. LNCS, vol. 1403, pp. 561–575. Springer, Heidelberg (1998)

20. Chaum, D.: Blind signatures for untraceable payments. In: Chaum, D., Rivest, R.L., Sherman, A.T. (eds) CRYPTO 1982, pp. 199–203. Plenum Press, New York (1982)

21. Chaum, D.: Blind signature system. In: Chaum, D. (ed.) CRYPTO 1983, p. 153. Plenum Press, New York (1983)

22. Fiat, A., Shamir, A.: How to prove yourself: practical solutions to identification and signature problems. In: Odlyzko, A.M. (ed.) CRYPTO 1986. LNCS, vol. 263, pp. 186–194. Springer, Heidelberg (1987)

23. Galbraith, S.D., Paterson, K.G., Smart, N.P.: Pairings for cryptographers. Discrete Applied Mathematics 156(16), 3113–3121 (2008)

24. Goldwasser, S., Micali, S., Rivest, R.L.: A digital signature scheme secure against adaptive chosen-message attacks. SIAM J. Comput. 17(2), 281–308 (1988)

25. Groth, J., Sahai, A.: Efficient non-interactive proof systems for bilinear groups. In: Smart, N.P. (ed.) EUROCRYPT 2008. LNCS, vol. 4965, pp. 415–432. Springer, Heidelberg (2008)

26. Izabachène, M., Libert, B.: Divisible E-Cash in the standard model. In: Abdalla, M., Lange, T. (eds.) Pairing 2012. LNCS, vol. 7708, pp. 314–332. Springer, Heidelberg (2013)

27. Nakanishi, T., Sugiyama, Y.: Unlinkable divisible electronic cash. In: Okamoto, E., Pieprzyk, J.P., Seberry, J. (eds.) ISW 2000. LNCS, vol. 1975, pp. 121–134. Springer, Heidelberg (2000)

28. Okamoto, T.: An efficient divisible electronic cash scheme. In: Coppersmith, D. (ed.) CRYPTO 1995. LNCS, vol. 963, pp. 438–451. Springer, Heidelberg (1995)

29. Okamoto, T., Ohta, K.: Universal electronic cash. In: Feigenbaum, J. (ed.) CRYPTO 1991. LNCS, vol. 576, pp. 324–337. Springer, Heidelberg (1992)

30. Schnorr, C.-P.: Efficient identification and signatures for smart cards. In: Brassard, G. (ed.) CRYPTO 1989. LNCS, vol. 435, pp. 239–252. Springer, Heidelberg (1990)

31. Stadler, M.A., Piveteau, J.-M., Camenisch, J.L.: Fair blind signatures. In: Guillou, L.C., Quisquater, J.-J. (eds.) EUROCRYPT 1995. LNCS, vol. 921, pp. 209–219. Springer, Heidelberg (1995)

Anonymous Transferable E-Cash

Foteini Baldimtsi[1](✉), Melissa Chase[2],
Georg Fuchsbauer[3], and Markulf Kohlweiss[2]

[1] Boston University, Boston, USA
foteini@cs.bu.edu
[2] Microsoft Research, Bengaluru, India
melissac@microsoft.com
[3] Institute of Science and Technology Austria, Klosterneuburg, Austria
georg.fuchsbauer@ist.ac.at, markulf@microsoft.com

Abstract. Cryptographic e-cash allows off-line electronic transactions between a bank, users and merchants in a secure and anonymous fashion. A plethora of e-cash constructions has been proposed in the literature; however, these traditional e-cash schemes only allow coins to be transferred once between users and merchants. Ideally, we would like users to be able to transfer coins between each other multiple times before deposit, as happens with physical cash.

"Transferable" e-cash schemes are the solution to this problem. Unfortunately, the currently proposed schemes are either completely impractical or do not achieve the desirable anonymity properties without compromises, such as assuming the existence of a trusted "judge" who can trace all coins and users in the system. This paper presents the first efficient and fully anonymous transferable e-cash scheme without any trusted third parties. We start by revising the security and anonymity properties of transferable e-cash to capture issues that were previously overlooked. For our construction we use the recently proposed malleable signatures by Chase et al. to allow the secure and anonymous transfer of coins, combined with a new efficient double-spending detection mechanism. Finally, we discuss an instantiation of our construction.

Keywords: Electronic payments · Transferable e-cash · Malleable signatures · Double-spending detection

1 Introduction

Electronic payment systems are everywhere and average users take their two main properties, security and privacy, for granted even though they may be built on shaky foundations. Payments made with debit or credit cards do not provide any privacy guarantee for users since the corresponding financial institution can

Work done as an intern in Microsoft Research Redmond and as a student at Brown University, where supported by NSF grant 0964379.
Supported by the European Research Council, ERC Starting Grant (259668-PSPC).

J. Katz (Ed.): PKC 2015, LNCS 9020, pp. 101–124, 2015.
DOI: 10.1007/978-3-662-46447-2_5

track all their transactions. Starting with Chaum [Cha83], the cryptographic community has worked on electronic analogues to physical money (e-cash) that guarantee secure and private payments [Cha83, CFN88, Bra93, CHL05, BCKL09]. A typical e-cash system consists of three types of entities: the bank, users and merchants. Users withdraw electronic coins from the bank and spend them to merchants, who then deposit them at the bank. E-cash systems should satisfy two main properties (1) *unforgeability*: an adversarial user cannot spend more e-coins than he withdrew; and (2) *anonymity*: nobody (including the bank) can link spending transactions to each other or to specific withdrawal transactions.

Unlike physical cash, electronic coins are easy to duplicate, so a mechanism is needed to ensure that a user cannot spend one coin multiple times. Two solutions were proposed in the literature: the first is *online* e-cash [Cha83], in which the merchants are constantly connected to the bank and can therefore check whether a coin has already been deposited before accepting it. In order to overcome the strong requirement of a permanent connection to the bank, a second solution is to use a *double-spending* mechanism [CFN88]. As long as a user is honest, his anonymity is guaranteed, but if he tries to cheat the system by spending one e-coin multiple times then his identity is revealed.

Unfortunately, in traditional e-cash users can only transfer their coins to merchants, who must then deposit them at the bank. It would be natural to allow users to transfer coins to other users (or merchants), who should be able to further transfer the received coins, and so on. Moreover, it would be desirable if these transfers could be done without being connected to the bank, i.e., offline. One of the main advantages of such a transferability property is that it would decrease the communication cost between the bank and the users. Moreover, it would allow for more real-world scenarios. Consider the example of coins of different denominations. A store, which is offline, wants to give back change to a customer, using coins previously received. In order to do so, coins need to be transferable multiple times. Transferability of e-cash was proposed in the 1990s and the desired security properties have been analyzed; however, all schemes proposed so far do not satisfy the proposed security and privacy requirements, or they are only of theoretical interest, such as [CG08].

Arguably, this was partly because e-cash fell out of fashion as it became clear that traditional banks were unlikely to support cryptographic currencies and that credit cards and centralized payment services offering little privacy are broadly accepted for online payments. Recently, with bitcoin [Nak08] demonstrating how to bypass the banks, there has been renewed interest in e-cash, as existing techniques from anonymous e-cash are likely to be applicable to the bitcoin world as well [MGGR13, BCG+14].

Related Work. Transferable e-cash was originally proposed by Okamoto and Ohta [OO89, OO91], who gave e-cash schemes that satisfy various properties such as divisibility and transferability but only provide weak levels of anonymity. While an adversary cannot link a withdrawal to a payment, he can link two payments by the same user, a property called *weak anonymity* (WA). Chaum and Pedersen [CP92] proved that (1) transferred coins have to grow in size and (2) an unbounded adversary can always recognize coins he owned when seeing them spent later. Moreover, they extended the scheme due to van Antwerpen [vAE90] to allow coin transfer. The resulting scheme satisfies *strong anonymity* (SA), guaranteeing that an adversary cannot decide whether two payments were made by the same user. However, he can recognize coins he observed in previous transactions. Strong anonymity is also satisfied by the schemes constructed in [Bla08, CGT08].

Anonymity for transferable e-cash has been a pretty subtle notion to define. In 2008 Canard and Gouget [CG08] gave the first formal treatment of anonymity properties for transferable e-cash. In addition to weak and strong anonymity, which do not yield the guarantees one would intuitively expect, they defined *full anonymity* (FA): an adversary acting as a malicious bank cannot link a coin previously (passively) observed to a coin he receives as a legitimate user (Observe-then-Receive). They also define *perfect anonymity* (PA): an adversary, acting as a malicious bank, cannot link a coin previously owned to a coin he receives and showed that $PA \Rightarrow FA \Rightarrow SA \Rightarrow WA$. Chaum and Pedersen [CP92] showed that perfect anonymity cannot be achieved against unbounded adversaries. Canard and Gouget [CG08] prove that it cannot be achieved against bounded adversaries either. They therefore introduce two modifications of perfect anonymity, which are incomparable to FA, namely PA1: an adversary, controlling the bank, cannot link a coin previously owned to a coin he passively observes being transferred between two honest users (Spend-then-Observe); and PA2 (Spend-then-Receive): an adversary cannot link a coin previously owned to a coin he receives, assuming the bank is honest. (If the adversary controls the bank, this notion is not achievable due to the impossibility results mentioned above.) In the same paper they present a construction which satisfies all achievable anonymity properties, but is only of theoretical interest due to its inefficiency as it relies on metaproofs and thus Cook-Levin reductions.

The first practical scheme that satisfies FA, PA1 and PA2 is the scheme due to Fuchsbauer et al. [FPV09]; however, it has two main drawbacks: (1) the users have to store the data of all transactions they were involved in to prove innocence in case of fraud; and (2) when a double-spending is detected, all users up to the double-spender lose their anonymity. Blazy et al. [BCF+11] addressed these problems and propose a new scheme using commuting signatures [Fuc11], which overcomes the above drawbacks by assuming the existence of a trusted entity called the *judge*. This entity is responsible for the tracing of double-spenders, but can also trace all coins and users in the system at any time. This clearly contradicts one of the main goals of e-cash: as long as users do not double-spend, they remain anonymous. (In addition, it is not clear whether their scheme satisfies PA2; see Section 4.4.)

Our Contributions

We present the first transferable e-cash scheme that satisfies all of the anonymity properties from the literature (FA, PA1, PA2) and a new anonymity notion that we introduce. Moreover, it does not assume any trusted party and does not rely on a Cook-Levin reduction or heuristics like the random-oracle model. Our contributions include new definitions, a construction based on malleable signatures and a double-spending detection mechanism potentially of independent interest.

Definitions. We provide a formal treatment of the security and anonymity properties of transferable e-cash in a game-based fashion, since many of the previous definitions were informal and/or incomplete. Moreover, we define a new anonymity requirement that was not captured before. Namely, we introduce a strengthening of Spend-then-Receive anonymity (a.k.a. PA2), which offers anonymity guarantees against a malicious bank. While it is unavoidable that an adversary impersonating the bank can link a coin he previously owned to one he receives, we require that he should not learn anything about which honest users possessed the coin in between. This was not guaranteed in previous definitions.

Construction. In traditional e-cash systems a coin withdrawn from the bank typically consists of the bank's signature σ on a unique serial number, SN. When spending the coin with a merchant, a double-spending tag DS is computed, which encodes the identity of the spender. The merchant then deposits $c = (\text{SN}, \sigma, \text{DS})$ at the bank. If two coins c, c' with the same serial number but with different double-spending tags DS, DS' are deposited, these tags together will reveal the identity of the user who double-spent. For transferable e-cash, the owner of a coin should be able to transfer the coin/signature she received from the bank to another user in such a way that the transferred coin is valid, carries all the information necessary to detect double-spending, and preserves anonymity. Thus, we need a digital signature scheme that allows a user to compute a "fresh" version of a valid signature (unlinkable to the original one to ensure anonymity) and to extend the current signature to include more information (such as a double-spending tag for the new owner).

A recent proposal of a signature scheme that satisfies the above properties is due to Chase et al. [CKLM14]. They propose *malleable* signatures, an extension of digital signatures, where anyone can transform a signature on a message m into a signature on m', as long as $T(m) = m'$ for some allowed transformation T. They then use malleable signatures to construct delegatable anonymous credentials. Our transferable e-cash scheme is inspired by their construction; however, the security against double-spending required in offline e-cash and the subtleties of the resulting anonymity guarantees introduce many technical challenges and make our construction much more involved.

In our construction, a coin withdrawn by the bank is signed using a malleable signature scheme. When a user wishes to transfer a coin to another user, he computes a mauled signature on a valid transformation of the coin. A valid transformation guarantees that the transferred coin is indeed owned by the sender (i.e. the sender's secret key corresponds to the information encoded in the coin) and the new coin/signature created will encode the right information of the receiver. The serial number and the double-spending tags are encrypted under the bank's public key, allowing it to check for double-spending on deposit. Moreover, the encryptions are re-randomized in every transfer, which ensures anonymity. We propose an instantiation, detailed in the full version [BCFK15], that can be proved secure under standard assumptions: Decision Linear (DLIN) and Symmetric External Decision Diffie-Hellman (SXDH).

Double-Spending Detection. Double-spending detection for transferable e-cash is a complex issue: it needs to ensure that the right user is accused while preserving the anonymity of honest owners of the coin. We propose an efficient double-spending detection mechanism, which is independent of our scheme and could be used by other transferable e-cash schemes, e.g., to provide an offline payment mechanism for users who have committed a sufficient quantity of bitcoins as a deposit. Our mechanism allows us to satisfy the new Spend-then-Receive anonymity property and still use an efficient proof mechanism. Ours is the only construction that does so apart from [CG08], which is only theoretical.[1]

2 Definitions for Transferable E-Cash

We adapt the definitions for transferable e-cash given by [CG08, BCF+11] and strengthen them in several aspects; in particular, we introduce an additional anonymity notion. Following the paradigm of previous work, we present the security and anonymity properties in a "game-based" fashion. This allows for comparisons with older definitions and results in modular security proofs for proposed schemes. We note that a simulation-based security definition for transferable e-cash that captures all properties considered so far is an interesting open problem.

In a transferable e-cash scheme there are two types of parties: the bank $\mathcal{B}$ and users $\mathcal{U}_i$. Coins are denoted by c and each coin is uniquely identifiable via a serial number SN, which will be retrieved by the bank during deposit to check if the same coin was deposited twice. We let $\mathcal{DCL}$ denote the list of deposited coins; if multiple coins with the same serial number were deposited, we keep all of them in $\mathcal{DCL}$.

We modify previous definitions in that we add a protocol for user registration[2] and we merge the Deposit and Identify protocols. A transferable e-cash scheme consists of the following algorithms (probabilistic unless otherwise stated):

ParamGen(1^λ) on input the security parameter λ outputs the system parameters *par*. (We assume that λ can be deduced from *par*.) *par* is a default input to the remaining algorithms.

BKeyGen() and UKeyGen() are executed by $\mathcal{B}$ and a user $\mathcal{U}$ respectively and output $(sk_\mathcal{B}, pk_\mathcal{B})$ and $(sk_\mathcal{U}, pk_\mathcal{U})$. The bank's key $sk_\mathcal{B}$ might be divided into two parts: $sk_\mathcal{W}$ for registrations and withdrawals and $sk_\mathcal{D}$ for deposits. During BKeyGen the list $\mathcal{DCL}$ is initialized to be empty.

Registration($\mathcal{B}[sk_\mathcal{W}, pk_\mathcal{U}], \mathcal{U}[sk_\mathcal{U}, pk_\mathcal{B}]$) is a protocol between the bank and a user. At the end the user receives a certificate $cert_\mathcal{U}$; both parties output either ok or $\bot$ in case of error.

---

[1] The construction in [BCF+11] does not satisfy the new Spend-then-Receive property if the judge is not assumed to be honest. If the judge is honest, it is not clear whether the notion is satisfied, as is the case for the original Spend-then-Receive notion (a.k.a. PA2); see Section 4.4.

[2] For Identification to be meaningful, we must guarantee not only that we can identify a doublespender's public key, but also that that public key corresponds to a legitimate identity, i.e. that it has been registered with the bank.

Withdraw($\mathcal{B}[sk_\mathcal{W}, pk_\mathcal{U}], \mathcal{U}[sk_\mathcal{U}, pk_\mathcal{B}]$) is a protocol between the bank and a user. The user either outputs a coin c or $\bot$. $\mathcal{B}$'s output is ok or $\bot$ in case of error.

Spend($\mathcal{U}_1[c, sk_{\mathcal{U}_1}, cert_{\mathcal{U}_1}, pk_\mathcal{B}], \mathcal{U}_2[sk_{\mathcal{U}_2}, pk_\mathcal{B}]$) is a protocol in which $\mathcal{U}_1$ spends/ transfers the coin c to $\mathcal{U}_2$. At the end, $\mathcal{U}_2$ either outputs a coin c' and ok or it outputs $\bot$; $\mathcal{U}_1$ either marks the coin c as spent and outputs ok, or it outputs $\bot$ in case of error.

Deposit($\mathcal{U}[c, sk_\mathcal{U}, cert_\mathcal{U}, pk_\mathcal{B}], \mathcal{B}[sk_\mathcal{D}, pk_\mathcal{U}, \mathcal{DCL}]$) is a protocol where a user $\mathcal{U}$ deposits a coin c at the bank. We split the deposit protocol into three subroutines. First CheckCoin checks whether the coin c is consistent, and if not outputs $\bot$. Else, $\mathcal{B}$ runs CheckDS, which outputs the serial number SN of the deposited coin. $\mathcal{B}$ checks whether $\mathcal{DCL}$ already contains an entry for SN. If not, $\mathcal{B}$ adds SN to $\mathcal{DCL}$, credits $\mathcal{U}$'s account and returns "success" and $\mathcal{DCL}$. Otherwise, the coin was double-spent: the subroutine DetectDS is run on the two coins and outputs ($pk_\mathcal{U}, \Pi$), where $pk_\mathcal{U}$ is the public key of the accused user, and Π is a proof that the registered user who owns $pk_\mathcal{U}$ double-spent the coin. Note that Π should reveal nothing about the coin itself.

VerifyGuilt($pk_\mathcal{U}, \Pi$) is a deterministic algorithm that can be executed by anyone. It outputs 1 if the proof verifies and 0 otherwise.

Notice that in our definition a transferable e-cash scheme is *stateless* since there is no common state information shared between the algorithms. This means that a coin withdrawn will not be affected by the order in which withdrawals happen, i.e. whether it was the first or the n-th coin the bank issues to a specific user. Moreover, when a user $\mathcal{U}_2$ receives a coin from a user $\mathcal{U}_1$, the transferred coin will only depend on $\mathcal{U}_1$'s original coin (not on other coins received by $\mathcal{U}_2$ or transferred by $\mathcal{U}_1$). Thus, the bank and the users do not need to remember anything about past transactions—for transfer the coin itself will be sufficient.

Global Variables. In order to formally define the security properties of transferable e-cash, we first define some global variables and oracles which will be used in the security games. In the **user list**, $\mathcal{UL}$, we store all information about users, keys and certificates. Its entries are of the form ($i, pk, sk, cert, uds$), where uds indicates how many times user $\mathcal{U}_i$ double-spent (this counter is used in the exculpability definition). If user i is corrupted (i.e. the adversary knows the secret key of this user) then $sk = \bot$; if it has not been registered then $cert = \bot$. We keep a counter, n, of the total number of generated/registered users which is initialized to 0.

In the **coin list**, $\mathcal{CL}$, we keep information about the coins created in the system. For each *original* coin withdrawn we store a tuple ($j, owner, c, fc, fd, cds, origin$), where j is its index in $\mathcal{CL}$, $owner$ stores the index i of the user who withdrew the coin[3] and c is the coin itself. The flag fc indicates whether the coin has been corrupted[4] and the flag fd indicates whether the coin has been

---

[3] We do not store the coins withdrawn by the adversary.

[4] A *corrupted coin* is defined as a coin that was under the adversary's control at some point. Once a coin is flagged as *corrupted*, it cannot be "un-flagged", even if it is later under the control of an honest user.

deposited. We also keep a counter, *cds*, of how many times this *specific instance* of the coin has been spent, which is initialized as $cds = 0$. In *origin* we write "$\mathcal{B}$" if the coin was issued by the honest bank and "$\mathcal{A}$" if the adversary issued it when impersonating the bank.

When a coin is transferred to another honest user, we add a new entry to $\mathcal{CL}$ as follows: $(j, owner, c, cds, pointer)$, where j is the position in $\mathcal{CL}$, *owner* shows the current owner, c is the new, *transferred* coin and *cds* indicates how many times the coin has been spent. In *pointer* we store a pointer j' indicating which original coin this transferred coin corresponds to. Once a transferred coin is deposited or corrupted, we mark the original coin's flags fc, fd appropriately. The last list is the **list of deposited coins**, $\mathcal{DCL}$. To make explicit the user or coin to which a variable belongs, we write, e.g., pk_i or $pointer_j$ respectively.

We now define oracles used in the security definitions. If during the oracle execution an algorithm fails (outputs $\perp$) then the oracle also stops. Otherwise the call to the oracle is considered *successful* (for the deposit oracles a successful call is one that also didn't detect any double-spending). We define several oracles for each operation, depending on which parties are controlled by the adversary.

Oracles for Creation, Registration and Corruption of Users. The adversary can instruct the creation of honest users, corrupt users, and invoke or participate in registration:

Create() sets $n = n + 1$, executes $(sk_n, pk_n) \leftarrow$ UKeyGen(), sets $\mathcal{UL}[n] = (n, pk_n, sk_n, \perp, 0)$ and outputs pk_n.

BRegister(pk) plays the bank side of the Register protocol and interacts with $\mathcal{A}$. If $pk \notin \mathcal{UL}$ then set $n = n + 1$ and $\mathcal{UL}[n] = (n, pk, \perp, \perp, 0)$; else abort.

URegister(i), for $i \leq n$, plays the user side of the Register protocol and adds *cert* to the corresponding field of $\mathcal{UL}$.

Register(i), for $i \leq n$, simulates both sides of the Register protocol. If user i was not registered then add *cert* to the corresponding field of $\mathcal{UL}$.

Corrupt(i, S), for $i \leq n$, allows the adversary to corrupt user i and a subset, S, of his coins[5]. If $sk_i = \perp$ (i.e. this user is already corrupted) then abort. The set S must consist of coin indices in $\mathcal{CL}$. For every $j \in S$ look up the j-th entry of $\mathcal{CL}$ and if $owner \neq i$ then ignore this coin and remove it from S. The oracle first outputs sk_i and then updates $\mathcal{UL}$ by setting $sk_i = \perp$ to mark this user as corrupted. Then, the coins in the set S are given to the adversary $\mathcal{A}$ and are marked as corrupted i.e. the flag fc of the corresponding *original* coin is set $fc = 1$. Note that if $\mathcal{A}$ tries to corrupt unregistered users, this doesn't give him any extra power. Also, once a user is corrupted he is considered to be an *adversarial* user and thus $\mathcal{A}$ will be running in his place. This means that $\mathcal{A}$ cannot run honest-user oracles on corrupted users, i.e. oracles With, UWith, Rcv, S&R, URegister.

---

[5] S allows us to capture the case, for example, where the honest user has not deleted all of his spent coins. (Ideally all coins should be deleted immediately after spending, but we want to define security even in the case where this does not happen.) S would include the user's unspent coins and any spent coins that have not been deleted.

Withdrawal Oracles

BWith() plays the bank side of the Withdraw protocol. Note that coins belonging to $\mathcal{A}$ are not added to the coin list $\mathcal{CL}$.

UWith(i) plays user i in a Withdraw protocol, where the bank is controlled by the adversary. Upon obtaining a coin c, it increases the current size ℓ of $\mathcal{CL}$ by 1 and adds (ℓ, $owner = i, c, fc = 0, fd = 0, cds = 0, origin = \mathcal{A}$) to $\mathcal{CL}$.

With(i) simulates a complete Withdraw protocol execution playing both $\mathcal{B}$ and user i. It increases the current size ℓ of $\mathcal{CL}$ by 1, adds (ℓ, $owner = i, c, fc = 0, fd = 0, cds = 0, origin = \mathcal{B}$) to $\mathcal{CL}$, and outputs the transcript.

Spend and Deposit Oracles

Rcv(i) lets $\mathcal{A}$ spend a coin to honest user i. It plays the role of $\mathcal{U}_2$ with user i's secret key in the Spend protocol. A new entry (j, $owner = i, c, fc = 1, fd = 0, cds = 0, origin = \mathcal{A}$) is added to $\mathcal{CL}$. Coins received from the adversary are considered as *original* coins in $\mathcal{CL}$.

Spd(j) enables $\mathcal{A}$ to receive coin number j in $\mathcal{CL}$. If the coin belongs to a corrupted user it aborts. Otherwise, it plays the role of user $\mathcal{U}_1$ in the Spend protocol with the secret key of the owner i of coin j. It increases the coin spend counter cds of entry j in $\mathcal{CL}$ by 1. If cds was already greater than zero (i.e., this specific user has already spent this coin) then the double-spending counter, uds, of the owner of coin j is increased by one. Finally, whenever a coin is received by $\mathcal{A}$, we mark the *original* instance of this coin as corrupted, i.e., we set $fc = 1$.

S&R(i, j) is the Spend-and-Receive oracle that allows $\mathcal{A}$ to passively observe the spending of coin j by its owner to user i (both of whom must not be corrupted). It increases the current size ℓ of $\mathcal{CL}$ by 1 and adds (ℓ, $owner = i, c, cds = 0, pointer$) to $\mathcal{CL}$, where $pointer = j$ if j is an *original* coin and $pointer = pointer_j$ if it is a *transferred* coin. It also increases the coin spend counter cds_j in entry j by 1. If cds_j was already greater than zero then the double-spending counter uds of the spender is also increased by 1.

BDepo() simulates the bank in the Deposit protocol interacting with $\mathcal{A}$ playing the role of a user. It updates $\mathcal{DCL}$ accordingly, and in case of a double-spending, outputs the resulting pk, Π.

UDepo(j) simulates the role of the owner (who must not be corrupted) of coin j in the Deposit protocol, interacting with the adversary playing the bank. It increases the spend counter cds_j in entry j in $\mathcal{CL}$ by 1. If cds_j was already greater than zero then the double-spending counter uds of the owner of coin j is increased by 1. It also marks $fd = 1$ for the original coin.

Depo(j) simulates a Deposit of coin j between an honest bank and the owner of j (who must not be corrupted). It increases cds_j in entry j of $\mathcal{CL}$ by 1. If cds_j was already greater than zero then uds of the owner of coin j is increased by one. It also marks $fd = 1$ in the original coin and adds the coin to $\mathcal{DCL}$, and in case of a double-spending, outputs the resulting pk, Π.

Let $\mathtt{size}(c)$ be a function that outputs the size of a coin. A withdrawn coin has size 1 and after a transfer the size increases by 1. We say that coins c_1 and c_2 are *compatible*, (denoted $\mathtt{comp}(c_1, c_2) = 1$), if $\mathtt{size}(c_1) = \mathtt{size}(c_2)$. We need this property, since transferred coins necessarily grow in size [CP92] and thus an adversary may break anonymity by distinguishing coins of different sizes.

2.1   Security Properties

We define the security properties of transferable e-cash by refining previous definitions by [CG08] and [BCF+11]. In the beginning of security games with an honest bank the challenger typically runs $par \leftarrow \mathtt{ParamGen}(1^\lambda)$ and $(sk_\mathcal{B}, pk_\mathcal{B}) \leftarrow \mathtt{BKeyGen}()$, which we merge into one algorithm $\mathtt{AllGen}$.

Unforgeability. This notion protects the bank in that an adversary should not be able to spend more coins than the number of coins he withdrew. In [BCF+11] an adversary can interact with honest users and wins the unforgeability game if he withdrew fewer coins than he successfully deposited.

We simplify the definition noticing that it is not necessary for the adversary to create or corrupt *honest* users (or instruct them to withdraw, spend, receive and deposit), since the adversary could simulate these users itself. An unforgeability definition *without* honest user oracles thus implies the definition *with* these oracles given in [BCF+11]. This also captures the scenario of coin theft in which the adversary steals coins of honest users, as he also has access to these coins in the simulation. Note here that we can only require that the adversary be caught if he spends more coins than he withdrew, *and if those coins are deposited*. Without drastically changing the approach of offline ecash, it seems impossible to catch a double-spending until the coins are finally deposited.

To define unforgeability we consider the following experiment:

Experiment $\mathbf{Expt}_\mathcal{A}^{\mathrm{unforg}}(\lambda)$;
   $(par, sk_\mathcal{B}, pk_\mathcal{B}) \leftarrow \mathtt{AllGen}(1^\lambda)$;
   $\mathcal{A}^{\mathtt{BRegister},\mathtt{BWith},\mathtt{BDepo}}(par, pk_\mathcal{B})$;
   Let q_W, q_D be the number of successful calls to $\mathtt{BWith}$, $\mathtt{BDepo}$ respectively;
   If $q_W < q_D$ then return 1;
   Return $\perp$.

Definition 1 (Unforgeability). *A transferable e-cash system is* unforgeable *if for any probabilistic polynomial-time (PPT) adversary $\mathcal{A}$, we have $\mathbf{Adv}_\mathcal{A}^{\mathrm{unforg}}(\lambda)$, defined as $\Pr[\mathbf{Expt}_\mathcal{A}^{\mathrm{unforg}}(\lambda) = 1]$, is negligible in λ.*

Identification of Double-Spenders. No collection of users should be able to spend a coin twice (double-spend) without revealing one of their identities along with a valid proof of guilt. Consider the following experiment where, analogously to the unforgeability definition, we do not give the adversary access to honest user oracles since he can simulate them himself.

Experiment $\mathbf{Expt}_{\mathcal{A}}^{\text{ident}}(\lambda)$

    $(par, sk_{\mathcal{B}}, pk_{\mathcal{B}}) \leftarrow \texttt{AllGen}(1^{\lambda});$

    $\mathcal{A}^{\texttt{BRegister,BWith,BDepo}}(par, pk_{\mathcal{B}});$

    Let (pk_{i^*}, Π_G) be the output of the last call to $\texttt{BDepo}$ to find a doublespending;

    Return 1 if any of the following hold:

      − $\texttt{VerifyGuilt}(pk_{i^*}, \Pi_G) = 0;$

      − $pk_{i^*} \notin \mathcal{UL};$

    Return $\perp$.

Definition 2 (Double-spender identification). *A transferable e-cash system is secure against double-spending if for any PPT adversary $\mathcal{A}$ we have that* $\mathbf{Adv}_{\mathcal{A}}^{\text{ident}}(\lambda) := \Pr[\mathbf{Expt}_{\mathcal{A}}^{\text{ident}}(\lambda) = 1]$ *is negligible in λ.*

Exculpability. Exculpability ensures that the bank, even when colluding with malicious users, cannot wrongly accuse honest users of double-spending. Specifically, it guarantees that an adversarial bank cannot output a double-spending proof Π^* that verifies for an honest user's public key if that user never double-spent. Our definition follows the one from [BCF+11], but we allow the adversary to generate the bank keys himself, thus truly modeling a malicious bank. The adversary must output the index of the user accused of double-spending and a corresponding proof. The game is formalized as follows.

Experiment $\mathbf{Expt}_{\mathcal{A}}^{\text{excul}}(\lambda)$

    $par \leftarrow \texttt{ParamGen}(1^{\lambda});$

    $(pk_{\mathcal{B}}) \leftarrow \mathcal{A}(par);$

    $(i^*, \Pi^*) \leftarrow \mathcal{A}^{\texttt{Create,URegister,Corrupt,UWith,Rcv,Spd,S\&R,UDepo}};$

    If $\texttt{VerifyGuilt}(pk_{i^*}, \Pi^*) = 1$ and $sk_{i^*} \neq \perp$ and $uds_{i^*} = 0$ then return 1;

    Return $\perp$.

Definition 3 (Exculpability). *A transferable e-cash system is exculpable if for any stateful PPT adversary $\mathcal{A}$, we have that* $\mathbf{Adv}_{\mathcal{A}}^{\text{excul}}(\lambda) := \Pr[\mathbf{Expt}_{\mathcal{A}}^{\text{excul}}(\lambda) = 1]$ *is negligible in λ.*

In the full version [BCFK15] we also discuss a stronger version of exculpability that guarantees that a user cannot be accused of double-spending *more* coins than he did.

2.2 Anonymity Properties

We first consider the three anonymity notions given in [CG08, BCF+11]:

Observe-then-Receive Full Anonymity (OtR-FA). The adversary, controlling the bank, cannot link a coin he receives as an adversarial user or as the bank to a previously (passively) observed transfer between honest users. This covers both the case where the adversary receives a coin as a user during a transfer and the case where he receives a coin as the bank during deposit.

Spend-then-Observe Full Anonymity (StO-FA). The adversary, controlling the bank, cannot link a (passively) observed coin transferred between two honest users to a coin he has already owned as a "legitimate" user.

Spend-then-Receive Full Anonymity (StR-FA). When the bank is honest, the adversary cannot recognize a coin he previously owned when he receives it again.

These three notions are incomparable as proved in [CG08]. The games formalizing these notions are fairly similar to those in [BCF+11]. A difference is that we define *coin* indistinguishability, which implies the *user* indistinguishability properties considered in [BCF+11]. We also allow $\mathcal{A}$ to pick the secret keys himself, in particular that of the adversarial bank (in contrast to [CG08,BCF+11], where the bank's keys are created by experiment). We begin by defining the appropriate experiment for each notion.

In the OtR game the adversary outputs two indices of coins owned by honest users and receives one of them, either as a Spend (by setting $v = 0$) or as a Deposit (setting $v = 1$). The adversary must not receive the coin a second time (he could otherwise distinguish them as he controls the bank), which the game ensures by resetting the flags fc, fd to 0 and checking that they remain that way.

Experiment $\mathbf{Expt}_{\mathcal{A},b}^{\text{OtR-fa}}(\lambda)$

> $par \leftarrow \mathsf{ParamGen}(1^\lambda)$; $pk_{\mathcal{B}} \leftarrow \mathcal{A}(par)$;
> $(j_0, j_1, v) \leftarrow \mathcal{A}^{\text{Create,URegister,Corrupt,UWith,Rcv,Spd,S\&R,UDepo}}$;
> If $\mathsf{comp}(j_0, j_1) \neq 1$ or $fc_{j_0} = 1$ or $fc_{j_1} = 1$ or $fd_{j_0} = 1$ or $fd_{j_1} = 1$
>   then return $\perp$;
> If $v = 0$ then simulate $\mathsf{Spd}(j_b)$ to $\mathcal{A}$;
> Else if $v = 1$ then simulate $\mathsf{UDepo}(j_b)$;
> Else return $\perp$;
> Reset the flags to $fd_{j_0} = 0$, $fd_{j_1} = 0$, $fc_{j_0} = 0$, $fc_{j_1} = 0$;
> $b^* \leftarrow \mathcal{A}^{\text{Create,URegister,Corrupt,With,Rcv,Spd,S\&R,UDepo}}$;
> If $fd_{j_0} = 1$ or $fd_{j_1} = 1$ or $fc_{j_0} = 1$ or $fc_{j_1} = 1$ then abort;
> Return b^*.

For the StO game we use a modified Spend&Receive oracle S&R*: for the coin c being transfered, it creates a new entry in $\mathcal{CL}$ in the form of an *original* coin whose origin is marked to be *Challenger* while $owner = i$, $fd = 0$, and $fc = 0$. If the adversary tries to corrupt, receive or deposit this coin (or a transferred coin whose "original coin" in $\mathcal{CL}$ is this coin) then we abort.

Experiment $\mathbf{Expt}_{\mathcal{A},b}^{\text{StO-fa}}(\lambda)$

> $par \leftarrow \mathsf{ParamGen}(1^\lambda)$; $pk_{\mathcal{B}} \leftarrow \mathcal{A}(par)$;
> $(j_0, j_1, i) \leftarrow \mathcal{A}^{\text{Create,URegister,Corrupt,UWith,Rcv,Spd,S\&R,UDepo}}$;
> For $\beta = 0, 1$, let u_β be index of the owner of coin j_β (i.e., $owner_{j_\beta} = u_\beta$);
> If $\mathsf{comp}(j_0, j_1) \neq 1$ or $sk_{U_{j_0}} = \perp$ or $sk_{U_{j_1}} = \perp$ or $sk_i = \perp$ then return $\perp$;
> Run $out \leftarrow \mathsf{S\&R}^*(j_b, i)$;
> $b^* \leftarrow \mathcal{A}^{\text{Create,URegister,Corrupt,UWith,Rcv,Spd,S\&R,UDepo}}(out)$;
> If the coin with origin *Challenger* has $fd = 1$ or $fc = 1$ then abort;
> Return b^*.

In the StR game we assume that the bank is honest, or at least that $\mathcal{A}$ does not know the deposit key $sk_{\mathcal{D}}$. The adversary picks two coins of the same size, with indices j_0, j_1, whose owners are uncorrupted. We then transfer the coin j_b to $\mathcal{A}$ for a randomly selected bit b and his goal is to guess b. When he runs again, we have to make sure that no one deposits j_0 or j_1; otherwise he could trivially win by depositing his coin and checking whether a double-spending occurred. We therefore use two modified oracles BDepo' and Depo', which check whether the deposited coin collides with coin j_0 or j_1. If it does, we deposit j_0, j_1 and his coin and return cumulative results so that the results will be independent of b.

BDepo'(j), Depo'(j) run the CheckCoin subroutine of Deposit as prescribed by BDepo(j) and Depo(j) respectively. If OK, initialize $\mathcal{DCL}' = \emptyset$ and simulate Deposit for coins j_0, j_1 and then CheckDS for the coin $\mathcal{A}$ deposits in both cases using $\mathcal{DCL}'$ instead.

If double-spending is detected then simulate Deposit for the coins j_0, j_1 and CheckDS, DetectDS for $\mathcal{A}$'s coin; each time reverting to the original $\mathcal{DCL}$. Only then add the three coins to $\mathcal{DCL}$. Return the set of public keys returned DetectDS for all three coins, together with one proof Π for each key. If there are multiple proofs, use the one from $\mathcal{A}$'s coin.

Else run CheckDS, DetectDS with $\mathcal{DCL}$ for $\mathcal{A}$'s coin, add the coin to $\mathcal{DCL}$, and return the result of DetectDS if there was a double-spending.

Experiment $\mathbf{Expt}_{\mathcal{A},b}^{\text{StR-fa}}(\lambda)$

$(par, sk_B = (sk_\mathcal{W}, sk_\mathcal{D}), pk_B) \leftarrow \text{AllGen}(1^\lambda);$

$(j_0, j_1) \leftarrow \mathcal{A}^{\text{Create,URegister,Corrupt,UWith,Rcv,Spd,S\&R,BDepo,Depo}}(par, sk_\mathcal{W}, pk_B);$

For $\beta = 0, 1$, let u_β be index of the owner of coin j_β (i.e., $owner_{j_\beta} = u_\beta$);

If $\text{comp}(j_0, j_1) \neq 1$ or $sk_{u_0} = \bot$ or $sk_{u_1} = \bot$ then return $\bot$;

Simulate $\text{Spd}(j_b)$ to $\mathcal{A}$;

$b^* \leftarrow \mathcal{A}^{\text{Create,URegister,Corrupt,UWith,Rcv,Spd,S\&R,BDepo',Depo'}};$

Return b^*.

In addition to these three notions, we introduce a new, strong, user-indistinguishability notion of anonymity that we call *Spend-then-Receive**: although the adversary, when controlling the bank, can tell whenever he receives a coin he owned before, he should not be able to learn anything about the identities of the users that owned the coin in between. We define this as an indistinguishability game in which the adversary picks a pair of users, to one of whom (according to bit b) the coins are transferred. The goal is to guess this bit b.[6]

---

[6] Note that it is important that the game below allows for many different values of k, as it is not clear how security for an experiment where $k = 1$ would imply security for higher values of k. To see this, consider the case where the adversary selects $k = 2$, and then plays a game where he either gives a coin to $\mathcal{U}_1$, who gives it to $\mathcal{U}_2$, who gives it back to $\mathcal{A}$, or he gives a coin to $\mathcal{U}_2$, who gives it to $\mathcal{U}_1$, who gives it back to $\mathcal{A}$ (i.e. he chooses $(i_0, i_1) = (\mathcal{U}_1, \mathcal{U}_2)$ the first time, and $(i_0, i_1) = (\mathcal{U}_2, \mathcal{U}_1)$ the second time). Now, it is not at all clear how to reduce this game to a game where $k = 1$, because any natural hybrid reduction would require the reduction to have control of either $\mathcal{U}_1$ or $\mathcal{U}_2$.

Experiment $\mathbf{Expt}^{\mathrm{StR*-fa}}_{\mathcal{A},b}(\lambda)$

$\quad par \leftarrow \mathtt{ParamGen}(1^{\lambda}); \quad pk_{\mathcal{B}} \leftarrow \mathcal{A}(par);$

$\quad (i_0, i_1, 1^k) \leftarrow \mathcal{A}^{\mathtt{Create},\mathtt{URegister},\mathtt{Corrupt},\mathtt{UWith},\mathtt{Rcv},\mathtt{Spd},\mathtt{S\&R},\mathtt{UDepo}};$

$\quad$ If $sk_{i_0} = \bot$ or $sk_{i_1} = \bot$ then return $\bot$;

$\quad$ Run $\mathtt{Rcv}(i_b)$ with $\mathcal{A}$;

$\quad$ Let c_1 be the received coin and let j_1 be its index in $\mathcal{CL}$;

$\quad$ Repeat the following two steps for $\alpha = 1, \ldots, k-1$:

$\qquad (i_0, i_1) \leftarrow \mathcal{A}$; If $sk_{i_0} = \bot$ or $sk_{i_1} = \bot$ then return $\bot$;

$\qquad$ Run $\mathtt{S\&R}(i_b, j_\alpha)$;

$\qquad$ Let $c_{\alpha+1}$ be the received coin and let $j_{\alpha+1}$ be its index in $\mathcal{CL}$;

$\quad$ Run $\mathtt{Spd}(j_k)$ with $\mathcal{A}$;

$\quad b^* \leftarrow \mathcal{A}^{\mathtt{Create},\mathtt{URegister},\mathtt{Corrupt},\mathtt{UWith},\mathtt{Rcv},\mathtt{Spd},\mathtt{S\&R},\mathtt{UDepo}};$

$\quad$ If for any of the coins $c_1, \ldots, c_k$ we have $cds > 1$ then output $\bot$;

$\quad$ If any of the owners of $c_1, \ldots, c_k$ is corrupted then output $\bot$;

$\quad$ Return b^*.

Definition 4. *(Anonymity) A transferable e-cash scheme is fully anonymous if for any stateful PPT adversary $\mathcal{A}$ we have that*

$$\mathbf{Adv}^{\mathrm{StR*-fa}}_{\mathcal{A}}(\lambda) := \Pr[(\mathbf{Expt}^{\mathrm{StR*-fa}}_{\mathcal{A},1}(\lambda) = 1] - \Pr[(\mathbf{Expt}^{\mathrm{StR*-fa}}_{\mathcal{A},0}(\lambda) = 1]$$

is negligible in λ (and analogously for $\mathbf{Expt}^{\mathrm{OtR-fa}}_{\mathcal{A},b}$, $\mathbf{Expt}^{\mathrm{StO-fa}}_{\mathcal{A},b}$, and $\mathbf{Expt}^{\mathrm{StR-fa}}_{\mathcal{A},b}$).

3 Double-Spending Detection

In our construction every coin in the system contains a serial number $\mathtt{SN} = \mathtt{SN}_1 \| \ldots \| \mathtt{SN}_k$ where $\mathtt{SN}_1$ was generated by the user who withdrew the coin, $\mathtt{SN}_2$ was generated by the second user who received the coin and so on. Moreover, a coin contains a set of double-spending tags $\mathtt{DS} = \mathtt{DS}_1 \| \ldots \| \mathtt{DS}_{k-1}$ which allows the bank to identify the user that double-spent whenever a coin is deposited twice. (To satisfy Spend-then-Receive anonymity, these values will be encrypted so that only the bank can see them.)

We first describe the properties of serial numbers and double-spending tags needed for our transferable e-cash construction. We then give concrete instantiations in Section 3.2.

3.1 Properties of Serial Numbers and Double-Spending Tags

As we will see in Section 3.2, for transferable e-cash it seems essential that the generation of $\mathtt{SN}_i$ uses both randomness chosen by the i-th receiver and the secret key of that user. We thus define a *serial-number function*, $f_{\mathtt{SN}}$, which on input a random nonce and a secret key (n_i, sk_i) outputs the serial-number component $\mathtt{SN}_i$ of the coin. We require a form of collision-resistance, which guarantees that different (n_i, sk_i) generate different $\mathtt{SN}$. Formally:

Definition 5 (Serial Number Function). *A serial number function $f_{\mathtt{SN}}$ for parameters $\mathtt{Gen}_{SN}$ takes as input parameters $par_{SN} \leftarrow \mathtt{Gen}_{SN}$, a nonce* and a secret key (n_i, sk_i), and outputs a serial number SN_i. (We omit par_{SN} when it is clear from context.) It is called collision-resistant if given $par_{SN} \leftarrow Gen_{SN}$, it is hard to find $(sk_i, n_i) \neq (sk'_i, n'_i)$ such that $f_{SN}(par_{SN}, n_i, sk_i) = f_{SN}(par_{SN}, n'_i, sk'_i)$.

We also define a *double-spending tag function*, f_{DS}, that takes as input the nonce n_i, that the coin owner $\mathcal{U}_i$ had picked when receiving the coin, $\mathcal{U}_i$'s secret key sk_i and SN_{i+1}, which was computed by the receiver of the coin. It might also take as input some additional user identifying information, ID_i. The output is a double-spending tag that reveals nothing about the owner, $\mathcal{U}_i$, unless she transfers the same coin to more than one user (i.e. double-spends). In that case, the bank can, given a database of public keys of all the users (and associated info ID for each one) identify the user that double-spent and produce a proof accusing her.

Definition 6 (Double-Spending Tag). A *double-spending tag function* f_{DS} *for parameters* Gen_{SN} *and key-generation algorithm* KeyGen *takes as input* par_{SN} *and* $(ID_i, n_i, sk_i, SN_{i+1})$ *and outputs the double-spending tag* DS_i.

- f_{DS} *is 2-show extractable if whenever we compute* DS_i *and* DS'_i *for the same* $(par_{SN}, ID_i, n_i, sk_i)$ *but different* $SN_{i+1} \neq SN'_{i+1}$, *there exists an efficient function* $f_{DetectDS}$ *that on input* DS_i *and* DS'_i *and a list of identifiers* $\mathcal{I}$ *such that* $(ID_i, pk_i) \in \mathcal{I}$ *for a* pk_i *corresponding to* sk_i *(according to* KeyGen*), efficiently extracts* (pk_i, Π) *where* Π *is an accepting proof for* pk_i.
- f_{DS} *is exculpable if, given a randomly generated public key* pk_i *produced by* KeyGen, *and* $par_{SN} \leftarrow Gen_{SN}$, *it is hard to compute an accepting proof,* Π, *for* pk_i. *More formally, consider the following game:* $par_{SN} \leftarrow Gen_{SN}$; $(pk_i, sk_i) \leftarrow$ KeyGen; $\Pi \leftarrow \mathcal{A}(par_{SN}, pk_i)$. *The adversary wins if* Π *is an accepting proof for* pk_i. *Exculpability means that any PPT adversary wins this game with at most negligible probability.*

Finally, we want to be able to guarantee anonymity notions even against a malicious bank who gets to see the serial numbers and double-spending tags for deposited coins. Thus, we require that as long as the nonce n_i is fresh and random, these values reveal nothing about the other values, such as sk and ID, used to generate them.[7]

Definition 7 (Anonymity of Double-Spending Tags). A *double-spending tag function* f_{DS} *and a serial number function* f_{SN} *are anonymous if for all* $ID_i, sk_i, SN_{i+1}, ID'_i, sk'_i, SN'_{i+1}$ *the following holds: If* $par_{SN} \leftarrow Gen_{SN}$ *and* n_i *is chosen at random then* $(par_{SN}, f_{SN}(par_{SN}, n_i, sk_i), f_{DS}(par_{SN}, ID_i, n_i, sk_i, SN_{i+1}))$ *and* $(par_{SN}, f_{SN}(par_{SN}, n_i, sk'_i), f_{DS}(par_{SN}, ID'_i, n_i, sk'_i, SN'_{i+1}))$ *are computationally indistinguishable.*

---

[7] This means that f_{SN} must be a commitment scheme. However the anonymity property we require here is stronger than commitment hiding in that indistinguishability is required to hold even given the additional double-spending value also computed using the same random string n_i.

3.2 A Double-Spending Detection Mechanism

Here we propose a concrete instantiation for the functions f_{SN}, f_{DS} used to generate the serial numbers and double-spending tags. To give some intuition, we first consider the natural translation of traditional (non-transferable) e-cash double-spending techniques [CFN88], and show why this is not sufficient in the transferable setting. Assume that $\mathcal{U}_i$ transfers a coin to $\mathcal{U}_{i+1}$ executing **Spend**. Let $SN_{i+1} = n_{i+1}$ be the nonce that $\mathcal{U}_{i+1}$ randomly picks and sends to $\mathcal{U}_i$. Then $\mathcal{U}_i$ would compute the double-spending tag as $DS_i = pk_i^{n_{i+1}} F(n_i)$, where $F(n_i)$ is hard to compute, except for the user that has chosen n_i.

Assume that $\mathcal{U}_i$ double-spends the coin by transferring it to users $\mathcal{U}_{i+1}$ and $\mathcal{U}'_{i+1}$ and that both instances of the coin get eventually deposited at the bank. The bank receives two coins starting with SN_1, so it looks for the first difference in the serial numbers SN and SN', which is $SN_{i+1} \neq SN'_{i+1}$, pointing to $\mathcal{U}_i$ as the double-spender. Using the tags DS_i and DS'_i, the bank can now compute $pk_i = (DS_i(DS'_i)^{-1})^{1/(n_{i+1}-n'_{i+1})}$. But what if a coin was double-spent and the receivers picked the same nonce n_{i+1}? We consider two cases:

Case 1: $\mathcal{U}_i$ double-spends the coin to the *same* user $\mathcal{U}_{i+1}$ and in both transactions $\mathcal{U}_{i+1}$ picks the same nonce n_{i+1}. When the coins are deposited the first difference occurs at position $i + 2$ and the bank will therefore accuse $\mathcal{U}_{i+1}$ of double-spending. However, user $\mathcal{U}_{i+1}$ can easily avoid being wrongly accused of double-spending by picking a fresh nonce each time he receives a coin.

Case 2: $\mathcal{U}_i$ transfers the same coin to *different* users with pk_{i+1} and pk'_{i+1} who pick the same nonce n_{i+1} when receiving the coin. As before, the bank's serial numbers will diverge at position $i + 2$. However, in this case computation of a public key will fail, as DS_{i+1} and DS'_{i+1} contain different public keys.

The second scenario could be exploited by a collusion of $\mathcal{U}_i, \mathcal{U}_{i+1}$ and $\mathcal{U}'_{i+1}$ to commit a double-spending without being traceable for it. We therefore need to ensure that different users cannot produce the same SN_{i+1} when receiving a coin. We ensure this by making SN_{i+1} dependent on the user's secret key, as formalized in Definition 5. We could easily achieve this by using a collision-resistant hash function, but in e-cash schemes users must prove well-formedness of SN and DS. We therefore want to keep the algebraic structure of the above example in order to use efficient proof systems.

Our Construction. The parameters par_{SN} describe an asymmetric pairing group (q, G_1, G_2, G_T, e) of prime order q and six random generators of G_1: $(g_1, g_2, h_1, h_2, \tilde{h}_1, \tilde{h}_2)$. We assume that secret keys and the info ID are elements of $\mathbb{Z}_q$. User $\mathcal{U}_{i+1}$ chooses the nonce n_{i+1} randomly from $\mathbb{Z}_q$ and computes SN_{i+1} as

$$f_{SN}(n_{i+1}, sk_{i+1}) = \{N_{i+1} = g_1^{n_{i+1}}, \ M_{i+1} = g_2^{sk_{i+1} \cdot n_{i+1}}\} .$$

When $\mathcal{U}_i$ receives $SN_{i+1} = (N_{i+1}, M_{i+1})$, she forms the double-spending tags as:

$$f_{DS}(ID_i, n_i, sk_i, (N_{i+1}, M_{i+1})) = \begin{cases} A_i = N_{i+1}^{ID_i} h_1^{n_i}, \ B_i = M_{i+1}^{ID_i} h_2^{n_i} \\ \tilde{A}_i = N_{i+1}^{sk_i} \tilde{h}_1^{n_i}, \ \tilde{B}_i = M_{i+1}^{sk_i} \tilde{h}_2^{n_i} \end{cases}$$

We show that this construction satisfies the properties defined in Section 3.1. First, the function f_{SN} function is *collision-resistant*: in order to have $N_{i+1} = N'_{i+1}$ the adversary must pick $n_{i+1} = n'_{i+1}$, but then $M_{i+1} = M'_{i+1}$ can only be achieved if $sk_{i+1} = sk'_{i+1}$.

Next we consider double-spending. The bank stores a database of pairs (pk, ID) for all registered users with pk and ID unique to each user. When a coin is deposited, the bank retrieves the serial number $\mathrm{SN} = \mathrm{SN}_1 \| \ldots \| \mathrm{SN}_k$. If a coin was deposited before with $\mathrm{SN} \neq \mathrm{SN}'$ but $\mathrm{SN}_1 = \mathrm{SN}'_1$, the bank looks for the first pair such that $\mathrm{SN}_{i+1} = (N_{i+1}, M_{i+1}) \neq \mathrm{SN}'_{i+1} = (N'_{i+1}, M'_{i+1})$ in order to detect where the double-spending happened. Depending on whether the N-values or the M-values are different, the bank checks for which $ID \in \mathcal{DB}_B$ the following holds:

$$(A_i(A'_i)^{-1}) \overset{?}{=} (N_{i+1}(N'_{i+1})^{-1})^{ID} \quad \text{or} \quad (B_i(B'_i)^{-1}) \overset{?}{=} (M_{i+1}(M'_{i+1})^{-1})^{ID}$$

This is a relatively cheap operation that can be implemented efficiently. (In our e-cash construction in Section 4, ID will be the user's position in the registered user list.) In our scheme KeyGen outputs $pk_i = \hat{g}^{sk_i}$ for a fixed generator $\hat{g}$ of G_2. When the bank finds an ID that satisfies the equation above, it looks up in its database the associated public key and checks whether the following pairing is satisfied:

$$e(\tilde{A}_i(\tilde{A}'_i)^{-1}, \hat{g}) = e(N_{i+1}(N'_{i+1})^{-1}, pk_i) \tag{1}$$

or similar for $\tilde{B}_i, \tilde{B}'_i, M_{i+1}, M'_{i+1}$ in case $N_{i+1} = N'_{i+1}$ (in which case we must have $M_{i+1} \neq M'_{i+1}$). If these checks fail for all pk, ID in the database, the bank outputs $(\bot, \bot)$, but this should never happen. The function f_{DetectDS} on input $\mathrm{DS}_i, \mathrm{DS}'_i, \mathcal{DB}_B$ outputs pk and $\Pi = (\mathrm{DS}_i, \mathrm{DS}'_i)$. The verification for this proof just checks equation (1). Thus, our f_{DS} function is 2-show extractable.

It remains to be shown that our system $(f_{\mathrm{SN}}, f_{\mathrm{DS}})$ is anonymous and exculpable. In the following lemma (whose proof is in the full version [BCFK15]) we show that both properties follow from SXDH:

Lemma 1. *The above constructions of a double-spending tag function f_{DS} and a serial number function f_{SN} are anonymous as defined in Definition 7 assuming that DDH holds in G_1. Moreover, the double-spending function is exculpable if DDH holds in G_2.*

Note that we could just use Equation (1) to detect double-spending (and discard the values A_i, B_i in f_{DS}). This would however be less efficient, since the bank would have to compute one pairing for every database entry. On the other hand, if exculpability is not required, we could discard the values $\tilde{A}_i, \tilde{B}_i$ from f_{DS}.

4   Transferable E-Cash Based on Malleable Signatures

We now describe a generic construction of a transferable e-cash scheme using malleable signatures. Assume the existence of a malleable signature scheme

(MSGen, MSKeyGen, MSign, MSVerify, MSigEval) with allowed transformation class $\mathcal{T}$ (as defined below), a signature scheme (SignGen, SKeyGen, Sign, Verify), a randomizable public-key encryption scheme (EKeyGen, Enc, REnc, Dec), a commitment scheme (ComSetup, Com), a zero knowledge proof system $\langle P, V \rangle$ and a hard[8] relation R_{pk}. We also assume the existence of the functions $f_{\mathsf{SN}}, f_{\mathsf{DS}}, f_{\mathsf{DetectDS}}$ for Gen_{SN} as defined in Section 3.1.

The bank's withdrawal key consists of $(vk_B^{(MS)}, sk_B^{(MS)}) \leftarrow \mathsf{MSKeyGen}(1^\lambda)$ and $(vk_B^{(S)}, sk_B^{(S)}) \leftarrow \mathsf{SKeyGen}(1^\lambda)$; the deposit key is $(pk_\mathcal{D}, sk_\mathcal{D}) \leftarrow \mathsf{EKeyGen}(1^\lambda)$. Users have key pairs $(pk_\mathcal{U}, sk_\mathcal{U}) \in R_{pk}$ and when registering they receive a certificate $cert_\mathcal{U} = \mathsf{Sign}_{sk_B^{(S)}}(pk_\mathcal{U}, I_\mathcal{U})$, where $I_\mathcal{U}$ is their joining order.

We recall the properties of malleable signatures, the central building block for our construction, and refer to the full version [BCFK15] for the definitions of commitment schemes and re-randomizable encryption.

4.1 Malleable Signatures

A malleable (or homomorphic) signature scheme [ABC+12, ALP12, CKLM14] allows anyone to compute a signature on a message m' from a signature on m as long as m and m' satisfy some predicate. Moreover, the resulting signature on m' reveals no extra information about the parent message m.

We adapt the definition by Chase et al. [CKLM14], who instead of a predicate consider a set of allowed *transformations*. A malleable signature scheme consists of the algorithms KeyGen, Sign, Verify and SigEval, of which the first three constitute a standard signature scheme. SigEval transforms multiple message/signature pairs into a new signed message: on input the verification key vk, messages $\vec{m} = (m_1, \ldots, m_n)$, signatures $\vec{\sigma} = (\sigma_1, \ldots, \sigma_n)$, and a transformation T on messages, it outputs a signature σ' on the message $T(\vec{m})$.

Definition 8 (Malleability). *A signature scheme* (KeyGen, Sign, Verify) *is malleable with respect to a set of transformations* $\mathcal{T}$ *if there exists an efficient algorithm* SigEval *that on input* $(vk, T, \vec{m}, \vec{\sigma})$, *where* $(vk, sk) \xleftarrow{\$} \mathsf{KeyGen}(1^\lambda)$, Verify$(vk, \sigma_i, m_i) = 1$ *for all* i, *and* $T \in \mathcal{T}$, *outputs a signature* σ' *for the message* $m := T(\vec{m})$ *such that* Verify$(vk, \sigma', m) = 1$.

In order to capture strong unforgeability and context-hiding notions, [CKLM14] provide simulation-based definitions for malleable signatures. *Simulatability* requires the existence of a simulator, which without knowing the secret key can simulate signatures that are indistinguishable from standard ones.[9] Moreover, a simulatable and malleable signature scheme is *context-hiding* if a transformed signature is indistinguishable from a simulated signature on the transformed message. A malleable signature scheme is *unforgeable* if an adversary can only derive signatures of messages that are allowed transformations of signed messages. In the full version [BCFK15] we present the corresponding formal definitions.

---

[8] Informally, a relation R is said to be hard if for $(x, w) \in R$, a PPT adversary $\mathcal{A}$ given x will output w_A s.t. $(x, w_A) \in R$ with only negligible probability.

[9] This requires a trusted setup; for details see the full version [BCFK15].

Chase et al. [CKLM14] describe a construction of malleable signatures based on controlled-malleable NIZKs [CKLM12] which they instantiate under the Decision Linear assumption [BBS04].

4.2 Allowed Transformations

In a malleable signature scheme we define a class of allowed transformations, and then unforgeability must guarantee that all valid signatures are generated either by the signer or by applying one of the allowed transformations to another valid signature. We will define two different types of transformations: T_{CWith} is used when a user withdraws a coin from the bank, and T_{CSpend} is used when a coin is transferred from one user to another.

Coin Spend Transformation. A coin that has been transferred i times (counting withdrawal as the first transfer) will have the following format:

$$c = (par, (C_{\overline{SN_i}}, C_{\overline{DS_{i-1}}}), (n_i, R_{SN_i}), \sigma) ,$$

where par denotes the parameters of the transferable e-cash scheme and $C_{\overline{SN_i}} = C_{SN_1} \parallel \cdots \parallel C_{SN_i}$, $C_{\overline{DS_{i-1}}} = C_{DS_1} \parallel \cdots \parallel C_{DS_{i-1}}$, for $C_{SN_j} = \mathsf{Enc}(SN_j)$ and $C_{DS_j} = \mathsf{Enc}(DS_j)$ respectively (all encryptions are w.r.t. $pk_{\mathcal{D}}$). By DS_{i-1} we denote the double-spending tag that was computed by user $\mathcal{U}_{i-1}$ when she transferred the coin to user $\mathcal{U}_i$; n_i is a nonce picked by $\mathcal{U}_i$ when he received the coin, and R_{SN_i} is the randomness used to compute the encryption of SN_i, i.e., $C_{SN_i} = \mathsf{Enc}(SN_i; R_{SN_i})$. Finally, σ is a malleable signature on $(C_{\overline{SN_i}}, C_{\overline{DS_{i-1}}})$.

Assume now that user $\mathcal{U}_i$ wants to transfer the coin c to $\mathcal{U}_{i+1}$. First, $\mathcal{U}_{i+1}$ picks a nonce n_{i+1} and sends $SN_{i+1} = f_{SN}(n_{i+1}, sk_{i+1})$ to $\mathcal{U}_i$. Then, $\mathcal{U}_i$ computes the new signature as (with T defined below):

$$\sigma' = \mathsf{MSigEval}(par, vk_B^{(MS)}, T, (C_{\overline{SN_i}}, C_{\overline{DS_{i-1}}}), \sigma) .$$

The transferred coin that $\mathcal{U}_{i+1}$ eventually obtains has the form:

$$c' = (par, (C_{\overline{SN_{i+1}}}, C_{\overline{DS_i}}), (n_{i+1}, R_{SN_{i+1}}), \sigma') .$$

Note that the value n_{i+1} is only known to $\mathcal{U}_{i+1}$ and he will have to use it when he wants to further transfer the coin, while the randomness $R_{SN_{i+1}}$, used to encrypt SN_{i+1}, was sent by $\mathcal{U}_i$. What is left is to define the transformation $T \in T_{CSpend}$, which takes as input $m = (C_{\overline{SN_i}}, C_{\overline{DS_{i-1}}})$ and outputs $T(m) = (C_{\overline{SN_{i+1}}}, C_{\overline{DS_i}})$.

A transformation of this type is described by the following values: (i.e. this is the information that one must "know" in order to apply the transformation)

$$\langle T \rangle = \big((sk_i, I_i, cert_i), (n_i, R_{SN_i}, R_{SN_{i+1}}, R_{DS_i}, R), SN_{i+1}\big) ,$$

where R is a random string that will be used to randomize $(C_{\overline{SN_i}}, C_{\overline{DS_{i-1}}})$ as part of the computation of the new signature. The output of T, as defined by these values, on input $m = (C_{\overline{SN_i}}, C_{\overline{DS_{i-1}}})$ is then computed as follows:

1. If $\text{SN}_i \neq f_{\text{SN}}(n_i, sk_i)$ or $\text{Enc}(\text{SN}_i; R_{\text{SN}_i}) \neq C_{\text{SN}_i}$ then output $\bot$.
2. The new part of the serial number is encoded using randomness $R_{\text{SN}_{i+1}}$:
   $C_{\text{SN}_{i+1}} = \text{Enc}(\text{SN}_{i+1}; R_{\text{SN}_{i+1}})$.
3. The new part of the double-spending tag is first computed using f_{DS} and then encrypted: $\text{DS}_i = f_{\text{DS}}(I_i, n_i, sk_i, \text{SN}_{i+1})$; $C_{\text{DS}_i} = \text{Enc}(\text{DS}_i; R_{\text{DS}_i})$.
4. These encryptions are appended to the re-randomizations of $C_{\overline{\text{SN}_i}}$ and $C_{\overline{\text{DS}_{i-1}}}$:

$$C_{\overline{\text{SN}_{i+1}}} = \text{REnc}(C_{\text{SN}_1}; R_1) \parallel \ldots \parallel \text{REnc}(C_{\text{SN}_i}; R_i) \parallel C_{\text{SN}_{i+1}}$$
$$C_{\overline{\text{DS}_i}} = \text{REnc}(D_{\text{DS}_1}; R_1') \parallel \ldots \parallel \text{REnc}(C_{\text{DS}_{i-1}}; R_{i-1}') \parallel C_{\text{DS}_i}$$

where $R_1, \ldots, R_i, R_1', \ldots, R_{i-1}'$ are all parts of the randomness R included in the description of the transformation.

We define $\mathcal{T}_{CSpend}$ as the set of all transformations of this form such that:

1. The certificate $cert_i$ is valid (verifiable under the bank's verification key) and corresponds to the secret key sk_i and some additional info I_i.
2. The random values $R_{\text{SN}_i}, R_{\text{SN}_{i+1}}, R_{\text{DS}_i}, R$ picked by $\mathcal{U}_i$ belong to the correct randomness space as defined by the encryption scheme.

Coin Withdrawal Transformation. A coin that was just withdrawn has a different format from a coin that has already been transferred, as there is no need to include double-spending tags for either the bank or the user (we ensure that each coin withdrawn is a different coin). While a transfer between users requires that the user spending the coin apply a transformation (as described above), in a withdrawal the user receiving the coin will be the one to transform the signature. When a user $\mathcal{U}_i$ withdraws a coin from the bank, she picks a nonce n_1, computes a commitment $com = \text{Com}(n_1, sk_i; open)$ on n_1 and her secret key and sends it to the bank. (For the user to remain anonymous it is important that the bank does not learn n_1.) The bank computes $\sigma = \text{MSign}(sk_B^{(MS)}, com)$ and sends it to the user. The latter computes $\text{SN}_1 = f_{\text{SN}}(n_1, sk_i)$, chooses randomness R_{SN_1}, sets $C_{\text{SN}_1} = \text{Enc}(\text{SN}_1; R_{\text{SN}_1})$ and computes a new signature $\sigma' = \text{MSigEval}(par, vk_B^{(MS)}, T, com, \sigma)$, which yields the coin defined as $c = (par, C_{\text{SN}_1}, (n_1, R_{\text{SN}_1}), \sigma')$. A transformation $T \in \mathcal{T}_{CWith}$, which takes as input $m = com$ and outputs $T(m) = C_{\text{SN}_1}$ is described by $\langle T \rangle = ((sk_i, I_i, cert_i), (n_1, open), R_{\text{SN}_1}, \text{SN}_1)$. We define

$$T(com) = \begin{cases} C_{\text{SN}_1} = \text{Enc}(\text{SN}_1; R_{\text{SN}_1}) & \text{if } \text{Com}(n_1, sk_i; open) = com \\ & \text{and } \text{SN}_1 = f_{\text{SN}}(sk_i, n_1) \\ \bot & \text{otherwise.} \end{cases}$$

We define $\mathcal{T}_{CWith}$ to be the set of all transformations of this form such that:

1. The certificate $cert_i$ is valid (i.e. it verifies under the bank's verification key) and correspond to the secret key sk_i and I_i.
2. Randomness R_{SN_1} belongs to the appropriate randomness space.

The class of allowed transformations $\mathcal{T}_{tec}$: We allow users to apply a transformation in $\mathcal{T}_{CWith}$ followed by any number of transformations in $\mathcal{T}_{CSpend}$. Thus, we define the allowed class of transformations for the malleable signature scheme used in our transferable e-cash to be the closure of $\mathcal{T}_{tec} = \mathcal{T}_{CWith} \cup \mathcal{T}_{CSpend}$.

4.3 A Transferable E-Cash Construction

Below we describe a transferable e-cash scheme based on malleable signatures. For our construction we assume *secure channels* for all the communications, thus an adversary cannot overhear or tamper with the transferred messages.

ParamGen(1^λ): Compute $par_{MS} \leftarrow$ MSGen(1^λ), $par_{SN} \leftarrow$ Gen$_{SN}$(1^λ), $par_{com} \leftarrow$ ComSetup(1^λ). Output $par := (1^\lambda, par_{MS}, par_{com}, par_{SN})$.

UKeyGen(par): Output a random pair ($pk_{\mathcal{U}}, sk_{\mathcal{U}}$) sampled from R_{pk}.

BKeyGen(par): Run ($vk_B^{(MS)}, sk_B^{(MS)}$) $\leftarrow$ MSKeyGen(1^λ) and ($vk_B^{(S)}, sk_B^{(S)}$) $\leftarrow$ SKeyGen(1^λ) and define the bank's withdrawal keys as $pk_{\mathcal{W}} = (vk_B^{(MS)}, vk_B^{(S)})$ and $sk_{\mathcal{W}} = (sk_B^{(MS)}, sk_B^{(S)})$. Sample a deposit key ($pk_{\mathcal{D}}, sk_{\mathcal{D}}$) $\leftarrow$ EKeyGen(1^λ) and output (($pk_{\mathcal{W}}, sk_{\mathcal{W}}$), ($pk_{\mathcal{D}}, sk_D$)). The bank maintains a list $\mathcal{UL}$ of all registered users and a list $\mathcal{DCL}$ of deposited coins.

Registration($\mathcal{B}[sk_{\mathcal{W}}, pk_{\mathcal{U}}], \mathcal{U}[sk_{\mathcal{U}}, pk_{\mathcal{W}}]$): If $pk_{\mathcal{U}} \in \mathcal{UL}$, the bank outputs $\perp$. Otherwise, it computes $cert_{\mathcal{U}} = \text{Sign}_{sk_B^{(S)}}(pk_{\mathcal{U}}, ID_{\mathcal{U}})$, where $ID_{\mathcal{U}} = |\mathcal{UL}| + 1$, adds ($pk_{\mathcal{U}}, cert, ID_{\mathcal{U}}$) to the user list $\mathcal{UL}$ and returns ($cert_{\mathcal{U}}, ID_{\mathcal{U}}$).

Withdraw($\mathcal{B}[sk_{\mathcal{W}}, pk_{\mathcal{U}}], \mathcal{U}[sk_{\mathcal{U}}, pk_{\mathcal{W}}]$): The user picks a nonce n_1 and sends $com = \text{Com}(n_1, sk_{\mathcal{U}}; open)$. $\mathcal{B}$ computes $\sigma \leftarrow \text{MSign}(par_{MS}, sk_B^{(MS)}, com)$, sends it to the user and outputs ok. If MSVerify($par_{MS}, pk_B^{(MS)}, \sigma, com$) = 0, the user outputs $\perp$; otherwise she sets $\text{SN}_1 = f_{\text{SN}}(n_1, sk_{\mathcal{U}})$, chooses randomness R_{SN_1} and computes $C_{\text{SN}_1} = \text{Enc}(\text{SN}_1; R_{\text{SN}_1})$. Then she sets $\langle T \rangle = ((sk_i, cert_i), (n_1, open), R_{\text{SN}_1}, \text{SN}_1)$ and computes the new signature $\sigma' = \text{MSigEval}(par_{MS}, vk_B^{(MS)}, T, com, \sigma)$. The output is the coin $c = (par, C_{\text{SN}_1}, (n_1, R_{\text{SN}_1}), \sigma')$.

Spend($\mathcal{U}_1[c, sk_{\mathcal{U}_1}, cert_{\mathcal{U}_1}, pk_{\mathcal{W}}], \mathcal{U}_2[sk_{\mathcal{U}_2}, pk_{\mathcal{W}}]$): Parse the coin as

$$c = \left(par, (C_{\overline{\text{SN}_i}}, C_{\overline{\text{DS}_{i-1}}}), (n_i, R_{\text{SN}_i}), \sigma\right) .$$

$\mathcal{U}_2$ picks a nonce n_{i+1}, computes $\text{SN}_{i+1} = f_{\text{SN}}(n_{i+1}, sk_{\mathcal{U}_2})$ and sends it to $\mathcal{U}_1$. $\mathcal{U}_1$ computes the double-spending tag $\text{DS}_i = f_{\text{DS}}(ID_{\mathcal{U}}, n_i, sk_{\mathcal{U}_i}, \text{SN}_{i+1})$ and defines the transformation

$$\langle T \rangle = \left((sk_{\mathcal{U}_1}, cert_{\mathcal{U}_1}), (n_i, R_{\text{SN}_i}, R_{\text{SN}_{i+1}}, R_{\text{DS}_i}, R), \text{SN}_{i+1}\right) .$$

Next, he computes $C_{\text{SN}_{i+1}} = \text{Enc}(\text{SN}_{i+1}; R_{\text{SN}_{i+1}})$ and $C_{\text{DS}_i} = \text{Enc}(\text{DS}_i; R_{\text{DS}_i})$, which he appends to the randomized ciphertext contained in c:

$$C_{\overline{\text{SN}_{i+1}}} = \text{REnc}(C_{\text{SN}_1}; R_1) \| \ldots \| \text{REnc}(C_{\text{SN}_i}; R_i) \| C_{\text{SN}_{i+1}}$$

$$C_{\overline{\text{DS}_i}} = \text{REnc}(D_{\text{DS}_1}; R_1') \| \ldots \| \text{REnc}(C_{\text{DS}_{i-1}}; R_{i-1}') \| C_{\text{DS}_i}$$

$\mathcal{U}_1$ computes $\sigma' = \mathsf{MSigEval}\big(par, vk_B^{(MS)}, T, (C_{\overline{\mathrm{SN}_{i+1}}}, C_{\overline{\mathrm{DS}_i}}), \sigma\big)$ and then sends $(\sigma', R_{i+1}, (C_{\overline{\mathrm{SN}_{i+1}}}, C_{\overline{\mathrm{DS}_i}}))$ to $\mathcal{U}_2$.

If $\mathsf{MSVerify}\big(par_{MS}, pk_B^{(MS)}, \sigma', (C_{\overline{\mathrm{SN}_{i+1}}}, C_{\overline{\mathrm{DS}_i}})\big) = 0$ then $\mathcal{U}_2$ aborts. Otherwise, $\mathcal{U}_2$ outputs $c' = \big(par, (C_{\overline{\mathrm{SN}_{i+1}}}, C_{\overline{\mathrm{DS}_i}}), (n_{i+1}, R_{\mathrm{SN}_{i+1}}), \sigma'\big)$.

$\mathsf{Deposit}(\mathcal{U}[c, sk_{\mathcal{U}}, cert_{\mathcal{U}}, pk_B], \mathcal{B}[sk_{\mathcal{D}}, pk_{\mathcal{U}}, \mathcal{DCL}])$:   First, $\mathcal{U}$ runs a   Spend   protocol   with   the   bank   being   the   receiver: $\mathsf{Spend}(\mathcal{U}[c, sk_{\mathcal{U}}, cert_{\mathcal{U}_1}, pk_{\mathcal{W}}], \mathcal{B}[\bot, pk_{\mathcal{W}}])$ (the bank can set the secret key to $\bot$, as it will not transfer this coin). If the protocol did not abort, $\mathcal{B}$ holds a valid coin $c = \big(par, (C_{\overline{\mathrm{SN}_i}}, C_{\overline{\mathrm{DS}_{i-1}}}), (n_i, R_{\mathrm{SN}_i}), \sigma\big)$. Next, using $sk_{\mathcal{D}}$, $\mathcal{B}$ decrypts the serial number $\overline{\mathrm{SN}_i} = \mathrm{SN}_1 \parallel \cdots \parallel \mathrm{SN}_i$ and the double-spending tags $\overline{\mathrm{DS}_{i-1}} = \mathrm{DS}_1 \parallel \cdots \parallel \mathrm{DS}_{i-1}$. It checks if in $\mathcal{DCL}$ there exists another coin c' with $\mathrm{SN}_1' = \mathrm{SN}_1$; if not, it adds the coin to $\mathcal{DCL}$.

Otherwise, a double-spending must have happened and the bank looks for the first position d, where $\mathrm{SN}_d' \neq \mathrm{SN}_d$. (Except with negligible probability such a position exists, since SN_i was chosen by the bank.) It applies the double-spending detection function f_{DetectDS} on the corresponding double-spending tags DS_{d-1} and DS_{d-1}'. If f_{DetectDS} outputs $\bot$ then $\mathcal{B}$ aborts. Otherwise, it outputs $(pk_{\mathcal{U}}, \Pi) = f_{\mathsf{DetectDS}}(\mathrm{DS}_{d-1}, \mathrm{DS}_{d-1}', \mathcal{UL})$.

$\mathsf{VerifyGuilt}(pk_{\mathcal{U}}, \Pi)$: it outputs 1 if the proof Π verifies and 0 otherwise.

The proof of the following can be found in the full version [BCFK15].

Theorem 1. *If the malleable signature scheme* (MSGen, MSKeyGen, MSign, MSVerify, MSigEval) *is simulatable, simulation-unforgeable and simulation-hiding w.r.t.* $\mathcal{T}$, *the signature scheme* (SKeyGen, Sign, Verify) *is existentially unforgeable, the randomizable public-key encryption scheme* (EKeyGen, Enc, REnc, Dec) *is semantically secure and statistically re-randomizable, and the commitment scheme* (ComSetup, Com) *is computationally hiding and perfectly binding, then the construction in Section 4.3 describes a secure and anonymous transferable e-cash scheme as defined in Section 2.*

4.4 Why Malleable Signatures

Let us discuss why our construction requires the use of this powerful primitive. Malleable signatures satisfy a strong notion of unforgeability, called *simulation unforgeability* (See the full version [BCFK15]). In brief, it requires that an adversary who can ask for simulated signatures and then outputs a valid message/signature pair (m^*, σ^*) must have derived the pair from received signatures. This is formalized by requiring that there exists an extractor that from (m^*, σ^*) extracts messages $\vec{m}$ that were all queried to the signing oracle and a transformation T such that $m^* = T(\vec{m})$.

Among the anonymity notions considered in the literature, Spend-then-Receive (StR) anonymity (defined on page 111) is the hardest to achieve. Recall that it formalizes that an adversary should not be able to recognize a coin he had already owned before. Intuitively, our scheme satisfies it, since a coin only consists of ciphertexts, which are re-randomized, and a malleable signature, which can be simulated. However, when formally proving the notion we have to provide a Deposit oracle, which we have to simulate when reducing to the security of the encryptions. Here we make use of the properties of malleable signatures, which allow us to extract enough information to check for double-spendings—even after issuing simulated signatures (see the proof of Theorem 1 in the full version [BCFK15]).

The scheme by Blazy et al. [BCF+11] also claims to achieve StR anonymity. In their scheme a coin contains Groth-Sahai (GS) commitments $\vec{c}$ to the serial number, additional (ElGamal) encryptions $\vec{d}$ of it and a GS proof that the values in $\vec{c}$ and $\vec{d}$ are equal. The bank detects double-spending by decrypting $\vec{d}$. In their proof of StR anonymity by game hopping, they first replace the GS commitments and proofs by perfectly hiding ones and then simulate the proofs. (Double-spending can still be checked via the values $\vec{d}$.) Finally they argue that in the "challenge spending via Spd in the experiment, we replace the commitments/encryptions d_{n_i} [...] by random values."

It is not clear how this can be done while still simulating the Deposit oracle, which must check for double-spendings: a simulator breaking security of the encryptions would not know the decryption key required to extract the serial number from $\vec{d}$. (One would have to include additional encryptions of the serial number and use them for extraction—however, for this approach to work, the proof guaranteeing that the encryptions contain the same values would have to be simulation-sound (cf. [Sah99]), which contradicts the fact that they must be randomizable.)

5   Instantiation

In order to instantiate our scheme we need to make concrete choices for a malleable signature scheme which supports the allowable transformations $\mathcal{T}_{CSpend}$ and $\mathcal{T}_{CWith}$, a signature scheme for the signing of certificates, a randomizable public-key encryption scheme, a commitment scheme (ComSetup, Com) and a zero-knowledge proof system $\langle P, V \rangle$.

Chase et al. [CKLM14] provide a generic construction of malleable signatures based on cm-NIZKs [CKLM12], which suits our requirements. There exist two constructions of cm-NIZKs, both due to Chase et al.: the first [CKLM12] is based in Groth-Sahai proofs [GS08], the second [CKLM13] is less efficient but simpler and is based on succinct non-interactive arguments of knowledge (SNARKs) and fully homomorphic encryption. The SNARK-based construction directly gives a feasibility result, as long as there is some constant maximum on the number of times a given coin can be transferred. To achieve an efficient instantiation, one could instead use the Groth-Sahai instantiation.

In the full version [BCFK15] we present an instantiation of our construction based on Groth-Sahai. We show that our relation and transformations are *CM-friendly*, which means that all of the objects (instances, witnesses and transformations) can be represented as elements of a bilinear group so that the system is compatible with Groth-Sahai proofs. To achieve that we need to slightly modify our construction, in order to map elements of $\mathbb{Z}_p$ (like n_i, sk_i, I_i) into the pairing group for the transformation. (This can be done fairly simply, without affecting security.) Finally, for the remaining building blocks, we use the structure-preserving signature [AFG+10] due to Abe et al. [ACD+12] and El Gamal encryption scheme [ElG85] for both encryption and commitments.

References

[ABC+12]   Ahn, J.H., Boneh, D., Camenisch, J., Hohenberger, S., Shelat, A., Waters, B.: Computing on authenticated data. In: Cramer, R. (ed.) TCC 2012. LNCS, vol. 7194, pp. 1–20. Springer, Heidelberg (2012)

[ACD+12]   Abe, M., Chase, M., David, B., Kohlweiss, M., Nishimaki, R., Ohkubo, M.: Constant-Size structure-preserving signatures: generic constructions and simple assumptions. In: Wang, X., Sako, K. (eds.) ASIACRYPT 2012. LNCS, vol. 7658, pp. 4–24. Springer, Heidelberg (2012)

[AFG+10]   Abe, M., Fuchsbauer, G., Groth, J., Haralambiev, K., Ohkubo, M.: Structure-Preserving signatures and commitments to group elements. In: Rabin, T. (ed.) CRYPTO 2010. LNCS, vol. 6223, pp. 209–236. Springer, Heidelberg (2010)

[ALP12]   Attrapadung, N., Libert, B., Peters, T.: Computing on authenticated data: new privacy definitions and constructions. In: Wang, X., Sako, K. (eds.) ASIACRYPT 2012. LNCS, vol. 7658, pp. 367–385. Springer, Heidelberg (2012)

[BBS04]   Boneh, D., Boyen, X., Shacham, H.: Short group signatures. In: Franklin, M. (ed.) CRYPTO 2004. LNCS, vol. 3152, pp. 41–55. Springer, Heidelberg (2004)

[BCF+11]   Blazy, O., Canard, S., Fuchsbauer, G., Gouget, A., Sibert, H., Traoré, J.: Achieving optimal anonymity in transferable E-Cash with a judge. In: Nitaj, A., Pointcheval, D. (eds.) AFRICACRYPT 2011. LNCS, vol. 6737, pp. 206–223. Springer, Heidelberg (2011). http://crypto.rd.francetelecom.com/publications/p121

[BCFK15]   Baldimtsi, F., Chase, M., Fuchsbauer, G., Kohlweiss, M.: Anonymous transferable e-cash. Cryptology ePrint Archive (2015). http://eprint.iacr.org/

[BCG+14]   Ben-Sasson, E., Chiesa, A., Garman, C., Green, M., Miers, I., Tromer, E., Virza, M.: Zerocash: Decentralized anonymous payments from bitcoin. In: IEEE S&P (2014)

[BCKL09]   Belenkiy, M., Chase, M., Kohlweiss, M., Lysyanskaya, A.: Compact E-Cash and simulatable VRFs revisited. In: Shacham, H., Waters, B. (eds.) Pairing 2009. LNCS, vol. 5671, pp. 114–131. Springer, Heidelberg (2009)

[Bla08]   Blanton, M.: Improved conditional E-Payments. In: Bellovin, S.M., Gennaro, R., Keromytis, A.D., Yung, M. (eds.) ACNS 2008. LNCS, vol. 5037, pp. 188–206. Springer, Heidelberg (2008)

[Bra93]   Brands, S.: Untraceable off-line cash in wallets with observers (extended abstract). In: Stinson, D.R. (ed.) CRYPTO 1993. LNCS, vol. 773, pp. 302–318. Springer, Heidelberg (1994)

[CFN88]   Chaum, D., Fiat, A., Naor, M.: Untraceable electronic cash. In: Goldwasser, S. (ed.) CRYPTO 1988. LNCS, vol. 403, pp. 319–327. Springer, Heidelberg (1990)

[CG08]   Canard, S., Gouget, A.: Anonymity in transferable E-cash. In: Bellovin, S.M., Gennaro, R., Keromytis, A.D., Yung, M. (eds.) ACNS 2008. LNCS, vol. 5037, pp. 207–223. Springer, Heidelberg (2008)

[CGT08] Canard, S., Gouget, A., Traoré, J.: Improvement of efficiency in (unconditional) anonymous transferable E-Cash. In: Tsudik, G. (ed.) FC 2008. LNCS, vol. 5143, pp. 202–214. Springer, Heidelberg (2008)

[Cha83] Chaum, D.: Blind signature system. In: CRYPTO (1983)

[CHL05] Camenisch, J.L., Hohenberger, S., Lysyanskaya, A.: Compact E-Cash. In: Cramer, R. (ed.) EUROCRYPT 2005. LNCS, vol. 3494, pp. 302–321. Springer, Heidelberg (2005)

[CKLM12] Chase, M., Kohlweiss, M., Lysyanskaya, A., Meiklejohn, S.: Malleable proof systems and applications. In: Pointcheval, D., Johansson, T. (eds.) EUROCRYPT 2012. LNCS, vol. 7237, pp. 281–300. Springer, Heidelberg (2012)

[CKLM13] Chase, M., Kohlweiss, M., Lysyanskaya, A., Meiklejohn, S.: Succinct malleable NIZKs and an application to compact shuffles. In: Sahai, A. (ed.) TCC 2013. LNCS, vol. 7785, pp. 100–119. Springer, Heidelberg (2013)

[CKLM14] Chase, M., Kohlweiss, M., Lysyanskaya, A., Meiklejohn, S.: Malleable signatures: New definitions and delegatable anonymous credentials. In: IEEE CSF (2014)

[CP92]   Chaum, D., Pedersen, T.P.: Transferred cash grows in size. In: Rueppel, R.A. (ed.) EUROCRYPT 1992. LNCS, vol. 658, pp. 390–407. Springer, Heidelberg (1993)

[ElG85] El Gamal, T.: A public key cryptosystem and a signature scheme based on discrete logarithms. In: Blakely, G.R., Chaum, D. (eds.) CRYPTO 1984. LNCS, vol. 196, pp. 10–18. Springer, Heidelberg (1985)

[FPV09] Fuchsbauer, G., Pointcheval, D., Vergnaud, D.: Transferable constant-size fair E-Cash. In: Garay, J.A., Miyaji, A., Otsuka, A. (eds.) CANS 2009. LNCS, vol. 5888, pp. 226–247. Springer, Heidelberg (2009)

[Fuc11] Fuchsbauer, G.: Commuting signatures and verifiable encryption. In: Paterson, K.G. (ed.) EUROCRYPT 2011. LNCS, vol. 6632, pp. 224–245. Springer, Heidelberg (2011)

[GS08]   Groth, J., Sahai, A.: Efficient non-interactive proof systems for bilinear groups. In: Smart, N.P. (ed.) EUROCRYPT 2008. LNCS, vol. 4965, pp. 415–432. Springer, Heidelberg (2008)

[MGGR13] Miers, I., Garman, C., Green, M., Rubin, A.D.: Zerocoin: Anonymous distributed e-cash from bitcoin. In: IEEE S&P (2013)

[Nak08] Nakamoto, S.: Bitcoin: A peer-to-peer electronic cash (2008). http://bitcoin.org/bitcoin.pdf

[OO89]   Okamoto, T., Ohta, K.: Disposable zero-knowledge authentications and their applications to untraceable electronic cash. In: Brassard, G. (ed.) CRYPTO 1989. LNCS, vol. 435, pp. 481–496. Springer, Heidelberg (1990)

[OO91]   Okamoto, T., Ohta, K.: Universal electronic cash. In: Feigenbaum, J. (ed.) CRYPTO 1991. LNCS, vol. 576, pp. 324–337. Springer, Heidelberg (1992)

[Sah99] Sahai, A.: Non-malleable non-interactive zero knowledge and adaptive chosen-ciphertext security. In: FOCS (1999)

[vAE90] van Antwerpen, H.: Off-line Electronic Cash. Eindhoven University of Technology (1990)

Cryptanalysis

Collision of Random Walks and a Refined Analysis of Attacks on the Discrete Logarithm Problem

Shuji Kijima[1] and Ravi Montenegro[2(✉)]

[1] Graduate School of Information Science and Electrical Engineering,
Kyushu University, Fukuoka 819-0395, Japan
kijima@inf.kyushu-u.ac.jp
[2] Department of Mathematical Sciences, University of Massachusetts Lowell,
Lowell, MA 01854, USA
ravi_montenegro@uml.edu

Abstract. Some of the most efficient algorithms for finding the discrete logarithm involve pseudo-random implementations of Markov chains, with one or more "walks" proceeding until a collision occurs, i.e. some state is visited a second time. In this paper we develop a method for determining the expected time until the first collision. We use our technique to examine three methods for solving discrete-logarithm problems: Pollard's Kangaroo, Pollard's Rho, and a few versions of Gaudry-Schost. For the Kangaroo method we prove new and fairly precise matching upper and lower bounds. For the Rho method we prove the first rigorous non-trivial lower bound, and under a mild assumption show matching upper and lower bounds. Our Gaudry-Schost results are heuristic, but improve on the prior limited understanding of this method. We also give results for parallel versions of these algorithms.

1 Introduction

Given a cyclic group $G = \langle g \rangle$ and an element $h \in G$, the discrete-logarithm problem asks to find a solution x to $h = g^x$. Shoup showed that for a generic cyclic group this requires $\Omega(\sqrt{|G|})$ group operations [17], although this bound can be beaten for many representations of such groups. The discrete-logarithm problem over a random group of elliptic curves seems to be as hard as this lower bound, which has led to its use in cryptosystems.

Several methods have been proposed which use a pseudo-random "walk" to achieve heuristic run time equal to Shoup's lower bound. Each step of these walks will involve a single group operation and so the number of steps (run time) will equal the number of group operations until discrete logarithm is found, aside from a small amount of pre-computation. In this paper we give a fairly general method for understanding the performance of such methods, and in particular

R. Montenegro—Supported by a Japan Society for Promotion of Science (JSPS) Fellowship while a guest at Kyushu University.

© International Association for Cryptologic Research 2015
J. Katz (Ed.): PKC 2015, LNCS 9020, pp. 127–149, 2015.
DOI: 10.1007/978-3-662-46447-2_6

for understanding the extent to which they will be slower than predicted by simple heuristics. We use our method to show very precise estimates on run time of three such methods: Pollard's Rho, Pollard's Kangaroo, and Gaudry-Schost. These methods have been used for attacks on problems of cryptographic significance. For instance, a parallelized Pollard's Rho method was used in an attack on Certicom's challenge problem ECC2K-130 [2], while an attack based on Gaudry-Schost was used to break a proposed EMVco protocol to replace the chip-and-pin system used in over 1.6 billion payments cards [3].

1.1 Description of Algorithms

Before describing our results we review the algorithms being considered. Methods of detecting collisions, such as via distinguished points or Floyd's cycle finding method, will not be discussed.

For Pollard's Rho, partition G into 3 roughly equal sized pieces S_1, S_2, S_3, and define an iterating function

$$F(X) = \begin{cases} Xg & \text{if } X \in S_1, \\ Xh & \text{if } X \in S_2, \\ X^2 & \text{if } X \in S_3. \end{cases}$$

Let $X_0 = h = g^x$ and repeatedly iterate with $X_{i+1} = F(X_i)$. Continue until the first time that some $X_i = X_j$, known as a "collision." If we keep track of the exponent $X_i = g^{a_i + b_i x}$ then $g^{a_i + b_i x} = g^{a_j + b_j x}$. The discrete logarithm is then $x \equiv (a_i - a_j)(b_j - b_i)^{-1} \mod |G|$, except in the rare degenerate case when $b_i \equiv b_j \mod |G|$. Teske suggests an "additive" version that is faster in practice. For a fixed integer r define r step types s_1, s_2, ..., s_r by choosing α_k, β_k uniformly at random from $\{0, 1, \ldots, |G| - 1\}$ and setting $s_k = g^{\alpha_k} h^{\beta_k} = g^{\alpha_k + \beta_k x}$. Then take r partitions S_1, S_2, ..., S_r, set $F(X) = X s_k$ on S_k, and proceed as before. One way to parallelize is to start M processors at different randomly chosen states: $g^\alpha h^\beta = g^{\alpha + \beta x}$ with $\alpha, \beta \in [0, |G| - 1]$. These may be re-randomized every time a distinguished point is encountered (see Gaudry-Schost below and [19]).

Pollard's Kangaroo method applies when it is known that $x \in [a, a + N)$ for some $a, N \leq |G|$. Set $X_0 = h = g^x$ and $Y_0 = g^{a + \lfloor N/2 \rfloor}$. Take $d + 1$ partitions S_0, S_1, ..., S_d, set $F(X) = X g^{2^k}$ on S_k, and repeatedly iterate both processes with $X_{i+1} = X_i F(X_i)$ and $Y_{i+1} = Y_i F(Y_i)$. Once some $X_i = Y_j$, say at $X_i = g^{x+\alpha}$ and $Y_j = g^{a + \lfloor N/2 \rfloor + \beta}$, then $x \equiv a + \lfloor N/2 \rfloor + \beta - \alpha \mod |G|$, and the discrete logarithm is found. The processes X_i and Y_j are known as the wild and tame kangaroos respectively.

In the Gaudry-Schost method the discrete logarithm x is known to lie in a hypercube $[a, b]^n$ with volume $N = (b - a + 1)^n$. We discuss only the $n = 1$ version here, although our technique applies in higher dimensions as well. Let A be a region centered at the unknown discrete logarithm x, let B be a duplicate of this region but centered at a predetermined value within the hypercube such as the centerpoint, and let D be a set of *distinguished points* covering roughly a θ

fraction of group elements. For a pre-specified integer r and average step size m choose r step types $s_1, s_2, \ldots, s_r$ uniformly at random from $[1, 2m)$, and partition the space into r pieces $S_1, S_2, \ldots, S_r$. Use iterating function $F(X) = X g^{s_i}$ if $X \in S_i$, except for the θ fraction of the time that X is a distinguished point and F transitions to a point chosen uniformly at random in A or B. Proceed until some $X_i = Y_j$, say with $X_i = g^{x+\alpha}$ and $Y_j = g^{\beta}$, at which point the discrete logarithm is $x \equiv \beta - \alpha \mod |G|$. This will usually be in $A \cap B$, but could be slightly outside this region. One way to parallelize is to start $M/2$ processors at different randomly chosen states in A, and $M/2$ in B.

1.2 Heuristic Run Time

The attacks just described involve pseudo-random processes on G which proceed until a *collision*: either a single walk proceeds until it visits a state (group element) it has previously been to, or two walks proceed until each has visited a common state (group element). If we treat these as truly random processes then there are natural heuristic arguments for their run time.

Pollard's Rho resembles a random walk which proceeds until some state is visited twice. If each transition were a uniform random sample from G then the birthday paradox would suggest run time of $\sqrt{\frac{\pi}{2}|G|} \approx 1.25\sqrt{|G|}$. However, because the process only has 3 transition types, consecutive states are highly dependent and the true run time is about 30% slower. Teske's additive version is significantly slower when there are $r = 3$ transition types, but is nearly as good as the birthday heuristic when r is large, e.g. $r = 16$. Several improvements have been made on this basic heuristic, see Section 2.1. The parallel version with M processors generates samples M times faster, and so is M times faster.

Pollard's Kangaroo resembles two random walks which proceed until they visit some common state. Let $d \sim \log_2 \sqrt{N} + \log_2(\log_2 \sqrt{N}) - 2$ be such that the average transition size is $m = \frac{1}{d+1} \sum_{k=0}^{d} 2^k \approx \frac{1}{2}\sqrt{N}$. After a warmup of around $\mathbb{E}T = \mathbb{E}\frac{|X_0 - Y_0|}{m} = \frac{N}{4m} = \frac{1}{2}\sqrt{N}$ steps, the walk starting with smaller exponent of $X_0 = g^x$ and $Y_0 = g^{a+N/2}$ will have caught up to the initial location of the other walk. Each walk visits a $1/m$ fraction of states, so at each subsequent step there is probability $p \approx 1/m$ of a "collision," for expected runtime of about $2(\mathbb{E}T + m) \approx 2\sqrt{N}$. However, because the process only has $(d+1)$ transition types there are dependencies and the probability of a collision varies significantly from step to step, with probability often 0.

The Gaudry-Schost method resembles two random walks, one in A and one in B, where each step produces a sample from $A \cap B$ with probability roughly $\frac{|A \cap B|}{|A|}$. A generalized birthday problem [14] suggests that each walk should take $\frac{1}{2}\sqrt{\pi |A \cap B|}$ samples from $A \cap B$ until collision, for an expected run time of $2 \frac{|A|}{|A \cap B|} \frac{1}{2}\sqrt{\pi |A \cap B|}$ transitions. But again, consecutive states are highly dependent unless a distinguished point was just visited. Once again, the parallel version generates samples M times faster.

The largest flaw in each heuristic is that consecutive states are highly dependent. One solution might be if Rho, for instance, used an iterating function

$F : G \rightarrow G$ that outputs a pseudo-random uniform sample from the entirety of G. However, computing random values of $g^\alpha h^\beta$ is slow. Even if in an average of only two group operations sufficed, finding the discrete logarithm would take $2 \times 1.25\sqrt{|G|}$ group operations, versus $1.6\sqrt{|G|}$ for Pollard's Rho and under $1.3\sqrt{|G|}$ for Teske's additive version. So the dependencies in these algorithms are an important component of their fast run time. An improved method for understanding the effects of dependencies could thus help to minimize their negative effects.

1.3   New Results

Each algorithm considered here is entirely deterministic once the partition function (hash) has been chosen. Indeed, the deterministic nature is necessary for efficient detection of collisions. However, the hash is usually chosen to "look" random, and so all attempts to explain these algorithms have treated the iterative process as if it were entirely random until the first collision. Our results will make this assumption as well, even those we describe as "rigorous." Since our concern is with when that collision occurs, not what happens after it, we also treat these as fully random walks, even after collision. As such we will use the language of random walks, so that "state" refers to a group element and "run time" refers to the number of iterations taken. After some precomputation each iteration requires exactly one group operation, and so run time will be equivalent to counting group operations, except when a distinguished point is hit in Gaudry-Schost.

The heuristic arguments just described neglect dependencies between consecutive states. One way of avoiding this problem is to only consider a subset of states all of which are τ steps apart, where τ denotes the number of steps required to lose this dependency, so that X_j is nearly independent of X_i when $|j - i| \geq \tau$. However, this would give results which are very weak since a large fraction of possible collisions are being ignored.

A different approach is to try to measure the extent of the dependency. Consider how many times two independent random walks can be expected to collide (visit common states) if they start at the same state and proceed τ steps until they have lost their initial dependency. We find that this quantity alone is sufficient to explain the extent to which Pollard's Kangaroo and Pollard's Rho fail to match heuristic bounds. It also explains the vast majority of the slow down for Gaudry-Schost, although boundary effects along $\partial(A \cap B)$ also come into play. The precise quantity we consider is the following:

Definition 1. *The* collision number C_τ *is the expected number of collisions when two independent copies of a random walk start at the same state, chosen uniformly at random, and proceed for τ steps.*

Consider the Kangaroo method. This is generally thought to be well understood, in the sense that the heuristic of $2\sqrt{N}$ matches asymptotic behavior. However, even on groups as large as $|G| = 10^{12}$ the Kangaroo method runs about 3% slower than predicted by heuristic. We use the collision number to prove a bound which more-or-less eliminates this error (see Figure 1).

Theorem 2 (Pollard's Kangaroo). *Given a cyclic group G, the Kangaroo method with power-of-two jumps for computing the discrete logarithm in an interval of size $N = o(|G|)$ has expected run time*

$$2\,\mathbb{E}\min\{k : \exists i, j \leq k,\, X_i = Y_j\} = \left(2 + \frac{2}{\log_2 N} + \frac{14}{(\log_2 N)^2} + O((\log N)^{-3})\right)\sqrt{N}.$$

This extends to transitions other than powers of two if $2 + \frac{2}{\log_2 N} + \cdots$ is replaced by $1 + C_\tau$.

For Pollard's Rho method we show the first rigorous non-trivial lower bound on runtime.

Theorem 3 (Pollard's Rho). *Given a cyclic group G of prime order N, the Rho method with r step types has expected run time of*

$$\mathbb{E}\min\{i : \exists j \leq i - \tau),\, X_i = X_j\} \geq (1 + O(1/N))\sqrt{\frac{\pi}{2}\frac{N}{1 - 1/r}}$$

where $\tau = O(\log^2 N)$ for Pollard's process and $\tau = O(N^{2/(r-1)})$ for Teske's.

This neglects the $o(1)$ fraction of potential collisions $X_i = X_j$ with $i - j < \tau$, except for Teske's process with $r \leq 5$.

Under a fairly mild assumption we can determine the precise run time.

Heuristic 4 (Pollard's Rho) *Given a cyclic group G of prime order N, Pollard's Rho method has expected run time of*

$$\mathbb{E}\min\{i : \exists j < i,\, X_i = X_j\} = (1.62555 + O(1/N))\sqrt{N}.$$

Teske's additive version with $r \geq 6$ step types has

$$\mathbb{E}\min\{i : \exists j \leq i,\, X_i = X_j\} = (1 + O(1/N))\sqrt{\frac{\pi}{2}\frac{N}{1 - (1/r + 1/r^2 + 2/r^3 + O(1/r^4))}}.$$

Parallel versions with M threads will take $1/M$ times as long.

Simulation data matches this to 4 decimals points , so the heuristic is almost certainly correct.

The final process we consider is the Gaudry-Schost method. This has boundary effects which complicate any attempt at a rigorous proof, and there are too many variants to analyze them all here. In order to present the ideas without complicating things excessively we have chosen to analyze one of the simpler cases [6].

Heuristic 5 (Gaudry-Schost) *Galbraith and Ruprai's Gaudry-Schost method for computing the discrete logarithm on an interval of size N with r step types, distinguished point probability θ at each state, and average step size $m = c\theta N$ with c small (e.g. $c = 0.01$), has expected run time*

$$2\mathbb{E}\min\{k : \exists i, j \leq k, X_i = Y_j\}$$

$$= (1 + O(1/N))\frac{2}{3^{1/2}}\sqrt{\pi\frac{N}{1 - (1/r + 1/r^2 + 2/r^3 + O(1/r^4))}}.$$

Parallel versions with M threads will take $1/M$ times as long.

This indicates a slowdown by $\sqrt{\mathcal{C}_\tau} = 1/\sqrt{1 - (1/r + 1/r^2 + 2/r^3 + O(1/r^4))}$ over previous heuristics based on the birthday problem. We test our method on a more complicated case of Gaudry-Schost, namely Galbraith, Pollard, and Ruprai's [5] improved 3 walk Gaudry-Schost method for discrete logarithm on an interval of width N. Our heuristic predicts the runtime within 0.3% of that found in simulations.

The paper proceeds as follows. In Section 2 we discuss past results on collision times and also give an overview of our new method for studying collision times. We apply this method to Pollard's Kangaroo in Section 3, to Pollard's Rho in Section 4, and to Gaudry-Schost in Section 5. Section 6 includes discussion on computation of $\mathcal{C}_\tau$, while Section 7 consolidates our simulation data confirming the high degree of accuracy in our results.

2   Methods of Studying Collision Time

The attacks considered in this paper depend on iterative processes which proceed until some group element has been visited twice, a "collision." In Section 1.2 we gave simple heuristics for understanding the time until the first collision. In Section 1.3 we justified treating the attacks as if they involved random walks. Under this assumption several improvements have been made on the basic heuristic arguments, and we discuss here both those improvements and our new approach to studying collision time.

We use some notation here that may be unfamiliar: $f = o(g)$ if $\lim_{x\to\infty}\frac{f(x)}{g(x)} = 0$, while $f = O(g)$ if $\lim_{x\to\infty}\frac{f(x)}{g(x)} \leq C$ for some constant C, and $f = O^*(g)$ indicates that logarithmic terms are being ignored, e.g. if $f = O(x^3 \log x)$ then $f = O^*(x^3)$.

2.1   Past Work

Of the three methods we consider, Pollard's Rho has been studied most heavily. A heuristic based on the birthday problem suggests that it will take an average of $\sqrt{\frac{\pi}{2}N} = 1.2533\sqrt{|G|}$ steps until a collision. However, experimental data finds the run time to be slower than this, and sometimes significantly so. Blackburn and Murphy [4] borrow an idea of Brent and Pollard to give an improved heuristic, that for a process with r step types the collision time will be $\sqrt{\frac{\pi}{2} \frac{N}{1-1/r}}$. Teske gives a heuristic suggesting that her additive version has run time $O(\sqrt{N})$ when there are $r \geq 5$ step types [18]. The first rigorous result for a Rho method is Miller and Venkatesan's proof of order $O^*(\sqrt{N})$ for Pollard's Rho [12]. Kim, Montenegro, Peres and Tetali [10] improve this to $O(\sqrt{N \mathcal{C}_\tau})$, with Pollard's Rho having expected collision time of $\leq (52.5 + o(1))\sqrt{N}$. Bailey et al. [1] extend Blackburn and Murphy's method to the case where steps do not all have equal probabilities. Bernstein and Lange [2] take a very different approach to the problem and yet also arrive at our Heuristic 4 for the special case of Teske's additive walks.

Pollard's Kangaroo method on an interval $[a, a + N)$ is based on a principle known as the Kruskal Count, which suggests a run time of $(2+o(1))\sqrt{N}$. Pollard gives a very convincing argument that $(2 + o(1))\sqrt{N}$ steps suffice, although it was not quite rigorous. Montenegro and Tetali give the first rigorous result that $(2 + o(1))\sqrt{N}$ steps suffices [13]. However, their upper and lower bounds do not agree on the error term, or even whether the run time is greater or less than $2\sqrt{N}$.

For the Gaudry-Schost method nothing has been shown rigorously, and simulations disagree somewhat with heuristic. This method is complicated by having several variables: the number of generators, the average step size, and the number of distinguished points. Our result is thus the first attempt at a bound better than what can be obtained by a simple generalized birthday problem, and yet it is quite accurate, predicting runtime within 0.3% of what we find in simulations.

2.2   Our Approach

We take a similar approach to each algorithm. First, choose the appropriate heuristic from Section 1.2. This would be more-or-less rigorous if the probability of a collision between every pair of states X_i and X_j were independent, but this is clearly not the case.

We revise the heuristic by replacing each individual state X_i by a long segment S_i of some L consecutive states, preceded by a short randomization segment R_i of τ states to ensure that S_i is independent of the earlier segments. In particular, let $a_0 = 0$, $b_0 = a_0 + \tau$, $a_\ell = b_{\ell-1} + L$, $b_\ell = a_\ell + \tau$.

$$R_\ell = \{X_{a_\ell}, \dots, X_{b_\ell}\}$$
$$S_\ell = \{X_{b_\ell}, \dots, X_{a_{\ell+1}}\} \tag{1}$$

By construction segments S_i and S_j will be independent when $i \neq j$. If $\tau \ll L$ almost no collisions will involve randomization segments R_i, while if L is much less than the expected collision time almost no collisions will involve a segment S_i with itself, leaving almost all collisions to be between distinct segments S_i and S_j. It is generally not hard to modify the heuristic of Section 1.2 to determine a new and precise estimate of collision time. The hard part is in adding rigor.

First, although $\mathcal{C}_\tau$ is fairly easy to estimate numerically it is very difficult to find τ and $\mathcal{C}_\tau$ rigorously. Second, it can be difficult to show that there is indeed a negligible chance of collisions between a segment S_i and itself, or of a collision involving an R_i segment. Most of the technical work required for rigor is left to the full version of this paper or cited from prior research, as it is tedious and not very enlightening.

The simplest approach to parallelization involves starting M threads at M independent initial points, and recording visits to distinguished points until some distinguished point is visited a second time. For fixed values of L and τ each thread will generate a new nearly-independent segment every $(\tau + L)$ steps, and so this form of parallelization produces segments M times faster, and expected collision time is $1/M$ times as long.

Our approach is inspired by our past work [10,13], and indeed we borrow several of the more tedious results from those papers. However, a critical difference is that we now partition the walk by design, with a conscious goal to rework prior heuristics. In our past work the walk was partitioned as well, but that was an artifact of the proof failing to work up to the full collision time. As a result the partitioning felt unnecessary, the method of proof was harder to follow, and the results were less precise than obtained in this paper.

3   Pollard's Kangaroo Method

We begin by studying Pollard's Kangaroo method, as the argument is somewhat simpler and sharper than in the Rho or Gaudry-Schost cases.

Collision in the random walk is equivalent to collision in the exponent of g, i.e. $g^\alpha = g^\beta$ iff $\alpha \equiv \beta \mod |G|$. This induces an additive form of the process: let $X_0 = x$, $Y_0 = a + N/2$, and transitions are of the form $X_{i+1} = X_i + 2^k$ mod $|G|$ and $Y_{i+1} = Y_i + 2^\ell \mod |G|$, where $k, \ell \in \{0, 1, \ldots, d\}$. Furthermore, we are most interested in the case when N is much smaller than the group size $|G|$, and so wrap-around effects mod $|G|$ can safely be neglected. This lets us simplify further: assume that $|X_0 - Y_0| \le N/2$ and take iterations of the form $X_{i+1} = X_i + 2^k$ and $Y_{i+1} = Y_i + 2^\ell$. The Kangaroo process is then a monotone increasing walk on the integers $\mathbb{Z}$ with $X_{i+1} = X_i + 2^k$, $Y_{i+1} = Y_i + 2^\ell$. Due to this simplification, our upper bound will be valid for all N, but the lower bound holds only when $N = o(|G|)$.

The goal is to determine the expected time of the first collision between these processes:

$$\mathbb{E} \min\{k : \exists i, j \le k, X_i = Y_j\}.$$

Because both processes are run simultaneously, the total number of steps taken is twice this.

The non-rigorous part of the heuristic in Section 1.2 is the claim that collisions occur with probability $p \approx 1/m$, and so $p^{-1} \approx m$ steps are required until a collision. We replace this by a claim that there is a $p = (1 + o(1)) L/m^2$ probability of segment S_i including a state visited by the tame kangaroo, and so an average of p^{-1} segments are needed until a collision. The expected run time of the Kangaroo method is then $\frac{N}{4m} + (\tau + L)p^{-1}$.

This argument neglects potential collisions involving the R_i segments, and so it is only an upper bound. To show a lower bound we set $L = |S_i| = \sqrt[4]{N}$ and $\tau = |R_i| = O((\log N)^6)$, so that $\tau = o(L)$ and the R_i segments are involved in only a $o(1)$ fraction of potential collisions. We show in the full version of the paper that the R_i segments have a negligible probability of being the location of the first collision.

Why this value for τ? The re-randomization portion R_i is intended to make the probability of a collision in S_i be independent of the outcome of earlier segments. One approach to this would be to have τ be the mixing time, i.e. the number of steps required to produce a uniform random sample from G. However, this is too pessimistic as the Kangaroo method for $N \ll |G|$ might even solve for the discrete logarithm in fewer steps than the mixing time. Instead we require a local mixing property. The follow property, defined by Montenegro and Tetali [13], suffices:

Definition 6. *Consider two independent instances of the same monotone increasing Markov chain on the infinite state space $\mathbb{Z}$, i.e. walks $X_0, X_1, \ldots$ and $Y_0, Y_1, \ldots$ such that $\forall i : X_{i+1} > X_i$ and $\forall j : Y_{j+1} > Y_j$. If the Markov chain has average step size m then the* intersection mixing time $T(\epsilon)$ *is the smallest integer with*

$$\forall i \geq T(\epsilon), \forall Y_0 \leq X_0 : \frac{1-\epsilon}{m} \leq \mathsf{P}\left(X_i \in \{Y_0, Y_1, \ldots, Y_k, \ldots\}\right) \leq \frac{1+\epsilon}{m}.$$

In our analysis the walks in Definition 6 will correspond to the wild and tame kangaroos defined at the beginning of this section. Intersection mixing time was studied in [13] where Lemma 3.1 shows that the Kangaroo walk with steps $\{2^k\}_{k=0}^d$, when treated as a monotone walk on $\mathbb{Z}$, satisfies $T(2/(d+1)) \leq 64(d+1)^5$. Mixing type results typically have a dropoff similar to $T(\epsilon) = T(1/e)\log(1/\epsilon)$. Since $d \sim 0.5 \log_2 N + O(\log\log N)$ this suggests that

$$T(1/N) = O\left((d+1)^5 \frac{\log N}{\log D}\right) = O((d+1)^6) = O((\log N)^6).$$

Indeed, the proof in [13] can be easily modified to show this.

It remains to determine the probability that a collision occurs in a segment S_k. The following relation will be used to show this. Given a non-negative random variable Q:

$$\mathsf{P}\left(Q > 0\right) = \frac{\mathbb{E}Q}{\mathbb{E}(Q \mid Q > 0)}.$$

Let CS_i denote the number of collisions between the tame walk and segment S_i in (1). Each state within S_i has probability $(1 + O(1/N))/m$ of colliding with the tame walk. It follows from additivity of expectation that

$$\mathbb{E}\mathrm{CS}_i = (1 + O(1/N))\frac{L}{m}.$$

We next bound the conditional $\mathbb{E}(\mathrm{CS}_i \mid \mathrm{CS}_i > 0)$. The first collision is part of a sequence of $\mathcal{C}_\tau$ collisions on average, after which each step has probability at most $(1 + 1/N)/m$ of colliding with the tame walk.

$$\mathbb{E}(\mathrm{CS}_i \mid \mathrm{CS}_i > 0) \le (1 + 1/N)\left(\mathcal{C}_\tau + \frac{L - \tau}{m}\right)$$

To lower bound the expectation, observe that each step of the walk in S_i is equally likely to have a collision, and so the probability that $X_i \in S_i$ is the first collision is decreasing in i. As such, with probability at least $1 - \tau/L$ the collision occurs before the final τ states, in which case it is part of a sequence of $\mathcal{C}_\tau$ collisions on average, potentially followed by even more. Then

$$\mathbb{E}(\mathrm{CS}_i \mid \mathrm{CS}_i > 0) \ge (1 - 1/N)\left(1 - \frac{\tau}{L}\right)\mathcal{C}_\tau .$$

Combining these various equalities leads to the conclusions:

$$\Rightarrow \ \mathbb{E}(\mathrm{CS}_i \mid \mathrm{CS}_i > 0) = \left(1 + O\left(\frac{L}{m} + \frac{\tau}{L} + \frac{1}{N}\right)\right)\mathcal{C}_\tau$$

$$\Rightarrow \ p = \mathsf{P}\left(\mathrm{CS}_i > 0\right) = \left(1 + O\left(\frac{L}{m} + \frac{\tau}{L} + \frac{1}{N}\right)\right)\frac{L}{m\,\mathcal{C}_\tau} \tag{2}$$

The identity for $\mathsf{P}\left(\mathrm{CS}_i > 0\right)$ is independent of the outcome on earlier segments, up to a small error due to the big-O term, and so as was discussed earlier the number of segments until a collision is p^{-1}. Let $L = \sqrt[4]{N}$, and recall that $\tau = O(\log^6 N)$ and $m = \Theta(\sqrt{N})$. The expected collision time of the original process is

$$(L + \tau)p^{-1} = (L + \tau)\left(1 + O\left(\frac{L}{m} + \frac{\tau}{L} + \frac{1}{N}\right)\right)\frac{m\,\mathcal{C}_\tau}{L} = (1 + O^*(1/\sqrt[4]{N}))\,m\,\mathcal{C}_\tau .$$

We leave it to the full version of the paper to prove that the answer does not change when potential collisions in the re-randomization segments R_i are considered.

When $m = \frac{1}{2}\sqrt{N}$ the expected number of transitions by the wild kangaroo is

$$\mathbb{E}\frac{|X_0 - Y_0|}{m} + (1 + O^*(1/\sqrt[4]{N}))\,m\,\mathcal{C}_\tau = \frac{1 + \mathcal{C}_\tau + O^*(1/\sqrt[4]{N})}{2}\sqrt{N} .$$

The tame kangaroo travels an equal number of steps. Counting both kangaroos gives Theorem 2.

In Figure 1 we compare our Theorem 2 to the old heuristic of $2\sqrt{N}$ and simulation data with an (absolute) margin of error of $\pm 0.01\sqrt{N}$. These show our bound to be very accurate when $N > 1000$.

4   Pollard's Rho Method

The analysis for the Rho method is not much different, but a bit more preliminary work is required, and the result will not be as precise. Our solution focuses on the case when each step type has equal probability, with a few comments at the end about generalizing to the non-uniform case. We focus on the non-parallel case because the parallel case follows immediately from this, as discussed in Section 2.2.

Pollard's Rho is equivalent to an additive walk on exponents which starts at some X_0 with $0 \leq X_0 < |G|$, and has transitions $\mathsf{P}(X_{i+1} = X_i + 1) = \mathsf{P}(X_{i+1} = X_i + x) = \mathsf{P}(X_{i+1} = 2X_i) = 1/3$. Teske's version has transitions $\mathsf{P}(X_{i+1} = X_i + s_k) = 1/r$. Note that Pollard's Rho is a process with $r = 3$ transition types. We use the additive walk on exponents in our analysis.

The goal of this section is to determine the expected time of the first collision between these processes:

$$\mathbb{E}\min\{i : \exists j < i, X_i = X_j\}$$

The non-rigorous part of the heuristic in Section 1.2 is in treating every X_i as if it were an independent uniform random sample from G, and so $p = \mathsf{P}(X_i = X_j) = 1/|G|$ when $i \neq j$, and there are an average $\sqrt{\frac{\pi}{2}p^{-1}}$ samples until collision. We replace this by a claim that every S_i and S_j are pairwise independent, with $p = \mathsf{P}(S_i \cap S_j \neq \emptyset) \approx 1/A$ for some A, and so the expected number of segments until a collision is around $\sqrt{\frac{\pi}{2}}p^{-1} = \sqrt{\frac{\pi}{2}A}$. The expected run time of the Rho method is then $(L + \tau)\sqrt{\frac{\pi}{2}A}$.

This ignores potential collisions involving an R_i or an S_i with itself. However, if $\tau = o(L)$ then collisions involving an R_i segment make up only an $o(1)$ fraction of potential collisions. Likewise, collisions within an S_i are only an $o(1)$ fraction of potential collisions if $L = o(\sqrt{N})$. For the sake of rigor we show in the full version of the paper that these in fact have only a negligible probability of being the location of the first collision.

What is the appropriate value for τ? The re-randomization portion R_i is intended to make S_i independent of earlier segments. It suffices that the first state in S_i be an independent nearly uniform random sample.

$$\forall v, w \in V : \frac{1 - 1/N}{N} \leq \mathsf{P}^\tau(v, w) \leq \frac{1 + 1/N}{N}.$$

The minimum value of τ for which this holds is called "L^∞ mixing time." Montenegro, Kim, and Tetali [9] showed that for Pollard's Rho walk $\tau = O(\log^3 N)$, while Hildebrand [8,18] showed that for Teske's additive walk $\tau = O^*(N^{2/(r-1)})$. A slightly weaker notion of mixing should be used for Teske's process when $r < 6$, but we do not consider it here.

We now turn to the proof of Theorem 3. This uses a generalization of the birthday problem. Consider a family of events $E_1, E_2, \ldots$ such that $\mathsf{P}(E_1) = 0$ and $\mathsf{P}(E_k \mid \neg E_{k-1}) = (1 + o(1))\frac{k-1}{A}$. Then

$$\mathbb{E}\min\{t : E_t\} = (1 + O(1/A))\sqrt{\frac{\pi}{2}A}.$$

We prove a more general form of this in the Appendix.

Let CS_t denote the number of collisions between the first t segments S_1, S_2, ..., S_t. We will take E_t as the event that $\mathrm{CS}_t > 0$, and so we need to determine $\mathsf{P}\,(E_t \mid \neg E_{t-1})$.

Consider segment S_t. It starts at $X_{(t-1)L+t\tau}$, which is a sample within $\epsilon = 1/N$ of uniform, independent of earlier rounds. It proceeds as a random path containing L states. Assume for now that all transitions are equally likely, so that all paths are equally likely as well; we discuss the non-uniform case at the end of the section. There are $N \times r^{L-1}$ possible paths, and each will have probability between $\frac{1 \pm 1/N}{N r^{L-1}}$. In order to have $\mathrm{CS}_t > 0$ the path must collide with one of the $\leq (t-1)L$ points appearing in $S_1, S_2, \ldots, S_{t-1}$, denote this as X_j. There are L positions in the path at which the collision could occur, denote the chosen location as X_i, and r^{L-1} possibilities for the remainder of the path, so at most $(t-1)L^2 r^{L-1}$ potential S_t segments include collisions. It follows that

$$\mathsf{P}\,(\mathrm{CS}_t > 0 \mid \mathrm{CS}_{t-1} = 0) \leq \frac{(t-1)L^2 r^{L-1}(1+1/N)}{N r^{L-1}(1-1/N)} = \frac{(t-1)(1+O(1/N))}{N/L^2}$$

$$\Rightarrow\ \mathbb{E}\min\{t : \mathrm{CS}_t > 0\} \geq (1+O(L^2/N))\sqrt{\frac{\pi}{2}\frac{N}{L^2}}$$

Each round introduced $\tau + L$ new states, so this suggests run time of

$$\mathbb{E}\min\{i : \exists j < i,\, X_i = X_j\} \gtrsim (\tau + L)(1+O(L^2/N))\sqrt{\frac{\pi}{2}\frac{N}{L^2}}$$

$$= (1+O(L^2/N)+O(\tau/L))\sqrt{\frac{\pi}{2}N}$$

This is just the birthday heuristic. We can improve on this by reducing double-counting of paths. In the construction just given, once X_i and X_j have been decided on, do not construct paths with $X_{i-1} = X_{j-1}$, as these paths will be counted anyway. This reduces the number of segments with $X_i = X_j$ from r^{L-1} to $(r-1)r^{L-2}$, unless X_i or X_j is the first state in their respective segment. This results in:

$$\mathsf{P}\,(\mathrm{CS}_t > 0 \mid \mathrm{CS}_{t-1} = 0) \leq \frac{(1-1/L)^2(1-1/r)(t-1)L^2 r^{L-1}}{N r^{L-1}}\frac{1+1/N}{1-1/N}$$

$$= (1+O(1/L)+O(1/N))\frac{(t-1)(1-1/r)L^2}{N}$$

$$\Rightarrow\ \mathbb{E}\min\{t : \mathrm{CS}_t > 0\} \geq (1+O(L^2/N))\sqrt{\frac{\pi}{2}\frac{N}{L^2(1-1/r)}}$$

$$\Rightarrow\ \mathbb{E}\min\{i : \exists j < i,\, X_i = X_j\} \gtrsim (1+O(L^2/N)+O(\tau/L))\sqrt{\frac{\pi}{2}\frac{N}{1-1/r}}$$

In the full version of the paper we make the final line rigorous, with the added condition that $j \leq i - \tau$, and so $\gtrsim$ can (almost) be replaced by $\geq$.

The bound can be made more-or-less sharp, but at the cost of rigor. A path with first collision at $X_i = X_j$ will have an average of C_τ collisions in the next τ steps, and so we counted colliding paths C_τ times each on average. The number of colliding paths is only $(1 - \tau/L)/C_\tau$ of our original rough estimate.

$$P\left(\mathrm{CS}_t > 0 \mid I_t = 0\right) \approx \frac{(t-1)\,L^2\,r^{L-1}/C_\tau}{N\,r^{L-1}} \frac{1 + O(1/N)}{1 - O(1/N)}$$

$$= \frac{(t-1)\,L^2}{C_\tau N}\,(1 + O(1/N))$$

$$\Rightarrow \mathbb{E}\min\{t : \mathrm{CS}_t > 0\} \approx (1 + O(L^2/N))\sqrt{\frac{\pi}{2}\,\frac{N\,C_\tau}{L^2}}$$

$$\Rightarrow \mathbb{E}\min\{i : \exists j < i,\, X_i = X_j\} \approx (1 + O(L^2/N) + O(\tau/L))\sqrt{\frac{\pi}{2}\,N\,C_\tau}$$

The non-rigor here is in ignoring the effects of the condition $\mathrm{CS}_{t-1} = 0$ on the expected number of collisions after $X_i = X_j$. However, given that only an $O(1/\sqrt{N})$ fraction of states will be covered before the expected collision time this effect should be quite minimal. Indeed, the simulations data discussed in Section 7 show that our heuristic has 4 or more digits of accuracy.

The approximation $C_\tau \geq C_1$ gives our earlier weaker, but rigorous, result, so this is an extension of what we know to be true. Pollard's walk has $\tau = O(\log^3 N)$ [9] and so when $L = \sqrt[3]{N}$ we get run time $(1 + O^*(1/\sqrt[3]{N}))\sqrt{\frac{\pi}{2}\,N\,C_\tau}$. Teske's additive walks have $\tau = O(N^{2/(r-1)})$ [18] and so if $r \geq 6$ then $L = N^{0.5-\epsilon}$ for small ϵ will suffice to show run time of $(1 + o(1))\sqrt{\frac{\pi}{2}\,N\,C_\tau}$, while if $r = 5$ then $L = \sqrt{N}$ will show $O\left(\sqrt{\frac{\pi}{2}\,N\,C_\tau}\right)$. These are consistent with Teske's observation that the walk slows considerably when $r \leq 4$.

Remark 7. When the transitions have non-uniform probabilities nearly everything just argued still applies, because in our construction of colliding paths we allow all possible transitions to occur. The sole exception is the $1 - 1/r$ correction. In this case it suffices to replace $1/r$ by the smallest transition probability. That is of course pessimistic, but is difficult to avoid in a rigorous argument. The C_τ bound does not suffer this weakness and again seems to be sharp.

5   Gaudry-Schost

There are many variations of the Gaudry-Schost method, with versions to solve multi-dimensional discrete logarithms, to speed up the algorithm by making the regions non-hypercubes, to speed up by considering collision of 3 or 4 walks on differing regions, etc [5–7]. Our technique can be applied in each of these settings, but for simplicity we will consider only the simplest case, an early one-dimensional version [7]. We comment on a few other versions at the end of this section and in Section 7.

The non-rigorous part of the heuristic is in ignoring the dependence between states such as X_i and X_{i+1}. We resolve this by breaking the X and Y walks into segments S_i^X and S_j^X that are independent. The most natural choice for segments is to let S_i^X denote the states visited by walk X between the $(i-1)^{st}$ and i^{th} distinguished points, including the ith, and define S_i^Y and R_i^Y similarly. This implicitly sets $R_i^X = \emptyset$. The length $|S_i|$ is a random variable with geometric distribution $\mathsf{P}\left(|S_i| = \ell\right) = (1-\theta)^{\ell-1}\theta$ and expectation $\mathbb{E}|S_i| = \theta^{-1}$.

As before, we consider the probability that two segments collide, this time segments S_i^X and S_j^Y. To simplify the discussion we ignore boundary effects and assume that all segments are in $A \cap B$, since this is the only area in which collisions can occur. There are two main types of boundary effects: when walk X crosses into B it effectively increases the size of $A \cap B$, which improves the runtime, but when it crosses into A^c it effectively increases the size of A which decreases the runtime. A careful analysis finds that these effects almost exactly cancel out.

Let E_t denote the number of times that one of the first t segments for X intersects one of the first t segments for Y. As in the analysis of the Kangaroo method, we will use the relation that for a non-negative random variable $\mathsf{P}\left(Q > 0\right) = \frac{\mathbb{E}Q}{\mathbb{E}(Q\,|\,Q>0)}$.

First, consider the chance that S_t^X intersects with one of the first $(t-1)$ segments of the Y walk.

$$\mathsf{P}\left(S_t^X \cap \left(\cup_{j=1}^{t-1} S_j^Y\right) \neq \emptyset \mid E_{t-1} = 0\right) \approx \frac{\theta^{-1} \times (t-1)\frac{\theta^{-1}}{|A\cap B|}}{\mathcal{C}_\tau}$$

$$= \frac{t-1}{\theta^2 \mathcal{C}_\tau\,|A \cap B|}$$

Next, consider the chance that S_t^Y intersects with one of the first t segments of the X walk, if it has not collided already:

$$\mathsf{P}\left(S_t^Y \cap \left(\cup_{j=1}^{t} S_j^X\right) \neq \emptyset \mid E_{t-1} = 0 \wedge S_t^X \cap \left(\cup_{j=1}^{t-1} S_j^Y\right) = \emptyset\right) \approx \frac{\theta^{-1} \times t\frac{\theta^{-1}}{|A\cap B|}}{\mathcal{C}_\tau}$$

$$= \frac{t}{\theta^2 \mathcal{C}_\tau\,|A \cap B|}$$

Then

$$\mathsf{P}\left(E_t > 0 \mid E_{t-1} = 0\right) \approx \frac{t-1}{\theta^2 \mathcal{C}_\tau\,|A \cap B|} + \left(1 - \frac{t-1}{\theta^2 \mathcal{C}_\tau\,|A \cap B|}\right)\frac{t}{\theta^2 \mathcal{C}_\tau\,|A \cap B|} \tag{3}$$

The two-walk birthday problem generalizes to say that if E_t is a non-negative random variable such that

$$\mathsf{P}\left(E_t > 0 \mid E_{t-1} = 0\right) = \frac{t-1}{\mathcal{N}} + \left(1 - \frac{t-1}{\mathcal{N}}\right)\frac{t}{\mathcal{N}}$$

then

$$\mathbb{E}\min\{t : E_t > 0\} = (1 + O(1/\mathcal{N}))\frac{1}{2}\sqrt{\pi\mathcal{N}}.$$

Equation (3) satisfies the condition when $\mathcal{N} = \theta^2 C_\tau |A \cap B|$, and so each walk requires an average of $\frac{1}{2} \sqrt{\pi \mathcal{N}}$ segments in $A \cap B$. If we ignore boundary effects, then each segment from the X walk has probability $\frac{|A \cap B|}{|A|}$ of being in $A \cap B$, while each segment from Y has probability $\frac{|A \cap B|}{|B|}$ of this. So drawing the required number of samples from $A \cap B$ requires an average of

$$\frac{|A|}{|A \cap B|} \frac{1}{2} \sqrt{\pi \theta^2 C_\tau |A \cap B|}$$

segments from X and a similar number from the Y process. Each segment involved an average of θ^{-1} steps of the walk, so the number of steps of the walks is

$$\frac{|A| + |B|}{2|A \cap B|} \sqrt{\pi C_\tau |A \cap B|}.$$

For instance, Galbraith and Ruprai's improved version of Gaudry-Schost [6] uses regions with $|A|/|A \cap B| = |B|/|A \cap B| = 2$ and $|A \cap B| = N/3$. This leads to a runtime estimate of $\frac{2}{3^{1/2}} \sqrt{\pi C_\tau N}$, which is a factor $\sqrt{C_\tau}$ times slower than previous predictions. Our simulations find that this is within 0.3% of the correct runtime. See Section 7 for further details.

6   The Collision Number

Almost all of our bounds consider the collision number C_τ. We remind the reader of its definition.

Definition 8. *The* collision number C_τ *is the expected number of collisions when two independent copies of a random walk start at the same state, chosen uniformly at random, and proceed for τ steps.*

The fact that this is an average case behavior means that we can ignore the possibility of bad start values, as these are rare. Determining this value exactly is still generally prohibitive, but upper and lower bounds of arbitrary precision are possible.

The simplest approximation on the collision number is the lower bound $C_\tau \geq C_\ell$ for $\ell \leq \tau$. When $C_\tau \geq C_0 = 1$ is used our bounds simply reduce to the heuristic results of Section 1.2. When $C_\tau \geq C_1 = 1 + 1/r$ is used the Rho heuristic of Heuristic 4 reduces to Theorem 3; this also gives Blackburn and Murphy's heuristic. When $C_\tau \geq C_2$ is used then we start producing new results.

For small terms such as C_2 it is typically possible to compute the value exactly by hand. We give a few examples below.

Another method of estimating C_τ is to observe that most collisions will occur quickly, and once a collision does occur then it should be followed by roughly another C_τ collisions. Hence, if p_ℓ is the probability of a collision within a small number of steps ℓ then

$$C_\tau \geq 1 + p_\ell C_\tau$$

$$\Rightarrow C_\tau \geq \frac{1}{1 - p_\ell} \qquad (4)$$

For very small ℓ this can be computed by hand, but it is usually better to involve a computer. The values produced by this estimate are quite accurate.

Simulation data shown in Section 7 shows that our heuristics are very precise. The methods of computing each C_τ will not differ much, so we only give detailed work for Pollard's Rho while keeping the work short for Pollard's Kangaroo and Gaudry-Schost.

Example 9 (Pollard's Kangaroo). Consider p_1. This requires both walks to make the same initial transition $X_1 = X_0 + 2^k = Y_1$, so $p_1 = 1/(d+1)$ and

$$C_\tau \geq \frac{1}{1 - p_1} = 1 + \frac{1}{d} = 1 + \frac{2}{\log_2 N}$$

Consider p_2. This requires both to make the same initial transition, or do the first two steps in reversed order, or one walk does the same step twice making it add up to the other walk's value. Then

$$p_2 = \frac{1}{d+1} + \binom{d+1}{2} \frac{1}{(d+1)^4} + 2d \frac{1}{(d+1)^3}$$

$$= \frac{2}{\log_2 N} + \frac{10}{(\log_2 N)^2} + O((\log N)^{-3}).$$

As $N \to \infty$ this goes to zero, so we can use the relation $1/(1-p) \to 1 + p + p^2 + \cdots$. This gives the relation

$$C_\tau \geq 1 + \frac{2}{\log_2 N} + \frac{14}{(\log_2 N)^2} + O((\log N)^{-3}).$$

This is quite accurate. See Section 7 for a plot using a version of this bound.

Example 10 (Teske's Additive Walks). For Teske's additive version of Pollard's Rho there are r step types of the form $X \to X + s_i$. Consider the probability that two independent walks with $X_0 = Y_0$ intersect within $\ell = 3$ steps:

$P(\exists i, j \leq 3, X_i = Y_j \mid X_0 = Y_0)$
$= P(X_1 = Y_1 \mid X_0 = Y_0) + P(X_2 = Y_2, X_1 \neq Y_1 \mid X_0 = Y_0)$
$\quad + P(X_3 = Y_3, X_2 \neq Y_2, X_1 \neq Y_1 \mid X_0 = Y_0)$
$= P(X_1 = X_0 + s_i = Y_0 + s_i = Y_1)$
$\quad + P(X_2 = X_0 + s_i + s_j = Y_0 + s_j + s_i = Y_2, i \neq j \mid X_0 = Y_0)$
$\quad + P(X_3 = X_0 + s_i + s_j + s_k = Y_0 + s_j + s_k + s_i, i \neq j \neq k \neq i, \mid X_0 = Y_0)$
$= \frac{1}{r} + {}_r P_2 \frac{1}{r^2} \frac{1}{r^2} + \frac{3\,{}_r P_3 + 2\,{}_r P_2}{r^6}$
$= \frac{1}{r} + \frac{1}{r^2} + \frac{2}{r^3} + O(1/r^4)$

It follows that

$$C_\tau \approx \frac{1}{1 - p_3} = \frac{1}{1 - \left(\frac{1}{r} + \frac{1}{r^2} + \frac{2}{r^3} + O(1/r^4)\right)} = 1 + \frac{1}{r} + \frac{2}{r^2} + \frac{4}{r^3} + O(1/r^4)$$

See Section 7 for discussion of the accuracy of this.

Example 11 (Gaudry-Schost). The step types were chosen uniformly at random from an interval, and so with high probability a collision will occur in a short number of steps iff the same steps are taken by both walks, or the same steps are taken but with the order re-arranged. This is just what happens with Teske's additive walks, and so we may borrow the work done when we examined her methods. Namely,

$$\mathcal{C}_\tau \approx \frac{1}{1-p_3} = \frac{1}{1-\left(\frac{1}{r}+\frac{1}{r^2}+\frac{2}{r^3}+O(1/r^4)\right)} = 1 + \frac{1}{r} + \frac{2}{r^2} + \frac{4}{r^3} + O(1/r^4)$$

7 Sharpness of our Results

We have consolidated our simulation details here. All of these show that our results are extremely precise.

We note that our simulations are done in a non-standard way. Our goal is to study performance of various methods for finding the discrete logarithm, not to study the strengths or weaknesses of specific hash functions or representations of a cyclic group. As a result we study walks on the exponents, not the group. For instance, the walk $X_0 = h = g^x$, $X_1 = hg$, $X_2 = (hg)^2$ is equivalent to $x \to x+1 \to 2x+2 \mod |G|$. The hash used to do a walk on the exponent was based on the Mersenne Twister [11], as it is a fast source of pseudo-randomness. Several variations on this hash were tested, and it was confirmed that run time was similar in each case.

We first consider Pollard's Kangaroo with power of two steps.

Example 12 (Pollard's Kangaroo). When $N = |G| = 10^9$ Figure 1 shows that there is still a significant gap between simulation data and prior heuristics, but that our new result almost exactly matches the simulation results.

Pollard's degree 3 process is a useful test cases as its performance deviates from simple heuristic much more than does Teske's improved process.

Example 13 (Pollard's Rho). Very large simulations show that $\mathcal{C}_\tau = 1.68221 \pm 0.00001$. A computer can be used to enumerate all possible paths of length $\ell \le 20$. This gives the estimate $\mathcal{C}_\tau \approx \frac{1}{1-p_5} = 1.65237$, while $\mathcal{C}_\tau \approx \frac{1}{1-p_{10}} = 1.67730$, and $\mathcal{C}_\tau \approx \frac{1}{1-p_{20}} = 1.68203$. So even p_{10} was sufficient to give an estimate of $\mathcal{C}_\tau$ within 0.3% of the true value.

This can be seen more clearly visually. Figure 2 shows simulation data for runtime and finds that it is consistently around $1.6254\sqrt{N}$. Figure 3 shows that $\mathcal{C}_t$ approaches $\mathcal{C}_\tau$ fairly quickly in t, with $\mathcal{C}_{20} \approx \mathcal{C}_\tau$, and leads to a runtime prediction of $1.6256\sqrt{N}$.

We next consider Teske's r-adding version of the Rho method.

Example 14 (Teske's additive walks).
Teske estimates average collision time of the 20-adding walk is around $1.292\sqrt{N}$ steps [18]. We did a much larger run of 75 million simulations and

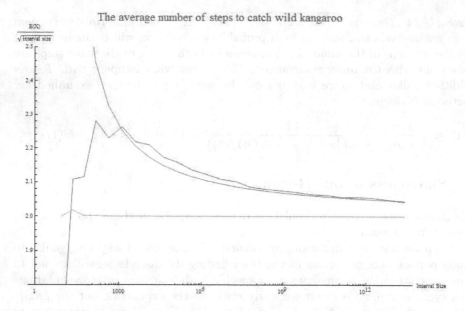

Fig. 1. Standard heuristic (flat line), our bound (smooth curve), simulation data with margin of error $\pm 0.01\sqrt{N}$ (jagged plot)

found a 95% confidence interval of $1.2877\sqrt{N}$ to $1.2880\sqrt{N}$. This suggests that collision time is about 3% slower than the $1.2533\sqrt{N}$ steps predicted by the birthday heuristic.

To apply our heuristic, recall from Section 6 that

$$C_\tau \approx \frac{1}{1 - p_3} = \frac{1}{1 - \left(\frac{1}{r} + \frac{1}{r^2} + \frac{2}{r^3} + O(1/r^4)\right)}$$

When $r = 20$ this leads to an estimate on collision time of $1.2877\sqrt{N}$, which is already within the 95% confidence interval given by simulation data. An exact enumeration of walks of length $\ell = 5$ increases the estimate only negligibly to $1.287765\sqrt{N}$ steps, at $\ell = 10$ to $1.287770\sqrt{N}$ steps, and the sampling based estimate at length $\ell = 100$ gave an estimate of $(1.287769 \pm 0.000003)\sqrt{N}$ with 95% confidence.

So in this case a mere 3 steps already explains 99.7% of the 20-additive walk's deviation from the birthday heuristic, and by 5 steps the estimate is essentially sharp.

Last of all, we compare simulation data to our heuristic for Gaudry-Schost.

Example 15. Galbraith, Pollard, and Rubrai [5] discuss 3 and 4-walk versions with even better runtime than Pollard's Kangaroo method. The same argument used to give a heuristic bound for Gaudry-Schost shows that this will have a $\sqrt{C_\tau}$ slowdown over their predicted runtime. They consider an interval of side

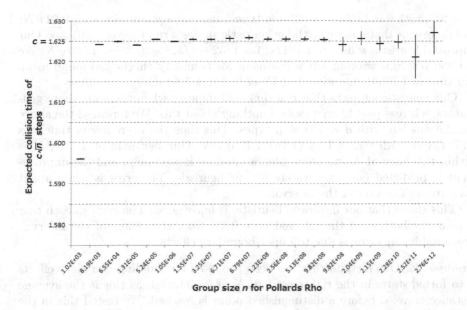

Fig. 2. Run time of Pollard's Rho: Simulations estimate $(1.6254 \pm 0.0004)\sqrt{N}$ steps

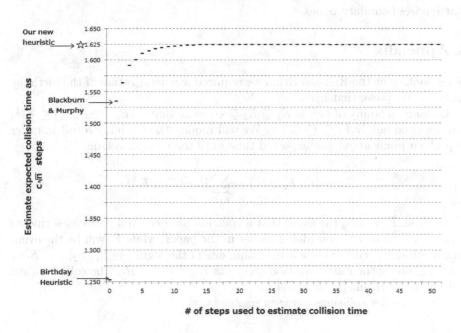

Fig. 3. Run time of Pollard's Rho: Heuristic predicts $1.6256\sqrt{N}$ steps

$N = 2^{40}$, with $\theta = 1/500$, $r = 32$ step types, and average step size $m = 0.01\,\theta\,N$, and determine that a basic birthday heuristic suggests run time of $1.761\sqrt{N}$. Our improved heuristic will be $\approx 1.761/\sqrt{1 - 1/32 - 1/32^2 - 2/32^3} = 1.790\sqrt{N}$. We did 250,000 runs without any adjustment for boundary effects and found mean run time of $1.79501\sqrt{N}$ with 95% CI of $(1.791, 1.799)\sqrt{N}$.

Our heuristic suggests that run time will improve when there are more generators, whereas past heuristics said nothing about this. We repeated the above simulations but with $d = 128$ step types. This time the average run time was $1.77113\sqrt{N}$ with 95% CI of $(1.767, 1.775)\sqrt{N}$. Our heuristic of $1.768\sqrt{N}$ is within this interval. Using more generators does indeed help, and the improvement is predicted fairly accurately by our heuristic. The error is again about 0.3% from the center of the interval.

This shows that our improved heuristic is fairly good. The error in each case is near the bottom of the CI, and only 0.3% from the center of the interval. Presumably any error is due to minor boundary effects.

Example 16. One method that has been proposed for avoiding boundary effects is to forbid starts in the rightmost $0.01\,N$ of an interval, as this is the average distance traveled before a distinguished point is reached. We tested this in the case above, with $r = 32$, and found mean run time of $1.79721\sqrt{N}$ with 95% CI of $(1.793, 1.801)\sqrt{N}$. This is not a statistically significant difference from the case that ignores boundary issues.

A Appendix

When looking at the Rho algorithm we required a generalization of the birthday problem. We prove that here.

Consider a family of events $E_1 \subseteq E_2 \subseteq \cdots$ such that $\mathsf{P}\,(E_k \mid \neg E_{k-1}) \leq \frac{k-1}{A}$, and a second family $F_1 \subseteq F_2 \subseteq \cdots$. We will modify the birthday result in order to prove a result about the expected time until some event is true.

$$\mathbb{E}\min\{t : E_t \cup F_t\} = \sum_{t=0}^{\infty} \mathsf{P}\,(\neg(E_t \cup F_t))$$

In our case, E_t will be the event that a collision has occurred between segments $S_1, S_2, \ldots, S_t$, as was considered earlier in the paper, while F_t will be the event that a collision occurred elsewhere: within one of the segments $S_1, S_2, \ldots, S_t$ or involving one of the randomization segments $R_1, R_2, \ldots, R_t$. The collision time will be $(L + T)\mathbb{E}\min\{t : E_t \cup F_t\}$.

First consider collisions between segments.

$$\mathsf{P}\,(\neg E_t) = \mathsf{P}\,(\neg E_1) \prod_{k=2}^{t} \mathsf{P}\,(\neg E_k \mid \neg E_{k-1})$$

$$\geq 1 \prod_{k=2}^{t}(1 - \frac{k-1}{A})$$

This is exactly the probability that occurs in the birthday problem when there are A days in the year, and so

$$\mathbb{E}\min\{t: E_t\} = \sum_{t=0}^{\infty} \mathsf{P}\left(\neg E_t\right) \geq (1 + O(1/A)) \sqrt{\frac{\pi}{2} A} \tag{5}$$

It follows that for any value of T

$$\mathbb{E}\min\{t: E_t \cup F_t\} = \sum_{t=0}^{\infty} \mathsf{P}\left(\neg (E_t \cup F_t)\right)$$

$$\geq \sum_{t=0}^{T-1} \mathsf{P}\left(\neg E_t\right) - \sum_{t=0}^{T-1} \mathsf{P}\left(F_t\right)$$

$$\geq (1 + O(1/A)) \sqrt{\frac{\pi}{2} A} - \sum_{t=T}^{\infty} 1 \prod_{k=2}^{t} (1 - \frac{k-1}{A}) - \sum_{t=0}^{T-1} \mathsf{P}\left(F_t\right)$$

The tail probability in the first sum can be estimated as

$$\sum_{t=T}^{\infty} 1 \prod_{k=2}^{t} (1 - \frac{k-1}{A}) \leq \sum_{t=T}^{\infty} \exp\left(-\sum_{k=2}^{t} \frac{k-1}{A}\right)$$

$$= \sum_{t=T}^{\infty} \exp\left(-t(t-1)/2A\right)$$

$$\leq \sum_{t=T}^{\infty} \int_{t-2}^{t-1} e^{-x^2/2A} \, dx$$

$$= \int_{T-2}^{\infty} e^{-x^2/2A} \, dx$$

$$\leq \int_{(T-2)/\sqrt{A}}^{\infty} \frac{u}{(T-2)/\sqrt{A}} e^{-u^2/2} \left(\sqrt{A}\, du\right)$$

$$= \frac{A}{T-2} e^{-(T-2)^2/2A}$$

The final inequality involved the substitution $u = x/\sqrt{A}$ and the relation $u \geq \frac{T-2}{\sqrt{A}}$.. When $T \geq 2 + \sqrt{A}\log A$ then this is $o(1)$. Then

$$\mathbb{E}\min\{t: E_t \cup F_t\} \geq (1 + O(1/A)) \sqrt{\frac{\pi}{2} A} - \frac{A^{3/2}}{T-2} e^{-(T-2)^2/2A} - \sum_{t=0}^{T-1} \mathsf{P}\left(F_t\right) \ .$$

We found in Section 4 that $A = \frac{N}{L^2(1-1/r)}$ can be shown rigorously, while $A = \frac{NC_r}{L^2}$ can be shown heuristically.

References

1. Bailey, D., Batina, L., Bernstein, D., Birkner, P., Bos, J., Chen, H.-C., Cheng, C.-M., Van Damme, G., de Meulenaer, G., Perez, L.J.D., Fan, J., Güneysu, T., Gürkaynak, F., Kleinjung, T., Lange, T., Mentens, N., Niederhagen, R., Paar, C., Regazzoni, F., Schwabe, P., Uhsade, L., Van Herrewege, A., Yang, B-Y.: "Breaking ECC2K-130," Cryptology ePrint Archive, Report 2009/541 (2009). https://eprint.iacr.org/2009/541
2. Bernstein, D.J., Lange, T.: Two grumpy giants and a baby. In: ANTS X: Proceedings of the 10th International Symposium on Algorithmic Number Theory. Mathematical Sciences Publishers (2013)
3. Blackburn, S., Scott, S.: The discrete logarithm problem for exponents of bounded height. In: ANTS XI: Proceedings of the 11th International Symposium on Algorithmic Number Theory. LMS J. Comput. Math **17**, 148–156 (2014)
4. Blackburn, S., Murphy, S.: The number of partitions in Pollard Rho, Unpublished note : Later made available as Technical report RHUL-MA-2011-11 (Department of Mathematics, p. 2011. University of London, Royal Holloway (1998)
5. Galbraith, S.D., Pollard, J.M., Ruprai, R.S.: Computing discrete logarithms in an interval. Math. Comp. **82**, 1181–1195 (2013)
6. Galbraith, S., Ruprai, R.S.: An improvement to the Gaudry-Schost algorithm for multidimensional discrete logarithm problems. In: Parker, M.G. (ed.) Cryptography and Coding 2009. LNCS, vol. 5921, pp. 368–382. Springer, Heidelberg (2009)
7. Gaudry, P., Schost, É.: A low-memory parallel version of Matsuo, Chao, and Tsujii's algorithm. In: Buell, D.A. (ed.) ANTS 2004. LNCS, vol. 3076, pp. 208–222. Springer, Heidelberg (2004)
8. Hildebrand, M.: On the Chung-Diaconis-Graham random process. Electron. Comm. Probab. **11**, 347–356 (2006)
9. Kim, J-H., Montenegro, R., Tetali, P.: Near Optimal Bounds for Collision in Pollard Rho for Discrete Log. In: IEEE Proc. of the Symposium on Foundations of Computer Science (FOCS 2007), pp. 215–223 (2007)
10. Kim, J.-H., Montenegro, R., Peres, Y., Tetali, P.: A Birthday Paradox for Markov chains, with an optimal bound for collision in the Pollard Rho Algorithm for Discrete Logarithm. The Annals of Applied Probability **20**(2), 495–521 (2010)
11. Matsumoto, M., Nishimura, T.: Mersenne twister: a 623-dimensionally equidistributed uniform pseudo-random number generator. ACM Transactions on Modeling and Computer Simulation **8**(1), 3–30 (1998)
12. Miller, S.D., Venkatesan, R.: Spectral analysis of Pollard rho collisions. In: Hess, F., Pauli, S., Pohst, M. (eds.) ANTS 2006. LNCS, vol. 4076, pp. 573–581. Springer, Heidelberg (2006)
13. Montenegro, R., Tetali, P.: How long does it take to catch a wild kangaroo?. In: Proc. of 41st ACM Symposium on Theory of Computing (STOC 2009), pp. 553–559 (2009). Citations refer to an improved version at http://arxiv.org/pdf/0812.0789v2.pdf
14. Nishimura, K., Shibuya, M.: Probability to meet in the middle. Journal of Cryptology **2**(1), 13–22 (1990)
15. Pollard, J.: Monte Carlo methods for index computation mod p. Mathematics of Computation **32**(143), 918–924 (1978)
16. Pollard, J.: Kangaroos, Monopoly and Discrete Logarithms. Journal of Cryptology **13**(4), 437–447 (2000)

17. Shoup, V.: Lower bounds for discrete logarithms and related problems. In: Fumy, W. (ed.) EUROCRYPT 1997. LNCS, vol. 1233, pp. 256–266. Springer, Heidelberg (1997)
18. Teske, E.: Speeding up Pollard's rho method for computing discrete logarithms. In: Buhler, J.P. (ed.) ANTS 1998. LNCS, vol. 1423, pp. 541–554. Springer, Heidelberg (1998)
19. Rosini, M.D.: Applications. In: Rosini, M.D. (ed.) Macroscopic Models for Vehicular Flows and Crowd Dynamics: Theory and Applications. UCS, vol. 12, pp. 217–226. Springer, Heidelberg (2013)

A Polynomial-Time Key-Recovery Attack on MQQ Cryptosystems

Jean-Charles Faugère[1,2,3]([✉]), Danilo Gligoroski[4], Ludovic Perret[1,2,3],
Simona Samardjiska[4,5], and Enrico Thomae[6]

[1] INRIA, Paris-Rocquencourt Center, Paris, France
jean-charles.faugere@inria.fr, ludovic.perret@lip6.fr
[2] Sorbonne Universités, UPMC Univ Paris 06, Équipe PolSys,
LIP6, 75005 Paris, France
[3] LIP6, CNRS, UMR 7606, 75005 Paris, France
[4] Department of Telematics, NTNU, Trondheim, Norway
{danilog,simonas}@item.ntnu.no
[5] FCSE, UKIM, Skopje, Macedonia
[6] Operational Services, Frankfurt, Germany
enrico.thomae@rub.de

Abstract. We investigate the security of the family of MQQ public key cryptosystems using multivariate quadratic quasigroups (MQQ). These cryptosystems show especially good performance properties. In particular, the MQQ-SIG signature scheme is the fastest scheme in the ECRYPT benchmarking of cryptographic systems (eBACS). We show that both the signature scheme MQQ-SIG and the encryption scheme MQQ-ENC, although using different types of MQQs, share a common algebraic structure that introduces a weakness in both schemes. We use this weakness to mount a successful polynomial time key-recovery attack that finds an equivalent key using the idea of so-called *good keys*. In the process we need to solve a MinRank problem that, because of the structure, can be solved in polynomial-time assuming some mild algebraic assumptions. We highlight that our theoretical results work in characteristic 2 which is known to be the most difficult case to address in theory for MinRank attacks and also without any restriction on the number of polynomials removed from the public-key. This was not the case for previous MinRank like-attacks against $\mathcal{MQ}$ schemes. From a practical point of view, we are able to break an MQQ-SIG instance of 80 bits security in less than 2 days, and one of the more conservative MQQ-ENC instances of 128 bits security in little bit over 9 days. Altogether, our attack shows that it is very hard to design a secure public key scheme based on an easily invertible MQQ structure.

Keywords: MQ cryptography · MQQ cryptosystems · Equivalent keys · Good keys · MinRank · Gröbner bases

© International Association for Cryptologic Research 2015
J. Katz (Ed.): PKC 2015, LNCS 9020, pp. 150–174, 2015.
DOI: 10.1007/978-3-662-46447-2_7

1   Introduction

Multivariate quadratic ($\mathcal{MQ}$) public key schemes are cryptosystems based (in part) on the NP-hard problem of solving polynomial systems of quadra-tic equations over finite fields, also known as the $\mathcal{MQ}$-problem. Until the mid 2000's, $\mathcal{MQ}$ cryptography was developing very rapidly, producing many interesting and versatile design ideas such as C* [24], HFE [33], SFLASH [12], UOV [26], TTM [29], TTS [42]. However, many of them were soon successfully cryptanalysed, and the biggest surprise was probably the break of SFLASH in 2007 [15], shortly after it was chosen by the NESSIE European Consortium [31] as one of the three recommended public key signature schemes. As a consequence, the confidence in $\mathcal{MQ}$ cryptosystems declined, and so did the research in this area as well.

Now, several years later, it seems that there have emerged new important reasons for renewal of the interest in a new generation of $\mathcal{MQ}$ schemes. In the past two years, the algorithms for solving the Discrete Logarithm (DL) problem underwent an extraordinary development (for instance, but not limited to [1]). This clearly illustrates the risk to not consider alternatives to classical assumptions based on number theory. In parallel, two of the most important standardization bodies in the world, NIST and ETSI have recently started initiatives for developing cryptographic standards not based on number theory, with a particular focus on primitives resistant to quantum algorithms [16,32].

A common characteristic of all $\mathcal{MQ}$ schemes is the construction of the public key as $\mathcal{P} = T \circ \mathcal{F} \circ S$ where $\mathcal{F}$ is some easily invertible quadratic mapping, masked by two bijective affine transformations S and T. A consequence of these construction is that some specific properties of the secret-key can be recovered on the public-key. In particular, one of the most important characteristic of $\mathcal{MQ}$ schemes that allows a successful key-recovery is connected to unexpected high rank defect on the matrices associated to the public-key. The attacks on TTM [11], STS [37,38], Rainbow [7,14], HFE and MultiHFE [5,6,25,27] are all in essence based on the problem of finding a low rank linear combination of matrices, known as MinRank in cryptography [10]. This problem is NP-hard [10] and was used to design a zero-knowledge authentication scheme [13]. Although NP-hard, the instances of MinRank arising from $\mathcal{MQ}$ schemes are often easy, thus providing a powerful tool for finding equivalent keys in canonical form.

1.1   Our Contribution

In this paper, we are concerned with the security analysis of a particular family of $\mathcal{MQ}$ (Multivariate Quadratic) cryptosystems, namely the MQQ schemes proposed in 2008 [21]. In these schemes the secret map $\mathcal{F}$ is derived from multivariate quadratic quasigroups (MQQ), which makes the inversion of $\mathcal{F}$ especially efficient. A message-recovery attack was proposed in [30], and later in [19], it was proven that a direct attack [30] can be done in polynomial-time. In [22], the authors proposed a signature scheme, called MQQ-SIG, based on the same idea and secure against direct attacks, as well as claimed to be CMA secure. They made heavy use of the minus modifier, known from HFE-[33], to repair MQQ.

Finally, in [23] the authors proposed an enhanced variant of the MQQ encryption scheme, called MQQ-ENC. The MQQ-SIG signature scheme is the fastest scheme in signing in the ECRYPT Benchmarking of Cryptographic Systems (eBACS) SUPERCOP [4], and is therefore very appealing for practical use.

We show in this paper that this family of designs has a fundamental weakness which allows us to mount an efficient key-recovery attack on all known constructions based on MQQ. More precisely, we can recover a key, equivalent to the secret-key, by solving simultaneous instances of MinRank (Theorem 3) problems, which due to the structure of the schemes can be solved in polynomial-time. To do so, we first assume that the field is not too big. That is to say, we assume that $q = \mathcal{O}(n)$ which is indeed the case for most of the parameters proposed so far for MQQ cryptosystems. Of independent interest, we show that the simultaneous MinRank problem is equivalent to a rectangular MinRank (Corollary 1) problem. For the complexity of our attack, we summarize the first result below:

Theorem 1. *Let $\omega, 2 \leqslant \omega < 3$ be the linear algebra constant. Let $\mathcal{P} = T \circ \mathcal{F} \circ S$ be the public mapping of MQQ-SIG or MQQ-ENC consisting of $n - r$ polynomials in n variables over $\mathbb{F}_q$ (with $\mathrm{Char}(\mathbb{F}_q) = 2$). $\mathcal{F}$ is a set of quadratic polynomials derived from multivariate quadratic quasigroups (MQQ), while S and T are invertible matrices used to mask the structure of $\mathcal{F}$. Then, the last columns of S and T (up to equivalence) can be recovered in $\mathcal{O}(n^\omega)$. More generally, a key equivalent to the secret-key in MQQ-SIG or MQQ-ENC can be found by solving $n - r$ MinRank instances with $N - r$ matrices from $\mathbb{F}_q^{N \times (N-r)}$ where $N, r + 2 \leqslant N \leqslant n - 1$. If $q = \mathcal{O}(n)$ then each MinRank can be solved in polynomial-time assuming a mild regularity condition on the public matrices. Under this condition and assuming $q = \mathcal{O}(n)$, we can recover a key equivalent to the secret-key in*

$$\mathcal{O}(n^{\omega+3}), \text{ with probability } 1 - 1/q.$$

The genericity assumption required in the previous result is that the rank defect in the skew-symmetric matrices derived from the public polynomials is a not too big constant. We have implemented our attack in practice and verified that this assumption is reasonable. We highlight that our theoretical results work in characteristic 2 which is known to be the most difficult case to address in theory [5,6,25] for MinRank attacks. Also, we emphasize that our attack works without any restriction on the number of polynomials removed from the public-key (the minus modifier). This was not the case for previous MinRank like-attacks against $\mathcal{MQ}$ schemes.

If we relax the condition on the size of q, we can still bound the complexity (although, we require a slightly stronger assumption).

Theorem 2 (informal version of Theorem 5). *Let $\omega, 2 \leqslant \omega < 3$ be the linear algebra constant. Let $\mathcal{P} = T \circ \mathcal{F} \circ S$ be the public mapping of MQQ-SIG or MQQ-ENC consisting of $n - r$ polynomials in n variables over $\mathbb{F}_q$ (with $\mathrm{Char}(\mathbb{F}_q) = 2$). Assuming that the kernels of the skew-symmetric matrices derived from the public-key behave as random subspaces and a genericity* *condition on the MinRank modeling, then we can recover a key, equivalent to the secret-key, in*

$$\mathcal{O}\left(n^{3\,\omega+1}\right), with\ probability\ \left(1-\tfrac{1}{q}\right)\left(1-\tfrac{1}{q^{n-3}}\right). \tag{1}$$

The assumption used in Theorem 2 means that we can restrict our attention to a sub-system of our modeling of the simultaneous MinRank (Theorem 3) such that the sub-system is bi-linear with a block of variables of constant size. If the sub-system behaves as a generic affine bi-linear system, this implies that the maximum degree reached during a Gröbner basis computation is constant [17]. This is what we observed in practice.

Indeed, in order to verify our assumptions and the correctness of the attack, we implemented the attack in Magma (Ver. 2.19-10 [8]). The results obtained confirm the computed theoretical complexity. Using the implementation, we demonstrated that our attack is very efficient by practically breaking instances with recommended parameters. For example, we recovered an equivalent key for MQQ-SIG 160, of claimed security of $\mathcal{O}(2^{80})$, in 2^{48} operations, *i.e.* in less than 2 days. Similarly, for MQQ-ENC 128 defined over $\mathbb{F}_4$ with claimed security of $\mathcal{O}(2^{128})$, we recovered an equivalent key in $2^{50.6}$ operations which took a little bit over 9 days. We also emphasize that the practical results obtained, almost perfectly match the theoretical complexity bound (1) derived in Section 7.1.

Altogether, our attack shows that it is very hard to design a secure scheme based on an easily invertible MQQ structure. It seems that using MQQs successfully in future $\mathcal{MQ}$ designs may require deep insight from quasigroup theory, in order to obtain the necessary security while preserving the attractive performance level.

1.2 Organization of the Paper

The paper is organized as follows. In Sect. 2 we present the necessary preliminaries about $\mathcal{MQ}$ cryptosystems. We also recall the MinRank problem and the known tools for solving it, as well as the concepts of equivalent keys and good keys. In Sect. 3 we describe the cryptosystems from the MQQ family, and in Sect. 4 we uncover the algebraic structure that the two systems, MQQ-SIG and MQQ-ENC share, and that shows the weaknesses of the cryptosystems. Sect. 5 is devoted to the presentation of the main idea behind our key recovery attack on both MQQ-ENC and MQQ-SIG. We further point out the difference in the attack in odd and even characteristic fields, and present the necessary modifications of the attack for even characteristic fields. As a result of the analysis, in Sect. 6 we conclude that the problem of finding good keys can be modeled as a special instance of MinRank for rectangular matrices. The complexity analysis of our attack is given in Sect. 7. We conclude the paper in Sect. 8.

2 Preliminaries

2.1 Basic Notations

Throughout this paper, $\mathbb{F}_q$ will denote the finite field of q elements, $\mathcal{M}_{n\times m}(\mathbb{F}_q)$ will denote the set of $n \times m$ matrices over $\mathbb{F}_q$ and $\mathrm{GL}_n(\mathbb{F}_q)$ will denote the general linear group of degree n over $\mathbb{F}_q$. First, we briefly recall the general principle of $\mathcal{MQ}$ public key cryptosystems. This will allow to fix some notations. The public key of an $\mathcal{MQ}$ cryptosystem is usually given by a multivariate quadratic map $\mathcal{P} : \mathbb{F}_q^n \to \mathbb{F}_q^m$, that is

$$
\mathcal{P}(x_1,\ldots,x_n) := \begin{pmatrix} p_1(x_1,\ldots,x_n) = \displaystyle\sum_{1\leqslant i\leqslant j\leqslant n} \widetilde{\gamma}_{i,j}^{(1)} x_i x_j + \sum_{i=1}^{n} \widetilde{\beta}_i^{(1)} x_i + \widetilde{\alpha}^{(1)} \\ \vdots \\ p_m(x_1,\ldots,x_n) = \displaystyle\sum_{1\leqslant i\leqslant j\leqslant n} \widetilde{\gamma}_{i,j}^{(m)} x_i x_j + \sum_{i=1}^{n} \widetilde{\beta}_i^{(m)} x_i + \widetilde{\alpha}^{(m)} \end{pmatrix}
$$

for some coefficients $\widetilde{\gamma}_{i,j}^{(s)}, \widetilde{\beta}_i^{(s)}$, and $\widetilde{\alpha}^{(s)} \in \mathbb{F}_q$.

In our attack, we will see that w.l.o.g. we can restrict our attention to the homogeneous components of highest degree, i.e. to the quadratic components. Classically, a quadratic form can be written as $p_s(x_1,\ldots,x_n) := \displaystyle\sum_{1\leq i\leq j\leq n} \widetilde{\gamma}_{i,j}^{(s)} x_i x_j = x^{\mathsf{T}}\mathfrak{P}^{(s)}x$, where $x := (x_1,\ldots,x_n)^{\mathsf{T}}$ and $\mathfrak{P}^{(s)}$ is an $n \times n$ matrix describing the degree-2 homogeneous component of p_s. The public key $\mathcal{P}$ is obtained by obfuscating a structured central map $\mathcal{F} : x \in \mathbb{F}_q^n \to (f_1(x),\ldots,f_m(x)) \in \mathbb{F}_q^m$. We denote by $\mathfrak{F}^{(s)}$ an $n \times n$ matrix describing the homogeneous quadratic part of f_s. In order to hide the structured central map, we choose two secret linear[1] transformations $S \in \mathrm{GL}_n(\mathbb{F}_q)$, $T \in \mathrm{GL}_m(\mathbb{F}_q)$ and define the public key as $\mathcal{P} := T \circ \mathcal{F} \circ S$.

Remark 1. It is known that the matrix of a quadratic form is constructed differently depending on the parity of the field characteristic. In odd characteristic, $\mathfrak{P}^{(s)}$ is a symmetric matrix, i.e. $\mathfrak{P}_{i,j}^{(s)} := \widetilde{\gamma}_{i,j}^{(s)}/2$ for $i \neq j$ and $\mathfrak{P}_{i,i}^{(s)} := \widetilde{\gamma}_{i,i}^{(s)}$. Over fields $\mathbb{F}_q$ of characteristic 2, we cannot choose $\mathfrak{P}^{(s)}$ in this manner, since $(\widetilde{\gamma}_{i,j} + \widetilde{\gamma}_{j,i})x_i x_j = 2\widetilde{\gamma}_{i,j}x_i x_j = 0$ for $i \neq j$. Instead, let $\widetilde{\mathfrak{P}}^{(s)}$ be the upper-triangular representation of p_s, i.e. $\widetilde{\mathfrak{P}}_{i,j}^{(s)} = \widetilde{\gamma}_{i,j}^{(s)}$ for $i \leq j$. The symmetric form is obtained by $\mathfrak{P}^{(s)} := \widetilde{\mathfrak{P}}^{(s)} + \widetilde{\mathfrak{P}}^{(s)\mathsf{T}}$. In this case only the upper-triangular part represents the according polynomial, and all elements on the diagonal are zero. This implies that for $x, y \in \mathbb{F}_q^n$ the symmetric bilinear form $x^{\mathsf{T}}\mathfrak{P}^{(s)}y$ is alternating and has even rank.

2.2 The MinRank Problem

The problem of finding a low rank linear combination of matrices is a basic linear algebra problem [10] known as MinRank in cryptography [13]. The MinRank problem over a finite field $\mathbb{F}_q$ is as follows.

MinRank (MR)

---

[1] Note that S and T can actually be chosen to be affine. We restrict ourselves to linear secrets for the sake of simplicity. However, we mention that the attack can be simply adapted to work in the affine case (see [27,34]).

Input: $n, m, r, k \in \mathbb{N}$, where $n < m$ and $M_0, M_1, \ldots, M_k \in \mathcal{M}_{n \times m}(\mathbb{F}_q)$.

Question: Find – if any – a k-tuple $(\lambda_1, \ldots, \lambda_k) \in \mathbb{F}_q^k$ such that:

$$\text{Rank}\left(\sum_{i=1}^{k} \lambda_i M_i - M_0 \right) \leqslant r.$$

In Appendix A, we review some known techniques for solving MinRank.

2.3 Good Keys

Our attack relies on so-called *equivalent keys* introduced by Wolf and Preneel [40,41]. We briefly recall below the concept of equivalent keys, and then present *good keys* which are at the core of our attack.

Let $\mathcal{F} = \{f_1, \ldots, f_m\} \subset \mathbb{F}_q[x_1, \ldots, x_n]^m$. For $k, 1 \leqslant k \leqslant m$, we denote by $I^{(k)} \subseteq \{x_i x_j \mid 1 \leqslant i \leqslant j \leqslant n\}$ a subset of the degree-2 monomials. We define $\mathcal{F}|_I = \{f_1|_{I^{(1)}}, \ldots, f_m|_{I^{(m)}}\}$ where $f_k|_{I^{(k)}} := \sum_{x_i x_j \in I^{(k)}} \gamma_{i,j}^{(k)} x_i x_j$ is the projection of f_k to $I^{(k)}$.

Definition 1. *Let* $(\mathcal{F}, S, T), (\mathcal{F}', S', T') \in \mathbb{F}_q[x_1, \ldots, x_n]^m \times \text{GL}_n(\mathbb{F}_q) \times \text{GL}_m(\mathbb{F}_q)$. *We say that* $(\mathcal{F}, S, T)$ *and* $(\mathcal{F}', S', T')$ *are equivalent keys, denoted by* $(\mathcal{F}, S, T) \simeq (\mathcal{F}', S', T')$, *if and only if* $(T \circ \mathcal{F} \circ S = T' \circ \mathcal{F}' \circ S') \wedge \left(\mathcal{F}|_I = \mathcal{F}'|_I \right)$, *that is,* $\mathcal{F}$ *and* $\mathcal{F}'$ *share the same structure when restricted to a fixed set* $I = \{I^{(1)}, \ldots, I^{(m)}\}$.

Since the relation $\simeq$ given by Definition 1 is an equivalence relation [40], the set of all keys S, T can be partitioned into several equivalence classes. For a large fraction of all equivalence classes, we can find special representatives S' and T' with fixed entries at certain values.

For ease of notation, let $\overline{S} := S^{-1}$ and $\overline{T} := T^{-1}$. Obviously $\mathcal{P} = T \circ \mathcal{F} \circ S$, implies that $\mathcal{F} = \overline{T} \circ \mathcal{P} \circ \overline{S}$. This leads to the equality below on the quadratic forms:

$$\mathfrak{F}^{(k)} = \overline{S}^{\mathsf{T}} \left(\sum_{j=1}^{m} \overline{t}_{k,j} \mathfrak{P}^{(j)} \right) \overline{S}, \ \forall k, 1 \leqslant k \leqslant m. \tag{2}$$

The corresponding system of equations is as follows:

$$\mathfrak{F}_{i,j}^{(k)} = \sum_{x=1}^{m} \sum_{y=1}^{n} \sum_{z=1}^{n} \mathfrak{P}_{y,z}^{(x)} \overline{t}_{k,x} \overline{s}_{y,i} \overline{s}_{z,j}. \tag{3}$$

Due to the structure of the secret mapping $\mathfrak{F}$, we know that certain coefficients in $\mathfrak{F}^{(i)}$ are systematically zero. This allows then to obtain cubic equations on the components of $\overline{S}$ and $\overline{T}$. In general, the system of equations has too many variables for being solved efficiently in this form.

The concept of equivalent keys allows to reduce the number of variables by introducing two linear maps $(\Sigma, \Omega) \in \text{GL}_m(\mathbb{F}_q) \times \text{GL}_n(\mathbb{F}_q)$ such that $\mathcal{P} = T \circ$

$\Sigma^{-1} \circ \Sigma \circ \mathcal{F} \circ \Omega \circ \Omega^{-1} \circ S$. If $\mathcal{F}$ and $\mathcal{F}' := \Sigma \circ \mathcal{F} \circ \Omega$ share the same structure (cf. Def. 1), then $T' := T\Sigma^{-1}$ and $S' = \Omega^{-1}S$ will be equivalent keys. Depending on Σ and Ω we can define a canonical form of the secret-keys and typically fix large parts of T and S (see [39–41]). We note that it may happen that such a canonical key does not exist. For example, the Unbalanced Oil and Vinegar Scheme has such an equivalent key with probability roughly $1 - 1/q$ [36].

The idea of *good keys* [37] is to further decrease the number of unknowns or unfixed coefficients in (S', T'). Here, we do not aim to preserve all the zero coefficients of $\mathcal{F}$, but just some of them. This way, we have more freedom to choose Σ and Ω and thus further reduce the number of variables. On the other hand, we can generate less equations. Finding the best trade-off is not obvious and strongly depends on the underlying structure of $\mathcal{F}$. Formally, we define good keys through the following definition.

Definition 2 ([37]).   *Let* $(\mathcal{F}, S, T), (\mathcal{F}', S', T')$ *be in* $\mathbb{F}_q[x_1, \ldots, x_n]^m \times \mathrm{GL}_n(\mathbb{F}_q) \times \mathrm{GL}_m(\mathbb{F}_q)$. *Let* $I = \{I^{(1)}, \ldots, I^{(m)}\}$ *and* $J = \{J^{(1)}, \ldots, J^{(m)}\}$ *such that* $J^{(k)} \subsetneq I^{(k)}$ *for all* $k, 1 \leqslant k \leqslant m$ *with at least one* $J^{(k)} \neq \emptyset$. *We shall say that* $(\mathcal{F}', S', T') \in \mathbb{F}_q[x_1, \ldots, x_n]^m \times \mathrm{GL}_n(\mathbb{F}_q) \times \mathrm{GL}_m(\mathbb{F}_q)$ *is a* good key *for* $(\mathcal{F}, S, T)$ *if and only if:*

$$\left(T \circ \mathcal{F} \circ S = T' \circ \mathcal{F}' \circ S'\right) \wedge \left(\mathcal{F}|_J = \mathcal{F}'|_J\right).$$

3   MQQ Cryptosystems

The Multivariate Quadratic Quasigroup (MQQ) scheme was proposed in 2008 [21]. The underlying idea is to use bijective multivariate quadratic maps obtained through the existence of left and right inverses in some quasigroup, in order to build the trapdoor map $\mathcal{F}$.

Definition 3. *Let Q be a set and* $\mathfrak{q} : Q \times Q \to Q$ *be a binary operation on Q. We call $(Q, \mathfrak{q})$ a left (resp. right) quasigroup if*

$$\forall \overline{u}, \overline{v} \in Q, \exists! \, \overline{x}, \overline{y} \in Q : \mathfrak{q}(\overline{u}, \overline{x}) = \overline{v} \quad (resp. \, \mathfrak{q}(\overline{y}, \overline{u}) = \overline{v}).$$

If $(Q, \mathfrak{q})$ is both left and right quasigroup, then we simply call it a quasigroup.

Clearly, $\mathfrak{q}$ defines a bijective map if we fix some $\overline{u} \in Q$. Hence, we can define two inverse operations $\mathfrak{q}_\backslash(\overline{u}, \overline{v}) = \overline{x}$ and $\mathfrak{q}_/(\overline{v}, \overline{u}) = \overline{y}$, called left and right parastrophe, respectively. A *multivariate quadratic quasigroup* (MQQ) is a special quasigroup, that can be described through a multivariate quadratic map over some finite field $\mathbb{F}_q$. In [21], $\mathbb{F}_2$ is used to built such MQQs of order 2^d, with parameter $d = 5$ and bilinear maps $\mathfrak{q}$. The central map $\mathcal{F}$ is constructed using a so called quasigroup string transformation of the MQQs, in order to scale the number of variables.

Definition 4. *Let* $Q := \mathbb{F}_q^d$ *and* $\mathfrak{q}_i : Q \times Q \to Q$ *be such that* $(Q, \mathfrak{q}_i)$ *forms a quasigroup for $1 \leqslant i \leqslant \ell$ and some parameter ℓ which allows to scale the scheme*

*later on. We fix some element $\overline{u} \in Q$, call it leader and define $\mathcal{F} : \mathbb{F}_q^{\ell d} \to \mathbb{F}_q^{\ell d}$
through*

$$
\begin{aligned}
(f_1, & \quad \ldots, f_d \ ) := \mathfrak{q}_1(\overline{u}, \overline{x}_1), \\
(f_{d+1}, & \quad \ldots, f_{2d}) := \mathfrak{q}_2(\overline{x}_1, \overline{x}_2), \\
& \quad \vdots \qquad\qquad \vdots \\
(f_{(\ell-1)d+1}, & \ \ldots, f_{\ell d}) := \mathfrak{q}_\ell(\overline{x}_{\ell-1}, \overline{x}_\ell).
\end{aligned}
$$

In order to find pre-images of $\mathcal{F}$, we use the corresponding left-parastrophe operations of $\mathfrak{q}_1, \ldots, \mathfrak{q}_\ell$. In addition, the authors of [21] used the Dobbertin bijection to deal with the linear part of $\mathcal{F}$ that comes from $\mathfrak{q}_1(\overline{u}, \overline{x}_1)$ for some fixed $\overline{u} \in Q$ and the fact that they chose bilinear maps $\mathfrak{q}_i$.

Unfortunately, this trapdoor provided a lot of structure so the MQQ encryption scheme was broken by a direct attack on the public key [30]. Faugère *et al.* showed in [19] that the degree of regularity of the equations generated by the pubic key can be bounded from above by a small constant. Thus, the complexity of a direct Gröbner basis attack is polynomial.

3.1 MQQ-SIG Signature Scheme

Recently, in [22] a signature scheme was proposed, called MQQ-SIG, which is based on the same idea but makes heavy use of the minus modifier, known from HFE-[33]. MQQ-SIG does not use the Dobbertin bijection and the construction of the quasigroup is different and given by the map $\mathfrak{q} : \mathbb{F}_2^d \times \mathbb{F}_2^d \to \mathbb{F}_2^d$:

$$
\mathfrak{q}(\overline{x}, \overline{y}) := B \cdot (I + A_0) \cdot B_2 \cdot \overline{y} + B \cdot B_1 \cdot \overline{x} + \overline{c}, \tag{4}
$$

where $\overline{x} := (x_1, x_2, \ldots, x_d)^\mathsf{T}, \overline{y} := (y_1, y_2, \ldots, y_d)^\mathsf{T}, \overline{c} \in \mathbb{F}_2^d$ and $B_1, B_2, B \in \mathrm{GL}_d(\mathbb{F}_2)$ are arbitrary. $A_0 = [\, 0 \quad U_1 \cdot B_1 \cdot \overline{x} \quad U_2 \cdot B_1 \cdot \overline{x} \quad \ldots \quad U_{d-1} \cdot B_1 \cdot \overline{x} \,]$, is a $d \times d$ block matrix where $U_i, i \in \{1, \ldots d-1\}$ are upper triangular matrices over $\mathbb{F}_2$ having all elements 0 except the elements in the rows from $\{1, \ldots, i\}$ that are strictly above the main diagonal.

A key feature of the MQQ-SIG scheme is the application of the minus modifier. In particular, $n/2$ of the equations are removed in the public key $\mathcal{P}$, in order to prevent direct algebraic and MinRank attacks. Therefore, we obtain a signature expansion of factor two for messages of length $n/2$. Further the public key is rather large, since it is defined over $\mathbb{F}_2$. In order to reduce the size of the public key the designers decided to split the message in two and sign it using the same trapdoor function twice. The proposed parameters are $n \in \{160, 192, 224, 256\}$ for the trapdoor function for security levels of $2^{80}, 2^{96}, 2^{112}, 2^{128}$ binary operations respectively, and $d = 8$ for the order 2^d of the quasigroup.

3.2 MQQ-ENC Encryption Scheme

The encryption scheme MQQ-ENC was recently proposed in [23], and it follows the same line of design as its predecessors. Again, the internal mapping $\mathcal{F}$ is a quasigroups string transformation and the affine secrets S and T are built from two circulant matrices. The minus modifier is used again, but since it is an encryption scheme, only a small fixed number r of polynomials is removed. This destroys the bijectivity of $\mathcal{P}$, so to enable correct decryption a universal hash function is used, and decryption is performed by going through all possible pre-images of $\mathcal{P}$. Compared to its predecessors, MQQ-ENC can be defined over any small field $\mathbb{F}_{p^k}$ and instead of bilinear quasigroups, the authors used more general left quasigroups, *i.e.* mappings that are bijections only in the second variable.

Lemma 1 ([35]). *Let p be prime and $k > 0$ be an integer. For all $s, 1 \leqslant s \leqslant d$, we define the component $\mathfrak{q}_s \in \mathbb{F}_{p^k}[x_1, \ldots, x_d, y_1, \ldots, y_d]$ by:*

$$\mathfrak{q}_s(x_1, \ldots, x_d, y_1, \ldots, y_d) := p_s(y_s) + \sum_{1 \leqslant i, j \leqslant d} \alpha_{i,j}^{(s)} x_i x_j + \sum_{s < i, j \leqslant d} \beta_{i,j}^{(s)} y_i y_j$$

$$+ \sum_{1 \leqslant i \leqslant d, s < j \leqslant d} \gamma_{i,j}^{(s)} x_i y_j + \sum_{1 \leqslant i \leqslant d} \delta_i^{(s)} x_i + \sum_{s < i \leqslant d} \epsilon_i^{(s)} y_i + \eta^{(s)}, \quad (5)$$

where $p_s(y_s) \in \{a^{(s)} y_s, a^{(s)} y_s^2\}$ for even p, and $p_s(y_s) = a^{(s)} y_s$ for odd p, for some $a^{(s)} \neq 0$. The function $\mathfrak{q} = (\mathfrak{q}_1, \mathfrak{q}_2, \ldots, \mathfrak{q}_d) : \mathbb{F}_{p^k}^{2d} \to \mathbb{F}_{p^k}^d$, as defined in (5), defines a left multivariate quadratic quasigroup (LMQQ) $(\mathbb{F}_{p^k}^d, \mathfrak{q})$ of order p^{kd}.

Lemma 2. *Let $(\mathbb{F}_{p^k}^d, \mathfrak{q})$ be an LMQQ as defined by Lemma 1. Let D and D_y be $d \times d$ nonsingular matrices and $\bar{c}, \bar{c}_y$ vectors of dimension d over $\mathbb{F}_{p^k}$. Then $\hat{\mathfrak{q}}(\bar{x}, \bar{y}) := D \cdot \mathfrak{q}(\bar{x}, D_y \cdot \bar{y} + \bar{c}_y) + \bar{c}$ is again an LMQQ of order p^{kd}. We say that $\hat{\mathfrak{q}}$ is linearly isotopic to $\mathfrak{q}$.*

The recommended values for the parameters n, k, r, d, p for a security level of 2^{128} are $d = 8$, $p = 2$ and $(n, k, r) \in \{(256, 1, 8), (128, 2, 4), (64, 4, 2), (32, 8, 1)\}$.

4   The Algebraic Structure of MQQ-ENC and MQQ-SIG

We explain the algebraic structure that both MQQ-ENC and MQQ-SIG share. This is the weaknesses that we are going to exploit to mount our attack.

First of all, we note that the trapdoor of MQQ-SIG can be seen as a very special case of MQQ-ENC when defined over $\mathbb{F}_2$. Indeed, the quasigroup string transformation only makes use of the left translation (the bijection in the second variable) of a quasigroup $\mathfrak{q}$, *i.e.* the additional bijectivity in the first variable is unnecessary. Thus, we can regard the MQQs used in MQQ-SIG as left quasigroups without loss of generality. Even more, it can be shown (cf. Proposition 1) that the MQQs used in MQQ-SIG are linearly isotopic to quasigroups that can be represented in the form given in Lemma 1, with some additional constraints on the coefficients.

Proposition 1 ([35]). *Let $(\mathbb{F}_2^d, \hat{\mathfrak{q}})$ be a quasigroup used in MQQ-SIG. Then $\hat{\mathfrak{q}}$ can be represented by $\hat{\mathfrak{q}}(\overline{x}, \overline{y}) = B \cdot \mathfrak{q}(B_1 \cdot \overline{x}, B_2 \cdot \overline{y}) + \overline{c}$ for some invertible matrices B, B_1, B_2, a vector $\overline{c}$, and $\mathfrak{q} = (\mathfrak{q}_1, \mathfrak{q}_2, \dots, \mathfrak{q}_d)$ with*

$$\mathfrak{q}_s(\overline{x}, \overline{y}) = x_s + y_s + \sum_{s < i,j \leqslant d} \gamma_{i,j}^{(s)} x_i y_j + \sum_{s < i \leqslant d} \delta_i^{(s)} x_i + \sum_{s < i \leqslant d} \epsilon_i^{(s)} y_i + \eta^{(s)},$$

for all $1 \leq s \leq d$ and coefficients $\gamma_{i,j}^{(s)}, \delta_i^{(s)}, \epsilon_i^{(s)}, \eta^{(s)} \in \mathbb{F}_{p^k}$.

In the sequel, we will investigate the more general trapdoor of MQQ-ENC, since all the properties of MQQ-ENC apply to MQQ-SIG as well. In order to avoid redundancy and to provide a clear and simple algebraic description, we exploit the following simplification. In the central map $\mathcal{F}$ the authors used LMQQs constructed through Lemma 2, and not directly LMQQs from Lemma 1. This was done to mask the otherwise triangular structure of the LMQQs from Lemma 1. However, the linear isotopy, can actually be absorbed by S and T. First of all, as we are only considering quadratic coefficients later on, we can safely ignore $\overline{c}_y$ and $\overline{c}$. Further, the linear transformation D can be absorbed by T, *i.e.* instead of using $\hat{\mathfrak{q}}$ and the original T, we work with $\mathfrak{q}$ and $T \cdot (I_{\frac{n}{d}} \otimes D)$, with $\otimes$ the matrix tensor product of the $\frac{n}{d}$ dimensional identity matrix and D. The same holds for the transformation of variables S. Instead of working with $\mathfrak{q}$ and the original transformation S, we work with $(I_{\frac{n}{d}} \otimes D_y^{-1}) \cdot S$ and $\tilde{\mathfrak{q}}(\overline{x}_1, \overline{x}_2) := \mathfrak{q}(D_y^{-1} \overline{x}_1, \overline{x}_2)$. As there is no structure hidden in the first component of $\mathfrak{q}$, all the systematical zeros in $\tilde{\mathfrak{q}}$ and $\mathfrak{q}$ equal and thus we can assume a central map $\mathcal{F}$ with $\mathfrak{q}$ according to Lemma 1. Writing the quadratic part of $\mathfrak{q}_s = x^\mathsf{T} \mathfrak{Q}^{(s)} x$ in its quadratic form with $x = (x_1, \dots, x_d, y_1, \dots, y_d)^\mathsf{T}$, we can illustrate the matrix $\mathfrak{Q}^{(s)}$ by Figure 1.

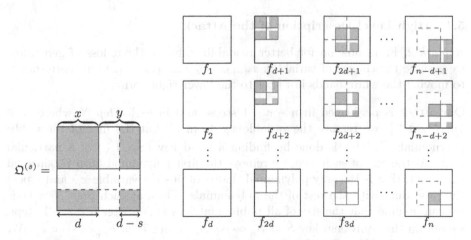

Fig. 1. The quadratic form $\mathfrak{Q}^{(s)}$ of $\mathfrak{q}_s$. Gray parts denote arbitrary values, white parts denote systematic zeros.

Fig. 2. Matrices of the quadratic forms of the central map $\mathcal{F}$ of MQQ-ENC. Gray parts denote some arbitrary values, whereas white parts denote systematic zeros.

Note that both in odd and even characteristic, the coefficient of y_s^2 does not occur in $\mathfrak{Q}^{(s)}$. In odd characteristic, $p_s(y_s) = a^{(s)} y_s$, *i.e.* it is always linear. For characteristic 2, we have either $p_s(y_s) = a^{(s)} y_s$ or $p_s(y_s) = a^{(s)} y_s^2$, but nevertheless, it is again always linear, and the representation of $\mathfrak{Q}^{(s)}$ has systematic zeros on the main diagonal. The central polynomials f_s (Definition 4), with $s, 1 \leqslant s \leqslant m$ are illustrated in Figure 2.

Another simplification can be made regarding the secret affine transformations S and T. First of all, we neglect linear terms, as we do not use them and they also never interfere with the coefficients of quadratic monomials. Thus we can assume S and T to be linear transformations. Note that using coefficients of linear terms could only speed up the attack, as long as they are not all chosen uniformly at random. Second, in [23] as well as in [22], the authors did not choose S and T purely at random but as a combination of two circulant matrices. This structure was meant to reduce the key size and speed up the decryption process. We note that we do not use this special structure to speed up our attack. As we are recovering $(I_{\frac{n}{d}} \otimes D_y^{-1}) \cdot S$ instead of S and $T \cdot (I_{\frac{n}{d}} \otimes D)$ instead of T, for some randomly chosen D and D_y, we lose most of the structure anyway. Therefore we assume to recover some random matrices in the sequel. Note that this gives a worst case complexity of our attack.

5 Key-Recovery Attack

In this part, we present an efficient algebraic key-recovery attack on MQQ-ENC and MQQ-SIG. To do so, we combine a MinRank attack and good keys in order to recover the columns of S and T.

5.1 High Level Description of the Attack

Remark 2. From now on for better readability, but without loss of generality, we assume the change of variables: $x_{n-id+j} \mapsto x_{n-id+d-j+1}$. (This corresponds to moving the white bands in Fig. 1 to the lower right corner.)

Our attack is performed in $n - r - 1$ steps, and in each *Step N*, where $N \in \{n, \ldots r + 2\}$, we remove the variable x_N from all but the first of the public polynomials $\mathcal{P}$. This is done by finding a good key $(\overline{S}'_N, \overline{T}'_N)$ of a particular form. At the end of each step, we remove the first polynomial form $\mathcal{P}$, since, at this point, that is the only polynomial that contains the variable x_N and repeat the procedure with the rest of the polynomials. Thus, at each *Step N*, w.l.o.g. we can assume that the size of all public matrices is N. After $n - r - 1$ steps, we obtain the equivalent key $\overline{S}' = \overline{S}'_n \circ \cdots \circ \overline{S}'_{r+2}$ and $\overline{T}' = \overline{T}'_{r+2} \circ \cdots \circ \overline{T}'_n$. We can summarize the steps of our attack in Alg. 1.

Algorithm 1 High Level Description of the Key-Recovery Attack

---

Input: $n - r$ public polynomials $\mathcal{P}$ in n variables.

  for $N := n$ down to $r + 2$ do

    Consider that all public polynomials involve $\leqslant N$ variables.

  Step N:

      Find a good key $(\overline{S}'_N, \overline{T}'_N)$.

      Transform the public key as $\mathcal{P} \leftarrow \overline{T}'_N \circ \mathcal{P} \circ \overline{S}'_N$,

      and if $N < n$ remove the first polynomial from $\mathcal{P}$.

  end for;

Output: The equivalent key $\overline{S}' = \overline{S}'_n \circ \cdots \circ \overline{S}'_{r+2}$ and $\overline{T}' = \overline{T}'_{r+2} \circ \cdots \circ \overline{T}'_n$.

5.2   Detailed Description of the Attack

We describe in this part the steps performed in Alg. 1. We consider first the case $N = n$ which is a bit different from the others steps.

Step $n = N$. How to recover a linear component of the secret-key. Let $\mathcal{P}$ be the $n - r$ public polynomials in n variables of an MQQ scheme. From now on, we denote by $\mathfrak{P}^{(1)}, \ldots, \mathfrak{P}^{(n-r)}$ the corresponding public matrices. As explained, the public-key is constructed as $\mathcal{P} = T \circ \mathcal{F} \circ S$ where $\mathcal{F}$ is a set of quadratic polynomials constructed as in Sect. 3 and S and T are two bijective linear maps used to mask the structure of $\mathcal{P}$. We denote by $\mathfrak{F}^{(1)}, \ldots, \mathfrak{F}^{(n)}$ the quadratic forms of $\mathcal{F}$.

We explain how to recover one column of the secret transformation S using good keys. This corresponds to the first step performed in Alg. 1 and will allow to remove the variable x_n. Recall from Subsect. 2.3 that we are looking for two linear maps $(\Sigma, \Omega) \in \mathrm{GL}_m(\mathbb{F}_q) \times \mathrm{GL}_n(\mathbb{F}_q)$ such that

$$\mathcal{P} = T \circ \Sigma^{-1} \circ \Sigma \circ \mathcal{F} \circ \Omega \circ \Omega^{-1} \circ S.$$

and $\mathcal{F}' := \Sigma \circ \mathcal{F} \circ \Omega$ preserves some of the structure of $\mathcal{F}$ (cf. Def. 2). Then, $T' := T\Sigma^{-1}$ and $S' = \Omega^{-1}S$ will be good keys.

A crucial observation for MQQ-ENC is that the central polynomials f_i, do not contain the monomials $x_n x_i$ for any $i, 1 \leqslant i < n$. This means that we preserve some structure even if we choose $\Sigma = T$ and thus a good key $T' = I$. In order to preserve the corresponding systematic zero coefficients, Ω is allowed to map every variable to every variable, except x_n. We can then choose the good key S', or more precisely $\overline{S}' := S'^{-1} = \overline{S}\Omega$, to be of the form given in Figure 3.

Obviously, a good key $\overline{S}'$ – according to Figure 3 – almost always exists. We can choose the first $n - 1$ columns of Ω equal to the first $n - 1$ columns of S. However, there is a small probability for Ω to not be invertible, in which case, a good key does not exist.

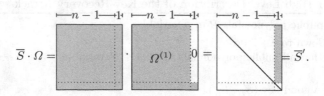

Fig. 3. Unique transformation Ω to obtain the good key $\overline{S}'$

Lemma 3. *If $\overline{S}_{n,n} = 0$, then a good key $\overline{S}'$ as given in Figure 3 does not exist.*

Proof. Due to the structure of Ω in Figure 3, we have $\overline{S}_{n,n}\Omega_{n,n} = \overline{S}'_{n,n}$. Thus, $\overline{S}_{n,n} = 0$ implies that $\overline{S}'_{n,n} = 0$ and $\overline{S}'$ can not be invertible.   □

Remark 3. To guarantee that a good key as in Figure 3 exists with high probability, we can randomize the public quadratic forms $\mathfrak{P}^{(1)}, \ldots, \mathfrak{P}^{(m)}$ with a random invertible matrix $S_{rand} \in \mathrm{GL}_n(\mathbb{F}_q)$. That is, we construct a new equivalent set of public polynomials $\mathfrak{P}^{(i)}_{rand}$:

$$\mathfrak{P}^{(i)}_{rand} := S_{rand}^{\mathsf{T}}\mathfrak{P}^{(i)}S_{rand} = (SS_{rand})^{\mathsf{T}}\left(\sum_{j=1}^{n} t_{i,j}\mathfrak{F}^{(j)}\right)SS_{rand}.$$

Since $S_{\ell,\ell} = 0$ holds with probability $1/q$, the average number of randomizations to obtain a nonzero entry at position (ℓ, ℓ) is $q/(q-1)$. From now on, we will always assume that – up to randomization – good keys as in Figure 3 exist.

Using a good key $\overline{T}' = I$ and $\overline{S}'$ as in Figure 3, the algebraic system (3) can be rewritten as:

$$\mathfrak{F}'^{(k)}_{i,j} = \sum_{y=1}^{n}\sum_{z=1}^{n}\mathfrak{P}^{(k)}_{y,z}\overline{s}'_{y,i}\overline{s}'_{z,j}.$$

We constructed $\mathcal{F}' := \Sigma \circ \mathcal{F} \circ \Omega$ such that the monomial $x_n x_i$ does not appear for any $i, 1 \leqslant i < n$. This yields $\mathfrak{F}'^{(k)}_{n,j} = 0$, for all $k, 1 \leqslant k \leqslant m$, and $j, 1 \leqslant j < n$. Also, for all $j \neq n$, we have that $\overline{s}'_{z,j} = 0$ for $z \neq j$ and $\overline{s}'_{j,j} = 1$ due to the structure of $\overline{S}'$. This yields a system of $m(n-1)$ linear equations in $(n-1)$ variables (since $\overline{s}'_{n,n} = 1$), given by

$$\sum_{y=1}^{n}\mathfrak{P}^{(k)}_{y,j}\overline{s}'_{y,n} = 0, \text{ for all } k, 1 \leqslant k \leqslant m, \text{ and } j, 1 \leqslant j < n.$$

After solving the system, we obtain the good key S'. We can then transform the public polynomials $\mathcal{P}$ with the change of variables $\overline{S}'x$, i.e.:

$$\mathcal{P} \circ \overline{S}' = T \circ \Sigma^{-1} \circ \Sigma \circ \mathcal{F} \circ \Omega \circ \Omega^{-1} \circ S \circ \overline{S}' = \mathcal{F}'.$$

From the previous discussion, the transformed public polynomials $\mathcal{P} \circ \overline{S}'$ do not contain the variable x_n in any of the quadratic terms.

Remark 4. To ease the notation, we continue to denote the obtained transformed polynomials and their matrix representations as before (we regard $\mathcal{P} \circ \overline{S}'$ as being the public $\mathcal{P}$). Since we removed the variable x_n, we can consider that now the dimension of the public matrices $\mathfrak{P}^{(i)}$ is $n-1$. We explain now how to remove the variables $x_{n-1}, x_{n-2} \ldots$ down to x_{r+2}.

Step $N \in \{n-1, \ldots, r+2\}$ – Using MinRank to recover the entire secret key. We assume that the dimension of all public matrices $\mathfrak{P}^{(i)}$ is $N \in \{n-1, \ldots, r+2\}$. Observe that the variable x_N occurs in at most one polynomial of the central map $\mathcal{F}$, namely f_N (cf. Figure 2). This suggests to find a linear combination of two public polynomials, w.l.o.g. p_1 and p_k, with $k, 1 < k \leqslant m$ such that x_N no longer occurs, so we want to find $\lambda \in \mathbb{F}_q$ such that:

$$\mathfrak{P}^{(k)} + \lambda \mathfrak{P}^{(1)} = S^\mathsf{T} \left(\sum_{j=1}^{N-1} (t_{k,j} + \lambda t_{k,j}) \mathfrak{F}^{(j)} \right) S. \qquad (6)$$

To recover such linear combination, we exploit the fact that the rank is invariant under a bijective linear transformation of variables, i.e. for all k, $\mathrm{Rank}(\mathfrak{P}^{(k)}) = \mathrm{Rank}(S^\mathsf{T} \mathfrak{P}^{(k)} S)$. Thus, we can use the rank as distinguisher to recover parts of $\overline{T}$. More precisely, we need to solve the following MinRank instance:

$$\text{Find } \lambda \in \mathbb{F}_q \text{ such that } \mathrm{Rank}\left(\mathfrak{P}^{(k)} + \lambda \mathfrak{P}^{(1)}\right) < N. \qquad (7)$$

The good key $(\overline{S}'_N, \overline{T}'_N)$ given in Fig. 4 is a solution of (7). Indeed, using the two public polynomials $\mathfrak{P}^{(1)}, \mathfrak{P}^{(k)}$ and thanks to (3), we obtain the following system of $N-1$ quadratic equations in $N-1$ variables:

$$\mathfrak{F}'^{(k)}_{i,j} = \sum_{y=1}^{N} \sum_{z=1}^{N} \left(\mathfrak{P}^{(k)}_{y,z} + \lambda \mathfrak{P}^{(1)}_{y,z}\right) \overline{s}'_{y,i} \overline{s}'_{z,j}.$$

By construction, $\mathfrak{F}'^{(k)}_{N,j} = 0$ for all $j, 1 \leqslant j < N$. Also, for all $j < N$ and $z \neq j$ we have that $\overline{s}'_{z,j} = 0$ and $\overline{s}'_{j,j} = 1$. This gives

$$\sum_{y=1}^{N} \left(\mathfrak{P}^{(k)}_{y,j} + \lambda \mathfrak{P}^{(1)}_{y,j}\right) \overline{s}'_{y,N} = 0, \text{ for all } j, \ 1 \leqslant j < n. \qquad (8)$$

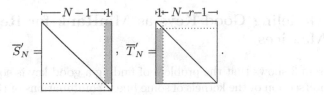

Fig. 4. The good key $(\overline{S}'_N, \overline{T}'_N)$

Applying the same reasoning for all of the public matrices $\mathfrak{P}^{(k)}$, $1 < k \leqslant N-r+1$ we obtain the good key $(\overline{S}'_N, \overline{T}'_N)$. The correctness of the procedure follows from the next theorem.

Theorem 3. *Let N be the number of variables in the $N - r + 1$ public polynomials of MQQ-ENC (or MQQ-SIG) during step $N \in \{n - 1, \ldots, r + 2\}$. Let $\overline{s}' = (\overline{s}'_{1,N}, \overline{s}'_{2,N}, \ldots, \overline{s}'_{N-1,N}, 1)$ and $\overline{t}' = (1, \overline{t}'_{2,1}, \overline{t}'_{3,1}, \ldots, \overline{t}'_{N-r+1,1})$ be unknown vectors. Thus, it holds that $(\overline{s}'_0, \overline{t}'_0)$ is a solution of:*

$$\overline{s}' \left(\mathfrak{P}^{(k)} + \overline{t}'_{k,1} \mathfrak{P}^{(1)} \right) = \mathbf{0}_{1 \times N}, \quad \forall k, 1 < k \leqslant N - r + 1 \tag{9}$$

if and only if $(\overline{S}'_N, \overline{T}'_N)$ is a good key for MQQ-ENC (respectively MQQ-SIG), where $\overline{S}'_N$ is obtained from the identity matrix I_N by replacing the last column with $\overline{s}'_0$, and $\overline{T}'_N$ is obtained from I_N by replacing the first column with $\overline{t}'_0$.

Proof. From (2), we have that:

$$\mathfrak{F}'^{(k)} = \overline{S}'^{\mathsf{T}}_N \left(\mathfrak{P}^{(k)} + \overline{t}'_{k,1} \mathfrak{P}^{(1)} \right) \overline{S}'_N, \quad \forall k, 1 < k \leqslant N - r + 1, \text{ or equivalently :}$$

$$\mathfrak{F}'^{(k)}_{i,j} = \sum_{y=1}^{N} \sum_{z=1}^{N} \left(\mathfrak{P}^{(k)}_{y,z} + \overline{t}'_{k,1} \mathfrak{P}^{(1)}_{y,z} \right) \overline{s}'_{y,i} \overline{s}'_{z,j}, \forall 1 < k \leqslant N - r + 1.$$

Thus, if $(\overline{S}'_N, \overline{T}'_N)$ is a good key, then $\mathfrak{F}'^{(k)}_{i,N} = 0$ (or equivalently $\mathfrak{F}'^{(k)}_{N,i} = 0$) for every $1 \leqslant i < N$. By construction, for every $1 \leqslant i < N$, $\overline{s}'_{y,i} = 0$, for all $y \neq i$, and $\overline{s}'_{i,i} = 1$. Hence, $(\overline{S}'_N, \overline{T}'_N)$ is a good key if and only if for every i, k, s.t. $1 \leqslant i < N$ and $1 < k \leqslant N - r + 1$ it holds that:

$$\sum_{z=1}^{N} \left(\mathfrak{P}^{(k)}_{i,z} + \overline{t}'_{k,1} \mathfrak{P}^{(1)}_{i,z} \right) \overline{s}'_{z,N} = 0.$$

The last system is equivalent to (9), so the claim follows.   □

Remark 5. Note that Theorem 3 can be applied to *Step n* as well. In this case it is known that $\overline{t}'_{k,1} = 0$, so instead of a system of quadratic equations we obtain a system of linear equations as explained in the previous part. So, *Step $n = N$* is actually just an easier sub-case of the others steps.

6   Modeling Good Keys as MinRank for Rectangular Matrices

Theorem 3 shows that the problem of finding a good key is equivalent to finding the intersection of the kernels of some linear combinations of the public matrices. This can be nicely modeled as a special instance of the MinRank problem for rectangular matrices.

Corollary 1. *Let* N, $\bar{s}'$ *and* $\bar{t}'$ *be as in Theorem 3. Let*

$$\mathfrak{P} = [\mathfrak{P}^{(2)}|\mathfrak{P}^{(3)}|\ldots|\mathfrak{P}^{(N-r+1)}]_{N \times N(N-r)}, \quad \mathfrak{P}_i = [\mathbf{0}|\ldots|\mathbf{0}|\mathfrak{P}^{(1)}|\mathbf{0}|\ldots|\mathbf{0}]_{N \times N(N-r)}$$

be block matrices, where $\mathfrak{P}^{(1)}$ *is the i-th block in* $\mathfrak{P}_i$. *It holds that finding a good key* $(\overline{S}'_N, \overline{T}'_N)$ *of the form given in Theorem 3 for* MQQ-ENC *(or* MQQ-SIG*) is equivalent to solving the MinRank instance defined below:*

$$\text{Find } \bar{t}'_{2,1}, \ldots, \bar{t}'_{N-r+1,1} \in \mathbb{F}_q \ \text{ s.t. } \ \text{Rank}\left(\mathfrak{P} + \sum_{k=2}^{N-r+1} \bar{t}'_{k,1}\mathfrak{P}_k\right) < N. \quad (10)$$

Proof. Using the Kipnis-Shamir modeling, the MinRank instance (10) can be expressed exactly as the system (9). The claim follows from Theorem 3.   □

In Alg. 2, we summarize our key-recovery attack on MQQ-ENC and MQQ-SIG based on the results from Theorem 3, Remark 5 and Corollary 1.

Algorithm 2 Key Recovery

Input: $n - r$ public polynomials $\mathcal{P}$ in n variables.

for $N := n$ down to $r + 2$ do

Consider the dimension of all public matrices $\mathfrak{P}^{(i)}$ to be N.

If $N = n$, set $b = 0$, otherwise set $b = 1$.

Step *Rectangular MinRank*(N):

Let $\bar{s}' = (\bar{s}'_{1,N}, \bar{s}'_{2,N}, \ldots, \bar{s}'_{N-1,N}, 1)$ and $\bar{t}' = (\bar{t}'_{2,1}, \bar{t}'_{3,1}, \ldots, \bar{t}'_{N-r+b,1})$

be unknown vectors.

Find a good key $(\overline{S}'_N, \overline{T}'_N)$ by solving the system (9) in $(\bar{s}', \bar{t}')$:

$$\bar{s}'\left(\mathfrak{P} + \sum_{k=2}^{N-r+b} \bar{t}'_{k,1}\mathfrak{P}_k\right) = \mathbf{0}_{1 \times N(N-r)}, \text{where if } b = 0, \text{ then } \bar{t}' = (0, 0, \ldots, 0);$$

for $\mathfrak{P} = [\mathfrak{P}^{(2)}|\mathfrak{P}^{(3)}|\ldots|\mathfrak{P}^{(N-r+1)}]_{1 \times N(N-r)}$ and

$\mathfrak{P}_i = [\mathbf{0}|\ldots|\mathbf{0}|\mathfrak{P}^{(1)}|\mathbf{0}|\ldots|\mathbf{0}]_{1 \times N(N-r)}$ with $\mathfrak{P}^{(1)}$ being the i-th block in $\mathfrak{P}_i$.

Transform the public key: $\mathcal{P} \leftarrow \overline{T}'_N \circ \mathcal{P} \circ \overline{S}'_N$,

If $b = 1$ remove the first polynomial from $\mathcal{P}$ ($\mathcal{P}$ now contains $N - r$ polynomials).

end for;

Output: The equivalent keys $\overline{S}' = \overline{S}'_n \circ \cdots \circ \overline{S}'_{r+2}$ and $\overline{T}' = \overline{T}'_{r+2} \circ \cdots \circ \overline{T}'_n$.

---

7 Complexity of the Key-Recovery Attack

In this part, we show that the complexity of our attack is polynomial. To do so, we present a complexity analysis of the Alg. 2. We also present experimental results which confirm our theoretical results.

7.1   Theoretical Complexity

The goal of this part is to bound the complexity of solving the algebraic equations (9) arising at each step of Alg. 2. As we will see from the experimental results (Sect. 7.2), it appears that the system (9) can be solved efficiently in practice. In particular, the maximum degree reached during the Gröbner basis computation is bounded by a small constant, 3. We will now theoretically explain this fact. A strategy for bounding the complexity of solving (9) is to consider a subset of the equations. In particular, the equations of (9) derived from a given $k, 1 < k \leqslant N - r + 1$ correspond to a Kipnis-Shamir modeling of the MinRank problem (7). To give intuition, we consider a pair of matrices $\left(\mathfrak{P}^{(1)}, \mathfrak{P}^{(k)}\right)$ such that $\mathfrak{P}^{(1)}$ is invertible. Setting $\mathfrak{P}^* = \mathfrak{P}^{(k)}\left(\mathfrak{P}^{(1)}\right)^{-1}$, we obtain that (7) is equivalent to:

$$\text{Find } \lambda \in \mathbb{F}_q \text{ such that } \text{Det}(\mathfrak{P}^* - \lambda I_N) = 0. \tag{11}$$

We can compute the roots of the characteristic polynomial, which are the eigenvalues of $\mathfrak{P}^* - \lambda I_N$, and the corresponding eigenvectors. All such pairs will vanish the k-th equation of (9). We can then substitute each possible eigenvector in the other equations and solve the linear system involving the remaining unknowns. We have found a part of the secret-key as soon as the linear system is consistent. However, the complexity of this approach will depend on the multiplicity of the eigenvalues. If all the roots of (11) are simple, then the approach described, allows to solve the system (9) in polynomial-time.

Remark 6. In characteristic 2, the previous discussion does not directly apply since the matrix representation of a public polynomial has always an even rank (cf. Remark 1). In particular, the situation is as follows:

- When N is even, the rank of the skew-symmetric matrices $\mathfrak{P}^{(1)}$ and $\mathfrak{P}^{(k)}$ is $\leqslant N$. A drop of the rank will likely yield $\text{Rank}\left(\mathfrak{P}^{(k)} + \lambda\mathfrak{P}^{(1)}\right) = N - 2$. In this case, we can expect that the MinRank problem has unique solution λ. For this λ, the dimension of $\text{Ker}\left(\mathfrak{P}^{(k)} + \lambda\mathfrak{P}^{(1)}\right)$ is 2 (in this case, (11) would have a root of multiplicity > 1). Since $\overline{s}'_{N,N} = 1$ in (8), we obtain q solutions for the good key $\overline{S}'_N$.
- For odd N, the rank of the matrices $\mathfrak{P}^{(1)}$ and $\mathfrak{P}^{(k)}$ is $\leqslant N - 1$, which means that (7) is satisfied for any λ. In this case, since $\overline{s}'_{N,N} = 1$, for each $\lambda \in \mathbb{F}_q$ we get a unique solution for the good key $\overline{S}'_N$ if the rank defect is minimum, just one.

To analyse the complexity of this simple approach, we introduce:

Definition 5. *Let $\mathbb{F}_q$ be a field of characteristic 2 and $(A, B) \in \mathbb{F}_q^{N \times N} \times \mathbb{F}_q^{N \times N}$ be a pencil [20] of skew-symmetric matrices. We shall say that the pencil is generic if for all $\lambda_0 \in \mathbb{F}_q, \text{Ker}\left(A + \lambda_0 B\right)$ is of dimension $\leqslant 2$ if N is even and $\leqslant 1$ otherwise.*

If N is odd, a generic pencil (A, B) means that the pencil is always of maximal possible rank. If N is even, the pencil is generic if the rank defect, if any, is minimal, just one.

Remark 7. For the parameter sets of the MQQ cryptosystems, we can assume with high probability that the pencils from the public matrices are generic. Indeed, let $\lambda(q,n) = \prod_{i=1}^{n}\left(1 - 1/q^i\right)$ be the probability that a $n \times n$ matrix over $\mathbb{F}_q$ is invertible. It is known from [28] (and recalled in [9, Section10]) that the probability that a skew-symmetric matrix is of maximal rank $(n-1)$ when n is odd is $\mathrm{Pr}_{\mathrm{odd}} = \frac{\lambda(q,n)}{\lambda(q^2,(n-1)/2)}\frac{1}{1-1/q}$ and the probability that it is of rank $\geqslant n-2$ when n is even is: $\mathrm{Pr}_{\mathrm{even}} = \frac{\lambda(q,n)}{\lambda(q^2,(n-1)/2)}\left(1 + \frac{q^n-1}{q^{n-2}(q^2-1)(q-1)}\right)$. Having this in mind, we get that the probability that the pencils in question are generic is $(\mathrm{Pr}_{\mathrm{odd}})^q$ or $(\mathrm{Pr}_{\mathrm{even}})^q$, depending on the parity of n. In either case, for the parameter sets of MQQ-ENC and MQQ-SIG (as in Section 7.2), it can be checked that the probability is bigger than 0.7.

We first assume that the field q is not too big, typically $q = \mathcal{O}(n)$. This is indeed the case for most of the parameters proposed so far for MQQ cryptosystems.

Theorem 4. *Let $N \in \{n-1,\ldots,r+2\}$ and let $\mathbb{F}_q$ be a field of characteristic 2 such that $q = \mathcal{O}(n)$. Let $\mathfrak{P}^{(1)},\ldots,\mathfrak{P}^{(N-r+1)} \in \mathbb{F}_q^{N\times N}$ be the skew-symmetric matrices occurring in Algorithm 2 at step Rectangular MinRank(N). If there exists $i_0, 2 \leqslant i_0 \leqslant (N-r+1)$ such that the pencil $(\mathfrak{P}^{(1)},\mathfrak{P}^{(i_0)})$ is generic, then, the system (9) of Theorem 3 can be solved with probability $1 - 1/q$ in $\mathcal{O}(n^{\omega+2})$ operations, where $2 \leqslant \omega < 3$ is the linear algebra constant. In total, and under the assumptions, there exists an algorithm which recovers a key equivalent to the secret-key in*

$$\mathcal{O}\left(n^{\omega+3}\right) \text{ operations with probability } 1 - 1/q.$$

The proof can be found in Appendix B. Theorem 4 can be extended even if we assume that there exists a pencil of matrices for which the rank defect is small, that is, a constant. More generally, for arbitrary q and N, we show that we can get a complexity which is independent of the field size and polynomial in the number of variables. More precisely, the following result holds (proof in Appendix B).

Theorem 5. *Let $\mathbb{F}_q$ be an arbitrary field of characteristic 2 and let $N \in \{n-1,\ldots,r+2\}$. We assume that the system (9) of Theorem 3 is not harder to solve than a generic affine bi-linear system (Theorem 7). Let the matrices $\mathfrak{P}^{(1)},\ldots,\mathfrak{P}^{(N-r+1)} \in \mathbb{F}_q^{N\times N}$ be as in Algorithm 2. If there exist $i_0, i_1 \in \{2,\ldots,(N-r+1)\}$ such that the pencils $(\mathfrak{P}^{(1)},\mathfrak{P}^{(i_0)})$, and $(\mathfrak{P}^{(1)},\mathfrak{P}^{(i_1)})$ are generic, and if we assume that the corresponding kernels behave like random, then, for all $N \in \{n-1,\ldots,r+2\}$, the system (9) of Theorem 3 can be solved in $\mathcal{O}(N^{3\omega})$, with $2 \leqslant \omega < 3$ the linear algebra constant. In total, and under the assumptions, there exists an algorithm which recovers a key equivalent to the secret-key in*

$$\mathcal{O}(n^{3\omega+1}) \text{ field operations with probability } \left(1 - \tfrac{1}{q}\right)\left(1 - \tfrac{1}{q^{n-3}}\right).$$

7.2   Experimental Results

For the parameter sets proposed for MQQ-ENC [23] and MQQ-SIG [22] the results from Theorem 5 lead to the complexities given in Table 1 and Table 2. They have been calculated using the more precise formula $C(n,r,q) = \sum_{N=r+2}^{n-1} \binom{N+4}{3}^{\omega}$.

Table 1. Theoretical complexities, in terms of field operations, of the key recovery attack on MQQ-ENC compared to the original decryption algorithm. All of the parameters are for claimed security of $\mathcal{O}(2^{128})$.

Table 2. Theoretical complexities, in terms of field operations, of the key recovery attack on MQQ-SIG compared to the claimed security level

2^k	k	n	r	d	Decryption	Key Recovery
2	1	256	8	8	2^{25}	$2^{56.3}$
4	2	128	4	8	2^{23}	$2^{48.2}$
16	4	64	2	8	2^{21}	$2^{40.3}$
256	8	32	1	8	2^{20}	$2^{32.5}$

Security	n	d	Key Recovery
2^{80}	160	8	$2^{50.8}$
2^{96}	192	8	$2^{52.9}$
2^{112}	224	8	$2^{54.7}$
2^{128}	256	8	$2^{56.2}$

We have implemented the attack in Magma (Version 2.19-10 [8]) on a workstation with 32 cores based on Intel Xeon 2.27GHz, with 1TB of RAM memory. The results of the practical attack are summarized in Table 3 and Table 4.

Table 3. Results of the practical attack on MQQ-ENC

2^k	k	n	r	d	Key Recovery Theoretical	Key Recovery Practical		
						cycles	sec	d_{max}
2	1	64	8	8	$2^{40.3}$	$2^{43.4}$	5421	3
2	1	96	8	8	$2^{44.9}$	$2^{47.8}$	111844	3
4	2	64	4	8	$2^{40.3}$	$2^{43.7}$	6978	3
4	2	96	4	8	$2^{44.9}$	$2^{47.8}$	109258	3
4	2	128	4	8	$2^{48.2}$	$2^{50.6}$	787214	3
16	4	32	2	8	$2^{32.5}$	$2^{34.7}$	14	3
16	4	48	2	8	$2^{37.0}$	$2^{38.9}$	251	3
16	4	64	2	8	$2^{40.3}$	$2^{41.6}$	1783	3

From the tables, we can see that all our experiments, for both MQQ-ENC, and MQQ-SIG, confirmed that the maximum degree reached during the Gröbner basis computation (d_{max}) of the system (9) is 3, consistent with Theorem 4. Furthermore, the results are almost a perfect match with the theoretical calculations of Theorem 5.

Table 4. Results of the practical attack on MQQ-SIG

n	r	d	Key Recovery Theoretical	Key Recovery Practical		
				cycles	sec	d_{max}
64	32	8	$2^{40.3}$	$2^{40.1}$	560	3
96	48	8	$2^{44.9}$	$2^{43.2}$	4822	3
128	64	8	$2^{48.2}$	$2^{46.0}$	34376	3
160	80	8	$2^{50.8}$	$2^{48.0}$	120882	3

8 Conclusion

Mounting a successful key recovery attack against MQQ-ENC and MQQ-SIG using good keys, we have yet again shown that MinRank is a fundamental problem in $\mathcal{MQ}$ cryptography. We have, however, also shown that it is necessary to take into account the parity of the characteristic of the field when using Min-Rank to reveal the good key. Because of the different representation of quadratic polynomials over fields of characteristic 2, the attack, otherwise valid over odd characteristic fields, can not be directly applied. Interestingly, this has often been overlooked in the literature. By unveiling the pitfalls in the attack of the MQQ schemes arising from the even characteristic of the field, our analysis shows that the same modification is necessary when attacking similar $\mathcal{MQ}$ schemes over fields of characteristic 2 using MinRank.

Acknowledgments. We thank the anonymous referees for detailed comments which greatly improved this work. Jean-Charles Faugère, and Ludovic Perret have been partially supported by the HPAC grant (ANR-11-BS02-013) of the French National Research Agency. Simona Samardjiska has been partially supported by FCSE, UKIM, Macedonia and the COINS Research School of Computer and Information Security, Norway.

A The MinRank Problem

The MinRank problem over a finite field $\mathbb{F}_q$ is defined as follows.
MinRank (MR)
Input: $n, m, r, k \in \mathbb{N}$, where $n < m$ and $M_0, M_1, \ldots, M_k \in \mathcal{M}_{n \times m}(\mathbb{F}_q)$.
Question: Find – if any – a k-tuple $(\lambda_1, \ldots, \lambda_k) \in \mathbb{F}_q^k$ such that:

$$\text{Rank}\left(\sum_{i=1}^{k} \lambda_i M_i - M_0 \right) \leqslant r.$$

Kipnis and Shamir [27] proposed to model the MinRank problem as a multi-variate polynomial system of equations. The basic idea of the modeling is that the matrix $\left(\sum_{i=1}^{k} \lambda_i M_i - M_0 \right)$ has rank $\leqslant r$ if and only if there exists a set of $n - r$ independent vectors in its left kernel. Writing this set as a matrix in echelon form, yields a system of $n(n - r)$ equations in $r(n - r) + k$ variables given in matrix form:

$$\begin{pmatrix} 1 & x_{1,1} & \cdots & x_{1,r} \\ & \ddots & \vdots & \vdots \\ & 1 & x_{n-r,1} & \cdots & x_{n-r,r} \end{pmatrix} \cdot \left(\sum_{i=1}^{k} \lambda_i M_i - M_0 \right) = \mathbf{0}_{n \times n}. \tag{12}$$

Note that, over a finite field, the set of unknown independent vectors can be written in such a systematic form with high probability. Initially, relineariza-tion [27] was used to solve this algebraic system. The authors of [18] proposed instead to use Gröbner bases tools to solve this system. In addition, [18] noticed that the system has a specific structure: it is formed by bilinear equations [17].

We recall the complexity of the F_5 algorithm for computing a grevlex Gröbner basis of a polynomial system as given in [2,3].

Theorem 6. *The complexity of computing a Gröbner basis of a zero-dimensional (i.e. with a finite number of solutions in the algebraic closure of the coefficient field) polynomial system of m equations in n variables with F_5 is*

$$\mathcal{O}\left(m \cdot \binom{n + d_{\mathrm{reg}}}{d_{\mathrm{reg}}}^{\omega} \right),$$

where d_{reg} is the degree of regularity of the ideal and $2 \leqslant \omega \leqslant 3$ the linear algebra constant.

Informally, d_{reg} is the maximum degree reached during a Gröbner basis compu-tation. It has to be noticed that if the degree of regularity does not depend on the number of variables, the complexity then becomes polynomial in n.

From Theorem 6, we can see that in order to estimate the complexity of finding the MinRank solution with this modeling, we need a good estimate of the degree of regularity of the system (12). Using the fact that (12) is an affine bilinear system, the following tight bound can be appropriately used for the purpose.

Theorem 7 ([17]). *Let X and Y be two blocks of variables of sizes n_X and n_Y respectively. We shall say $f \in \mathbb{K}[X, Y]$ is bilinear if $f(\alpha X, \beta Y) = \alpha \beta f(X, Y)$ for all $(\alpha, \beta) \in \mathbb{K} \times \mathbb{K}$. For the grevlex ordering, the degree of regularity of a generic affine bilinear zero-dimensional system over $\mathbb{K}[X, Y]$ is upper bounded by*

$$d_{\mathrm{reg}} \leqslant \min(n_X, n_Y) + 1.$$

In particular, this result implies that computing the Gröbner basis of generic affine bilinear zero-dimensional system with $\min(n_X, n_Y) \in \mathcal{O}(1)$ can be done in polynomial-time.

B Complexity Theorems Proofs

B.1 Proof of Theorem 4

Proof. W.L.O.G., we can assume that $i_0 = 2$ (up to re-ordering the equations). Let λ_2 be a root of the degree-N univariate polynomial $\mathrm{Det}\left(\mathfrak{P}^{(2)} + X \cdot \mathfrak{P}^{(1)}\right)$. We denote by $K_2 = \mathrm{Ker}\left(\mathfrak{P}^{(2)} + \lambda_2 \mathfrak{P}^{(1)}\right)$ the corresponding kernel.

We first assume that N is odd. By the genericity assumption, we know that K_2 is of dimension one. Since $\overline{s}'_{N,N} = 1$ in (8), each K_2 yields an unique $\overline{s_2}'$ (stated differently, $\overline{s_2}'$ is the vector generating K_2 in a systematic basis). There is at most $q = \mathcal{O}(n)$ distinct values for $\overline{s_2}'$. We then plug each $\overline{s_2}'$ in (9) which reduces then to a system of linear equation in the $\overline{t}'$. We know that there is at least one $\overline{s_2}'$ which leads to a consistent system. If $N < n$ is odd, we can then solve (9) in $\mathcal{O}(n^{\omega+1})$.

When N is even, the situation is very similar. The only difference is that K_2 is of dimension 2. Since $\overline{s}'_{N,N} = 1$ in (8), each K_2 yields $q = \mathcal{O}(n)$ distinct $\overline{s_2}'$. There is at most $N < n$ distinct values for $\overline{s_2}'$. As before, we plug each possible $\overline{s_2}'$ in (9) which yields a system of linear equation in the $\overline{t}'$. Thus, if N is even, we can then solve (9) in $\mathcal{O}(n^{\omega+2})$.

Note that because of Lemma 3, the system will give a solution with probability $\frac{q-1}{q}$, so we need to randomize the public polynomials on average $\frac{q}{q-1}$ times.

The whole procedure needs to be repeated for every N starting from $n-1$ down to $r+2$. Note that in the first iteration, when $N = n$, we actually solve only a linear system of equations. $\qquad\square$

B.2 Proof of Theorem 5

Proof. Denote by $\binom{n}{k}_q = \frac{(q^n-1)(q^n-q)\ldots(q^n-q^{k-1})}{(q^k-1)(q^k-q)\ldots(q^k-q^{k-1})}$ the Gaussian binomial coefficient, that gives the number of k-dimensional subspaces of an n-dimensional vector space.

The main idea of the proof is to show that in (9) it is enough to consider only two coordinates of $\overline{t}'$ in order to get a unique solution for $\overline{s}'$ with overwhelming probability. Namely, it is enough to consider only the equations corresponding to $i_0 = 2, i_1 = 3$ (w.l.o.g. up to reordering of equations):

$$\overline{s}'\left(\mathfrak{P}^{(2)} + \overline{t}'_{2,1}\mathfrak{P}^{(1)}\right) = \mathbf{0}_{1\times N}, \tag{13}$$

$$\overline{s}'\left(\mathfrak{P}^{(3)} + \overline{t}'_{3,1}\mathfrak{P}^{(1)}\right) = \mathbf{0}_{1\times N}. \tag{14}$$

For odd N, for both $i \in \{2,3\}$ we have that $\mathrm{Dim}(\mathrm{Ker}(\mathfrak{P}^{(i)} + \lambda\mathfrak{P}^{(1)})) = 1$ for every $\lambda \in \mathbb{F}_q$. Denote the set $\{\mathrm{Ker}(\mathfrak{P}^{(2)} + \lambda\mathfrak{P}^{(1)})|\lambda \in \mathbb{F}_q\}$ by R_2, and the set $\{\mathrm{Ker}(\mathfrak{P}^{(3)}+\lambda\mathfrak{P}^{(1)})|\lambda \in \mathbb{F}_q\}$ by R_3. We know that, if there exists a good key, it will be a vector in the vector space that is the intersection $R_2 \cap R_3$. The probability that the intersection contains another vector space by chance is $|R_1|\cdot|R_2|/\binom{N}{1}_q \approx q^{(3-N)}$, which is very small for big enough N. Similarly, for even N, there exist

λ_2, λ_3 such that for both $i \in \{2, 3\}$, $\mathrm{Dim}(\mathrm{Ker}(\mathfrak{P}^{(i)} + \lambda_i \mathfrak{P}^{(1)})) = 2$. Now, if a good key exists, it will be in the intersection of the kernels and all other elements in the intersection will be linearly dependent of the good key. Hence, in this case the probability that we get a solution of the system that is not a good key is the same as the probability that the two kernels coincide, which equals $1/\binom{N}{2}_q \approx q^{(4-2N)}$. This again is very small. Thus, in total, with probability of $1 - \frac{1}{q^{N-3}}$, it is enough to use only equations (13) and (14).

The task now reduces to solving a bilinear system of equations of bidegree $(1, 1)$, over $\mathbb{F}_q[\overline{t}'_{i_0,1}, \overline{t}'_{i_1,1}, \overline{s}'_{1,N}, \ldots, \overline{s}'_{N-1,N}]$. From Theorem 7, such system can be solved in $\mathcal{O}\left(\binom{N+4}{3}^\omega\right)$.

Again because of Lemma 3, we need to randomize the public polynomials on average $\frac{q}{q-1}$ times. The step of solving the system (9) needs to be repeated for every N starting from $n - 1$ down to $r + 2$. Note that, when $N = n$, we actually solve only a linear system of equations, which is of smaller complexity.

In total, asymptotically, since we have $\mathcal{O}(n)$ steps of complexity $\mathcal{O}(\binom{n+4}{3}^\omega)$, we obtain the total complexity of the attack. □

References

1. Barbulescu, R., Gaudry, P., Joux, A., Thomé, E.: A heuristic quasi-polynomial algorithm for discrete logarithm in finite fields of small characteristic. In: Nguyen, P.Q., Oswald, E. (eds.) EUROCRYPT 2014. LNCS, vol. 8441, pp. 1–16. Springer, Heidelberg (2014)
2. Bardet, M., Faugère, J.C., Salvy, B.: On the complexity of Gröbner basis computation of semi-regular overdetermined algebraic equations. In: Proc. of International Conference on Polynomial System Solving (ICPSS), pp. 71–75 (2004)
3. Bardet, M., Faugère, J.C., Salvy, B., Yang, B.Y.: Asymptotic behaviour of the degree of regularity of semi-regular polynomial systems. In: Proc. of MEGA 2005, Eighth Int. Symposium on Effective Methods in Algebraic Geometry (2005)
4. Bernstein, D.J., Lange, T. (eds.): eBACS: ECRYPT Benchmarking of Cryptographic Systems (2014). http://bench.cr.yp.to
5. Bettale, L., Faugère, J.-C., Perret, L.: Cryptanalysis of multivariate and odd-characteristic HFE variants. In: Catalano, D., Fazio, N., Gennaro, R., Nicolosi, A. (eds.) PKC 2011. LNCS, vol. 6571, pp. 441–458. Springer, Heidelberg (2011)
6. Bettale, L., Faugre, J.C., Perret, L.: Cryptanalysis of HFE, multi-HFE and variants for odd and even characteristic. Designs, Codes and Cryptography 69(1), 1–52 (2013)
7. Billet, O., Gilbert, H.: Cryptanalysis of rainbow. In: De Prisco, R., Yung, M. (eds.) SCN 2006. LNCS, vol. 4116, pp. 336–347. Springer, Heidelberg (2006)
8. Bosma, W., Cannon, J., Playoust, C.: The Magma Algebra System. I. The User Language. J. Symbolic Comput. 24(3–4), 235–265 (1997). Computational algebra and number theory (London, 1993)
9. Bouillaguet, C.: Etudes d'hypothèses algorithmiques et attaques de primitives cryptographiques. Ph.D. thesis, Paris Diderot, France (2011)
10. Buss, W., Frandsen, G., Shallit, J.: The computational complexity of some problems of linear algebra. Journal of Computer and System Sciences (1999)

11. Goubin, L., Courtois, N.T.: Cryptanalysis of the TTM Cryptosystem. In: Okamoto, T. (ed.) ASIACRYPT 2000. LNCS, vol. 1976, p. 44. Springer, Heidelberg (2000)
12. Courtois, N., Goubin, L., Patarin, J.: Sflash, a fast asymmetric signature scheme for low-cost smartcards - primitive specification and supporting documentation. https://www.cosic.esat.kuleuven.ac.be/nessie/workshop/
13. Courtois, N.T.: Efficient zero-knowledge authentication based on a linear algebra problem minrank. In: Boyd, C. (ed.) ASIACRYPT 2001. LNCS, vol. 2248, p. 402. Springer, Heidelberg (2001)
14. Ding, J., Yang, B.-Y., Chen, C.-H.O., Chen, M.-S., Cheng, C.-M.: New differential-algebraic attacks and reparametrization of rainbow. In: Bellovin, S.M., Gennaro, R., Keromytis, A.D., Yung, M. (eds.) ACNS 2008. LNCS, vol. 5037, pp. 242–257. Springer, Heidelberg (2008)
15. Dubois, V., Fouque, P.-A., Shamir, A., Stern, J.: Practical cryptanalysis of SFLASH. In: Menezes, A. (ed.) CRYPTO 2007. LNCS, vol. 4622, pp. 1–12. Springer, Heidelberg (2007)
16. ETSI: 2nd Quantum-Safe Crypto Workshop in partnership with the IQC. http://www.etsi.org/news-events/events/770-etsi-crypto-workshop-2014   (Retrieved: September 2014)
17. Faugère, J.C., Din, M.S.E., Spaenlehauer, P.J.: Gröbner bases of bihomogeneous ideals generated by polynomials of bidegree (1, 1): Algorithms and complexity. J. Symb. Comput. **46**(4), 406–437 (2011)
18. Faugère, J.-C., Levy-dit-Vehel, F., Perret, L.: Cryptanalysis of minrank. In: Wagner, D. (ed.) CRYPTO 2008. LNCS, vol. 5157, pp. 280–296. Springer, Heidelberg (2008)
19. Faugère, J.-C., Ødegård, R.S., Perret, L., Gligoroski, D.: Analysis of the MQQ public key cryptosystem. In: Heng, S.-H., Wright, R.N., Goi, B.-M. (eds.) CANS 2010. LNCS, vol. 6467, pp. 169–183. Springer, Heidelberg (2010)
20. Gantmacher, F.: The Theory of Matrices, Vol. 1. Chelsea (1959)
21. Gligoroski, D., Markovski, S., Knapskog, S.J.: Multivariate quadratic trapdoor functions based on multivariate quadratic quasigroups. In: Proc. of the American Conference on Applied Mathematics, MATH, pp. 44–49. World Scientific and Engineering Academy and Society (WSEAS) (2008)
22. Gligoroski, D., Ødegård, R.S., Jensen, R.E., Perret, L., Faugère, J.-C., Knapskog, S.J., Markovski, S.: MQQ-SIG. In: Chen, L., Yung, M., Zhu, L. (eds.) INTRUST 2011. LNCS, vol. 7222, pp. 184–203. Springer, Heidelberg (2012)
23. Gligoroski, D., Samardjiska, S.: The Multivariate Probabilistic Encryption Scheme MQQ-ENC. In: SCC (2012)
24. Imai, H., Matsumoto, T.: Algebraic methods for constructing asymmetric cryptosystems. In: Calmet, J. (ed.) Algebraic Algorithms and Error-Correcting Codes. LNCS, vol. 229, pp. 108–119. Springer, Heidelberg (1985)
25. Jiang, X., Ding, J., Hu, L.: Kipnis-shamir attack on HFE revisited. In: Pei, D., Yung, M., Lin, D., Wu, C. (eds.) Inscrypt 2007. LNCS, vol. 4990, pp. 399–411. Springer, Heidelberg (2008)
26. Kipnis, A., Patarin, J., Goubin, L.: Unbalanced oil and vinegar signature schemes. In: Stern, J. (ed.) EUROCRYPT 1999. LNCS, vol. 1592, p. 206. Springer, Heidelberg (1999)
27. Kipnis, A., Shamir, A.: Cryptanalysis of the HFE public key cryptosystem by relinearization. In: Wiener, M. (ed.) CRYPTO 1999. LNCS, vol. 1666, p. 19. Springer, Heidelberg (1999)
28. MacWilliams, J.: Orthogonal matrices over finite fields. Orthogonal matrices over finite fields. The American Mathematical Monthly **76**(2), 152–164 (1969)

29. Moh, T.T.: A public key system with signature and master key functions. Communications in Algebra **27**(5), 2207–2222 (1999)
30. Mohamed, M.S.E., Ding, J., Buchmann, J., Werner, F.: Algebraic attack on the MQQ public key cryptosystem. In: Garay, J.A., Miyaji, A., Otsuka, A. (eds.) CANS 2009. LNCS, vol. 5888, pp. 392–401. Springer, Heidelberg (2009)
31. NESSIE: New european schemes for signatures, integrity, and encryption (2003). https://www.cosic.esat.kuleuven.be/nessie/ (Retrieved: September 2014)
32. NIST: Workshop on Cybersecurity in a Post-Quantum World. http://www.nist.gov/itl/csd/ct/post-quantum-crypto-workshop-2015.cfm (Retrieved: September 2014)
33. Patarin, J.: Hidden Fields Equations (HFE) and Isomorphisms of Polynomials (IP): Two New Families of Asymmetric Algorithms. In: Maurer, U.M. (ed.) EUROCRYPT 1996. LNCS, vol. 1070, pp. 33–48. Springer, Heidelberg (1996)
34. Perret, L.: A fast cryptanalysis of the isomorphism of polynomials with one secret problem. In: Cramer, R. (ed.) EUROCRYPT 2005. LNCS, vol. 3494, pp. 354–370. Springer, Heidelberg (2005)
35. Samardjiska, S., Chen, Y., Gligoroski, D.: Algorithms for construction of Multivariate Quadratic Quasigroups (MQQs) and their parastrophe operations in arbitrary galois fields. J. Inf. Assurance and Security **7**(3), 146–172 (2012)
36. Thomae, E.: About the Security of Multivariate Quadratic Public Key Schemes. Ph.D. thesis, Ruhr-University Bochum, Germany (2013)
37. Thomae, E., Wolf, C.: Cryptanalysis of enhanced TTS, STS and all its variants, or: why cross-terms are important. In: Mitrokotsa, A., Vaudenay, S. (eds.) AFRICACRYPT 2012. LNCS, vol. 7374, pp. 188–202. Springer, Heidelberg (2012)
38. Wolf, C., Braeken, A., Preneel, B.: On the security of stepwise triangular systems. Designs, Codes and Cryptography **40**(3), 285–302 (2006)
39. Wolf, C., Preneel, B.: Equivalent keys in HFE, C*, and variations. In: Dawson, E., Vaudenay, S. (eds.) Mycrypt 2005. LNCS, vol. 3715, pp. 33–49. Springer, Heidelberg (2005)
40. Wolf, C., Preneel, B.: Large superfluous keys in multivariate quadratic asymmetric systems. In: Vaudenay, S. (ed.) PKC 2005. LNCS, vol. 3386, pp. 275–287. Springer, Heidelberg (2005)
41. Wolf, C., Preneel, B.: Equivalent keys in multivariate quadratic public key systems. Journal of Mathematical Cryptology **4**, 375–415 (2011)
42. Yang, B.-Y., Chen, J.-M., Chen, Y.-H.: TTS: high-speed signatures on a low-cost smart card. In: Joye, M., Quisquater, J.-J. (eds.) CHES 2004. LNCS, vol. 3156, pp. 371–385. Springer, Heidelberg (2004)

A Polynomial-Time Attack on the BBCRS Scheme

Alain Couvreur[2,3]([✉]), Ayoub Otmani[4], Jean-Pierre Tillich[1],
and Valérie Gauthier–Umaña[5]

[1] INRIA, Secret Team, 78153 Le Chesnay Cedex, France
jean-pierre.tillich@inria.fr
[2] INRIA, Grace Team, 1 rue H. d'Estienne d'Orves, 91120 Palaiseau Cedex, France
[3] École Polytechnique, Grace Team and LIX, CNRS UMR 7161,
Allée H. D'Estienne d'Orves, 91120 Palaiseau Cedex, France
alain.couvreur@lix.polytechnique.fr
[4] LITIS, University of Rouen, 76821 Mont-Saint-Aignan, France
ayoub.otmani@univ-rouen.fr
[5] Faculty of Natural Sciences and Mathematics, Department of Mathematics,
Universidad Del Rosario, Bogotá, Colombia
gauthier.valerie@urosario.edu.co

Abstract. The BBCRS scheme is a variant of the McEliece public-key
encryption scheme where the hiding phase is performed by taking the
inverse of a matrix which is of the form $T + R$ where T is a sparse
matrix with average row/column weight equal to a very small quantity
m, usually $m < 2$, and R is a matrix of small rank $z \geqslant 1$. The rationale of this new transformation is the reintroduction of families of codes,
like generalized Reed-Solomon codes, that are famously known for rep-
resentin insecure choices. We present a key-recovery attack when $z = 1$
and m is chosen between 1 and $1 + R + O(\frac{1}{\sqrt{n}})$ where R denotes the code
rate. This attack has complexity $O(n^6)$ and breaks all the parameters
suggested in the literature.

Keywords: Code-based cryptography · Distinguisher · Generalized
Reed-Solomon codes · Key-recovery · Component-wise product of codes

Introduction

Post-Quantum Cryptography. All public key cryptographic primitives used
in practice such as RSA, ElGamal scheme, DSA or ECDSA rely either on the
difficulty of factoring or computing the discrete logarithm and would therefore
be broken by Shor's algorithm [24] if a large enough quantum computer could be
built. Moreover, even if a large enough quantum computer might not be built in
the next five years, it should be mentioned that tremendous progress has been
made for computing the discrete logarithm over finite fields of small characteristic
with the quasi-polynomial time algorithm of [5]. This lack of diversity in public

© International Association for Cryptologic Research 2015
J. Katz (Ed.): PKC 2015, LNCS 9020, pp. 175–193, 2015.
DOI: 10.1007/978-3-662-46447-2_8

key cryptography has been identified as a major concern in the field of information security. For all these reasons, it would be very desirable to be ready to replace these schemes by others that would rely on other hard problems. However only few other proposals have emerged which are essentially hash-based signature schemes, lattice-based, code-based and multivariate quadratic based schemes. They are either based on the problem of solving multivariate equations over a finite field, the problem of finding a short vector in a lattice and the problem of decoding a linear code. Those problems are known for being NP-hard and are therefore believed to be immune to the quantum computer threat.

The McEliece Cryptosystem. Among those, one of the most promising scheme is the McEliece public key cryptosystem [20]. It is also one of the oldest public-key cryptosystem. It uses a family of codes for which there is a fast decoding algorithm (the binary Goppa code family here) which is used in the decryption process whereas an attacker has only a random generator matrix of the Goppa code which reveals nothing about the algebraic structure of the Goppa code that is used in the decoding process. He has therefore to decode a generic linear code for which only exponential time decoding algorithms are known. The main advantage of this system is to have very fast encryption and decryption functions. Depending on how the parameters are chosen for a fixed security level, this cryptosystem is about five times faster for encryption and about 10 to 100 times faster for decryption than RSA [8]. Furthermore, it has withstood many attacking attempts. After more than thirty five years now, it still belongs to the very few public key cryptosystems which remain unbroken.

The Use of Reed-Solomon Codes in a McEliece Scheme. Goppa codes are subfield subcodes of Generalized Reed-Solomon codes (GRS codes in short). This means that a Goppa code defined over $\mathbb{F}_q$ is actually the set of codewords of a GRS code defined over an extension field $\mathbb{F}_{q^\mu}$ (we say that μ is the extension degree of the Goppa code) whose coordinates all belong to the subfield $\mathbb{F}_q$. Actually the fast decoding process of Goppa codes is the decoder of the underlying GRS code. Roughly speaking, a Goppa code of length n and dimension $n - 2t\mu$ defined over $\mathbb{F}_q$ can correct t errors[1] and is a subfield subcode of a GRS code that can also correct t errors which is of the same length n but has a larger dimension $n - 2t$ and is defined over $\mathbb{F}_{q^\mu}$. In this sense, the underlying GRS code has a better error correction capacity than the Goppa code. This raises the issue of using GRS codes instead of Goppa codes in the McEliece system. The better decoding capacity of GRS codes translates into smaller public key sizes for the McEliece scheme which is actually one of the main drawback of this scheme. This approach has been tried in Niederreiter's scheme (whose security is equivalent to the McEliece scheme) but has encountered a dreadful fate when the Sidelnikov-Shestakov attack appeared [25].

Baldi et al. Approach for Reviving GRS Codes. In their Journal of Cryptology article [2], Baldi *et al.* have suggested a new way of using GRS codes in this context. Instead of using directly such a code, they multiplied it by the

---

[1] But the dimension can be increased to $n - t\mu$ in the binary case.

inverse of the sum $T + R$ where T is a sparse matrix and R is a low rank matrix. By doing this, the attacker sees a code which is radically different from a GRS code but the legitimate user can still use the underlying GRS decoder. This thwarts the Sidelnikov-Shestakov attack completely. However the decoding capacity of the resulting code is basically scaled down by a factor of $\frac{1}{m}$ where m denotes the average weight of rows of the matrix T. It should be noted that the very same approach has also been tried for the Low-Density-Parity-Check code family, LDPC in short, which is notoriously known for being insecure in a McEliece scheme [3,4,22]. In this case, they did not even use the low rank matrix and despite of this fact the resulting public code obtained by this multiplication is not an LDPC code anymore (it becomes a moderate-density-parity-check code) and it seems now that if the attacker wants to break this scheme he has to be able to solve a generic decoding problem [21]. There are therefore good reasons to believe that this approach can be powerful for disguising the secret code structure.

An Earlier Attempt. Baldi *et al.* [1] first used this approach with T being a permutation matrix. In this case $m = 1$ and nothing is lost in term of decoding capacity compared to a GRS decoder. In other words, this allows to decrease the public key size as if we had a GRS code in the McEliece cryptosystem. This first attempt got broken in [11,12]. Roughly speaking the reason of this attack in this case can be traced back to two facts (i) it turns out that the resulting code is still close to the underlying GRS code: the intersection of the public code with the secret GRS code is of co-dimension one; (ii) there is a very powerful way of distinguishing a GRS code [12] from a random code by computing the dimension of its square which can be used to unravel the algebraic structure of the public code. On the other hand, when the degree of sparseness of T is > 1 the resulting code does not have a large intersection with a GRS code and there was some hope to obtain a secure scheme.

Our Contribution: an Attack Which Works in the Regime $1 < m < 2$. In the present article we will show that despite the fact that the public code is far from being a GRS code, a similar trick that has already been used to attack successfully in [14] some wild Goppa codes proposed in [7] when the degree of extension is only 2 can also be used in this context. It consists in computing the dimension of the square of shortenings of the public code. Because of the hidden structure of the public code, the squares of some of its shortenings have a smaller dimension than the squares of shortened random codes of the same dimension. This distinguisher is then used to unravel the structure of the matrix T. This gives an attack of polynomial time complexity which can be used to break the examples given in [2]. Several were broken in a few hours, and others in a few days. As an illustration, Example 1 given in [2] with a claimed 90-bit security can be broken in 2.75 hours on a computer equipped with Xeon 2.27GHz processor and 72 Gb of RAM. This attack works up to values of m of order $1 + R + O(\frac{1}{\sqrt{n}})$, where R is the rate of the public code. The attack we present here can obviously be thwarted by taking values for m greater than 2, but in this case, since the price to pay is a decrease of the decoding capacity by a factor of more than 2, we do not obtain better public key sizes than the ones we obtain by using Goppa codes, or more generally alternant codes of extension degree 2, provided we choose non wild Goppa codes in order to avoid the attack of [14]. The complexity of the present attack is similar to that of [11], namely $O(n^6)$ where n is the code length. More precisely, this attack starts with two steps of respective complexity $O(n^3)$ and $O(n^5)$ and then applying the attack of [11] whose complexity is $O(n^6)$ operations in the base field.

Note. Due to space limitation, several proofs are omitted. A longer ver- sion of the present paper including the missing proofs can be found online.

1   GRS Codes and the Square Code Construction

We recall in this section a few relevant results and definitions from coding theory and bring in the fundamental notion of square code construction.

Definition 1 (Generalized Reed-Solomon code). *Let k and n be integers such that $1 \leqslant k < n \leqslant q$ where q is a prime power. The code $\mathbf{GRS}_k\,(\boldsymbol{x}, \boldsymbol{y})$ of dimension k is associated to a pair $(\boldsymbol{x}, \boldsymbol{y})$ where $\boldsymbol{x}$ is an n-tuple of distinct elements of $\mathbb{F}_q$ and $\boldsymbol{y} \in (\mathbb{F}_q^\times)^n$, is defined as:*

$$\mathbf{GRS}_k\,(\boldsymbol{x}, \boldsymbol{y}) \stackrel{def}{=} \Big\{(y_1 p(x_1), \dots, y_n p(x_n)) \mid p \in \mathbb{F}_q[X], \deg p < k\Big\}.$$

The first work that suggested to use GRS codes in a public-key encryption scheme was [23]. But Sidelnikov and Shestakov [25] showed that for any GRS code it is possible to recover in polynomial time a pair $(\boldsymbol{x}, \boldsymbol{y})$ defining it, which is all that is needed to decode efficiently such codes and is therefore enough to break any McEliece type cryptosystem [20] that uses GRS codes.

Definition 2 (Componentwise products). *Given two vectors $\boldsymbol{a} = (a_1, \dots, a_n)$ and $\boldsymbol{b} = (b_1, \dots, b_n) \in \mathbb{F}_q^n$, we denote by $\boldsymbol{a} \star \boldsymbol{b}$ the componentwise product*

$$\boldsymbol{a} \star \boldsymbol{b} \stackrel{def}{=} (a_1 b_1, \dots, a_n b_n).$$

The star product $\boldsymbol{a} \star \boldsymbol{b}$ should be distinguished from a more common operation, namely the canonical inner product:

$$\boldsymbol{a} \cdot \boldsymbol{b} \stackrel{def}{=} \sum_{i=1}^{n} a_i b_i.$$

Definition 3 (Product of codes & square code). *Let $\mathscr{A}$ and $\mathscr{B}$ be two codes of length n. The star product code denoted by $\mathscr{A} \star \mathscr{B}$ of $\mathscr{A}$ and $\mathscr{B}$ is the vector space spanned by all products $\boldsymbol{a} \star \boldsymbol{b}$ where $\boldsymbol{a}$ and $\boldsymbol{b}$ range over $\mathscr{A}$ and $\mathscr{B}$ respectively. When $\mathscr{B} = \mathscr{A}$ then $\mathscr{A} \star \mathscr{A}$ is called the square code of $\mathscr{A}$ and is rather denoted by $\mathscr{A}^2$.*

Proposition 1. *Let $\mathscr{A}$ be a code of length n, then*

$$\dim(\mathscr{A}^2) \leqslant \min\left\{ n, \binom{\dim(\mathscr{A}) + 1}{2} \right\}.$$

Proposition 2. *Let $\mathscr{A} \subset \mathbb{F}_q^n$ be a code of dimension k. The complexity of the computation of a basis of $\mathscr{A}^2$ is $O(k^2 n^2)$ operations in $\mathbb{F}_q$.*

See for instance [11], for proofs of Propositions 1 and 2.

The importance of the square code construction becomes clear when we compare the dimension of the square of structured codes like GRS codes with the dimension of the square of a random code. Roughly speaking, given a code of dimension k, the dimension of its square is linear in k if it is a GRS code and quadratic if it is a random code as explained in the two following propositions.

Proposition 3. $\mathbf{GRS}_k(\boldsymbol{x}, \boldsymbol{y})^2 = \mathbf{GRS}_{2k-1}(\boldsymbol{x}, \boldsymbol{y} \star \boldsymbol{y})$.

Proof. See for instance [18, Proposition 10].

Remark 1. This property can also be used in the case $2k - 1 > n$. To see this, consider the dual of the Reed-Solomon code, which is itself a generalized Reed-Solomon code [17, Theorem 4, p.304].

Theorem 1. *Let $\mathscr{A}$ be a random code of length n and dimension k such that $n > \binom{k+1}{2}$. Then, for all integer $\ell < \binom{k+1}{2}$,*

$$Prob\left(\dim \mathscr{A}^2 \leqslant \binom{k+1}{2} - \ell \right) = O\left(q^{-\ell} \cdot q^{-\left(n - \binom{k+1}{2}\right)} \right), \qquad (k \to +\infty).$$

Proof. See [10].

Remark 2. A slightly weaker result was already obtained in the papers [15,16] (see also [19]).

For this reason, $\mathbf{GRS}_k(\boldsymbol{x}, \boldsymbol{y})$ can be distinguished from a random linear code of the same dimension by computing the dimension of the associated square code. In [15,16], this phenomenon was already observed for q-ary alternant codes (in particular Goppa codes) at very high rates whose duals are distinguishable from random codes by the very same manner. Subsequently, the very same phenomenon lead to attacks on GRS based cryptosystems [11,12], to a polynomial time attack on Wild Goppa codes over quadratic extensions [14] and to a polynomial time attack on algebraic geometry codes [13].

Historically, the star product of codes has been used for the first time by Wieschebrink to cryptanalyze a McEliece-like scheme [6] based on subcodes of Reed-Solomon codes [26]. The use of the star product here is nevertheless different from the way it is used in [26]. In Wieschebrink's paper, the star product is used to identify, given a certain low codimensional subcode $\mathscr{C}$ of a GRS code $\mathbf{GRS}_k(\boldsymbol{x}, \boldsymbol{y})$, a possible pair $(\boldsymbol{x}, \boldsymbol{y})$. This is achieved by computing $\mathscr{C}^2$ which turns out to be $\mathbf{GRS}_k(\boldsymbol{x}, \boldsymbol{y})^2 = \mathbf{GRS}_{2k-1}(\boldsymbol{x}, \boldsymbol{y} \star \boldsymbol{y})$ with a high probability. The Sidelnikov and Shestakov algorithm is then used on $\mathscr{C}^2$ to recover a possible $(\boldsymbol{x}, \boldsymbol{y} \star \boldsymbol{y})$ pair to describe $\mathscr{C}^2$ as a GRS code, and hence, a pair $(\boldsymbol{x}, \boldsymbol{y})$ is deduced for which $\mathscr{C} \subset \mathbf{GRS}_k(\boldsymbol{x}, \boldsymbol{y})$.

2   Description of the Scheme

The BBCRS public-key encryption scheme given in [2] can be summarized as follows:

Secret Key
- G_{sec} is a generator matrix of a GRS code of length n and dimension k over $\mathbb{F}_q$.
- $Q \stackrel{\text{def}}{=} T + R$ where T is an $n \times n$ non-singular sparse matrix with elements in $\mathbb{F}_q$ and average row weight $m \ll n$. Note that m is not necessarily an integer. For example $m = 1.4$ means that 40% of the rows of T have weight equal to 2 and the other 60% have weight equal to 1.
- R is a rank-z matrix over $\mathbb{F}_q$ such that Q is invertible. In other words there exist $\boldsymbol{\alpha} \stackrel{\text{def}}{=} (\alpha_1, \ldots, \alpha_n)$ and $\boldsymbol{\beta} \stackrel{\text{def}}{=} (\beta_1, \ldots, \beta_n)$ such that $R \stackrel{\text{def}}{=} \boldsymbol{\alpha}^T \boldsymbol{\beta}$ and α_i and β_i are $z \times 1$ full rank matrices defined over $\mathbb{F}_q$ for all $i \in \{1, \ldots, n\}$ and $z \leqslant n$.
- S is a $k \times k$ random invertible matrix over $\mathbb{F}_q$.

Public Key
$$G_{pub} \stackrel{\text{def}}{=} S^{-1} G_{sec} Q^{-1}. \tag{1}$$

Encryption. The ciphertext $c \in \mathbb{F}_q^n$ of a plaintext $m \in \mathbb{F}_q^k$ is obtained by drawing at random e in $\mathbb{F}_q^n$ of weight less than or equal to $\frac{n-k}{2m}$ (recall that m denotes the density of the matrix T) and computing $c \stackrel{\text{def}}{=} mG_{pub} + e$.

Decryption. It consists in performing the three following steps:

1. Guessing the value of eR.
2. Calculating $c' \stackrel{\text{def}}{=} cQ - eR = mS^{-1}G_{sec} + eQ - eR = mS^{-1}G_{sec} + eT$ and using the decoding algorithm of the GRS code to recover mS^{-1} from the knowledge of c'.
3. Multiplying the result of the decoding by S to recover m.

Remark 3. In [2], the authors suggest to take $m = 1 + \frac{n-k-3}{n} \approx 2 - R$ for the density of T.

Further Details on the Construction of the Matrix T. We deal with the case $m \leqslant 2$. According to [2] the matrix T is constructed[2] as follows.

1. Choose a permutation matrix P. Replace each 1 by a random element of $\mathbb{F}_q^\times$.
2. Set $t \stackrel{\text{def}}{=} \lfloor \frac{n-k}{2} \rfloor$, $\delta_t \stackrel{\text{def}}{=} t - \lfloor \frac{t}{m} \rfloor$ and $\ell \stackrel{\text{def}}{=} \lfloor (m-1)n \rfloor$. Choose a random set $\mathcal{C}$ of δ_t columns and a random set $\mathcal{J}_2$ of ℓ rows of P.
3. For all $i \in \mathcal{J}_2$, we denote by $\pi(i)$ the integer such that $P_{i,\pi(i)} \neq 0$. For each $i \in \mathcal{J}_2$, choose a random element $j \in \mathcal{C} \setminus \pi(i)$ and add a random element of $\mathbb{F}_q^\times$ at position (i, j).

---

[2] Actually, the authors propose three constructions for T and express a clear preference for the one described in the present article.

We also tested another construction allowing to have row and column weight upper bounded by 2. The sparse matrix T is constructed as $T = T_1 + T_2$ where:

- T_1 is of the form $T_1 = D_1 P_1$, where D_1 is diagonal invertible and P_1 is a permutation matrix;
- $T_2 = D_2 P_2$, where D_2 is diagonal with $(m-1)n$ nonzero diagonal coefficients and P_2 is a permutation matrix;
- The matrices do not overlap, that is, there is no pair (i, j) with $1 \leqslant i, j \leqslant n$ such that both $(T_1)_{ij}$ and $(T_2)_{ij}$ are nonzero.

Our attack works for both choices of the matrix T. The experimental results in Sec. 6 rely on the first construction for T.

2.1 Previous Attacks and Discussion on the Parameters

The BBCRS scheme has been subject to an attack [11] in the case $m = 1$, *i.e.* the matrix T is a permutation matrix and $z = 1$, *i.e.* the matrix R has rank 1. The attack presented here holds for $m < 1 + R + O(\frac{1}{\sqrt{n}})$ and $z = 1$. The relevance of choosing higher m or z is discussed in Section 7.

The attack of the present article uses in its last step the attack [11] on the original system [1].

2.2 Notation

It will be convenient to bring the following notation.

- $\mathscr{C}_{\mathrm{pub}}$ is the code with generator matrix G_{pub};
- $\mathscr{C}_{\mathrm{sec}}$ is the GRS code with generator matrix G_{sec}, we assume that it is specified by its dual (which is itself a GRS code) as $\mathscr{C}_{\mathrm{sec}}^{\perp} = \mathbf{GRS}_{n-k}(x, y)$;
- $\mathcal{J}_1$ is the set of positions which correspond to rows of T of Hamming weight 1. The elements of $\mathcal{J}_1$ are called the *positions of degree* 1. For any row $i \in \mathcal{J}_1$ of T, we define $j(i)$ as the unique column of T for which $T_{ij(i)} \neq 0$;
- $\mathcal{J}_2$ is the set of positions which correspond to rows of T of Hamming weight 2. The positions in $\mathcal{J}_2$ are called the *positions of degree* 2. When i belongs to $\mathcal{J}_2$, let j_1 and j_2 be the columns of T for which we have $T_{ij_1} \neq 0$ and $T_{ij_2} \neq 0$. We define similarly $j(i)$ as the set $\{j_1, j_2\}$ in this case.

2.3 Structure of the Public Code

The following result explains how $\mathscr{C}_{\mathrm{pub}}$ and $\mathscr{C}_{\mathrm{sec}}$ and their duals are related.

Lemma 1

$$\mathscr{C}_{pub} = \mathscr{C}_{sec}(T + R)^{-1} \tag{2}$$
$$\mathscr{C}_{pub}^{\perp} = \mathscr{C}_{sec}^{\perp}(T + R)^{T}. \tag{3}$$

Proof The first equality follows immediately from (1), whereas the second one was is observed in [2, p.6, Equation (8)] where a parity-check matrix for the public code $\mathscr{C}_{\mathrm{pub}}$ is expressed in terms of a parity-check matrix of the secret code. This can be proved as follows. For all $c \in \mathscr{C}_{\mathrm{sec}}$, $c' \in \mathscr{C}_{\mathrm{sec}}^{\perp}$,

$$(c(\boldsymbol{T} + \boldsymbol{R})^{-1}) \cdot (c'(\boldsymbol{T} + \boldsymbol{R})^{T}) = (c(\boldsymbol{T} + \boldsymbol{R})^{-1}(\boldsymbol{T} + \boldsymbol{R})) \cdot c' = c \cdot c' = 0.$$

Moreover, since $\boldsymbol{Q} = \boldsymbol{T} + \boldsymbol{R}$ is invertible, we get $\dim \mathscr{C}_{\mathrm{sec}}^{\perp}(\boldsymbol{T} + \boldsymbol{R})^{T} + \dim \mathscr{C}_{\mathrm{sec}}(\boldsymbol{T} + \boldsymbol{R})^{-1} = n$, hence the codes are dual to each other.

3   The Fundamental Tool: Shortening and Puncturing the Dual of the Public Code

Puncturing and shortening will play a fundamental role in the attack. Recall that for a given code $\mathscr{C} \subset \mathbb{F}_q^n$ and a subset $\mathcal{I}$ of code positions the *punctured* code $\mathcal{P}_{\mathcal{I}}(\mathscr{C})$ and *shortened* code $\mathcal{S}_{\mathcal{I}}(\mathscr{C})$ are defined as:

$$\mathcal{P}_{\mathcal{I}}(\mathscr{C}) \overset{\mathrm{def}}{=} \{(c_i)_{i \notin \mathcal{I}} \mid c \in \mathscr{C}\};$$
$$\mathcal{S}_{\mathcal{I}}(\mathscr{C}) \overset{\mathrm{def}}{=} \{(c_i)_{i \notin \mathcal{I}} \mid \exists c = (c_i)_i \in \mathscr{C} \text{ such that } \forall i \in \mathcal{I}, \ c_i = 0\}.$$

Given a subset $\mathcal{I}$ of the set of coordinates of a vector $\boldsymbol{u}$, we denote by $\mathcal{P}_{\mathcal{I}}(\boldsymbol{u})$ the vector $\boldsymbol{u}$ *punctured* at $\mathcal{I}$, that is to say, *indexes that are in $\mathcal{I}$ are removed*.

First let us recall the influence of these operations on GRS codes.

Lemma 2. *Let $\boldsymbol{x}, \boldsymbol{y}$ be two n–tuples of element sof $\mathbb{F}_q$ such that $\boldsymbol{x}$ has pairwise distinct entries and $\boldsymbol{y}$ has only nonzero entries. Let $k < n$ and $\mathcal{I} \subseteq \{1, \ldots, n\}$. Then*

$$\mathcal{P}_{\mathcal{I}}(\mathbf{GRS}_k(\boldsymbol{x}, \boldsymbol{y})) = \mathbf{GRS}_k(\mathcal{P}_{\mathcal{I}}(\boldsymbol{x}), \mathcal{P}_{\mathcal{I}}(\boldsymbol{y})) \tag{4}$$
$$\mathcal{S}_{\mathcal{I}}(\mathbf{GRS}_k(\boldsymbol{x}, \boldsymbol{y})) = \mathbf{GRS}_{k-|\mathcal{I}|}(\mathcal{P}_{\mathcal{I}}(\boldsymbol{x}), \boldsymbol{y}_{\mathcal{I}}), \tag{5}$$

for some $\boldsymbol{y}_{\mathcal{I}} \in \mathbb{F}_q^{n-|\mathcal{I}|}$ depends only on $\boldsymbol{y}$ and $\mathcal{I}$.

Next, with these notions at hand, it follows that the dual of the public code punctured in $\mathcal{J}_2$ is very close to a GRS code. We will also need to understand the structure of versions of this code which are shortened in positions belonging to $\mathcal{J}_1$ and then punctured in $\mathcal{J}_2$. It turns out that these codes too are close to GRS codes. First of all, puncturing $\mathscr{C}_{\mathrm{pub}}^{\perp}$ in the positions belonging to $\mathcal{J}_2$ gives "almost" a GRS code, as shown by:

Lemma 3. *Let $\boldsymbol{u} = (u_i)_{i \in \mathcal{J}_1}$ and $\boldsymbol{v} = (v_i)_{i \in \mathcal{J}_1}$ be vectors in $\mathbb{F}_q^{n-|\mathcal{J}_2|}$ defined by*

$$u_i = x_{j(i)}$$
$$v_i = T_{ij(i)} y_{j(i)}.$$

Let $\mathscr{D} \overset{\mathrm{def}}{=} \mathscr{C}_{\mathrm{sec}}^{\perp} \boldsymbol{T}^T$, then

$$\mathcal{P}_{\mathcal{J}_2}(\mathscr{D}) \subseteq \mathbf{GRS}_{n-k}(\boldsymbol{u}, \boldsymbol{v}). \tag{6}$$

Lemma 4. *Let λ and μ be vectors of $\mathbb{F}_q^n$ such that $\boldsymbol{R}^T = \lambda^T \mu$ and let $\mathscr{C}_{sec}^\perp(\lambda) \overset{def}{=} \mathscr{C}_{sec}^\perp \cap < \lambda >^\perp$, $\mathscr{C}_{pub}^\perp(\lambda) \overset{def}{=} \mathscr{C}_{sec}^\perp(\lambda)(\boldsymbol{T}^T + \boldsymbol{R}^T)$. Then,*

$$\mathcal{P}_{\mathcal{J}_2}\left(\mathscr{C}_{pub}^\perp(\lambda)\right) \subseteq \mathbf{GRS}_{n-k}\left(\boldsymbol{u}, \boldsymbol{v}\right), \tag{7}$$

Moreover if $\mathcal{J}_1$ contains an information set[3] of $\mathscr{C}_{sec}^\perp \boldsymbol{T}^T$ and $\boldsymbol{T}^T$ is invertible, then there exist $\boldsymbol{a}$ and $\boldsymbol{b}$ in $\mathbb{F}_q^{n-|\mathcal{J}_2|}$ such that for any $\boldsymbol{c}$ in $\mathcal{P}_{\mathcal{J}_2}\left(\mathscr{C}_{pub}^\perp\right)$, there exists a vector $\boldsymbol{p}$ in $\mathbf{GRS}_{n-k}\left(\boldsymbol{u}, \boldsymbol{v}\right)$ for which

$$\boldsymbol{c} = \boldsymbol{p} + (\boldsymbol{p} \cdot \boldsymbol{b})\boldsymbol{a}. \tag{8}$$

In particular, $\mathcal{P}_{\mathcal{J}_2}\left(\mathscr{C}_{pub}^\perp\right) \subseteq \mathbf{GRS}_{n-k}\left(\boldsymbol{u}, \boldsymbol{v}\right) + < \boldsymbol{a} >$.

If we puncture with respect to $\mathcal{J}_2$ shortened versions of $\mathscr{C}_{pub}^\perp$ in positions belonging to $\mathcal{J}_1$, then we observe a similar phenomenon, namely

Lemma 5. *Let $\mathcal{I}_1$ be a subset of code positions which is a subset of $\mathcal{J}_1$. Let $s \overset{def}{=} |\mathcal{I}_1|$ and assume that $s \leqslant n-k$. Then there exist vectors $\boldsymbol{a}, \boldsymbol{u}, \boldsymbol{v}$ in $\mathbb{F}_q^{n-s-|\mathcal{J}_2|}$ such that:*

$$\mathcal{P}_{\mathcal{J}_2}\left(\mathcal{S}_{\mathcal{I}_1}\left(\mathscr{C}_{pub}^\perp\right)\right) \subseteq \mathscr{E} + < \boldsymbol{a} > \tag{9}$$

and $\mathscr{E}$ is a subcode of $\mathbf{GRS}_{n-k-s}\left(\boldsymbol{u}, \boldsymbol{v}\right)$.

4 Key-Recovery Attack

4.1 Outline

Our key-recovery attack starts with a parity-check matrix $\boldsymbol{H_{pub}}$ of the (public) code $\mathscr{C}_{\mathrm{pub}}$. The main goal is to recover matrices $\boldsymbol{T}$ and $\boldsymbol{R}$, where $\boldsymbol{H_{pub}}(\boldsymbol{T}^T + \boldsymbol{R}^T)^{-1}$ is a parity check matrix of a GRS code, $\boldsymbol{T}$ is a low density square matrix and $\boldsymbol{R}$ a rank 1 matrix. Recall that in our terminology, rows of $\boldsymbol{T}$ belonging to $\mathcal{J}_1$ are positions of degree 1, and those in $\mathcal{J}_2$ are positions of degree 2. It implies, thanks to (3), that some columns of $\boldsymbol{H_{pub}}$ belong to $\mathcal{J}_1$ and the others are in $\mathcal{J}_2$.

Our attack is composed of three mains steps having the following objectives:

1. Detecting columns of $\boldsymbol{H_{pub}}$ that belong to $\mathcal{J}_2$, and then deducing those of $\mathcal{J}_1$.
2. Transforming columns of $\mathcal{J}_2$ into degree 1 columns by linear combinations with columns of $\mathcal{J}_1$.

---

[3] In coding theory, an *information set* of a code $\mathscr{C}$ of dimension k is a set of k positions $\mathcal{I}$ such that the knowledge of a codeword $\boldsymbol{c} \in \mathscr{C}$ on the positions in $\mathcal{I}$ determines entirely the codeword. Equivalently, if $\boldsymbol{G}$ denotes a $k \times n$ generator matrix of the code, then the $k \times k$ submatrix of $\boldsymbol{G}$ given by extracting the columns indexed by $\mathcal{I}$ is invertible.

3. At this stage, the public code has been transformed into another code $\mathscr{C}$ such that there exists a secret GRS code $\mathscr{C}'_{\text{sec}}$ and a matrix $\Pi + \boldsymbol{R}'$ where Π is a permutation matrix and $\boldsymbol{R}'$ is rank-1 matrix such that:

$$\mathscr{C} = \mathscr{C}'_{\text{sec}}(\Pi + \boldsymbol{R}'). \tag{10}$$

The third step consists then in applying the attack developed in [11] which is purposely devised to recover a pair $(\Pi, \boldsymbol{R}')$ from $\mathscr{C}$ as outlined in Section 2.1.

The purpose of the next sections is to describe more precisely the first two steps of the attack.

4.2   A Distinguisher of the Public Code

The attack uses in a crucial way a distinguisher which discriminates the public code from a random code of the same dimension. It is based on square code considerations. The point is the following: if we shorten the dual $\mathscr{C}_{\text{pub}}^{\perp}$ of the public code in a large enough set of positions $\mathcal{I}$, then the square code $\left(\mathcal{S}_{\mathcal{I}}\left(\mathscr{C}_{\text{pub}}^{\perp}\right)\right)^2$ has dimension strictly smaller than that of $\left(\mathcal{S}_{\mathcal{I}}\left(\mathscr{C}_{\text{rand}}^{\perp}\right)\right)^2$ where $\mathscr{C}_{\text{rand}}$ is a random code of the same dimension as $\mathscr{C}_{\text{pub}}$. The code $\left(\mathcal{S}_{\mathcal{I}}\left(\mathscr{C}_{\text{rand}}^{\perp}\right)\right)^2$ has dimension which is typically $\min\left\{n - |\mathcal{I}|, \binom{k_{\mathcal{I}}+1}{2}\right\}$ where $k_{\mathcal{I}}$ stands for the dimension of $\mathcal{S}_{\mathcal{I}}\left(\mathscr{C}_{\text{rand}}^{\perp}\right)$. In general, $k_{\mathcal{I}}$ is equal to $n-k-|\mathcal{I}|$ since $\dim \mathscr{C}_{\text{rand}}^{\perp} = \dim \mathscr{C}_{\text{pub}}^{\perp} = n-k$ whereas we generally have:

$$\dim \left(\mathcal{S}_{\mathcal{I}}\left(\mathscr{C}_{\text{pub}}^{\perp}\right)\right)^2 \leqslant 3(n - k) + |\mathcal{J}_2| - 3|\mathcal{I}| - 1. \tag{11}$$

In other words, when $3(n-k)+|\mathcal{J}_2|-3|\mathcal{I}|-1 < \min\left\{n - |\mathcal{I}|, \binom{k_{\mathcal{I}}+1}{2}\right\}$ we expect to distinguish $\mathscr{C}_{\text{pub}}$ from a random code of the same dimension. We write here "generally" because there are some exceptional cases where such an inequality does not hold. However in the case when $\mathcal{I} \subset \mathcal{J}_1$, this inequality always holds.

Proposition 4. *Let* $\mathcal{I} \subseteq \mathcal{J}_1$, *then* $\dim \left(\mathcal{S}_{\mathcal{I}}\left(\mathscr{C}_{pub}^{\perp}\right)\right)^2 \leqslant 3(n-k)-3|\mathcal{I}|-1+|\mathcal{J}_2|$.

Remark 4. It turns out that a similar inequality also generally holds when $\mathcal{I}$ contains degree 2 positions. However in this case, the situation is more complicated and it might happen in rare cases that this upper-bound is not met but, roughly speaking, when it happens, the actual result remains *close* to this upper bound. Experimentally, we observed that (11) was satisfied even when $\mathcal{I}$ contained positions of $\mathcal{J}_2$.

Remark 5. The use of shortening is important since in general the (dual) public code itself is non distinguishable because its square equals the whole ambient space. However, for a part of the parameters proposed in [2], the dual public code is distinguishable from a random code without shortening. See §6 for further details.

4.3 Description of the Attack

First Step – Distinguishing Between Positions in $\mathcal{J}_1$ and $\mathcal{J}_2$. Roughly speaking the attack builds upon an algorithm which allows to distinguish between a position of degree 1 and a position of degree 2. It turns out now that once we are able to distinguish the public code from a random one by shortening it in a set of positions $\mathcal{I}$ such that:

$$\dim \left(\mathcal{S}_{\mathcal{I}} \left(\mathscr{C}_{\mathrm{pub}}^{\perp} \right) \right)^2 < \min \left\{ n - |\mathcal{I}|, \binom{n - k - |\mathcal{I}| + 1}{2} \right\}, \tag{12}$$

we can puncture $\mathcal{S}_{\mathcal{I}} \left(\mathscr{C}_{\mathrm{pub}}^{\perp} \right)$ in a position i that does not belong to $\mathcal{I}$ and this allows to distinguish degree 1 positions from degree 2 positions. The dimension of the square code of this punctured code will differ drastically when i is a degree 1 position (or a certain type of degree 2 position) or a "usual" degree 2 position. When i is a degree 1 position it turns out that

$$\dim \left(\mathcal{S}_{\mathcal{I}} \left(\mathscr{C}_{\mathrm{pub}}^{\perp} \right) \right)^2 = \dim \left(\mathcal{P}_i \left(\mathcal{S}_{\mathcal{I}} \left(\mathscr{C}_{\mathrm{pub}}^{\perp} \right) \right) \right)^2, \tag{13}$$

whereas for "usual" degree 2 positions we observe that

$$\dim \left(\mathcal{S}_{\mathcal{I}} \left(\mathscr{C}_{\mathrm{pub}}^{\perp} \right) \right)^2 = \dim \left(\mathcal{P}_i \left(\mathcal{S}_{\mathcal{I}} \left(\mathscr{C}_{\mathrm{pub}}^{\perp} \right) \right) \right)^2 + 1. \tag{14}$$

Sometimes (in the "non usual" cases), we can have positions of degree 2 for which

$$\dim \left(\mathcal{S}_{\mathcal{I}} \left(\mathscr{C}_{\mathrm{pub}}^{\perp} \right) \right)^2 = \dim \left(\mathcal{P}_i \left(\mathcal{S}_{\mathcal{I}} \left(\mathscr{C}_{\mathrm{pub}}^{\perp} \right) \right) \right)^2$$

as for degree 1 positions. This happens for instance if shortening in $\mathcal{I}$ "induces" a degree 1 position in i. This arises mostly when the position i of degree 2 is such that $j(i) = \{j_1, j_2\}$ where either $j_1 = j(i')$ or $j_2 = j(i')$ for a position i' of degree 1 that belongs to $\mathcal{I}$. This phenomenon really depends on the choice of $\mathcal{I}$. However, by choosing several random subsets $\mathcal{I}$ we quickly find a shortening set $\mathcal{I}$ for which the degree 2 position we want to test behaves as predicted in (14).

Procedure to Compute $\mathcal{J}_2$

- Choose a set of random subsets $\mathcal{I}_1, \ldots, \mathcal{I}_s$ (in our experimentations we always chose $s \approx 20$) whose cardinals satisfy (12).
- For $i = 1, \ldots, s$ compute $\mathcal{S}_{\mathcal{I}_i} \left(\mathscr{C}_{\mathrm{pub}}^{\perp} \right)^2$ and call $\mathcal{J}_2(i)$ this set of positions satisfying

$$\dim \mathcal{S}_{\mathcal{I}_i} \left(\mathscr{C}_{\mathrm{pub}}^{\perp} \right)^2 \neq \dim \mathcal{P}_j \left(\mathcal{S}_{\mathcal{I}_i} \left(\mathscr{C}_{\mathrm{pub}}^{\perp} \right)^2 \right).$$

- Set $\mathcal{J}_2 = \mathcal{J}_2(1) \cup \cdots \cup \mathcal{J}_2(s)$.

Second Step – Transforming Degree 2 Positions into Degree 1 Ones

Proposition 5. *Let $i_1 \in \mathcal{J}_1$ and $i_2 \in \mathcal{J}_2$ be a position associated to i_1. Let $D(\alpha, i_1, i_2)$ be an $n \times n$ matrix which is the identity matrix with an additional entry in column i_2 and row i_1 that is equal to α. Define $\mathscr{C} \stackrel{def}{=} \mathscr{C}_{pub}^{\perp} D_{\alpha, i_1, i_2}$. If $\alpha = -\frac{T_{i_2 j_1}}{T_{i_1 j_1}}$, then there exists $\mathbf{R}'$ of rank at most one such that*

$$\mathscr{C} = \mathscr{C}_{sec}^{\perp}(\mathbf{T}'^T + \mathbf{R}'^T) \tag{15}$$

where $\mathbf{T}'$ differs from $\mathbf{T}$ only in row i_2 and column j_1, the corresponding entry being now equal to 0.

This proposition is exploited as follows, we first compute for a degree 1 position i_1 the set of degree 2 positions i_2 such that $j(i_1) \in j(i_2)$. These positions i_2 can be detected by checking if i_2 has now become a degree 1 position for $\mathcal{S}_{\{i_1\}}\left(\mathscr{C}_{pub}^{\perp}\right)$ (this is the case if and only if $j(i_1) \in j(i_2)$). Once such a pair (i_1, i_2) has been found we try all possible values for $\alpha \in \mathbb{F}_q^{\times}$ until we obtain a code $\mathscr{C}$ for which the corresponding $\mathbf{T}'$ contains a row of index i_2 which is now of Hamming weight 1. That is to say: i_2 became a position of degree 1 for $\mathscr{C}$. This can be easily checked by using the previous technique to distinguish between a position of degree 1 or 2.

In other words, when we are successful, we obtain a new code $\mathscr{C}$ for which there is one more row of weight 1. We iterate this process by replacing $\mathscr{C}_{pub}^{\perp}$ by $\mathscr{C}$ and $\mathcal{J}_1$ by $\mathcal{J}_1 \cup \{i_2\}$ until we do not find such pairs (i_1, i_2). For the values of m chosen in [2] and with rows of $\mathbf{T}$ which were all of weight 1 or 2 we ended up with $\mathbf{T}'$ which was a permutation matrix and a code $\mathscr{C}$ which was linked to the secret code by

$$\mathscr{C} = \mathscr{C}_{sec}^{\perp}(\Pi + \mathbf{R}')$$

where Π is a permutation matrix and $\mathbf{R}'$ a matrix of rank at most 1. To finish the attack, we just apply the attack described in [11, Sec.4] to recover $\mathscr{C}_{sec}$.

Case of Remaining Degree-2 Positions

It could happen that the previously decribed method is unsufficient to transform every degree 2 position into a degree 1. It could for instance happen if there is a position i of degree 2 such that for all position i' of degree 1, $j(i') \notin j(i)$. In such a situation, no position of degree 1 can be used to eliminate this position of degree 2.

This problem can be addressed as soon as the set of positions of degree 1 contains an information set of the code. We describe the strategy to conclude the attack in such a situation.

Let $\mathscr{C}$ be the code obtained after performing the two steps of the attack and assume that there remains as nonempty set $\mathcal{J}_2$ of positions of degree 2, which are known (since they have been identified during the first step of the attack). Here is the strategy

1. Puncture $\mathscr{C}$ at $\mathcal{J}_2$. The punctured code is of the form

$$\mathscr{C}'(I + R') \tag{16}$$

   where $\mathscr{C}'$ is a GRS code, I is the identity matrix and R' a rank 1 matrix.
2. Perform the attack of [11] on $\mathcal{P}_{\mathcal{J}_2}(\mathscr{C})$. We get the knowledge of a support x' a multiplier y' and a rank 1 matrix R' such that

$$\mathscr{C}' = \mathbf{GRS}_k(x', y')(I + R').$$

   Moreover, we are able to identify the polynomials $P_1, \ldots, P_k$ yielding the rows of the public matrix G_{pub}.
3. For all $x \in \mathbb{F}_q$ which is not in the support x' of $\mathscr{C}'$, compute the column

$$\begin{pmatrix} P_1(x) \\ P_2(x) \\ \vdots \\ P_k(x) \end{pmatrix}$$

   and join it to the matrix G_{pub}. By this manner we get new positions of degree 1 which can be used to eliminate the remaining positions of degree 2.

Remark 6. In our experiments, this situation never happened: we have always eliminated all the degree 2 positions using Proposition 5.

5   Limits and Complexity of the Attack

5.1   Choosing Appropriately the Cardinality of $\mathcal{I}$

By definition of the density m, the sets $\mathcal{J}_1$ and $\mathcal{J}_2$ have respective cardinalities $(2 - m)n$ and $(m - 1)n$. In what follows, we denote by R the rate of the public code namely $R = k/n$. Let us recall that the attack shortens the dual of a public code which is of dimension $n - k$. The cardinality of $\mathcal{I}$ is denoted by a. We list the constraints we need to satisfy for the success of the attack.

1. The shortened code should be reduced to the zero space, which implies that $a < n - k$.
2. The code punctured at $\mathcal{J}_2$ must contain an information set, that is to say:

$$n - k \leqslant |\mathcal{J}_1|. \tag{17}$$

   It is clear that (17) is equivalent to $m \leqslant 1 + R$.
3. The computed square code in Proposition 4 should also be different from the full space which implies:

$$3(n - k - a) + |\mathcal{J}_2| - 1 < n - a \tag{18}$$

One can easily check that (18) is equivalent to:

$$a \geqslant \frac{1}{2}\Big((1 + m)n - 3k\Big). \tag{19}$$

4. Finally, to have good chances that the dimension of the square code reaches the upper bound given by Proposition 4, we also need:

$$3(n - k - a) + |\mathcal{J}_2| - 1 < \binom{n - k - a + 1}{2} \tag{20}$$

which is equivalent to the inequality:

$$a^2 + \left(5 - 2(n - k)\right)a + (n - k)^2 - 5(n - k) + 2(1 - m)n \geqslant 0 \tag{21}$$

Considering (21) as an inequality involving a degree-2 polynomial in a, we can check that its discriminant is equal to $\Delta \overset{\text{def}}{=} 8(m - 1)n + 25$, so that its roots are a_0 and a_1 where:

$$a_0 \overset{\text{def}}{=} n - k - \frac{5}{2} - \frac{1}{2}\sqrt{\Delta} \quad \text{and} \quad a_1 \overset{\text{def}}{=} n - k - \frac{5}{2} + \frac{1}{2}\sqrt{\Delta}. \tag{22}$$

Let us recall that in order to have (21) satisfied, we should have $a \leqslant a_0$ or $a \geqslant a_1$. Because of the constraint $a < n - k$ and since $a_1 > n - k$, the only case to study is $a \leqslant a_0$. Combining (19) with $a \leqslant a_0$, we obtain:

$$\frac{1}{2}\left((1 + m)n - 3k\right) \leqslant a_0.$$

which is equivalent to the following inequality involving this time a degree-2 polynomial in m:

$$n^2 m^2 + 2n(1 - n - k)m + 2kn + k^2 - 10k + n^2 - 2n \geqslant 0. \tag{23}$$

The discriminant of this polynomial is $n^2(8k + 1)$ and the roots are:

$$m_0 \overset{\text{def}}{=} 1 + R - \frac{1}{n} - \sqrt{\frac{8}{n}R + \frac{1}{n^2}} \quad \text{and} \quad m_1 \overset{\text{def}}{=} 1 + R - \frac{1}{n} + \sqrt{\frac{8}{n}R + \frac{1}{n^2}}.$$

Because of the fact that $m \leqslant 1 + R$ from (17), and since $m_1 > 1 + R$, we conclude that the attack can be applied as long as $m \leqslant m_0$, that is to say:

$$m \leqslant 1 + R - \frac{1}{n} - \sqrt{\frac{8}{n}R + \frac{1}{n^2}}. \tag{24}$$

5. Finally, the last step of the attack consists in performing the attack of [11].

Remark 7. This upper-bound is roughly $1 + R$. In [2], the authors suggest to choose $m \approx 2 - R$ for rates $R > \frac{1}{2}$, which is well within the reach of the present attack.

5.2 Estimating the Complexity

As explained in Proposition 2, the square of a code of dimension k and length n can be computed in $O(n^2k^2)$. Let us study the costs of the steps of the attack.

- **Step 1. Finding the positions of degree 2.** For a constant number of subsets $\mathcal{I}$ of length $a \leqslant a_0$ where a_0 is defined in (22), we shorten $\mathscr{C}_{\mathrm{pub}}^{\perp}$ and compute its square. If a is close to a_0 then, the shortened code has dimension $n - k - a = O(\sqrt{n})$. Hence, the computation of its square costs $O(n^3)$. Thus this first step costs $O(n^3)$ operations in $\mathbb{F}_q$.
- **Step 2. Transforming degree-2 positions into degree 1 positions.** This is the most expensive part of the attack. For a given position $i_1 \in \mathcal{J}_1$, the computation of positions i_2 of degree 2 such that[4] $j(i_1) \in j(i_2)$ consists essentially in shortening the dual public code at i_1 and applying to the shortened code the first step. This costs $O(n^3)$. Then, the application of Proposition 5 to transform i_2 requires to proceed to at most q linear combinations and, for each one, to check whether the position became of degree 1. Each check has mostly the same cost as the first step, that is $O(n^3)$. Thus, the overall cost to reduce one position of degree 2 is $O(n^4)$ and hence the cost of this second step is $O(n^5)$.
- **Step 3.** According to [11], it is in $O(n^6)$.

6 Experimental Results

Table 1 gathers experimental results obtained when the attack is programmed in Magma V2.20-3 [9]. The attacked parameters are taken from [2, Tables 3 & 4] The timings given are obtained with Intel® Xeon 2.27GHz and 72 Gb of RAM. Our programs are far from being optimized and probably improved programs could provide better timings and memory usage.

The running times for codes of length 346 are below 5 hours and those for codes of length 546 can be a bit longer than one day. The total memory usage remains below 100Mb for codes of length 346 and 500Mb for codes of length 546.

Remark 8. Since the algorithms include many random choices, the identification of pairs (i_1, i_2), where $i_1 \in \mathcal{J}_1$ and $i_2 \in \mathcal{J}_2$ such that $j(i_1) \in j(i_2)$ might happen quickly or be rather long. This explains the important gaps between different running times.

Remark 9. Actually some parameters proposed in [2] were directly distinguishable without even shortening. This holds for $(q, n, k) = (347, 346, 268)$, $(q, n, k) = (347, 346, 284)$ and $(q, n, k) = (547, 546, 428)$ with m respectively equal to 1.217, 1.171 and 1.211. This explains why the first step is quicker for these examples.

---

[4] Equivalently, there exists an integer j such that $T_{i_1,j} \neq 0$ and $T_{i_2,j} \neq 0$.

Table 1. Running times

(q, n, k, z)	m	Step 1	Step 2
(347, 346, 180, 1)	1.471	15s	18513s ($\approx$5 hours)
(347, 346, 188, 1)	1.448	8s	10811s ($\approx$3 hours)
(347, 346, 204, 1)	1.402	10s	8150s ($\approx$2.25 hours)
(347, 346, 228, 1)	1.332	15s	9015s ($\approx$2.5 hours)
(347, 346, 252, 1)	1.263	36s	10049s ($\approx$2.75 hours)
(347, 346, 268, 1)	1.217	3s	14887s ($\approx$4 hours)
(347, 346, 284, 1)	1.171	3s	7165s ($\approx$2 hours)
(547, 546, 324, 1)	1.401	60s	58778s ($\approx$16 hours)
(547, 546, 340, 1)	1.372	83s	72863s ($\approx$20 hours)
(547, 546, 364, 1)	1.328	100s	72343s ($\approx$20 hours)
(547, 546, 388, 1)	1.284	170s	85699s ($\approx$24 hours)
(547, 546, 412, 1)	1.240	15s	157999s ($\approx$43 hours)
(547, 546, 428, 1)	1.211	15s	109970s ($\approx$30,5 hours)

Remark 10. The examples $[346, 180]_{347}$ and $[346, 188]_{347}$ do not satisfy (24). However, they are distinguishable by shortening and squaring and the attack works on them. Because of some cancellation phenomenon for positions of degree 2 which we do not control, it may happen that the upper bound in Proposition 4 is not sharp and that some shortenings of $\mathscr{C}_{\text{pub}}^{\perp}$ turn out to be distinguishable while our formulas could not anticipate it.

The above remark is of interest since it points out that our attack might work for values of m above $1 + R$.

7 Concluding Remarks

The papers [1–4] can be seen as an attempt of replacing the permutation matrix in the McEliece scheme by a more complicated transformation. Instead of having as in the McEliece scheme a relation between the secret code $\mathscr{C}_{\text{sec}}$ and the public code $\mathscr{C}_{\text{pub}}$ of the form $\mathscr{C}_{\text{sec}} = \mathscr{C}_{\text{pub}}\Pi$ where Π is a permutation matrix, it was chosen in [3,4] that

$$\mathscr{C}_{\text{sec}} = \mathscr{C}_{\text{pub}}\boldsymbol{T}$$

where $\boldsymbol{T}$ is a sparse matrix of density m or as

$$\mathscr{C}_{\text{sec}} = \mathscr{C}_{\text{pub}}(\boldsymbol{T} + \boldsymbol{R})$$

where $\boldsymbol{T}$ is as before and $\boldsymbol{R}$ is of very small rank z (the case of rank 1 being probably the only practical way of choosing this rank as will be discussed below) as in [1,2]. It was advocated that this allows to use for the secret code $\mathscr{C}_{\text{sec}}$, codes which are well known to be weak in the usual McEliece cryptosystem such as LDPC codes [3,4] or GRS codes [1,2]. Interestingly enough, it turns out that for LDPC codes this basically amounts choosing a McEliece system where the density of the parity-check matrix is increased by a large amount and the error-correction capacity is decreased by the same multiplicative constant. The latter approach has been studied in [21], it leads to schemes with slightly larger decoding complexity but that have at least partial security proofs.

In the case of GRS codes, the first attempt [1] of choosing for T a permutation matrix was broken in [11, Sec.4]. It was suggested later on [2] that this attack can be avoided by choosing T of larger density. In order to reduce the public key size when compared to the McEliece scheme based on Goppa codes, rather moderate values of m between 1 and 2 ($m = 1.4$ for instance) were chosen in [2]. We show here that the parameters proposed in [2] can be broken by a new attack computing first the dimension of the square code of shortened versions of the dual of the public code and using this to reduce the problem to the original problem [1] when T is a permutation matrix. This attack can be avoided by choosing larger values for m and/or z, but this comes at a certain cost as we now show.

Increasing z. Increasing $z = 1$ to larger values of z avoids the attack given here, though some of the ideas of [11] might be used in this new context to get rid of the R part in the scheme and might lead to an attack of reasonable complexity when $z = 2$ by trying first to guess several codewords which lie in the code $\mathscr{C} \stackrel{\text{def}}{=} \mathscr{C}_{\text{sec}}^{\perp} T^T \cap \mathscr{C}_{\text{pub}}^{\perp}$ (this code is of codimension at least z in $\mathscr{C}_{\text{pub}}^{\perp}$). Once $\mathscr{C}$ is found, we basically have to recover T and the approach used in this paper can be applied to it. To avoid such an attack, rather large values of z have to be chosen, but the decryption cost becomes prohibitive by doing so. Indeed, decryption time is of order $q^z C$ where C is the decoding complexity of the underlying GRS code. Choosing $z = 2$ is of questionable practical interest and $z > 2$ becomes probably unreasonable.

Increasing m. Choosing values for m close enough to 2 will avoid the attack presented here. However this also reduces strongly the gain in key size when compared to the McEliece scheme based on Goppa or alternant codes. Indeed, assume for simplicity $m = 2$. We can use in such a case for the secret code a GRS code over $\mathbb{F}_q$ of dimension $k = n - 2t$ and add errors of weight $\leqslant \frac{t}{2}$ in the BBCRS scheme. The public key size of such a scheme is however not better than choosing in the McEliece scheme a Goppa code of the same dimension $n - 2t$ but which is the subfield subcode of a GRS code over $\mathbb{F}_{q^2}$ of dimension $n - t$, and which can also correct $\frac{t}{2}$ errors. This Goppa code has the very same parameters and provides the same security level. For this reason, one loses the advantages of using GRS codes when choosing m close to 2. Thus, to have interesting key sizes and to resist to our attack m should be smaller than 2 and larger than $1 + R$. One should however be careful, since, as explained in §6, it is still unclear whether the attack fails for m closely above $1 + R$.

On the other hand, it might be interesting for theoretical reasons to understand better the security of the BBCRS scheme for larger values of m. There might be a closer connection than what it looks between the BBCRS scheme with density m and the usual McEliece scheme with (possibly non-binary) Goppa codes of extension degree m. The connection is that the case $m = 2$ is in both cases the limiting case where the distinguishing approach of [11,14] might work (in [14], the attack only works because wild Goppa codes are studied and this brings an additional power to the distinguishing attack). It should also be added that it might be interesting to study the choice of $\mathscr{C}_{sec}$ being an LDPC code and $\mathscr{C}_{sec} = \mathscr{C}_{pub}(T + R)$ since here adding R of small rank can also change rather drastically the property of $\mathscr{C}_{pub}$ being an LDPC code (which is at the heart of the key attacks on McEliece schemes based on LDPC codes).

References

1. Baldi, M., Bianchi, M., Chiaraluce, F., Rosenthal, J., Schipani, D.: Enhanced public key security for the McEliece cryptosystem. preprint (2011). arXiv:1108.2462v2
2. Baldi, M., Bianchi, M., Chiaraluce, F., Rosenthal, J., Schipani, D.: Enhanced public key security for the McEliece cryptosystem. J. of Cryptology (2014). http://link.springer.com/article/10.1007/s00145-014-9187-8 and also ArXiv:1108.2462v4 (published online: August 15, 2014)
3. Baldi, M., Bodrato, M., Chiaraluce, F.: A new analysis of the McEliece cryptosystem based on QC-LDPC codes. In: Ostrovsky, R., De Prisco, R., Visconti, I. (eds.) SCN 2008. LNCS, vol. 5229, pp. 246–262. Springer, Heidelberg (2008)
4. Baldi, M., Chiaraluce, G.F.: Cryptanalysis of a new instance of McEliece cryptosystem based on QC-LDPC codes. In: IEEE International Symposium on Information Theory, pp. 2591–2595. Nice (March 2007)
5. Barbulescu, R., Gaudry, P., Joux, A., Thomé, E.: A heuristic quasi-polynomial algorithm for discrete logarithm in finite fields of small characteristic. In: Nguyen, P.Q., Oswald, E. (eds.) EUROCRYPT 2014. LNCS, vol. 8441, pp. 1–16. Springer, Heidelberg (2014)
6. Berger, T.P., Loidreau, P.: How to mask the structure of codes for a cryptographic use. Des. Codes Cryptogr. **35**(1), 63–79 (2005)
7. Bernstein, D.J., Lange, T., Peters, C.: Wild McEliece. In: Selected Areas in Cryptography, pp. 143–158 (2010)
8. Biswas, B., Sendrier, N.: McEliece cryptosystem implementation: theory and practice. In: Buchmann, J., Ding, J. (eds.) PQCrypto 2008. LNCS, vol. 5299, pp. 47–62. Springer, Heidelberg (2008)
9. Bosma, W., Cannon, J.J., Playoust, C.: The Magma algebra system I: The user language. J. Symbolic Comput. **24**(3/4), 235–265 (1997)
10. Cascudo, I., Cramer, R., Mirandola, D., Zémor, G.: Squares of random linear codes. arXiv:1407.0848v1
11. Couvreur, A., Gaborit, P., Gauthier-Umaña, V., Otmani, A., Tillich, J.P.: Distinguisher-based attacks on public-key cryptosystems using Reed-Solomon codes. Des. Codes Cryptogr., pp. 1–26 (2014)
12. Couvreur, A., Gaborit, P., Gauthier-Umaña, V., Otmani, A., Tillich, J.P.: Distinguisher-based attacks on public-key cryptosystems using Reed-Solomon codes. In: International Workshop on Coding and Cryptography, WCC 2013. Bergen, Norway (April 15–19, 2013)
13. Couvreur, A., Márquez-Corbella, I., Pellikaan, R.: A polynomial time attack against algebraic geometry code based public key cryptosystems. In: IEEE International Symposium on Information Theory (ISIT 2014). Honolulu, US (2014)

14. Couvreur, A., Otmani, A., Tillich, J.P.: Polynomial time attack on wild McEliece over quadratic extensions. In: Nguyen, P.Q., Oswald, E. (eds.) EUROCRYPT 2014. LNCS, vol. 8441, pp. 17–39. Springer, Heidelberg (2014)
15. Faugère, J.C., Gauthier, V., Otmani, A., Perret, L., Tillich, J.P.: A distinguisher for high rate McEliece cryptosystems. In: Proceedings of the Information Theory Workshop 2011. ITW 2011, pp. 282–286. Paraty, Brasil (2011)
16. Faugère, J.C., Gauthier-Umaña, V., Otmani, A., Perret, L., Tillich, J.P.: A distinguisher for high-rate McEliece cryptosystems. IEEE Trans. Inform. Theory **59**(10), 6830–6844 (2013)
17. MacWilliams, F.J., Sloane, N.J.A.: The Theory of Error-Correcting Codes, 5th edn. North-Holland, Amsterdam (1986)
18. Márquez-Corbella, I., Martínez-Moro, E., Pellikaan, R.: The non-gap sequence of a subcode of a generalized Reed-Solomon code. Des. Codes Cryptogr. **66**(1–3), 317–333 (2013)
19. Márquez-Corbella, I., Pellikaan, R.: Error-correcting pairs for a public-key cryptosystem. preprint (2012)
20. McEliece, R.J.: A Public-Key System Based on Algebraic Coding Theory, pp. 114–116. Jet Propulsion Lab (1978), dSN Progress Report 44
21. Misoczki, R., Tillich, J.P., Sendrier, N., Barreto, P.S.L.M.: MDPC-McEliece: New McEliece variants from moderate density parity-check codes. In: ISIT, pp. 2069–2073 (2013)
22. Monico, C., Rosenthal, J., Shokrollahi, A.: Using low density parity check codes in the McEliece cryptosystem. In: IEEE International Symposium on Information Theory (ISIT 2000), p. 215. Sorrento, Italy (2000)
23. Niederreiter, H.: Knapsack-type cryptosystems and algebraic coding theory. Problems Control Inform. Theory **15**(2), 159–166 (1986)
24. Shor, P.W.: Algorithms for quantum computation: Discrete logarithms and factoring. In: Goldwasser, S. (ed.) Proceedings of the 35th Annual Symposium on the Foundations of Computer Science, pp. 124–134. IEEE Computer Society, Los Alamitos (1994)
25. Sidelnikov, V., Shestakov, S.: On the insecurity of cryptosystems based on generalized Reed-Solomon codes. Discrete Math. Appl. **1**(4), 439–444 (1992)
26. Wieschebrink, C.: Cryptanalysis of the niederreiter public key scheme based on GRS subcodes. In: Sendrier, N. (ed.) PQCrypto 2010. LNCS, vol. 6061, pp. 61–72. Springer, Heidelberg (2010)

Algebraic Cryptanalysis of a Quantum Money Scheme: The Noise-Free Case

Marta Conde Pena[1]([⊠]), Jean-Charles Faugère[2,3,4], and Ludovic Perret[2,3,4]

[1] Institute of Physical and Information Technologies (ITEFI) – Spanish National Research Council (CSIC), Madrid, Spain
marta.conde@iec.csic.es
[2] Sorbonne Universités, UPMC Univ Paris 06, POLSYS, UMR 7606, LIP6, 75005 Paris, France
[3] INRIA, Paris-Rocquencourt Center, POLSYS Project, Paris, France
[4] CNRS, UMR 7606, LIP6, 75005 Paris, France
jean-charles.faugere@inria.fr, ludovic.perret@lip6.fr

Abstract. We investigate the Hidden Subspace Problem (HSP_q) over $\mathbb{F}_q$:

Input : $p_1, \ldots, p_m, q_1, \ldots, q_m \in \mathbb{F}_q[x_1, \ldots, x_n]$ of degree $d \geq 3$ (and $n \leq m \leq 2n$).
Find : a subspace $A \subset \mathbb{F}_q{}^n$ of dimension $n/2$ (n is even) such that

$$p_i(A) = 0 \ \forall i \in \{1, \ldots, m\} \text{ and } q_j(A^\perp) = 0 \ \forall j \in \{1, \ldots, m\},$$

where $A^\perp$ denotes the orthogonal complement of A with respect to the usual scalar product in $\mathbb{F}_q$.

This problem underlies the security of the first public-key quantum money scheme that is proved to be cryptographically secure under a non quantum but classic hardness assumption. This scheme was proposed by S. Aaronson and P. Christiano [1] at STOC'12. In particular, it depends upon the hardness of HSP_2. More generally, Aaronson and Christiano left as an open problem to study the security of the scheme for a general field $\mathbb{F}_q$. We present a randomized polynomial-time algorithm that solves the HSP_q for $q > d$ with success probability $\approx 1 - 1/q$. So, the quantum money scheme extended to $\mathbb{F}_q$ is not secure for big q. Finally, based on experimental results and a structural property of the polynomials that we prove, we conjecture that there is also a randomized polynomial-time algorithm solving the HSP_2 with high probability. To support our theoretical results we also present several experimental results confirming that our algorithms are very efficient in practice. We emphasize that [1] proposes a non-noisy and a noisy version of the public-key quantum money scheme. The noisy version of the quantum money scheme remains secure.

1 Introduction

The no-cloning theorem in quantum mechanics states the impossibility of creating identical copies of an unknown arbitrary quantum money state. In [20],

© International Association for Cryptologic Research 2015
J. Katz (Ed.): PKC 2015, LNCS 9020, pp. 194–213, 2015.
DOI: 10.1007/978-3-662-46447-2_9

Wiesner suggested to take advantage of this physical law in order to construct a scheme for (quantum) money that could not be counterfeited. The initial work of Wiesner has been then followed by several papers that try to improve the initial idea of [20], i.e. [5,17,18]. This line of research culminated with the proposal of Aaronson and Christiano [1] at STOC'12 who proposed a public-key quantum money scheme.

A public-key quantum money scheme is a scheme in which anyone with a quantum device can verify if a banknote is valid rather than only the bank that issued it (in contrast to [20]). A public-key quantum money scheme based on knot theory was introduced in [12]. However, its security is not well understood. The scheme proposed by Aaronson and Christiano in [1] is the first that is public-key and proved to be cryptographically secure under a classical (as in non-quantum) hardness assumption. The scheme is based on hiding two orthogonal subspaces by expressing each of them as the common zeros of a set of appropriate random multivariate non-linear polynomials. In particular, its security relies on the assumption that the following problem is hard:

Hidden Subspaces Problem (HSP_q)
Input : polynomials $p_1, \ldots, p_m, q_1, \ldots, q_m \in \mathbb{F}_q[x_1, \ldots, x_n]$ of degree $d \geq 3$, $n \leq m \leq 2n$.
Find : a subspace $A \subset \mathbb{F}_q{}^n$ of dimension $n/2$ (n is even) such that

$$p_i(A) = 0 \ \forall i \in \{1, \ldots, m\} \text{ and } q_j(A^\perp) = 0 \ \forall j \in \{1, \ldots, m\},$$

where $A^\perp$ denotes the orthogonal complement of A with respect to the standard scalar product in $\mathbb{F}_q$.

We emphasize that in [1] the authors propose a non-noisy and a noisy version of the public-key quantum money scheme. In this paper we only consider the noise-free version of the quantum money scheme.

In particular, the non-noisy version of the quantum money scheme relies on the HSP_2 and Aaronson and Christiano conjecture that it cannot be solved in polynomial time. They also state as an open problem the study of the scheme extended to a general field $\mathbb{F}_q$, which brings up the question of the hardness of HSP_q.

We analyze the hardness of the HSP_q. The main idea is to model the problem as a set of algebraic equations. Expressing elements as the common zeros of a set of random multivariate non-linear polynomials is the core of algebraic attacks, e.g. [11,15,16]. However, in this case we can exploit that there are two sets of public polynomials whose sets of zeros are two subspaces orthogonal to each other.

Aside from this quantum money scheme, the HSP_q has also interest as a general computer algebra problem closely related to the isomorphism of polynomials [19]. Given $\mathbf{p} = T \circ \mathbf{p}' \circ S$, where $\mathbf{p} = (p_1, \ldots, p_m), \mathbf{p}' = (p'_1, \ldots, p'_m) \in \mathbb{F}_q[x_1, \ldots, x_n]^m$ and T, S are affine invertible transformations, the *Isomorphism of Polynomials* (IP) problem consists on recovering T and S. The HSP_q can be seen as a slight modification of the isomorphism of polynomials problem where $\mathbf{p} = \mathbf{0}$, T is the identity transformation and S is linear but not invertible.

1.1 Main Results

Our results mostly rely on Gröbner bases and linear algebra techniques. This is because we are capable of identifying the solution of the HSP_q as the unique solution of an overdetermined system of multivariate equations in $N = n^2/4$ unknowns (Section 3.1, Proposition 5). The properties of this system are different for $q = 2$ and for $q > d$, so we study separately both cases.

Our first main result (Section 3) solves an open problem presented in [1], which is the study of the HSP_q for $q \neq 2$. From the algebraic equations describing HSP_q we observe that we can extract a set of linear equations (Lemma 3). Due to the shape of the linear equations, we can prove that sufficiently many linearly independent ones can be extracted. This gives:

Theorem 1 (Section 3.2). *Let $N = n^2/4$. There is a randomized polynomial-time algorithm solving HSP_q, for $q > d$, with complexity $\mathcal{O}(N^\omega) = \mathcal{O}(n^{2\omega})$, where $2 \leq \omega \leq 3$ is the linear algebra constant, and success probability*

$$\frac{\gamma_q(n/2)\gamma_q(m)}{\gamma_q(m - n/2)},$$

$\gamma_q(k)$ being the probability that a random $k \times k$ matrix with entries in $\mathbb{F}_q$ is invertible. For n big enough, the success probability is $\approx 1 - 1/q$.

In Section 3.3 we report experimental results demonstrating that HSP_q, with $q > d$, can be solved very efficiently. For $n \leq 20$, the algorithm requires less than 0.1 s. for various q. We have implemented the algorithm using the MAGMA software [6]. The code is provided with the submission so that the results can be reproduced or conducted for bigger values of n.

Our second result is concerned with the HSP_2 (Section 4). In this case our system does not contain, except with a small probability, linear equations and so the approach needs to be different. Still, in the case of the HSP_2 we have an algebraic system of equations which is very overdetermined.

Proposition 1 (Section 4). *Let $\big(\mathbf{p} = (p_1, \ldots, p_m), \mathbf{q} = (q_1, \ldots, q_m)\big) \in \mathbb{F}_2[x_1, \ldots, x_n]^m \times \mathbb{F}_2[x_1, \ldots, x_n]^m$ be degree-d multivariate polynomials. Let $A \subset \mathbb{F}_2^n$ be a vector subspace of dimension $n/2$. If A is a solution of HSP_2 on $(\mathbf{p}, \mathbf{q}) \in \mathbb{F}_2[x_1, \ldots, x_n]^m \times \mathbb{F}_2[x_1, \ldots, x_n]^m$, then we can construct an algebraic system of equations Sys_{HSP_2} over $\mathbb{F}_2$ in $N = n^2/4$ variables with at most $2m \left[\binom{n/2}{1} + \binom{n/2}{2} + \ldots + \binom{n/2}{d} \right]$ equations such that a systematic basis of A vanishes Sys_{HSP_2} with probability $\gamma_2(n/2)$, where $\gamma_2(n/2)$ denotes the probability that a random $n/2 \times n/2$ matrix with entries in $\mathbb{F}_2$ is invertible. For n big enough, this is $\approx 1/2$.*

So, we can still hope that the computation of a Gröbner basis of the system will be efficient. In Section 4.1 we run experiments to confirm this intuition. It appears that Sys_{HSP_2} is much easier to solve than a semi-regular system of the same size. The MAGMA code of this part is also provided with the submission. Typically, we can solve in practice Sys_{HSP_2} for $n \leq 18$ and $d = 3$ in less than

3 hours (for smaller n, we can solve in few minutes). For $n = 18$, we have to solve a system of degree-3 equations with 81 variables. In practice we observed that the maximum degree reached during the computation of a Gröbner basis of $\mathrm{Sys}_{\mathrm{HSP}_2}$ is bounded above by a small constant. Based on this observation we conjecture then that:

Conjecture 1. The degree of regularity is bounded above by $d + 1$.

If this conjecture is true the following result is obtained:

Theorem 2. *Let $N = n^2/4$. There is a randomized polynomial-time algorithm solving HSP_2 with a complexity of $\mathcal{O}(N^{\omega(d+1)}) = \mathcal{O}(n^{2\omega(d+1)})$, where $2 \leq \omega \leq 3$ is the linear algebra constant, and success probability $\gamma_2(n/2)$, where $\gamma_2(k)$ denotes the probability that a random $k \times k$ matrix with entries in $\mathbb{F}_2$ is invertible. For n big enough, the success probability of the algorithm is $\approx 1/2$.*

To support our assumption we analyze in Section 5 the structure of $\mathrm{Sys}_{\mathrm{HSP}_2}$. We prove a structural property (due to the orthogonality of the hidden subspaces) that allows to obtain equations of degree lower than d from the public polynomials $\mathrm{Sys}_{\mathrm{HSP}_2}$ by performing simple manipulations on the initial system. In particular:

Proposition 2. *We can easily generate $\mathcal{O}(m^2)$ equations of degree $d - 1$ which are linear combinations of the equations from $\mathrm{Sys}_{\mathrm{HSP}_2}$.*

This means that a Gröbner computation on $\mathrm{Sys}_{\mathrm{HSP}_2}$ will generate at the very first step many equations of lower degree. This is known as a fall of degree and it is typically a behaviour which is not occurring in a random (i.e. semi-regular) system of equations. So, it is a first step towards proving our conjecture.

1.2 Organization of the Paper

In Section 2 we introduce some notation that will be used throughout the paper, we recall the basics of Gröbner bases and we describe the non-noisy version of the quantum money scheme of [1]. The first part of Section 3 is concerned with the general modeling of the HSP_q as a system of multivariate non-linear equations, and the second part is dedicated to obtain the algorithm of the first Theorem. Sections 4 and 5 are dedicated to the HSP_2. In Section 4 we explain precisely why the behaviour of HSP_q is different for $q = 2$ and for $q > d$, we report experimental results and we derive our conjecture which, if true, results in the second Theorem. Section 5 is the most technical one, in which we explain that equations of degree $< d$ can be obtained due to the orthogonality of the hidden subspaces.

2   Preliminaries

We first recall some basics of Gröbner bases as the main tool to approach non-linear systems. Then we describe precisely our target problem and its relation with the quantum money scheme proposed in [1]. Before that we fix some general notation: we denote by $\mathbb{F}_q$ the finite field with q elements, we set $\mathbf{x} = (x_1, \ldots, x_n)$ and $\mathbb{F}_q[\mathbf{x}] = \mathbb{F}_q[x_1, \ldots, x_n]$ to be the polynomial ring over $\mathbb{F}_q$ in the unknowns $x_1, \ldots, x_n$. We denote by $\mathrm{M}(\mathbb{F}_q[\mathbf{x}])$ the set of monomials in $\mathbb{F}_q[\mathbf{x}]$, $\mathrm{M}(\mathbb{F}_2[\mathbf{x}])$ refers to the set of square-free monomials in $\mathbb{F}_2[\mathbf{x}]$ and $\mathrm{M}_s(\mathbb{F}_q[\mathbf{x}])$ refers to the set of monomials of degree s in $\mathbb{F}_q[\mathbf{x}]$. As usual, $\mathcal{M}_{k,\ell}(\mathbb{F}_q)$ denotes the set of $k \times \ell$ matrices with entries in $\mathbb{F}_q$, $\mathcal{M}_k(\mathbb{F}_q)$ denotes the square matrices of order k with entries in $\mathbb{F}_q$, and $\mathrm{GL}_k(\mathbb{F}_q)$ the set of invertible matrices in $\mathcal{M}_k(\mathbb{F}_q)$.

2.1 Basics of Computer Algebra

As systems of multivariate non-linear equations are the key component of this work we recall some aspects of Gröbner bases computations [8–10]. Given a polynomial ideal over $\mathbb{F}_q$, say $\mathcal{I} = \langle f_1, \ldots, f_s \rangle = \{\sum_{i=1}^{s} f_i h_i \mid h_1, \ldots, h_s \in \mathbb{F}_q[\mathbf{x}]\}$, Gröbner bases provide a way to obtain the variety $V_q(\mathcal{I}) = \{x \in \mathbb{F}_q \mid f_i(\mathbf{x}) = 0, \text{ for all } 1 \leq i \leq s\}$ by transforming the initial generators of the ideal into new generators with better properties, in the sense that computing the variety becomes simpler (this "better" set of generators is precisely the Gröbner basis).

The classic method to compute Gröbner bases is Buchberger's algorithm [8–10], but more efficient methods, such as F_4 [13] and F_5 [14], have been proposed. F_5 is considered to be one of the most efficient algorithms up to date for computing Gröbner bases. It uses linear algebra techniques and suppresses useless computations carried out in Buchberger's algorithm.

For increasing values of $\tilde{d}$, the F_5 algorithm successively reduces to row echelon form matrices of the form

$$A_{\tilde{d}} = \begin{matrix} m_1 f_{i_1} \\ m_2 f_{i_2} \\ \cdots \end{matrix} \begin{pmatrix} \cdots & \cdots & \cdots \\ \cdots & \cdots & \cdots \\ \cdots & \cdots & \cdots \end{pmatrix} \tag{1}$$

where the columns are indexed by the monomials ordered decreasingly with respect to $<$, and m_j are monomials such that $\deg(m_j f_{i_j}) \leq \tilde{d}$. At some point, for some d, the reduced row echelon form of the matrix A_d contains a Gröbner basis. This maximum degree d reached during a F_5 computation is called the *degree of regularity* and it is an important parameter when assessing the running time of a Gröbner basis computation.

Systems verifying certain hypotheses are called semi-regular [3,4], and they are interesting due to two reasons. Firstly, because if a system is chosen at random it turns out to be semi-regular with high probability, and secondly because the degree of regularity is known for this kind of systems. In fact, if $\{f_1, \ldots, f_s\} \subset \mathbb{F}_q[\mathbf{x}]$ is a semi-regular system, where each f_i has degree d_i, its degree of regularity is given by the index of the first non-positive coefficient of the power series

$$\sum_{k \geq 0} c_k z^k = \frac{\prod_{i=1}^{s}(1 - z^{d_i})}{(1 - z)^n}. \tag{2}$$

The time complexity of computing a Gröbner basis [2] is roughly given by the time spent carrying out the row echelon reduction of A_d, which is $\mathcal{O}((\#A_d)^\omega)$, where $2 \leq \omega \leq 3$ is the linear algebra constant. Since the size of the matrix A_d can be roughly approximated by $\mathcal{O}(n^d)$, this gives an overall complexity of $\mathcal{O}(n^{\omega d})$.

2.2 Definition of the Problem

From now on we will always assume that n is even. Recall that we are focusing on analyzing the hardness of the following problem:

Hidden Subspaces Problem (HSP_q)
Input : $p_1, \ldots, p_m, q_1, \ldots, q_m \in \mathbb{F}_q[\mathbf{x}]$ of degree $d \geq 3$ ($n \leq m \leq 2n$).
Find : a subspace $A \subset \mathbb{F}_q{}^n$ of dimension $n/2$ such that

$$p_i(A) = 0 \ \forall i \in \{1, \ldots, m\} \text{ and } q_j(A^\perp) = 0 \ \forall j \in \{1, \ldots, m\},$$

where $A^\perp$ denotes the orthogonal complement of A with respect to the standard scalar product in $\mathbb{F}_q$.

As mentioned in the introduction, HSP_q arises in relation to the security of the non-noisy version of the quantum money scheme proposed in [1]. The private key of this scheme is a subspace $A \subset \mathbb{F}_q{}^n$, and the polynomials $p_1, \ldots, p_m \in \mathbb{F}_q[\mathbf{x}]$ (vanishing on A) and $q_1, \ldots, q_m \in \mathbb{F}_q[\mathbf{x}]$ (vanishing on $A^\perp$) are the public key. To output money, the bank queries an oracle to obtain a basis of A and using this description of the subspace it generates a quantum state \$ which is the banknote. The verifying process is based on the fact that it is easy to check whether a given element is a zero of a polynomial or not.

The recovery of A compromises the security of the scheme, so it becomes crucial that the HSP_q cannot be easily solved. It is conjectured in [1] that, for big enough d, there is no polynomial-time algorithm that solves HSP_2 with success probability $\Omega\left(2^{-n/2}\right)$.

Before proceeding any further we need to detail how the keys are generated. This is specified in [1]. The generation of a uniformly random subspace is clear by just choosing a full rank matrix in $\mathcal{M}_{n/2,n}(\mathbb{F}_q)$. The generation of a uniformly random polynomial vanishing on a given subspace can be done in $\mathcal{O}(n^d)$-time:

Lemma 1 ([1]). *Denote by $I_{d,A}$ the set of polynomials of degree d that vanish on A, by $e_i \in \mathbb{F}_q{}^n$ the vector that has a 1 in its i-th position and 0 elsewhere, and by E the subspace generated by the vectors $e_1, \ldots, e_{n/2}$. We have:*

1. *A polynomial is in $I_{d,E}$ if and only if each of its monomials is divisible by an element in the set $\{x_{n/2+1}, \ldots, x_n\}$.*

2. *If L is an invertible linear transformation on $I_{d,A}$, the function $p(\boldsymbol{x}) \rightarrow p(\boldsymbol{x}L)$ maps $I_{d,A}$ to $I_{d,AL^{-1}}$.*

Applying this lemma, one can generate polynomials vanishing on the appropriate subspace in the following way:

Proposition 3. *(Vanishing polynomial) The generation of a uniformly random polynomial of degree d vanishing on a given subspace A consists of the following two steps:*

1. *Generate a polynomial $p(\boldsymbol{x})$ of degree d vanishing on E: by lemma 1(1), this is done including each monomial of degree d or lower independently and with probability $1/2$ if it is divisible by an element in the set $\{x_{n/2+1}, \ldots, x_n\}$.*
2. *Transform the polynomial $p(\boldsymbol{x})$ into one vanishing on A: considering the matrix L of change of basis (i.e., $E = AL$), the polynomial $p(\boldsymbol{x}L)$ vanishes on A by lemma 1(2).*

We have performed all our experiments using Proposition 3.

3   The HSP_q, for $q > d$

We analyze the hardness of the HSP_q for $q > d$. This is an open problem in [1] that arises when studying the security of the quantum money scheme extended to a general field $\mathbb{F}_q$. We conclude that the quantum money scheme extended to $\mathbb{F}_q$ is not secure for big q. First we show that, with a certain probability, the HSP_q can be modeled by a suitable set of non-linear equations. Then we prove that, with very high probability, enough linear equations that are linearly independent can be extracted from it. This results in a randomized polynomial-time algorithm for the HSP_q $(q > d)$.

3.1   General Modeling of HSP_q

In this part we show that the HSP_q can be rather naturally modeled as a set of algebraic equations. The first straightforward modeling presented is however not optimal as it includes many equivalent solutions. We show how we can use the structure of our problem to remove the unnecessary solutions.

We abuse notation and denote by A either a subspace of $\mathbb{F}_q^n$ of dimension $n/2$ or a matrix in $\mathcal{M}_{n/2,n}(\mathbb{F}_q)$ whose rows are the elements of a basis of the subspace A.

Proposition 4. *Let $\left(\mathbf{p} = (p_1, \ldots, p_m), \mathbf{q} = (q_1, \ldots, q_m)\right) \in \mathbb{F}_q[\boldsymbol{x}]^m \times \mathbb{F}_q[\boldsymbol{x}]^m$ be a degree-d instance of HSP_q. Let $(y_1, \ldots, y_{n/2})$ be variables and $G = (g_{i,j})_{1 \le i \le n/2, 1 \le j \le n}$, $G^{\perp} = (g_{i,j}^{\perp})_{1 \le i \le n/2, 1 \le j \le n}$ be formal matrices of size $n/2 \times n$. We consider the system:*

$$\mathrm{SysNaive}_{\mathrm{HSP}_q} = \{\mathrm{Coeff}(p_i, t), \mathrm{Coeff}(q_j, t) \mid \forall i, j \in \{1, \ldots, m\}, \forall t \in M(\mathbb{F}_q[y_1, \ldots, y_{n/2}])\} \quad (3)$$

where $\mathrm{Coeff}(p_i, t)$ *denotes the coefficient of* $t \in \mathrm{M}(\mathbb{F}_q[g_{1,1}, \ldots, g_{n/2,n}])$ *in* $p_i((y_1, \ldots, y_{n/2}) \cdot G)$ *and* $\mathrm{Coeff}(q_j, t)$ *the coefficient of* $t \in \mathrm{M}(\mathbb{F}_q[g_{1,1}^\perp, \ldots, g_{n/2,n}^\perp])$ *in* $q_j((y_1, \ldots, y_{n/2}) \cdot G^\perp)$. $\mathrm{SysNaive_{HSP_q}}$ *is a system of* $\mathcal{O}(n^{d+1})$ *algebraic equations over* $\mathbb{F}_q$ *in* n^2 *variables (the entries of* G *and* $G^\perp$).

Let $A \subset \mathbb{F}_q^n$ *be a vector subspace of dimension* $n/2$. *If* A *is a solution of* HSP_q *on* $(\mathbf{p}, \mathbf{q}) \in \mathbb{F}_q[\boldsymbol{x}]^m \times \mathbb{F}_q[\boldsymbol{x}]^m$ *then the components of* A *and* $A^\perp$ *vanish all the equations* $\mathrm{SysNaive_{HSP_q}}$.

Proof. This is an immediate consequence of the fact that every element of the subspace A (resp. $A^\perp$) can be expressed as $(y_1, \ldots, y_{n/2})A$ (resp. $(y_1, \ldots, y_{n/2})A^\perp$). As a consequence, all the coefficients of the polynomials $p_i((y_1, \ldots, y_{n/2}) \cdot A)$ (resp. $p_i((y_1, \ldots, y_{n/2}) \cdot A^\perp)$) must be equal to zero.   □

It is easy to see that $\mathrm{SysNaive_{HSP_q}}$ has many solutions which are equivalent. If a vector subspace $A \subset \mathbb{F}_q^n$ is a solution of HSP_q, then any basis of A will be a solution $\mathrm{SysNaive_{HSP_q}}$. It is then natural to define a canonical form of the solutions of HSP_q.

Lemma 2. *Let* $(\mathbf{p} = (p_1, \ldots, p_m), \mathbf{q} = (q_1, \ldots, q_m)) \in \mathbb{F}_q[\boldsymbol{x}]^m \times \mathbb{F}_q[\boldsymbol{x}]^m$ *be a degree-d instance of* HSP_q. *Let* $A \subset \mathbb{F}_q^n$ *be a vector subspace of dimension* $n/2$. *If* A *is a solution of* HSP_q *on* $(\mathbf{p}, \mathbf{q}) \in \mathbb{F}_q[\boldsymbol{x}]^m \times \mathbb{F}_q[\boldsymbol{x}]^m$, *then for any* $S \in \mathrm{GL}_{n/2}(\mathbb{F}_q)$, $S \cdot A$ *is a solution of* HSP_q *on* $(\mathbf{p}, \mathbf{q}) \in \mathbb{F}_q[\boldsymbol{x}]^m \times \mathbb{F}_q[\boldsymbol{x}]^m$.

Proof. For all $i, 1 \leq i \leq m$, $p_i((y_1, \ldots, y_{n/2})S \cdot A) = 0$ holds as a consequence of S being invertible. Also, since $(SA)^\perp = A^\perp$ (as $A^\perp(SA)^T = A^\perp A^T S^T = 0$ considering that $A^\perp A^T = 0$), it also holds that $q_j((y_1, \ldots, y_{n/2})(SA)^\perp) = 0$ for all $j, 1 \leq j \leq m$.   □

A direct consequence of Lemma 2 is that we can assume, with high probability, that a vector space solution A of HSP_q is given in systematic form. This is, we can suppose that $A = (I|G)$, where $G \in \mathrm{GL}_{n/2}(\mathbb{F}_q)$ and I is the $n/2 \times n/2$ identity matrix. If A has such a form then $A^\perp = (-G^T|I)$.

Fact 1. *We recall that the probability that a random matrix in* $\mathcal{M}_n(\mathbb{F}_q)$ *is invertible is given by:*

$$\gamma_q(n) = \prod_{i=1}^{n} \left(1 - \frac{1}{q^i}\right).$$

It is well known that:

$$\lim_{n \to \infty} \gamma_q(n) = 1 - \frac{1}{q} + \mathcal{O}\left(\frac{1}{q^2}\right).$$

For big values of q, $\gamma_q(n/2)$ *is close to 1, which justifies the restriction on the shape of the subspace* A.

We can now improve the modeling thanks to a canonical form of the solutions. We remove all the solutions of $\mathrm{SysNaive_{HSP_q}}$ which correspond to equivalent bases. To do so, we generate a similar system of equations but with a smaller number of variables.

Proposition 5. *Let* $\left(\mathbf{p} = (p_1, \ldots, p_m), \mathbf{q} = (q_1, \ldots, q_m)\right) \in \mathbb{F}_q[\boldsymbol{x}]^m \times \mathbb{F}_q[\boldsymbol{x}]^m$
be a degree-d instance of HSP_q. *Let* $(y_1, \ldots, y_{n/2})$ *be variables and* $G = (g_{i,j})_{1 \leq i \leq n/2, 1 \leq j \leq n/2}$ *be a formal matrix of size* $n/2 \times n/2$ *and* $N = n^2/4$. *We consider the system:*

$$\mathrm{Sys}_{\mathrm{HSP}_q} = \{\mathrm{Coeff}(p_i, t), \mathrm{Coeff}(q_j, t) \mid \forall i, j \in \{1, \ldots, m\}, \forall t \in M\left(\mathbb{F}_q[y_1, \ldots, y_{n/2}]\right)\} \quad (4)$$

where $\mathrm{Coeff}(p_i, t)$ *denotes the coefficient of* $t \in \mathrm{M}(\mathbb{F}_q\left[g_{1,1}, \ldots, g_{n/2,n/2}\right])$
in $p_i\left((y_1, \ldots, y_{n/2}) \cdot (I|G)\right)$, *and* $\mathrm{Coeff}(q_j, t)$ *the coefficient of* $t \in$
$\mathrm{M}(\mathbb{F}_q[g_{1,1}, \ldots, g_{n/2,n/2}])$ *in* $q_j\left((y_1, \ldots, y_{n/2}) \cdot (-G^T|I)\right)$. $\mathrm{Sys}_{\mathrm{HSP}_q}$ *is a system of*
$\mathcal{O}(n^{d+1})$ *algebraic equations over* $\mathbb{F}_q$ *in* N *variables (the entries of* G).
    Let $A \subset \mathbb{F}_q^n$ *be a vector subspace of dimension* $n/2$. *If* A *is a solution of* HSP_q
on $(\mathbf{p}, \mathbf{q}) \in \mathbb{F}_q[\boldsymbol{x}]^m \times \mathbb{F}_q[\boldsymbol{x}]^m$, *then* A *admits with probability* $\gamma_q(n/2)$ *a basis in*
systematic form whose components vanish all the equations $\mathrm{Sys}_{\mathrm{HSP}_q}$.

Proof. This follows easily from Lemma 2 and Proposition 4.   □

So, Lemma 2 permitted to divide by 4 the number of variables that we have to consider.

3.2   Randomized Polynomial-Time Algorithm for HSP_q, with $q > d$

According to Proposition 5, solving HSP_q is equivalent with high probability (w.h.p) to solve the non-linear system $\mathrm{Sys}_{\mathrm{HSP}_q}$. In this part we show that the non-linear system can be solved in polynomial-time. This is due to the fact that we can extract from $\mathrm{Sys}_{\mathrm{HSP}_q}$ sufficiently many linear equations that are linearly independent. These sufficiently many equations can be obtained with high probability considering only the polynomials $p_1, \ldots, p_m$ vanishing on A.

Lemma 3. *Let* $\left(\mathbf{p} = (p_1, \ldots, p_m), \mathbf{q} = (q_1, \ldots, q_m)\right) \in \mathbb{F}_q[\boldsymbol{x}]^m \times \mathbb{F}_q[\boldsymbol{x}]^m$ *be a*
degree-d instance of HSP_q. *Let* $p_i^{(1)}$ *(resp.* $q_i^{(1)}$) *be the homogeneous component*
of degree 1 *of* p_i *(resp.* q_i), *that is:*

$$p_i^{(1)} = \sum_{j=1}^{n} \lambda_{i,j}^p x_j, \quad \text{where } \lambda_{i,1}, \ldots, \lambda_{i,n} \in \mathbb{F}_q,$$

$$q_i^{(1)} = \sum_{j=1}^{n} \lambda_{i,j}^q x_j, \quad \text{where } \lambda_{i,1}, \ldots, \lambda_{i,n} \in \mathbb{F}_q.$$

For $i \in \{1, \ldots, m\}$ *and* $k \in \{1, \ldots, n/2\}$, *the linear equations:*

$$\begin{cases} \sum_{j=1}^{n/2} \lambda_{i,j+n/2}^p g_{k,j} + \lambda_{i,k}^p \\ \sum_{j=1}^{n/2} -\lambda_{i,j}^q g_{j,k} + \lambda_{i,k+n/2}^q \end{cases}$$

are in $\mathrm{Sys}_{\mathrm{HSP}_q}$.

Proof. Let $G = (g_{i,j})_{1 \leq i,j \leq n/2}$ be a formal matrix. If we expand the products $(y_1, \ldots, y_{n/2})(I|G)$ and $(y_1, \ldots, y_{n/2})(-G^T|I)$, we can see that $\mathrm{Sys}_{\mathrm{HSP}_q}$ is obtained from the coefficients of:

$$
\begin{cases}
p_i \left(y_1, \ldots, y_{n/2}, \displaystyle\sum_{t=1}^{n/2} g_{t,1} y_t, \ldots, \sum_{t=1}^{n/2} g_{t,n/2} y_t \right), \forall i, 1 \leq i \leq m, \\
q_j \left(\displaystyle\sum_{t=1}^{n/2} -g_{1,t} y_t, \ldots, \sum_{t=1}^{n/2} -g_{n/2,t} y_t, y_1, \ldots, y_{n/2} \right), \forall j, 1 \leq j \leq m.
\end{cases}
\tag{5}
$$

Since $q > d$ and so there are no reductions modulo the field equations, it is clear that the equations $\mathrm{Coeff}(p_i, y_1), \ldots, \mathrm{Coeff}(p_i, y_{n/2}), \mathrm{Coeff}(q_i, y_1), \ldots, \mathrm{Coeff}(q_i, y_{n/2})$ are linear for all $i \in \{1, \ldots, m\}$. Taking into account the expressions of $p_i^{(1)}$ and $q_i^{(1)}$ as well as (5), we have that for $k = 1, 2, \ldots, n/2$:

$$
\mathrm{Coeff}(p_i, y_k) = \lambda_{i,k}^p + \sum_{j=1}^{n/2} \lambda_{i,j+n/2}^p g_{k,j},
$$

$$
\mathrm{Coeff}(q_i, y_k) = \lambda_{i,k+n/2}^q - \sum_{j=1}^{n/2} \lambda_{i,j}^q g_{j,k},
$$

as required. □

Let $N = n^2/4$. Since $m \geq n$, the system of linear equations in Lemma 3 is already overdetermined with at most $2mn/2 = mn \geq 4N$ linear equations versus N unknowns. We show now that among these (at most) mn linear equations there are, with high probability, at least N linearly independent ones, enough to solve it.

Lemma 4. *Let* $(\mathbf{p} = (p_1, \ldots, p_m), \mathbf{q} = (q_1, \ldots, q_m)) \in \mathbb{F}_q[\boldsymbol{x}]^m \times \mathbb{F}_q[\boldsymbol{x}]^m$ *be a degree-d instance of* HSP_q. *With probability* $\frac{\gamma_q(m)}{\gamma_q(m-n/2)}$, *we can extract from* $\mathrm{Sys}_{\mathrm{HSP}_q}$ *at least* $N = n^2/4$ *linear equations that are linearly independent.*

Proof. The $mn \times N$ matrix of coefficients associated to the linear system specified in Lemma 3, whose columns are the unknowns $g_1, \ldots, g_{n/2}, \ldots, g_{N-n/2}, \ldots, g_N$, is the following:

$$
\begin{pmatrix}
\cdots & & \cdots & & \cdots & & \cdots & & \cdots & & \cdots & & \cdots \\
\lambda_{i,n/2+1}^p & \cdots & \lambda_{i,n}^p & 0 & \cdots & 0 & \cdots & 0 & \cdots & 0 \\
0 & \cdots & 0 & \lambda_{i,n/2+1}^p & \cdots & \lambda_{i,n}^p & \cdots & 0 & \cdots & 0 \\
\cdots & & \cdots & & \cdots & & \cdots & & \cdots & & \cdots \\
0 & \cdots & 0 & 0 & \cdots & 0 & \cdots & \lambda_{i,n/2+1}^p & \cdots & \lambda_{i,n}^p \\
\cdots & & \cdots & & \cdots & & \cdots & & \cdots & & \cdots \\
-\lambda_{j,1}^q & \cdots & 0 & -\lambda_{j,2}^q & \cdots & 0 & \cdots & -\lambda_{j,n/2}^q & \cdots & 0 \\
\cdots & & \cdots & & \cdots & & \cdots & & \cdots & & \cdots \\
0 & \cdots & -\lambda_{j,1}^q & 0 & \cdots & -\lambda_{j,2}^q & \cdots & 0 & \cdots & -\lambda_{j,n/2}^q \\
\cdots & & \cdots & & \cdots & & \cdots & & \cdots & & \cdots
\end{pmatrix}.
$$

We restrict our attention to the following $mn/2 \times N$ submatrix containing the equations $\mathrm{Coeff}(p_i, y_j)$ only, for $i \in \{1, \ldots, m\}$ and $j \in \{1, \ldots, n/2\}$:

$$
\begin{pmatrix}
\cdots & & \cdots & \cdots & & \cdots & & \cdots & & \cdots & & \cdots & \cdots & \cdots \\
\lambda^p_{i,n/2+1} & \cdots & \lambda^p_{i,n} & 0 & \cdots & 0 & \cdots & & 0 & & \cdots & 0 \\
0 & \cdots & 0 & \lambda^p_{i,n/2+1} & \cdots & \lambda^p_{i,n} & \cdots & & 0 & & \cdots & 0 \\
\cdots & & \cdots & \cdots & & \cdots & & \cdots & & \cdots & & \cdots \\
0 & \cdots & 0 & 0 & \cdots & 0 & \cdots & \lambda^p_{i,n/2+1} & \cdots & \lambda^p_{i,n} \\
\cdots & & \cdots & & \cdots & & \cdots & & \cdots & & \cdots
\end{pmatrix},
$$

We see that due to its particular shape it has rank N if there exists an $n/2 \times n/2$ invertible submatrix in the following $m \times n/2$ matrix:

$$
\begin{pmatrix}
\lambda^p_{1,n/2+1} & \lambda^p_{1,n/2+2} & \cdots & \lambda^p_{1,n} \\
\lambda^p_{2,n/2+1} & \lambda^p_{2,n/2+2} & \cdots & \lambda^p_{2,n} \\
\cdots & \cdots & \cdots & \cdots \\
\lambda^p_{m,n/2+1} & \lambda^p_{m,n/2+2} & \cdots & \lambda^p_{m,n}
\end{pmatrix}.
\tag{6}
$$

this is, if the matrix (6) is of maximum rank. Since the coefficients of the matrix are uniformly random, the probability that an $m \times n/2$ matrix has maximum rank is, according to [7], precisely

$$
\frac{(1 - \frac{1}{q}) \ldots (1 - \frac{1}{q^m})}{(1 - \frac{1}{q}) \ldots (1 - \frac{1}{q^{m-n/2}})} = \frac{\gamma_q(m)}{\gamma_q(m - n/2)}.
$$

$\square$

Considering that the shape of A is of the restricted form we assumed with probability $\gamma_q(n/2)$ and that the system above can be solved successfully with probability $\frac{\gamma_q(m)}{\gamma_q(m-n/2)}$, the following theorem sums up the results of this section:

Theorem 3. *Let $q > d$. There is a randomized polynomial-time algorithm solving* HSP_q *in:*

$$
\mathcal{O}(n^{2\omega}),
$$

where $2 \le \omega \le 3$ is the linear algebra constant, and with success probability

$$
\frac{\gamma_q(n/2)\gamma_q(m)}{\gamma_q(m - n/2)}.
$$

The success probability of our algorithm can be asymptotically approximated by $1 - 1/q$.

Proof. The algorithm to solve HSP_q is the following:

Input: $p_1, \ldots, p_m, q_1, \ldots, q_m \in \mathbb{F}_q[\mathbf{x}]$ of degree $d \geq 3$.
Construct the first set of equations of the linear system of Lemma 3.
Solve it.
Return this solution.

Taking into account that $\gamma_q(n) = \prod_{i=1}^{n} \left(1 - \frac{1}{q^i}\right)$ and that $\lim_{n \to \infty} \gamma_q(n) = 1 - \frac{1}{q} + \mathcal{O}\left(\frac{1}{q^2}\right)$,

$$\lim_{n \to \infty} \frac{\gamma_q(n/2)\gamma_q(m)}{\gamma_q(m - n/2)} = 1 - \frac{1}{q} + \mathcal{O}\left(\frac{1}{q^2}\right)$$

follows, and so the asymptotic success probability of our algorithm increases as we increase q. $\qquad \square$

3.3   Experimental Results

We report here our experimental results for HSP_q, with $q > d$, obtained with the algorithm of Theorem 3. We have implemented the algorithm using the MAGMA software [6]. In the tables below, $\mathtt{NextPrime}(k)$ is the Magma function that outputs the least prime number greater than k. Also, $\mathrm{Time}_{\mathrm{gen}}$ is the time needed to generate the instances, and Time is the time spent solving the linear system. Finally, $N = n^2/4$ is the number of unknowns in the linear system.

$d = 3$					
n	q	N	$\mathrm{Time}_{\mathrm{gen}}$	Time	Memory
10	5	25	1 s	0.00 s.	13MB
12	5	36	2 s	0.00 s.	12MB
20	5	100	135.1 s	0.02 s	481MB
10	$\mathrm{NextPrime}(2^{16})$	25	1 s	0.00 s	11MB
12	$\mathrm{NextPrime}(2^{16})$	36	4 s	0.00 s	12MB
20	$\mathrm{NextPrime}(2^{16})$	100	244.7 s	0.03 s	77MB

$d = 4$					
n	q	N	$\mathrm{Time}_{\mathrm{gen}}$	Time	Memory
10	5	25	8 s	0.00 s	16MB
12	5	36	40 s	0.00 s	16MB
10	$\mathrm{NextPrime}(2^{16})$	25	18 s	0.0 s	22MB
12	$\mathrm{NextPrime}(2^{16})$	36	107 s	0.0 s	22MB
20	$\mathrm{NextPrime}(2^{16})$	100	5154.050 s	0.02 s	300MB

As expected from Theorem 3 the algorithm is very efficient. Note that even for small q, all experiments performed succeeded as the probability of obtaining sufficiently many linearly independent linear equations, $\gamma_q(m)/\lambda_q(m - n/2)$, tends to 1 very quickly even for small values of q. Note that the running time of our algorithm is clearly dominated by the time spent in generating the instance. This is done in polynomial time[1] , so we can infer from the experiments that the algorithm runs in polynomial time, which is coherent with the theoretical results obtained.

4   An Efficient Algorithm for Solving HSP$_2$

We consider in this part the special case of HSP$_2$. As in Proposition 5, we can model HSP$_2$ by a set of algebraic equations. However, the system for $q = 2$ will have a different structure than Sys$_{\text{HSP}_q}$ due to reductions modulo the field equations that we now have to consider. In particular, it is no longer possible to extract linear equations. As a consequence, we have to adopt a different strategy for solving HSP$_2$. First we adapt the modeling for HSP$_2$ adding the field equations:

Proposition 6. *Let $\big(\mathbf{p} = (p_1, \ldots, p_m), \mathbf{q} = (q_1, \ldots, q_m)\big) \in \mathbb{F}_2[\boldsymbol{x}]^m \times \mathbb{F}_2[\boldsymbol{x}]^m$ be a degree-d instance of* HSP$_2$*. Let $\big(y_1, \ldots, y_{n/2}\big)$ be variables and $G = (g_{i,j})_{1 \leq i,j \leq n/2}$ be a formal matrix and $N = n^2/4$. We consider the system:*

$$\text{Sys}_{\text{HSP}_2} = \{\text{Coeff}(p_i, t), \text{Coeff}(q_j, t) \mid \forall i, j \in \{1, \ldots, m\}, \forall t \in M\left(\mathbb{F}_2[y_1, \ldots, y_{n/2}]\right)\} \cup \tag{7}$$
$$\{g_{i,j}^2 - g_{i,j} \mid 1 \leq i, j \leq n/2\}$$

where $\text{Coeff}(p_i, t)$ denotes the coefficient of $t \in M(\mathbb{F}_2\left[g_{1,1}, \ldots, g_{n/2,n/2}\right])$ in $p_i((y_1, \ldots, y_{n/2}) \cdot (I|G))$, and $\text{Coeff}(q_j, t)$ the coefficient of $t \in M(\mathbb{F}_2[g_{1,1}, \ldots, g_{n/2,n/2}])$ in $q_j((y_1, \ldots, y_{n/2}) \cdot (G^T|I))$. $\text{Sys}_{\text{HSP}_2}$ is a system of at most $2m \left[\binom{n/2}{1} + \binom{n/2}{2} + \ldots + \binom{n/2}{d}\right]$ algebraic equations over $\mathbb{F}_2$ in N variables (the entries of G).

Let $A \subset \mathbb{F}_2^n$ be a vector subspace of dimension $n/2$. If A is a solution of HSP$_2$ *on $(\mathbf{p}, \mathbf{q}) \in \mathbb{F}_2[\boldsymbol{x}]^m \times \mathbb{F}_2[\boldsymbol{x}]^m$, then A admits with probability $\gamma_2(n/2)$ a basis in systematic form whose components vanish all the equations $\text{Sys}_{\text{HSP}_2}$.*

Proof. Direct application of Proposition 5 and the fact that

$$\#(\text{M}(\mathbb{F}_2[y_1, \ldots, y_{n/2}]) = \binom{n/2}{1} + \ldots + \binom{n/2}{d}.$$

$\square$

Note that the equations of $\text{Sys}_{\text{HSP}_2}$ are of degree d with high probability for big enough parameters. Indeed, let $G = (g_{i,j})_{1 \leq i,j \leq n/2}$ be a formal matrix of size $n/2 \times n/2$ and recall that $\text{Sys}_{\text{HSP}_2}$ is obtained from the coefficients of:

$$\begin{cases} p_i\left(y_1, \ldots, y_{n/2}, \sum_{t=1}^{n/2} g_{t,1}y_t, \ldots, \sum_{t=1}^{n/2} g_{t,n/2}y_t\right), \forall i, 1 \leq i \leq m, \\ q_j\left(\sum_{t=1}^{n/2} -g_{1,t}y_t, \ldots, \sum_{t=1}^{n/2} -g_{n/2,t}y_t, y_1, \ldots, y_{n/2}\right), \forall j, 1 \leq j \leq m. \end{cases}$$

---

[1] Note that the generation of the instance is rather slow in practice, probably due to a non-optimal implementation of the `Evaluate` function in MAGMA for symbolic polynomials.

Since we reduce modulo the field equations, the coefficient of a linear term is obtained from the linear terms of p_i and q_j but also from the coefficients of higher degree terms reduced modulo the field equations. So, it is expected with a high probability that $\text{Sys}_{\text{HSP}_2}$ has no linear equations.

However, although $\text{Sys}_{\text{HSP}_2}$ is non-linear it is greatly overdetermined. Thus we can expect that computing a Gröbner basis of $\text{Sys}_{\text{HSP}_2}$ can still be done efficiently.

4.1   Experimental Results and Interpretation

The goal of this part is to show that $\text{Sys}_{\text{HSP}_2}$ is indeed much easier to solve than a semi-regular system of the same size. Recall that if a system is semi-regular, its degree of regularity is given by the first non-positive coefficient of the power series specified in (2).

We report experiments run on a 2.93 GHz Intel PC with 128 Gb. of RAM with the MAGMA software [6] (V2.19-1) for the most disadvantageous choice of parameters (this is, $m = n$). We recall that MAGMA implements the F_4 algorithm ([13]) for computing Gröbner bases.

The notation used in the table is the following: n the number of variables of the public polynomials, $N = n^2/4$ is the number of unknowns of the system in proposition 6, U_{eqs} is the upper bound on the number of equations as specified in proposition 6, d_{reg} is the degree of regularity observed in practice, and $d_{\text{reg}}^{\text{sg}}$ is the theoretical degree of regularity treating the system as if it was semi-regular. The

$d = 3$						
n	N	U_{eqs}	$d_{\text{reg}}^{\text{sg}}$	d_{reg}	Time	Memory
8	16	224	4	3	1 s	17MB
10	25	500	5	3	1 s	20MB
12	36	984	5	3	2 s	55MB
14	49	1764	5	4	136 s	3Gb
16	64	2944	6	4	2.30 min	8GB
18	81	4725	7	4	2h20	80GB

$d = 4$						
n	N	U_{eqs}	$d_{\text{reg}}^{\text{sg}}$	d_{reg}	Time	Memory
8	16	240	6	4	1 s	20MB
10	25	600	6	4	1 s	50MB
12	36	1344	7	5	38 s	840MB
14	49	2744	8	5	66 min	8GB

first thing we observe is that the number of equations of our system coincides with the upper bound for the maximum number of possible equations. The experiments show that solving these systems is easier than if they were random: the degree of regularity observed in practice is indeed lower than the expected one, which suggests that there is an underlying structure that can be exploited. Furthermore, the degree of regularity stays bounded, so we conjecture the following:

Conjecture 1. The degree of regularity is bounded above by $d + 1$.

If our conjecture is true, there is a randomized polynomial-time algorithm for HSP_2 as follows:

Theorem 4. *Assuming Conjecture 1, there is a randomized polynomial-time algorithm (the computation of a Gröbner basis) solving degree-d instances of* HSP_2 *with a complexity of*

$$\mathcal{O}(n^{2\omega(d+1)}),$$

where $2 \leq \omega \leq 3$ *is the linear algebra constant, and success probability* $\gamma_2(n/2)$.

5   Structural Low Degree Equations

The goal of this part is to provide theoretical arguments supporting Conjecture 1. That is, we show that the system of algebraic equations of Proposition 6 has a very particular structure. We prove that suitable linear combinations of the equations will lead to equations of a lower degree. This is actually the first computation performed by a Gröbner basis algorithm on the system of Proposition 6. As a consequence, solving the system of degree d-equations from Proposition 6 reduces to solve a system with equations of degree d and degree $d - 1$. This is typically a behaviour which is not occurring in a random (i.e. semi-regular) system of equations and so it is a first step towards proving Conjecture 1.

Let $(p, q) \in \mathbb{F}_2[\mathbf{x}] \times \mathbb{F}_2[\mathbf{x}]$ be polynomials of degree d such that p vanishes on a vector subspace $A \subset \mathbb{F}_2^n$ of dimension $n/2$ and q vanishes on the orthogonal space $A^\perp$. Let $N_d = \binom{n/2}{d}$. We order lexicographically the monomials of degree d in the rings

$$\mathbb{F}_2\left[y_1, \ldots, y_{n/2}\right], \mathbb{F}_2\left[x_{n/2+1}, \ldots, x_n\right], \text{ and } \mathbb{F}_2\left[x_1, \ldots, x_{n/2}\right].$$

We then denote by $t_1 < \ldots < t_{N_d}, m_1 < \ldots < m_{N_d}$ and $m^\perp{}_1 < \ldots < m^\perp{}_{N_d}$ the respective monomials in ascending order. This way we can write

$$\begin{cases} p = \alpha_1 m_1 + \ldots + \alpha_{N_d} m_{N_d} + \tilde{p}, \ \alpha_1, \ldots, \alpha_{N_d} \in \mathbb{F}_2, \tilde{p} \in \mathbb{F}_2[\mathbf{x}] \setminus \mathrm{M}_d(\mathbb{F}_2[x_{\frac{n}{2}+1}, \ldots, x_n]), \\ q = \beta_1 m^\perp{}_1 + \ldots + \beta_{N_d} m^\perp{}_{N_d} + \tilde{q}, \ \beta_1, \ldots, \beta_{N_d} \in \mathbb{F}_2, \tilde{q} \in \mathbb{F}_2[\mathbf{x}] \setminus \mathrm{M}_d(\mathbb{F}_2[x_1, \ldots, x_{n/2}]). \end{cases} \quad (8)$$

Recall that the notation $\mathrm{Coeff}(p, t)$ refers to the coefficient of $t \in \mathrm{M}(\mathbb{F}_2[g_{1,1}, \ldots, g_{n/2,n/2}])$ occurring in $p((y_1, \ldots, y_{n/2})(I|G))$, and $\mathrm{Coeff}(q, t)$ refers to the coefficient of $t \in \mathrm{M}(\mathbb{F}_2[g_{1,1}, \ldots, g_{n/2,n/2}])$ occurring in $p((y_1, \ldots, y_{n/2})(G^T|I))$. We will denote by $\mathrm{Coeff}(p, t)^{(d)}$ the homogeneous component of degree d of $\mathrm{Coeff}(p, t)$.

Let $t \in \mathrm{M}_d(\mathbb{F}_2[y_1, \ldots, y_{n/2}])$, and we can deduce from (5) that $\mathrm{Coeff}(\tilde{p}, t)^{(d)} = 0 = \mathrm{Coeff}(\tilde{q}, t)^{(d)}$. Then, the homogeneous component of degree d of $\mathrm{Coeff}(p, t)$ (resp. $\mathrm{Coeff}(q, t)$) is equal to the sum of the contributions with terms of degree d that each monomial m_i (resp. $m_j^\perp$) present in (8) makes to, respectively, $\mathrm{Coeff}(p, t)^{(d)}$ and $\mathrm{Coeff}(q, t)^{(d)}$, this is,

$$\mathrm{Coeff}(p, t)^{(d)} = \alpha_1 \mathrm{Coeff}(m_1, t)^{(d)} + \ldots + \alpha_{N_d} \mathrm{Coeff}(m_{N_d}, t)^{(d)},$$

$$\mathrm{Coeff}(q, t)^{(d)} = \beta_1 \mathrm{Coeff}(m^\perp{}_1, t)^{(d)} + \ldots + \beta_{N_d} \mathrm{Coeff}(m^\perp{}_{N_d}, t)^{(d)}.$$

The fact that G and G^T have the same entries (in different positions) and are involved in the evaluations of $p_i((y_1, \ldots, y_{n/2})(I|G))$ and $q_j((y_1, \ldots, y_{n/2})(G^T|I))$

produces certain relations between expressions of the form $\text{Coeff}(m_i, t_1)^{(d)}$ and expressions of the form $\text{Coeff}(m^\perp_j, t_2)^{(d)}$ for appropriate $t_1, t_2 \in M_d(\mathbb{F}_2[y_1, \ldots, y_{n/2}])$. These relations are detailed in the following result:

Proposition 7. *Let $(p, q) \in \mathbb{F}_2[\boldsymbol{x}] \times \mathbb{F}_2[\boldsymbol{x}]$ be polynomials of degree d such that p vanishes on a vector subspace $A \subset \mathbb{F}_2^n$ of dimension $n/2$ and q vanishes on the orthogonal space $A^\perp$. Let $N_d = \binom{n/2}{d}$. For all $i, j \in \{1, \ldots, N_d\}$, it holds that:*

$$\text{Coeff}(m_i, t_j)^{(d)} = \text{Coeff}(m^\perp_j, t_i)^{(d)},$$

where $t_1 < \ldots < t_{N_d}, m_1 < \ldots < m_{N_d}$, and $m^\perp_1 < \ldots < m^\perp_{N_d}$ are ordered increasingly in the sets of monomials $M_d(\mathbb{F}_2[y_1, \ldots, y_{n/2}]), M_d(\mathbb{F}_2[x_{n/2+1}, \ldots, x_n])$, and $M_d(\mathbb{F}_2[x_1, \ldots, x_{n/2}])$ respectively. Also, $\text{Coeff}(m_i, t_j)$ (resp. $\text{Coeff}(m^\perp_j, t_i)$) denotes the coefficient of $t_j \in M_d(\mathbb{F}_2[y_1, \ldots, y_{n/2}])$ (resp. $t_i \in M_d(\mathbb{F}_2[y_1, \ldots, y_{n/2}])$) in $m_i((y_1, \ldots, y_{n/2})(I|G))$ (resp. $m^\perp_j((y_1, \ldots, y_{n/2})(G^T|I))$). Finally, the expression $\text{Coeff}(m_i, t_j)^{(d)}$ (resp. $\text{Coeff}(m^\perp_j, t_i)^{(d)}$) denotes the homogeneous component of degree d of $\text{Coeff}(m_i, t_j)$ (resp. $\text{Coeff}(m^\perp_j, t_i)$).

Proof. Given $i, j \in \{1, \ldots, N_d\}$, we have that $t_i = y_{i_1} y_{i_2} \cdots y_{i_d}, t_j = y_{j_1} y_{j_2} \cdots y_{j_d}$, for some $i_1, i_2, \ldots, i_d$, $j_1, j_2, \ldots, j_d \in \{1, \ldots, n/2\}$. On the one hand:

$$\text{Coeff}(m_i, t_j)^{(d)} = \text{Coeff}\left(\prod_{k=1}^{d} x_{i_k + n/2}, y_{j_1} y_{j_2} \cdots y_{j_d}\right)^{(d)}.$$

Observing the system (5), this is the coefficient of $y_{j_1} y_{j_2} \cdots y_{j_d}$ in the product

$$\prod_{k=1}^{d} \sum_{\ell=0}^{n/2-1} g_{\ell+1, i_k} y_{\ell+1},$$

which, after expanding it, equals

$$\sum_{\pi \text{ permutation over } \{1, \ldots, d\}} \prod_{k=1}^{d} g_{j_{\pi(k)}, i_k}. \tag{9}$$

On the other hand,

$$\text{Coeff}(m^\perp_j, t_i)^{(d)} = \text{Coeff}\left(\prod_{k=1}^{d} x_{j_k}, y_{j_1} y_{j_2} \cdots y_{j_d}\right)^{(d)}.$$

Again, observing the system (5), this is the coefficient of $y_{i_1} y_{i_2} \cdots y_{i_d}$ in the product

$$\prod_{k=1}^{d} \sum_{\ell=1}^{n/2} g_{j_k, \ell} y_\ell$$

which, again after expanding it, equals

$$\sum_{\pi \text{ permutation over } \{1,\ldots,d\}} \prod_{k=1}^{d} g_{j_k, i_{\pi(k)}}. \tag{10}$$

Now (10) and (9) clearly coincide since

$$\sum_{\pi \text{ permutation over } \{1,\ldots,d\}} \prod_{k=1}^{d} g_{j_k, i_{\pi(k)}} = \sum_{\pi \text{ permutation over } \{1,\ldots,d\}} \prod_{k=1}^{d} g_{j_{\pi^{-1}(\pi(k))}, i_{\pi(k)}} =$$

$$\sum_{\pi^{-1} \text{ permutation over } \{1,\ldots,d\}} \prod_{k=1}^{d} g_{j_{\pi^{-1}(k)}, i_k}.$$

□

We can use this proposition to identify the suitable linear combinations that are of degree $d-1$:

Theorem 5. *Let the notations be as in Proposition 7. There exist* $i, j \in \{1, \ldots, N_d\}$ *such that the equation*

$$\text{Coeff}(p, t_j) + \text{Coeff}(q, t_i) + \sum_{\{k \neq i \mid \alpha_k \neq 0\}} \text{Coeff}(q, t_k) + \sum_{\{\ell \neq j \mid \beta_\ell \neq 0\}} \text{Coeff}(p, t_\ell)$$

is of degree $d-1$.

Proof. Denote by i, j the smallest indexes such that $\alpha_i, \beta_j \neq 0$. Using Proposition 7,

$$\text{Coeff}(m_i, t_j)^{(d)} = \text{Coeff}(m^\perp{}_j, t_i)^{(d)}.$$

Now, for every $k \neq i$ such that $\alpha_k \neq 0$ and for all $\ell \neq j$ such that $\beta_\ell \neq 0$, using Proposition 7 we get the following equalities:

$$\text{Coeff}(m_k, t_j)^{(d)} = \text{Coeff}(m^\perp{}_j, t_k)^{(d)}, \quad \text{Coeff}(m^\perp{}_\ell, t_i)^{(d)} = \text{Coeff}(m_i, t_\ell)^{(d)}, \text{ and}$$

$$\text{Coeff}(m^\perp{}_\ell, t_k)^{(d)} = \text{Coeff}(m_k, t_\ell)^{(d)}.$$

Now adding up both the left-hand side and the right-hand side of all the four equalities, we obtain

$$\text{Coeff}(m_i, t_j)^{(d)} + \sum_{\{k \neq i \mid \alpha_k \neq 0\}} \text{Coeff}(m_k, t_j)^{(d)} + \sum_{\{\ell \neq j \mid \beta_\ell \neq 0\}} \text{Coeff}(m^\perp{}_\ell, t_i)^{(d)} +$$

$$+ \sum_{\{\ell \neq j, k \neq i \mid \alpha_k \neq 0, \beta_\ell \neq 0\}} \text{Coeff}(m^\perp{}_\ell, t_k)^{(d)} + \text{Coeff}(m^\perp{}_j, t_i)^{(d)} + \sum_{\{k \neq i \mid \alpha_k \neq 0\}} \text{Coeff}(m^\perp{}_j, t_k)^{(d)} +$$

$$+ \sum_{\{\ell \neq j \mid \beta_\ell \neq 0\}} \text{Coeff}(m_i, t_\ell)^{(d)} + \sum_{\{\ell \neq j, k \neq i \mid \alpha_k \neq 0, \beta_\ell \neq 0\}} \text{Coeff}(m_k, t_\ell)^{(d)} = 0.$$

The left-hand side of this equality is the homogeneous component of degree d of

$$\text{Coeff}(p, t_j) + \text{Coeff}(q, t_i) + \sum_{\{k \neq i \mid \alpha_k \neq 0\}} \text{Coeff}(q, t_k) + \sum_{\{\ell \neq j \mid \beta_\ell \neq 0\}} \text{Coeff}(p, t_\ell)$$

which means that we cancelled out the terms of degree d and so the required equation is of degree $d - 1$. □

This result can be used to generate low-degree equations:

Corollary 1. *Let* $\big(\mathbf{p} = (p_1, \ldots, p_m), \mathbf{q} = (q_1, \ldots, q_m)\big) \in \mathbb{F}_2[\boldsymbol{x}]^m \times \mathbb{F}_2[\boldsymbol{x}]^m$ *be a degree-d instance of* HSP_2. *We can easily generate* $\mathcal{O}(m^2)$ *equations of degree $d - 1$. These equations are linear combinations of the degree-d equations of* $\text{Sys}_{\text{HSP}_2}$.

Proof. We apply simply Theorem 5 to each pair of polynomials $(p_i, q_j) \in \mathbb{F}_2[\mathbf{x}] \times \mathbb{F}_2[\mathbf{x}]$. From the proof of Theorem 5, it is clear that these equations are linear combinations of the equations from $\text{Sys}_{\text{HSP}_2}$. □

To conclude this part, we include below experimental results about the number of equations of degree $d - 1$ generated as Corollary 1 which are linearly independent. In the table, we denote by $\#\text{eqs}_{\text{pr}}$ the number of linearly independent equations obtained in practice and by $\#\text{eqs}_{\text{th}}$ the maximum number of linearly independent equations that can be obtained, which is m^2.

	$d = 3$		$d = 4$	
	$\#\text{eqs}_{\text{pr}}$	$\#\text{eqs}_{\text{th}}$	$\#\text{eqs}_{\text{pr}}$	$\#\text{eqs}_{\text{th}}$
$m = n = 10$	99	100	71	100
$m = n = 12$	144	144	144	144
$m = n = 14$	196	196	196	196
$m = n = 16$	256	256	256	256

We observe that the behaviour is unstable for small values of the parameters. This is partially due to the fact that if a polynomial p_i (resp. q_j) does not have terms of degree d in $\mathbb{F}_2[x_{n/2+1}, \ldots, x_n]$ (resp. $\mathbb{F}_2[x_1, \ldots, x_{n/2}]$), then we do not get equations of degree $d - 1$ applying Theorem 5 to the pair (p_i, q_k) for all $k \in \{1, \ldots, m\}$ (resp. from the pair (p_k, q_j) for all $k \in \{1, \ldots, m\}$). This happens with probability $1/2^{\binom{n/2}{d}}$, which is not too small for low parameters. So, for small parameters it is possible that we obtain a number of equations of degree $d - 1$ lower than m^2. However, if this is the case there still are equations of degree $d - 1$ (or lower) produced by the terms of degree $d - 1$ (or lower). We see that the behavior becomes stable for big enough values of the parameters m, n obtaining as many equations of degree $d - 1$ as possible, this is, m^2.

6   Conclusions

In this paper we presented a very efficient attack for HSP_q with $q > d$. The case $q \leq d$ is not treated, but as there are reductions modulo the field equations taking place, the behaviour might be similar to the one over $\mathbb{F}_2$ (Section 4). Since the asymptotic probability of success of this algorithm is $1 - 1/q$, the quantum money scheme extended to $\mathbb{F}_q$ is not secure for big q. We also provided some experimental and theoretical arguments that support the conjecture that HSP_2 can be solved in polynomial time. In both cases, we only considered public polynomials chosen randomly as described in [1]. For other choices of public polynomials with a certain structure (for instance, homogeneous polynomials of degree d, ...) the hardness of HSP remains open. Another interesting open question is the hardness of the noisy version of the scheme, which is related to the study of the noise-free version when $m = \mathcal{O}(1)$ (in this paper, we considered $m = \mathcal{O}(n)$).

Acknowledgments. We thank Scott Aaronson and the anonymous referees for detailed comments which greatly improved this work. Jean-Charles Faugère and Ludovic Perret have been partially supported supported the HPAC grant (ANR-11-BS02-013) of the French National Research Agency.

References

1. Aaronson, S., Christiano, P.: Quantum money from hidden subspaces. In: Proceedings of the 44th Symposium on Theory of Computing Conference, STOC 2012, New York, NY, USA, May 19–22, pp. 41–60 (2012)
2. Bardet, M., Faugère, J.-C., Salvy, B.: On the Complexity of the F5 Gröbner basis Algorithm. Journal of Symbolic Computation, 1–24
3. Bardet, M., Faugère, J.-C., Salvy, B.: On the complexity of Gröbner basis computation of semi-regular overdetermined algebraic equations. In: Proc. of International Conference on Polynomial System Solving (ICPSS), pp. 71–75 (2004)
4. Bardet, M., Faugère, J.-C., Salvy, B., Yang, B.-Y.: Asymptotic behaviour of the degree of regularity of semi-regular polynomial systems. In: Proc. of MEGA 2005, Eighth International Symposium on Effective Methods in Algebraic Geometry (2005)
5. Bennett, C.H., Brassard, G., Breidbard, S., Wiesner, S.: Quantum cryptography, or unforgeable subway tokens. In: Proceedings of CRYPTO, pp. 267–275 (1982)
6. Bosma, W., Cannon, J.J., Playoust, C.: The Magma algebra system I: The user language. Journal of Symbolic Computation **24**(3–4), 235–265 (1997)
7. Brent, R.P., McKay, B.D.: Determinants and rank of random matrices over $\mathbb{Z}_m$. Discrete Math. **66**, 35–50 (1987)
8. Buchberger, B.: Ein Algorithmus zum Auffinden der Basiselemente des Restklassenringes nach einem nulldimensionalen Polynomideal. PhD thesis, University of Innsbruck (1965)
9. Buchberger, B.: Bruno Buchberger's PhD thesis 1965: An algorithm for finding the basis elements of the residue class ring of a zero dimensional polynomial ideal. J. Symb. Comput. **41**(3–4), 475–511 (2006)
10. Buchberger, B.: Comments on the translation of my phd thesis. J. Symb. Comput. **41**(3–4), 471–474 (2006)

11. Courtois, N., Meier, W.: Algebraic attacks on stream ciphers with linear feedback. In: Biham, E. (ed.) EUROCRYPT 2003. LNCS, vol. 2656, pp. 345–359. Springer, Heidelberg (2003)
12. Farhi, E., Gosset, D., Hassidim, A., Lutomirski, A., Shor, P.W.: Quantum money from knots, pp. 276–289 (2012)
13. Faugère, J.-C.: A new efficient algorithm for computing Gröbner bases (F_4). Journal of Pure and Applied Algebra **139**, 61–88 (1999)
14. Faugère, J.-C.: A new efficient algorithm for computing Gröbner bases without reduction to zero (F_5). In: ACM Press (ed.) International Symposium on Symbolic and Algebraic Computation, ISAAC 2002, pp. 75–83 (2002)
15. Faugère, J.-C., Joux, A.: Algebraic cryptanalysis of hidden field equation (HFE) cryptosystems using Gröbner bases. In: Boneh, D. (ed.) CRYPTO 2003. LNCS, vol. 2729, pp. 44–60. Springer, Heidelberg (2003)
16. Faugère, J.-C., Perret, L.: Polynomial equivalence problems: algorithmic and theoretical aspects. In: Vaudenay, S. (ed.) EUROCRYPT 2006. LNCS, vol. 4004, pp. 30–47. Springer, Heidelberg (2006)
17. Gavinsky, D.: Quantum money with classical verification, pp. 42–52 (2012)
18. Mosca, M., Stebila, D.: Quantum coins. Error-Correcting Codes, Finite Geometry and Cryptography **523**, 35–47 (2010)
19. Patarin, J.: Hidden fields equations (HFE) and isomorphisms of polynomials (IP): two new families of asymmetric algorithms. In: Maurer, U.M. (ed.) EUROCRYPT 1996. LNCS, vol. 1070, pp. 33–48. Springer, Heidelberg (1996)
20. Wiesner, S.: Conjugate coding. ACM SIGACT News **15**(1), 78–88 (1983)

Digital Signatures I

Digital Signatures from Strong RSA
Without Prime Generation

David Cash[1]([✉]), Rafael Dowsley[2], and Eike Kiltz[3]

[1] Department of Computer Science, Rutgers University, New Brunswick, NJ, USA
david.cash@cs.rutgers.edu
[2] Institute of Theoretical Informatics,
Karlsruhe Institute of Technology, Karlsruhe, Germany
rafael.dowsley@kit.edu
[3] Horst Görtz Institute for IT-Security,
Ruhr-Universität Bochum, Bochum, Germany
eike.kiltz@rub.de

Abstract. We construct a signature scheme that is proved secure, without random oracles, under the strong RSA assumption. Unlike other efficient strong-RSA based schemes, the new scheme does not generate large prime numbers during signing. The public key size and signature size are competitive with other strong RSA schemes, but verification is less efficient. The new scheme adapts the prefix signing technique of Hohenberger and Waters (CRYPTO 2009) to work without generating primes.

Keywords: Digital signatures · Strong RSA

1 Introduction

Digital signatures are amongst the most widely deployed cryptographic primitives, with several efficient, standardized schemes that are implemented and used in common functionalities like HTTPS. Theoretical constructions study the extent to which digital signatures can be proved secure under mild hardness assumptions, like the existence of one-way functions, giving us good evidence for the possibility of constructing secure schemes.

As is often the case with provable security, however, the proved-secure schemes with the best security guarantees are not nearly as efficient as the (unbroken) schemes that are used in practice, where applications require fast signing and verification along with short public-keys and short signatures. The best provable security evidence (when it is available) for practical schemes comes from security proofs that use the random oracle model [3], where one models a hash function as a random function. Of course, in practice we use a non-random function like SHA-256, a reality that leads some theoretical limitations of these results [7,12]. From an assurance standpoint it is desirable to have security proofs without random oracles in order to lessen the possibility that a proved-secure scheme will be broken when implemented. From a theoretical standpoint it is interesting to know what is achievable without the random oracle.

© International Association for Cryptologic Research 2015
J. Katz (Ed.): PKC 2015, LNCS 9020, pp. 217–235, 2015.
DOI: 10.1007/978-3-662-46447-2_10

OUR CONTRIBUTION. In this paper we continue a line of work on designing efficient signature schemes that are proved secure, without a random oracle, under the strong RSA assumption [2]. Unlike other such schemes, ours does not need to generate large prime numbers during signing and avoids this by embedding the strong RSA problem into the scheme in a different way.

Recall that the strong RSA problem requires an adversary, on input (N, y) where $N = pq$ for large random primes p, q, and $y \in \mathbb{Z}_N^*$ is random, to compute (e, x) satisfying $x^e = y \mod N$ and $e > 1$. The structure of the problem suggests a natural approach for embedding it into digital signatures, where the public key is N and a signature will consist of (e, x), where e is computed at signing time and x is an e-th root of a value y that depends on the public key and the message. In order to apply known techniques that prevent an adversary from assembling several signatures into a new signature, the e that is generated is typically required to be a large prime or a product of large primes.

Our construction instead works with e set to be a product of several composite numbers so that the likelihood of one of them being divisible by a large prime factor is large. In order to avoid making e extremely large, we adapt techniques from prior work, including the "prefix signing" of Hohenberger and Waters [19] and analysis techniques for dealing with composite numbers in RSA signatures due to Gennaro, Halevi, and Rabin [14]. A sketch of our approach and the techniques we use is given below in the next sub-section.

It is desirable to avoid prime generation in signing because it is typically an expensive operation and is a step which is not intrinsic for the signing algorithm. While our scheme does this with a relatively simple signing procedure and with public key and signature sizes competitive with prior schemes, it has a much slower verification algorithm. Like all other signature schemes that do not use random oracles in their security proofs, our construction is not competitive with practical schemes and we do not recommend it for consideration in applications. Instead, we aim to have a conceptual contribution towards the goal of practical schemes from conservative hardness assumptions without random oracles.

In order to more precisely describe our contribution, we first need to recall some prior work.

STANDARD MODEL RSA SIGNATURES. We focus on signatures whose security is based on the (strong) RSA problem without a random oracle. While there exists a number of different schemes [5,6,8,11,13,14,17–19,21–23], they all have in common that the signing algorithm has to generate one or more primes (of some large size). The prime generation can either be deterministic (via some hash function h from messages to primes) or according to the uniform distribution. In both cases the prime generation remains an expensive step whose elimination is desirable.

Concretely, the strong-RSA based signature schemes from [6,11,13,18,22,23] compute a signature on message m as $\sigma(m) = (\mathsf{H}(m)^{1/e} \mod N, e)$, where e is a random prime and H is some (algebraic) hash function that depends on the specific scheme; the (weakly secure) scheme by Gennaro et al. [14] defines

$\sigma(m) = g^{1/h(m)} \bmod N$ where h is a hash function that hashes into primes.[1] The signature scheme by Hohenberger and Waters [19] as well as the one by Hofheinz et al. [17] are based on the (weaker) RSA assumption and define $\sigma(m) = g^{1/\prod_{i=1}^{n} h_i(m)} \bmod N$, where h_i are independent hash functions that hash into primes. Designing a standard-model signature scheme whose signing algorithm does not rely on the generation of prime numbers is an open problem explicitly mentioned in [17].

1.1   Our Contributions

Our new scheme is relatively simple, so we describe it right away. Its public key consists of $N = pq$ where p and q are large safe primes[2], a number $h \in \mathbb{Z}_N^*$, and a key of a pseudorandom function $F_K(\cdot)$. For the time being, we assume that $F_K(\cdot)$ takes variable-length inputs, and always outputs odd numbers of some given length. Signatures on a message $m \in \{0,1\}^\ell$ are defined via

$$\mathsf{Sign}(m) = h^{1/e} \bmod N, \qquad \text{where } e = \prod_{i=1}^{\ell} F_K(m[1...i]) \cdot \prod_{i=1}^{d} F_K(m \| i). \quad (1)$$

Here $m[1..i]$ is the i-bit prefix of m, d is a parameter that factors into the concrete security, and $m \| i$ means m with an encoding of the number i appended. (Signatures can be computed using the secret key, the factorization of $N = pq$.) We stress that we are using the outputs of the $F_K(\cdot)$, which are random odd numbers that are likely to be composite. This is the main difficulty in proving security. Theorem 5 shows that this scheme achieves a type of weak security under the strong RSA assumption in the standard model. Full security (unforgeability against chosen-message attack) can be achieved by adding a chameleon hash function - see [20] or the full version of [19].

INTUITION. Let us sketch how our scheme adapts and differs from prior proof techniques. The notion of weak security for signature schemes means that the adversary gets only one parallel signing query on chosen messages before seeing the public key. Then it is given the public key, along with the requested signatures, and must generate a signature on a new message $\widehat{m}$. See the next section for a formal definition, via the game wCMA.

We start with a very high level explanation of why all of the prefixes of m are processed using F_K and multiplied together. Consider a rooted full binary tree of depth ℓ, with all nodes assigned a label from $\{0,1\}^{\leq \ell}$ according to the left/right steps to that node from the root. The prefixes of a message are exactly the labels on the nodes encountered on the root-to-message path.

Then we can see the requested messages from the adversary's parallel signing query as leaves in the tree, and the union of all root-to-message paths is a subtree.

---

[1] For GHR signatures, the weaker condition *collision intractability* is sufficient for h. However, the only known way to instantiate h in the standard model is to hash into primes [10,14,21].

[2] A safe prime is an odd prime number p such that $p' = (p-1)/2$ is also prime.

Now for any message $\widehat{m}$ not in this subtree, the root-to-$\widehat{m}$ path must have some first node that is not in the subtree. In fact, we can show that *all* paths to messages not in the subtree must pass through one of a small number of "exit nodes".

The Hohenberger-Waters signature scheme was designed to take advantage of this structure by guessing which exit node would be used by the message on which the adversary forges a message. If the guess is correct, then, using hash functions that output only primes, they can arrange to program in an instance of the (non-strong) RSA problem. Since the number of exit nodes is polynomial, this guess is correct with non-negligible probability, resulting in an acceptable loss in the success probability during the reduction.

We also exploit this structure, but instead we do not guess which exit node will be used. Instead, we arrange so that we can solve the strong RSA problem no matter which exit node is used by the adversary during forging. Examining the proof reveals that this amounts to hoping that several (composite) numbers output by $F_K(\cdot)$ on different inputs will *all* have large prime factors (i.e, they are non-smooth). A naive analysis of this technique in which one hopes that with overwhelming probability all exit nodes are non-smooth gives very bad parameters. So instead of hoping that every exit node helps us solve the problem with overwhelming probability, we show that it is enough for each exit node to help us (i.e., have a large prime factor) with only constant probability. We can show that this is in fact enough, because when a node does not help, we can discard it and look at both its children, recursively repeating this process. Analyzing this behavior is the main difficulty in our proof.

While the idea of using the fact that a number x is not α-smooth is not new in cryptography (see below for related work), it is clear that the straightforward approach of requiring x to be α-smooth with negligible probability would normally result in very bad protocol parameters since the gap between x and α would have to be too big. Our scheme derives its advantage because the reduction can tolerate the random numbers having large prime factors with only constant probability via the recursive tree searching, allowing us to save in parameters (i.e. use smaller numbers), at the expense of the d extra evaluations and multiplications. Consider the set of message queried by the adversary and the subtree formed by all their root-to-message paths. The central idea of the security proof is that for any message $\widehat{m}$ not in this subtree (i.e., all the messages for which a forgery would be acceptable), there should be at least one random number in $\widehat{m}$'s root-to-message path which is not in the subtree of queried messages and has a large prime factor. If all the numbers associated to the exit nodes were such that they had a large prime factor, the proof would be done. But we only require the random numbers to have a large prime factor with constant probability, thus for all exit nodes which do not have a large prime factor, we need to analyze both of its children, and follow the same procedure recursively for the children. Our analysis of this recursive tree searching shows that with overwhelming probability all message $\widehat{m}$ not in the subtree of queried messages will have at least one random number in $\widehat{m}$'s root-to-message path which is not in the subtree and has a large prime factor. The d extra evaluations are due to the exit nodes close to the bottom of the tree. After establishing this fact, the analysis proceeds to show that the existence of this large prime factor can be used to extract solutions to the strong RSA problem from a forged signature. Note that while the Hohenberger-Waters signature scheme is based on the (weaker) RSA assumption, we need to base our scheme on the strong RSA assumption because we cannot simply guess the exit node and program the RSA instance there.

1.2 Efficiency

The public key contains the modulus N, $h \in \mathbb{Z}_N^*$, and a key of a PRF. Recall the definition of a signature from Equation (1). The cost of computing a signature $\sigma(m)$ is dominated by one full exponentiation modulo N to compute $h^{1/e}$. While signing is quite efficient, the cost of signature verification is substantially higher. If the PRF outputs numbers between 1 and $2^n - 1$, the verification has to perform one modular exponentiation of an exponent e which is of an $n(\ell+d)$ bit number. (Note that verification can't reduce e modulo $\varphi(N)$ since that value is only contained in the secret key.) Our security analysis of Theorem 5 and Section 4 give an upper bound in the numbers ℓ, d, and n such that our system is secure. Concretely, for 80 bits security (and assuming that the Dickmann function, $\rho(u)$, is a good approximation for the probability of a random number between 1 and x being $x^{1/u}$-smooth) we can have $\ell = 160$, $n = 200$ and $d = 80$, in which case verification has to perform one exponentiation modulo N with an exponent of size $200(160+80) = 48000$ bits. This analysis is for the weakly secure scheme. The fully secure scheme adds one Chameleon Hash and therefore one exponentiation during signing and verification.

Overall, our new signature scheme offers fast and simple signing combined with a small public key, but has relatively slow verification. More importantly, it is the first scheme that does not need to generate primes or run primality tests during the signing process. We believe that this departure from prime generation dependency is a possible direction for future improvements in the quest for more practical signature schemes which are provable secure in the standard model and can also be useful in other contexts.

1.3 Related Work

The key idea that large random numbers are somewhat likely to have large prime factors and that large random numbers can replace large prime numbers are not new in cryptography. In 1999, Gennaro, Halevi, and Rabin [14], in the process of proving the security of their signature scheme, analyzed the probability that a specific random number is smooth and then showed that if such number is non-smooth then the probability that it divides the product (of a polynomial number) of random numbers is negligible, thus establishing an essential step of the security proof of their signature scheme. We adapt their analysis technique in order to extract solutions to the strong RSA problem in our reduction.

Subsequently, in the context of elliptic-curve signatures, Coron, Handschuh and Naccache [9] avoided point counting (i.e., the need of the participants to know the number of points on the curve and a big factor of it) by first using curves over larger underlying fields. As in our case, a naive analysis of the smoothness property, i.e., requiring the number of curve points to be smooth with negligible probability, would result in very bad parameters for the protocol. Hence the authors only increased the size of the underlying field such that the probability that the curve is smooth is low. Next, they iterated the protocol over many independent random curves in order to guarantee that, with overwhelming probability, at least one curve is non-smooth. Hence their modified signature scheme for avoiding point counting consists of many parallel instances of the original signature scheme and therefore had a considerable slowdown around a factor of 500 [9]. If we used the same approach and signed the messages multiple times with Hohenberger-Waters-style signatures in the hope that for all exit nodes, in at least one instance its associated number would be non-smooth, then this would result in a considerable protocol slowdown.

We stress that even though our signatures are syntactically related to the schemes by Hohenberger and Waters [19] and Gennaro et al. [14], the main difference is that in our scheme the hash functions h_i (instantiated via a PRF F_K) do not output primes.

2   Preliminaries

NOTATION. When convenient, we identify a vector with the set of its entries, i.e. a vector $\mathbf{m}$ with Q entries will be identified with $\{\mathbf{m}[1], \ldots, \mathbf{m}[Q]\}$. We denote by $x \leftarrow_\$ X$ the action of selecting a random element of a set X and calling it x. Most of our security definitions and proofs will use code-based games in the style of Bellare and Rogaway [4]. These games are algorithms that start by running an INITIALIZE procedure, if present, and giving the output to the adversary. Then the adversary queries the oracles provided by the games, and finally halts, with its output becoming the input to FINALIZE. The game output is the output of FINALIZE. We denote by G^A the event that G outputs true when running with A. In the code, all boolean flags are implicitly initialized to false and all tables are initially populated with $\bot$.

SIGNATURE SCHEMES. A signature scheme $\Pi = (\mathsf{KeyGen}, \mathsf{Sign}, \mathsf{Verify})$ consists of three algorithms that satisfy the following syntax requirements. Algorithm KeyGen takes the security parameter λ as input and outputs a public/secret key pair, denoted (pk, sk). Sign takes as input a secret key sk, a message $m \in \{0,1\}^\ell$, and outputs a signature σ or $\bot$ (our security definitions will imply that it should only output $\bot$ with very small probability). Verify takes as input a public key pk, a message m, and a signature σ and outputs accept or reject. We require that, for all (pk, sk) output by $\mathsf{KeyGen}(1^\lambda)$, all messages $m \in \{0,1\}^\ell$, and all $\sigma \neq \bot$ output by $\mathsf{Sign}(sk, m)$, $\mathsf{Verify}(pk, m, \sigma)$ accepts.

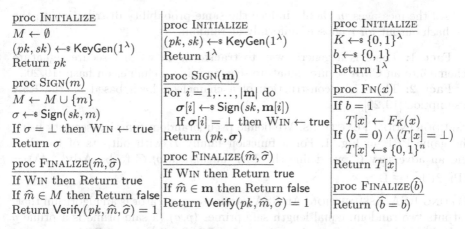

Fig. 1. Games CMA (left), wCMA (middle), and PRF (right). In wCMA the adversary is only allowed one query to SIGN.

SECURITY NOTIONS FOR SIGNATURE SCHEMES. We will target existential unforgeability under chosen message attacks. We define security using the game CMA in Fig. 1. For a signature scheme $\Pi = (\mathsf{KeyGen}, \mathsf{Sign}, \mathsf{Verify})$ and an adversary A, define the *CMA advantage of A* to be $\mathbf{Adv}^{\mathrm{cma}}_{\Pi,A}(\lambda) = \Pr[\mathrm{CMA}^A]$. Note that, in a slight departure from the standard definition, the adversary wins when the signature scheme outputs $\bot$.

While existential unforgeability under chosen message attacks is our ultimate target, we will mostly deal with an intermediate notion called existential unforgeability under *weak* chosen message attacks, which is defined via the game wCMA in Fig. 1. In this game, the adversary is only allowed one SIGN query, which is issued before the adversary sees the public key. We define the *wCMA advantage of A* to be $\mathbf{Adv}^{\mathrm{wcma}}_{\Pi,A}(\lambda) = \Pr[\mathrm{wCMA}^A]$.

CHAMELEON HASH FUNCTIONS. A hash function $\mathsf{HF} = (\mathsf{K}, \mathsf{HE})$ is a tuple of polynomial-time algorithms. Algorithm K takes the security parameter λ as input and outputs a key K. The hash evaluation algorithm HE takes a key K and some input x and computes $y \leftarrow \mathsf{HE}(K, x)$. A collision-resistance adversary H, given $K \leftarrow \mathsf{K}(1^\lambda)$ as input, outputs (x, x'). The adversary advantage, $\mathbf{Adv}^{\mathrm{cr}}_{\mathsf{HF},H}(\lambda)$, is given by the probability that the outputted (x, x') satisfy $(x \neq x') \wedge (\mathsf{HE}(K, x) = \mathsf{HE}(K, x'))$. A chameleon hash [20] is a collision-resistant hash function with additional properties.

- The hash evaluation algorithm HE takes a pair consisting of a message m and randomness r as input.
- The algorithm K, in addition to K, also generates a secret trapdoor information, HT. There should be an efficient algorithm that when given messages m_1, m_2, randomness r_1 and HT as input, finds r_2 such that $\mathsf{HE}(K, (m_1, r_1)) = \mathsf{HE}(K, (m_2, r_2))$.

– All the messages m should induce the same probability distribution on the hash output for r chosen uniformly at random.

Fact 1: There is a generic way to transform an wCMA secure signature scheme into an CMA secure signature scheme using a chameleon hash [19, 20].

Fact 2: There is a construction of a chameleon hash based on the RSA assumption [19, 20].

PSEUDORANDOM FUNCTIONS. We define pseudorandom function security using the game PRF in Fig. 1. For a function family F with outputs of length n and an adversary C, we define the *PRF advantage of* C to be $\mathbf{Adv}_{F,C}^{\mathrm{prf}}(\lambda) = 2\Pr[\mathrm{PRF}^C] - 1$.

STRONG RSA ASSUMPTION. An RSA parameter generator is an algorithm that, outputs two random, equal length safe primes (p, q) (a safe prime is a prime p such that $p' = (p-1)/2$ is also prime). Let $\mathsf{RSAGen}(1^\lambda)$ be an RSA parameter generator. We define the advantage of an adversary C against the strong RSA assumption with RSAGen [2, 24], $\mathbf{Adv}_{\mathsf{RSAGen},C}^{\mathrm{srsa}}(\lambda)$, as the probability that C given (N, y), where $(p, q) \leftarrow \mathsf{RSAGen}(1^\lambda)$ and $N = pq$ and $y \leftarrow_{\$} \mathbb{Z}_N^*$ as input, returns (e, x) such that $e > 1$ and $x^e = y \mod N$.

FACTS FROM NUMBER THEORY. Let α be a positive integer. An integer x is called α-smooth if all prime factors of x are less than or equal to α. We will denote by $\varepsilon(\alpha, n)$ the probability that a random number between 0 and $2^n - 1$ is α-smooth. Define the function

$$L_x[a] = \exp\left((a + o(1))\sqrt{\log x \log\log x}\right).$$

The probability that a random integer between one and x is $L_x[a]$-smooth is $L_x\left[\frac{-1}{2a}\right]$ (see [10]). We will also use the following lemma from [16].

Lemma 1. *Given* $x, y \in \mathbb{Z}_N^*$ *and* $a, b \in \mathbb{Z}$ *such that* $x^a = y^b$, *one can efficiently compute* $z \in \mathbb{Z}_N^*$ *such that* $z = y^{\frac{\gcd(a,b)}{a}}$.

STRINGS. We will write $\{0, 1\}^{\leq \ell}$ for $\cup_{i=0}^{\ell}\{0, 1\}^i$. For a string $x \in \{0, 1\}^{\leq \ell}$ we write $\mathsf{Pref}(x)$ for the set of all prefixes of x, including the empty string and x. We extend this notation to prefixes of sets in the obvious way.

The following definition formalizes the notion of "exit nodes" from the introduction.

Definition 2. *Let* $M \subseteq \{0, 1\}^\ell$ *be non-empty. A minimal non-prefix of* M *is a string* $x \in \{0, 1\}^{\leq \ell}$ *such that* $x \notin \mathsf{Pref}(M)$ *but* $x' \in \mathsf{Pref}(M)$, *where* x' *is* x *with the last bit deleted. We denote the set of minimal non-prefixes of* M *by* $\mathsf{MNP}(M)$.

Note that the empty string is never in $\mathsf{MNP}(M)$ because it is always in $\mathsf{Pref}(M)$. The following lemma is implicit in [19].

Lemma 3. *Let* $M \subseteq \{0, 1\}^\ell$ *be non-empty. Then we have:*

- For all $i = 1, \ldots, \ell$, $|\mathsf{MNP}(M) \cap \{0,1\}^i| \leq |M|$, so $|\mathsf{MNP}(M)| \leq \ell|M|$. Moreover, $\mathsf{MNP}(M)$ can be computed in time linear in $\ell|M|$.
- For any $y \notin M$, $\mathsf{Pref}(y) \cap \mathsf{MNP}(M)$ consists of exactly one string.

CHERNOFF BOUND. We will use the following standard multiplicative Chernoff bound.

Lemma 4. Let $Y_1, \ldots, Y_\ell$ be independent Bernoulli random variables such that $\Pr[Y_i = 1] = \varepsilon$ for all i, and let $Y = Y_1 + \cdots Y_\ell$. Then for all $\delta > 0$,

$$\Pr[Y > (1 + \delta)\varepsilon\ell] < \left(\frac{e^\delta}{(1 + \delta)^{1+\delta}} \right)^{\varepsilon\ell}.$$

3   Signature Scheme

The signature scheme works as follows. Let λ be the security parameter and let $n = n(\lambda)$, $\ell = \ell(\lambda)$ and $d = d(\lambda)$ be functions of the security parameter. The scheme signs messages from $\{0,1\}^\ell$, but this can be extended using a collision resistant hash function.

Fix an RSA parameter generator RSAGen and a function family F that maps $\{0,1\}^{\leq \ell'}$ to odd numbers between 0 and $2^n - 1$ (i.e., bitstrings with the last bit set), where $\ell' = \ell + \lceil \log d \rceil$. We associate with each message $m \in \{0,1\}^\ell$ a set of strings $S(m) \subseteq \{0,1\}^{\leq \ell'}$ given by

$$S(m) = \mathsf{Pref}(m) \cup \{m \,\|\, i : i \in [d]\}. \tag{2}$$

That is, $S(m)$ consists of all of the prefixes of m, including the empty string and m itself, along with d strings that are formed by appending to m (an encoding of) an integer between 1 and d.

KeyGen(1^n): Run $(p,q) \leftarrow_\$ \mathsf{RSAGen}(1^\lambda)$, then set $N = pq$. Select $h \leftarrow_\$ \mathbb{Z}_N^*$ and a key $K \leftarrow_\$ \{0,1\}^\lambda$ for the function family F. The public key is $pk = (N, h, K)$ and the secret key is $sk = (pk, p, q)$.
Sign(sk, m): Compute the set $S(m)$. For each $s \in S(m)$, let $e_s \leftarrow F_K(s)$ (recall that F outputs odd numbers), and set $e \leftarrow \prod_{s \in S(m)} e_s$. If e is not coprime with $\phi(N)$, then output $\bot$. Otherwise, solve the equation

$$\sigma = h^{1/e} \mod N,$$

for σ using the factorization of N. Then output the signature σ. Note that the probability of outputting $\bot$ is negligible in the security parameter.
Verify(pk, m, σ): Compute the set $S(m)$, and for each $s \in S(m)$ let $e_s \leftarrow F_K(s)$. Then let $e \leftarrow \prod_{s \in S(m)} e_s$, and finally accept if

$$\sigma^e = h \mod N$$

and otherwise reject.

proc SIGN(**m**)   // G_0, $\boxed{G_1}$
$(p, q) \leftarrow\!\!{\scriptstyle\$} \ \mathsf{RSAGen}(1^\lambda)$; $N \leftarrow pq$
$p' \leftarrow (p-1)/2$; $q' \leftarrow (q-1)/2$
$h \leftarrow\!\!{\scriptstyle\$} \ \mathbb{Z}_N^*$; $K \leftarrow\!\!{\scriptstyle\$} \ \{0,1\}^\lambda$
$pk \leftarrow (N, h, K)$
If BadSet$^{F_K(\cdot)}$(**m**) then
  bad $\leftarrow$ true ; $\boxed{\text{LOSE} \leftarrow \text{true}}$
For each $j = 1, \ldots, Q$ do
  $e_j \leftarrow \prod_{s \in S(\mathbf{m}[j])} F_K(s)$
  If $\gcd(e_j, p'q') > 1$ then
    $\boldsymbol{\sigma}[j] \leftarrow \perp$
  Else $\boldsymbol{\sigma}[j] \leftarrow h^{1/e_j} \bmod N$
Return $(pk, \boldsymbol{\sigma})$

proc FINALIZE$(\widehat{m}, \widehat{\sigma})$ // G_0, G_1, G_2
$\widehat{e} \leftarrow \prod_{s \in S(\widehat{m})} F_K(s)$
If $\gcd(\widehat{e}, p'q') > 1$ then return false
If LOSE then return false
Return $\perp \in \boldsymbol{\sigma} \vee ((\widehat{\sigma}^{\widehat{e}} = h) \wedge (\widehat{m} \notin \mathbf{m}))$

proc SIGN(**m**)   // G_2
$(p, q) \leftarrow\!\!{\scriptstyle\$} \ \mathsf{RSAGen}(1^\lambda)$; $N \leftarrow pq$
$p' \leftarrow (p-1)/2$; $q' \leftarrow (q-1)/2$
$y \leftarrow\!\!{\scriptstyle\$} \ \mathbb{Z}_N^*$; $K \leftarrow\!\!{\scriptstyle\$} \ \{0,1\}^\lambda$
If BadSet$^{F_K(\cdot)}$(**m**) then LOSE $\leftarrow$ true
For each $j = 1, \ldots, Q$ do
  $e_j \leftarrow \prod_{s \in S(\mathbf{m}[j])} F_K(s)$
$e^* \leftarrow \prod_{j=1}^Q e_j$
$h \leftarrow y^{e^*} \bmod N$; $pk \leftarrow (N, h, K)$
For each $j = 1, \ldots, Q$ do
  If $\gcd(e_j, p'q') > 1$ then
    $\boldsymbol{\sigma}[j] \leftarrow \perp$
  Else
    $e_j' \leftarrow e^*/e_j$; $\boldsymbol{\sigma}[j] \leftarrow y^{e_j'} \bmod N$
Return $(pk, \boldsymbol{\sigma})$

proc SIGN(**m**)   // G_3
Choose a random function π
If BadSet$^\pi$(**m**) then
  bad $\leftarrow$ true

proc FINALIZE$(\widehat{m}, \widehat{\sigma})$ // G_3
Return bad

Fig. 2. Games G_0, G_1, G_2, G_3 for the proof of Theorem 5. G_1 includes the boxed code and G_0 does not. BadSet is described below.

3.1   Security Proof

Theorem 5. *Let F be a function family with outputs of length n, RSAGen be a RSA parameter generator, and Π be the signature scheme associated to F and RSAGen via the construction above. Let α be such that $\varepsilon(\alpha, n) \leq 1/4$. Then for all adversaries A that request Q signatures, there exist efficient adversaries B, C such that*

$$\mathbf{Adv}_{\Pi,A}^{\mathrm{wcma}}(\lambda) \leq \mathbf{Adv}_{F,C}^{\mathrm{prf}}(\lambda) + \mathbf{Adv}_{\mathsf{RSAGen},B}^{\mathrm{srsa}}(\lambda)$$
$$+ Q\left(2^{-2d+1} + 2\ell^3(\ell+d)Q/\alpha + \ell^2(e/4)^\ell\right). \tag{3}$$

where e is the base of the natural logarithm.

Recall that $\varepsilon(\alpha, n)$ is the probability that a random number between 0 and $2^n - 1$ is α-smooth. In Section 4, we will provide example instantiations of the parameters n, ℓ, and d.

Proof: We use the games in Fig. 2. These games use as subroutine an oracle algorithm BadSet, which we describe now. Algorithm BadSet takes as input a vector of messages $\mathbf{m} \subseteq \{0,1\}^\ell$, expects access to an oracle $\mathcal{O}$ mapping $\{0,1\}^*$ to $\mathbb{Z}_N$, and outputs true or false. It works as follows.

$\mathsf{BadSet}^{\mathcal{O}}(\mathbf{m})$ first computes $e^* \leftarrow \prod_{m \in \mathbf{m}} \prod_{t \in S(m)} \mathcal{O}(t)$, and then computes the set $\mathsf{MNP}(\mathbf{m})$. Then for each $x \in \mathsf{MNP}(\mathbf{m})$, it runs the recursive subroutine $\mathsf{Check}^{\mathcal{O}}(x)$. If any of these runs returns true, then BadSet returns true, and otherwise it returns false.

$\underline{\mathsf{Check}^{\mathcal{O}}(x)}$
    If $\mathcal{O}(x) \nmid e^*$ then
        Return false
    If $|x| = \ell$ then
        If $\mathcal{O}(x \| i) \nmid e^*$ for some $i = 1, \ldots, d$ then
            Return false
        Else
            Return true
    If $|x| < \ell$ then
        Return $\mathsf{Check}^{\mathcal{O}}(x \| 0) \vee \mathsf{Check}^{\mathcal{O}}(x \| 1)$

We add the rule that, if any call to $\mathsf{Check}^{\mathcal{O}}(x)$ results in more than $2\ell^2$ recursive calls, then $\mathsf{BadSet}^{\mathcal{O}}(\mathbf{m})$ halts the computation and returns true.

We now turn to relating the games. Game G_0 is just an implementation of the game wCMA with an extra bad flag that is set when BadSet returns true. The purpose of this flag will become clear later - it is meant to catch cases where, after issuing its signing query, the adversary could find a message for which a forgery is easily created by assembling the given signatures.

Game G_1 is the same as G_0, except that when the bad flag is set it returns false to the adversary. We have

$$\mathbf{Adv}^{\mathrm{wcma}}_{\Pi,A}(\lambda) = \Pr[G_0^A] \tag{4}$$

$$\Pr[G_0^A] \leq \Pr[G_1^A] + \Pr[\mathsf{BAD}(G_0^A)]. \tag{5}$$

The inequality follows by the fundamental lemma of game playing since G_0 and G_1 are identical-until-bad.

We will bound the summands in (5) individually. We first deal with $\Pr[G_1^A]$. To this end, we use G_2, which employs the now-standard technique of computing the public key and signatures "backwards" without changing their distribution - instead, the changes are meant to help the reduction to the SRSA problem. G_2 computes h by choosing a random element of $\mathbb{Z}_N^*$, y, and raising it to the product of all the exponents used during signing. Since the adversary wins if this product is not relatively prime to $p'q'$, the resulting h is a uniformly random element of $\mathbb{Z}_N^*$ (or both games output true). Subsequently, signatures can be computed using y and the exponents using the identity

$$h^{1/e_j} = y^{(\prod_{i=1}^n e_i)/e_j} = y^{\prod_{i \neq j} e_i}.$$

We have

$$\Pr[G_1^A] = \Pr[G_2^A].$$

We claim there exists an efficient adversary B such that

$$\Pr[G_2^A] \leq \mathbf{Adv}_{\mathsf{RSAGen},B}^{\mathrm{srsa}}(\lambda).$$

Naturally, B is designed to take advantage of the changes made in G_2. B takes as input (N, y) and attempts to compute some $x \in \mathbb{Z}_N^*$ and $e > 1$ such that $x^e = y$ mod N. It gives the adversary the security parameter, and then the adversary queries SIGN with a vector of messages $\mathbf{m}$. B then computes

> $K \leftarrow_\$ \{0,1\}^\lambda$
> If $\mathsf{BadSet}^{F_K(\cdot)}(\mathbf{m})$ then halt with output $\bot$
> For each $j = 1, \ldots, Q$ do
> $\quad e_j \leftarrow \prod_{s \in S(\mathbf{m}[j])} F_K(s)$
> $e^* \leftarrow \prod_{j=1}^Q e_j$
> $h \leftarrow y^{e^*} \bmod N$; $pk \leftarrow (N, h, K)$
> For each $j = 1, \ldots, Q$ do
> $\quad$ If $N > \gcd(2e_j + 1, N) > 1$ then $\boldsymbol{\sigma}[j] \leftarrow \bot$; use e_j to factor N
> $\quad$ Else $e_j' \leftarrow e^*/e_j$; $\boldsymbol{\sigma}[j] \leftarrow y^{e_j'} \bmod N$
> Return $(pk, \boldsymbol{\sigma})$

B runs A until it outputs $(\widehat{m}, \widehat{\sigma})$. We claim that whenever A would have won G_2, B will solve its SRSA instance. First, if it occurs that $\bot \in \boldsymbol{\sigma}$ in G_2, then B will have factored N in the computation above, thus B can use the factorization to solve the SRSA problem. Note that $\gcd(2e_j + 1, N) > 1$ if and only if $\gcd(e_j, p'q') > 1$.

If instead the output of A satisfies $\widehat{\sigma}^{\widehat{e}} = h \bmod N$ and $\widehat{m} \notin \mathbf{m}$, then B uses the output of A to solve the SRSA instance. Now the fact that $\mathsf{BadSet}^{F_K(\cdot)}(\mathbf{m})$ must have returned false become relevant: We claim it implies that $\widehat{e} = \prod_{s \in S(\widehat{m})} F_K(s)$ does not divide e^*. To see this, let x be the unique prefix of $\widehat{m}$ in $\mathsf{MNP}(\mathbf{m})$. Then $\mathsf{Check}^{F_K}(x)$ must have returned false, meaning that, for one of the $s \in S(\widehat{m})$, $F_K(s)$ did not divide e^*. If one of these did not divide e^*, then certainly product did not, as desired.

Given that $\widehat{e}$ does not divide e^*, we can apply Lemma 1. More specifically, $\widehat{\sigma}, \widehat{e}, y, e^*$ satisfy $\widehat{\sigma}^{\widehat{e}} = y^{e^*} \bmod N$, and we can compute $z \in \mathbb{Z}_N^*$ satisfying $z^{\widehat{e}/\gcd(\widehat{e}, e^*)} = y \bmod N$. We have $\widehat{e}/\gcd(\widehat{e}, e^*) > 1$, so $(z, \widehat{e}/\gcd(\widehat{e}, e^*))$ is a valid solution to the SRSA instance. This establishes the claim.

Returning to our bound on the advantage of A and now considering Game G_3, substitutions give

$$\mathbf{Adv}_{\Pi,A}^{\mathrm{wcma}}(\lambda) \leq \mathbf{Adv}_{\mathsf{RSAGen},B}^{\mathrm{srsa}}(\lambda) + \Pr[\mathrm{BAD}(G_0^A)] \tag{6}$$

$$= \mathbf{Adv}_{\mathsf{RSAGen},B}^{\mathrm{srsa}}(\lambda) + \Pr[G_3^A] + (\Pr[\mathrm{BAD}(G_0^A)] - \Pr[G_3^A]). \tag{7}$$

We complete the proof by showing

$$\Pr[\mathrm{BAD}(G_0^A)] - \Pr[G_3^A] \leq \mathbf{Adv}_{F,C}^{\mathrm{prf}}(\lambda) \tag{8}$$

and

$$\Pr[G_3^A] \leq Q \left(2^{-2d+1} + 2\ell^3(\ell+d)Q/\alpha + \ell^2(e/4)^\ell\right). \tag{9}$$

We first prove (8). The adversary C works as follows. It has access to an oracle FN which returns "real" evaluations of F or random samples. It runs A on input 1^λ. When A queries SIGN with a message vector $\mathbf{m}$, C evaluates $\mathsf{BadSet}^{\mathcal{O}}(\mathbf{m})$, where all of the calls to $\mathcal{O}$ are answered using the FN oracle provided to C. Finally, C outputs the value returned by BadSet. It is easy to see that C satisfies (8).

Proving (9) requires more work. It follows from the next lemma, which will complete the proof of the theorem.

Lemma 6. *Let* $\ell' = \ell + \lceil \log d \rceil$ *and* π *be a random function from* $\{0,1\}^{\leq \ell'}$ *to* $\{0,1\}^n$*. Let* BadSet^π *be defined as above. For* $\alpha > 0$*, let* $\varepsilon = \varepsilon(\alpha,n)$ *be the probability that a random number between* 0 *and* $2^n - 1$ *is* α*-smooth. Then for any* $\mathbf{m} \subseteq \{0,1\}^\ell$ *and* $\alpha, n > 0$ *such that* $\varepsilon(\alpha,n) \leq 1/4$,

$$\Pr[\mathsf{BadSet}^\pi(\mathbf{m})] \leq Q \left(2^{-2d+1} + 2\ell^3(\ell+d)Q/\alpha + \ell^2(e/4)^\ell\right).$$

For the proof, we define an alternative, more restrictive version of BadSet, called SmoothSet. SmoothSet will not be efficiently computable, but we stress that this is inconsequential for our claims below. SmoothSet takes the same input and has access to the same oracle. On input $\mathbf{m}$, $\mathsf{SmoothSet}^\pi$ first computes $e^* \leftarrow \prod_{m \in \mathbf{m}} \prod_{t \in S(m)} \pi(t)$, and then computes the set $\mathsf{MNP}(\mathbf{m})$. Then it runs $\mathsf{FindPrimes}^\pi(x)$ for each $x \in \mathsf{MNP}(\mathbf{m})$, which is the following algorithm that returns a set of prime numbers.

$\mathsf{FindPrimes}^\pi(x)$

    If $\exists$ prime $p > \alpha$ s.t. $p \mid \pi(x)$ then
        Choose one p meeting such criteria and return $\{p\}$
    If $|x| = \ell$ then
        If $\exists$ prime $p > \alpha, i \in [d]$ s.t. $p \mid \pi(x \| i)$ then
            Choose one p meeting such criteria and return $\{p\}$
        Else
            Return $\{\bot\}$
    If $|x| < \ell$ then Return $\mathsf{FindPrimes}^\pi(x \| 0) \cup \mathsf{FindPrimes}^\pi(x \| 1)$

We add the rule that, if any call to $\mathsf{FindPrimes}^\pi(x)$ results in more than $2\ell^2$ recursive calls, then $\mathsf{SmoothSet}^\pi(\mathbf{m})$ halts the computation and returns true. $\mathsf{SmoothSet}^\pi(\mathbf{m})$ takes the union of all the sets returned by calls to $\mathsf{FindPrimes}^\pi(x)$. If $\bot$ was returned at any point, or if any of the returned primes divide e^*, then it returns true. Otherwise, it returns false.

We first argue that whenever $\mathsf{BadSet}^\pi(\mathbf{m})$ returns true due to the halting condition (i.e., if some call $\mathsf{Check}^\pi(x)$ results in more than $2\ell^2$ recursive calls) then $\mathsf{SmoothSet}^\pi(\mathbf{m})$ also returns true. Note that in such cases either $\mathsf{SmoothSet}^\pi(\mathbf{m})$

also returns true due to the halting condition or for at least one called value x there were less recursive calls in $\mathsf{FindPrimes}^\pi(x)$ than in $\mathsf{Check}^\pi(x)$. But then there exists some value $u = x \,\|\, v$ such that: (i) $\mathsf{FindPrimes}^\pi(u)$ was called and did not generate any recursive call but (ii) $\mathsf{Check}^\pi(u)$ generated recursive calls. (i) implies that $\mathsf{FindPrimes}^\pi(u)$ outputted some prime $p > \alpha$ such that $p \mid \pi(u)$ and (ii) implies that $\pi(u) \mid e^*$. Therefore these two facts together imply that $p \mid e^*$ and so $\mathsf{SmoothSet}^\pi(\mathbf{m})$ returns true by definition.

The other case in which $\mathsf{BadSet}^\pi(\mathbf{m})$ returns true is if there is an $x \in \mathsf{MNP}(\mathbf{m})$ and $y \in \{0,1\}^{\ell - |x|}$ such that

$$\forall s \in \mathsf{Pref}(y), \quad \pi(x \,\|\, s) \mid e^*$$

and

$$\forall i = 1, \ldots, d, \quad \pi(x \,\|\, y \,\|\, i) \mid e^*.$$

But then it also holds that $\forall s \in \mathsf{Pref}(y)$ all prime factors of $\pi(x \,\|\, s)$ divide e^* and $\forall i = 1, \ldots, d$ all prime factors of $\pi(x \,\|\, y \,\|\, i)$ divide e^* and hence $\mathsf{SmoothSet}^\pi(\mathbf{m})$ also returns true. So we have

$$\Pr[\mathsf{BadSet}^\pi(\mathbf{m})] \leq \Pr[\mathsf{SmoothSet}^\pi(\mathbf{m})].$$

Thus it suffices to bound the latter probability. We recall that $\mathsf{SmoothSet}^\pi(\mathbf{m})$ returns true if, and only if, for some $x \in \mathsf{MNP}(\mathbf{m})$, $\mathsf{FindPrimes}^\pi(x)$ returns $\bot$ or performs more than $2\ell^2$ recursions or one of the returned primes divides e^*.

We first bound the probability that $\bot$ is in the set returned by a call to $\mathsf{FindPrimes}^\pi(x)$. This will happen if there is an $x \in \mathsf{MNP}(\mathbf{m})$ and $y \in \{0,1\}^{\ell - |x|}$ such that

$$\forall s \in \mathsf{Pref}(y), \quad \pi(x \,\|\, s) \text{ is } \alpha\text{-smooth}$$

and

$$\forall i = 1, \ldots, d, \quad \pi(x \,\|\, y \,\|\, i) \text{ is } \alpha\text{-smooth}.$$

For a particular x and y this happens with probability $\varepsilon^{|y|+d} = \varepsilon^{\ell - |x| + d}$. A union bound over all x and y show that $\bot$ is in a set with probability at most

$$\sum_{x \in \mathsf{MNP}(\mathbf{m})} \sum_{y \in \{0,1\}^{\ell - |x|}} \varepsilon^{\ell - |x| + d} = \sum_{x \in \mathsf{MNP}(\mathbf{m})} 2^{\ell - |x|} \varepsilon^{\ell - |x| + d}$$

$$\leq \sum_{i=1}^{\ell} Q 2^{\ell - i} \varepsilon^{\ell - i + d}$$

$$= Q\varepsilon^d \sum_{i=0}^{\ell-1} (2\varepsilon)^i < 2Q\varepsilon^d \leq Q 2^{-2d+1}$$

For the first inequality we used Lemma 3, and for the second we used the assumption that $\varepsilon \leq 1/4$ and applied the formula for summing a geometric series.

Next we need the following lemma that gives an upper bound on the number of recursive calls generated by $\mathsf{FindPrimes}^\pi(x)$ (i.e., this lemma bounds the probability that the halting condition makes SmoothSet return true due to this x). Note that since each call adds at most one element to the returned set, this will also bound the size of the returned set.

Lemma 7. *Let π be a random function from $\{0,1\}^*$ to $\{0,1\}^n$, $\alpha > 0$, and $\varepsilon = \varepsilon(\alpha, n) \leq 1/4$ be the probability that a random number between 0 and $2^n - 1$ is α-smooth. Then, for any $x \in \mathsf{MNP}(\mathbf{m})$, the probability that $\mathsf{FindPrimes}^\pi(x)$ generates more than $2\ell^2$ recursive calls is at most $\ell(e/4)^\ell$.*

Using Lemma 7, it is possible to complete the proof of Lemma 6. Suppose that $\mathsf{FindPrimes}^\pi(x)$ returns a set of at most $2\ell^2$ primes without ever returning $\bot$. The probability that each of the primes p divides e^* is at most the probability that p divides one of the $Q(\ell + d)$ random factors used in the product defining e^*. This probability is $1/p < 1/\alpha$, because both numbers are random and independent. A union bound over the factors shows that a given prime divides e^* with probability at most $Q(\ell + d)/\alpha$; another union bound over the (at most) $2\ell^2$ primes gives a bound of $2Q\ell^2(\ell + d)/\alpha$.

Finally, we sum the probability that $\mathsf{FindPrimes}^\pi(x)$ returns $\bot$ and the probabilities that $\mathsf{FindPrimes}^\pi(x)$ performs more than $2\ell^2$ recursions or one of the returned primes divides e^* for an $x \in \mathsf{MNP}(\mathbf{m})$ (there are at most $Q\ell$ by Lemma 3) in order to conclude the proof of Lemma 6 and hence of Theorem 5.

Proof of Lemma 7: Fix any $x \in \mathsf{MNP}(\mathbf{m})$. We bound the number of recursive calls in the computation of $\mathsf{FindPrimes}^\pi(x)$: Since each call adds at most one element to the returned set, this will also bound the size of that set. We consider the number of calls to FindPrimes on inputs of each length. Let X_i the number of calls on inputs of length i that are generated due to the computation of $\mathsf{FindPrimes}^\pi(x)$. We will show that with high probability, $X_i < 2\ell$ for all i, which gives $\sum_{i=1}^\ell X_i < 2\ell^2$.

$$\Pr[X_1, \ldots, X_\ell \leq 2\ell] = 1 - \Pr[\exists X_i : X_i > 2\ell]$$

$$= 1 - \sum_{i=1}^\ell \Pr[X_i > 2\ell | X_1, \ldots, X_{i-1} \leq 2\ell]$$

We proceed to prove that for all i

$$\Pr[X_i > 2\ell | X_1, \ldots, X_{i-1} \leq 2\ell] < (e/4)^\ell. \tag{10}$$

Let j be the length of x. Then we have that $X_1, \ldots, X_j \leq 1$ with probability 1. Now consider the other X_i. Since each call results in at most two calls at the input with one bit appended, we have $X_i \leq 2X_{i-1}$ for all $i = j + 1, \ldots, \ell$. We have that

$$\Pr[X_i > 2\ell | X_1, \ldots, X_{i-1} \le 2\ell] = \Pr\left[X_i > 2\ell \,\middle|\, \begin{array}{l} X_1, \ldots, X_{i-2} \le 2\ell \\ \wedge\, X_{i-1} < \ell \end{array}\right]$$

$$+ \Pr\left[X_i > 2\ell \,\middle|\, \begin{array}{l} X_1, \ldots, X_{i-2} \le 2\ell \\ \wedge\, \ell \le X_{i-1} \le 2\ell \end{array}\right].$$

In the right-hand side the first probability is 0 because $X_i \le 2X_{i-1} < 2\ell$. We are left to bound the the second term. Now we use the observation that X_i is the sum of $\ell' = X_{i-1}$ (with $2\ell \ge \ell' \ge \ell$) Bernoulli random variables with expectation 2ε, allowing us to apply the Chernoff bound in Lemma 4 giving

$$\Pr[X_i > 2\ell | X_1, \ldots, X_{i-1} \le 2\ell] = \Pr[X_i > 2\ell | X_1, \ldots, X_{i-1} \le 2\ell \wedge X_{i-1} \ge \ell]$$

$$= \Pr\left[X_i > \left(\frac{\ell}{\varepsilon\ell'}\right) 2\varepsilon\ell' \,\middle|\, \begin{array}{l} X_1, \ldots, X_{i-1} \le 2\ell \\ \wedge\, X_{i-1} \ge \ell \end{array}\right]$$

$$< \left(\frac{(e)^{\frac{\ell}{\varepsilon\ell'} - 1}}{\left(\frac{\ell}{\varepsilon\ell'}\right)^{\frac{\ell}{\varepsilon\ell'}}}\right)^{2\varepsilon\ell'}$$

$$= \frac{e^{2\ell - 2\varepsilon\ell'}}{\left(\frac{\ell}{\varepsilon\ell'}\right)^{2\ell}}$$

$$= \frac{e^{2\ell - 2\ell(\varepsilon\ell'/\ell)}}{\left(\frac{\ell}{\varepsilon\ell'}\right)^{2\ell}}$$

where we used the fact that $\frac{\ell}{\varepsilon\ell'} > 1$ for $\varepsilon \le 1/4$ in order to apply the Chernoff bound. Now letting $\beta = \frac{\varepsilon\ell'}{\ell}$

$$\frac{e^{2\ell - 2\ell(\varepsilon\ell'/\ell)}}{\left(\frac{\ell}{\varepsilon\ell'}\right)^{2\ell}} = \left(e^{1-\beta}\beta\right)^{2\ell}$$

We note that $0 < \beta < 1/2$ since $2\ell \ge \ell' \ge \ell$ and $0 < \varepsilon \le 1/4$, and that this is an increasing function of β for the range $0 < \beta < 1/2$. Therefore the worst case is

$$\Pr[X_i > 2\ell | X_1, \ldots, X_{i-1} \le 2\ell] < \left(\frac{\sqrt{e}}{2}\right)^{2\ell}$$

$$= \left(\frac{e}{4}\right)^{\ell}$$

Note that this bound can be made stronger if the upper bound of ε is decreased. This proves Inequality 10 and then summing the probabilities over the l different lengths we conclude the proof of the lemma. ∎

4 Setting the Parameters

From Theorem 5 we have

$$\mathbf{Adv}_{\Pi,A}^{\mathrm{wcma}}(\lambda) \leq \mathbf{Adv}_{F,C}^{\mathrm{prf}}(\lambda) + \mathbf{Adv}_{\mathsf{RSAGen},B}^{\mathrm{srsa}}(\lambda)$$

$$+ Q\left(2^{-2d+1} + 2\ell^3(\ell+d)Q/\alpha + \ell^2(e/4)^\ell\right).$$

Now we consider the case in which we want to give concrete upper bounds on the advantage of any wCMA adversary A. Using the previous equation we would like to have

$$2^{-\lambda} \geq \mathbf{Adv}_{F,C}^{\mathrm{prf}}(\lambda) + \mathbf{Adv}_{\mathsf{RSAGen},B}^{\mathrm{srsa}}(\lambda) + Q\left(2^{-2d+1} + 2\ell^3(\ell+d)Q/\alpha + \ell^2(e/4)^\ell\right)$$

$$= \mathbf{Adv}_{F,C}^{\mathrm{prf}}(\lambda) + \mathbf{Adv}_{\mathsf{RSAGen},B}^{\mathrm{srsa}}(\lambda) + Q2^{-2d+1} + 2Q^2\ell^3(\ell+d)/\alpha + Q\ell^2(e/4)^\ell$$

for some security parameter λ. To obtain such bound, we will upper bound each of the five terms by $2^{-\lambda}/8$. For the first two terms, we only need to setup the function family F and the RSA parameter generator RSAGen in such a way that for any polynomial-time adversaries C and B we have

$$\mathbf{Adv}_{F,C}^{\mathrm{prf}}(\lambda) < 2^{-\lambda}/8$$

and

$$\mathbf{Adv}_{\mathsf{RSAGen},B}^{\mathrm{srsa}}(\lambda) < 2^{-\lambda}/8$$

For bounding

$$Q2^{-2d+1} < 2^{-\lambda}/8$$

we only need to set

$$d > \frac{\lambda + 4 + \log(Q)}{2}$$

Having fixed the value of d, we can now bound

$$2Q^2\ell^3(\ell+d)/\alpha < 2^{-\lambda}/8$$

by setting

$$\alpha > 2^{\lambda+4}Q^2\ell^3(\ell+d).$$

Now the value of α will determine the value of n, since we need $\varepsilon(\alpha, n) \leq 1/4$. To set the value of n we will use the Dickman function. The Dickman function $\rho(u)$ is an asymptotical approximation for the probability of a random number between 1 and x being $x^{1/u}$-smooth. Assuming that the Dickman function gives a good approximation in the range of interest, we can use the fact that $\rho(2.2) < 0.221$ [15] and set $n = \log(\alpha^{2.2})$ (i.e., we are choosing numbers up to $\alpha^{2.2}$) in order to obtain $\varepsilon(\alpha, \log(\alpha^{2.2})) < 1/4$ as required by Theorem 5.

SOUNDNESS OF USING DICKMAN APPROXIMATION. As mentioned by Bach and Peralta [1] no discrepancy has been observed between the values predicted by the ρ function and the real smoothness probabilities, in the range of interest to algorithm designers. In addition, for small values of u (the case that we are interested), counts of smooth number have shown that the error of the approximation is as low as 2% even for values of x as low as 10^{15} (i.e., for numbers between 1 and 10^{15}, considering $10^{15/u}$-smoothness). Tables available in [1].

Acknowledgments. The third author was supported by a Sofja Kovalevskaja Award of the Alexander von Humboldt Foundation and the German Federal Ministry for Education and Research. Part of this work was done while the first two authors were visiting Ruhr-University Bochum, supported by the Sofja Kovalevskaja Award.

References

1. Bach, E., Peralta, R.: Asymptotic semismoothness probabilities. Math. Comput. **65**(216), 1701–1715 (1996)
2. Barić, N., Pfitzmann, B.: Collision-free accumulators and fail-stop signature schemes without trees. In: Fumy, W. (ed.) EUROCRYPT 1997. LNCS, vol. 1233, pp. 480–494. Springer, Heidelberg (1997)
3. Bellare, M., Rogaway, P.: Random oracles are practical: A paradigm for designing efficient protocols. In: Ashby, V. (ed.) ACM CCS 93, pp. 62–73. ACM Press, Nov. (1993)
4. Bellare, M., Rogaway, P.: The security of triple encryption and a framework for code-based game-playing proofs. In: Vaudenay, S. (ed.) EUROCRYPT 2006. LNCS, vol. 4004, pp. 409–426. Springer, Heidelberg (2006)
5. Böhl, F., Hofheinz, D., Jager, T., Koch, J., Seo, J.H., Striecks, C.: Practical signatures from standard assumptions. In: Johansson, T., Nguyen, P.Q. (eds.) EUROCRYPT 2013. LNCS, vol. 7881, pp. 461–485. Springer, Heidelberg (2013)
6. Camenisch, J.L., Lysyanskaya, A.: Signature schemes and anonymous credentials from bilinear maps. In: Franklin, M. (ed.) CRYPTO 2004. LNCS, vol. 3152, pp. 56–72. Springer, Heidelberg (2004)
7. Canetti, R., Goldreich, O., Halevi, S.: The random oracle methodology, revisited (preliminary version). In: 30th ACM STOC, pp. 209–218. ACM Press, May 1998
8. Catalano, D., Fiore, D., Warinschi, B.: Adaptive pseudo-free groups and applications. In: Paterson, K.G. (ed.) EUROCRYPT 2011. LNCS, vol. 6632, pp. 207–223. Springer, Heidelberg (2011)
9. Coron, J.-S., Handschuh, H., Naccache, D.: ECC: Do We Need to Count? In: Lam, K.-Y., Okamoto, E., Xing, C. (eds.) ASIACRYPT 1999. LNCS, vol. 1716, pp. 122–134. Springer, Heidelberg (1999)
10. Coron, J.-S., Naccache, D.: Security Analysis of the Gennaro-Halevi-Rabin Signature Scheme. In: Preneel, B. (ed.) EUROCRYPT 2000. LNCS, vol. 1807, p. 91. Springer, Heidelberg (2000)
11. Cramer, R., Shoup, V.: Signature schemes based on the strong RSA assumption. In ACM CCS 99, pp. 46–51. ACM Press, November 1999
12. Dodis, Y., Oliveira, R., Pietrzak, K.: On the generic insecurity of the full domain hash. In: Shoup, V. (ed.) CRYPTO 2005. LNCS, vol. 3621, pp. 449–466. Springer, Heidelberg (2005)
13. Fischlin, M.: The Cramer-Shoup strong-RSA signature scheme revisited. In: Desmedt, Y. (ed.) PKC 2003, volume of. LNCS, vol. 2567, pp. 116–129. Springer, Heidelberg (2003)

14. Gennaro, R., Halevi, S., Rabin, T.: Secure Hash-and-Sign Signatures without the Random Oracle. In: Stern, J. (ed.) EUROCRYPT 1999. LNCS, vol. 1592, p. 123. Springer, Heidelberg (1999)
15. Granville, A.: Smooth numbers: computational number theory and beyond. Algorithmic Number Theory **44**, 267–323 (2008)
16. Guillou, L.C., Quisquater, J.-J.: A Practical Zero-Knowledge Protocol Fitted to Security Microprocessor Minimizing Both Transmission and Memory. In: Günther, C.G. (ed.) EUROCRYPT 1988. LNCS, vol. 330, pp. 123–128. Springer, Heidelberg (1988)
17. Hofheinz, D., Jager, T., Kiltz, E.: Short Signatures from Weaker Assumptions. In: Lee, D.H., Wang, X. (eds.) ASIACRYPT 2011. LNCS, vol. 7073, pp. 647–666. Springer, Heidelberg (2011)
18. Hofheinz, D., Kiltz, E.: Programmable Hash Functions and Their Applications. In: Wagner, D. (ed.) CRYPTO 2008. LNCS, vol. 5157, pp. 21–38. Springer, Heidelberg (2008)
19. Hohenberger, S., Waters, B.: Short and Stateless Signatures from the RSA Assumption. In: Halevi, S. (ed.) CRYPTO 2009. LNCS, vol. 5677, pp. 654–670. Springer, Heidelberg (2009)
20. Krawczyk, H., Rabin, T.: Chameleon signatures. In NDSS 2000. The Internet Society, February 2000
21. Kurosawa, K., Schmidt-Samoa, K.: New online/offline signature schemes without random oracles. In: Yung, M., Dodis, Y., Kiayias, A., Malkin, T. (eds.) PKC 2006. LNCS, vol. 3958, pp. 330–346. Springer, Heidelberg (2006)
22. Zhu, H.: New digital signature scheme attaining immunity to adaptive chosen-message attack. Chinese Journal of Electronics **10**(4), 484–486 (2001)
23. Zhu, H.: A formal proof of zhus signature scheme. Cryptology ePrint Archive, Report 2003/155, 2003. http://eprint.iacr.org/
24. Fujisaki, E., Okamoto, T.: Statistical zero knowledge protocols to prove modular polynomial relations. In: Kaliski Jr, B.S. (ed.) CRYPTO 1997. LNCS, vol. 1294, pp. 16–30. Springer, Heidelberg (1997)

Short Signatures with Short Public Keys from Homomorphic Trapdoor Functions

Jacob Alperin-Sheriff[✉]

School of Computer Science, Georgia Institute of Technology, Atlanta, GA, USA
jmas6@cc.gatech.edu

Abstract. We present a lattice-based stateless signature scheme provably secure in the standard model. Our scheme has a *constant* number of matrices in the public key and a single lattice vector (plus a tag) in the signatures. The best previous lattice-based encryption schemes were the scheme of Ducas and Micciancio (CRYPTO 2014), which required a logarithmic number of matrices in the public key and that of Bohl et. al (J. of Cryptology 2014), which required a logarithmic number of lattice vectors in the signature. Our main technique involves using fully homomorphic computation to compute a degree d polynomial over the tags hidden in the matrices in the public key. In the scheme of Ducas and Micciancio, only functions *linear* over the tags in the public key matrices were used, which necessitated having d matrices in the public key.

As a matter of independent interest, we extend Wichs' (eprint 2014) recent construction of homomorphic trapdoor functions into a primitive we call puncturable homomorphic trapdoor functions (PHTDFs). This primitive abstracts out most of the properties required in many different lattice-based cryptographic constructions. We then show how to combine a PHTDF along with a function satisfying certain properties (to be evaluated homomorphically) to give an eu-scma signature scheme.

1 Introduction

Lattice-based cryptography has made great strides since the original work of Ajtai [AD97, Ajt96]. In many areas, it holds its own in comparison to cryptography based on various quantum-insecure number-theoretic problems such as RSA and Diffie-Hellman. Variants of the very efficient commercial NTRUEncrypt scheme have been proved secure under worst-case lattice problems [HPS98, SS11]. Moreover, lattice-based cryptography has led to cryptographic primitives such as fully homomorphic encryption (FHE) which have not been realized at all under classical number-theoretic hardness assumptions [Gen09].

J. Alperin-Sheriff—This material is based upon work supported by DARPA under agreement number FA8750-11-C-0096. Any opinions, findings, and conclusions or recommendations expressed in this material are those of the author(s) and do not necessarily reflect the views of DARPA or U.S. Government. The U.S. Government is authorized to reproduce and distribute reprints for Governmental purposes notwithstanding any copyright notation thereon.

© International Association for Cryptologic Research 2015
J. Katz (Ed.): PKC 2015, LNCS 9020, pp. 236–255, 2015.
DOI: 10.1007/978-3-662-46447-2_11

In the area of digital signatures, lattice-based cryptography is also able to hold its own–in the random oracle model. The work in this area [Lyu09,Lyu12, GLP12,DDLL13,BG14] has led to signature schemes which are very efficient. Signing is about as fast as in state-of-the-art schemes providing comparable security (in the random oracle model) based on quantum-insecure problems, and verification is much faster. On the downside, the key and signatures are quite a bit larger.

The gap in key size is even more pronounced for stateless signatures in the standard model. In state-of-the-art schemes based on the security of standard number-theoretic assumptions as RSA and decisional Bilinear Diffie-Hellman (BDH), [Wat09,HW09] both the public key and signatures contain only a constant number of "basic" elements (elements of $\mathbb{Z}_N^*$ in the RSA scheme, group elements in the BDH-based scheme). This results in the public key and signatures having size *linear* $(O(\lambda))$ in the security parameter. By contrast, even when using "compact" algebraic lattices [Mic02], the "basic" elements in lattice-based cryptography (matrices of a certain size in $\mathbb{Z}_q$ for the public key, where q can usually be polynomial in λ, vectors of a certain size in $\mathbb{Z}_q$ for the signatures) have size quasilinear $(\tilde{O}(\lambda))$ in the security parameter. Moreover, the best known schemes require either a logarithmic number of "basic" elements in the public key [DM14] or a logarithmic number of "basic" elements in signatures [BHJ+14].

The efficient RSA-based scheme cited above [HW09] uses the well-studied prefix-guessing technique for achieving static security in signature schemes. In this technique, the simulator samples from the polynomially-sized set of shortest prefixes not found in the messages received from the adversary and then sets up the scheme so that a forgery on a message with that prefix lets the simulator solve RSA. A short public key is achieved by embedding trapdoors for all prefixes of the messages received by the adversary into the public key. The efficient BDH-based scheme [Wat09] is a generic transformation from an efficient fully secure identity-based encryption scheme. The techniques used in the RSA scheme does not appear to have an easy realization in the lattice setting, and since the most efficient known lattice-based fully secure identity-based encryption scheme requires a linear number of "basic" elements in the public key [ABB10], it also does not appear to be a productive avenue of investigation for improving efficiency in signatures. Instead of attempting to use these techniques, we turn to an area where lattice-based cryptography has proven to be particularly versatile: homomorphic computation.

1.1 Our Results

We present the first standard model construction of a lattice-based stateless signature scheme with short signatures and a *constant* number of matrices in the public key. The constant number of matrices does come at a price, as our scheme requires a significantly larger SIS parameter β (and correspondingly, a larger modulus q) to achieve similar levels of security to previous schemes. See Figure 1.1 for a detailed comparison to previous works.

Scheme	Pub. Key $R_q^{1\times k}$ mat.	Secret Key $R_q^{k\times k}$ mat.	Signature R_q^k vec.	Reduction loss	SIS param β
[LM08] (Trees)	1	1	$\log n$	Q	$\tilde{\Omega}(n^2)$
[CHKP10]	n	n	n	Q	$\tilde{\Omega}(n^{3/2})$
[Boy10, MP12]	n	n	1	Q	$\tilde{\Omega}(n^{7/2})$, $\tilde{\Omega}(n^{5/2})$
[BHJ+14]	1	1	d	$(Q^2/\epsilon)^c$	$\tilde{\Omega}(n^{5/2})$
[DM14]	d	1	1	$(Q^2/\epsilon)^c$	$\tilde{\Omega}(n^{7/2})$
This work	1	1	1	$(Q^2/\epsilon)^c$	$\tilde{\Omega}(d^{2d}\cdot n^{11/2})$

In the above table, we have ignored constant factors to avoid clutter. The comparison is in the ring setting because as written, [LM08, DM14] have no realization over general lattices. Here, $R_q = \mathbb{Z}_q[X]/\langle f(X)\rangle$ for some cyclotomic polynomial f of degree n, the modulus $q \geq \beta\sqrt{n}\omega(\sqrt{\log n})$, and $k = O(\log q)$. Q is the number of signatures queries made by the adversary and ϵ is its success probability. For those schemes using the confined guessing technique, d is a value satisfying $2Q^2/\epsilon < 2^{\lfloor c^d\rfloor}$ for an arbitrary constant $c > 1$ (which governs a trade-off between public key size and the reduction loss). The reduction loss is the ratio ϵ'/ϵ between the success probability ϵ' of the reduction and the success probability ϵ of the adversary. In order to be secure against any PPT adversary succeeding with non-negligible probability, we need $d = \omega(\log\log n)$. For our scheme, we can choose d to be as large as $O(\log(n)/\log(\log(n)))$ and still end up with a polynomial-sized SIS parameter β. However, it does have the downside that, choosing $d = \log(n)$, as in previous works using confined guessing, results in a SIS parameter of size $n^{\tilde{\Omega}(\log\log n)}$.

Fig. 1. Comparison to previous standard-model lattice-based signature schemes in the ring setting

Our starting point is the recent scheme of Ducas and Micciancio [DM14], which combines the confined guessing technique of Böhl et al. [BHJ+14] with the "vanishing trapdoors" technique of Boyen [Boy10]. We provide two improvents to the scheme:

Instantiation Over General Lattices. The Ducas-Micciancio scheme only works in the ring-based setting. The reason for this is that, as written, the scheme requires that their tags (represented as matrices) commute with a certain structured matrix $\mathbf{G} \in \mathbb{Z}_q^{n\times m}$ under multiplication. Over general lattices, the only tags which commute with $\mathbf{G}$ are scalar tags, and there are only a (small) polynomial number of these tags which are "short", while a superpolynomial number are required for the construction. As a result, they were forced to use the ring setting, where their tag space can be represented as ring elements, which do in fact commute with $\mathbf{G}$.

To resolve this non-commutativity issue, we recall a technique which appears to have first been explicitly presented by [Xag13], although it appears earlier implicitly in an earlier work in the area of fully homomorphic encryption [BV11]. This technique involves a function which we denote (somewhat abusively) as $\mathbf{G}^{-1}(\mathbf{U})$, where the output of the function is a $\{0,1\}^{m\times m}$ matrix $\mathbf{X}$ such that $\mathbf{GX} = \mathbf{U}$. As a result, in order to multiply a tag $\mathbf{H}$ "commutatively" with

$\mathbf{G}$, we simply compute $\mathbf{G} \cdot \mathbf{G}^{-1}(\mathbf{HG}) = \mathbf{HG}$. As a further benefit, in the actual construction, the multiplication causes the size of the trapdoor to grow according to the norm of the tag, which forced them to use tags from a set with small norm. As $\mathbf{G}^{-1}(\mathbf{X})$ has small norm regardless of the size of $\mathbf{X}$, our scheme is not subject to this restriction in terms of tag choice.

Homomorphic Computation of Trapdoors. Lattice-based signature schemes using the "vanishing trapdoors" technique of Boyen ([Boy10, MP12, DM14]) involve homomorphically evaluating a function $g = g_{(\mu,T)}$ over tags $\hat{t}_i$ statistically hidden in matrices $(\mathbf{A}_0, \mathbf{A}_1, \ldots, \mathbf{A}_d)$ in the public key, where the function g to be evaluated is from a function family indexed by the message μ being signed and (possibly) some additional set of tags T sampled randomly. The output of this function is a matrix $\mathbf{A}_{(\mu,T)}$, with an associated trapdoor, the size of which grows in a manner depending on the function g being evaluated. The trapdoor can be used by the signer to sample short vectors from some coset of a lattice constructed using $\mathbf{A}_{(\mu,T)}$ whenever the tag hidden in $\mathbf{A}_{(\mu,T)}$ is *invertible*; these preimages are combined with the tags T to form the signature. However, when the tag hidden is 0, we refer to $\mathbf{A}_{(\mu,T)}$ as *punctured*, because in this case we can no longer sample short vectors, and in fact, $\mathbf{A}_{(\mu,T)}$ can be used to embed a challenge for the SIS problem.

In order to make the signature scheme secure, the function family g must be such that we can choose two sets of $d + 1$ tags $\hat{T}_1, \hat{T}_2$ to hide in the matrices in the public key such that the tags satisfy certain properties. The first set of tags is used in the actual signature scheme, and they must be such that for any message μ and tags T, the tag associated with matrix $\mathbf{A}_{(\mu,T)}$ is *invertible*. The second set of tags is used in the security reduction, and they must be such that we can (with non-negligible probability) produce a signature for each of the adversary's queried messages while ensuring that a forgery output by the adversary will result in a punctured $\mathbf{A}_{\mu^*,T^*}$ with non-negligible probability.

In these previous schemes, the function g being computed was *linear* over the $d + 1$ tags in the public key. We use a technique from recent works works by Boneh et al. [BGG+14] and Wichs et al. [GVW14] to allow us to homomorphically compute a degree d polynomial over these tags. This lets us use just two tagged matrices in the public key instead of d. Computation in these works was defined in terms of basic operations of addition, multiplication, addition-with-constant, and multiplication-by-constant. However, naive evaluation of computation over homomorphic trapdoors results in larger growth in the size of the trapdoor than is necessary. To reduce the growth of the trapdoor, we use the "right-associativity" technique for multiplication. This technique was developed by Brakerski and Vaikuntanathan [BV14] and by Alperin-Sheriff and Peikert [ASP14] in the context of bootstrapping the GSW homomorphic encryption scheme [GSW13]. Those two papers only used the technique with $\{0, 1\}$ messages (tags in our context) which resulted in "quasi-additive" noise growth in the size of the (implicit) trapdoors. Here, we show that for tags of bounded size at most d, the technique allows us to homomorphically evaluate a degree d polynomial while causing the trapdoors to grow by a $d^d \operatorname{poly}(n)$ factor.

Puncturable Homomorphic Trapdoor Functions. As a side contribution, we abstract out the properties required to construct "vanishing trapdoor"-based cryptographic primitives, including signatures, identity-based encryption and attribute-based encryption, into a primitive we call puncturable homomorphic trapdoor functions (PHTDFs). These functions are an extension of the Wichs et al. definition of homomorphic trapdoor functions [GVW14]. A PHTDF consists of a tagged function space a_i with corresponding trapdoors r_i. One can homomorphically compute functions g of these a_i, r_i to get a tagged function a^* and (if one knows the trapdoors for the original a_i) trapdoor r^*. Whenever the tag associated with a^* is invertible, one can use the trapdoor r^* to invert the function $f_{pk,a^*,x}$, where $x \in \mathcal{X}$ are indices.

For security, we require that for a punctured a^*, it should be difficult to find collisions $x \neq x'$, u, u' such that $f_{pk,a^*,x}(u) = f_{pk,a^*,x'}(u')$, even given oracle access to an inverter for $f_{pk,a_i,x}$ for arbitrary a_i with invertible tags and arbitrary x.

We do not expect realizations of PHTDFs under the various classical assumptions (just as we do not expect realizations of fully homomorphic cryptography in general from those assumptions). However, we believe that building our signature scheme generically using a PHTDF makes the proof of security easier to follow. Perhaps more importantly, we believe that viewing "vanishing trapdoor"-based cryptographic primitives under this framework and focusing on the function g to be computed may lead to realizations of these primitives with smaller public keys.

Organization. The remainder of the paper is organized as follows. In Section 2 we recall some preliminary information about lattice-based cryptography. In Section 3 we define and construct puncturable homomorphic trapdoor functions (PHTDFs). In Section 4 we show how to use a PHTDF to construct a secure signature scheme given that the function g being homomorphically computed satisfies certain properties. In Section 5 we provide our main result, the explicit construction and analysis of the function g.

Acknowledgements. I would like to thank Léo Ducas and Daniele Micciancio for some helpful correspondence regarding their signature scheme in the early stages of this work. Thanks are also due to the anonymous PKC '15 reviewers and to my advisor Chris Peikert for their helpful comments.

2   Preliminaries

We write $[d]$ for a positive integer d to denote the set $\{1, \ldots, d\}$. We denote vectors over $\mathbb{Z}$ with lower-case bold letters (e.g. $\mathbf{x}$), and matrices by upper-case bold letters (e.g. $\mathbf{A}$). For an integer $q \geq 2$, we let $\mathbb{Z}_q$ denote the ring of integers modulo q. We represent the elements of $\mathbb{Z}_q$ as integers in $(-q/2, q/2]$ and define $|x| \in \mathbb{Z}_q$ by taking the absolute value of the representative in this range. We say that a function is *negligible*, written $\mathrm{negl}(n)$, if it vanishes faster than the inverse of any polynomial in n. For a matrix $\mathbf{X} \in \mathbb{R}^{n \times k}$, the *largest singular value* (also known as the *spectral norm*) of $\mathbf{X}$ is defined as $s_1(\mathbf{X}) = \max_{\|\mathbf{u}\|=1} \|\mathbf{X}\mathbf{u}\|$.

2.1   Signatures

We briefly recall the standard definitions of digital signature schemes. A *signature scheme* SIG is a triple (Gen, Sign, Ver) of PPT (probabilistic polynomial time) algorithms, together with a message space $\mathcal{M} = \mathcal{M}_\lambda$. It is correct if, for all messages $\mu \in \mathcal{M}_\lambda$, $\mathsf{Ver}(vk, \mu, \sigma) = 1$ holds true, except with negligible probability in λ over the choice of $(sk, vk) \leftarrow \mathsf{Gen}(1^\lambda)$ and $\sigma \leftarrow \mathsf{Sign}(sk, \mu)$.

We now recall the standard security definitions for digital signature schemes. Existential unforgeability under static chosen-message attack, or eu-scma, is as follows: the adversary $\mathcal{A}$ first outputs a list of message $\mu_1, \ldots, \mu_Q$ to be signed, for some $Q = \mathrm{poly}(n)$. The challenger then generates keys $(vk, sk) \leftarrow \mathsf{Gen}$ and signatures $\sigma_i \leftarrow \mathsf{Sign}(sk, \mu_i)$ for each $i \in [Q]$, and sends vk and $\{\sigma_i\}_{i \in [Q]}$ to $\mathcal{A}$. Finally, $\mathcal{A}$ outputs an attempted forged signature (μ^*, σ^*). In order to satisfy eu-scma security, the probability that $\mu^* \neq \mu_i$ for any $i \in [Q]$ and that $\mathsf{Ver}(vk, \mu^*, \sigma^*) = 1$ accepts should be negligible in the security parameter λ.

Existential unforgeability under *adaptive* chosen-message attack (eu-acma security) is defined in a similar manner. The difference is that under this notion, $\mathcal{A}$ receives the verification key vk before making any queries, and is allowed to make queries one at a time, receiving back a signature before having to make its next query.

A standard technique for achieving adaptive security from static security is chameleon hashing [KR00]. An efficient construction (which has an immediate analog over general lattices) requiring a constant number of matrices was given by Ducas and Micciancio [DM14]. As a result, we can use it to make our eu-scma signature scheme adaptively secure without increasing the asymptotic size of our public key by more than a constant factor.

2.2   Lattices and Gaussians

A (full-rank) m-dimensional *integer lattice* Λ is an additive subgroup of $\mathbb{Z}^m$ with finite index. This work is concerned with the family of integer lattices whose cryptographic importance was first demonstrated by Ajtai [Ajt96]. For integers $n \geq 1$, modulus $q \geq 2$, an m-dimensional lattice from this family is specified by an "arity check" matrix $\mathbf{A} \in \mathbb{Z}_q^{n \times m}$:

$$\Lambda^\perp(\mathbf{A}) = \{\mathbf{x} \in \mathbb{Z}^m : \mathbf{A}\mathbf{x} = \mathbf{0} \in \mathbb{Z}_q^n\} \subseteq \mathbb{Z}^m.$$

For $\mathbf{y}$ in the subgroup of $\mathbb{Z}_q^n$ generated by the columns of $\mathbf{A}$, we define the coset

$$\Lambda_{\mathbf{y}}^\perp(\mathbf{A}) = \{\mathbf{x} \in \mathbb{Z}^m : \mathbf{A}\mathbf{x} = \mathbf{y} \bmod q\} = \Lambda^\perp(\mathbf{A}) + \bar{\mathbf{x}},$$

where $\bar{\mathbf{x}} \in \mathbb{Z}^m$ is an arbitrary solution to $\mathbf{A}\bar{\mathbf{x}} = \mathbf{y}$.

We briefly recall Gaussian distributions over lattices (for more details see [MR04, GPV08]). For $s > 0$ and dimension $m \geq 1$, the Gaussian function $\rho_s : \mathbb{R}^m \to (0, 1]$ is defined as $\rho_s(\mathbf{x}) = \exp(-\pi \|\mathbf{x}\|^2 / s^2)$. For a coset $\Lambda + \mathbf{c}$ of a lattice Λ, the *discrete Gaussian distribution* $D_{\Lambda+\mathbf{c}, s}$ (centered at zero) assigns probability proportional to $\rho_s(\mathbf{x})$ to each vector in the coset, and probability zero elsewhere.

We will need several standard facts about discrete Gaussians over lattices. First, for $\epsilon > 0$ the *smoothing parameter* [MR04] $\eta_\epsilon(\Lambda)$ of an n-dimensional lattice is a positive real value. We will not need its precise definition in this work. Instead, we recall the few relevant facts that we need; for more details, see, e.g., [MR04, GPV08, MP12].

Lemma 2.1. *Let $m \geq Cn \lg q$ for some constant $C > 1$.*

1. *For any $\omega(\sqrt{\log n})$ function, we have $\eta_\epsilon(\mathbb{Z}^n) \leq \omega(\sqrt{\log n})$ for some negligible $\epsilon(n) = \mathrm{negl}(n)$.*

2. *With all but $\mathrm{negl}(n)$ probability over the uniformly random choice of $\mathbf{A} \in \mathbb{Z}_q^{n \times m}$, the following holds: For $\mathbf{e} \leftarrow D_{\mathbb{Z}^m, r}$ where $r = \omega(\sqrt{\log n})$, the distribution of $\mathbf{y} = \mathbf{A}\mathbf{e} \bmod q$ is within $\mathrm{negl}(n)$ statistical distance of uniform, and the conditional distribution of $\mathbf{e}$ given $\mathbf{y}$ is $D_{\Lambda_{\mathbf{y}}^\perp(\mathbf{A}), r}$.*

3. *For any m-dimensional lattice Λ, any $\mathbf{c} \in \mathbb{Z}^m$, and any $r \geq \eta_\epsilon(\Lambda)$ where $\epsilon(n) = \mathrm{negl}(n)$, we have $\|D_{\Lambda+\mathbf{c}, r}\| \leq r\sqrt{m}$ with all but $\mathrm{negl}(n)$ probability. In addition, for $\Lambda = \mathbb{Z}$ we have $|D_{\mathbb{Z}, r}| \leq r \cdot \omega(\sqrt{\log n})$ except with $\mathrm{negl}(n)$ probability.*

4. *For any $r > 0$, and for $\mathbf{R} \leftarrow D_{\mathbb{Z}, r}^{n \times k}$, we have $s_1(\mathbf{R}) \leq r \cdot O(\sqrt{n} + \sqrt{k})$ except with $\mathrm{negl}(n)$ probability.*

5. *Let $\Lambda \subset \mathbb{R}^m$ be a lattice and $r \geq 2\eta_\epsilon(\Lambda)$ for some $\epsilon \in (0, 1)$. Then for any $\mathbf{c} \in \mathbb{R}^n$, $\mathbf{y} \in \Lambda + \mathbf{c}$, we have $\Pr[D_{\Lambda+\mathbf{c}, r} = \mathbf{y}] \leq 2^{-n} \cdot \frac{1+\epsilon}{1-\epsilon}$.*

The SIS Problem. For $\beta > 0$, the *short integer solution* problem $\mathsf{SIS}_{n,q,\beta}$ is an average-case version of the approximate shortest vector problem on $\Lambda^\perp(\mathbf{A})$. Given a uniformly random matrix $\mathbf{A} \in \mathbb{Z}_q^{n \times m}$ for any $m = \mathrm{poly}(n)$, the problem is to find a nonzero vector $\mathbf{z} \in \mathbb{Z}^m$ such that $\mathbf{A}\mathbf{z} = \mathbf{0} \bmod q$ and $\|\mathbf{z}\| \leq \beta$. For $q \geq \beta\sqrt{n}\omega(\sqrt{\log n})$, it has been shown that solving this problem with non-negligible success probability over the random choice of $\mathbf{A}$ is at least as hard as probabilistically approximating the classic Shortest Independent Vectors Problem (SIVP) on n-dimensional lattices to within $\tilde{O}(\beta\sqrt{n})$ factors in the *worst case*. [Ajt96, MR04, GPV08]

2.3   Trapdoors for Lattices

In this section, we recall the efficient trapdoor construction and associated sampling algorithm of Micciancio and Peikert [MP12], which is at the heart of our signature scheme. This construction uses a universal public "gadget" matrix $\mathbf{G} \in \mathbb{Z}_q^{n \times w}$ for which there is an efficient discrete Gaussian sampling algorithm for any parameter $r \geq \omega(\sqrt{\log n}) \geq \eta_\epsilon(\Lambda^\perp(\mathbf{G}))$ (for some $\epsilon(n) = \mathrm{negl}(n)$), i.e., an algorithm that, given any $\mathbf{y} \in \mathbb{Z}_q^n$ and r, outputs a sample from $D_{\Lambda_{\mathbf{y}}^\perp(\mathbf{G}), r}$. For concreteness, as in [MP12] we take $\mathbf{G} = \mathbf{I}_n \otimes [1, 2, 4, \ldots, 2^{k-1}] \in \mathbb{Z}_q^{n \times nk}$ for $k = \lceil \lg q \rceil$. We will somewhat abuse notation by writing $\mathbf{G}^{-1}(\mathbf{v})$ to denote computing the lexically first (using $0 < 1$) binary vector $\mathbf{x} \in \{0,1\}^{nk}$ such that $\mathbf{G}\mathbf{x} = \mathbf{v}$; the vector will be unique if $q = 2^{\ell}$, but for other moduli (including the ones used in our scheme), there will potentially be more than one such vector.

Following [MP12], we say that an integer matrix $\mathbf{R} \in \mathbb{Z}^{(m) \times nk}$ is a $\mathbf{G}$-trapdoor with tag $\mathbf{H}$ for $\mathbf{A} \in \mathbb{Z}_q^{n \times (m+nk)}$ if $\mathbf{A} \begin{bmatrix} \mathbf{R} \\ \mathbf{I} \end{bmatrix} = \mathbf{H}\mathbf{G}$ for some invertible matrix $\mathbf{H} \in \mathbb{Z}_q^{n \times n}$. If $\mathbf{H} = \mathbf{0}$, we say that $\mathbf{R}$ is a "punctured" trapdoor for $\mathbf{A}$. We require the following two lemmas regarding these trapdoors.

Lemma 2.2 ([MP12]). *There is a probabilistic polynomial time algorithm* $\mathsf{GenTrap}(\bar{\mathbf{A}}, \mathbf{H}, r)$ *that on input a matrix* $\bar{\mathbf{A}} \in \mathbb{Z}_q^{n \times m}$, *a matrix* $\mathbf{H} \in \mathbb{Z}_q^{n \times n}$ *and parameter* $r \geq \omega(\sqrt{\log(n)})$, *outputs a matrix* $\mathbf{A} := [\bar{\mathbf{A}} \mid -\bar{\mathbf{A}}\mathbf{R} + \mathbf{H}\mathbf{G}] \in \mathbb{Z}_q^{n \times (m+nk)}$ *which is statistically close to uniform over the choice of* $\mathbf{R}$ *as well as a matrix* $\mathbf{R} \in \mathbb{Z}_q^{m \times nk}$ *such that if* $\mathbf{H}$ *is invertible,* $\mathbf{R}$ *is a* $\mathbf{G}$-trapdoor with tag $\mathbf{H}$ *for* $\mathbf{A}$, *while if* $\mathbf{H} = \mathbf{0}$, *then* $\mathbf{R}$ *is a punctured trapdoor.*

Lemma 2.3 ([MP12]). *Let* $\mathbf{R}$ *be a* $\mathbf{G}$-trapdoor for $\mathbf{A} \in \mathbb{Z}_q^{n \times m}$. *There is an efficient randomized algorithm* $\mathsf{SampleD}(\mathbf{A}, \mathbf{u}, \mathbf{R}, r)$ *that, given* $\mathbf{R}$, *any* $\mathbf{u} \in \mathbb{Z}_q^n$, *and any* $r \geq s_1(\mathbf{R}) \cdot \omega(\sqrt{\log n}) \geq \eta_\epsilon(\Lambda^{\perp}(\mathbf{A}))$ *(for some* $\epsilon(n) = \mathrm{negl}(n)$*), samples from a distribution within* $\mathrm{negl}(n)$ *distance of* $D_{\Lambda_{\mathbf{u}}^{\perp}(\mathbf{A}), r}$.

3 Puncturable Homomorphic Trapdoor Functions

In this section we define and describe our construction of puncturable homomorphic trapdoor functions, a primitive that abstracts out the properties required for our signature scheme, as well as those for many other lattice-based cryptographic primitives.

3.1 Definition

Our definition is an extension of the Wichs et al. definition of homomorphic trapdoor functions [GVW14]. A *puncturable homomorphic trapdoor function* (PHTDF) scheme consists of six polynomial-time algorithms $(\mathsf{Gen}, \mathsf{GenTrap}, f, \mathsf{Invert}, \mathsf{Eval}_{pk}^{td}, \mathsf{Eval}_{pk}^{func})$ with the following syntax:

$pk \leftarrow \mathsf{Gen}(1^\lambda)$ generates the public key. The parameter λ also defines a tag space $\mathcal{T}$, a trapdoor space $\mathcal{R}$, a tagged function space $\mathcal{A}$,[1] an index space $\mathcal{X}$, an input space $\mathcal{U}$ and an output space $\mathcal{V}$. We also need an efficiently sampleable key distribution $D_\mathcal{R}$ over $\mathcal{R}$, a parameterized input distribution $D_{\mathcal{U},s}$ over $\mathcal{U}$ and a tag set distribution $D_{\mathcal{T}^\ell}$ over $\mathcal{T}^\ell$. We also need to be able to sample $\mathcal{V}$ uniformly at random.

$(a, r) \leftarrow \mathsf{GenTrap}(pk, t)$ generates a trapdoor $r \leftarrow D_\mathcal{R}$ for $(pk, a \in \mathcal{A})$, with t the tag *associated with* a. We need the distribution of a to be statistically close to uniform over $\mathcal{A}$. We define the auxiliary function $\mathsf{Tag}(pk, a, r)$ to output $t \in \mathcal{T}$ if t is the tag associated with a and r is a trapdoor for a.

---

[1] Technically, the function space is also parameterized by the public key and the index space.

$f_{pk,a,x} : \mathcal{U} \to \mathcal{V}$ is a deterministic function (not necessarily injective) indexed by $x \in \mathcal{X}$, and $pk, a \in \mathcal{A}$.

$\mathsf{Invert}_{r,pk,a,x,s} : \mathcal{V} \to \mathcal{U}$ is a *puncturable* probabilistic inverter indexed by $x \in \mathcal{X}$, $r \in \mathcal{R}$ and $pk, a \in \mathcal{A}$. The parameter $s \in \mathbb{R}$ relates to some property $\mathsf{Prop} : \mathcal{U} \to \mathbb{R}$ of the desired inverse when the function space is not injective. We need to be able to find an inverse u such that $\mathsf{Prop}(u) \leq s$ (with overwhelming probability) whenever the tag t associated with a is *invertible* and whenever the trapdoor r is strong enough to invert with parameter s. If these conditions are not fulfilled, it outputs $\bot$.

$r^* \leftarrow \mathsf{Eval}_{pk}^{td}(g, \{(a_i, r_i)\}_{i \in [\kappa]}, T), a^* \leftarrow \mathsf{Eval}_{pk}^{func}(g, \{a_i\}_{i \in [\kappa]}, T)$ are deterministic trapdoor/function homomorphic evaluation algorithms. The algorithms take as input some function $g : \mathcal{T}^\kappa \times \mathcal{T}^\ell \to \mathcal{T}$, a set of tags $T = \{t_j\}_{j \in [\ell]} \in \mathcal{T}$, as well as values $a_i \in \mathcal{A}$, $r_i \in \mathcal{R}$. The outputs are $r^* \in \mathcal{R}$ and $a^* \in \mathcal{A}$.

Correctness of Evaluation. Let $(pk) \leftarrow \mathsf{Gen}(1^\lambda)$, $\hat{T} = \{\hat{t}_i \in \mathcal{T}\}_{i \in [\kappa]}$, $T = \{t_j \in \mathcal{T}\}_{j \in [\ell]}$, $(r_i, a_i) \leftarrow \mathsf{GenTrap}(pk, \hat{t}_i)$. Let $g : \mathcal{T}^\kappa \times \mathcal{T}^\ell \to \mathcal{T}$ and let $t^* := g(\hat{T}, T)$. We require that for

$$r^* \leftarrow \mathsf{Eval}_{pk}^{td}(g, \{(a_i, r_i)\}_{i \in [\kappa]}, T), \quad a^* \leftarrow \mathsf{Eval}_{pk}^{func}(g, \{a_i\}_{i \in [\kappa]}, T)$$

we have that r^* is a trapdoor for (pk, a^*), and that t^* is the tag associated with a^*.

Leveled relaxation: In a *leveled* fully homomorphic scheme, each trapdoor $r_i \in \mathcal{R}$ has an associated level of noise $\beta_i \in \mathbb{R}$. The noise level β^* of the homomorphically computed key r^* is larger than the initial noise levels, and depends in concrete instantiations on the function g (and the method by which it is computed), the initial trapdoors r_i, and the tags $\hat{t}_i \in \mathcal{T}$. If the noise level $\beta^* > \beta_{max}$ for some threshold β_{max}, the trapdoor will not be strong enough to compute $\mathsf{Invert}_{r,pk,a,x,s}$, thus limiting the type of functions g that can be computed.

Definition 3.1. *We call a function g admissible with parameter s on the set of tags $\hat{T} := \{t_i\}_{i \in [\kappa]}$, if, whenever, the initial trapdoors r_i have noise levels $\beta_i \leq \beta_{init} = \omega(\sqrt{\log n})$, r^* will have noise level $\beta^* \leq s/\omega(\sqrt{\log n})$ with overwhelming probability.*

In our concrete construction below, the trapdoors will be matrices $\mathbf{R}_i$, and we measure the noise level using the spectral norm $s_1(\mathbf{R}_i)$.

Distribution Equivalence of Inversion. We require the following statistical indistinguishability for $pk \leftarrow \mathsf{Gen}(1^\lambda)$, trapdoor/function pair (r, a) with an invertible tag t:

$$(pk, r, a, x, u, v) \stackrel{s}{\approx} (pk, r, a, x, u', v')$$

where $x \in \mathcal{X}$ is arbitrary, $u \leftarrow D_{\mathcal{U},s}$, $v := f_{pk,a,x}(u)$, $v' \leftarrow \mathcal{V}$ and $u' \leftarrow \mathsf{Invert}_{r,pk,a,x,s}(v')$.

Security for PHTDFs. Our security definition allows us to use a PHTDF easily as a building block in our construction of a secure signature scheme. Roughly, we need it to be difficult, given two *punctured* trapdoor functions $a^{(1)}, a^{(2)}$ computed using a function $g : T^\kappa \times T^\ell \to T$ admissible with parameter s, to find a collision $u, u', x, x' \in \mathcal{U}$, with $x \neq x' \in \mathcal{X}$ such that $f_{pk,a^{(1)},x}(u) = f_{pk,a^{(2)},x'}(u')$, even given oracle access to inversion queries for non-punctured functions a' computed using that same function g.

The security game between an adversary $\mathcal{A}$ and a challenger $\mathcal{C}$ is parameterized by a security parameter λ, as well as a function $g : T^\kappa \times T^\ell \to T$ and set of tags $\hat{T} := \{t_i\}_{i \in [\kappa]}$ such that g is admissible with some parameter s on the set of tags $\hat{T}$:

1. $\mathcal{C}$ runs $pk \leftarrow \mathsf{Gen}(1^\lambda)$ and then computes $(a_i, r_i) \leftarrow \mathsf{GenTrap}(pk, \hat{t}_i)$ for each $i \in [\kappa]$. $\mathcal{A}$ is given pk and $\{a_i\}$.
2. $\mathcal{A}$ may make inversion queries. To query, $\mathcal{A}$ sends some $v \in \mathcal{V}$, $x \in \mathcal{X}$ and some $T' := \{t'_j\}_{j \in [\ell]}$ such that $g(\hat{T}, T')$ is *invertible*. $\mathcal{C}$ computes $r' \leftarrow \mathsf{Eval}_{pk}^{td}(g, \{(a_i, r_i)\}, T')$ as well as $a' \leftarrow \mathsf{Eval}_{pk}^{func}(g, \{a_i\}, T')$, samples $u \leftarrow \mathsf{Invert}_{r', pk, a', x, s}(v)$ and returns u to $\mathcal{A}$.
3. $\mathcal{A}(1^\lambda)$ outputs tag sets $T^{(1)} := \{t_j^{(1)}\}, T^{(2)} := \{t_j^{(2)}\} \in T^\ell$ which satisfy $g(\hat{T}, T^{(1)}) = g(\hat{T}, T^{(2)}) = 0$, as well as $(u^{(1)}, u^{(2)} \in \mathcal{U}, x^{(1)} \neq x^{(2)} \in \mathcal{X})$, and wins if $f_{pk,a^{(1)},x^{(1)}}(u^{(1)}) = f_{pk,a^{(2)},x^{(2)}}(u^{(2)})$, where $\mathsf{Prop}(u^{(1)}), \mathsf{Prop}(u^{(2)}) \leq s$ and $a^{(b)} \leftarrow \mathsf{Eval}_{pk}^{func}(g, \{(a_i)\}, T^{(b)})$ for $b \in \{1, 2\}$.

We say the PHTDF satisfies $(\lambda, g, \{t_i\})$-collision resistance when punctured (CRP) security if every PPT adversary has a negligible probability of success in the above game.

3.2   Construction: Basic Algorithms

Our explicit lattice-based construction of PHTDFs is as follows. While our construction is written over general lattices, it may be instantiated easily in the ring setting. We have a lattice dimension parameter $n := \lambda$ and a prime modulus $q > 2$. Other parameters include $\bar{m} = O(n \log q)$, $k = \lceil \log_2 q \rceil$, $r = \omega(\sqrt{\log n})$, $m = \bar{m} + nk$. We let $\mathcal{A} = \mathbb{Z}_q^{n \times nk}$, $\mathcal{R} = \mathbb{Z}_q^{\bar{m} \times nk}$, $D_\mathcal{R} = D_{\mathbb{Z},r}^{\bar{m} \times nk}$, $\mathcal{X} = \{-1, 0, 1\}^{\bar{m}}$, $\mathcal{U} = \mathbb{Z}_q^m$, $D_{\mathcal{U},s} = D_{\mathbb{Z},s}^m$, $\mathcal{V} = \mathbb{Z}_q^n$.

Tags. We first consider the general lattice setting. For a degree-n polynomial $f(x)$, the ring $R_q = \mathbb{Z}_q[x]/\langle f(x) \rangle$ has a standard embedding into $\mathrm{M}_n(\mathbb{Z}_q)$ [ABB10]. The embedding sets the ith row of the matrix $\mathbf{H}$ corresponding to $g(x) \in R_q$ to the coefficients (in increasing order of degree) of $x^{i-1} g(x) \bmod R_q$. By choosing $f(x)$ to be irreducible over $\mathbb{Z}_q$, we ensure that R_q is a field, and set $T = R_q$. In this setting, there are some operations that can only be done over the subring of scalar elements $\{t\mathbf{I}_n\} \subset T$, because for technical reasons, the tags must be commutative under multiplication with respect to arbitrary matrices.

When using our construction in the ring setting, some care must be taken in constructing the embedding; see [DM14] for an instantiation of a tag space that will work for our scheme as well.

$\mathsf{Gen}(1^\lambda)$: Choose $\bar{\mathbf{A}}, \mathbf{B} \leftarrow \mathbb{Z}_q^{n \times \bar{m}}$, and output $pk = (\bar{\mathbf{A}}, \mathbf{B})$.

$\mathsf{GenTrap}(\bar{\mathbf{A}} \in \mathbb{Z}_q^{n \times \bar{m}}, \mathbf{H} \in \mathcal{T})$: Output $(\mathbf{A} = [\bar{\mathbf{A}} \mid \mathbf{C}], \mathbf{R}) \leftarrow \mathsf{GenTrap}(\bar{\mathbf{A}}, \mathbf{H}, r)$ using Lemma 2.2.

$\mathsf{Tag}_{pk=\bar{\mathbf{A}}}(\mathbf{C} \in \mathbb{Z}_q^{n \times nk}, \mathbf{R})$: Compute $\mathbf{X} = [\bar{\mathbf{A}} \mid \mathbf{C}] \left[{\mathbf{R} \atop \mathbf{I}} \right]$. If $\mathbf{X} = \mathbf{HG}$ for some $\mathbf{H}$, output $\mathbf{H}$.

$f_{\mathbf{A}=[\bar{\mathbf{A}}|\mathbf{C}], \mathbf{x} \in \mathcal{X}}(\mathbf{u} \in \mathcal{U})$: Let $\mathbf{z} = (\mathbf{u}, \mathbf{x}) \in \mathbb{Z}_q^{m+\bar{m}}$. Output $\mathbf{v} := [\mathbf{A} \mid \mathbf{B}]\mathbf{z}$.

$\mathsf{Invert}_{\mathbf{A}=[\bar{\mathbf{A}}|\mathbf{C}], \mathbf{R} \in \mathcal{R}, \mathbf{x} \in \mathcal{X}, s \in \mathbb{R}}(\mathbf{v} \in \mathcal{V})$: Compute $\mathbf{H} = \mathsf{Tag}(\mathbf{A}, \mathbf{R})$. If $\mathbf{H} = 0$ or $\mathbf{H} = \perp$ or if the parameter $s < s_1(\mathbf{R}) \cdot \omega(\sqrt{\log n})$, output $\perp$. Otherwise, output $\mathbf{u} \leftarrow \mathsf{SampleD}(\mathbf{A}, \mathbf{v} - \mathbf{Bx}, \mathbf{R}, s)$ using Lemma 2.3. We define $\mathsf{Prop}(\mathbf{u}) := \|\mathbf{u}\|/\sqrt{\bar{m}}$, so that by Lemma 2.1, with overwhelming probability over the randomness of $\mathsf{SampleD}$, $\mathsf{Prop}(\mathbf{u}) \leq s$.

As long as $s \geq s_1(\mathbf{R}) \cdot \omega(\sqrt{\log n})$, distributional equivalence of inversion follows immediately from Lemma 2.1

3.3 Construction: Homomorphic Computation

We define the algorithms $\mathsf{Eval}_{pk}^{td}, \mathsf{Eval}_{pk}^{func}$ by showing how to compute basic operations. Note that in our actual construction in Section 5, instead of naively composing addition and multiplication, we extend a technique used by Brakerski and Vaikuntanathan [BV14] and Alperin-Sheriff and Peikert [ASP14] regarding *chaining homomorphic multiplications* that was originally developed in the context of bootstrapping the GSW [GSW13] encryption scheme. These techniques carry over immediately, because the only difference between the form of a GSW ciphertext and the form of our trapdoor functions is that in the former case, the matrix $\mathbf{A}$ in the public key is an LWE instance $\mathbf{A} = \left[{\bar{\mathbf{A}} \atop \mathbf{b}^t = \mathbf{s}^t \bar{\mathbf{A}} + \mathbf{e}^t} \right]$, while in our case it is truly uniform.

In the descriptions of the basic homomorphic operations on tags below, $\mathbf{C}_i \in \mathcal{A}$ is a trapdoor function, $\mathbf{C}_i := \bar{\mathbf{A}} \mathbf{R}_i + t_i \mathbf{G}$.

Homomorphic addition ($\mathbf{C}_1 \boxplus \mathbf{C}_2$) of two functions is defined as $\mathbf{C}^* \leftarrow \mathbf{C}_1 + \mathbf{C}_2$. The operation induces $\mathbf{R}^* \leftarrow \mathbf{R}_1 + \mathbf{R}_2$ on the trapdoors. The tags t_1, t_2 may be any elements in $\mathcal{T}$.

Homomorphic multiplication ($\mathbf{C}_1 \boxdot \mathbf{C}_2$) is defined as $\mathbf{C}^* \leftarrow \mathbf{C}_1 \cdot \mathbf{G}^{-1}(\mathbf{C}_2)$, and is *right associative*. The operation induces $\mathbf{R}^* \leftarrow \mathbf{R}_1 \mathbf{G}^{-1}(\mathbf{C}_2) + t_1 \mathbf{R}_2$ on the trapdoors. Here the tag t_1 must be a scalar (of the form $t_1 \mathbf{I}_n$), while t_2 can be any element of $\mathcal{T}$. Unlike in the GSW scheme, we need to compute $\mathbf{G}^{-1}(\mathbf{C}_2)$ in the deterministic manner described in Section 2.3.

Multiplication by a constant ($\mathbf{C} \boxdot \mathbf{H}$) is defined as $\mathbf{C}^* \leftarrow \mathbf{C} \cdot \mathbf{G}^{-1}(\mathbf{HG})$. The operation induces $\mathbf{R}^* \leftarrow \mathbf{R}\mathbf{G}^{-1}(\mathbf{HG})$ on the trapdoor. The constant tag $\mathbf{H}$ may be any element in $\mathcal{T}$, but the tag t associated with $\mathbf{C}$ must be a scalar.

Addition of a constant ($\mathbf{C} \boxplus \mathbf{H}$) is defined as $\mathbf{C}^* \leftarrow \mathbf{C} + \mathbf{HG}$. This operation does not affect the trapdoor, which remains $\mathbf{R}$. Both the constant tag $\mathbf{H}$ and the tag t associated with $\mathbf{C}$ may be any element in $\mathcal{T}$.

3.4 Construction: Security

We now prove the security of our PHTDF construction under the SIS assumption.

Theorem 3.1. *Let g be admissible with parameter s for $\hat{T} := \{t_i\}_{i\in[\kappa]}$. Assuming the $\mathsf{SIS}_{n,q,\beta}$ assumption holds for $\beta := O(s^2\sqrt{n\log q})$, the scheme satisfies $CRP_{n,g,\hat{T}}$ security.*

Proof. Let g be admissible with parameter s for $\hat{T} := \{t_i\}_{i\in[\kappa]}$. Now, assume there exists an adversary $\mathcal{A}$ that wins the PHTDF security game for the above scheme with non-negligible probability δ with respect to g and $\hat{T}$. We consider an alternate game where we change our PHTDF by setting $\mathbf{B} = \bar{\mathbf{A}}\mathbf{S}$ for $\mathbf{S} \leftarrow D^{\bar{m}\times\bar{m}}_{\mathbb{Z},\omega(\sqrt{\log n})}$ instead of choosing it uniformly at random. By Lemma 2.1, this change is statistically indistinguishable and it does not affect our ability to invert, so that the adversary $\mathcal{A}$ still wins with non-negligible probability.

We now give a reduction to SIS. The reduction uses the challenge matrix $\bar{\mathbf{A}}$ as the public key. It then computes $(\mathbf{C}_i, \mathbf{R}_i) \leftarrow \mathsf{GenTrap}(\bar{\mathbf{A}}, t_i, \omega(\sqrt{\log n}))$. We can invert with parameter s on any trapdoor function and trapdoor $\mathbf{C}', \mathbf{R}'$ output by $\mathsf{Eval}^{func}_{pk}, \mathsf{Eval}^{td}_{pk}$ when computing g homomorphically on $\hat{T}$ and arbitrary other tags $T' := \{t'_j\}_{j\in[\ell]}$ as long as $g(\hat{T}, T')$ is invertible, so we can properly answer all of $\mathcal{A}$'s inversion queries.

With non-negligible probability δ, $\mathcal{A}$ eventually outputs tag sets $T^{(1)} := \{t^{(1)}_j\}_{j\in[\ell]}$, $T^{(2)} := \{t^{(2)}_j\}_{j\in[\ell]}$ such that $g(\hat{T}, T^{(1)}) = g(\hat{T}, T^{(2)}) = 0$ along with $(\mathbf{u}^{(1)} = (\mathbf{u}^{(1)}_1 \in \mathbb{Z}^{\bar{m}}_q, \mathbf{u}^{(1)}_2 \in \mathbb{Z}^{nk}_q), \mathbf{x}^{(1)}), (\mathbf{u}^{(2)} = (\mathbf{u}^{(2)}_1 \in \mathbb{Z}^{\bar{m}}_q, \mathbf{u}^{(2)}_2 \in \mathbb{Z}^{nk}_q), \mathbf{x}^{(2)})$ such that $\mathsf{Prop}(\mathbf{u}^{(1)}), \mathsf{Prop}(\mathbf{u}^{(2)}) \leq s$, $\mathbf{x} \neq \mathbf{x}'$ and $f_{\mathbf{A}^{(1)}=[\bar{\mathbf{A}}|\mathbf{C}^{(1)}],\mathbf{x}^{(1)}}(\mathbf{u}^{(1)}) = f_{\mathbf{A}^{(2)}=[\bar{\mathbf{A}}|\mathbf{C}^{(2)}],\mathbf{x}^{(2)}}(\mathbf{u}^{(2)})$, where $\mathbf{C}^{(b)} := \mathsf{Eval}^{func}_{pk}(g, \{t_i\}, \{t^{(b)}_j\})$. Since g is admissible with parameter s, we have $\mathbf{C}^{(b)} = \bar{\mathbf{A}}\mathbf{R}^{(b)}$, where $s_1(\mathbf{R}^{(b)}) \leq s/\omega(\sqrt{\log n})$. Let

$$\mathbf{v} := \mathbf{u}^{(1)}_1 - \mathbf{u}^{(2)}_1 + \mathbf{R}^{(1)}\mathbf{u}^{(1)}_2 - \mathbf{R}^{(2)}\mathbf{u}^{(2)}_2 + \mathbf{S}(\mathbf{x}^{(1)} - \mathbf{x}^{(2)})$$

Recalling the definition of f, we then have that $\bar{\mathbf{A}}\mathbf{v} = \mathbf{0}$.

Since $\mathsf{Prop}(\mathbf{u}^{(1)}), \mathsf{Prop}(\mathbf{u}^{(2)}) \leq s$, by Lemma 2.1 with overwhelming probability $\|\mathbf{R}^{(b)}\mathbf{u}^{(b)}_2\| \leq O(s^2(\sqrt{\bar{m}+nk})) \leq O(s^2\sqrt{n\log q})$. The other terms in $\mathbf{v}$ can be bounded at or below $O(s^2\sqrt{n\log q})$, so

$$\|\mathbf{v}\| \leq O(s^2(\sqrt{n\log q})) \leq \beta$$

Thus, in order to show that we have in fact solved SIS, we need only show that with non-negligible probability, $\mathbf{v} \neq \mathbf{0}$. To do so, we let $\mathbf{x}^* = \mathbf{x}^{(1)} - \mathbf{x}^{(2)}$ and choose some entry of $\mathbf{x}^*$ that is nonzero (since $\mathbf{x}^{(1)} \neq \mathbf{x}^{(2)}$, such an entry exists); without loss of generality we may say it is x^*_1. Now, let $\mathbf{s}$ be the first column of $\mathbf{S}$, let $\mathbf{b}$ be the first column of $\mathbf{B}$, and fix the last $\bar{m} - 1$ columns of $\mathbf{S}$ as well as $\mathbf{u}^{(b)}, \mathbf{R}^{(b)}$. Then we have $\mathbf{v} = \mathbf{0}$ only if $\mathbf{s} \cdot x^*_1 = \mathbf{y}$ for some fixed $\mathbf{y}$. Over the view of the adversary, $\mathbf{s}$ is distributed as a discrete Gaussian of parameter larger than $2\eta_\epsilon(\Lambda^\perp(\bar{\mathbf{A}}))$ for an $\epsilon = \mathsf{negl}(n)$ over the coset $\Lambda^\perp_{\mathbf{b}}(\bar{\mathbf{A}})$. As a result, by Lemma 2.1 we have $\mathbf{s} = \mathbf{y}/x_1^*$ with only negligible probability, so that with probability $\delta - \mathrm{negl}(n)$, $\mathbf{v} \neq \mathbf{0}$ and we have solved SIS.

4   Signatures from PHTDFs

Here we show how to construct a statically secure (eu-scma) signature scheme using a PHTDF, in a manner that encompasses both our signature scheme and that of Ducas and Micciancio. The reduction itself depends directly on the properties of the *admissible* function g that is homomorphically computed in the Sign and Ver algorithms. We recall that one can apply the efficient generic transformation using chameleon hash functions to achieve full (eu-acma) security.

4.1   Required Properties of the Function g and Tags

In order for our construction to work, we need to be able to choose two different sets of tags $\hat{T} = \{t_i \in T\}$, one set for the actual scheme and one set for the security reduction, to use when calling $(a_i, r_i) \leftarrow \mathsf{GenTrap}(pk, \hat{t}_i)$. In particular, when $g : T^\kappa \times T^\ell \to T$ is homomorphically evaluated $Q = \mathrm{poly}(n)$ times on the fixed set of tags $\hat{T}$ and on sampled sets of tags $T := \{t_j\} \leftarrow D_{T^\ell}$, we need the following properties to be fulfilled:

Actual Scheme The tag homomorphically computed by g must always be invertible.

Security Reduction Here, we need two different properties to be satisfied with non-negligible probabilities:

1. At most one of the Q sets of tags $T_i \leftarrow D_{T^\ell}$ (corresponding to signature queries by the adversary) may result in $g(\hat{T}, T_i) = 0$.
2. $\mathcal{A}$ chooses tags $T^* := \{t_j^*\}$ for his forgery such that $g(\hat{T}, T^*) = 0$.

4.2   Generic Signature Scheme from PHTDFs

We now present our generic signature scheme constructed from a PHTDF. It is parameterized by a security parameter λ as well as a family of functions $\{g : T^\kappa \times T^\ell \to T\} \in \mathcal{G}$ admissible with parameter s and sets of tags $\hat{T} := \{\hat{t}_i \in T\}_{i \in [\kappa]}$, which allow us to satisfy the properties in Section 4.1 for the actual scheme, and $\hat{T}^* := \{\hat{t}_i^* \in T\}_{i \in [\kappa]}$, which allow us to satisfy the properties for the security reduction. The specific choice of function will depend on a parameter $d = \omega(\log\log n)$ (so that $2^{\lfloor c^d \rfloor}$ for some constant $c > 1$ is superpolynomially large), which in our concrete construction of g corresponds to the degree of a polynomial. Below, we assume that d is fixed and so the specific function g in the family is determined.

We also have some requirements for the index space $\mathcal{X}$. In particular, we need there to exist a collision-resistant hash function $h : \{0,1\}^* \to \mathcal{X}$ such that there is some $x^* \in \mathcal{X}$ that is not in the range of h, i.e. no μ exists such that $h(\mu) = x^*$. In our concrete instantiation, we can satisfy this property by choosing a collision-resistant hash function which maps into $\{0,1\}^{\bar{m}}$ (in which case any $x^* \in \mathcal{X} = \{-1,0,1\}^{\bar{m}}$ with a negative element is not in the range of h and is therefore not a valid hash of any message).

$\mathsf{Gen}(1^\lambda)$: Compute $pk_{\mathrm{PHTDF}} \leftarrow \mathrm{PHTDF}.\mathsf{Gen}(1^\lambda)$, and then let $v \leftarrow \mathcal{V}$, $\{(a_i, r_i) \leftarrow \mathrm{PHTDF}.\mathsf{GenTrap}(pk_{\mathrm{PHTDF}}, t_i)\}_{i \in [\kappa]}$. We set $vk = (pk_{\mathrm{PHTDF}}, \{a_i\}_{i \in [\kappa]}, v)$, $sk = (\{r_i\}_{i \in [\kappa]})$.

$\mathsf{Sign}(sk, x = h(\mu) \in \mathcal{X})$: Sample $T := \{t'_j\} \leftarrow D_{T^\ell}$, and compute
   $r^* \leftarrow \mathsf{Eval}_{pk}^{td}(g, \{(a_i, r_i)\}_{i \in [\kappa]}, T)$ and $a^* \leftarrow \mathsf{Eval}_{pk}^{func}(g, \{a_i\}_{i \in [\kappa]}, T)$. Let $u \leftarrow$
   $\mathsf{Invert}_{r^*, pk, a^*, x, s}(v)$, and output $\sigma = (u, T)$.

$\mathsf{Ver}(vk, x = h(\mu) \in \mathcal{X}, \sigma = (u, T \in T^\ell))$: Compute $a^* \leftarrow \mathsf{Eval}_{pk}^{func}(g, \{a_i\}_{i \in [\kappa]}, T)$,
   and verify that $f_{pk, a^*, x}(u) = v$ and that $\mathsf{Prop}(u) \le s$.

Correctness. We immediately have that the scheme is correct, since in the actual scheme the homomorphically computed tag will always be invertible, and a u output by $\mathsf{Invert}_{r^*, pk, a^*, x, s}(v)$ will always satisfy $f_{pk, a^*, x}(u) = v$, and will with overwhelming probability satisfy that $\mathsf{Prop}(u) \le s$.

Security Reduction. We prove that this signature scheme satisfies eu-scma security assuming the underlying PHTDF satisfies $(\lambda, g, \hat{T})$-CRP security for g admissible with parameter s on a set of tags $\hat{T} := \{t_i\}_{i \in [\kappa]}$.

Theorem 4.1. *Let g be admissible with parameter s on a set of tags $\hat{T} := \{\hat{t}_i\}$ which allow us to satisfy the properties for the security reduction described in Section 4.1 with non-negligible probabilities $\epsilon_1 := \epsilon_1(Q, d, \delta), \epsilon_2 := \epsilon_2(Q, \delta)$ respectively against an eu-scma adversary $\mathcal{A}$ making Q signature queries and succeeding with probability δ. Then there exists an algorithm $\mathcal{S}^{\mathcal{A}}$ that breaks the $(\lambda, g, \hat{T})$-CRP security of the underlying PHTDF with probability $\epsilon^* = (\delta - (1 - \epsilon_1))\epsilon_2$, and so the above signature scheme is eu-scma secure.*

Proof. We assume we have an adversary $\mathcal{A}$ against the eu-scma security game who makes Q signature queries and succeeds in outputting a successful forgery with probability δ. The simulator $\mathcal{S}$ first receives the Q messages $(x^{(j)} = h(\mu^{(j)}) \in \mathcal{X})$ from the adversary. Next, it samples Q sets of tags $T_i := \{t_{ij}\}_{j \in [\ell]} \leftarrow D_{T^\ell}$. With probability ϵ_1, at most one set of these tags will result in $g(\hat{T}, T_i) = 0$. If there is more than one such set of tags, the simulator aborts (this happens with probability at most $(1 - \epsilon_1)$). Otherwise, it invokes the $(\lambda, g, \{t_i\})$-CRP security game, receiving back pk_{PHTDF} and $A := \{a_i\}_{i \in [\kappa]}$.

Now, if there exists a T_i such that $g(\hat{T}, T_i) = 0$, we set $T^\diamond := T_i$ and $x^\diamond := x^{(i)}$. Otherwise, we choose some tag set[2] $\bar{T} \in T^\ell$ ourselves such that $g(\hat{T}, \bar{T}) = 0$ and sample some $\bar{x}$ from the set of elements in $\mathcal{X}$ not in the range of the hash function h. We then set $T^\diamond := \bar{T}$, $\mu^\diamond := \bar{\mu}$. We then compute $a \leftarrow \mathsf{Eval}_{pk}^{func}(g, A, T^\diamond)$, sample $u^\diamond \leftarrow D_{\mathcal{U}}$, and set $v \leftarrow f_{pk, a, \mu^\diamond}(u^\diamond)$; the signature for message $\mu^\diamond$ is $\sigma^\diamond =$

---

[2] Note that such a tag set must exist since g and $\hat{T}$ allow us to fulfill the second required property for the security reduction.

$(u^{\diamond}, T^{\diamond})$. By the distribution equivalence of inversion property of the PHTDF, this is statistically indistinguishable from having chosen $v \leftarrow \mathcal{V}$.

We have thus "programmed" in a signature for the tag/hashed message pair $(T^{\diamond}, x^{\diamond})$. For the rest of the messages, $g(\hat{T}, T_i)$ is invertible, so $\mathcal{S}$ is able to compute signatures for hashed messages $x^{(i)} = h(\mu^{(i)})$ by making inversion queries on $v, x^{(i)}, T_i$, receiving back u_i and setting $\sigma_i = (u_i, T_i)$ to be the signature. $\mathcal{S}$ then sends the verification key $(pk_{\mathrm{PHTDF}}, \{a_i\}, v)$ and the signatures σ_i to the adversary $\mathcal{A}$, thus successfully simulating the public key and signatures in a manner indistinguishable from an actual attack.

Now, conditioned on having made it this far, since the second needed property for the security reduction is satisfied by g and $\hat{T}$, with probability ϵ_2 the tag T^* used by the adversary in a successful forgery ($\sigma^* = (u^*, T^*), x^* = h(\mu^*)$) with $\mu^* \notin \{\mu^{(i)}\}_{i \in [Q]}$ will be such that $g(\hat{T}, T^*) = 0$. Letting $a^b \leftarrow \mathrm{Eval}_{pk}^{func}(g, \{a_i\}, T^{(b)})$ for $b \in \{*, \diamond\}$, we have that

$$f_{pk_{\mathrm{PHTDF}}, a^*, x^*}(u^*) = f_{pk_{\mathrm{PHTDF}}, a^{\diamond}, x^{\diamond}}(u^{\diamond}) = v,$$

and that $\mathrm{Prop}(u^*), \mathrm{Prop}(u^{\diamond}) \leq s$. If $x^{\diamond} = x^{(i)}$ for some i, then by the collision-resistance of h, $x^{\diamond} \neq x^*$, while if $x^{\diamond}$ was chosen from outside the range of h, then we immediately have that $x^{\diamond} \neq x^* = h(\mu^*)$. As a result, we have that $x^{\diamond} \neq x^*$, so that we have broken the $(\lambda, g, \hat{T})$-CRP security of the underlying PHTDF.

5   Lattice-Based Instantiation of the Function g

We now give the main result of our paper, the lattice-based instantiation of a function g to be homomorphically evaluated in our signature scheme, and the method of choosing tags for it that allow us to fulfill the properties described in Section 4.1.

Theorem 5.1. *Let g be as defined in Algorithm 1, $c > 1$ be a constant. Let $d = \omega(\log \log n)$, and let $\beta \geq O(d^{2d} n^{11/2} \log^{13/2} q)$. Assume there exists an eu-scma adversary making Q signature queries that succeeds with probability ϵ against the signature scheme of Section 4 instantiated with the lattice-based PHTDF of Section 3, where $2Q^2/\epsilon \leq 2^{\lfloor c^d \rfloor}$. Then there exists an algorithm $\mathcal{S}^{\mathcal{A}}$ that solves $\mathrm{SIS}_{n,q,\beta}$ with probability $\frac{\delta^{1+c}}{4Q^{2c}} - \mathrm{negl}(n)$.*

The remainder of this section is devoted to proving those parts of this theorem we have not already shown in Theorem 3.1 and Theorem 4.1.

5.1   Tag Instantiations

We define the explicit distribution $T \leftarrow D_{\mathcal{T}^\ell}$ used as the "tag" part of the signatures from Section 4.2, following the instantiation of Ducas and Micciancio. Recall that our tag space is, in the general setting, an embedding of $\mathrm{GF}(q^n)$ (represented as $R_q := \mathbb{Z}_q[x]/\langle f(x) \rangle$ for $f(x)$ irreducible over $\mathbb{Z}_q$) into $\mathbb{Z}_q^{n \times n}$. Each tag set consists of d elements, where $d = \omega(\log \log n)$. However, these d elements each correspond to specific subsets of coefficients of a degree $e := 2^d = O(n)$ polynomial in R_q (the tag prefixes below), so that in the signatures, we can represent the entire set of tags with a single polynomial in R_q. As a result, our signatures remain short.

Concretely, for the constant $c > 1$ mentioned in the theorem statement above, we define sets of tag prefixes $\mathcal{T}_i = \{0,1\}^{c_i}$ of lengths $c_0 = 0$, $c_i = \lfloor c^i \rfloor$ for $i \in [d]$. For *full tags* $t \in \mathcal{T} = \mathcal{T}_d$ and $i \leq d$, we write $t_{\leq i} \in \mathcal{T}_i$ for its prefix of length c_i and $t_{[i]}$ for the difference $t_{\leq i}(x) - t_{\leq i-1}(x) \in R_q$.

We technically have more freedom than the previous work when it comes to identifying tag prefixes with ring elements, as we do not need our tag prefixes to satisfy geometric properties. Instead, the critical requirement is that for any two distinct tag prefixes $t, t' \in \mathcal{T}_i$, the difference $t(X) - t'(X)$ is *invertible* over R_q. However, for simplicity, we may nonetheless use the identification described therein, where a tag prefix $t = [t_0, \ldots, t_{c_i-1}] \in \mathcal{T}_i$ is mapped to the ring element $t(X) = \sum_{j<c_i} t_j X^j \in R_q$.

As in the Ducas-Micciancio scheme, to choose how to tag the homomorphic trapdoor matrices $\mathbf{A}_i$ in the public key, we have a confined guessing stage [BHJ+14] where we let $i^* \leq d$ be the smallest index such that $2Q^2/\epsilon \leq |\mathcal{T}_{i^*}|$, where Q is the number of signature queries made by the adversary and ϵ is the adversary's probability of success in the eu-scma security game. Note that such an index exists, since $2Q^2/\epsilon \leq 2^{\lfloor c^d \rfloor} = |\mathcal{T}_d|$. This choice of i^* guarantees that for Q tags $\{t^{(j)}\}_{j \in Q}$ chosen uniformly at random from $\mathcal{T}$, their prefixes $\{t_{\leq i^*}^{(j)}\}$ of length c_{i^*} will all be distinct except with probability at most $\delta/2$. For our construction of g, this guarantees that $g(\hat{T}, t^{(j)}) = 0$ for at most one tag (the first security property from Section 4.1). We then choose a prefix $t_{\leq i^*}^{\diamond} \in \mathcal{T}_{i^*}$ uniformly at random, with the hope that the tag t^* in the forgery output by the adversary is such that $t_{\leq i^*}^{\diamond} = t_{\leq i^*}^*$ (so that for our construction, we will have that $g(\hat{T}, t^*) = 0$, satisfying the second security property). By keeping the adversary's view statistically independent of our choice of prefix, we will have that $t_{\leq i^*}^{\diamond} = t_{\leq i^*}^*$ with probability $1/|\mathcal{T}_{i^*}|$. Following the proof of security for the generic signature scheme in Section 4.2, if one of the tags $t^{(j)}$ is such that $t_{\leq i^*}^{(j)} = t_{\leq i^*}^{\diamond}$, we set $t^{\diamond} = t^{(j)}$, and if not, we choose the full tag $t^{\diamond}$ uniformly at random from the set of tags with prefix $t_{\leq i^*}^{\diamond}$. Our choice of i^* guarantees that $2^{c_{i^*}-1} < \frac{2Q^2}{\delta} \leq 2^{c_{i^*}} = |\mathcal{T}_{i^*}|$. We also have that $c_{i^*} \leq c^{i^*} = c(c^{i^*-1}) < c(c_{i^*-1} + 1)$. As a result, we have that $|\mathcal{T}_{i^*}| \leq 2^{c(c_{i^*-1}+1)} \leq (\frac{4Q^2}{\delta})^c$, so that the second security property is fulfilled with probability at least $(\frac{\delta}{4Q^2})^c$.

In the various previous "vanishing trapdoor"-based signature schemes, the public key contained $d+1$ trapdoor functions a_i, and the function g computed homomorphically was *linear* over the $d+1$ associated tags $\hat{T} = (\hat{t}_0, \hat{t}_1, \ldots, \hat{t}_d)$. Specifically, letting $T = (t_1, \ldots, t_d) \leftarrow D_{\mathcal{T}^d}$, the function g was

$$g(\hat{T}, T) := t_0 + \sum_{i \in [d]} \hat{t}_i t_i.$$

To achieve the required properties for the actual scheme, they set $\hat{t}_0 = 1$, $\hat{t}_i = 0$ for $i \in [d]$, so that the homomorphically computed tag $g(\hat{T}, \cdot) = 1$ was always invertible. In the security reduction, they let $t^*_{\leq i^*}$ be the prefix of length i^* on which they hoped the adversary will forge. Then they set $\hat{t}_0 = -t^*_{\leq i^*}$, $\hat{t}_i = 1$ for $1 \leq i \leq i^*$ and $\hat{t}_i = 0$ for $i^* < i \leq d$.

In our scheme, we have only two trapdoor functions $a_0 = \mathbf{A}_0, \tilde{a} = \tilde{\mathbf{A}}$ in the public key, and compute *degree-$(d-1)$ polynomials*. We set the associated tags $\hat{t}_0, \tilde{t}$ as follows:

Actual Scheme: Let $\hat{t}_0 = 1$, $\tilde{t} = 0$.
Security Reduction: Let $t^*_{\leq i^*}$ be the prefix of length i^* on which we hope the adversary will forge. Then we let $\hat{t}_0 = -t^*_{\leq i^*}$, $\tilde{t} = i^*$.

5.2   Computation of g

To help compute g, in Gen we add to the public key d the coefficients of degree $d-1$ polynomials $p_1, \ldots, p_d \in \mathbb{Z}_q[x]$ with the following behavior:

$$p_i(x) := \begin{cases} 1 & 1 \leq x \leq i \\ 0 & i < x \leq d \end{cases} = \sum_{j \in \{0, d-1\}} c_{ij} x^j$$

Since $\mathbb{Z}_q$ is a finite field, these polynomials have a unique realization as degree $d-1$ polynomials over $\mathbb{Z}_q$, and their coefficients can easily be computed using Lagrange interpolation; see, i.e. [Sha79]. The total number of bits required to store the coefficients is $d^2 \log q = o(n)$, so they do not increase the asymptotics of the public key (and technically the coefficients may be computed on the fly from d and q alone).

We can now give a concrete definition of the function g in terms of input tags $\hat{t}_0, \tilde{t}$ (which will be associated with the trapdoors as discussed in the previous section) and $T = (t_1, \ldots, t_d)$. We have

$$g(\hat{T} = (\hat{t}_0, \tilde{t}), T) := \hat{t}_0 + \sum_{i \in [d]} (p_i(\tilde{t}) t_i).$$

To reduce the space required and the noise growth of the trapdoors when evaluating g homorphically on input $(\hat{T} = (\hat{t}_0, \tilde{t}), T \leftarrow D_{T^d})$ using the PHTDF from Section 3, we instead compute g in a slightly different manner. In the clear, we view g in an alternative (but identical) form (recall that c_{ij} is the jth coefficient of the polynomial p_i described above):

$$g(\hat{T} = (\hat{t}_0, \tilde{t}), T) := \hat{t}_0 + \sum_{j=0}^{d-1} \left(\tilde{t}^j \sum_{i \in [d]} (c_{ij} t_i) \right).$$

Homomorphically, we evaluate g using Algorithm 1. In the algorithm, $\mathbf{S}_i$ is the trapdoor for $\mathbf{B}_i$, $\hat{t}_0$ is the tag for $\mathbf{A}_0$, $\tilde{t}$ is the tag for $\tilde{\mathbf{A}}$.

Correctness of the algorithm follows by inspection.

Algorithm 1. $\mathsf{Eval}_{pk}^{func}(g, \mathbf{A}_0, \tilde{\mathbf{A}}, T)$ and $\mathsf{Eval}_{pk}^{td}(g, (\mathbf{A}_0, \mathbf{R}_0), (\tilde{\mathbf{A}}, \tilde{\mathbf{R}}, T))$

$\mathbf{B}_0 \leftarrow (\sum_{i \in d} c_{i0} t_i)\mathbf{G}$	$\mathbf{S}_0 \leftarrow \mathbf{0}$
$\mathbf{B}_1 \leftarrow \mathbf{G}$	$\mathbf{S}_1 \leftarrow \mathbf{0}$
for $j \in [d-1]$ **do**	
$\quad \mathbf{B}_1 \leftarrow \tilde{\mathbf{A}} \boxdot \mathbf{B}_1$	$\mathbf{S}_1 \leftarrow \tilde{\mathbf{R}}\mathbf{G}^{-1}(\mathbf{B}_1) + \tilde{t}\mathbf{S}_1$
$\quad \mathbf{B}_2 \leftarrow \mathbf{B}_1 \boxdot (\sum_{i \in [d]} c_{ij} t_i)$	$\mathbf{S}_2 \leftarrow \mathbf{S}_1 \mathbf{G}^{-1}(\sum_{i \in [d]} c_{ij} t_i \mathbf{G})$
$\quad \mathbf{B}_0 \leftarrow \mathbf{B}_0 \boxplus \mathbf{B}_2$	$\mathbf{S}_0 \leftarrow \mathbf{S}_0 + \mathbf{S}_2$
end for	
$\mathbf{B}_0 \leftarrow \mathbf{B}_0 \boxplus \mathbf{A}_0$	$\mathbf{S}_0 \leftarrow \mathbf{S}_0 + \mathbf{R}_0$
return $\mathbf{B}_0$	**return** $\mathbf{S}_0$

5.3 Noise Growth Analysis

We now proceed to analyze the noise growth of the trapdoor $\mathbf{S}_0$ for $\mathbf{B}_0$ in Algorithm 1. The following theorem covers the tag settings in both the actual scheme and the security reduction.

Theorem 5.2. *Let $\tilde{\mathbf{A}} \in \mathbb{Z}_q^{n \times \bar{m}}$ for $\bar{m} = O(n \log q)$. Let $r = \omega(\sqrt{\log n})$. Sample $(\mathbf{A}_0, \mathbf{R}_0) \leftarrow \mathsf{GenTrap}(\bar{\mathbf{A}}, \hat{t}_0 \mathbf{I}, r)$ for some $\hat{t}_0 \in \mathbb{Z}_q$, $(\tilde{\mathbf{A}}, \tilde{\mathbf{R}}) \leftarrow \mathsf{GenTrap}(\bar{\mathbf{A}}, \tilde{t}\mathbf{I}, r)$ for some $\tilde{t} \leq d \in \mathbb{Z}_q$. Then the noise level in the trapdoor $\mathbf{S}_0$ for $\mathbf{B}_0$ returned by Algorithm 1 is at most $d^d r O(n^{5/2} \log^3 q)$. In particular, the function g as evaluated by Algorithm 1 is admissible with parameter $s = d^d O(n^{5/2} \log^3 q)$.*

Proof. Let $\mathbf{S}_i$ denote the trapdoor for $\mathbf{B}_i$ in Algorithm 1. We denote by $\mathbf{B}_{i,j}$, $\mathbf{S}_{i,j}$ the value of $\mathbf{B}_i, \mathbf{S}_i$ at the end of the jth iteration. We have that at the end of the jth iteration,

$$\mathbf{S}_{1,j} = \tilde{\mathbf{R}}\left(\sum_{\ell=0}^{j-1} \tilde{t}^\ell \mathbf{G}^{-1}(\mathbf{B}_{1,j-\ell-1})\right),$$

so that $s_1(\mathbf{S}_{1,j}) \leq j \cdot d^{j-1} nk \cdot s_1(\mathbf{R}) \leq d^j r \cdot O(n^{3/2} \log^2 q)$. As a result, we have that $s_1(\mathbf{S}_{2,j}) \leq d^j r \cdot O(n^{5/2} \log^3 q)$. Since the final value of $\mathbf{S}_0$ is just $\sum_{j \in [d-1]} \mathbf{S}_{2,j} + \mathbf{R}_0$, we have that at the end of the algorithm,

$$s_1(\mathbf{S}_0) \leq d^d r O(n^{5/2} \log^3 q).$$

References

[ABB10] Agrawal, S., Boneh, D., Boyen, X.: Efficient Lattice (H)IBE in the standard model. In: Gilbert, H. (ed.) EUROCRYPT 2010. LNCS, vol. 6110, pp. 553–572. Springer, Heidelberg (2010)

[AD97] Ajtai, M., Dwork, C.: A public-key cryptosystem with worst-case/average-case equivalence. In: STOC, pp. 284–293 (1997)

[Ajt96] Ajtai, M.: Generating hard instances of lattice problems. Quaderni di Matematica **13**, 1–32 (2004). Preliminary version in STOC 1996

[ASP14] Alperin-Sheriff, J., Peikert, C.: Faster bootstrapping with polynomial error. In: Garay, J.A., Gennaro, R. (eds.) CRYPTO 2014, Part I. LNCS, vol. 8616, pp. 297–314. Springer, Heidelberg (2014)

[BG14] Bai, S., Galbraith, S.D.: An improved compression technique for signatures based on learning with errors. In: Benaloh, J. (ed.) CT-RSA 2014. LNCS, vol. 8366, pp. 28–47. Springer, Heidelberg (2014)

[BGG+14] Boneh, D., Gentry, C., Gorbunov, S., Halevi, S., Nikolaenko, V., Segev, G., Vaikuntanathan, V., Vinayagamurthy, D.: Fully key-homomorphic encryption, arithmetic circuit ABE and compact garbled circuits. In: Nguyen, P.Q., Oswald, E. (eds.) EUROCRYPT 2014. LNCS, vol. 8441, pp. 533–556. Springer, Heidelberg (2014)

[BHJ+14] Böhl, F., Hofheinz, D., Jager, T., Koch, J., Striecks, C.: Confined guessing: New signatures from standard assumptions. Journal of Cryptology, 1–33 (2014)

[Boy10] Boyen, X.: Lattice mixing and vanishing trapdoors: a framework for fully secure short signatures and more. In: Nguyen, P.Q., Pointcheval, D. (eds.) PKC 2010. LNCS, vol. 6056, pp. 499–517. Springer, Heidelberg (2010)

[BV11] Brakerski, Z., Vaikuntanathan, V.: Efficient fully homomorphic encryption from (standard) LWE. In: FOCS, pp. 97–106 (2011)

[BV14] Brakerski, Z., Vaikuntanathan, V.: Lattice-based FHE as secure as PKE. In: Innovations in Theoretical Computer Science, ITCS 2014, Princeton, January 12–14, 2014, pp. 1–12 (2014)

[CHKP10] Cash, D., Hofheinz, D., Kiltz, E., Peikert, C.: Bonsai trees, or how to delegate a Lattice basis. In: Gilbert, H. (ed.) EUROCRYPT 2010. LNCS, vol. 6110, pp. 523–552. Springer, Heidelberg (2010)

[DDLL13] Ducas, L., Durmus, A., Lepoint, T., Lyubashevsky, V.: Lattice signatures and Bimodal Gaussians. In: Canetti, R., Garay, J.A. (eds.) CRYPTO 2013, Part I. LNCS, vol. 8042, pp. 40–56. Springer, Heidelberg (2013)

[DM14] Ducas, L., Micciancio, D.: Improved Short Lattice Signatures in the Standard Model. In: Garay, J.A., Gennaro, R. (eds.) CRYPTO 2014, Part I. LNCS, vol. 8616, pp. 335–352. Springer, Heidelberg (2014)

[Gen09] Gentry, C.: Fully homomorphic encryption using ideal lattices. In: STOC, pp. 169–178 (2009)

[GLP12] Güneysu, T., Lyubashevsky, V., Pöppelmann, T.: Practical Lattice-based cryptography: a signature scheme for embedded systems. In: Prouff, E., Schaumont, P. (eds.) CHES 2012. LNCS, vol. 7428, pp. 530–547. Springer, Heidelberg (2012)

[GPV08] Gentry, C., Peikert, C., Vaikuntanathan, V.: Trapdoors for hard lattices and new cryptographic constructions. In: STOC, pp. 197–206 (2008)

[GSW13] Gentry, C., Sahai, A., Waters, B.: Homomorphic encryption from learning with errors: conceptually-simpler, asymptotically-faster, attribute-based. In: Canetti, R., Garay, J.A. (eds.) CRYPTO 2013, Part I. LNCS, vol. 8042, pp. 75–92. Springer, Heidelberg (2013)

[GVW14] Gorbunov, S., Vaikuntanathan, V., Wichs, D.: Leveled fully homomorphic signatures from standard lattices. Cryptology ePrint Archive, Report 2014/897 (2014) http://eprint.iacr.org/

[HPS98] Hoffstein, J., Pipher, J., Silverman, J.H.: NTRU: a ring-based public key cryptosystem. In: Buhler, J.P. (ed.) ANTS 1998. LNCS, vol. 1423, pp. 267–288. Springer, Heidelberg (1998)

[HW09] Hohenberger, S., Waters, B.: Short and stateless signatures from the RSA assumption. In: Halevi, S. (ed.) CRYPTO 2009. LNCS, vol. 5677, pp. 654–670. Springer, Heidelberg (2009)

[KR00] Krawczyk, H., Rabin, T.: Chameleon signatures. In: NDSS (2000)

[LM08] Lyubashevsky, V., Micciancio, D.: Asymptotically efficient Lattice-based digital signatures. In: Canetti, R. (ed.) TCC 2008. LNCS, vol. 4948, pp. 37–54. Springer, Heidelberg (2008)

[Lyu09] Lyubashevsky, V.: Fiat-Shamir with aborts: applications to Lattice and factoring-based signatures. In: Matsui, M. (ed.) ASIACRYPT 2009. LNCS, vol. 5912, pp. 598–616. Springer, Heidelberg (2009)

[Lyu12] Lyubashevsky, V.: Lattice signatures without trapdoors. In: Pointcheval, D., Johansson, T. (eds.) EUROCRYPT 2012. LNCS, vol. 7237, pp. 738–755. Springer, Heidelberg (2012)

[Mic02] Micciancio, D.: Generalized compact knapsacks, cyclic lattices, and efficient one-way functions. Computational Complexity 16(4), 365–411 (2007). Preliminary version in FOCS 2002

[MP12] Micciancio, D., Peikert, C.: Trapdoors for lattices: Simpler, tighter, faster, smaller. In: Pointcheval, D., Johansson, T. (eds.) EUROCRYPT 2012. LNCS, vol. 7237, pp. 700–718. Springer, Heidelberg (2012)

[MR04] Micciancio, D., Regev, O.: Worst-case to average-case reductions based on Gaussian measures. SIAM J. Comput. 37(1), 267–302 (2007). Preliminary version in FOCS 2004

[Sha79] Shamir, A.: How to share a secret. Commun. ACM 22(11), 612–613 (1979)

[SS11] Stehlé, D., Steinfeld, R.: Making NTRU as secure as worst-case problems over ideal Lattices. In: Paterson, K.G. (ed.) EUROCRYPT 2011. LNCS, vol. 6632, pp. 27–47. Springer, Heidelberg (2011)

[Wat09] Waters, B.: Dual system encryption: realizing fully secure IBE and HIBE under simple assumptions. In: Halevi, S. (ed.) CRYPTO 2009. LNCS, vol. 5677, pp. 619–636. Springer, Heidelberg (2009)

[Xag13] Xagawa, K.: Improved (hierarchical) inner-product encryption from Lattices. In: Kurosawa, K., Hanaoka, G. (eds.) PKC 2013. LNCS, vol. 7778, pp. 235–252. Springer, Heidelberg (2013)

Tightly-Secure Signatures from Chameleon Hash Functions

Olivier Blazy[1]([✉]), Saqib A. Kakvi[2], Eike Kiltz[2], and Jiaxin Pan[2]

[1] XLim, Université de Limoges, Limoges, France
olivier.blazy@unilim.fr
[2] Horst Görtz Institute for IT-Security and Faculty of Mathematics,
Ruhr-University Bochum, Bochum, Germany
{saqib.kakvi,eike.kiltz,jiaxin.pan}@rub.de

Abstract. We give a new framework for obtaining signatures with a tight security reduction from standard hardness assumptions. Concretely, we show that any Chameleon Hash function can be transformed into a (binary) tree-based signature scheme with tight security. The transformation is in the standard model, i.e., it does not make use of any random oracle. For specific assumptions (such as RSA, Diffie-Hellman and Short Integer Solution (SIS)) we further manage to obtain a more efficient flat-tree construction. Our framework explains and generalizes most of the existing schemes as well as providing a generic means for constructing tight signature schemes based on arbitrary assumptions, which improves the standard Merkle tree transformation. Moreover, we obtain the first tightly secure signature scheme from the SIS assumption and several schemes based on Diffie-Hellman in the standard model.

Some of our signature schemes can (using known techniques) be combined with Groth-Sahai proof methodology to yield tightly secure and efficient simulation-sound NIZK proofs of knowledge and CCA-secure encryption in the multi-user/-challenge setting under classical assumptions.

Keywords: Signature · Standard model · Tight reduction · Chameleon hash

1 Introduction

Digital Signatures are one of the most fundamental cryptographic primitives. They are used as a building block in numerous high-level cryptographic protocols. Their security is commonly proven in terms of a security reduction showing that any successful adversary $\mathcal{A}$ attacking the scheme can be transformed into a successful adversary $\mathcal{B}$ breaking the underlying hard intractability assumption. Naturally, we would desire that $\mathcal{B}$'s success $\varepsilon_{\mathcal{B}}$ is approximately the same as $\mathcal{A}$'s success $\varepsilon_{\mathcal{A}}$ in attacking the system and also the running times of $\mathcal{A}$ and $\mathcal{B}$ are approximately the same. Such a scheme is said to have a tight security reduction and does not require to compensate reduction's security loss with increased parameters.

© International Association for Cryptologic Research 2015
J. Katz (Ed.): PKC 2015, LNCS 9020, pp. 256–279, 2015.
DOI: 10.1007/978-3-662-46447-2_12

Signature schemes with a tight security reduction are known based on standard intractability assumptions such as the RSA [6] or the (bilinear) Computational Diffie-Hellman (CDH) assumption [25]. However, their security can only be proven in the random oracle model [5] with all its limitations (e.g., [14,21]).

STANDARD MODEL SIGNATURES. We now discuss signature schemes in the standard model (i.e., without using random oracles). On the one hand, there exist signature schemes with a tight security reduction (e.g., [18,44]) but they usually rely on specific relatively strong "q assumptions," such as the Strong (or, Flexible) RSA assumption [20] and the q-Diffie-Hellman Inversion Assumption (q-CDHI) [10].[1] On the other hand, known signature schemes from "standard assumptions" (i.e., general assumptions such as the one-wayness of trapdoor permutations [22,27,43] or more specific assumptions such as the RSA assumption [31,32] , the CDH assumption [45], or the Short Integer Solution (SIS) assumption [15,38]) have non-tight security reductions, meaning their security reduction loses a multiplicative factor of q, which is the maximal number of established signatures. Since q can be as large as 2^{40}, this security loss can have a dramatic impact on the scheme's parameters.

To the best of our knowledge, there are only a few exceptions to the above. The flat d-ary tree-based signature scheme by Cramer and Damgård [19] from almost two decades ago is based on a standard assumption (the RSA assumption) and (even though not explicitly mentioned in [19]) the security reduction is tight. In follow-up papers [16] and [13] extend their methods to an assumption related to factoring and CDH, respectively. Hofheinz and Jager [30] proposed a binary tree-based construction from the Linear (LIN) assumption. More recently, works on identity-based encryption [9,17] imply tight signatures from LIN.

1.1 Our Contributions

OVERVIEW. In this work we revisit the question of construction standard-model signatures with a tight security reduction. Our main result shows that, surprisingly, *tightly-secure* signatures can be constructed from any Chameleon Hash function CHF. Our transformation is based on binary trees and hence a signature contains λ Chameleon Hashes plus λ elements from the randomness space of CHF, where λ is the security parameter. As tightly secure Chameleon Hash functions exist from generic primitives such as claw-free permutations (CFP) [35], Σ protocols [4] and specific assumptions such as the RSA [32], the factoring (FAC) [35], and the discrete logarithm (DLOG) [35] assumptions, we immediately obtain a number of new signature schemes with tight security reductions. We improve the well-known Merkle tree construction [37] and its variant [41] in the sense that our signature size is the same as the original Merkle tree construction, but our security loss is independent of the number of signing queries.

---

[1] In q-assumptions an adversary is provided with q (polynomially many) random "solved instances" and has to compute a new solved instance. Examples are the strong RSA and the q-Diffie-Hellman Inversion assumptions. Both are considerably stronger than their "non-q" counterparts.

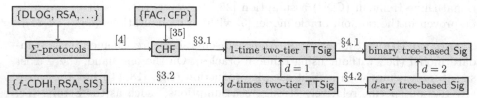

Fig. 1. Schematic overview of our constructions from the assumption level (left) over two-tier signatures (middle) to signatures (right). All implications have a tight security reduction, except the dotted line which loses a factor of d.

In fact, our transformation can be generalized to flat-tree signatures with improved efficiency. From a general primitive called d-time two-tier signatures TTSig (a generalization of two-tier signatures [7] to any $d \geq 1$), we build flat d-ary (instead of binary, 2-ary) trees via our second transformation d-Tree, such that a signature only contains $O(\lambda/\log d)$ many elements. Whereas Chameleon Hash functions only imply *one-time* two-tier signatures, for specific assumptions such as RSA, CDH and SIS we are able to construct efficient d-time two-tier signatures, hence also d-ary tree signatures. Our reduction loses a factor of d which is still (almost) tight as d is generally assumed to be small and, in particular, is independent of the number of signing queries. See Figure 1 for a schematic overview of our transformations.

We stress that while all our schemes are only secure in a non-adaptive sense (a.k.a. weak security), they can be transformed into adaptively secure signature schemes using a Chameleon Hash or a one-time signature, without losing efficiency or tightness (such transformations have been used several times [11,33,35,40]).

Interestingly, our framework also offers a theoretical explanation of almost all known tightly secure signature schemes. Our d-ary transformation d-Tree instantiated with an RSA-based d-times two-tier signature essentially equals the scheme by Cramer and Damgård [19]. The scheme by Hofheinz and Jager [30] can be obtained by using a Chameleon Hash function based on the LIN assumption (which is given in the full version [8]), it can in fact be generalized by building a chameleon hash based on any of the matrix assumptions from [23]. The CDH-based signature scheme from [13] is a less efficient version of our construction from the f-CDHI assumption with the parameters $f = 1$. Table 1 gives an overview over all known tightly secure signature schemes from standard assumptions. Some of our schemes are also (almost) structure preserving, a property with important applications, which we will discuss later.

DETAILS. First, we transform a Chameleon Hash into a two-tier signature and then, we show how to transform the latter into a binary tree-based signature scheme.

The concept of d-time two-tier signatures is a natural generalization of (one-time, $d = 1$) two-tier signatures introduced by Bellare and Shoup [7]. A two-tier signature scheme is like a standard signature scheme except that the public

Table 1. Comparison between known tightly-secure signature schemes from standard (non-q) assumptions, where λ is the security parameter

Scheme	Origin	Assumption	|pk|	Signature size	Loss	Structure preserving
BinTree+CHF$_{\text{DLOG}}$	new	DLOG	$O(1) \times \mathbb{G}$	$O(\lambda) \times (\mathbb{G} + \mathbb{Z}_p)$	$O(1)$	almost
BinTree+CHF$_{\text{FAC}}$	new	FAC	$O(1) \times \mathbb{Z}_N$	$O(\lambda) \times \mathbb{Z}_N$	$O(1)$	--
BinTree+CHF$_{\text{RSA}}$	new	RSA	$O(1) \times \mathbb{Z}_N$	$O(\lambda) \times \mathbb{Z}_N$	$O(1)$	--
BinTree+CHF$_{\text{LIN}}$	[30]	LIN	$O(1) \times \mathbb{G}$	$O(\lambda) \times (\mathbb{G} + \mathbb{Z}_p)$	$O(1)$	$\checkmark$
d-Tree+TTSig$_{f\text{-CDHI}}$	new	f-CDHI	$O(d/f) \times \mathbb{G}$	$O(\lambda/\log(d)) \times (\mathbb{G} + \mathbb{Z}_p)$	$O(d)$	almost
d-Tree+TTSig$_{\text{RSA}}$	[19]	RSA	$O(d) \times \mathbb{Z}_N$	$O(\lambda/\log(d)) \times \mathbb{Z}_N$	$O(d)$	--
d-Tree+TTSig$_{\text{SIS}}$	new	SIS	$O(d) \times \mathbb{Z}_p^{(\lambda \times \lambda \log(p))}$	$O(\lambda/\log(d)) \times \mathbb{Z}_p^{\lambda \log(p)}$	$O(d)$	--
BKP14	[9]	k-LIN	$O(\lambda k^2) \times \mathbb{G}$	$O(k) \times \mathbb{G}$	$O(\lambda)$	almost
CW13	[17]	k-LIN	$O(\lambda k^2) \times \mathbb{G}$	$O(k) \times \mathbb{G}$	$O(\lambda)$	almost

(secret) key is split into fixed primary part ppk (psk) and a variable secondary part spk (ssk). In terms of security we require that an adversary possessing the primary public key and having access to an oracle generating q independent secondary public keys, together with d signatures for each of oracle queries, cannot forge a fresh signature relative to one of the established public keys. The challenge will be to construct a d-time two-tier signature scheme with a tight (i.e., independent of q) security reduction from a standard assumption.

- Any Chameleon Hash implies a 1-time two-tier signature scheme. While it is well-known that a Chameleon Hash implies a (standard) 1-time signature [40], the novelty of our observation lies in the tight security reduction for two-tier signatures.
- We give constructions of d-time two-tier signatures for any $d \geq 2$ with a tight security reduction from a number of standard number theoretic assumptions such as the RSA, the SIS, the CDH and the f-CDHI^2 ($1 \leq f \leq d$) assumption. The important feature of our new constructions is the constant number of elements in the secondary public key while maintaining the tight reduction.
- We show that d-time two-tier signatures imply d-ary tree-based signatures with a tight security reduction. In our construction the verification/signing keys are the primary public/secret key of the d-times two-tier signature scheme. The signer implicitly maintains a d-ary authenticated tree of height $k = \lambda/\log(d)$, where λ is the security parameter. Each internal node is assigned a secondary public/secret key, the secret key is used to authenticate the key of the d distinct children via a signature. To sign a message, the signer picks the next unused leaf and outputs the authenticated path to the leaf plus a signature of the message under the leaf's secret key.

APPLICATIONS. We remark that some of our tightly secure signature schemes are almost structure preserving (cf. Table 1) in the sense that they do not satisfy the structure preserving definition in [2], but, following a similar method as Hofheinz and Jager [30], these schemes can be used to build tightly-secure simulation-sounds NIZK and tightly-secure encryption in the multi-user/multi-challenge

---

^{2} The f-CDHI assumption is a generalization of CDH and states that given $g, g^x, \ldots g^{x^f}$, it is hard to compute $g^{1/x}$. Note that f is small (constant) in our applications and does not depend on the number of signing queries.

setting. A discussion of this can be found in Appendix B. We also note that our results can be used to improve the Key Agreement of Bader et al. [3].

OPEN PROBLEMS. Since our signature schemes contain $O(\lambda/\log d)$ many group elements, they cannot be considered to be practical. More recently, Blazy, Kiltz and Pan [9] and Chen and Wee [17] proposed tightly secure identity-based encryptions from the LIN assumption independently, which imply tightly secure signature schemes with constant signature size. However, it is not clear how to extend their methods to constructing tight signatures based on the RSA assumption or any lattice assumption. Thus, obtaining a tightly secure signature scheme from the standard RSA assumption or any lattice assumption whose signatures only contain a *constant number* of group elements remains an open problem.

2   Preliminaries

2.1   Notation

We denote our security parameter as λ. For all $n \in \mathbb{N}$, we denote by 1^n the n-bit string of all ones. For any element x in a set S, we use $x \in_R S$ to indicate that we choose x uniformly random in S. All algorithms may be randomized. For any algorithm A, we define $x \leftarrow_s A(a_1, \ldots, a_n)$ as the execution of A with inputs $a_1, \ldots, a_n$ and fresh randomness and then assigning the output to x.

A list of classical security definitions and assumptions (CDH, f-CDHI, SIS, RSA) that we require for our results can be found in Appendix A.

2.2   Signatures

We first recall the definition of a digital signature scheme.

Definition 1 (Signature scheme). *A digital signature scheme* Sig *with message space* $\mathcal{M}$ *is defined as a triple of probabilistic polynomial time (PPT) algorithms* Sig = (Gen, Sign, Verify):
- Gen *takes as an input the unary representation of our security parameter* 1^λ *and outputs a signing key* sk *and verification key* pk.
- Sign *takes as input a signing key* sk, *message* m *and outputs a signature* σ.
- Verify *is a deterministic algorithm, which on input of a public key and a message-signature pair* (m, σ) *outputs 1 (accept) or 0 (reject).*

Sig *is perfectly correct if for any* $\lambda \in \mathbb{N}$, *all* $(\text{pk}, \text{sk}) \leftarrow_s \text{Gen}(1^\lambda)$, *all* $m \in \mathcal{M}$, *and all* $\sigma \leftarrow_s \text{Sign}(\text{sk}, m)$ *that* $\text{Verify}(\text{pk}, m, \sigma) = 1$.

Some of the signature schemes we present are stateful. This means that the signer maintains a state that is updated after each execution of the signing algorithm. Fortunately, our stateful schemes can be transformed to be stateless by using the technique from [26].

Table 2. EUF-NCMA and EUF-CMA experiments for the signature scheme

Experiment $\mathsf{Exp}^{\mathsf{EUF\text{-}NCMA}}_{\mathsf{Sig},\mathcal{F},q}(\lambda)$	**Experiment** $\mathsf{Exp}^{\mathsf{EUF\text{-}CMA}}_{\mathsf{Sig},\mathcal{F},q}(\lambda)$
$\mathcal{Q} := (m_1, \ldots, m_q) \leftarrow_{\$} \mathcal{F}(1^\lambda);$	$(\mathsf{pk}, \mathsf{sk}) \leftarrow_{\$} \mathsf{Gen}(1^\lambda);$
$(\mathsf{pk}, \mathsf{sk}) \leftarrow_{\$} \mathsf{Gen}(1^\lambda);$	$(m^*, \sigma^*) \leftarrow_{\$} \mathcal{F}^{\mathsf{OSign}(\cdot)}(\mathsf{pk})$, where the oracle
$\sigma_i \leftarrow_{\$} \mathsf{Sign}(\mathsf{sk}, m_i)$ for $i = 1, \ldots, q;$	$\mathsf{OSign}(\cdot) := \mathsf{Sign}(\mathsf{sk}, \cdot)$
$(m^*, \sigma^*) \leftarrow_{\$} \mathcal{F}(\mathsf{pk}, \sigma_1, \ldots, \sigma_q);$	If $\mathsf{Verify}(\mathsf{pk}, m^*, \sigma^*) = 1$ and $m^* \notin \mathcal{Q} := \{m_1, \ldots, m_q\}$
If $\mathsf{Verify}(\mathsf{pk}, m^*, \sigma^*) = 1$ and $m^* \notin \mathcal{Q}$	where m_i is the i-th query, then return 1;
then return 1, else return 0.	else return 0.

Definition 2 (Security of signatures). *Signature scheme* Sig *is* (t, ε, q)-*existential unforgeable under non-adaptive chosen-message attacks (*EUF-NCMA*) iff*

$$\Pr[\mathsf{Exp}^{\mathsf{EUF\text{-}NCMA}}_{\mathsf{Sig},\mathcal{F},q}(\lambda) = 1] \leq \varepsilon$$

holds for any PPT adversary $\mathcal{F}$ *with running time* t, *where* $\mathsf{Exp}^{\mathsf{EUF\text{-}NCMA}}_{\mathsf{Sig},\mathcal{F},q}(\lambda)$ *is defined in Table 2. The existential unforgeability under chosen-message attacks is defined in the similar way.*

We also consider a stronger security notion than EUF, namely strong unforgeability, SUF. In the strong unforgeability experiment, the adversary is allowed to forge a new signature on a message for which he has already seen a signature on. To accommodate this, we adjust our list $\mathcal{Q} := \{(m_1, \sigma_1), \ldots, (m_q, \sigma_q)\}$. Furthermore for the valid forgery, we require $(m^*, \sigma^*) \notin \mathcal{Q}$. This stronger notion applies for both adaptive and non-adaptive definitions, which we refer to as SUF-CMA and SUF-NCMA respectively.

2.3 Two-Tier Signatures

We now present a generalization of two-tier signature schemes, due to Bellare and Shoup [7]. In a two-tier signature scheme, the key generation algorithm is split into two algorithms, the primary and secondary key generation algorithms. The primary key is static and used for all signatures. The secondary key is ephemeral and used for only one or many messages. To generate the signature, we need both a primary and secondary key. In the original definition [7], each secondary key was allowed to be used to sign exactly once. We generalize to allow each secondary key to be used to sign at most d messages. We refer to this generalization as the d-time two-tier signature, the constructions presented in [7] are 1-time two-tier signatures.

Definition 3 (d-time two-tier signature scheme). *A two-tier signature* TTSig *is defined as a quadruple of probabilistic algorithms* (PriGen, SecGen, TTSign, TTVerify)*:*

- *PriGen$(1^\lambda, d)$ outputs a primary signing key* psk *and primary verification key* ppk.
- *SecGen(ppk, psk) outputs a fresh secondary verification and signing key pair* (spk, ssk).
- *TTSign(psk, ssk, m) outputs a signature* σ. *We denote the stateful variant by* TTSign(psk, ssk, m; j) *where* j *is the state.*

- TTVerify(ppk, spk, m, σ) *deterministically outputs 1 (accept) or 0 (reject).*
  We denote the stateful variant by TTVerify(ppk, spk, $m, \sigma; j$) *where j is the state.*

Correctness is defined in a natural way as in Definition 1.

Definition 4 (Security of two-tier signatures). *A two-tier signature* TTSig *is (t, q, d, ε)-existential unforgeable under non-adaptively chosen-message attacks* (TT-EUF-NCMA) *iff*

$$\Pr[\mathsf{Exp}_{\mathsf{Sig},\mathcal{F},q}^{\mathsf{TT\text{-}EUF\text{-}NCMA}}(\lambda, d) = 1] \leq \varepsilon$$

holds for any PPT adversary $\mathcal{F}$ with running time t, where $\mathsf{Exp}_{\mathsf{Sig},\mathcal{F},q}^{\mathsf{TT\text{-}EUF\text{-}NCMA}}(\lambda, d)$ is defined in Table 3. The existential unforgeability under (adaptively) chosen-message attacks (TT-EUF-CMA) is defined in the similar way.

Table 3. TT-EUF-NCMA and TT-EUF-CMA experiments for the two-tier signature scheme

Experiment $\mathsf{Exp}_{\mathsf{TTSig},\mathcal{F},q}^{\mathsf{TT\text{-}EUF\text{-}NCMA}}(\lambda, d)$	**Experiment** $\mathsf{Exp}_{\mathsf{Sig},\mathcal{F},q}^{\mathsf{TT\text{-}EUF\text{-}CMA}}(\lambda, d)$
$(\mathsf{ppk}, \mathsf{psk}) \leftarrow_\$ \mathsf{PriGen}(1^\lambda, d)$;	$(\mathsf{ppk}, \mathsf{psk}) \leftarrow_\$ \mathsf{PriGen}(1^\lambda, d)$;
$(m^*, \sigma^*, i^*) \leftarrow_\$ \mathcal{F}^{\mathsf{NTTSign}(\cdot)}(\mathsf{ppk})$;	$(m^*, \sigma^*, i^*) \leftarrow_\$ \mathcal{F}^{\mathsf{OSKey}(), \mathsf{TTSign}(\cdot, \cdot)}(\mathsf{ppk})$;
If TTVerify(ppk, $\mathsf{spk}_{i^*}, m^*, \sigma^*$) = 1 and $m^* \notin \mathcal{Q}_{i^*}$	If TTVerify(ppk, $\mathsf{spk}_{i^*}, m^*, \sigma^*$) = 1 and $m^* \notin \mathcal{Q}_{i^*}$
then return 1, else return 0.	then return 1, else return 0.
	Oracle OSKey()
	$i = i + 1$ and $j_i = 0$;
	$(\mathsf{spk}_i, \mathsf{ssk}_i) \leftarrow_\$ \mathsf{SecGen}(\mathsf{ppk}, \mathsf{psk})$;
	Return spk_i.
Oracle NTTSign($m_1, \ldots, m_d$)	**Oracle** TTSign(i', m)
$i = i + 1$ and $(\mathsf{spk}_i, \mathsf{ssk}_i) \leftarrow_\$ \mathsf{SecGen}(\mathsf{ppk}, \mathsf{psk})$;	$j_{i'} = j_{i'} + 1$; $m_{j_{i'}} := m$
$\sigma_j \leftarrow_\$ \mathsf{TTSign}(\mathsf{psk}, \mathsf{ssk}_i, m_j)$ for $j = 1, \ldots, d$;	If $j_{i'} > d$ or $(\mathsf{spk}_{i'}, \mathsf{ssk}_{i'})$ is undefined then return $\bot$;
Store $(m_1, \ldots, m_d)$ in the list $\mathcal{Q}_i$;	$\sigma \leftarrow_\$ \mathsf{TTSign}(\mathsf{psk}, \mathsf{ssk}_{i'}, m_{j_{i'}})$ and store $m_{j_{i'}}$ in $\mathcal{Q}_{i'}$;
Return $(\mathsf{spk}_i, \sigma_1, \ldots, \sigma_d)$.	Return σ.

We also define the strong unforgeability of two-tier signatures, in both the adaptive case, TT-SUF-CMA, and the non-adaptive case, TT-SUF-NCMA, analogously as to how we defined it for standard signatures.

2.4 Chameleon Hash Functions

A Chameleon Hash Function is defined as CHF = (CHGen, CHash, Coll):
- CHGen(1^λ) outputs the hash key chk and the trapdoor td.
- CHash(chk, m, r) outputs the hash value h.
- Coll(td, $(m, r), \hat{m}$) outputs a randomness $\hat{r}$ such that CHash(chk, m, r) = CHash(chk, $\hat{m}, \hat{r}$).

The standard security notion for Chameleon Hashes is collision resistance (coll). Formally, CHF is (t, ε)-coll if for the adversary $\mathcal{A}$ running in time at most t we have:

$$\Pr\left[\begin{array}{l} (\mathsf{chk}, \mathsf{td}) \leftarrow_\$ \mathsf{CHGen}(1^\lambda); ((m_1, r_1), (m_2, r_2)) \leftarrow_\$ \mathcal{A}(\mathsf{chk}) \\ \wedge \mathsf{CHash}(\mathsf{chk}, m_1, r_1) = \mathsf{CHash}(\mathsf{chk}, m_2, r_2) \wedge (m_1, r_1) \neq (m_2, r_2) \end{array}\right] \leq \varepsilon.$$

However, any user in possession of the trapdoor td is able to find a collision using Coll. Additionally, Chameleon Hash functions have the uniformity property, which means the hash value leaks nothing about the message input. Formally, for all pair of messages m_1 and m_2 and the randomly chosen r, the probability distributions of the random variables $\mathsf{CHash}(\mathsf{chk}, m_1, r)$ and $\mathsf{CHash}(\mathsf{chk}, m_2, r)$ are computationally indistinguishable.

3   Constructions of Two-Tier Signatures

In this section we show different constructions of d-time two-tier signatures for $d = 1$ (Section 3.1) and $d \geq 2$ (Section 3.2).

3.1   Construction from Any Chameleon Hash Function

We construct a non-adaptively strongly secure one-time two-tier signature $\mathsf{TTSig}_{\mathsf{CHF}} = (\mathsf{PriGen}, \mathsf{SecGen}, \mathsf{TTSign}, \mathsf{TTVerify})$ from any Chameleon Hash $\mathsf{CHF} = (\mathsf{CHGen}, \mathsf{CHash}, \mathsf{Coll})$ with message space $\mathcal{M}$ and randomness space $\mathcal{R}$.

- $\mathsf{PriGen}(1^\lambda)$: Generate a Chameleon Hash key and the corresponding trapdoor $(\mathsf{chk}, \mathsf{td}) \leftarrow_\$ \mathsf{CHGen}(1^\lambda)$. Define $\mathsf{ppk} = \mathsf{chk}$ and $\mathsf{psk} = \mathsf{td}$.
- $\mathsf{SecGen}(\mathsf{ppk}, \mathsf{psk})$: Pick random $\hat{\sigma} \in_R \mathcal{R}$ and compute $h = \mathsf{CHash}(\mathsf{ppk}, \hat{m}, \hat{\sigma})$, for an arbitrary public $\hat{m} \in \mathcal{M}$ (possibly $\hat{m} = 0$). Define $\mathsf{spk} = h$ and $\mathsf{ssk} = \hat{\sigma}$.
- $\mathsf{TTSign}(\mathsf{psk}, \mathsf{ssk}, m)$: The signer uses the trapdoor of the chameleon hash to compute a collision as $\sigma = \mathsf{Coll}(\mathsf{psk}, \hat{m}, \hat{\sigma}, m)$, which means $\mathsf{CHash}(\mathsf{ppk}, m, \sigma) = \mathsf{spk}$. The signature on m is $\sigma \in \mathcal{R}$.
- $\mathsf{TTVerify}(\mathsf{ppk}, \mathsf{spk}, m, \sigma)$: Check if $\mathsf{CHash}(\mathsf{ppk}, m, \sigma) = \mathsf{spk}$.

Correctness of the scheme follows by correctness of the Chameleon Hash function.

Theorem 1. *If* CHF *is a* (t, ε)-coll *Chameleon Hash function, then for any* $q \in \mathbb{N}$, $\mathsf{TTSig}_{\mathsf{CHF}}$ *is a* $(t', q, 1, \varepsilon')$-TT-SUF-NCMA *signature where* $\varepsilon' = \varepsilon$ *and* $t' = t - O(q)$.

Proof. Let $\mathcal{F}$ be a PPT adversary that $(t', q, 1, \varepsilon')$-breaks the TT-SUF-NCMA security of $\mathsf{TTSig}_{\mathsf{CHF}}$. Then we construct an adversary $\mathcal{B}$ that (t, ε)-breaks the collision resistance of CHF. Formally, $\mathcal{B}$ is given the challenge Chameleon Hash key chk and asked to come up with two distinct inputs $(m, r) \neq (m', r')$ such that $\mathsf{CHash}(\mathsf{chk}, m, r) = \mathsf{CHash}(\mathsf{chk}, m', r')$.

SIMULATION. $\mathcal{B}$ simulates $\mathsf{PriGen}(1^\lambda)$ as follows: it sets $\mathsf{ppk} = \mathsf{chk}$ and returns ppk to $\mathcal{F}$. Now $\mathcal{B}$ does not have the Chameleon Hash trapdoor and psk is empty.

Upon receiving the ith message m_i from $\mathcal{F}$, $\mathcal{B}$ simulates $\mathtt{NTTSign}(m_i)$ as follows: it picks a random $\sigma_i \in_R \mathcal{R}$ and computes $h_i = \mathsf{CHash}(\mathsf{ppk}, m_i, \sigma_i)$. Define the secondary public key $\mathsf{spk}_i = h_i$ and return spk_i and the signature σ_i.

The simulation is identical to the real execution. Firstly, chk is from the Chameleon Hash challenge and, thus, the simulation of PriGen is identical to the definition. Secondly, in the original definition $\mathsf{spk}_i = \mathsf{CHash}(\mathsf{ppk}, 0, r_i)$, while $\mathsf{spk}_i = \mathsf{CHash}(\mathsf{ppk}, m_i, \sigma_i)$ in the simulation. These two distributions are identical based on the uniformity property of CHF. Thirdly, it is easy to see the simulated signatures are well-formed.

EXTRACTING THE COLLISION. Once $\mathcal{F}$ outputs a forgery (m^*, σ^*, i^*), $\mathcal{B}$ aborts if spk_{i^*} is undefined. Otherwise, $\mathcal{B}$ checks if $\mathsf{CHash}(\mathsf{ppk}, m_{i^*}, \sigma_{i^*}) = \mathsf{spk}_{i^*} = \mathsf{CHash}(\mathsf{ppk}, m^*, \sigma^*)$. If that is the case, then $\mathcal{B}$ returns the collision $((m^*, \sigma^*), (m_{i^*}, \sigma_{i^*}))$. By the strong unforgeability of $\mathsf{TTSig}_{\mathsf{CHF}}$, $(m^*, \sigma^*) \neq (m_{i^*}, \sigma_{i^*})$. Thus, if $\mathcal{F}$ outputs a successful forgery then $\mathcal{B}$ finds a collision for the Chameleon Hash with probability $\varepsilon = \varepsilon'$. $\qquad\square$

3.2 Direct Constructions of d-Time Two-Tier Signatures

The construction from Section 3.1 can be extended to yield a d-time two-tier signature scheme for any $d \geq 1$ but the size of the secondary public-key is linear in d which is not useful for constructing efficient flat-tree signatures. In this section, we present stateful d-time two-tier signature schemes with *constant size* secondary key, from the f-CDHI, and SIS assumptions. Two more constructions from RSA and factoring are given in the full version [8].

Construction from f-CDHI. The construction from this section has an additional parameter $1 \leq f \leq d$ which offers a trade-off between the size of ppk ($O(d/f)$ group elements) and the underlying hardness assumption f-CDHI relative to a pairing group generator algorithm PGroupGen. (See Appendix A for a formal definition of f-CDHI.) We now present the stateful d-time two-tier signature scheme $\mathsf{TTSig}_{f\text{-CDHI}} = (\mathsf{PriGen}, \mathsf{SecGen}, \mathsf{TTSign}, \mathsf{TTVerify})$ from f-CDHI with message space $\mathbb{Z}_p$. For simplicity we assume there exists an integer c such that $c \cdot f = d$.

- $\mathsf{PriGen}(1^\lambda, d)$: generates a pairing group $\mathcal{PG} = (\mathbb{G}, g, p, \mathbb{G}_T, e) \leftarrow_\$$ $\mathsf{PGroupGen}(1^\lambda)$, picks random scalars $x_0, \ldots, x_c \in_R \mathbb{Z}_p$ and computes $h_i = g^{x_i}$ for $i = 0 \ldots, c$ and defines $\mathsf{psk} = (x_0, \ldots, x_c)$, $\mathsf{ppk} = (\mathcal{PG}, (h_0, \ldots, h_c))$.
- $\mathsf{SecGen}(\mathsf{psk}, \mathsf{ppk})$: picks a random $u \in_R \mathbb{G}$, and defines $\mathsf{spk} = u$, the secondary signing key is empty.
- $\mathsf{TTSign}(\mathsf{psk}, \mathsf{ssk}, m_j; j)$: to sign the $j = (\alpha \cdot f + \beta)$-th message m_j ($j \in 1, d$, $\alpha \in 0, c$, $\beta \in 0, f - 1$), compute $\sigma_j = (g^{m_j} u)^{1/(x_\alpha + \beta)}$.
- $\mathsf{TTVerify}(\mathsf{ppk}, \mathsf{spk}, m_j, \sigma_j; j)$: parses $j = \alpha \cdot f + \beta$ and checks if $e(\sigma, h_\alpha \cdot g^\beta) = e(g^{m_j} \cdot u, g)$.

It is easy to verify correctness.

Theorem 2. *If the f-CDHI assumption is (t, ε)-hard, then for any $q \in \mathbb{N}$, $\mathsf{TTSig}_{d, f\text{-CDHI}}$ is a (t', q, d, ε')-TT-EUF-NCMA signature scheme where $\varepsilon' = d\varepsilon$ and $t' = t - O(dq)$.*

We stress that f is a fixed small parameter of the scheme. In particular, as 1-CDHI is equivalent to CDH, $\mathsf{TTSig}_{1\text{-CDHI}}$ is secure under the standard CDH assumption, which is equivalent to the scheme from [13].

Proof. Let $\mathcal{F}$ be an adversary that (t', q, d, ε')-breaks the TT-EUF-NCMA security of $\mathsf{TTSig}_{f\text{-CDHI}}$. Then we construct an adversary $\mathcal{B}$ that (t, ε)-breaks the f-CDHI Assumption. Adversary $\mathcal{B}$ takes as input a pairing group description $\hat{\mathcal{PG}} = (\mathbb{G}, \mathbb{G}_T, \hat{g}, p, e)$ and a f-CDHI-challenge $(\hat{g}, \hat{g}^x, \ldots, \hat{g}^{x^f})$. Its goal is to compute $\hat{g}^{\frac{1}{x}}$.

- To simulate PriGen, $\mathcal{B}$ picks a random $j' \in_R [1, d]$, which defines uniquely α', β' as the quotient and modulo in the euclidean division of j' by f. $\mathcal{B}$ computes $g = \hat{g}^{\prod_{b \neq \beta'}(x+b-\beta')}$ $(b \in [0, f-1])$ from f-CDHI-challenge and chooses c random scalars $(x_0, \ldots, x_{\alpha'-1}, x_{\alpha'+1}, \ldots, x_c) \in_R \mathbb{Z}_p^c$, where $c = d/f$ as defined in the scheme, and for all $\alpha \in [0, c]$ computes:

$$h_\alpha = \begin{cases} g^{x-\beta'} & \text{if } \alpha = \alpha' \text{ (Implicitely, } x_{\alpha'} := x - \beta') \\ g^{x_\alpha} & \text{otherwise} \end{cases}$$

The primary public-key is $\mathsf{ppk} = (\mathcal{PG} = (\mathbb{G}, g, p, \mathbb{G}_T, e, g), (h_0, \ldots, h_c))$.

- When receiving the i-th NTTSign query $(i \in [1, q])$ on $\boldsymbol{m}_i = (m_{i,1}, \ldots, m_{i,d})$:
  1. SecGen: $\mathcal{B}$ picks a random scalar $r_i \in_R \mathbb{Z}_p$ and defines $\mathsf{spk}_i = u_i = \hat{g}^{r_i \prod_{b=1}^{f}(x+b-\beta')} h_{\alpha'}^{-m_{i,j'}}$.

  2. TTSign: $\mathcal{B}$ then computes the signature vector $\boldsymbol{\sigma}_i = (\sigma_{i,1}, \ldots, \sigma_{i,d})$ on $\boldsymbol{m}_i$ via

$$\sigma_{i,j} = (u_i \cdot h_\alpha^{m_{i,j}})^{\frac{1}{x_\alpha + \beta}}$$

$$= \begin{cases} g^{r_i} & \text{if } j = j' \\ \hat{g}^{r_i \prod_{b \neq \beta}(x+b-\beta')} \hat{g}^{(m_{i,j}-m_{i,j'})(x-\beta')\prod_{b \neq \beta,\beta'}(x+b-\beta')} & \text{if } \alpha = \alpha' \wedge \beta \neq \beta' \\ u_i^{1/(x_\alpha+\beta)} h_\alpha^{m_{i,j}/(x_\alpha+\beta)} & \text{otherwise} \end{cases}$$

where $j = \alpha \cdot f + \beta$ and $\alpha \in [0, c]$ and $\beta \in [0, f-1]$. Since x_α (for $\alpha \neq \alpha'$) is chosen by $\mathcal{B}$, the last equation can be computed. It is easy to see the simulated distribution is identical to the real scheme, since $\hat{g}$ from f-CDHI challenge is a random generator of $\mathbb{G}$.

Eventually, the adversary $\mathcal{F}$ outputs a forgery σ^* on a message m^* for some previously established spk_{i^*} $(i^* \in [1, q])$. With probability $1/d$ the forgery is for the j'-th index. As σ^* is valid we have

$$\sigma^* = (u_{i^*} h_{\alpha'}^{m^*})^{1/(x_{\alpha'}+\beta')} = \hat{g}^{r_{i^*} \prod_{b \neq \beta'}(x+b-\beta')} (\hat{g}^{(x-\beta')\cdot(m^*-m_{i,j'})\cdot \prod_{b \neq \beta'}(x+b-\beta')})^{1/x}$$

As we know $m^*, m_{i,j'}, r_i$, and $m^* \neq m_{i,j'}$ this allows to compute the helper value

$$(\sigma^*/g^{r_{i^*}})^{1/(m^*-m_{i,j'})} = (\hat{g}^{(x-\beta')\prod_{b \neq \beta'}(x+b-\beta')})^{1/x}.$$

The helper value can be written as $\hat{g}^{\frac{\mathrm{poly}(x)}{x}}$, where $\mathrm{poly}(x)$ admits $\{\beta' - b : b \in [1, f] \wedge b \neq \beta'\} \cup \{\beta'\}$ as roots. Using partial fraction decomposition, it can be rewritten as $\hat{g}^{\mathrm{poly}'(x)} \hat{g}^{\frac{\beta' \prod_{b \neq \beta'}(\beta'-b)}{x}}$ where poly' is a polynomial of degree $f-1$. Due to its degree, $\hat{g}^{\mathrm{poly}'(x)}$ can be efficiently computed from the challenge, so $\mathcal{B}$ can recover $g^{\frac{1}{x}}$ to solve the f-CDHI challenge with probability $\varepsilon = \varepsilon'/d$. $\qquad\square$

Construction from SIS. Useful facts about lattice are recalled in Appendix A. Our scheme is defined as follows:

Let $k = \lceil \log p \rceil = O(\log \lambda)$, $\bar{m} = O(\lambda k)$ and $m = \bar{m} + \lambda k$ be the dimension of the signature. Let $\mathcal{D} = D_{\mathbb{Z}^{\bar{m} \times \lambda k}, \omega(\sqrt{\log \lambda})}$ be the Gaussian distribution over $\mathbb{Z}^{\bar{m} \times \lambda k}$ with parameter $\omega(\sqrt{\log \lambda})$ and let $s = O(\sqrt{\lambda k})$ be a Gaussian parameter. Then the signature scheme $\mathsf{TTSig}_{\mathsf{SIS}} = (\mathsf{PriGen}, \mathsf{SecGen}, \mathsf{TTSign}, \mathsf{TTVerify})$ with message space $\{0,1\}^\ell$ is defined as follows:

- $\mathsf{PriGen}(1^\lambda, d)$: pick a random matrix $\mathbf{A}_0 \in_R \mathbb{Z}_p^{\lambda \times \ell}$. For $i = 1, \ldots, d$, sample $(\mathbf{A}_i, \mathbf{R}_i) \leftarrow_{\$} \mathsf{GenTrap}^{\mathcal{D}}(1^\lambda, 1^m, p)$. Define $\mathsf{ppk} = (\mathbf{A}_0, \mathbf{A}_1, \ldots, \mathbf{A}_d)$ and $\mathsf{psk} = (\mathbf{R}_1, \ldots, \mathbf{R}_d)$.
- $\mathsf{SecGen}(\mathsf{psk}, \mathsf{ppk}, d)$: choose a random vector $\mathbf{u} \in_R \mathbb{Z}_p^\lambda$. Define $\mathsf{spk} = \mathbf{u}$ and $\mathsf{ssk} = \{\}$ is empty.
- $\mathsf{TTSign}(\mathsf{psk}, \mathsf{ssk}, \mathbf{m}_j; j)$: to sign the j-th message $\mathbf{m}_j \in \{0,1\}^\ell$, compute the syndrome $\mathbf{y}_j = \mathbf{u} - \mathbf{A}_0 \mathbf{m}_j$. Then sample $\boldsymbol{\sigma}_j \in \mathbb{Z}^m$ from $D_{\Lambda_{\mathbf{y}_j}^\perp(\mathbf{A}_j), s \cdot \omega(\sqrt{\log \lambda})}$, $\boldsymbol{\sigma}_j \leftarrow_{\$} \mathsf{SampleD}(\mathbf{R}_j, \mathbf{A}_j, \mathbf{y}_j, s)$.
- $\mathsf{TTVerify}(\mathsf{ppk}, \mathsf{spk}, \mathbf{m}_j, \boldsymbol{\sigma}_j; j)$: accept if $\|\boldsymbol{\sigma}_j\| \leq s \cdot \omega(\sqrt{\log \lambda}) \cdot \sqrt{m}$ and $\mathbf{A}_j \boldsymbol{\sigma}_j = \mathbf{u} - \mathbf{A}_0 \mathbf{m}_j$; otherwise, reject.

Correctness of the scheme follows as explained in Lemmas 2 and 1.

Theorem 3. *If* $\mathsf{SIS}_{p,\beta}$ *is* (t, ε)-*hard for* $\beta = \sqrt{\ell + s^2 \cdot \omega(\log \lambda) \cdot m)}$, *then for any* $q \in \mathbb{N}$, $\mathsf{TTSig}_{\mathsf{SIS}}$ *is a* (t', q, d, ε')-*TT-SUF-NCMA signature scheme where* $\varepsilon' = d\varepsilon + \mathsf{negl}(\lambda)$ *and* $t' = t - O(d \cdot q)$.

Proof. Let $\mathcal{F}$ be a PPT adversary that (t', q, d, ε')-breaks the TT-SUF-NCMA security of $\mathsf{TTSig}_{\mathsf{SIS}}$. Then we construct an adversary $\mathcal{B}$ that (t, ε)-breaks the $\mathsf{SIS}_{p,\beta}$ problem. $\mathcal{B}$ is given a $\mathsf{SIS}_{p,\beta}$ instance $\mathbf{A} = [\mathbf{A}'|\mathbf{A}''] \in_R \mathbb{Z}_p^{\lambda \times m'}$ where $m' = \ell + m$ and $\mathbf{A}' \in_R \mathbb{Z}_p^{\lambda \times \ell}$ and $\mathbf{A}'' \in_R \mathbb{Z}_p^{\lambda \times m}$.

SIMULATION. $\mathcal{B}$ simulates $\mathsf{PriGen}(1^\lambda, d)$: it guesses a random $i^* \in_R \{1, \ldots, d\}$ and defines $\mathbf{A}_0 = \mathbf{A}'$ and $\mathbf{A}_{i^*} = \mathbf{A}''$. For $i \neq i^*$, $\mathcal{B}$ generates $\mathbf{A}_i$ and $\mathbf{R}_i$ as in the real scheme. Then $\mathcal{B}$ sends $\mathsf{ppk} = (\mathbf{A}_0, \ldots, \mathbf{A}_d)$ to $\mathcal{F}$.

Upon receiving the d messages $(\mathbf{m}_1, \ldots, \mathbf{m}_d)$ from $\mathcal{F}$, $\mathcal{B}$ simulates the corresponding signatures and the secondary verification key: it samples a $\boldsymbol{\sigma}_{i^*}$ from the Gaussian $D_{\mathbb{Z}^m, s \cdot \omega(\sqrt{\log \lambda})}$ and computes $\mathbf{u} = [\mathbf{A}_0|\mathbf{A}_{i^*}] \cdot \begin{bmatrix} \mathbf{m}_{i^*} \\ \boldsymbol{\sigma}_{i^*} \end{bmatrix}$ and defines $\mathsf{spk} = \mathbf{u}$. $\mathcal{B}$ uses $\mathbf{R}_i$ to compute $\boldsymbol{\sigma}_i$ as in the real scheme for $i \neq i^*$. Then $\mathcal{B}$ responds $\mathcal{F}$ with the signatures $\{\boldsymbol{\sigma}_1, \ldots, \boldsymbol{\sigma}_d\}$ and the secondary verification key spk.

The simulation is statistically close to the real execution. According to Lemma 1, the simulated $\mathbf{A}_{i^*}$ is $\mathsf{negl}(\lambda)$-far from the real distribution. It is easy to see the signatures $\boldsymbol{\sigma}_i$ for $i \neq i^*$ are identical to the scheme definition. It remains to show the simulated joint distribution $\{\mathsf{spk}, \boldsymbol{\sigma}_{i^*}\}$ is statistically close to the real distribution. Firstly, in the real scheme, spk is uniformly random over $\mathbb{Z}_p^\lambda$. In the simulation, $\mathsf{spk} = \mathbf{u} = \mathbf{A}_0 \mathbf{m}_{i^*} + \mathbf{A}_{i^*} \boldsymbol{\sigma}_{i^*}$, where $\boldsymbol{\sigma}_{i^*} \in D_{\mathbb{Z}^m, s \cdot \omega(\sqrt{\log \lambda})}$ and $s \cdot \omega(\sqrt{\log \lambda}) = O(\sqrt{\lambda k})\omega(\sqrt{\log \lambda}) > \omega(\sqrt{\log m})$. By Lemma 3, for all but a $2p^{-\lambda}$ fraction of all $\mathbf{A}_{i^*} \in \mathbb{Z}_p^{\lambda \times m}$, $\mathbf{A}_{i^*} \boldsymbol{\sigma}_{i^*}$ is statistically close to uniform over

$\mathbb{Z}_p^\lambda$, which implies spk is statistically close to the real distribution. Secondly, in the real scheme, $\boldsymbol{\sigma}_{i^*}$ is sampled from the Gaussian $D_{\Lambda_{\mathbf{y}_{i^*}}^{\perp}(\mathbf{A}_{i^*}), s \cdot \omega(\sqrt{\log \lambda})}$ where $\mathbf{y}_{i^*} = \mathbf{u} - \mathbf{A}_0 \mathbf{m}_{i^*}$. In the simulation, $\boldsymbol{\sigma}_{i^*}$ is sampled from $D_{\mathbb{Z}^m, s \cdot \omega(\sqrt{\log \lambda})}$ and it is easy to see $\boldsymbol{\sigma}_{i^*} \in \Lambda_{\mathbf{y}_{i^*}}^{\perp}(\mathbf{A}_{i^*})$, since $\mathbf{A}_{i^*} \boldsymbol{\sigma}_{i^*} = \mathbf{u} - \mathbf{A}_0 \mathbf{m}_{i^*} = \mathbf{y}_{i^*}$. Thus, the simulated $\boldsymbol{\sigma}_{i^*}$ is identical to the real scheme.

EXTRACTING $\mathsf{SIS}_{p,\beta}$ SOLUTION. Once $\mathcal{F}$ outputs a forgery $(\mathbf{m}^*, \boldsymbol{\sigma}^*)$, $\mathcal{B}$ aborts if $(\mathbf{m}^*, \boldsymbol{\sigma}^*)$ is not valid under $\mathbf{A}_{i^*}$. Otherwise, since $(\mathbf{m}^*, \boldsymbol{\sigma}^*)$ is valid signature, we have

$$[\mathbf{A}_0 | \mathbf{A}_{i^*}] \cdot \begin{bmatrix} \mathbf{m}^* \\ \boldsymbol{\sigma}^* \end{bmatrix} = \mathbf{u} = [\mathbf{A}_0 | \mathbf{A}_{i^*}] \cdot \begin{bmatrix} \mathbf{m}_{i^*} \\ \boldsymbol{\sigma}_{i^*} \end{bmatrix}.$$

Define $\mathbf{z} = \begin{bmatrix} \mathbf{m}^* \\ \boldsymbol{\sigma}^* \end{bmatrix} - \begin{bmatrix} \mathbf{m}_{i^*} \\ \boldsymbol{\sigma}_{i^*} \end{bmatrix}$. By the strong unforgeability of $\mathsf{TTSig}_{\mathsf{SIS}}$, $(\mathbf{m}^*, \boldsymbol{\sigma}^*) \neq (\mathbf{m}_{i^*}, \boldsymbol{\sigma}_{i^*})$ and thus $\mathbf{z} \neq \mathbf{0}$. We claim $\mathbf{z}$ is the solution to the $\mathsf{SIS}_{p,\beta}$ problem instance $\mathbf{A}$, since

$$\mathbf{A} \cdot \mathbf{z} = \mathbf{A} \cdot \left(\begin{bmatrix} \mathbf{m}^* \\ \boldsymbol{\sigma}^* \end{bmatrix} - \begin{bmatrix} \mathbf{m}_{i^*} \\ \boldsymbol{\sigma}_{i^*} \end{bmatrix} \right) = [\mathbf{A}_0 | \mathbf{A}_{i^*}] \cdot \left(\begin{bmatrix} \mathbf{m}^* \\ \boldsymbol{\sigma}^* \end{bmatrix} - \begin{bmatrix} \mathbf{m}_{i^*} \\ \boldsymbol{\sigma}_{i^*} \end{bmatrix} \right) = \mathbf{0}.$$

and $\|\mathbf{z}\|^2 \leq \ell + s^2 \omega(\sqrt{\log \lambda})^2 m = \beta^2$ by the triangle inequality. The successful probability of $\mathcal{B}$ is $\varepsilon = \frac{\varepsilon'}{d} - \mathsf{negl}(\lambda)$ and its running time is $t = t' + O(d \cdot q)$. □

4 Generic Constructions of Non-adaptive Signatures

In this section, we give two constructions of non-adaptively secure signature scheme Sig from any non-adaptively secure two-tier signature TTSig. The first construction is from a one-time two-tier signature scheme and the second construction is from a d-time two-tier signature scheme. Both constructions have tight security. The basic idea behind our constructions is as follows.

BASIC IDEA. In our constructions, the signer implicitly holds a tree. Each node has an out-degree d and the depth of the tree is h. Every node, including the leaves, $v \in \{1, \ldots, d\}^{\leq h}$ has a label L_v which is a secondary public key of TTSig. All nodes can be computed "on the fly." Each leaf is used to sign a single message. We have $d^h = 2^\lambda$ (or, equivalently, $h \log d = \lambda$), where the scheme can sign up to 2^λ messages.

When signing message m, the signer takes the leftmost unused leaf $v_h \in \{1, \ldots, d\}^h$ in the tree and generates the label $L_{v_h} \leftarrow_{\$} \mathsf{SecGen}(\mathsf{ppk}, \mathsf{psk})$. Define $L_{v_{h+1}} = m$. Then the path from the root v_0 to v_h is computed. For each undefined node v_i on the path, the signer assigns label $L_{v_i} \leftarrow_{\$} \mathsf{SecGen}(\mathsf{ppk}, \mathsf{psk})$. After that, every node on the path is signed using the label (i.e., the secondary secret key) of its parent. In this step, we have different signing methods depending on whether $d = 1$ or $d \geq 2$.

- $d = 1$: The signer holds a binary Merkle tree. When signing the nodes on the path, the signer takes the node v_i in the top-down manner and signs both children of v_i under L_{v_i}, $\sigma_{i+1} \leftarrow_{\$} \mathsf{Sign}(\mathsf{psk}, \mathsf{ssk}_{v_i}, \mathsf{Child}_l \| \mathsf{Child}_r)$ where ssk_{v_i}

is the secondary secret key associated with node v_i, and Child$_l$ and Child$_r$ are the left and right children of node v_i respectively. This construction can be viewed as a generalization of the tree-based signature by Hofheinz and Jager [30].

- $d \geq 2$: The signer holds a flat-tree with out-degree d. When signing the nodes on the path, the signer takes the node v_i in the top-down manner. Assume the jth child Child$_j$ of v_i is on the path. Then the signer uses ssk$_{v_i}$ to sign Child$_j$, $\sigma_{i+1} \leftarrow_\$ \mathsf{Sign}(\mathsf{psk}, \mathsf{ssk}_{v_i}, \mathsf{Child}_j)$.

The signer outputs the path and the two-tier signatures on the path as the signature of m. Details are given in the definitions of the schemes.

Note that both of our schemes are stateful. One can use the technique of Goldreich [26] to make them stateless. Precisely, the randomness used to generate secondary secret key ssk$_{v_i}$ for each node v_i will be derived by a pseudo-random function. Another pseudo-random function will be used to determine the leaf used to sign a given message. As this technique is quite standard for Merkle-tree-based signatures, we skip the details here and refer the reader to Section 3.2.3 of [34].

Moreover, it is well-known that a non-adaptively secure signature can be tightly transferred to be an adaptively secure signature by using a Chameleon Hash [35]. This is explicitly proven in the full version of [33].

4.1 Construction from any One-Time Two-Tier Signature

Let $\mathsf{TTSig} = (\mathsf{PriGen}, \mathsf{SecGen}, \mathsf{TTSign}, \mathsf{TTVerify})$ be a one-time two-tier signature scheme with message space $\{0,1\}^*$. The stateful signature scheme $\mathsf{BinTree}[\mathsf{TTSig}] = (\mathsf{Gen}, \mathsf{Sign}, \mathsf{Verify})$ is based on a binary tree of height $h = \lambda$ and is defined as follows. Figure 2 shows the nodes involved in signing the i-th message m.

- $\mathsf{Gen}(1^\lambda)$: Generate a primary key $(\mathsf{ppk}, \mathsf{psk}) \leftarrow_\$ \mathsf{PriGen}(1^\lambda, 1)$. The label of the root node ϵ is also generated $(\mathsf{spk}_\epsilon, \mathsf{ssk}_\epsilon) \leftarrow_\$ \mathsf{SecGen}(\mathsf{ppk}, \mathsf{psk})$ and $L_\epsilon = \mathsf{spk}_\epsilon$. Define the verification key $\mathsf{pk} = (\mathsf{ppk}, \mathsf{spk}_\epsilon)$ and the signing key $\mathsf{sk} = (\mathsf{psk}, \mathsf{ssk}_\epsilon)$.
- $\mathsf{Sign}(\mathsf{sk}, m)$: To sign a message m, the signer proceeds in two steps:
  - **Node generation step**: The signer takes the leftmost unused leaf $v_h \in \{0,1\}^h$ and searches the binary path $(v_0, v_1, v_2, \ldots, v_h)$ from the root $v_0 = \epsilon$ to v_h, i.e., v_i is the i-th prefix of v_h. For each node v_i on the path (including the leaf v_h), if v_i's label L_{v_i} is not defined, then the signer generates $(\mathsf{spk}_{v_i}, \mathsf{ssk}_{v_i}) \leftarrow_\$ \mathsf{SecGen}(\mathsf{ppk}, \mathsf{psk})$ and assigns $L_{v_i} = \mathsf{spk}_{v_i}$. For the sibling $\bar{v}_i$ of v_i, the corresponding secondary public key and secret key are generated in the same way, $(\mathsf{spk}_{\bar{v}_i}, \mathsf{ssk}_{\bar{v}_i}) \leftarrow_\$ \mathsf{SecGen}(\mathsf{ppk}, \mathsf{psk})$ and $L_{\bar{v}_i} = \mathsf{spk}_{\bar{v}_i}$.
  - **Path authentication step**: Define $M_h = m$. For each node v_i ($i = h - 1, \ldots, 0$) on the path, define the message associated with v_i by $M_i = L_{v_i||0}||L_{v_i||1}$, where $L_{v_i||0}$ and $L_{v_i||1}$ are labels of the left and right children of v_i respectively. Then the signer computes the signatures on the path as $\sigma_i = \mathsf{TTSign}(\mathsf{psk}, \mathsf{ssk}_{v_i}, M_i)$ for $i = 0, \ldots, h$.

The signer returns $\sigma = (v_h, M_0, \ldots, M_{h-1}, \sigma_0, \ldots, \sigma_h)$ as the signature of m.

– Verify(pk, m, σ): A signature $\sigma = (v_h, M_0, \ldots, M_{h-1}, \sigma_0, \ldots, \sigma_h)$ on the message m is verified in the natural way. Define $M_h = m$. Note that each M_{i-1} ($i = 1, \ldots, h$) contains the secondary public keys of v_{i-1}'s children, $L_{v_{i-1}\|0}$ and $L_{v_{i-1}\|1}$. Hence, we check if $\mathsf{TTVerify}(\mathsf{ppk}, L_{v_i}, M_i, \sigma_i) = 1$. If that is true for $i = 0, \ldots, h$, then it outputs 1, otherwise 0.

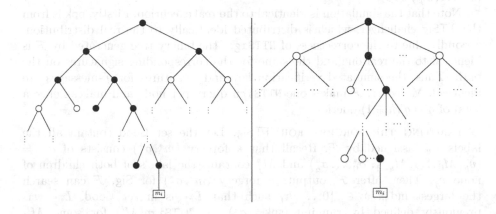

Fig. 2. Nodes in black are used in the i-th Signature with BinTree[TTSig], left and d-Tree[TTSig], right

The following theorem shows the non-adaptively security of BinTree[TTSig] is tightly reduced to the security of the one-time two-tier signature TTSig.

Theorem 4. *If* TTSig *is* $(t, q, 1, \varepsilon)$-TT-EUF-NCMA *secure, then* Sig $=$ BinTree[TTSig] *is* (t', ε', q')-EUF-NCMA *secure, where* $t' = t - O(hq')$, $\varepsilon' = \varepsilon$, *and* $q' = \frac{q}{h+1}$.

Proof. Let $\mathcal{F}'$ be a PPT adversary that breaks the EUF-NCMA-security of Sig with success probability ε' and time complexity t' and makes q' times non-adaptive message queries. Then we construct an adversary $\mathcal{F}$ to $(t, q, 1, \varepsilon)$-breaks the TT-EUF-NCMA security of TTSig with the parameters given above. First, $\mathcal{F}$ is given a challenge TTSig primary public key ppk.

SIMULATION. Recall that $\mathcal{F}'$ is an adversary for non-adaptive security, which means $\mathcal{F}'$ will output q' messages $m_1, \ldots, m_{q'}$ before seeing the verification key. In the following we explain how $\mathcal{F}$ generates the signatures on each m_i and the verification key of Sig without knowing the real signing key of TTSig.

$\mathcal{F}$ generates the binary tree in a bottom-up fashion by using the oracle NTTSign (note that the number of leaves are the same as the number of the signing queries q' and, thus, all the leaves are defined after signing q' messages). For each i-th query to NTTSign ($1 \leq i \leq q'$), $\mathcal{F}$ does the following:

– For a leaf $v_h^{(i)}$, $\mathcal{F}$ defines $M_h^{(i)} = m_i$ and queries $(\mathsf{spk}_{v_h^{(i)}}, \sigma_h^{(i)}) \leftarrow_\$$ NTTSign($M_h^{(i)}$). Define $L_{v_h^{(i)}} = \mathsf{spk}_{v_h^{(i)}}$.

- For an internal node v_j (for each $0 \leq j \leq h-1$), $\mathcal{F}$ defines $M_j^{(i)} = L_{v_{j-1}\|0}\|L_{v_{j-1}\|1}$. $\mathcal{F}$ queries $(\mathsf{spk}_{v_j}, \sigma_j^{(i)}) \leftarrow_\$ \mathtt{NTTSign}(M_j^{(i)})$. Define $L_{v_j} = \mathsf{spk}_{v_j}$.
- The signature σ_i on m_i is $(v_h^{(i)}, M_0^{(i)}, \dots, M_{h-1}^{(i)}, \sigma_0^{(i)}, \dots, \sigma_h^{(i)})$.

Finally, $\mathcal{F}$ returns the verification key $\mathsf{pk} = (\mathsf{ppk}, \mathsf{spk}_\epsilon)$ and the signatures $(\sigma_1, \dots, \sigma_{q'})$ to $\mathcal{F}'$.

Note that the simulation is identical to the real execution. Firstly, ppk is from the TTSig challenger, which is distributed identically to the real distribution. Secondly, due to the correctness of $\mathtt{NTTSign}$, the binary tree generated by $\mathcal{F}$ is identical to the real one and the same for the corresponding signatures on the path. Thus, the simulated verification key and signatures for q'-messages are identical. Moreover, $\mathcal{F}$ makes one $\mathtt{NTTSign}$ query per node and makes hence a total of $q = q'(h+1)$ queries.

EXTRACTING THE FORGERY FOR TTSig. Let the set Good contain all the labels L_{v_j} assigned by $\mathcal{F}$. Recall that a forgery (m^*, σ^*) consists of $\sigma^* = (v_h^*, M_0^*, \dots, M_{h-1}^*, \sigma_0^*, \dots \sigma_h^*)$ and M_j^* contains the labels of both children of node v_j^*. Then, after $\mathcal{F}'$ outputs a forgery (m^*, σ^*) for Sig, $\mathcal{F}$ can search the largest index $\delta \in \{0, \dots, h\}$ such that $L_{v_\delta^*}$ is in set Good. $L_{v_\delta^*}$ was previously defined by running $(\mathsf{spk}_{v_\delta^*}, \sigma_\delta) \leftarrow \mathtt{NTTSign}(M')$ for some M'. If (m^*, σ^*) is a valid EUF-NCMA forgery, $\mathcal{F}$ can find $(M_\delta^*, \sigma_\delta^*)$ such that $\mathsf{TTVerify}(\mathsf{ppk}, \mathsf{spk}_{v_\delta^*}, M_\delta^*, \sigma_\delta^*) = 1$ where $M_\delta^* \neq M'$.

Thus, $\mathcal{F}$ can break the TT-EUF-NCMA security of TTSig with probability $\varepsilon = \varepsilon'$. A similar argument can be applied to prove the strong EUF-NCMA security of Sig when TTSig is strongly TT-EUF-NCMA secure.   □

4.2   Construction from any d-Time Two-Tier Signature

Let $\mathsf{TTSig} = (\mathsf{PriGen}, \mathsf{SecGen}, \mathsf{TTSign}, \mathsf{TTVerify})$ be a d-time two-tier signature with message space $\{0,1\}^*$. The stateful signature scheme $d\text{-Tree}[\mathsf{TTSig}] = (\mathsf{Gen}, \mathsf{Sign}, \mathsf{Verify})$ is defined as follows, once again you can refer to Figure 2 to see the nodes involved:

- $\mathsf{Gen}(1^\lambda)$: It generates a d-time primary key, $(\mathsf{ppk}, \mathsf{psk}) \leftarrow_\$ \mathsf{PriGen}(1^\lambda, d)$. The label of the root $v_0 = \epsilon$ is also generated $(\mathsf{spk}_\epsilon, \mathsf{ssk}_\epsilon) \leftarrow_\$ \mathsf{SecGen}(\mathsf{ppk}, \mathsf{psk})$ and $L_\epsilon := \mathsf{spk}_\epsilon$. Define the verification key $\mathsf{pk} := (\mathsf{ppk}, \mathsf{spk}_\epsilon)$ and the signing key $\mathsf{sk} := (\mathsf{psk}, \mathsf{ssk}_\epsilon)$.
- $\mathsf{Sign}(\mathsf{sk}, m)$: To sign a message m, the signer proceeds in two steps:
  - Nodes generation step: The signer takes the leftmost unused leaf $v_h \in \{1, \dots, d\}^h$ and searches the path $(v_0, \dots, v_h)$ from the root $v_0 = \epsilon$ to v_h. Define $L_{v_h} := m$ and for each internal node v_i on the path, if v_i's label L_{v_i} is not defined, then the signer generates $(\mathsf{spk}_{v_i}, \mathsf{ssk}_{v_i}) \leftarrow_\$ \mathsf{SecGen}(\mathsf{ppk}, \mathsf{psk})$ and assigns $L_{v_i} := \mathsf{spk}_{v_i}$.
  - Path authentication step: Each L_{v_i} $(i = 1, \dots, h)$ on the path is signed under $L_{v_{i-1}} = \mathsf{spk}_{v_{i-1}}$, $\sigma_i \leftarrow_\$ \mathsf{TTSign}(\mathsf{psk}, \mathsf{ssk}_{v_{i-1}}, L_{v_i}; j)$ where $v_i = v_{i-1}\|j$ and $1 \leq j \leq d$. The d-time TTSign is a stateful algorithm and j is the state.

The signer returns $\sigma = (v_h, L_{v_1}, \ldots, L_{v_{h-1}}, \sigma_1, \ldots, \sigma_h)$ as the signature of m.

- Verify(pk, m, σ): Parse $\sigma = (v_h, L_{v_1}, \ldots, L_{v_h}, \sigma_1, \ldots, \sigma_h)$. The verifier defines $L_{v_h} := m$ and checks if TTVerify(ppk, $L_{v_{i-1}}, L_{v_i}, \sigma_i; j) = 1$ for all $i = 1, \ldots, h$, where $v_{i+1} = v_i || j$ $(1 \le j \le d)$. If that is true, then it outputs 1, otherwise 0. Here the d-time TTVerify is a stateful algorithm and j is the state.

The following theorem tightly reduces the non-adaptively security of d-Tree[TTSig] to the one of the d-time two-tier signature TTSig.

Theorem 5. *If* TTSig *is* (t, q, d, ε)-TT-EUF-NCMA *secure, then* Sig = d-Tree[TTSig] *is* (t', ε', q')-EUF-NCMA *secure, where* $t' = t - O(hq')$, $\varepsilon' = \varepsilon$, *and* $q' = \frac{q}{h}$.

Proof. The security proof is a generalization of the proof of the Cramer-Damgård scheme [19], and it is rather similar to the proof of Theorem 4. Therefore we only sketch it. The major difference between Sig and BinTree[TTSig] is that each internal node v in Sig uses a d-time signature to sign its d-many children one by one, while in BinTree[TTSig] each internal node v can only sign its both children one-time.

Assume $\mathcal{F}'$ (t', ε', q')-breaks EUF-NCMA-security of Sig. Then we construct $\mathcal{F}$ break TT-EUF-NCMA security of TTSig:

SIMULATION. Similar to the proof of Theorem 4, given q' messages, $\mathcal{F}$ can simulate all the tree nodes and the signature on the path by asking the d-time signing oracle NTTSign in a bottom-up fashion. By the correctness of NTTSign, it is easy to see the simulation is identical to the Sig definition. Moreover, $\mathcal{F}$ makes one NTTSign query per node and makes hence a total of $q = q' \cdot h$ queries.

EXTRACTING THE FORGERY FOR TTSig. After $\mathcal{F}'$ outputs a success forgery (m^*, σ^*), $\mathcal{F}$ defines $L_{v^*_{h+1}} := m^*$ and finds the forgery for TTSig following the same step in the proof of Theorem 4. Thus, $\varepsilon = \varepsilon'$. □

A   Hardness Assumptions

We now define the hardness assumptions that we have used in our results.

GROUP GENERATOR ALGORITHMS. We define an algorithm GroupGen, that on input of 1^λ gives us $\mathcal{G} = (\mathbb{G}, g, p)$, such that $\mathbb{G} = \langle g \rangle$ is a multiplicative group of order p and $\log p = \lambda$.

Let PGroupGen be an algorithm that on input 1^λ outputs a description of a bilinear group $\mathcal{PG} = (\mathbb{G}, \mathbb{G}_T, g, p, e)$ such that $\mathbb{G} = \langle g \rangle$ and $\mathbb{G}_T$ are two cyclic groups of prime-order p and $e : \mathbb{G} \times \mathbb{G} \to \mathbb{G}_T$ is a bilinear pairing satisfying the following properties:

1. $\mathbb{G}_T = \langle e(g, g) \rangle$ (in particular $e(g, g) \neq 1$).
2. $\forall a, b \in \mathbb{Z}_p$, $e(g^a, g^b) = e(g, g)^{ab}$.

We now discuss the computational assumptions that we use in this setting. All the assumptions below are defined relative to either GroupGen or PGroupGen. For compactness, we use the Setup algorithm, which can be in either setting.

LINEAR ASSUMPTION. The linear assumption, denoted by LIN, states that given three random generators g, h, k of $\mathbb{G}$ and a tuple (g^u, h^v, k^c) where $u, v \in_R \mathbb{Z}_p$ and $c = u + v$ or random in $\mathbb{Z}_p$, it is hard for the adversary $\mathcal{A}$ to guess $c = u + v$ or c is random. LIN is said to be (t, ε)-hard if for all adversaries $\mathcal{A}$ running in time at most t, we have

$$\Pr\left[\mathcal{A}(g, h, k, (g^u, h^v, k^c))_\$ \rightarrow \text{`}c = u + v\text{' or not}\right] \leq \varepsilon.$$

COMPUTATIONAL DIFFIE-HELLMAN ASSUMPTION. The Computational Diffie-Hellman Assumption, denoted by CDH, states that given $\mathcal{G} = (\mathbb{G}, g, p)$ and elements g^a, g^b, it is hard to compute g^{ab}. CDH is said to be (t, ε)-hard if for all adversaries $\mathcal{A}$ running in time at most t, we have

$$\Pr\left[\mathcal{G} \leftarrow_\$ \mathsf{Setup}(1^\lambda), a, b \in_R \mathbb{Z}_p : g^{ab} \leftarrow_\$ \mathcal{A}(\mathcal{G}, g^a, g^b)\right] \leq \varepsilon.$$

f-COMPUTATIONAL DIFFIE-HELLMAN INVERSION ASSUMPTION. The f- Computational Diffie-Hellman Inversion Assumption, denoted by f-CDHI, states that given $\mathcal{G} = (\mathbb{G}, g, p)$ and elements $g^x, g^{x^2}, g^{x^3}, \ldots g^{x^f}$, it is hard to compute $(g^{\frac{1}{x}})$. f-CDHI is said to be (t, ε)-hard if for all adversaries $\mathcal{A}$ running in time at most t, we have

$$\Pr\left[\mathcal{G} \leftarrow_\$ \mathsf{Setup}(1^\lambda), x \in_R \mathbb{Z}_p : g^{\frac{1}{x}} \leftarrow_\$ \mathcal{A}(\mathcal{G}, g^x, g^{x^2}, g^{x^3}, \ldots g^{x^f})\right] \leq \varepsilon.$$

We note that 1-CDHI is tightly equivalent to CDH.

RSA ASSUMPTION. The RSA Assumptions, denoted by RSA, states that given (N, e, x^e), where N is a random λ-bit RSA modulus generated by an algorithm $\mathsf{RSAGen}(1^\lambda)$ and $x \in_R \mathbb{Z}_N^*$, it is hard to compute x. RSA is said to be (t, ε)-hard, if for all adversaries $\mathcal{A}$ running in time at most t, we have:

$$\Pr\left[(N, e) \leftarrow_\$ \mathsf{RSAGen}(1^\lambda), x \in_R \mathbb{Z}_N^* : x = \mathcal{A}(N, e, x^e)\right] \leq \varepsilon.$$

LATTICES AND SIS ASSUMPTION. for integers λ, m and for a prime p, let $\mathbf{A} \in \mathbb{Z}_p^{\lambda \times m}$. The m-dimensional integer lattice $\Lambda^\perp(\mathbf{A})$ is defined as

$$\Lambda^\perp(\mathbf{A}) := \{\mathbf{z} \in \mathbb{Z}^m : \mathbf{A}\mathbf{z} = \mathbf{0} \bmod p\}.$$

For any $\mathbf{u} \in \mathbb{Z}_p^\lambda$, define the coset

$$\Lambda_{\mathbf{u}}^\perp(\mathbf{A}) := \{\mathbf{z} \in \mathbb{Z}^m : \mathbf{A}\mathbf{z} = \mathbf{u} \bmod p\}.$$

The *short integer solution* problem $\mathsf{SIS}_{p,\beta}$ $(\beta > 0)$ is an average-case version of the approximate shortest vector problem on $\Lambda^\perp(\mathbf{A})$. It states that, given a uniformly random $\mathbf{A} \in \mathbb{Z}_p^{\lambda \times m}$ for $m = \mathrm{poly}(\lambda)$, find a non-zero $\mathbf{z} \in \Lambda^\perp(\mathbf{A})$ and $\|\mathbf{z}\| \leq \beta$, where $\|\cdot\|$ is the Euclidean norm. $\mathsf{SIS}_{p,\beta}$ is (t, ε)-hard if all adversaries with running time t have a success probability of at most ε. It has been shown if $p \geq \beta\sqrt{\lambda} \cdot \omega(\sqrt{\log \lambda})$ then solving $\mathsf{SIS}_{p,\beta}$ is at least as hard as approximating the

Shortest Independent Vectors Problem within approximation factor $\tilde{O}(\beta\sqrt{\lambda})$ in worst case [24,39].

Let $D_{\mathbb{Z}^m,s}$ be the Gaussian distribution over $\mathbb{Z}^m$ with center $\mathbf{0}$ and parameter s and, similarly, let $D_{\Lambda^\perp(\mathbf{A}),s}$ be the Gaussian distribution over $\Lambda^\perp(\mathbf{A})$ with center $\mathbf{0}$ and parameter s.

The following lemmas are useful for the definition and the security proof of our scheme.

Lemma 1 (Theorem 5.1 of [38]). *There is an efficient randomized algorithm* $\mathsf{GenTrap}^{\mathcal{D}}(1^\lambda, 1^m, p)$ *that, given any integers* $\lambda \geq 1$, $p \geq 2$, *and sufficiently large* $m = O(\lambda \log p)$, *outputs a parity-check matrix* $\mathbf{A} \in \mathbb{Z}_p^{\lambda \times m}$ *and a trapdoor* $\mathbf{R}$ *such that the distribution of* $\mathbf{A}$ *is* $\mathsf{negl}(\lambda)$-*far from uniform and* $\mathbf{R}$ *is sampled from the Gaussian* $\mathcal{D}$.

Moreover, for any $\mathbf{y} \in \mathbb{Z}_p^\lambda$ *and large enough* $s = O(\sqrt{\lambda \log p})$, *there is an efficient randomized algorithm* $\mathsf{SampleD}(\mathbf{R}, \mathbf{A}, \mathbf{y}, s)$ *that samples from a distribution with* $\mathsf{negl}(\lambda)$ *statistical distance of* $D_{\Lambda_{\mathbf{y}}^\perp(\mathbf{A}),s\cdot\omega(\sqrt{\log\lambda})}$.

Lemma 2 (Lemma 4.4 of [39]). *Let* $\mathbf{x} \leftarrow D_{\Lambda^\perp(\mathbf{A}),s}$ *where* $\mathbf{A} \in \mathbb{Z}_p^{\lambda \times m}$. *Then the probability that* $\|\mathbf{x}\| > s\sqrt{m}$ *is negligible in* λ.

Lemma 3 (Corollary 5.4 of [24]). *Let* λ *be a positive integer and* p *be a prime, and let integer* $m \geq 2\lambda \log p$. *Then for all but a* $2p^{-\lambda}$ *fraction of all* $\mathbf{A} \in \mathbb{Z}_p^{\lambda \times m}$ *and for any* $s \geq \omega(\sqrt{\log m})$, *the distribution of the syndrome* $\mathbf{y} = \mathbf{A}\mathbf{x}$ mod p *is statically close to uniform over* $\mathbb{Z}_p^\lambda$, *where* $\mathbf{x}$ *is from* $D_{\mathbb{Z}^m,s}$.

B   Applications

In this appendix we show some applications of our almost structure-preserving signature scheme $\mathsf{Sig}_{d,f\text{-CDHI}} = d\text{-}\mathsf{Tree}[\mathsf{TTSig}_{f\text{-CDHI}}]$ and we get a more efficient tightly-secure CCA encryption in the multi-user and multi-challenge setting.

A Structure-Preserving signature over a bilinear group [2] considers signatures fully compatible with the Groth-Sahai methodology. Such signatures assume that messages, signatures and verification keys are in the same space ($\mathbb{G}$) and that verification can be expressed as simple pairing product equations.

When someone wants to commit to a signature, the naive approach consists in computing the signature, and then committing individually to each component of the signature. However, in many signature schemes, like ours, parts of the signature do not require the knowledge of the secret key and therefore do not require to be committed.[3] In the following, we relax the definition of structure preserving signatures and consider signatures where the verification equation is a pairing product equation in the elements that have to be committed. (To be more specific, we will allow hash values and scalars to appear in the verification equation as long as they are uncommitted/public values.)

---

[3] A good illustration consists in considering a Waters signature: $\sigma_1 = \mathsf{sk}F(m)^s, \sigma_2 = g^s$, committing σ_1 into C_1 is enough to completely hide the signature. (C_1, σ_2) leaks no information on the validity of the signature.

In a symmetric bilinear group $\mathcal{PG} = (p, \mathbb{G}, g, \mathbb{G}_T, e)$, a Pairing-Product Equation is an equation of the form: $\prod_{i=1}^{n} e(X_i, A_i) \cdot \prod_{i=1}^{n} \prod_{j=i}^{n} e(X_i, X_j)^{\gamma_{i,j}} = t_T$, where A_i are public group elements in $\mathbb{G}$, $\gamma_{i,j}$ are public scalars in $\mathbb{Z}_p$, t_T is a public element in the target group $\mathbb{G}_T$, and X_i are variables in $\mathbb{G}$. In [29], the authors have shown how to build Non-Interactive Zero-Knowledge Proofs of Knowledge of solutions of such equations and have proven that their construction can be improved in the linear case ($\gamma = 0$).

B.1   Tight Simulation-Sound NIZK in Pairing Groups

In this subsection, we revisit a technique introduced in [28,36] to obtain simulation-sound NIZK (also used in [30]) and instantiate it with our new signature scheme $\mathsf{Sig}_{d,f\text{-CDHI}}$.

A Simulation-Sound Non-Interactive Zero-Knowledge (SSNIZK) Proofs of Knowledge, is a standard NIZK where the soundness holds even if the simulator is given simulated proofs.

We build SSNIZK Proofs of Knowledge to prove that variables X verify a set of Pairing-Product Equations $\mathcal{S}$, for which we combine our non-adaptive signature scheme, a one-time two-tier signature (to make it adaptively secure) and Groth-Sahai Proofs of Knowledge [29].

The verification of the validity of our signature can be viewed as several linear Pairing-Product Equations. This will allow us to greatly improve the efficiency of the SSNIZK Proof of Knowledge.

Roadmap of the Technique. To construct a Simulation-Sound proof that some variables X verify a set $\mathcal{S}$ of equations, one uses the following roadmap assuming the crs contains $\mathsf{crs}_{\mathsf{GS}}$, a verification key pk for the Structure-Preserving Signature scheme Sig, and the prover already possesses a pair of primary keys psk, ppk for a one-time two-tier signature scheme $\mathcal{S}_1$.

1. Generates a secondary signing/verification key pair (ssk, spk) for the one-time two-tier signature
2. Commits to a random tuple of elements R corresponding to a signature (the tuple should be random, but the size and type of elements committed should be consistent with what is expected from a signature).
3. Generates a Groth-Sahai proof π, that either X verifies this set $\mathcal{S}$, or that R is a valid signature under pk in the crs of the verification key spk of the one-time signature scheme.
4. He then sends this Groth-Sahai proof π, the verification key of the one-time signature, a one-time signature under psk, ssk of everything.

Referring to [30], it can be shown that this scheme is Zero-Knowledge under the indistinguishability of the two types of Groth-Sahai crs, and that both the simulation-soundness and the soundness come from the unforgeability of two kind of signatures. The reductions inherit the tightness of the underlying signature schemes.

Instantiation from f-CDHI and Efficiency Comparison. We now use our non-adaptive structure-preserving signature scheme based on f-CDHI (obtained by combining the d-time two-tier signature presented in Section 3.2, and the transformation from 4.2), together with the Strong one-time two-tier signature based on DLOG (see Section 3.1 with a DLOG-based Chameleon Hash), we obtain:

- $\mathcal{ZK}.\mathsf{Setup}(1^\lambda)$: generates a crs consisting of a bilinear group $(p, \mathbb{G}, g, \mathbb{G}_T, e)$, an extra generator $\tilde{g}$ for the $\mathsf{ppk}_{\mathcal{S}_1}$ of the one-time signature scheme, a collision resistant Hash Function $\mathcal{H}$, a Groth-Sahai CRS crs_{GS} and the verification key $\mathsf{pk} = g^x_{i \in 1,c}$ for a Structure-Preserving Signature Scheme, which is also strongly unforgeable. The prover possesses a pair ($\mathsf{psk} = \alpha, \mathsf{ppk} = \tilde{g} = g^\alpha$).
- $\mathcal{ZK}.\mathsf{Prove}(\mathsf{crs}, \mathcal{S}, X)$: where X is a set of variables satisfying the set of equations $\mathcal{S}$. First this samples a fresh secondary key pair for the strong adaptive one-time two-tier signature scheme: a pair $(\mathsf{ssk}_{\mathcal{S}_1} = (\eta, \mu), \mathsf{spk}_{\mathcal{S}_1} = \tilde{g}^\eta g^\mu)$ for $\eta, \mu \in_R \mathbb{Z}_p$.
  It then computes a Groth-Sahai proof π_{GS} stating that either X satisfies $\mathcal{S}$, or that σ is a valid signature on $\mathsf{spk}_{\mathcal{S}_1}$, by picking a fresh leaf in the signature tree, and generating a commitment σ of random values emulating a signature on the path (random group elements $\mathsf{spk}_i \in_R \mathbb{G}$ for the nodes of the tree on the path, reusing those already chosen on the shared path in previous proofs), a random scalar t for the one-time signature of $\mathsf{spk}_{\mathcal{S}_1}$ on the leaf, and $h+1$ commitments to fictive signature S_i of spk_{i+1} valid under spk_i. The proof consists of $h+1$ proofs of linear pairing product equations, so $3h + 3$ group elements only where h is the depth of the tree ($h = \lambda / \log(d)$). It then sends $\pi = \pi_{GS}, \mathsf{spk}_{\mathcal{S}_1}, \sigma_{\mathsf{spk}_{\mathcal{S}_1}}(\pi_{GS})$.
- $\mathcal{ZK}.\mathsf{Verify}(\mathsf{crs}, \mathcal{S}, \pi)$, checks the validity of the one-time two-tier signature, and then the validity of the Groth-Sahai proof.

The principal difference between this approach and the one in [30] resides in the signature scheme, in particular the sizes thereof. Their signature requires 10 group elements per node; to hide the signature, 6 of them have to be committed, resulting in 22 elements per node. The verification equation is a quadratic pairing product-equation, hence the sub-proof requires 9 group elements per node. The proof on the committed signature requires overall roughly 31λ group elements.

Recently, Abe et al. [1] have presented an optimization on this initial construction. They evaluated the cost of their corresponding part as roughly $21\lambda + 27$. (They presented several construction, but the others are either less efficient and/or not tight)

On the other hand, our signature based on f-CDHI requires two group elements per node (the child verification key and the signature itself) and one group element and a scalar for the last node. We need to hide one of these elements for each node. This means that we need 4 elements per node, and 3 group elements and a scalar for the last one. As explained previously, the verification equation can be viewed in this case as a linear pairing-product equation so on each node the proof consists of 3 group elements. We end up with a proof on the committed signature consisting of $(7\lambda)/\log(d) + 7$ group elements and 1 scalar. This is where, the trade-off comes into play, for a fair comparison to previous schemes, we need a signature relying on an equivalent assumption, as they are based on LIN, we need to rely on CDH, so $f = 1\text{-CDHI}$, we also want to have a reasonable sized CRS, so minimize d/f, and take $d = 2$. In the end, we can show that by increasing the CRS size by one element, we manage to reduce the size of the proofs by a factor 3.

B.2   Tight Multi-Challenge (and Multi-User) IND-CCA Scheme

IND-CCA encryption is a very useful primitive, but in some contexts, one may wish to give even more power to the adversary, he might be allowed to give q challenge tuples and only answer on one of them, or he might ask the challenges to be run on μ encryption keys. There is a transformation based on the Naor-Yung paradigm [42] which allows to create a (μ, q)-CCA-Encryption from a (μ, q)-Structure-Preserving CPA-Encryption[4], and a SSNIZK in pairing groups.

This technique is described in more details in [30], where they show how to obtain a tight reduction to the CPA-encryption and the SSNIZK.

Roadmap of the Technique. To encrypt a message M, one obeys the following roadmap (assuming a crs containing two encryption keys ek_1, ek_2 for an IND-CPA scheme.):

1. Generates two CPA-encryptions of M, one under each two encryption keys in the CRS.
2. Uses the Simulation-Sound NIZK to generate a proof that those two ciphertexts C_1 and C_2 encrypt the same message with respect to the encryption keys.
3. The CCA ciphertext then consists of the two ciphertexts and this proof.

To decrypt the message, one simply has to check the validity of the proof and to decrypt one of the CPA encryptions.

Instantiations. The solution presented in [30] uses Linear Encryption [12] for the CPA-encryption. Our SS-NIZK construction works on bilinear groups, so is also compatible with this encryption scheme.

The overall size of the CCA-Encryption is 6 group elements for the two encryptions, 2 for the verification key and the one-time signature, and several elements for the OR proof. The OR proof needs 4 commitments and 5 linear multiscalar multiplications proof to handle the equality of ciphertexts, an extra commitment for the OR, and a commitment and proof of validity of the signature.

---

[4] A structure-preserving encryption scheme has public keys, messages, and ciphertexts that consist entirely of group elements, and both the encryption and decryption algorithms perform only group operations.

The signature and its proof of validity are the larger part of the encryption, and as explained before our construction for that is at least 3 times more efficient than the original one. So our CCA-encryption inherits this efficiency and is nearly 3 times more efficient than theirs while our construction is still tight.

Acknowledgments. We thank Mihir Bellare for his valuable comments. Part of this work was done while Olivier Blazy was employed at Ruhr-University Bochum. All authors were (partially) funded by a Sofja Kovalevskaja Award of the Alexander von Humboldt Foundation and the German Federal Ministry for Education and Research. Jiaxin Pan was also partially funded by the German Israeli Foundation.

References

1. Abe, M., David, B., Kohlweiss, M., Nishimaki, R., Ohkubo, M.: Tagged one-time signatures: tight security and optimal tag size. In: Kurosawa, K., Hanaoka, G. (eds.) PKC 2013. LNCS, vol. 7778, pp. 312–331. Springer, Heidelberg (2013)
2. Abe, M., Fuchsbauer, G., Groth, J., Haralambiev, K., Ohkubo, M.: Structure-preserving signatures and commitments to group elements. In: Rabin, T. (ed.) CRYPTO 2010. LNCS, vol. 6223, pp. 209–236. Springer, Heidelberg (2010)
3. Bader, C., Hofheinz, D., Jager, T., Kiltz, E., Li, Y.: Tightly-secure authenticated key exchange. Cryptology ePrint Archive, Report 2014/797 (2014)
4. Bellare, M., Ristov, T.: A characterization of chameleon hash functions and new, efficient designs. Journal of Cryptology **27**(4), 799–823 (October 2014)
5. Bellare, M., Rogaway, P.: Random oracles are practical: A paradigm for designing efficient protocols. In: Ashby, V. (ed.) ACM CCS 1993, pp. 62–73. ACM Press, November 1993
6. Bellare, M., Rogaway, P.: The exact security of digital signatures - how to sign with RSA and Rabin. In: Maurer, U.M. (ed.) EUROCRYPT 1996. LNCS, vol. 1070, pp. 399–416. Springer, Heidelberg (1996)
7. Bellare, M., Shoup, S.: Two-tier signatures, strongly unforgeable signatures, and Fiat-Shamir without random oracles. In: Okamoto, T., Wang, X. (eds.) PKC 2007. LNCS, vol. 4450, pp. 201–216. Springer, Heidelberg (2007)
8. Blazy, O., Kakvi, S., Kiltz, E., Pan. J.: Tightly-secure signatures from chameleon hash functions. Cryptology ePrint Archive, Report 2014/1021 (2014)
9. Blazy, O., Kiltz, E., Pan, J.: (Hierarchical) Identity-based encryption from affine message authentication. In: Garay, J.A., Gennaro, R. (eds.) CRYPTO 2014, Part I. LNCS, vol. 8616, pp. 408–425. Springer, Heidelberg (2014)
10. Boneh, D., Boyen, X.: Short signatures without random oracles. In: Cachin, C., Camenisch, J.L. (eds.) EUROCRYPT 2004. LNCS, vol. 3027, pp. 56–73. Springer, Heidelberg (2004)
11. Boneh, D., Boyen, X.: Short signatures without random oracles and the SDH assumption in bilinear groups. Journal of Cryptology **21**(2), 149–177 (April 2008)
12. Boneh, D., Boyen, X., Shacham, H.: Short group signatures. In: Franklin, M. (ed.) CRYPTO 2004. LNCS, vol. 3152, pp. 41–55. Springer, Heidelberg (2004)
13. Boneh, D., Mironov, I., Shoup, V.: A secure signature scheme from bilinear maps. In: Joye, M. (ed.) CT-RSA 2003. LNCS, vol. 2612, pp. 98–110. Springer, Heidelberg (2003)
14. Canetti, R., Goldreich, O., Halevi, S.: The random oracle methodology, revisited (preliminary version). In: 30th ACM STOC, pp. 209–218. ACM Press, May 1998

15. Cash, D., Hofheinz, D., Kiltz, E., Peikert, C.: Bonsai trees, or how to delegate a lattice basis. In: Gilbert, H. (ed.) EUROCRYPT 2010. LNCS, vol. 6110, pp. 523–552. Springer, Heidelberg (2010)

16. Catalano, D., Gennaro, R.: Cramer-damgård signatures revisited: Efficient flat-tree signatures based on factoring. In: Vaudenay, S. (ed.) PKC 2005. LNCS, vol. 3386, pp. 313–327. Springer, Heidelberg (2005)

17. Chen, J., Wee, H.: Fully, (almost) tightly secure IBE and dual system groups. In: Canetti, R., Garay, J.A. (eds.) CRYPTO 2013, Part II. LNCS, vol. 8043, pp. 435–460. Springer, Heidelberg (2013)

18. Chevallier-Mames, B., Joye, M.: A practical and tightly secure signature scheme without hash function. In: Abe, M. (ed.) CT-RSA 2007. LNCS, vol. 4377, pp. 339–356. Springer, Heidelberg (2006)

19. Cramer, R., Damgård, I.B.: New generation of secure and practical RSA-based signatures. In: Koblitz, N. (ed.) CRYPTO 1996. LNCS, vol. 1109, pp. 173–185. Springer, Heidelberg (1996)

20. Cramer, R., Shoup, V.: Signature schemes based on the strong RSA assumption. In: ACM CCS 1999, pp. 46–51. ACM Press, November 1999

21. Dodis, Y., Oliveira, R., Pietrzak, K.: On the generic insecurity of the full domain hash. In: Shoup, V. (ed.) CRYPTO 2005. LNCS, vol. 3621, pp. 449–466. Springer, Heidelberg (2005)

22. Dwork, C., Naor, M.: An efficient existentially unforgeable signature scheme and its applications. In: Desmedt, Y.G. (ed.) CRYPTO 1994. LNCS, vol. 839, pp. 234–246. Springer, Heidelberg (1994)

23. Escala, A., Herold, G., Kiltz, E., Ràfols, C., Villar, J.: An algebraic framework for Diffie-Hellman assumptions. In: Canetti, R., Garay, J.A. (eds.) CRYPTO 2013, Part II. LNCS, vol. 8043, pp. 129–147. Springer, Heidelberg (2013)

24. Gentry, C., Peikert, C., Vaikuntanathan, V.: Trapdoors for hard lattices and new cryptographic constructions. In: Ladner, R.E., Dwork, C. (eds.) 40th ACM STOC, pp. 197–206. ACM Press, May 2008

25. Goh, E.-J., Jarecki, S., Katz, J., Wang, N.: Efficient signature schemes with tight reductions to the Diffie-Hellman problems. Journal of Cryptology 20(4), 493–514 (October 2007)

26. Goldreich, O.: Two remarks concerning the Goldwasser-Micali-Rivest signature scheme. In: Odlyzko, A.M. (ed.) CRYPTO 1986. LNCS, vol. 263, pp. 104–110. Springer, Heidelberg (1987)

27. Goldwasser, S., Micali, S., Rivest, R.L.: A digital signature scheme secure against adaptive chosen-message attacks. SIAM Journal on Computing 17(2), 281–308 (April 1988)

28. Groth, J.: Simulation-sound NIZK proofs for a practical language and constant size group signatures. In: Lai, X., Chen, K. (eds.) ASIACRYPT 2006. LNCS, vol. 4284, pp. 444–459. Springer, Heidelberg (2006)

29. Groth, J., Sahai, A.: Efficient non-interactive proof systems for bilinear groups. In: Smart, N.P. (ed.) EUROCRYPT 2008. LNCS, vol. 4965, pp. 415–432. Springer, Heidelberg (2008)

30. Hofheinz, D., Jager, T.: Tightly secure signatures and public-key encryption. In: Safavi-Naini, R., Canetti, R. (eds.) CRYPTO 2012. LNCS, vol. 7417, pp. 590–607. Springer, Heidelberg (2012)

31. Hofheinz, D., Jager, T., Kiltz, E.: Short signatures from weaker assumptions. In: Lee, D.H., Wang, X. (eds.) ASIACRYPT 2011. LNCS, vol. 7073, pp. 647–666. Springer, Heidelberg (2011)

32. Hohenberger, S., Waters, B.: Realizing hash-and-sign signatures under standard assumptions. In: Joux, A. (ed.) EUROCRYPT 2009. LNCS, vol. 5479, pp. 333–350. Springer, Heidelberg (2009)
33. Hohenberger, S., Waters, B.: Short and stateless signatures from the RSA assumption. In: Halevi, S. (ed.) CRYPTO 2009. LNCS, vol. 5677, pp. 654–670. Springer, Heidelberg (2009)
34. Katz, J.: Digital Signatures. Springer (2010)
35. Krawczyk, H., Rabin, T.: Chameleon signatures. In: NDSS 2000. The Internet Society, February 2000
36. Lindell, Y.: A simpler construction of CCA2-secure public-key encryption under general assumptions. In: Biham, E. (ed.) EUROCRYPT 2003. LNCS, vol. 2656, pp. 241–254. Springer, Heidelberg (2003)
37. Merkle, R.C.: A certified digital signature. In: Brassard, G. (ed.) CRYPTO 1989. LNCS, vol. 435, pp. 218–238. Springer, Heidelberg (1990)
38. Micciancio, D., Peikert, C.: Trapdoors for lattices: simpler, tighter, faster, smaller. In: Pointcheval, D., Johansson, T. (eds.) EUROCRYPT 2012. LNCS, vol. 7237, pp. 700–718. Springer, Heidelberg (2012)
39. Micciancio, D., Regev, O.: Worst-case to average-case reductions based on gaussian measures. In: 45th FOCS, pp. 372–381. IEEE Computer Society Press, October 2004
40. Mohassel, P.: One-time signatures and chameleon hash functions. In: Biryukov, A., Gong, G., Stinson, D.R. (eds.) SAC 2010. LNCS, vol. 6544, pp. 302–319. Springer, Heidelberg (2011)
41. Naor, M., Yung, M.: Universal one-way hash functions and their cryptographic applications. In: 21st ACM STOC, pp. 33–43. ACM Press, May 1989
42. Naor, M., Yung, M.: Public-key cryptosystems provably secure against chosen ciphertext attacks. In: 22nd ACM STOC, pp. 427–437. ACM Press, May 1990
43. Rompel, J.: One-way functions are necessary and sufficient for secure signatures. In: 22nd ACM STOC, pp. 387–394. ACM Press, May 1990
44. Schäge, S.: Tight proofs for signature schemes without random oracles. In: Paterson, K.G. (ed.) EUROCRYPT 2011. LNCS, vol. 6632, pp. 189–206. Springer, Heidelberg (2011)
45. Waters, B.: Efficient identity-based encryption without random oracles. In: Cramer, R. (ed.) EUROCRYPT 2005. LNCS, vol. 3494, pp. 114–127. Springer, Heidelberg (2005)

Password-Based Authentication

Two-Server Password-Authenticated Secret Sharing UC-Secure Against Transient Corruptions

Jan Camenisch[1]([✉]), Robert R. Enderlein[1,2], and Gregory Neven[1]

[1] IBM Research – Zurich, Säumerstrasse 4, 8803 Rüschlikon, Switzerland
jca@zurich.ibm.com
[2] Department of Computer Science, ETH Zürich, 8092 Zürich, Switzerland

Abstract. Protecting user data entails providing authenticated users access to their data. The most prevalent and probably also the most feasible approach to the latter is by username and password. With password breaches through server compromise now reaching billions of affected passwords, distributing the password files and user data over multiple servers is not just a good idea, it is a dearly needed solution to a topical problem. Threshold password-authenticated secret sharing (TPASS) protocols enable users to share secret data among a set of servers so that they can later recover that data using a single password. No coalition of servers up to a certain threshold can learn anything about the data or perform an offline dictionary attack on the password. Several TPASS protocols have appeared in the literature and one is even available commercially. Although designed to tolerate server corruptions, unfortunately none of these protocols provide details, let alone security proofs, about how to proceed when a compromise actually occurs. Indeed, they consider static corruptions only, which for instance does not model real-world adaptive attacks by hackers. We provide the first TPASS protocol that is provably secure against adaptive server corruptions. Moreover, our protocol contains an efficient recovery procedure allowing one to re-initialize servers to recover from corruption. We prove our protocol secure in the universal-composability model where servers can be corrupted adaptively at any time; the users' passwords and secrets remain safe as long as both servers are not corrupted at the same time. Our protocol does not require random oracles but does assume that servers have certified public keys.

Keywords: Universal composability · Threshold cryptography · Passwords · Transient corruptions

1 Introduction

Properly protecting our digital assets still is a major challenge today. Because of their convenience, we protect access to our data almost exclusively by passwords, despite their inherent weaknesses. Indeed, not a month goes by without the announcement of another major password breach in the press. In 2013, hundreds of millions of passwords were stolen through server compromises, including massive breaches at Adobe, Evernote, LivingSocial, and Cupid Media. In

© International Association for Cryptologic Research 2015
J. Katz (Ed.): PKC 2015, LNCS 9020, pp. 283–307, 2015.
DOI: 10.1007/978-3-662-46447-2_13

August 2014, more than one billion passwords from more than 400,000 websites were reported stolen by a single crime ring. Barring some technical blunders on the part of Adobe, most of these passwords were properly salted and hashed. But even the theft of password hashes is detrimental to the security of a system. Indeed, the combination of weak human-memorizable passwords (NIST estimates sixteen-character passwords to contain only 30 bits of entropy [5]) and the blazing efficiency of brute-force dictionary attacks (currently testing up to 350 billion guesses per second on a rig of 25 GPUs [20]) mean that any password of which a hash was leaked should be considered cracked.

Stronger password hash functions [32] only give a linear security improvement, in the sense that the required effort from the attacker increases at most with the same factor as the honest server is willing to spend on password verification. Since computing password hashes is the attacker's core business, but only a marginal activity to a respectable web server, the former probably has the better hardware and software for the job.

A much better approach to password-based authentication, first suggested by Ford and Kaliski [19], is to distribute the capability to test passwords over multiple servers. The idea is that no single server by itself stores enough information to allow it to test whether a password is correct and therefore to allow an attacker to mount an offline dictionary attack after having stolen the information. Rather, each server stores an information-theoretic share of the password and engages in a cryptographic protocol with the user and the other servers to test password correctness. As long as less than a certain threshold of servers are compromised, the password and the stored data remain secure.

Building on this approach, several threshold password-authenticated key exchange (TPAKE) protocols have since appeared in the literature [4,16,19,24–26,28,34], where, if the password is correct, the user shares a different secret key with each of the servers after the protocol. Finally addressing the problem of protecting user data, threshold password-authenticated secret sharing (TPASS) protocols [1,9,10,25] combine data protection and user authentication into a single protocol. They enable the password-authenticated user to reconstruct a strong secret, which can then be used for further cryptographic purposes, e.g., decrypting encrypted data stored in the cloud. An implementation of the protocol by Brainard et al. [4] is commercially available as EMC's *RSA Distributed Credential Protection* (DCP) [17].

Unfortunately, none of the protocols proposed to date provide a satisfying level of security. Indeed, for protocols that are meant to resist server compromise, the research papers are surprisingly silent about what needs to be done when a server actually gets corrupted and how to recover from such an event. The work by Di Raimondo and Gennaro [16] is the only one to mention the possibility to extend their protocol to provide proactive security by refreshing the shares between time periods; unfortunately, no details are provided. The RSA DCP product description [17] mentions a re-randomization feature that "can happen proactively on an automatic schedule or reactively, making information taken from one server useless in the event of a detected breach." This feature is not described in any of the underlying research papers [4, 34], however, and neither is a security proof known. Taking only protocols with provable security guarantees into account, the existing ones can protect against servers that are malicious from the beginning, but do not offer any guarantees against adaptive corruptions. The latter is a much more realistic setting, modelling for instance servers getting compromised by malicious hackers. This state of affairs is rather troubling, given that the main threats to password security today, and arguably, the whole *raison d'être* of TPAKE/TPASS schemes, come from the latter type of attacks.

One would hope to be able to strengthen existing protocols with ideas from proactive secret sharing [21] to obtain security against adaptive corruptions, but this task is not straightforward and so far neither the resulting protocol details nor the envisaged security properties have ever been spelled out. Indeed, designing cryptographic protocols secure against adaptive corruptions is much more difficult than against static corruptions. One difficulty thereby is that in the security proof the simulator must generate network traffic for honest parties *without* knowing their inputs, but, once the party is corrupted, must be able to produce realistic state information that is consistent with the now revealed actual inputs as well as the previously simulated network traffic. Generic multiparty computation protocols secure against adaptive corruption can be applied, but these are too inefficient. In fact, evaluating a single multiplication gate in the most efficient two-party computation protocol secure against adaptive corruptions [7] is more than three times slower than a full execution of the dedicated protocol we present here.

Our Contributions. We provide the first threshold password-authenticated secret sharing protocol that is provably secure against *adaptive* corruptions, assuming data can be securely erased, which in this setting is a standard and also realistic assumption. Our protocol is a two-server protocol in the public-key setting, meaning that servers have trusted public keys, but users do not. We do not require random oracles. We also describe a *recovery procedure* that servers can execute to recover from corruption and to renew their keys assuming a trusted backup is available. The security of the password and the stored secret is preserved as long as both servers are never corrupted simultaneously.

We prove our protocol secure in the universal composability (UC) framework [11, 12]. The very relevant advantages of composable security notions for the particular case of password-based protocols have been argued before [10, 13]; we briefly summarize them here. In composable notions, the passwords for honest users, as well as their password attempts, are provided by the environment. Passwords and password attempts can therefore be distributed arbitrarily and even dependently, reflecting real users who may choose the same or similar passwords for different accounts. It also correctly models typos made by honest users when entering their passwords: all property-based notions in the literature limit the adversary to seeing transcripts of honest users authenticating with their correct password, so in principle security breaks down as soon as a user mistypes the password. Finally, composable definitions absorb the inherent polynomial success probability of the adversary into the functionality. Thus, security is retained when the protocol is composed with other protocols, in particular, protocols that use the stored secret as a key. In contrast, composition of property-based notions with non-negligible success probabilities is problematic because the adversary's advantage may be inflated. Also, strictly speaking, the security provided by property-based notions is guaranteed only if a protocol is used in isolation.

Our construction uses the same basic approach as the TPASS protocols of Brainard et al. [4] and Camenisch et al. [10]. During the setup phase, the user generates shares of his key and password and sends them to the servers (together with some commitments that will later be used in the retrieve phase). During the retrieve phase, the servers run a subprotocol with the user to verify the latter's password attempt using the commitments and shares obtained during setup. If the verification succeeds, the servers send the shares of the key back to the user, who can then reconstruct the key. Furthermore, the correctness of all values exchanged is enforced by zero-knowledge proofs. Like the recent work of Camenisch et al. [9], we do not require the user to share the password during the retrieve phase but run a dedicated protocol to verify whether the provided password equals the priorly shared one. This offers additional protection for the user's password in case he mistakenly tries to recover his secret from servers different from the ones he initially shared his secret with. During setup, the user can be expected to carefully choose his servers, but retrieval happens more frequently and possibly from different devices, leaving more room for error.

The novelty of our protocol lies in how we transform the basic approach into an efficient protocol secure against an adaptive adversary. The crux here is that parties should never be committed to their inputs but at the same time must prove that they perform their computation correctly. We believe that the techniques we use in our protocol to achieve this are of independent interest when building other protocols that are UC-secure against adaptive corruptions. First, instead of using (binding) encryptions to transmit integers between parties, we use a variant of Beaver and Haber's non-committing encryption based on one-time pads (OTP) [3]: the sender first commits to a value with a mixed trapdoor commitment scheme [7] and then encrypts both the value and the opening with the OTP. This enables the recipient to later prove statements about the encrypted value. Second, our three-party password-checking protocol achieves efficiency by transforming commitments with shared opening information into an Elgamal-like encryption of the same value under a shared secret key. To be able to simulate the servers' state if they get corrupted during the protocol execution, each pair of parties needs to temporarily re-encrypt the ciphertext with a key shared between them.

Finally, we note that our protocol is well within reach of a practical implementation: users and servers have to perform a few hundred exponentiations each, which translates to an overall computation time of less than 0.1 seconds per party.

2   Our Ideal Functionality $\mathcal{F}_{2\text{pass}}$

We now describe on a high level our ideal functionality $\mathcal{F}_{2\text{pass}}$ for two-server password-authenticated secret sharing, secure against transient corruptions.

$\mathcal{F}_{2pass}$ processes the instructions as follows. $\mathcal{F}_{2pass}$ accepts inputs and messages only for a specific sid. It further checks that the sid has the correct format. Whenever $\mathcal{F}_{2pass}$ receives an input from a party it will eventually send a message to $\mathcal{A}$ containing the identity of the party, the type of input, sid, qid, and—if applicable—sends out delayed messages. [a]

Setup: The user inputs $\langle \text{Setup}, sid, qid = \text{"Setup"}, p, k \rangle$ to $\mathcal{F}_{2pass}$ and the two servers each input[b] $\langle \text{ReadySetup}, sid, qid = \text{"Setup"} \rangle$ to $\mathcal{F}_{2pass}$. $\mathcal{F}_{2pass}$ then sends a public delayed message $\langle \text{Done}, sid, qid \rangle$ to the user and each of the two servers.

Retrieve: To start, the user inputs $\langle \text{Retrieve}, sid, qid, a \rangle$ to $\mathcal{F}_{2pass}$, and the two servers each input $\langle \text{ReadyRetrieve}, sid, qid \rangle$ to $\mathcal{F}_{2pass}$. $\mathcal{F}_{2pass}$ waits for a message $\langle \text{Lock}, sid, qid \rangle$ from $\mathcal{A}$, and then replies whether the user's password attempt was correct by sending $\langle \text{Lock}, sid, qid, b \rangle$ to $\mathcal{A}$—where $b = 1$ if $a = p$ and $b = 0$ otherwise. $\mathcal{F}_{2pass}$ then sends a public delayed message $\langle \text{Delivered}, sid, qid, b \rangle$ to the two servers, and a private delayed message $\langle \text{Deliver}, sid, qid, k' \rangle$ to the user, where $k' = k$ if $a = p$, and $k' = \varepsilon$ otherwise.

Corrupt: When a party becomes corrupt, the party's ideal peer will input $\langle \text{Corrupt}, sid \rangle$ to $\mathcal{F}_{2pass}$. Recall that $\mathcal{A}$ thereafter obtains control of the corrupted party's input to and output from $\mathcal{F}_{2pass}$. $\mathcal{A}$ may prevent a subsequent Refresh query from succeeding in case the server later recovers from corruption—in a real protocol, $\mathcal{A}$ may tamper with the server's internal state. If both servers are corrupted at the same time (or corrupted in sequence with no Refresh query in between), $\mathcal{F}_{2pass}$ will send (k, p) to $\mathcal{A}$ and allow $\mathcal{A}$ to provide arbitrary replacement values. That is, $\mathcal{A}$ can force $\mathcal{F}_{2pass}$ to return arbitrary values to the user if the latter interacts with two corrupted servers in a Retrieve query.

Recover: When a party recovers from corruption, the party's ideal peer will input $\langle \text{Recover}, sid \rangle$ to $\mathcal{F}_{2pass}$. $\mathcal{F}_{2pass}$ then stops accepting input and messages for all currently running Setup and Retrieve queries, and will not accept any further Setup and Retrieve queries until a Refresh query suceeds.

Refresh: To start a Refresh query, each server inputs $\langle \text{Refresh}, sid, qid \rangle$ to $\mathcal{F}_{2pass}$. While this query is in progress, no further Setup, Retrieve, and Refresh queries are accepted, and currently running queries are dropped. Once it has received a message from both servers, $\mathcal{F}_{2pass}$ sends $\langle \text{RefreshDone}, sid, qid \rangle$ as public delayed messages to the two servers. $\mathcal{F}_{2pass}$ then resumes accepting new queries. Note that while a server was corrupted, $\mathcal{A}$ might have prevented it from completing this Refresh query.

Hijack: Just after a user provided its first input to $\mathcal{F}_{2pass}$ in a Setup or Retrieve query and before $\mathcal{A}$ sends anything to $\mathcal{F}_{2pass}$ for the same query, $\mathcal{A}$ has the option of stealing the id of the query by sending a $\langle \text{HijackSetup}, sid, qid, p, k \rangle$ or $\langle \text{HijackRetrieve}, sid, qid, a \rangle$ message, respectively, to $\mathcal{F}_{2pass}$. In that case, $\mathcal{F}_{2pass}$ ignores the user's first message and runs the query with $\mathcal{A}$ instead of the user, with the qid chosen by the user but input—(p, k) or a—provided by $\mathcal{A}$.

---

[a] Messages from an ideal functionality to a party are direct outputs, unless they are specified to be delayed outputs. In the latter case, $\mathcal{F}_{2pass}$ notifies $\mathcal{A}$ it wishes to send the message and waits for a confirmation by $\mathcal{A}$ before actually sending out the message. A public delayed output means that $\mathcal{A}$ learns the message; a private message means that $\mathcal{A}$ will learn only the type of the message and the recipient.

[b] The GNUC coventions forbid that $\mathcal{F}_{2pass}$ sends a message to the servers at this point, as the servers might not yet exist.

Fig. 1. High-level definition of $\mathcal{F}_{2pass}$. See the text for explanations, and see the full version [6] for the full formalization.

We provide the formal definition of $\mathcal{F}_{2pass}$ in the GNUC variant [22] of the UC framework [11] in the full version [6]. $\mathcal{F}_{2pass}$ is reminiscent of similar functionalities by Camenisch et al. [9,10], the main differences being our modifications to handle transient corruptions. We compare the ideal functionalities in the full version [6].

The functionality $\mathcal{F}_{2pass}$ involves two servers, $\mathcal{P}$ and $\mathcal{Q}$, and a plurality of users. We chose to define $\mathcal{F}_{2pass}$ for a single user account, specified by the session id sid. Multiple accounts can be realized by multiple instances of $\mathcal{F}_{2pass}$ or with a multi-session realization of $\mathcal{F}_{2pass}$. The session identifier sid consists of $(pid_\mathcal{P}, pid_\mathcal{Q}, (\mathbb{G}, q, g), uacc, ssid)$, i.e., the identity of the two servers, the description of a group of prime order q with generator g, the name of the user account $uacc$ (any string), and an arbitrary suffix $ssid$. Only the parties with identities $pid_\mathcal{P}$ and $pid_\mathcal{Q}$ can provide input in the role of $\mathcal{P}$ and $\mathcal{Q}$, respectively, to $\mathcal{F}_{2pass}$. When starting a fresh query, any party can provide input in the role of a user to $\mathcal{F}_{2pass}$; for subsequent inputs in that query, $\mathcal{F}_{2pass}$ ensures it comes from the same party; additionally, $\mathcal{F}_{2pass}$ does not disclose the identity of the user to the servers.

$\mathcal{F}_{2pass}[sid]$ reacts to a set of instructions, each requiring the parties to send multiple inputs to $\mathcal{F}_{2pass}$ in a specific order. The main instructions are Setup, Retrieve, and Refresh. Additionally $\mathcal{F}_{2pass}$ reacts to instructions modelling dishonest behavior, namely Corrupt, Recover, and Hijack. $\mathcal{F}_{2pass}$ may process multiple queries (instances of instructions) concurrently. A query identifier qid is used to distinguish between separate executions of the main instructions. We now provide a summary of the instructions. We refer to Figure 1 for a high-level definition of $\mathcal{F}_{2pass}$ and to the full version [6] for the full formalization.

With the *Setup* instruction, a user sets up the user account by submitting a key k and a password p to $\mathcal{F}_{2pass}$ for storage, protected under the password. This instruction can be run only once, which we enforce by fixing qid to "Setup". With the *Retrieve* instruction, any user can then retrieve that k provided her submitted password attempt a is correct, i.e., $a = p$, and the servers are willing to participate in this query. Giving the server the choice to refuse to participate in a query is important to counter online password guessing attacks. $\mathcal{F}_{2pass}$ allows for the adaptive corruption of users and servers with the *Corrupt* instruction, and for recovery from corruption of servers at any time with the *Recover* instruction. Servers should run the *Refresh* instruction whenever they recover from corruption or at regular intervals; in the real protocol, the two servers re-randomize their state in this instruction and thereby clear the residual knowledge $\mathcal{A}$ might have. If both servers are corrupted at the same time or sequentially with no Refresh in between, the adversary $\mathcal{A}$ will learn the current key and password (k, p) and is allowed to set them to different values. Finally, recall that in our realization of $\mathcal{F}_{2pass}$, the first message from the user to the servers is not authenticated. $\mathcal{A}$ can therefore learn the qid from that message, drop the message, and send his own message to the servers with that qid. We model this attack in $\mathcal{F}_{2pass}$ with the *Hijack* instruction. Servers will not notice this attack, but the user will conclude his query failed.

Our $\mathcal{F}_{2\mathrm{pass}}$ functionality gives the following security guarantees: k and p are protected from $\mathcal{A}$ as long as at least one server is honest and no corrupt user is able to correctly guess the password. Furthermore, if at least one server is honest, no offline password guessing attacks are possible. Honest servers can limit online guessing attacks by limiting Retrieve queries after too many failed attempts. Finally, an honest user's password attempt a remains hidden even if a Retrieve query is directed at two corrupt servers.

3 Preliminaries

In this section, we introduce the notation used throughout this paper, give the ideal functionalities and cryptographic building blocks we use as subroutines in our construction, and provide a refresher on corruption models in the UC framework.

3.1 Notation

Let $\eta \geq 80$ be the security parameter. Let ε denote the empty string. If $\mathbb{S}$ is a set, then $s \xleftarrow{\$} \mathbb{S}$ means we set s to a random element of that set. If A is a probabilistic polynomial-time (PPT) algorithm, then $y \xleftarrow{\$} \mathrm{A}(x)$ means we assign y to the output of $\mathrm{A}(x)$ when run with fresh random coins on input x. If s is a bitstring, then by $|s|$ we denote the length of s. If $\mathcal{U}$ and $\mathcal{P}$ are parties, and Sub is a two-party protocol, then by $(out_{\mathcal{U}}; out_{\mathcal{P}}) \xleftarrow{\$} \langle \mathcal{U}.\mathrm{Sub}(in_{\mathcal{U}}), \mathcal{P}.\mathrm{Sub}(in_{\mathcal{P}}) \rangle (in_{\mathcal{U}\mathcal{P}})$ we denote the simultaneous execution of the protocol by the two parties, on common input $in_{\mathcal{U}\mathcal{P}}$, with $\mathcal{U}$'s additional private input $in_{\mathcal{U}}$, with $\mathcal{P}$'s additional private input $in_{\mathcal{P}}$, and where $\mathcal{U}$'s output is $out_{\mathcal{U}}$ and $\mathcal{P}$'s output is $out_{\mathcal{P}}$. We use an analogue notation for three-party protocols.

We use the following arrow-notation: $\xrightarrow{\quad publicData \quad}$ to denote the transmission of public data over a channel that the two parties have already established between themselves (we discuss how such a channel is established in more detail later). When we write ($\circledcirc : dataToErase$) next to such an arrow, we mean that the value $dataToErase$ is securely erased before the public data is transmitted. When we write $[secretData]_\blacksquare$ on such an arrow, we mean that $secretData$ is sent in a non-committing encrypted form. All these transmissions must be secure against adaptive corruptions in the erasure model.

3.2 Ideal Functionalities that we Use as Subroutines

We now describe the ideal functionalities we use as subroutines in our construction. These are authenticated channels ($\mathcal{F}_{\mathrm{ac}}$), one-side-authenticated channels ($\mathcal{F}_{\mathrm{osac}}$), zero-knowledge proofs of existence ($\mathcal{F}_{\mathrm{gzk}}$), and common reference strings ($\mathcal{F}_{\mathrm{crs}}^D$).

Authenticated Channels. Let $\mathcal{F}_{\mathrm{ac}}[sid]$ be a single-use authenticated channel [22]. In our construction, we allow only servers to communicate among themselves using $\mathcal{F}_{\mathrm{ac}}[sid]$. We recall the formal definition in the full version [6].

One-Side-Authenticated Channels. Let $\mathcal{F}_{osac}[sid]$ be a multi-use channel where only one party, the server, authenticates himself towards the other party, the client. The server has the guarantee that in a given session all messages come from the same client. Note that the first message from the client to the server is not authenticated and can be modified (*hijacked*) by the adversary—the original client will be excluded from the rest of the interaction. We provide a formal definition in the full version [6]. We also refer to the work of Barak et al. [2] for a formal treatment of communication without or with partial authentication. A realization of $\mathcal{F}_{osac}[sid]$ is out of scope, but not hard to construct.

Zero-Knowledge Proofs of Knowledge and Existence. Let $\mathcal{F}_{gzk}[sid]$ be the zero-knowledge functionality supporting proofs of existence [8], also called "gullible" zero-knowledge proofs. These proofs of existence are cheaper than the corresponding proofs of knowledge, but they impose limitations on the simulator $\mathcal{S}$ in the security proof. In a realization of $\mathcal{F}_{gzk}$, the prover reveals the statement to be proven only in the *last* message. This is crucial for our construction, as this allows the prover to *erase* ($\circledast$) witnesses and other data before disclosing the statement to be proven. We recall the formal definition [8] in the full version [6].

Notation. When specifying the predicate to be proven, we use a combination of the Camenisch-Stadler notation [15] and the notation introduced by Camenisch, Krenn, and Shoup [8]; for example: $\mathcal{F}_{gzk}[sid]\{(\lambda\alpha, \beta \; ; \; \exists\gamma) : y = g^\gamma \wedge z = g^\alpha k^\beta h^\gamma\}$ is used for proving the existence of the discrete logarithm to the base g, and of a representation of z to the bases g, k, and h such that the h-part of this representation is equal to the discrete logarithm of y to the base g. Furthermore, knowledge of the g-part and the k-part of the representation is proven. Variables quantified by λ (knowledge) can be extracted by the simulator $\mathcal{S}$ in the security proof, while variables quantified by $\exists$ (existence) cannot.

By writing a proof on an arrow: $\xrightarrow{\quad \pi_0 \quad}$ we denote the performance of such an interactive zero-knowledge proof protocol secure against adaptive corruptions with erasures. If additional public or secret data is written on the arrow, or data to be erased besides the arrow, then this data is transmitted with, or erased before, respectively, the last message of the proof protocol (cf. §3.1). The predicate of the proof may depend on that data.

Proofs with two verifiers. Let $\mathcal{F}_{gzk}^{2v}[sid]$ be the three-party ideal functionality to denote the parallel execution of two independent zero-knowledge proofs with the same prover and same specification, but two different verifiers. The prover waits for a reply from both verifiers before sending out the last message of each proof. This gives the prover the opportunity to erase the same witnesses in both proofs. We provide a formal definition in the full version [6]. The proof that the special composition theorem by Camenisch, Krenn, and Shoup [8] holds also for $\mathcal{F}_{gzk}^{2v}$ is very similar to the proof that it holds for $\mathcal{F}_{gzk}$ and is omitted.

Common Reference String. Let $\mathcal{F}_{crs}^D[sid]$ be a common reference string (CRS) functionality, which provides a CRS distributed according to some distribution D. We make use of two distributions in this paper: $\mathcal{F}_{crs}^{G^3}$ provides a uniform CRS over $\mathbb{G}^3$ and $\mathcal{F}_{crs}^{gzk}$ provides a CRS as required by Camenisch et al.'s protocol π, the intended realization of $\mathcal{F}_{gzk}$ [8]. We provide a formal definition in the full version [6].

3.3 Cryptographic Building Blocks of Our Construction

Our construction makes use of two cryptographic building blocks: a CCA2-secure encryption scheme, and a homomorphic mixed trapdoor commitment scheme.

CCA2-Secure Encryption. We denote the key generation function $(pk, sk, kgr) \xleftarrow{\$} \mathrm{Gen}(1^\eta)$, where kgr is the randomness that was used to generate the key pair. We denote the encryption function $(e, er) \xleftarrow{\$} \mathrm{Enc}(pk, pt, l)$ that takes as input a public key pk, a plaintext $pt \in \{0,1\}^*$, and a label $l \in \{0,1\}^*$; and outputs the ciphertext e and the randomness er used to encrypt. The corresponding decryption function $pt \xleftarrow{\$} \mathrm{Dec}(sk, e, l)$ takes as input the secret key sk, the ciphertext e, and the label l. We require the scheme to be secure against adaptive chosen ciphertext attacks [33]. An example of such an encryption scheme is Cramer-Shoup encryption in a hybrid setting over a group $\mathbb{G}$ of prime order q [15, §5.2]. To accommodate the label l in the encryption function, it must be added as an additional input to the hash function used during encryption.

Homomorphic Mixed Trapdoor (HMT) Commitment. An HMT commitment scheme [7] is a computationally binding equivocable homomorphic commitment scheme, constructed from Pedersen commitments [31]. It works well with proofs of *existence* using $\mathcal{F}_{gzk}$, resulting in an efficiency gain in our protocol compared to a construction using plain Pedersen commitments, which would have to use proofs of *knowledge*. We provide a high-level overview of HMT commitments here and recall the definition of HMT commitments in the full version [6].

HMT commitments operate in a group $\mathbb{G}$ of prime order q (with generator g) where the decision Diffie-Hellman (DDH) problem is hard. They implicitly use a CRS (h, y, w) provided by $\mathcal{F}_{crs}^{\mathbb{G}^3}$. By $(c, o) \xleftarrow{\$} \mathrm{Com}(s)$ we denote the function that takes as input a value $s \in \mathbb{Z}_q$ to be committed, and outputs a commitment c and an opening $o \in \mathbb{Z}_q$ to the commitment. We will also use the notation $c \leftarrow \mathrm{Com}(s, o)$, where the opening is chosen outside the function. The commitments are homomorphic with respect to addition over $\mathbb{Z}_q$: i.e., $c*c' = \mathrm{Com}(s+s', o+o')$. With a trapdoor to the CRS it is possible to efficiently equivocate commitments. Finally, we note that it is possible to extract a Pedersen commitment pc from a commitment c, we denote this operation by $pc := y^s h^o \leftarrow \mathrm{PedC}(c)$.

3.4 Corruption in the UC Model

The UC model defines several types of party corruptions, the most important being *static*, *adaptive*, and *transient* corruptions. In protocols secure against static party corruptions, parties are either honest or corrupt from the start of the protocol and do not change their corruption status. In protocols secure against adaptive corruptions, parties can become corrupted at any time; once corrupted, they remain so for the rest of the protocol. Finally, transient corruptions [11] are similar to the adaptive corruptions, but parties can *recover* from corruption and regain their security.

In the following we discuss the modelling of transient corruptions in the UC framework, how one can use ideal functionalities designed for adaptive corruptions in a protocol designed for transient corruptions, and finally we discuss a particular problem that appears in protocols secure against adaptive or transient corruptions: the selective decommitment problem.

Modelling Transient Corruptions in Real/Hybrid Protocols. We now recall how corruption and recovery is modelled in real/hybrid protocols.

Corruption of a party. When a party becomes corrupted, all of its internal state excluding the parts that were explicitly erased ($\oslash$) is handed over to the adversary $\mathcal{A}$. $\mathcal{A}$ then controls that party. The ideal functionalities that were used as subroutines are notified of the corruption, and may provide additional information or capabilities to $\mathcal{A}$. Note that $\mathcal{A}$ can always choose to let a corrupted party follow the honest protocol, but passively monitor the party's internal state.

Recovery from corruption. $\mathcal{A}$ may cede control from a party. When doing that, $\mathcal{A}$ may specify a new internal state for the party. We then say that the party formally recovered. In real life, a party might know it recovered if it detected a breach and has restored from backup.

In most protocols however, formal recovery is not enough: the adversary still knows parts of the internal state of the formally recovered party. To allow the party to effectively recover its security, it must take additional steps, e.g., notify its subroutines (and stop using the subroutines that cannot handle recovery) and run a protocol-specific *Refresh* instruction. The party might thereby drop all currently running queries.

A party initiates a Refresh query to modify its internal state so that firstly it is synchronized with the other protocol participants, and so that secondly $\mathcal{A}$'s knowledge of the old state does not interfere with security of the new state. Parties should initiate a Refresh query when they formally recover from corruption. (If parties cannot detect formal recovery, they should run Refresh periodically.) The Refresh query might fail if the state of the party is inconsistent with that of the others. The party might also not necessarily recover its security even after succesful completion of the query, e.g., because all other participants are corrupted. Note that the security of a party is fully restored (if at all) only after Refresh completes: in the grey zone bewteen formal recovery and completion of Refresh, the party must not run any queries other than Refresh.

Using Ideal Functionalities Designed for the Adaptive type in a Transient-Secure Hybrid Protocol. Protocols secure against transient corruptions may use ideal functionalities as subroutines that were designed to handle adaptive corruptions, e.g., $\mathcal{F}_{\mathrm{ac}}$, $\mathcal{F}_{\mathrm{osac}}$, $\mathcal{F}_{\mathrm{gzk}}$, and $\mathcal{F}_{\mathrm{gzk}}^{\mathrm{2v}}$: upon formal recovery, the party must stop using all instances of these ideal functionalities. Thereby, it has to abort all currently running queries. Thereafter, it has to use fresh instances of these ideal functionalities for running the Refresh query, and all subsequent queries.

The Selective Decommitment Problem. Hofheinz demonstrated that it is impossible to prove any protocol secure against adaptive corruptions (and thus, against transient corruptions) that uses perfectly binding commitments or (binding) encryptions to commit to or to encrypt the parties' input, respectively [23]. Let us expand on this. For example, assume that in a protocol a user $\mathcal{U}$ with an input i must send out a binding commitment c or an encryption e depending on i, e.g., $(c, o) = \mathrm{Com}(i)$ or $(e, er) = \mathrm{Enc}(pk, i, l)$. The simulator $\mathcal{S}$ in the security proof must be able to simulate the honest $\mathcal{U}$ without knowing her input i, i.e., $\mathcal{S}$ must send c or e to the adversary $\mathcal{A}$, containing some value that is most likely different from i. If $\mathcal{U}$ then gets corrupted, $\mathcal{S}$ must produce an internal state for $\mathcal{U}$, namely the opening o or the randomness er used to encrypt and—if applicable—the secret key sk, that is consistent with both her real input i and the values c or e already sent out to the adversary. However, due to the binding nature of the commitment and encryption, and unless it could predict i, $\mathcal{S}$ cannot find an internal state for $\mathcal{U}$ consistent with these values and therefore the security proof will not go through.

We explain how we avoid the selective decommitment problem in our protocol in Section 4.2.

4 Our Construction of TPASS Secure against Transient Corruptions

In this section we present our realization $\Pi_{2\mathrm{pass}}$ of the $\mathcal{F}_{2\mathrm{pass}}$ ideal functionality in the $(\mathcal{F}_{\mathrm{crs}}^{\mathbb{G}^3}, \mathcal{F}_{\mathrm{osac}}, \mathcal{F}_{\mathrm{ac}}, \mathcal{F}_{\mathrm{gzk}}, \mathcal{F}_{\mathrm{gzk}}^{2\mathrm{v}})$-hybrid setting. Our $\Pi_{2\mathrm{pass}}$ protocol further uses a CCA2-secure cryptosystem and an HMT commitment scheme. As for $\mathcal{F}_{2\mathrm{pass}}$, we describe $\Pi_{2\mathrm{pass}}$ for a single user account only, i.e., each instance of $\Pi_{2\mathrm{pass}}$ uses a fixed sid.

We start this section by discussing the high-level ideas of our construction. We then elaborate on the novel core ideas in our construction, before providing the detailed construction, and we comment on a multi-session version of $\Pi_{2\mathrm{pass}}$ that uses a constant size CRS. We finish by providing an estimate of the computational and communication complexity of $\Pi_{2\mathrm{pass}}$ in both the standard and random oracle models, and compare it with the complexity of related work.

4.1 High Level Approach of Our TPASS Protocol

Our protocol $\Pi_{2\mathrm{pass}}$ implements the Setup, Retrieve, and Refresh instructions of $\mathcal{F}_{2\mathrm{pass}}$. An adversary can hijack a Setup or Retrieve query through the $\mathcal{F}_{\mathrm{osac}}$ subroutine. The other instructions of $\mathcal{F}_{2\mathrm{pass}}$ are purely conceptual for the security proof. At a high level, the realizations of the Setup and Retrieve instructions of $\Pi_{2\mathrm{pass}}$ are reminiscent of the schemes by Camenisch et al. [9,10] and Brainard et al. [4]: during Setup, the user generates shares of his key and password and sends them to the servers (together with some commitments that will later be used in Retrieve). During Retrieve, the servers run a subprotocol with the user to verify the latter's password attempt using the commitments and shares obtained in Setup. If the verification succeeds, the servers send the shares of the key back to the user, who can then reconstruct the key. Furthermore, the correctness of all values exchanged is enforced by zero-knowledge proofs. To deal with transient corruptions, our $\Pi_{2\text{pass}}$ needs to implement the Refresh instruction, which allows the servers to re-randomize their shares of the key and password and thereby to re-secure their states when one of them is recovering from corruption. Naturally, prior schemes do not have a Refresh instruction as they do not provide security against transient corruptions.

The novelties of our construction arise from how we turn this basic approach into a scheme that is secure against adaptive and transient corruptions and at the same time efficient enough to be considered for practical deployment.

4.2   Key Ideas of Our TPASS Protocol

We now present the key ideas that make it possible for our TPASS protocol to be secure against transient corruptions. These ideas are novel and of independent interest.

Three-Party Computation for Determining Equality to Zero. The core subprotocol ChkPwd is depicted in Figure 2. To check if the password attempt a input by the user during a Retrieve query matches the stored password $p = p_{\mathcal{P}} + p_{\mathcal{Q}}$, the user and the two servers engage in a three-party computation to check if $\delta := p_{\mathcal{P}} + p_{\mathcal{Q}} - a \overset{?}{=} 0$, where $p_{\mathcal{P}}$ and $p_{\mathcal{Q}}$ are the shares stored by the respective servers. For efficiency reasons, it does not make sense to base that protocol on a generic multiparty computation protocol. Indeed, running one Retrieve query in our protocol is more than 3.7 times faster than evaluating a single multiplication gate in the best generic two-party computation protocol that is secure against adaptive corruptions [7] (see the full version [6]).

The first observation is that a commitment in the HMT scheme we use essentially consists of a *pair* of Pedersen commitments. Thus, while all components need to be considered to prove that a commitment is formed correctly, it is often sufficient to consider just one component later when doing computations with them. Now, based on this, a first idea for the desired subprotocol would be as follows. The servers' commitments $cp_{\mathcal{P}}$ and $cp_{\mathcal{Q}}$ to the shares of the password are distributed to all the parties, who then generate a commitment on the sum of the two shares using the homomorphic property of HMT commitments, and extract the first component thereof to obtain a value

$$C := \text{PedC}(cp_{\mathcal{P}} * cp_{\mathcal{Q}}) = y^{p_{\mathcal{P}} + p_{\mathcal{Q}}} h^{op_{\mathcal{P}} + op_{\mathcal{Q}}},$$

where y and h are part of the CRS. That value is an equivocable Pedersen commitment to $p := p_{\mathcal{P}} + p_{\mathcal{Q}}$ with equivocation trapdoor $\log_y h$. Given C, the user subtracts his password attempt a from that commitment:

$$B := Cy^{-a} = y^{\delta} h^{op_{\mathcal{P}} + op_{\mathcal{Q}}}.$$

We now consider the Elgamal "ciphertext" $(A := h^{-1}, B)$, which is an encryption of y^{δ} under the shared secret key $(-op_{\mathcal{P}} - op_{\mathcal{Q}})$ with fixed randomness -1. This ciphertext is then passed from $\mathcal{U}$ to $\mathcal{P}$, from $\mathcal{P}$ to $\mathcal{Q}$, and then from $\mathcal{Q}$ back to $\mathcal{P}$, where at each step, the sender exponentiates that ciphertext by a non-zero random number $r_{\mathcal{U}}$, $r_{\mathcal{P}}$, and $r_{\mathcal{Q}}$, respectively, thereby multiplying the plaintext by that random number. Also, if possible, the sender will partially decrypt the ciphertext by removing $op_{\mathcal{P}}$ or $op_{\mathcal{Q}}$: $\mathcal{U}$ computes

$$(A_u, D_u) := (A^{ru}, B^{ru}) = (h^{-ru}, y^{\delta * ru} h^{(op_P + op_Q)ru})$$

and sends it to $\mathcal{P}$, $\mathcal{P}$ computes

$$(A_P, D_P) := (A_u^{rp}, D_u^{rp} A_P^{op_P}) = (h^{-ru_{rp}}, y^{\delta * ru_{rp}} h^{op_Q ru_{rp}})$$

and sends it to $\mathcal{Q}$, and $\mathcal{Q}$ computes

$$(A_Q, B_Q) := (A_P^{rQ}, D_P^{rQ} A_Q^{op_Q}) = (h^{-ru_{rp}r_Q}, y^{\delta * ru_{rp}r_Q})$$

and sends it to $\mathcal{P}$. If in the end the result B_Q is the neutral element, then $\delta = 0$, and the password was correct.

Unfortunately, this first idea doesn't quite work: if $\delta = 0$, D_u fixes a value for $(op_P + op_Q)$ and D_P fixes a value for op_Q. Thus cp_P and cp_Q, together with D_u and D_P form unequivocable statistically binding commitments to p_P and p_Q. This causes a selective decommitment problem. Our solution is to blind the values D_u and D_P with non-committing random shifts s_{uP}, s_{uQ}, and s_{PQ} as follows, thereby circumventing the problem. $\mathcal{U}$ chooses s_{uP} and s_{uQ}, and sends them to $\mathcal{P}$ and $\mathcal{Q}$, respectively, in a non-committing manner. $\mathcal{U}$ then generates B_u by multiplying D_u with the blinding factor $A_u^{s_{uP} + s_{uQ}}$, i.e.,

$$(A_u, B_u) := (A^{ru}, B^{ru} A_u^{s_{uP} + s_{uQ}}) = (h^{-ru}, y^{\delta * ru} h^{(op_P + op_Q - s_{uP} - s_{uQ})ru})$$

and sends B_u instead of D_u to $\mathcal{P}$. The ciphertext (A_u, B_u) is now encrypted under the shared key $(s_{uP} + s_{uQ} - op_P - op_Q)$. Similarly, $\mathcal{P}$ chooses s_{PQ} and sends it to $\mathcal{Q}$. $\mathcal{P}$ generates B_P like D_P but uses B_u instead of D_u in the formula and multiplies the result by $A_P^{-s_{uP} + s_{PQ}}$, i.e.,

$$(A_P, B_P) := (A_u^{rp}, B_u^{rp} A_P^{op_P - s_{uP} + s_{PQ}}) = (h^{-ru_{rp}}, y^{\delta * ru_{rp}} h^{(op_Q - s_{uQ} - s_{PQ})ru_{rp}})$$

and sends B_P to $\mathcal{Q}$ instead of D_P, i.e., the ciphertext (A_P, B_P) is now encrypted under the shared key $(s_{uQ} + s_{PQ} - op_Q)$. Finally $\mathcal{Q}$ computes B_Q differently by replacing D_P by B_P in the formula and multiplying the result by $A_Q^{-s_{uQ} - s_{PQ}}$, i.e.,

$$(A_Q, B_Q) := (A_P^{rQ}, B_P^{rQ} A_Q^{op_Q - s_{uQ} - s_{PQ}}) = (h^{-ru_{rp}r_Q}, y^{\delta * ru_{rp}r_Q}).$$

At the end of each step, the parties prove to each other in zero-knowledge that they computed their values correctly; whereby the parties use the trick explained in the next paragraph to refer to s_{uP}, s_{uQ}, and s_{PQ} in the proofs. These proofs also allow the simulator to extract a, p_P, p_Q, op_P, op_Q, and $(s_{uP} + s_{PQ})$ in the security proof.

Transmission of Secrets for Later use in Proofs. In the protocol just described, $\mathcal{U}$ must send the value s_{uP} to $\mathcal{P}$ in a non-committing manner and all parties must be able to prove knowledge of that same value in subsequent zero-knowledge proofs. Simply having $\mathcal{U}$ encrypt s_{uP} is not sufficient, because $\mathcal{P}$ can later not prove knowledge of the encrypted s_{uP} in proofs. A similar situation also arises in other parts of our protocol, for example in the Setup instruction when $\mathcal{U}$ must send a share p_P to the password to $\mathcal{P}$ in a non-committing manner.

In a setting that considers only static corruptions, such problems are often solved by requiring $\mathcal{U}$ to send a Pedersen commitment cs_{uP} to s_{uP} to all parties, and to send s_{uP} and the opening os_{uP} to the commitment to $\mathcal{P}$, encrypted under $\mathcal{P}$'s public key. Thus, with cs_{uP}, $\mathcal{P}$ can later prove that it correctly used s_{uP} in its computations.

When dealing with adaptive or transient corruptions, this does not work: the encryption of s_{uP} causes a selective decommitment problem. Instead, we have $\mathcal{U}$ generate an equivocable commitment cs_{uP} to s_{uP} with opening os_{uP}, then

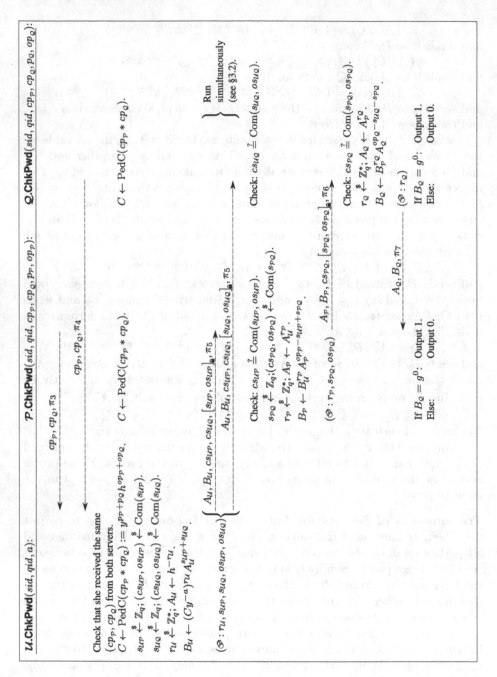

Fig. 2. Subroutine ChkPwd: the servers check if $\mathcal{U}$'s password attempt a is equal to the password $p_\mathcal{P} + p_\mathcal{Q}$. See the next figure for the instantiation of the zero-knowledge proofs.

establish a one-time pad (OTP) with $\mathcal{P}$, and then encrypt both $s_{u\mathcal{P}}$ and $os_{u\mathcal{P}}$ with the OTP. $\mathcal{U}$ then sends the resulting ciphertext to $\mathcal{P}$ in any convenient manner (in this specific example, $\mathcal{U}$ sends it as part of proof protocol π_5 in Figure 2 that actually uses the values $s_{u\mathcal{P}}$, $os_{u\mathcal{P}}$, and $cs_{u\mathcal{P}}$ in some indirect form; in the Setup instruction where she needs to send $p_{\mathcal{P}}$ to $\mathcal{P}$ in a non-committing manner, $\mathcal{U}$ sends the ciphertext to $\mathcal{P}$ directly). Afterwards, $\mathcal{P}$ can refer to $s_{u\mathcal{P}}$ in zero-knowledge proofs by means of $cs_{u\mathcal{P}}$, e.g., $\mathcal{F}_{\mathrm{gzk}}[sid]\{(\exists s_{u\mathcal{P}}, os_{u\mathcal{P}}) : cs_{u\mathcal{P}} = \mathrm{Com}(s_{u\mathcal{P}}, os_{u\mathcal{P}})\}$. This approach will allow $\mathcal{S}$ to equivocate $s_{u\mathcal{P}}$, provided that no extra dependencies on the opening $os_{u\mathcal{P}}$ are introduced in other protocol steps (the first idea of the three-party protocol above describes the problems when such an extra dependency is introduced on $op_{\mathcal{P}}$).

$\pi_3 := \mathcal{F}_{\mathrm{gzk}}[sid, qid, 3]\{(\nexists p_{\mathcal{P}}, op_{\mathcal{P}}) : cp_{\mathcal{P}} = \mathrm{Com}(p_{\mathcal{P}}, op_{\mathcal{P}})\}.$

$\pi_4 := \mathcal{F}_{\mathrm{gzk}}[sid, qid, 4]\{(\nexists p_{\mathcal{Q}}, op_{\mathcal{Q}}) : cp_{\mathcal{Q}} = \mathrm{Com}(p_{\mathcal{Q}}, op_{\mathcal{Q}})\}.$

$\pi_5 := \mathcal{F}_{\mathrm{gzk}}^{2\mathrm{v}}[sid, qid, cp_{\mathcal{P}}, cp_{\mathcal{Q}}, 5]\{(\nexists a, \sigma \; ; \; \exists \rho, \beta) :$

$\qquad h = A_{\mathcal{U}}^{\rho} \wedge C = (B_{\mathcal{U}}^{-1})^{\rho} y^a h^{\sigma} \wedge (cs_{u\mathcal{P}} * cs_{u\mathcal{Q}}) = \mathrm{Com}(\sigma, \beta)$

$\qquad \}$, where $\sigma := s_{u\mathcal{P}} + s_{u\mathcal{Q}}, \rho := -1/r_{\mathcal{U}}$, and $\beta := os_{u\mathcal{P}} + os_{u\mathcal{Q}}.$

$\mathcal{U}$ runs two proofs, one with $\mathcal{P}$ and one with $\mathcal{Q}$, in parallel: she performs the erasures and sends out the last message of both proofs only *after* she received the second message of the proof from both servers (see *Proofs with two verifiers* in §3.2).

$\pi_6 := \mathcal{F}_{\mathrm{gzk}}[sid, qid, cp_{\mathcal{P}}, cp_{\mathcal{Q}}, cs_{u\mathcal{P}}, cs_{u\mathcal{Q}}, A_{\mathcal{U}}, B_{\mathcal{U}}, 6]\{(\exists p_{\mathcal{P}}, op_{\mathcal{P}}, r_{\mathcal{P}}, \sigma, \beta) :$

$\qquad A_{\mathcal{P}} = A_{\mathcal{U}}^{r_{\mathcal{P}}} \wedge A_{\mathcal{P}} \neq g^0 \wedge B_{\mathcal{P}} = B_{\mathcal{U}}^{r_{\mathcal{P}}} A_{\mathcal{P}}^{op_{\mathcal{P}} + \sigma} \wedge$

$\qquad cp_{\mathcal{P}} = \mathrm{Com}(p_{\mathcal{P}}, op_{\mathcal{P}}) \wedge (cs_{\mathcal{P}\mathcal{Q}} * cs_{u\mathcal{P}}^{-1}) = \mathrm{Com}(\sigma, \beta)$

$\qquad \}$, where $\sigma := s_{\mathcal{P}\mathcal{Q}} - s_{u\mathcal{P}}$ and $\beta := os_{\mathcal{P}\mathcal{Q}} - os_{u\mathcal{P}}.$

$\pi_7 := \mathcal{F}_{\mathrm{gzk}}[sid, qid, cs_{\mathcal{P}\mathcal{Q}}, A_{\mathcal{P}}, B_{\mathcal{P}}, 7]\{(\exists p_{\mathcal{Q}}, op_{\mathcal{Q}}, r_{\mathcal{Q}}, \sigma, \beta) :$

$\qquad A_{\mathcal{Q}} = A_{\mathcal{P}}^{r_{\mathcal{Q}}} \wedge A_{\mathcal{Q}} \neq g^0 \wedge B_{\mathcal{Q}} = B_{\mathcal{P}}^{r_{\mathcal{Q}}} A_{\mathcal{Q}}^{op_{\mathcal{Q}} - \sigma} \wedge$

$\qquad cp_{\mathcal{Q}} = \mathrm{Com}(p_{\mathcal{Q}}, op_{\mathcal{Q}}) \wedge (cs_{u\mathcal{Q}} * cs_{\mathcal{P}\mathcal{Q}}) = \mathrm{Com}(\sigma, \beta)$

$\qquad \}$, where $\sigma := s_{u\mathcal{Q}} + s_{\mathcal{P}\mathcal{Q}}$ and $\beta := os_{u\mathcal{Q}} + os_{\mathcal{P}\mathcal{Q}}.$

Fig. 3. Instantiation of zero-knowledge proofs for ChkPwd

4.3   Detailed Construction of $\Pi_{2\mathrm{pass}}$ in the Standard Model (with Erasures)

We now give the full details of the instructions of our protocol and their respective subprotocols. Let us start with five remarks. First, we implicitly assume that all parties query $\mathcal{F}_{\mathrm{crs}}^{\mathsf{G}^3}$ to obtain a CRS (h, y, w) whenever they need it. Second, all commitments Com must be realized with HMT commitments (see §3.3). Using Pedersen commitments instead would require expensive zero-knowledge proofs of *knowledge* in the protocol, thereby massively increasing the computational complexity. Third, we assume that for each query the user establishes a single instance of a one-side-authenticated channel $\mathcal{F}_{osac}[(sid, qid), \mathcal{P}]$ and $\mathcal{F}_{osac}[(sid, qid), \mathcal{Q}]$ with each respective server; all communication denoted by arrows: ---➤, and all communication inside the zero-knowledge functionalities $\mathcal{F}_{gzk}$ and $\mathcal{F}_{gzk}^{2v}$ happen through that instance.[1] The two servers communicate with each other through regular authenticated channels $\mathcal{F}_{ac}[(sid, qid), \mathcal{P}, \mathcal{Q}, ssid]$. Fourth, parties can send data in a non-committing and confidential manner, i.e., secure against adaptive corruptions, by using the secureSend subroutine depicted in Figure 4. We denote such communication by: $[secretData]_{\bullet}$ (cf. §3.1). The parties establish a one-time pad (OTP) with each other, encrypt the data with that OTP, and erase the OTP before sending the ciphertext [3]. Fifth, we implicitly assume that a party aborts a query without output if any check fails.

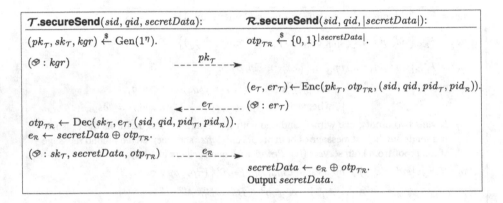

Fig. 4. Subroutine secureSend, the realization of $\underset{\xrightarrow{\hspace{1cm}}}{[secretData]_{\bullet}}$: a party $\mathcal{T}$ (user or server) sends $secretData$ to $\mathcal{R}$ (user or server) in a non-committing encrypted form.

The Setup Instruction. Recall that the goal of the Setup instruction is for a user to set up an account $uacc$ with the two servers $\mathcal{P}$ and $\mathcal{Q}$ and store a key $k \in \mathbb{Z}_q$ protected under a password $p \in \mathbb{Z}_q$ therein. The servers will silenty abort a Setup query if the user account has already been established.

When a user $\mathcal{U}$ receives an input $\langle$Setup, $sid = (pid_{\mathcal{P}}, pid_{\mathcal{Q}}, (\mathbb{G}, q, g), uacc, ssid), qid = $ "Setup"$, p, k \rangle$ from the environment $\mathcal{Z}$, she starts a Setup query. Each of the servers starts a Setup query when he receives an input $\langle$ReadySetup, $sid, qid \rangle$ from $\mathcal{Z}$. As the first step of the Setup query, $\mathcal{U}$ distributes shares of k and p to both servers using the Share subprotocol. In that subprotocol, the user establishes an OTP with each server and encrypts the shares with the respective OTPs in order to circumvent the *selective decommitment problem* [23]. Finally, the servers store their shares as their internal state and send an acknowledgement back to the user. See Figure 5. At the end of the Setup query, each of the three parties outputs $\langle$Done, $sid, qid \rangle$ to $\mathcal{Z}$.

---

[1] Refer to Barak et al. [2] for details about modelling communication with partial authentication in the UC model.

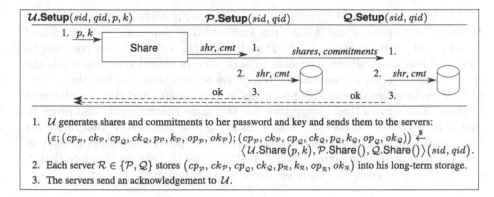

1. $\mathcal{U}$ generates shares and commitments to her password and key and sends them to the servers:
$$(\varepsilon; (cp_\mathcal{P}, ck_\mathcal{P}, cp_\mathcal{Q}, ck_\mathcal{Q}, p_\mathcal{P}, k_\mathcal{P}, op_\mathcal{P}, ok_\mathcal{P}); (cp_\mathcal{P}, ck_\mathcal{P}, cp_\mathcal{Q}, ck_\mathcal{Q}, p_\mathcal{Q}, k_\mathcal{Q}, op_\mathcal{Q}, ok_\mathcal{Q})) \xleftarrow{\$}$$
$$\langle \mathcal{U}.\mathsf{Share}(p,k), \mathcal{P}.\mathsf{Share}(), \mathcal{Q}.\mathsf{Share}() \rangle (sid, qid).$$

2. Each server $\mathcal{R} \in \{\mathcal{P}, \mathcal{Q}\}$ stores $(cp_\mathcal{P}, ck_\mathcal{P}, cp_\mathcal{Q}, ck_\mathcal{Q}, p_\mathcal{R}, k_\mathcal{R}, op_\mathcal{R}, ok_\mathcal{R})$ into his long-term storage.

3. The servers send an acknowledgement to $\mathcal{U}$.

Fig. 5. Setup instruction: $\mathcal{U}$ distributedly stores a key k protected under a password p on two servers $\mathcal{P}$ and $\mathcal{Q}$.

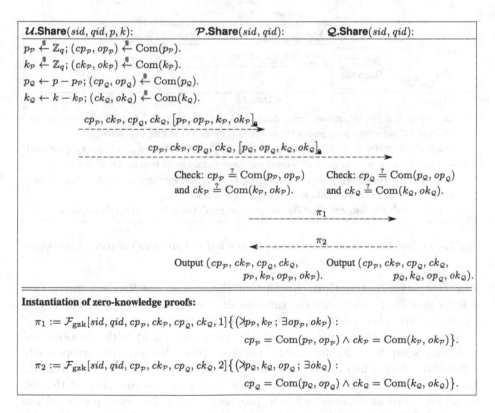

Instantiation of zero-knowledge proofs:

$\pi_1 := \mathcal{F}_{\mathrm{gzk}}[sid, qid, cp_\mathcal{P}, ck_\mathcal{P}, cp_\mathcal{Q}, ck_\mathcal{Q}, 1]\{(\lambda p_\mathcal{P}, k_\mathcal{P} ; \exists op_\mathcal{P}, ok_\mathcal{P}) :$
$$cp_\mathcal{P} = \mathrm{Com}(p_\mathcal{P}, op_\mathcal{P}) \wedge ck_\mathcal{P} = \mathrm{Com}(k_\mathcal{P}, ok_\mathcal{P})\}.$$

$\pi_2 := \mathcal{F}_{\mathrm{gzk}}[sid, qid, cp_\mathcal{P}, ck_\mathcal{P}, cp_\mathcal{Q}, ck_\mathcal{Q}, 2]\{(\lambda p_\mathcal{Q}, k_\mathcal{Q}, op_\mathcal{Q} ; \exists ok_\mathcal{Q}) :$
$$cp_\mathcal{Q} = \mathrm{Com}(p_\mathcal{Q}, op_\mathcal{Q}) \wedge ck_\mathcal{Q} = \mathrm{Com}(k_\mathcal{Q}, ok_\mathcal{Q})\}.$$

Fig. 6. Subroutine Share: $\mathcal{U}$ generates shares to her password p and key k, and sends them to the servers.

The Share subprotocol Setup uses is depicted in Figure 6. In that subprotocol $\mathcal{U}$ splits her inputs p and k into random additive shares $p_\mathcal{P} + p_\mathcal{Q} := p$ and $k_\mathcal{P} + k_\mathcal{Q} := k$, and sends $(p_\mathcal{P}, k_\mathcal{P})$ to $\mathcal{P}$ and sends $(p_\mathcal{Q}, k_\mathcal{Q})$ to $\mathcal{Q}$. She commits to all shares and sends all commitments to both servers; additionally she sends the openings for a server's shares to the respective server; thus enabling the servers to later perform zero-knowledge proofs about their shares and the commitments to them. The servers then ensure they got the same commitments and prove to each other that they know their shares. In π_2, $\mathcal{Q}$ also proves to $\mathcal{P}$ that he knows the opening $op_\mathcal{Q}$ corresponding to his share of the password: this is needed so that $\mathcal{S}$ can properly simulate $B_\mathcal{P} = (A_\mathcal{P})^{s_{u_\mathcal{Q}} + s_{P_\mathcal{Q}} - op_\mathcal{Q}}$ in ChkPwd (we note that $\mathcal{S}$ does not need to know the value $op_\mathcal{P}$ from π_1 at this point).

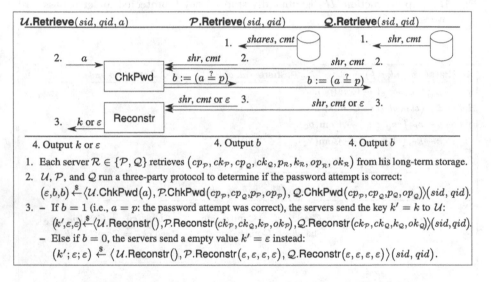

Fig. 7. Retrieve instruction: $\mathcal{U}$ retrieves the key k if she provides the correct password.

The Retrieve Instruction. Recall that the goal of the Retrieve instruction is for a user (not necessarily the same as during Setup) to retrieve the key k, contingent upon her holding a correct password attempt $a \in \mathbb{Z}_q$.

When a user $\mathcal{U}$ receives an input $\langle$Retrieve, $sid, qid, a\rangle$ with the same sid as during Setup from $\mathcal{Z}$, she starts a Retrieve query. Each of the servers starts a Retrieve query when he receives an input $\langle$ReadyRetrieve, $sid, qid\rangle$ from $\mathcal{Z}$. The servers may refuse to service the query if they for instance suspect that an online password guessing attack is in progress, e.g., if they have processed too many failed Retrieve queries for that user account already. As many policies for throttling down can be envisaged, we decided not to include the policy in our model but rather to let $\mathcal{Z}$ decide: if the server should refuse service, $\mathcal{Z}$ does not provide the initial input $\langle$ReadyRetrieve, $sid, qid\rangle$. The Retrieve instruction runs as follows and is depicted in Figure 7. The servers start a Retrieve query by

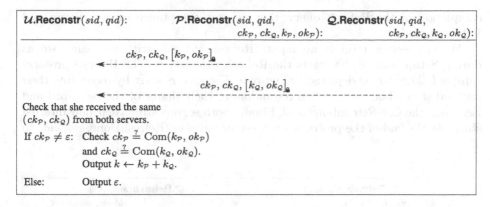

Fig. 8. Subroutine Reconstr: the servers send their commitments and shares of the key to $\mathcal{U}$ so that she may reconstruct her key k.

retrieving their internal state. The user and the servers then engage in a three-party computation to determine whether $\delta := p_\mathcal{P} + p_\mathcal{Q} - a \overset{?}{=} 0$, i.e., whether the password attempt is correct, using the ChkPwd subprotocol. If the password is correct, the servers send their shares of the key back to the user using the Reconstr subprotocol; if wrong, they send back ε. At the end of the Retrieve query, $\mathcal{U}$ outputs $\langle \text{Deliver}, sid, qid, k' \rangle$ to $\mathcal{Z}$, and each server outputs $\langle \text{Delivered}, sid, qid, b \rangle$ to $\mathcal{Z}$—where $k' = k$ and $b = 1$ if the password attempt was correct, else $k' = \varepsilon$ and $b = 0$.

We now describe the two subprotocols that the Retrieve instruction uses. ChkPwd was already explained in §4.2 and was depicted in Figure 2. Reconstr is depicted in Figure 8. In this subprotocol, each server sends his share of the key ($k_\mathcal{P}$ or $k_\mathcal{Q}$) and the corresponding opening to $\mathcal{U}$. Both servers also send her the two commitments to the shares of the key. The user checks that she received the same commitments from both servers, that the shares and openings are correct, and reconstructs the key $k := k_\mathcal{P} + k_\mathcal{Q}$. The servers may send ε instead to denote a failed password attempt; in that case $\mathcal{U}$ outputs ε.

In both the ChkPwd and the Reconstr subprotocols, $\mathcal{U}$ needs to send data in a non-committing and confidential manner to $\mathcal{P}$. Instead of generating the OTPs for each subprotocol separately, the two parties could generate a single OTP of double the length in one operation and use the first half of the OTP during ChkPwd and the second half during Reconstr. This optimization would save one key generation (for the CCA2-secure cryptosystem), one encryption, and one decryption. The same optimization can be applied between $\mathcal{U}$ and $\mathcal{Q}$.

The Refresh Instruction. In the Refresh instruction, the servers re-randomize their shares and generate new commitments to them. This ensures that $\mathcal{A}$ no longer has any knowledge about the internal state of a party who recovered from corruption. Servers execute a Refresh query immediately after they formally recover from corruption (see §3.4). Upon starting a Refresh query, the servers abort all running Setup and Retrieve queries and stop accepting new ones. Upon completion of the Refresh query, they resume acceptance of new Setup and Retrieve queries.

When a server receives an input $\langle \text{Refresh}, sid, qid \rangle$ with the same sid as during Setup from $\mathcal{Z}$, he starts the Refresh instruction. The Refresh protocol runs as follows and is depicted in Figure 9. The servers start by recovering their internal state. The servers then re-randomize their shares of the password and key using the ComRefr subprotocol. Finally both servers store their new internal state. At the end of the protocol, each server outputs $\langle \text{RefreshDone}, sid, qid \rangle$ to $\mathcal{Z}$.

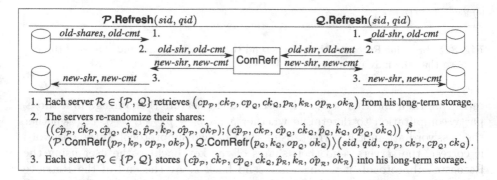

Fig. 9. Refresh instruction: the servers re-randomize their internal state.

The Refresh instruction uses the ComRefr subprotocol, depicted in Figure 10, the goal of which is for both servers $\mathcal{P}$ and $\mathcal{Q}$ to re-randomize their respective shares $(p_\mathcal{P}, k_\mathcal{P})$ and $(p_\mathcal{Q}, k_\mathcal{Q})$. $\mathcal{P}$ randomly selects two offsets $\mathring{p}$ and $\mathring{k}$ and subtracts them from his shares. $\mathcal{P}$ then commits to the offsets and his new shares. $\mathcal{P}$ proves to $\mathcal{Q}$ that all operations were done correctly. As part of the proof, $\mathcal{P}$ sends all the commitments and a ciphertext that contains the offsets and the corresponding openings encrypted under an OTP to $\mathcal{Q}$. $\mathcal{Q}$ likewise updates his shares and generates new commitments to them. $\mathcal{Q}$ proves to $\mathcal{P}$ that all operations were done honestly and that he knows the opening $\mathring{op}_\mathcal{Q}$ corresponding to his new share of the password (for the same reason as in Share: $\mathcal{S}$ needs $\mathring{op}_\mathcal{Q}$ when simulating $B_\mathcal{P}$ in ChkPwd). As part of the proof, $\mathcal{Q}$ sends the new commitments to $\mathcal{P}$.

4.4 Constructing a Multi-session $\Pi_{2\text{pass}}$ with Constant-Size CRS

In order to handle multiple user accounts, one can run multiple independent sessions of $\Pi_{2\text{pass}}$. With that first approach, security is guaranteed by direct application of the UC composition theorem. Each session however needs an independent copy of $\mathcal{F}_{\text{crs}}^{\mathbb{G}^3}$. In the full version [6] we argue that using the *same* instance of $\mathcal{F}_{\text{crs}}^{\mathbb{G}^3}$ for all the otherwise independent sessions is secure as well. Informally, the second approach works because the CRS is used chiefly by the HMT commitments, which are all bound to sid by the zero-knowledge proofs. Further, the

$\mathcal{P}.\mathbf{ComRefr}(sid, qid, cp_\mathcal{P}, ck_\mathcal{P}, cp_\mathcal{Q}, ck_\mathcal{Q},$ $\mathcal{Q}.\mathbf{ComRefr}(sid, qid, cp_\mathcal{P}, ck_\mathcal{P}, cp_\mathcal{Q}, ck_\mathcal{Q},$

            $p_\mathcal{P}, k_\mathcal{P}, op_\mathcal{P}, ok_\mathcal{P})$: $p_\mathcal{Q}, k_\mathcal{Q}, op_\mathcal{Q}, ok_\mathcal{Q})$:

$\mathring{p} \xleftarrow{\$} \mathbb{Z}_q; (\mathring{cp}, \mathring{op}) \xleftarrow{\$} \mathrm{Com}(\mathring{p}).$

$\mathring{k} \xleftarrow{\$} \mathbb{Z}_q; (\mathring{ck}, \mathring{ok}) \xleftarrow{\$} \mathrm{Com}(\mathring{k}).$

$\hat{p}_\mathcal{P} \leftarrow p_\mathcal{P} - \mathring{p}; (\hat{cp}_\mathcal{P}, \hat{op}_\mathcal{P}) \xleftarrow{\$} \mathrm{Com}(\hat{p}_\mathcal{P}).$

$\hat{k}_\mathcal{P} \leftarrow k_\mathcal{P} - \mathring{k}; (\hat{ck}_\mathcal{P}, \hat{ok}_\mathcal{P}) \xleftarrow{\$} \mathrm{Com}(\hat{k}_\mathcal{P}).$

$(\oslash : p_\mathcal{P}, k_\mathcal{P}, \mathring{p}, \mathring{k}, op_\mathcal{P}, ok_\mathcal{P}, \mathring{op}, \mathring{ok})$ $\xrightarrow{\;\;\mathring{cp}, \mathring{ck}, \hat{cp}_\mathcal{P}, \hat{ck}_\mathcal{P}, [\mathring{p}, \mathring{op}, \mathring{k}, \mathring{ok}]_\mathbb{a}, \pi_8\;\;}$

                             Check: $\mathring{cp} \overset{?}{=} \mathrm{Com}(\mathring{p}, \mathring{op})$ and $\mathring{ck} \overset{?}{=} \mathrm{Com}(\mathring{k}, \mathring{ok}).$

                             $\hat{p}_\mathcal{Q} \leftarrow p_\mathcal{Q} + \mathring{p}; (\hat{cp}_\mathcal{Q}, \hat{op}_\mathcal{Q}) \xleftarrow{\$} \mathrm{Com}(\hat{p}_\mathcal{Q}).$

                             $\hat{k}_\mathcal{Q} \leftarrow k_\mathcal{Q} + \mathring{k}; (\hat{ck}_\mathcal{Q}, \hat{ok}_\mathcal{Q}) \xleftarrow{\$} \mathrm{Com}(\hat{k}_\mathcal{Q}).$

       $\xleftarrow{\;\;\hat{cp}_\mathcal{Q}, \hat{ck}_\mathcal{Q}, \pi_9\;\;}$ $(\oslash : p_\mathcal{Q}, k_\mathcal{Q}, \mathring{p}, \mathring{k}, op_\mathcal{Q}, ok_\mathcal{Q}, \mathring{op}, \mathring{ok})$

Output $(\hat{cp}_\mathcal{P}, \hat{ck}_\mathcal{P}, \hat{cp}_\mathcal{Q}, \hat{ck}_\mathcal{Q}, \hat{p}_\mathcal{P}, \hat{k}_\mathcal{P}, \hat{op}_\mathcal{P}, \hat{ok}_\mathcal{P}).$ Output $(\hat{cp}_\mathcal{P}, \hat{ck}_\mathcal{P}, \hat{cp}_\mathcal{Q}, \hat{ck}_\mathcal{Q}, \hat{p}_\mathcal{Q}, \hat{k}_\mathcal{Q}, \hat{op}_\mathcal{Q}, \hat{ok}_\mathcal{Q}).$

Instantiation of zero-knowledge proofs:

$\pi_8 := \mathcal{F}_{\mathrm{gzk}}[sid, qid, cp_\mathcal{P}, ck_\mathcal{P}, cp_\mathcal{Q}, ck_\mathcal{Q}, 8]\{(\nmid p_\mathcal{P}, k_\mathcal{P} ; \exists op_\mathcal{P}, ok_\mathcal{P}, \alpha, \beta):$

$cp_\mathcal{P} = \mathrm{Com}(p_\mathcal{P}, op_\mathcal{P}) \wedge (\hat{cp}_\mathcal{P} * \mathring{cp}) = \mathrm{Com}(p_\mathcal{P}, \alpha) \wedge ck_\mathcal{P} = \mathrm{Com}(k_\mathcal{P}, ok_\mathcal{P}) \wedge (\hat{ck}_\mathcal{P} * \mathring{ck}) = \mathrm{Com}(k_\mathcal{P}, \beta)$

                                       $\}$, where $\alpha := \hat{op}_\mathcal{P} + \mathring{op}$ and $\beta := \hat{ok}_\mathcal{P} + \mathring{ok}.$

$\pi_9 := \mathcal{F}_{\mathrm{gzk}}[sid, qid, \mathring{cp}, \mathring{ck}, \hat{cp}_\mathcal{P}, \hat{cp}_\mathcal{Q}, 9]\{(\nmid \hat{p}_\mathcal{Q}, \hat{k}_\mathcal{Q}, \hat{op}_\mathcal{Q} ; \exists \hat{ok}_\mathcal{Q}, \alpha, \beta,):$

$\hat{cp}_\mathcal{Q} = \mathrm{Com}(\hat{p}_\mathcal{Q}, \hat{op}_\mathcal{Q}) \wedge \hat{ck}_\mathcal{Q} = \mathrm{Com}(\hat{k}_\mathcal{Q}, \hat{ok}_\mathcal{Q}) \wedge (cp_\mathcal{Q} * \mathring{cp}) = \mathrm{Com}(\hat{p}_\mathcal{Q}, \alpha) \wedge (ck_\mathcal{Q} * \mathring{ck}) = \mathrm{Com}(\hat{k}_\mathcal{Q}, \beta)$

                                       $\}$, where $\alpha := op_\mathcal{Q} + \mathring{op}$ and $\beta := ok_\mathcal{Q} + \mathring{ok}.$

Fig. 10. Subroutine ComRefr: the servers generate new commitments and shares of the password and key based on the old ones.

JUC theorem [14] guarantees that all instances in the realizations of $\mathcal{F}_{\mathrm{gzk}}$ and $\mathcal{F}_{\mathrm{gzk}}^{2v}$ can use the same instance of $\mathcal{F}_{\mathrm{crs}}^{\mathrm{gzk}}$.

4.5 Computational and Communication Complexity in the Standard Model

The sum of the computation time of all parties for Setup, Retrieve, and Refresh queries is less than 0.08, 0.16, and 0.09 seconds for 80/1248-bit security[2] on modern computers,[3] and the communication complexity is 5, 7, and 3 round trips (when combining messages wherever possible), respectively. For the Setup instruction, 43 elements of $\mathbb{Z}_q$, 56 elements of $\mathbb{G}$, 12 elements of $\mathbb{Z}_n$, and 4 elements of $\mathbb{Z}_{n^2}$ are transmitted over plain/TCP channels in our preferred embodiment, corresponding to roughly 5.2 kilobytes for 80/1248-bit security when $\mathbb{G}$ is an elliptic curve. For the Retrieve instruction, 73.5, 99, 16, and 6 elements of $\mathbb{Z}_q, \mathbb{G}, \mathbb{Z}_n$, and $\mathbb{Z}_{n^2}$ are transmitted respectively (8 kB). For the Refresh instruction, 34, 46, 10, and 4 elements of $\mathbb{Z}_q, \mathbb{G}, \mathbb{Z}_n$, and $\mathbb{Z}_{n^2}$ are transmitted respectively

---

[2] The subgroup size $|q|$ is 2*80 bits and the RSA modulus size $|n|$ is 1248 bits.

[3] When using the GNU MP (GMP) bignum library on 64-bit Linux on a computer with an Intel Core i7 Q720 1.60GHz CPU.

(4.5 kB). Due to the fact that our protocol is secure against adaptive corruptions, it is computationally more expensive than a standard-model instantiation of the CLN protocol [10] (i.e., with *interactive* zero-knowledge proofs): our Retrieve queries are about 10 and 2.6 times slower for users and servers, respectively; and more data is transferred; however the number of round trips is identical. See the full version [6] for a detailed analysis.

4.6   Construction of $\varPi_{2\text{pass}}$ in the Random-Oracle Model

Our $\varPi_{2\text{pass}}$ can be improved in several ways when security in the random-oracle model only is sufficient. First, one can transform all interactive zero-knowledge proofs into non-interactive ones using the Fiat-Shamir transformation [18] in combination with encryption to a public key in the CRS for online extraction [30]. Second, one can replace our secureSend protocol by Nielsen's NINCE [29]. Third, one can use faster encryption and signature algorithms. This improves the computational complexity of our Setup, Retrieve, and Refresh queries by only about 15%, 25%, and 6% but the number of communication rounds is now much smaller: 3, 3, and 2 round trips, respectively. Compared to CLN [10], the computational complexity of our Retrieve queries are then about 11 and 3.7 times larger for users and servers, respectively; the number of round trips is the same. Compared to 1-out-of-2 CLLN [9], the computational complexity of our Retrieve queries are about 2.6 and 4.1 times larger for users and servers, respectively, but need 2 round trips less: if the network delay is large then our protocol is faster than CLLN. See the full version [6] for a detailed analysis.

5   Proof Sketch

For reasons of space, we provide the security proof in the full version [6] and explain only the main ideas here.

We use the standard approach for proving the security of UC protocols: we construct a straight-line simulator S such that for all polynomial-time bounded environments and all polynomial-time bounded adversaries A it holds that the environment Z cannot distinguish its interaction with A and $\varPi_{2\text{pass}}$ in the ($\mathcal{F}_{\text{crs}}^{\text{G}^3}$, $\mathcal{F}_{\text{osac}}$, $\mathcal{F}_{\text{ac}}$, $\mathcal{F}_{\text{gzk}}$, $\mathcal{F}_{\text{gzk}}^{2\text{v}}$)-hybrid *real* world from its interaction with S and $\mathcal{F}_{2\text{pass}}$ in the *ideal* world. We prove this statement by defining a sequence of intermediate *hybrid* worlds (the first one being the real world and the last one the ideal world) and showing that Z cannot distinguish between any two consecutive hybrid worlds.

The main difficulties in constructing S (and accordingly in designing our protocol to allow us to address those difficulties) are as follows: *1)* S has to extract the inputs of all corrupted parties from the interaction with them; *2)* S has to compute and send commitments and ciphertexts to the corrupted parties on behalf of the honest parties without knowing the latter's inputs, i.e., S needs to commit and encrypt dummy values; *3)* but when an honest party gets corrupted mid-protocol, S has to provide A with the full *non-erased* intermediate state of that party, in particular the opening of commitments that were sent out and the randomness used to compute encryptions that were sent out (if these value need to be retained by a party).

To address the first difficulty, recall that parties are required to perform proofs of *knowledge* of their shares upon their first use in the protocol. S can therefore recover the inputs of all corrupted parties with the help of $\mathcal{F}_{gzk}$ and $\mathcal{F}_{gzk}^{2v}$. The commitments and proofs of *existence* with $\mathcal{F}_{gzk}$ and $\mathcal{F}_{gzk}^{2v}$ ensure that the corrupted parties are unable to alter their inputs mid-protocol.

The second and third difficulty we address as follows. In general, S runs honest parties with random input and adjusts their internal state as follows when it learns the correct values. When S is told by $\mathcal{F}_{2pass}$ whether the password attempt was correct in a Retrieve query, it can generate credible values $B_{\mathcal{U}}$, $B_{\mathcal{P}}$, and $B_{\mathcal{Q}}$ in the ChkPwd subroutine because S can recover the opening values *op* from dishonest servers through $\mathcal{F}_{gzk}$ and $\mathcal{F}_{gzk}^{2v}$. When a user gets corrupted during Setup, or both servers get corrupted, S can recover the actual password and key associated with the user account from $\mathcal{F}_{2pass}$ and then needs to equivocate all relevant commitments and encryptions sent earlier to the corrupted parties. This is also the case when a user gets corrupted during Retrieve, where S is also allowed to recover the actual password attempt. S can equivocate such commitments, with the help of the trapdoor, and equivocate the ciphertexts containing the openings of commitments it sent between two honest parties by altering the one-time pads. By the time a one-time pad is used, the decryption keys and randomness used to establish it have been erased and so they can be changed to equivocate. Additionally, S never needs to reveal the randomness used inside the ChkPwd subroutine, in particular because $\mathcal{F}_{gzk}$ and $\mathcal{F}_{gzk}^{2v}$ allow for the erasure of witnesses *before* delivering the statement to be proven to the other party. The rest of the security proof is rather straightforward.

6   Conclusion

We presented the first TPASS protocol secure against adaptive corruptions and where servers can recover from corruptions in a provably secure way. Our protocol involves two servers, and security for the user is guaranteed as long as at most one server is corrupted at any time. Our protocol is efficient enough to be well within reach of a practical implementation. Designing an efficient protocol in the more general t-out-of-n setting is an interesting open problem.

Acknowledgments. We are grateful to the anonymous reviewers of all earlier versions of this paper for their comments, and thank Anja Lehmann for many helpful discussions. This work was supported by the European Community through the Seventh Framework Programme (FP7), under grant agreement n°321310 for the project PERCY.

References

1. Bagherzandi, A., Jarecki, S., Saxena, N., Lu, Y.: Password-protected secret sharing. In: ACM CCS 2011, pp. 433–444 (2011)
2. Barak, B., Canetti, R., Lindell, Y., Pass, R., Rabin, T.: Secure computation without authentication. In: Shoup, V. (ed.) CRYPTO 2005. LNCS, vol. 3621, pp. 361–377. Springer, Heidelberg (2005)
3. Beaver, D., Haber, S.: Cryptographic protocols provably secure against dynamic. In: Rueppel, R.A. (ed.) EUROCRYPT 1992. LNCS, vol. 658, pp. 307–323. Springer, Heidelberg (1993)
4. Brainard, J., Juels, A., Kaliski, B., Szydlo, M.: A new two-server approach for authentication with short secrets. In: USENIX SECURITY 2003, pp. 201–214 (2003)
5. Burr, W., Dodson, D., Newton, E., Perlner, R., Polk, W., Gupta, S., Nabbus, E.: Electronic authentication guideline. NIST Special Publication 800–63-1 (2011)
6. Camenisch, J., Enderlein, R.R., Neven, G.: Two-Server Password-Authenticated Secret Sharing UC-Secure Against Transient Corruptions. IACR Cryptology ePrint Archive, 2015:006
7. Camenisch, J., Enderlein, R.R., Shoup, V.: Practical and employable protocols for UC-secure circuit evaluation over $\mathbb{Z}_n$. In: Crampton, J., Jajodia, S., Mayes, K. (eds.) ESORICS 2013. LNCS, vol. 8134, pp. 19–37. Springer, Heidelberg (2013)
8. Camenisch, J., Krenn, S., Shoup, V.: A framework for practical universally composable zero-knowledge protocols. In: Lee, D.H., Wang, X. (eds.) ASIACRYPT 2011. LNCS, vol. 7073, pp. 449–467. Springer, Heidelberg (2011)
9. Camenisch, J., Lehmann, A., Lysyanskaya, A., Neven, G.: Memento: How to reconstruct your secrets from a single password in a hostile environment. In: Garay, J.A., Gennaro, R. (eds.) CRYPTO 2014, Part II. LNCS, vol. 8617, pp. 256–275. Springer, Heidelberg (2014)
10. Camenisch, J., Lysyanskaya, A., Neven, G.: Practical yet universally composable two-server password-authenticated secret sharing. In: ACM CCS 2012, pp. 525–536 (2012)
11. Canetti, R.: Universally Composable Security: A New Paradigm for Cryptographic Protocols. IACR Cryptology ePrint Archive, 2000:67
12. Canetti, R.: Universally composable security: A new paradigm for cryptographic protocols. In: FOCS 2001, pp. 136–145 (2001)
13. Canetti, R., Halevi, S., Katz, J., Lindell, Y., MacKenzie, P.: Universally composable password-based key exchange. In: Cramer, R. (ed.) EUROCRYPT 2005. LNCS, vol. 3494, pp. 404–421. Springer, Heidelberg (2005)
14. Canetti, R., Rabin, T.: Universal composition with joint state. In: Boneh, D. (ed.) CRYPTO 2003. LNCS, vol. 2729, pp. 265–281. Springer, Heidelberg (2003)
15. Cramer, R., Shoup, V.: A practical public key cryptosystem provably secure against adaptive chosen ciphertext attack. In: Krawczyk, H. (ed.) CRYPTO 1998. LNCS, vol. 1462, pp. 13–25. Springer, Heidelberg (1998)
16. Di Raimondo, M., Gennaro, R.: Provably secure threshold password-authenticated key exchange. In: Biham, E. (ed.) EUROCRYPT 2003. LNCS, vol. 2656, pp. 507–523. Springer, Heidelberg (2003)
17. EMC Corporation. RSA Distributed Credential Protection. http://www.emc.com/security/rsa-distributed-credential-protection.htm
18. Fiat, A., Shamir, A.: How to prove yourself: practical solutions to identification and signature problems. In: Odlyzko, A.M. (ed.) CRYPTO 1986. LNCS, vol. 263, pp. 186–194. Springer, Heidelberg (1987)

19. Ford, W., Kaliski, B.: Server-assisted generation of a strong secret from a password. In: IEEE International Workshops on Enabling Technologies: Infrastructure for Collaborative Enterprises (WETICE 2000), pp. 176–180 (2000)
20. Gosney, J.: Password cracking HPC. In: Passwords 12 Conference (2012)
21. Herzberg, A., Jarecki, S., Krawczyk, H., Yung, M.: Proactive secret sharing or: how to cope with perpetual leakage. In: Coppersmith, D. (ed.) CRYPTO 1995. LNCS, vol. 963, pp. 339–352. Springer, Heidelberg (1995)
22. Hofheinz, D., Shoup, V.: GNUC: A new universal composability framework. IACR Cryptology ePrint Archive, 2011:303
23. Hofheinz, D.: Possibility and impossibility results for selective decommitments. J. Cryptology **24**(3), 470–516 (2011)
24. Jablon, D.P.: Password authentication using multiple servers. In: Naccache, D. (ed.) CT-RSA 2001. LNCS, vol. 2020, pp. 344–360. Springer, Heidelberg (2001)
25. Jarecki, S., Kiayias, A., Krawczyk, H.: Round-optimal password-protected secret sharing and t-pake in the password-only model. In: Sarkar, P., Iwata, T. (eds.) ASIACRYPT 2014, Part II. LNCS, vol. 8874, pp. 233–253. Springer, Heidelberg (2014)
26. Katz, J., MacKenzie, P., Taban, G., Gligor, V.: Two-server password-only authenticated key exchange. J. of Computer and System Sciences **78**(2), 651–669 (2012)
27. Krenn, S.: Bringing zero-knowledge proofs of knowledge to practice. PhD thesis (2012)
28. MacKenzie, P.D., Shrimpton, T., Jakobsson, M.: Threshold password-authenticated key exchange. In: Yung, M. (ed.) CRYPTO 2002. LNCS, vol. 2442, pp. 385–400. Springer, Heidelberg (2002)
29. Nielsen, J.B.: Separating random oracle proofs from complexity theoretic proofs: the non-committing encryption case. In: Yung, M. (ed.) CRYPTO 2002. LNCS, vol. 2442, pp. 111–126. Springer, Heidelberg (2002)
30. Paillier, P.: Public-key cryptosystems based on composite degree residuosity classes. In: Stern, J. (ed.) EUROCRYPT 1999. LNCS, vol. 1592, pp. 223–238. Springer, Heidelberg (1999)
31. Pedersen, T.P.: Non-interactive and information-theoretic secure verifiable secret sharing. In: Feigenbaum, J. (ed.) CRYPTO 1991. LNCS, vol. 576, pp. 129–140. Springer, Heidelberg (1992)
32. Provos, N., Mazières, D.: A future-adaptable password scheme. In: USENIX 1999, FREENIX Track, pp. 81–91 (1999)
33. Rackoff, C., Simon, D.R.: Non-interactive zero-knowledge proof of knowledge and chosen ciphertext attack. In: Feigenbaum, J. (ed.) CRYPTO 1991. LNCS, vol. 576, pp. 433–444. Springer, Heidelberg (1992)
34. Szydlo, M., Kaliski, B.: Proofs for two-server password authentication. In: Menezes, A. (ed.) CT-RSA 2005. LNCS, vol. 3376, pp. 227–244. Springer, Heidelberg (2005)

Adaptive Witness Encryption and Asymmetric Password-Based Cryptography

Mihir Bellare[1]([✉]) and Viet Tung Hoang[2,3]

[1] Department of Computer Science and Engineering,
University of California San Diego, San Diego, USA
mihir@eng.ucsd.edu
[2] Department of Computer Science, Georgetown University,
Washington DC, USA
[3] Department of Computer Science, University of Maryland,
Washington DC, USA

Abstract. We show by counter-example that the soundness security requirement for witness encryption given by Garg, Gentry, Sahai and Waters (STOC 2013) does not suffice for the security of their own applications. We introduce adaptively-sound (AS) witness encryption to fill the gap. We then introduce asymmetric password-based encryption (A-PBE). This offers gains over classical, symmetric password-based encryption in the face of attacks that compromise servers to recover hashed passwords. We distinguish between invasive A-PBE schemes (they introduce new password-based key-derivation functions) and non-invasive ones (they can use existing, deployed password-based key-derivation functions). We give simple and efficient invasive A-PBE schemes and use AS-secure witness encryption to give non-invasive A-PBE schemes.

1 Introduction

This paper introduces (1) witness encryption with adaptive soundness security and (2) asymmetric password-based encryption (A-PBE). We show how to use (1) to achieve (2) as well as other goals.

The Problem. The security of Internet communication remains ubiquitously based on client passwords. Standards such as the widely implemented PKCS#5 —equivalently, RFC 2898 [33]— specify password-based encryption (PBE). From the client password pw, one derives a hashed password $hpw = \mathsf{PH}(sa, pw)$, where sa is a random, user-specific public salt, and PH is a deterministic password-hashing function. (In the standards, $\mathsf{PH}(sa, pw) = H^t(sa|pw)$ where t is an iteration count and H^t denotes the t-fold iteration of cryptographic hash function H.) The server holds hpw while the client holds (sa, pw). Now the server will encrypt under hpw using any symmetric encryption scheme, for example CBC-AES. The client can recompute hpw from (sa, pw) and decrypt using this key.

This classical form of PBE is *symmetric*: encryption and decryption are both done under the same key hpw. But this means that anyone who knows hpw can

© International Association for Cryptologic Research 2015
J. Katz (Ed.): PKC 2015, LNCS 9020, pp. 308–331, 2015.
DOI: 10.1007/978-3-662-46447-2_14

decrypt. This is a serious vulnerability in practice because of server compromise leading to exposure of hashed passwords. The Heartbleed attack of April 2014, allowing an attacker to read large chunks of server memory that can contain sensitive client information including hashed passwords, is a recent and prominent instance. Other high-profile attacks that compromised servers to expose client information include Target (December 2013), Adobe (October 2013), LinkedIn (June 2012), RSA (March 2011), Sony (2011) and TJ Maxx (2007). According to CNBC, there were over 600 breaches in 2013 alone.

We emphasize that the problem here is not the possibility of password-recovery via a dictionary attack based on the hashed password. The problem is that S-PBE (symmetric PBE) is vulnerable *even if the password is well chosen to resist dictionary attack*. This is because possession of the hashed password is already and directly enough to decrypt any prior communications. So under S-PBE, even well-chosen passwords do not provide security in the face of server compromise.

A-PBE. We propose asymmetric password-based encryption (A-PBE). Here, encryption is done under the hashed password hpw, decryption is done under the password pw, and *possession of hpw does not allow decryption*. This offers significantly higher security in the face of the most important attack, namely server compromise exposing the hashed password hpw.

This paper initiates a foundational treatment of A-PBE including definitions and both "invasive" and "non-invasive" schemes. At first it may appear that definitionally A-PBE is just like PKE and brings nothing new, but this is not true. Not just is security based on passwords, but in practice users pick related passwords, for example varying a base password by appending the name of the website, resulting in encryption under related keys. Our definition extends the S-PBE framework of [10]. Our security model explicitly considers encryption under *multiple* passwords, assumed to be individually unpredictable —otherwise security is not possible— but arbitrarily related to each other.

We give two proven-secure A-PBE schemes that we call APBE1 and APBE2. Their attributes are summarized in Fig. 1. APBE1 is simple, natural and as efficient as possible, but what we call invasive, is that it specifies its own password-hashing function PH. APBE2 is non-invasive, meaning able to use any, given password-hashing function. In particular it can work with in-use, standardized password hashing functions such as PKCS#5 [33] or bcrypt [34]. If one has the flexibility of changing PH and the associated password hashes then the first solution is preferable. The second solution may be easier to deploy in the face of the legacy constraint of millions of existing, PKCS#5 hashed passwords.

APBE1. We specify and analyze the following simple and natural scheme for A-PBE that we call APBE1. PH, given sa, pw, applies to them a deterministic function EX to derive a string r, uses this as coin tosses for a key-generation algorithm PKE.Kg of some standard PKE scheme to get (pk, sk), and outputs $hpw = pk$ as the hashed password. Encryption is under the encryption algorithm PKE.Enc of the PKE scheme keyed with $hpw = pk$. Since PH is deterministic,

Scheme	Invasive	Assumptions
APBE1	Yes	PKE, RIP-secure hash
APBE2	No	AS-secure WE RIP-secure password hash with large stretch
		XS-secure WE ROW-secure password hash with arbitrary stretch

Fig. 1. Our A-PBE schemes. Both achieve our notion of security for related, unpredictable passwords. APBE1 has a dedicated password hash (invasive) while APBE2 can work with an arbitrary, legacy one (non-invasive). The first analysis of APBE2 assumes the password hash has large stretch, a restriction dropped in the second analysis under a stronger form of WE.

decryption under (sa, pw) can re-execute PH to get (sk, pk) and then use sk to decrypt under PKE.

A natural choice for EX is a randomness extractor [32] with seed sa. But recall that we require A-PBE to be secure even under multiple, related passwords. To achieve this, outputs of EX must be independent even if the input passwords are related, and an extractor does not guarantee this. Indeed it is not possible for this to be true information theoretically, meaning if the "independence" is required to be statistical. We instead target computational independence of the outputs of EX. We define an appropriate security goal for EX that we call related-input pseudorandomness (RIP) [29] and show that this together with security of the base PKE scheme suffices for the security of the A-PBE scheme. In practice, EX can be efficiently instantiated via HMAC [5].

Non-invasive A-PBE. APBE1 prescribes its own password-hashing algorithm under which the hashed password hpw is a public key of some existing PKE scheme. In current practice, however, the hashed password is derived via the iterated hashing password-hash function of PKCS#5 [33] or alternatives such as bcrypt [34]. Right now millions of passwords are in use with these particular password-hashing functions. In the face of this legacy constraint, deployment of A-PBE would be eased by a scheme that could encrypt under an existing, given hashed password, regardless of its form. We ask whether such non-invasive A-PBE is achievable.

This turns out to be challenging, even in principle, let alone in practice. In all known PKE schemes, the secret and public keys have very specific structure and are related in very particular ways. How can we encrypt asymmetrically with the public key being just an arbitrary hash of the secret key?

The answer is witness encryption (WE), introduced by Garg, Gentry, Sahai and Waters (GGSW) [20]. We will use WE to achieve non-invasive A-PBE. For this purpose, however, we will need WE schemes satisfying an extension of the soundness security notion of GGSW [20] that we introduce and call adaptive soundness security. We define and achieve WE with adaptive soundness and apply it to achieve non-invasive A-PBE as we now discuss.

SS-Secure Witness Encryption. In a WE scheme [20] for a language $L \in$ **NP**, the encryption function WE.Enc takes a unary representation 1^λ of the security parameter $\lambda \in \mathbb{N}$, a string $x \in \{0,1\}^*$ and a message m to return a ciphertext c. If $x \in L$ then decryption is possible given a witness w for the membership of x in L. If $x \notin L$ then the message remains private given the ciphertext. The soundness security (SS) requirement of GGSW [20] formalized the latter by asking that for any PT adversary A, any $x \notin L$ and any equal-length messages m_0, m_1, there is a negligible function ν such that

$$\Pr[A(\mathsf{WE.Enc}(1^\lambda, x, m_1)) = 1] - \Pr[A(\mathsf{WE.Enc}(1^\lambda, x, m_0)) = 1] \le \nu(\lambda)$$

for all $\lambda \in \mathbb{N}$.

AS-Secure Witness Encryption. Our (new) adaptive soundness (AS) requirement lets the adversary A, on input 1^λ, pick and return x, m_0, m_1 to the game. The latter picks a random challenge bit b and returns $\mathsf{WE.Enc}(1^\lambda, x, m_b)$ to A, who now responds with a guess b' as to the value of b. The AS-advantage of A is defined as the probability that $(b = b')$ and $x \notin L$. We require that any PT A have negligible advantage. We note that due to the check that $x \notin L$, our game may not be polynomial time but this does not hinder our applications.

It may at first seem that adaptivity does not add strength, since soundness security already quantifies over all x, m_0, m_1. But in fact we show that AS is strictly stronger than SS. Namely we show in Proposition 2 that AS always implies SS but SS does not necessarily imply AS. That is, any WE scheme that is AS secure is SS secure, but there exist WE schemes that are SS secure and not AS secure. Intuitively, the reason AS is strictly stronger is that SS does not allow x, m_0, m_1 to depend on λ. Our separation result modifies a SS-secure WE scheme to misbehave when $|x| \ge f(\lambda)$ for a certain poly-logarithmic function f of the security parameter. SS is preserved because for each x only finitely many values of λ trigger the anomaly. The proof that AS is violated uses the fact that **NP** $\subseteq$ **EXP**, the constructed adversary nonetheless being polynomial time.

Having strengthened the goal, we must revisit achievability. GGHRSW [18] give an elegant and conceptually simple construction of SS-secure WE from indistinguishability obfuscation (iO). In Theorem 3 we show that the same construction achieves the stronger AS goal. Recent work has provided constructions of iO improved both along the assumptions and efficiency fronts [2,3,16,24], leading to corresponding improvements for AS-secure WE. Thus AS-secure WE can be achieved without loss of efficiency or added assumptions compared to SS-secure WE.

APBE2. Our APBE2 scheme lets L be the language of pairs $(sa, \mathsf{PH}(sa, pw))$ over the choices of sa, pw, the witness being pw. A-PBE encryption of m using the hashed password as the public key will be AS-secure witness encryption of m under $x = (sa, hpw)$. Decryption will use the witness pw.

This solution is non-invasive, as it does not prescribe or require any particular design for PH. Rather, it takes PH as given, and shows how to encrypt with public key the hashed password obtained from PH. In this way, PH can in particular be the iterated hash design of the PKCS#5 standard [33] that already underlies millions of usages of passwords, or any other practical, legacy design. Of course, for security, we will need to make an assumption about the security of PH, but that is very different from prescribing its design. Our assumption is the same RIP security as discussed above. We note that this assumption is already, even if implicitly, made in practice for the security of in-use S-PBE, where the hashed passwords are the keys, and is shown by [10] to hold for PKCS#5 in the ROM, so it is a natural and reasonable assumption.

SS Revisited. GGSW [20,21] present constructions of PKE, IBE and ABE schemes from witness encryption, claiming that these constructions are secure assuming soundness security of the WE scheme. The need for adaptive security of our A-PBE scheme leads to the natural question of why we need a stronger condition than GGSW [20,21]. The answer is that they need it too. We point out that the theorems of GGSW [20,21] claiming security of their applications under SS are incorrect, and that SS does not in fact suffice for the security of their schemes. We do this by presenting counter-examples (cf. Section 4). Taking their PRG-based PKE construction as a representative example, we provide a WE scheme which satisfies SS yet, if used in their construction, the resulting PKE scheme will provide no security at all. We then show that the gap can be filled by using AS. Namely, we show that their PKE scheme is secure if the underlying WE scheme is AS secure and the PRG is secure. Analogous results hold for GGSW's applications to IBE and ABE. Intuitively, the weakness of SS that compromises the applications of GGSW [20,21] is that a WE scheme may satisfy SS yet behave totally insecurely, for example returning the message in the clear, when $|x| = \lambda$. But in applications, x will have length related to λ, so SS is not enough. AS does not have this weakness because x can depend on λ.

Better Security for APBE2. Define the stretch of a password-hashing function as the difference between its output length and input length, and denote it by s. Our result of Theorem 5 proving the security of APBE2 requires that 2^{-s} is negligible, meaning the output length is somewhat more than the input length. This captures situations in which passwords are, say 12-character ASCII strings (input length is 78-bit) and the password hashing function is iterated SHA1 (output length is 160-bit). However, when passwords are longer, say 24-character, then passwords should offer more security. To fill this gap we offer a second analysis of the security of APBE2 that removes the restriction on the stretch, allowing it now to be arbitrary. For this purpose we strengthen the assumption on the WE scheme from AS to a notion of adaptive extractability we call XS. As a side benefit, the prior assumption on the password hashing function (RIP security, asking that password hashes are pseudorandom) is reduced to ROW security, asking merely that the password hashing function is one way.

XS is an adaptive variant of the notion of extractability from GKPVZ [26]. XS asks that, given an adversary violating the security of the encryption under $x \in \{0, 1\}^*$, one can extract a witness w for the membership of $x \in L$, even when x depends on the security parameter. We show that XS implies AS and also that XS-secure WE can be achieved based on extractable (aka. differing-input) obfuscations [1, 4, 14].

Some works [15, 19] cast doubts on the achievability of extractable witness encryption or extractable iO with *arbitrary auxiliary inputs*. Our result however requires a very particular auxiliary input and the attacks in these works do not apply.

A-PBE as PKE. The standard model for public-key encryption (PKE) is that the user (receiver) publishes a public encryption key and stores the corresponding secret key securely. In practice, however, the secret key is often not stored in computer memory but instead derived from a password stored in human memory. Reasons this is advantageous include *security* and *mobility*. Computer-stored keys are vulnerable to exfiltration by malware. Meanwhile, users tend to have numerous devices including cellphones and tablets on which they want to decrypt. They may also use web-based services such as gmail on untrusted client machines. Passwords are more flexible and secure than stored keys in such settings.

A-PBE captures this more real-world PKE model. Our definitions allow us to evaluate security in the setting of actual use, namely when secret keys are possibly correlated passwords. Our schemes provide solutions with provable guarantees. We note that A-PBE is the model of the recently proposed gmail end-to-end encryption system, evidencing practical relevance of the goal.

Password-Based Signatures. Beyond A-PBE, we view this paper as initiating a study of asymmetric password-based cryptography. In this light we also introduce and treat password-based signatures with both invasive and non-invasive solutions to mirror the case of A-PBE.

Password-based authentication is currently done using a MAC keyed by the hashed password. It is thus subject to the same weakness as S-PBE, namely that compromise of the server through Heartbleed or other attacks leads to compromise of hashed passwords, resulting in compromise of the authentication. In the password-based signatures we suggest, one signs under the password pw and verifies under the hashed password $hpw = \mathsf{PH}(sa, pw)$. Possession of the hashed password does not compromise security.

We can give a simple solution analogous to the one for A-PBE, namely apply a RIP function EX to the password and salt to get coins; run a key-generation of a standard digital signature scheme on these to get a signing key and verification key; set the password hash to the verification key; to sign given the password, re-generate the signing and verifying keys and sign under the former. This, however is invasive, prescribing its own password-hashing function. It is a good choice if one has the flexibility of implementing a new password hashing function, but as discussed above, deployment in the face of legacy PKCS#5 password hashes motivates asking whether a non-invasive solution, meaning one that can utilize any given password hashing function, is possible. As with A-PBE, this is a much more challenging question. We can show how to obtain a non-invasive password-based signature scheme by using key-versatile signatures [9].

The latter are effectively witness signatures meeting strong simulatability and extractability conditions [9,17] and allow us to obtain password-based signatures analogous to how we obtained A-PBE from WE. The only assumption needed on the password hashing function PH is that it is one-way.

Discussion and GGSW Updates. A good definition for WE should have two properties: (1) *Usability*, meaning it suffices to prove security of applications, and (2) *Achievability*, meaning proposed and natural constructions, which in this case mainly means the iO-based one of GGHRSW [18], can be shown to meet the definition. Our AS definition has both properties, making it viable. We have shown that SS lacked the usability property.

Here we have referred to the original GGSW STOC paper [20] and the corresponding original full ePrint version [21]. Subsequent to seeing prior versions of our paper, the GGSW authors updated their paper on ePrint [22,23]. They acknowledge the gap we found. They also propose their own, modified definitions in an attempt to fill this gap.

Beyond (and despite) the fact that these updated definitions are subsequent to ours, they remain problematic. We showed that their first proposed definition, which we call SS2 [22], is unachievable. (Because the negligible function is not allowed to depend on the adversary. See Appendix A.) We communicated this to the authors. They then updated SS2 to SS3 [23]. But we explain in Appendix A that SS3 has limitations with regard to achievability. While one might of course propose still further modifications to their definition it is not clear why this is a productive route for the community in the face of the fact that, with AS, we have —and had prior to the GGSW updates— a definition that provides both usability and achievability.

Recently KNY [31] gave a definition, that we call SS5, in the quantifier style of SS1, SS2 and SS3. We discuss it also in Appendix A where we show that it is unachievable. (Because, like SS2, the negligible function doesn't depend on the adversary.)

These developments are an indication that neither the gap we find, nor the AS definition we propose to fill it, are trivial, that quantifier-based definitions are error-prone, and that our counter-examples for SS remain important to understand and guide definitional choices. Demonstrating the last, beyond [22,23], further work subsequent to ours, and definitionally influenced by ours, includes [25].

We believe the idea of witness encryption is important and useful and we view our work as advancing its cause. Precision in definitions, proofs and details is particularly important in our field because we claim proven security. Reaching such precision can require iteration and definitional adjustments and increments, and our work, in this vein, helps towards greater impact and clarity for the area of witness encryption.

2   Preliminaries

By $\lambda \in \mathbb{N}$ we denote the security parameter and by 1^λ its unary representation. We denote the number of coordinates of a vector $\mathbf{x}$ by $|\mathbf{x}|$, and the length of a string $x \in \{0,1\}^*$ by $|x|$. Algorithms are randomized unless otherwise indicated. Running time is worst case. "PT" stands for "polynomial-time," whether for randomized algorithms or deterministic ones. If A is an algorithm, we let $y \leftarrow A(x_1, \ldots; r)$ denote running A with random coins r on inputs $x_1, \ldots$ and assigning the output to y. We let $y \leftarrow_{\$} A(x_1, \ldots)$ be the resulting of picking r at random and letting $y \leftarrow A(x_1, \ldots; r)$. We say that $f : \mathbb{N} \rightarrow \mathbb{R}$ is negligible if for every positive polynomial p, there exists $n_p \in \mathbb{N}$ such that $f(n) < 1/p(n)$ for all $n > n_p$. An adversary is an algorithm or a tuple of algorithms.

We use the code based game playing framework of [11]. For an example of a game see Fig. 2. By $\mathrm{G}^A(\lambda)$ we denote the event that the execution of game G with adversary A and security parameter λ results in output true, the game output being what is returned by GAME.

Unpredictability. Let $A = (A_1, \ldots)$ be a tuple of algorithms where A_1, on input the unary representation 1^λ of the security parameter $\lambda \in \mathbb{N}$, returns a vector **pw**. Let $\mathrm{Guess}_A(\lambda)$ denote the maximum, over all i, pw, of $\Pr[\mathbf{pw}[i] = pw]$, the probability over $\mathbf{pw} \leftarrow_{\$} A_1(\lambda)$. We say that A is *unpredictable* if the function $\mathrm{Guess}_A(\cdot)$ is negligible.

3 Adaptive Witness Encryption

We begin by recalling the notion of witness encryption of GGSW [20] and their soundness security requirement. We then give a different security notion called adaptive soundness. We show that it is strictly stronger than the original, which means we must address achieving it. We show that it is achievable via indistinguishability obfuscation.

NP Relations. For R: $\{0,1\}^* \times \{0,1\}^* \rightarrow \{\mathsf{true}, \mathsf{false}\}$, we let $\mathsf{R}(x) = \{ w : \mathsf{R}(x,w) \}$ be the *witness set* of $x \in \{0,1\}^*$. We say R is an **NP**-relation if it is computable in PT and there is a polynomial R.wl: $\mathbb{N} \rightarrow \mathbb{N}$, called the witness length of R, such that $\mathsf{R}(x) \subseteq \{0,1\}^{\mathsf{R.wl}(|x|)}$ for all $x \in \{0,1\}^*$. We let $\mathcal{L}(\mathsf{R}) = \{ x : \mathsf{R}(x) \neq \emptyset \} \in \mathbf{NP}$ be the language defined by R.

WE Syntax and Correctness. A witness encryption (WE) scheme WE for $L = \mathcal{L}(\mathsf{R})$ defines a pair of PT algorithms WE.Enc, WE.Dec. Algorithm WE.Enc takes as input the unary representation 1^λ of a security parameter $\lambda \in \mathbb{N}$, a string $x \in \{0,1\}^*$, and a message $m \in \{0,1\}^*$, and outputs a ciphertext c. Algorithm WE.Dec takes as input a string w and a ciphertext c, and outputs $m \in \{0,1\}^* \cup \{\bot\}$. Correctness requires that $\mathsf{WE.Dec}(w, \mathsf{WE.Enc}(1^\lambda, x, m)) = m$ for all $\lambda \in \mathbb{N}$, all $x \in L$, all $w \in \mathsf{R}(x)$ and all $m \in \{0,1\}^*$.

Soundness Security. The soundness security (SS) condition of GGSW [20] says that for any PT adversary A, any $x \in \{0,1\}^* \setminus L$ and any equal-length $m_0, m_1 \in \{0,1\}^*$, there is a negligible function ν such that for all $\lambda \in \mathbb{N}$ we have

$$\Pr[A(\mathsf{WE.Enc}(1^\lambda, x, m_1)) = 1] - \Pr[A(\mathsf{WE.Enc}(1^\lambda, x, m_0)) = 1] < \nu(\lambda) . \quad (1)$$

GAME $\mathrm{AS}_{\mathsf{WE},L}^A(\lambda)$

$(x, m_0, m_1, \mathrm{St}) \leftarrow_\$ A(1^\lambda)$; $b \leftarrow_\$ \{0,1\}$; $c \leftarrow_\$ \mathsf{WE}(1^\lambda, x, m_b)$; $b' \leftarrow_\$ A(\mathrm{St}, c)$

Return $((b = b') \wedge (x \notin L))$

Fig. 2. Game AS defining adaptive soundness of witness encryption scheme WE

In the following, it is useful to let $\mathsf{Adv}_{\mathsf{WE},L,x,m_0,m_1,A}^{\mathrm{ss}}(\lambda)$ denote the probability difference in (1). Then the soundness condition can be succinctly and equivalently stated as follows: WE is SS[L]-secure if for any PT adversary A, any $x \in \{0,1\}^* \setminus L$ and any equal-length $m_0, m_1 \in \{0,1\}^*$, the function $\mathsf{Adv}_{\mathsf{WE},L,x,m_0,m_1,A}^{\mathrm{ss}}(\cdot)$ is negligible. It is convenient, in order to succinctly and precisely express relations between notions, to let SS[L] denote the set of all correct witness encryption schemes that are SS[L]-secure.

Adaptive Soundness. Our security definition associates to witness encryption scheme WE, language $L \in \mathbf{NP}$, adversary A and $\lambda \in \mathbb{N}$ the game $\mathrm{AS}_{\mathsf{WE},L}^A(\lambda)$ of Fig. 2. Here the adversary, on input 1^λ, produces instance x, messages m_0, m_1, and state information St. It is required that $|m_0| = |m_1|$. The game picks a random challenge bit b and computes a ciphertext c via $\mathsf{WE}.\mathsf{Enc}(1^\lambda, x, m_b)$. The adversary is now given c, along with its state information St, and outputs a prediction b' for b. The game returns true if the prediction is correct, meaning $b = b'$, and also if $x \notin L$. We let $\mathsf{Adv}_{\mathsf{WE},L,A}^{\mathrm{as}}(\lambda) = 2\Pr[\mathrm{AS}_{\mathsf{WE},L}^A(\lambda)] - 1$. We say that WE has adaptive soundness security for L, or is AS[L]-secure, if for every PT A the function $\mathsf{Adv}_{\mathsf{WE},L,A}^{\mathrm{as}}(\cdot)$ is negligible. We let AS[L] denote the set of all correct witness encryption schemes that are AS[L]-secure.

Due to the check that $x \notin L$, our game does not necessarily run in PT. This, however, will not preclude applicability. The difference between AS and SS is that in the former, x, m_0, m_1 can depend on the security parameter and on each other. Given that SS quantifies over all x, m_0, m_1, this may not at first appear to make any difference. But we will see that it does and that AS is strictly stronger than SS.

AS is a game-based definition while SS is phrased in a more "quantifier-based" style that mimics the soundness condition in interactive proofs [28]. The game-based AS notion is better suited for applications because the latter are also underlain by game-based definitions. Indeed we'll see that SS does not suffice for applications.

A Useful Transform. In several proofs, we'll employ the following transform. Given a WE scheme $\mathsf{WE} \in \mathsf{SS}[L]$ and a PT function $f \colon \mathbb{N} \to \mathbb{N}$, our transform returns another WE scheme WE_f. The constructed scheme, formally specified in Fig. 3, misbehaves, returning the message in the clear, when $|x| \geq f(\lambda)$, and otherwise behaves like WE. The following says that if f is chosen to satisfy certain conditions then SS[L]-security is preserved, meaning $\mathsf{WE}_f \in \mathsf{SS}[L]$. In our uses of the transform we will exploit the fact that WE_f will fail to have other security properties or lead to failure of applications that use it.

$\mathsf{WE}_f.\mathsf{Enc}(1^\lambda, x, m)$	$\mathsf{WE}_f.\mathsf{Dec}(w, c)$
If $|x| \geq f(\lambda)$ then return $(0, m)$	$(b, t) \leftarrow c$
Else return $(1, \mathsf{WE}.\mathsf{Enc}(1^\lambda, x, m))$	If $b = 0$ then return t else return
	$\mathsf{WE}.\mathsf{Dec}(w, t)$

Fig. 3. Witness encryption scheme WE_f for $L \in \mathbf{NP}$, derived from $\mathsf{WE} \in \mathsf{SS}[L]$ and a PT-computable function $f : \mathbb{N} \to \mathbb{N}$

Lemma 1. Let $L \in \mathbf{NP}$ and $\mathsf{WE} \in \mathsf{SS}[L]$. Let $f : \mathbb{N} \to \mathbb{N}$ be a non-decreasing, PT-computable function such that $\lim_{\lambda \to \infty} f(\lambda) = \infty$. Consider witness encryption scheme WE_f derived from WE and f as shown in Fig. 3. Then $\mathsf{WE}_f \in \mathsf{SS}[L]$.

Proof. Let A be a PT adversary. Let $x \in \{0,1\}^* \setminus L$ and let $m_0, m_1 \in \{0,1\}^*$ have equal length. Let PT adversary B, on input ciphertext c, return $b' \leftarrow A((1, c))$. Let $S(x) = \{\lambda \in \mathbb{N} : f(\lambda) \leq |x|\}$. Then for all $\lambda \in \mathbb{N} \setminus S(x)$ we have $\mathsf{Adv}^{\mathsf{ss}}_{\mathsf{WE}, L, x, m_0, m_1, B}(\lambda) = \mathsf{Adv}^{\mathsf{ss}}_{\mathsf{WE}_f, L, x, m_0, m_1, A}(\lambda)$. The assumption that $\mathsf{WE} \in \mathsf{SS}[L]$ means that $\mathsf{Adv}^{\mathsf{ss}}_{\mathsf{WE}, L, x, m_0, m_1, B}(\cdot)$ is negligible. But the assumptions on f mean that the set $S(x)$ is finite. Consequently, the function $\mathsf{Adv}^{\mathsf{ss}}_{\mathsf{WE}_f, L, x, m_0, m_1, A}(\cdot)$ is negligible as well. □

Relations. We show that adaptive soundness implies soundness but not vice versa, meaning adaptive soundness is a strictly stronger requirement.

Proposition 2. Let $L \in \mathbf{NP}$. Then: (1) $\mathsf{AS}[L] \subseteq \mathsf{SS}[L]$, and (2) If $\{0,1\}^* \setminus L$ is infinite and $\mathsf{SS}[L] \neq \emptyset$ then $\mathsf{SS}[L] \not\subseteq \mathsf{AS}[L]$.

Claim (1) above says that any witness encryption scheme WE that is $\mathsf{AS}[L]$-secure is also $\mathsf{SS}[L]$-secure. Claim (2) says that the converse is not true. Namely, there is a witness encryption scheme WE such that WE is $\mathsf{SS}[L]$-secure but not $\mathsf{AS}[L]$-secure. This separation assumes some $\mathsf{SS}[L]$-secure witness encryption scheme exists, for otherwise the claim is moot. It also assumes that the complement of L is not trivial, meaning is infinite, which is true if L is $\mathbf{NP}$-complete and $\mathbf{P} \neq \mathbf{NP}$, hence is not a strong assumption.

Proof (Proposition 2). For part (1), assume we are given WE that is $\mathsf{AS}[L]$-secure. We want to show that WE is $\mathsf{SS}[L]$-secure. Referring to the definition of soundness security, let A be a PT adversary, let $x \in \{0,1\}^* \setminus L$ and let $m_0, m_1 \in \{0,1\}^*$ have equal length. We want to show that the function $\mathsf{Adv}^{\mathsf{ss}}_{\mathsf{WE}, L, x, m_0, m_1, A}(\cdot)$ is negligible. We define the adversary B_{x, m_0, m_1} as follows: Let $B_{x, m_0, m_1}(1^\lambda)$ return $(x, m_0, m_1, \varepsilon)$ and let $B_{x, m_0, m_1}(t, c)$ return $b' \leftarrow_\$ A(c)$. Here, B_{x, m_0, m_1} has x, m_0, m_1 hardwired in its code, and, in its first stage, it returns them, along with $\mathsf{St} = \varepsilon$ as state information. In its second stage, it simply runs A. Note that even though B_{x, m_0, m_1} has hardwired information, this information is finite and not dependent on the security parameter, so the hardwiring does not require non-uniformity. Now it is easy to see that for all $\lambda \in \mathbb{N}$ we have $\mathsf{Adv}^{\mathsf{as}}_{\mathsf{WE}, L, B_{x, m_0, m_1}}(\lambda) = \mathsf{Adv}^{\mathsf{ss}}_{\mathsf{WE}, L, x, m_0, m_1, A}(\lambda)$. The assumption that WE is $AS[L]$-secure means that $\mathsf{Adv}^{as}_{WE,L,B_{x,m_0,m_1}}(\cdot)$ is negligible, hence so is $\mathsf{Adv}^{ss}_{WE,L,x,m_0,m_1,A}(\cdot)$, as desired.

For part (2), the assumption $SS[L] \neq \emptyset$ means there is some $WE \in SS[L]$. By way of Lemma 1, we can modify it to $WE_f \in SS[L]$ as specified in Fig. 3, where $f : \mathbb{N} \to \mathbb{N}$ is some non-decreasing, PT-computable function such that $\lim_{\lambda \to \infty} f(\lambda) = \infty$. Now we want to present an attacker A violating $AS[L]$-security of WE_f. The difficulty is that A needs to find $x \notin L$ of length $f(\lambda)$, but $L \in \mathbf{NP}$ and A must be PT. We will exploit the fact that $\mathbf{NP} \subseteq \mathbf{EXP}$ and pick f to be a poly-logarithmic function related to the exponential time to decide L, so that if there exists an $x \notin L$ of length $f(\lambda)$ then A can find it by exhaustive search in PT. Our assumption that the complement of L is infinite means that A succeeds on infinitely many values of λ.

Proceeding to the details, since $L \in \mathbf{NP} \subseteq \mathbf{EXP}$, there is a constant $d \geq 1$ and a deterministic algorithm M such that for every $x \in \{0,1\}^*$, we have $M(x) = 1$ if and only if $x \in L$, and M's running time is $\mathcal{O}(2^{|x|^d})$. Define f by $f(\lambda) = \lfloor \lg^{1/d}(\lambda) \rfloor$ for all $\lambda \in \mathbb{N}$. Let $WE \in SS[L]$ and let WE_f be the witness encryption scheme derived from WE and f as specified in Fig. 3. By Lemma 1, $WE_f \in SS[L]$. Now we show that $WE_f \notin AS[L]$. Let $m_0, m_1 \in \{0,1\}^*$ be arbitrary, distinct, equal-length messages. Consider the following adversary A:

$\underline{A(1^\lambda)}$	$\underline{A(t,c)}$
$k \leftarrow f(\lambda)$; $x \leftarrow 0^k$	$(b,m) \leftarrow c$
For all $s \in \{0,1\}^k$ do	If $((b=0) \wedge (m = m_1))$ then return 1
$\quad$ If $(M(s) \neq 1)$ then $x \leftarrow s$	Return 0
Return $(x, m_0, m_1, \varepsilon)$	

Each execution of M takes time $\mathcal{O}(2^{k^d}) = \mathcal{O}(\lambda)$. The For loop goes through all $s \in \{0,1\}^k$ in lexicographic order and thus M is executed at most $2^k \leq \lambda$ times. So A is PT. For any $\lambda \in \mathbb{N}$, if $\{0,1\}^{f(\lambda)} \setminus L \neq \emptyset$ then $\mathsf{Adv}^{as}_{WE_f,L,A}(\lambda) = 1$. Since $\{0,1\}^* \setminus L$ is infinite, f is non-decreasing, and $\lim_{t \to \infty} f(t) = \infty$, there are infinitely many values λ such that $\mathsf{Adv}^{as}_{WE_f,L,A}(\lambda) = 1$, and thus $WE_f \notin AS[L]$, as claimed. $\qquad\square$

Indistinguishability Obfuscation. We say that two circuits C_0 and C_1 are *functionally equivalent*, denoted $C_0 \equiv C_1$, if they have the same size, the same number n of inputs, and $C_0(x) = C_1(x)$ for every input $x \in \{0,1\}^n$. An obfuscator P defines PT algorithms $\mathsf{P.Ob}, \mathsf{P.Ev}$. Algorithm $\mathsf{P.Ob}$ takes as input the unary representation 1^λ of a security parameter λ and a circuit C, and outputs a string c. Algorithm $\mathsf{P.Ev}$ takes as input strings c, x and returns $y \in \{0,1\}^* \cup \{\bot\}$. We require that for any circuit C, any input x, and any $\lambda \in \mathbb{N}$, it holds that $\mathsf{P.Ev}(x, \mathsf{P.Ob}(1^\lambda, C)) = C(x)$. We say that P is iO-secure if $\mathsf{Adv}^{io}_{\mathsf{P},A}(\lambda) = 2\Pr[\mathrm{IO}^A_{\mathsf{P}}(\lambda)] - 1$ is negligible for every PT adversary A, where game IO is defined at Fig. 4. This definition is slightly different from the notion in [4,18]—the adversary is non-uniform and must produce functionally equivalent circuits C_0 and C_1—but the former definition is implied by the latter.

$$\begin{array}{|l|}
\hline
\text{GAME } \mathrm{IO}_\mathsf{P}^A(\lambda) \\
\hline
(C_0, C_1, \mathrm{St}) \leftarrow_\$ A(1^\lambda) \; ; \; b \leftarrow_\$ \{0,1\} \; ; \; c \leftarrow_\$ \mathsf{P.Ob}(1^\lambda, C_b) \\
b' \leftarrow_\$ A(\mathrm{St}, c) \; ; \; \text{Return } (b = b') \wedge (C_0 \equiv C_1) \\
\hline
\end{array}$$

Fig. 4. Game IO defining security of an indistinguishability obfuscator P

Achieving AS-Security. Our AS security notion is strictly stronger than the SS one of GGSW [20], but we'll show that the iO-based WE scheme of [18] is AS-secure. Proceeding to the details, let R be an **NP**-relation. For each $x, m \in \{0,1\}^*$, let $R_{x,m}$ be a circuit that, on input $w \in \{0,1\}^{\mathsf{R.wl}(|x|)}$, returns m if $\mathsf{R}(x, w)$ and returns $0^{|m|}$ otherwise. Let P be an indistinguishability obfuscator, defining a PT obfuscation algorithm P.Ob and a PT evaluation algorithm P.Ev. We define WE scheme $\mathsf{WE_R}[\mathsf{P}]$ as follows: algorithm $\mathsf{WE_R}[\mathsf{P}].\mathsf{Enc}(1^\lambda, x, m)$ returns $c \leftarrow_\$ \mathsf{P.Ob}(1^\lambda, R_{x,m})$; and algorithm $\mathsf{WE_R}[\mathsf{P}].\mathsf{Dec}(w, c)$ returns $m \leftarrow_\$ \mathsf{P.Ev}(w, c)$.

Theorem 3. Let R be an **NP**-relation and let $L = \mathcal{L}(\mathsf{R})$. Let P be an indistinguishability obfuscator. Construct $\mathsf{WE_R}[\mathsf{P}]$ as above. If P is iO-secure then $\mathsf{WE_R}[\mathsf{P}] \in \mathrm{AS}[L]$.

Proof. Let A be a PT adversary attacking the $\mathrm{AS}[L]$-security of $\mathsf{WE_R}[\mathsf{P}]$. Wlog, assume that A produces distinct m_0 and m_1. Note that $R_{x,m_0} \equiv R_{x,m_1}$ if and only if $x \notin L$. Consider the following PT adversary B attacking iO-security of P:

$$\begin{array}{l|l}
\underline{B(1^\lambda)} & \underline{B(\mathrm{St}, c)} \\
(x, m_0, m_1, \mathrm{St}) \leftarrow_\$ A(1^\lambda) & b' \leftarrow_\$ A(\mathrm{St}, c) \; ; \; \text{Return } b' \\
\text{Return } (R_{x,m_0}, R_{x,m_1}, \mathrm{St}) &
\end{array}$$

Then $\Pr[\mathrm{AS}_{\mathsf{WE_R}[\mathsf{P}], L}^A(\cdot)] = \Pr[\mathrm{IO}_\mathsf{P}^B(\cdot)]$ and thus $\mathsf{Adv}_{\mathsf{WE_R}[\mathsf{P}], L, A}^{\mathsf{as}}(\cdot) = \mathsf{Adv}_{\mathsf{P}, B}^{\mathsf{io}}(\cdot)$. $\square$

4 Insufficiency of Soundness Security

GGSW [20] present constructions of several primitives from witness encryption, including PKE, IBE and ABE for all circuits. They claim security of these constructions assuming soundness security of the underlying witness-encryption scheme. We observe here that these claims are wrong. Taking their PRG-based PKE scheme as a representative example, we present a counter-example, namely a witness-encryption scheme satisfying soundness security such that the PKE scheme built from it is insecure. Similar counter-examples can be built for the other applications in GGSW [20]. Briefly, the problem is that a witness encryption scheme could fail to provide any security when $|x|$ is equal to, or related in some specific way to, the security parameter, yet satisfy SS security because the latter requirement holds x fixed and lets λ go to ∞. We show that the gap can be filled, and all the applications of GGSW recovered, by using adaptive soundness in place of soundness security. We'll begin by recalling the well-known notions of PRG and PKE.

GAME $\mathrm{PRG}_G^A(\lambda)$	GAME $\mathrm{INDCPA}_{\mathsf{PKE}}^A(\lambda)$
$s \leftarrow\!\!\text{\$}\ \{0,1\}^\lambda$; $x_1 \leftarrow G(s)$	$(pk, sk) \leftarrow\!\!\text{\$}\ \mathsf{PKE.Kg}(1^\lambda)$; $b \leftarrow\!\!\text{\$}\ \{0,1\}$
$x_0 \leftarrow\!\!\text{\$}\ \{0,1\}^{\ell(\lambda)}$; $b \leftarrow\!\!\text{\$}\ \{0,1\}$	$b' \leftarrow\!\!\text{\$}\ A^{\mathrm{LR}}(1^\lambda, pk)$; Return $(b = b')$
$b' \leftarrow\!\!\text{\$}\ A(1^\lambda, x_b)$; Return $(b = b')$	$\underline{\mathrm{LR}(m_0, m_1)}$
	$c \leftarrow\!\!\text{\$}\ \mathsf{PKE.Enc}(pk, m_b)$; Return c

Fig. 5. Left: Game PRG defining security of a pseudorandom generator G. Here $\ell : \mathbb{N} \to \mathbb{N}$ is the expansion factor of G. **Right:** Game INDCPA defining INDCPA security of a PKE scheme PKE. For each oracle query, the messages $m_0, m_1 \in \{0,1\}^*$ must have the same length.

$\mathsf{PKE.Kg}(1^\lambda)$	$\mathsf{PKE.Enc}(pk, m)$	$\mathsf{PKE.Dec}(sk, c)$
$sk \leftarrow\!\!\text{\$}\ \{0,1\}^\lambda$; $x \leftarrow G(sk)$	$(\lambda, x) \leftarrow pk$	Return $\overline{\mathsf{WE}}.\mathsf{Dec}(c, sk)$
$pk \leftarrow (\lambda, x)$; Return (pk, sk)	Return $\overline{\mathsf{WE}}.\mathsf{Enc}(1^\lambda, x, m)$	

Fig. 6. GGSW's PKE scheme $\mathsf{PKE}[G, \overline{\mathsf{WE}}]$, where G is a length-doubling PRG and $\overline{\mathsf{WE}}$ is a witness encryption scheme for $L_G = \{\ G(s)\ :\ s \in \{0,1\}^*\ \}$.

Primitives. A pseudorandom generator (PRG) [12,37] is a PT deterministic algorithm G that takes any string $s \in \{0,1\}^*$ as input and return a string $G(s)$ of length $\ell(|s|)$, where the function $\ell : \mathbb{N} \to \mathbb{N}$ is call the *expansion factor* of G. We say that G is secure if $\mathsf{Adv}_{A,G}^{\mathsf{prg}}(\lambda) = 2\Pr[\mathrm{PRG}_A^G(\lambda)] - 1$ is negligible, for every PT adversary A, where game PRG is defined in Fig. 5.

A public-key encryption (PKE) scheme PKE defines PT algorithms PKE.Kg, PKE.Enc, PKE.Dec, the last deterministic. Algorithm PKE.Kg takes as input 1^λ and outputs a public encryption key pk and a secret decryption key sk. Algorithm PKE.Enc takes as input pk and a message $m \in \{0,1\}^*$, and outputs a ciphertext c. Algorithm $\mathsf{PKE.Dec}(sk, c)$8 outputs $m \in \{0,1\}^* \cup \{\bot\}$. Scheme PKE is INDCPA-secure [6,27] if $\mathsf{Adv}_{\mathsf{PKE},A}^{\mathsf{ind\text{-}cpa}}(\cdot) = 2\Pr[\mathrm{INDCPA}_{\mathsf{PKE}}^A(\cdot)] - 1$ is negligible for every PT adversary A, where game INDCPA is defined in Fig. 5.

SS does not Suffice for GGSW's PKE Scheme. Let G be a PRG that is length doubling, meaning $|G(s)| = 2|s|$ for every $s \in \{0,1\}^*$. Let $L_G = \{\ G(s)\ :\ s \in \{0,1\}^*\ \}$. This language is in **NP**. Let $\overline{\mathsf{WE}} \in \mathrm{SS}[L_G]$ be a $\mathrm{SS}[L_G]$-secure WE scheme. The PKE scheme $\mathsf{PKE}[G, \overline{\mathsf{WE}}]$ of GGSW is shown in Fig. 6. We claim that $\mathrm{SS}[L_G]$-security of $\overline{\mathsf{WE}}$ is insufficient for PKE to be INDCPA-secure. We show this by counter-example, meaning we give an example of a particular WE scheme $\overline{\mathsf{WE}} \in \mathrm{SS}[L_G]$ such that $\mathsf{PKE}[G, \overline{\mathsf{WE}}]$ is not INDCPA. We assume there exists some $\mathsf{WE} \in \mathrm{SS}[L_G]$, else the question is moot. Let $f(\lambda) = 2\lambda$ for every $\lambda \in \mathbb{N}$. Now let $\overline{\mathsf{WE}} = \mathsf{WE}_f$ be the WE scheme of Fig. 3 obtained from WE and f. Lemma 1 tells us that $\mathsf{WE}_f \in \mathrm{SS}[L_G]$. Now we claim that $\mathsf{PKE}[G, \mathsf{WE}_f]$ is not INDCPA. The reason is that when $\mathsf{PKE.Enc}(pk, m)$ runs $\mathsf{WE}_f.\mathsf{Enc}(1^\lambda, x, m)$, we have $|x| = 2\lambda = f(\lambda)$. By definition of $\mathsf{WE}_f.\mathsf{Enc}$, the latter returns $(0, m)$ as the ciphertext, effectively sending the message in the clear.

AS Security Suffices for GGSW's PKE. We now show that the gap can be filled using AS. That is, we prove that if G is a secure PRG and $\overline{\mathsf{WE}}$ is $\mathsf{AS}[L_G]$-secure, then $\mathsf{PKE}[G, \mathsf{WE}]$ is INDCPA-secure:

Theorem 4. Let $G : \{0,1\}^* \to \{0,1\}^*$ be a length-doubling PRG. Let $L_G = \{ G(s) : s \in \{0,1\}^* \}$. If G is a secure PRG and $\overline{\mathsf{WE}} \in \mathsf{AS}[L_G]$ then $\mathsf{PKE}[G, \overline{\mathsf{WE}}]$ is INDCPA-secure.

The proof is in [7]. It follows the template of the proof of GGSW [20]. First one uses the PRG security of G to move to a game where x is random. Since G is length doubling, such an x is not in L_G with high probability. At this point GGSW [20] (incorrectly) claim that the result follows from the $\mathsf{SS}[L_G]$-security of $\overline{\mathsf{WE}}$. We instead use the $\mathsf{AS}[L_G]$-security of $\overline{\mathsf{WE}}$, providing a reduction with an explicit construction of an AS adversary.

To obtain similar counter-examples showing the inadequacy of SS for the other applications of GGSW (namely IBE and ABE for all circuits), one can follow the template of our PKE attack, by choosing a lower bound $f(\lambda)$ for the length of the string $x = X(\lambda)$ given to the witness encryption. Since $X(\lambda)$ is generated from some cryptographic primitive π (for example, in IBE, π is a unique signature scheme), the security of π requires that $X(\lambda)$ have super-logarithmic length. Hence there is a constant $C > 0$ such that $|X(\lambda)| \geq C \lg(\lambda)$ for all $\lambda \in \mathbb{N}$, and therefore we can let $f(\lambda) = \lfloor C \lg(\lambda) \rfloor$.

5   Asymmetric Password-Based Encryption

In this Section we introduce the new primitive of asymmetric password-based encryption (A-PBE). We then provide a non-invasive, WE-based A-PBE scheme we call APBE2, with two security analyses. First we prove security of APBE2 under AS-security of the WE scheme. Then under XS-security of the WE scheme we provide another proof that shows the scheme to admit better "stretch," leading to better security for some real password distributions. In [7] we provide a simple and fast, but invasive, A-PBE scheme, called APBE1. Our model and definitions are of interest beyond our schemes because they capture PKE in the real-world setting where secret keys are based on passwords and may thus be related.

A-PBE Syntax and Security. An *asymmetric password-based encryption* (A-PBE) scheme F specifies PT algorithms F.Ph, F.Enc, F.Dec, the first and the last deterministic. It also specifies a password-length function F.pl : $\mathbb{N} \to \mathbb{N}$, a salt-length function F.sl : $\mathbb{N} \to \mathbb{N}$, and a hash-length function F.hl : $\mathbb{N} \to \mathbb{N}$. Algorithm F.Ph takes as input the unary representation 1^λ of security parameter λ, a salt $sa \in \{0,1\}^{\mathsf{F.sl}(\lambda)}$, and a password $pw \in \{0,1\}^{\mathsf{F.pl}(\lambda)}$, and returns a hashed password $hpw = \mathsf{F.Ph}(1^\lambda, sa, pw) \in \{0,1\}^{\mathsf{F.hl}(\lambda)}$. Algorithm F.Enc takes as input $1^\lambda, hpw, sa$ and a message $m \in \{0,1\}^*$, and outputs a ciphertext c. Finally, given (pw, c), algorithm F.Dec returns $m \in \{0,1\}^* \cup \{\bot\}$. We require that

$$\mathsf{F.Dec}\big(pw, \mathsf{F.Enc}(1^\lambda, \mathsf{F.Ph}(1^\lambda, sa, pw), sa, m)\big) = m$$

for every $m \in \{0,1\}^*, \lambda \in \mathbb{N}, sa \in \{0,1\}^{\mathsf{F.sl}(\lambda)}$, and $pw \in \{0,1\}^{\mathsf{F.pl}(\lambda)}$.

GAME $\text{APBE}_\mathsf{F}^A(\lambda)$	GAME $\text{RIP}_\mathsf{H}^A(\lambda)$
$\mathbf{pw} \leftarrow\!\!\$\ A_1(1^\lambda)\ ;\ b \leftarrow\!\!\$\ \{0,1\}$	$\mathbf{pw} \leftarrow\!\!\$\ A_1(1^\lambda)\ ;\ b \leftarrow\!\!\$\ \{0,1\}$
For $i = 1$ to $|\mathbf{pw}|$ do	For $i = 1$ to $|\mathbf{pw}|$ do
$\quad \mathbf{sa}[i] \leftarrow\!\!\$\ \{0,1\}^{\mathsf{F.sl}(\lambda)}$	$\quad \mathbf{sa}[i] \leftarrow\!\!\$\ \{0,1\}^{\mathsf{H.kl}(\lambda)}$
$\quad \mathbf{hpw}[i] \leftarrow \mathsf{F.Ph}(1^\lambda, \mathbf{sa}[i], \mathbf{pw}[i])$	$\quad \mathbf{hpw}[i] \leftarrow \mathsf{H}(1^\lambda, \mathbf{sa}[i], \mathbf{pw}[i])$
$b' \leftarrow\!\!\$\ A_2^{\text{LR}}(1^\lambda, \mathbf{sa}, \mathbf{hpw})$	$\quad$ If $b = 0$ then $\mathbf{hpw}[i] \leftarrow\!\!\$\ \{0,1\}^{\mathsf{H.ol}(\lambda)}$
Return $(b = b')$	$b' \leftarrow\!\!\$\ A_2(1^\lambda, \mathbf{sa}, \mathbf{hpw})\ ;\ $ Return $(b = b')$
$\underline{\text{LR}(m_0, m_1, i)}$	
$c \leftarrow\!\!\$\ \mathsf{F.Enc}(1^\lambda, \mathbf{hpw}[i], \mathbf{sa}[i], m_b)$	
Return c	

Fig. 7. Left: Game APBE defining security of an A-PBE scheme F. **Right:** Game RIP defining RIP security for a hash family H.

An adversary A is a pair of PT algorithms (A_1, A_2). Adversary $A_1(1^\lambda)$ generates a vector of passwords $\mathbf{pw}$, each entry a $\mathsf{F.pl}(\lambda)$-bit string. It is required that A is unpredictable as defined in Section 2. Note that passwords —entries of the vector $\mathbf{pw}$— may be correlated, even though each individually is unpredictable, to capture the fact that individual users often pick related passwords for their different accounts. We say that A-PBE scheme F is secure if $\mathsf{Adv}_{\mathsf{F},A}^{\text{apbe}}(\cdot) = 2\Pr[\text{APBE}_\mathsf{F}^A(\cdot)] - 1$ is negligible for every PT unpredictable adversary A, where game $\text{APBE}_\mathsf{F}^A(\lambda)$ is defined in Fig. 7. In this game, $A_1(1^\lambda)$ first generates its vector $\mathbf{pw}$ of passwords. The game picks a challenge bit $b \leftarrow\!\!\$\ \{0,1\}$ and a vector of random salts $\mathbf{sa}$. Adversary A_2 is given $\mathbf{sa}$ and the vector $\mathbf{hpw}$ of hashed passwords. It can then query its oracle LR with equal-length, distinct messages m_0, m_1, and an index i, to get $\mathsf{F.Enc}(1^\lambda, \mathbf{hpw}[i], \mathbf{sa}[i], m_b)$. Finally A_2 outputs a prediction b' for b. The game returns true if the prediction is correct, meaning $b = b'$, and false otherwise.

Achieving A-PBE. If we have the luxury of prescribing our own password hashing function PH then we can provide a fast and simple A-PBE scheme, that we call APBE1, based on any PKE scheme. See [7]. However, this solution is invasive, asking for the deployment of a new PH, which may not be possible due to existing legacy passwords and password-hashing functions. We thus ask if it is possible to design a secure A-PBE scheme that is non-invasive. This means we take F.Ph as given and aim to achieve security by making reasonable assumptions about its security without prescribing its design, assumptions that in particular are met by the F.Ph function of PKCS#5 or other standards. This turns out to be more challenging. We now provide the APBE2 scheme that accomplishes this using WE.

Non-invasive A-PBE. We view ourselves as given a function family H with key, input and output length functions H.kl, H.il, H.ol. Our goal is to design an A-PBE scheme F such that F.Ph is H. In particular, we could let H be the password

$F[H,WE].Ph(1^\lambda, sa, pw)$	$F[H,WE].Enc(1^\lambda, hpw, sa, m)$	$F[H,WE].Dec(pw, c)$
$hpw \leftarrow H(1^\lambda, sa, pw)$	$x \leftarrow (1^\lambda, sa, hpw)$	$m \leftarrow WE.Dec(pw, c)$
Return hpw	$c \leftarrow\!\!\text{\$}\, WE(1^\lambda, x, m)$	Return m
	Return c	

Fig. 8. A-PBE scheme $F = APBE2[H, WE]$ associated to hash family H and witness encryption scheme WE for L_H

---

hashing function family from PKCS#5 [33] or bcrypt [34], thereby obtaining A-PBE without change in the existing hashed passwords. We begin by reviewing the security assumption on H.

Related-Input Pseudorandomness. Let H be a function family. This means that H is a deterministic, PT function taking 1^λ, a key $k \in \{0,1\}^{H.kl(\lambda)}$ and an input $x \in \{0,1\}^{H.il(\lambda)}$ to return $H(1^\lambda, k, x) \in \{0,1\}^{H.ol(\lambda)}$. Here $H.kl, H.il, H.ol: \mathbb{N} \to \mathbb{N}$ are the key, input and output lengths associated to H, respectively. We say that H is related-input pseudorandom (RIP) if $Adv_{H,A}^{rip}(\cdot) = 2\Pr[RIP_H^A(\cdot)] - 1$ is negligible for every PT unpredictable adversary $A = (A_1, A_2)$, where game RIP_H^A is shown in Fig. 7. Informally, this means that the hashed passwords should be indistinguishable from random strings, even in the presence of the salts. We note that this is exactly the property needed for classical S-PBE (symmetric PBE) to be secure, for it uses the hashed password as the symmetric key. Thus, the assumption can be viewed as already made and existing, even if implicitly, in current usage of passwords for S-PBE. We note that RIP security of H is implied by UCE security of H relative to statistically unpredictable sources [8].

The APBE2 Scheme. Let

$$L_H = \{ (1^\lambda, sa, H(1^\lambda, sa, pw)) : \lambda \in \mathbb{N}, \ sa \in \{0,1\}^{H.kl(\lambda)}, \ pw \in \{0,1\}^{H.il(\lambda)} \} .$$

This language is in **NP**. Let WE be a witness encryption scheme for L_H. We associate to H and WE the A-PBE scheme $F = APBE2[H, WE]$ specified in Fig. 8. We let $F.pl = H.il$, $F.sl = H.kl$ and $F.hl = H.ol$. The construction lets the salt play the role of the key for H, the password being the input and the hashed password the output.

Security of APBE2 under AS. Theorem 5 below says that if H is RIP and WE is $AS[L_H]$-secure then $APBE2[H, WE]$ is a secure A-PBE scheme. The proof is in [7].

Theorem 5. Let H be a function family such that $2^{H.il(\cdot)-H.ol(\cdot)}$ is a negligible function. If H is RIP and $WE \in AS[L_H]$ then $F = APBE2[H, WE]$ is a secure A-PBE scheme.

The key feature of this result is that it is non-invasive, meaning it puts conditions on the hash family H that suffice for security rather than mandating any

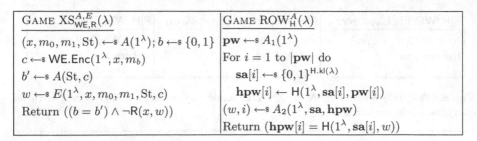

Fig. 9. **Left:** Game XS defining extractable security of witness encryption scheme WE. **Right:** Game ROW defining ROW security of H.

particular design of H. Practical and standardized key-derivation functions may be assumed to satisfy concrete versions of these asymptotic conditions.

Arbitrary Stretch. Define the stretch $H.s(\cdot) = H.ol(\cdot) - H.il(\cdot)$ of password hashing function H as the difference between its output length and its input length. Theorem 5 requires that $2^{-H.s(\cdot)}$ is negligible, meaning the output length of the hash must be somewhat longer than the input length. This captures situations in which passwords are, say 12-character ASCII strings (input length is 78-bit) and H is iterated SHA1 (output length is 160-bit). However, when passwords are longer, say 24-character, then Theorem 5 doesn't apply. This is unsatisfying, because intuitively, longer passwords should offer better security. In this section, we formalize a stronger security requirement for witness encryption called XS that allows us to remove the assumption on the stretch of H.

XS-Secure Witness Encryption. The security requirements for SS and AS are for $x \notin L$, no security requirement being made if $x \in L$. Extractable witness encryption [26] is a requirement for all $x \in \{0,1\}^*$, asking that if the adversary violates privacy of encryption under x then one can extract a witness for the membership of $x \in L$. Intuitively, the only way to violate privacy is to know a witness. We provide a formalization of extraction security that we call XS. It strengthens the formalization of GKPVZ [26] in being adaptive, in the vein of AS, but weakens it by not involving auxiliary inputs. The formalizations also differ in other details.

Let R be an **NP**-relation and let $L = \mathcal{L}(R)$. Let WE be a witness encryption scheme for L. We say that WE is XS[L]-secure if for any PT adversary A there is a corresponding PT algorithm E such that $\mathsf{Adv}^{xs}_{WE,R,A,E}(\lambda) = 2\Pr[XS^{A,E}_{WE,R}(\lambda)] - 1$ is negligible, where game $XS^{A,E}_{WE,R}$ is defined at the leftpanel of Fig. 9. Let XS[L] denote the set of correct, XS[L]-secure witness encryption schemes for L.

Intuitively, XS[L] security implies AS[L] security for any $L \in \mathbf{NP}$, because in the former notion, if the adversary produces $x \notin L$ then no witness exists, so no extractor E (even a computationally unbounded one) can find one. Proposition 6 below formally confirms this. The proof is in [7].

Proposition 6. *For any* **NP**-relation R, *it holds that* XS[$\mathcal{L}(R)$] $\subseteq$ AS[$\mathcal{L}(R)$].

Extractable obfuscation (xO), also known as differing-input obfuscation, was defined in [1,4,14]. BCP [14] show that it implies extractable witness encryption meeting the definition of GKPVZ [26]. In [7], we give an alternative definition of xO and show that it implies $XS[\mathcal{L}(R)]$-secure witness encryption, for any **NP** relation R. The construction is the same $WE_R[P]$ in Section 3, where the obfuscator P is assumed to be xO-secure, instead of just being iO-secure.

Related-Input One-Wayness. We now formalize another hardness assumption, related-input one-wayness, on hash function family H. Informally we demand that if the adversary is given the hashed passwords and the salts, it can't compute a preimage of any hashed password. This is exactly the intuitive requirement for password-hashing functions: if passwords are well-chosen to resist dictionary attacks, then no adversary should be able to recover some password from the hashed ones. It's a variant of the notion of one-wayness under correlated products of [35]. Formally, we say that H is related-input one-way (ROW) if $Adv_{H,A}^{row}(\lambda) = Pr[ROW_H^A(\lambda)]$ is negligible for all PT unpredictable adversary $A = (A_1, A_2)$, where game ROW_H^A is shown at the right panel of Fig. 9.

Security of APBE2 under XS. The following establishes the security of $F = APBE2[H, WE]$ without any restrictions or assumptions on the stretch of H. See [7] for the proof.

Theorem 7. If H is ROW and $WE \in XS[L_H]$ then $F = APBE2[H, WE]$ is a secure A-PBE scheme.

A   Further Versions of SS

A good definition for WE security should have two properties: (1) *Usability*, meaning it should suffice to prove security of applications, and (2) *Achievability*, meaning it should be provably achieved by the natural constructs, which in this case means the iO-based one of GGHRSW [18]. Our AS definition has both properties. We have shown that SS [20,21] lacks (1).

After seeing a prior version of our work, GGSW updated the ePrint version of their paper [22]. Here they acknowledge the gaps we find. They then propose their own modification of SS, that we call SS2, in an attempt to fill the gaps. This was unnecessary because AS had already been put forth and shown to fill the gap, but GGSW appeared to want a definition in their quantifier-based style rather than our game-based style. They viewed the problem in SS as arising from the "order of quantification" and attempted to address it by changing this order. SS2 quantified the negligible function first, making it universal. We explain below that SS2 is unachievable, meaning no WE scheme can be SS2 secure. (More precisely our result is that SS2-secure WE is unachievable for any **NP**-complete language unless the polynomial-time hierarchy collapses. Our proof uses the fact that statistically-secure WE is not achievable [20].) We pointed this out to GGSW in a personal communication. They acknowledged this and further updated their definition to one we call SS3 [22], which used another order of quantification. Below we show that SS3 remains limited in terms of achievability. This is because it does not seem possible to show that the iO-based WE construction of GGHRSW [18] meets it under the definition of iO-security that is commonly used in other applications of iO [13,30,36] and that we have shown suffices for AS-secure WE.

The updated GGSW papers [22,23] characterize the gap we find as having to do with the "order of quantifiers" in the SS definition, and their fixes attempt to change quantifier order. However, the issue is not quantifier order but, more subtly, the relation between x and λ. More broadly, game-based definitions are a better fit in this domain than quantifier-based ones. This is because applications one wants to achieve with WE, as well as primitives one wants to use to achieve WE, are both themselves underlain by game-based definitions. Reductions are thus facilitated, and less error-prone, with a game-based WE definition. A quantifier-based one leads to mismatches. In particular, under certain quantifier orders, one gets definitions like SS that do not provide usability, and when one changes the order, one gets definitions like SS3 that are too strong and challenge achievability. Intuitively, the latter is because the quantification ends up demanding security even on inputs that no adversary could ever find. This does not mean a viable quantifier-based definition is impossible. Indeed, below, we suggest SS4, a quantifier-based definition of WE that recovers achievability under weak iO in the non-uniform case. But the game-based AS is simpler and more user friendly, and does not require non-uniformity to be achieved under weak iO.

Below we also consider a recent definition of soundness security of KNY [31]. We call it SS5. It is similar to SS2 and consequently also unachievable.

The above indicates that the problems we find with SS, and the fix we deliver with AS, are not trivial. Certainly it is easy, once the problem has been pointed out, to propose alternatives, but our work remains important in having pointed out the need for alternatives and in guiding the choice of, and verifying, these alternatives.

We believe that WE is an important and useful notion and that our work helps advance its cause via precise definitions that satisfy the usability and achievability conditions above. We believe it is important for our field that work like this is published, and that such work is not damaging for the GGSW authors but rather advances the primitive they proposed.

SS2. WE scheme WE is SS2[L]-secure according to [22] if there exists a negligible function $\nu : \mathbb{N} \to \mathbb{N}$ such that for any PT adversary A, any $x \in \{0,1\}^* \backslash L$, any equal-length $m_0, m_1 \in \{0,1\}^*$, and any $\lambda \in \mathbb{N}$ we have

$$
\mathsf{Adv}^{\mathsf{ss2}}_{\mathsf{WE}, L, x, m_0, m_1, A}(\lambda)
$$
$$
= \Pr[A(\mathsf{WE.Enc}(1^\lambda, x, m_1)) = 1] - \Pr[A(\mathsf{WE.Enc}(1^\lambda, x, m_0)) = 1] < \nu(\lambda) .
$$

We claim this notion is unachievable, meaning, *no* WE scheme is SS2[L]-secure. The reason is that ν is universal and in particular not allowed to depend on the adversary. More formally let L be an **NP**-complete language. Let WE by any WE scheme and let ν be any negligible function. We show that if the polynomial-time hierarchy does not collapse then there is a PT adversary A as well as $x \in \{0,1\}^* \backslash L$, equal-length m_0, m_1 and $\lambda \in \mathbb{N}$ such that $\mathsf{Adv}^{ss2}_{\mathsf{WE},L,x,m_0,m_1,A}(\lambda) \geq \nu(\lambda)$. This shows that WE is not SS2[L]-secure.

For probability distribution functions $\mu, \mu' : D \rightarrow [0,1]$, let

$$\|\mu - \mu'\| = \frac{1}{2} \sum_{x \in D} |\mu(x) - \mu'(x)|$$

be the statistical distance between μ and μ'. For any λ, x, m let $\mu_{\lambda,x,m}$ be the distribution of $\mathsf{WE.Enc}(1^\lambda, x, m)$. Results from GGSW [20] imply that, unless the polynomial hierarchy collapses, there exists a string $x' \in \{0,1\}^* \backslash L$, equal-length messages m_0', m_1' and a constant $\lambda_0 \in \mathbb{N}$ such that $\|\mu_{\lambda_0,x',m_1'} - \mu_{\lambda_0,x',m_0'}\| \geq \nu(\lambda_0)$. Consider the following adversary A. On input a ciphertext c, if c is not in the domain of $\mu_{\lambda_0,x',m_1'}$ then A outputs a random guess. Otherwise, A outputs 1 if $\mu_{\lambda_0,x',m_1'}(c) > \mu_{\lambda_0,x',m_0'}(c)$, and outputs 0 otherwise. Note that the test as to whether c is in the domain of $\mu_{\lambda_0,x',m_1'}$ only takes polynomial time because λ_0, x', m_1' are fixed, and all computations related to them are constant time, and similarly for computations of $\mu_{\lambda_0,x',m_0'}(\cdot)$. Thus A runs in polynomial time. But $\mathsf{Adv}^{ss2}_{\mathsf{WE},L,x',m_0',m_1',A}(\lambda_0) = \|\mu_{\lambda_0,x',m_1'} - \mu_{\lambda_0,x',m_0'}\| \geq \nu(\lambda_0)$.

SS3. A WE scheme WE is SS3[L]-secure [23] if for any PT adversary A, there exists a negligible function $\nu : \mathbb{N} \rightarrow \mathbb{N}$ such that for any $x \in \{0,1\}^* \backslash L$ and any $\lambda \in \mathbb{N}$,

$$\mathsf{Adv}^{ss3}_{\mathsf{WE},L,x,A}(\lambda)$$
$$= \Pr[A(\mathsf{WE.Enc}(1^\lambda, x, 1)) = 1] - \Pr[A(\mathsf{WE.Enc}(1^\lambda, x, 0)) = 1] < \nu(\lambda) .$$

A first nit is that this considers only encryption of a 1-bit message but for applications one has to encrypt many bits, and it is not stated how security is defined in this case. More importantly, however, SS3 has limitations with regard to achievability. Specifically, it seems unlikely one can show that iO implies SS3[L]-secure WE via the natural GGHRSW construction that worked for both SS and AS and under the definition of iO that is used for other applications [13,30,36] and we have shown suffices for AS-secure WE. We now explain, referring to our formulation of the definition in Section 3. Let L be an **NP** language. In Section 3 we recalled the GGHRSW construction WE = $\mathsf{WE_R}[\mathsf{P}]$ of a WE scheme from an indistinguishability obfuscator P. Now assume we are given an arbitrary PT adversary A attacking the SS3[L]-security of WE. To prove security, we need to build an adversary B attacking the iO-security of P. Adversary B, given 1^λ, needs to efficiently find and output circuits of the form $R_{x,m}$ that we defined in Section 3, where x intuitively is an input where the WE security "breaks." But how is B to find such an x efficiently? There seems to be no way. Even if we allow B to be non-uniform, its advice string has length polynomial in λ, and thus it can't tell what is the "best" x because the set $\{0,1\}^* \backslash L$ is infinite. In the case of AS, this was not a problem because A handed back an x on which it succeeded. Also for the original SS, it is not a problem because the entire claim pertains to only one, fixed x that can be assumed known to B. An approach we might consider for SS3 is the following. Given any string $x \notin L$, we can build an adversary B_x such that $\mathsf{Adv}^{ss3}_{\mathsf{WE},L,x,A}(\lambda) \leq \mathsf{Adv}^{io}_{\mathsf{P},B_x}(\lambda)$ for all $\lambda \in \mathbb{N}$. Now the assumed iO security gives us a negligible function ν_x such that $\mathsf{Adv}^{io}_{\mathsf{P},B_x}(\cdot) < \nu_x(\cdot)$. But the SS3 notion wants a single negligible function ν that is independent of x. It's unclear how to get ν from the set $\{ \nu_x : x \notin L \}$ since the latter set is infinite. One natural idea is to set $\nu(\lambda) = \sup_{x \notin L}\{\nu_x(\lambda)\}$. But this doesn't work. For example, consider $\nu_x(\lambda) = 1$ if $\lambda < |x|$, and $\nu_x(\lambda) = 0$ otherwise. For any fixed x, the function ν_x is negligible, but $\nu(\lambda) = 1$ for every $\lambda \in \mathbb{N}$, meaning ν is not negligible. So one appears to need to construct an iO adversary B independent of x, but it is unclear how to do that.

We note the proof does seem possible under some stronger notions of iO from [18]. However, iO is a strong assumption no matter what and it is desirable that applications use as weak a form of it as possible. Also in further work subsequent to ours, GLW [25] claim to achieve SS3 via a direct construction. However, this requires sub-exponential hardness assumptions. (They call it complexity leveraging.) Beyond this, trying to achieve SS3 is an unnecessary route to follow, since AS already provides the properties we want, namely it suffices for applications and is achieved even under weak iO.

SS4. As we have seen, the game-based AS definition fulfills the usability and achievability conditions for a good definition. However, GGSW appear to want a quantifier-based definition in the style of SS. But their SS2, SS3 attempts have been inadequate. Here we accordingly suggest a quantifier-based definition that we call SS4 which does satisfy, usability and is less limited than SS3 with regard to achievability, namely weak iO does suffice for it, as long as this is assumed for non-uniform adversaries. In particular it is implied by the non-uniform generalization of AS and thus can be built from weak, non-uniform iO by our results. We explain why it suffices for the PKE application of GGSW.

We say that a WE scheme WE is SS4[L]-secure if for any PT adversary A and any polynomial $\ell : \mathbb{N} \to \mathbb{N}$, there exists a negligible function $\nu : \mathbb{N} \to \mathbb{N}$ such that, for any string $x \in \{0,1\}^* \backslash L$, and any $\lambda \in \mathbb{N}$, if $|x| \leq \ell(\lambda)$ then

$$\mathsf{Adv}^{ss4}_{\mathsf{WE},L,\ell,x,A}(\lambda)$$
$$= \Pr[A(1^\lambda, x, \mathsf{WE.Enc}(1^\lambda, x, 1)) = 1] - \Pr[A(1^\lambda, x, \mathsf{WE.Enc}(1^\lambda, x, 0)) = 1]$$
$$< \nu(\lambda) .$$

We now show this notion is implied by non-uniform AS. Given any SS4 adversary A and any polynomial ℓ, one can build another non-uniform AS adversary B as follows. For each $\lambda \in \mathbb{N}$, let $x_\lambda \in \{0,1\}^* \backslash L$ be a string such that $|x_\lambda| \leq \ell(\lambda)$ and $\mathsf{Adv}^{ss4}_{\mathsf{WE},L,\ell,x,A}(\lambda) \leq \mathsf{Adv}^{ss4}_{\mathsf{WE},L,\ell,x_\lambda,A}(\lambda)$ for all $x \in \{0,1\}^* \backslash L$ with $|x| \leq \ell(\lambda)$. Adversary $B(1^\lambda)$ outputs $(x_\lambda, 0, 1, \varepsilon)$, and $B(\mathsf{St}, c)$ runs $A(1^\lambda, x_\lambda, c)$. Then for any string $x \in \{0,1\}^* \backslash L$, $\lambda \in \mathbb{N}$, if $|x| \leq \ell(\lambda)$ then

$$\mathsf{Adv}^{as}_{\mathsf{WE},B}(\lambda) = \mathsf{Adv}^{ss4}_{\mathsf{WE},L,\ell,x_\lambda,A}(\lambda) \geq \mathsf{Adv}^{ss4}_{\mathsf{WE},L,\ell,x,A}(\lambda) .$$

We now briefly explain why SS4 is enough for GGSW's PKE scheme, but under message space $\{0, 1\}$, because SS4 only allows encrypting a single bit. The IND-CPA adversary is assumed to make only a single query $(0, 1)$. The proof will follow the template in [7] but with a change in constructing WE adversary D from an INDCPA adversary A. Let $\ell(\lambda) = 2\lambda$ for every $\lambda \in \mathbb{N}$. Adversary $D(1^\lambda, x, c)$ runs $A(1^\lambda, pk)$ with $pk = (\lambda, x)$. When the latter makes its query, the former returns c. Finally, D outputs the same guess as A.

For both SS3 and SS4, in the PKE application, to encrypt an n-bit message, one has to make n calls to WE to encrypt n bits individually, exacerbating the inefficiency of the scheme. If one modifies SS3 and SS4 for encrypting equal-length m_0, m_1 of arbitrary length instead of $m_0 = 0$ and $m_1 = 1$, then the PKE still can only encrypt bit-by-bit. The reason is that, an INDCPA adversary A is allowed to choose any equal-length m_0, m_1 but in SS3 and SS4, the WE adversary D has no control of the messages m_0, m_1, and thus one can't construct D from A. This again shows that AS is superior to SS3 and SS4 in terms of usability.

SS5. In a recent paper, KNY [31] define the following variant of SS, which we call SS5. A scheme is SS5[L]-secure if for any security parameter λ, any equal-length messages $m_0, m_1 \in \{0, 1\}^{\text{poly}(\lambda)}$, any PT adversary A, and any $x \notin L$, we have

$$\mathsf{Adv}^{ss5}_{\mathsf{WE}, L, x, m_0, m_1, A}(\lambda)$$
$$= \Pr[A(\mathsf{WE}.\mathsf{Enc}(1^\lambda, x, m_1) = 1] - \Pr[A(\mathsf{WE}.\mathsf{Enc}(1^\lambda, x, m_0)) = 1] < \mathsf{negl}(\lambda) \ .$$

This definition doesn't specify where to place the (existential) quantifier for the negligible function negl, but the only meaningful position in the context of what is written is to place it prior to the (universal) quantification of the security parameter. (We certainly don't want a different negligible function for every value of λ.) But if so, the function negl is independent of the adversary A. The same argument against SS2 can be used to show that SS5 is unachievable.

SS5 again demonstrates that quantifier-based notions for WE are error-prone. KNY's definition [31] is problematic, although it is subsequent to our work and all of GGSW's revisions.

Acknowledgments. We thank Krysztof Pietrzak and Georg Fuchsbauer for discussions about witness encryption. Bellare is supported in part by NSF grants CNS-0904380, CCF-0915675, CNS-1116800 and CNS-1228890. Part of the work was done when Hoang was working at UCSD, and supported in part by NSF grants CNS-0904380, CCF-0915675, CNS-1116800 and CNS-1228890.

References

1. Ananth, P., Boneh, D., Garg, S., Sahai, A., Zhandry, M.: Differing-inputs obfuscation and applications. Cryptology ePrint Archive, Report 2013/689 (2013). http://eprint.iacr.org/2013/689
2. Ananth, P.V., Gupta, D., Ishai, Y., Sahai, A.: Optimizing obfuscation: avoiding barrington's theorem. In: Ahn, G.-J., Yung, M., Li, N. (eds.) ACM CCS 2014, pp. 646–658. ACM Press, November 2014

3. Barak, B., Garg, S., Kalai, Y.T., Paneth, O., Sahai, A.: Protecting obfuscation against algebraic attacks. In: Nguyen, P.Q., Oswald, E. (eds.) EUROCRYPT 2014. LNCS, vol. 8441, pp. 221–238. Springer, Heidelberg (2014)
4. Barak, B., Goldreich, O., Impagliazzo, R., Rudich, S., Sahai, A., Vadhan, S.P., Yang, K.: On the (im)possibility of obfuscating programs. In: Kilian, J. (ed.) CRYPTO 2001. LNCS, vol. 2139, pp. 1–18. Springer, Heidelberg (2001)
5. Bellare, M., Canetti, R., Krawczyk, H.: Keying hash functions for message authentication. In: Koblitz, N. (ed.) CRYPTO 1996. LNCS, vol. 1109, pp. 1–15. Springer, Heidelberg (1996)
6. Bellare, M., Desai, A., Pointcheval, D., Rogaway, P.: Relations among notions of security for public-key encryption schemes. In: Krawczyk, H. (ed.) CRYPTO 1998. LNCS, vol. 1462, pp. 26–45. Springer, Heidelberg (1998)
7. Bellare, M., Hoang, V.T.: Adaptive witness encryption and asymmetric password-based cryptography. Cryptology ePrint Archive, Report 2013/704 (2013). http://eprint.iacr.org/2013/704
8. Bellare, M., Hoang, V.T., Keelveedhi, S.: Instantiating random oracles via UCEs. In: Canetti, R., Garay, J.A. (eds.) CRYPTO 2013, Part II. LNCS, vol. 8043, pp. 398–415. Springer, Heidelberg (2013)
9. Bellare, M., Meiklejohn, S., Thomson, S.: Key-versatile signatures and applications: RKA, KDM and joint Enc/Sig. In: Nguyen, P.Q., Oswald, E. (eds.) EUROCRYPT 2014. LNCS, vol. 8441, pp. 496–513. Springer, Heidelberg (2014)
10. Bellare, M., Ristenpart, T., Tessaro, S.: Multi-instance security and its application to password-based cryptography. In: Safavi-Naini, R., Canetti, R. (eds.) CRYPTO 2012. LNCS, vol. 7417, pp. 312–329. Springer, Heidelberg (2012)
11. Bellare, M., Rogaway, P.: The security of triple encryption and a framework for code-based game-playing proofs. In: Vaudenay, S. (ed.) EUROCRYPT 2006. LNCS, vol. 4004, pp. 409–426. Springer, Heidelberg (2006)
12. Blum, M., Micali, S.: How to generate cryptographically strong sequences of pseudorandom bits. SIAM Journal on Computing 13(4), 850–864 (1984)
13. Boneh, D., Zhandry, M.: Multiparty key exchange, efficient traitor tracing, and more from indistinguishability obfuscation. In: Garay, J.A., Gennaro, R. (eds.) CRYPTO 2014, Part I. LNCS, vol. 8616, pp. 480–499. Springer, Heidelberg (2014)
14. Boyle, E., Chung, K.-M., Pass, R.: On extractability obfuscation. In: Lindell, Y. (ed.) TCC 2014. LNCS, vol. 8349, pp. 52–73. Springer, Heidelberg (2014)
15. Boyle, E., Pass, R.: Limits of extractability assumptions with distributional auxiliary input. Cryptology ePrint Archive, Report 2013/703 (2013). http://eprint.iacr.org/2013/703
16. Brakerski, Z., Rothblum, G.N.: Virtual black-box obfuscation for all circuits via generic graded encoding. In: Lindell, Y. (ed.) TCC 2014. LNCS, vol. 8349, pp. 1–25. Springer, Heidelberg (2014)
17. Chase, M., Lysyanskaya, A.: On signatures of knowledge. In: Dwork, C. (ed.) CRYPTO 2006. LNCS, vol. 4117, pp. 78–96. Springer, Heidelberg (2006)
18. Garg, S., Gentry, C., Halevi, S., Raykova, M., Sahai, A., Waters, B.: Candidate indistinguishability obfuscation and functional encryption for all circuits. In: 54th FOCS, pp. 40–49. IEEE Computer Society Press, October 2013
19. Garg, S., Gentry, C., Halevi, S., Wichs, D.: On the implausibility of differing-inputs obfuscation and extractable witness encryption with auxiliary input. In: Garay, J.A., Gennaro, R. (eds.) CRYPTO 2014, Part I. LNCS, vol. 8616, pp. 518–535. Springer, Heidelberg (2014)

20. Garg, S., Gentry, C., Sahai, A., Waters, B.: Witness encryption and its applications. In: Boneh, D., Roughgarden, T., Feigenbaum, J. (eds.) 45th ACM STOC, pp. 467–476. ACM Press, June 2013
21. Garg, S., Gentry, C., Sahai, A., Waters, B.: Witness encryption and its applications. Cryptology ePrint Archive, Report 2013/258, version 20130508:202916, May 8, 2013
22. Garg, S., Gentry, C., Sahai, A., Waters, B.: Witness encryption and its applications. Cryptology ePrint Archive, Report 2013/258, version 20140211:224937, February 11, 2014
23. Garg, S., Gentry, C., Sahai, A., Waters, B.: Witness encryption and its applications. Cryptology ePrint Archive, Report 2013/258, version 20140418:025904, April 18, 2014
24. Gentry, C., Lewko, A., Sahai, A., Waters, B.: Indistinguishability obfuscation from the multilinear subgroup elimination assumption. Cryptology ePrint Archive, Report 2014/309 (2014). http://eprint.iacr.org/2014/309
25. Gentry, C., Lewko, A., Waters, B.: Witness encryption from instance independent assumptions. In: Garay, J.A., Gennaro, R. (eds.) CRYPTO 2014, Part I. LNCS, vol. 8616, pp. 426–443. Springer, Heidelberg (2014)
26. Goldwasser, S., Kalai, Y.T., Popa, R.A., Vaikuntanathan, V., Zeldovich, N.: How to run turing machines on encrypted data. In: Canetti, R., Garay, J.A. (eds.) CRYPTO 2013, Part II. LNCS, vol. 8043, pp. 536–553. Springer, Heidelberg (2013)
27. Goldwasser, S., Micali, S.: Probabilistic encryption. Journal of Computer and System Sciences 28(2), 270–299 (1984)
28. Goldwasser, S., Micali, S., Rackoff, C.: The knowledge complexity of interactive proof systems. SIAM Journal on Computing 18(1), 186–208 (1989)
29. Goyal, V., O'Neill, A., Rao, V.: Correlated-input secure hash functions. In: Ishai, Y. (ed.) TCC 2011. LNCS, vol. 6597, pp. 182–200. Springer, Heidelberg (2011)
30. Hohenberger, S., Sahai, A., Waters, B.: Replacing a random oracle: full domain hash from indistinguishability obfuscation. In: Nguyen, P.Q., Oswald, E. (eds.) EUROCRYPT 2014. LNCS, vol. 8441, pp. 201–220. Springer, Heidelberg (2014)
31. Komargodski, I., Naor, M., Yogev, E.: Secret-sharing for NP. In: Sarkar, P., Iwata, T. (eds.) ASIACRYPT 2014, Part II. LNCS, vol. 8874, pp. 254–273. Springer, Heidelberg (2014)
32. Nisan, N., Zuckerman, D.: Randomness is linear in space. Journal of Computer and System Sciences 52(1), 43–52 (1996)
33. PKCS #5: Password-based cryptography standard (RFC 2898). RSA Data Security Inc, Version 2.0, September 2000
34. Provos, N., Mazières, D.: A future-adaptable password scheme. In: USENIX Annual Technical Conference, FREENIX Track, pp. 81–91 (1999)
35. Rosen, A., Segev, G.: Chosen-ciphertext security via correlated products. In: Reingold, O. (ed.) TCC 2009. LNCS, vol. 5444, pp. 419–436. Springer, Heidelberg (2009)
36. Sahai, A., Waters, B.: How to use indistinguishability obfuscation: deniable encryption, and more. In: Shmoys, D.B. (ed.) 46th ACM STOC, pp. 475–484. ACM Press, May/June 2014
37. Yao, A.C.-C.: Theory and applications of trapdoor functions (extended abstract). In: 23rd FOCS, pp. 80–91. IEEE Computer Society Press, November 1982

Public-Key Encryption Indistinguishable Under Plaintext-Checkable Attacks

Michel Abdalla[✉], Fabrice Benhamouda, and David Pointcheval

ENS, CNRS, INRIA, and PSL, 45 rue d'Ulm, 75005 Paris, France
{michel.abdalla,fabrice.benhamouda,david.pointcheval}@ens.fr

Abstract. Indistinguishability under adaptive chosen-ciphertext attack (IND-CCA) is now considered the *de facto* security notion for public-key encryption. However, the security guarantee that it offers is sometimes stronger than what is needed by certain applications. In this paper, we consider a weaker notion of security for public-key encryption, termed indistinguishability under plaintext-checking attacks (IND-PCA), in which the adversary is only given access to an oracle which says whether or not a given ciphertext encrypts a given message. After formalizing the IND-PCA notion, we then design a new public-key encryption scheme satisfying it. The new scheme is a more efficient variant of the Cramer-Shoup encryption scheme with shorter ciphertexts and its security is also based on the plain Decisional Diffie-Hellman (DDH) assumption. Additionally, the algebraic properties of the new scheme also allow for proving plaintext knowledge using Groth-Sahai non-interactive zero-knowledge proofs or smooth projective hash functions. Finally, in order to illustrate the usefulness of the new scheme, we further show that, for many password-based authenticated key exchange (PAKE) schemes in the Bellare-Pointcheval-Rogaway security model, one can safely replace the underlying IND-CCA encryption schemes with our new IND-PCA one. By doing so, we were able to reduce the overall communication complexity of these protocols and obtain the most efficient PAKE schemes to date based on the plain DDH assumption.

1 Introduction

Public-key encryption (PKE) is one of the most fundamental primitives in cryptography, allowing users to exchange messages privately without the need for pre-established secrets. The basic security notion for (probabilistic) public-key encryption is indistinguishability of encryptions under chosen-plaintext attacks (IND-CPA) [18], also known as semantic security. Informally speaking, this notion states that any passive adversary capable of eavesdropping on the communication between two parties should not be able to obtain any information about the encrypted messages.

While IND-CPA security may suffice for certain applications, it does not provide any guarantee against active attacks, in which the adversary may modify existing ciphertexts or inject new ones into the communication and obtain information about the decrypted messages. In fact, as shown by Bleichenbacher [9]

J. Katz (Ed.): PKC 2015, LNCS 9020, pp. 332–352, 2015.
DOI: 10.1007/978-3-662-46447-2_15

in his attack against RSA PKCS #1, one can sometimes break an existing PKE scheme simply by knowing whether an existing ciphertext is valid or not.

In order to address the problem of active attacks, several notions of security have been proposed, such as indistinguishability under non-adaptive chosen-ciphertext attack (IND-CCA1) [28], indistinguishability under adaptive chosen-ciphertext attack (IND-CCA2 or IND-CCA) [30], non-malleability under chosen-plaintext attack (NM-CPA) or adaptive chosen-ciphertext attack (NM-CCA) [13,14]. Among these, as shown by Bellare *et al.* [5], the IND-CCA notion is the strongest one and implies all of the other ones. Unlike the IND-CPA notion, the IND-CCA security notion states that the adversary should not be capable to learning any information about the underlying message of a given ciphertext even when given access to the decryption of other ciphertexts of its choice.

Indistinguishabiliy Under Plaintext-Checkable Attacks. Even though IND-CCA is now considered the *de facto* security notion for public-key encryption, the security guarantee that it offers is sometimes stronger than what is needed by certain applications. Since stronger security guarantees usually result in a loss of efficiency, different security goals, such as oneway-ness, and different attack capabilities, such as plaintext-checkable attacks [29], have been considered as alternatives to the IND-CCA security notion. While in oneway-ness, the goal of the adversary is to recover the underlying encrypted message, in plaintext-checkable attacks, the adversary is given access to a plaintext-checking oracle that answers, on a given pair (m, c), whether c encrypts m or not.

In this paper, we first revisit the notion of oneway-ness under plaintext-checkable attacks (OW-PCA) by Okamoto and Pointcheval [29] and describe an indistinguishability-based variant for it. In the new notion, termed indistin-guishability under plaintext-checkable attacks (IND-PCA), the adversary should not be able to learn any information about an encrypted message even when given access to a plaintext-checking oracle. As we show in Section 2, the new notion is also equivalent to the IND-CCA notion when the message space is small (polynomial in the security parameter) since it is possible to enumerate all the possible messages in this case.

A New IND-PCA Encryption Scheme. After defining the IND-PCA notion, our first main contribution is to design a new public-key encryption scheme which for-mally meets the new notion. The new scheme is a more efficient variant of the Cramer-Shoup encryption scheme [11], whose ciphertext consists of only 3 group elements. Like the Cramer-Shoup encryption scheme, the security of new scheme is also based on the plain Decisional Diffie-Hellman (DDH) assumption [27].

In addition to being quite efficient, the new scheme can also be used with Groth-Sahai Non-Interactive Zero-Knowledge Proofs [20] and smooth projective hash functions (SPHF) [12], for proving plaintext knowledge. To illustrate this fact, we design two different constructions of SPHFs for the new scheme, each providing a different security-efficiency trade-off.

Since IND-PCA implies IND-CCA for short messages, the new scheme can also replace IND-CCA schemes in applications where the message space is small. This is the case, for instance, when bits have to be encrypted as in [2].

Applications to PAKE. After proposing the new scheme, our second main contribution is to show that, for many password-based authenticated key exchange (PAKE) in the Bellare-Pointcheval-Rogaway (BPR) security model [6], one can safely replace the underlying IND-CCA encryption schemes with an IND-PCA one. In particular, we revisit the frameworks by Gennaro and Lindell [17], by Groce and Katz [19], and by Katz and Vaikuntanathan [26], and show that one can replace the underlying IND-CCA encryption schemes in their constructions with an IND-PCA encryption scheme. In all of these cases, we were able to reduce the overall communication complexity of the original protocols by at least one group element.

More precisely, in the case of the Gennaro-Lindell framework [17], which is a generalization of the PAKE scheme by Katz, Ostrovsky, and Yung [23], we were able to obtain a quite clean 2-flow protocol with 7 group elements in total, instead of 8 group elements in 3 flows [22] or 10 group elements in 3 flows in [16,24,25]. The security of the new scheme is based on the DDH in the underlying group and assumes a trusted common reference string (CRS). In addition to avoiding the use of IND-CCA encryption schemes, our instantiation also avoids the use of one-time signatures and message authentication codes. Although it was already known that one of the two ciphertexts could be generated using an IND-CPA encryption scheme [4,10,22], IND-CCA security was always required for the generation of the other ciphertext in all concrete instantiations of the KOY/GL framework.

In the case of the Groce-Katz (GK) framework [19], which is a generalization of the PAKE scheme by Jiang and Gong [21] that additionally provides mutual authentication, we were able to obtain a scheme with a total communication complexity of 7 group elements instead of the original 8 by using an IND-PCA encryption scheme to generate the second flow. Moreover, in cases where mutual authentication is not needed, one could further improve the overall efficiency of these protocols by removing the third flow. The resulting scheme would only have 2 flows and require the exchange of 6 group elements in total. The security of the new scheme is based on the plain DDH assumption and on the security of the underlying pseudorandom number generator and assumes a trusted CRS.

Finally, in the case of Katz-Vaikuntanathan (KV) framework [26], we were able to obtain a PAKE scheme with a total communication complexity of 10 group elements instead of the current 12 in [8]. As in [8,26], our new scheme only has a single round of communication and assumes a trusted CRS. Its security proof is based on the plain DDH assumption.

Organization. Section 2 recalls standard definitions for public-key encryption and smooth projective hash proof functions (SPHFs) and describes some of the most classic instantiations of these primitives. Section 3 introduces our new

IND-PCA encryption scheme and the associated SPHFs along with its security proof. The new scheme is a variant of the Cramer-Shoup encryption scheme [11] with shorter ciphertexts. Section 4 presents the security models for password-based authenticated key exchange (PAKE) used in our security proofs. Section 5 describes three PAKE constructions based on the frameworks by Gennaro and Lindell [17], by Groce and Katz [19], and by Katz and Vaikuntanathan [26], whose security proofs appear in the full version [1].

2 Public-Key Encryption

2.1 Definition

A (labeled) public-key encryption scheme is defined by three algorithms:

- KG$(1^{\mathfrak{K}})$ generates a key pair: a public key pk and a secret key sk;
- Enc$^\ell$(pk, M; r) encrypts the message M under the key pk with label ℓ, using the random coins r;
- Dec$^\ell$(sk, C) decrypts the ciphertext C, using the secret key sk, with label ℓ.

The correctness requires that for all key pairs (pk, sk), all labels ℓ, all random coins r and all messages M,

$$\mathsf{Dec}^\ell(\mathsf{sk}, \mathsf{Enc}^\ell(\mathsf{pk}, M; r)) = M.$$

The main security notion is the so-called *indistinguishability of ciphertexts*, depicted in Fig. 1, in which the adversary chooses two messages M_0 and M_1 and a label ℓ^* (FIND phase), and then has to guess which of the two has been encrypted in the challenge ciphertext $C^* = \mathsf{Enc}^{\ell^*}(\mathsf{pk}, M_b; r)$ for a random bit b (GUESS phase). The adversary has access to an oracle ORACLE which may update some list of forbidden challenges CTXT, and it wins if and only if he guessed correctly the bit b (i.e., it outputs $b' = b$) and (ℓ^*, C^*) is not in CTXT. The advantages are:

$$\mathsf{Adv}^{\mathsf{ind}}_{\mathsf{ES}}(\mathcal{A}) = \Pr[\mathsf{Exp}^{\mathsf{ind}-1}_{\mathsf{ES},\mathcal{A}}(\mathfrak{K}) = 1] - \Pr[\mathsf{Exp}^{\mathsf{ind}-0}_{\mathsf{ES},\mathcal{A}}(\mathfrak{K}) = 1]$$

$$\mathsf{Adv}^{\mathsf{ind}}_{\mathsf{ES}}(t, q) = \max_{\mathcal{A} \leq t, q}\{\mathsf{Adv}^{\mathsf{ind}}_{\mathsf{ES}}(\mathcal{A})\},$$

$\mathsf{Exp}^{\mathsf{ind}-b}_{\mathsf{ES},\mathcal{A}}(\mathfrak{K})$
  CTXT $\leftarrow$ empty list
  (pk, sk) $\leftarrow$ KG$(\mathfrak{K})$
  $(\ell^*, M_0, M_1) \leftarrow \mathcal{A}(\mathsf{FIND} : \mathsf{pk}, \mathsf{ORACLE}(\cdot))$
  $C^* \leftarrow \mathsf{Enc}^{\ell^*}(\mathsf{pk}, M_b)$
  $b' \leftarrow \mathcal{A}(\mathsf{GUESS} : C^*, \mathsf{ORACLE}(\cdot))$
  if $(\ell^*, C^*) \in$ CTXT then return 0
  else return b'

Fig. 1. Indistinguishability Security Notions for Labeled Public-Key Encryption (IND-CPA when ORACLE $=\perp$, IND-PCA when ORACLE = OPCA, and IND-CCA when ORACLE = OCCA)

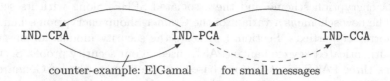

Fig. 2. Relations between IND-CPA, IND-PCA, and IND-CCA (normal arrows are implications, strike out arrows are separations)

where $\mathcal{A} \leq t, q$ are adversaries running within time t and asking at most q queries to ORACLE.

Depending on the definition of ORACLE, one gets three different security notions:

- if ORACLE $=\bot$, the adversary just has access to the public key, and one gets the IND-CPA notion, CPA meaning *Chosen-Plaintext Attack*;
- if ORACLE(ℓ, C) outputs the decryption of C under the label ℓ (Dec$^\ell$(sk, C)) and adds (ℓ, C) to CTXT, one gets the IND-CCA notion, CCA meaning *Chosen-Ciphertext Attack*;
- if ORACLE(ℓ, C, M) just answers whether the decryption of C under the label ℓ is M and adds (ℓ, C) to CTXT, one gets the IND-PCA notion, PCA meaning *Plaintext-Checking Attack*, as proposed in [29].

2.2 Relations with the IND-CPA and IND-CCA Security Notions

It is well known that IND-CCA implies IND-CPA (i.e., an encryption scheme IND-CCA-secure is IND-CPA-secure), and it is clear that IND-PCA implies IND-CPA. Let us now show that relations between IND-CPA, IND-PCA, IND-CCA are as depicted in Fig. 2. In all this paper, when we speak of small messages, we mean that it is possible to enumerate all the possible messages (i.e., the message space has a cardinal polynomial in the security parameter).

IND-CCA $\implies$ IND-PCA. One just has to remark that the OPCA oracle can be simulated by the OCCA oracle, and the restrictions are compatible (the same list CTXT will be generated): given a query (ℓ, M, C) to the OPCA oracle, the simulator can simply ask for (ℓ, C) to the OCCA oracle. This perfectly simulates the OPCA oracle.

IND-PCA $\implies$ IND-CCA, for Small Messages. In case of small messages for the encryption scheme, we remark that the OCCA oracle can be simulated by the OPCA oracle, and the restrictions are compatible too: given a query (ℓ, C) to the OCCA oracle, the simulator can simply ask for (ℓ, M, C) to the OPCA oracle, for all the messages M (we insist that by small messages, we mean we can enumerate them in polynomial time).If no message M matches, the simulator outputs $\bot$, otherwise it outputs the unique matching message (since the encryption is perfectly binding, at most one message can match). This perfectly simulates the OCCA oracle.

2.3   Classical Schemes

ElGamal Encryption Scheme [15]. The ElGamal (EG) encryption scheme is defined as follows, in a cyclic group $\mathbb{G}$ of prime order p, with a generator g:

- EG.KG($1^\mathfrak{K}$) generates the secret key $\mathsf{sk} = x \xleftarrow{\$} \mathbb{Z}_p$ and the public key $\mathsf{pk} = y = g^x$;
- EG.Enc($\mathsf{pk} = y, M; r$), for a group element $M \in \mathbb{G}$ and a scalar $r \in \mathbb{Z}_p$, generates the ciphertext $C = (u = g^r, e = y^r M)$;
- EG.Dec($\mathsf{sk} = x, C = (u, e)$) computes $M = e/u^x$.

This encryption scheme is well-known to be IND-CPA under the DDH assumption, which states that it is hard to distinguish a Diffie-Hellman tuple (g^a, g^b, g^{ab}) from a random tuple (g^a, g^b, g^c), for random scalars $a, b, c \xleftarrow{\$} \mathbb{Z}_q$:

$$\mathsf{Adv}_{\mathsf{EG}}^{\mathsf{ind-cpa}}(t) \leq \mathsf{Adv}_{\mathbb{G}}^{\mathsf{ddh}}(t).$$

Cramer-Shoup Encryption Scheme [11]. The labeled Cramer-Shoup (CS) encryption scheme is defined as follows, in a cyclic group $\mathbb{G}$ of prime order p, with two generators g_1, g_2, together with a hash function H_{CS} randomly drawn from a collision-resistant[1] hash function family $\mathcal{H}$ from the set $\{0,1\}^* \times \mathbb{G}^2$ to the set $\mathbb{G}\backslash\{1\}$:

- CS.KG($1^\mathfrak{K}$) generates the secret key $\mathsf{sk} = (s, a, b, a', b') \xleftarrow{\$} \mathbb{Z}_p$ and the public key $\mathsf{pk} = (h = g_1^s, c = g_1^a g_2^b, d = g_1^{a'} g_2^{b'})$;
- CS.Enc$^\ell$($\mathsf{pk} = (h, c, d), M; r$), for a label ℓ, a group element $M \in \mathbb{G}$ and a scalar $r \in \mathbb{Z}_p$, generates the ciphertext $C = (u_1 = g_1^r, u_2 = g_2^r, e = h^r M, v = (cd^\xi)^r)$, where $\xi = H_{\mathsf{CS}}(\ell, u_1, u_2, e)$;
- CS.Dec$^\ell$($\mathsf{sk} = (s, a, b, a', b'), C = (u_1, u_2, e, v)$) first checks whether $v = u_1^{a+\xi a'} \cdot u_2^{b+\xi b'}$, for $\xi = H_{\mathsf{CS}}(\ell, u_1, u_2, e)$. If the equality holds, it outputs $M = e/u_1^s$, otherwise it outputs $\bot$.

This encryption scheme is well-known to be IND-CCA under the DDH assumption and the collision-resistance of the hash function family:

$$\mathsf{Adv}_{\mathsf{CS}}^{\mathsf{ind-cca}}(t, q_d) \leq 2\mathsf{Adv}_{\mathbb{G}}^{\mathsf{ddh}}(t) + \mathsf{Succ}_{\mathcal{H}}^{\mathsf{coll}}(t) + 3q_d/p,$$

where q_d is the number of queries to the OCCA oracle.

Remark 1. A family $\mathcal{H}$ of hash functions from a set X to a set Y is said (t, ε)-collision-resistant if for any adversary $\mathcal{A}$ running within time t, on a random element $H \xleftarrow{\$} \mathcal{H}$, its probability to output $x \neq x'$ such that $H(x) = H(x')$ is bounded by ε. We denote $\mathsf{Succ}_{\mathcal{H}}^{\mathsf{coll}}(t)$ the best success probability any adversary can get within time t.

---

[1] Second-preimage resistance is actually sufficient.

2.4   Smooth Projective Hash Functions

Projective hash function families were first introduced by Cramer and Shoup [12]. Here we use the formalization from [8]: Let X be the domain of these functions and let L be a certain subset of this domain (a language). A key property of these functions is that, for words C in L, their values can be computed by using either a *secret* hashing key hk or a *public* projection key hp but with a witness w of the fact that C is indeed in L. More precisely, a smooth projective hash function (SPHF) over $L \subseteq X$ is defined by four algorithms.

- HashKG(L) generates a hashing key hk for the language L;
- ProjKG(hk, L, C) derives the projection key hp, possibly depending on the word C;
- Hash(hk, L, C) outputs the hash value from the hashing key, for any word $C \in X$;
- ProjHash(hp, L, C, w) outputs the hash value from the projection key hp, and the witness w, for a word $C \in L$.

On the one hand, the *correctness* of the SPHF assures that if $C \in L$ with w a witness of this fact, then Hash(hk, L, C) = ProjHash(hp, L, C, w). On the other hand, the security is defined through the *smoothness*, which guarantees that, if $C \notin L$, Hash(hk, L, C) is *statistically* indistinguishable from a random element, even knowing hp.

Note that HashKG and ProjKG can just depend partially on L (i.e., can only depend on a superset $\hat{L}$): we then note HashKG($\hat{L}$) and ProjKG(hk, $\hat{L}$, C). In addition, if ProjKG does not depend on C, and verify a slightly stronger smoothness property (called adaptive smoothness, which holds even if C is chosen after hp), we say the SPHF is a KVSPHF. Otherwise, it is said to be a GLSPHF. A KVSPHF is stronger than a GLSPHF (in particular, a KVSPHF is a GLSPHF), and some applications require KVSPHF.

More precisely, if ProjKG does not use C and, if for any function from the set of projection keys to $X \setminus L$, on the probability space hk $\xleftarrow{\$}$ HashKG(L), hp $\leftarrow$ ProjKG(hk, L, $\perp$), the distributions $\{(\mathsf{hp}, H) \mid H \leftarrow \mathsf{Hash}(\mathsf{hk}, L, C)\}$ and $\{(\mathsf{hp}, H) \mid H \xleftarrow{\$} \Pi\}$ are ε-close, where Π is the output set of the hash function, then the SPHF is an ε-smooth KVSPHF. If ProjKG uses C (or not) and if, for any $C \notin L$, on the probability space hk $\xleftarrow{\$}$ HashKG(L), hp $\leftarrow$ ProjKG(hk, L, C), the distributions $\{(\mathsf{hp}, H) \mid H \leftarrow \mathsf{Hash}(\mathsf{hk}, L, C)\}$ and $\{(\mathsf{hp}, H) \mid H \xleftarrow{\$} \Pi\}$ are ε-close, then the SPHF is an ε-smooth GLSPHF. See [8] for more details on GLSPHF and KVSPHF.

Let us now recall SPHFs for the ElGamal and Cramer-Shoup encryption schemes, proposed in [8,12,17].

ElGamal Encryption Scheme. EG admits an efficient KVSPHF for the language $L_M = \{C \mid \exists r,\ C = \mathsf{EG.Enc}(\mathsf{pk}, M; r)\}$, with $L = \mathbb{G}^2$ the superset of the ciphertexts:

$$\mathsf{hk} = \mathsf{HashKG}(L) = (\alpha, \beta) \xleftarrow{\$} \mathbb{Z}_p^2 \qquad \mathsf{hp} = \mathsf{ProjKG}(\mathsf{hk}, L, \perp) = g^\alpha y^\beta$$

$$H = \mathsf{Hash}(\mathsf{hk}, L_M, C) = u^\alpha (e/M)^\beta \qquad H' = \mathsf{ProjHash}(\mathsf{hp}, L_M, C, r) = \mathsf{hp}^r$$

Cramer-Shoup Encryption Scheme. CS admits an efficient GLSPHF for the language $L_M^\ell = \{C \mid \exists r, C = \mathsf{CS.Enc}^\ell(\mathsf{pk}, M; r)\}$, with L the superset of the ciphertexts:

$$\mathsf{hk} = \mathsf{HashKG}(L) = (\alpha, \beta, \gamma, \delta) \xleftarrow{\$} \mathbb{Z}_p^4$$
$$\mathsf{hp} = \mathsf{ProjKG}(\mathsf{hk}, L, C) = g_1^\alpha g_2^\beta h^\gamma (cd^\xi)^\delta$$
$$H = \mathsf{Hash}(\mathsf{hk}, L_M^\ell, C) = u_1^\alpha u_2^\beta (e/M)^\gamma v^\delta$$
$$H' = \mathsf{ProjHash}(\mathsf{hp}, L_M^\ell, C, r) = \mathsf{hp}^r,$$

where $\xi = H_{\mathsf{CS}}(\ell, u_1, u_2, e)$.

CS also admits an efficient KVSPHF for the language L_M^ℓ [8]:

$$\mathsf{hk} = \mathsf{HashKG}(L) = (\alpha_1, \alpha_2, \beta, \gamma, \delta) \xleftarrow{\$} \mathbb{Z}_p^5$$
$$\mathsf{hp} = \mathsf{ProjKG}(\mathsf{hk}, L, C) = (\mathsf{hp}_1 = g_1^{\alpha_1} g_2^\beta h^\gamma c^\delta, \mathsf{hp}_2 = g_1^{\alpha_2} d^\delta)$$
$$H = \mathsf{Hash}(\mathsf{hk}, L_M^\ell, C) = u_1^{\alpha_1 + \xi \alpha_2} u_2^\beta (e/M)^\gamma v^\delta$$
$$H' = \mathsf{ProjHash}(\mathsf{hp}, L_M^\ell, C, r) = (\mathsf{hp}_1 \mathsf{hp}_2^\xi)^r,$$

where $\xi = H_{\mathsf{CS}}(\ell, u_1, u_2, e)$.

3   The Short Cramer-Shoup Encryption Scheme

The labeled Short Cramer-Shoup (SCS) encryption scheme is a variant of the above Cramer-Shoup encryption scheme, but with one less element. It is defined as follows, in a cyclic group $\mathbb{G}$ of prime order p, with a generator g, together with a hash function H_{SCS} randomly drawn from a collision-resistant[2] hash function family $\mathcal{H}$ from the set $\{0,1\}^* \times \mathbb{G}^2$ to the set $\mathbb{G} \setminus \{1\}$:

- SCS.KG($1^\Re$) generates the secret key $\mathsf{sk} = (s, a, b, a', b') \xleftarrow{\$} \mathbb{Z}_p$ and the public key $\mathsf{pk} = (h = g^s, c = g^a h^b, d = g^{a'} h^{b'})$;
- SCS.Enc$^\ell$($\mathsf{pk} = (h, c, d), M; r$), for a label ℓ, a group element $M \in \mathbb{G}$ and a scalar $r \in \mathbb{Z}_p$, generates the ciphertext $C = (u = g^r, e = h^r M, v = (cd^\xi)^r)$, where $\xi = H_{\mathsf{SCS}}(\ell, u, e)$;
- SCS.Dec$^\ell$($\mathsf{sk} = (s, a, b, a', b'), C = (u, e, v)$) first computes $M = e/u^s$ and checks whether $v = u^{a + \xi a'} (e/M)^{b + \xi b'}$, for $\xi = H_{\mathsf{SCS}}(\ell, u, e)$. If the equality holds, it outputs M, otherwise it outputs $\bot$.

We show below it is IND-PCA under the DDH and the collision-resistance assumptions:
$$\mathsf{Adv}_{\mathsf{SCS}}^{\mathsf{ind-pca}}(t) \leq \mathsf{Adv}_{\mathbb{G}}^{\mathsf{ddh}}(t) + \mathsf{Succ}_{\mathcal{H}}^{\mathsf{coll}}(t) + 2(q_p + 1)/p,$$

where q_p is the number of queries to the OPCA oracle. But before that, we build a GLSPHF and a KVSPHF for the SCS scheme.

---

[2] Second-preimage resistance is actually enough, as for the original Cramer-Shoup encryption scheme.

3.1 Smooth Projective Hash Functions

Let us now define smooth projective hash functions. We use the formalization from [8] to explain where these SPHFs come from. The reader not acquainted with it may skip the definitions via matrix/vectors and just look at the resulting GLSPHF and KVSPHF.

GLSPHF. The following matrix and vectors lead to an SPHF for the language $L_M^\ell = \{C \mid \exists r, \ C = \mathsf{SCS.Enc}^\ell(\mathsf{pk}, M; r)\}$, with L the superset of the ciphertexts:

$$\Gamma(C) = (\ g \quad h \quad cd^\xi\ ) \qquad \begin{aligned} \boldsymbol{\lambda} &= (r) \\ \boldsymbol{\lambda} \cdot \Gamma &= (g^r, h^r, (cd^\xi)^r) \\ \Theta(C) &= (u, e/M, v) \end{aligned}$$

where $\xi = H_{\mathsf{SCS}}(\ell, u, e)$. The matrix Γ depends on ξ, and thus on the word C. Hence, this is a GLSPHF:

$$\mathsf{hk} = \mathsf{HashKG}(L) = (\alpha, \beta, \gamma) \xleftarrow{\$} \mathbb{Z}_p^3 \qquad \mathsf{hp} = \mathsf{ProjKG}(\mathsf{hk}, L, C) = g^\alpha h^\beta (cd^\xi)^\gamma$$

$$H = \mathsf{Hash}(\mathsf{hk}, L_M^\ell, C) = u^\alpha (e/M)^\beta v^\gamma \qquad H' = \mathsf{ProjHash}(\mathsf{hp}, L_M^\ell, C, r) = \mathsf{hp}^r$$

KVSPHF. We could also use the following matrix and vectors:

$$\Gamma(C) = \begin{pmatrix} g & 1 & h & c \\ 1 & g & 1 & d \end{pmatrix} \qquad \begin{aligned} \boldsymbol{\lambda} &= (r) \\ \boldsymbol{\lambda} \cdot \Gamma &= (g^r, g^{\xi r}, h^r, (cd^\xi)^r) \\ \Theta(C) &= (u, u^\xi, e/M, v) \end{aligned}$$

where $\xi = H_{\mathsf{SCS}}(\ell, u, e)$. The matrix Γ does not depend anymore on ξ, nor on the word C in general. Hence, this is a KVSPHF:

$$\mathsf{hk} = \mathsf{HashKG}(L) = (\alpha_1, \alpha_2, \beta, \gamma) \xleftarrow{\$} \mathbb{Z}_p^4$$

$$\mathsf{hp} = \mathsf{ProjKG}(\mathsf{hk}, L, C) = (\mathsf{hp}_1 = g^{\alpha_1} h^\beta c^\gamma, \mathsf{hp}_1 = g^{\alpha_2} d^\gamma)$$

$$H = \mathsf{Hash}(\mathsf{hk}, L_M^\ell, C) = u^{\alpha_1 + \alpha_2 \xi}(e/M)^\beta v^\gamma$$

$$H' = \mathsf{ProjHash}(\mathsf{hp}, L_M^\ell, C, r) = (\mathsf{hp}_1 \mathsf{hp}_2^\xi)^r$$

3.2 IND-PCA Security Proof

Let us now prove the IND-CPA security as advertised at the beginning of this section. We first recall the security game in Game $\mathbf{G_0}$, and present a series of indistinguishable games to show the advantage of the adversary is negligible [7,31].

Game $\mathbf{G_0}$: The adversary $\mathcal{A}$ is given a public key $\mathsf{pk} = (h = g^s, c = g^a h^b, d = g^{a'} h^{b'})$, generated with the secret key $\mathsf{sk} = (s, a, b, a', b') \xleftarrow{\$} \mathbb{Z}_p^5$, as well as an unlimited access to an OPCA oracle with input a tuple (ℓ, M, C) that consists of a ciphertext C and an alleged plaintext M with the label ℓ. This oracle answers whether C really encrypts M or not. At some point, the adversary outputs a label ℓ^* and two message M_0 and M_1, and receives the encryption $C^* = (u^*, e^*, v^*)$ of M_δ with the label ℓ^*. After more calls to the OPCA oracle, the adversary outputs a bit δ', its guess on the bit δ. Note that the adversary is not allowed to query the OPCA oracle on any tuple (ℓ^*, M, C^*).

More precisely, C^* is generated with a random scalar $r^* \xleftarrow{\$} \mathbb{Z}_p$, as $C^* = (u^* = g^{r^*}, e^* = h^{r^*} M_\delta, v^* = (cd^{\xi^*})^{r^*})$, where $\xi^* = H_{\mathsf{SCS}}(\ell^*, u^*, e^*)$. The OPCA oracle, on input $(\ell, M, C = (u, e, v))$, unless $(\ell, C) = (\ell^*, C^*)$, checks both equations: $e \stackrel{?}{=} u^s M$ and $v \stackrel{?}{=} u^{a+\xi a'} \cdot (e/M)^{b+\xi b'}$, for $\xi = H_{\mathsf{SCS}}(\ell, u, e)$. Then, $\mathsf{Adv}_{\mathbf{G}_0}(\mathcal{A}) = \mathsf{Adv}_{\mathsf{SCS}}^{\mathsf{ind\text{-}pca}}(\mathcal{A})$.

Game $\mathbf{G}_1$: In this game, we reject all queries $(\ell, M, C = (u, e, v))$ to the OPCA oracle, where $(\ell, u, e) \neq (\ell^*, u^*, e^*)$ but $\xi^* = \xi$. This game is computationally indistinguishable from the previous one under the collision-resistance of H_{SCS}: $|\mathsf{Adv}_{\mathbf{G}_1}(\mathcal{A}) - \mathsf{Adv}_{\mathbf{G}_0}(\mathcal{A})| \leq \mathsf{Succ}_{\mathcal{H}}^{\mathsf{coll}}(t)$, where t is approximately the running time of $\mathcal{A}$.

Game $\mathbf{G}_2$: We first simplify the simulation of the OPCA oracle: it just checks the second equation: $v \stackrel{?}{=} u^{a+\xi a'} \cdot (e/M)^{b+\xi b'}$, for $\xi = H_{\mathsf{SCS}}(\ell, u, e)$, so that we do not need to know s in this game anymore. It can only make a difference if this equation is satisfied while the first was not: this means that $e = u^{s'} M$ and $v = u^{a+\xi a'} \cdot (e/M)^{b+\xi b'}$, for $\xi = H_{\mathsf{SCS}}(\ell, u, e)$, with $h = g^s$ and $\Delta_s = s'-s \neq 0$. However, we can see that the probability for v to satisfy the above equation while e does not is negligible (actually upper-bounded by $1/p$) since a, a', b, b' are unknown. See a more complex case in Game $\mathbf{G}_6$, where even more information is available to the adversary. One thus gets $|\mathsf{Adv}_{\mathbf{G}_2}(\mathcal{A}) - \mathsf{Adv}_{\mathbf{G}_1}(\mathcal{A})| \leq q_p/p$, where q_p is the number of queries to the OPCA oracle.

Game $\mathbf{G}_3$: We are now given a Diffie-Hellman tuple $(g, X = g^x, Y = g^y, Z = g^z)$, with $z = xy$. We set $h \leftarrow X$ (which means that $s = x$), but let the rest of the setup as before: $a, b, a', b' \xleftarrow{\$} \mathbb{Z}_p$ and $\delta \xleftarrow{\$} \{0, 1\}$. This is possible since we do not know s anymore since Game $\mathbf{G}_2$. For the challenge ciphertext, we set $u^* \leftarrow Y$ (which means that $r^* = y$) and $e^* \leftarrow Z M_\delta$. For v^*, since we do not know r^*, we use the verification equation: $v^* \leftarrow Y^{a+\xi^* a'} \cdot Z^{b+\xi^* b'}$, for $\xi^* = H_{\mathsf{SCS}}(\ell^*, u^*, e^*)$. Since $z = xy$, we have a perfect simulation of v^* as in the previous game, hence $\mathsf{Adv}_{\mathbf{G}_3}(\mathcal{A}) = \mathsf{Adv}_{\mathbf{G}_2}(\mathcal{A})$:

$$v^* = g^{y(a+\xi^* a')+xy(b+\xi^* b')} = (g^{(a+xb)} \cdot g^{\xi^*(a'+xb')})^y$$
$$= ((g^a h^b) \cdot (g^{a'} h^{b'})^{\xi^*})^y = (cd^{\xi^*})^{r^*}.$$

Game $\mathbf{G}_4$: We are now given a random tuple $(g, X = g^x, Y = g^y, Z = g^z)$, with z independently chosen. The simulation is the same as in the previous game: $|\mathsf{Adv}_{\mathbf{G}_4}(\mathcal{A}) - \mathsf{Adv}_{\mathbf{G}_3}(\mathcal{A})| \leq \mathsf{Adv}^{\mathsf{ddh}}(t)$, where t is essentially the running time of the adversary $\mathcal{A}$.

Game $\mathbf{G}_5$: We now choose z uniformly at random in $\mathbb{Z}_p \setminus \{xy\}$ instead of $\mathbb{Z}_p$. This game is statistically indistinguishable from the previous one. Hence we have: $|\mathsf{Adv}_{\mathbf{G}_5}(\mathcal{A}) - \mathsf{Adv}_{\mathbf{G}_4}(\mathcal{A})| \leq 1/p$.

Game $\mathbf{G}_6$: We now randomly choose $g \xleftarrow{\$} \mathbb{G}$, and $x, y, z \xleftarrow{\$} \mathbb{Z}_p$ (with $z \neq xy$) to define the random tuple $(g, X = g^x, Y = g^y, Z = g^z)$ as in the previous game, but with the knowledge of the exponents. We thus know again $s = x$. We can go back with the full simulation of the OPCA oracle: it additionally checks whether $e = u^s M$ or not. It can again make a difference if this equation is not satisfied while the other one was: this means that $e = u^{s'} M$ and $v = u^{a+\xi a'} \cdot (e/M)^{b+\xi b'}$, for $\xi = H_{\mathsf{SCS}}(\ell, u, e)$, with $h = g^s$ and $\Delta_s = s'-s \neq 0$. First, if $(\ell, u, e) = (\ell^*, u^*, e^*)$ but $v \neq v^*$, since that implies $\xi = \xi^*$, we can safely answer negatively. We thus now have to deal with the cases $(\ell, u, e) \neq (\ell^*, u^*, e^*)$, where $\xi^* \neq \xi$ (since we have already dealt with collisions in ξ and ξ^* in Game $\mathbf{G_1}$).

As in Game $\mathbf{G_2}$, we have to show that the probability for v to satisfy the above equation while e does not is negligible since a, b, a', b' are unknown. This is a bit more subtle than in Game $\mathbf{G_2}$, since more relations are available to the adversary. This proof would thus also apply for the Game $\mathbf{G_2}$. Anyway, with the given relations, any v could be possible: a powerful adversary might know, where $u = g^r$ and $\Delta_z = z - xy$,

$$\begin{cases} c & = g^a h^b \\ d & = g^{a'} h^{b'} \\ v^* & = u^{*a+\xi^* a'} \cdot (e^*/M_\delta)^{b+\xi^* b'} \\ & = g^{y(a+\xi^* a')} \cdot g^{z(b+\xi^* b')} \\ v & = u^{a+\xi a'} \cdot (e/M)^{b+\xi b'} \\ & = g^{r(a+\xi a')} \cdot g^{rs'(b+\xi b')} \end{cases}$$

$$\begin{cases} \log_g c & = a + s \cdot b \\ \log_g d & = a' + s \cdot b' \\ \log_g v^* & = y \cdot (a + \xi^* a') + z(b + \xi^* b') \\ & = y \cdot (\log_g c + \xi^* \log_g d) + \Delta_z \cdot (b + \xi^* b') \\ \log_g v & = r \cdot (a + \xi a') + rs'(b + \xi b') \\ & = r \cdot (\log_g c + \xi \log_g d + \Delta_s \cdot (b + \xi b')) \end{cases}$$

This system can be turned into

$$\begin{pmatrix} \log_g c \\ \log_g d \\ \log_g v^* - y \cdot (\log_g c + \xi^* \log_g d) \\ \log_g v - r \cdot (\log_g c + \xi \log_g d) \end{pmatrix} = \begin{pmatrix} 1 & 0 & s & 0 \\ 0 & 1 & 0 & s \\ 0 & 0 & \Delta_z & \Delta_z \xi^* \\ 0 & 0 & r\Delta_s & r\Delta_s \xi \end{pmatrix} \cdot \begin{pmatrix} a \\ a' \\ b \\ b' \end{pmatrix}$$

where the determinant is clearly $\Delta_z \Delta_s (\xi^* - \xi)$. Since we assumed $z \neq xy$, $\Delta_z \neq 0$, and no collision on the hash function H_{SCS}, the determinants are all non-zero, in which cases the expected values for v are unpredictable, hence $|\mathsf{Adv}_{\mathbf{G_6}}(\mathcal{A}) - \mathsf{Adv}_{\mathbf{G_5}}(\mathcal{A})| \leq q_p/p$, where q_p is the number of queries to the OPCA oracle.

Game $\mathbf{G_7}$: We now choose v^* at random, independently of Y and Z.

To show this does not change anything, we first show that what $\mathcal{A}$ sees does never depend on the four variables a, b, a', b', but only depends on $\alpha = a + xb$ and $\beta = a' + xb'$, except for v^*: The only information $\mathcal{A}$ has from a, b, a', b' comes from the answers of the OPCA oracle, where we first check that $e \stackrel{?}{=} u^x M$

and then, if that equality holds, that $v \stackrel{?}{=} u^{a+\xi a'} \cdot (e/M)^{b+\xi b'}$. But when $e = u^x M$, $u^{a+\xi a'} \cdot (e/M)^{b+\xi b'} = u^{(a+\xi a')+x(b+\xi b')} = u^{(a+xb)+\xi(a'+xb')} = u^{\alpha+\xi\beta}$, therefore the second verification can be replaced by $v \stackrel{?}{=} u^{\alpha+\xi\beta}$, which only depends on α and β.

If we denote $v^* = g^\gamma$, we have $\gamma = y(a + \xi^* a) + z(b + \xi^* b')$, which is linearly independent of α and β (when a, a', b, b' are unknowns) since $z \neq xy$, and so γ looks completely random to the adversary, and so does v^* too: $\mathsf{Adv}_{\mathbf{G}_7}(\mathcal{A}) = \mathsf{Adv}_{\mathbf{G}_6}(\mathcal{A})$.

Game $\mathbf{G}_8$: We now choose z uniformly at random in $\mathbb{Z}_p$ instead of $\mathbb{Z}_p \setminus \{xy\}$. This game is statistically indistinguishable from the previous one. Hence we have: $|\mathsf{Adv}_{\mathbf{G}_8}(\mathcal{A}) - \mathsf{Adv}_{\mathbf{G}_7}(\mathcal{A})| \leq 1/p$.

Game $\mathbf{G}_9$: We now choose e^* at random, independently of Z and M_δ.

To show this does not change anything either, we review the previous game:

- the simulator chooses random scalars x, y, z to define the random tuple $(g, X = g^x, Y = g^y, Z = g^z)$, as well as random scalars α, β to define $c = g^\alpha, d = g^\beta$, and $\delta \stackrel{\$}{\leftarrow} \{0, 1\}$;
- for the OPCA oracle on $(\ell, M, C = (u, e, v))$, one checks $e \stackrel{?}{=} u^x M$ and $v \stackrel{?}{=} u^{\alpha+\xi\beta}$, for $\xi = H_{\mathsf{SCS}}(\ell, u, e)$;
- for the challenge ciphertext, one sets $u^* \leftarrow Y$, $e^* \leftarrow ZM_\delta$, and $v^* \stackrel{\$}{\leftarrow} \mathbb{G}$.

Since Z was used in e^* only (and nowhere else), a random Z or a random e^* are indistinguishable: $\mathsf{Adv}_{\mathbf{G}_9}(\mathcal{A}) = \mathsf{Adv}_{\mathbf{G}_8}(\mathcal{A})$. In addition, δ does not appear anywhere, hence $\mathsf{Adv}_{\mathbf{G}_9}(\mathcal{A}) = 0$.

4 PAKE Security Models

In this section, we recall the BPR security model [6] and the extension proposed by Abdalla, Fouque, and Pointcheval (AFP) [3]. Then, in the next section, we will present several protocols secure in the basic BPR model, but also in the AFP model and with forward-secrecy.

4.1 The Bellare-Pointcheval-Rogaway Security Model

Users and Passwords. Each client $C \in \mathcal{C}$ holds a password π_C, while each server $S \in \mathcal{S}$ holds passwords $\pi_{S,C}$ for each client C.

Protocol Execution. The adversary $\mathcal{A}$ can create several concurrent instances U^i of each user $U \in \mathcal{C} \cup \mathcal{S}$, and can interact with them via the following oracle queries:

- Execute(C^i, S^j): this query models a passive attack in which the adversary eavesdrops on honest executions between a client instance C^i and a server instance S^j. The output of this query consists of the messages that are exchanged during an honest execution of the protocol between C^i and S^j (i.e., the transcript of the protocol);

- $\mathtt{Send}(U^i, U'^j, M)$: this query models an active attack, in which the adversary may intercept a message and modify it, create a new message, or simply replay or forward an existing message, to the user instance U'^j in the name of the user instance U^i. The output of this query is the message that U'^j would generate after receiving M. A specific message $\mathtt{Start}$ can be sent to a client, in the name of a server, to initiate a session between this client and this server;
- $\mathtt{Reveal}(U)$: this query models the misuse of the session key that has been established. The output of this query is the session key, if it has been set.
- $\mathtt{Corrupt}(C)$: this query models the client corruption. The output of this query is the password π_C.
- $\mathtt{Corrupt}(S, C, \pi)$: this query models the server corruption. The output of this query is the stored password $\pi_{S,C}$. In addition, if $\pi \neq \bot$, $\pi_{S,C}$ is then changed to π.

This is a slight variant of the so-called *weak corruption* model in BPR, since the long term secrets (passwords) only are leaked, and not the internal states, in case of corruption. But contrarily to BPR, in case of server corruption, we also leak the password even in case of a password change request. However, this does not affect the security notion since, in both the original BPR model and in ours, any corruption query makes the password *corrupted*, and so the $\mathtt{Test}$-query is not allowed anymore on instances of these players (see below), since they are no longer fresh.

Partnering. Before actually defining the secrecy of the session key, and thus implicit authentication, we need to introduce the notion of partnering: Two instances are partnered if they have matching transcripts, which means that, for one user, its view is a part of the view of the other user. One should note that the last flow can be dropped by the adversary, without letting the sender know. The sender of this last flow thus thinks that the receiver got the message and still computes the session key.

Security. To actually define the semantic security of a PAKE scheme, the adversary $\mathcal{A}$ has access to a challenge oracle $\mathtt{Test}(U^i)$, available only once, to evaluate the indistinguishability of a specific session key. A random bit b is chosen and the $\mathtt{Test}$-query, for some user instance U^i is answered as follows: if $b = 1$, return the session key of U^i, and otherwise, return a random session key. At the end of the game, the adversary $\mathcal{A}$ has to output a bit b', as a guess for b. The success probability Succ of $\mathcal{A}$ is the probability that $b' = b$, while its advantage is defined by $\mathsf{Adv} = 2 \cdot \mathsf{Succ} - 1$.

Note that there are natural restrictions for the $\mathtt{Test}$-query: the tested instance must be *fresh*, which means that this is not a trivial case, where trivial cases are no key or known key. More precisely, there are two definitions of freshness, whether we consider the forward-secrecy, or not:

- basic freshness: an instance U^i is fresh (fresh) if,
  - a session key has been defined;
  - no Reveal-query has been asked to U^i, or to his partner, if there is one;
  - the password of the client C has not been corrupted (either via a query Corrupt(C) or via a query Corrupt$(\cdot, C, \cdot)$), where $C = U$ is U is a client or U^i's partner is an instance C^j of C
- forward-secure freshness: similar to basic freshness except for the last part, where only corruptions before U^i defined his key can make this instance unfresh.

In case of Test-query to an unfresh instance, the answer is $\perp$, which means that the adversary cannot have any advantage in these cases. A PAKE is considered BPR-secure if the advantage of any adversary $\mathcal{A}$, running within time t, in the previous experiment is bounded by $q_s \times 2^{-m} + \mathsf{negl}(\mathfrak{K})$, where q_s is the number of active sessions (handled with Send queries), and m is the min-entropy of the password distribution. Intuitively this means that to win, the adversary has to do an on-line dictionary attack, which only enables it to test one password per session.

4.2 The Abdalla-Fouque-Pointcheval Security Model

It extends the model with multiple Test-queries, which are all answered with the same bit b. Queries asked to unfresh instances are answered by $\perp$.

5 PAKE Constructions

In this section, we present three PAKE constructions: the first one follows the Gennaro-Lindell (GL) framework [17]. The second one follows the Groce-Katz (GK) framework [19], and the third one follows the one-round Katz-Vaikuntanathan (KV) framework [26]. They all make use of public-key encryption schemes that admit SPHFs on the languages of the ciphertexts of a given message.

5.1 Public-Key Encryption Schemes

In all our constructions, we will consider a labeled IND-PCA encryption scheme ES $=$ (KG, Enc, Dec) and an IND-CPA encryption scheme ES$'$ $=$ (KG$'$, Enc$'$, Dec$'$) so that SPHFs (either GLSPHFs or KVSPHFs according to the protocol) exist for the following families of languages:

$$L_\pi^\ell = \{c \mid \exists r,\ c = \mathsf{Enc}^\ell(\mathsf{pk}, \pi; r)\} \qquad L_\pi' = \{c \mid \exists r,\ c = \mathsf{Enc}'(\mathsf{pk}', \pi; r)\},$$

with the global parameters and the public keys pk and pk$'$ in the common reference string CRS. We also suppose that HashKG and ProjKG, for both L_π^ℓ and L_π', do not depend on π nor ℓ, and thus, just (respectively) on the supersets

$$L = \{c \mid \exists \ell, \exists \pi, \exists r,\ c = \mathsf{Enc}^\ell(\mathsf{pk}, \pi; r)\} \quad L' = \{c \mid \exists \pi, \exists r,\ c = \mathsf{Enc}'(\mathsf{pk}', \pi; r)\}.$$

5.2 GL-PAKE Construction and GL-SPOKE

GL-PAKE. Our first two-flow construction is depicted in Fig. 3, where $\times$ is a commutative operation between hash values such that if A is a uniform hash value and B is any hash value, $A \times B$ is uniform (often hash values live in a group and $\times$ is just the group law). The session key generated by the client is denoted K_C, while the one generated by the server is denoted K_S.

Client C (π_C)	CRS: (parameters, pk, pk')	Server S $(\pi_{S,C})$
$\mathsf{hk}_C \overset{\$}{\leftarrow} \mathsf{HashKG}(L')$		
$\mathsf{hp}_C \leftarrow \mathsf{ProjKG}(\mathsf{hk}_C, L', \bot)$		
$\ell = (C, S, \mathsf{hp}_C)$		
$r_C \overset{\$}{\leftarrow}\,;\; c_C \leftarrow \mathsf{Enc}^\ell(\mathsf{pk}, \pi_C; r_C)$	$\xrightarrow{\quad \mathsf{hp}_C, c_C \quad}$	$\ell = (C, S, \mathsf{hp}_C)$
		$r_S \overset{\$}{\leftarrow}\,;\; c_S \leftarrow \mathsf{Enc}'(\mathsf{pk}', \pi_{S,C}; r_S)$
		$\mathsf{hk}_S \overset{\$}{\leftarrow} \mathsf{HashKG}(L^\ell_{\pi_{S,C}})$
	$\xleftarrow{\quad \mathsf{hp}_S, c_S \quad}$	$\mathsf{hp}_S \leftarrow \mathsf{ProjKG}(\mathsf{hk}_S, L^\ell_{\pi_{S,C}}, c_C)$
$H'_C \leftarrow \mathsf{ProjHash}(\mathsf{hp}_S, L^\ell_{\pi_C}, c_C, r_C)$		$H'_S \leftarrow \mathsf{ProjHash}(\mathsf{hp}_C, L'_{\pi_{S,C}}, c_S, r_S)$
$H_S \leftarrow \mathsf{Hash}(\mathsf{hk}_C, L'_{\pi_C}, c_S)$		$H_C \leftarrow \mathsf{Hash}(\mathsf{hk}_S, L^\ell_{\pi_{S,C}}, c_C)$
$K_C \leftarrow H'_C \times H_S$		$K_S \leftarrow H'_S \times H_C$

Fig. 3. Generic GL-PAKE Construction

It requires an IND-CPA encryption scheme ES' with a KVSPHF, and an IND-PCA encryption scheme ES with a GLSPHF. In the full version [1], we prove the following result, with perfectly-smooth SPHFs, which applies for the basic freshness in the BPR setting, or for the forward-secure freshness in the AFP setting with static corruptions only:

$$\mathsf{Adv}(\mathcal{A}) \le q_s \times 2^{-m} + (q_e + q_s) \times (\mathsf{Adv}^{\mathsf{ind\text{-}cpa}}_{\mathsf{ES'}}(t) + \mathsf{Adv}^{\mathsf{ind\text{-}pca}}_{\mathsf{ES}}(t)) + \frac{q_e q_s}{2^{2n}},$$

where q_e and q_s are the number of Execute and Send-queries, n is the entropy of both the projected keys and the ciphertexts, and m is the entropy of the passwords.

GL-SPOKE: GL – Simple Password-Only Key Exchange (Fig. 4). Combining our new Short Cramer-Shoup encryption scheme, with the basic ElGamal encryption scheme, we obtain the most efficient PAKE with implicit authentication.

It is based on the plain DDH assumption, and consists of 4 group elements to be sent by the client and 3 group elements by the server. They both have to compute 10 exponentiations.

Using the above security bounds for the encryption schemes, one gets, for the basic freshness in the BPR setting, or for the forward-secure freshness in the AFP setting with static corruptions:

$$\mathsf{Adv}(t) \le q_s \times 2^{-m} + 2Q \times (\mathsf{Adv}^{\mathsf{ddh}}_{\mathbb{G}}(t) + \mathsf{Succ}^{\mathsf{coll}}_{\mathcal{H}}(t)) + \frac{2Q^2}{p},$$

Client C (π_C)	Server S $(\pi_{S,C})$
CRS: (param $= (\mathbb{G}, p, q)$, pk $= (h, c, d) \in \mathbb{G}^3$, pk$' = y \in \mathbb{G}$)	

$(\alpha', \beta') \xleftarrow{\$} \mathbb{Z}_p^2$; $t' \leftarrow g^{\alpha'} y^{\beta'} \in \mathbb{G}$

$r \xleftarrow{\$} \mathbb{Z}_p$

$(u \leftarrow g^r, e \leftarrow h^r g^{\pi_C}, v \leftarrow (cd^\xi)^r) \in \mathbb{G}^3,$

$\quad$ with $\xi \leftarrow H_{\mathsf{SCS}}(C, S, t', u, e)$ $\xrightarrow{\quad t', (u, e, v) \quad}$

$\hspace{6cm} (\alpha, \beta, \gamma) \xleftarrow{\$} \mathbb{Z}_p^3$

$\hspace{6cm} t \leftarrow g^\alpha h^\beta (cd^\xi)^\gamma \in \mathbb{G}$

$\hspace{6cm}$ with $\xi \leftarrow H_{\mathsf{SCS}}(C, S, t', u, e)$

$\hspace{6cm} r' \xleftarrow{\$} \mathbb{Z}_p$

$\xleftarrow{\quad t, (u', e') \quad}$ $\quad (u' \leftarrow g^{r'}, e' \leftarrow y^{r'} g^{\pi_{S,C}}) \in \mathbb{G}^2$

$H'_C \leftarrow t^{r}$; $H_S \leftarrow u'^{\alpha'} (e'/g^{\pi_C})^{\beta'}$ $\hspace{3cm} H'_S \leftarrow t'^{r'}$; $H_C \leftarrow u^\alpha (e/g^{\pi_{S,C}})^\beta v^\gamma$

$K_C \leftarrow H'_C \times H_S$ $\hspace{6.5cm} K_S \leftarrow H'_S \times H_C$

Fig. 4. GL-SPOKE

where q_s is the number of Send-queries, Q is the global number of oracle queries, and m is the min-entropy of the passwords.

We remark that one encrypted g^π where π is the password, instead of π. This makes it hard to recover π from the decryption of a ciphertext, but that is not a problem in the proofs, where one only needs to check whether a ciphertext contains a given password or not.

Client C (π_C)	CRS: (parameters, pk, pk$'$)	Server S $(\pi_{S,C})$

$r_C \xleftarrow{\$}$; $c_C \leftarrow \mathsf{Enc}'(\mathsf{pk}', \pi_C; r_C)$ $\xrightarrow{\quad c_C \quad}$

$\hspace{6cm}$ hk $\xleftarrow{\$}$ HashKG$(L'_{\pi_{S,C}})$

$\hspace{6cm}$ hp $\leftarrow$ ProjKG(hk, $L'_{\pi_{S,C}}, c_C$)

$\hspace{6cm} H \leftarrow$ Hash(hk, $L'_{\pi_{S,C}}, c_C$)

$\hspace{6cm} (K_S, r_S) \leftarrow$ PRG(H)

$\hspace{6cm} \ell = (C, S, c_C, \mathsf{hp})$

$H' \leftarrow$ ProjHash(hp, L_{π_C}, c_C, r_C) $\xleftarrow{\quad \mathsf{hp}, c_S \quad}$ $c_S \leftarrow \mathsf{Enc}^\ell(\mathsf{pk}, \pi_{S,C}; r_S)$

$(K_C, r'_S) \leftarrow$ PRG(H')

$\ell = (C, S, c_C, \mathsf{hp})$

$c'_S \leftarrow \mathsf{Enc}^\ell(\mathsf{pk}, \pi_C; r'_S)$

If $c'_S \neq c_S$, abort

Fig. 5. Generic GK-PAKE Construction

5.3 GK-PAKE Construction and GK-SPOKE

GK-PAKE. Our second two-flow construction is depicted in Fig. 5. It additionally provides explicit server authentication to the client. It requires an IND-CPA encryption scheme ES' with a GLSPHF, and an IND-PCA encryption scheme ES (no need of SPHF for it). It also makes use of a Pseudo-Random Generator PRG, which on a random input returns a longer output that looks indistinguishable to random.

In the full version [1], we prove the following result, with perfectly-smooth SPHFs, which applies for the basic freshness in the BPR setting, or for the forward-secure freshness in the AFP setting with static corruptions only:

$$\mathsf{Adv}(\mathcal{A}) \leq q_s \times 2^{-m} + (q_e + q_s) \times (\mathsf{Adv}_{\mathsf{ES}'}^{\mathsf{ind\text{-}cpa}}(t) + \mathsf{Adv}_{\mathsf{ES}}^{\mathsf{ind\text{-}pca}}(t) + \mathsf{Adv}_{\mathsf{PRG}}^{\mathsf{prg}}(t)) + \frac{q_e q_s}{2^{2n}},$$

where q_e and q_s are the number of Execute and Send-queries, n is the entropy of both the projected keys and the ciphertexts, and m is the entropy of the passwords.

GK-SPOKE: GK – Simple Password-Only Key Exchange (Fig. 6). Combining our new Short Cramer-Shoup encryption scheme, with the basic ElGamal encryption scheme, we obtain the most efficient PAKE known so far: It is based on the plain DDH assumption, and consists of 2 group elements to be sent by the client and 4 group elements by the server. They both have to compute less than 9 exponentiations.

It also uses a PRG from $\mathbb{G}$ to $\{0,1\}^k \times \mathbb{Z}_p$, where k is the bit-length of the eventual common session key. In practice, one would just need a randomness extractor to extract a seed, and then one extends the seed to get the session key K and the random coins r for the encryption scheme.

Using the above security bounds for the encryption schemes, one gets, for the basic freshness in the BPR setting, or for the forward-secure freshness in the AFP setting with static corruptions:

$$\mathsf{Adv}(t) \leq q_s \times 2^{-m} + 2Q \times (\mathsf{Adv}_{\mathbb{G}}^{\mathsf{ddh}}(t) + \mathsf{Succ}_{\mathcal{H}}^{\mathsf{coll}}(t) + \mathsf{Succ}_{\mathsf{PRG}}^{\mathsf{prg}}(t)) + \frac{2Q^2}{p},$$

where q_s is the number of Send-queries, Q is the global number of oracle queries, and m is the min-entropy of the passwords.

Client C (π_C)	Server S ($\pi_{S,C}$)
CRS: (param $= (\mathbb{G}, p, q)$, pk $= (h, c, d) \in \mathbb{G}^3$, pk$' = y \in \mathbb{G}$)	

$r' \xleftarrow{\$} \mathbb{Z}_p$
$(u' \leftarrow g^{r'}, e' \leftarrow y^{r'} g^{\pi_C}) \in \mathbb{G}^2$
$\qquad\qquad \xrightarrow{\quad (u', e') \quad}$
$\qquad\qquad\qquad (\alpha', \beta') \xleftarrow{\$} \mathbb{Z}_p^2 ; \; t' \leftarrow g^{\alpha'} y^{\beta'} \in \mathbb{G}$
$\qquad\qquad\qquad H_C \leftarrow u'^{\alpha'} (e'/g^{\pi_{S,C}})^{\beta'}$
$\qquad\qquad\qquad (K_S, r) \leftarrow \mathsf{PRG}(H_C)$
$\qquad\qquad\qquad (u \leftarrow g^r, e \leftarrow h^r g^{\pi_{S,C}}, v \leftarrow (cd^\xi)^r) \in \mathbb{G}^3,$
$\qquad\qquad \xleftarrow{\quad t', (u, e, v) \quad} \;$ with $\xi \leftarrow H_{\mathsf{SCS}}(C, S, u', e', t', u, e)$
$H_C' \leftarrow t'^{r'}$
$(K_C, r'') \leftarrow \mathsf{PRG}(H_C')$
$(u'' \leftarrow g^{r''}, e'' \leftarrow h^{r''} g^{\pi_C}, v'' \leftarrow (cd^{\xi''})^{r''}) \in \mathbb{G}^3,$
$\quad$ with $\xi'' \leftarrow H_{\mathsf{SCS}}(C, S, u', e', t', u'', e'')$
If $(u'', e'', v'') \neq (u, e, v)$, abort

Fig. 6. GK-SPOKE

Client C (π_C)	CRS: (parameters, pk, pk$'$)	Server S ($\pi_{S,C}$)

$\mathsf{hk}_C \xleftarrow{\$} \mathsf{HashKG}(L')$; $\mathsf{hp}_C \leftarrow \mathsf{ProjKG}(\mathsf{hk}_C, L', \bot)$

$\ell_C = (C, S, \mathsf{hp}_C)$; $r_C \xleftarrow{\$}$; $c_C \leftarrow \mathsf{Enc}^{\ell_C}(\mathsf{pk}, \pi_C; r_C)$ $\xrightarrow{\mathsf{hp}_C, c_C}$

$\ell_S = (S, C, \mathsf{hp}_S)$ $\xleftarrow{\mathsf{hp}_S, c_S}$

$H'_C \leftarrow \mathsf{ProjHash}(\mathsf{hp}_S, L^{\ell_C}_{\pi_C}, c_C, r_C)$

$H_S \leftarrow \mathsf{Hash}(\mathsf{hk}_C, L^{\ell_S}_{\pi_C}, c_S)$

$K_C \leftarrow H'_C \times H_S$

Fig. 7. Generic KV-PAKE Construction

5.4   KV-PAKE Construction and KV-SPOKE

KV-PAKE. Our third construction is a one-round PAKE, depicted in Fig. 7, from the client point of view, but the server does exactly the same thing, since this is a one-round protocol, where the two flows can be sent independently to each other.

It requires an IND-PCA encryption scheme ES with a KVSPHF. In the full version [1], we prove the following result, which applies for the basic freshness in the BPR setting, or for the forward-secure freshness in the AFP setting with static corruptions only:

$$\mathsf{Adv}(\mathcal{A}) \leq q_s \times 2^{-m} + (2q_e + q_s) \times \mathsf{Adv}^{\mathsf{ind\text{-}pca}}_{\mathsf{ES}}(t) + \frac{q_e q_s}{2^{2n}},$$

where q_e and q_s are the number of Execute and Send-queries, n is the entropy of both the projected keys and the ciphertexts, and m is the entropy of the passwords.

KV-SPOKE: KV – Simple Password-Only Key Exchange (Fig. 8). Using our new Short Cramer-Shoup encryption scheme and its associated KVSPHF, we obtain the most efficient one-round PAKE known so far: It is based on the plain DDH assumption, and consists of 5 group elements to be sent by the each user. They both have to compute 14 exponentiations.

Client C (π_C)		Server S ($\pi_{S,C}$)
	CRS: (param $= (\mathbb{G}, p, q)$, pk $= (h, c, d) \in \mathbb{G}^3$)	

$(\alpha'_1, \alpha'_2, \beta', \gamma') \xleftarrow{\$} \mathbb{Z}^4_p$

$(t'_1 \leftarrow g^{\alpha'_1} h^{\beta'} c^{\gamma'}, t'_2 \leftarrow g^{\alpha'_2} d^{\gamma'}) \in \mathbb{G}^2$

$r \xleftarrow{\$} \mathbb{Z}_p$; $(u \leftarrow g^r, e \leftarrow h^r g^{\pi_C}, v \leftarrow (cd^\xi)^r) \in \mathbb{G}^3$,

$\qquad$ with $\xi \leftarrow H_{\mathsf{SCS}}(C, S, t'_1, t'_2, u, e)$ $\xrightarrow{t'_1, t'_2, (u, e, v)}$
$\qquad\qquad\qquad\qquad\qquad\qquad\qquad\qquad\qquad$ $\xleftarrow{t_1, t_2, (u', e', v')}$

$H'_C \leftarrow (t_1 t^\xi_2)^r$

$H_S \leftarrow u'^{\alpha'_1 + \xi' \alpha'_2} (e'/g^{\pi_C})^{\beta'} v'^{\gamma'}$

$\qquad$ with $\xi' \leftarrow H_{\mathsf{SCS}}(S, C, t_1, t_2, u', e')$

$K_C \leftarrow H'_C \times H_S$

Fig. 8. KV-SPOKE

Using the above security bounds for the encryption schemes, one gets, for the basic freshness in the BPR setting, or for the forward-secure freshness in the AFP setting with static corruptions:

$$\mathsf{Adv}(t) \leq q_s \times 2^{-m} + 4Q \times (\mathsf{Adv}_{\mathbb{G}}^{\mathsf{ddh}}(t) + \mathsf{Succ}_{\mathcal{H}}^{\mathsf{coll}}(t)) + \frac{2Q^2}{p},$$

where q_s is the number of Send-queries, Q is the global number of oracle queries, and m is the min-entropy of the passwords.

Acknowledgments. This work was supported in part by the French ANR-12-INSE-0014 SIMPATIC Project, the CFM Foundation, and the European Research Council under the European Community's Seventh Framework Programme (FP7/2007-2013 Grant Agreement no. 339563 – CryptoCloud).

References

1. Abdalla, M., Benhamouda, F., Pointcheval, D.: Public-key encryption scheme indistinguishable under plaintext-checkable attacks. Cryptology ePrint Archive, Report 2014/609 (2014). http://eprint.iacr.org/2014/609
2. Abdalla, M., Chevalier, C., Pointcheval, D.: Smooth projective hashing for conditionally extractable commitments. In: Halevi, S. (ed.) CRYPTO 2009. LNCS, vol. 5677, pp. 671–689. Springer, Heidelberg (2009)
3. Abdalla, M., Fouque, P.-A., Pointcheval, D.: Password-based authenticated key exchange in the three-party setting. In: Vaudenay, S. (ed.) PKC 2005. LNCS, vol. 3386, pp. 65–84. Springer, Heidelberg (2005)
4. Abdalla, M., Pointcheval, D.: A scalable password-based group key exchange protocol in the standard model. In: Lai, X., Chen, K. (eds.) ASIACRYPT 2006. LNCS, vol. 4284, pp. 332–347. Springer, Heidelberg (2006)
5. Bellare, M., Desai, A., Pointcheval, D., Rogaway, P.: Relations among notions of security for public-key encryption schemes. In: Krawczyk, H. (ed.) CRYPTO 1998. LNCS, vol. 1462, pp. 26–45. Springer, Heidelberg (1998)
6. Bellare, M., Pointcheval, D., Rogaway, P.: Authenticated key exchange secure against dictionary attacks. In: Preneel, B. (ed.) EUROCRYPT 2000. LNCS, vol. 1807, p. 139. Springer, Heidelberg (2000)
7. Bellare, M., Rogaway, P.: Code-based game-playing proofs and the security of triple encryption. Cryptology ePrint Archive, Report 2004/331 (2004). http://eprint.iacr.org/2004/331
8. Benhamouda, F., Blazy, O., Chevalier, C., Pointcheval, D., Vergnaud, D.: New techniques for SPHFs and efficient one-round PAKE protocols. In: Canetti, R., Garay, J.A. (eds.) CRYPTO 2013, Part I. LNCS, vol. 8042, pp. 449–475. Springer, Heidelberg (2013)
9. Bleichenbacher, D.: Chosen ciphertext attacks against protocols based on the RSA encryption standard PKCS #1. In: Krawczyk, H. (ed.) CRYPTO 1998. LNCS, vol. 1462, pp. 1–12. Springer, Heidelberg (1998)
10. Canetti, R., Halevi, S., Katz, J., Lindell, Y., MacKenzie, P.: Universally composable password-based key exchange. In: Cramer, R. (ed.) EUROCRYPT 2005. LNCS, vol. 3494, pp. 404–421. Springer, Heidelberg (2005)

11. Cramer, R., Shoup, V.: A practical public key cryptosystem provably secure against adaptive chosen ciphertext attack. In: Krawczyk, H. (ed.) CRYPTO 1998. LNCS, vol. 1462, pp. 13–25. Springer, Heidelberg (1998)

12. Cramer, R., Shoup, V.: Universal hash proofs and a paradigm for adaptive chosen ciphertext secure public-key encryption. In: Knudsen, L.R. (ed.) EUROCRYPT 2002. LNCS, vol. 2332, pp. 45–64. Springer, Heidelberg (2002)

13. Dolev, D., Dwork, C., Naor, M.: Non-malleable cryptography (extended abstract). In: 23rd ACM STOC, pp. 542–552. ACM Press, May 1991

14. Dolev, D., Dwork, C., Naor, M.: Nonmalleable cryptography. SIAM Journal on Computing 30(2), 391–437 (2000)

15. El Gamal, T.: A public key cryptosystem and a signature scheme based on discrete logarithms. In: Blakely, G.R., Chaum, D. (eds.) CRYPTO 1984. LNCS, vol. 196, pp. 10–18. Springer, Heidelberg (1985)

16. Gennaro, R.: Faster and shorter password-authenticated key exchange. In: Canetti, R. (ed.) TCC 2008. LNCS, vol. 4948, pp. 589–606. Springer, Heidelberg (2008)

17. Gennaro, R., Lindell, Y.: A framework for password-based authenticated key exchange. In: Biham, E. (ed.) EUROCRYPT 2003. LNCS, vol. 2656, pp. 524–543. Springer, Heidelberg (2003). http://eprint.iacr.org/2003/032.ps.gz

18. Goldwasser, S., Micali, S.: Probabilistic encryption. Journal of Computer and System Sciences 28(2), 270–299 (1984)

19. Groce, A., Katz, J.: A new framework for efficient password-based authenticated key exchange. In: Al-Shaer, E., Keromytis, A.D., Shmatikov, V. (eds.) ACM CCS 2010, pp. 516–525. ACM Press, October 2010

20. Groth, J., Sahai, A.: Efficient non-interactive proof systems for bilinear groups. In: Smart, N.P. (ed.) EUROCRYPT 2008. LNCS, vol. 4965, pp. 415–432. Springer, Heidelberg (2008)

21. Jiang, S., Gong, G.: Password based key exchange with mutual authentication. In: Handschuh, H., Hasan, M.A. (eds.) SAC 2004. LNCS, vol. 3357, pp. 267–279. Springer, Heidelberg (2004)

22. Katz, J., MacKenzie, P.D., Taban, G., Gligor, V.D.: Two-server password-only authenticated key exchange. In: Ioannidis, J., Keromytis, A.D., Yung, M. (eds.) ACNS 2005. LNCS, vol. 3531, pp. 1–16. Springer, Heidelberg (2005)

23. Katz, J., Ostrovsky, R., Yung, M.: Efficient password-authenticated key exchange using human-memorable passwords. In: Pfitzmann, B. (ed.) EUROCRYPT 2001. LNCS, vol. 2045, pp. 475–494. Springer, Heidelberg (2001)

24. Katz, J., Ostrovsky, R., Yung, M.: Forward secrecy in password-only key exchange protocols. In: Cimato, S., Galdi, C., Persiano, G. (eds.) SCN 2002. LNCS, vol. 2576, pp. 29–44. Springer, Heidelberg (2003)

25. Katz, J., Ostrovsky, R., Yung, M.: Efficient and secure authenticated key exchange using weak passwords. Journal of the ACM 57(1), 78–116 (2009)

26. Katz, J., Vaikuntanathan, V.: Round-optimal password-based authenticated key exchange. In: Ishai, Y. (ed.) TCC 2011. LNCS, vol. 6597, pp. 293–310. Springer, Heidelberg (2011)

27. Naor, M., Reingold, O.: Number-theoretic constructions of efficient pseudo-random functions. In: 38th FOCS, pp. 458–467. IEEE Computer Society Press, October 1997

28. Naor, M., Yung, M.: Public-key cryptosystems provably secure against chosen ciphertext attacks. In: 22nd ACM STOC, pp. 427–437. ACM Press, May 1990

29. Okamoto, T., Pointcheval, D.: REACT: rapid enhanced-security asymmetric cryptosystem transform. In: Naccache, D. (ed.) CT-RSA 2001. LNCS, vol. 2020, pp. 159–175. Springer, Heidelberg (2001)

30. Rackoff, C., Simon, D.R.: Non-interactive zero-knowledge proof of knowledge and chosen ciphertext attack. In: Feigenbaum, J. (ed.) CRYPTO 1991. LNCS, vol. 576, pp. 433–444. Springer, Heidelberg (1992)
31. Shoup, V.: Sequences of games: a tool for taming complexity in security proofs. Cryptology ePrint Archive, Report 2004/332 (2004). http://eprint.iacr.org/2004/332

Pairing-Based Cryptography

Strongly-Optimal Structure Preserving Signatures from Type II Pairings: Synthesis and Lower Bounds

Gilles Barthe[1]($\boxtimes$), Edvard Fagerholm[1,2], Dario Fiore[1],
Andre Scedrov[2], Benedikt Schmidt[1], and Mehdi Tibouchi[3]

[1] IMDEA Software Institute, Madrid, Spain
{gilles.barthe,dario.fiore,benedikt.schmidt}@imdea.org
[2] University of Pennsylvania, Philadelphia, USA
{edvardf,scedrov}@math.upenn.edu
[3] NTT Secure Platform Laboratories, Tokyo, Japan
tibouchi.mehdi@lab.ntt.co.jp

Abstract. Recent work on structure-preserving signatures studies optimality of these schemes in terms of the number of group elements needed in the verification key and the signature, and the number of pairing-product equations in the verification algorithm. While the size of keys and signatures is crucial for many applications, another important aspect to consider for performance is the time it takes to verify a given signature. By far, the most expensive operation during verification is the computation of pairings. However, the concrete number of pairings that one needs to compute is not captured by the number of pairing-product equations considered in earlier work.

To fill this gap, we consider the question of what is the minimal number of pairings that one needs to compute in the verification of structure-preserving signatures. First, we prove lower bounds for schemes in the Type II setting that are secure under chosen message attacks in the generic group model, and we show that three pairings are necessary and that at most one of these pairings can be precomputed. We also extend our lower bound proof to schemes secure under random message attacks and show that in this case two pairings are still necessary.

Second, we build an automated tool to search for schemes matching our lower bounds. The tool can generate automatically and exhaustively all valid structure-preserving signatures within a user-specified search space, and analyze their (bounded) security in the generic group model. Interestingly, using this tool, we find a new randomizable structure-preserving signature scheme in the Type II setting that is optimal with respect to the lower bound on the number of pairings, and also minimal with respect to the number of group operations that have to be computed during verification.

1 Introduction

Structure-preserving signatures [3] (SPS) are signature schemes defined over groups with a bilinear map in which messages, public keys and signatures are all

© International Association for Cryptologic Research 2015
J. Katz (Ed.): PKC 2015, LNCS 9020, pp. 355–376, 2015.
DOI: 10.1007/978-3-662-46447-2_16

group elements, and the verification algorithm consists of evaluating so-called "pairing-product equations" (i.e., products of pairings of the aforementioned group elements). One of the main motivations of considering such specific signature schemes is that they are remarkably useful in the modular design of several cryptographic protocols, notably in combination with non-interactive zero-knowledge (NIZK) proofs of knowledge about group elements, and more specifically with the celebrated Groth-Sahai proof system [24]. In a nutshell, Groth-Sahai proofs allow one to prove knowledge of a set of group elements satisfying a certain pairing-product equation. For instance, by using SPS with Groth-Sahai proofs one can create a NIZK proof showing knowledge of a valid signature on some message (perhaps satisfying certain properties) without disclosing the message, the signature or both. This is only a basic example, though. Indeed, the combination of SPS with Groth-Sahai proofs has been shown to be a powerful tool for the modular design of several cryptographic protocols, such as blind signatures [3,20], group signatures [3,20,27], homomorphic signatures [10,26], oblivious transfer [14,22], tightly-secure encryption [1,25], and more.

Realization of SPS has been considered over the three possible bilinear groups settings introduced in the classification of Galbraith, Paterson and Smart [21]; the type of a pairing $e : \mathbb{G}_1 \times \mathbb{G}_2 \to \mathbb{G}_T$ depends on whether the two source groups are the same, i.e., $\mathbb{G}_1 = \mathbb{G}_2$ (*Type I*), or there is a one-way, efficiently computable homomorphism $\psi : \mathbb{G}_2 \to \mathbb{G}_1$ (*Type II*), or there is no known efficiently computable homomorphism in either direction between $\mathbb{G}_2$ and $\mathbb{G}_1$ (*Type III*). However, more recent work has focused on proving lower bounds on the complexity of SPS, and exhibiting optimal constructions that match lower bounds. The common measures of complexity adopted in all these works are the number of group elements in the public key, the number of group elements in the signature, and the number of pairing-product equations in the verification algorithm. Considering these measures, it has been shown in [4,8] that in both the Type I and the Type III settings SPS require at least 3 group elements in the signatures and 2 verification equations. However, the Type II setting has been shown to (surprisingly) deviate from these bounds: SPS in the Type II setting require at least 2 group elements in the signatures and admit a *single* verification equation [7]. Moreover, for SPS in the Type II setting, it has been shown that the lower bound for the number of group elements in the verification key is 2. Together with showing such lower bounds, these works [4,7,8] have proposed SPS schemes matching these (optimal) measures.

1.1   Our Contribution

We continue the study of the efficiency of SPS schemes by focusing on another important measure that, to the best of our knowledge, has not been considered in any previous work: the number of pairing computations that need to be performed by the verifier. Previous work [4,7,8] considers verifier efficiency only in terms of the number of pairing-product equations. Such a number, however, does not tell much about the number of pairings that the verifier needs to compute, and thus about the concrete verification running time. So, considering that pairings are definitely the most expensive operation in this process, here we refine this question and ask what is the *minimal* number of pairings necessary in the verification of SPS, and in particular of schemes with optimal bandwidth (i.e., 2 elements in the signatures and 2 elements in the verification key). Indeed, even though having fewer elements in the public key and in the signature intuitively leads to fewer pairings, in practice it is unclear what is the minimal number of pairings that is needed.

In this paper we initiate this study focusing on the Type II setting, and our contribution is mainly twofold. First, we show lower bounds on the number of pairings necessary in the pairing-product verification equation. Second, we build a synthesis tool that automates the generation and security analysis of SPS schemes, and we leverage our tool in order to find new SPS schemes that match our new lower bounds and improve over previous work. In the following paragraphs, we discuss our contribution in more detail.

NEW OPTIMALITY MEASURES AND LOWER BOUNDS. First, we show lower bounds for the number of pairings in the pairing-product verification equation of SPS in the Type II setting. We prove that, when considering schemes that are already optimal with respect to previously considered measures (i.e., two group elements in the verification key, two group elements in the signature, and a single verification equation), *three* pairings are necessary for achieving security against chosen-message attacks, whereas *two* pairings are necessary for achieving security against random-message attacks.

More specifically, we refine our analysis and distinguish between, what we call, offline and online pairings. Informally speaking, *offline pairings* are pairings that involve only group elements in the public key or in the public parameters, whereas *online pairings* involve the message and/or elements of the signature. In other words, offline pairings are computed in every signature verification (when using the same verification key) and thus can be precomputed "offline" and be re-used in an arbitrary number of verifications. In contrast, online pairings involve elements, such as the message and the signature, that inherently change every time, and thus must be computed "online". So, given this notion of online and offline pairings, we ask how many of the three necessary pairings can be computed offline. Such question is indeed quite relevant for practical purposes since online pairings are those that really matter (e.g., think of the case in which one verifies several signatures with the same verification key). We answer this question by proving that, for schemes secure against chosen-message attacks, among the three pairings, *at most one* can be precomputed, i.e., two online pairings are necessary. For schemes that are secure against random-message attacks, instead two online pairings are always necessary. We call schemes matching these bounds *strongly-optimal*.

Once established these bounds, we address the question of constructing strongly-optimal SPS schemes. First, we consider schemes secure against chosen-message attacks: we look at the previous work (in the Type II setting) and observe that there already exists a strongly-unforgeable SPS matching our lower bounds [7]. Yet there is no known SPS scheme that is re-randomizable and allows for only two online pairings in verification. As discussed in [7], re-randomizable schemes are useful because one of the group elements in the signature is uniformly random. This property is convenient in some applications, e.g., anonymization protocols, as one of the signature elements can be revealed in the clear without leaking information on what was the original signature. So, as an additional contribution, in this paper we show a new re-randomizable SPS scheme that is strongly-optimal and improves over the re-randomizable scheme proposed in [7] by requiring one less online pairing. Then we take into consideration schemes secure against random-message attacks (RMA) for which there is no strongly-optimal candidate in the previous work. We fill this gap by showing a simple, strongly-optimal, RMA-secure SPS. We note that although random-message security is a weak notion, it has been shown useful in applications such as constructing adaptive oblivious transfer [22] and in a transformation for obtaining chosen-message secure SPS [1]. By using our strongly-optimal RMA-secure SPS scheme, all these applications can benefit of its improved efficiency.

AUTOMATED SYNTHESIS OF SPS. As emerges from the previous discussion, optimality results (at least in the single-dimensional form in which they have been developed so far) are insufficient in rich settings such as structure-preserving signatures where many meaningful measures of efficiency can be considered (e.g., verification time, key or signature size). Therefore, an attractive approach for achieving a broad range of optimality results is to perform an exhaustive search of valid SPS within user-defined parameters. In the second part of our work, we develop a synthesis tool that takes as input a user-defined budget, consisting of the number of pairings, group elements, etc. that can be used by the construction, and generates all possible expressions within this budget. Broadly speaking, our tool then uses an extension of the Generic Group Analyzer reported in [12], to generate, whenever it exists, a verification equation for the signature algorithm. Finally, our tool proves or disproves security of candidate schemes in the generic group model for the case when the adversary makes a bounded number of signing queries. Through this approach, we generate an exhaustive database, by exploring more than 2000 candidate SPS schemes, that can then be mined for different efficiency criteria. For instance, our database contains our new scheme with optimal number of online/offline pairings as well as the SPS schemes in the Type II setting that were previously proposed in [7]. Beyond its intrinsic interest, the database can also be used to validate or refute empirically new conjectures on SPS. For example, it is interesting to mention that our work on proving the new lower bounds was motivated by observing that among the schemes generated by our tool none of the ones secure against chosen-message attacks can be verified with only two pairings. More generally, our tool suggests the feasibility and interest to develop synthesis methods for structure-preserving cryptography. We believe that our methods can be extended to the Type I and Type III settings (however exhaustive search will be more difficult to attain because secure schemes must use two verification equations, which results in an exponential growth in the search space), and to other forms of structure-preserving cryptography, such as structure-preserving commitments [3] and encryption [15].

1.2 Other Related Work

STRUCTURE-PRESERVING SIGNATURES. While the notion of structure-preserving signature was first given by Abe et al. in [3], the first construction was proposed earlier by Groth [23], though its efficiency is far from being truly practical (it consists of hundreds of group elements). Green and Hohenberger [22] proposed SPS that are proved secure only against random-message attacks. Cathalo, Libert and Yung [16] constructed a scheme that is structure-preserving in a relaxed sense since it has a verification key which includes elements of the target group.

The study of lower bounds for SPS was put forward by Abe et al. [4] who showed that SPS in the Type III setting require at least three group elements in the signature and two pairing-product equations, and also proposed schemes matching these bounds that are only proven secure in the generic bilinear group model. Next, Abe et al. [5] refined the result in [4] considering schemes whose security can be proved under a non-interactive assumption using a black-box reduction. For this case they show that any scheme with only 3 elements in the signature cannot be proved secure under a non-interactive assumption. Optimal schemes in the symmetric (Type I) setting have been explored more recently by Abe et al. [8] who show that Type I SPS schemes require 3 elements in the signature and 2 verification equations (i.e., the same bounds as in Type III). Furthermore, the same work [8] proposes a general scheme that works in all three bilinear settings, and thus shows a Type II scheme with 3 elements in the signature and 2 verification equations. Finally, the recent work of Abe et al. [7] focused on the Type II setting and showed that in this setting the lower bounds are (surprisingly) different. Namely, Type II SPS schemes require 2 elements in the signature, a single verification equation, and 2 elements in the verification key (the latter being the first lower bound for the size of the verification key).

All the optimal schemes in [4,7,8] are proved secure directly in the generic bilinear group model. Another line of work investigated efficient SPS that can be proved secure under standard assumptions. Hofheinz and Jager [25] and Abe et al. [1,2] proposed schemes based on the decision linear assumption. The efficiency of these schemes, however, does not meet that of the schemes secure in the generic group model.

Finally, Chatterjee and Menezes [18] re-considered the result of Abe et al. [7] for Type II SPS in light of the current state-of-the-art implementations of Type II vs. Type III pairings. They start from the observation that implementations of Type III pairings are currently more efficient than the ones of Type II pairings. Then they note that Type II SPS, albeit optimal in terms of the number of signature elements and number of verification equations, are not as efficient as their Type III counterparts (i.e., the SPS schemes that can be obtained through a semi-generic transformation from Type II to Type III [17]).[1] Although this is a valid point when considering concrete efficiency, we believe that the exploration of Type II SPS is still quite interesting. For example, they have a simpler structure that leads to a smaller search space when looking for new schemes. Yet, given a Type II scheme, one can always translate it to the Type III setting if concrete efficiency is a concern, e.g., using the approach from [17].

COMPUTER-AIDED CRYPTOGRAPHY. In contrast to computer-aided tools for verifying cryptographic proofs, which have existed for some time, computer-aided tools for synthesizing new constructions are very recent. Barthe et al. [11] develop an automated tool, called ZooCrypt, for synthesizing padding-based encryption schemes; their tool uses a dedicated logic with an efficient proof search procedure to prove chosen-plaintext or chosen-ciphertext security, and an efficient method for finding attacks on insecure schemes. Because the search space for reasonably-sized constructions is small (about 10^6 well-typed schemes), simple trimming techniques are sufficient to cover the full search space efficiently. Malozemoff, Katz, and Green [28] develop an automated tool for proving security of modes of operations; the security of candidate schemes is proved using a type system, but no attack is exhibited for insecure schemes.

Akinyele, Green, and Hohenberger [9] develop two synthesis tools for pairing-based cryptography. Their tool AutoGroup converts schemes in the Type I setting into schemes in the Type III setting, whereas their tool AutoStrong transforms an existentially unforgeable signature into a strongly unforgeable one, using SMT solvers to check whether the original signature satisfies a criterion allowing an efficient transformation. The idea of automatically transforming constructions from the symmetric to the asymmetric setting was further considered by Abe, Groth, Ohkubo and Tango [6], who develop an automated transformation of Type I protocols into Type III protocols.

Automating proofs in the generic group model has been recently considered by Barthe et al. [12] who propose a tool that enables to automatically analyze the validity of cryptographic assumptions in the generic (multilinear) group model. The tool developed in this work actually builds on the techniques of [12] in order to perform the security analysis of SPS in the generic bilinear group model.

Finally, in a concurrent and independent work, De Ruiter [19] recently proposed a tool for analyzing the security of structure-preserving signatures. The proposed tool provides a security analysis of SPS similar to the one we provide, even though the security arguments in [19] do not have a full formalization in the generic group model. Additionally, we note that our tool is not limited to the security analysis of SPS, but also includes the novel synthesis component which allows to automatically generate SPS schemes.

---

[1] One main issue that leads to such difference of performance here is that testing group membership in $\mathbb{G}_2$ (which is required in the signature verification) is significantly more expensive in Type II than in Type III groups.

2   Preliminaries

2.1   Bilinear Groups

A *bilinear group description* is a tuple $(p, \mathbb{G}_1, \mathbb{G}_2, \mathbb{G}_T, e, \psi, G, H)$ where p is a prime number, $\mathbb{G}_1, \mathbb{G}_2, \mathbb{G}_T$ are cylic groups of order p, G, H are generators of $\mathbb{G}_1$ and $\mathbb{G}_2$ respectively, $\psi \colon \mathbb{G}_2 \to \mathbb{G}_1$ is the homomorphism sending H to G (so that $\psi(H^x) = G^x$ for all $x \in \mathbb{Z}$), and $e \colon \mathbb{G}_1 \times \mathbb{G}_2 \to \mathbb{G}_T$ is a nondegenerate bilinear pairing, meaning that $e(G, H)$ generates $\mathbb{G}_T$ and $e(G^x, H^y) = e(G, H)^{xy}$ for all $x, y \in \mathbb{Z}$.

A *bilinear group generator* $\mathcal{G}$ is an efficient algorithm which, on input of a security parameter 1^λ, returns a bilinear group description $(p, \mathbb{G}_1, \mathbb{G}_2, \mathbb{G}_T, e, \psi, G, H)$ with $p = 2^{\Omega(\lambda)}$ and efficient algorithms for computing group operations and the bilinear map e, and deciding equality of group elements and membership in the groups.

Furthermore, following Galbraith, Paterson and Smart [21], we say that the result is a Type I bilinear group if the homomorphism ψ is efficiently computable and efficiently invertible (in which case we can simplify identify $\mathbb{G}_1$ and $\mathbb{G}_2$), a Type II bilinear group if ψ is efficiently computable but not efficiently invertible (i.e. it is a one-way function) and a Type III bilinear group if ψ is neither efficiently computable nor invertible. This paper mainly focuses on the Type II setting.

Generic Algorithms. In a bilinear group $(p, \mathbb{G}_1, \mathbb{G}_2, \mathbb{G}_T, e, \psi, G, H)$ generated by $\mathcal{G}$ we refer to deciding group membership, computing group operations in $\mathbb{G}_1$, $\mathbb{G}_2$ or $\mathbb{G}_T$, comparing group elements and evaluating the homomorphism or the bilinear map as the generic bilinear group operations. The signature schemes we construct only use generic bilinear group operations.

As is customary in the literature, we denote group elements in $\mathbb{G}_1$ and $\mathbb{G}_2$ by uppercase letters such as $M, R, S, V, W, \ldots$, and their discrete logarithms with respect to base G or H using the corresponding lowercase letters $m, r, s, v, w, \ldots$ In particular, for an element $X \in \mathbb{G}_2$, we have $\psi(X) = G^x$, and for $(Y, Z) \in \mathbb{G}_1 \times \mathbb{G}_2$, we have $e(Y, Z) = e(G, H)^{yz}$. Furthermore, we will often express pairings equations, such as $e(X, Y)^{a_1} = e(W, Z)^{a_2} \cdot e(T, H)^{a_3}$, as a quadratic polynomial involving the corresponding exponents, i.e., $a_1 xy = a_2 wz + a_3 t$.

2.2   Structure-Preserving Signature Schemes

We study structure-preserving signature schemes (SPS) [3] on bilinear groups generated by group generator $\mathcal{G}$. We refer to the full version of this paper [13] for basic definitions about signature schemes. In a structure preserving signature scheme the verification key, the messages and the signatures consist only of group elements from $\mathbb{G}_1$ and $\mathbb{G}_2$ and the verification algorithm evaluates the signature by deciding group membership of elements in the signature, using the homomorphism ψ and by evaluating pairing product equations, which are equations of the form:

$$\prod_i \prod_j e(X_i, Y_j)^{a_{ij}} = 1,$$

where $X_1, X_2, \ldots \in \mathbb{G}_1$, $Y_1, Y_2, \ldots \in \mathbb{G}_2$ are group elements appearing in PP, VK, M and Σ (where in the Type II setting it may hold $Y_i = \Psi(X_j)$ for some i, j) and the elements $a_{ij} \in \mathbb{Z}_p$ are constants stored in PP. More precisely:

Definition 1 (Structure-preserving signatures). *A signature scheme (Setup, KeyGen, Sign, Verify) is said to be structure-preserving with respect to some bilinear group generator $\mathcal{G}$ if*

- *PP consists of a bilinear group $(p, \mathbb{G}_1, \mathbb{G}_2, \mathbb{G}_T, e, \psi, G, H)$ generated by $\mathcal{G}$ and constants in $\mathbb{Z}_p$,*
- *the verification key consists of group elements in $\mathbb{G}_1$ and $\mathbb{G}_2$,*
- *the messages consist of group elements in $\mathbb{G}_1$ and $\mathbb{G}_2$,*
- *the signatures consist of group elements in $\mathbb{G}_1$ and $\mathbb{G}_2$,*
- *the signing algorithm only uses generic group operations,[2] and*
- *the verification algorithm only needs to decide membership in $\mathbb{G}_1$ and $\mathbb{G}_2$, use the homomorphism ψ, and evaluate pairing product equations.*

2.3 Known Lower Bounds on Type II SPS

A number of lower bounds on signature size, verification key size and the number of verification equations have been established for secure structure-preserving signature schemes and one-time signature schemes. In particular, Abe et al. [7] establish many such bounds in the Type II setting. As some of our results rely heavily on those bounds, we recall them below. Note that membership tests are not counted as "verification equations", although some of them may require an amortizable (aka offline) pairing computation in practical instantiations.

First, just as Type I and Type III SPS, Type II SPS for messages in $\mathbb{G}_1$ require two verification equations:

Lemma 1 ([7, Theorem 3]). *A structure-preserving signature scheme for messages in $\mathbb{G}_1$ must have at least two verification equations. This holds even for one-time signatures with security against random message attack.*

Since this paper will mostly focus on schemes with a single verification equation, we will therefore consider signatures on messages in $\mathbb{G}_2$, which can have a single verification equation. In that case, Abe et al. obtain a lower bound on verification key size, and show that all signature elements must be in $\mathbb{G}_2$.

---

[2] Technically, this condition was not required in the original definition of Abe et al. [3], but all known constructions satisfy this property and it is required for the proofs of most lower bounds to go through. Since an SPS scheme with a non-generic signing algorithm would be very unnatural and surprising, it seems appropriate to include genericity of the signer in the definition (see also the discussion in [7, §2.3]).

Lemma 2 ([7, Theorem 4 and Lemma 1]). *A structure-preserving signature scheme with a single verification equation must have at least two group elements in the verification key, and can have no non-redundant signature element in $\mathbb{G}_1$. This holds even for one-time signatures secure under random message attack.*

Finally, signatures in a secure Type II SPS scheme must consist of at least two elements (although that property does not hold for one-time signatures), and three elements for messages in $\mathbb{G}_1$ (idem).

Lemma 3 ([7, Theorem 5]). *An EUF-RMA-secure structure-preserving signature scheme must have at least 2 group elements for messages in $\mathbb{G}_2$ and at least 3 group elements for messages in $\mathbb{G}_1$.*

3   Lower Bounds on the Number of Pairings in the Type II Setting

In this section we show lower bounds for the number of pairings in the pairing-product verification equations of SPS in the Type II setting. In particular, in our analysis we consider SPS schemes that already match the lower bounds shown in [7], i.e., they have 2 group elements in the verification key, 2 group elements in the signature and the verification consists of a single pairing-product equation (as well as possible group membership tests).

To have a more refined and practically interesting analysis, we distinguish between pairings according to whether they can be precomputed from the public key or not. In the former case we call a pairing *offline* while in the latter case *online*.

3.1   Main Result

Having defined the notion of online and offline pairings, we are now ready to state our main result. It shows that any optimal-size SPS scheme requires at least three pairings for verification, and two of these pairings must be online ones.

Theorem 1 (Main result). *Any EUF-CMA-secure structure-preserving signature scheme in the Type II setting with 1 verification pairing-product equation, 2 group elements in the verification key and 2 elements in the signature requires at least 3 pairings in the pairing-product equation, and at least 2 of them must be online pairings.*

To prove the theorem, we distinguish between three cases according to which groups the two elements V, W of the verification key belong to, i.e., (i) $V, W \in \mathbb{G}_2$, (ii) $V, W \in \mathbb{G}_1$, and (iii) $V \in \mathbb{G}_1, W \in \mathbb{G}_2$.

The first case is rather simple and is addressed in the following lemma which shows that there exists no such structure-preserving signature scheme.

Lemma 4. *There is no secure structure-preserving signature scheme in the Type II setting with a single verification equation and a verification key consisting entirely of elements of* $\mathbb{G}_2$.

Proof. We know by Lemma 2 and Lemma 3 that the signatures and messages all have to be in $\mathbb{G}_2$. Since all inputs are in $\mathbb{G}_2$ the scheme would also be secure in the Type I setting and must therefore be insecure since Type I SPS require two pairing product equations for security [8, Theorem 4]. □

The second case is somewhat more involved, and mainly addressed by the following lemma, proved in Section 3.3 below.

Lemma 5. *An EUF-CMA-secure structure-preserving signature scheme in the Type II setting with 1 verification pairing-product equation, 2 group elements $V, W \in \mathbb{G}_1$ in the verification key and 2 group elements in the signature requires at least 3 pairings in the pairing-product equation.*

That result establishes that 3 pairings are needed, so all that remains to show is that 2 of them must be online. This follows immediately from the following observation.

Lemma 6. *In a Type II structure-preserving signature scheme where all verification key elements are in $\mathbb{G}_1$, it is possible to compute all the offline pairings in a verification pairing-product equation using a single pairing evaluation. More generally, $\ell + 1$ pairing evaluations are sufficient if the verification key contains ℓ elements in $\mathbb{G}_2$.*

Proof. Indeed, if the verification key is $(V_1, \ldots, V_k, U_1, \ldots, U_\ell) \in \mathbb{G}_1^k \times \mathbb{G}_2^\ell$, then any product of offline pairings can be expanded into an expression of the form $\prod_{i,j} e(X_i, Y_j)^{c_{ij}}$ where Y_j runs through $H, U_1, \ldots, U_\ell$ (since these are the only elements of $\mathbb{G}_2$ in the verification key and the public parameters) and X_i runs through $G, V_1, \ldots, V_k, \psi(U_1), \ldots, \psi(U_\ell)$. By rewriting the product as:

$$\prod_j e\Big(\prod_i X_i^{c_{ij}}, Y_j\Big)$$

we can compute it with at most $\ell + 1$ pairing evaluations as required. □

Finally, to complete the proof of Theorem 1, we only need to prove it when the verification key consists of one element of $\mathbb{G}_1$ and one element of $\mathbb{G}_2$. This case, which is somewhat less interesting as such a scheme is less space efficient than when all key elements are in $\mathbb{G}_1$, but turns out to be more technically challenging, is dealt with in details in the full version of this paper [13].

3.2 Gaps in Bounds Between EUF-RMA and EUF-CMA-Security

Following Lemma 5, in the setting when $(V, W) \in \mathbb{G}_1^2$ the bound of Theorem 1 holds only for EUF-CMA-secure SPS schemes. This however is not the case in the setting when the verification key is of the form $(V, W) \in \mathbb{G}_1 \times \mathbb{G}_2$: as discussed in the full version of this paper [13], the bound of Theorem 1 holds even for EUF-RMA-secure SPS schemes. In what follows we establish a slightly weaker general lower bound on the number of pairings in the single pairing-product equation of minimal EUF-RMA-secure SPS schemes in the setting when $(V, W) \in \mathbb{G}_1^2$.

Theorem 2. *Any EUF-RMA-secure structure-preserving signature scheme in the Type II setting with 1 verification pairing-product equation requires at least 2 pairings in the pairing-product equation, and both of them must be online pairings.*

Proof. It suffices to show that a Type II SPS scheme with a single verification equation (and which we can assume without loss of generality signs one-element messages) cannot be EUF-RMA-secure if the pairing-product equation consists of only one online pairing (and any number of offline pairings).

To see this, denote by $(S_1, \ldots, S_k)$ the signature vector (which is in $\mathbb{G}_2^k$ without loss of generality by Lemma 2), and observe that the pairing product equation must be of the form:

$$\prod_{i,j} e(X_i, Y_j) = e\left(\psi(M)^{a_0} \cdot \prod_{i=1}^{k} \psi(S_i)^{a_i} \cdot Z, M^{b_0} \cdot \prod_{j=1}^{k} S_j^{b_j} \cdot T \right)$$

where the pairings on the left-hand side are offline (and hence the X_i's and Y_j's do not depend on the message or the signature), and Z, T are elements which also do not depend on the message or the signature. But then we can do the change of variables:

$$(R', S') = \left(\psi(M)^{a_0} \cdot \prod_{i=1}^{k} \psi(S_i)^{a_i}, M^{b_0} \cdot \prod_{j=1}^{k} S_j^{b_j} \right)$$

and then (R', S') provides a two-element EUF-RMA-secure signature scheme whose verification equation is just:

$$\prod_{i,j} e(X_i, Y_j) = e(R' \cdot Z, S' \cdot T),$$

and in particular does not depend on the message: this is a contradiction.   □

We see that the bounds given by Theorem 1 and Theorem 2 show a gap. Namely, there could exist an EUF-RMA-secure scheme with precisely two online pairings and no offline pairing. We confirm that both lower bounds are indeed tight, by providing an EUF-RMA-secure SPS with precisely two online pairings in Section 5.2.

3.3   Proof of Lemma 5

Proof. The proof proceeds by contradiction showing that having a scheme with only 2 pairings in the single pairing-product equation is impossible. Let us first recall that in this setting we have a message $M \in \mathbb{G}_2$, verification keys $V, W \in \mathbb{G}_1$ and signature elements $R, S \in \mathbb{G}_2$. As usual, we denote their discrete logarithms by the corresponding lower case letters. We may write the general verification equation in terms of the discrete logarithms of M, R, S, V, W as follows:

$$
\begin{aligned}
(c_1m + c_2r + c_3s + c_4v + v_5w + c_6)(d_1m + d_2r + d_3s + d_4) = \\
(e_1m + e_2r + e_3s + e_4v + e_5w + e_6)(f_1m + f_2r + f_3s + f_4),
\end{aligned}
\tag{1}
$$

where the products represent a pairing, the left factor in each product represent the element in $\mathbb{G}_1$ and the right factor the element in $\mathbb{G}_2$ of each pairing.

Now if we define the vectors $X_1 = (c_1, \ldots, c_6), X_2 = (e_1, \ldots, e_6), Y_1 = (d_1, \ldots, d_4), Y_2 = (f_1, \ldots, f_4)$ over $\mathbb{Z}_p$ and the matrix:

$$
E = X_1^t Y_1 - X_2^t Y_2,
$$

then the verification equation (1) can be rewritten as

$$
(m, r, s, v, w, 1) \cdot E \cdot (m, r, s, 1)^t = 0.
$$

A simple observation shows that if $\operatorname{Ker} E$ contains a vector $(x_1, \ldots, x_4)$, where $x_4 \neq 0$, then we may scale to $x_4 = 1$ and then

$$
m = x_1, \ r = x_2, \ s = x_3
$$

is a valid key-only attack forgery (since the kernel of E can be computed entirely from the public parameters). It follows that if the scheme is secure, then $\operatorname{Ker} E \subset \{(x_1, \ldots, x_4) \mid x_4 = 0\}$. However, this implies that the following system

$$
\begin{cases}
d_1m + d_2r + d_3s = -d_4 \\
f_1m + f_2r + f_3s = -f_4
\end{cases}
$$

lacks a solution. Up to exchanging the roles of Y_1 and Y_2 without loss of generality, this implies that $Y_1 = cY_2 + (0, 0, 0, \lambda)$ for some constants c, λ, and hence:

$$
E = X_1^t Y_1 - X_2^t Y_2 = X_1^t \big(cY_2 + (0,0,0,\lambda)\big) - X_2^t Y_2 = (\lambda X_1)^t \cdot (0,0,0,1) - (X_2 - cX_1)^t Y_2.
$$

Therefore, after relabeling the coefficients, we may assume that $Y_1 = (0, 0, 0, 1)$ and the verification equation (1) can be rewritten as

$$
\begin{aligned}
c_1m + c_2r + c_3s + c_4v + c_5w + c_6 = \\
(e_1m + e_2r + e_3s + e_4v + e_5w + e_6)(f_1m + f_2r + f_3s + f_4),
\end{aligned}
\tag{2}
$$

Now if $(c_4, c_5) = \lambda(e_4, e_5)$ or $(e_4, e_5) = \lambda(c_4, c_5)$, then we may replace the verification key by a single element $t = e_4v + e_5w$ or $t = c_4v + c_5w$, which is insecure by Lemma 2. It follows that

$$
\det \begin{pmatrix} c_4 & c_5 \\ e_4 & e_5 \end{pmatrix} \neq 0
$$

and we may do a linear change of variables

$$\begin{pmatrix} v' \\ w' \end{pmatrix} = \begin{pmatrix} c_4 & c_5 \\ e_4 & e_5 \end{pmatrix} \begin{pmatrix} v \\ w \end{pmatrix} + \begin{pmatrix} c_6 \\ e_6 \end{pmatrix},$$

so that the verification equation (2) becomes, after renaming coefficients,

$$c_1 m + c_2 r + c_3 s + v = (e_1 m + e_2 r + e_3 s + w)(f_1 m + f_2 r + f_3 s + f_4). \tag{3}$$

Note that the vectors $(c_2, c_3), (e_2, e_3), (f_2, f_3)$ cannot all be collinear, because otherwise we may again compress the signature into one group element, which we already know is impossible.

Next, we look at the matrix

$$N = \begin{pmatrix} e_2 & e_3 \\ f_2 & f_3 \end{pmatrix}$$

and distinguish two cases depending on the determinant.

On one hand, if $\det N \neq 0$, then as before, a change of variables let us write the verification equation (3) in the form

$$c_1 m + c_2 r + c_3 s + v = (r + w)s.$$

Since m must be used in the verification equation, we know that $c_1 \neq 0$. An easy calculation then shows that if (m, r, s) is a triple satisfying the verification equation for the keys v, w, then so does $(m - (c_2 - s)/c_1, r + 1, s)$. This gives us a forgery unless $c_2 = s$ for a non-negligible set of signatures. However, if this happens, then s would be a redundant signature element. From Lemma 3 we know that the scheme must be insecure.

On the other hand, if $\det N = 0$, we have the two cases $(e_2, e_3) = \lambda(f_2, f_3)$ or $(f_2, f_3) = 0$. If $(f_2, f_3) = 0$, then

$$\det \begin{pmatrix} c_2 & c_3 \\ e_2 & e_3 \end{pmatrix} \neq 0$$

or otherwise $(c_2, c_3), (e_2, e_3), (f_2, f_3)$ would be collinear. It follows that the verification equation (3) reduces to

$$r + v = (s + w)(f_1 m + f_4).$$

and since $f_1 \neq 0$, as the message must be used, we may query $m_1 = -f_1^{-1} f_4$ getting back a signature (r_1, s_1), where $r_1 = -v$. Now make another query with $m_2 = f_1^{-1}(1 - f_4)$ to get back a signature (r_2, s_2). Then

$$r_2 + v = s_2 + w \Rightarrow w = r_2 + v - s_2 = r_2 - r_1 - s_2,$$

so with two *chosen-message* queries the attacker can transfer V, W to $\mathbb{G}_2$ and then we know the scheme cannot be secure (concretely, $(R_1, R_1 R_2^{-1} S_2) = (V^{-1}, W^{-1})$ is a valid signature on any message). Therefore, we must have that map $\mathbb{G}_1 \times \mathbb{G}_2 \to \mathbb{G}_T$. iso $\mathbb{G}_2 \to \mathbb{G}_1$.

input $[V]$ in $\mathbb{G}_1$. input $[W]$ in $\mathbb{G}_2$.

oracle $o(M : \mathbb{G}_2) = $ sample R; return $[R, (1 + W^2 + M * V) * R^{-1}]$ in $\mathbb{G}_2$.

win $(M' : \mathbb{G}_2, R' : \mathbb{G}_2, S' : \mathbb{G}_2) = (S' * R' = 1 + W^2 + V * M' \wedge \forall i : M' \neq M_i)$.

Fig. 1. Example of input for analyzing EUF-CMA security of an SPS scheme using our extended version of the GGA tool

$(e_2, e_3) = \lambda(f_2, f_3)$. Again using the fact that $(c_2, c_3), (e_2, e_3), (f_2, f_3)$ are not collinear, we must have

$$\det \begin{pmatrix} c_2 & c_3 \\ f_2 & f_3 \end{pmatrix} \neq 0.$$

It follows that we may do a change of variables $s' = f_1 m + f_2 r + f_3 s + f_4$ and $r' = c_1 m + c_2 r + c_3 s$ and by the collinearity of (e_2, e_3) and (f_2, f_3) the verification equation (3) becomes of the form

$$r + v = (e_1 m + e_3 s + w + e_6) s$$

and now if (m, r, s) is a valid signature, then so is $(m + 1/e_1, r + s, s)$, which is a valid forgery, since m must be used in the verification equation and hence $e_1 \neq 0$. Also, note that in the latter case, the attack can be performed in the random-message security game.   □

4   Synthesis of Schemes

Our tool[3] for the synthesis of SPS schemes consists of two components. The first component takes the description of a search space and generates all included SPS schemes. The second component classifies a given scheme by performing a proof and attack search.

4.1   Generation of Schemes

For our generation algorithm, we consider SPS schemes with generic *KeyGen* and *Sign* algorithms and assume all random values are sampled uniformly.

Our definition of an SPS scheme consists of
 - the employed group type and the supported message space $\mathbb{G}_1^k \times \mathbb{G}_2^l$,
 - the randomly sampled values $u_i \in \mathbb{Z}_p$ used in *KeyGen*,
 - the verification keys $V_i = G^{f_i(\boldsymbol{u})} \in \mathbb{G}_1$ and $W_i = H^{g_i(\boldsymbol{u})} \in \mathbb{G}_2$,
 - the randomly sampled values $r_i \in \mathbb{Z}_p$ used in *Sign*,

---

[3] Available at https://www.easycrypt.info/GGA

  - the signature elements $S_i = G^{s_i(u,r,m)} \in \mathbb{G}_1$ and $T_i = H^{t_i(u,r,m)} \in \mathbb{G}_2$, and

  - the pairing-product equations used by *Verify*.

Here, f_i and g_i are arbitrary rational functions in the random variables u. Similarly, s_i and t_i are rational functions in the random variables u, r and the discrete logarithms m of the messages such that there exists a corresponding generic signing algorithm, i.e., S_i and T_i can be computed without knowing the discrete logarithms of the messages.

A search space description characterizes a finite set of SPS schemes and consists of (1) the group type, (2) the number of messages, verification key elements, and signature elements in $\mathbb{G}_1$ and $\mathbb{G}_2$, (3) the number of random values sampled in *KeyGen* and *Sign*, and (4) a description of the rational expressions that can be used for f_i, g_i, s_i, and t_i.

There are two ways to characterize the allowed rational expressions. First, the tool can take a set of Laurent polynomials with placeholders and allowed values for these placeholders, and generate all instances. Second, the tool accepts a set of constraints that specify bounds on the number of additions, the size of coefficients, and the degree of monomials. Then, it generates all Laurent polynomials that satisfy these constraints.

Given a search space description and concrete polynomials for the verification keys and the signature elements, the tool can compute the (strongest) verification equation as follows. Using distinct variables $Z_1, Z_2, \ldots$ for all group elements in the verification keys, signature elements, and messages, enumerate all products over these variables that can be computed by applying the homomorphisms and the bilinear map. This yields a sequence of monomials $M_1, M_2, \ldots$ over the the variables Z_i denoting products in $\mathbb{G}_T$ that can be computed from the input of the verification algorithm using Ψ and e. To characterize the linear relations between the elements in $\mathbb{G}_T$ corresponding to the monomials M_i, we associate a rational expression F_i over u, r, m to M_i by evaluating the monomial for $Z_i := h_i(u, r, m)$ where h_i is the exponent of the group element associated with Z_i. Finally, we use linear algebra to compute a basis of the linear relations between the F_i and map them back to verification equations using M_i.

4.2   Proof and Attack Search

We classify generated schemes using a proof and attack search based on an extension of the generic group analyzer developed by Barthe et al. [12]. The generic group analyzer (GGA) is a tool that automatically analyzes cryptographic assumptions in generic group models. To analyze SPS schemes, we use GGA's support for the generic bilinear group model. Here, the adversary is given blackbox access (using handles) to elements in the groups $\mathbb{G}_1$, $\mathbb{G}_2$, and $\mathbb{G}_T$ and provided with oracles for performing the group operations and applying the bilinear map and the efficiently computable homomorphisms. The GGA tool also supports a restricted class of interactive assumptions that enable the analysis of signature schemes that sign messages in $\mathbb{Z}_p$, but does not support oracles that take group elements. To analyze such interactive assumptions, the

GGA tool exploits that the signing oracle queries are essentially non-adaptive. More concretely, since the signing oracle takes elements in $\mathbb{Z}_p$ and returns handles to group elements, the adversary can only use these returned handles to compute the forgery, but the arguments to signing oracle queries cannot depend on the results of earlier oracle queries. This allows the GGA tool to treat oracle return values like initially known values by using parameters to model the oracle arguments in $\mathbb{Z}_p$. Another reason why the GGA cannot be directly applied to most SPS schemes is that there is no support for Laurent polynomials, which are required to model signing algorithms that invert elements of $\mathbb{Z}_p$.

To overcome these limitations, we have extended the GGA tool with support for both features and our extension can now analyze assumptions, such as the one shown in Figure 1, that were out of scope of the original version. To support signing oracles that take handles to group elements, the adversary knowledge can contain polynomials with parameters that are used to model oracle arguments in $\mathbb{Z}_p$ and in the groups $\mathbb{G}_*$. The parameters introduced to model known group elements correspond to coefficients of linear combinations, i.e., we exploit that every known group element is a linear combination of initially known group elements, group elements returned by earlier oracle queries, or the result of applying a pairing or an isomorphism to such group elements. To compute a basis for all known group elements after q oracle queries, we recursively extend the knowledge after i queries with the results of an additional query, starting with the initial knowledge.

The definition in Figure 1 specifies the EUF-CMA security experiment for an SPS scheme in the Type II setting. The verification keys are specified in the second line, the signing algorithm is given in the third line, and the winning condition (including the verification equation) is given in the last line. Here, group elements are specified by giving their exponent polynomials and the variables V and W are assumed to be randomly sampled. For such an input and a bound on the number q of performed oracle queries, the tool either returns an attack or a proof that the scheme is q-EUF-CMA secure in the generic group model. We note that our tool can be invoked with any specified value of q, though in this specific setting of SPS it runs efficiently only with small values.

5   Synthesized Schemes

In this section we will present and discuss the SPS schemes that we obtained by searching using our tool described in Section 4.

5.1   A Summary of Our Search

We have performed an exhaustive search for Type II schemes with keys $V, W \in \mathbb{G}_1$, message $M \in \mathbb{G}_2$, and signature $T, S \in \mathbb{G}_2$ such that: V and W are random; $T = H^r \cdot U$ where r is random and U does not involve r; the exponent polynomials of S, i.e., $s(r, v, w, m)$, have coefficients in $\{0, 1\}$. The results of our search are presented in Table 1. We use "Proof" to denote that our tool could prove at

Table 1. Synthesis results for Type II with keys $V, W \in \mathbb{G}_1$, message $M \in \mathbb{G}_2$, and signature $T, S \in \mathbb{G}_2$. The value r in the exponent of T is always chosen as a random element in $\mathbb{Z}_p$.

Search Space		Schemes		Results (for eq. cl.)		
Verification equation	First sig. elt.	total	eq. cl.	Noverif	Attack	Proof
$s = f(t, v, w, m)$	$T = H^r$	212	57	0	55	1
$s\, t = f(t, v, w, m)$	$T = H^r$	224	67	0	55	12
$s\,(t-w) = f(t, v, w, m)$	$T = H^{r+w}$	1344	774	651	103	14
$s\, w = f(t, v, w, m)$	$T = H^r$	224	126	0	120	3
		2004	1024	651	333	30

least 2-EUF-CMA security. Among the SPS schemes that are found, we identify equivalent schemes according to the following notion: we say two schemes Σ and Σ' are in the same equivalence class if Σ can be obtained from Σ' by applying invertible affine transformations to the verification keys, the messages, and the signature elements. This implies the existence of reductions from the security of Σ to the security of Σ' and vice-versa. As a simple example, consider a scheme that is obtained from another scheme by first multiplying the message M with G and then applying the original signing algorithm. Overall, except for 10 of the 1024 analyzed schemes, our tool either finds an attack, proves at least 2-EUF-CMA security, or proves that there is no verification equation. For the 10 schemes, the tool either returned unknown or timed out[4].

5.2 New SPS Schemes

Among the schemes that we found using our tool, we highlight two of them that are of particular interest, as well as a counterpart of the first one in the Type III setting.

A Strongly-Optimal Randomizable SPS. The first scheme is an SPS which is randomizable and matches the lower bound of Theorem 1, i.e., it can be verified using one offline and two online pairings. This scheme improves over the previously known randomizable schemes (in particular over the one recently proposed in [7]) as the latter requires three online pairings. This new scheme is presented in Fig. 2, and its security, stated as follows, is proved in the full version of this paper [13].

Theorem 3. *The signature scheme in Fig. 2 is EUF-CMA-secure in the generic bilinear group model.*

This scheme can be translated to Type III groups using the transformation in [17], which essentially consists in "duplicating" R, i.e., to give $R = G^r \in \mathbb{G}_1$

---

[4] We used a timeout of 30 seconds.

Setup(1^k): return $PP = (p, \mathbb{G}_1, \mathbb{G}_2, \mathbb{G}_T, e, \psi, G, H) \leftarrow \mathcal{G}(1^k)$.
KeyGen(PP): choose random $v, w \leftarrow \mathbb{Z}_p$ and return $VK = (V, W)$, $SK = (v, w)$
     where $V = G^v$ and $W = G^w$.
Sign(PP, SK, M): given $M \in \mathbb{G}_2$, choose a random $r \leftarrow \mathbb{Z}_p^*$ and return (R, S)
     where $R = H^r$ and $S = (M^v H^w)^{1/r}$.
Rerand$(PP, VK, M, (R, S))$: pick a random $\alpha \leftarrow \mathbb{Z}_p^*$ and compute a randomized
     signature (R', S') as $R' = R^\alpha$ and $S' = S^{1/\alpha}$.
Verify$(PP, VK, M, (R, S))$: accept if and only if $M, R, S \in \mathbb{G}_2$ and

$$e(\psi(R), S) = e(V, M) \cdot e(W, H).$$

Fig. 2. Our strongly-optimal re-randomizable SPS

and $T = H^r \in \mathbb{G}_2$, and adding a pairing-product equation to check that R, T have the same discrete logarithm, i.e., $e(R, H) = e(G, T)$. Such transformed scheme however requires one offline and four online pairings in the pairing-product equations. In what follows we propose a slightly different way to transform our scheme in the Type III setting which yields a solution requiring only three online pairings. The basic idea is that in the previous transformation T is not used in the first pairing-product equation, and its utility is to force the adversary to show that it knows the discrete log of R (or obtained (R, T) by applying a linear operation on a pair received by the challenger). We obtain the same functionality by letting the signer compute $T = H^{1/r}$. This allows us to test "equality of r between R and T" by checking $e(R, T) = e(G, H)$. The last pairing, however, involves only the generators and can thus be computed offline. A precise description of the resulting scheme is provided in Fig. 3, and the security result, stated below, is proved in the full version of this paper [13].

Theorem 4. *The signature scheme in Fig. 3 is EUF-CMA-secure in the generic bilinear group model.*

A Strongly-Optimal RMA-Secure SPS. Our second new SPS scheme, presented in Fig. 4, is secure against random-message attacks, and achieves the lower bound of only two pairings in the pairing-product equation (both necessarily online) for EUF-RMA-secure schemes, as stated in Theorem 2. In particular, it *beats* the lower bound of Theorem 1 that holds for EUF-CMA-secure schemes.

This scheme is also perfectly randomizable, with the simple randomization algorithm that sends a signature (R, S) on M to $(R \cdot H^t, S \cdot M^t)$ for some uniformly random t.

As an interesting note, we observe that the verification equation of this scheme is exactly the only possible one, according to our impossibility proof. Indeed, while our Lemma 5 holds for SPS schemes that are EUF-CMA-secure, the actual proof relies on EUF-RMA-security in all cases but one. For that particular case, in which we show a chosen-message attack, the verification equation is

---

Setup(1^k): return $PP = (p, \mathbb{G}_1, \mathbb{G}_2, \mathbb{G}_T, e, G, H) \leftarrow \mathcal{G}(1^k)$.

KeyGen(PP): choose random $v, w \leftarrow \mathbb{Z}_p$ and return $VK = (V, W)$, $SK = (v, w)$
    where $V = G^v$ and $W = G^w$.

Sign(PP, SK, M): given $M \in \mathbb{G}_2$, choose a random $r \leftarrow \mathbb{Z}_p^*$ and return $(R, T, S) \in$
    $\mathbb{G}_1 \times \mathbb{G}_2^2$ where $R = G^r$, $T = H^{1/r}$ and $S = (M^v H^w)^{1/r}$.

Rerand$(PP, VK, M, (R, T, S))$: pick a random $\alpha \leftarrow \mathbb{Z}_p^*$ and compute a randomized
    signature (R', T', S') as $R' = R^\alpha$, $T' = T^{1/\alpha}$ and $S' = S^{1/\alpha}$.

Verify$(PP, VK, M, (R, T, S))$: accept if and only if $R \in \mathbb{G}_1$, $M, T, S \in \mathbb{G}_2$ and

$$e(R, S) = e(V, M) \cdot e(W, H) \quad \text{and} \quad e(R, T) = e(G, H).$$

Fig. 3. A re-randomizable SPS in Type III groups

Setup(1^k): return $PP = (p, \mathbb{G}_1, \mathbb{G}_2, \mathbb{G}_T, e, \psi, G, H) \leftarrow \mathcal{G}(1^k)$.

KeyGen(PP): choose random $v, w \leftarrow \mathbb{Z}_p$ and return $VK = (V, W)$, $SK = (v, w)$
    where $V = G^v$ and $W = G^w$.

Sign(PP, SK, M): given $M \in \mathbb{G}_2$, choose a random $r \leftarrow \mathbb{Z}_p$ and return (R, S)
    where $R = H^r$ and $S = M^{r+v} H^{-w}$.

Verify$(PP, VK, M, (R, S))$: accept if and only if $M, R, S \in \mathbb{G}_2$ and

$$e(\psi(S) \cdot W, H) = e(R \cdot V, M).$$

Fig. 4. Our RMA-secure SPS with two pairings

---

of the form $s + w = (r + v)(f_1 m + f_4)$ for some constants f_1, f_4, up to invertible linear transformations on the verification key and signature elements.

The security of this scheme, stated below, is proved in the full version of this paper [13].

Theorem 5. *The signature scheme in Fig. 4 is EUF-RMA-secure in the generic bilinear group model.*

6 Conclusion

In this work, we considered a new measure for the efficiency of SPS, that is, the number of pairings required in the verification equation. With respect to this measure, we proved lower bounds and proposed new schemes matching these bounds in the Type II setting. In order to find schemes, we built a synthesis tool that automates the generation and security analysis of SPS. Currently, our methods only support security proofs with respect to a bounded number of signing queries. Developing new methods that support security proofs with respect to an unbounded number of queries for SPS is an interesting open problem that requires new techniques. Another direction left open by our work is to obtain similar results for the Type I and Type III setting. In contrast to the Type II setting, the Type I and Type III settings are more complex since they need more than one verification equation [4,8]. For synthesis, this causes a significant blowup of the search space, while for the minimality result, our proofs exploit that there is exactly one equation.

Acknowledgments. This work is supported in part by ONR grant N00014-12-1-0914, Madrid regional project S2009TIC-1465 PROMETIDOS, and Spanish projects TIN2009-14599 DESAFIOS 10 and TIN2012-39391-C04-01 Strongsoft. Additional support for Scedrov and Fagerholm is from the AFOSR MURI "Science of Cyber Security: Modeling, Composition, and Measurement" and from NSF Grant CNS-0830949. The research of Fiore and Schmidt has received funds from the European Commissions Seventh Framework Programme Marie Curie Cofund Action AMAROUT II (grant no. 291803).

References

1. Abe, M., Chase, M., David, B., Kohlweiss, M., Nishimaki, R., Ohkubo, M.: Constant-size structure-preserving signatures: generic constructions and simple assumptions. In: Wang, X., Sako, K. (eds.) ASIACRYPT 2012. LNCS, vol. 7658, pp. 4–24. Springer, Heidelberg (2012)
2. Abe, M., David, B., Kohlweiss, M., Nishimaki, R., Ohkubo, M.: Tagged one-time signatures: tight security and optimal tag size. In: Kurosawa, K., Hanaoka, G. (eds.) PKC 2013. LNCS, vol. 7778, pp. 312–331. Springer, Heidelberg (2013)
3. Abe, M., Fuchsbauer, G., Groth, J., Haralambiev, K., Ohkubo, M.: Structure-preserving signatures and commitments to group elements. In: Rabin, T. (ed.) CRYPTO 2010. LNCS, vol. 6223, pp. 209–236. Springer, Heidelberg (2010)
4. Abe, M., Groth, J., Haralambiev, K., Ohkubo, M.: Optimal structure-preserving signatures in asymmetric bilinear groups. In: Rogaway, P. (ed.) CRYPTO 2011. LNCS, vol. 6841, pp. 649–666. Springer, Heidelberg (2011)
5. Abe, M., Groth, J., Ohkubo, M.: Separating short structure-preserving signatures from non-interactive assumptions. In: Lee, D.H., Wang, X. (eds.) ASIACRYPT 2011. LNCS, vol. 7073, pp. 628–646. Springer, Heidelberg (2011)
6. Abe, M., Groth, J., Ohkubo, M., Tango, T.: Converting cryptographic schemes from symmetric to asymmetric bilinear groups. In: Garay, J.A., Gennaro, R. (eds.) CRYPTO 2014, Part I. LNCS, vol. 8616, pp. 241–260. Springer, Heidelberg (2014)
7. Abe, M., Groth, J., Ohkubo, M., Tibouchi, M.: Structure-preserving signatures from type II pairings. In: Garay, J.A., Gennaro, R. (eds.) CRYPTO 2014, Part I. LNCS, vol. 8616, pp. 390–407. Springer, Heidelberg (2014)
8. Abe, M., Groth, J., Ohkubo, M., Tibouchi, M.: Unified, minimal and selectively randomizable structure-preserving signatures. In: Lindell, Y. (ed.) TCC 2014. LNCS, vol. 8349, pp. 688–712. Springer, Heidelberg (2014)
9. Akinyele, J.A., Green, M., Hohenberger, S.: Using SMT solvers to automate design tasks for encryption and signature schemes. In: Sadeghi, A.-R., Gligor, V.D., Yung, M. (eds.) ACM CCS 2013: 20th Conference on Computer and Communications Security, pp. 399–410. ACM Press, November 2013
10. Attrapadung, N., Libert, B., Peters, T.: Efficient completely context-hiding quotable and linearly homomorphic signatures. In: Kurosawa, K., Hanaoka, G. (eds.) PKC 2013. LNCS, vol. 7778, pp. 386–404. Springer, Heidelberg (2013)

11. Barthe, G., Crespo, J.M., Grégoire, B., Kunz, C., Lakhnech, Y., Schmidt, B., Zanella Béguelin, S.: Fully automated analysis of padding-based encryption in the computational model. In: Sadeghi, A.-R., Gligor, V.D., Yung, M. (eds.) ACM CCS 2013: 20th Conference on Computer and Communications Security, pp. 1247–1260. ACM Press, November 2013
12. Barthe, G., Fagerholm, E., Fiore, D., Mitchell, J., Scedrov, A., Schmidt, B.: Automated analysis of cryptographic assumptions in generic group models. In: Garay, J.A., Gennaro, R. (eds.) CRYPTO 2014, Part I. LNCS, vol. 8616, pp. 95–112. Springer, Heidelberg (2014)
13. Barthe, G., Fagerholm, E., Fiore, D., Scedrov, A., Schmidt, B., Tibouchi, M.: Strongly-optimal structure preserving signatures from type II pairings: synthesis and lower bounds. Cryptology ePrint Archive (2015). Full version of this paper. http://eprint.iacr.org/
14. Camenisch, J., Dubovitskaya, M., Enderlein, R.R., Neven, G.: Oblivious transfer with hidden access control from attribute-based encryption. In: Visconti, I., De Prisco, R. (eds.) SCN 2012. LNCS, vol. 7485, pp. 559–579. Springer, Heidelberg (2012)
15. Camenisch, J., Haralambiev, K., Kohlweiss, M., Lapon, J., Naessens, V.: Structure preserving CCA secure encryption and applications. In: Lee, D.H., Wang, X. (eds.) ASIACRYPT 2011. LNCS, vol. 7073, pp. 89–106. Springer, Heidelberg (2011)
16. Cathalo, J., Libert, B., Yung, M.: Group encryption: non-interactive realization in the standard model. In: Matsui, M. (ed.) ASIACRYPT 2009. LNCS, vol. 5912, pp. 179–196. Springer, Heidelberg (2009)
17. Chatterjee, S., Menezes, A.: On cryptographic protocols employing asymmetric pairings - the role of Ψ revisited. Discrete Applied Mathematics **159**(13), 1311–1322 (2011)
18. Chatterjee, S., Menezes, A.: Type 2 structure-preserving signature schemes revisited. Cryptology ePrint Archive, Report 2014/635 (2014). http://eprint.iacr.org/2014/635
19. de Ruiter, J.: Automated algebraic analysis of structure-preserving signature schemes. Cryptology ePrint Archive, Report 2014/590 (2014). http://eprint.iacr.org/2014/590
20. Fuchsbauer, G., Vergnaud, D.: Fair blind signatures without random oracles. In: Bernstein, D.J., Lange, T. (eds.) AFRICACRYPT 2010. LNCS, vol. 6055, pp. 16–33. Springer, Heidelberg (2010)
21. Galbraith, S.D., Paterson, K.G., Smart, N.P.: Pairings for cryptographers. Discrete Appl. Math. **156**(16), 3113–3121 (2008)
22. Green, M., Hohenberger, S.: Universally composable adaptive oblivious transfer. In: Pieprzyk, J. (ed.) ASIACRYPT 2008. LNCS, vol. 5350, pp. 179–197. Springer, Heidelberg (2008)
23. Groth, J.: Simulation-sound NIZK proofs for a practical language and constant size group signatures. In: Lai, X., Chen, K. (eds.) ASIACRYPT 2006. LNCS, vol. 4284, pp. 444–459. Springer, Heidelberg (2006)
24. Groth, J., Sahai, A.: Efficient non-interactive proof systems for bilinear groups. In: Smart, N.P. (ed.) EUROCRYPT 2008. LNCS, vol. 4965, pp. 415–432. Springer, Heidelberg (2008)
25. Hofheinz, D., Jager, T.: Tightly secure signatures and public-key encryption. In: Safavi-Naini, R., Canetti, R. (eds.) CRYPTO 2012. LNCS, vol. 7417, pp. 590–607. Springer, Heidelberg (2012)

26. Libert, B., Peters, T., Joye, M., Yung, M.: Linearly homomorphic structure-preserving signatures and their applications. In: Canetti, R., Garay, J.A. (eds.) CRYPTO 2013, Part II. LNCS, vol. 8043, pp. 289–307. Springer, Heidelberg (2013)
27. Libert, B., Peters, T., Yung, M.: Group signatures with almost-for-free revocation. In: Safavi-Naini, R., Canetti, R. (eds.) CRYPTO 2012. LNCS, vol. 7417, pp. 571–589. Springer, Heidelberg (2012)
28. Malozemoff, A.J., Katz, J., Green, M.D.: Automated analysis and synthesis of block-cipher modes of operation. In: CSF 2014 (2014)

A Profitable Sub-prime Loan: Obtaining the Advantages of Composite Order in Prime-Order Bilinear Groups

Allison Lewko[1](✉) and Sarah Meiklejohn[2]

[1] Columbia University, New York, USA
alewko@cs.columbia.edu
[2] University College London, London, UK
s.meiklejohn@ucl.ac.uk

Abstract. Composite-order bilinear groups provide many structural features that are useful for both constructing cryptographic primitives and enabling security reductions. Despite these convenient features, however, composite-order bilinear groups are less desirable than prime-order bilinear groups for reasons of both efficiency and security. A recent line of work has therefore focused on translating these structural features from the composite-order to the prime-order setting; much of this work focused on two such features, projecting and canceling, in isolation, but a result due to Seo and Cheon showed that both features can be obtained simultaneously in the prime-order setting.

In this paper, we reinterpret the construction of Seo and Cheon in the context of dual pairing vector spaces (which provide canceling as well as useful parameter hiding features) to obtain a unified framework that simulates all of these composite-order features in the prime-order setting. We demonstrate the strength of this framework by providing two applications: one that adds dual pairing vector spaces to the existing projection in the Boneh-Goh-Nissim encryption scheme to obtain leakage resilience, and another that adds the concept of projecting to the existing dual pairing vector spaces in an IND-CPA-secure IBE scheme to "boost" its security to IND-CCA1. Our leakage-resilient BGN application is of independent interest, and it is not clear how to achieve it from pure composite-order techniques without mixing in additional vector space tools. Both applications rely solely on the Symmetric External Diffie Hellman assumption (SXDH).

1 Introduction

Since their introduction in 2005 by Boneh, Goh, and Nissim [9], composite-order bilinear groups have been used to construct a diverse set of advanced cryptographic primitives, including (hierarchical) identity-based encryption [30, 32], group signatures [12,13], functional encryption [26,29], and attribute-based encryption [31]. The main assumptions used to prove the security of such schemes are variants of the *subgroup decision* assumption, which (in the simplest case)

© International Association for Cryptologic Research 2015
J. Katz (Ed.): PKC 2015, LNCS 9020, pp. 377–398, 2015.
DOI: 10.1007/978-3-662-46447-2_17

states that, for a bilinear group G of order $N = pq$, without an element of order q it should be hard to distinguish a random element of G from a random element of order p. Such assumptions crucially rely on the hardness of factoring N.

Beyond this basic assumption and its close variants, many of these schemes have exploited additional structural properties that are inherent in composite-order bilinear groups. Two such properties, *projecting* and *canceling*, were formally identified by Freeman [18]; projecting requires (roughly) that there exists a trapdoor projection map from G into its p-order subgroup (and a related map in the target group G_T), and canceling requires that elements in the p-order and q-order subgroups cancel each other out (i.e., yield the identity when paired). Additionally, Lewko [27] identified another property, *parameter hiding*, that requires (again, roughly) that elements in the p-order subgroup reveal nothing about seemingly correlated elements in the q-order subgroup.

While therefore quite attractive and rich from a structural standpoint, the use of composite-order bilinear groups comes with a number of drawbacks, both in terms of efficiency and security. Until a recent construction of Boneh, Rubin, and Silverberg [11], all known composite-order bilinear groups were on supersingular, or Type-1 [19], curves. Even in the prime-order setting, supersingular curves are already less efficient than their ordinary counterparts: speed records for the former [4,42] are approximately six times slower than speed records for the latter [5]. In the composite-order setting, it is furthermore necessary to increase the size of the modulus by at least a factor of 10 (from 160 to at least 1024 bits) in order to make the assumption that N is hard to factor plausible. Operations performed in composite-order bilinear groups are therefore significantly slower; for example, Guillevic [22] recently observed that computing a pairing was 254 times slower. (This slowdown also extends to the non-supersingular construction of Boneh et al., and indeed to any composite-order bilinear group.) Furthermore, from a security standpoint, a number of recent results [1,2,21,23,25] demonstrate that it is possible to efficiently compute discrete logarithms in common types of supersingular curves, so that one must be significantly more careful when working over supersingular curves than when working over their non-supersingular counterparts.

One natural question to ask is: to what extent is it possible to obtain the structural advantages of composite-order bilinear groups without the disadvantages? Although the structural properties described above might seem specific to composite-order groups, both Freeman and Lewko are in fact able to express them rather abstractly and then describe how to construct prime-order bilinear groups in which each of these individual properties are met; they also show how to translate the subgroup decision assumption into a generalized version, that in prime-order groups is implied by either Decision Linear [8] or Symmetric External Diffie Hellman (SXDH) [6]. Lewko's approach is based on the framework of dual pairing vector spaces, as developed by Okamoto and Takashima [38,39]. This framework has been particularly useful for enabling translations of cryptosystems employing the dual system encryption methodology in their security reductions.

In contrast, Meiklejohn, Shacham, and Freeman [36] showed that it was impossible to achieve projecting and canceling simultaneously under a "natural" usage of Decision Linear; as a motivation, they presented a blind signature scheme that seemingly relied upon both projecting and canceling for its proof of security. Recently, Seo and Cheon [44] showed that it was actually possible to achieve both projecting and canceling simultaneously in prime-order groups, and Seo [43] explored both possibility and impossibility results for projecting. To derive hardness of subgroup decision in their setting, however, Seo and Cheon rely on a non-standard assumption and show that this implies the hardness of subgroup decision only in a very limited case. They also provide a prime-order version of the Meiklejohn et al. blind signature that is somewhat divorced from their setting: rather than prove its security directly using projecting and canceling, they instead alter the blind signature, introduce a new property called *translating*, and then show that the modified blind signature is secure not in the projecting and canceling setting, but rather in a separate projecting and translating setting.

Subsequently, Herold et al. [24] presented a new translation framework called "polynomial spaces" that achieves projecting in a natural and elegant way, and can also be augmented to simultaneously achieve canceling. Like the prior result of Seo and Cheon, they employ a non-standard hardness assumption to obtain subgroup decision hardness when projecting and canceling are both supported. Interestingly, their approach does not seem to provide a way of achieving just canceling with subgroup decision problems relying on standard assumptions like SXDH or DLIN, as is achieved by dual pairing vector spaces. Integrating the benefits of dual pairing vector spaces into something like the polynomial spaces approach remains a worthwhile goal for future work. The framework in [24] also extends to the setting of multilinear groups, as do approaches based on eigenspaces, as demonstrated for example in [20].

Our Contributions. In this paper, we present in Section 3 an abstract presentation of the projecting and canceling pairing due to Seo and Cheon [44]. Our presentation is based on dual pairing vector spaces (DPVS) [38,39], and it can be parameterized to yield projection properties of varying strength. This perspective yields several advantages. First, all the power of DPVS is embedded inside this construction and can thus be exploited as in prior works. Second, we observe that many instances of subgroup decision problems in this framework are implied by the relatively simple SXDH assumption.

The advantages of our perspective are most clear for our BGN application, which we present in Section 4. If one starts with the goal of making the composite-order BGN scheme leakage resilient (i.e., providing provable security even when some bits of the secret key may have been leaked), the first obstacle one faces is the uniqueness of secret keys. Since the secret key is a factorization of the group order, there is only one secret key for each public key, making the common kind of hash proof argument for leakage resilience (as codified by Naor and Segev [37], for example) inapplicable. The DPVS techniques baked into our projecting and canceling prime-order construction remove this barrier quite naturally by allowing secret keys to be vectors that still serve as projection maps but can now be sampled from subspaces containing exponentially many potential keys. This demonstrates the benefits of adding canceling and parameter hiding to applications that are designed around projection.

As an additional application, in Section 5, we present an IND-CCA1-secure identity-based encryption (IBE) scheme that uses canceling, parameter hiding, and weak projecting properties in its proof of security. Although efficient constructions of IND-CCA2-secure IBE schemes have been previously obtained by combining IND-CPA-secure HIBE schemes with signatures [15], we nevertheless view our IBE construction as a demonstration of the applicability of our unified framework. Furthermore, our new construction does not aim to amplify security by adding new primitives; instead, it explores the existing security of the IND-CPA-secure IBE due to Boneh and Boyen [7] (which cannot be IND-CCA2 secure, as it has re-randomizable ciphertexts), and observes that, by modifying the scheme in a rather organic way and exploiting the (weak) projecting and canceling properties of the setting, we can prove IND-CCA1 security directly. Hence, we view this as an exploration of the security properties that can be proved solely from the minimalistic spirit of the Boneh-Boyen scheme.

Our two applications serve as a proof of concept for the usefulness of obtaining projecting and canceling simultaneously in the prime-order setting, and a demonstration of how to leverage such properties while relying only on relatively simple assumptions like SXDH. We believe that the usefulness of our framework extends beyond these specific examples, and we intend our work to facilitate future applications of these combined properties.

Our Techniques. To obtain a more user-friendly interpretation of the projecting and canceling pairing construction over prime-order groups, we begin by observing that it is essentially a concatenation of DPVS. Dual pairing vector spaces were first used in prime-order bilinear groups by Okamoto and Takashima [38,39] and have since been employed in many works, in particular to instantiate dual system technique [45] in the prime-order setting [27,29,40]. These previous uses of DPVS typically relied on the canceling property, variants of subgroup decision problems, and certain parameter hiding properties that are present by design in DPVS. One particularly nice feature of DPVS constructions is that a large family of useful subgroup decision variants can be proven to follow from standard assumptions like SXDH for asymmetric groups and DLIN for symmetric groups; viewing the construction of a projecting and canceling pairing as a natural extension of DPVS therefore has the twin benefits that it provides a clear guide on how to derive certain subgroup decision variants from standard assumptions, and that it comes with all the built-in tools that DPVS offers.

In particular, DPVS includes a suite of vector-space-based tools for proving leakage resilience, similar to ones used in previous works [14,16,17,34,35,37]. This enables us to combine the projecting-supported limited homomorphic functionality of the BGN encryption scheme with provable leakage resilience. DPVS also supports a toolkit developed for dual system proofs (e.g., [29,40,41]), which is what enables us to boost our IBE to full IND-CCA1 security with just the addition of projection.

2 Definitions and Notation

In this section, we define bilinear groups and the three functional properties we would like them to satisfy: projecting, canceling, and parameter hiding. For the first two, we use the definitions of Freeman [18] (albeit in a somewhat modified form); for parameter hiding, on the other hand, we come up with a new formal framework. In addition to these functional properties, we consider the notion of subgroup decision in bilinear groups, in which a random element of a subgroup should be indistinguishable from a random element of the full group. The variant we define, called generalized correlated subgroup decision, is very general: in addition to seeing random elements of subgroups, we allow an attacker to see elements *correlated* across subgroups (e.g., elements of different subgroups with correlated randomness), and require that it is still difficult for him to distinguish between correlated elements of different subgroups. We then see in Section 3 that many specific instances of this general notion are implied by more standard notions of subgroup decision in prime-order groups.

2.1 Bilinear Groups

In what follows, we refer to a *bilinear group* as a tuple $\mathcal{G} = (N, G, H, G_T, e, \mu)$, where N is either prime or composite, $|G| = |H| = kN$ and $|G_T| = \ell N$ for some $k, \ell \in \mathbb{N}$, and $e : G \times H \to G_T$ is a bilinear map; i.e., e is an efficient map that satisfies both *bilinearity* ($e(x^a, y^b) = e(x, y)^{ab}$ for all $x \in G$, $y \in H$, $a, b \in \mathbb{Z}/N\mathbb{Z}$) and *non-degeneracy* (if $e(x, y) = 1$ for all $x \in G$ then $y = 1$ and if $e(x, y) = 1$ for all $y \in H$ then $x = 1$). In some bilinear groups, we may additionally include generators g and h of G and H respectively (if G and H are cyclic), information about meaningful subgroups of G and H, or some auxiliary information μ that allows for efficient membership testing in G and H (and possibly more). In what follows, we refer to the algorithm that is used to generate such a $\mathcal{G}$ as BilinearGen. Beyond the security parameter, BilinearGen takes in an additional parameter n that specifies the number of desired subgroups; i.e., for $(N, G, H, G_T, e, \mu) \xleftarrow{\$} \mathsf{BilinearGen}(1^k, n)$, we have $G = \oplus_{i=1}^n G_i$ and $H = \oplus_{i=1}^n H_i$ (where typically G_i and H_i are cyclic).

In terms of functional properties of bilinear groups, we first define both *projecting* and *canceling*; our definitions are modified versions of the ones originally given by Freeman [18]. We give three flavors of projecting. The first, *weak projecting*, considers projecting into a single subgroup of the source group, without requiring a corresponding map in the target group. The second, which we call simply *projecting*, most closely matches the definition given by Freeman, and considers projecting into a single subgroup in both the source and target groups. Lastly, we define *full* projecting, which considers projecting into every subgroup individually. As we will see in Section 3, we can satisfy all of these flavors by tweaking appropriate parameters in our prime-order construction.

Definition 2.1 (Weak Projecting). *A bilinear group $\mathcal{G} = (N, G, H, G_T, e, \mu)$ is* weakly projecting *if there exist decompositions $G = G_1 \oplus G_2$ and $H = H_1 \oplus H_2$,* and projection maps π_G and π_H such that $\pi_G(x_1) = x_1$ for all $x_1 \in G_1$ and $\pi_G(x_2) = 1$ for all $x_2 \in G_2$, and similarly $\pi_H(y_1) = y_1$ for all $y_1 \in H_1$ and $\pi_H(y_2) = 1$ for all $y_2 \in H_2$.

Definition 2.2 (Projecting). *A bilinear group* $\mathcal{G} = (N, G, H, G_T, e, \mu)$ *is projecting if there exist subgroups* $G' \subset G$, $H' \subset H$, *and* $G'_T \subset G_T$ *such that there exist non-trivial maps* $\pi_G : G \to G'$, $\pi_H : H \to H'$, *and* $\pi_T : G_T \to G'_T$ *such that* $\pi_T(e(x, y)) = e(\pi_G(x), \pi_H(y))$ *for all* $x \in G$, $y \in H$.

Definition 2.3 (Full projecting). *A bilinear group* $\mathcal{G} = (N, G, H, G_T, e, \mu)$ *is fully projecting if there exists some* $n \in \mathbb{N}$ *and decompositions* $G = \oplus_{i=1}^n G_i$, $H = \oplus_{i=1}^n H_i$, *and* $G_T = \oplus_{i=1}^n G_{T,i}$, *and non-trivial maps* $\pi_{Gi} : G \to G_i$, $\pi_{Hi} : H \to H_i$, *and* $\pi_{Ti} : G_T \to G_{T,i}$ *for all* i *such that* $\pi_{Ti}(e(x, y)) = e(\pi_{Gi}(x), \pi_{Hi}(y))$ *for all* $x \in G$, $y \in H$.

Definition 2.4 (Canceling). *A bilinear group* $\mathcal{G} = (N, G, H, G_T, e, \mu)$ *is canceling if there exists some* $n \in \mathbb{N}$ *and decompositions* $G = \oplus_{i=1}^n G_i$ *and* $H = \oplus_{i=1}^n H_i$ *such that* $e(x_i, y_j) = 1$ *for all* $x_i \in G_i$, $y_j \in H_j$, $i \neq j$.

2.2 Parameter Hiding

Beyond projecting and canceling, we aim to define *parameter hiding*. As mentioned in the introduction, this property roughly says that elements in one subgroup should not reveal anything about related elements in other subgroups, and was previously used, without a formal definition, by Lewko [27]. In essence, parameter hiding in composite-order groups is a simple consequence of the Chinese Remainder Theorem, which tells us that if we sample a random value modulo $N = pq$, its reductions modulo p and q are uncorrelated. In the prime-order setting, a form of parameter hiding can be instantiated from dual pairing vector spaces, leveraging the fact that if one commits to only certain parts of dual orthonormal bases over $\mathbb{F}_p^n$, there is remaining ambiguity in the hidden basis vectors.

The main difficulty in providing a formal definition for parameter hiding is that it is not as self-contained a feature as projecting and canceling: elements within subgroups may be related to elements in other subgroups in a myriad of ways, and their relation to one another may depend both on the form of the element (which can involve any function on the exponents) and on the subgroups. We therefore do not try to consider all types of correlations, but instead focus on one simple type, defined as follows:

Definition 2.5. *For a bilinear group* $\mathcal{G} = (N, G = \oplus_{i=1}^n G_i, H = \oplus_{i=1}^n H_i, G_T, e, \{g_i\}_{i=1}^n, \{h_i\}_{i=1}^n)$, *an element* $x \in \mathbb{Z}/N\mathbb{Z}$, *and indices* $1 \leq i_1, i_2 \leq n$, *an x-correlated sample from the subgroup* $G_{i_1} \oplus G_{i_2}$ *is an element of the form* $g_{i_1}^\alpha \cdot g_{i_2}^{\alpha x}$ *for* $\alpha \xleftarrow{\$} \mathbb{Z}/N\mathbb{Z}$.

We also consider correlated samples in H, but for convenience we define a *y*-correlated sample from the subgroup $H_{i_1} \oplus H_{i_2}$ to be an element of the form

$h_{i_1}^{\beta y} \cdot h_{i_2}^{\beta}$ for $\beta \xleftarrow{\$} \mathbb{Z}/N\mathbb{Z}$. Although we choose this type of correlation mainly for ease of exposition (and because we encounter it in Section 5), our discussion below could be adjusted to accommodate more general types of correlation, which would remain compatible with our prime-order construction in Section 3.

Intuitively then, parameter hiding says that, under certain restrictions about which subgroup elements one is allowed access to, the distributions over x-correlated samples and random samples should in fact be the same, even when x is known. (We need some restrictions because there may be testable relationships between the images of various generators in the target group.) To consider the distributions we can use — i.e., what additional information we might give out besides the samples — we consider distributions $\mathcal{D}$ parameterized by sets $S_G^{\mathsf{ph}} = \{S_{G,\mathrm{gen}}^{\mathsf{ph}}, S_{G,\mathrm{sam}}^{\mathsf{ph}}, S_{G,\mathrm{cor}}^{\mathsf{ph}}\}$, $S_H^{\mathsf{ph}} = \{S_{H,\mathrm{gen}}^{\mathsf{ph}}, S_{H,\mathrm{sam}}^{\mathsf{ph}}, S_{H,\mathrm{cor}}^{\mathsf{ph}}\}$, and C; intuitively, S_G^{ph} and S_H^{ph} tell us which elements to include in the distribution, and C tells us which correlated samples to change to random. Formally, these sets are defined as follows:

- $S_{G,\mathrm{gen}}^{\mathsf{ph}}$ indicates which subgroup generators to include: For all $s_i \in S_{G,\mathrm{gen}}^{\mathsf{ph}}$, include g_{s_i} in $\mathcal{D}$.
- $S_{G,\mathrm{sam}}^{\mathsf{ph}}$ is a multiset that indicates which random samples to include: For all $t_i = (t_{1,i}, \ldots, t_{m_i,i}) \in S_{G,\mathrm{sam}}^{\mathsf{ph}}$, include a random sample from $G_{t_{1,i}} \oplus \ldots \oplus G_{t_{m_i,i}}$ in $\mathcal{D}$.
- $S_{G,\mathrm{cor}}^{\mathsf{ph}}$ is a set that indicates which correlated samples to include: For all $c_i = (x_i, c_{1,i}, c_{2,i}) \in S_{G,\mathrm{cor}}^{\mathsf{ph}}$, include $g_{c_{1,i}}^a \cdot g_{c_{2,i}}^{ax_i}$ in $\mathcal{D}$, where $a \xleftarrow{\$} \mathbb{Z}/N\mathbb{Z}$.
- S_H^{ph} is defined analogously to S_G^{ph}.
- C indicates which correlated samples to change: For all $c_i = (b_i, c_i') \in C$, if $b_i = 0$ then $c_i' \in S_{G,\mathrm{cor}}^{\mathsf{ph}}$ and if $b_i = 1$ then $c_i' \in S_{H,\mathrm{cor}}^{\mathsf{ph}}$; i.e., we require that $C \subseteq \{0 \times S_{G,\mathrm{cor}}^{\mathsf{ph}}\} \cup \{1 \times S_{H,\mathrm{cor}}^{\mathsf{ph}}\}$.

Given all these sets, we now require that they are *well-behaved* in the following two ways: (1) for any changed x-correlated sample, do not reveal the corresponding subgroup generators on either side of the pairing, and (2) do not change correlated samples for the same value x in the same subgroups on opposite sides of the pairing. Formally, we express these requirements as

- Don't include generators for switched samples: For all $(b_i, (x_i, c_{1,i}, c_{2,i})) \in C$, $s_j \in S_{G,\mathrm{gen}}^{\mathsf{ph}}$, and $s_\ell \in S_{H,\mathrm{gen}}^{\mathsf{ph}}$, $s_j \neq c_{1,i}, c_{2,i}$ and $s_\ell \neq c_{1,i}, c_{2,i}$.
- Don't switch x-correlated samples in overlapping subgroups of G and H: For all $(0, (x_i, c_{1,i}, c_{2,i})), (1, (x_j, c_{1,j}, c_{2,j})) \in C$, either $x_i \neq x_j$ or $c_{1,i} \neq c_{1,j}, c_{2,j}$ and $c_{2,i} \neq c_{1,j}, c_{2,j}$.

To see why these restrictions can be necessary, consider trying to establish that an x-correlated sample in $G_1 \oplus G_2$ is identical to a random sample in $G_1 \oplus G_2$, and suppose we are given h_1 and h_2. If we are given $g_1^\alpha g_2^{\alpha x}$ (for some random, unknown α), then — assuming we are using a canceling pairing — we can compute $e(g_1, h_1)^\alpha$ and $e(g_2, h_2)^{\alpha x}$. When working with specific instantiations, there may be a known relationship between $e(g_1, h_1)$ and $e(g_2, h_2)$. (In fact, for our IBE construction, $e(g_1, h_1) = e(g_2, h_2)^{-1}$.) In this case, if x is known then we can test for an x-correlation in the target group, and hence distinguish an x-correlated sample from a random one. Similarly, if we have x-correlated samples $g_1^\alpha g_2^{\alpha x}$ and $h_1^{\beta x} h_2^\beta$, then pairing these yields the identity, which distinguishes them from random.

Definition 2.6 (Parameter Hiding). *We say that a group $\mathcal{G} = (N, G, H, G_T, e, \mu)$ satisfies parameter hiding with respect to a well-behaved distribution $\mathcal{D} = (S_G^{ph}, S_H^{ph}, C)$ if $\mathcal{D}$ is identical to the distribution in which the correlated samples indicated by C are replaced with random samples.*

Example 1. As an example, consider the distribution $\mathcal{D}$ defined by $S_G^{ph} = \{\{1, 2\}, \emptyset, \{(x, 1, 2), (x, 3, 4)\}\}$, $S_H^{ph} = \{\{1, 2, 5, 6\}, \{(3, 4), (3, 4)\}, \{(y, 1, 2), (y, 3, 4)\}\}$, and $C = \{(0, (x, 3, 4)), (1, (y, 3, 4)\}$ for any $x, y \in \mathbb{Z}/N\mathbb{Z}$ such that $x \neq y$; we can easily check that these sets are well-behaved in the sense defined above. Then parameter hiding holds for $\mathcal{G} = (N, G, H, G_T, e, \mu)$ if for $a, b, c, d, s, t, u, v, w, z \overset{\$}{\leftarrow} \mathbb{Z}/N\mathbb{Z}$,

$$(N, G, H, G_T, e, \mu, g_1, g_2, h_1, h_2, h_5, h_6, h_3^a h_4^b, h_3^c h_4^d, h_1^{ty} h_2^t, h_3^{zy} h_4^z, g_1^s g_2^{sx}, g_3^w g_4^{wx})$$

is *identical* to

$$(N, G, H, G_T, e, \mu, g_1, g_2, h_1, h_2, h_5, h_6, h_3^a h_4^b, h_3^c h_4^d, h_1^{ty} h_2^t, h_3^v h_4^z, g_1^s g_2^{sx}, g_3^w g_4^u).$$

In our uses of parameter hiding in Section 5, we restrict ourselves to this one example. Again, this is due to the difficulty of providing a fully general definition of parameter hiding, as certain types of correlated samples require more entropy than others. We nevertheless do not find it to be overly limiting to consider this one example, as it keeps our constructions in Section 5 simple and tailored to the requirements that we need. We also use a variant of parameter hiding in the proof for our leakage-resilient BGN variant presented in Section 4. Here, the flexibility in the hidden parameters is leveraged to allow the simulator to a leak on a secret key before fully committing to a complete basis (i.e., before determining how to form an appropriate ciphertext).

2.3   Generalized Correlated Subgroup Decision

Beyond functional properties of bilinear groups, we must also consider the types of security guarantees we can provide. The assumption we define, generalized correlated subgroup decision, considers indistinguishability between subgroups in a very general way: given certain subgroup generators and "correlated" elements across subgroups (i.e., elements in different subgroups that use the same randomness), it should still be hard to distinguish between elements of other subgroups. Formally, we consider sets $S_G^{sgh} = \{S_{G,\text{gen}}^{sgh}, S_{G,\text{sam}}^{sgh}\}$, $S_H^{sgh} = \{S_{H,\text{gen}}^{sgh}, S_{H,\text{sam}}^{sgh}\}$, $T_1 = \{(\ell_1, \lambda_1), \ldots, (\ell_m, \lambda_m)\}$, and $T_2 = \{(\ell'_1, \lambda'_1), \ldots, (\ell'_{m+1}, \lambda'_{m+1})\}$, and an indicator bit b. (We assume without loss of generality that T_2 is the larger set.) Intuitively, S_G^{sgh} and S_H^{sgh} tell us which group elements an adversary is given, and (T_1, T_2, b) tell us what the challenge terms should look like. We have the following requirements:

- $S_{G,\mathrm{gen}}^{\mathsf{sgh}}$ indicates which subgroup generators to include: Give out g_{s_i} for all $s_i \in S_{G,\mathrm{gen}}^{\mathsf{sgh}}$.
- $S_{G,\mathrm{sam}}^{\mathsf{sgh}}$ indicates which samples to include: For each

$$t_i = ((\ell_{1,i}, \lambda_{1,i}), \ldots, (\ell_{m_i,i}, \lambda_{m_i,i})) \in S_{G,\mathrm{sam}}^{\mathsf{sgh}}$$

, give out $g_{\ell_{1,i}}^{a_1} \cdot \ldots \cdot g_{\ell_{m_i,i}}^{a_{m_i}}$ and $g_{\lambda_{1,i}}^{a_1} \cdot \ldots \cdot g_{\lambda_{m_i,i}}^{a_{m_i}}$ for $a_1, \ldots, a_{m_i} \xleftarrow{\$} \mathbb{Z}/N\mathbb{Z}$. These elements are *correlated*, in that the same randomness is used for both.
- The bit b indicates which group the challenge element comes from: $b = 0$ indicates G, and $b = 1$ indicates H.
- The sets T_1 and T_2 must differ in exactly one pair; i.e., there must exist a unique pair P such that $P \notin T_1$ but $P \in T_2$. For this pair $P = (\ell, \lambda)$, we cannot give out the subgroup generators on either side of the pairing, so we require $s_i \neq \ell$ and $s_i \neq \lambda$ for any $s_i \in S_{G,\mathrm{gen}}^{\mathsf{sgh}}$ or $s_i \in S_{H,\mathrm{gen}}^{\mathsf{sgh}}$.

If $P \in t_i$ for some $t_i \in S_{G,\mathrm{sam}}^{\mathsf{sgh}} \cup S_{H,\mathrm{sam}}^{\mathsf{sgh}}$, then $T_1 \cap t_i \neq \emptyset$; i.e., P can appear only in random samples that also contain another component in the challenge term. Then, assuming $b = 0$ (and replacing g with h if $b = 1$), our challenge elements are of the form $T := (g_{\ell_1}^{a_1} \cdot \ldots \cdot g_{\ell_m}^{a_m}, g_{\lambda_1}^{a_1} \cdot \ldots \cdot g_{\lambda_m}^{a_m})$ and

$$T' := (g_{\ell_{1'}}^{a_1} \cdot \ldots \cdot g_{\ell_{m+1}'}^{a_{m+1}}, g_{\lambda_1'}^{a_1} \cdot \ldots \cdot g_{\lambda_{m+1}'}^{a_{m+1}}) \text{ for } a_1, \ldots a_{m+1} \xleftarrow{\$} \mathbb{Z}/N\mathbb{Z}.$$

Assumption 2.1 (Generalized Correlated Subgroup Decision). *For all tuples* $(S_G^{\mathsf{sgh}}, S_H^{\mathsf{sgh}}, T_1, T_2, b)$ *satisfying the requirements specified above and for any* $n \in \mathbb{N}$, *for any PPT adversary* $\mathcal{A}$ *given* $\mathcal{G} \xleftarrow{\$} \mathsf{BilinearGen}(1^k, n)$ *and the elements specified by* S_G^{sgh} *and* S_H^{sgh}, *it is hard to distinguish between values* T *defined by* (b, T_1) *and values* T' *defined by* (b, T_2).

As an example, consider the case in which $n = 6$ and $S_G^{\mathsf{sgh}} = \{\{1, 2\}, \{((1, 2), (3, 4))\}\}$, $S_H^{\mathsf{sgh}} = \{\{1, 2, 5, 6\}, \{((1, 2), (3, 4)), ((3, 4), (5, 6))\}\}$, $T_1 = \{(1, 2), (5, 6)\}$, $T_2 = \{(1, 2), (3, 4), (5, 6)\}$, and $b = 0$. In this case, the concrete assumption is: Given $\mathcal{G}$ and generators $g_1, g_2, h_1, h_2, h_5, h_6$, correlated samples from $G_1 \oplus G_3$ and $G_2 \oplus G_4$, correlated samples from $H_1 \oplus H_3$ and $H_2 \oplus H_4$, and correlated samples from $H_3 \oplus H_5$ and $H_4 \oplus H_6$, it should be hard to distinguish correlated samples from $G_1 \oplus G_5$ and $G_2 \oplus G_6$ from correlated samples from $G_1 \oplus G_3 \oplus G_5$ and $G_2 \oplus G_4 \oplus G_6$.

3 A Prime-Order Bilinear Group Satisfying All Features

Our ultimate goal in this section is to define a prime-order bilinear group that satisfies all three of the properties defined in the previous section: projecting, canceling, and parameter hiding; additionally, we want to require that subgroup decision is hard in this group. Our construction can be viewed as an abstraction of the construction of Seo and Cheon [44], which they prove satisfies (regular) projecting, canceling, and a somewhat restrictive notion of subgroup decision. In contrast, our construction satisfies canceling and parameter hiding, is flexible enough to achieve any of the three flavors of projecting we defined in the previous section (depending on the parameter choices), and comes equipped with reductions for more general instances of subgroup decision.

Notationally, we augment the bilinear groups $\mathcal{G}$ discussed in the previous section: we now focus only on the case when the group order is some prime p, and consider $\mathbb{G} = (p, B_1, B_2, B_T, E, \mu)$ built on top of $\mathcal{G} = (p, G, H, G_T, e)$; this means B_1, B_2, and B_T may contain multiple copies of G, H, and G_T respectively, and that the map E uses e as a component. Because we are moving to bigger spaces, we also include a value μ that allows us to test membership in B_1 and B_2; as an example, consider $B_1 \subset G \times G$. Then, while an efficient membership test for G implies one for $G \times G$, additional information μ may be necessary to allow one to (efficiently) test for membership in B_1.

Our construction crucially uses dual pairing vector spaces, which were introduced by Okamoto and Takashima [38,39] and have been previously used to provide pairings $E : G^n \times H^n \to G_T$, built on top of pairings $e : G \times H \to G_T$, that satisfy the canceling property. As we cannot have a cyclic target space if we want to satisfy projecting, however, we instead need a map whose image is G_T^d for some $d > 1$. Intuitively, we achieve this by piecing together d "blocks," where each block is an instance of a dual pairing vector space; the construction of Seo and Cheon is then obtained as the special case in which $d = n$, and regular dual pairing vector spaces are obtained with $d = 1$. We begin with a key definition:

Definition 3.1 (Dual Orthonormal). *Two bases* $\mathbb{B} = (\boldsymbol{b}_1, \ldots, \boldsymbol{b}_n)$ *and* $\mathbb{B}^* = (\boldsymbol{b}_1^*, \ldots, \boldsymbol{b}_n^*)$ *of* $\mathbb{F}_p^n$ *are* dual orthonormal *if* $\boldsymbol{b}_j \cdot \boldsymbol{b}_j^* \equiv 1 \bmod p$ *for all* j, $1 \leq j \leq n$, *and* $\boldsymbol{b}_j \cdot \boldsymbol{b}_k^* \equiv 0 \bmod p$ *for all* $j \neq k$.

We note that one can efficiently sample a random pair of dual orthonormal bases $(\mathbb{B}, \mathbb{B}^*)$ by sampling first a random basis $\mathbb{B}$ and then solving uniquely for $\mathbb{B}^*$ using linear algebra over $\mathbb{F}_p$; we denote this sampling process as $(\mathbb{B}, \mathbb{B}^*) \xleftarrow{\$} Dual(\mathbb{F}_p^n)$. By repeating this sampling process d times, we can obtain a tuple $((\mathbb{B}_1, \mathbb{B}_1^*), \ldots, (\mathbb{B}_d, \mathbb{B}_d^*))$ of d pairs of dual orthonormal bases of $\mathbb{F}_p^n$. We denote the vectors of $\mathbb{B}_i$ as $(\boldsymbol{b}_{1,i} \ldots, \boldsymbol{b}_{n,i})$, and the vectors of $\mathbb{B}_i^*$ as $(\boldsymbol{b}_{1,i}^*, \ldots, \boldsymbol{b}_{n,i}^*)$. We then give the following definition:

Definition 3.2 (Concatenation). *The* concatenation *of bases* $(\mathbb{B}_1, \ldots, \mathbb{B}_d)$ *of* $\mathbb{F}_p^n$ *is a collection of* n *vectors* $(\boldsymbol{v}_1, \ldots, \boldsymbol{v}_n)$ *in* $\mathbb{F}_p^{dn}$, *where each* $\boldsymbol{v}_j := \boldsymbol{b}_{j,1} || \ldots || \boldsymbol{b}_{j,d}$. *Alternatively, we can view each* $\boldsymbol{v}_j$ *as a* $d \times n$ *matrix, where the* i-*th row is* $\boldsymbol{b}_{j,i}$. *We denote the concatenation of* $(\mathbb{B}_1, \ldots, \mathbb{B}_d)$ *as* $\mathsf{Concat}(\mathbb{B}_1, \ldots, \mathbb{B}_d)$.

To begin our construction, we build off $\mathcal{G} = (p, G, H, G_T, e, g, h)$, where g and h are generators of G and H respectively, and consider groups $B_1 \subset G^{dn}$ and $B_2 \subset H^{dn}$. Notationally, we write an element of B_1 as g^A, where $A =$

$(\alpha_{i,j})_{i,j=1}^{d,n}$ is a $d \times n$ matrix and $g^A := (g^{\alpha_{1,1}}, \ldots, g^{\alpha_{1,j}}, \ldots, g^{\alpha_{1,n}}, g^{\alpha_{2,1}}, \ldots, g^{\alpha_{d,n}})$. We similarly write elements of B_2 as h^B for a $d \times n$ matrix $B = (\beta_{ij})_{i,j=1}^{d,n}$, and furthermore define the bilinear map $E : B_1 \times B_2 \to G_T^d$ as

$$E(g^A, h^B) := \left(\prod_{k=1}^n e(g^{\alpha_{1,k}}, h^{\beta_{1,k}}), \ldots, \prod_{k=1}^n e(g^{\alpha_{d,k}}, h^{\beta_{d,k}}) \right). \tag{1}$$

Observe that the i-th coordinate of the image is equal to $e(g, h)^{A_i \cdot B_i \bmod p}$, where A_i and B_i denote the i-th rows of A and B respectively. Then, to begin to see how our construction will satisfy projecting and canceling, we have the following lemma:

Lemma 3.1. *Let* $(v_1, \ldots, v_n) = \mathsf{Concat}(\mathbb{B}_1, \ldots, \mathbb{B}_d)$ *and* $(v_1^*, \ldots, v_n^*) = \mathsf{Concat}(\mathbb{B}_1^*, \ldots, \mathbb{B}_d^*)$, *where* $(\mathbb{B}_i, \mathbb{B}_i^*)$ *are dual orthonormal bases of* $\mathbb{F}_p^n$. *Then*

$$E(g^{v_j}, h^{v_j^*}) = (e(g, h), \ldots, e(g, h)) \; \forall j \quad and \quad E(g^{v_j}, h^{v_k^*}) = (1_T, \ldots, 1_T) \; \forall j \neq k.$$

Proof. By definition of the pairing,

$$E(g^{v_j}, h^{v_k^*}) = \left(e(g, h)^{b_{j,1} \cdot b_{k,1}^*}, \ldots, e(g, h)^{b_{j,d} \cdot b_{k,d}^*} \right)$$

for any j and k. If $j = k$, then the fact that $(\mathbb{B}_i, \mathbb{B}_i^*)$ are dual orthonormal for all i implies by definition that $b_{j,i} \cdot b_{j,i}^* \equiv 1 \bmod p$ for all i and j, and thus $E(g^{v_j}, h^{v_j^*}) = (e(g, h), \ldots, e(g, h))$. For the second property, we again use the definition of dual orthonormal bases to see that $b_{j,i} \cdot b_{k,i}^* \equiv 0 \bmod p$ for all $j \neq k$, and thus $E(g^{v_j}, h^{v_k^*}) = (1_T, \ldots, 1_T)$. $\qquad\square$

While Lemma 3.1 therefore shows us directly how to obtain canceling, for projecting we are still mapping into a one-dimensional image. To obtain more dimensions, it turns out we need only perform some additional scalar multiplication. We give the following definition:

Definition 3.3 (Scaling). *Define* $C = (c_{i,j})_{i,j=1}^{d,n}$ *to be a* $n \times d$ *matrix of entries over* $\mathbb{F}_p \setminus \{0\}$. *Given bases* $(\mathbb{B}_1, \ldots, \mathbb{B}_d)$ *of* $\mathbb{F}_p^n$, *we define the* scaling *of these bases by* C *to be new bases* $(\mathbb{D}_1, \ldots, \mathbb{D}_d)$, *where* $\mathbb{D}_i = (c_{1,i} b_{1,i}, \ldots, c_{n,i} b_{n,i})$ *for all* i, $1 \leq i \leq d$. *We denote the scaling of* $(\mathbb{B}_1, \ldots, \mathbb{B}_d)$ *by* C *as* $\mathsf{Scale}(C, \mathbb{B}_1, \ldots, \mathbb{B}_d)$.

Intuitively then, we use the entries in the i-th column of C to scale the vectors in the basis $\mathbb{B}_i$ and obtain the basis $\mathbb{D}_i$. As we still have $b_{j,i} \cdot b_{k,i}^* \equiv 0 \bmod p$ for $j \neq k$, multiplication by a scalar will not affect this and we still satisfy canceling. The scalar values do, however, build in extra dimensions into the image of our pairing, as demonstrated by the following lemma:

Lemma 3.2. *Let* $(\mathbb{B}_1, \ldots, \mathbb{B}_d)$ *and* $(\mathbb{B}_1^*, \ldots, \mathbb{B}_d^*)$ *be sets of bases for* $\mathbb{F}_p^n$ *such that* $(\mathbb{B}_i, \mathbb{B}_i^*)$ *are dual orthonormal for all* i. *Define* $(v_1, \ldots, v_n) := \mathsf{Concat}(\mathbb{D}_1, \ldots, \mathbb{D}_d)$

and $(\boldsymbol{v}_1^*, \ldots, \boldsymbol{v}_n^*) := \mathsf{Concat}(\mathbb{B}_1^*, \ldots, \mathbb{B}_d^*)$, *where* $(\mathbb{D}_1, \ldots, \mathbb{D}_d) = \mathsf{Scale}(C, \mathbb{B}_1, \ldots, \mathbb{B}_d)$ *for some* $C \in M_{n \times d}(\mathbb{F}_p)$. *Then*

$$E(g^{\boldsymbol{v}_j}, h^{\boldsymbol{v}_j^*}) = (e(g,h)^{c_{j,1}}, \ldots, e(g,h)^{c_{j,d}}) \ \forall j \quad and$$
$$E(g^{\boldsymbol{v}_j}, h^{\boldsymbol{v}_k^*}) = (1_T, \ldots, 1_T) \ \forall j \neq k.$$

Proof. y definition of the pairing,

$$E(g^{\boldsymbol{v}_j}, h^{\boldsymbol{v}_k^*}) = \left(e(g,h)^{c_{j,1}\boldsymbol{b}_{j,1} \cdot \boldsymbol{b}_{k,1}^*}, \ldots, e(g,h)^{c_{j,d}\boldsymbol{b}_{j,d} \cdot \boldsymbol{b}_{k,d}^*} \right)$$

for any j and k. If $j = k$, then the fact that $(\mathbb{B}_i, \mathbb{B}_i^*)$ are dual orthonormal for all i implies by definition that $\boldsymbol{b}_{j,i} \cdot \boldsymbol{b}_{j,i}^* \equiv 1 \bmod p$ for all i and j, and thus $c_{j,i}\boldsymbol{b}_{j,i} \cdot \boldsymbol{b}_{j,i}^* \equiv c_{j,i} \bmod p$ and $E(g^{\boldsymbol{v}_j}, h^{\boldsymbol{v}_j^*}) = (e(g,h)^{c_{j,1}}, \ldots, e(g,h)^{c_{j,d}})$. For the second property, we again use the definition of dual orthonormal bases to see that $\boldsymbol{b}_{j,i} \cdot \boldsymbol{b}_{k,i}^* \equiv 0 \bmod p$ for all $j \neq k$, and thus $c_{j,i}\boldsymbol{b}_{j,i} \cdot \boldsymbol{b}_{k,i}^* \equiv 0 \bmod p$ and $E(g^{\boldsymbol{v}_j}, h^{\boldsymbol{v}_k^*}) = (1_T, \ldots, 1_T)$. $\square$

We are now ready to give our full construction of an algorithm BilinearGen', parameterized by integers n and d, and a distribution $\mathcal{D}_{n,d}$ on $n \times d$ matrices, to achieve a setting $\mathbb{G} = (p, B_1, B_2, B_T, E, \mu)$ such that $B_1 \subset G^{dn}$, $B_2 \subset H^{dn}$, and $B_T = G_T^d$. We present this construction in Algorithm 1, and demonstrate that it satisfies projecting, canceling, parameter hiding, and subgroup decision.

The generality of this construction stems from the choices of d, n, and $\mathcal{D}$; in fact, by choosing different values for these parameters, we can satisfy each of the different flavors of projecting from Section 2. To satisfy fully projecting, we choose C from a distribution over matrices of full rank n and use $d \geq n$. If we use a less restrictive distribution, we obtain weaker projection capabilities and a more efficient construction (as we can have $d < n$) when projecting onto all subgroups individually is not needed: to achieve (regular) projecting, we can use $d > 1$ and pick C to be of rank > 1, and to achieve weak projecting we can in fact use $d = 1$ and pick C to be the vector consisting of all 1 entries. (This last case is equivalent to working in regular dual pairing vector spaces.)

Theorem 3.1. *For all values of* $n \geq 2$, *the bilinear group* $\mathbb{G} \xleftarrow{\$} \mathsf{BilinearGen}'(1^k, n, d, \mathcal{D}_{d,n})$ *satisfies canceling, fully projecting as defined in Definition 2.3 for* $d \geq n$ *when* $\mathcal{D}_{d,n}$ *is defined over full-rank matrices, projecting as defined in Definition 2.2 for* $d > 1$ *when* $\mathcal{D}_{d,n}$ *is defined over matrices of rank* > 1, *and weak projecting as defined in Definition 2.1 for* $d = 1$.

Proof. Given that our construction was specifically designed to satisfy the conditions for Lemma 3.2, we immediately obtain canceling. To satisfy projecting, we additionally need to construct the projection maps π_{ij} and argue that they satisfy the requirements of Definition 2.3 (in the case that C is full rank). By the way our subgroups are defined, each projection map π_{1i} within the group B_1 must map an arbitrary element $g^{a_1 \boldsymbol{v}_1 + \cdots + a_n \boldsymbol{v}_n}$ of B_1 to $g^{a_i \boldsymbol{v}_i} \in B_{1,i}$; similarly, π_{2i} must map $h^{a_1^* \boldsymbol{v}_1^* + \cdots + a_n^* \boldsymbol{v}_n^*} \in B_2$ to $h^{a_i^* \boldsymbol{v}_i^*} \in B_{2,i}$. For π_{1i}, we observe that it

---

Algorithm 1. BilinearGen′: generate a bilinear group $\mathbb{G}$ that satisfies projecting and canceling

---

Input: $d, n \in \mathbb{N}$; distribution $\mathcal{D}_{d,n}$ over matrices in $M_{n \times d}(\mathbb{F}_p)$; security parameter 1^k.

1. $(p, G, H, G_T, e) \xleftarrow{\$} \mathsf{BilinearGen}(1^k, 1)$.
2. Pick values g and h such that $G = \langle g \rangle$ and $H = \langle h \rangle$.
3. Sample d pairs $(\mathbb{B}_i, \mathbb{B}_i^*) \xleftarrow{\$} Dual(\mathbb{F}_p^n)$ to obtain two sets $(\mathbb{B}_1, \ldots, \mathbb{B}_d)$ and $(\mathbb{B}_1^*, \ldots, \mathbb{B}_d^*)$ of bases of $\mathbb{F}_p^n$, where $(\mathbb{B}_i, \mathbb{B}_i^*)$ are dual orthonormal.
4. Sample $C = (c_{ij})_{i,j=1}^{d,n} \xleftarrow{\$} \mathcal{D}$ and compute $(\mathbb{D}_1, \ldots, \mathbb{D}_d) := \mathsf{Scale}(C, \mathbb{B}_1, \ldots, \mathbb{B}_d)$.
5. For all i, $1 \leq i \leq n$, define $B_{1,i} := \langle g^{v_i} \rangle$ and $B_{2,i} := \langle h^{v_i^*} \rangle$, where $(v_1, \ldots, v_n) := \mathsf{Concat}(\mathbb{D}_1, \ldots, \mathbb{D}_d)$ and $(v_1^*, \ldots, v_n^*) := \mathsf{Concat}(\mathbb{B}_1^*, \ldots, \mathbb{B}_d^*)$.
6. Define $B_1 := \oplus_{i=1}^n B_{1,i} \subset G^{dn}$, $B_2 := \oplus_{i=1}^n B_{2,i} \subset H^{dn}$, and $B_T := G_T^d$. Define the pairing $E : B_1 \times B_2 \to B_T$ as in Equation 1.
7. Finally, to be able to check that an element $g^M \in G^{dn}$ for $M = (m_{ij})_{i,j=1}^{d,n}$ is an element of B_1, we observe that the vectors $v_1, \ldots, v_n$ span an n-dimensional subspace $\mathbb{V}$ of $\mathbb{F}_p^{dn}$. Thus, there must be another subspace, call it $\mathbb{W}$, of dimension $dn - n$, that contains all vectors in $\mathbb{F}_p^n$ that are orthogonal to vectors in $\mathbb{V}$. Given $\mu_2 := (h^{w_1}, \ldots, h^{w_{(d-1)n}})$, where the $\{w_i\}_{i=1}^{(d-1)n}$ are a basis of $\mathbb{W}$, one can therefore efficiently check if $g^M \in B_1$ by checking if $E(g^M, h^{w_i}) = (1_T, \ldots, 1_T)$ for all i, $1 \leq i \leq (d-1)n$.
Analogously, given $\mu_1 := (g^{w_1^*}, \ldots, g^{w_{(d-1)n}^*})$, one can check if $h^A \in B_2$ by checking if $E(g^{w_i^*}, h^A) = (1_T, \ldots, 1_T)$, where $\{w_i^*\}_{i=1}^{(d-1)n}$ are a basis for the subspace $\mathbb{W}^*$ of $\mathbb{F}_p^n$ consisting of vectors orthogonal to vectors in the span of $v_1^*, \ldots, v_n^*$.
8. Output $\mathbb{G} := (p, B_1, B_2, B_T, E, (\mu_1, \mu_2))$.

---

can be computed efficiently by anyone knowing v_i and another vector in $\mathbb{F}_p^{dn}$ that is orthogonal to v_k for all $k \neq i$. The situation for π_{2i} is analogous.

As for the projection maps $\pi_{T,i}$ required for the target space, we define $\pi_{T,i}$ to map an element $e(g, h)^{a_1 C_1 + \cdots + a_n C_n}$ to $e(g, h)^{a_i C_i}$, where we recall C_i denotes the i-th row of the scaling matrix C (C_i is thus a vector in $\mathbb{F}_p^d$ for all i).

Finally, we show that the required associativity property holds, namely that $E(\pi_{1,i}(g^M), \pi_{2,i}(h^A)) = \pi_{T,i}(E(g^M, h^A))$ for all elements $g^M \in B_1$, $h^A \in B_2$, and for all i, $1 \leq i \leq d$. To see this, observe that $g^M \in B_1$ implies that $g^M = g^{\alpha_1 v_1 + \cdots + \alpha_n v_n}$ for some $\alpha_1, \ldots, \alpha_n \in \mathbb{F}_p$, and similarly that $h^A = h^{\beta_1 v_1^* + \cdots + \beta_n v_n^*}$. We therefore have that

$$E(\pi_{1,i}(g^M), \pi_{2,i}(h^A)) = E(g^{\alpha_i v_i}, h^{\beta_i v_i^*}) = e(g, h)^{\alpha_i \beta_i C_i},$$

where this last equality follows from Lemma 3.2. On the other hand, we have that

$$\pi_{T,i}(E(g^M, h^A)) = \pi_{T,i}(\prod_{k=1}^n e(g, h)^{\alpha_k \beta_k C_k}) = e(g, h)^{\alpha_i \beta_i C_i},$$

and the two quantities are therefore equal.

A similar argument applies to obtaining more limited projections when C has lower rank.   □

It remains to prove that our construction also satisfies parameter hiding and subgroup hiding. For the latter property, our definition in Section 2.3 is highly general and we cannot prove that all instances of generalized correlated subgroup decision reduce to any one assumption. Instead, we show that certain "nice" instances of the assumption follow from SXDH.

Before we define a nice instance, we first restrict our attention to the case where $n = 8$, $d = 1$, C is a matrix with all 1 entries. For succinctness here and in later sections, we use $\mathsf{BasicGen}(1^k) = \mathsf{BilinearGen}'(1^k, 8, 1, \mathcal{D})$, where $\mathcal{D}$ produces matrices with all 1 entries; i.e., we use $\mathsf{BasicGen}$ to produce the specific setting in which we are interested in Section 5.

We consider two variants of this setting, which differ only in the auxiliary information μ. For μ as defined above in Algorithm 1, we show that the required instances of the correlated subgroup decision assumption are implied by SXDH. We additionally consider a case where μ is augmented to contain the following three pieces of information: (1) the vectors $\boldsymbol{v}_7$, $\boldsymbol{v}_8$, $\boldsymbol{v}_7^*$, and $\boldsymbol{v}_8^*$; (2) a random basis for the span of $(\boldsymbol{v}_1, \ldots, \boldsymbol{v}_6)$ inside $\mathbb{F}_p^8$; and (3) a random basis for the span of $(\boldsymbol{v}_1^*, \ldots, \boldsymbol{v}_6^*)$ inside $\mathbb{F}_p^8$. With this μ, one can then perform a membership test for $G_1 \oplus \ldots \oplus G_6$ on some element $g^{\boldsymbol{v}}$ by computing a basis for the orthogonal space of the span of $(\boldsymbol{v}_1, \ldots, \boldsymbol{v}_6)$, pairing against h raised to these vectors, and taking a dot product in $\mathbb{F}_p^8$. While this additional information in μ makes some instances of subgroup decision easy, instances entirely within $G_1 \oplus \ldots \oplus G_6$ and $H_1 \oplus \ldots H_6$ are still implied by SXDH. To refer to this instance with augmented μ in what follows, we call it the *augmented construction*. Now, by "nice," we mean that the instance of the assumption behaves as follows: if the challenge terms are in H (the situation is analogous if they are in G), then there is a single pair in S that is common to the challenge sets T_1 and T_2 that appears in all tuples in $S_{G,\mathrm{sam}}^{\mathrm{sgh}}$ that also contain the differing pair. In other words, the given correlated samples from the opposite side of the challenge that include the differing space must also be attached to a particular space that is guaranteed to be present in the challenge term. As we will see, this feature turns out to be convenient for reducing to SXDH, as demonstrated by the following lemmas. For the augmented construction, we additionally restrict to instances where each correlated sample t_i in $S_{G,\mathrm{sam}}^{\mathrm{sgh}}$ or $S_{H,\mathrm{sam}}^{\mathrm{sgh}}$ is contained within the set $S := \{(1,2), (3,4), (5,6)\}$ (this is to avoid the additional information in μ from compromising the hardness).

Lemma 3.3. *For the augmented construction, the nice instances of the generalized correlated subgroup decision assumption, where additionally each correlated sample t_i in $S_{G,sam}^{sgh}$ or $S_{H,sam}^{sgh}$ is contained within the set $\{(1,2), (3,4), (5,6)\}$, are implied by the SXDH assumption.*

Proof. We consider a nice instance of the generalized correlated subgroup decision assumption parameterized by sets S_G^{sgh} and S_H^{sgh} containing singletons and tuples of the pairs $(1,2)$, $(3,4)$, $(5,6)$ and challenge sets T_1 and T_2 differing by one pair. We assume without loss of generality that the differing pair is $(3,4)$, that $(1,2)$ is a common pair to both T_1, T_2, and the challenge terms are in G.

We assume we are given an SXDH challenge of the form (g, h, g^a, g^b, T), where $T = g^{ab}$ or is random in G. We will simulate the specified instance of the generalized correlated subgroup decision assumption. We first choose a random dual orthonormal bases pair $\mathbb{F}, \mathbb{F}^*$ for $\mathbb{F}_p^8$. We then implicitly define $\mathbb{B}, \mathbb{B}^*$ as follows:

$$b_1 = a f_3 + f_1, \ b_2 = a f_4 + f_2, \ b_3 = f_3, \ b_4 = f_4,$$

$$b_5 = f_5, \ b_6 = f_6, \ b_7 = f_7, \ b_8 = f_8$$

$$b_1^* = f_1^*, \ b_2^* = f_2^*, \ b_3^* = f_3^* - a f_1^*, \ b_4^* = f_4^* - a f_2^*,$$

$$b_5^* = f_5^*, \ b_6^* = f_6^*, \ b_7^* = f_7^*, \ b_8^* = f_8^*.$$

We note that $(\mathbb{B}, \mathbb{B}^*)$ are properly distributed, since applying a linear transformation to randomly sampled dual orthonormal bases while preserving orthonormality produces equivalently distributed bases. We observe that v_7, v_8, v_7^*, v_8^* are known, as are the spans of $\{v_1, \ldots, v_6\}$ and $\{v_1^*, \ldots, v_6^*\}$. Thus we can produce the specified auxiliary information μ.

Since we have h, g, g^a, we can produce all generators *except* h_3, h_4. Since $(3, 4)$ is the differing pair for the challenges, these generators cannot be required. Since all generators are known on the G side, any correlated samples in G are easy to produce. To produce correlated samples for tuples containing $(1, 2)$ and $(3, 4)$ in H, we simply choose random exponents $t', z \in \mathbb{F}_p$ and implicitly set $t = az + t'$. We can then produce

$$h_1^t h_3^z = h^{t' f_1^* + z f_3^*}, \ h_2^t h_4^z = h^{-t' f_2^* - z f_4^*}.$$

To produce the challenge terms, we compute

$$T^{f_3} (g^b)^{f_1}, \ T^{f_4} (g^b)^{f_2}.$$

If $(5, 6)$ is also common to T_1, T_2, we can use the generators g_5, g_6 to add on properly distributed terms in these subgroups as well. $\qquad \square$

The same proof can also be applied more generally when μ is *not* augmented, resulting in:

Lemma 3.4. *For* $\mathbb{G} \overset{\$}{\leftarrow} \mathsf{BasicGen}(1^k)$, *all nice instances of the generalized correlated subgroup decision assumption are implied by SXDH.*

Finally, we prove that parameter hiding holds for the augmented construction as well.

Lemma 3.5. *Parameter hiding, as in Example 1, holds for the augmented construction.*

Proof. This is essentially Lemmas 3 and 4 in [27], and is a consequence of the following observation. We consider sampling a random pair of dual orthonormal bases $\mathbb{F}, \mathbb{F}^*$ of $\mathbb{F}_p^8$, and let A be an invertible 2×2 matrix over $\mathbb{F}_p$. We consider the 8×2 matrix F whose columns are equal to f_3 and f_4. Then FA is also an 8×2 matrix, and we form a new basis $\mathbb{B}$ from $\mathbb{F}$ and A by taking these columns in place of f_3, f_4. To form the dual basis $\mathbb{B}^*$, we similarly multiply the matrix with columns f_3^*, f_4^* by the transpose of A^{-1}. It is noted in [27] that the resulting distribution of $\mathbb{B}, \mathbb{B}^*$ is equivalent to choosing this pair randomly, and in particular, this distribution is independent of the choice of A. Lemma 4 in [27] observes that if we take $x \neq y$ and define $\boldsymbol{x}$ to be the transpose of $(1, x)$ and $\boldsymbol{y}$ to be the transpose of $(y, -1)$, then choosing random scalars γ, λ in $\mathbb{F}_p$ and a random matrix A over $\mathbb{F}_p$ yields that the joint distribution of $\lambda A^{-1} \boldsymbol{x}$ and $\gamma A^T \boldsymbol{y}$ is negligibly close to the uniform distribution over $\mathbb{F}_p^2 \times \mathbb{F}_p^2$. This is precisely our parameter hiding requirement, where A represents the ambiguity in our precise choice of the generators $\boldsymbol{b}_3, \boldsymbol{b}_4, \boldsymbol{b}_3^*, \boldsymbol{b}_4^*$, conditioned on the span of $\{\boldsymbol{b}_3, \boldsymbol{b}_4\}$ and the span of $\{\boldsymbol{b}_3^*, \boldsymbol{b}_4^*\}$ being known (in addition to the other individual $\boldsymbol{b}_i$ and $\boldsymbol{b}_i^*$ vectors for $i \notin \{3, 4\}$). □

Finally, although we do not use any non-nice instances of the generalized correlated subgroup decision assumption in this work, it is interesting to ask which of the more complex instances can be reduced to SXDH or other static assumptions. For values of $d > 1$, the additional structure required to achieve projecting seems to make directly reducing a large space of assumptions to SXDH difficult. Nonetheless, we are able to rely only on SXDH for our projecting leakage-resilient BGN variant through the use of hybrid transitions that incrementally change the rank of the scaling matrix C. We leave it as an interesting question for future work to further explore the minimal assumptions for supporting a broader class of subgroups decision variants.

4   A Leakage-Resilient BGN Variant

A very elegant use of the projecting property in the composite-order setting is the public key encryption scheme of Boneh, Goh, and Nissim [9], a scheme that is designed to allow arbitrary additions and one multiplication of ciphertexts. The basic group operation is used for ciphertext addition, while the bilinear map is applied during ciphertext multiplication. The secret key is then a projection map (which equates to a factorization of the group order) that allows the decryptor to strip off the blinding factors of the underlying ciphertexts, even after their interaction has migrated to the target group.

While these limited homomorphic properties make the BGN scheme appealing, the rigid structure of keys can be a source of frustration when one attempts to augment its functionality or security guarantees. Having the secret key reveal a factorization of the group order means that different users must generate different groups, and it additionally means that the secret key is uniquely determined (information-theoretically) from the public key. This presents a challenge, for instance, if one wants to design a variant with provable guarantees of leakage resilience.

Proofs of leakage resilience for public key encryption schemes typically follow a strategy inspired by the hash proof paradigm of Naor and Segev [37]. This paradigm starts with a scheme that has many possible secret keys for each public key. A hybrid argument is used, where the first step changes to a malformed — or *invalid* — ciphertext, that decrypts to different messages under the different secret keys associated to a fixed public key. A bound on the total leakage of the secret key is then used to argue that the adversary cannot tell which of the many possible secret keys the challenger is holding. Thus, even though the challenger may be holding a secret key that decrypts the challenge ciphertext correctly, he may as well be a holding a key that decrypts it to a random message. It is then possible to argue that the scheme remains secure under leakage.

If we wish to apply this kind of proof strategy to a version of the BGN scheme, we first need a way of allowing many secret keys for each public key. The DPVS framework we described in the previous section provides a natural answer. In this framework, the projection map is no longer a factorization, but rather a vector that comes from a suitably high-dimensional space to allow for many possibilities. This makes it rather easy to imagine a BGN variant that preserves the somewhat-homomorphic properties of ciphertexts, yet allows for an exponential number of secret keys per public key.

It is already well-known that applying DPVS and similar techniques for designing vector spaces in the exponent is a useful approach for achieving leakage resilience. For example, Lewko et al. [35] demonstrated that leakage resilience can be incorporated quite easily into dual system encryption proofs by combining mechanisms for canceling, parameter hiding, and the fact that the dot product of sufficiently long vectors over $\mathbb{F}_p$ has convenient information-theoretic properties (roughly, the dot product modulo p is a good two-source extractor). The same high level of compatibility exists between our framework and the pre-existing leakage resilience techniques, thus allowing us to repurpose the same linear algebraic underpinnings that implement projecting and canceling in our framework to achieve leakage resilience for a BGN-type scheme.

4.1 The Scheme

As in the original BGN scheme, we will assume that the message space is small to allow efficient decryption. We use our framework from Section 3 with $n = d = 4$. For the matrix distribution $\mathcal{D}$, we consider all matrices whose second and third rows form a rank-1 submatrix. The setting we then work in is $\mathbb{G} \xleftarrow{\$} \mathsf{BilinearGen}'(1^k, 4, 4, \mathcal{D})$. Rather than use this framework generically, as we do in Section 5, we re-purpose the matrix C and basis vectors $(v_1, v_2, v_3, v_4), (v_1^*, v_2^*, v_3^*, v_4^*) \in \mathbb{F}_p^{16}$ — defined in Step 4 and Step 5 of Algorithm 1 respectively — and use them explicitly in our construction and proofs. Below, we use C_i to denote the i-th row of the scaling matrix C (for $i \in \{1, 2, 3, 4\}$).

- Setup($\mathbb{G}$): Pick $r, r^* \xleftarrow{\$} \mathbb{F}_p$ and define $u := \sum_i v_i$, $u^* := \sum_i v_i^*$, $w := rv_2$, and $w^* := r^*v_2^*$. Choose y uniformly at random from the set of vectors in $\mathbb{F}_p^4$ such that $y \cdot C_2 = 0$, noting that $y \cdot C_3 = 0$ then holds automatically as well. Output $pk = (g, g^u, g^w, h^{u^*}, h^{w^*})$ and $sk = \left(y, sk_T = e(g, h)^{y \cdot (\sum_i C_i)}\right)$. Note that, by construction, $y \cdot (\sum_i C_i) = y \cdot (C_1 + C_4)$ and, by Lemma 3.2, $E(g^u, h^{u^*}) = \left(e(g, h)^{\sum_j c_{j,1}}, \ldots, e(g, h)^{\sum_j c_{j,4}}\right)$.

- Enc(pk, m): We have two types of ciphertexts: Type A and Type B. If we want to be able to perform homomorphic operations on *any* pair of ciphertexts, a single ciphertext could include both types. To form a Type A ciphertext, choose $s \xleftarrow{\$} \mathbb{F}_p$ and compute $\mathsf{ct}_A := g^{mu+sw}$. To form a Type B ciphertext, choose $s^* \xleftarrow{\$} \mathbb{F}_p$ and compute $\mathsf{ct}_B := h^{mu^*+s^*w^*}$. Output $\mathsf{ct} = (\mathsf{ct}_A, \mathsf{ct}_B)$. (Or just ct_A or ct_B, depending on the desired homomorphic properties.)
- Eval($pk, \mathsf{ct}_1, \mathsf{ct}_2$): We describe two evaluation cases: addition of Type A ciphertexts (the operations are analogous for Type B ciphertexts), and multiplication of a Type A and Type B ciphertext (which can then be further added in the target space B_T).

  First pick a random value $t \xleftarrow{\$} \mathbb{F}_p$. If ct_1 and ct_2 are Type A, then return $\mathsf{ct} = \mathsf{ct}_1 \cdot \mathsf{ct}_2 \cdot g^{tw}$. If ct_1 is Type A and ct_2 is Type B, then return $\mathsf{ct} = E(\mathsf{ct}_1, \mathsf{ct}_2) \cdot E(g^w, h^{w^*})^t$.
- Dec(sk, ct): To decrypt a ciphertext $(\mathsf{ct}_1, \mathsf{ct}_2, \mathsf{ct}_3, \mathsf{ct}_4) \in G_T^4$, compute

$$\prod_{i=1}^{4} \mathsf{ct}_i^{y_i} = sk_T^m.$$

Using knowledge of sk_T, exhaustively search for m (this is possible since we have a small message space). If ct is Type A, then compute $\mathsf{ct}' = E(\mathsf{ct}, \mathsf{Enc}(pk, 1))$ and decrypt ct' (and analogously for a Type B ciphertext).

To see that decryption is correct, observe that

$$\prod_i \mathsf{ct}_i^{y_i} = \prod_i e(g, h)^{m y_i \sum_j c_{j,i}} = e(g, h)^{m \sum_i \sum_j y_i c_{j,i}}$$

$$= e(g, h)^{m \sum_j \sum_i y_i c_{j,i}} = e(g, h)^{m \sum_j \boldsymbol{y} \cdot C_j}$$

$$= sk_T^m.$$

To see that evaluation is correct, observe that if ct_1 encrypts m_1 and ct_2 encrypts m_2 then

$$\mathsf{ct} = g^{m_1 u + s_1 w} \cdot g^{m_2 u + s_2 w} \cdot g^{tw} = g^{(m_1+m_2)u + (s_1+s_2+t)w},$$

which is a properly distributed Type A encryption of $m_1 + m_2$. Pairing a Type A ct_1 and a Type B ct_2 similarly yields a properly distributed encryption of $m_1 m_2$ in the target space, just as in BGN.

4.2   Security Analysis

The security model we use is leakage against non-adaptive memory attacks, as defined by Akavia et al. [3, Definition 3]. Briefly, the attacker first declares a leakage function f mapping secret keys to $\{0, 1\}^\ell$ for a suitably small ℓ. The attacker then receives pk and $f(sk)$, and proceeds as in a standard IND-CPA game; i.e., it outputs two messages m_0 and m_1, receives an encryption of m_b, and wins if it correctly guesses b. As in the case of the original BGN scheme, it suffices to argue security for challenge ciphertexts generated in G/H, as security for the ciphertexts generated via the multiplicative homomorphism follows from the security of ciphertexts in the base groups. While there are several other interesting models for leakage-resilient PKE security, we choose to work with this one, as it is clean and simple and thus allows us to give a concise demonstration of the use of our framework.

Theorem 4.1. *If SXDH holds in* $\mathbb{G}$ *and* $\ell \leq \log(p-1) - 2k$, *the above construction is leakage resilient with respect to non-adaptive memory attacks.*

As in the typical hash proof system paradigm, we first define invalid ciphertexts that have more blinding randomness than honestly generated ciphertexts. Initially, these are still decrypted consistently by the set of secret keys corresponding to a fixed public key. After having transitioned to a game with an invalid challenge ciphertext, however, we gradually adjust the respective distributions of secret keys and ciphertexts to arrive at a game where, in the adversary's view, it seems that the secret key decrypts the ciphertext randomly.

In the course of these game transitions, we use SXDH in multiple ways. First we use it to change from an honest to an invalid ciphertext by bringing in an additional blinding factor in a new subgroup. This is just a "nice" instance of subgroup decision. We will also use it to make changes to the rank of particular submatrices inside the scaling matrix C. This technique is inspired by the observation in [10] that DDH implies a rank-1 matrix in the exponent is hard to distinguish from a rank-2 matrix. To make the crucial switch from a secret key that properly decrypts the challenge ciphertext to a key that decrypts it incorrectly, we rely on an information-theoretic argument leveraging a form of parameter hiding, along with the leakage bound. Essentially, the simulator uses the remaining ambiguity in the underlying parameters (conditioned on the public key) to help it create an invalid challenge ciphertext after supplying the leakage. The proof of Theorem 4.1 can be found in the full version of our paper [28].

5   An IBE with IND-CCA1 Security

In this section, we discuss how to obtain an IND-CCA1-secure identity-based encryption scheme. Although IND-CCA2-secure IBE schemes have already been constructed, we view this as a demonstration of our techniques rather than an application of independent interest.

Our technique for proving IND-CCA1 security extends from the observation due to Lewko and Waters [33] that dual system proofs can be interpreted as a reduction from a full security game to a weak game in which the attacker does not have access to the public parameters. Using this technique, we first define such a weak game for IND-CCA1 security, and then prove that our IBE construction satisfies it. Next, leveraging a weak form of projection, we reduce the full IND-CCA1 security to this weaker notion by first expanding the system to have extra components in a space that is not reflected in the public parameters, and then projecting to play the weak game in that space.

In the full version of our paper [28], we formulate our IBE and proof in a unified framework that can be instantiated in either prime-order groups or in composite-order groups. In the prime-order setting, we obtain the following result:

Theorem 5.1. *If SXDH holds in* $\mathbb{G} \xleftarrow{\$} \mathsf{BilinearGen}'(1^k, 8, 1, \mathcal{D})$, *where* $\mathcal{D}$ *produces the vector* $\mathbf{1}$, *then the instantiation of our IBE construction is IND-CCA1 secure.*

References

1. Adj, G., Menezes, A., Oliveira, T., Rodríguez-Henríquez, F.: Weakness of $\mathbb{F}_{3^{6\cdot509}}$ for discrete logarithm cryptography. In: Cao, Z., Zhang, F. (eds.) Pairing 2013. LNCS, vol. 8365, pp. 20–44. Springer, Heidelberg (2014)
2. Adj, G., Menezes, A., Oliveira, T., Rodríguez-Henríquez, F.: Computing discrete logarithms in $f_{3^{6\cdot137}}$ and $f_{3^{6\cdot163}}$ using magma. Cryptology ePrint Archive, Report 2014/057 (2014). http://eprint.iacr.org/2014/057
3. Akavia, A., Goldwasser, S., Vaikuntanathan, V.: Simultaneous hardcore bits and cryptography against memory attacks. In: Reingold, O. (ed.) TCC 2009. LNCS, vol. 5444, pp. 474–495. Springer, Heidelberg (2009)
4. Aranha, D.F., Beuchat, J.-L., Detrey, J., Estibals, N.: Optimal eta pairing on supersingular genus-2 binary hyperelliptic curves. In: Dunkelman, O. (ed.) CT-RSA 2012. LNCS, vol. 7178, pp. 98–115. Springer, Heidelberg (2012)
5. Aranha, D.F., Karabina, K., Longa, P., Gebotys, C.H., López, J.: Faster explicit formulas for computing pairings over ordinary curves. In: Paterson, K.G. (ed.) EUROCRYPT 2011. LNCS, vol. 6632, pp. 48–68. Springer, Heidelberg (2011)
6. Ballard, L., Green, M., de Medeiros, B., Monrose, F.: Correlation-resistant storage via keyword-searchable encryption. Cryptology ePrint Archive, Report 2005/417 (2005). http://eprint.iacr.org/
7. Boneh, D., Boyen, X.: Efficient selective-ID secure identity-based encryption without random oracles. In: Cachin, C., Camenisch, J.L. (eds.) EUROCRYPT 2004. LNCS, vol. 3027, pp. 223–238. Springer, Heidelberg (2004)
8. Boneh, D., Boyen, X., Shacham, H.: Short group signatures. In: Franklin, M. (ed.) CRYPTO 2004. LNCS, vol. 3152, pp. 41–55. Springer, Heidelberg (2004)
9. Boneh, D., Goh, E.-J., Nissim, K.: Evaluating 2-DNF formulas on ciphertexts. In: Kilian, J. (ed.) TCC 2005. LNCS, vol. 3378, pp. 325–341. Springer, Heidelberg (2005)
10. Boneh, D., Halevi, S., Hamburg, M., Ostrovsky, R.: Circular-secure encryption from decision Diffie-Hellman. In: Wagner, D. (ed.) CRYPTO 2008. LNCS, vol. 5157, pp. 108–125. Springer, Heidelberg (2008)
11. Boneh, D., Rubin, K., Silverberg, A.: Finding ordinary composite order elliptic curves using the Cocks-Pinch method. Journal of Number Theory **131**(5), 832–841 (2011)
12. Boyen, X., Waters, B.: Compact group signatures without random oracles. In: Vaudenay, S. (ed.) EUROCRYPT 2006. LNCS, vol. 4004, pp. 427–444. Springer, Heidelberg (2006)

13. Boyen, X., Waters, B.: Full-domain subgroup hiding and constant-size group signatures. In: Okamoto, T., Wang, X. (eds.) PKC 2007. LNCS, vol. 4450, pp. 1–15. Springer, Heidelberg (2007)
14. Brakerski, Z., Kalai, Y.T., Katz, J., Vaikuntanathan, V.: Overcoming the hole in the bucket: public-key cryptography resilient to continual memory leakage. In: 51st FOCS, Las Vegas, Nevada, USA, 23–26 October 2010, pp. 501–510. IEEE Computer Society Press (2010)
15. Canetti, R., Halevi, S., Katz, J.: A forward-secure public-key encryption scheme. In: Biham, E. (ed.) EUROCRYPT 2003. LNCS, vol. 2656, pp. 255–271. Springer, Heidelberg (2003)
16. Dodis, Y., Haralambiev, K., López-Alt, A., Wichs, D.: Cryptography against continuous memory attacks. In: 51st FOCS, Las Vegas, Nevada, USA, 23–26 October 2010, pp. 511–520. IEEE Computer Society Press (2010)
17. Dodis, Y., Lewko, A.B., Waters, B., Wichs, D.: Storing secrets on continually leaky devices. In: Ostrovsky, R. (ed.) 52nd FOCS, Palm Springs, California, USA, 22–25 October 2011, pp. 688–697. IEEE Computer Society Press (2011)
18. Freeman, D.M.: Converting pairing-based cryptosystems from composite-order groups to prime-order groups. In: Gilbert, H. (ed.) EUROCRYPT 2010. LNCS, vol. 6110, pp. 44–61. Springer, Heidelberg (2010)
19. Galbraith, S., Paterson, K., Smart, N.: Pairings for cryptographers. Discrete Applied Mathematics 156(16), 3113–3121 (2008)
20. Gentry, C., Lewko, A., Waters, B.: Witness encryption from instance independent assumptions. In: Garay, J.A., Gennaro, R. (eds.) CRYPTO 2014, Part I. LNCS, vol. 8616, pp. 426–443. Springer, Heidelberg (2014)
21. Göloğlu, F., Granger, R., McGuire, G., Zumbrägel, J.: On the function field sieve and the impact of higher splitting probabilities. In: Canetti, R., Garay, J.A. (eds.) CRYPTO 2013, Part II. LNCS, vol. 8043, pp. 109–128. Springer, Heidelberg (2013)
22. Guillevic, A.: Comparing the pairing efficiency over composite-order and prime-order elliptic curves. In: Jacobson, M., Locasto, M., Mohassel, P., Safavi-Naini, R. (eds.) ACNS 2013. LNCS, vol. 7954, pp. 357–372. Springer, Heidelberg (2013)
23. Hayashi, T., Shimoyama, T., Shinohara, N., Takagi, T.: Breaking pairing-based cryptosystems using η_T pairing over $gf(3^{97})$. In: Wang, X., Sako, K. (eds.) ASIACRYPT 2012. LNCS, vol. 7658, pp. 43–60. Springer, Heidelberg (2012)
24. Herold, G., Hesse, J., Hofheinz, D., Ràfols, C., Rupp, A.: Polynomial spaces: a new framework for composite-to-prime-order transformations. In: Garay, J.A., Gennaro, R. (eds.) CRYPTO 2014, Part I. LNCS, vol. 8616, pp. 261–279. Springer, Heidelberg (2014)
25. Joux, A.: Faster index calculus for the medium prime case application to 1175-bit and 1425-bit finite fields. In: Johansson, T., Nguyen, P.Q. (eds.) EUROCRYPT 2013. LNCS, vol. 7881, pp. 177–193. Springer, Heidelberg (2013)
26. Katz, J., Sahai, A., Waters, B.: Predicate encryption supporting disjunctions, polynomial equations, and inner products. In: Smart, N.P. (ed.) EUROCRYPT 2008. LNCS, vol. 4965, pp. 146–162. Springer, Heidelberg (2008)
27. Lewko, A.: Tools for simulating features of composite order bilinear groups in the prime order setting. In: Pointcheval, D., Johansson, T. (eds.) EUROCRYPT 2012. LNCS, vol. 7237, pp. 318–335. Springer, Heidelberg (2012)
28. Lewko, A., Meiklejohn, S.: A profitable sub-prime loan: obtaining the advantages of composite order in prime-order bilinear groups. Cryptology ePrint Archive, Report 2013/300 (2013). http://eprint.iacr.org/2013/300

29. Lewko, A., Okamoto, T., Sahai, A., Takashima, K., Waters, B.: Fully secure functional encryption: attribute-based encryption and (hierarchical) inner product encryption. In: Gilbert, H. (ed.) EUROCRYPT 2010. LNCS, vol. 6110, pp. 62–91. Springer, Heidelberg (2010)
30. Lewko, A., Waters, B.: New techniques for dual system encryption and fully secure HIBE with short ciphertexts. In: Micciancio, D. (ed.) TCC 2010. LNCS, vol. 5978, pp. 455–479. Springer, Heidelberg (2010)
31. Lewko, A., Waters, B.: Decentralizing attribute-based encryption. In: Paterson, K.G. (ed.) EUROCRYPT 2011. LNCS, vol. 6632, pp. 568–588. Springer, Heidelberg (2011)
32. Lewko, A., Waters, B.: Unbounded HIBE and attribute-based encryption. In: Paterson, K.G. (ed.) EUROCRYPT 2011. LNCS, vol. 6632, pp. 547–567. Springer, Heidelberg (2011)
33. Lewko, A., Waters, B.: New proof methods for attribute-based encryption: achieving full security through selective techniques. In: Safavi-Naini, R., Canetti, R. (eds.) CRYPTO 2012. LNCS, vol. 7417, pp. 180–198. Springer, Heidelberg (2012)
34. Lewko, A.B., Lewko, M., Waters, B.: How to leak on key updates. In: Fortnow, L., Vadhan, S.P. (eds.) 43rd ACM STOC, San Jose, California, USA, 6–8 June 2011, pp. 725–734. ACM Press (2011)
35. Lewko, A., Rouselakis, Y., Waters, B.: Achieving leakage resilience through dual system encryption. In: Ishai, Y. (ed.) TCC 2011. LNCS, vol. 6597, pp. 70–88. Springer, Heidelberg (2011)
36. Meiklejohn, S., Shacham, H., Freeman, D.M.: Limitations on transformations from composite-order to prime-order groups: the case of round-optimal blind signatures. In: Abe, M. (ed.) ASIACRYPT 2010. LNCS, vol. 6477, pp. 519–538. Springer, Heidelberg (2010)
37. Naor, M., Segev, G.: Public-key cryptosystems resilient to key leakage. In: Halevi, S. (ed.) CRYPTO 2009. LNCS, vol. 5677, pp. 18–35. Springer, Heidelberg (2009)
38. Okamoto, T., Takashima, K.: Homomorphic encryption and signatures from vector decomposition. In: Galbraith, S.D., Paterson, K.G. (eds.) Pairing 2008. LNCS, vol. 5209, pp. 57–74. Springer, Heidelberg (2008)
39. Okamoto, T., Takashima, K.: Hierarchical predicate encryption for inner-products. In: Matsui, M. (ed.) ASIACRYPT 2009. LNCS, vol. 5912, pp. 214–231. Springer, Heidelberg (2009)
40. Okamoto, T., Takashima, K.: Fully secure functional encryption with general relations from the decisional linear assumption. In: Rabin, T. (ed.) CRYPTO 2010. LNCS, vol. 6223, pp. 191–208. Springer, Heidelberg (2010)
41. Okamoto, T., Takashima, K.: Adaptively attribute-hiding (hierarchical) inner product encryption. In: Pointcheval, D., Johansson, T. (eds.) EUROCRYPT 2012. LNCS, vol. 7237, pp. 591–608. Springer, Heidelberg (2012)
42. Scott, M.: On the efficient implementation of pairing-based protocols. In: Chen, L. (ed.) IMACC 2011. LNCS, vol. 7089, pp. 296–308. Springer, Heidelberg (2011)
43. Seo, J.H.: On the (im)possibility of projecting property in prime-order setting. In: Wang, X., Sako, K. (eds.) ASIACRYPT 2012. LNCS, vol. 7658, pp. 61–79. Springer, Heidelberg (2012)
44. Seo, J.H., Cheon, J.H.: Beyond the limitation of prime-order bilinear groups, and round optimal blind signatures. In: Cramer, R. (ed.) TCC 2012. LNCS, vol. 7194, pp. 133–150. Springer, Heidelberg (2012)
45. Waters, B.: Dual system encryption: realizing fully secure IBE and HIBE under simple assumptions. In: Halevi, S. (ed.) CRYPTO 2009. LNCS, vol. 5677, pp. 619–636. Springer, Heidelberg (2009)

Digital Signatures II

Simpler Efficient Group Signatures from Lattices

Phong Q. Nguyen[1,2], Jiang Zhang[3], and Zhenfeng Zhang[3(✉)]

[1] INRIA, Paris, France
pnguyen@di.ens.fr,
http://www.di.ens.fr/~pnguyen
[2] Institute for Advanced Study, Tsinghua University, Beijing, China
[3] Trusted Computing and Information Assurance Laboratory,
State Key Laboratory of Computer Science, Institute of Software,
Chinese Academy of Sciences, Beijing, China
jiangzhang09@gmail.com, zfzhang@tca.iscas.ac.cn

Abstract. A group signature allows a group member to anonymously sign messages on behalf of the group. In the past few years, new group signatures based on lattice problems have appeared: the most efficient lattice-based constructions are due to Laguillaumie *et al.* (Asiacrypt '13) and Langlois *et al.* (PKC '14). Both have at least $O(n^2 \log^2 n \log N)$-bit group public key and $O(n \log^3 n \log N)$-bit signature, where n is the security parameter and N is the maximum number of group members. In this paper, we present a simpler lattice-based group signature, which is more efficient by a $O(\log N)$ factor in both the group public key and the signature size. We achieve this by using a new non-interactive zero-knowledge (NIZK) proof corresponding to a simple identity-encoding function. The security of our group signature can be reduced to the hardness of SIS and LWE in the random oracle model.

1 Introduction

In a group signature, each group member has a private key that is certified with its identity by the group manager. By using its private key, each group member is able to sign messages on behalf of the group without compromising its identity to the signature verifier. Group signatures provide users a nice tradeoff between authenticity and anonymity (*i.e.*, given a signature, the verifier is assured that someone in the group signed a message, but cannot determine which member of the group signed). However, such a functionality allows malicious group members to damage the whole group without being detected, *e.g.* signing some unauthorized/illegal messages. To avoid this, the group manager usually has a secret key which can be used to break anonymity.

Several real-life applications require properties of group signatures. For example, in trusted computing, a trusted platform module (TPM) usually has to attest

The work is supported in part by China's 973 program (No. 2013CB338003, 2013CB834205) and the National Natural Science Foundation of China (No. 61133013, 61170278, 91118006).

J. Katz (Ed.): PKC 2015, LNCS 9020, pp. 401–426, 2015.
DOI: 10.1007/978-3-662-46447-2_18

certain statements w.r.t. the current configurations of the host device to a remote party (*i.e.* the verifier) via a signature on corresponding messages. After the attestation, the verifier is assured that some remote device that contains a TPM authorized the messages. For user privacy, the signature is often required not to reveal the identity of the TPM. In fact, a variant of group signatures (namely, direct anonymous attestation (DAA) [26,33]) has been implemented in TPM 1.2 [40] and TPM 2.0 [41] by the Trusted Computing Group. Another promising application is vehicle safety communications [42], where group signatures can protect the privacy of users so that a broadcast message does not reveal the current location/speed of the vehicle. Besides, other applications of group signatures are found in anonymous communications, e-commerce systems *etc.*

Since their introduction by Chaum and van Heyst [32], group signatures have attracted much attention from the research community. Bellare, Micciancio and Warinschi (BMW) [11] formalized the security of group signatures for static groups (where the group members are fixed in the system setup phase) in two main notions, *i.e.*, *full anonymity* and *full traceability*. Informally, *full anonymity* requires that an adversary without the group manager secret key should not be able to determine the signer's identity from a signature, even if it can access an open oracle that returns the identity of any other (valid) signature. And *full traceability* implies that no collusion of group members can create a valid signature which cannot be traced back to one of them (by the group manager using the group manager secret key). Bellare *et al.* [11] also gave a theoretical construction based on the existence of trapdoor permutations. In a weak variant of the BMW model where the adversary against anonymity is not given access to the open oracle (*i.e.*, CPA-anonymity), Boneh *et al.* [16] constructed a short group signature scheme based on the Strong Diffie-Hellman (SDH) [15] and Decision Linear (DLIN) [16] assumptions in the random oracle model [13]. Besides, many papers focused on designing various group signatures based on different assumptions [1,9,20,21,28,38,39,45,46].

In recent years, lattice cryptography has attracted significant interest, due to several potential benefits: asymptotic efficiency, worst-case hardness assumptions, and security against quantum computers. A natural goal is to find lattice-based counterparts of all classical cryptographic schemes. In 2010, Gordon *et al.* [37] made the first step in constructing secure group signatures from lattices. They elegantly combined several powerful lattice-based tools [36,54,57] to build a group signature scheme where the sizes of both the group public key and signature was linear in the maximum number N of group members. Later, Camenisch el al. [29] proposed a variant of [37] with improvements both in efficiency (*i.e.*, shorter group public key) and security (*i.e.*, stronger adversary against anonymity), but the signature size of their scheme was still linear in N. Recently, two papers [43,44] have significantly decreased the signature size. By first representing the identity of group members as a bit-string [19], and then applying the "encrypt-and-prove" paradigm of [11,37], Laguillaumie *et al.* [43] constructed an efficient lattice-based group signature where both the sizes of the group public key and the signature are proportional to $\log N$ (*i.e.*, with bit-length slightly greater than $O(n^2 \log^2 n \log N)$ and $O(n \log^3 n \log N)$, respectively). Using similar identity representations together with the non-interactive zero-knowledge (NIZK) proof in [47], Langlois et al. [44] proposed a nice scheme without encryption, which achieves almost the same asymptotical efficiency as that of [43], and provides an additional property called verifier-local revocation [18]. Another interesting group signature is due to Benhamouda et al. [14], for which privacy holds under a lattice-based assumption but the security is discrete-logarithm-based, i.e. it is not a pure lattice-based group signature.

A current and independent work of Ling, Nguyen and Wang [48] also try to design an efficient lattice-based group signature scheme. Specifically, by first constructing a nice Stern-type [58] NIZK protocol, they propose a scheme which excels previous ones in [43,44] by a constant factor in terms of efficiency, i.e., all the sizes are still proportional to $\log N$. Besides, they also show how to transform their basic scheme into the setting of ideal lattices, which can save a factor of n in the size of group public key.

1.1 Our Results

In this paper, we present a new lattice-based group signature. Compared to the best previous lattice-based schemes [37,43,44], it is both simpler and more efficient, saving a $O(\log N)$ factor in both sizes of the group public key and the signature. As in [43], we first present a simple CPA-anonymous scheme, which can be easily extended to support CCA-anonymity (please refer to the full version). The security of both our schemes is provably based on the hardness of the Small Integer Solutions (SIS) and Learning with Errors (LWE) problems in the random oracle model, which are both as hard as several worst-case lattice problems, such as SIVP_γ for some polynomial factor $\gamma = poly(n)$.

In Table 1, we give a rough comparison with related lattice-based group signatures in terms of the size of the group public-key, the group user secret key and the signature. There, n denotes the security parameter, and N is the maximum number of group users. The other two parameters m and q are both polynomial in n (and N), and are usually determined by the underlying lattices used by those schemes. The integer t used in [43,44] and our scheme is a repetition parameter for obtaining NIZKs with negligible soundness error. For a security parameter n, one can set $t = \omega(\log n)$ and $m = O(n \log n)$. The choice of q might be slightly different in those schemes either for security or for functionality. For example, q is explicitly required to be larger than N in our scheme. We note that this requirement might also be satisfied in the previous three schemes for most applications. Besides, even if $N < q$ does not hold in previous schemes, the sizes of the group public-key and the signature in our scheme are still asymptotically shorter (since both N and q are polynomials in n, and $\log N = O(\log q)$ holds).

Since the schemes in [37,43] and ours follow a general "encrypt-and-prove" paradigm in [11], we also give a comparison of computational costs between the schemes in [37,43] and ours at a very high level, i.e., in terms of the number of the underlying encryptions and basic NIZK proofs, in Table 2. We note that such a comparison is less interesting to the scheme in [44], since it departs from the

Table 1. Rough Comparison of Overheads

Schemes	Group public-key	User secret-key	Signature	Security
GKV10 [37]	$O(nmN \log q)$	$O(nm \log q)$	$O(nmN \log q)$	CPA-anonymity
LLLS13 [43]	$O(nm \log N \log q)$	$O(nm \log q)$	$O(tm \log N \log q)$	CCA-anonymity
LLNW14 [44]	$O(nm \log N \log q)$	$O(m \log N \log q)$	$O(tm \log N \log q \log \beta)^\star$	CCA-anonymity
Our scheme	$O(nm \log q)$	$O(nm \log q)$	$O(t(m + \log N) \log q)^{\star\star}$	CCA-anonymity

$\star$ $\beta = \omega(\sqrt{n \log q \log n}) \log m$ is the integer norm bound in [44].
$\star\star$ Since N is always a polynomial in n (thus in m), this term is actually bounded by $O(tm \log q)$. Besides, we note that group signatures supporting opening should have a signature in bit-size at least logarithmic in N [11].

general paradigm and does not make use of any encryption. Although all three schemes use (almost) the same encryption (namely [57]), the NIZKs are very different. Concretely, Gordon *et al.* [37] used a N-OR variant of the witness-indistinguishable (WI) proof system for the gap version of the closest vector problem in [54], while the NIZKs used in [43] and ours are derived from the more efficient protocol [50] for the ISIS problem. In Table 2, we simply compare the complexity of each algorithm of the schemes in [37,43] and ours, with respect to the number of basic operations in terms of encryptions and basic NIZKs.

Table 2. Rough Comparison of Computational Costs (The encryption and decryption of Regev's LWE-based encryption [57] are denoted by enc. and dec., respectively. The proof and verification of the corresponding basic NIZKs in [50,54] are denoted by pro. and ver., respectively).

Schemes	Sign (enc.,pro.,ver.,dec.)	Verify (enc.,pro.,ver.,dec.)	Open (enc.,pro.,ver.,dec.)
GKV10 [37]	$(N, O(N), -, -)$	$(-, -, O(N), -)$	$(-, -, -, N/2)$
LLLS13 [43]	$(1 + \log N, O(\log N), -, -)$	$(-, -, O(\log N), -)$	$(-, -, -, 1 + \log N)$
Our scheme	$(1, \leq 5, -, -)$	$(-, -, \leq 5, -)$	$(-, -, -, 1)$

However, we note that we do not provide a full comparison with all the schemes in [37,43,44], which would require at least a concrete analysis of the security reduction (running time, lattice approximation factor, success probability, *etc.*), which is usually not explicitly given in the literature.

1.2   Techniques

At a high level, the two constructions in [37,43] and our scheme use the same general paradigm as that of [11]. Roughly speaking, the group manager first generates the group public key gpk and group manager secret key $gmsk$. For a user with identity $i \in \{1, \ldots, N\}$ (recall that N is the maximum number of group members, and is fixed at the system setup), the group manager computes the user's secret key gsk_i corresponding to an encoded "public key" $H(gpk, i)$, where H is an encoding function that (uniquely) encodes the group user's identity i in

gsk_i. When signing a message m, the group user proves to the verifier that he has a secret key gsk_i for some $i \in \{1, \ldots, N\}$ (*i.e.*, to prove that he is a legal member of the group). The hardness of this general paradigm usually lies in the choices of an appropriate encoding function $H(gpk, i)$ and a compatible non-interactive zero-knowledge (NIZK) for the membership relations determined by $H(gpk, i)$.

Gordon *et al.* [37] used a simple projective encoding function $H(gpk, i)$ and a NIZK extended from [54] to construct the first lattice-based group signature. Informally, the group public key gpk consists of N independent public keys of the GPV signature [36], *i.e.*, $gpk = (pk_1, \ldots, pk_N)$ where pk_j is an integer matrix over $\mathbb{Z}_q$ for some positive $q \in \mathbb{Z}$, and all $j \in \{1, \ldots, N\}$. The encoding function simply outputs the i-th element of gpk, *i.e.*, $H(gpk, i) := pk_i$. Due to the particular choice of $H(gpk, i)$, both the group public key and the signature of [37] have a size linear in N.

At Asiacrypt '13, by using an efficient encoding function inspired by Boyen's lattice-based signature [19] and a NIZK derived from [50], Laguillaumie *et al.* [43] proposed a more efficient lattice-based group signature. Roughly speaking, the group public key gpk consists of $\ell = \lfloor \log N \rfloor + 1$ independent matrices over $\mathbb{Z}_q$, *i.e.*, $gpk = (\mathbf{A}_1, \ldots, \mathbf{A}_\ell)$. The encoding function is defined as $H(gpk, i) := \sum_{j=1}^{\ell} i_j \mathbf{A}_j$, where $(i_1, \ldots, i_l) \in \mathbb{Z}_2^\ell$ is the binary decomposition of i. We also note that Langlois *et al.* [44] constructed a lattice-based group signature with verifier-local revocation by using the same identity encoding function but a different NIZK from [47]. Both schemes [43, 44] decreased the sizes of the group public key and the signature to proportional to $\log N$.

An Efficient Identity Encoding. We use a more efficient and compact way to encode the group member's identity, by building upon the encoding technique introduced by Agrawal *et al.* [2] for identity-based encryption (IBE). Let the group public key gpk consist of three matrices over $\mathbb{Z}_q^{n \times m}$ for some positive integers n, m, q, *i.e.*, $gpk = (\mathbf{A}_1, \mathbf{A}_{2,1}, \mathbf{A}_{2,2})$. We define $H(gpk, i) = \hat{\mathbf{A}}_i :=$ $(\mathbf{A}_1 \| \mathbf{A}_{2,1} + G(i)\mathbf{A}_{2,2})$ where $G(\cdot)$ is a function from $\mathbb{Z}_N$ to $\mathbb{Z}_q^{n \times n}$. Then, the secret key of user i is a short basis of the classical q-ary lattice Λ_i determined by $H(gpk, i) = \hat{\mathbf{A}}_i$, where $\Lambda_i := \{\mathbf{e} \in \mathbb{Z}^m \ \text{s.t.} \ \hat{\mathbf{A}}_i \mathbf{e} = \mathbf{0} \mod q\}$. When signing a message, user i samples a short vector $\mathbf{e}_i$ from Λ_i (by using the short basis of Λ_i) and encrypts it using Regev's encryption [57]. Then, he proves to the verifier that $\mathbf{e}_i$ is a short vector in a lattice determined by $H(gpk, i)$ for some $i \in \{1, \ldots, N\}$. But we do not know an efficient lattice-based NIZK suitable for the membership relation determined by $H(gpk, i)$.

Fortunately, since the maximum number of group members N is always bounded by a polynomial in the security parameter n, we actually do not need an encoding function as powerful as for IBE [2], where there are possibly exponentially many users. We simplify the encoding function by defining $H(gpk, i) := (\mathbf{A}_1 \| \mathbf{A}_{2,1} + i\mathbf{A}_{2,2})$. (A similar combination of matrices has been used in a different way in [4, 17, 35] to construct functional encryption.) Namely, the identity function $G(i) := i$ is used instead of a function $G : \mathbb{Z}_N \to \mathbb{Z}_q^{n \times n}$. For collision resistance, we require that $N < q$. Since N is usually fixed at the system setup in group signatures for static groups such as [37,43,44] and ours, one can simply set q big enough (but still a polynomial in n) to satisfy the requirement. Hereafter, we assume that $N < q$ always holds.

This encoding function provides two main benefits:

- Only three matrices are needed for the encoding function, which provides a short group public key. By comparison, there are respectively at least $O(N)$ and $O(\log N)$ matrices needed in [37] and [43].
- It gives a simple membership relation, which allows to construct an efficient NIZK proof for the relation (please see next paragraph). In [37,43], the NIZKs for relatively complex membership relations are obtained by involving many encryptions, which results in schemes with large computational costs and signature sizes.

A New Non-interactive Zero-Knowledge (NIZK). Recall that the secret key of user i is a short basis $\mathbf{T}_i$ of the q-ary lattice Λ_i determined by $\hat{\mathbf{A}}_i = (\mathbf{A}_1 \| \mathbf{A}_{2,1} + i\mathbf{A}_{2,2})$. To sign a message, user i first samples a short vector $(\mathbf{x}_1, \mathbf{x}_2)$ by using Gentry *et al.*'s Gaussian sampling algorithm [36] such that $\mathbf{A}_1\mathbf{x}_1 + (\mathbf{A}_{2,1} + i\mathbf{A}_{2,2})\mathbf{x}_2 = 0 \mod q$. Then, he generates an LWE encryption $\mathbf{c}$ of $\mathbf{x}_1$. The final signature σ consists of $\mathbf{c}, \mathbf{x}_2$, a proof π_1 that $\mathbf{c}$ encrypts $\mathbf{x}_1$ correctly, and a proof π_2 that there exists a tuple $(\mathbf{x}_1, i)$ satisfying $\mathbf{A}_1\mathbf{x}_1 + i\mathbf{A}_{2,2}\mathbf{x}_2 = -\mathbf{A}_{2,1}\mathbf{x}_2 \mod q$, namely, $\sigma = (\mathbf{c}, \mathbf{x}_2, \pi_1, \pi_2)$.

The nice properties of the sampling algorithm in [31,36] guarantee that the public $\mathbf{x}_2$ is statistically indistinguishable for all user $i \in \{1, \ldots, N\}$, namely, the verifier cannot determine the signer's identity i solely from $\mathbf{x}_2$, however, he can efficiently determine it from $(\mathbf{x}_1, \mathbf{x}_2)$, that's why we choose to encrypt $\mathbf{x}_1$. The proof of π_1 can be generated by using the duality of LWE and Small Integer Solutions (SIS) [51], and the NIZK proof for SIS [50] in a standard way. Thanks to our new identity encoding function $H(gpk, i)$ and the public $\mathbf{x}_2$, we manage to design a NIZK proof (*i.e.*, π_2) for the statement $\mathbf{A}_1\mathbf{x}_1 + i\mathbf{A}_{2,2}\mathbf{x}_2 = -\mathbf{A}_{2,1}\mathbf{x}_2 \mod q$ based on the hardness of SIS.

Formally, we introduce a new problem called split-SIS, which is a variant of SIS (and might be of independent interest). Given a split-SIS instance $\mathbf{A}_1, \mathbf{A}_{2,2} \in \mathbb{Z}_q^{n \times m}$, the algorithm is asked to output a triple $(\mathbf{x}_1, \mathbf{x}_2, h)$ such that $\mathbf{x}_1, \mathbf{x}_2 \in \mathbb{Z}^m$ have small norms, and $h < q = poly(n)$ is a positive integer satisfying $\mathbf{A}_1\mathbf{x}_1 + h\mathbf{A}_{2,2}\mathbf{x}_2 = 0 \mod q$. We first show that the split-SIS problem (associated with an appropriate solution space) is polynomially equivalent to the standard SIS problem. Then, we derive a family of hash functions

$$\mathcal{H} = \left\{ \begin{array}{l} f_{\mathbf{A}_1, \mathbf{A}_{2,2}}(\mathbf{x}_1, \mathbf{x}_2, h) = (\mathbf{A}_1\mathbf{x}_1 + h\mathbf{A}_{2,2}\mathbf{x}_2 \mod q, \mathbf{x}_2) : \\ \qquad\qquad\qquad (\mathbf{x}_1, \mathbf{x}_2, h) \in \mathbb{Z}^m \times \mathbb{Z}^m \times \mathbb{Z} \end{array} \right\}_{\mathbf{A}_1, \mathbf{A}_{2,2} \in \mathbb{Z}_q^{n \times m}}$$

from our split-SIS problem, and prove that the hash function family $\mathcal{H}$ with appropriate domain is *one-way*, *collision-resistant*, and *statistically hiding* with respect to the third input (*i.e.*, h). Combining those useful properties with the observation that $\mathbf{A}_1\mathbf{x}_1 + h\mathbf{A}_{2,2}\mathbf{x}_2 = (\mathbf{A}_1 \| \mathbf{A}_{2,2}\mathbf{x}_2)(\mathbf{x}_1; h) \mod q$, we manage to adapt a Σ-protocol for $\mathcal{H}$ from existing protocols for standard ISIS problems [43, 49, 50], which can in turn be transformed into a NIZK using the Fiat-Shamir transformation in the random oracle model. This finally helps us obtain a lattice-based group signature scheme with $O(tm \log q)$-bit signature, where the repetition parameter $t = \omega(\log n)$ is due to our NIZK as in [43, 44].

In order to open a signature $\sigma = (\mathbf{c}, \mathbf{x}_2, \pi_1, \pi_2)$, the group manager only has to decrypt $\mathbf{c}$ to obtain $\mathbf{x}_1$, and computes an integer $h < q$ satisfying $\mathbf{A}_1 \mathbf{x}_1 + h \mathbf{A}_{2,2} \mathbf{x}_2 = -\mathbf{A}_{2,1} \mathbf{x}_2 \mod q$. Note that such an integer is unique if $\mathbf{A}_{2,2} \mathbf{x}_2 \neq \mathbf{0}$ $\mod q$ for prime q. Replacing the CPA-encryption of $\mathbf{x}_1$ with a CCA one (i.e., by applying the CHK transformation [30] to the IBEs [2, 36]), we obtain a CCA-anonymous group signature at a minimal price of doubling the sizes of the group public key and the signature.

1.3 On Membership Revocation

A group signature with opening allows the group manager to break the anonymity of any valid signature, however, it cannot prevent a malicious group member from using his certificate. In practice, it may be desirable to support membership revocation, e.g., to revoke the certificate of a malicious group member such that he cannot sign any message in the future. Actually, membership revocation is an important and complex problem and has been extensively studied in the literature [10, 18, 25, 27, 45, 46]. In [44], Langlois et al. constructed a lattice-based group signature with verifier-local revocation, which was the first lattice-based group signatures supporting membership revocation and achieved the same asymptotic efficiency as that of [43]. For now, we do not know how to construct a simpler and efficient group signature with membership revocation from lattices.

1.4 Roadmap

After some preliminaries, we recall several useful tools and algorithms on lattices in Section 3. In Section 4, we introduce the split-SIS problems, and construct a NIZK proof for the split-SIS problems. We finally present our CPA-anonymous group signature scheme in Section 5. The description of our CCA-anonymous group signature scheme is deferred to the full version.

2 Preliminaries

2.1 Notation

The set of real numbers (integers) is denoted by $\mathbb{R}$ ($\mathbb{Z}$, resp.). By $\leftarrow_R$ we denote randomly choosing elements from some distribution (or the uniform distribution over some finite set). For a variable x following some distribution D, we denote it by $x \backsim D$. For any integer $N \in \mathbb{Z}$, we denote by $[N]$ the set of integers $\{0, 1, \ldots, N - 1\}$. Vectors are in column form and denoted by bold lower-case letters (e.g., $\mathbf{x}$). We view a matrix simply as the set of its column vectors and denoted by bold capital letters (*e.g.*, $\mathbf{X}$). Denote the l_2 and l_∞ norm by $\|\cdot\|$ and $\|\cdot\|_\infty$, respectively. Define the norm of a matrix $\mathbf{X}$ as the norm of its longest column (*i.e.*, $\|\mathbf{X}\| = \max_i \|\mathbf{x}_i\|$). If the columns of $\mathbf{X} = (\mathbf{x}_1, \ldots, \mathbf{x}_k)$ are linearly independent, let $\widetilde{\mathbf{X}} = (\widetilde{\mathbf{x}}_1, \ldots, \widetilde{\mathbf{x}}_k)$ denote the Gram-Schmidt orthogonalization of vectors $\mathbf{x}_1, \ldots, \mathbf{x}_k$ taken in that order. For $\mathbf{X} \in \mathbb{R}^{n \times m}$ and $\mathbf{Y} \in \mathbb{R}^{n \times m'}$, $(\mathbf{X}\|\mathbf{Y}) \in \mathbb{R}^{n \times (m+m')}$ denotes the concatenation of the columns of $\mathbf{X}$ followed by the columns of $\mathbf{Y}$. Similarly, for $\mathbf{X} \in \mathbb{R}^{n \times m}$ and $\mathbf{Y} \in \mathbb{R}^{n' \times m}$, $(\mathbf{X}; \mathbf{Y}) \in \mathbb{R}^{(n+n') \times m}$ is the concatenation of the rows of $\mathbf{X}$ followed by the rows of $\mathbf{Y}$.

Throughout this paper, we let n be the natural security parameter, so that all quantities are implicitly dependent on n. The function log denotes the natural logarithm. We will frequently use the standard notation of O, ω for classifying the growth of functions. If $f(n) = O(g(n) \cdot \log^c(n))$ for some constant c, we write $f(n) = \tilde{O}(g(n))$. By $poly(n)$ we denote some arbitrary $f(n) = O(n^c)$ for some c. We say that a function $f(n)$ is negligible if for every positive c, we have $f(n) < n^{-c}$ for sufficiently large n. We denote an arbitrary such function by $negl(n)$, and say that a probability is overwhelming if it is $1 - negl(n)$.

2.2   Group Signatures

We recall the definition and security model of group signatures. A (static) group signature scheme $\mathcal{GS}$ consists of a tuple of four Probabilistic Polynomial Time (PPT) algorithms (KeyGen, Sign, Verify, Open):

– KeyGen($1^n, 1^N$): Take the security parameter n and the maximum number of group members N as inputs, output the group public key gpk, the group manager secret key $gmsk$ and a vector of users' keys $\mathbf{gsk} = (gsk_1, \ldots, gsk_N)$, where gsk_j is the j-th user's secret key for $j \in \{1, \ldots, N\}$.
– Sign(gpk, gsk_j, M): Take the group public key gpk, the j-th user's secret key gsk_j, and a message $M \in \{0,1\}^*$ as inputs, output a signature σ of M.
– Verify(gpk, M, σ): Take the group public key gpk, a message $M \in \{0,1\}^*$ and a string σ as inputs, return 1 if σ is a valid signature of M, else return 0.
– Open($gpk, gmsk, M, \sigma$): Take the group public key gpk, the group manager secret key $gmsk$, a message $M \in \{0,1\}^*$, and a valid signature σ of M as inputs, output an index $j \in \{1, \ldots, N\}$ or a special symbol $\perp$ in case of opening failure.

For correctness, we require that for any $(gpk, gmsk, \mathbf{gsk}) \leftarrow$ KeyGen($1^n, 1^N$), any $j \in \{1, \ldots, N\}$, any message $M \in \{0,1\}^*$, and any $\sigma \leftarrow$ Sign(gpk, gsk_j, M), the following conditions hold with overwhelming probability:

$$\mathsf{Verify}(gpk, M, \sigma) = 1 \ and \ \mathsf{Open}(gpk, gmsk, M, \sigma) = j$$

For group signatures, there are two security notions: anonymity and traceability [11]. The first notion, informally, says that anyone without the group manager secret key cannot determine the owner of a valid signature. The second notion says a set C of group members cannot collude to create a valid signature such that the Open algorithm fails to trace back to one of them. In particular, this notion implies that any non-group member cannot create a valid signature.

Experiment $\mathbf{Exp}_{\mathcal{GS},\mathcal{A}}^{\mathrm{anon}}(n, N)$
$\quad (gpk, gmsk, \mathbf{gsk}) \leftarrow \mathsf{KeyGen}(1^n, 1^N)$
$\quad (st, i_0, i_1, M^*) \leftarrow \mathcal{A}^{\mathsf{Open}(\cdot, \cdot)}(gpk, \mathbf{gsk})$
$\quad b \leftarrow_R \{0, 1\}$
$\quad \sigma^* \leftarrow \mathsf{Sign}(gpk, gsk_{i_b}, M^*)$
$\quad b' \leftarrow \mathcal{A}^{\mathsf{Open}(\cdot, \cdot)}(st, \sigma^*)$
$\quad$ If $b = b'$ return 1, else return 0

Experiment $\mathbf{Exp}_{\mathcal{GS},\mathcal{A}}^{\mathrm{trace}}(n, N)$
$\quad (gpk, gmsk, \mathbf{gsk}) \leftarrow \mathsf{KeyGen}(1^n, 1^N)$
$\quad (M^*, \sigma^*) \leftarrow \mathcal{A}^{\mathsf{Sign}(\cdot, \cdot), \mathsf{Corrupt}(\cdot)}(gpk, gmsk)$
$\quad$ If $\mathsf{Verify}(gpk, M^*, \sigma^*) = 0$ then return 0
$\quad$ If $\mathsf{Open}(gmsk, M^*, \sigma^*) = \perp$ then return 1
$\quad$ If $\exists j^* \in \{1, \ldots, N\}$ such that
$\qquad \mathsf{Open}(gpk, gmsk, M^*, \sigma^*) = j^*$ and $j^* \notin C$,
$\qquad$ and (j^*, M^*) was not queried to $\mathsf{Sign}(\cdot, \cdot)$ by $\mathcal{A}$,
$\qquad$ then return 1, else return 0

Fig. 1. Security games for group signatures

Definition 1 (Full anonymity). *For any (static) group signature scheme $\mathcal{GS}$, we associate to an adversary $\mathcal{A}$ against the full anonymity of $\mathcal{GS}$ experiment $\mathbf{Exp}_{\mathcal{GS},\mathcal{A}}^{\mathrm{anon}}(n, N)$ in the left-side of Fig. 1, where the Open$(\cdot, \cdot)$ oracle takes a valid message-signature pair (M, σ) as inputs, outputs the index of the user whose secret key is used to create σ. In the guess phase, the adversary $\mathcal{A}$ is not allowed to make an Open query with inputs (M^*, σ^*). We define the advantage of $\mathcal{A}$ in the experiment as*

$$\mathrm{Adv}_{\mathcal{GS},\mathcal{A}}^{\mathrm{anon}}(n, N) = \left| \Pr[\mathbf{Exp}_{\mathcal{GS},\mathcal{A}}^{\mathrm{anon}}(n, N) = 1] - \frac{1}{2} \right|.$$

A group signature $\mathcal{GS}$ is said to be fully anonymous if the advantage $\mathrm{Adv}_{\mathcal{GS},\mathcal{A}}^{\mathrm{anon}}(n, N)$ is negligible in n, N for any PPT adversary $\mathcal{A}$.

In a weak definition of anonymity (*i.e.*, CPA-anonymity), the adversary is not given access to an open oracle. In this paper, we first present a CPA-anonymous scheme, then we extend it to satisfy full/CCA anonymity.

Definition 2 (Full traceability). *For any (static) group signature scheme $\mathcal{GS}$, we associate to an adversary $\mathcal{A}$ against the full traceability of $\mathcal{GS}$ experiment $\mathbf{Exp}_{\mathcal{GS},\mathcal{A}}^{\mathrm{trace}}(n, N)$ in the right-side of Fig. 1, where the Sign$(\cdot, \cdot)$ oracle takes a user index i and a message M as inputs, returns a signature of M by using gsk_i. The Corrupt$(\cdot)$ oracle takes a user index i as input, returns gsk_i, and C is a set of user indexes that $\mathcal{A}$ submitted to the Corrupt$(\cdot)$ oracle. The advantage of $\mathcal{A}$ in the experiment is defined as*

$$\mathrm{Adv}_{\mathcal{GS},\mathcal{A}}^{\mathrm{trace}}(n, N) = \Pr[\mathbf{Exp}_{\mathcal{GS},\mathcal{A}}^{\mathrm{trace}}(n, N) = 1].$$

A group signature $\mathcal{GS}$ is said to be fully traceable if the advantage $\mathrm{Adv}_{\mathcal{GS},\mathcal{A}}^{\mathrm{trace}}(n, N)$ is negligible in n, N for any PPT adversary $\mathcal{A}$.

3   Lattices and Discrete Gaussians

An m-rank lattice $\Lambda \subset \mathbb{R}^n$ is the set of all integral combinations of m linearly independent vectors $\mathbf{B} = (\mathbf{b}_1, \ldots, \mathbf{b}_m) \in \mathbb{R}^{n \times m}$, i.e., $\Lambda = \mathcal{L}(\mathbf{B}) = \left\{ \sum_{i=1}^m x_i \mathbf{b}_i : x_i \in \mathbb{Z} \right\}$. The dual lattice of Λ is defined to be $\Lambda^* = \left\{ \mathbf{x} \in \text{span}(\Lambda) : \forall\, \mathbf{v} \in \Lambda, \langle \mathbf{x}, \mathbf{v} \rangle \in \mathbb{Z} \right\}$.

For $\mathbf{x} \in \Lambda$, define the Gaussian function $\rho_{s,\mathbf{c}}(\mathbf{x})$ over $\Lambda \subseteq \mathbb{Z}^n$ centered at $\mathbf{c} \in \mathbb{R}^n$ with parameter $s > 0$ as $\rho_{s,\mathbf{c}}(\mathbf{x}) = \exp\left(-\pi \|\mathbf{x} - \mathbf{c}\|^2 / s^2 \right)$. Letting $\rho_{s,\mathbf{c}}(\Lambda) = \sum_{\mathbf{x} \in \Lambda} \rho_{s,\mathbf{c}}(\mathbf{x})$, define the discrete Gaussian distribution over Λ as $D_{\Lambda,s,\mathbf{c}}(\mathbf{y}) = \frac{\rho_{s,\mathbf{c}}(\mathbf{y})}{\rho_{s,\mathbf{c}}(\Lambda)}$, where $\mathbf{y} \in \Lambda$. The subscripts s and $\mathbf{c}$ are taken to be 1 and $\mathbf{0}$ (respectively) when omitted. For large enough s, almost all the elements from $D_{\Lambda,s,\mathbf{c}}$ are not far from $\mathbf{c}$.

Lemma 1 ([36,53]). *For any n-dimensional lattice Λ with basis $\mathbf{B} \in \mathbb{R}^{n \times n}$, vector $\mathbf{c} \in \mathbb{R}^n$, and reals $\epsilon \in (0,1)$, $s \geq \|\widetilde{\mathbf{B}}\| \cdot \omega(\sqrt{\log n})$, we have $\Pr_{\mathbf{x} \leftarrow_R D_{\Lambda,s,\mathbf{c}}}[\|\mathbf{x} - \mathbf{c}\| > s\sqrt{n}] \leq \frac{1-\epsilon}{1+\epsilon} \cdot 2^{-n}$.*

For any $\alpha \in \mathbb{R}^+$, integer $q \in \mathbb{Z}$, let Ψ_α be the distribution over $\mathbb{T} = \mathbb{R}/\mathbb{Z}$ of a normal variable with mean 0 and standard deviation $\alpha/\sqrt{2\pi}$, reduced modulo 1. The discrete distribution $\bar{\Psi}_\alpha$ over $\mathbb{Z}_q$ is the random variable $\lfloor q \cdot X \rceil \bmod q$, where $X \leftarrow_R \Psi_\alpha$. For simplicity, we denote $\chi_\alpha := \bar{\Psi}_\alpha$.

Lemma 2 ([3]). *Let $\mathbf{e}$ be some vector in $\mathbb{Z}^m$ and let $\mathbf{y} \leftarrow_R \chi_\alpha^m$. Then the quantity $|\mathbf{e}^T \mathbf{y}|$ treated as an integer in $[0, q-1]$ satisfies $|\mathbf{e}^T \mathbf{y}| \leq \|\mathbf{e}\| q \alpha \omega(\sqrt{\log m}) + \|\mathbf{e}\| \sqrt{m}/2$ with all but negligible probability in m. In particular, if $x \leftarrow_R \chi_\alpha$ is treated as an integer in $[0, q-1]$ then $|x| \leq q \alpha \omega(\sqrt{\log m}) + 1/2$ with all but negligible probability in m.*

We also need the following three useful facts from the literature:

Lemma 3 ([36]). *Let n be a positive integer, q be a prime, and $m \geq 2n \log q$. Then for all but a $2q^{-n}$ fraction of all $\mathbf{A} \in \mathbb{Z}_q^{n \times m}$ and for any $s \geq \omega(\sqrt{\log m})$, the distribution of $\mathbf{u} = \mathbf{A}\mathbf{e} \bmod q$ is statistically close to uniform over $\mathbb{Z}_q^n$, where $\mathbf{e} \leftarrow_R D_{\mathbb{Z}^m, s}$.*

3.1   Learning with Errors (LWE) and Small Integer Solutions (SIS)

Let $n \in \mathbb{Z}^+$ and $q = q(n)$ be integers, $\alpha \in \mathbb{R}^+$, χ_α be some discrete Gaussian distribution over $\mathbb{Z}_q$, and $\mathbf{s} \in \mathbb{Z}_q^n$ be some vector. Define $A_{\mathbf{s}, \chi_\alpha} \subseteq \mathbb{Z}_q^n \times \mathbb{Z}_q$ as the distribution of the variable $(\mathbf{a}, \mathbf{a}^T \mathbf{s} + x)$, where $\mathbf{a} \leftarrow_R \mathbb{Z}_q^n$, $x \leftarrow_R \chi_\alpha$, and all the operations are performed in $\mathbb{Z}_q$. For m independent samples $(\mathbf{a}_1, y_1), \ldots, (\mathbf{a}_m, y_m)$ from $A_{\mathbf{s}, \chi_\alpha}$, we denote it in matrix form $(\mathbf{A}, \mathbf{y}) \in \mathbb{Z}_q^{n \times m} \times \mathbb{Z}_q^m$, where $\mathbf{A} = (\mathbf{a}_1, \ldots, \mathbf{a}_m)$ and $\mathbf{y} = (y_1, \ldots, y_m)^T$. We say that an algorithm solves $\text{LWE}_{q, \chi_\alpha}$ if, for randomly chosen $\mathbf{s} \in \mathbb{Z}_q^n$, given polynomial samples from $A_{\mathbf{s}, \chi_\alpha}$ it outputs s with overwhelming probability. The decisional variant of LWE is that, for a uniformly chosen $\mathbf{s} \leftarrow_R \mathbb{Z}_q^n$, an algorithm is asked to distinguish $A_{\mathbf{s},\chi_\alpha}$ from the uniform distribution over $\mathbb{Z}_q^n \times \mathbb{Z}_q$ (with only polynomial samples). For certain modulus q, the average-case decisional LWE problem is polynomially equivalent to its worst-case search version [8,55,57].

Proposition 1 ([57]). *Let $\alpha = \alpha(n) \in (0,1)$ and let $q = q(n)$ be a prime such that $\alpha q > 2\sqrt{n}$. If there exists an efficient (possibly quantum) algorithm that solves LWE_{q,χ_α}, then there exists an efficient quantum algorithm for approximating SIVP in the l_2 norm, in the worst case, to within $\tilde{O}(n/\alpha)$ factors.*

The Small Integer Solution (SIS) problem was introduced by Ajtai [5], but its name is due to Micciancio and Regev [53], who improved Ajtai's connection between SIS and worst-case lattice problems.

Definition 3 (Small Integer Solution). *The Small Integer Solution (SIS) problem in l_2 norm is: Given an integer q, a uniformly random matrix $\mathbf{A} \in \mathbb{Z}_q^{n \times m}$, and a real β, find a non-zero integer vector $\mathbf{e} \in \mathbb{Z}^m$ such that $\mathbf{Ae} = \mathbf{0}$ (mod q) and $\|\mathbf{e}\| \leq \beta$.*

Definition 4 (Inhomogeneous Small Integer Solution). *The Inhomogeneous Small Integer Solution (ISIS) problem in l_2 norm is: Given an integer q, a uniformly random matrix $\mathbf{A} \in \mathbb{Z}_q^{n \times m}$, a random syndrome $\mathbf{u} \in \mathbb{Z}_q^n$, and real $\beta \in \mathbb{R}$, find an integer vector $\mathbf{e} \in \mathbb{Z}^m$ such that $\mathbf{Ae} = \mathbf{u}$ (mod q) and $\|\mathbf{e}\| \leq \beta$.*

The ISIS problem is an inhomogenous variant of SIS. Both problems were shown to be as hard as certain worst-case lattice problems.

Proposition 2 ([36]). *For any polynomially bounded $m, \beta = poly(n)$ and prime $q \geq \beta \cdot \omega(\sqrt{n \log n})$, the average-case problems $SIS_{q,m,\beta}$ and $ISIS_{q,m,\beta}$ are as hard as approximating SIVP in the worst case to within certain $\gamma = \beta \cdot \tilde{O}(\sqrt{n})$ factors.*

3.2 q-ary Lattices and Trapdoors

Let $\mathbf{A} \in \mathbb{Z}_q^{n \times m}$ for some positive integers n, m and q. Consider the following two integer lattices:

$$\Lambda_q^\perp(\mathbf{A}) = \left\{ \mathbf{e} \in \mathbb{Z}^m \ s.t. \ \mathbf{Ae} = 0 \mod q \right\}$$

$$\Lambda_q(\mathbf{A}) = \left\{ \mathbf{y} \in \mathbb{Z}^m \ s.t. \ \exists \mathbf{s} \in \mathbb{Z}^n, \ \mathbf{A}^T\mathbf{s} = \mathbf{y} \mod q \right\}$$

The two q-ary lattices defined above are dual when properly scaled, namely $\Lambda_q^\perp(\mathbf{A}) = q\Lambda_q(\mathbf{A})^*$ and $\Lambda_q(\mathbf{A}) = q\Lambda_q^\perp(\mathbf{A})^*$. Moreover, for any $h \in \mathbb{Z}_q^*$, we have: $\Lambda_q^\perp(\mathbf{A}) = \Lambda_q^\perp(h\mathbf{A})$.

In 1999, Ajtai [6] showed how to sample an essentially uniform matrix $\mathbf{A}$ together with a short basis of $\Lambda_q^\perp(\mathbf{A})$. This trapdoor generation algorithm has been significantly improved in [7,52].

Proposition 3 ([7]). *For any $\delta_0 > 0$, there is a PPT algorithm* TrapGen *that, on input a security parameter n, an odd prime $q = poly(n)$, and integer $m \geq (5 + 3\delta_0)n \log q$, outputs a statistically $(mq^{-\delta_0 n/2})$-close to uniform matrix $\mathbf{A} \in \mathbb{Z}_q^{n \times m}$ and a basis $\mathbf{T_A} \subset \Lambda_q^{\perp}(\mathbf{A})$ such that with overwhelming probability $\|\mathbf{T_A}\| \leq O(n \log q)$ and $\|\tilde{\mathbf{T}}_\mathbf{A}\| \leq O(\sqrt{n \log q}) = O(\sqrt{m})$. In particular, if let $\delta_0 = \frac{1}{3}$, we can choose $m \geq \lceil 6n \log q \rceil$.*

The following proposition is implied by [31, Lem.3.2andLem.3.3] which shows that there is an efficient algorithm to extract a random basis for $(\mathbf{A}\|\mathbf{B})$ by using a short basis of $\mathbf{A}$ such that the new basis statistically hides the information of its input basis.

Proposition 4 ([31]). *There is a PPT algorithm* ExtRndBasis *which takes a matrix $\mathbf{A}' = (\mathbf{A}\|\mathbf{B}) \in \mathbb{Z}_q^{n \times (m+m')}$, a basis $\mathbf{T_A} \in \mathbb{Z}_q^{m \times m}$ of $\Lambda_q^{\perp}(\mathbf{A})$, an arbitrary matrix $\mathbf{B} \in \mathbb{Z}_q^{n \times m'}$, and a real $s \geq \|\tilde{\mathbf{T}}_\mathbf{A}\| \cdot \omega(\sqrt{\log m})$ as inputs, outputs a random basis $\mathbf{T_{A'}}$ of $\Lambda_q^{\perp}(\mathbf{A}')$ satisfying $\|\mathbf{T_{A'}}\| \leq s(m + m')$ and $\|\tilde{\mathbf{T}}_{\mathbf{A}'}\| \leq s\sqrt{m + m'}$.*

Equipped with the above proposition, and the proof technique of [2, Th.4], we obtain the following useful proposition:

Proposition 5. *Let $q > 2, m > n$, there is a PPT algorithm* ExtBasisRight *which takes matrix $\mathbf{A}' = (\mathbf{C}\|\mathbf{A}\|\mathbf{AR} + \mathbf{B}) \in \mathbb{Z}_q^{n \times (2m+m')}$, a uniformly and randomly chosen $\mathbf{R} \in \{-1, 1\}^{m \times m}$, a basis $\mathbf{T_B}$ of $\Lambda_q^{\perp}(\mathbf{B})$, arbitrary $\mathbf{C} \in \mathbb{Z}_q^{n \times m'}$ and a Gaussian parameter $s > \|\tilde{\mathbf{T}}_\mathbf{B}\| \cdot \sqrt{m}\omega(\log m)$, outputs a basis $\mathbf{T_{A'}}$ of $\Lambda_q^{\perp}(\mathbf{A}')$ satisfying $\|\mathbf{T_{A'}}\| \leq s(2m + m')$ and $\|\tilde{\mathbf{T}}_{\mathbf{A}'}\| \leq s\sqrt{2m + m'}$.*

Proof. As shown in the proof of [2, Th.4], we can use $\mathbf{T_B}$ to efficiently sample a basis $\mathbf{T}_{\hat{\mathbf{A}}}$ for the matrix $\hat{\mathbf{A}} = (\mathbf{A}\|\mathbf{AR} + \mathbf{B})$ satisfying $\|\tilde{\mathbf{T}}_{\hat{\mathbf{A}}}\| \leq \|\tilde{\mathbf{T}}_\mathbf{B}\| \cdot \sqrt{m}\omega(\sqrt{\log m})$, then we can apply Proposition 4 to obtain a basis $\mathbf{T_{A'}}$ for $\mathbf{A}' = (\mathbf{C}\|\hat{\mathbf{A}})$ satisfying $\|\tilde{\mathbf{T}}_{\mathbf{A}'}\| \leq s\sqrt{2m + m'}$. Besides, by the property of the ExtRndBasis algorithm, the claim still holds no matter how the (columns of) matrix $\mathbf{C}$ appears in $\mathbf{A}'$. □

The following SuperSamp algorithm allows us to sample a random matrix $\mathbf{B}$ together with a short basis such that the columns of $\mathbf{B}$ lie in a prescribed affine subspace of $\mathbb{Z}_q^n$.

Proposition 6 ([43]). *Let $q > 2, m > \lceil 6n \log q + n \rceil$, there is a PPT algorithm* SuperSamp *which takes matrices $\mathbf{A} \in \mathbb{Z}_q^{n \times m}$ and $\mathbf{C} \in \mathbb{Z}_q^{n \times n}$ as inputs, and outputs an almost uniform matrix $\mathbf{B} \in \mathbb{Z}_q^{n \times m}$ such that $\mathbf{AB}^T = \mathbf{C}$, and a basis $\mathbf{T_B}$ of $\Lambda_q^{\perp}(\mathbf{B})$ satisfying $\|\mathbf{T}_B\| \leq m^{1.5} \cdot \omega(\sqrt{\log m})$ and $\|\tilde{\mathbf{T}}_B\| \leq m \cdot \omega(\sqrt{\log m})$.*

Given a basis of $\Lambda_q^{\perp}(\mathbf{A})$, there is an efficient algorithm to solve the (I)SIS problem as follows.

Proposition 7 ([36]). *There is a PPT algorithm* SamplePre *that, given a basis $\mathbf{T_A}$ of $\Lambda_q^{\perp}(\mathbf{A})$, a real $s \geq \|\tilde{\mathbf{T}}_\mathbf{A}\| \cdot \omega(\sqrt{\log m})$ and a vector $\mathbf{u} \in \mathbb{Z}_q^n$, outputs a vector $\mathbf{e} \sim D_{\mathbb{Z}^m, s}$ satisfying $\mathbf{Ae} = \mathbf{u}$.*

3.3 Non-interactive Zero-Knowledge Proofs of Knowledge

In 2013, Laguillaumie *et al.* [43] adapted the protocol of [49,50] to obtain a zero-knowledge proof of knowledge for the ISIS problem in the random oracle model. Concretely, there is a non-interactive zero-knowledge proof of knowledge (NIZKPoK) for the ISIS relations

$$R_{\mathrm{ISIS}} = \{(\mathbf{A}, \mathbf{y}, \beta; \mathbf{x}) \in \mathbb{Z}_q^{n \times m} \times \mathbb{Z}_q^n \times \mathbb{R} \times \mathbb{Z}^m : \mathbf{A}\mathbf{x} = \mathbf{y} \text{ and } \|\mathbf{x}\| \le \beta\}.$$

In particular, there is a knowledge extractor which, given two valid proofs with the same commitment message but two different challenges, outputs a witness $\mathbf{x}'$ satisfying $\|\mathbf{x}'\| \le O(\beta m^2)$ and $\mathbf{A}\mathbf{x}' = \mathbf{y}$. By using the duality between LWE and ISIS, there exists an NIZKPoK for the LWE relation:

$$R_{\mathrm{LWE}} = \{(\mathbf{A}, \mathbf{b}, \alpha; \mathbf{s}) \in \mathbb{Z}_q^{n \times m} \times \mathbb{Z}_q^m \times \mathbb{R} \times \mathbb{Z}_q^n : \|\mathbf{b} - \mathbf{A}^T\mathbf{s}\| \le \alpha q \sqrt{m}\}.$$

Actually, as noted in [51], given a random matrix $\mathbf{A} \in \mathbb{Z}_q^{n \times m}$ such that the columns of $\mathbf{A}$ generate $\mathbb{Z}_q^n$ (this holds with overwhelming probability for a uniformly random $\mathbf{A} \in \mathbb{Z}_q^{n \times m}$), one can compute a matrix $\mathbf{G} \in \mathbb{Z}_q^{(m-n) \times m}$ such that 1) the columns of $\mathbf{G}$ generate $\mathbb{Z}_q^{m-n}$; 2) $\mathbf{G}\mathbf{A}^T = \mathbf{0}$. Thus, to prove $(\mathbf{A}, \mathbf{b}, \alpha; \mathbf{s}) \in R_{\mathrm{LWE}}$, one can instead prove the existence of $\mathbf{e}$ such that $\|\mathbf{e}\| \le \alpha q \sqrt{m}$ and $\mathbf{G}\mathbf{e} = \mathbf{G}\mathbf{b}$. In particular, in the construction of our group signature we need to prove that for given $(\mathbf{A}, \mathbf{b}) \in \mathbb{Z}_q^{n \times m} \times \mathbb{Z}_q^m$, there exist short vectors $(\mathbf{e}, \mathbf{x})$ such that $\|\mathbf{e}\| \le \alpha q \sqrt{m}$, $\|\mathbf{x}\| \le \beta$ and $\mathbf{b} = \mathbf{A}^T\mathbf{s} + p\mathbf{e} + \mathbf{x}$ for some $\mathbf{s} \in \mathbb{Z}_q^n$, where $p \ge (\alpha q \sqrt{m} + \beta)m^2$. Similarly, this can also be achieved by proving the existence of short vectors $\mathbf{e}$ and $\mathbf{x}$ such that $p\mathbf{G}\mathbf{e} + \mathbf{G}\mathbf{x} = \mathbf{G}\mathbf{b}$ using the NIZKPoK for ISIS relations. Formally, denoting $\gamma = \max(\alpha q \sqrt{m}, \beta)$, there exists an NIZKPoK for the extended-LWE (eLWE) relations

$$R_{\mathrm{eLWE}} = \{(\mathbf{A}, \mathbf{b}, \gamma; \mathbf{s}, \mathbf{e}, \mathbf{x}) \in \mathbb{Z}_q^{n \times m} \times \mathbb{Z}_q^m \times \mathbb{R} \times \mathbb{Z}_q^n \times \mathbb{Z}^{2m} :$$
$$\mathbf{b} = \mathbf{A}^T\mathbf{s} + p\mathbf{e} + \mathbf{x} \text{ and } \|\mathbf{e}\| \le \gamma \text{ and } \|\mathbf{x}\| \le \gamma\}.$$

4 Split-SIS Problems

Given uniformly random matrices $(\mathbf{A}_1, \mathbf{A}_2) \in \mathbb{Z}_q^{n \times m} \times \mathbb{Z}_q^{n \times m}$, integer $N = N(n)$ and $\beta = \beta(n)$, an algorithm solving the split-$\mathrm{SIS}_{q,m,\beta,N}$ problem is asked to output a tuple $(\mathbf{x} = (\mathbf{x}_1; \mathbf{x}_2), h) \in \mathbb{Z}^{2m} \times \mathbb{Z}$ such that

- $\mathbf{x}_1 \ne \mathbf{0}$ or $h\mathbf{x}_2 \ne \mathbf{0}$
- $\|\mathbf{x}\| \le \beta$, $h \in [N]$, and $\mathbf{A}_1\mathbf{x}_1 + h\mathbf{A}_2\mathbf{x}_2 = \mathbf{0}$.

Recall that the standard $\mathrm{SIS}_{q,m',\beta}$ problem asks an algorithm to find a root of the hash function $f_{\mathbf{A}}(\mathbf{x}) = \mathbf{A}\mathbf{x} = \mathbf{0} \bmod q$ for a uniformly chosen matrix $\mathbf{A}$ and a "narrow" domain $\hat{D}_{m',\beta} := \{\mathbf{x} \in \mathbb{Z}^{m'} : \|\mathbf{x}\| \le \beta\}$. While for the split-$\mathrm{SIS}_{q,m,\beta,N}$ problem, the algorithm is allowed to "modify" the function by defining $f_{\mathbf{A}'}(\mathbf{x}') = \mathbf{A}'\mathbf{x}'$ for $\mathbf{A}' = (\mathbf{A}_1 \| \mathbf{A}_2\mathbf{x}_2)$ with arbitrarily $\mathbf{x}_2 \in \hat{D}_{m,\beta}$, and outputs a root $\mathbf{x}' = (\mathbf{x}_1, h) \in \hat{D}_{m,\beta} \times [N]$. Intuitively, the split-$\mathrm{SIS}_{q,m,\beta,N}$ problem is not harder than $\text{SIS}_{q,2m,\beta}$ problem. Since if $\mathbf{x} = (\mathbf{x}_1, \mathbf{x}_2)$ is a solution of the $\text{SIS}_{q,2m,\beta}$ instance $\mathbf{A} = (\mathbf{A}_1 \| \mathbf{A}_2)$, $(\mathbf{x}, 1)$ is a solution of the split-$\text{SIS}_{q,m,\beta,N}$ instance $(\mathbf{A}_1, \mathbf{A}_2)$ with $N \geq 1$.

However, for prime $q = q(n)$, and $N = N(n) < q$ of a polynomial in n, we show in the following theorem that the split-$\text{SIS}_{q,m,\beta,N}$ problem is at least as hard as $\text{SIS}_{q,2m,\beta}$. Thus, the average-case hardness of the split-SIS problem is based on the worst-case hardness of SIVP by Proposition 2.

Theorem 1 (Hardness of Split-SIS Problems). *For any polynomial $m = m(n), \beta = \beta(n), N = N(n)$, and any prime $q \geq \beta \cdot \omega(\sqrt{n \log n}) > N$, the split-$\text{SIS}_{q,m,\beta,N}$ problem is polynomially equivalent to $\text{SIS}_{q,2m,\beta}$ problem. In particular, the average-case split-$\text{SIS}_{q,m,\beta,N}$ is as hard as approximating the SIVP problem in the worst case to within certain $\gamma = \beta \cdot \widetilde{O}(\sqrt{n})$ factors.*

Proof. The direction from split-$\text{SIS}_{q,m,\beta,N}$ to $\text{SIS}_{q,2m,\beta}$ is obvious. We now prove the other direction. Assume that there is an algorithm $\mathcal{A}$ that solves split-$\text{SIS}_{q,m,\beta,N}$ with probability ϵ, we now construct an algorithm $\mathcal{B}$ that solves $\text{SIS}_{q,2m,\beta}$ with probability at least ϵ/N (recall that N is a polynomial in n). Formally, given a $\text{SIS}_{q,2m,\beta}$ instance $\hat{\mathbf{A}} = (\hat{\mathbf{A}}_1 \| \hat{\mathbf{A}}_2) \in \mathbb{Z}_q^{n \times 2m}$, $\mathcal{B}$ randomly chooses an integer $h^* \leftarrow_R [N]$. If $h^* = 0$, $\mathcal{B}$ sets $\mathbf{A} = \hat{\mathbf{A}}$. Otherwise, $\mathcal{B}$ sets $\mathbf{A} = (h^* \hat{\mathbf{A}}_1 \| \hat{\mathbf{A}}_2)$. Since q is a prime and $N < q$ (*i.e.*, $h^* \neq 0$ is invertible in $\mathbb{Z}_q$), we have that $\mathbf{A}$ is uniformly distributed over $\mathbb{Z}_q^{n \times 2m}$. Then, $\mathcal{B}$ gives $\mathbf{A} = (\mathbf{A}_1 \| \mathbf{A}_2)$ to $\mathcal{A}$, and obtains a solution $(\mathbf{x} = (\mathbf{x}_1; \mathbf{x}_2), h) \in \mathbb{Z}^{2m} \times [N]$ satisfying $\mathbf{A}_1 \mathbf{x}_1 + h \mathbf{A}_2 \mathbf{x}_2 = \mathbf{0}$. If $h^* \neq h$, $\mathcal{B}$ aborts. (Since h^* is randomly chosen from $[N]$, the probability $\Pr[h^* = h]$ is at least $1/N$.) Otherwise, $\mathcal{B}$ returns $\mathbf{y} = (\mathbf{x}_1; \mathbf{0})$ if $h^* = 0$, else returns $\mathbf{y} = \mathbf{x}$. The first claim follows from the fact that $\mathbf{y} \neq \mathbf{0}$, $\|\mathbf{y}\| \leq \beta$ and $\hat{\mathbf{A}} \mathbf{y} = \mathbf{0}$. Combining this with Proposition 2, the second claim follows. $\square$

4.1   A Family of Hash Functions from Split-SIS Problems

We define a new family of hash functions based on the split-SIS problem, which plays a key role in reducing the sizes of the group public key and the signature in our construction. Formally, for integers n, m, prime q, and polynomial $\beta = \beta(n) \geq \omega(\sqrt{\log m})$, $N = N(n) < q$, we define $D_{m,\beta} = \{\mathbf{x} \leftarrow_R D_{\mathbb{Z}^m,\beta} : \|\mathbf{x}\| \leq \beta \sqrt{m}\}$, and a hash function family $\mathcal{H}_{n,m,q,\beta,N} = \{f_{\mathbf{A}} : D_{m,\beta,N} \to \mathbb{Z}_q^n \times D_{m,\beta}\}_{\mathbf{A} \in \mathbb{Z}_q^{n \times 2m}}$, where $D_{m,\beta,N} := D_{m,\beta} \times D_{m,\beta} \times [N]$. For index $\mathbf{A} = (\mathbf{A}_1 \| \mathbf{A}_2) \in \mathbb{Z}_q^{n \times 2m}$, and input $(\mathbf{x}_1, \mathbf{x}_2, h) \in D_{m,\beta,N}$, the hash value $f_{\mathbf{A}}(\mathbf{x}_1, \mathbf{x}_2, h) := (\mathbf{A}_1 \mathbf{x}_1 + h \mathbf{A}_2 \mathbf{x}_2, \mathbf{x}_2) \in \mathbb{Z}_q^n \times D_{m,\beta}$. In the following, we show three properties of $\mathcal{H}_{n,m,q,\beta,N}$, which are useful to construct zero-knowledge proofs for the function in $\mathcal{H}_{n,m,q,\beta,N}$.

Theorem 2 (One-Wayness). *For parameters $m > 2n \log q$, $\beta = \beta(n) > 2 \cdot \omega(\sqrt{\log m})$, prime $q = q(n)$, and polynomial $N = N(n) < q$, if the split-$\text{SIS}_{q,m,\sqrt{5m}\beta,N}$ problem is hard, then the family of hash functions $\mathcal{H}_{n,m,q,\beta,N}$ is one-way.*

Proof. Assume that there is an algorithm $\mathcal{A}$ that breaks the one-wayness of $\mathcal{H}_{n,m,q,\beta,N}$, we construct an algorithm $\mathcal{B}$ that solves the split-$\text{SIS}_{q,m,\sqrt{5m}\beta,N}$

problem. Actually, given a split-$SIS_{q,m,\sqrt{5m}\beta,N}$ instance $\mathbf{A} = (\mathbf{A}_1 \| \mathbf{A}_2) \in \mathbb{Z}_q^{n \times 2m}$, $\mathcal{B}$ randomly chooses $(\mathbf{x}_1, \mathbf{x}_2) \in D_{\mathbb{Z}^m,\beta} \times D_{\mathbb{Z}^m,\beta}$ and $h \leftarrow_R [N]$, and computes $\mathbf{y} = f_\mathbf{A}(\mathbf{x}_1, \mathbf{x}_2, h) = (\mathbf{A}_1\mathbf{x}_1 + h\mathbf{A}_2\mathbf{x}_2, \mathbf{x}_2)$. Then, it gives $(\mathbf{A}, \mathbf{y})$ to $\mathcal{A}$, and obtains $(\mathbf{x}_1', \mathbf{x}_2', h')$ satisfying $(\mathbf{A}_1\mathbf{x}_1' + h'\mathbf{A}_2\mathbf{x}_2', \mathbf{x}_2') = \mathbf{y}$. Finally, if $h \geq h'$, $\mathcal{B}$ outputs $(\hat{\mathbf{x}}_1, \hat{\mathbf{x}}_2, \hat{h}) = (\mathbf{x}_1 - \mathbf{x}_1', \mathbf{x}_2, h - h')$. Else, $\mathcal{B}$ outputs $(\hat{\mathbf{x}}_1, \hat{\mathbf{x}}_2, \hat{h}) = (\mathbf{x}_1' - \mathbf{x}_1, \mathbf{x}_2, h' - h)$.

It is easy to check that $\mathbf{A}_1\hat{\mathbf{x}}_1 + \hat{h}\mathbf{A}_2\hat{\mathbf{x}}_2 = \mathbf{0} \mod q$, $\hat{h} \in [N]$, and $\|(\hat{\mathbf{x}}_1; \hat{\mathbf{x}}_2)\| \leq \sqrt{5m}\beta$ with overwhelming probability by the standard tail inequality of the Gaussian distribution $D_{\mathbb{Z}^m,\beta}$. We finish this proof by showing that $\Pr[\hat{\mathbf{x}}_1 = \mathbf{0}]$ is negligible in n. Note that $\mathcal{A}$ can only obtain the information about $\mathbf{x}_1$ from $\mathbf{A}_1\mathbf{x}_1$. By [36, Lem.5.2], this only leaks the distribution $\mathbf{t} + D_{\Lambda_q^\perp(\mathbf{A}_1),\beta,-\mathbf{t}}$ for any $\mathbf{t}$ satisfying $\mathbf{A}_1\mathbf{t} = \mathbf{A}_1\mathbf{x}_1$. Namely, $\mathbf{x}_1$ should be uniformly distributed over $\mathbf{t} + D_{\Lambda_q^\perp(\mathbf{A}_1),\beta,-\mathbf{t}}$ from the view of $\mathcal{A}$. Combining this with [56, Lem.2.16], we have $\Pr[\mathbf{x}_1 = \mathbf{x}_1']$ is negligible in n. In other words, we have $\Pr[\hat{\mathbf{x}} \neq \mathbf{0}] = 1 - negl(n)$, which completes the proof. $\quad\square$

Since $f_\mathbf{A}(\mathbf{x}_1, \mathbf{0}, h) = f_\mathbf{A}(\mathbf{x}_1, \mathbf{0}, 0)$ holds for all $h \in [N]$, the function $\mathcal{H}_{n,m,q,\beta,N}$ with domain $D_{m,\beta,N} := D_{m,\beta} \times D_{m,\beta} \times [N]$ are not collision-resistant. However, if we slightly restrict the domain of $\mathcal{H}_{n,m,q,\beta,N}$ to exclude the above trivial case, we can prove that the family of $\mathcal{H}_{n,m,q,\beta,N}$ is collision-resistant. Formally, we slightly restrict the domain of $\mathcal{H}_{n,m,q,\beta,N}$ to be $D'_{m,\beta,N} = \{(\mathbf{x}_1, \mathbf{x}_2, h) \in D_{m,\beta,N} : \mathbf{x}_2 \neq \mathbf{0}\}$.

Theorem 3 (Collision-Resistance). *For parameter $m = m(n), \beta = \beta(n)$, prime $q = q(n)$, and polynomial $N = N(n) < q$, if the split-$SIS_{q,m,\sqrt{5m}\beta,N}$ problem is hard, then the family of hash functions $\mathcal{H}_{n,m,q,\beta,N}$ with domain $D'_{m,\beta,N}$ is collision-resistant.*

Proof. Assume there is a PPT algorithm $\mathcal{A}$ that can find collisions of $\mathcal{H}_{n,m,q,\beta,N}$ with non-negligible probability ϵ, we construct an algorithm $\mathcal{B}$ solving split-$SIS_{q,m,\sqrt{5m}\beta,N}$ with the same probability. Concretely, after obtaining a split-$SIS_{q,m,\sqrt{5m}\beta,N}$ instance $\mathbf{A} = (\mathbf{A}_1 \| \mathbf{A}_2)$, $\mathcal{B}$ directly gives $\mathbf{A}$ to $\mathcal{A}$, and obtains a pair of collisions $(\mathbf{x}_1, \mathbf{x}_2, h) \in D'_{m,\beta,N}$ and $(\mathbf{x}_1', \mathbf{x}_2', h') \in D'_{m,\beta,N}$ satisfying $(\mathbf{x}_1, \mathbf{x}_2, h) \neq (\mathbf{x}_1', \mathbf{x}_2', h')$ and $f_\mathbf{A}(\mathbf{x}_1, \mathbf{x}_2, h) = f_\mathbf{A}(\mathbf{x}_1', \mathbf{x}_2', h')$. Note that in this case, we must have $\mathbf{x}_2 = \mathbf{x}_2' \neq \mathbf{0}$. If $h \geq h'$, $\mathcal{B}$ returns $(\hat{\mathbf{x}}_1, \hat{\mathbf{x}}_2, \hat{h}) = (\mathbf{x}_1 - \mathbf{x}_1', \mathbf{x}_2, h - h')$, else it returns $(\hat{\mathbf{x}}_1, \hat{\mathbf{x}}_2, \hat{h}) = (\mathbf{x}_1' - \mathbf{x}_1, \mathbf{x}_2, h' - h)$. By the assumption that $(\mathbf{x}_1, \mathbf{x}_2, h) \neq (\mathbf{x}_1', \mathbf{x}_2', h')$, the inequality $(\hat{\mathbf{x}}_1, \hat{h}) \neq \mathbf{0}$ holds in both cases, *i.e.*, we always have $\hat{\mathbf{x}}_1 \neq \mathbf{0}$ or $\hat{h}\hat{\mathbf{x}}_2 \neq \mathbf{0}$. The claim follows from the fact that $\|(\hat{\mathbf{x}}_1; \hat{\mathbf{x}}_2)\| \leq \sqrt{5m}\beta$ and $\hat{h} \in [N]$. $\quad\square$

Finally, we show that the family of hash functions $\mathcal{H}_{n,m,q,\beta,N}$ statistically hides its third input.

Theorem 4. *Let parameter $m > 2n \log q, \beta = \beta(n) > \omega(\sqrt{\log m})$, prime $q = q(n)$, and polynomial $N = N(n)$. Then, for a randomly chosen $\mathbf{A} = (\mathbf{A}_1 \| \mathbf{A}_2) \in \mathbb{Z}_q^{n \times 2m}$, and arbitrarily $\mathbf{x}_2$ with norm $\|\mathbf{x}_2\| \leq \beta\sqrt{m}$, the statistical distance between the following two distributions:*

$$\{(\mathbf{A}, f_\mathbf{A}(\mathbf{x}_1, \mathbf{x}_2, h), h) : \mathbf{x}_1 \leftarrow_R D_{m,\beta}, h \leftarrow_R [N]\}$$

and

$$\{(\mathbf{A}, (\mathbf{u}, \mathbf{x}_2), h) : \mathbf{u} \leftarrow_R \mathbb{Z}_q^n, h \leftarrow_R [N]\}$$

is negligible in n.

Proof. Since the second output of $f_{\mathbf{A}}(\mathbf{x}_1, \mathbf{x}_2, h)$ (*i.e.*, $\mathbf{x}_2$) is independent from the choices of h, we only have to show that, for arbitrarily $\mathbf{x}_2$ and h, the distribution $\{\mathbf{A}_1\mathbf{x}_1 + h\mathbf{A}_2\mathbf{x}_2 : \mathbf{x}_1 \leftarrow_R D_{m,\beta}\}$ is statistically close to uniform over $\mathbb{Z}_q^n$. Actually, using the fact that $\beta \geq \omega(\sqrt{\log m})$ together with Lemma 3, we have that the distribution of $\mathbf{A}_1\mathbf{x}_1$ is statistically close to uniform over $\mathbb{Z}_q^n$ when $\mathbf{x}_1 \leftarrow_R D_{\mathbb{Z}^m,\beta}$. The claim of this theorem follows from the fact that the statistical distance between $D_{\mathbb{Z}^m,\beta}$ and $D_{m,\beta}$ is negligible, and that the distribution $\{\mathbf{u} + h\mathbf{A}_2\mathbf{x}_2 : \mathbf{u} \leftarrow_R \mathbb{Z}_q^n\}$ is exactly the uniform distribution over $\mathbb{Z}_q^n$ for arbitrary $\mathbf{x}_2 \in D_{m,\beta}, h \in [N]$. $\square$

4.2   Zero-Knowledge Proof of Knowledge for the Hash Functions

In this subsection, we present a proof of knowledge protocol for the family of hash functions $\mathcal{H}_{n,m,q,\beta,N}$. Concretely, given a matrix $\mathbf{A} = (\mathbf{A}_1\|\mathbf{A}_2)$, a vector $\mathbf{y} = (\mathbf{y}_1, \mathbf{y}_2) \in \mathbb{Z}_q^n \times \mathbb{Z}^m$ with $0 < \|\mathbf{y}_2\| \leq \beta\sqrt{m}$, the prover can generate a proof of knowledge of $\mathbf{x} = (\mathbf{x}_1, \mathbf{x}_2, h) \in \mathbb{Z}^{2m+1}$ satisfying $\|\mathbf{x}_1\| \leq \beta\sqrt{m}$, $h \in [N]$ and $f_{\mathbf{A}}(\mathbf{x}_1, \mathbf{x}_2, h) = (\mathbf{A}\mathbf{x}_1 + h\mathbf{A}_2\mathbf{x}_2, \mathbf{x}_2) = \mathbf{y}$. Since $\mathbf{x}_2$ must be equal to $\mathbf{y}_2$, the protocol is actually a proof of knowledge for the relation

$$R_{\text{split-SIS}} = \{(\mathbf{A}, \mathbf{y}, \beta, N; \mathbf{x}_1, h) \in \mathbb{Z}_q^{n \times 2m} \times (\mathbb{Z}_q^n \times \mathbb{Z}^m) \times \mathbb{R} \times \mathbb{Z} \times \mathbb{Z}^m \times \mathbb{Z} :$$
$$\mathbf{A}_1\mathbf{x}_1 + h\mathbf{A}_2\mathbf{y}_2 = \mathbf{y}_1, \|\mathbf{x}_1\| \leq \beta\sqrt{m} \text{ and } h \in [N]\}.$$

Intuitively, we can adapt a variant of the protocols for ISIS relations in [43,49,50] for our purpose, since one can rewrite $\mathbf{y}_1 = \mathbf{A}_1\mathbf{x}_1 + h\mathbf{A}_2\mathbf{y}_2 = (\mathbf{A}_1\|\mathbf{A}_2\mathbf{y}_2)(\mathbf{x}_1; h)$. However, this may not work when $N \gg \beta$. Since the basic idea of [43,49,50] is to use randomness from a "large width" distribution (compared to the distribution of the witness) to hide the distribution of the witness, the width of the randomness distribution should be sufficiently larger than N in our case, which might lead to a proof without soundness guarantee.

Fortunately, we can borrow the "bit-decomposition" technique from [22–24] to deal with large N. The idea is to decompose $h \in [N]$ into a vector of small elements, and then prove the existence of such a vector for h. Formally, for any $h \in [N]$, we compute the representation of h in base $\bar{\beta} = \lfloor\beta\rfloor$, namely, a ℓ-dimension vector $\mathbf{v}_h = (v_0, \ldots, v_{\ell-1}) \in \mathbb{Z}^\ell$ such that $0 \leq v_i \leq \bar{\beta} - 1$ and $h = \sum_{i=0}^{\ell-1} v_i\bar{\beta}^i$, where $\ell = \lceil\log_{\bar{\beta}} N\rceil$. Denote $\mathbf{b} = \mathbf{A}_2\mathbf{y}_2$, compute $\mathbf{D} = (\mathbf{b}, \bar{\beta}\mathbf{b}, \ldots, \bar{\beta}^{\ell-1}\mathbf{b}) \in \mathbb{Z}_q^{n \times \ell}$. It is easy to check that for any vector $\mathbf{e} \in \mathbb{Z}^\ell$, there exists a $h' \in \mathbb{Z}_q$ such that $\mathbf{D}\mathbf{e} = h'\mathbf{b} \mod q$. ($h' \in \mathbb{Z}_q$ is unique if $\mathbf{b} \neq \mathbf{0}$.) In particular, we have that $\mathbf{y}_1 = \hat{\mathbf{A}}\hat{\mathbf{x}}$, where $\hat{\mathbf{A}} = (\mathbf{A}_1\|\mathbf{D}) \in \mathbb{Z}_q^{n \times (m+\ell)}$, $\hat{\mathbf{x}} = (\mathbf{x}_1; \mathbf{v}_h) \in \mathbb{Z}^{m+\ell}$ and $\|\hat{\mathbf{x}}\| \leq \beta\sqrt{m+\ell}$. Since $\bar{\beta} > 2$ and N is a polynomial in n, we have $\ell \ll m$ and $\|\hat{\mathbf{x}}\| < \eta = \beta\sqrt{2m}$.

We first present a Σ-protocol for the function family $\mathcal{H}_{n,m,q,\beta,N}$, which repeats a basic protocol with single-bit challenge $t = \omega(\log n)$ times in parallel. As in [43,50], the basic protocol makes use of the rejection sampling technique to achieve zero-knowledge. Formally, let $\gamma = \eta \cdot m^{1.5}$, denote $\zeta(\mathbf{z}, \mathbf{y}) = 1 - \min(\frac{D_{\mathbb{Z}^{m+\ell},\gamma}(\mathbf{z})}{M_l \cdot D_{\mathbb{Z}^{m+\ell},\mathbf{y},\gamma}(\mathbf{z})}, 1)$, where $\mathbf{y}, \mathbf{z} \in \mathbb{Z}^{m+\ell}$, and the constant $M_l \leq 1 + O(\frac{1}{m})$ is set according to Lemma 4.5 in [50], the protocol is depicted in Fig 2.

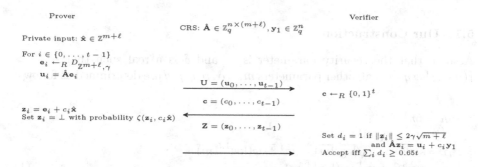

Fig. 2. Σ-protocol for $R_{\text{split-SIS}}$

By [50, Th.4.6], we have $\Pr[\mathbf{z}_i \neq \perp] \approx \frac{1}{M_l} = 1 - O(\frac{1}{m})$ for each $i \in \{0, \ldots, t-1\}$. In addition, $\Pr[\|\mathbf{z}_i\| \leq 2\gamma\sqrt{m+\ell} \mid \mathbf{z}_i \neq \perp] = 1 - negl(m)$ by [50, Lem.4.4]. A simple calculation shows that the completeness error of the protocol is at most $2^{-\Omega(t)}$ (when m is sufficiently large, e.g., $m > 100$). Besides, the protocol has the property of special Honest-Verifier Zero Knowledge (HVZK). Namely, given a challenge c_i, there exists a simulator $\mathcal{S}$ that outputs a distribution $(\mathbf{u}_i, c_i, \mathbf{z}_i)$ statistically close to the real transcript distribution. Concretely, $\mathcal{S}$ first chooses $\mathbf{z}_i \leftarrow_R D_{\mathbb{Z}^{m+\ell},\gamma}$, and computes $\mathbf{u}_i = \hat{\mathbf{A}}\mathbf{z}_i - c_i\mathbf{y}_1 \mod q$. Then, it sets $\mathbf{z}_i = \perp$ with probability $1 - \frac{1}{M_l}$, and outputs $(\mathbf{u}_i, c_i, \mathbf{z}_i)$. By Theorem 4, the term $\hat{\mathbf{A}}\mathbf{z}_i(\mod q)$ is statistically close to uniform over $\mathbb{Z}_q^n$, thus the distribution of $\mathbf{u}_i$ is statistically close to that in the real proof. Moreover, by [50, Th.4.6], the distribution of $\mathbf{z}_i$ is also statistically close to that in the real transcripts.

Finally, since the binary challenges (*i.e.*, $\mathbf{c}$) are used, the above protocol has the property of special soundness. Actually, given two transcripts $(\mathbf{U}, \mathbf{c}, \mathbf{Z})$ and $(\mathbf{U}, \mathbf{c}', \mathbf{Z}')$ with distinct challenges $\mathbf{c} \neq \mathbf{c}'$, one can extract a "weak" witness $\mathbf{x}' = \mathbf{z}_i - \mathbf{z}_i'$ for some i satisfying $\hat{\mathbf{A}}\mathbf{x}' = \mathbf{y}_1$ and $\|\mathbf{x}'\| \leq 4\gamma\sqrt{2m}$.

Applying the "Fiat-Shamir Heuristic" [34] in a standard way, one can obtain an NIZKPoK by computing $\mathbf{c} = H(\rho, \mathbf{U})$, where $H : \{0,1\}^* \rightarrow \{0,1\}^t$ is modeled as a random oracle, and ρ represents all the other auxiliary inputs, e.g., a specified message M to be signed. Finally, due to the nice property of Σ-protocol, one can easily combine the protocol to prove EQ-relation, OR-relation, and AND-relation, we omit the details.

5   A Simple and Efficient Group Signature from Lattices

In this section, we present our CPA-anonymous lattice-based group signature, which can be easily extended to support CCA anonymity by replacing the underlying encryption with a CCA one. We defer the full-anonymous scheme to the full version.

5.1   Our Construction

Assume that the security parameter is n, and δ is a real such that $n^{1+\delta} > \lceil (n+1)\log q+n \rceil$, all other parameters $m, s, \alpha, \beta, \eta, p, q$ are determined as follows:

$$
\begin{aligned}
m &= 6n^{1+\delta} \\
s &= m \cdot \omega(\log m) \\
\beta &= s\sqrt{2m} \cdot \omega(\sqrt{\log 2m}) = m^{1.5} \cdot \omega(\log^{1.5} m) \\
p &= m^{2.5}\beta = m^4 \cdot \omega(\log^{1.5} m) \\
q &= m^2 \cdot \max(pm^{2.5} \cdot \omega(\log m), 4N) = m^{2.5}\max(m^6 \cdot \omega(\log^{2.5} m), 4N) \\
\alpha &= 2\sqrt{m}/q \\
\eta &= \max(\beta, \alpha q)\sqrt{m} = m^2 \cdot \omega(\log^{1.5} m)
\end{aligned}
\tag{1}
$$

Now, we present our group signature $\mathcal{GS} = ($KeyGen, Sign, Verify, Open$)$:

- KeyGen($1^n, 1^N$): Take the security parameter n and the maximum number N of group members as inputs, set an integer $m \in \mathbb{Z}$, primes $p, q \in \mathbb{Z}$, and $s, \alpha, \beta, \eta \in \mathbb{R}$ as above, and choose a hash function $H : \{0,1\}^* \to \{0,1\}^t$ (modeled as random oracle) for the NIZKPoK proof, where $t = \omega(\log n)$. Then, the algorithm proceeds as follows:
  1. Compute $(\mathbf{A}_1, \mathbf{T}_{\mathbf{A}_1}) \leftarrow$ TrapGen(n, m, q), and randomly choose $\mathbf{A}_{2,1}$, $\mathbf{A}_{2,2} \leftarrow_R \mathbb{Z}_q^{n \times m}$.
  2. Compute $(\mathbf{B}, \mathbf{T}_{\mathbf{B}}) \leftarrow$ SuperSamp$(n, m, q, \mathbf{A}_1, \mathbf{0})$.
  3. For $j = 1, \ldots, N$, define $\bar{\mathbf{A}}_j = (\mathbf{A}_1 \| \mathbf{A}_{2,1} + j\mathbf{A}_{2,2})$, extract a basis $\mathbf{T}_{\bar{\mathbf{A}}_j} \leftarrow$ ExtRndBasis$(\bar{\mathbf{A}}_j, \mathbf{T}_{\mathbf{A}_1}, s)$ such that $\|\widetilde{\mathbf{T}}_{\bar{\mathbf{A}}_j}\| \le s\sqrt{2m}$.
  4. Define the group public key $gpk = \{\mathbf{A}_1, \mathbf{A}_{2,1}, \mathbf{A}_{2,2}, \mathbf{B}\}$, the group manager secret key $gmsk = \mathbf{T}_{\mathbf{B}}$, and the group member's secret keys $\mathbf{gsk} = \{gsk_j = \mathbf{T}_{\bar{\mathbf{A}}_j}\}_{j \in \{1, \ldots, N\}}$
- Sign(gpk, gsk_j, M): Take the group public key $gpk = \{\mathbf{A}_1, \mathbf{A}_{2,1}, \mathbf{A}_{2,2}, \mathbf{B}\}$, the j-th user's secret key $gsk_j = \mathbf{T}_{\bar{\mathbf{A}}_j}$, and a message $M \in \{0,1\}^*$ as inputs, proceed as follows:
  1. Compute $(\mathbf{x}_1, \mathbf{x}_2) \leftarrow$ SamplePre$(\bar{\mathbf{A}}_j, \mathbf{T}_{\bar{\mathbf{A}}_j}, \beta, \mathbf{0})$, where $\mathbf{x}_1, \mathbf{x}_2 \in D_{\mathbb{Z}^m, \beta}$.
  2. Choose $\mathbf{s} \leftarrow_R \mathbb{Z}_q^n$, $\mathbf{e} \leftarrow_R \chi_\alpha^m$, and compute

$$
\mathbf{c} = \mathbf{B}^T \mathbf{s} + p\mathbf{e} + \mathbf{x}_1
$$

  3. Generate a NIZKPoK proof π_1 of $(\mathbf{s}, \mathbf{e}, \mathbf{x}_1)$ such that $(\mathbf{B}, \mathbf{c}, \eta; \mathbf{s}, \mathbf{e}, \mathbf{x}_1) \in R_{\text{eLWE}}$.

4. Let $\bar{\beta} := \lfloor \beta \rfloor$ and $\ell = \lceil \log_{\bar{\beta}} N \rceil$, define $\mathbf{b} = \mathbf{A}_{2,2}\mathbf{x}_2$, and $\mathbf{D} = (\mathbf{b}, \bar{\beta}\mathbf{b}, \ldots, \bar{\beta}^{\ell-1}\mathbf{b}) \in \mathbb{Z}_q^{n\times\ell}$. Generate a NIZKPoK π_2 of $\mathbf{x}_1, \mathbf{e}$, and $\mathbf{v}_j = (v_0, \ldots, v_{\ell-1}) \in \mathbb{Z}_{\bar{\beta}}^\ell$ of $j \in [N]$ such that,

$$
\begin{aligned}
\mathbf{A}_1\mathbf{c} + \mathbf{A}_{2,1}\mathbf{x}_2 &= (p\mathbf{A}_1)\mathbf{e} - \mathbf{D}\mathbf{v}_j, \text{ and} \\
\mathbf{A}_1\mathbf{c} &= (p\mathbf{A}_1)\mathbf{e} + \mathbf{A}_1\mathbf{x}_1
\end{aligned}
\tag{2}
$$

where the challenge is computed by $H(\mathbf{c}, \mathbf{x}_2, \pi_1, M, \mathbf{Com})$, and $\mathbf{Com}$ is the commitment message for the NIZKPoK proof of π_2. (Note that the proof, i.e., π_2, is actually a standard composition of our protocol in Section 4.2 and the protocol for R_{ISIS} [43,50] according to the nice property of the underlying Σ-protocol. More discussions are given in the full version.)

5. Output the signature $\sigma = (\mathbf{c}, \mathbf{x}_2, \pi_1, \pi_2)$.

- Verify(gpk, M, σ): Parse $\sigma = (\mathbf{c}, \mathbf{x}_2, \pi_1, \pi_2)$, return 1 if $\|\mathbf{x}_2\| \leq \beta\sqrt{m}$, $\mathbf{A}_{2,2}\mathbf{x}_2 \neq \mathbf{0}$, and the proofs π_1, π_2 are valid, else return 0.
- Open$(gpk, gmsk, M, \sigma)$: Parse $gpk = \{\mathbf{A}_1, \mathbf{A}_{2,1}, \mathbf{A}_{2,2}, \mathbf{B}\}$ and $gmsk = \mathbf{T_B}$, compute $\mathbf{x}_1$ by decrypting $\mathbf{c}$ using $\mathbf{T_B}$. Then, compute $\mathbf{y}_0 = \mathbf{A}_{2,2}\mathbf{x}_2$ and $\mathbf{y}_1 = -\mathbf{A}_1\mathbf{x}_1 - \mathbf{A}_{2,1}\mathbf{x}_2$. If $\mathbf{y}_0 \neq \mathbf{0}$ and there is a $j \in \mathbb{Z}_q^*$ such that $\mathbf{y}_1 = j \cdot \mathbf{y}_0 \bmod q$, output j, else output $\perp$.

Remark 1. One can decrypt $\mathbf{c}$ by first computing $\mathbf{T_B}^T \cdot \mathbf{c} = \mathbf{T_B}^T(p\mathbf{e} + \mathbf{x}_1) \bmod q$. If $\|\mathbf{T_B}^T(p\mathbf{e} + \mathbf{x}_1)\|_\infty < q/2$, one can expect that $\mathbf{T_B}^T(p\mathbf{e} + \mathbf{x}_1) = (\mathbf{T_B}^T\mathbf{c} \bmod q)$ holds over $\mathbb{Z}$. Thus, $\hat{\mathbf{x}} = (p\mathbf{e} + \mathbf{x}_1)$ can be solved by using Gaussian elimination over $\mathbb{Z}$ since $\mathbf{T_B} \in \mathbb{Z}^{m\times m}$ is full-rank. Finally, $\mathbf{x}_1 = \hat{\mathbf{x}} \bmod p$ can be successfully recovered if $\|\mathbf{x}_1\|_\infty < p/2$.

For the correctness of our group signature scheme, we have the following theorem.

Theorem 5. *Assume n is the security parameter, and all other parameters $m, s, \alpha, \beta, \eta, p, q$ are functions of n defined as in (1), where p, q are primes. Then, the group signature $\mathcal{GS}$ is correct, and the group public key and the signature have bit-length $4nm\log q$ and $O(tm\log q)$, respectively, where $t = \omega(\log n)$.*

Proof. Since we set $m = 6n^{1+\delta} > \lceil 6n\log q + n \rceil$, the two algorithms TrapGen and SuperSamp can work correctly with overwhelming probability. In particular, we have $\|\tilde{\mathbf{T}}_{\mathbf{A}_1}\| \leq O(\sqrt{m})$, and $\|\mathbf{T_B}\| \leq m^{1.5} \cdot O(\sqrt{\log m})$ by Proposition 3 and Proposition 6. By Proposition 4, we have $\|\tilde{\mathbf{T}}_{\bar{\mathbf{A}}_j}\| \leq s\sqrt{2m}$ for all $i \in \{1, \ldots, N\}$ with overwhelming probability. Since the group public key only contains four matrices over $\mathbb{Z}_q^{n\times m}$, it has bit-size $4nm\log q = O(nm\log q)$.

For the Sign algorithm, since $\beta = s\sqrt{2m} \cdot \omega(\sqrt{\log 2m}) \geq \|\tilde{\mathbf{T}}_{\bar{\mathbf{A}}_j}\| \cdot \omega(\sqrt{\log 2m})$, we have $\mathbf{x}_1, \mathbf{x}_2 \rightsquigarrow D_{\mathbb{Z}^m, \beta}$ by the correctness of the SamplePre algorithm in [36], and $\|\mathbf{x}_i\| \leq \beta\sqrt{m}$ with overwhelming probability. In addition, since $\mathbf{e}$ is chosen from χ_α, we have $\|\mathbf{e}\| \leq \alpha q\sqrt{m}$ with overwhelming probability. By the choices of $\eta = \max(\beta, \alpha q)\sqrt{m}$, the algorithm can successfully generate the proofs π_1 and π_2. For the bit-length of the signature $\sigma = (\mathbf{c}, \mathbf{x}_2, \pi_1, \pi_2)$, we know that both the bit-length of $\mathbf{c}$ and $\mathbf{x}_2$ are at most $m \log q$. In addition, if we set the repetition parameter $t = \omega(\log n)$ for the proof π_1 and π_2, the bit-length of π_1 and π_2 are at most $(3m - n)t \log q$ and $(2m + 2n + \ell)t \log q$, respectively. Thus, the total bit-length of the signature σ is less than $2m \log q + (5m + n + \ell)t \log q = O(t(m + \log N) \log q) = O(tm \log q)$ since $\ell = \lceil \log_{\bar{\beta}} N \rceil \ll n$ and $m = O(n \log q)$.

Note that $\mathbf{x}_2 \backsim D_{\mathbb{Z}^{2m}, \beta}$,[1] therefore $\Pr[\mathbf{A}_{2,2}\mathbf{x}_2 = \mathbf{0}] \leq O(q^{-n})$ by Lemma 3. Moreover, by the completeness of π_1 and π_2, the algorithm Verify will work correctly with overwhelming probability. As for the Open algorithm, we only have to show that we can correctly decrypt $\mathbf{x}_1$ from $\mathbf{c}$ by using $\mathbf{T_B}$. Since $\mathbf{T}_B^T \cdot \mathbf{c} = \mathbf{T}_B^T(p\mathbf{e} + \mathbf{x}_1) \mod q$ holds, one can expect that $\mathbf{T}_B^T(p\mathbf{e} + \mathbf{x}_1) = (\mathbf{T}_B^T\mathbf{c} \mod q)$ holds over $\mathbb{Z}$ if $\|\mathbf{T}_B^T(p\mathbf{e} + \mathbf{x}_1)\|_\infty < q/2$. Thus, one can solve $\hat{\mathbf{x}} = (p\mathbf{e} + \mathbf{x}_1)$ by Gaussian elimination over $\mathbb{Z}$ since $\mathbf{T_B} \in \mathbb{Z}^{m \times m}$ is full-rank. Moreover, by the choices of p and β, we have $\|\mathbf{x}_1\|_\infty \leq \|\mathbf{x}_1\| < p$, therefore $\mathbf{x}_1$ can be recovered by computing $\hat{\mathbf{x}} \mod p$. We finish this proof by showing that $\|\mathbf{T}_B^T(p\mathbf{e} + \mathbf{x}_1)\|_\infty < q/2$. Actually, by Lemma 2 and Lemma 1, we have $\|p\mathbf{e} + \mathbf{x}_1\| \leq 3m^6 \cdot \omega(\log^3 m)$. By Proposition 6, we have $\|\mathbf{T_B}\| \leq m^{1.5} \cdot \omega(\sqrt{\log m})$. It is easy to check that $\|\mathbf{T}_B^T(p\mathbf{e} + \mathbf{x}_1)\|_\infty \leq 3m^8 \cdot \omega(\log^{3.5} m) \ll q$, which satisfies the requirement. $\qquad\square$

5.2 The Security

For security, namely CPA-anonymity and full traceability, we have the following two theorems.

Theorem 6. *CPA-Anonymity] Under the LWE assumption, our group signature $\mathcal{GS}$ is CPA-anonymous in the random oracle model.*

Proof. We prove Theorem 6 via a sequence of games.

In game G_0, the challenger honestly generates the group public key $gpk = \{\mathbf{A}_1, \mathbf{A}_{2,1}, \mathbf{A}_{2,2}, \mathbf{B}\}$, the group manager secret key $gmsk = \mathbf{T_B}$, and the group member's secret key $\mathbf{gsk} = \{gsk_j = \mathbf{T}_{\bar{\mathbf{A}}_j}\}_{j \in \{1,\dots,N\}}$ by running the KeyGen algorithm. Then, it gives $(gpk, \mathbf{gsk})$ to the adversary $\mathcal{A}$, and obtains a message M, and two user indexes $i_0, i_1 \in \{1, \dots, N\}$. Finally, the challenger randomly chooses a bit $b \leftarrow_R \{0, 1\}$, computes $\sigma^* = (\mathbf{c}^*, \mathbf{x}_2^*, \pi_1^*, \pi_2^*) \leftarrow \mathsf{Sign}(gpk, gsk_{i_b}, M)$, and returns σ^* to $\mathcal{A}$.

In Game G_1, the challenger behaves almost the same as in G_0, except that it uses the NIZKPoK simulators (by appropriately programming the random oracle) to generate π_1^*, π_2^*. By the property of the NIZKPoKs, G_1 is computationally indistinguishable from G_0.

In Game G_2, the challenger behaves almost the same as in G_1, except that it first chooses $\mathbf{x}_2^*$ from $D_{\mathbb{Z}^m, \beta}$, and then uses $\mathbf{T}_{\mathbf{A}_1}$ to extract $\mathbf{x}_1^*$ such that

---

[1] As noted by Cash *et al.* [31], the output distribution of the SamplePre algorithm in [36] is statistically close to the distribution $(\mathbf{x}_1, \mathbf{x}_2)$ that samples as follows: randomly choose $\mathbf{x}_2 \leftarrow_R D_{\mathbb{Z}^m, s}$, and then compute $\mathbf{x}_1$ using $\mathbf{T}_{\mathbf{A}_1}$ to satisfy the condition $\mathbf{A}_1\mathbf{x}_1 + (\mathbf{A}_{2,1} + j\mathbf{A}_{2,2})\mathbf{x}_2 = \mathbf{0}$. We note that this is also the reason why we do not encrypt $\mathbf{x}_2$ as in [43], since it leaks little information about j without $\mathbf{x}_1$.

$\bar{\mathbf{A}}_{i_b}(\mathbf{x}_1^*; \mathbf{x}_2^*) = \mathbf{0}$. By the property of the SamplePre algorithm from [31,36], Game G_2 is statistically close to Game G_1

In Game G_3, the challenger behaves almost the same as in G_2, except that it computes $\mathbf{c}^* = \mathbf{u} + \mathbf{x}_1^*$ with a randomly chosen $\mathbf{u} \leftarrow_R \mathbb{Z}_q^m$.

Lemma 4. *Under the LWE assumption, Game G_3 is computationally indistinguishable from Game G_2.*

Proof. Assume there is an algorithm $\mathcal{A}$ which distinguishes G_2 from G_3 with non-negligible probability. Then, there is an algorithm $\mathcal{B}$ that breaks the LWE assumption. Formally, given a LWE tuple $(\hat{\mathbf{B}}, \hat{\mathbf{u}}) \in \mathbb{Z}_q^{n \times m} \times \mathbb{Z}_q^m$, $\mathcal{B}$ sets $\mathbf{B} = p\hat{\mathbf{B}}$, and computes $(\mathbf{A}_1, \mathbf{T}_{\mathbf{A}_1}) \leftarrow \mathsf{SuperSamp}(n, m, q, \mathbf{B}, \mathbf{0})$. Then, it chooses $\mathbf{A}_{2,1}, \mathbf{A}_{2,2} \leftarrow_R \mathbb{Z}_q^{n \times m}$. For $j = 1, \ldots, N$, define $\bar{\mathbf{A}}_j = (\mathbf{A}_1 \| \mathbf{A}_{2,1} + j\mathbf{A}_{2,2})$, extract a random basis $\mathbf{T}_{\bar{\mathbf{A}}_j} \leftarrow \mathsf{ExtRndBasis}(\bar{\mathbf{A}}_j, \mathbf{T}_{\mathbf{A}_1}, s)$. Finally, $\mathcal{B}$ gives the group public key $gpk = \{\mathbf{A}_1, \mathbf{A}_{2,1}, \mathbf{A}_{2,2}, \mathbf{B}\}$, and the group members' secret keys $\mathbf{gsk} = \{gsk_j = \mathbf{T}_{\bar{\mathbf{A}}_j}\}_{j \in \{1, \ldots, N\}}$ to $\mathcal{A}$. Note that the distributions of $gpk, \mathbf{gsk}$ are statistically close to that in Game G_2 and G_3 by Proposition 4.

When generating the challenge signature, $\mathcal{B}$ behaves the same as the challenger in G_2, except that it computes $\mathbf{c} = p\hat{\mathbf{u}} + \mathbf{x}_1^*$. We note that if $(\hat{\mathbf{B}}, \hat{\mathbf{u}})$ is a LWE tuple with respect to the error distribution χ_α, $\mathbf{c}$ is the same as in G_2. Otherwise, we have that $p\hat{\mathbf{u}}$ is uniformly distributed over $\mathbb{Z}_q^m$ (since p, q are primes, and $p < q$), which shows that $\mathbf{c}$ has the same distribution as in G_3. If $\mathcal{A}$ can distinguish G_2 from G_3 with advantage ϵ, then $\mathcal{B}$ can break the LWE assumption with advantage $\epsilon - negl(k)$.   □

In Game G_4, the challenger behaves almost the same as in G_3, except that it randomly chooses $\mathbf{c}^* \leftarrow_R \mathbb{Z}_q^m$.

Lemma 5. *In Game G_4, the probability that $b' = b$ is exactly $1/2$.*

Proof. The claim follows from the fact that the signature σ^* in G_4 is independent from the choice of i_b.   □

Theorem 7. *Traceability] Under the SIS assumption, our group signature $\mathcal{GS}$ is fully traceable in the random oracle model.*

Proof. Assume that there is an adversary $\mathcal{A}$ that breaks the full traceability of $\mathcal{GS}$, we construct an algorithm $\mathcal{B}$ breaking the SIS assumption. Formally, $\mathcal{B}$ is given a matrix $\hat{\mathbf{A}} \in \mathbb{Z}_q^m$ and tries to find a solution $\hat{\mathbf{x}} \in \mathbb{Z}_q^m$ such that $\|\hat{\mathbf{x}}\| \leq poly(m)$ and $\hat{\mathbf{A}}\hat{\mathbf{x}} = \mathbf{0}$.

Setup. $\mathcal{B}$ randomly chooses $\mathbf{R} \leftarrow_R \{-1, 1\}^{m \times m}$ and $j^* \leftarrow_R \{-4m^{2.5}N + 1, \ldots, 4m^{2.5}N - 1\}$, and computes $(\mathbf{A}_{2,2}, \mathbf{T}_{\mathbf{A}_{2,2}}) \leftarrow \mathsf{TrapGen}(n, m, q)$. Then, it sets $\mathbf{A}_1 = \hat{\mathbf{A}}$ and $\mathbf{A}_{2,1} = \mathbf{A}_1\mathbf{R} - j^*\mathbf{A}_{2,2}$. Finally, compute $(\mathbf{B}, \mathbf{T}_{\mathbf{B}}) \leftarrow \mathsf{SuperSamp}(n, m, q, \mathbf{A}_1, \mathbf{0})$, and give the group public key $gpk = \{\mathbf{A}_1, \mathbf{A}_{2,1}, \mathbf{A}_{2,2}, \mathbf{B}\}$, and the group manager secret key $gmsk = \mathbf{T}_{\mathbf{B}}$ to the adversary $\mathcal{A}$.

Secret Key Queries. Upon receiving the secret key query for user j from $\mathcal{A}$, $\mathcal{B}$ aborts if $j = j^*$ or $j \notin \{1, \ldots, N\}$. Otherwise, it defines $\bar{\mathbf{A}}_j = (\mathbf{A}_1 \| \mathbf{A}_{2,1} + j^* \mathbf{A}_{2,2}) = (\mathbf{A}_1 \| \mathbf{A}_1 \mathbf{R} + (j - j^*) \mathbf{A}_{2,2})$, extracts a random basis $\mathbf{T}_{\bar{\mathbf{A}}_j} \leftarrow \mathsf{ExtBasisRight}(\bar{\mathbf{A}}_j, \mathbf{R}, \mathbf{T}_{\mathbf{A}_{2,2}}, s)$,[2] and returns it to $\mathcal{A}$.

Sign Queries. Upon receiving a signing query for message M under user j from $\mathcal{A}$, $\mathcal{B}$ returns $\perp$ if $j \notin \{1, \ldots, N\}$. Else if $j = j^*$, $\mathcal{B}$ generates a signature on M using the NIZKPoK simulators for π_1 and π_2 (*i.e.*, by simply choosing $\mathbf{c} \leftarrow_R \mathbb{Z}_q^m$ and $\mathbf{x}_2 \leftarrow_R D_{\mathbb{Z}^m, s}$). Otherwise, it generates the signature by first extracting the j-th user's secret key as in answering the secret key queries.

Forge. Upon receiving a forged valid signature $\sigma = (\mathbf{c}, \mathbf{x}_2, \pi_1, \pi_2)$ with probability ϵ, $\mathcal{B}$ extracts the knowledge $\mathbf{e}, \mathbf{x}_1$ and $\mathbf{v}_j$ with norm at most $4\eta m^2$ by programming the random oracle twice to generate two different "challenges". By the forking lemma of [12], $\mathcal{B}$ can succeed with probability at least $\epsilon(\epsilon/q_h - 2^{-t})$, where q_h is the maximum number of hash queries of $\mathcal{A}$. Then, $\mathcal{B}$ decrypts $\mathbf{c}$ using $\mathbf{T}_{\mathbf{B}}$, and obtains $(\mathbf{e}', \mathbf{x}_1')$, and distinguishes the following cases:

- If $(\mathbf{x}_1', \mathbf{e}') \neq (\mathbf{x}_1, \mathbf{e})$, we have $\mathbf{A}_1 \mathbf{c} = p\mathbf{A}_1 \mathbf{e} + \mathbf{A}_1 \mathbf{x}_1 = p\mathbf{A}_1 \mathbf{e}' + \mathbf{A}_1 \mathbf{x}_1'$. Thus, $\hat{\mathbf{x}} = p(\mathbf{e} - \mathbf{e}') + (\mathbf{x}_1 - \mathbf{x}_1')$ is a solution of the SIS problem, $\mathcal{B}$ returns $\hat{\mathbf{x}}$ as its own solution. Note that in this case, we have $\|\hat{\mathbf{x}}\| \leq 8(p+1)\eta m^2 = m^8 \cdot \omega(\log^3 m)$.

- Otherwise, if $(\mathbf{x}_1', \mathbf{e}') = (\mathbf{x}_1, \mathbf{e})$, we have $\mathbf{A}_1 \mathbf{x}_1 + \mathbf{A}_{2,1} \mathbf{x}_2 + j\mathbf{A}_{2,2} \mathbf{x}_2 = \mathbf{0}$ according to equation (2) of π_2, where $j = \sum_{i=0}^{\ell-1} v_i \bar{\beta}^i$ and $\mathbf{v}_h = (v_0, \ldots, v_{\ell-1})$. A simple calculation indicates that $|j| < 4m^{2.5} N < q$ (we note that $\|\mathbf{v}_h\| \leq 4\eta m^2 = 4\beta m^{2.5}$). Since $\mathbf{A}_{2,2} \mathbf{x}_2 \neq \mathbf{0}$ and q is a prime, the open algorithm will always output j, namely, it will never output $\perp$. In addition, if $j \neq j^*$, $\mathcal{B}$ aborts. Otherwise, $\mathcal{B}$ returns $\hat{\mathbf{x}} = \mathbf{x}_1 + \mathbf{R}\mathbf{x}_2$ as its own solution.

  Since j^* is randomly chosen from $\{-4m^{2.5}N + 1, \ldots, 4m^{2.5}N - 1\}$, the probability that $j^* = j$ is at least $\frac{1}{8m^{2.5}N}$. Conditioned on $j^* = j$, we have $\mathbf{A}_1 \mathbf{x}_1 + \mathbf{A}_{2,1} \mathbf{x}_2 + j\mathbf{A}_{2,2} \mathbf{x}_2 = \mathbf{A}_1 \mathbf{x}_1 + \mathbf{A}_1 \mathbf{R}\mathbf{x}_2 = \mathbf{0}$, which shows that $\hat{\mathbf{x}} = \mathbf{x}_1 + \mathbf{R}\mathbf{x}_2$ is a solution of the SIS problem, in particular, we have $\|\hat{\mathbf{x}}\| \leq \eta m^{2.5} \cdot \omega(\sqrt{\log m}) = m^{4.5}\omega(\log^2 m)$ by [2, Lem.5].

In all, the probability that $\mathcal{B}$ solves the SIS problem is at least $\frac{\epsilon(\epsilon/q_h - 2^{-t})}{8m^{2.5}N}$, which is non-negligible if ϵ is non-negligible. Moreover, since the norm of $\hat{\mathbf{x}}$ is at most $m^8 \cdot \omega(\log^3 m)$ and $q \geq m^{8.5} \cdot \omega(\log^{2.5} m)$, we have that the security of our scheme is based on the hardness of the SIVP problem in the worst case to within a polynomial approximation factor, by Proposition 2. $\square$

Acknowledgments. We would like to thank Kang Yang for his helpful comments on the related work of group signatures, and the anonymous reviewers of PKC 2015 for kind suggestions on our paper. We are also grateful to Sherman Chow for bringing their work to our attention.

---

[2] Recall that $\mathbf{T}_{\mathbf{A}_{2,2}}$ is also a short basis of $\Lambda_q^{\perp}(j \cdot \mathbf{A}_{2,2})$ for all $j \neq 0 \mod q$.

References

1. Abe, M., Fuchsbauer, G., Groth, J., Haralambiev, K., Ohkubo, M.: Structure-preserving signatures and commitments to group elements. In: Rabin, T. (ed.) CRYPTO 2010. LNCS, vol. 6223, pp. 209–236. Springer, Heidelberg (2010)
2. Agrawal, S., Boneh, D., Boyen, X.: Efficient lattice (H)IBE in the standard model. In: Gilbert, H. (ed.) EUROCRYPT 2010. LNCS, vol. 6110, pp. 553–572. Springer, Heidelberg (2010)
3. Agrawal, S., Boneh, D., Boyen, X.: Lattice basis delegation in fixed dimension and shorter-ciphertext hierarchical IBE. In: Rabin, T. (ed.) CRYPTO 2010. LNCS, vol. 6223, pp. 98–115. Springer, Heidelberg (2010)
4. Agrawal, S., Freeman, D.M., Vaikuntanathan, V.: Functional encryption for inner product predicates from learning with errors. In: Lee, D.H., Wang, X. (eds.) ASIACRYPT 2011. LNCS, vol. 7073, pp. 21–40. Springer, Heidelberg (2011)
5. Ajtai, M.: Generating hard instances of lattice problems (extended abstract). In: 28th Annual ACM Symposium on Theory of Computing (STOC), pp. 99–108. ACM, New York (1996)
6. Ajtai, M.: Generating hard instances of the short basis problem. In: Wiedermann, J., Van Emde Boas, P., Nielsen, M. (eds.) ICALP 1999. LNCS, vol. 1644, pp. 1–9. Springer, Heidelberg (1999)
7. Alwen, J., Peikert, C.: Generating shorter bases for hard random lattices. In: STACS, pp. 75–86 (2009)
8. Applebaum, B., Cash, D., Peikert, C., Sahai, A.: Fast cryptographic primitives and circular-secure encryption based on hard learning problems. In: Halevi, S. (ed.) CRYPTO 2009. LNCS, vol. 5677, pp. 595–618. Springer, Heidelberg (2009)
9. Ateniese, G., Camenisch, J.L., Joye, M., Tsudik, G.: A practical and provably secure coalition-resistant group signature scheme. In: Bellare, M. (ed.) CRYPTO 2000. LNCS, vol. 1880, pp. 255–270. Springer, Heidelberg (2000)
10. Ateniese, G., Song, D., Tsudik, G.: Quasi-efficient revocation of group signatures. In: Blaze, M. (ed.) FC 2002. LNCS, vol. 2357, pp. 183–197. Springer, Heidelberg (2002)
11. Bellare, M., Micciancio, D., Warinschi, B.: Foundations of group signatures: formal definitions, simplified requirements, and a construction based on general assumptions. In: Biham, E. (ed.) EUROCRYPT 2003. LNCS, vol. 2656, pp. 614–629. Springer, Heidelberg (2003)
12. Bellare, M., Neven, G.: Multi-signatures in the plain public-key model and a general forking lemma. In: 13th ACM Conference on Computer and Communications Security (CCS), pp. 390–399. ACM, New York (2006)
13. Bellare, M., Rogaway, P.: Random oracles are practical: a paradigm for designing efficient protocols. In: 1st ACM Conference on Computer and Communications Security (CCS), pp. 62–73. ACM Press (1993)
14. Benhamouda, F., Camenisch, J., Krenn, S., Lyubashevsky, V., Neven, G.: Better zero-knowledge proofs for lattice encryption and their application to group signatures. In: Sarkar, P., Iwata, T. (eds.) ASIACRYPT 2014. LNCS, vol. 8873, pp. 551–572. Springer, Heidelberg (2014)
15. Boneh, D., Boyen, X.: Short signatures without random oracles. In: Cachin, C., Camenisch, J.L. (eds.) EUROCRYPT 2004. LNCS, vol. 3027, pp. 56–73. Springer, Heidelberg (2004)
16. Boneh, D., Boyen, X., Shacham, H.: Short group signatures. In: Franklin, M. (ed.) CRYPTO 2004. LNCS, vol. 3152, pp. 41–55. Springer, Heidelberg (2004)

17. Boneh, D., Nikolaenko, V., Segev, G.: Attribute-based encryption for arithmetic circuits. Cryptology ePrint Archive, Report 2013/669 (2013)

18. Boneh, D., Shacham, H.: Group signatures with verifier-local revocation. In: 11th ACM Conference on Computer and Communications Security (CCS), pp. 168–177. ACM, New York (2004)

19. Boyen, X.: Lattice mixing and vanishing trapdoors: a framework for fully secure short signatures and more. In: Nguyen, P.Q., Pointcheval, D. (eds.) PKC 2010. LNCS, vol. 6056, pp. 499–517. Springer, Heidelberg (2010)

20. Boyen, X., Waters, B.: Compact group signatures without random oracles. In: Vaudenay, S. (ed.) EUROCRYPT 2006. LNCS, vol. 4004, pp. 427–444. Springer, Heidelberg (2006)

21. Boyen, X., Waters, B.: Full-domain subgroup hiding and constant-size group signatures. In: Okamoto, T., Wang, X. (eds.) PKC 2007. LNCS, vol. 4450, pp. 1–15. Springer, Heidelberg (2007)

22. Brakerski, Z., Gentry, C., Vaikuntanathan, V.: Fully homomorphic encryption without bootstrapping. In: Innovations in Theoretical Computer Science, ITCS, pp. 309–325 (2012)

23. Brakerski, Z., Vaikuntanathank, V. : Efficient fully homomorphic encryption from (standard) LWE. In: IEEE 52nd Annual Symposium on Foundations of Computer Science (FOCS), pp. 97–106 (2011)

24. Brakerski, Z., Vaikuntanathan, V.: Lattice-based FHE as secure as PKE. In: 5th Conference on Innovations in Theoretical Computer Science (ITCS), pp. 1–12. ACM, New York (2014)

25. Bresson, E., Stern, J.: Efficient revocation in group signatures. In: Kim, K. (ed.) PKC 2001. LNCS, vol. 1992, pp. 190–206. Springer, Heidelberg (2001)

26. Brickell, E., Camenisch, J., Chen, L.: Direct anonymous attestation. In: 11th ACM Conference on Computer and Communications Security (CCS), pp. 132–145. ACM Press (2004)

27. Camenisch, J.L., Lysyanskaya, A.: Dynamic accumulators and application to efficient revocation of anonymous credentials. In: Yung, M. (ed.) CRYPTO 2002. LNCS, vol. 2442, pp. 61–76. Springer, Heidelberg (2002)

28. Camenisch, J.L., Lysyanskaya, A.: Signature schemes and anonymous credentials from bilinear maps. In: Franklin, M. (ed.) CRYPTO 2004. LNCS, vol. 3152, pp. 56–72. Springer, Heidelberg (2004)

29. Camenisch, J., Neven, G., Rückert, M.: Fully anonymous attribute tokens from lattices. In: Visconti, I., De Prisco, R. (eds.) SCN 2012. LNCS, vol. 7485, pp. 57–75. Springer, Heidelberg (2012)

30. Canetti, R., Halevi, S., Katz, J.: Chosen-ciphertext security from identity-based encryption. In: Cachin, C., Camenisch, J.L. (eds.) EUROCRYPT 2004. LNCS, vol. 3027, pp. 207–222. Springer, Heidelberg (2004)

31. Cash, D., Hofheinz, D., Kiltz, E., Peikert, C.: Bonsai trees, or how to delegate a lattice basis. In: Gilbert, H. (ed.) EUROCRYPT 2010. LNCS, vol. 6110, pp. 523–552. Springer, Heidelberg (2010)

32. Chaum, D., van Heyst, E.: Group signatures. In: Davies, D.W. (ed.) EUROCRYPT 1991. LNCS, vol. 547, pp. 257–265. Springer, Heidelberg (1991)

33. Chen, L., Li, J.: Flexible and scalable digital signatures in TPM 2.0. In: 20th ACM Conference on Computer and Communications Security (CCS), pp. 37–48. ACM Press (2013)

34. Fiat, A., Shamir, A.: How to prove yourself: practical solutions to identification and signature problems. In: Odlyzko, A.M. (ed.) CRYPTO 1986. LNCS, vol. 263, pp. 186–194. Springer, Heidelberg (1987)

35. Gentry, C., Gorbunov, S., Halevi, S., Vaikuntanathan, V., Vinayagamurthy, D.: How to compress (reusable) garbled circuits. Cryptology ePrint Archive, Report 2013/687 (2013)
36. Gentry, C., Peikert, C., Vaikuntanathan, V.: Trapdoors for hard lattices and new cryptographic constructions. In: 40th Annual ACM Symposium on Theory of Computing (STOC), pp. 197–206. ACM, New York (2008)
37. Gordon, S.D., Katz, J., Vaikuntanathan, V.: A group signature scheme from lattice assumptions. In: Abe, M. (ed.) ASIACRYPT 2010. LNCS, vol. 6477, pp. 395–412. Springer, Heidelberg (2010)
38. Groth, J.: Simulation-sound NIZK proofs for a practical language and constant size group signatures. In: Lai, X., Chen, K. (eds.) ASIACRYPT 2006. LNCS, vol. 4284, pp. 444–459. Springer, Heidelberg (2006)
39. Groth, J.: Fully anonymous group signatures without random oracles. In: Kurosawa, K. (ed.) ASIACRYPT 2007. LNCS, vol. 4833, pp. 164–180. Springer, Heidelberg (2007)
40. T.C. Group. TCG TPM specification 1.2. (2003).
    http://www.trustedcomputinggroup.org
41. T.C. Group. TCG TPM specification 2.0. (2013).
    http://www.trustedcomputinggroup.org/resources/tpm_library_specification
42. I.P.W. Group, VSC Project. Dedicated short range communications (DSRC) (2003)
43. Laguillaumie, F., Langlois, A., Libert, B., Stehlé, D.: Lattice-based group signatures with logarithmic signature size. In: Sako, K., Sarkar, P. (eds.) ASIACRYPT 2013, Part II. LNCS, vol. 8270, pp. 41–61. Springer, Heidelberg (2013)
44. Langlois, A., Ling, S., Nguyen, K., Wang, H.: Lattice-based group signature scheme with verifier-local revocation. In: Krawczyk, H. (ed.) PKC 2014. LNCS, vol. 8383, pp. 345–361. Springer, Heidelberg (2014)
45. Libert, B., Peters, T., Yung, M.: Group signatures with almost-for-free revocation. In: Safavi-Naini, R., Canetti, R. (eds.) CRYPTO 2012. LNCS, vol. 7417, pp. 571–589. Springer, Heidelberg (2012)
46. Libert, B., Peters, T., Yung, M.: Scalable group signatures with revocation. In: Pointcheval, D., Johansson, T. (eds.) EUROCRYPT 2012. LNCS, vol. 7237, pp. 609–627. Springer, Heidelberg (2012)
47. Ling, S., Nguyen, K., Stehlé, D., Wang, H.: Improved zero-knowledge proofs of knowledge for the ISIS problem, and applications. In: Kurosawa, K., Hanaoka, G. (eds.) PKC 2013. LNCS, vol. 7778, pp. 107–124. Springer, Heidelberg (2013)
48. Ling, S., Nguyen, K., Wang, H.: Group signatures from lattices: simpler, tighter, shorter, ring-based. In: Katz, J. (ed.) PKC 2015. LNCS, vol. 9020, pp. xx-yy. Springer, Heidelberg (2015)
49. Lyubashevsky, V.: Lattice-based identification schemes secure under active attacks. In: Cramer, R. (ed.) PKC 2008. LNCS, vol. 4939, pp. 162–179. Springer, Heidelberg (2008)
50. Lyubashevsky, V.: Lattice signatures without trapdoors. In: Pointcheval, D., Johansson, T. (eds.) EUROCRYPT 2012. LNCS, vol. 7237, pp. 738–755. Springer, Heidelberg (2012)
51. Micciancio, D., Mol, P.: Pseudorandom knapsacks and the sample complexity of LWE search-to-decision reductions. In: Rogaway, P. (ed.) CRYPTO 2011. LNCS, vol. 6841, pp. 465–484. Springer, Heidelberg (2011)
52. Micciancio, D., Peikert, C.: Trapdoors for lattices: simpler, tighter, faster, smaller. In: Pointcheval, D., Johansson, T. (eds.) EUROCRYPT 2012. LNCS, vol. 7237, pp. 700–718. Springer, Heidelberg (2012)

53. Micciancio, D., Regev, O.: Worst-case to average-case reductions based on gaussian measures. SIAM J. Comput. **37**, 267–302 (2007)
54. Micciancio, D., Vadhan, S.P.: Statistical zero-knowledge proofs with efficient provers: lattice problems and more. In: Boneh, D. (ed.) CRYPTO 2003. LNCS, vol. 2729, pp. 282–298. Springer, Heidelberg (2003)
55. Peikert, C.: Public-key cryptosystems from the worst-case shortest vector problem: extended abstract. In: 41st Annual ACM Symposium on Theory of Computing (STOC), pp. 333–342. ACM, New York (2009)
56. Peikert, C., Rosen, A.: Efficient collision-resistant hashing from worst-case assumptions on cyclic lattices. In: Halevi, S., Rabin, T. (eds.) TCC 2006. LNCS, vol. 3876, pp. 145–166. Springer, Heidelberg (2006)
57. Regev, O.: On lattices, learning with errors, random linear codes, and cryptography. In: 37 Annual ACM Symposium on Theory of Computing (STOC), pp. 84–93. ACM, New York (2005)
58. Stern, J.: A new paradigm for public key identification. IEEE Transactions on Information Theory **42**(6), 1757–1768 (1996)

Group Signatures from Lattices: Simpler, Tighter, Shorter, Ring-Based

San Ling[✉], Khoa Nguyen, and Huaxiong Wang

Division of Mathematical Sciences, School of Physical and Mathematical Sciences,
Nanyang Technological University, Singapore, Singapore
{lingsan,khoantt,hxwang}@ntu.edu.sg

Abstract. We introduce a lattice-based group signature scheme that provides several noticeable improvements over the contemporary ones: simpler construction, weaker hardness assumptions, and shorter sizes of keys and signatures. Moreover, our scheme can be transformed into the ring setting, resulting in a scheme based on ideal lattices, in which the public key and signature both have bit-size $\widetilde{\mathcal{O}}(n \cdot \log N)$, for security parameter n, and for group of N users. Towards our goal, we construct a new lattice-based cryptographic tool: a statistical zero-knowledge argument of knowledge of a valid message-signature pair for Boyen's signature scheme (Boyen, PKC'10), which potentially can be used as the building block to design various privacy-enhancing cryptographic constructions.

1 Introduction

Group signatures [CvH91] have been an active research topic in public-key cryptography. Such schemes allow users of a group to anonymously sign messages on behalf of the whole group (*anonymity*). On the other hand, in cases of disputes, there is a tracing mechanism which can link a given signature to the identity of the misbehaving user (*traceability*). These two appealing features allow group signatures to find applications in various real-life scenarios, such as digital right management, anonymous online communications, e-commerce systems, and much more. On the theoretical front, designing secure and efficient group signature schemes is interesting and challenging, since those advanced constructions usually require a sophisticated combination of carefully chosen cryptographic ingredients: digital signatures, encryptions, and zero-knowledge protocols. Over the last two decades, numerous group signature schemes have been proposed (e.g., [CS97, ACJT00, BMW03, BBS04, BS04, Gro07, LPY12]).

In recent years, lattice-based cryptography, possessing nice features such as provable security under worst-case hardness assumptions, conjectured resistance against quantum computers and asymptotic efficiency, has become one of the most trendy research directions, especially after the emergence of fully-homomorphic encryption schemes from lattices, pioneered by Gentry [Gen09]. Along with other primitives, lattice-based group signatures has received noticeable attention. Prior to our work, several schemes were proposed, each of

© International Association for Cryptologic Research 2015
J. Katz (Ed.): PKC 2015, LNCS 9020, pp. 427–449, 2015.
DOI: 10.1007/978-3-662-46447-2_19

which has its own strengths and weaknesses. The first group signature from lattices was introduced by Gordon et al. [GKV10]. While their scheme is of great theoretical interest, its public key and signature have sizes $N \cdot \widetilde{\mathcal{O}}(n^2)$, for security parameter n, and for group of N users. In terms of efficiency, this is a noticeable disadvantage when the group is large, e.g., group of all employees of a big company. Camenisch et al. [CNR12] later proposed lattice-based anonymous attribute tokens system - a generalization of group signature. Their scheme supports CCA-anonymity, a stronger security requirement than the relaxed notion CPA-anonymity achieved by [GKV10], but the signature size is still linear in N. The linear-size barrier was finally overcome by Laguillaumie et al. [LLLS13], who designed a scheme featuring public key and signature sizes $\log N \cdot \widetilde{\mathcal{O}}(n^2)$. Yet, their scheme requires large parameters (e.g., $q = \log N \cdot \widetilde{\mathcal{O}}(n^8)$), and its anonymity and traceability properties have to rely on the hardness of $\mathsf{SIVP}_{\log N \cdot \widetilde{\mathcal{O}}(n^8)}$ and $\mathsf{SIVP}_{\log N \cdot \widetilde{\mathcal{O}}(n^{7.5})}$, respectively. Thus, the scheme produces significant overheads in terms of hardness assumptions, considering the fact that it is constructed based on Boyen's signature [Boy10] and the Dual-Regev encryption [GPV08] which rely on much weaker assumptions. Recently, Langlois et al. [LLNW14] introduced a lattice-based group signature scheme with verifier-local revocation, that also achieves logarithmic signature size. However, their scheme only satisfies a weak security model suggested by Boneh et al. [BBS04]. As in the schemes from [GKV10, CNR12, LLLS13], we consider the currently strongest model for static groups provided by Bellare et al. [BMW03].

The present state of lattice-based group signatures raises several interesting open questions. One of them is whether it is possible to design a scheme in the BMW model that simultaneously achieves signature size $\log N \cdot \widetilde{\mathcal{O}}(n)$ and weak hardness assumptions. Another open question, pointed out in [LLLS13], is to construct group signatures based on the ring variants of the Small Integer Solutions (SIS) and Learning with Errors (LWE) problems. This would make a noticeable step towards practice, since in those schemes, the public key size can be as small as $\log N \cdot \widetilde{\mathcal{O}}(n)$. Furthermore, we remark that the design approach of [GKV10, CNR12, LLLS13] are relatively complex. First, in all of these schemes, the encryption layer (needed for enabling traceability) has to be initialized in accordance with the signature layer (used for key generation), which, to some extent, limits the choice of encryption mechanisms. In addition, the encryption layer requires the costly generation of at least $\mathcal{O}(\log N)$ matrices in $\mathbb{Z}_q^{n \times m}$, and the signer has to encrypt at least $\log N \cdot \widetilde{\mathcal{O}}(n)$ bits, which leads to a growth in public key and signature sizes. Moreover, these schemes have to employ involved zero-knowledge protocols to prove the well-formedness of the obtained ciphertexts: in [GKV10, CNR12], the main protocols are obtained by OR-ing N proofs, while in [LLLS13], $\log N + 2$ different proofs are needed. This somewhat unsatisfactory situation highlights the challenge of simplifying the design of lattice-based group signatures.

Our Contributions and Summary of Our Techniques

In this work, we reply positively to all the open questions discussed above. Specifically, we introduce a lattice-based group signature scheme in the random oracle model (in Section 4), which simultaneously achieves the following features:

- The public key and signature have sizes $\log N \cdot \widetilde{\mathcal{O}}(n^2)$ and $\log N \cdot \widetilde{\mathcal{O}}(n)$, respectively [1]. In comparison with [LLLS13], the key is around 4 times smaller, and the signature contains a shorter ciphertext.
- The scheme relies on relatively weak hardness assumptions: it is CCA-anonymous and traceable if $\mathsf{SIVP}_{\log N \cdot \widetilde{\mathcal{O}}(n^2)}$ is hard in the worst-case. In contrast to [LLLS13], the scheme produces no overhead in terms of security: its anonymity and traceability properties rely exactly on the hardness assumptions of the underlying encryption scheme and signature scheme, respectively.

Furthermore, our scheme can be transformed into the ring setting, resulting in a scheme based on ideal lattices (in Section 5), in which the key and signature both have size $\widetilde{\mathcal{O}}(n \cdot \log N)$. In Table 1, we summarize the features of our two schemes in comparison with the existing ones.

Table 1. Comparison among lattice-based group signature schemes, for security parameter n, and groups of N users. The [GKV10] scheme and our scheme in Section 5 only satisfy the CPA-anonymity notion, while the schemes from [CNR12] and [LLLS13], and our scheme in Section 4 support the stronger notion CCA-anonymity.

Scheme	[GKV10]	[CNR12]	[LLLS13]	Section 4	Section 5
Signature size	$N \cdot \widetilde{\mathcal{O}}(n^2)$	$N \cdot \widetilde{\mathcal{O}}(n^2)$	$\log N \cdot \widetilde{\mathcal{O}}(n)$	$\log N \cdot \widetilde{\mathcal{O}}(n)$	$\log N \cdot \widetilde{\mathcal{O}}(n)$
Public key size	$N \cdot \widetilde{\mathcal{O}}(n^2)$	$N \cdot \widetilde{\mathcal{O}}(n^2)$	$\log N \cdot \widetilde{\mathcal{O}}(n^2)$	$\log N \cdot \widetilde{\mathcal{O}}(n^2)$	$\log N \cdot \widetilde{\mathcal{O}}(n)$
Anonymity assumption	$\mathsf{SIVP}_{\widetilde{\mathcal{O}}(n^2)}$	$\mathsf{SIVP}_{\widetilde{\mathcal{O}}(n^2)}$	$\mathsf{SIVP}_{\log N \cdot \widetilde{\mathcal{O}}(n^8)}$	$\mathsf{SIVP}_{\log N \cdot \widetilde{\mathcal{O}}(n^2)}$	$\mathsf{SVP}^{\infty}_{\log N \cdot \widetilde{\mathcal{O}}(n^{3.5})}$
Traceability assumption	$\mathsf{SIVP}_{\widetilde{\mathcal{O}}(n^{1.5})}$	$\mathsf{SIVP}_{\widetilde{\mathcal{O}}(n^2)}$	$\mathsf{SIVP}_{\log N \cdot \widetilde{\mathcal{O}}(n^{7.5})}$	$\mathsf{SIVP}_{\log N \cdot \widetilde{\mathcal{O}}(n^2)}$	$\mathsf{SVP}^{\infty}_{\log N \cdot \widetilde{\mathcal{O}}(n^2)}$

Another contribution of this work is that our schemes are obtained via a simple design approach. We rely on Boyen's signature scheme [Boy10], and consider group of $N = 2^{\ell}$ users, where each user is identified by a string $d \in \{0,1\}^{\ell}$, as in [LLLS13]. Yet, in our scheme, the user's secret key is simply a Boyen signature $\mathbf{z} \in \mathbb{Z}^{2m}$ on d (in [LLLS13], it is a matrix in $\mathbb{Z}^{2m \times 2m}$ - which is $2m = \widetilde{\mathcal{O}}(n)$ times longer). To sign a message on behalf of the group, the user first encrypts his identity d to obtain a ciphertext $\mathbf{c}$, and then generates a zero-knowledge argument to prove that he possesses a valid message-signature pair $(d, \mathbf{z})$ for

---

[1] It was noted by Bellare et al. [BMW03], that the dependency of keys and signatures sizes on $\log N$ is unavoidable for group signature schemes in the their model.

Boyen's signature scheme, and that $\mathbf{c}$ is a correct encryption of d. The protocol then is repeated to make the soundness error negligibly small, and then is made non-interactive using the Fiat-Shamir heuristic. The group signature is simply the pair $(\mathbf{c}, \Pi)$, where Π is the obtained non-interactive argument. To verify a signature, one checks Π, and to open it, the group manager decrypts $\mathbf{c}$. We remark that in our design, the signer has to encrypt only $\ell = \log N$ bits. Furthermore, the underlying encryption scheme is totally independent of the underlying standard signature (i.e., Boyen's signature in this case). This provides us a flexible choice of encryption schemes.

1. In the scheme in Section 4, to achieve CCA-anonymity, we rely on a CCA-secure encryption scheme, obtained by the standard technique of combining a one-time signature scheme and an identity-based encryption (IBE) scheme [BCHK07]. In particular, we employ the IBE scheme by Gentry et al. [GPV08] to gain efficiency in the random oracle model.
2. In the ring-based scheme in Section 5, since our main goal is efficiency, we employ the CPA-secure encryption scheme from [LPR13], for which the public key and ciphertext consist of only 2 ring elements.

In the process, we introduce a new lattice-based cryptographic tool: a statistical zero-knowledge argument of knowledge of a valid message-signature pair for Boyen's signature scheme. We remark that previous protocols in lattice-based cryptography (e.g., [MV03][Lyu08][LNSW13]) only allow to prove in zero-knowledge the possession of a signature on a *publicly given* message. The challenging part is to hide *both* the signature and message from the verifier, which we overcome by a non-trivial technique described in Section 3. We believe that our new protocol is of independent interest. Indeed, apart from group signatures, such protocols are essential for designing various privacy-enhancing constructions, such as anonymous credentials [CL01], compact e-cash [CHL05], policy-based signatures [BF14], and much more.

Comparison to Related Work. In a concurrent and independent work, Nguyen, Zhang and Zhang [NZZ15], based on a new zero-knowledge protocol corresponding to a simple identity-encoding function, also obtain a simpler lattice-based group signature than [GKV10, LLLS13]. In [NZZ15], the public key and signature sizes are shorter by a $\mathcal{O}(\log N)$ factor than in previous works, and are shorter than ours. On the other hand, the user's secret key in [NZZ15] is still a matrix in $\mathbb{Z}^{2m \times 2m}$ (as in [LLLS13]), and the scheme requires larger parameters, e.g., $q = m^{2.5} \max(m^6 \omega(\log^{2.5} m), 4N)$, as well as stronger security assumptions than ours.

2   Preliminaries

NOTATIONS. For integer $n \geq 1$, we denote by $[n]$ the set $\{1, \ldots, n\}$. The set of all permutations of k elements is denoted by $\mathcal{S}_k$. We assume that all vectors are column vectors. The concatenation of vectors $\mathbf{x} \in \mathbb{R}^m$ and $\mathbf{y} \in \mathbb{R}^k$ is denoted by $(\mathbf{x}\|\mathbf{y})$. We denote the column concatenation of matrices $\mathbf{A} \in \mathbb{R}^{n \times m}$ and $\mathbf{B} \in \mathbb{R}^{n \times k}$ by $[\mathbf{A}|\mathbf{B}]$. The identity matrix of order k is denoted by $\mathbf{I}_k$. If S is a finite set, $y \xleftarrow{\$} S$ means that y is chosen uniformly at random from S.

2.1 Group Signatures

Definition 1 ([BMW03]). A group signature scheme is a tuple of 4 polynomial-time algorithms:

- KeyGen: This algorithm takes as input $1^n, 1^N$, where $n \in \mathbb{N}$ is the security parameter and $N \in \mathbb{N}$ is the number of group users, and outputs a triple (gpk, gmsk, gsk), where gpk is the group public key; gmsk is the group manager's secret key; and gsk $= \{\text{gsk}[i]\}_{i \in \{0,\dots,N-1\}}$, where for $i \in \{0,\dots,N-1\}$, gsk$[i]$ is the secret key for user of index i.
- Sign: This algorithm takes as input gsk$[i]$ for some $i \in \{0,\dots,N-1\}$, and a message M, and returns a group signature Σ.
- Verify: This algorithm takes as input gpk, a message M, a purported signature Σ on M, and returns either 1 (Valid) or 0 (Invalid).
- Open: This algorithm takes as input gmsk, a message M, a signature Σ, and returns an index $i \in \{0,\dots,N-1\}$, or $\perp$ (to indicate failure).

Correctness. The correctness requirement for a group signature is as follows. For all $n, N \in \mathbb{N}$, all (gpk, gmsk, gsk) produced by KeyGen$(1^n, 1^N)$, all $i \in \{0,\dots,N-1\}$, and all $M \in \{0,1\}^*$,

$$\text{Verify}\big(\text{gpk}, M, \text{Sign}(\text{gsk}[i], M)\big) = 1 \ \wedge \ \text{Open}\big(\text{gmsk}, M, \text{Sign}(\text{gsk}[i], M)\big) = i.$$

Security. A secure group signature must satisfy two security notions:

- *Traceability* requires that all signatures, even those produced by a coalition of group users and the group manager, can be traced back to a member of the coalition.
- *Anonymity* requires that, signatures generated by two distinct group users are computationally indistinguishable to an adversary knowing all the user secret keys. In Bellare et al.'s model [BMW03], the anonymity adversary is granted access to an opening oracle (CCA-anonymity). Boneh et al. [BBS04] later proposed a relaxed notion, where the adversary cannot query the opening oracle (CPA-anonymity).

Formal definitions of the above notions are provided in Appendix A.

2.2 Average-Case Lattices Problems and Their Ring Variants

We first recall the definitions and hardness results for average-case problems SIS, LWE.

Definition 2 ([Ajt96, GPV08]). The $\text{SIS}^p_{n,m,q,\beta}$ problem is as follows: Given uniformly random matrix $\mathbf{A} \in \mathbb{Z}_q^{n \times m}$, find a non-zero vector $\mathbf{x} \in \mathbb{Z}^m$ such that $\|\mathbf{x}\|_p \leq \beta$ and $\mathbf{Ax} = \mathbf{0} \bmod q$.

If $m, \beta = \mathsf{poly}(n)$, and $q > \sqrt{n}\beta$, then the $\mathsf{SIS}^\infty_{n,m,q,\beta}$ problem is at least as hard as SIVP_γ for some $\gamma = \beta \cdot \widetilde{O}(\sqrt{nm})$ (see [GPV08, MP13]).

Definition 3 ([Reg05]). Let $n, m \geq 1$, $q \geq 2$, and let χ be a probability distribution on $\mathbb{Z}$. For $\mathbf{s} \in \mathbb{Z}_q^n$, let $A_{\mathbf{s},\chi}$ be the distribution obtained by sampling $\mathbf{a} \xleftarrow{\$} \mathbb{Z}_q^n$ and $e \hookleftarrow \chi$, and outputting $(\mathbf{a}, \mathbf{a}^T \cdot \mathbf{s} + e) \in \mathbb{Z}_q^n \times \mathbb{Z}_q$. The $\mathsf{LWE}_{n,q,\chi}$ problem asks to distinguish m samples chosen according to $A_{\mathbf{s},\chi}$ (for $\mathbf{s} \xleftarrow{\$} \mathbb{Z}_q^n$) and m samples chosen according to the uniform distribution over $\mathbb{Z}_q^n \times \mathbb{Z}_q$.

If q is a prime power, $b \geq \sqrt{n}\omega(\log n)$, $\gamma = \widetilde{O}(nq/b)$, then there exists an efficient sampleable b-bounded distribution χ (i.e., χ outputs samples with norm at most b with overwhelming probability) such that $\mathsf{LWE}_{n,q,\chi}$ is as least as hard as SIVP_γ (see [Reg05, Pei09, MM11, MP12]).

We now recall the ring variants of the SIS and LWE, as well as their hardness results. Let $f = x^n + 1$, where n is a power of 2, and let $q > 2$ be prime. Let $\mathsf{R} = \mathbb{Z}[x]/\langle f \rangle$ and $\mathsf{R}_q = \mathsf{R}/q\mathsf{R}$. (As an additive group, $\mathcal{R}_q$ is isomorphic to $\mathbb{Z}_q^n$.) For an element $a = c_0 + c_1 x + \ldots + c_{n-1}x^{n-1} \in \mathsf{R}$, we define $\|a\|_\infty = \max_i(|c_i|)$. For a vector $\mathbf{a} = (a_1, \ldots, a_m) \in \mathsf{R}^m$, we define $\|\mathbf{a}\|_\infty = \max_j(\|a_j\|_\infty)$. To avoid ambiguity, we will denote the multiplication operation of two ring elements by the symbol $\otimes$.

Definition 4 ([LM06, PR06, LMPR08]). The Ring-$\mathsf{SIS}_{n,m,q,\beta}$ problem is as follows: Given a uniformly random $\mathbf{a} = (a_1, \ldots, a_m) \in \mathsf{R}_q^m$, find a non-zero vector $\mathbf{x} = (x_1, \ldots, x_m) \in \mathsf{R}_q^m$ such that $\|\mathbf{a}\|_\infty \leq \beta$ and $\mathbf{a}\mathbf{x} = a_1 \otimes x_1 + \ldots a_m \otimes x_m = 0 \bmod q$.

For $m > \frac{\log q}{\log(2\beta)}$, $\gamma = 16\beta mn \log^2 n$, and $q \geq \frac{\gamma\sqrt{n}}{4\log n}$, the Ring-$\mathsf{SIS}_{n,m,q,\beta}$ problem is at least as hard as $\mathsf{SVP}^\infty_\gamma$ in any ideal in the ring R (see [LM06]).

Definition 5 ([LPR10]). Let $n, m \geq 1$, $q \geq 2$, and let χ be a probability distribution on $\mathcal{R}$. For $s \in \mathcal{R}_q$, let $A_{s,\chi}$ be the distribution obtained by sampling $a \xleftarrow{\$} \mathcal{R}_q$ and $e \hookleftarrow \chi$, and outputting the pair $(a, a \otimes s + e) \in \mathcal{R}_q \times \mathcal{R}_q$. The Ring-$\mathsf{LWE}_{n,m,q,\chi}$ problem asks to distinguish m samples chosen according to $A_{s,\chi}$ (for $s \xleftarrow{\$} \mathcal{R}_q$) and m samples chosen according to the uniform distribution over $\mathcal{R}_q \times \mathcal{R}_q$.

Let $q = 1 \bmod 2n$, $b \geq \omega(\sqrt{n \log n})$ and $\gamma = n^2(q/b)(nm/\log(nm))^{1/4}$. Then there exists an efficient sampleable b-bounded distribution χ such that the Ring-$\mathsf{LWE}_{n,m,q,\chi}$ problem is at least as hard as $\mathsf{SVP}^\infty_\gamma$ in any ideal in the ring R (see [LPR10]).

Note that the hardness of LWE is not affected if the secret $\mathbf{s}$ is sampled from χ [ACPS09]. The same holds for Ring-LWE (see [LPR13]). This is called the "Hermite Normal Form" (HNF) of these problems.

2.3 Boyen's "Lattice-mixing" Signature Scheme and Its Ring-Based Variant

Boyen's signature scheme [Boy10] is a lattice analogue of Water's pairing-based signature [Wat05]. Here we consider its improved version provided in [MP12]. The scheme uses the following parameters: n is the security parameter, ℓ is the message length, $q = \mathsf{poly}(n)$ is sufficiently large, $m \geq 2n \log q$, $\sigma = \Omega(\sqrt{\ell n \log q}$ $\log n)$ and $\beta = \sigma \omega(\sqrt{\log m})$. The public key is a tuple $(\mathbf{A}, \mathbf{A}_0, \dots, \mathbf{A}_\ell, \mathbf{u})$, and the signing key is a trapdoor $\mathbf{T_A}$, where:

- Matrix $\mathbf{A}$ is statistically close to uniform over $\mathbb{Z}_q^{n \times m}$ and its trapdoor $\mathbf{T_A} \in \mathbb{Z}^{m \times m}$ is a short basis for the lattice $\Lambda^\perp(\mathbf{A}) = \{\mathbf{x} \in \mathbb{Z}^m : \mathbf{A} \cdot \mathbf{x} = \mathbf{0} \bmod q\}$. The pair $(\mathbf{A}, \mathbf{T_A})$ is generated by a PPT algorithm $\mathsf{GenTrap}(n, m, q)$ (see [GPV08, AP11, MP12]).
- Matrices $\mathbf{A}_0, \dots, \mathbf{A}_\ell \in \mathbb{Z}_q^{n \times m}$ and vector $\mathbf{u} \in \mathbb{Z}_q^n$ are uniformly random.

To sign a message $d = (d_1, \dots, d_\ell) \in \{0,1\}^\ell$, the signer forms matrix $\mathbf{A}_{(d)} = [\mathbf{A} \,|\, \mathbf{A}_0 + \sum_{i=1}^\ell d_i \mathbf{A}_i] \in \mathbb{Z}_q^{n \times 2m}$, then runs the deterministic algorithm $\mathsf{ExtBasis}$ $(\mathbf{T_A}, \mathbf{A}_{(d)})$ from [CHKP10] to obtain a short basis $\mathbf{T}_{(d)}$ for the lattice $\Lambda^\perp(\mathbf{A}_{(d)})$. Finally the signer runs the probabilistic algorithm $\mathsf{SamplePre}(\mathbf{T}_{(d)}, \mathbf{A}_{(d)}, \mathbf{u}, \sigma)$ from [GPV08] to output a signature $\mathbf{z} \in \mathbb{Z}^{2m}$ satisfying $\|\mathbf{z}\|_\infty \leq \beta$ and $\mathbf{A}_{(d)}\mathbf{z} = \mathbf{u} \bmod q$. It follows from the improved security reduction in [MP12] that scheme is unforgeable under adaptive chosen-message attack if the $\mathsf{SIS}_{n,m,q,\beta'}^\infty$ problem is hard for some $\beta' = \ell \widetilde{\mathcal{O}}(n)$. Therefore, for the given parameters, the security of the scheme can be based on the worst-case hardness of $\mathsf{SIVP}_{\ell \cdot \widetilde{\mathcal{O}}(n^2)}$.

The public key in Boyen's signature has size $\ell \mathcal{O}(nm \log q) = \ell \widetilde{\mathcal{O}}(n^2)$, but can be reduced to $\ell \widetilde{\mathcal{O}}(n)$ by transforming the scheme into the ring setting, because the parameter m then can be set as $m = \Omega(\log q)$. This can be done rather straightforwardly, thanks to the constructions of the algorithms $\mathsf{GenTrap}$, $\mathsf{SamplePre}$, and $\mathsf{ExtBasis}$ for ideal lattices given by Stehlé et al. [SSTX09]. For an element $a \in \mathcal{R}_q$, define $\mathsf{rot}(a) \in \mathbb{Z}_q^{n \times n}$ as the matrix whose i-th column is $x^i \otimes a$, for $i = 0, \dots, n-1$. For a vector $\mathbf{a} = (a_1, \dots, a_m) \in \mathcal{R}_q^m$, define $\mathsf{rot}(\mathbf{a}) = [\mathsf{rot}(a_1) \,|\, \dots \,|\, \mathsf{rot}(a_m)] \in \mathbb{Z}_q^{n \times nm}$.

In the ring variant of Boyen's signature, the public key is a tuple $(\mathbf{a}, \mathbf{a}_0, \dots, \mathbf{a}_\ell,$ $u) \in (\mathcal{R}_q^m)^{\ell+2} \times \mathcal{R}_q$, and the signing key is a trapdoor $\mathbf{T_a} \in \mathbb{Z}^{nm \times nm}$ for $\Lambda^\perp(\mathsf{rot}(\mathbf{a}))$. Similarly, a signature on message $d \in \{0,1\}^\ell$ is a small-norm vector $\mathbf{z} \in \mathcal{R}^{2m}$ such that $[\mathbf{a} \,|\, \mathbf{a}_0 + \sum_{i=1}^\ell d_i \mathbf{a}_i] \mathbf{z} = u \bmod q$. By adapting the security reduction from [MP12] into the ring setting, the security of the scheme can be based on the average-case hardness of the $\mathsf{Ring\text{-}SIS}_{n,m,q,\beta'}$ problem for some $\beta' = \ell \widetilde{\mathcal{O}}(n)$, which in turn can be based on the worst-case hardness of the $\mathsf{SVP}_{\ell \cdot \widetilde{\mathcal{O}}(n^2)}^\infty$ problem on ideal lattices.

2.4 Zero-Knowledge Argument Systems for Lattices

We will work with statistical zero-knowledge argument systems, namely, inter-active protocols where the soundness property only holds for *computationally bounded* cheating provers, while the zero-knowledge property holds against *any* cheating verifier. More formally, let the set of statements-witnesses $R = \{(y, w)\} \in \{0, 1\}^* \times \{0, 1\}^*$ be an NP relation. A two-party game $\langle P, V \rangle$ is called an interactive argument system for the relation R with soundness error e if the following two conditions hold:

- Completeness. If $(y, w) \in R$ then $\Pr\left[\langle P(y, w), V(y) \rangle = 1\right] = 1$.
- Soundness. If $(y, w) \notin R$, then $\forall$ PPT P^*: $\Pr[\langle P^*(y, w), V(y) \rangle = 1] \leq e$.

An interactive argument system is called statistical zero-knowledge if for any $V^*(y)$, there exists a PPT simulator $\mathcal{S}(y)$ producing a simulated transcript that is statistically close to the one of the real interaction between $P(y, w)$ and $V^*(y)$. A related notion is argument of knowledge, which requires the witness-extended emulation property. For protocols consisting of 3 moves (i.e., commitment-challenge-response), witness-extended emulation is implied by *special soundness* [Gro04], where the latter assumes that there exists a PPT extractor which takes as input a set of valid transcripts with respect to all possible values of the 'challenge' to the same 'commitment', and outputs w' such that $(y, w') \in R$.

Statistical zero-knowledge arguments of knowledge (sZKAoK) are usually constructed using a statistically hiding and computationally binding string commitment scheme. Kawachi et al. [KTX08] designed such commitment scheme from lattices, where the binding property relies on the hardness of $\mathsf{SIVP}_{\widetilde{\mathcal{O}}(n)}$. Using this primitive, Ling et al. [LNSW13] proposed a Stern-type [Ste96] sZKAoK for the Inhomogeneous SIS relation:

$$R_{\mathsf{ISIS}} = \left\{ ((\mathbf{A} \in \mathbb{Z}_q^{n \times m}; \mathbf{u} \in \mathbb{Z}_q^n), \mathbf{x} \in \mathbb{Z}^m) : \|\mathbf{x}\|_\infty \leq \beta \wedge \mathbf{A}\mathbf{x} = \mathbf{u} \bmod q \right\}.$$

The core technique in Ling et al.'s work is called Decomposition-Extension. This technique is as follows. Letting $p = \lfloor \log \beta \rfloor + 1$, Ling et al. observe that an integer $x \in [0, \beta]$ if and only if there exist $x_1, \ldots, x_p \in \{0, 1\}$ such that $x = \sum_{j=1}^p \beta_j x_j$, where the sequence of integers $\beta_1, \ldots, \beta_p$ is determined as follows:

$$\beta_1 = \lceil \beta/2 \rceil; \beta_2 = \lceil (\beta - \beta_1)/2 \rceil; \beta_3 = \lceil (\beta - \beta_1 - \beta_2)/2 \rceil; \ldots; \beta_p = 1.^2$$

This observation allows the prover to efficiently decompose $\mathbf{x} \in [-\beta; \beta]^m$ into $\tilde{\mathbf{x}}_1, \ldots, \tilde{\mathbf{x}}_p \in \{-1, 0, 1\}^m$ such that $\sum_{j=1}^p \beta_j \tilde{\mathbf{x}}_j = \mathbf{x}$. To argue the possession of the $\tilde{\mathbf{x}}_j$'s in zero-knowledge, the prover extends $\tilde{\mathbf{x}}_j$ to $\mathbf{x}_j \in \mathsf{B}_{3m}$, where B_{3m} is the set of all vectors in $\{-1, 0, 1\}^{3m}$ having exactly m coordinates equal 0; m coordinates equal to 1; and m coordinates equal to -1. This set has a helpful property: if π is a permutation of $3m$ elements, then $\mathbf{x}_j \in \mathsf{B}_{3m}$ if and only if $\pi(\mathbf{x}_j) \in \mathsf{B}_{3m}$. Then in the framework of Stern's 3-move protocol, the prover is able to demonstrate that:

---

^{2} We note that the same sequence of integers was previously used by Lipmaa et al. [LAN02] in the context of range proofs, but under a different representation: $\beta_j = \lfloor (\beta + 2^{j-1})/2^j \rfloor$ for each $j \in [p]$.

1. For each j, a random permutation of $\mathbf{x}_j$ belongs to B_{3m}, which implies that $\mathbf{x}_j \in \mathsf{B}_{3m}$, and thus, $\tilde{\mathbf{x}}_j \in \{-1, 0, 1\}^m$. This will convinces the verifier that $\mathbf{x} \in [-\beta, \beta]^m$.

2. $\mathbf{A}^* \sum_{j=1}^{p} \beta_j(\mathbf{x}_j + \mathbf{r}_j) - \mathbf{u} = \mathbf{A}^* \sum_{j=1}^{p} \beta_j \mathbf{r}_j \bmod q$, where $\mathbf{A}^* \in \mathbb{Z}_q^{n \times 3m}$ is the extended matrix obtained by appending $2m$ "dummy" zero-columns to $\mathbf{A}$, and $\mathbf{r}_1, \ldots, \mathbf{r}_p \in \mathbb{Z}_q^{3m}$ are uniformly "masking" vectors for the $\mathbf{x}_j$'s. This equation implies $\mathbf{A}\mathbf{x} = \mathbf{A}^* \sum_{j=1}^{p} \beta_j \mathbf{x}_j = \mathbf{u} \bmod q$.

3 New Zero-Knowledge Protocols for Lattice-Based Cryptography

In this section, we first present a sZKAoK of a valid message-signature pair $(d, \mathbf{z})$ for Boyen's signature scheme ([Boy10], see also Section 2.3). Then we provide a lattice-based verifiable encryption protocol to show that a given ciphertext correctly encrypts d. The combined protocol of these two ones, which will serve as the building block in both constructions of our group signatures, is described in detail in Section 3.3.

3.1 ZKAoK of a Valid Message-Signature Pair for Boyen's Signature Scheme

Suppose that the verification key for Boyen's signature scheme is a tuple $(\mathbf{A}, \mathbf{A}_0, \ldots, \mathbf{A}_\ell, \mathbf{u})$. Our goal is to design a statistical ZKAoK of a pair $(d, \mathbf{z}) \in \{0, 1\}^\ell \times \mathbb{Z}^{2m}$ satisfying $\|\mathbf{z}\|_\infty \leq \beta$ and $\mathbf{A}_{(d)}\mathbf{z} = \mathbf{u} \bmod q$, where $\mathbf{A}_{(d)} = \begin{bmatrix} \mathbf{A} \mid \mathbf{A}_0 + \sum_{i=1}^{\ell} d_i \mathbf{A}_i \end{bmatrix} \in \mathbb{Z}_q^{n \times 2m}$. We first observe that obtaining a ZKAoK of a Boyen signature on a *given* message d is relatively straightforward: one can just run a zero-knowledge protocol for an ISIS solution (e.g., [MV03,Lyu08,LNSW13]) on public input $(\mathbf{A}_{(d)}, \mathbf{u})$, and prover's witness $\mathbf{z}$. However, constructing a ZKAoK of a message-signature pair $(d, \mathbf{z})$ is challenging, because on one hand, the prover has to convince the verifier that $\mathbf{A}_{(d)}\mathbf{z} = \mathbf{u} \bmod q$, while on the other hand, *both* $\mathbf{z}$ and d should be kept *secret* from the verifier.

Our first step towards solving the above challenge is making the public verification matrix independent of d. Let $\overline{\mathbf{A}} = \begin{bmatrix} \mathbf{A} \mid \mathbf{A}_0 \mid \mathbf{A}_1 \mid \ldots \mid \mathbf{A}_\ell \end{bmatrix} \in \mathbb{Z}_q^{n \times (\ell+2)m}$, and let $\mathbf{z} = (\mathbf{x} \| \mathbf{y})$, where $\mathbf{x}, \mathbf{y} \in \mathbb{Z}^m$, then we have:

$$\mathbf{u} = \mathbf{A}_{(d)}\mathbf{z} = \mathbf{A}\mathbf{x} + \mathbf{A}_0\mathbf{y} + \sum_{j=1}^{\ell} \mathbf{A}_i(d_i \mathbf{y}) = \overline{\mathbf{A}}\,\overline{\mathbf{z}} \bmod q,$$

where $\overline{\mathbf{z}} \in \mathbb{Z}^{(\ell+2)m}$ has the form $\overline{\mathbf{z}} = (\mathbf{x} \| \mathbf{y} \| d_1\mathbf{y} \| \ldots \| d_\ell \mathbf{y})$. Now our goal is: Given $(\overline{\mathbf{A}}, \mathbf{u})$, arguing in zero-knowledge the possession of $\overline{\mathbf{z}} \in \mathbb{Z}^{(\ell+2)m}$ such that:

1. "$\|\overline{\mathbf{z}}\|_\infty \leq \beta$ and $\overline{\mathbf{A}}\,\overline{\mathbf{z}} = \mathbf{u} \bmod q$." This part can be done using the Decomposition-Extension technique from [LNSW13] for an ISIS solution. Specifically, we transform $\mathbf{x}$ and $\mathbf{y}$ into $p = \lfloor \log \beta \rfloor + 1$ vectors $\mathbf{x}_1, \ldots, \mathbf{x}_p \in \mathsf{B}_{3m}$ and $\mathbf{y}_1, \ldots, \mathbf{y}_p \in \mathsf{B}_{3m}$, respectively.

2. "$\bar{\mathbf{z}}$ has the form $\bar{\mathbf{z}} = (\mathbf{x}\|\mathbf{y}\|d_1\mathbf{y}\|\dots\|d_\ell\mathbf{y})$ for certain secret $d \in \{0,1\}^\ell$." At a high level, in order to argue that $d \in \{0,1\}^\ell$, we first extend d to $d^* = (d_1, \dots, d_\ell, d_{\ell+1}, \dots, d_{2\ell}) \in \mathsf{B}_{2\ell}$, where $\mathsf{B}_{2\ell}$ is the set of all vectors in $\{0,1\}^{2\ell}$ having Hamming weight ℓ, and then show that a random permutation of d^* belongs to the set $\mathsf{B}_{2\ell}$, which implies that the original $d \in \{0,1\}^\ell$.

Now, for simplicity of description of our technique, we introduce the following notations:

- For permutations $\pi, \psi \in \mathsf{S}_{3m}$; $\tau \in \mathsf{S}_{2\ell}$, and for $\mathbf{t} = (\mathbf{t}_{-1}\|\mathbf{t}_0\|\mathbf{t}_1\|\dots\|\mathbf{t}_{2\ell}) \in \mathbb{Z}_q^{(2\ell+2)3m}$ consisting of $(2\ell + 2)$ blocks of size $3m$, we define:

$$F_{\pi,\psi,\tau}(\mathbf{t}) = \big(\pi(\mathbf{t}_{-1})\|\psi(\mathbf{t}_0)\|\psi(\mathbf{t}_{\tau(1)})\|\psi(\mathbf{t}_{\tau(2)})\|\dots\|\psi(\mathbf{t}_{\tau(2\ell)})\big).$$

  Namely, $F_{\pi,\psi,\tau}(\mathbf{t})$ is a composition of 3 permutations. It *rearranges* the order of the 2ℓ blocks $\mathbf{t}_1, \mathbf{t}_2, \dots, \mathbf{t}_{2\ell}$ according to τ, and then *permutes* block $\mathbf{t}_{-1}$ according to π, and the other $(2\ell + 1)$ blocks according to ψ.
- Given $e = (e_1, e_2, \dots, e_{2\ell}) \in \{0,1\}^{2\ell}$, we say that vector $\mathbf{t} \in \mathsf{VALID}(e)$ if $\mathbf{t} \in \{-1,0,1\}^{(2\ell+2)3m}$, and there exist certain $\mathbf{v}, \mathbf{w} \in \mathsf{B}_{3m}$ such that $\mathbf{t} = (\mathbf{v}\|\mathbf{w}\|e_1\mathbf{w}\|e_2\mathbf{w}\|\dots\|e_{2\ell}\mathbf{w})$.

We now describe our technique. We define the sequence of integers $\beta_1, \dots, \beta_p$ as in [LNSW13], and let:

$$\mathbf{A}^* = [\mathbf{A}|0^{n\times 2m}|\mathbf{A}_0|0^{n\times 2m}|\mathbf{A}_1|0^{n\times 2m}|\dots|\mathbf{A}_\ell|0^{n\times 2m}|0^{n\times 3m\ell}] \in \mathbb{Z}_q^{n\times(2\ell+2)3m}, \quad (1)$$

$$\mathbf{z}_j = (\mathbf{x}_j\|\mathbf{y}_j\|d_1\mathbf{y}_j\|\dots\|d_\ell\mathbf{y}_j\|d_{\ell+1}\mathbf{y}_j\|\dots\|d_{2\ell}\mathbf{y}_j) \in \{-1,0,1\}^{(2\ell+2)3m}, \forall j \in [p]. \quad (2)$$

We then have: $\mathbf{A}^*(\sum_{j=1}^p \beta_j \mathbf{z}_j) = \mathbf{u} \bmod q$, and $\mathbf{z}_j \in \mathsf{VALID}(d^*)$ for all $j \in [p]$. In Stern's framework, we proceed as follows:

- To argue that $\mathbf{A}^*(\sum_{j=1}^p \beta_j \mathbf{z}_j) = \mathbf{u} \bmod q$, we instead show that

$$\mathbf{A}^* \sum_{j=1}^p \beta_j(\mathbf{z}_j + \mathbf{r}_{\mathbf{z}}^{(j)}) - \mathbf{u} = \mathbf{A}^*(\sum_{j=1}^p \beta_j \mathbf{r}_{\mathbf{z}}^{(j)}) \bmod q,$$

  where $\mathbf{r}_{\mathbf{z}}^{(1)}, \dots, \mathbf{r}_{\mathbf{z}}^{(p)} \in \mathbb{Z}_q^{n\times(2\ell+2)3m}$ are uniformly random "masking" vectors for the $\mathbf{z}_j$'s.
- We sample a uniformly random permutation $\tau \in \mathsf{S}_{2\ell}$, and for each $j \in [p]$, sample uniformly random $\pi_j, \psi_j \in \mathsf{S}_{3m}$, and send $\mathbf{t}_d = \tau(d^*)$ together with $\mathbf{t}_{\mathbf{z}}^{(j)} = F_{\pi_j,\psi_j,\tau}(\mathbf{z}_j)$, for all j. Seeing that $\mathbf{t}_d \in \mathsf{B}_{2\ell}$, and $\mathbf{t}_{\mathbf{z}}^{(j)} \in \mathsf{VALID}(\mathbf{t}_d)$, the verifier will be convinced that $\mathbf{z}_j \in \mathsf{VALID}(d^*)$ while learning no additional information about $\mathbf{z}_j$ or d^*.

Based on the above discussion, we can build a ZKAoK of a valid message-signature pair for Boyen's signature scheme. For convenience, we will present the details in the combined protocol in Section 3.3.

3.2   A Lattice-Based Verifiable Encryption Protocol

We consider two lattice-based encryption schemes:

1. The GPV-IBE scheme [GPV08] based on LWE, to be employed in the group signature in Section 4.
2. The LPR encryption scheme [LPR13] based on Ring-LWE, to be employed in the ring-based group signature in Section 5.

We observe that, in both of these schemes, if one encrypts a plaintext $d \in \{0,1\}^\ell$ using the HNF variants of LWE and Ring-LWE, respectively, then the relation among the related objects can be expressed as:

$$\mathbf{Pe} + (\,0^{k_1-\ell}\,\|\,\lfloor q/2 \rfloor d\,) = \mathbf{c} \bmod q,$$

where $\mathbf{P} \in \mathbb{Z}_q^{k_1 \times k_2}$ is a matrix obtained from the public key, $\mathbf{c} \in \mathbb{Z}_q^{k_1}$ is a ciphertext, $\mathbf{e} \in \mathbb{Z}^{k_2}$ is the encryption randomness satisfying $\|\mathbf{e}\|_\infty \le b$. Here k_1, k_2, b are certain parameters depending on the underlying scheme.

Our goal is to construct a verifiable encryption protocol for both of the mentioned above schemes, namely, a protocol such that: given $(\mathbf{P}, \mathbf{c})$, the prover, possessing $(\mathbf{e}, d)$, can argue in zero-knowledge that $\mathbf{c}$ is a correct encryption of d. We observe that, this task can be achieved as follows:

- To argue that $d \in \{0,1\}^\ell$, we can use the same technique as in the previous section, i.e., extend d to $d^* \in \mathsf{B}_{2\ell}$, then use a random permutation.
- To argue that $\mathbf{e} \in \mathbb{Z}^{k_2}$ and $\|\mathbf{e}\|_\infty \le b$, we form vectors $\mathbf{e}_1, \dots, \mathbf{e}_{\bar{p}} \in \mathsf{B}_{3k_2}$, where $\bar{p} = \lfloor \log b \rfloor + 1$, then use random permutations to show $\mathbf{e}_j \in \mathsf{B}_{3k_2}$.
- Next, we define the matrices $\mathbf{P}^* \in \mathbb{Z}_q^{k_1 \times 3k_2}$, $\mathbf{Q} \in \{0, \lfloor q/2 \rfloor\}^{k_1 \times 2\ell}$, where:

$$\mathbf{P}^* = \left[\mathbf{P}\,|\,0^{k_1 \times 2k_2}\right]; \quad \mathbf{Q} = \begin{pmatrix} 0^{(k_1-\ell) \times \ell} & | & 0^{(k_1-\ell) \times \ell} \\ ---- & & ---- \\ \lfloor q/2 \rfloor \mathbf{I}_\ell & | & 0^{\ell \times \ell} \end{pmatrix}. \tag{3}$$

We then have that:

$$\mathbf{P}^*\Big(\sum_{j=1}^{\bar{p}} b_j \mathbf{e}_j\Big) + \mathbf{Q}d^* = \mathbf{Pe} + (\,0^{k_1-\ell}\,\|\,\lfloor q/2 \rfloor d\,) = \mathbf{c} \bmod q. \tag{4}$$

In Stern's framework, to argue that (4) is true, we instead show that:

$$\mathbf{P}^*\Big(\sum_{j=1}^{\bar{p}} b_j(\mathbf{e}_j + \mathbf{r_e}^{(j)})\Big) + \mathbf{Q}(d^* + \mathbf{r}_d) - \mathbf{c} = \mathbf{P}^*\Big(\sum_{j=1}^{\bar{p}} b_j \mathbf{r_e}^{(j)}\Big) + \mathbf{Q}\mathbf{r}_d \bmod q,$$

where $\mathbf{r_e}^{(j)} \in \mathbb{Z}_q^{3k_2}$, for every $j \in [\bar{p}]$, and $\mathbf{r}_d \in \mathbb{Z}_q^{2\ell}$ are masking vectors.

3.3   The Combined Protocol

We now describe in detail the combined protocol that allows the prover to argue that it knows a valid message-signature pair $(d, \mathbf{z})$ for Boyen's signature scheme, and that a given ciphertext correctly encrypts d. The associated relation $\mathrm{R_{gs}}(n, \ell, q, m, k_1, k_2, \beta, b)$ is defined as follows.

Definition 6

$$R_{gs} = \Big\{ \big((A, A_0, \ldots, A_\ell \in \mathbb{Z}_q^{n \times m}; u \in \mathbb{Z}_q^n; P \in \mathbb{Z}_q^{k_1 \times k_2}; c \in \mathbb{Z}_q^{k_1}); d \in \{0,1\}^\ell;$$

$$z \in \mathbb{Z}^{2m}; e \in \mathbb{Z}^{k_2} \big) : \big(\|z\|_\infty \leq \beta \wedge \Big[A \mid A_0 + \sum_{i=1}^\ell d_i A_i \Big] z = u \bmod q \big) \bigwedge$$

$$\bigwedge \big(\|e\|_\infty \leq b \wedge Pe + (0^{k_1-\ell} \| \lfloor q/2 \rfloor d) = c \bmod q \big). \Big\}$$

Let COM be the statistically hiding and computationally binding string commitment scheme from [KTX08]. Let $p = \lfloor \log \beta \rfloor + 1$ and $\bar{p} = \lfloor \log b \rfloor + 1$ and define two sequences of integers $\beta_1, \ldots, \beta_p$ and $b_1, \ldots, b_{\bar{p}}$ as in sections [LNSW13]. The inputs of two parties are as follows:

- The common input is $(A, A_0, \ldots, A_\ell, u, P, c)$. Both parties form matrices A^*, P^*, Q as described in (1) and (3).
- The prover's witness is (d, z, e). Using the techniques above, the prover extends d to some $d^* \in B_{2\ell}$ and forms vectors $z_1, \ldots, z_p \in \mathsf{VALID}(d^*)$, and $e_1, \ldots, e_{\bar{p}} \in B_{3k_2}$. The obtained vectors satisfy:

$$A^* \big(\sum_{j=1}^p \beta_j z_j \big) = u \bmod q \; \wedge \; P^* \big(\sum_{j=1}^{\bar{p}} b_j e_j \big) + Q d^* = c \bmod q.$$

The interaction between P and V is described in Figure 1.

The following theorem summarizes the properties of our protocol.

Theorem 1. *Let* COM *be a statistically hiding and computationally binding string commitment scheme. Then the protocol in Figure 1 is a statistical* ZKAoK *for the relation* $R_{gs}(n, \ell, q, m, k_1, k_2, \beta, b)$. *Each round of the protocol has perfect completeness, soundness error* $2/3$, *and communication cost* $(\mathcal{O}(\ell m) \log \beta + \mathcal{O}(k_2) \log b) \log q$.

The proof of Theorem 1 employs the standard proof technique for Stern-type protocols. It is given in the full version [LNW15].

4   An Improved Lattice-Based Group Signature Scheme

4.1   Description of Our Scheme

We first specify the parameters of the scheme. Let n be the security parameter, and let $N = 2^\ell = \mathsf{poly}(n)$ be the maximum expected number of group users. Then we choose other scheme parameters such that Boyen's signature scheme and the GPV-IBE scheme function properly, and are secure. Specifically, let modulus $q = \mathcal{O}(\ell \cdot n^2)$ be prime, dimension $m \geq 2n \log q$, and Gaussian parameter $s = \omega(\log m)$. The infinity norm bound for signatures from Boyen's scheme is integer $\beta = \widetilde{\mathcal{O}}(\sqrt{\ell n})$. The norm bound for LWE noises is integer b such that $q/b = \ell \widetilde{\mathcal{O}}(n)$.

Choose hash functions $\mathcal{H}_1 : \{0,1\}^* \to \mathbb{Z}_q^{n \times \ell}$ and $\mathcal{H}_2 : \{0,1\}^* \to \{1,2,3\}^t$, to be modeled as random oracles, and select a one-time signature scheme $\mathcal{OTS} = (\mathsf{OGen}, \mathsf{OSign}, \mathsf{OVer})$. Let χ be a b-bounded distribution over $\mathbb{Z}$.

Our group signature scheme is described as follows:

1. **Commitment:** P samples

$$\begin{cases} \mathbf{r}_{\mathbf{z}}^{(1)}, \ldots, \mathbf{r}_{\mathbf{z}}^{(p)} \xleftarrow{\$} \mathbb{Z}_q^{(2\ell+2)3m}; \ \mathbf{r}_{\mathbf{e}}^{(1)}, \ldots, \mathbf{r}_{\mathbf{e}}^{(\bar{p})} \xleftarrow{\$} \mathbb{Z}_q^{3k_2}; \ \mathbf{r}_d \xleftarrow{\$} \mathbb{Z}_q^{2\ell} \\ \tau \xleftarrow{\$} S_{2\ell}; \ \pi_1, \ldots, \pi_p, \psi_1, \ldots, \psi_p \xleftarrow{\$} S_{3m}; \ \phi_1, \ldots, \phi_{\bar{p}} \xleftarrow{\$} S_{3k_2}. \end{cases}$$

Then P sends the commitment $\text{CMT} = (\mathbf{c}_1, \mathbf{c}_2, \mathbf{c}_3)$ to V, where

$$\begin{cases} \mathbf{c}_1 = \text{COM}(\tau; \{\pi_j\}_{j=1}^p; \{\psi_j\}_{j=1}^p; \{\phi_j\}_{j=1}^{\bar{p}}; \mathbf{A}^*(\sum_{j=1}^p \beta_j \mathbf{r}_{\mathbf{z}}^{(j)}); \ \mathbf{P}^*(\sum_{j=1}^{\bar{p}} b_j \mathbf{r}_{\mathbf{e}}^{(j)}) + \mathbf{Q}\mathbf{r}_d), \\ \mathbf{c}_2 = \text{COM}(\{F_{\pi_j, \psi_j, \tau}(\mathbf{r}_{\mathbf{z}}^{(j)})\}_{j=1}^p; \{\phi_j(\mathbf{r}_{\mathbf{e}}^{(j)})\}_{j=1}^{\bar{p}}; \tau(\mathbf{r}_d)), \\ \mathbf{c}_3 = \text{COM}(\{F_{\pi_j, \psi_j, \tau}(\mathbf{z}_j + \mathbf{r}_{\mathbf{z}}^{(j)})\}_{j=1}^p; \{\phi_j(\mathbf{e}_j + \mathbf{r}_{\mathbf{e}}^{(j)})\}_{j=1}^{\bar{p}}; \tau(d^* + \mathbf{r}_d)). \end{cases}$$

2. **Challenge:** V sends a challenge $Ch \xleftarrow{\$} \{1, 2, 3\}$ to P.
3. **Response:** Depending on Ch, P computes the response RSP as follows:
   - Case $Ch = 1$: For each $j \in [p]$, let $\mathbf{t}_{\mathbf{z}}^{(j)} = F_{\pi_j, \psi_j, \tau}(\mathbf{z}_j)$ and $\mathbf{v}_{\mathbf{z}}^{(j)} = F_{\pi_j, \psi_j, \tau}(\mathbf{r}_{\mathbf{z}}^{(j)})$. For each $j \in [\bar{p}]$, let $\mathbf{t}_{\mathbf{e}}^{(j)} = \phi_j(\mathbf{e}_j)$ and $\mathbf{v}_{\mathbf{e}}^{(j)} = \phi_j(\mathbf{r}_{\mathbf{e}}^{(j)})$. Let $\mathbf{t}_d = \tau(d^*)$ and $\mathbf{v}_d = \tau(\mathbf{r}_d)$. Then the prover sends:

$$\text{RSP} = (\{\mathbf{t}_{\mathbf{z}}^{(j)}\}_{j=1}^p; \{\mathbf{v}_{\mathbf{z}}^{(j)}\}_{j=1}^p; \{\mathbf{t}_{\mathbf{e}}^{(j)}\}_{j=1}^{\bar{p}}; \{\mathbf{v}_{\mathbf{e}}^{(j)}\}_{j=1}^{\bar{p}}; \mathbf{t}_d; \mathbf{v}_d). \tag{5}$$

   - Case $Ch = 2$: For each $j \in [p]$, let $\widehat{\pi}_j = \pi_j$; $\widehat{\psi}_j = \psi_j$; and $\mathbf{w}_{\mathbf{z}}^{(j)} = \mathbf{z}_j + \mathbf{r}_{\mathbf{z}}^{(j)}$. For each $j \in [\bar{p}]$, let $\widehat{\phi}_j = \phi_j$; and $\mathbf{w}_{\mathbf{e}}^{(j)} = \mathbf{e}_j + \mathbf{r}_{\mathbf{e}}^{(j)}$. Let $\widehat{\tau} = \tau$ and $\mathbf{w}_d = d^* + \mathbf{r}_d$. Then the prover sends:

$$\text{RSP} = (\widehat{\tau}; \{\widehat{\pi}_j\}_{j=1}^p; \{\widehat{\psi}_j\}_{j=1}^p; \{\widehat{\phi}_j\}_{j=1}^{\bar{p}}; \{\mathbf{w}_{\mathbf{z}}^{(j)}\}_{j=1}^p; \{\mathbf{w}_{\mathbf{e}}^{(j)}\}_{j=1}^{\bar{p}}; \mathbf{w}_d). \tag{6}$$

   - Case $Ch = 3$: For each $j \in [p]$, let $\widetilde{\pi}_j = \pi_j$; $\widetilde{\psi}_j = \psi_j$; and $\mathbf{y}_{\mathbf{z}}^{(j)} = \mathbf{r}_{\mathbf{z}}^{(j)}$. For each $j \in [\bar{p}]$, let $\widetilde{\phi}_j = \phi_j$; and $\mathbf{y}_{\mathbf{e}}^{(j)} = \mathbf{r}_{\mathbf{e}}^{(j)}$. Let $\widetilde{\tau} = \tau$ and $\mathbf{y}_d = \mathbf{r}_d$. Then the prover sends:

$$\text{RSP} = (\widetilde{\tau}; \{\widetilde{\pi}_j\}_{j=1}^p; \{\widetilde{\psi}_j\}_{j=1}^p; \{\widetilde{\phi}_j\}_{j=1}^{\bar{p}}; \{\mathbf{y}_{\mathbf{z}}^{(j)}\}_{j=1}^p; \{\mathbf{y}_{\mathbf{e}}^{(j)}\}_{j=1}^{\bar{p}}; \mathbf{y}_d). \tag{7}$$

Verification: Receiving RSP, the verifier proceeds as follows:

- Case $Ch = 1$: Parse RSP as in (5). Check that $\mathbf{t}_d \in \mathsf{B}_{2\ell}$; $\mathbf{t}_{\mathbf{z}}^{(j)} \in \text{VALID}(\mathbf{t}_d)$, $\forall j \in [p]$; $\mathbf{t}_{\mathbf{e}}^{(j)} \in \mathsf{B}_{3k_2}$, $\forall j \in [\bar{p}]$; and that

$$\begin{cases} \mathbf{c}_2 = \text{COM}(\{\mathbf{v}_{\mathbf{z}}^{(j)}\}_{j=1}^p; \{\mathbf{v}_{\mathbf{e}}^{(j)}\}_{j=1}^{\bar{p}}; \mathbf{v}_d) \\ \mathbf{c}_3 = \text{COM}(\{\mathbf{t}_{\mathbf{z}}^{(j)} + \mathbf{v}_{\mathbf{z}}^{(j)}\}_{j=1}^p; \{\mathbf{t}_{\mathbf{e}}^{(j)} + \mathbf{v}_{\mathbf{e}}^{(j)}\}_{j=1}^{\bar{p}}; \mathbf{t}_d + \mathbf{v}_d). \end{cases}$$

- Case $Ch = 2$: Parse RSP as in (6). Check that:

$$\begin{cases} \mathbf{c}_1 = \text{COM}(\widehat{\tau}; \{\widehat{\pi}_j\}_{j=1}^p; \{\widehat{\psi}_j\}_{j=1}^p; \{\widehat{\phi}_j\}_{j=1}^{\bar{p}}; \\ \qquad \mathbf{A}^*(\sum_{j=1}^p \beta_j \mathbf{w}_{\mathbf{z}}^{(j)}) - \mathbf{u}; \ \mathbf{P}^*(\sum_{j=1}^{\bar{p}} b_j \mathbf{w}_{\mathbf{e}}^{(j)}) + \mathbf{Q}\mathbf{w}_d - \mathbf{c}), \\ \mathbf{c}_3 = \text{COM}(\{F_{\widehat{\pi}_j, \widehat{\psi}_j, \widehat{\tau}}(\mathbf{w}_{\mathbf{z}}^{(j)})\}_{j=1}^p; \{\widehat{\phi}_j(\mathbf{w}_{\mathbf{e}}^{(j)})\}_{j=1}^{\bar{p}}; \widehat{\tau}(\mathbf{w}_d)). \end{cases}$$

- Case $Ch = 3$: Parse RSP as in (7). Check that:

$$\begin{cases} \mathbf{c}_1 = \text{COM}(\widetilde{\tau}; \{\widetilde{\pi}_j\}_{j=1}^p; \{\widetilde{\psi}_j\}_{j=1}^p; \{\widetilde{\phi}_j\}_{j=1}^{\bar{p}}; \mathbf{A}^*(\sum_{j=1}^p \beta_j \mathbf{y}_{\mathbf{z}}^{(j)}); \ \mathbf{P}^*(\sum_{j=1}^{\bar{p}} b_i \mathbf{y}_{\mathbf{e}}^{(j)}) + \mathbf{Q}\mathbf{y}_d), \\ \mathbf{c}_2 = \text{COM}(\{F_{\widetilde{\pi}_j, \widetilde{\psi}_j, \widetilde{\tau}}(\mathbf{y}_{\mathbf{z}}^{(j)})\}_{j=1}^p; \{\widetilde{\phi}_j(\mathbf{y}_{\mathbf{e}}^{(j)})\}_{j=1}^{\bar{p}}; \widetilde{\tau}(\mathbf{y}_d)). \end{cases}$$

In each case, V outputs 1 if and only if all the conditions hold. Otherwise, it outputs 0.

Fig. 1. A zero-knowledge argument that the prover possesses a valid message-signature pair $(d, \mathbf{z})$ for Boyen's signature scheme, and that a given ciphertext correctly encrypts d.

KeyGen$(1^n, 1^N)$**:** This algorithm performs the following steps:

1. Generate verification key $(\mathbf{A}, \mathbf{A}_0, \ldots, \mathbf{A}_\ell, \mathbf{u})$ and signing key $\mathbf{T_A}$ for Boyen's signature scheme (see Section 2.3 for more details). Then for each $d = (d_1, \ldots, d_\ell) \in \{0,1\}^\ell$, use $\mathbf{T_A}$ to generate gsk$[d]$ as a Boyen signature on message d.
2. Generate encrypting and decrypting keys for the GPV-IBE scheme: Run algorithm GenTrap(n, m, q) from [GPV08] to output $\mathbf{B} \in \mathbb{Z}_q^{n \times m}$ together with a trapdoor basis $\mathbf{T_B}$ for $\Lambda^\perp(\mathbf{B})$.
3. Output

$$\mathsf{gpk} = \big((\mathbf{A}, \mathbf{A}_0, \ldots, \mathbf{A}_\ell, \mathbf{u}),\ \mathbf{B}\big);\ \mathsf{gmsk} = \mathbf{T_B};\ \mathsf{gsk} = \{\mathsf{gsk}[d]\}_{d \in \{0,1\}^\ell}.$$

Sign(gsk$[d]$, M)**:** Given gpk, to sign a message $M \in \{0,1\}^*$ using the secret key gsk$[d] = \mathbf{z}$, the user generates a key pair (ovk, osk) $\leftarrow$ OGen(1^n) for $\mathcal{OTS}$, and then performs the following steps:

1. Encrypt the index d with respect to "identity" ovk as follows. Let $\mathbf{G} = \mathcal{H}_1(\mathsf{ovk}) \in \mathbb{Z}_q^{n \times \ell}$. Sample $\mathbf{s} \hookleftarrow \chi^n; \mathbf{e}_1 \hookleftarrow \chi^m; \mathbf{e}_2 \hookleftarrow \chi^\ell$, then compute the ciphertext:

$$\big(\mathbf{c}_1 = \mathbf{B}^T\mathbf{s} + \mathbf{e}_1, \mathbf{c}_2 = \mathbf{G}^T\mathbf{s} + \mathbf{e}_2 + \lfloor q/2 \rfloor d\big) \in \mathbb{Z}_q^m \times \mathbb{Z}_q^\ell.$$

2. Generate a NIZKAoK Π to show the possession of a valid message-signature pair $(d, \mathbf{z})$ for Boyen's signature, and that $(\mathbf{c}_1, \mathbf{c}_2)$ is a correct GPV-IBE encryption of d with respect to "identity" ovk. This is done as follows:

   – Let $k_1 := m + \ell$ and $k_2 := n + m + \ell$, and form the following:

$$\mathbf{P} = \begin{pmatrix} \mathbf{B}^T & \\ -- & \mathbf{I}_{m+\ell} \\ \mathbf{G}^T & \end{pmatrix} \in \mathbb{Z}_q^{k_1 \times k_2};\ \mathbf{c} = \begin{pmatrix} \mathbf{c}_1 \\ \mathbf{c}_2 \end{pmatrix} \in \mathbb{Z}^{k_1};\ \mathbf{e} = \begin{pmatrix} \mathbf{s} \\ \mathbf{e}_1 \\ \mathbf{e}_2 \end{pmatrix} \in \mathbb{Z}^{k_2}, \quad (8)$$

   Then we have $\|\mathbf{e}\|_\infty \le b$, and $\mathbf{Pe} + \big(0^{k_1-\ell} \| \lfloor q/2 \rfloor d\big) = \mathbf{c} \bmod q$. Now one can observe that:

$$\big((\mathbf{A}, \mathbf{A}_0, \ldots, \mathbf{A}_\ell, \mathbf{u}, \mathbf{P}, \mathbf{c}), d, \mathbf{z}, \mathbf{e}\big) \in \mathrm{R}_{\mathsf{gs}}(n, \ell, q, m, k_1, k_2, \beta, b).$$

   – Run the protocol described in Section 3.3 with public parameter $(\mathbf{A}, \mathbf{A}_0, \ldots, \mathbf{A}_\ell, \mathbf{u}, \mathbf{P}, \mathbf{c})$ and prover's witness $(d, \mathbf{z}, \mathbf{e})$. The protocol is repeated $t = \omega(\log n)$ times to make the soundness error negligibly small, and then made non-interactive using the Fiat-Shamir heuristic as a triple $\Pi = \big(\{\mathrm{CMT}_j\}_{j=1}^t, \mathrm{CH}, \{\mathrm{RSP}_j\}_{j=1}^t\big)$, where

$$\mathrm{CH} = \{Ch_j\}_{j=1}^t = \mathcal{H}_2\big(M, \{\mathrm{CMT}_j\}_{j=1}^t, \mathbf{c}_1, \mathbf{c}_2\big).$$

3. Compute a one-time signature $sig = \mathsf{OSign}(\mathsf{osk}; \mathbf{c}_1, \mathbf{c}_2, \Pi)$.
4. Output the group signature $\Sigma = \big(\mathsf{ovk}, (\mathbf{c}_1, \mathbf{c}_2), \Pi, sig\big)$.

Verify(gpk, M, Σ) : This algorithm works as follows:

1. Parse Σ as $\big(\text{ovk}, (\mathbf{c}_1, \mathbf{c}_2), \Pi, sig\big)$. If $\text{OVer}(\text{ovk}; sig; (\mathbf{c}_1, \mathbf{c}_2), \Pi) = 0$, then return 0.
2. Parse Π as $\big(\{\text{CMT}_j\}_{j=1}^t, \{Ch_j\}_{j=1}^t, \{\text{RSP}_j\}_{j=1}^t\big)$.
   If $\big(Ch_1, \ldots, Ch_t\big) \neq \mathcal{H}_2\big(M, \{\text{CMT}_j\}_{j=1}^t, \mathbf{c}_1, \mathbf{c}_2\big)$, then return 0.
3. Compute $\mathbf{G} = \mathcal{H}_1(\text{ovk})$ and form $\mathbf{P}, \mathbf{c}$ as in (8). Then for $j = 1$ to t, run the verification step of the protocol from Section 3.3 with public input $\big(\mathbf{A}, \mathbf{A}_0, \ldots, \mathbf{A}_\ell, \mathbf{u}, \mathbf{P}, \mathbf{c}\big)$ to check the validity of RSP_j with respect to CMT_j and Ch_j. If any of the conditions does not hold, then return 0.
4. Return 1.

Open(gmsk, M, Σ) On input gmsk $= \mathbf{T_B}$ and $\Sigma = \big(\text{ovk}, (\mathbf{c}_1, \mathbf{c}_2), \Pi, sig\big)$, this algorithm decrypts $(\mathbf{c}_1, \mathbf{c}_2)$ as follows:

1. Extract the decryption key for "identity" ovk: Let $\mathbf{G} = [\mathbf{g}_1 | \ldots | \mathbf{g}_\ell] = \mathcal{H}_1(\text{ovk})$. Then for $i \in [\ell]$, sample $\mathbf{y}_i \hookleftarrow \text{SamplePre}(\mathbf{T_B}, \mathbf{B}, \mathbf{g}_i, s)$ (see [GPV08]), and let $\mathbf{Y} = [\mathbf{y}_1 | \ldots | \mathbf{y}_\ell] \in \mathbb{Z}^{m \times \ell}$.
2. Compute $d' = (d'_1, \ldots, d'_\ell) = \mathbf{c}_2 - \mathbf{Y}^T \mathbf{c}_1 \in \mathbb{Z}_q^\ell$. For each $i \in [\ell]$, if d'_i is closer to 0 than to $\lfloor q/2 \rfloor$ modulo q, then let $d_i = 0$; otherwise, let $d_i = 1$.
3. Return $d = (d_1, \ldots, d_\ell) \in \{0, 1\}^\ell$.

4.2   Analysis of the Scheme

Efficiency and Correctness. The given group signature scheme can be implemented in polynomial time. The bit-size of the NIZKAoK Π is roughly $t = \omega(\log n)$ times the communication cost of the interactive protocol in Section 3.3, which is $\widetilde{\mathcal{O}}(\ell n)$ for the chosen parameters. This is also the asymptotical bound on the size of the group signature Σ.

The correctness of algorithm Verify follows from the facts that every group user with a valid secret key is able to compute a satisfying witness for $\text{R}_{\text{gs}}(n, \ell, q, m, k_1, k_2, \beta, b))$, and that the underlying argument system is perfectly complete. Moreover, we set the parameters so that the GPV-IBE scheme is correct, which implies that algorithm Open is also correct.

Theorem 2 (CCA-anonymity). *Suppose that $\mathcal{OTS}$ is a strongly unforgeable one-time signature. In the random oracle model, the group signature described in Section 4.1 is CCA-anonymous if $\text{LWE}_{n,q,\chi}$ is hard.*

As a corollary, the CCA-anonymity of the scheme can be based the quantum worst-case hardness of SIVP_γ, with $\gamma = \widetilde{\mathcal{O}}(nq/b) = \ell \widetilde{\mathcal{O}}(n^2)$.

The proof of Theorem 2 uses the strong unforgeability of $\mathcal{OTS}$, the statistical zero-knowledge property of the underlying argument system, and the $\text{LWE}_{n,q,\chi}$ assumption. Due to the lack of space, the proof is provided in the full version [LNW15].

Theorem 3 (Traceability). *In the random oracle model, the group signature described in Section 4.1 is fully traceable if $\text{SIVP}_{\ell \cdot \widetilde{\mathcal{O}}(n^2)}$ is hard.*

Proof. Without loss of generality, we assume that the string commitment scheme COM used in the underlying NIZKAoK is computationally binding, because an adversary breaking its computational binding property can be used to solve $\mathsf{SIVP}_{\ell \cdot \widetilde{\mathcal{O}}(n^2)}$.

Let $\mathcal{A}$ be an PPT traceability adversary against our group signature scheme with advantage ϵ, we construct a PPT forger $\mathcal{F}$ for Boyen's signature scheme whose advantage is polynomially related to ϵ. Since the unforgeability of Boyen's signature scheme can be based on the hardness of $\mathsf{SIVP}_{\ell \cdot \widetilde{\mathcal{O}}(n^2)}$ [Boy10, MP12], this completes the proof.

$\mathcal{F}$ is given the verification key $(\mathbf{A}, \mathbf{A}_0, \ldots, \mathbf{A}_\ell, \mathbf{u})$ for Boyen's signature scheme. It generates a key-pair $(\mathbf{B}, \mathbf{T_B})$ for the GPV IBE scheme, and begins interacting with $\mathcal{A}$ by sending $\mathsf{gpk} = (\mathbf{A}, \mathbf{A}_0, \ldots, \mathbf{A}_\ell, \mathbf{u}, \mathbf{B})$ and $\mathsf{gsk} = \mathbf{T_B}$, the distribution of which is statistically close to that in the real game. Then $\mathcal{F}$ sets $CU = \emptyset$ and handles the queries from $\mathcal{A}$ as follows:

- Queries to $\mathcal{H}_1$ and $\mathcal{H}_2$ are handled by consistently returning uniformly random values in the respective ranges. If $\mathcal{A}$ makes $Q_{\mathcal{H}_2}$ queries to $\mathcal{H}_2$, then $\forall \kappa \leq Q_{\mathcal{H}_2}$, we let r_κ denote the answer to the κ-th query.
- Queries for the secret key $\mathsf{gsk}[d]$, for any $d \in \{0,1\}^\ell$: $\mathcal{F}$ queries its own signing oracle for Boyen's signature of d, and receives in return $\mathbf{z}_{(d)} \in \mathbb{Z}^{2m}$ such that $\|\mathbf{z}_{(d)}\|_\infty \leq \beta$ and $\mathbf{A}_{(d)}\mathbf{z}_{(d)} = \mathbf{u} \bmod q$, where $\mathbf{A}_{(d)}$ is computed in the usual way. Then $\mathcal{F}$ sets $CU := CU \cup \{d\}$ and sends $\mathbf{z}_{(d)}$ to $\mathcal{A}$.
- Queries for group signatures on arbitrary message: $\mathcal{F}$ returns with a simulated signature $\Sigma = (\mathsf{ovk}, (\mathbf{c}_1, \mathbf{c}_2), \Pi', sig)$, where $(\mathsf{ovk}, (\mathbf{c}_1, \mathbf{c}_2), sig)$ are faithfully generated, while the NIZKAoK Π' is simulated without using the valid secret key (as in experiment $G_3^{(b)}$ in the proof of anonymity). The zero-knowledge property of the underlying argument system guarantees that Σ is indistinguishable from a legitimate signature.

Eventually $\mathcal{A}$ outputs a message M^* and a forged group signature

$$\Sigma^* = \big(\mathsf{ovk}, (\mathbf{c}_1, \mathbf{c}_2), (\{\mathrm{CMT}_j\}_{j=1}^t, \{Ch_j\}_{j=1}^t, \{\mathrm{RSP}_j\}_{j=1}^t), sig\big),$$

which satisfies the requirements of the traceability game. Then $\mathcal{F}$ exploits the forgery as follows. First, one can argue that $\mathcal{A}$ must have queried $\mathcal{H}_2$ on input $(M, \{\mathrm{CMT}_j\}_{j=1}^t, \mathbf{c}_1, \mathbf{c}_2)$, since otherwise, the probability that $(Ch_1, \ldots, Ch_t) = \mathcal{H}_2(M, \{\mathrm{CMT}_j\}_{j=1}^t, \mathbf{c}_1, \mathbf{c}_2)$ is at most 3^{-t}. Therefore, with probability at least $\epsilon - 3^{-t}$, there exists certain $\kappa^* \leq Q_{\mathcal{H}_2}$ such that the κ^*-th oracle query involves the tuple $(M, \{\mathrm{CMT}_j\}_{j=1}^t, \mathbf{c}_1, \mathbf{c}_2)$. Next, $\mathcal{F}$ picks κ^* as the target forking point and replays $\mathcal{A}$ many times with the same random tape and input as in the original run. In each rerun, for the first $\kappa^* - 1$ queries, $\mathcal{A}$ is given the same answers $r_1, \ldots, r_{\kappa^*-1}$ as in the initial run, but from the κ^*-th query onwards, $\mathcal{F}$ replies with fresh random values $r'_{\kappa^*}, \ldots, r'_{q_{\mathcal{H}_2}} \xleftarrow{\$} \{1,2,3\}^t$. The Improved Forking Lemma of Pointcheval and Vaudenay [PV97, Lemma 7] implies that, with probability larger than $1/2$, algorithm $\mathcal{F}$ can obtain a 3-fork involving the tuple $(M, \{\mathrm{CMT}_j\}_{j=1}^t, \mathbf{c}_1, \mathbf{c}_2)$ after less than $32 \cdot Q_{\mathcal{H}_2}/(\epsilon - 3^{-t})$ executions of $\mathcal{A}$.

Now, let the answers of $\mathcal{F}$ with respect to the 3-fork branches be

$$r_{\kappa^*}^{(1)} = (Ch_1^{(1)}, \ldots, Ch_t^{(1)}); \; r_{\kappa^*}^{(2)} = (Ch_1^{(2)}, \ldots, Ch_t^{(2)}); \; r_{\kappa^*}^{(3)} = (Ch_1^{(3)}, \ldots, Ch_t^{(3)}).$$

A simple calculation shows that:

$$\Pr[\exists j \in \{1, \ldots, t\} : \; \{Ch_j^{(1)}, Ch_j^{(2)}, Ch_j^{(3)}\} = \{1, 2, 3\}] = 1 - (7/9)^t.$$

Conditioned on the existence of such j, one parses the 3 forgeries corresponding to the fork branches to obtain $(\mathrm{RSP}_j^{(1)}, \mathrm{RSP}_j^{(2)}, \mathrm{RSP}_j^{(3)})$. They turn out to be 3 *valid* responses to 3 different challenges for the same commitment CMT_j. Since COM is assumed to be computationally-binding, we can use the knowledge extractor of the underlying argument system to extract $(d^*, \mathbf{z}^*, \mathbf{s}^*, \mathbf{e}_1^*, \mathbf{e}_2^*) \in \{0,1\}^\ell \times \mathbb{Z}^{2m} \times \mathbb{Z}_q^n \times \mathbb{Z}^m \times \mathbb{Z}^\ell$ such that $\|\mathbf{z}^*\|_\infty \leq \beta$ and $\mathbf{A}_{(d^*)}\mathbf{z}^* = \mathbf{u} \bmod q$; and $\mathbf{s}^*, \mathbf{e}_1^*, \mathbf{e}_2^*$ has infinity norm bounded by b, and $\mathbf{B}^T\mathbf{s}^* + \mathbf{e}_1^* = \mathbf{c}_1 \bmod q$, $\mathbf{G}^T\mathbf{s}^* + \mathbf{e}_2^* + \lfloor q/2 \rfloor d^* = \mathbf{c}_2 \bmod q$, where $\mathbf{G} = \mathcal{H}_1(\mathsf{ovk})$. Now observe that, $(\mathbf{c}_1, \mathbf{c}_2)$ is a correct encryption of d^*, the opening algorithm $\mathsf{Open}(\mathbf{T_B}, M^*, \Sigma^*)$ must return d^*. It then follows from the requirements of the traceability game that $d^* \notin CU$. As a result, $(\mathbf{z}^*, d^*)$ is a valid forgery for Boyen's signature with respect to the verification key $(\mathbf{A}, \mathbf{A}_0, \ldots, \mathbf{A}_\ell, \mathbf{u})$. Furthermore, the above analysis shows that, if $\mathcal{A}$ has non-negligible success probability and runs in polynomial time, then so does $\mathcal{F}$. This concludes the proof.

5   A Ring-Based Group Signature Scheme

5.1   Description of the Scheme

Let $f = x^n + 1$, where $n = 2^k$ for $k \geq 2$, and let $N = 2^\ell = \mathsf{poly}(n)$ be the number of group users. Then we choose other scheme parameters such that the ring variant of Boyen's signature scheme and the LPR encryption scheme are correct and secure. Let $q = \mathcal{O}(\ell \cdot n^2)$ be a prime satisfying $q = 1 \bmod 2n$. Let $\mathcal{R} = \mathbb{Z}[x]/\langle f \rangle$ and $\mathcal{R}_q = \mathcal{R}/q\mathcal{R}$. Let $m = \mathcal{O}(\log q)$. The infinity norm bound for signatures from Boyen's scheme is integer $\beta = \widetilde{\mathcal{O}}(\sqrt{\ell n})$. The norm bound for Ring-LWE noises is integer b such that $q/b = \ell\widetilde{\mathcal{O}}(n^{1.5})$. Choose a hash function $\mathcal{H} : \{0,1\}^* \to \{1,2,3\}^t$ to be modeled as random oracles. Let χ be a b-bounded distribution over $\mathcal{R}$.

KeyGen$(1^n, 1^N)$: This algorithm performs the following steps:
1. Generate verification key $(\mathbf{a}, \mathbf{a}_0, \ldots, \mathbf{a}_\ell, u)$ and signing key $\mathbf{T_a}$ for the ring variant of Boyen's signature (see Section 2.3 for more details). Then for each $d = (d_1, \ldots, d_\ell) \in \{0,1\}^\ell$, generate $\mathsf{gsk}[d]$ as a ring-based Boyen's signature on message d.
2. Generate keys for the LPR encryption scheme: Sample $f \xleftarrow{\$} \mathcal{R}_q$ and $x, e \hookleftarrow \chi$. Then compute $g = f \otimes x + e \in \mathcal{R}_q$.
3. Output

$$\mathsf{gpk} = ((\mathbf{a}, \mathbf{a}_0, \ldots, \mathbf{a}_\ell, u), (f, g)); \quad \mathsf{gmsk} = x; \quad \mathsf{gsk} = \{\mathsf{gsk}[d]\}_{d \in \{0,1\}^\ell}.$$

Sign(gsk$[d], M$): Given gpk, to sign a message $M \in \{0,1\}^*$ using the secret key gsk$[d] = \mathbf{z} \in \mathcal{R}^{2m}$, the user performs the following steps:

1. Encrypt d: First extend d to $\bar{d} = (0^{n-\ell}\|d) \in \{0,1\}^n$ and view $\bar{d}$ as an element of $\mathcal{R}$ with coefficients $0, 1$. Then sample $s, e_1, e_2 \hookleftarrow \chi$, and compute the ciphertext:

$$(c_1 = f \otimes s + e_1, c_2 = g \otimes s + e_2 + \lfloor q/2 \rfloor \bar{d}) \in \mathcal{R}_q^2. \tag{9}$$

2. Generate a NIZKAoK Π to show the possession of a valid message-signature pair $(d, \mathbf{z})$ for the ring variant of Boyen's signature, and that (c_1, c_2) is a correct LPR encryption of $\bar{d}$. This is done as follows:

   - Let $\mathbf{A} = \mathsf{rot}(\mathbf{a}) \in \mathbb{Z}_q^{n \times nm}$, and $\mathbf{A}_i = \mathsf{rot}(\mathbf{a}_i) \in \mathbb{Z}_q^{n \times mn}$ for every $i = 0, \ldots, \ell$. Next, consider $\mathbf{z}$ as a vector in $\mathbb{Z}^{2mn}$ with infinity norm bounded by β, and consider u as vector $\mathbf{u} \in \mathbb{Z}_q^n$. Then one has
   $$\left[\mathbf{A} \mid \mathbf{A}_0 + \sum_{i=1}^{\ell} d_i \mathbf{A}_i\right] \mathbf{z} = \mathbf{u} \bmod q.$$
   Furthermore, let $\mathbf{P}_0 = [\mathsf{rot}(b) \mid \mathsf{rot}(g)]^T \in \mathbb{Z}_q^{2n \times n}$ and form $\mathbf{P} = \left[\mathbf{P}_0 \mid \mathbf{I}_{2n}\right] \in \mathbb{Z}_q^{2n \times 3n}$. Next, consider $\mathbf{c} = (c_1\|c_2)$ as a vector in $\mathbb{Z}_q^{2n}$, and $\mathbf{e} = (s\|e_1\|e_2)$ as a vector in $\mathbb{Z}^{3n}$. Then (9) can be equivalently written as: $\mathbf{c} = \mathbf{P}\mathbf{e} + (0^{2n-\ell} \| \lfloor q/2 \rfloor d) \bmod q$.
   The above transformation leads to the following observation:
   $$((\mathbf{A}, \mathbf{A}_0, \ldots, \mathbf{A}_\ell, \mathbf{u}, \mathbf{P}, \mathbf{c}), d, \mathbf{z}, \mathbf{e}) \in R_{gs}(n, \ell, q, m', k_1, k_2, \beta, b),$$
   where $m' = nm$, $k_1 = 2n$, and $k_2 = 3n$.
   - Run the protocol for $R_{gs}(n, \ell, q, m', k_1, k_2, \beta, b)$ in Section 3.3 with public input $(\mathbf{A}, \mathbf{A}_0, \ldots, \mathbf{A}_\ell, \mathbf{u}, \mathbf{P}, \mathbf{c})$ and prover's witness $(d, \mathbf{z}, \mathbf{e})$. The protocol is repeated $t = \omega(\log n)$ times to make the soundness error negligibly small, and then made non-interactive using Fiat-Shamir heuristic as $\Pi = (\{\mathrm{CMT}_j\}_{j=1}^t, \mathrm{CH}, \{\mathrm{RSP}_j\}_{j=1}^t)$, where $\mathrm{CH} = \{Ch_j\}_{j=1}^t = \mathcal{H}(M, \{\mathrm{CMT}_j\}_{j=1}^t, (c_1, c_2))$.

3. Output the group signature $\Sigma = ((c_1, c_2), \Pi)$.

Verify(gpk, M, Σ) This deterministic algorithm works as follows:

1. Parse Σ as $((c_1, c_2), (\{\mathrm{CMT}_j\}_{j=1}^t, \mathrm{CH}, \{\mathrm{RSP}_j\}_{j=1}^t))$. If $(Ch^{(1)}, \ldots, Ch^{(t)}) \neq \mathcal{H}(M, \{\mathrm{CMT}_j\}_{j=1}^t, (c_1, c_2))$, then return 0.

2. Then for $j = 1$ to t, run the verification step of the protocol from Section 3.3 with public input $(\mathbf{A}, \mathbf{A}_0, \ldots, \mathbf{A}_\ell, \mathbf{u}, \mathbf{P}, \mathbf{c})$ to check the validity of RSP_j with respect to CMT_j and Ch_j. If any of the conditions does not hold, then return 0.

3. Return 1.

Open(gmsk, M, Σ) Let gmsk$=x$ and $\Sigma = ((c_1, c_2), \Pi)$, proceed as follows:

1. Compute $\bar{d} = \mathbf{c}_2 - x \otimes \mathbf{c}_1 \in \mathcal{R}_q$. For each $i \in [n]$, if $\bar{d}_i$ is closer to 0 than to $\lfloor q/2 \rfloor$ modulo q, then let $\bar{d}_i = 0$; otherwise, let $\bar{d}_i = 1$.

2. If $\bar{d}$ is of the form $(0^{n-\ell}\|d)$, then return $d \in \{0,1\}^\ell$. Otherwise, return $\perp$.

5.2   Analysis

Efficiency and Correctness. The ring-based group signature can be implemented in polynomial time. The public key $((\mathbf{a}, \mathbf{a}_0, \ldots, \mathbf{a}_\ell, u), (f, g))$ has bit-size $\widetilde{\mathcal{O}}(\ell n)$. In comparison with the scheme from Section 4, a factor of $\mathcal{O}(n)$ is saved. The signature size is also bounded by $\widetilde{\mathcal{O}}(\ell n)$.

The correctness of algorithm Verify follows from the facts that every user with a valid secret key is able to compute a satisfying witness for $R_{gs}(n, \ell, q, nm, 2n, 3n, \beta, b)$, and that the underlying argument system is perfectly complete. We also set the parameters so that the LPR encryption scheme is correct, which implies that algorithm Open is also correct.

The anonymity and traceability properties of the scheme are stated in Theorem 4 and 5, respectively.

Theorem 4. *In the random oracle model, the group signature scheme described in Section 5.1 is CPA-anonymous if* $\mathsf{SVP}^\infty_{\ell \cdot \widetilde{\mathcal{O}}(n^{3.5})}$ *on ideal lattices in the ring $\mathcal{R}$ is hard in the worst case.*

The proof of Theorem 4 uses the fact that the underlying argument system is statistical zero-knowledge, and the assumed hardness of the HNF variant of Ring-LWE$_{n,q,\chi}$. The proof is given in the full version [LNW15].

Theorem 5. *In the random oracle model, the group signature scheme described in Section 5.1 is traceable if* $\mathsf{SVP}^\infty_{\ell \cdot \widetilde{\mathcal{O}}(n^2)}$ *on ideal lattices in the ring $\mathcal{R}$ is hard in the worst case.*

The proof of Theorem 5 is similar to that of Theorem 3, and is given in the full version [LNW15].

A   Security Requirements for Group Signatures

The presentation in this section follows the model of Bellare et al. [BMW03], and the relaxed anonymity notion proposed by Boneh et al. [BBS04].
ANONYMITY.   Consider the anonymity experiment $\mathbf{Exp}^{\text{t-anon}}_{\mathcal{GS},\mathcal{A}}(n, N)$ between a challenger $\mathcal{C}$ and an adversary $\mathcal{A}$, where $t \in (\mathsf{CPA}, \mathsf{CCA})$.

- $\mathcal{C}$ generates $(\mathsf{gpk}, \mathsf{gmsk}, \mathsf{gsk}) \leftarrow \mathsf{KeyGen}(1^n, 1^N)$, then gives $(\mathsf{gpk}, \mathsf{gsk})$ to $\mathcal{A}$.
- If $t = \mathsf{CCA}$, then $\mathcal{A}$ can query the opening oracle. On input a message M and a signature Σ, the oracle returns $\mathsf{Open}(\mathsf{gmsk}, M, \Sigma)$ to $\mathcal{A}$.
- $\mathcal{A}$ outputs two distinct identities i_0, i_1 and a message M^*. Then $\mathcal{C}$ picks a coin $b \xleftarrow{\$} \{0, 1\}$, and sends $\Sigma^* \leftarrow \mathsf{Sign}(\mathsf{gsk}[i_b], M^*)$ to $\mathcal{A}$.
- If $t = \mathsf{CCA}$, then $\mathcal{A}$ can query the opening oracle. On input (M, Σ), if $(M, \Sigma) = (M^*, \Sigma^*)$, then $\mathcal{C}$ outputs 0 and halts; otherwise it returns $\mathsf{Open}(\mathsf{gmsk}, M, \Sigma)$ to $\mathcal{A}$.
- $\mathcal{A}$ outputs $b' \in \{0, 1\}$. $\mathcal{C}$ outputs 1 if $b' = b$, or 0 otherwise.

Define $\mathbf{Adv}_{\mathcal{GS},\mathcal{A}}^{\text{t-anon}}(n, N) = \left| \Pr\left[\mathbf{Exp}_{\mathcal{GS},\mathcal{A}}^{\text{t-anon}}(n, N) = 1\right] - 1/2 \right|$. We say that the scheme is CPA-anonymous (resp., CCA-anonymous) if for all polynomial N, and all PPT adversary $\mathcal{A}$, the function $\mathbf{Adv}_{\mathcal{GS},\mathcal{A}}^{\text{CPA-anon}}(n, N)$ (resp., $\mathbf{Adv}_{\mathcal{GS},\mathcal{A}}^{\text{CCA-anon}}(n, N)$) is negligible in the security parameter n.

TRACEABILITY. Consider the traceability experiment $\mathbf{Exp}_{\mathcal{GS},\mathcal{A}}^{\text{trace}}(n, N)$ between a challenger $\mathcal{C}$ and an adversary $\mathcal{A}$.

- $\mathcal{C}$ runs KeyGen($1^n, 1^N$) to obtain (gpk, gmsk, gsk), then it sets $CU \leftarrow \emptyset$ and gives (gpk, gmsk) to $\mathcal{A}$.
- $\mathcal{A}$ can make the following queries adaptively, and in any order:
  - Key query: On input an index i, $\mathcal{C}$ adds i to CU, and returns gsk[i].
  - Signing query: On input i, M, $\mathcal{C}$ returns Sign(gsk[i], M).
- $\mathcal{A}$ outputs a message M, and a signature Σ. Then $\mathcal{C}$ proceeds as follows: If Verify(gpk, M, Σ) = 0 then return 0. If Open(gmsk, M, Σ) = $\perp$ then return 1. If $\exists i$ such that the following are true then return 1, else return 0:
  1. Open(gmsk, M, Σ) = $i \notin CU$,
  2. $\mathcal{A}$ has never made a signing query for i, M.

Define $\mathbf{Adv}_{\mathcal{GS},\mathcal{A}}^{\text{trace}}(n, N) = \Pr\left[\mathbf{Exp}_{\mathcal{GS},\mathcal{A}}^{\text{trace}}(n, N) = 1\right]$. We say that the scheme is fully traceable if for all polynomial N and all PPT adversary $\mathcal{A}$, the function $\mathbf{Adv}_{\mathcal{GS},\mathcal{A}}^{\text{trace}}(n, N)$ is negligible in the security parameter n.

Acknowledgments. This research is supported by the Singapore Ministry of Education under Research Grant MOE2013-T2-1-041. The authors would like to thank the anonymous reviewers of PKC 2015 for their helpful comments.

References

[ACJT00] Ateniese, G., Camenisch, J.L., Joye, M., Tsudik, G.: A practical and provably secure coalition-resistant group signature scheme. In: Bellare, M. (ed.) CRYPTO 2000. LNCS, vol. 1880, pp. 255–270. Springer, Heidelberg (2000)

[ACPS09] Applebaum, B., Cash, D., Peikert, C., Sahai, A.: Fast cryptographic primitives and circular-secure encryption based on hard learning problems. In: Halevi, S. (ed.) CRYPTO 2009. LNCS, vol. 5677, pp. 595–618. Springer, Heidelberg (2009)

[Ajt96] Ajtai, M.: Generating hard instances of lattice problems (extended abstract). In: STOC, pp. 99–108. ACM (1996)

[AP11] Alwen, J., Peikert, C.: Generating Shorter Bases for Hard Random Lattices. Theory Comput. Syst. **48**(3), 535–553 (2011)

[BBS04] Boneh, D., Boyen, X., Shacham, H.: Short group signatures. In: Franklin, M. (ed.) CRYPTO 2004. LNCS, vol. 3152, pp. 41–55. Springer, Heidelberg (2004)

[BCHK07] Boneh, D., Canetti, R., Halevi, S., Katz, J.: Chosen-ciphertext Security from Identity-based Encryption. SIAM J. C. **36**(5), 1301–1328 (2007)

[BF14] Bellare, M., Fuchsbauer, G.: Policy-based signatures. In: Krawczyk, H. (ed.) PKC 2014. LNCS, vol. 8383, pp. 520–537. Springer, Heidelberg (2014)

[BMW03] Bellare, M., Micciancio, D., Warinschi, B.: Foundations of group signatures: formal definitions, simplified requirements, and a construction based on general assumptions. In: Biham, E. (ed.) EUROCRYPT 2003. LNCS, vol. 2656, pp. 614–629. Springer, Heidelberg (2003)

[Boy10] Boyen, X.: Lattice mixing and vanishing trapdoors: a framework for fully secure short signatures and more. In: Nguyen, P.Q., Pointcheval, D. (eds.) PKC 2010. LNCS, vol. 6056, pp. 499–517. Springer, Heidelberg (2010)

[BS04] Boneh, D., Shacham, H.: Group signatures with verifier-local revocation. In: ACM CCS, pp. 168–177. ACM (2004)

[CHKP10] Cash, D., Hofheinz, D., Kiltz, E., Peikert, C.: Bonsai trees, or how to delegate a lattice basis. In: Gilbert, H. (ed.) EUROCRYPT 2010. LNCS, vol. 6110, pp. 523–552. Springer, Heidelberg (2010)

[CHL05] Camenisch, J.L., Hohenberger, S., Lysyanskaya, A.: Compact e-cash. In: Cramer, R. (ed.) EUROCRYPT 2005. LNCS, vol. 3494, pp. 302–321. Springer, Heidelberg (2005)

[CL01] Camenisch, J.L., Lysyanskaya, A.: An efficient system for non-transferable anonymous credentials with optional anonymity revocation. In: Pfitzmann, B. (ed.) EUROCRYPT 2001. LNCS, vol. 2045, pp. 93–118. Springer, Heidelberg (2001)

[CNR12] Camenisch, J., Neven, G., Rückert, M.: Fully anonymous attribute tokens from lattices. In: Visconti, I., De Prisco, R. (eds.) SCN 2012. LNCS, vol. 7485, pp. 57–75. Springer, Heidelberg (2012)

[CS97] Camenisch, J.L., Stadler, M.A.: Efficient group signature schemes for large groups (extended abstract). In: Kaliski Jr, B.S. (ed.) CRYPTO 1997. LNCS, vol. 1294, pp. 410–424. Springer, Heidelberg (1997)

[CvH91] Chaum, D., van Heyst, E.: Group signatures. In: Davies, D.W. (ed.) EUROCRYPT 1991. LNCS, vol. 547, pp. 257–265. Springer, Heidelberg (1991)

[Gen09] Gentry, C.: Fully homomorphic encryption using ideal lattices. In: STOC, pp. 169–178. ACM (2009)

[GKV10] Gordon, S.D., Katz, J., Vaikuntanathan, V.: A group signature scheme from lattice assumptions. In: Abe, M. (ed.) ASIACRYPT 2010. LNCS, vol. 6477, pp. 395–412. Springer, Heidelberg (2010)

[GPV08] Gentry, C., Peikert, C., Vaikuntanathan, V.: Trapdoors for hard lattices and new cryptographic constructions. In: STOC, pp. 197–206. ACM (2008)

[Gro04] Groth, J.: Evaluating security of voting schemes in the universal composability framework. In: Jakobsson, M., Yung, M., Zhou, J. (eds.) ACNS 2004. LNCS, vol. 3089, pp. 46–60. Springer, Heidelberg (2004)

[Gro07] Groth, J.: Fully anonymous group signatures without random oracles. In: Kurosawa, K. (ed.) ASIACRYPT 2007. LNCS, vol. 4833, pp. 164–180. Springer, Heidelberg (2007)

[KTX08] Kawachi, A., Tanaka, K., Xagawa, K.: Concurrently secure identification schemes based on the worst-case hardness of lattice problems. In: Pieprzyk, J. (ed.) ASIACRYPT 2008. LNCS, vol. 5350, pp. 372–389. Springer, Heidelberg (2008)

[LAN02] Lipmaa, H., Asokan, N., Niemi, V.: Secure vickrey auctions without threshold trust. In: Blaze, Matt (ed.) FC 2002. LNCS, vol. 2357, pp. 87–101. Springer, Heidelberg (2003)

[LLLS13] Laguillaumie, F., Langlois, A., Libert, B., Stehlé, D.: Lattice-based group signatures with logarithmic signature size. In: Sako, K., Sarkar, P. (eds.) ASIACRYPT 2013, Part II. LNCS, vol. 8270, pp. 41–61. Springer, Heidelberg (2013)

[LLNW14] Langlois, A., Ling, S., Nguyen, K., Wang, H.: Lattice-based group signature scheme with verifier-local revocation. In: Krawczyk, H. (ed.) PKC 2014. LNCS, vol. 8383, pp. 345–361. Springer, Heidelberg (2014)

[LM06] Lyubashevsky, V., Micciancio, D.: Generalized compact knapsacks are collision resistant. In: Bugliesi, M., Preneel, B., Sassone, V., Wegener, I. (eds.) ICALP 2006. LNCS, vol. 4052, pp. 144–155. Springer, Heidelberg (2006)

[LMPR08] Lyubashevsky, V., Micciancio, D., Peikert, C., Rosen, A.: SWIFFT: a modest proposal for FFT hashing. In: Nyberg, K. (ed.) FSE 2008. LNCS, vol. 5086, pp. 54–72. Springer, Heidelberg (2008)

[LNSW13] Ling, S., Nguyen, K., Stehlé, D., Wang, H.: Improved zero-knowledge proofs of knowledge for the ISIS problem, and applications. In: Kurosawa, K., Hanaoka, G. (eds.) PKC 2013. LNCS, vol. 7778, pp. 107–124. Springer, Heidelberg (2013)

[LNW15] Ling, S., Nguyen, K., Wang, H.: Group Signatures from Lattices Simpler Tighter Shorter Ring-based. IACR Cryptology ePrint Archive **2015**, 0xx (2015)

[LPR10] Lyubashevsky, V., Peikert, C., Regev, O.: On ideal lattices and learning with errors over rings. In: Gilbert, H. (ed.) EUROCRYPT 2010. LNCS, vol. 6110, pp. 1–23. Springer, Heidelberg (2010)

[LPR13] Lyubashevsky, V., Peikert, C., Regev, O.: On Ideal Lattices and Learning with Errors over Rings. J. ACM **60**(6), 43 (2013)

[LPY12] Libert, B., Peters, T., Yung, M.: Scalable group signatures with revocation. In: Pointcheval, D., Johansson, T. (eds.) EUROCRYPT 2012. LNCS, vol. 7237, pp. 609–627. Springer, Heidelberg (2012)

[Lyu08] Lyubashevsky, V.: Lattice-based identification schemes secure under active attacks. In: Cramer, R. (ed.) PKC 2008. LNCS, vol. 4939, pp. 162–179. Springer, Heidelberg (2008)

[MM11] Micciancio, D., Mol, P.: Pseudorandom knapsacks and the sample complexity of LWE search-to-decision reductions. In: Rogaway, P. (ed.) CRYPTO 2011. LNCS, vol. 6841, pp. 465–484. Springer, Heidelberg (2011)

[MP12] Micciancio, D., Peikert, C.: Trapdoors for lattices: simpler, tighter, faster, smaller. In: Pointcheval, D., Johansson, T. (eds.) EUROCRYPT 2012. LNCS, vol. 7237, pp. 700–718. Springer, Heidelberg (2012)

[MP13] Micciancio, D., Peikert, C.: Hardness of SIS and LWE with Small Parameters. IACR Cryptology ePrint Archive **2013**, 69 (2013)

[MV03] Micciancio, D., Vadhan, S.P.: Statistical zero-knowledge proofs with efficient provers: lattice problems and more. In: Boneh, D. (ed.) CRYPTO 2003. LNCS, vol. 2729, pp. 282–298. Springer, Heidelberg (2003)

[NZZ15] Nguyen, P.Q., Zhang, J., Zhang, Z.: Simpler efficient group signatures from lattices. In: Katz, J. (ed.) PKC 2015. LNCS, vol. 9020, pp. xx–yy. Springer, Heidelberg (2015)

[Pei09] Peikert, C.: Public-key cryptosystems from the worst-case shortest vector problem: extended abstract. In: STOC, pp. 333–342. ACM (2009)

[PR06] Peikert, C., Rosen, A.: Efficient collision-resistant hashing from worst-case assumptions on cyclic lattices. In: Halevi, S., Rabin, T. (eds.) TCC 2006. LNCS, vol. 3876, pp. 145–166. Springer, Heidelberg (2006)

[PV97]   Pointcheval, D., Vaudenay, S.: On Provable Security for Digital Signature Algorithms. Technical Report LIENS-96-17, Laboratoire d'Informatique de ENS (1997)

[Reg05]   Regev, O.: On lattices, learning with errors, random linear codes, and cryptography. In: STOC, pp. 84–93. ACM (2005)

[SSTX09]   Stehlé, D., Steinfeld, R., Tanaka, K., Xagawa, K.: Efficient public key encryption based on ideal lattices. In: Matsui, M. (ed.) ASIACRYPT 2009. LNCS, vol. 5912, pp. 617–635. Springer, Heidelberg (2009)

[Ste96]   Stern, J.: A New Paradigm for Public Key Identification. IEEE Transactions on Information Theory **42**(6), 1757–1768 (1996)

[Wat05]   Waters, B.: Efficient identity-based encryption without random oracles. In: Cramer, R. (ed.) EUROCRYPT 2005. LNCS, vol. 3494, pp. 114–127. Springer, Heidelberg (2005)

Secure Efficient History-Hiding Append-Only Signatures in the Standard Model

Benoît Libert[1]([✉]), Marc Joye[2], Moti Yung[3], and Thomas Peters[4]

[1] Laboratoire LIP, Ecole Normale Supérieure de Lyon, Lyon, France
benoit.libert@ens-lyon.fr
[2] Technicolor, Los Altos, USA
marc.joye@technicolor.com
[3] Columbia University and Google Inc., New York, USA
moti@cs.columbia.edu
[4] Ecole Normale Supérieure, Paris, France
thomas.peters@ens.fr

Abstract. As formalized by Kiltz *et al.* (ICALP '05), append-only signatures (AOS) are digital signature schemes where anyone can publicly append extra message blocks to an already signed sequence of messages. This property is useful, *e.g.*, in secure routing, in collecting response lists, reputation lists, or petitions. Bethencourt, Boneh and Waters (NDSS '07) suggested an interesting variant, called *history-hiding* append-only signatures (HH-AOS), which handles messages as sets rather than ordered tuples. This HH-AOS primitive is useful when the exact order of signing needs to be hidden. When free of subliminal channels (i.e., channels that can tag elements in an undetectable fashion), it also finds applications in the storage of ballots on an electronic voting terminals or in other archival applications (such as the record of petitions, where we want to hide the influence among messages). However, the only subliminal-free HH-AOS to date only provides heuristic arguments in terms of security: Only a proof in the idealized (non-realizable) random oracle model is given. This paper provides the first HH-AOS construction secure in the standard model. Like the system of Bethencourt *et al.*, our HH-AOS features constant-size public keys, no matter how long messages to be signed are, which is atypical (we note that secure constructions often suffer from a space penalty when compared to their random-oracle-based counterpart). As a second result, we show that, even if we use it to sign ordered vectors as in an ordinary AOS (which is always possible with HH-AOS), our system provides considerable advantages over existing realizations. As a third result, we show that HH-AOS schemes provide improved identity-based ring signatures (i.e., in prime order groups and with a better efficiency than the state-of-the-art schemes).

Keywords: Homomorphic signatures · Provable security · Privacy · Unlinkability · Standard model · Superset predicates · Archive integrity

J. Katz (Ed.): PKC 2015, LNCS 9020, pp. 450–473, 2015.
DOI: 10.1007/978-3-662-46447-2_20

1   Introduction

Append-only signatures (AOS), as introduced by Kiltz, Mityagin, Panjwani and Raghavan [37], are signature schemes where, given a signature on a multi-block message $(M_1, \ldots, M_n)$, anyone can publicly compute a signature on the message $(M_1, \ldots, M_n, M_{n+1})$, for any M_{n+1}. Kiltz *et al.* provided both generic constructions, based on any signature scheme, and concrete constructions based on specific assumptions. They further proved that AOS are equivalent to hierarchical identity-based signatures [30,47]. Importantly, the schemes of [37] are inherently history-preserving in that signed messages are *ordered* tuples.

In [14], Bethencourt, Boneh and Waters (BBW) noted that certain important applications of incremental signature nature require, in fact, a kind of AOS system that allows authenticating sets (i.e., without divulging any order among elements) rather than ordered tuples. They suggested a primitive, called *History-Hiding Append-Only Signatures* (HH-AOS) that can be seen as a special case of homomorphic signatures. It allows one to sign a set of messages in such a way that anyone can subsequently derive a signature on arbitrary supersets of the initial set. Bethencourt *et al.* used this primitive to design tamper-evident, history-hiding and subliminal-free mechanisms (by extending techniques due to Molnar *et al.* [42]) for storing ballots on e-voting terminals. To prevent anyone from injecting subliminal information (*e.g.*, by embedding some information in derived signatures), it is required that derived signatures be indistinguishable from original ones on the resulting superset. Independently, Moran, Naor and Segev [43] addressed the same problem using write-once memories rather than digital signatures. They described a deterministic vote-storage mechanism without relying on cryptographic techniques. Their solution fits within a line of work, initiated by Micciancio [41], on history-hiding data structures [41,44], which recently has been extended to applied systems [8]. While secure against unbounded adversaries, the Moran *et al.* technique [43] is significantly more memory-demanding than [14] and this overhead was proved inherent to deterministic techniques [43]. The HH-AOS approach of Bethencourt *et al.* [14] thus appears to remain the most promising method to reliably store n elements in a history-hiding, tamper-evident and scalable manner, namely, using only $O(n)$ memory.

It is worth noting that HH-AOS are a more powerful primitive than ordinary AOS: any HH-AOS can immediately be turned —by means of a hash-based order-embedding transformation— into an equally efficient regular append-only signature. HH-AOS schemes are thus more versatile as they can also be used in all the applications which append-only signatures were initially designed for.

RELATED WORK. Homomorphic signatures were first suggested by Desmedt [24] as a new concept useful in the validation of computer operation. Johnson *et al.* [36] provided security definitions and examples of set homomorphic signatures. Several such constructions in [5,6,36] allow for subset derivation (i.e., a signature on a set allows deriving a signature on arbitrary subsets of that set) but none of these works considers the dual superset homomorphism case.

The latter was investigated for the first time by Bethencourt *et al.* [14] who provided two HH-AOS realizations which both have some limitations pointed at by the original authors (in essence, demonstrating the associated difficulties with such a scheme). The first one is a generic construction, based on any signature, where the public key has linear size in the maximal size of sets to be signed. As a consequence, this construction requires the signer to determine an upper bound on the cardinality of sets when generating a key pair. Moreover, this generic construction is not free of subliminal channels. The reason is that it allows the party running the signature derivation algorithm to choose certain values pseudo-randomly (rather than truly randomly), which allows a distinguisher to infer some information on the derivation history of signatures.

The second construction of [14] is a subliminal-free system built upon the aggregate signature scheme of Boneh *et al.* [20]. It eliminates the disadvantages of the first scheme in that it provides constant-size public keys and removes the need for an *a priori* bound on the cardinality of authenticated sets. However, while practical, this second scheme is only shown secure in the random oracle model [11]. Recall that it is widely accepted that the random oracle methodology, while better than providing no proof whatsoever, is an idealization that may have no standard model instantiation. Indeed, at times, it is provably unrealizable, as was shown by a number of works (*e.g.*, [21]).

So far, the only apparent way to build a HH-AOS system in the standard model — let alone with constant-size public keys— is to take advantage of aggregate signatures [34,35] in order to instantiate the BBW system system [14] outside the random oracle idealization. (As explained in the full version of the paper [39], sequential aggregate signatures like [40] do not suffice for this.) This requires standard model instantiations [25,35] of Full Domain Hash [12]. As of now, this is only known under the recent "multi-linear maps" [27], which still have no practical realizations and serve as polynomial plausibility only. Even the recent results of Hohenberger *et al.* [35] rely on indistinguishability obfuscation [28], known to exist from multi-linear maps only. Thus, such possible ideas cannot yield practical schemes based on simple standard assumptions (like Diffie-Hellman or Decision Linear [16]). In addition, multi-linear maps are quite new, and the state of their secure implementation remains unclear.

OUR CONTRIBUTION. We describe the first efficient history-hiding append-only signature with constant-size public keys in the standard model (by "constant" we mean that it only depends on the security parameter, and not on the cardinality of sets to be signed). This new scheme further provides perfectly re-randomizable signatures, which guarantees the absence of subliminal channels.

Our scheme also provably satisfies a definition of unlinkability stronger than that of [14]. We actually re-cast the syntax of HH-AOS schemes in the definitional framework of Ahn *et al.* [5] for homomorphic signatures. The privacy notion of [5] mandates that derived signatures be statistically indistinguishable from original signatures, *even* when these are given to the distinguisher. In [6], Attrapadung *et al.* further strengthened the latter privacy notion by considering all valid-looking original signatures and not only those in the range of the signing algorithm.

Our construction is asymptotically as efficient as the original BBW realization. Even if we ignore its history-hiding property, it favorably compares to existing append-only signatures [37] in that it appears to be the only known AOS realization that simultaneously provides the following properties: (i) full security (i.e., unforgeability in a model where the adversary can adaptively choose its target message); (ii) constant-size public keys; and (iii) privacy in the sense of the strongest definition considered in [6]. In comparison, the certificate-based generic AOS scheme of [37] is easily seen not to reach the latter level of privacy. As for other fully secure constructions with short public keys, they are all obtained by applying the Naor transformation [17] to unbounded hierarchical identity-based encryption systems [38], which build on Waters' dual system encryption technique [49]. Since the latter always involves at least two distinct distributions of valid signatures (or private keys), it seems inherently incompatible with the information-theoretic privacy notion used in [6].

Our scheme is motivated by ideas that were used in [6] to construct a subset homomorphic signature (namely, a signature on a set authenticates the entire powerset of that set). These ideas, in turn, are augmented by other novel techniques and ideas. Like [6], we rely on the randomizability of Groth-Sahai proofs [32] to render signatures perfectly randomizable. However, superset predicates seem harder to handle than their subset counterpart. Indeed, if we disregard privacy properties, simple constructions[1] readily solve the subset case whereas no such thing is known to work for superset predicates, even when privacy is not a concern. Like [6], our approach proceeds by generating a fresh ephemeral public key $X = g^x$ for each set to be signed. The underlying private key is split into n additive shares $\{\omega_i\}_{i=1}^n$ such that $x = \sum_{i=1}^n \omega_i$, where n is the cardinality of the set. Each of these is then used to sign a set element m_i in the fashion of Boneh-Lynn-Shacham [19] signatures, by computing $H_{\mathbb{G}}(m_i)^{\omega_i}$ using a number theoretic hash function $H_{\mathbb{G}} : \{0,1\}^L \to \mathbb{G}$. Although BLS signatures are only known to be secure in the random oracle model (at least in their original form), we, in contrast, can prove the security of the scheme in the standard model as long as $H_{\mathbb{G}}$ is programmable [33] in the same way as the hash function used in [48]. At the same time, we depart from the security proof of [48] in that the programmability of $H_{\mathbb{G}}$ is used in a different way which is closer to the security proofs of Hofheinz and Kiltz [33]. Recall that programmable hash functions [33] are number theoretic hash functions where the hash value $H_{\mathbb{G}}(m)$ is linked to its representation $g^{a_m} h^{b_m}$ for given base elements $g, h \in \mathbb{G}$. While security proofs in the standard model often require $\log_g(H_{\mathbb{G}}(m))$ to be available in the forgery message and unavailable in signed messages, we proceed the other way around: at some crucial signing query $\mathsf{Msg} = \{m_1, \ldots, m_n\}$, we require $H_{\mathbb{G}}(m)$ not to depend on h for exactly one set element $m_i \in \mathsf{Msg}$.

RELATION TO IDENTITY-BASED RING SIGNATURES. Ring signatures, as introduced by Rivest, Shamir and Tauman [45] allow users to anonymously sign

---

[1] For example, as mentioned in [6, Section 5], one can merely sign each set using a new ephemeral public key that is certified by the long-term key.

messages on behalf of any *ad hoc* set of users that includes them. Their typical application is to allow a source to anonymously reveal a sensitive information while providing guarantees of trustworthiness.

While ring signatures are known from 2001, rigorous security definitions remained lacking until the work of Bender *et al.* [13] and efficient constructions in the standard model were only given by Shacham and Waters [46] and by Chandran *et al.* [22]. In the identity-based setting, constructing ring signatures remains a non-trivial problem as generic constructions from ordinary ring signatures do not appear to work.

Identity-based ring signatures are extensions of ring signatures [45] to the identity-based setting [47]. They are signature schemes wherein users can employ a private key derived from their identity to sign messages on behalf of any set of identities that includes theirs. The verifier is convinced that a signature was created by a ring member but does not learn anything else. Recently, Au *et al.* [7] described a fully secure identity-based ring signature in the standard model using composite order groups. Their scheme seems amenable for constructing a HH-AOS system. However, due to the use of the dual system technique [29], it cannot achieve the same level of privacy as our scheme (as we discuss later on). Interestingly, any HH-AOS scheme, in fact, gives an identity-based ring signature as the private key of some identity id can consist of a HH-AOS signature on the singleton $\{0\|id\}$ which allows the derivation of a signature on the set $\{0\|id, 0\|id_1, \ldots, 0\|id_n, 1\|M\|\mathcal{R}\}$, where M is the message and $\mathcal{R} = \{id, id_1, \ldots, id_n\}$ is the ring. As detailed in Section 4, we obtain fully secure identity-based ring signatures based on simple assumptions in prime order groups, which allow for a much better efficiency and a stronger flavor of anonymity than [7].

2   Background

2.1   Definitions for History-Hiding Append-Only Signatures

We first recall the original syntactic definition of history-hiding append-only signatures.

Definition 1 ([14]). *An **History-Hiding Append-Only Signatures** (HH-AOS) is a tuple of algorithms* (Keygen, Append, Verify) *with the following specifications.*

Keygen(λ): *takes as input a security parameter $\lambda \in \mathbb{N}$ and outputs a public key PK and a private key $SK = \Phi$ which consists of an initial signature Φ on the empty set $\emptyset$.*

Append(PK, Φ, S, m): *given a public key PK, a signature Φ for some set S and a message $m \in \{0,1\}^*$, this algorithm outputs $\bot$ if Φ is not a valid signature on the set S or if $m \in S$. Otherwise, it outputs a signature Φ' on the augmented set $S' = S \cup \{m\}$.*

Verify(PK, S, Φ): *given a public key PK, and a presented signature Φ for a given set S, this algorithm outputs 1 if Φ is a valid signature for S and 0 otherwise.*

CORRECTNESS. For any integers $\lambda \in \mathbb{N}$ and $n \in \mathsf{poly}(\lambda)$, all key pairs $(PK, SK) \leftarrow \mathsf{Keygen}(\lambda)$ and all sets $S = \{m_1, \ldots, m_n\}$, if $\Phi_0 = SK$, $S_0 = \emptyset$ and $\Phi_i \leftarrow \mathsf{Append}(PK, \Phi_{i-1}, S_i, m_i)$, where $S_i = S_{i-1} \cup \{m_i\}$, for $i = 1$ to n, then $\mathsf{Verify}(PK, S, \Phi_n) = 1$.

Bethencourt *et al.* [14] define two security properties of HH-AOS schemes which are called *append-only unforgeability* and *history-hiding*. These properties can be defined as follows.

Definition 2. *A HH-AOS scheme* (Keygen, Append, Verify) *is* ***append-only unforgeable*** *if no PPT adversary has non-negligible advantage in the following game:*

1. *The challenger generates a key pair* $(PK, SK) \leftarrow \mathsf{Keygen}(\lambda)$ *and hands* PK *to the adversary* $\mathcal{A}$.
2. *On polynomially occasions, the adversary* $\mathcal{A}$ *chooses a set* $S = \{m_1, \ldots, m_n\}$, *for some arbitrary* $n \in \mathsf{poly}(\lambda)$. *We assume w.l.o.g. that* $m_1, \ldots, m_n$ *are sorted in lexicographical order. For* $i = 1$ *to* n, *the challenger computes* $\Phi_i \leftarrow \mathsf{Append}(PK, \Phi_{i-1}, S_{i-1}, m_i)$, *where* $S_i = S_{i-1} \cup \{m_i\}$ *for each* $i \in \{1, \ldots, n\}$ *and with* $S_0 = \emptyset$, $\Phi_0 = SK$. *Then,* Φ_n *is returned to* $\mathcal{A}$.
3. $\mathcal{A}$ *outputs a pair* $(S^\star, \Phi^\star)$ *and wins if: (i)* $\mathsf{Verify}(PK, S^\star, \Phi^\star) = 1$; *(ii) If* $S_1, \ldots, S_q$ *denote the sets for which* $\mathcal{A}$ *obtained signatures at Step 2, then* $S_i \not\subseteq S^\star$ *for each* $i \in \{1, \ldots, q\}$. *The adversary's advantage is its probability of success, taken over all coin tosses.*

Definition 3. *A HH-AOS scheme* (Keygen, Append, Verify) *is* ***history-hiding*** *if no PPT adversary has non-negligible advantage in the following game:*

1. *The challenger generates a key pair* $(PK, SK) \leftarrow \mathsf{Keygen}(\lambda)$ *and gives* PK *to the adversary* $\mathcal{A}$.
2. *The adversary* $\mathcal{A}$ *chooses a set* $S = \{m_1, \ldots, m_n\}$, *for some* $n \in \mathsf{poly}(\lambda)$, *and two distinct permutations* $\pi_0, \pi_1 : \{1, \ldots, n\} \to \{1, \ldots, n\}$. *The challenger chooses a random bit* $b \xleftarrow{R} \{0, 1\}$ *and defines* $m_i' = \pi_b(m_i)$ *for each* $i \in \{1, \ldots, n\}$. *It computes* $\Phi_i \leftarrow \mathsf{Append}(PK, \Phi_{i-1}, S_{i-1}, m_i')$, *where* $S_i = S_{i-1} \cup \{m_i'\}$ *for each* $i \in \{1, \ldots, n\}$ *and with* $S_0 = \emptyset$, $\Phi_0 = SK$. *It returns* Φ_n *to* $\mathcal{A}$.
3. $\mathcal{A}$ *outputs a bit* $b' \in \{0, 1\}$ *and wins if* $b' = b$. *The adversary's advantage is the distance* $\mathbf{Adv}(\mathcal{A}) := |\Pr[b' = b] - 1/2|$.

While the above definition is sufficient for applications like vote storage [14], it can be strengthened in a number of ways. For example, the adversary could be granted access to a signing oracle before and after Step 2. Alternatively, the adversary could be given the private key SK at Step 1 of the game. Finally, we may also ask for security in the statistical (rather than computational) sense.

These stronger security properties will be naturally obtained by viewing HH-AOS schemes as a particular case of homomorphic signatures in the sense of the definitions of [5,6].

2.2 Definitions for Homomorphic Signatures

Definition 4 ([5]). *Let $\mathcal{M}$ be a message space and $2^{\mathcal{M}}$ be its powerset. Let $P : 2^{\mathcal{M}} \times \mathcal{M} \to \{0, 1\}$ be a predicate. A message m' is said **derivable** from $M \subset \mathcal{M}$ if $P(M, m') = 1$. As in [5], $P^i(M)$ is defined as the set of messages derivable from $P^{i-1}(M)$, where $P^0(M) := \{m' \in \mathcal{M} \mid P(M, m') = 1\}$. Finally, $P^*(M) := \cup_{i=0}^{\infty} P^i(M)$ denotes the set of messages iteratively derivable from M.*

Definition 5 ([5]). *A **P-homomorphic signature** for a predicate $P : 2^{\mathcal{M}} \times \mathcal{M} \to \{0, 1\}$ consists of a triple of algorithms (Keygen, SignDerive, Verify) such that:*

Keygen(λ): *takes in a security parameter $\lambda \in \mathbb{N}$ and outputs a key pair (sk, pk). As in [5], the private key sk is a signature on the empty tuple $\varepsilon \in \mathcal{M}$.*

SignDerive(pk, ($\{\sigma_m\}_{m \in M}, M$), m'): *is a possibly probabilistic algorithm that inputs a public key pk, a set of messages $M \subset \mathcal{M}$, a corresponding set of signatures $\{\sigma_m\}_{m \in M}$ and a derived message $m' \in \mathcal{M}$. If $P(M, m') = 0$, it outputs $\perp$. Otherwise, it outputs a derived signature σ'.*

Verify(pk, m, σ): *is a deterministic algorithm that takes as input a public key pk, a signature σ and a message m. It outputs 0 or 1.*

The empty tuple $\varepsilon \in \mathcal{M}$ satisfies $P(\varepsilon, m) = 1$ for each message $m \in \mathcal{M}$. Similarly to Ahn *et al.* [5], we define Sign(pk, sk, m) as the algorithm that runs[2] SignDerive(pk, (sk, ε), m) and outputs the result. For any $M = \{m_1, \ldots, m_k\} \subset \mathcal{M}$, we let Sign(sk, M) := $\{$Sign(sk, m_1), $\ldots$, Sign(sk, m_k)$\}$. Finally, we write Verify(pk, M, $\{\sigma_m\}_{m \in M}$) = 1 to say that Verify(pk, m, σ_m) = 1 for each $m \in M$.

CORRECTNESS. For all key pairs (pk, sk) $\leftarrow$ Keygen(λ), for any message set $M \subset \mathcal{M}$ and any single message $m' \in \mathcal{M}$ such that $P(M, m') = 1$, the following conditions have to be satisfied: (i) SignDerive(pk, (Sign(sk, M), M), m') $\neq \perp$; (ii) Verify(pk, m', SignDerive(pk, (Sign(sk, M), M), m')) = 1.

Definition 6 ([5]). *A P-homomorphic signature scheme is **unforgeable** if no PPT adversary has noticeable advantage in the game below:*

1. *The challenger generates a key pair (pk, sk) $\leftarrow$ Keygen(λ) and gives pk to the adversary $\mathcal{A}$. It initializes two initially empty tables T and Q.*
2. *$\mathcal{A}$ adaptively interleaves the following queries.*
   - *Signing queries: $\mathcal{A}$ chooses a message $m \in \mathcal{M}$. The challenger replies by choosing a handle h, runs $\sigma \leftarrow$ Sign(sk, m) and stores (h, m, σ) in a table T. The handle h is returned to $\mathcal{A}$.*
   - *Derivation queries: $\mathcal{A}$ chooses a vector of handles $\vec{h} = (h_1, \ldots, h_k)$ and a message $m' \in \mathcal{M}$. The challenger first retrieves the tuples $\{(h_i, m_i, \sigma_i)\}_{i=1}^k$ from the table T and returns $\perp$ if one of them is missing. Otherwise, it defines $M := (m_1, \ldots, m_k)$ and $\{\sigma_m\}_{m \in M} = \{\sigma_1, \ldots, \sigma_k\}$. If $P(M, m') = 1$, the challenger runs $\sigma' \leftarrow$ SignDerive(pk, ($\{\sigma_m\}_{m \in M}, M$), m'), chooses a handle h', stores (h', m', σ') in T and returns h' to $\mathcal{A}$.*

---

[2] The intuition here is that any message can be derived when the original signature contains the signing key.

– *Reveal queries:* $\mathcal{A}$ *chooses a handle* h. *If no entry of the form* $(\mathsf{h}, m', \sigma')$ *exists in* T, *the challenger returns* $\perp$. *Otherwise, it returns* σ' *to* $\mathcal{A}$ *and adds* (m', σ') *to the set* Q.

3. *The adversary* $\mathcal{A}$ *outputs a pair* (σ', m') *and wins if: (i)* $\mathsf{Verify}(\mathsf{pk}, m', \sigma') = 1$; *(ii) If* $M \subset \mathcal{M}$ *is the set of messages in* Q, *then* $m' \notin P^*(M)$.

Ahn *et al.* [5] considered a strong notion of unconditional privacy that requires the inability of distinguishing derived signatures from original ones, *even* when these are given along with the private key. In [5], it was showed that, if a scheme is strongly context hiding, then Definition 6 can be simplified by only providing the adversary with an ordinary signing oracle.

As noted in [6], specific applications may require an even stronger definition. The following definition makes sense when homomorphic signatures are randomizable and/or the verifier accepts several distributions of valid signatures.

Definition 7 ([6]). *An homomorphic signature* $(\mathsf{Keygen}, \mathsf{Sign}, \mathsf{SignDerive}, \mathsf{Verify})$ *is* ***completely context hiding*** *for the predicate* P *if, for all key pairs* $(\mathsf{pk}, \mathsf{sk}) \leftarrow \mathsf{Keygen}(\lambda)$, *for all message sets* $M \subset \mathcal{M}^*$ *and all messages* $m' \in M$ *such that* $P(M, m') = 1$, *for all signatures* $\{\sigma_m\}_{m \in M}$ *such that* $\mathsf{Verify}(\mathsf{pk}, M, \{\sigma_m\}_{m \in M}) = 1$, *the distribution* $\{(\mathsf{sk}, \{\sigma_m\}_{m \in M}, \mathsf{Sign}(\mathsf{sk}, m'))\}_{\mathsf{sk}, M, m'}$ *is statistically close to the distribution of* $\{(\mathsf{sk}, \{\sigma_m\}_{m \in M}, \mathsf{SignDerive}(\mathsf{pk}, (\{\sigma_m\}_{m \in M}, M), m'))\}_{\mathsf{sk}, M, m'}$.

We will be interested in HH-AOS systems, which can be seen as P-homomorphic signatures for superset predicates: namely, for any two messages $\mathsf{Msg}_1, \mathsf{Msg}_2 \in \mathcal{M}$, we have $P(\mathsf{Msg}_1, \mathsf{Msg}_2) = 1 \iff \mathsf{Msg}_1 \subseteq \mathsf{Msg}_2$. Note that a completely context-hiding homomorphic signature for superset predicates immediately implies a HH-AOS scheme satisfying a stronger privacy property than Definition 3.

In particular, our construction immediately implies an ordinary (i.e., non-history-hiding) AOS scheme that allows signing ordered tuples while enjoying a stronger form of privacy than in [37]. For example, if we consider the generic AOS [37], which builds on any digital signature, a signature on a vector $(m_1, \ldots, m_n)$ is a sequence $(\sigma_0, pk_1, \ldots, \sigma_n, pk_n, sk_n)$ where $\sigma_i = \mathsf{Sign}(sk_i, (m_{i+1} \| pk_{i+1}))$ for each $i \in \{0, \ldots, n-1\}$, $\{pk_i\}_{i=1}^n$ are fresh public keys generated by the signing algorithm and (pk_0, sk_0) is the long term key pair of the scheme. This construction is clearly not completely context-hiding because auxiliary public keys $\{pk_i\}_{i=1}^n$ appear in an original signature and all its derivatives.

Non-generic AOS schemes can be derived from specific HIBE schemes like the one of Boneh, Boyen and Goh [15] but, in the standard model, the public parameters have length linear in the maximal length of signed messages. For the time being, the only known way to construct a fully secure AOS without having to fix a pre-determined maximal message length is to apply Naor's IBE-to-signature transformation [17] to an unbounded HIBE scheme [38]. Unfortunately, the security proof will probably rely on the dual system technique [49] (see also [29]) which is hardly compatible with the privacy notion of Definition 7. The reason is that this technique involves several computationally indistinguishable classes of signatures satisfying the same equations although they have different distributions. The difficulty is that there is usually no way to publicly modify the class that a given signature belongs to, so that a signature and its derivatives must be of the same class. Hence, for any original signatures $\{\sigma_m\}_{m \in M}$ outside the range of Sign(sk, .), Definition 7 cannot be satisfied.

In contrast, using any completely context-hiding HH-AOS, we can obtain —seemingly for the first time— a completely context-hiding AOS scheme in the sense of Definition 7, which hides all information about the derivation history of a signature on an ordered tuple. The construction is detailed in the full version of the paper [39].

2.3 Programmable Hash Functions

A group hash function $H = (\mathsf{PHF.Gen}, \mathsf{PHF.Eval})$ is a pair of algorithms such that, for a security parameter $\lambda \in \mathbb{N}$, a key $\kappa \leftarrow \mathsf{PHF.Gen}(\lambda)$ is generated by the key generation algorithm. This key is used to evaluate the deterministic evaluation algorithm that, on input of a string $X \in \{0,1\}^L$, computes a hash value $H_{\kappa,\mathbb{G}}(X) = \mathsf{PHF.Eval}(\kappa, X) \in \mathbb{G}$, where $\mathbb{G}$ is a cyclic abelian group.

Definition 8 ([33]). *A group hash function* $H_{\mathbb{G}} : \{0,1\}^* \to \mathbb{G}$ *is* (m, n, γ, δ)-*programmable if there exist PPT algorithms* $(\mathsf{PHF.TrapGen}, \mathsf{PHF.TrapEval})$ *such that:*

- *For generators* $g, h \in \mathbb{G}$, *the trapdoor key generation algorithm* $(\kappa', tk) \leftarrow \mathsf{PHF.TrapGen}(\lambda, g, h)$ *outputs a key* κ' *and a trapdoor* tk *such that, for any* $X \in \{0,1\}^L$, $(a_X, b_X) \leftarrow \mathsf{PHF.TrapEval}(tk, X)$ *produces integers* a_X, b_X *such that* $H_{\kappa',\mathbb{G}}(X) = \mathsf{PHF.Eval}(\kappa', X) = g^{a_X} h^{b_X}$.
- *For all* $g, h \in \mathbb{G}$ *and for* $\kappa \leftarrow \mathsf{PHF.Gen}(\lambda)$, $(\kappa', tk) \leftarrow \mathsf{PHF.TrapGen}(\lambda, g, h)$, *the distributions of* κ *and* κ' *are statistically* γ-*close to each other.*
- *For all generators* $g, h \in \mathbb{G}$ *and all keys* κ' *produced by* $\mathsf{PHF.TrapGen}$, *for all* $X_1, \ldots, X_m \in \{0,1\}^L$, $Z_1, \ldots, Z_n \in \{0,1\}^L$ *such that* $X_i \neq Z_j$, *the corresponding* $(a_{X_i}, b_{X_i}) \leftarrow \mathsf{PHF.TrapEval}(tk, X_i)$ *and* $(a_{Z_i}, b_{Z_i}) \leftarrow \mathsf{PHF.TrapEval}(tk, Z_i)$ *are such that*

$$\Pr[b_{X_1} = \cdots = b_{X_m} = 0 \wedge b_{Z_1}, \ldots, b_{Z_n} \neq 0] \geq \delta\,,$$

where the probability is taken over the trapdoor tk *produced along with* κ'.

The hash function of [48] hashes L-bit strings $M = m_1 \cdots m_L \in \{0,1\}^L$ by mapping them to $H_{\kappa,\mathbb{G}}(M) = h_0 \cdot \prod_{i=1}^{L} h_i^{m_i}$ using public group elements $(h_0, \ldots, h_L)$. This function is known [48] to be a $(1, n, 0, \delta)$-programmable hash function where $\delta = 1/(8n(L+1))$, for any polynomial n. Using a different technique, Hofheinz and Kiltz [33] increased the probability δ to $O(1/(n\sqrt{L}))$.

2.4 Hardness Assumption

We consider bilinear maps $e : \mathbb{G} \times \mathbb{G} \to \mathbb{G}_T$ over groups of prime order p. In these groups, we assume the intractability of the following problem.

Definition 9 ([16]). *The **Decision Linear Problem** (DLIN) in a group* $\mathbb{G}$ *of prime order p is, given $(g^a, g^b, g^{ac}, g^{bd}, \eta)$, with $a, b, c, d \stackrel{R}{\leftarrow} \mathbb{Z}_p$, to decide if $\eta = g^{c+d}$ or $\eta \in_R \mathbb{G}$.*

2.5 Structure-Preserving Signatures Secure Against Random Message Attacks

Structure-preserving signatures [1,2] (SPS) are signature schemes where messages, signatures and public keys all consist of elements of an abelian group over which a bilinear map is efficiently computable. In addition, the verification algorithm proceeds by testing the validity of pairing product equations (as defined in Appendix A).

We use structure-preserving signatures satisfying a relaxed security notion, where the adversary obtains signatures on messages it has no control on. In the following syntax, a structure-preserving signature is a tuple of efficient algorithms (Setup, Keygen, Sign, Verify) where, on input of a security parameter, Setup produces common public parameters gk (which typically specify the chosen bilinear groups) to be used by all other algorithms. As for algorithms Keygen, Sign and Verify, they operate as in an ordinary digital signatures.

In our construction, we need an SPS scheme that satisfies a notion of *extended* random-message security defined by Abe *et al.* [3]. In the definition hereunder, $\mathcal{M}$ denotes an efficient message sampler that takes as input common public parameters gk and outputs a message m as well as the random coins τ used to sample it. In short, the definition requires the scheme to remain unforgeable even if the adversary obtains the random coins of $\mathcal{M}$.

Definition 10 ([3]). *A signature scheme* (Setup, Keygen, Sign, Verify) *provides **extended random-message security** (or XRMA security) with respect to a message sampler $\mathcal{M}$ if, for any PPT adversary $\mathcal{A}$ and any polynomial $q \in$ poly(λ), the adversary's advantage is negligible in the following game.*

1. *The challenger runs* gk $\leftarrow$ Setup(λ) *and* (pk, sk) $\leftarrow$ Keygen(gk). *For $j = 1$ to q, the challenger runs $(m_j, \tau_j) \leftarrow \mathcal{M}(gk)$ and computes $\sigma_j \leftarrow$ Sign(gk, sk, m_j). The adversary is given* (gk, pk, $\{(m_j, \tau_j, \sigma_j)\}_{j=1}^q$)
2. *The adversary $\mathcal{A}$ halts and outputs a pair $(m^\star, \sigma^\star)$. It is declared successful if* Verify(gk, pk, $m^\star, \sigma^\star$) = 1 *and $m^\star \notin \{m_1, \dots, m_q\}$. As usual, $\mathcal{A}$'s advantage is its probability of success taken over all coin tosses.*

As in [3], we will need an XRMA-secure SPS scheme where τ contains the discrete logarithms of the group elements that m is made of.

3   An Efficient HH-AOS Scheme

The scheme's design is motivated by [6] to construct a homomorphic subset signature, which is exactly the dual primitive of HH-AOS. Like the ring signature of [7], the scheme is also inspired by the Lewko-Waters unbounded HIBE system [38] in that the signature derivation algorithm implicitly transforms an n-out-of-n additive secret sharing into a $(n+1)$-out-of-$(n+1)$ additive sharing of the same secret. This transformation actually takes place in the exponent as the shares themselves are not directly available to the derivation algorithm. Lewko and Waters [38] used a similar technique in the key delegation algorithm of their HIBE scheme. However, we depart from [38] in that the construction relies on the partitioning paradigm (i.e., the reduction is unable to sign certain messages that are used to solve a hard problem in the reduction) rather than the dual system approach. The reason is that, as pointed out in [6], the latter makes it harder to construct completely context-hiding schemes.

The construction relies on the properties of the hash function of [48]. A programmable hash function [33] maps a message m to a group element so that the discrete logarithm of $H_{\mathbb{G}}(m) \in \mathbb{G}$ may be available with some probabilities. The hash function of [48] maps a L-bit string $m \in \{0,1\}^L$ to the group element $H_{\mathbb{G}}(m) = h_0 \cdot \prod_{i=1}^{L} h_i^{m[i]}$, for uniformly distributed public group elements $(h_0, \ldots, h_L) \in_R \mathbb{G}^{L+1}$. For any $m \in \{0,1\}^L$, it is possible to relate $H_{\mathbb{G}}(m)$ to exponents $a_m, b_m \in \mathbb{Z}_p$ such that $H_{\mathbb{G}}(m) = g^{a_m} h^{b_m}$. As defined in [33], a (m,n)-programmable hash function is a hash function such that, for all $X_1, \ldots, X_m \in \{0,1\}^L$, $Z_1, \ldots, Z_n \in \{0,1\}^L$ with $X_i \neq Z_j$, the probability that $\bigwedge_{i=1}^{m} b_{X_i} = 0$ and $\bigwedge_{j=1}^{n} b_{Z_j} \neq 0$ is non-negligible.

It is known [48] that Waters' hash function is $(1, q)$-programmable with probability $1/8q(L+1)$. If this hash function is used to instantiate the Boneh $et\ al.$ signatures [19] (for which a signature on m consists of $H_{\mathbb{G}}(m)^{sk}$, where sk is the private key), this allows proving its one-time security (i.e., its security in a game where the adversary is only allowed one signing query) in the standard model: the adversary's unique signing query m is answered by computing $H_{\mathbb{G}}(m)^{sk} = (g^{sk})^{a_m}$ from the public key g^{sk} if $b_m = 0$. If the adversary forges a signature on $m^\star$ such that $b_{m^\star} \neq 0$, the reduction can extract h^{sk} and solve a Diffie-Hellman instance.

Our idea is to sign a set $\mathsf{Msg} = \{m_i\}_{i=1}^n$ by generating a fresh one-time key pair $(x, g^x) \in \mathbb{Z}_p \times \mathbb{G}$ for a BLS-type signature. The one-time public key $X = g^x$ is certified using the long-term key of a structure-preserving signature. Finally, $\mathsf{Msg} = \{m_i\}_{i=1}^n$ is signed by picking $\omega_1, \ldots, \omega_n \overset{R}{\leftarrow} \mathbb{Z}_p$ such that $\sum_{i=1}^n \omega_i = x$ and generating pairs $(\sigma_{i,1}, \sigma_{i,2}) = (H_{\mathbb{G}}(m_i)^{\omega_i}, g^{\omega_i})$, so that the verifier can check that $\prod_{i=1}^n \sigma_{i,2} = X$ and $e(\sigma_{i,1}, g) = e(H_{\mathbb{G}}(m_i), \sigma_{i,2})$ for each i. This allows anyone to publicly add new elements to the set by transforming the sharing $\{\omega_i\}_{i=1}^n$ into a new sharing $\{\omega_i'\}_{i=1}^{n+1}$ of the same value. At the same time, it will be infeasible to publicly remove elements from the signed set.

To guarantee the full context-hiding security, we refrain from letting $(\sigma_{i,1}, \sigma_{i,2})$ appear in clear and replace them by perfectly-hiding Groth-Sahai commitments to $(\sigma_{i,1}, \sigma_{i,2})$ along with NIWI randomizable proofs (which are recalled Appendix A) showing that committed values satisfy the appropriate relations.

In the notations hereunder, for any $h \in \mathbb{G}$ and any vector of group elements $\vec{g} = (g_1, g_2, g_3) \in \mathbb{G}^3$, the vector $(e(h, g_1), e(h, g_2), e(h, g_3)) \in \mathbb{G}_T^3$ is denoted by $E(h, \vec{g})$.

Keygen(λ):

1. Choose a SPS scheme $\Pi^{\text{SPS}} = (\text{Setup}, \text{Keygen}, \text{Sign}, \text{Verify})$ allowing to sign messages consisting of a single group element. We denote by ℓ_{sps} and v_{sps} the number of group elements per signature and the number of verification equations, respectively, in this scheme. Generate common parameter $\text{gk} \leftarrow \Pi^{\text{SPS}}.\text{Setup}(\lambda)$ and a key pair $(sk_{\text{sps}}, pk_{\text{sps}}) \leftarrow \Pi^{\text{SPS}}.\text{Keygen}(\text{gk})$ for this scheme. We assume that gk includes the description of bilinear groups $(\mathbb{G}, \mathbb{G}_T)$ or prime order $p > 2^\lambda$ with a generator $g \in_R \mathbb{G}$.

2. Generate a Groth-Sahai CRS $\mathbf{f} = (\vec{f_1}, \vec{f_2}, \vec{f_3})$ for the perfect witness indistinguishability setting. Namely, choose $\vec{f_1} = (f_1, 1, g)$, $\vec{f_2} = (1, f_2, g)$, and $\vec{f_3} = \vec{f_1}^{\,\xi_1} \cdot \vec{f_2}^{\,\xi_2} \cdot (1, 1, g)^{-1}$, with $f_1, f_2 \overset{R}{\leftarrow} \mathbb{G}$, $\xi_1, \xi_2 \overset{R}{\leftarrow} \mathbb{Z}_p$.

3. Choose a vector $(h_0, h_1, \ldots, h_L) \overset{R}{\leftarrow} \mathbb{G}^{L+1}$ which defines the function $H_{\mathbb{G}} : \{0, 1\}^L \to \mathbb{G}$ that maps any $m \in \{0, 1\}^L$ to $H_{\mathbb{G}}(m) = h_0 \cdot \prod_{i=1}^{L} h_i^{m[i]}$.

The public key is defined to be $\text{pk} := \left(\text{gk}, \mathbf{f}, pk_{\text{sps}}, \{h_i\}_{i=0}^{L} \right)$ and the private key is $\text{sk} := sk_{\text{sps}}$. The public key defines $\Sigma = \{0, 1\}^L$.

Sign(sk, Msg): On input of a message $\text{Msg} = \{m_i\}_{i=1}^{n}$, where $m_i \in \{0, 1\}^L$ for each i, and the private key $\text{sk} = sk_{\text{sps}}$, do the following.

1. Generate a one-time public key $X = g^x$, with $x \overset{R}{\leftarrow} \mathbb{Z}_p$, and a Groth-Sahai commitment $\vec{C}_X = (1, 1, X) \cdot \vec{f_1}^{\,r_X} \cdot \vec{f_2}^{\,s_X} \cdot \vec{f_3}^{\,t_X}$, with $r_X, s_X, t_X \overset{R}{\leftarrow} \mathbb{Z}_p$.

2. Generate a structure-preserving signature $(\theta_1, \ldots, \theta_{\ell_{\text{sps}}}) \in \mathbb{G}^{\ell_{\text{sps}}}$ on the group element $X \in \mathbb{G}$. Then, for each $j \in \{1, \ldots, \ell_{\text{sps}}\}$, generate commitments $\vec{C}_{\theta_j} = (1, 1, \theta_j) \cdot \vec{f_1}^{\,r_{\theta_j}} \cdot \vec{f_2}^{\,s_{\theta_j}} \cdot \vec{f_3}^{\,t_{\theta_j}}$. Finally, generate NIWI arguments $\{\vec{\pi}_{\text{sps},j}\}_{j=1}^{v_{\text{sps}}}$ showing that committed variables $(X, \{\theta_j\}_{j=1}^{\ell_{\text{sps}}})$ satisfy the verification equations of the structure-preserving signature.

3. Choose $\omega_1, \ldots, \omega_n \overset{R}{\leftarrow} \mathbb{Z}_p$ subject to the constraint $\sum_{i=1}^{n} \omega_i = x$. Then, for $i = 1$ to n, compute $(\sigma_{i,1}, \sigma_{i,2}) = \left(H_{\mathbb{G}}(m_i)^{\omega_i}, g^{\omega_i} \right)$, where the messages are indexed in some pre-determined lexicographical order.[3] Then, for each $i \in \{1, \ldots, n\}$, compute Groth-Sahai commitments

$$\vec{C}_{\sigma_{i,1}} = (1, 1, \sigma_{i,1}) \cdot \vec{f_1}^{\,r_{i,1}} \cdot \vec{f_2}^{\,s_{i,1}} \cdot \vec{f_3}^{\,t_{i,1}},$$

$$\vec{C}_{\sigma_{i,2}} = (1, 1, \sigma_{i,2}) \cdot \vec{f_1}^{\,r_{i,2}} \cdot \vec{f_2}^{\,s_{i,2}} \cdot \vec{f_3}^{\,t_{i,2}}$$

to $\{(\sigma_{i,1}, \sigma_{i,2})\}_{i=1}^{n}$. Next, generate a NIWI argument $\vec{\pi}_i$ that $e(\sigma_{i,1}, g) = e(H_{\mathbb{G}}(m_i), \sigma_{i,2})$. This argument is

$$(\pi_{i,1}, \pi_{i,2}, \pi_{i,3}) = \left(g^{r_{i,1}} H_{\mathbb{G}}(m_i)^{-r_{i,2}}, g^{s_{i,1}} H_{\mathbb{G}}(m_i)^{-s_{i,2}}, g^{t_{i,1}} H_{\mathbb{G}}(m_i)^{-t_{i,2}} \right)$$

and satisfies the equation

$$E(g, \vec{C}_{\sigma_{i,1}}) = E(H_{\mathbb{G}}(m_i), \vec{C}_{\sigma_{i,2}}) \cdot$$
$$E(\pi_{i,1}, \vec{f_1}) \cdot E(\pi_{i,2}, \vec{f_2}) \cdot E(\pi_{i,3}, \vec{f_3}) . \quad (1)$$

---

[3] This follows an observation by Naor and Teague [44] who used lexicographical ordering to make sure that the representation does not depend on the order of insertions.

4. Finally, generate a NIWI proof $\vec{\pi}_{sum}$ that $X = \prod_{i=1}^{n} \sigma_{i,2}$. This proof is

$$(\pi_{s,1}, \pi_{s,2}, \pi_{s,3}) = \left(g^{r_X - \sum_{i=1}^{n} r_{i,2}}, \ g^{s_X - \sum_{i=1}^{n} s_{i,2}}, \ g^{t_X - \sum_{i=1}^{n} t_{i,2}}\right) \quad (2)$$

which satisfies $E(g, \vec{C}_X \cdot \prod_{i=1}^{n} \vec{C}_{\sigma_{i,2}}^{-1}) = E(\pi_{s,1}, \vec{f}_1) \cdot E(\pi_{s,2}, \vec{f}_2) \cdot E(\pi_{s,3}, \vec{f}_3)$.

Return $\sigma = (\vec{C}_X, \{\vec{C}_{\theta_j}\}_{j=1}^{\ell_{sps}}, \{\vec{\pi}_{sps,j}\}_{j=1}^{v_{sps}}, \{(m_i, \vec{C}_{\sigma_{i,1}}, \vec{C}_{\sigma_{i,2}}, \vec{\pi}_i)\}_{i=1}^{n}, \vec{\pi}_{sum})$.

SignDerive(pk, (σ, Msg), Msg'): Given the original message $\mathsf{Msg} = \{m_i\}_{i=1}^{n}$, return $\perp$ if $\mathsf{Msg}' \neq \mathsf{Msg} \cup \{m'\}$ for some $m' \in \Sigma$. Otherwise, parse σ as above and do the following.

1. Choose $\omega_1', \ldots, \omega_{n+1}' \xleftarrow{R} \mathbb{Z}_p$ subject to the constraint $\sum_{i=1}^{n+1} \omega_i' = 0$. For each index $i \in \{1, \ldots, n\}$, compute updated Groth-Sahai commitments $\vec{C}_{\sigma_{i,1}}' = (1, 1, H(m_i)^{\omega_i'}) \cdot \vec{C}_{\sigma_{i,1}}$ and $\vec{C}_{\sigma_{i,2}}' = (1, 1, g^{\omega_i'}) \cdot \vec{C}_{\sigma_{i,2}}$. Observe that the argument $\vec{\pi}_i = (\pi_{i,1}, \pi_{i,2}, \pi_{i,3})$ still satisfies the equation $E(g, \vec{C}_{\sigma_{i,1}}') = E(H_{\mathbb{G}}(m_i), \vec{C}_{\sigma_{i,2}}') \cdot E(\pi_{i,1}, \vec{f}_1) \cdot E(\pi_{i,2}, \vec{f}_2) \cdot E(\pi_{i,3}, \vec{f}_3)$ as it only depends on the randomness of commitments.

2. Set $\sigma_{n+1,1} = H_{\mathbb{G}}(m')^{\omega_{n+1}'}$ and $\sigma_{n+1,2} = g^{\omega_{n+1}'}$. Then, pick random $r_{n+1,1}, s_{n+1,1}, t_{n+1,1} \xleftarrow{R} \mathbb{Z}_p$, $r_{n+1,2}, s_{n+1,2}, t_{n+1,2} \xleftarrow{R} \mathbb{Z}_p$ and compute commitments

$$\vec{C}_{\sigma_{n+1,1}}' = (1, 1, \sigma_{n+1,1}) \cdot \vec{f}_1^{\,r_{n+1,1}} \cdot \vec{f}_2^{\,s_{n+1,1}} \cdot \vec{f}_3^{\,t_{n+1,1}}$$

$$\vec{C}_{\sigma_{n+1,2}}' = (1, 1, \sigma_{n+1,2}) \cdot \vec{f}_1^{\,r_{n+1,2}} \cdot \vec{f}_2^{\,s_{n+1,2}} \cdot \vec{f}_3^{\,t_{n+1,2}}$$

as well as a NIWI argument $\vec{\pi}_{n+1}$ showing that $e(\sigma_{n+1,1}, g) = e(H_{\mathbb{G}}(m'), \sigma_{n+1,2})$, which is obtained as

$$\left(g^{r_{n+1,1}} \cdot H_{\mathbb{G}}(m')^{-r_{n+1,2}}, g^{s_{n+1,1}} \cdot H_{\mathbb{G}}(m')^{-s_{n+1,2}}, \right.$$
$$\left. g^{t_{n+1,1}} \cdot H_{\mathbb{G}}(m')^{-t_{n+1,2}}\right).$$

3. Update $\vec{\pi}_{sum} = (\pi_{s,1}, \pi_{s,2}, \pi_{s,3})$ by computing

$$\vec{\pi}_{sum}' = (\pi_{s,1}', \pi_{s,2}', \pi_{s,3}')$$
$$= \left(\pi_{s,1} \cdot g^{-r_{n+1,2}}, \ \pi_{s,2} \cdot g^{-s_{n+1,2}}, \ \pi_{s,3} \cdot g^{-t_{n+1,2}}\right).$$

Note that $\vec{\pi}_{sum}'$ is a valid proof that $X = \prod_{i=1}^{n+1} \sigma_{i,2}$ since $\vec{\pi}_{sum}$ only depends on the randomness of commitments $\vec{C}_X, \{\vec{C}_{\sigma_{i,2}}\}_{i=1}^{n}$, which have not been randomized at this point.

4. Re-randomize the commitments $\vec{C}_X, \{\vec{C}_{\sigma_{i,1}}', \vec{C}_{\sigma_{i,2}}'\}_{i=1}^{n+1}, \{\vec{C}_{\theta_j}\}_{j=1}^{\ell_{sps}}$ and the proofs $\{\vec{\pi}_{sps,j}\}_{j=1}^{v_{sps}}, \{\vec{\pi}_i\}_{i=1}^{n+1}, \vec{\pi}_{sum}'$. Let $\vec{C}_X'', \{\vec{C}_{\sigma_{i,1}}'', \vec{C}_{\sigma_{i,2}}''\}_{i=1}^{n+1}, \{\vec{C}_{\theta_j}''\}_{j=1}^{\ell_{sps}}$ and the proofs $\{\vec{\pi}_{sps,j}''\}_{j=1}^{v_{sps}}, \{\vec{\pi}_i''\}_{i=1}^{n+1}, \vec{\pi}_{sum}''$ be the re-randomized commitment and proofs. Note that, in all of these commitments and proofs, the underlying exponents have been updated.

Return $\sigma' = (\vec{C}''_X, \{\vec{C}''_{\theta_j}\}_{j=1}^{\ell_{sps}}, \{\vec{\pi}''_{sps,j}\}_{j=1}^{v_{sps}}, \{(m_i, \vec{C}''_{\sigma_{i,1}}, \vec{C}''_{\sigma_{i,2}}, \vec{\pi}''_i)\}_{i=1}^{n+1}, \vec{\pi}''_{sum})$
after having re-organized the indexation of $\{(m_i, \vec{C}''_{\sigma_{i,1}}, \vec{C}''_{\sigma_{i,2}}, \vec{\pi}''_i)\}_{i=1}^{n+1}$
according to the lexicographical order for $\{m_i\}_{i=1}^{n+1}$.

Verify(pk, Msg, σ): given pk, and a message $\mathsf{Msg} = \{m_i\}_{i=1}^n$, where $m_i \in \Sigma$ for
each i, parse σ as above. Return 1 iff the following checks all succeed.

1. Return 0 if $\{\vec{\pi}_{sps,j}\}_{j=1}^{v_{sps}}$ are not valid proofs that committed group
   elements $(X, \{\theta_j\}_{j=1}^{\ell_{sps}})$ satisfy the verification equations of the structure-
   preserving signature.
2. Return 0 if, there exists $i \in \{1, \ldots, n\}$ such that $\vec{\pi}_i = (\pi_{i,1}, \pi_{i,2}, \pi_{i,3})$
   does not satisfy (1).
3. Return 0 if $\vec{\pi}_{sum} = (\pi_{s,1}, \pi_{s,2}, \pi_{s,3})$ is not a valid proof.

Note that message elements $\{m_i\}_{i=1}^n$ can be omitted from the signature if
the signature components $\{(\vec{C}_{\sigma_{i,1}}, \vec{C}_{\sigma_{i,2}}, \vec{\pi}_i)\}_{i=1}^n$ are organized according to the
lexicographical order of $\{m_i\}_{i=1}^n$.

As in [14], one can finalize the set and prevent any further insertions by
adding a special message of the form "finalize$\|$#Msg" to the current message
Msg, where #Msg denotes the cardinality of Msg. In this case, the verifier has to
return 0 if Msg contains an element of the form "finalize$\|x$", where $x \neq$ #Msg-1.
We also note that, as in [14], multi-sets can be supported by merely appending
a nonce to each added message in order to ensure uniqueness.

The scheme is unconditionally completely context-hiding because, except
$\{m_i\}_{i=1}^n$ (which are re-ordered to appear in lexicographical order at each derivation), signatures only consist of perfectly hiding commitments and NIWI proofs.
Moreover, in the WI setting, these are uniformly distributed in the space of
valid proofs (as stressed in [32][Section 10]). Since these proofs are also perfectly
randomizable at each derivation, the complete context-hiding property follows.

The unforgeability is proved under the DLIN assumption and the assumption
that the underlying SPS scheme is XRMA-secure. In one step, the proof of
Theorem 1 relies on the programmability of the Waters hash function [48].

The security proof assumes a theoretical upper bound n_{max} on the cardinality
of sets to be signed. However, we emphasize that this bound does not affect
the efficiency of the scheme whatsoever. In particular, the public key size is
independent of n_{max} and only depends on the security parameter.

Theorem 1. *The scheme is unforgeable assuming that the DLIN assumption
holds in $\mathbb{G}$ and that the structure-preserving signature is secure against extended
random message attacks.*

Proof. Since the scheme is completely context hiding, we can use a simplified
definition where the adversary only interacts with a signing oracle. The proof
uses a sequence of games where, for each $i \in \{0, 1, 2\}$, S_i denotes the event that
the adversary $\mathcal{A}$ wins in Game$_i$.

Game$_0$: This game is the real game. We denote by S_0 the event that the adversary $\mathcal{A}$ manages to output a successful forgery. By definition, $\mathcal{A}$'s advantage is $\Pr[S_0]$.

Game$_1$: We change the generation of the public key and choose $\mathbf{f} = (\vec{f}_1, \vec{f}_2, \vec{f}_3)$ as a perfectly sound Groth-Sahai CRS, for which even an unbounded adversary cannot prove false statements. More precisely, the challenger $\mathcal{B}$ sets up $\vec{f}_1 = (f_1, 1, g)$, $\vec{f}_2 = (1, f_2, g)$ and $\vec{f}_3 = \vec{f}_1^{\,\xi_1} \cdot \vec{f}_2^{\,\xi_2}$, with $f_1 = g^{\phi_1}$ and $f_2 = g^{\phi_2}$, for randomly chosen $\phi_1, \phi_2, \xi_1, \xi_2 \xleftarrow{R} \mathbb{Z}_p$. If this modification significantly increases the adversary's probability of success, we can build a distinguisher for the DLIN assumption (specifically, the DLIN distinguisher outputs 1 if the adversary is successful and a random bit otherwise). This implies that, under the DLIN assumption, this modification does not significantly affect $\mathcal{A}$'s behavior. We can thus write $|\Pr[S_1] - \Pr[S_0]| \leq \mathbf{Adv}^{\mathrm{DLIN}}(\mathcal{B})$.

Game$_2$: In this game, we can explicitly use the discrete logarithms $(\phi_1, \phi_2) = (\log_g(f_1), \log_g(f_2))$ that were defined in Game$_1$ since we are done with the DLIN assumption. When $\mathcal{A}$ outputs a forgery $\sigma^\star$, the challenger $\mathcal{B}$ uses (ϕ_1, ϕ_2) to extract $X^\star$ from the Groth-Sahai commitment $\vec{C}_X^\star$ contained in $\sigma^\star$ (recall that, due to the modification introduced in Game$_1$, $\vec{C}_X^\star$ is a perfectly binding commitment). We raise a failure event, called F_2, and let the challenger $\mathcal{B}$ abort if the extracted $X^\star$ was never involved in any signing query. Clearly, any occurrence of F_2 immediately contradicts the extended random-message security of the SPS system as the adversary only gets to see structure-preserving signatures on uniformly distributed group elements X. The reduction is similar to that of [3, Theorem 3] and relies on the XRMA security of the underlying SPS scheme for the same reason.[4] We can thus write $|\Pr[S_2] - \Pr[S_1]| \leq \Pr[F_2] \leq \mathbf{Adv}^{\mathrm{XRMA\text{-}SPS}}(\mathcal{B})$.

In Game$_2$, we will prove that, conditionally on $\neg F_2$, event S_2 can only occur with negligible probability if the Diffie-Hellman assumption holds. Let $(\sigma^\star, \mathsf{Msg}^\star = \{m_1^\star, \ldots, m_{n^\star}^\star\})$ denote $\mathcal{A}$'s forgery. If F_2 does not occur, the group element $X^\star$, which is extracted from the commitment $\vec{C}_X^\star$ contained in $\sigma^\star$, *was* used by $\mathcal{B}$ in some signing query. Letting $j \in \{1, \ldots, q\}$ denote the index of that query $\mathsf{Msg}_j = \{m_{j,1}, \ldots, m_{j,n_j}\}$, we know that that $\mathsf{Msg}_j \not\subseteq \mathsf{Msg}^\star$ since $\mathcal{A}$ would not be a successful forger otherwise. Consequently, there exists $\ell \in \{1, \ldots, n_j\}$ such that $m_{j,\ell} \notin \mathsf{Msg}^\star$. Assuming that signed messages $\mathsf{Msg}_1, \ldots, \mathsf{Msg}_q$ are sets of cardinality at most n_{max}, Lemma 1 constructs an algorithm $\mathcal{B}'$ breaking the Diffie-Hellman assumption with probability at least $\Pr[S_2|\neg F_2]/(16 \cdot q \cdot n_{max} \cdot (L + 1))$. The probability of event $S_2|\neg F_2$ can thus be bounded by $\Pr[S_2|\neg F_2] \leq 16 \cdot q \cdot n_{max} \cdot (L + 1) \cdot \mathbf{Adv}^{\mathrm{CDH}}(\mathcal{B}')$.

Since $\Pr[S_2] = \Pr[S_2 \wedge F_2] + \Pr[S_2 \wedge \neg F_2] \leq \Pr[F_2] + \Pr[S_2|\neg F_2]$, we find

$$\Pr[S_0] \leq \mathbf{Adv}^{\mathrm{DLIN}}(\mathcal{B}) + 2 \cdot \mathbf{Adv}^{\mathrm{RMA\text{-}SPS}}(\mathcal{B}) + 16 \cdot q \cdot n_{max} \cdot (L + 1) \cdot \mathbf{Adv}^{\mathrm{CDH}}(\mathcal{B}')$$

---

[4] In short, for each message X for which the XRMA challenger generates a signature, the reduction needs $x = \log_g(X)$ to properly run Step 3 of the signing algorithm.

which proves the announced result.   □

The programmability properties of the Waters hash function are used in the proof of Lemma 1. In a nutshell, the reduction will have to guess upfront which one-time public key X_{j^*} will be recycled in the adversary's forgery among those involved in responses to signing queries. When answering this signing query, the reduction will implicitly use the g^a part of its given Diffie-Hellman instance (g, g^a, g^b) to form the one-time public key X_{j^*}. In addition, if the input of the j^*-th signing query is $\mathsf{Msg}_{j^*} = \{m_{j^*,i}\}_{i=1}^{n_{j^*}}$, we know that at least one element of Msg_{j^*} will be outside the set $\mathsf{Msg}^* = \{m_i^*\}_{i=1}^{n^*}$ chosen by the adversary for its forgery. If we denote by $m_{j^*,\ell}$ an arbitrary message in $\mathsf{Msg}_{j^*} \backslash \mathsf{Msg}^*$, the reduction will be successful if $H_{\mathbb{G}}(m_{j^*,\ell}) = g^{a m_{j^*,\ell}}$, for some known $a_{m_{j^*,\ell}} \in \mathbb{Z}_p$, and $H_{\mathbb{G}}(m_i^*) = g^{a m_i^*} \cdot (g^b)^{b m_i^*}$ with $b_{m_i^*} \neq 0$ for each $i \in \{1, \dots, n^*\}$. The results of [33, 48] guarantee that these conditions are met with non-negligible probability.

Lemma 1. *In* Game$_2$, *if event* $S_2 | \neg F_2$ *occurs with noticeable probability then there exists an algorithm* $\mathcal{B}'$ *solving the CDH problem with probability at least* $\mathbf{Adv}^{\mathrm{CDH}}(\mathcal{B}') \geq \Pr[S_2 | \neg F_2] / (16 \cdot q \cdot n_{max} \cdot (L + 1))$, *where* n_{max} *is the maximal cardinality of signed subsets.*

Proof. Algorithm $\mathcal{B}'$ takes as input (g, g^a, g^b) and aims at computing g^{ab} using its interaction with the adversary in Game$_2$.

To this end, $\mathcal{B}'$ begins by choosing $(h_0, h_1, \dots, h_L) \in \mathbb{G}^{L+1}$ as in the security proof of Waters signatures [48]. Namely, for any string $m \in \{0,1\}^L$, the hash value $H_{\mathbb{G}}(m) = h_0 \cdot \prod_{i=1}^{L} h_i^{m[i]}$ can be written as $H_{\mathbb{G}}(m) = (g^b)^{J(m)} \cdot g^{K(m)}$ for certain integer-valued functions $J, K : \{0,1\}^L \to \mathbb{Z}_p$ that remain internal to the simulation. In the terminology of programmable hash functions [33], $H_{\mathbb{G}}$ will have to be $(1, 2n_{max} - 1)$-programmable with non-negligible probability δ. Concretely, using the technique of [48], the functions J and K are chosen so that, for any pairwise distinct inputs $m, m_1, \dots, m_{2n_{max}-1}$, we have $J(m) = 0 \bmod p$ and $J(m_i) \neq 0 \bmod p$ for each $i \in \{1, \dots, 2n_{max} - 1\}$ with non-negligible probability $\delta = 1/(16 \cdot n_{max} \cdot (L + 1))$.

Algorithm $\mathcal{B}'$ begins by drawing $j^* \xleftarrow{R} \{1, \dots, q\}$ and starts interacting with the forger $\mathcal{A}$.

Signing queries: For $j \in \{1, \dots, q\}$, we let $\mathsf{Msg}_j = \{m_{j,1}, \dots, m_{j,n_j}\}$, with $n_j \leq n_{max}$, be the j-th signing query made by $\mathcal{A}$. These queries are handled by considering two cases:

- If $j \neq j^*$, $\mathcal{B}'$ chooses a fresh $x_j \xleftarrow{R} \mathbb{Z}_p$, computes $X_j = g^{x_j}$ and answers the query by generating $\omega_1, \dots, \omega_{n_j} \xleftarrow{R} \mathbb{Z}_p$ such that $\sum_{i=1}^{n_j} \omega_i = x_j$. This allows answering the query faithfully, by generating commitments and proofs according to the specification of the signing algorithm.
- If $j = j^*$, $\mathcal{B}'$ implicitly defines $X_{j^*} = g^a$. At this point, $\mathcal{B}'$ considers each message $m_{j^*,i} \in \mathsf{Msg}_{j^*}$ and evaluates $J(m_{j^*,i})$ for each $i \in \{1, \dots, n_{j^*}\}$. If $J(m_{j^*,i}) \neq 0$ for all i, $\mathcal{B}'$ halts and declares failure. It also aborts if Msg_{j^*} contains more than *one* message $m_{j^*,i}$ such that $J(m_{j^*,i}) = 0$. (A

lower bound on the probability for $\mathcal{B}'$ not to abort will be determined later on). Otherwise, there exists a unique index $\ell \in \{1, \ldots, n_{j^\star}\}$ such that $J(m_{j^\star, \ell}) = 0$. In this case, we have $H_{\mathbb{G}}(m_{j^\star, \ell}) = g^{K(m_{j^\star, \ell})}$, so that $\mathcal{B}'$ can pick $\omega_1, \ldots, \omega_{\ell-1}, \omega_{\ell+1}, \ldots, \omega_{n_{j^\star}} \xleftarrow{R} \mathbb{Z}_p$ and set

$$\sigma_{i,1} = H_{\mathbb{G}}(m_i)^{\omega_i} \qquad \sigma_{i,2} = g^{\omega_i} \qquad \text{for } i \in \{1, \ldots, n_{j^\star}\} \setminus \{\ell\},$$

as well as

$$\sigma_{\ell,1} = \left((g^a) \cdot g^{-\sum_{i=1, i \neq \ell}^{n_{j^\star}} \omega_i}\right)^{K(m_{j^\star, \ell})} \qquad \sigma_{\ell,2} = (g^a) \cdot g^{-\sum_{i=1, i \neq \ell}^{n_{j^\star}} \omega_i} .$$

Note that $\{(\sigma_{i,1}, \sigma_{i,2})\}_{i=1}^{n_{j^\star}}$ have the correct distribution as they implicitly share $a = \log_g(X_{j^\star})$ in the exponent. Next, $\mathcal{B}'$ generates commitments and NIWI proofs as in the real signing algorithm.

Forgery: When $\mathcal{A}$ terminates, it outputs a set $\mathsf{Msg}^\star = \{m_i^\star\}_{i=1}^{n^\star}$ with a valid signature

$$\sigma^\star = \left(\vec{C}_X^\star, \{\vec{C}_{\theta_j}^\star\}_{j=1}^{\ell_{\mathsf{sps}}}, \{\vec{\pi}_{\mathsf{sps},j}^\star\}_{j=1}^{v_{\mathsf{sps}}}, \{(m_i^\star, \vec{C}_{\sigma_{i,1}}^\star, \vec{C}_{\sigma_{i,2}}^\star, \vec{\pi}_i^\star)\}_{i=1}^{n^\star}, \vec{\pi}_{sum}^\star\right) .$$

At this point, $\mathcal{B}'$ uses the extraction trapdoor $(\phi_1, \phi_2) = (\log_g(f_1), \log_g(f_2))$ of the commitment to obtain $X^\star$ and $\{\sigma_{i,1}^\star, \sigma_{i,2}^\star\}_{i=1}^{n^\star}$ from $\vec{C}_X^\star$ and $\{C_{\sigma_{i,1}}^\star, C_{\sigma_{i,2}}^\star\}_{i=1}^{n^\star}$, respectively. If one of the following events occurs, $\mathcal{B}'$ aborts and declares failure:

E.1 $X^\star \neq g^a$: This is the event that $\mathcal{B}'$ fails to correctly predict which one-time public key X_j would be re-used in $\mathcal{A}$'s forgery among those involved in signing queries.

E.2 $m_{j^\star, \ell} \in \mathsf{Msg}^\star$.

E.3 There exists $i \in \{1, \ldots, n^\star\}$ such that $J(m_i^\star) = 0$.

If none of these events occurs, the perfect soundness of the proof $\vec{\pi}_{sum}^\star$ guarantees that $\mathcal{B}'$ can compute

$$g^{ab} = \prod_{i=1}^{n^\star} \left(\frac{\sigma_{i,1}^\star}{\sigma_{i,2}^{\star K(m_i^\star)}}\right)^{\frac{1}{J(m_i^\star)}} .$$

We are thus left with assessing the probability for $\mathcal{B}'$ to avoid the failure state during the game.

Since the choice of $j^\star$ is independent of $\mathcal{A}$'s view, we do have $X^\star = g^a$ with probability at least $\Pr[\neg E_1] \geq 1/q$. Regarding E_2 and E_3, since $\mathsf{Msg}_{j^\star} \not\subseteq \mathsf{Msg}^\star$, we know that there exists $k \in \{1, \ldots, n_{j^\star}\}$ such that $m_{j^\star, k} \in \mathsf{Msg}_{j^\star} \setminus \mathsf{Msg}^\star$. If we define the set $\overline{\mathsf{Msg}} = (\mathsf{Msg}_{j^\star} \cup \mathsf{Msg}^\star) \setminus \{m_{j^\star, k}\}$, a sufficient condition for the desirable event $\neg E_2 \wedge \neg E_3$ to come about is to have

$$J(m_{j^\star, k}) = 0 \quad \text{and} \quad J(m) \neq 0 \ \forall m \in \overline{\mathsf{Msg}} . \tag{3}$$

Since the cardinality of $\overline{\mathsf{Msg}}$ is at most $2n_{max} - 1$, the results of [33,48] imply that condition (3) is satisfied with probability at least $1/(16 \cdot n_{max} \cdot (L+1))$. A lower bound on the probability that $\neg E_2 \wedge \neg E_3$ and that $\mathcal{B}'$ does not abort at the $j^\star$-th signing query is thus given by $1/(16 \cdot n_{max} \cdot (L+1))$. Taking into account the probability $\Pr[\neg E_1] \geq 1/q$, it comes that $\mathcal{B}'$ never aborts with probability at least $1/(16 \cdot q \cdot n_{max} \cdot (L+1))$. $\qquad \square$

For the time being, the most efficient XRMA-secure structure-preserving signature based on simple assumptions is the construction of Abe $et\ al.$ [4], where signatures consist of 8 group elements and the verifier has to compute one quadratic equation and three linear equations. Also, each one-time public key $X \in \mathbb{G}$ must be encoded as a triple (g^x, g_1^x, g_2^x), for public elements $(g_1, g_2) \in \mathbb{G}^2$ and where $x = \log_g(X)$. Hence, the commitment $\vec{C}_X$ must come along with two other similar commitments. If the SPS scheme of [4] is plugged into our HH-AOS construction, a set $\{m_i\}_{i=1}^n$ of cardinality n can be signed using $9n + 54$ group elements under the DLIN assumption (which implies the CDH assumption). Then, the bit-size of the signature amounts to $4608 \cdot n + 27648$ if each element of $\mathbb{G}$ has a 512-bit representation. In comparison with [14], our scheme only inflates signatures by a constant factor.

In Section 4 and in the full version of the paper [39], we discuss further implications of the above result to the setting of ring signatures and ordinary (i.e., history-preserving) append-only signatures, where it implies constructions for arbitrarily long rings or sets.

4   Generic Identity-Based Ring Signatures

An identity-based ring signature is a tuple of efficient algorithms (Setup, Keygen, Sign, Verify) with the following syntax.

Setup is a randomized algorithm that takes as input a security parameter $\lambda \in \mathbb{N}$ and outputs a master key pair (msk, mpk). Keygen is a possibly randomized algorithm that takes as input an identity id and returns a private key d_{id}. Algorithm Sign takes as input a list of identities $\mathcal{R} = \{id_1, \ldots, id_r\}$, a private key d_{id} for an identity such that $id \in \mathcal{R}$ and a message M to output a signature $\sigma \leftarrow$ Sign(mpk, $d_{id}, \mathcal{R}, M$). Algorithm Verify inputs mpk, a message M, a list of identities $\mathcal{R} = \{id_1, \ldots, id_r\}$ and a signature σ. It outputs 1 if σ is deemed valid for the message M and the ring $\mathcal{R}$ and 0 otherwise.

Identity-based ring signatures should satisfy two notions called $unforgeability$ and $anonymity$, which can be formalized as below.

Bellare, Namprempre, and Neven [10] showed how to construct identity-based signatures from any signatures. Galindo, Herranz, and Kiltz [26] extended the generic construction of [10] to several kinds of identity-based signatures with special properties but their results do not carry over to the ring signature case. Boneh and Hamburg [18] gave a generic way to build short identity-based ring signatures from their spatial encryption primitive. However, their instantiations require to choose a maximal ring size when the system is set up. It thus remains interesting to provide a generic construction allowing for full security and rings of arbitrary size.

UNFORGEABILITY. This notion is formalized by a game where the challenger generates a master key pair (mpk, msk), where mpk is given to the adversary. Throughout the game, the adversary $\mathcal{A}$ is allowed to make private key queries: it chooses an identity id and obtains a private key $d_{id} \leftarrow$ Keygen(msk, id).

The adversary is also granted access to a signing oracle: at each query, it chooses a triple $(id, M, \mathcal{R})$ and the challenger returns $\perp$ if $id \notin \mathcal{R}$ and $\sigma \leftarrow \mathsf{Sign}(d_{id}, M, \mathcal{R})$ otherwise. Eventually, the adversary outputs a triple $(\sigma^\star, M^\star, R^\star)$ and wins if: (i) $\mathsf{Verify}(\mathsf{mpk}, M^\star, R^\star, \sigma^\star) = 1$; (ii) $\mathcal{A}$ did not invoke the signing oracle on a tuple $(id, M^\star, \mathcal{R}^\star)$ for any identity $id \in \mathcal{R}^\star$; (iii) No private key query was made for any $id \in \mathcal{R}^\star$. Note that this model allows the adversary to adaptively choose the ring $\mathcal{R}^\star$ of identities involved in the forgery. In the weaker model of selective-ring security, the adversary would be forced to declare $\mathcal{R}^\star$ at the very beginning of the game, before seeing mpk.

FULL ANONYMITY. This property is defined via the following game. Initially, the challenger generates a pair $(\mathsf{mpk}, \mathsf{msk})$ and gives mpk and msk to the adversary $\mathcal{A}$. The adversary chooses a message M, a list of identities $\mathcal{R} = \{id_1, \ldots, id_r\}$, a pair of identities (id_0, id_1) and two private keys d_{id_0}, d_{id_1}. If $\{id_0, id_1\} \not\subseteq \mathcal{R}$ or if d_{id_0}, d_{id_1} are not valid private keys for the identities id_0 and id_1, respectively, the challenger returns $\perp$. Otherwise, it challenger flips a fair coin $d \xleftarrow{R} \{0, 1\}$ and returns $\sigma \leftarrow \mathsf{Sign}(\mathsf{mpk}, d_{id_d}, M, \mathcal{R})$. The adversary eventually outputs a bit $d' \in \{0, 1\}$ and wins if $d' = d$. As usual, the adversary's advantage is measured by the distance $\mathbf{Adv}(\mathcal{A}) := |\Pr[d' = d] - 1/2|$.

The above definition of anonymity could be strengthened (as done in [7]) by allowing the adversary to choose the random coins used by the challenger to generate $(\mathsf{mpk}, \mathsf{msk})$. Although the generic construction hereunder does not guarantee anonymity in the sense of this stronger definition, the specific instantiations obtained from our HH-AOS schemes can be proved secure in that sense.

We also remark that the above definition allows the adversary to come up with private keys d_{id_0}, d_{id_1} of its own in the challenge phase. The anonymity definition of [7] is different and rather allows the adversary to choose the random coins used in the generation of d_{id_0} and d_{id_1}. However, the definition of [7] still forces the challenger to generate d_{id_0} and d_{id_1} by running the legal key generation algorithm. In this aspect, our definition is stronger since it allows the adversary to choose any identity-based private keys d_{id_0}, d_{id_1} that satisfy the key sanity check (we assume w.l.o.g. that valid private keys are recognizable) without necessarily being in the range of the private key generation algorithm. It is easy to verify that the scheme of [7] does not provide unconditional anonymity in the sense of the above definition. The reason is its use of groups $\mathbb{G}$ of composite order $N = p_1 p_2 p_3$ and the fact that signatures and private keys live in the subgroup of order p_1: if an unbounded adversary chooses d_{id_0}, d_{id_1} so that d_{id_0} does not have a component of order p_2 but d_{id_1} does, this adversary can infer the challenger's bit by testing if the signature σ has a component of order p_2.

Our generic construction thus provides the first fully secure schemes allowing for rings of arbitrary size while satisfying our definition of anonymity. Let $\Pi = (\mathsf{Keygen}, \mathsf{Sign}, \mathsf{SignDerive}, \mathsf{Verify})$ be a completely context-hiding and unforgeable HH-AOS scheme. Using Π, we can generically construct an identity-based ring signature as follows.

Setup(λ): run (sk, pk) $\leftarrow$ Π.Keygen(λ) and output (msk, mpk) = (sk, pk).

Keygen(msk, id): given msk = sk, compute and return $d_{id} \leftarrow$ Π.Sign(sk, $\{0\|id\}$).

Sign(mpk, d_{id}, M, $\mathcal{R}$): return $\perp$ if $id \notin \mathcal{R}$. Otherwise, encode $\mathcal{R} = \{id_1, \ldots, id_r\}$
and the message M as a set $L = \{0\|id_1, \ldots, 0\|id_r, 1\|M\|\mathcal{R}\}$ of cardinality
$r + 1$. Then, use d_{id} to compute $\sigma \leftarrow$ Π.SignDerive(pk, $\{(d_{id}, \{0\|id\})\}, L)$,
which is possible since L is a superset of the singleton $\{0\|id\}$ by construc-
tion.

Verify(mpk, M, R, σ): given mpk = pk, the ring of identities $\mathcal{R} = \{id_1, \ldots, id_r\}$
and the message M, define the set $L = \{0\|id_1, \ldots, 0\|id_r, 1\|M\|\mathcal{R}\}$. Return
1 if Π.Verify(pk, L, σ) = 1 and 0 otherwise.

Note that, in order to guarantee the unforgeability of the scheme, the ring of
identities R must be appended to the actual message in the last element of L.
Otherwise, the adversary would be able to introduce extra identities in the ring
associated with any given signature.

Theorem 2. *The above identity-based ring signature scheme provides unforgeability against adaptive-ring attacks assuming that Π is an unforgeable HH-AOS.
Moreover, it provides full anonymity against unbounded adversaries if Π is a
completely context hiding HH-AOS scheme.*

Proof. The proof of unforgeability is straightforward as, given a ring signature
forger, one can clearly construct a forger against the underlying HH-AOS. We
thus focus on the anonymity property.

The proof of anonymity is also immediate. We consider a first game, called
Game$_0$, which is the actual attack game. We define Game$_1$ to be identical to
Game$_0$ except that we modify the way to compute the challenge signature in
the challenge phase. Namely, instead of computing the challenge signature as
$\sigma \leftarrow$ Π.SignDerive(pk, $\{(d_{id_d}, id_d)\}, L)$, the challenger computes a new signature
$\sigma \leftarrow$ Π.Sign(sk, L) on the set L. The complete context-hiding property guarantees
that $\mathcal{A}$'s view will not be affected by this change since σ has exactly the same
distribution in both games. However, in Game$_1$, the challenge signature σ does
not depend on the adversary's secret bit $d \in_R \{0, 1\}$, which is thus independent
of the adversary's view. $\square$

A   Groth-Sahai Proof Systems

In [32], Groth and Sahai described efficient non-interactive witness indistinguishable (NIWI) proof systems of which one instantiation relies on the DLIN assumption. This instantiation uses prime order groups and a common reference string
containing three vectors $\vec{f_1}, \vec{f_2}, \vec{f_3} \in \mathbb{G}^3$, where $\vec{f_1} = (f_1, 1, g)$, $\vec{f_2} = (1, f_2, g)$
for some $f_1, f_2 \in \mathbb{G}$. To commit to a group element $X \in \mathbb{G}$, the prover chooses
$r, s, t \xleftarrow{R} \mathbb{Z}_p^*$ and computes $\vec{C} = (1, 1, X) \cdot \vec{f_1}^r \cdot \vec{f_2}^s \cdot \vec{f_3}^t$. On a perfectly sound
common reference string, we have $\vec{f_3} = \vec{f_1}^{\xi_1} \cdot \vec{f_2}^{\xi_2}$ where $\xi_1, \xi_2 \in \mathbb{Z}_p^*$. Commitments $\vec{C} = (f_1^{r+\xi_1 t}, f_2^{s+\xi_2 t}, X \cdot g^{r+s+t(\xi_1+\xi_2)})$ are extractable as their distribution coincides with that of Boneh-Boyen-Shacham (BBS) ciphertexts [16] and

the committed X can be extracted using $\beta_1 = \log_g(f_1)$, $\beta_2 = \log_g(f_2)$. In the witness indistinguishability (WI) setting, the vector $\vec{f}_3$ is chosen outside the span of $(\vec{f}_1, \vec{f}_2)$, so that $\vec{C}$ is a perfectly hiding commitment. Under the DLIN assumption, the two kinds of CRS can be exchanged for one another without the adversary noticing.

To convince the verifier that committed variables satisfy a set of relations, the prover computes one commitment per variable and one proof element per equation. Such NIWI proofs can be efficiently generated for pairing-product equations, which are relations of the type

$$\prod_{i=1}^{n} e(\mathcal{A}_i, \mathcal{X}_i) \cdot \prod_{i=1}^{n} \cdot \prod_{j=1}^{n} e(\mathcal{X}_i, \mathcal{X}_j)^{a_{ij}} = t_T, \tag{4}$$

for variables $\mathcal{X}_1, \ldots, \mathcal{X}_n \in \mathbb{G}$ and constants $t_T \in \mathbb{G}_T$, $\mathcal{A}_1, \ldots, \mathcal{A}_n \in \mathbb{G}$, $a_{ij} \in \mathbb{Z}_p$, for $i, j \in \{1, \ldots, n\}$.

In pairing-product equations, proving a quadratic equation requires 9 group elements. Linear equations (i.e., where $a_{ij} = 0$ for all i, j in Eq. (4)) are slightly more economical to prove as they only cost 3 group elements each.

In [9], Belenkiy et al. showed that Groth-Sahai proofs are perfectly randomizable. Given commitments $\{\vec{C}_{\mathcal{X}_i}\}_{i=1}^{n}$ and a NIWI proof $\vec{\pi}_{\mathrm{PPE}}$ that committed $\{\mathcal{X}\}_{i=1}^{n}$ satisfy (4), anyone can publicly compute re-randomized commitments $\{\vec{C}_{\mathcal{X}_i'}\}_{i=1}^{n}$ and a re-randomized proof $\vec{\pi}'_{\mathrm{PPE}}$ of the same statement. Moreover, $\{\vec{C}_{\mathcal{X}_i'}\}_{i=1}^{n}$ and $\vec{\pi}'_{\mathrm{PPE}}$ are distributed as freshly generated commitments and proof. This property was used in, e.g., [23].

Acknowledgments. We thank the anonymous reviewers for useful comments. The first author's work was supported in part by the "Programme Avenir Lyon Saint-Etienne de l'Université de Lyon" in the framework of the programme "Inverstissements d'Avenir" (ANR-11-IDEX-0007). The last author's work was supported by the ERC grant CryptoCloud.

References

1. Abe, M., Haralambiev, K., Ohkubo, M.: Signing on elements in bilinear groups for modular protocol design. Cryptology ePrint Archive: Report 2010/133 (2010)
2. Abe, M., Fuchsbauer, G., Groth, J., Haralambiev, K., Ohkubo, M.: Structure-preserving signatures and commitments to group elements. In: Rabin, T. (ed.) CRYPTO 2010. LNCS, vol. 6223, pp. 209–236. Springer, Heidelberg (2010)
3. Abe, M., Chase, M., David, B., Kohlweiss, M., Nishimaki, R., Ohkubo, M.: Constant-size structure-preserving signatures: generic constructions and simple assumptions. In: Wang, X., Sako, K. (eds.) ASIACRYPT 2012. LNCS, vol. 7658, pp. 4–24. Springer, Heidelberg (2012)
4. Abe, M., David, B., Kohlweiss, M., Nishimaki, R., Ohkubo, M.: Tagged one-time signatures: tight security and optimal tag size. In: Kurosawa, K., Hanaoka, G. (eds.) PKC 2013. LNCS, vol. 7778, pp. 312–331. Springer, Heidelberg (2013)

5. Ahn, J.H., Boneh, D., Camenisch, J., Hohenberger, S., Shelat, A., Waters, B.: Computing on authenticated data. In: Cramer, R. (ed.) TCC 2012. LNCS, vol. 7194, pp. 1–20. Springer, Heidelberg (2012)
6. Attrapadung, N., Libert, B., Peters, T.: Computing on authenticated data: new privacy definitions and constructions. In: Wang, X., Sako, K. (eds.) ASIACRYPT 2012. LNCS, vol. 7658, pp. 367–385. Springer, Heidelberg (2012)
7. Au, M.-H., Liu, J., Susilo, W., Zhou, J.: Realizing fully secure unrestricted ID-based ring signature in the standard model from HIBE. IEEE Trans. Information Forensics and Security 8(12) (2013)
8. Bajaj, S., Sion, R.: HIFS: History independence for file systems. In: ACM-CCS 2013. ACM Press (2013)
9. Belenkiy, M., Camenisch, J., Chase, M., Kohlweiss, M., Lysyanskaya, A., Shacham, H.: Randomizable proofs and delegatable anonymous credentials. In: Halevi, S. (ed.) CRYPTO 2009. LNCS, vol. 5677, pp. 108–125. Springer, Heidelberg (2009)
10. Bellare, M., Namprempre, C., Neven, G.: Security proofs for identity-based identification and signature schemes. J. Cryptology 22(1) (2009); Cachin, C., Camenisch, J.L. (eds.) EUROCRYPT 2004. LNCS, vol. 3027, pp. 268–286. Springer, Heidelberg (2004)
11. Bellare, M., Rogaway, P.: Random oracles are practical: A paradigm for designing efficient protocols. In: ACM CCS 1993. ACM Press (1993)
12. Bellare, M., Rogaway, P.: The exact security of digital signatures - how to sign with RSA and rabin. In: Maurer, U.M. (ed.) EUROCRYPT 1996. LNCS, vol. 1070, pp. 399–416. Springer, Heidelberg (1996)
13. Bender, A., Katz, J., Morselli, R.: Ring signatures: stronger definitions, and constructions without random oracles. J. Crypotology 22(1) (2009); In: Halevi, S., Rabin, T. (eds.) TCC 2006. LNCS, vol. 3876, pp. 60–79. Springer, Heidelberg (2006)
14. Bethencourt, J., Boneh, D., Waters, D.: Cryptographic methods for storing ballots on a voting machine. In: NDSS 2007. Internet Society (2007)
15. Boneh, D., Boyen, X., Goh, E.-J.: Hierarchical identity based encryption with constant size ciphertext. In: Cramer, R. (ed.) EUROCRYPT 2005. LNCS, vol. 3494, pp. 440–456. Springer, Heidelberg (2005)
16. Boneh, D., Boyen, X., Shacham, H.: Short group signatures. In: Franklin, M. (ed.) CRYPTO 2004. LNCS, vol. 3152, pp. 41–55. Springer, Heidelberg (2004)
17. Boneh, D., Franklin, M.: Identity-based encryption from the weil pairing. J. Comput. 32(3) (2001); Kilian, J. (ed.) CRYPTO 2001. LNCS, vol. 2139, pp. 213–229. Springer, Heidelberg (2001)
18. Boneh, D., Hamburg, M.: Generalized identity based and broadcast encryption schemes. In: Pieprzyk, J. (ed.) ASIACRYPT 2008. LNCS, vol. 5350, pp. 455–470. Springer, Heidelberg (2008)
19. Boneh, D., Lynn, B., Shacham, H.: Short signatures from the weil pairing. In: Boyd, C. (ed.) ASIACRYPT 2001. LNCS, vol. 2248, pp. 514–532. Springer, Heidelberg (2001)
20. Boneh, D., Gentry, C., Lynn, B., Shacham, H.: Aggregate and verifiably encrypted signatures from bilinear maps. In: Biham, E. (ed.) EUROCRYPT 2003. LNCS, vol. 2656, pp. 416–432. Springer, Heidelberg (2003)
21. Canetti, R., Goldreich, O., Halevi, S.: The random oracle methodology, revisited. In: STOC 1998. ACM Press (1998)

22. Chandran, N., Groth, J., Sahai, A.: Ring signatures of sub-linear size without random oracles. In: Arge, L., Cachin, C., Jurdziński, T., Tarlecki, A. (eds.) ICALP 2007. LNCS, vol. 4596, pp. 423–434. Springer, Heidelberg (2007)
23. Chase, M., Kohlweiss, M., Lysyanskaya, A., Meiklejohn, S.: Malleable proof systems and applications. In: Pointcheval, D., Johansson, T. (eds.) EUROCRYPT 2012. LNCS, vol. 7237, pp. 281–300. Springer, Heidelberg (2012)
24. Desmedt, Y.: Computer security by redefining what a computer is. In: New Security Paradigms Workshop, NSPW 1993 (1993)
25. Freire, E.S.V., Hofheinz, D., Paterson, K.G., Striecks, C.: Programmable hash functions in the multilinear setting. In: Canetti, R., Garay, J.A. (eds.) CRYPTO 2013, Part I. LNCS, vol. 8042, pp. 513–530. Springer, Heidelberg (2013)
26. Galindo, D., Herranz, J., Kiltz, E.: On the generic construction of identity-based signatures with additional properties. In: Lai, X., Chen, K. (eds.) ASIACRYPT 2006. LNCS, vol. 4284, pp. 178–193. Springer, Heidelberg (2006)
27. Garg, S., Gentry, C., Halevi, S.: Candidate multilinear maps from ideal lattices. In: Johansson, T., Nguyen, P.Q. (eds.) EUROCRYPT 2013. LNCS, vol. 7881, pp. 1–17. Springer, Heidelberg (2013)
28. Garg, S., Gentry, C., Halevi, S., Raykova, M., Sahai, A., Waters, B.: Candidate indistinguishability obfuscation and functional encryption for all circuits. In: FOCS 2013. IEEE Computer Society (2013)
29. Gerbush, M., Lewko, A., O'Neill, A., Waters, B.: Dual form signatures: an approach for proving security from static assumptions. In: Wang, X., Sako, K. (eds.) ASIACRYPT 2012. LNCS, vol. 7658, pp. 25–42. Springer, Heidelberg (2012)
30. Gentry, C., Silverberg, A.: Hierarchical ID-based cryptography. In: Zheng, Y. (ed.) ASIACRYPT 2002. LNCS, vol. 2501, pp. 548–566. Springer, Heidelberg (2002)
31. Groth, J.: Simulation-sound NIZK proofs for a practical language and constant size group signatures. In: Lai, X., Chen, K. (eds.) ASIACRYPT 2006. LNCS, vol. 4284, pp. 444–459. Springer, Heidelberg (2006)
32. Groth, J., Sahai, A.: Efficient non-interactive proof systems for bilinear groups. In: Smart, N.P. (ed.) EUROCRYPT 2008. LNCS, vol. 4965, pp. 415–432. Springer, Heidelberg (2008)
33. Hofheinz, D., Kiltz, E.: Programmable hash functions and their applications. In: Wagner, D. (ed.) CRYPTO 2008. LNCS, vol. 5157, pp. 21–38. Springer, Heidelberg (2008)
34. Hohenberger, S., Sahai, A., Waters, B.: Full domain hash from (leveled) multilinear maps and identity-based aggregate signatures. In: Canetti, R., Garay, J.A. (eds.) CRYPTO 2013, Part I. LNCS, vol. 8042, pp. 494–512. Springer, Heidelberg (2013)
35. Hohenberger, S., Sahai, A., Waters, B.: Replacing a random oracle: full domain hash from indistinguishability obfuscation. In: Nguyen, P.Q., Oswald, E. (eds.) EUROCRYPT 2014. LNCS, vol. 8441, pp. 201–220. Springer, Heidelberg (2014)
36. Johnson, R., Molnar, D., Song, D., Wagner, D.: Homomorphic signature schemes. In: Preneel, B. (ed.) CT-RSA 2002. LNCS, vol. 2271, pp. 244–262. Springer, Heidelberg (2002)
37. Kiltz, E., Mityagin, A., Panjwani, S., Raghavan, B.: Append-only signatures. In: Caires, L., Italiano, G.F., Monteiro, L., Palamidessi, C., Yung, M. (eds.) ICALP 2005. LNCS, vol. 3580, pp. 434–445. Springer, Heidelberg (2005)
38. Lewko, A., Waters, B.: Unbounded HIBE and attribute-based encryption. In: Paterson, K.G. (ed.) EUROCRYPT 2011. LNCS, vol. 6632, pp. 547–567. Springer, Heidelberg (2011)

39. Libert, B., Joye, M., Yung, M., Peters, T.: Secure efficient history-hiding append-only signatures in the standard model. Cryptology ePrint Archive (2015). http:// eprint.iacr.org/

40. Lu, S., Ostrovsky, R., Sahai, A., Shacham, H., Waters, B.: Sequential aggregate signatures and multisignatures without random oracles. In: Vaudenay, S. (ed.) EUROCRYPT 2006. LNCS, vol. 4004, pp. 465–485. Springer, Heidelberg (2006)

41. Micciancio, D.: Oblivious data structures: Applications to cryptography. In: STOC 1997. ACM Press (1997)

42. Molnar, D., Kohno, T., Sastry, N., Wagner, D.: Tamper-evident, history-independent, subliminal-free data structures on PROM storage -or- How to store ballots on a voting machine. In: S&P 2006. IEEE Computer Society (2006)

43. Moran, T., Naor, M., Segev, G.: Deterministic history-independent strategies for storing information on write-once memories. In: Arge, L., Cachin, C., Jurdziński, T., Tarlecki, A. (eds.) ICALP 2007. LNCS, vol. 4596, pp. 303–315. Springer, Heidelberg (2007)

44. Naor, M., Teague, V.: Anti-persistence: History independent data structures. In: STOC 2001. ACM Press (2001)

45. Rivest, R.L., Shamir, A., Tauman, Y.: How to leak a secret. In: Boyd, C. (ed.) ASIACRYPT 2001. LNCS, vol. 2248, pp. 552–565. Springer, Heidelberg (2001)

46. Shacham, H., Waters, B.: Efficient ring signatures without random oracles. In: Okamoto, T., Wang, X. (eds.) PKC 2007. LNCS, vol. 4450, pp. 166–180. Springer, Heidelberg (2007)

47. Shamir, A.: Identity-based cryptosystems and signature schemes. In: Blakely, G.R., Chaum, D. (eds.) CRYPTO 1984. LNCS, vol. 196, pp. 47–53. Springer, Heidelberg (1985)

48. Waters, B.: Efficient identity-based encryption without random oracles. In: Cramer, R. (ed.) EUROCRYPT 2005. LNCS, vol. 3494, pp. 114–127. Springer, Heidelberg (2005)

49. Waters, B.: Dual system encryption: realizing fully secure IBE and HIBE under simple assumptions. In: Halevi, S. (ed.) CRYPTO 2009. LNCS, vol. 5677, pp. 619–636. Springer, Heidelberg (2009)

Efficient Constructions

One-Round Key Exchange with Strong Security: An Efficient and Generic Construction in the Standard Model

Florian Bergsma[✉], Tibor Jager, and Jörg Schwenk

Horst Görtz Institute for IT Security, Ruhr-University Bochum, Bochum, Germany
{florian.bergsma,tibor.jager,joerg.schwenk}@rub.de

Abstract. One-round authenticated key exchange (ORKE) is an established research area, with many prominent protocol constructions like HMQV (Krawczyk, CRYPTO 2005) and Naxos (La Macchia et al., ProvSec 2007), and many slightly different, strong security models. Most constructions combine ephemeral and static Diffie-Hellman Key Exchange (DHKE), in a manner often closely tied to the underlying security model.

We give a generic construction of ORKE protocols from general assumptions, with security in the standard model, and in a strong security model where the attacker is even allowed to learn the randomness or the long-term secret of either party in the target session. The only restriction is that the attacker must not learn *both* the randomness *and* the long-term secret of one party of the target session, since this would allow him to recompute all internal states of this party, including the session key.

This is the first such construction that does not rely on random oracles. The construction is intuitive, relatively simple, and efficient. It uses only standard primitives, namely non-interactive key exchange, a digital signature scheme, and a pseudorandom function, with standard security properties, as building blocks.

Keywords: One-round key exchange · eCK security · Provable security

1 Introduction

KEY EXCHANGE PROTOCOLS AND THEIR SECURITY. Interactive key exchange protocols are fundamental cryptographic building blocks. Two-party protocols, where two parties A and B exchange messages in order to establish a common secret k_{AB}, are particularly important in practice. Popular examples are SSL/TLS [13], SSH [34], and IPSec IKE [22].

Following the seminal works of Bellare and Rogaway (BR) [1] and Canetti and Krawczyk [8], security for such protocols is usually defined with respect to *active* attackers [23,25,32], which may intercept, read, alter, replay, or drop any

© International Association for Cryptologic Research 2015
J. Katz (Ed.): PKC 2015, LNCS 9020, pp. 477–494, 2015.
DOI: 10.1007/978-3-662-46447-2_21

message transmitted between parties (see Section 3.3 for a precise definition). An attacker in such a security model interacts with a collection of oracles $\pi_1^1, \ldots, \pi_d^\ell$, where all oracles $\pi_i^1, \ldots, \pi_i^d$ share the same long-term public and secret keys of party P_i. An adversary breaks the security of the protocol, if she is able to distinguish the session key k shared between two oracles π_i^s and π_j^t from a random value from the same distribution. To this end, the attacker may ask a Test(i, s)-query to oracle π_i^s. Oracle π_i^s returns either the real key k or a random value, each with probability $1/2$.

Typical security models also allow the attacker to *corrupt* selected parties, that is, to learn their long-term secret keys, or to *reveal keys*, that is, to learn the shared keys of sessions which are not related to the Test session. Stronger models [8,23,25,32] allow the attacker furthermore to learn the randomness used by an oracle (which is easy to define clearly), or even internal computation states (which are difficult to define precisely).

ONE-ROUND KEY EXCHANGE. In this paper we consider *one-round key exchange* (ORKE) protocols, where two parties are able to establish a key in a single round. Such protocols are particularly interesting, due to their simplicity and their efficiency in terms of messages exchanged between parties.

In a (public-key, two-party) ORKE protocol, only two messages are exchanged between two parties A and B. If (pk_A, sk_A) is the public key pair of A, and (pk_B, sk_B) that of B, key establishment proceeds as follows. Party A chooses a random nonce r_A, computes a message $m_A = f(sk_A, pk_B, r_A)$, and sends m_A to B. B chooses a random nonce r_B and responds with message $m_B = f(sk_B, pk_A, r_B)$ (cf. Section 3.2). Note that m_B does not depend on m_A, thus, messages m_A and m_B may be computed and sent *simultaneously* in one round. The key is computed by evaluating a function g with $g(sk_A, pk_B, r_A, m_B) = g(sk_B, pk_A, r_B, m_A)$.

SECURITY MODELS. Some combinations of adversarial queries lead to trivial attacks, these trivial attacks must of course be excluded from the security definition. For instance, in all models, the attacker is not allowed to simultaneously reveal the session key of an oracle π_i^s, and then ask a Test query to π_i^s, as this would trivially allow the adversary to correctly answer the Test query with probability 1. Moreover, the attacker must also not learn *both* the long-lived secret key (Corrupt) *and* the randomness (RevealRand) of an oracle involved in the Test-session, because then the attacker would learn the entire internal state of this oracle, and thus would be able to re-compute everything the oracle is able to compute, including the secret session key.

RESEARCH CHALLENGES. The strongest form of security that is possible to achieve in such a model is to allow corruptions and randomness reveals even against oracles involved in the Test-session, provided that the attacker does not reveal *both* the randomness and the long-term secret of one oracle. (Corruptions of parties are of course only allowed *after* the key has been established, as otherwise trivial man-in-the-middle attacks are possible.) *Is it possible to construct an ORKE protocol that achieves security in such a strong model?*

If a party is corrupted, the adversary can impersonate this party *in the future*. In some cases, the adversary can also break the security of session keys that have been generated *in the past* (e.g. if RSA key transport is used). The property that session keys computed before the corruption remain secure is known as *perfect forward secrecy* (PFS) [14,16]. In reaction to a conjecture of Krawczyk that ORKE protocols could only achieve a weaker form of PFS [24], Cremers showed that full PFS is generally achievable for ORKE protocols [11]. However until now, none of the proposed ORKE protocols has this property. *Can we construct an ORKE protocol that achieves perfect forward secrecy in such a strong model as eCK?*

CONTRIBUTIONS. In this paper, we make the following contributions:

- *Novel generic construction.* We give an intuitive, relatively simple and efficient construction of an ORKE protocol with provable security in a model that allows *all non-trivial combinations* of corrupt- and reveal-queries, even against the Test-session.
- *Non-DH ORKE instantiation.* Instantiating our protocol with the factoring based NIKE protocol by Freire *et al.* [15], this yields an ORKE protocol based on the hardness of factoring large integers. This provides an alternative to known constructions based on (decisional) Diffie-Hellman.
- *First ORKE with perfect forward security under standard assumptions.* Our protocol is the first one-round AKE protocol which provides perfect forward security without random oracles.
- *Well-established, general assumptions.* The construction is based on general assumptions, namely the existence of secure non-interactive key exchange (NIKE) protocols [9,15], (unique) digital signatures, and a pseudorandom function. For all building blocks we require standard security properties.
- *Security in the Standard Model.* The security analysis is completely in the standard model, that is, without resorting to the Random Oracle heuristic [2] and without relying on non-standard complexity assumptions.

THE ADVANTAGES OF GENERIC CONSTRUCTIONS. From a theoretical point of view, generic constructions show relations and implications between different types of cryptographic primitives. From a practical point of view, a generic protocol construction based on abstract building blocks allows to instantiate the protocol with *arbitrary* concrete instantiations of these building blocks — provided that they meet the required security properties. For instance, in order to obtain a *"post-quantum"*-instantiation of our protocol, it suffices to construct a NIKE scheme, digital signatures, and a PRF with *post-quantum* security and plug these primitives into the generic construction.

A common disadvantage of generic constructions is that they tend to be significantly less efficient than direct constructions. However, when instantiated with the NIKE schemes from [15], our protocol is already efficient enough to be deployed in practice. See Section 5 for an efficiency comparison to other ORKE protocols.

PRACTICAL MOTIVATION OF THE MODEL. Most cryptographic protocols inherently require "good" (i.e., independent and uniform) randomness to achieve their security goals. The availability of "good" random coins is simply assumed in the theoretical security analysis. However in practice, there are many famous examples where a flawed (i.e., low-entropy) generation of random numbers has led to serious security flaws. These include, for instance, the Debian OpenSSL bug,[1] the results of Lenstra *et al.* [28] and Heninger *et al.* [17] on the distribution of public keys on the Internet, or the case of certified smart cards considered by Bernstein *et al.* [3].

In our security model we allow the attacker to learn the *full* randomness of each party. Thus, even if this randomness is completely predictable, the protocol still provides security — as long as the long-lived secret keys of all parties are generated with good, "secret" randomness.

2 Related Work

AUTHENTICATED KEY EXCHANGE. An important line of research on the field of authenticated key exchange protocols started with Bellare and Rogaway [1] (the *BR* model) and Canetti and Krawczyk [8] (the *CK* model). The *CK* model is usually used to analyze one-round protocols, where authentication and key negotiation is performed very efficiently by two parties, only sending one message per party. Examples of such one-round protocols are MQV [27], KEA [26,30], or NAXOS [25]. HMQV [23], SMQV [32] were proposed to meet stronger security definitions. A comparison of different variants of the *CK* model can be found in [10,35]. Most constructions are proven secure in the Random Oracle Model (ROM) [2], with only a few exceptions [5,31,33].

PFS AND KCI ATTACKS. Perfect forward secrecy (PFS) is an important security goal for key-exchange protocols. Loosely speaking, PFS guarantees the secrecy of older session keys, even when the parties long-term key is compromised. Krawczyk [24] conjectured that no one-round protocol with implicit authentication can achieve full PFS in a *CK*-type model and introduced the notion of weak PFS (wPFS); this conjecture was refuted by Cremers *et al.* [11]. A protocol is wPFS secure, if the session key is indistinguishable from a random key and the parties long-term key is compromised if the adversary was *passive* during the session key negotiation [24, Section 3.2]. Similar to [11], we define rules for the security game to model and prove (full) PFS. In our security definition, the party corresponding to the tested oracle is allowed to be corrupted before the session completes. The only restriction to the corruption of parties in the test session is that the *intended partner* of the tested oracle is uncorrupted until the tested oracle accepts.

---

[1] https://www.debian.org/security/2008/dsa-1571

Another security goal of AKE protocols is security against *key-compromise impersonation* (KCI) attacks [24]. In a KCI attack, an adversary corrupts a party A and is able to authenticate herself to A as some uncorrupted party B. Since in the *eCK* model the adversary is always allowed to corrupt some party and learn the session randomness of the matching session, security in the *eCK* model naturally brings security against KCI attacks.

eCK MODELS. The term "extended Canetti-Krawczyk model" (eCK) was first introduced in [25]. The main difference to the CK model is that the RevealState-query (which has to be specified for each protocol) is replaced with a different query, namely RevealEphemeralExponent (which is a meaningful definition only for DH-based protocols, or other protocols where ephemeral exponents appear). In subsequent publications, the eCK model was often slightly modified, such that it is difficult to speak of "the" eCK model.

THE *eCK-PFS* SECURITY MODEL. In 2012 Cremers and Feltz introduced a variant of the extended Canetti-Krawczyk model to capture perfect forward security [11]. The major difference between the *eCK* and *eCK-PFS* security models is the definition of session identifiers. Cremers et al. introduced the notion of *origin sessions*, which solves technical problems with the session identifier definition from the original *eCK*-model [12].

We slightly enhanced the *eCK-PFS* model in order to better model PFS, by introducing an explicit counter of adversarial interactions as done by Jager et al. [20] for the *BR* security model. Thus, we have a clear order of events and we can formally validate if a party was corrupted *before* or after a session *accepted* another party as a communication partner.

3 Preliminaries

In this paragraph we will define non-interactive key exchange (NIKE) and one-round key exchange (ORKE) protocols and their security.

3.1 Secure Non-Interactive Key Exchange

Definition 1. *A non-interactive key exchange (NIKE) scheme consists of two deterministic algorithms* (NIKEgen, NIKEkey).

NIKEgen$(1^\lambda, r)$ *takes a security parameter λ and randomness $r \in \{0,1\}^\lambda$. It outputs a key pair (pk, sk). We write $(pk, sk) \xleftarrow{\$} $ NIKEgen(1^λ) to denote that* NIKEgen$(1^\lambda, r)$ *is executed with uniformly random $r \xleftarrow{\$} \{0,1\}^\lambda$.*
NIKEkey(sk_i, pk_j) *is a deterministic algorithm which takes as input a secret key sk_i and a public key pk_j, and outputs a key $k_{i,j}$.*

We say that a NIKE scheme is correct, *if for all $(pk_i, sk_i) \xleftarrow{\$} $ NIKEgen(1^λ) and $(pk_j, sk_j) \xleftarrow{\$} $ NIKEgen(1^λ) holds that* NIKEkey$(sk_i, pk_j) = $ NIKEkey(sk_j, pk_i).

A NIKE scheme is used by d parties $P_1, \ldots, P_d$ as follows. Each party P_i generates a key pair $(pk_i, sk_i) \leftarrow \mathsf{NIKEgen}(1^\lambda)$ and publishes pk_i. In order to compute the key shared by P_i and P_j, party P_i computes $k_{i,j} = \mathsf{NIKEkey}(sk_i, pk_j)$. Similarly, party P_j computes $k_{j,i} = \mathsf{NIKEkey}(sk_j, pk_i)$. Correctness of the NIKE scheme guarantees that $k_{i,j} = k_{j,i}$.

CKS-LIGHT SECURITY. The *CKS-light* security model for NIKE protocols is relatively simplistic and compact. We choose this model because other (more complex) NIKE security models like *CKS*, *CKS-heavy* and *m-CKS-heavy* are polynomial-time equivalent to *CKS-light*. See [15] for more details.

Security of a NIKE protocol NIKE is defined by a game **NIKE** played between an adversary $\mathcal{A}$ and a challenger. The challenger takes a security parameter λ and a random bit b as input and answers all queries of $\mathcal{A}$ until she outputs a bit b'. The challenger answers the following queries for $\mathcal{A}$:

- RegisterHonest(i). $\mathcal{A}$ supplies an index i. The challenger runs $\mathsf{NIKEgen}(1^\lambda)$ to generate a key pair (pk_i, sk_i) and records the tuple $(\mathbf{honest}, pk_i, sk_i)$ for later and returns pk_i to $\mathcal{A}$. This query may be asked *at most twice* by $\mathcal{A}$.
- RegisterCorrupt(pk_i). With this query $\mathcal{A}$ supplies a public key pk_i. The challenger records the tuple $(\mathbf{corrupt}, pk_i)$ for later.
- GetCorruptKey(i, j). $\mathcal{A}$ supplies two indexes i and j where pk_i was registered as corrupt and pk_j as honest. The challenger runs $k \leftarrow \mathsf{NIKEkey}(sk_j, pk_i)$ and returns k to $\mathcal{A}$.
- Test(i, j). The adversary supplies two indexes i and j that were registered honestly. Now the challenger uses bit b: if $b = 0$, then the challenger runs $k_{i,j} \leftarrow \mathsf{NIKEkey}(pk_i, sk_j)$ and returns the key $k_{i,j}$. If $b = 1$, then the challenger samples a random element from the key space, records it for later, and returns the key to $\mathcal{A}$.

The game **NIKE** outputs 1, denoted by $\mathbf{NIKE}_{\mathsf{NIKE}}^{\mathcal{A}}(\lambda) = 1$ if $b = b'$ and 0 otherwise. We say $\mathcal{A}$ wins the game if $\mathbf{NIKE}_{\mathsf{NIKE}}^{\mathcal{A}}(\lambda) = 1$.

Definition 2. *For any adversary $\mathcal{A}$ playing the above* **NIKE** *game against a NIKE scheme* NIKE, *we define the advantage of winning the game* **NIKE** *as*

$$\boldsymbol{Adv}_{\mathsf{NIKE}}^{CKS\text{-}light}(\mathcal{A}) = \Pr\left[\mathbf{NIKE}_{\mathsf{NIKE}}^{\mathcal{A}}(\lambda) = 1\right] - \frac{1}{2}$$

Let λ be a security parameter, NIKE *be a NIKE protocol and $\mathcal{A}$ an adversary. We say* NIKE *is a CKS-light-secure NIKE protocol, if for all probabilistic polynomial-time adversaries $\mathcal{A}$, the function $\boldsymbol{Adv}_{\mathsf{NIKE}}^{CKS\text{-}light}(\mathcal{A})$ is a negligible function in λ.*

3.2   One-Round Key Exchange Protocols

Definition 3. *A one-round key exchange (ORKE) scheme consists of three deterministic algorithms* (ORKEgen, ORKEmsg, ORKEkey).

- ORKEgen$(1^\lambda, r)$ *takes a security parameter λ and randomness $r \in \{0,1\}^\lambda$. It outputs a key pair (pk, sk). We write $(pk, sk) \xleftarrow{\$} $ ORKEgen(1^λ) to denote that* ORKEgen *is executed with uniformly random $r \xleftarrow{\$} \{0,1\}^\lambda$.*
- ORKEmsg(r_i, sk_i, pk_j) *takes as input randomness $r_i \in \{0,1\}^\lambda$, secret key sk_i and a public key pk_j, and outputs a message m_i.*
- ORKEkey(sk_i, pk_j, r_i, m_j) *takes as input a secret key sk_i, a public key pk_j, randomness r_i, and message m_j. It outputs a key k.*

We say that a ORKE scheme is correct, *if for all $(pk_i, sk_i) \xleftarrow{\$} $ ORKEgen(1^λ) and $(pk_j, sk_j) \xleftarrow{\$} $ ORKEgen(1^λ), and for all $r_i, r_j \xleftarrow{\$} \{0,1\}^\lambda$ holds that*

$$\text{ORKEkey}(sk_i, pk_j, r_i, m_j) = \text{ORKEkey}(sk_j, pk_i, r_j, m_i),$$

where $m_i := $ ORKEmsg(r_i, sk_i, pk_j) and $m_j := $ ORKEmsg(r_j, sk_j, pk_i).

A ORKE scheme is used by d parties $P_1, \ldots, P_d$ as follows. Each party P_i generates a key pair $(pk_i, sk_i) \xleftarrow{\$} $ ORKEgen(1^λ) and publishes pk_i. Then, two parties P_i, P_j can establish a shared key as follows (see Figure 1 for an illustration).

1. P_i chooses $r_i \xleftarrow{\$} \{0,1\}^\lambda$, computes $m_i := $ ORKEmsg(r_i, sk_i, pk_j), and sends m_i to P_j.
2. P_j chooses $r_j \xleftarrow{\$} \{0,1\}^\lambda$, computes $m_j := $ ORKEmsg(r_j, sk_j, pk_i), and sends m_j to P_i.
   (Both messages m_i and m_j may be sent simultaneously, as this is a *one-round* protocol).
3. The shared key is computed by party P_i as $k_{i,j} := $ ORKEkey(sk_i, pk_j, r_i, m_j). Similarly, party P_j computes $k_{j,i} = $ ORKEkey(sk_j, pk_i, r_j, m_i). Correctness of the ORKE scheme guarantees that $k_{i,j} = k_{j,i}$.

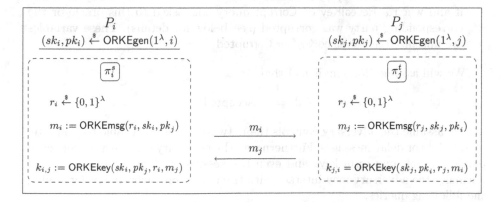

Fig. 1. Execution of an ORKE protocol

3.3   Secure One-Round Key Exchange

Security models for one-round key exchange have two major building blocks. The first defines the *execution environment* provided to an attacker on the AKE protocol. The second defines the rules of the game and the winning condition for an attacker.

Execution Environment. Consider a set of parties $\{P_1, \ldots, P_d\}$, $d \in \mathbb{N}$, where each party $P_i \in \{P_1, \ldots, P_d\}$ is a (potential) protocol participant and has a long-term key pair (pk_i, sk_i). To formalize several sequential and parallel executions of the protocol, each party P_i is modeled by a collection of ℓ oracles. Each oracle represents a process that executes one single instance of the protocol. All oracles representing party P_i have access to the same long-term key pair (pk_i, sk_i) of P_i and to all public keys $pk_1, \ldots, pk_d$. Moreover, each oracle π_i^s maintains as internal state the following variables:

- Accepted$_i^s \in \mathbb{N} \cup \{\texttt{reject}\}$. This variable indicates whether and when the oracle accepted. It is initialized to Accepted$_i^s = \texttt{reject}$.
- Key$_i^s \in \mathcal{K} \cup \{\emptyset\}$, where $\mathcal{K}$ is the keyspace of the protocol and $\emptyset$ is the empty string, initialized to Key$_i^s = \emptyset$.
- Partner$_i^s$ containing the intended communication partner. We assume that each party P_i is uniquely identified by its public key pk_i, and therefore use public keys as identities.[2] The variable is initialized to Partner$_i^s = \emptyset$.
- A variable $\mathcal{M}_{\text{out}}^{i,s}$ storing the message sent by an oracle and a variable $\mathcal{M}_{\text{in}}^{i,s}$ storing the received protocol message. Both are initialized as $\mathcal{M}_{\text{in}}^{i,s} = \mathcal{M}_{\text{out}}^{i,s} = \emptyset$.
- A variable Randomness$_i^s$, which contains a uniformly string from $\{0,1\}^\kappa$. This string corresponds to the local randomness of an oracle. It is never changed or modified by an oracle.
- Variables RevealedKey$_i^s$, Corrupted$_i \in \mathbb{N}$, which will be used to determine if and when a RevealKey or Corrupt query was asked to this oracle or the corresponding party was corrupted (see below for details). These variables are initialized as RevealedKey$_i^s = $ Corrupted$_i = \infty$.

We will assume (for simplicity) that

$$\text{Key}_i^s \neq \emptyset \iff \text{Accepted}_i^s \in \mathbb{N}.$$

We assume the adversary controls the network. Thus she is able to generate, manipulate or delay messages. Furthermore, the adversary can learn session keys, parties' secret long term keys and even the session randomness in our model. Formally the adversary may interact with the execution environment by issuing the following queries.

---

[2] In practice, several keys may be assigned to one identity. There are other ways to determine identities, for instance by using certificates. However, this is out of scope of this paper.

- Send$(i, s, m) \to m'$: The adversary sends message m to oracle π_i^s. Party P_i processes message m according to the protocol specification and its internal oracle state π_i^s, updates its state[3], and optionally outputs an outgoing message m'.

  There is a distinguished initialization message ini which allows the adversary to activate the oracle with certain information. In particular, the initialization message contains the identity P_j of the intended partner of this oracle.

- RevealKey(i, s): if this is the τ-th query issued by $\mathcal{A}$, then the challenger sets RevealedKey$_i^s := \tau$ and responds with the contents of variable Key$_i^s$. Recall that Key$_i^s \neq \emptyset$ iff Accepted$_i^s \in \mathbb{N}$.

- RevealRand(i, s): the challenger responds with the contents of Randomness$_i^s$.

- Corrupt(i, pk^*): if this is the τ-th query issued by $\mathcal{A}$ (in total), then the challenger sets the oracle state Corrupted$_i := \tau$ and responds with sk_i. Moreover, the public key pk_i is replaced (globally) with the adversarially-chosen key pk^*.[4]

- Test(i, s): This query may be asked only once throughout the game, it is answered as follows. Let $k_1 := $ Key$_i^s$ and $k_0 \xleftarrow{\$} \mathcal{K}$. If Accepted$_i^s \in \mathbb{N}$, the oracle flips a fair coin $b \xleftarrow{\$} \{0, 1\}$ and returns k_b. If Accepted$_i^s = $ reject or if Partner$_i^s = j$ and P_j is corrupted when Test is issued, terminate the game and output a random bit.

***eCK-PFS* Security Definition.** In the following we give the security definition for one-round key-exchange protocols in the extended Canetti-Krawczyk model with perfect forward security. Firstly we introduce the partnering definitions from Cremers and Feltz. Secondly we define the rules by which an adversary has to play the AKE game in the *eCK-PFS*-model. Finally we define the security for one-round key-exchange protocols in the model.

Definition 4 (Origin session). *Consider two parties P_i and P_j with oracles π_i^s and π_j^t. We say π_i^s has* origin session π_j^t, *if $\mathcal{M}_{in}^{i,s} = \mathcal{M}_{out}^{j,t}$, and denote this by $\pi_i^s \xleftarrow{os} \pi_j^t$.*

Alternatively we could say π_j^t is an origin session *of π_i^s, if $\mathcal{M}_{in}^{i,s} = \mathcal{M}_{out}^{j,t}$.*

Using the concept of origin sessions, we can define matching sessions as a symmetric relation of origin sessions: two sessions match, if they are origin sessions to each other. We capture this in the following definition.

Definition 5 (Matching session). *Consider two parties P_i and P_j with oracles π_i^s and π_j^t. We say π_i^s has a* matching session *to π_j^t (and vice versa), if π_i^s is an origin session of π_j^t and π_j^t is an origin session of π_i^s.*

---

[3] In particular, if π_i^s accepts after the τ-th query, set Accepted$_i^s = \tau$.

[4] Note, that the adversary does not 'take control' of oracles corresponding to a corrupted party. But he learns the long-term secret key, and can henceforth simulate these oracles.

The notions of origin and matching sessions will be used in Definition 6 to exclude trivial attacks from the security model: If $\mathsf{Test}(i, s)$ is asked, restrictions are imposed on oracle π_i^s itself, and on oracles and parties *from which the test oracle has received a message*. On the other hand, sessions and parties to which a message was sent from the test session do not necessary play any role in Definition 6, for example if the test session has no matching session.

AKE GAME. Consider the following security experiment $\mathbf{AKE}_\Pi^{\mathcal{A}}(\lambda)$ played between a challenger $\mathcal{C}$ and an adversary $\mathcal{A}$. The challenger receives the security parameter λ as an input and sets up all protocol parameters (like long term keys generation etc.). $\mathcal{C}$ simulates the protocol Π and keeps track of all variables of the execution environment. The adversary interacts by issuing any combination of the above mentioned queries. At some point of time during the game, she asks the Test_i^s query and gets a key k_b, which is either the exchanged key or a random key as described in the previous section. She may continue asking queries and finally outputs a bit b'. The game $\mathbf{AKE}$ outputs 1, denoted by $\mathbf{AKE}_\Pi^{\mathcal{A}}(\lambda) = 1$ if $b = b'$ and 0 otherwise.

Definition 6 (*eCK-PFS-rules*). *$\mathcal{A}$ plays the $\mathbf{AKE}$ game by eCK-PFS-rules, if the following conditions hold simultaneously when she issues $\mathsf{Test}(i, s)$:*

- *$\mathsf{Accepted}_i^s = \tau$ with $\tau \in \mathbb{N}$.*
- *$\mathcal{A}$ did not ask both $\mathsf{Corrupt}(i, pk^*)$ and $\mathsf{RevealRand}(i, s)$.*
- *If π_i^s has an origin session π_j^t, then it does not hold that both $\mathsf{Corrupted}_j \leq \tau$ and $\mathcal{A}$ asked $\mathsf{RevealRand}(j, t)$.*
- *If π_i^s has no origin session but intended partner $\mathsf{Partner}_i^s = j$, then it does not hold that $\mathsf{Corrupted}_j \leq \tau$.*

When $\mathcal{A}$ terminates and outputs a bit b', it also holds that $\mathcal{A}$ did not ask $\mathsf{RevealKey}(i, s)$ and (if π_i^s has a matching session to π_j^t) $\mathsf{RevealKey}(j, t)$.

We say $\mathcal{A}$ wins the AKE game, if $\mathbf{AKE}_\Pi^{\mathcal{A}}(\lambda) = 1$.

Definition 7 (*eCK-PFS-security*). *We define the advantage of $\mathcal{A}$ winning this game playing by eCK-PFS-rules as*

$$\boldsymbol{Adv}_\Pi^{eCK\text{-}PFS}(\mathcal{A}) = \Pr\left[\boldsymbol{AKE}_\Pi^{\mathcal{A}}(\lambda) = 1\right] - \frac{1}{2}.$$

Let λ be a security parameter, Π be an AKE protocol and $\mathcal{A}$ an adversary. We say Π is an eCK-secure AKE protocol, if it is correct and for all probabilistic polynomial-time adversaries $\mathcal{A}$ playing by eCK-PFS-rules, the function $\boldsymbol{Adv}_\Pi^{eCK\text{-}PFS}(\mathcal{A})$ is a negligible function in λ.

Remark 1. Note that this security definition includes perfect-forward secrecy and security against KCI attacks.

3.4 Further Building Blocks

DIGITAL SIGNATURES. A digital signature scheme consists of three polynomial-time algorithms $\mathsf{SIG} = (\mathsf{SIGgen}, \mathsf{SIGsign}, \mathsf{SIGvfy})$. The key generation algorithm $(sk, pk) \xleftarrow{\$} \mathsf{SIGgen}(1^\lambda)$ generates a public verification key pk and a secret signing key sk on input of security parameter λ. Signing algorithm $\sigma \xleftarrow{\$} \mathsf{SIGsign}(sk, m)$ generates a signature for message m. Verification algorithm $\mathsf{SIGvfy}(pk, \sigma, m)$ returns 1 if σ is a valid signature for m under key pk, and 0 otherwise.

Definition 8. *We say that* SIG *is deterministic, if* $\mathsf{SIGsign}$ *is deterministic.*

Consider the following security experiment played between a challenger $\mathcal{C}$ and an adversary $\mathcal{A}$.

1. The challenger generates a public/secret key pair $(sk, pk) \xleftarrow{\$} \mathsf{SIGgen}(1^\lambda)$, the adversary receives pk as input.
2. The adversary may query arbitrary messages m_i to the challenger. The challenger replies to each query with a signature $\sigma_i = \mathsf{SIGsign}(sk, m_i)$. Here i is an index, ranging between $1 \leq i \leq q$ for some $q \in \mathbb{N}$. Queries can be made adaptively.
3. Eventually, the adversary outputs a message/signature pair (m, σ).

Definition 9. *We define the advantage on an adversary* $\mathcal{A}$ *in this game as*

$$\mathbf{Adv}_{\mathsf{SIG}}^{sEUF\text{-}CMA}(\mathcal{A}) := \Pr\left[(m, \sigma) \xleftarrow{\$} \mathcal{A}^{\mathcal{C}(\lambda)}(pk) : \begin{array}{l} \mathsf{SIGvfy}(pk, m, \sigma) = 1, \\ (m, \sigma) \neq (m_i, \sigma_i) \; \forall i \end{array}\right]$$

SIG *is strongly secure* against *existential forgeries under adaptive chosen-message attacks (sEUF-CMA), if* $\mathbf{Adv}_{\mathsf{SIG}}^{sEUF\text{-}CMA}(\mathcal{A})$ *is a negligible function in* λ *for all probabilistic polynomial-time adversaries* $\mathcal{A}$.

Remark 2. Deterministic signatures with sEUF-CMA security can be constructed, for instance, from verifiable unpredictable or verifiable random functions with large input spaces [4,18,19,29].

PSEUDORANDOM FUNCTIONS. A *pseudo-random function* is an algorithm PRF. This algorithm implements a deterministic function $z = \mathsf{PRF}(k, x)$, taking as input a key $k \in \{0, 1\}^\lambda$ and some bit string x, and returning a string $z \in \{0, 1\}^\mu$.

Consider the following security experiment played between a challenger $\mathcal{C}$ and an adversary $\mathcal{A}$.

1. The challenger samples $k \xleftarrow{\$} \{0, 1\}^\lambda$ uniformly random.
2. The adversary may query arbitrary values x_i to the challenger. The challenger replies to each query with $z_i = \mathsf{PRF}(k, x_i)$. Here i is an index, ranging between $1 \leq i \leq q$ for some $q \in \mathbb{N}$. Queries can be made adaptively.
3. Eventually, the adversary outputs value x and a special symbol $\top$. The challenger sets $z_0 = \mathsf{PRF}(k, x)$ and samples $z_1 \xleftarrow{\$} \{0, 1\}^\mu$ uniformly random. Then it tosses a coin $b \xleftarrow{\$} \{0, 1\}$, and returns z_b to the adversary.

4. Finally, the adversary outputs a guess $b' \in \{0, 1\}$.

The Adversary wins the game, if she outputs b' such that $b = b'$.

Definition 10. *We denote the advantage of an adversary $\mathcal{A}$ in winning this game as*

$$\boldsymbol{Adv}_{\mathsf{PRF}}^{prf}(\mathcal{A}) = \Pr\left[b = b' \text{ for } b' \xleftarrow{\$} \mathcal{A}^{\mathcal{C}(\lambda)}(1^{\lambda})\right] - \frac{1}{2}$$

We say that PRF is a secure pseudo-random function, if for all probabilistic polynomial time adversaries $\mathcal{A}$ $\boldsymbol{Adv}_{\mathsf{PRF}}^{prf}(\mathcal{A})$ is a negligible function in λ.

4   Generic Construction of eCK-Secure Key Exchange

Let $\mathsf{SIG} = (\mathsf{SIGgen}, \mathsf{SIGsign}, \mathsf{SIGvfy})$ be a *deterministic* signature scheme, $\mathsf{NIKE} = (\mathsf{NIKEgen}, \mathsf{NIKEkey})$ be a NIKE scheme, and let PRF be a pseudo-random function. Let sort be an arbitrary function which takes as input two strings (m_i, m_j), and outputs them according to some order (e.g. lexicographically). That is,

$$\mathsf{sort}(m_i, m_j) := \begin{cases} (m_i, m_j), & \text{if } m_i \leq m_j, \\ (m_j, m_i), & \text{if } m_i > m_j, \end{cases}$$

where $\leq$ and $>$ are defined with respect to some (arbitrary) ordering. We construct an ORKE protocol $\Pi = (\mathsf{ORKEgen}, \mathsf{ORKEmsg}, \mathsf{ORKEkey})$ as follows (see also Figure 2).

$\mathsf{ORKEgen}(1^{\lambda})$ computes key pairs for the NIKE and digital signature scheme, respectively, as $(pk_i^{\mathsf{nike}}, sk_i^{\mathsf{nike}}) \xleftarrow{\$} \mathsf{NIKEgen}(1^{\lambda})$ and $(pk_i^{\mathsf{sig}}, sk_i^{\mathsf{sig}}) \xleftarrow{\$} \mathsf{SIGgen}(1^{\lambda})$, and outputs

$$(pk_i, sk_i) := ((pk_i^{\mathsf{nike}}, pk_i^{\mathsf{sig}}), (sk_i^{\mathsf{nike}}, sk_i^{\mathsf{sig}}))$$

$\mathsf{ORKEmsg}(r_i, sk_i, pk_j)$ parses $sk_i = (sk_i^{\mathsf{nike}}, sk_i^{\mathsf{sig}})$. Then it samples $r_i \xleftarrow{\$} \{0, 1\}^{\lambda}$ and runs the key generation algorithm $(pk_i^{\mathsf{tmp}}, sk_i^{\mathsf{tmp}}) \xleftarrow{\$} \mathsf{NIKEgen}(1^{\lambda}, r_i)$ to generate a key pair of the NIKE scheme. Then it computes a signature over pk_i^{tmp} as $\sigma_i \xleftarrow{\$} \mathsf{SIGsign}(sk_i^{\mathsf{sig}}, pk_i^{\mathsf{tmp}})$ and outputs the message $m_i := (pk_i^{\mathsf{tmp}}, \sigma_i)$.

$\mathsf{ORKEkey}(sk_i, (pk_j^{\mathsf{nike}}, pk_j^{\mathsf{sig}}), r_i, m_j)$ first parses its input as $m_j = (pk_j^{\mathsf{tmp}}, \sigma_j)$ and $sk_i = (sk_i^{\mathsf{nike}}, sk_i^{\mathsf{sig}})$. If

$$\mathsf{SIGvfy}(pk_j^{\mathsf{sig}}, pk_j^{\mathsf{tmp}}, \sigma_j) \neq 1,$$

then it outputs $\bot$. Otherwise it runs $(pk_i^{\mathsf{tmp}}, sk_i^{\mathsf{tmp}}) \xleftarrow{\$} \mathsf{NIKEgen}(1^{\lambda}, r_i)$ to re-compute sk_i^{tmp} from r_i. Finally it derives the key k as follows.

1. Compute $T := \mathsf{sort}(pk_i^{\mathsf{tmp}}, pk_j^{\mathsf{tmp}})$.

2. Compute

$$k_{\mathsf{nike,nike}} := \mathsf{PRF}(\mathsf{NIKEkey}(sk_i^{\mathsf{nike}}, pk_j^{\mathsf{nike}}), T), \tag{1}$$

$$k_{\mathsf{nike,tmp}} := \mathsf{PRF}(\mathsf{NIKEkey}(sk_i^{\mathsf{nike}}, pk_j^{\mathsf{tmp}}), T), \tag{2}$$

$$k_{\mathsf{tmp,nike}} := \mathsf{PRF}(\mathsf{NIKEkey}(sk_i^{\mathsf{tmp}}, pk_j^{\mathsf{nike}}), T), \tag{3}$$

$$k_{\mathsf{tmp,tmp}} := \mathsf{NIKEkey}(sk_i^{\mathsf{tmp}}, pk_j^{\mathsf{tmp}}). \tag{4}$$

3. Compute k as

$$k := k_{\mathsf{nike,nike}} \oplus k_{\mathsf{nike,tmp}} \oplus k_{\mathsf{tmp,nike}} \oplus k_{\mathsf{tmp,tmp}}$$

and output k.

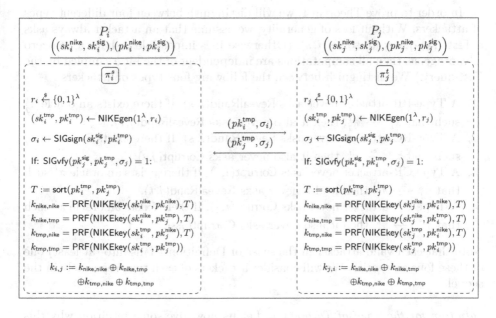

Fig. 2. Execution of protocol Π

Remark 3. In our generic construction Π we use a deterministic, strong existentially-unforgeable (*sEUF-CMA*) signature scheme. We could use a probabilistic signature scheme instead, but in this case we require a strong existentially-unforgeable *public coin* signature scheme.

The reason why we need *strong* existential unforgeability is the strictness of the matching conversation definition, which is also discussed in [7]. When using a probabilistic signature scheme, then we would need the public coin property to simulate RevealRand queries.

Even though such signatures may be easier or more efficiently to construct, we would not gain a better understanding of the reduction. Only the proofs would become harder to follow. For this reason we decided to use a deterministic scheme for simplicity.

Theorem 1. *From each attacker* $\mathcal{A}$, *we can construct attackers* $\mathcal{B}_{sig}$, $\mathcal{B}_{nike}^{(1)}$, $\mathcal{B}_{nike}^{(0)}$, *and* $\mathcal{B}_{prf}$ *such that*

$$\mathbf{Adv}_{\Pi}^{eCK}(\mathcal{A}) \leq 4 \cdot d^2\ell^2 \cdot \left(\mathbf{Adv}_{NIKE}^{CKS\text{-}light}(\mathcal{B}_{nike}^{(1)}) + \mathbf{Adv}_{PRF}^{prf}(\mathcal{B}_{prf}) \right)$$
$$+ 4 \cdot d \cdot \mathbf{Adv}_{SIG}^{sEUF\text{-}CMA}(\mathcal{B}_{sig}) + 4 \cdot \mathbf{Adv}_{NIKE}^{CKS\text{-}light}(\mathcal{B}_{nike}^{(0)})$$

The running time of $\mathcal{B}_{sig}$, $\mathcal{B}_{nike}^{(1)}$, $\mathcal{B}_{nike}^{(0)}$, *and* $\mathcal{B}_{prf}$ *is equal to the running time of* $\mathcal{A}$ *plus a minor overhead for the simulation of the security experiment for* $\mathcal{A}$.

In order to prove Theorem 1, we will distinguish between four different types of attackers. Without loss of generality, we assume that an attacker always asks a Test(i, s)-query for some (i, s). (Otherwise it is impossible to have a non-zero advantage, as then all computations are independent of the bit b sampled by the Test-query.) We distinguish between the following four types of attackers.

1. A Type-RR-attacker never asks RevealRand(i, s). If there exists an oracle π_j^t such that $\pi_i^s \xleftarrow{\text{os}} \pi_j^t$, then it also never asks RevealRand(j, t).
2. A Type-RC-attacker never asks RevealRand(i, s). If there exists an oracle π_j^t such that $\pi_i^s \xleftarrow{\text{os}} \pi_j^t$, then it also never asks Corrupt$(j, \cdot)$.
3. A Type-CR-attacker never asks Corrupt$(i, \cdot)$. If there exists an oracle π_j^t such that $\pi_i^s \xleftarrow{\text{os}} \pi_j^t$, then it also never asks RevealRand(j, t).
4. A Type-CC-attacker never asks Corrupt$(i, \cdot)$. If there exists an oracle π_j^t such that $\pi_i^s \xleftarrow{\text{os}} \pi_j^t$, then it also never asks Corrupt$(j, \cdot)$.

Note that each valid attacker in the sense of Definition 7 falls into (at least) one of these four categories. We will consider attackers of each type seperately in the sequel.

Intuition for the proof of Theorem 1. Let us now give some intuition why this classification of attackers will be useful for the security proof of Π. Recall that in protocol Π the key is computed as $k := k_{nike,nike} \oplus k_{nike,tmp} \oplus k_{tmp,nike} \oplus k_{tmp,tmp}$, where the keys $k_{nike,nike}, k_{nike,tmp}, k_{tmp,nike}, k_{tmp,tmp}$ are computed as described in Equations 1 to 4. The idea behind this construction is that in the proof we want to be able to reduce the indistinguishability of the ORKE-key k to the indistinguishability of a NIKE-key.

Recall that in the NIKE security experiment the attacker receives two challenge public-keys pk^{nike}, $pk^{nike'}$ from the challenger. In the reduction, we want to embed these keys into the view of the ORKE-attacker, such that we can embed the NIKE-challenge key into k while at the same time being able to answer all queries of the ORKE-attacker, in particular all Corrupt and RevealRand queries.

A Type-RR-attacker never asks RevealRand(i, s) and RevealRand(j, t) (if applicable). Thus, when considering Type-RR-attackers, then we can embed the NIKE-keys obtained from the NIKE-challenger as

$$pk_i^{\mathsf{tmp}} := pk^{\mathsf{nike}} \quad \text{and} \quad pk_j^{\mathsf{tmp}} := pk^{\mathsf{nike}'},$$

where pk_i^{tmp} and pk_j^{tmp} are the ephemeral keys generated by oracles π_i^s and π_j^t, respectively. Moreover, we embed the NIKE-challenge key k_{nike} as $k_{\mathsf{tmp,tmp}} := k_{\mathsf{nike}}$.

However, this embedding strategy does not work for Type-RC-attackers, because such an attacker might ask RevealRand(j, t). However, we know that a Type-RC attacker never asks a Corrupt$(j, \cdot)$, therefore we are able to embed the NIKE challenge public keys as

$$pk_i^{\mathsf{tmp}} := pk^{\mathsf{nike}} \quad \text{and} \quad pk_j^{\mathsf{nike}} := pk^{\mathsf{nike}'},$$

where pk_i^{tmp} is the ephemeral keys generated by π_i^s, and pk_j^{nike} is the long-term secret of party P_j. The NIKE-challenge key k_{nike} is in this case embedded as $k_{\mathsf{tmp,nike}} := \mathsf{PRF}(k_{\mathsf{nike}}, T)$. The additional PRF is necessary in this case, because the embedding involves a long-term secret of one party of the test session. This long-term secret is used in (potentially) many protocol executions involving party P_j. Similarly, CR- and CC-type attackers can be handled by embedding the NIKE challenge public- and session as appropriate for each case.

Thus, the four different types of attackers correspond exactly to all four possible combinations of Corrupt- and RevealRand-queries against the Test-session that the attacker is allowed (resp. not allowed) to ask in our security model.

The full proof of Theorem 1 can be found in Appendix A.

5   Efficiency Comparison with Other ORKE Protocols

In Table 1 we compare the efficiency of instantiations of our construction to other one-round key-exchange protocols. We count the number of exponentiations and pairing evaluations. We do not distinguish an exponentiation in a DH group from an exponentiation in an RSA group.

We see that our generic construction ORKE, if instantiated with the most efficient NIKE primitive from [15], will be almost as efficient as the NAXOS protocol if the Cremers-Feltz compiler is applied [11]. The efficient NIKE primitive is secure in the random oracle model, but its security is based on the factoring problem.

The very high number of pairing evaluations within the standard model instantiation results from the fact, that the underlying NIKE scheme needs 3 pairing evaluations for key computation and we have to compute 4 NIKE keys per key-exchange at each party.

Table 1. Efficiency comparison of popular one-round key-exchange protocols to our generic construction.
[1] A variant of the Bellare-Rogaway model [1] with modified partnering definition. No ephemeral states can be revealed.
[2] The NAXOS protocol after application of the Cremers-Feltz compiler [11].
[3] Our construction instantiated with a secure NIKE scheme in the random-oracle model.
[4] Our construction instantiated with a standard-model NIKE scheme

	Standard Model	PFS	weak PFS	KCI	exp. per party	pairing evaluations	Security model
$TS1$ [21]	✗	✗	✗	✗	1	-	BR^1
$TS3$ [21]	✓	✓	✓	✗	3	-	BR^1
MQV	✗	✗	✓	✗	1	-	CK
HMQV	✗	✗	✓	✓	2	-	CK
KEA	✗	✗	✓	✓	2	-	CK
P1 [6]	✓	✗	✗	✓	8	2	CK
P2 [6]	✓	✗	✓	✓	10	2	CK
NAXOS	✗	✗	✓	✓	4	-	eCK
Okamoto	✓ $+\pi$PRF	✗	✓	✓	8	-	eCK
$NAXOS^2_{pfs}$	✗	✓	✓	✓	4	-	$eCK\text{-}PFS$
$ORKE^3$	✗ (NIKE)	✓	✓	✓	5	-	$eCK\text{-}PFS$
$ORKE^4$	✓	✓	✓	✓	16	12	$eCK\text{-}PFS$

References

1. Bellare, M., Rogaway, P.: Entity authentication and key distribution. In: Stinson, D.R. (ed.) CRYPTO 1993. LNCS, vol. 773, pp. 232–249. Springer, Heidelberg (1994)
2. Bellare, M., Rogaway, P.: Random oracles are practical: A paradigm for designing efficient protocols. In: Ashby, V. (ed.) ACM CCS 1993: 1st Conference on Computer and Communications Security, pp. 62–73, Fairfax, Virginia, USA, November 3–5. ACM Press (1993)
3. Bernstein, D.J., Chang, Y.-A., Cheng, C.-M., Chou, L.-P., Heninger, N., Lange, T., van Someren, N.: Factoring RSA keys from certified smart cards: Coppersmith in the wild. In: Sako, K., Sarkar, P. (eds.) ASIACRYPT 2013, Part II. LNCS, vol. 8270, pp. 341–360. Springer, Heidelberg (2013)
4. Boneh, D., Montgomery, H.W., Raghunathan, A.: Algebraic pseudorandom functions with improved efficiency from the augmented cascade. In: Al-Shaer, E., Keromytis, A.D., Shmatikov, V. (eds.) ACM CCS 2010: 17th Conference on Computer and Communications Security, pp. 131–140, Chicago, Illinois, USA, October 4–8. ACM Press (2010)
5. Boyd, C., Cliff, Y., Nieto, J.M.G., Paterson, K.G.: Efficient one-round key exchange in the standard model. In: Mu, Y., Susilo, W., Seberry, J. (eds.) ACISP 2008. LNCS, vol. 5107, pp. 69–83. Springer, Heidelberg (2008)
6. Boyd, C., Cliff, Y., Nieto, J.M.G., Paterson, K.G.: One-round key exchange in the standard model. IJACT 1(3), 181–199 (2009)

7. Brzuska, C., Smart, N.P., Warinschi, B., Watson, G.J.: An analysis of the EMV channel establishment protocol. In: Sadeghi, A.-R., Gligor, V.D., Yung, M. (eds.) ACM CCS 2013: 20th Conference on Computer and Communications Security, pp. 373–386, Berlin, Germany, November 4–8. ACM Press (2013)

8. Canetti, R., Krawczyk, H.: Analysis of key-exchange protocols and their use for building secure channels. In: Pfitzmann, B. (ed.) EUROCRYPT 2001. LNCS, vol. 2045, pp. 453–474. Springer, Heidelberg (2001)

9. Cash, D., Kiltz, E., Shoup, V.: The twin Diffie-Hellman problem and applications. In: Smart, N.P. (ed.) EUROCRYPT 2008. LNCS, vol. 4965, pp. 127–145. Springer, Heidelberg (2008)

10. Cremers, C.: Examining indistinguishability-based security models for key exchange protocols: The case of CK, CK-HMQV, and eCK. In: Cheung, B.S.N., Hui, L.C.K., Sandhu, R.S., Wong, D.S. (eds.) ASIACCS 2011: 6th Conference on Computer and Communications Security, pp. 80–91, Hong Kong, China, March 22–24. ACM Press (2011)

11. Cremers, C., Feltz, M.: Beyond eCK: Perfect forward secrecy under actor compromise and ephemeral-key reveal. In: Foresti, S., Yung, M., Martinelli, F. (eds.) ESORICS 2012. LNCS, vol. 7459, pp. 734–751. Springer, Heidelberg (2012)

12. Cremers, C.J.F.: Formally and practically relating the CK, CK-HMQV, and eCK security models for authenticated key exchange. Cryptology ePrint Archive, Report 2009/253 (2009). http://eprint.iacr.org/2009/253

13. Dierks, T., Rescorla, E.: The Transport Layer Security (TLS) Protocol Version 1.2. RFC 5246 (Proposed Standard), Updated by RFCs 5746, 5878, 6176, August 2008

14. Diffie, W., van Oorschot, P.C., Wiener, M.J.: Authentication and authenticated key exchanges. Des. Codes Cryptography 2(2), 107–125 (1992)

15. Freire, E.S.V., Hofheinz, D., Kiltz, E., Paterson, K.G.: Non-interactive key exchange. In: Kurosawa, K., Hanaoka, G. (eds.) PKC 2013. LNCS, vol. 7778, pp. 254–271. Springer, Heidelberg (2013)

16. Günther, C.G.: An identity-based key-exchange protocol. In: Quisquater, J.-J., Vandewalle, J. (eds.) EUROCRYPT 1989. LNCS, vol. 434, pp. 29–37. Springer, Heidelberg (1990)

17. Heninger, N., Durumeric, Z., Wustrow, E., Alex Halderman, J.: Mining your ps and qs: Detection of widespread weak keys in network devices. In: Kohno, T. (ed.) Proceedings of the 21th USENIX Security Symposium, Bellevue, WA, USA, August 8–10, pp. 205–220. USENIX Association (2012)

18. Hohenberger, S., Waters, B.: Constructing verifiable random functions with large input spaces. In: Gilbert, H. (ed.) EUROCRYPT 2010. LNCS, vol. 6110, pp. 656–672. Springer, Heidelberg (2010)

19. Jager, T.: Verifiable random functions from weaker assumptions. Cryptology ePrint Archive, Report 2014/799 (2014). http://eprint.iacr.org/

20. Jager, T., Kohlar, F., Schäge, S., Schwenk, J.: On the security of TLS-DHE in the standard model. In: Safavi-Naini, R., Canetti, R. (eds.) CRYPTO 2012. LNCS, vol. 7417, pp. 273–293. Springer, Heidelberg (2012)

21. Jeong, I.R., Katz, J., Lee, D.-H.: One-round protocols for two-party authenticated key exchange. In: Jakobsson, M., Yung, M., Zhou, J. (eds.) ACNS 2004. LNCS, vol. 3089, pp. 220–232. Springer, Heidelberg (2004)

22. Kaufman, C., Hoffman, P., Nir, Y., Eronen, P., Kivinen, T.: Internet Key Exchange Protocol Version 2 (IKEv2). RFC 7296 (INTERNET STANDARD). Updated by RFC 7427, October 2014

23. Krawczyk, H.: HMQV: A high-performance secure Diffie-Hellman protocol. In: Shoup, V. (ed.) CRYPTO 2005. LNCS, vol. 3621, pp. 546–566. Springer, Heidelberg (2005)

24. Krawczyk, H.: HMQV: A high-performance secure Diffie-Hellman protocol. Cryptology ePrint Archive, Report 2005/176 (2005). http://eprint.iacr.org/2005/176

25. LaMacchia, B.A., Lauter, K., Mityagin, A.: Stronger security of authenticated key exchange. In: Susilo, W., Liu, J.K., Mu, Y. (eds.) ProvSec 2007. LNCS, vol. 4784, pp. 1–16. Springer, Heidelberg (2007)

26. Lauter, K., Mityagin, A.: Security analysis of KEA authenticated key exchange protocol. In: Yung, M., Dodis, Y., Kiayias, A., Malkin, T. (eds.) PKC 2006. LNCS, vol. 3958, pp. 378–394. Springer, Heidelberg (2006)

27. Law, L., Menezes, A., Minghua, Q., Solinas, J., Vanstone, S.: An efficient protocol for authenticated key agreement. Designs, Codes and Cryptography **28**(2), 119–134 (2003)

28. Lenstra, A.K., Hughes, J.P., Augier, M., Bos, J.W., Kleinjung, T., Wachter, C.: Public keys. In: Safavi-Naini, R., Canetti, R. (eds.) CRYPTO 2012. LNCS, vol. 7417, pp. 626–642. Springer, Heidelberg (2012)

29. Lysyanskaya, A.: Unique signatures and verifiable random functions from the DH-DDH separation. In: Yung, M. (ed.) CRYPTO 2002. LNCS, vol. 2442, pp. 597–612. Springer, Heidelberg (2002)

30. NIST. Skipjack and kea algorithm specifications (1998). http://csrc.nist.gov/groups/STM/cavp/documents/skipjack/skipjack.pdf

31. Okamoto, T.: Authenticated key exchange and key encapsulation in the standard model. In: Kurosawa, K. (ed.) ASIACRYPT 2007. LNCS, vol. 4833, pp. 474–484. Springer, Heidelberg (2007)

32. Sarr, A.P., Elbaz-Vincent, P., Bajard, J.-C.: A new security model for authenticated key agreement. In: Garay, J.A., De Prisco, R. (eds.) SCN 2010. LNCS, vol. 6280, pp. 219–234. Springer, Heidelberg (2010)

33. Yang, Z.: Efficient eCK-secure authenticated key exchange protocols in the standard model. In: Qing, S., Zhou, J., Liu, D. (eds.) ICICS 2013. LNCS, vol. 8233, pp. 185–193. Springer, Heidelberg (2013)

34. Ylonen, T., Lonvick, C.: The Secure Shell (SSH) Transport Layer Protocol. RFC 4253 (Proposed Standard). Updated by RFC 6668, January 2006

35. Yoneyama, K., Zhao, Y.: Taxonomical security consideration of authenticated key exchange resilient to intermediate computation leakage. In: Boyen, X., Chen, X. (eds.) ProvSec 2011. LNCS, vol. 6980, pp. 348–365. Springer, Heidelberg (2011)

Additively Homomorphic UC Commitments with Optimal Amortized Overhead

Ignacio Cascudo$^{(\boxtimes)}$, Ivan Damgård, Bernardo David, Irene Giacomelli,
Jesper Buus Nielsen, and Roberto Trifiletti

Department of Computer Science, Aarhus University, Aarhus, Denmark
{ignacio,ivan,bernardo,giacomelli,jbn,roberto}@cs.au.dk

Abstract. We propose the first UC secure commitment scheme with
(amortized) computational complexity linear in the size of the string
committed to. After a preprocessing phase based on oblivious transfer,
that only needs to be done once and for all, our scheme only requires a
pseudorandom generator and a linear code with efficient encoding. We
also construct an additively homomorphic version of our basic scheme
using VSS. Furthermore we evaluate the concrete efficiency of our schemes
and show that the amortized computational overhead is significantly
lower than in the previous best constructions. In fact, our basic scheme
has amortised concrete efficiency comparable with previous protocols in
the Random Oracle Model even though it is constructed in the plain
model.

1   Introduction

A commitment scheme is a very basic but nevertheless extremely powerful cryptographic primitive. Intuitively, a commitment scheme is a digital equivalent of
a secure box: it allows a prover P to commit to a secret s by putting it into
a locked box and giving it to a verifier V. Since the box is locked, V does not
learn s at commitment time and we say the commitment is *hiding*. Nevertheless,
P can later choose to give V the key to the box to let V learn s. Since P gave
away the box, he cannot change his mind about s after commitment time and
we say the commitment is *binding*.

Commitment schemes with stand-alone security (i.e., they only have the binding and hiding properties) can be constructed from any one-way function and

R. Trifiletti—The authors acknowledge support from the Danish National Research
Foundation and The National Science Foundation of China (under the grant
61361136003) for the Sino-Danish Center for the Theory of Interactive Computation
and from the Center for Research in Foundations of Electronic Markets (CFEM),
supported by the Danish Strategic Research Council within which part of this work
was performed. Partially supported by Danish Council for Independent Research
via DFF Starting Grant 10-081612. Partially supported by the European Research
Commission Starting Grant 279447.

© International Association for Cryptologic Research 2015
J. Katz (Ed.): PKC 2015, LNCS 9020, pp. 495–515, 2015.
DOI: 10.1007/978-3-662-46447-2_22

already this most basic form of commitments implies zero-knowledge proofs for all NP languages. Commitments with stand-alone security can be very efficient as they can be constructed from cheap symmetric cryptography such as pseudo-random generators [Nao91].

However, in many cases one would like a commitment scheme that composes well with other primitives, so that it can be used as a secure module that will work no matter which context it is used in. The strongest form of security we can ask for here is UC security [Can01]. UC commitments cannot be constructed without set-up assumptions such as a common reference string [CF01]. On the other hand, a construction of UC commitment in such models implies public-key cryptography [DG03] and even multiparty computation [CLOS02] (but see [DNO10] for a construction based only on one-way functions, under a stronger set-up assumption).

With this in mind, it is not surprising that constructions of UC commitments are significantly less efficient than those of stand-alone secure commitments. Until recently, the most efficient UC commitment schemes were based on the DDH assumption and required several exponentiations in a large group [Lin11, BCPV13]. Therefore, even though the communication complexity for committing to k strings was $O(k)$, the computational complexity was typically $\Omega(k^3)$.

However, in [DDGN14] and independently in [GIKW14], it was observed that even though we cannot build UC commitments without using public-key technology, we can still hope to confine the use of it to a once-and-for-all set-up phase, the cost of which can then be amortized over many uses of the commitment scheme.

While [GIKW14] focused on the rate of the commitment scheme, [DDGN14] concentrated on the computational complexity. More specifically, a UC commitment scheme was proposed based on the following idea: the committer will secret-share the string s to commit to using a linear secret sharing scheme (LSSS), encrypt the shares and send them to the receiver. The encryption is done in such a way that the receiver will be able to decrypt an unqualified subset (and hence will not learn s). However, the committer will not know which subset the receiver has seen. We can achieve this efficiently using a combination of oblivious transfers (done only in a set-up phase) and a pseudorandom generator. To open s, the committer will send s and the randomness used for the sharing and the receiver can then check if the resulting shares match those he already knows. Intuitively, we can hope this will be binding because any two sets of shares for different secrets must be different in many positions (they cannot agree on any qualified subset). Furthermore since the committer does not know which subset the receiver checks, it is likely that the receiver will see a mismatch for at least one of the sets of shares.

The most natural way to construct a suitable LSSS is to use the standard construction from a linear code $\mathcal{C}$, where we choose a random codeword subject to the condition that the secret s appears in the first k coordinates and the shares are then the values appearing in the rest of the codeword. This approach requires that both $\mathcal{C}$ and its dual have large minimum distance. But unfortunately, all known codes with linear time encoding have very bad dual codes. Therefore, [DDGN14] resorted to using Reed-Solomon codes which gives a complexity of $O(k \log k)$ for both parties.

Our contribution. In this paper, we propose a different way to construct an LSSS from a linear code $\mathcal{C}$: we encode the secret s in $\mathcal{C}$, and then additively share each entry in the codeword to form t shares, thus we get nt shares for a code of length n. We show that already for $t \geq 2$, using this LSSS in the above template construction results in a secure UC commitment scheme. Note that the LSSS we construct is not of the usual threshold type where any sufficiently large set can reconstruct, but instead we have a more general access structure where the qualified sets are those that can get enough entries in the underlying codeword to be able to decode.

Since we can now choose $\mathcal{C}$ without any conditions on the dual code, we can plug in known constructions of codes with linear time encoding and get complexity $O(k)$ for both parties. Furthermore we show a particular instantiation of the building blocks of our basic protocol for security parameter $\tau = 60$ and message length $k = 256$ that achieves an amortized computational complexity which is 5500 times lower than in the most efficient previous constructions [BCPV13, Lin11] (see Section 6 for details on the implementation). In fact, our basic scheme achieves amortised concrete effieciency comparable to previous schemes [HM04, DSW08] in the Random Oracle Model [BR93] even though it is constructed in the plain model. Concretely, it has an amortized computational cost 41% lower than the one of [HM04].

Commitment schemes can be even more useful if they are homomorphic. An additively homomorphic commitment scheme, for instance, has the following property: from commitments to s and s', the receiver can on his own compute a commitment to $s + s'$, such that if the committer opens this new commitment, $s + s'$ (and no other information on s, s') will be revealed. Our basic construction above is not additively homomorphic. The reason is that a corrupt committer may submit sets of values in the commit phase that are not consistent sharings of any value. Nevertheless, when some of these shares are added, we may get values that do in fact form valid commitments, and this may allow the committer to cheat. To solve this problem, we start from an idea that was introduced in [GIKW14]: they construct a very compact linear verifiable secret sharing scheme (VSS) from any LSSS. The idea is now that the committer will execute the VSS "in his head" and send to the receiver the resulting views of each VSS-player, encrypted in the same way as we encrypted shares before: the receiver can decrypt some subset of the views. The receiver will now be able to execute some of those consistency checks that honest players would normally do in the VSS, and will reject if anything is wrong. The hope is that this will force the committer to submit views from a correctly executed instance of the VSS, which in particular means that the sets of shares he submits will be consistent, thus implying the additive homomorphic property.

This idea was shown to work in [DDGN14], but unfortunately the proof works only if the underlying LSSS is a threshold scheme, and our LSSS is not threshold.

However, in this paper, we give a different proof showing that we do in fact get a secure commitment scheme if we choose the parameter t from our LSSS to be at least 3. This yields a UC secure and additively homomorphic commitment scheme with linear complexity, albeit with larger hidden constants than our first scheme. We also instantiate this scheme for concrete parameters, see Section 6.

It is interesting to note that there is strong relation between the way the VSS is used here and the "MPC-in-the-head" line of work [IPS09]. Roughly speaking, MPC-in-the-head is a general technique for turning a multiparty protocol into a 2-party protocol for the same purpose. A VSS is essentially a multiparty commitment scheme, so one can use the so-called IPS compiler on the VSS from [DDGN14] to get a UC secure commitment scheme. This commitment scheme is quite similar to (but not the same as) the one from [DDGN14]. Previously, the IPS compiler was only known to work for protocols with threshold security. However, our proof technique also applies to IPS, so from this point of view, our result is the first to show that the IPS compiler can also be used to transform a non-threshold multiparty protocol into a 2-party protocol. It is an interesting open problem to characterise the adversary structures for which it will work.

2   Preliminaries

2.1   Notation

We denote uniformly sampling a value r from a set D as $r \leftarrow D$ and $\{r_1, \ldots, r_n\} \leftarrow D$ indicates that we sample from D a uniformly random subset of n elements. We denote concatenation by $\|$ and vectors of elements of some field by bold symbols. For $z \in \mathbb{F}^k$, $z[i]$ denotes the i'th entry of the vector. We use 1-indexing, meaning that $z[1]$ is the first element of z and we write $[n] = \{1, 2, \ldots, n\}$. We will use π_k to denote the projection that outputs the first k coordinates of a vector, i.e. $\pi_k(z) = (z[1], \ldots, z[k])$. Finally we will denote by $e_{k,i}$ the row vector of k components whose i-th entry is 1 while all other entries are 0 and with 0_k the row vector of k components whose all entries are 0.

We say that a function ϵ is negligible in n if for every polynomial p there exists a constant c such that $\epsilon(n) < \frac{1}{p(n)}$ when $n > c$. Two ensembles $X = \{X_{\kappa,z}\}_{\kappa \in \mathbb{N}, z \in \{0,1\}^*}$ and $Y = \{Y_{\kappa,z}\}_{\kappa \in \mathbb{N}, z \in \{0,1\}^*}$ of binary random variables are said to be *indistinguishable*, denoted by $X \approx Y$, if for all z it holds that $\mid Pr[X_{\kappa,z} = 1] - Pr[Y_{\kappa,z} = 1] \mid$ is negligible in κ.

2.2   Universal Composability

The results presented in this paper are proven secure in the Universal Composability (UC) framework introduced by Canetti in [Can01]. We refer the reader to [Can01, CDD+14] for further details.

Adversarial Model: In this work we consider security against static adversaries, i.e. corruption may only take place *before* the protocols starts execution. We consider active adversaries who may deviate from the protocol in any arbitrary way.

Setup Assumption: It is known that UC commitment protocols (as well as most "interesting" functionalities) cannot be obtained in the plain model [CF01]. In order to overcome this impossibility, UC protocols require a setup assumption, that basically models a resource that is made available to all parties before execution starts. The security of our protocols is proved in the $\mathcal{F}_{\text{OT}}$-hybrid model [Can01,CLOS02], where all parties are assumed to have access to an ideal 1-out-of-2 OT functionality.

Ideal Functionalities: In Section 4, we construct a simple string commitment protocol that UC-realizes the functionality $\mathcal{F}_{\text{COM}}$ as presented in [CLOS02, CDD+14] In Section 5, we extend this simple scheme to allow homomorphic operations over commitments. The extended protocol UC-realizes the functionality $\mathcal{F}_{\text{HCOM}}$ defined in [CDD+14], that basically adds a command for adding two previously stored commitments and an abort command in the Commit Phase to $\mathcal{F}_{\text{COM}}$. The abort is necessary to deal with inconsistent commitments that could be sent by a corrupted party. In fact, our additively homomorphic commitment protocol is constructed in the $\mathcal{F}_{\text{OT}}^{t-1,t}$-hybrid model (*i.e.* assuming access to $(t-1)$-out-of-t OT where $t \geq 2$ is an integer parameter). Notice that $\mathcal{F}_{\text{OT}}^{t-1,t}$ is basically a special case of a k-out-of-n OT where $k = n - 1$, which can be subsequently reduced to the $\mathcal{F}_{\text{OT}}$-hybrid model via standard techniques [Nao91,BCR86,NP99]. We refer the reader to [CDD+14] for definitions of $\mathcal{F}_{\text{OT}}$ and $\mathcal{F}_{\text{OT}}^{t-1,t}$. Notice that $\mathcal{F}_{\text{OT}}$ can be efficiently UC-realized by the protocol in [PVW08], which can be used to instantiate the setup phase of our commitment protocols.

2.3   Linear Secret-Sharing Scheme

We briefly recall here the definition of linear secret-sharing scheme (LSSS) following the approach of [CDP12].

Definition 1. *A linear secret sharing scheme for N players $P_1, \ldots, P_N$ over the finite field $\mathbb{F}$ is defined by the pair $(k, \boldsymbol{M})$, where k is the length of a secret and $\boldsymbol{M}$ is a $N \times m$ matrix with entries in $\mathbb{F}$ (and $m > k$). If $k > 1$, then the scheme is called* packed. *The row number i of $\boldsymbol{M}$ is denoted by $\boldsymbol{m}_i$ and, if A is a subset of players, then $\boldsymbol{M}_A$ denotes the matrix consisting of rows $\boldsymbol{m}_i$ such that $P_i \in A$.*

In order to share a secret $\boldsymbol{s} \in \mathbb{F}^k$, the dealer of the LSSS given by $(k, \boldsymbol{M})$ takes a random column vector $\boldsymbol{f} \in \mathbb{F}^m$ such that $\pi_k(\boldsymbol{f}) = \boldsymbol{s}^\top$ and computes $\boldsymbol{c} = \boldsymbol{M} \cdot \boldsymbol{f}$. The column vector $\boldsymbol{c}$ is called the *share vector* of $\boldsymbol{s}$, and its i-th component $\boldsymbol{c}[i]$ is the share sent by the dealer to the player P_i.

Definition 2. *A subset of players A is called* unqualified *if the distribution of $\boldsymbol{M}_A \cdot \boldsymbol{f}$ is independent of $\boldsymbol{s}$, while a subset of players B is called* qualified *if $\boldsymbol{s}$ is uniquely determined from $\boldsymbol{M}_B \cdot \boldsymbol{f}$.*

It is the case that A is unqualified if and only if there exists, for each position j in $\boldsymbol{s}$, a column vector of m components $\boldsymbol{w}^{A,j}$ (called *sweeping vector*) such that $\boldsymbol{w}^{A,j} \in \ker(\boldsymbol{M}_A)$ and $\pi_k(\boldsymbol{w}^{A,j}) = \boldsymbol{e}_{k,j}^\top$. Similarly, B is qualified if and only if there exists, for each position j in s, a row vector of $|B|$ components $r_{B,j}$ (called *reconstruction vector*) such that $r_{B,j} \cdot M_B = e_{m,j}$.

Given two positive integers a and b, if any subset of players A with $|A| = a$ is unqualified, then we say that the LSSS has a-privacy. If any subset of players B with $|B| = b$ is qualified, then we say that the LSSS has b-reconstruction.

Example 1. The *additive secret-sharing scheme* for N players over $\mathbb{F}$ is the linear secret-sharing scheme where in order to share a secret $s \in \mathbb{F}$ among N players, the dealer chooses random values $s_1, \ldots, s_N$ in $\mathbb{F}$ such that $\sum_{i=1}^{N} s_i = s$ and sends the value s_i to player i. It is clear that the set of all the players can reconstruct the secret from the received values, while any set of at most $N-1$ players has no information on the value s held by the dealer. With the previous notation, this LSSS can be defined by the pair $(1, M)$, where M has the following N rows: $m_i = e_{N,i+1}$ for $i = 1, \ldots, N-1$ and $m_N = e_{N,1} - \sum_{i=1}^{N-1} m_i$.

3   Linear-Time Secret Sharing and Coding Scheme

In this section we describe the coding scheme $\mathcal{C}_t$ that stands in the core of our commitment protocols. We depart from *any* error correcting code and apply a simple transformation that yields a code that can also be seen as a linear secret sharing scheme for an specific access structure. Intuitively, this makes it possible to reveal a large fraction of a codeword generated by $\mathcal{C}_t$ without revealing any information on the encoded message.

Standard generic constructions of general linear secret sharing schemes from error correcting codes, require a code whose dual code has high minimum distance. On the other hand, our construction does not require any specific property from the underlying error correcting code. This conceptual difference is of fundamental importance for the asymptotic and concrete efficiencies of our constructions, since it allows a secret sharing scheme to be constructed from very efficient linear error correcting codes whose dual codes' minimum distance are mostly unfit for the standard generic constructions. In particular, our coding scheme $\mathcal{C}_t$ inherits the underlying code $\mathcal{C}$'s complexity. achieving linear-time encoding and/or decoding when constructed from appropriate codes [GI01, GI02, GI03, GI05, Spi96, DI14].

Intuitively, the encoding procedure $\mathsf{Enc}_t^{\mathcal{C}}$ of $\mathcal{C}_t$ first encodes a message m under the underlying code $\mathcal{C}$ obtaining a codeword v. In the next step, each element of v is secret shared into t shares under a simple additive secret sharing scheme (*i.e.* taking random vectors $v_1, \ldots, v_t$ such that $\sum_{i=1}^{t} v_i = v$). The final codeword c is defined as $c = (v_1[1], \ldots, v_t[1], \ldots, v_1[n], \ldots, v_t[n])^\top$, *i.e.*, each t successive elements of c sum up to the corresponding element of v. The decoding procedure $\mathsf{Dec}_t^{\mathcal{C}}$ basically reconstructs each element of v from c and then uses the decoding algorithm of $\mathcal{C}$ to decode v into the original message m.

Notice that only the encoding procedure $\mathsf{Enc}_t^{\mathcal{C}}$ is used in the actual commitment schemes, while the decoding procedure $\mathsf{Dec}_t^{\mathcal{C}}$ is used in the simulators. Moreover, $\mathcal{C}_t$ basically applies a linear transformation on codewords generated by the underlying code $\mathcal{C}$, since $\mathsf{Enc}_t^{\mathcal{C}}$ uses a LSSS to divide each component of the codeword into t shares. Hence, if $\mathcal{C}$ is linear, so is $\mathcal{C}_t$. Finally, we show in Remark 1 that $\mathsf{Enc}_t^{\mathcal{C}}$ itself can be seen as a LSSS. Intuitively, after a message $\boldsymbol{m}$ is encoded through $\mathsf{Enc}_t^{\mathcal{C}}$, an element $\boldsymbol{v}[i]$ of the underlying codeword can only be recovered if all shares $\boldsymbol{v}_1[i],\dots,\boldsymbol{v}_t[i]$ are known. Hence, no information on $\boldsymbol{m}$ is revealed as at least one share is missing for every underlying codeword element.

Before we formally outline the coding scheme $\mathcal{C}_t$ Figure 1, we need to define the auxiliary functions Σ_t and Λ_t:

- $\Sigma_t : \mathbb{F}^n \longrightarrow \mathbb{F}^{tn}$ is a randomized function that takes as input a row vector $\boldsymbol{v}$ in $\mathbb{F}^n$ and does the following: sample $\boldsymbol{v}_1,\dots,\boldsymbol{v}_{t-1} \leftarrow \mathbb{F}^n$ and compute $\boldsymbol{v}_t = \boldsymbol{v} - (\boldsymbol{v}_1 + \cdots + \boldsymbol{v}_{t-1})$. For $j = 1,\dots,n$, define $\boldsymbol{w}_j = \|_{i=1}^t \boldsymbol{v}_i[j] = (\boldsymbol{v}_1[j],\dots,\boldsymbol{v}_t[j])$ and set $\Sigma_t(\boldsymbol{v}) = \|_{j=1}^n \boldsymbol{w}_j = (\boldsymbol{w}_1,\dots,\boldsymbol{w}_n)$. Note that this means each consecutive t-tuple of $\Sigma_t(\boldsymbol{v})$ sums to the corresponding element in the vector $\boldsymbol{v}$.
- $\Lambda_t : \mathbb{F}^{tn} \to \mathbb{F}^n$ takes as input a vector $\boldsymbol{h}$ and adds each consecutive t components of $\boldsymbol{h}$. That is, $\Lambda_t(\boldsymbol{h})$ gives as output the row vector in $\mathbb{F}^n$ whose i'th component is $\sum_{j=1}^t \boldsymbol{h}[(i-1)t+j]$. Note that $\Lambda_t(\Sigma_t(\boldsymbol{m})) = \boldsymbol{m}$.

Coding Scheme $\mathcal{C}_t$

Let $\mathcal{C} : \mathbb{F}^k \to \mathbb{F}^n$ be a linear error correcting code over a field $\mathbb{F}$ of dimension k, length n and minimum distance d, and let $t \geq 2$ be a fixed integer. Let $\boldsymbol{m}$ be a row vector in $\mathbb{F}^k$ and $\boldsymbol{c}$ be a column vector in $\mathbb{F}^{tn}$ The coding scheme is composed by the pair of algorithms $(\mathsf{Enc}_t^{\mathcal{C}}, \mathsf{Dec}_t^{\mathcal{C}})$ described as follows:

- $\mathsf{Enc}_t^{\mathcal{C}}(\boldsymbol{m})$: the encoding procedure $\mathsf{Enc}_t^{\mathcal{C}} : \mathbb{F}^k \to \mathbb{F}^{tn}$ takes as input a message $\boldsymbol{m}$ and proceeds as follows:
  1. Encode $\boldsymbol{m}$ using $\mathcal{C}$, thus obtaining $\boldsymbol{v} = \mathcal{C}(\boldsymbol{m}) \in \mathbb{F}^n$.
  2. Use the randomized function $\Sigma_t(\boldsymbol{v})$ to additively secret share each component of the codeword $\boldsymbol{v}$ into t shares. Output the column vector $\boldsymbol{c} = \Sigma_t(\boldsymbol{v})^\top$. When we need to remember the randomness used in Σ_t, we will write $\mathsf{Enc}_t^{\mathcal{C}}(\boldsymbol{m}; \boldsymbol{v}_1,\dots,\boldsymbol{v}_{t-1})$.

Let $\tau = \lfloor \frac{d-1}{2} \rfloor$ and let $\mathcal{D} : \mathbb{F}^n \to \mathbb{F}^n \cup \{\bot\}$ be a τ-bounded decoding algorithm for the underlying code $\mathcal{C}$. That is, $\mathcal{D}$ either decodes a received word $\boldsymbol{r}$ into the unique codeword $\boldsymbol{c} \in \mathcal{C}$ at distance not more than τ from $\boldsymbol{r}$ (if such codeword exists) or indicates that no such codeword exists, declaring a decoder failure.

- $\mathsf{Dec}_t^{\mathcal{C}}(\boldsymbol{c})$: the decoding procedure $\mathsf{Dec}_t^{\mathcal{C}} : \mathbb{F}^{tn} \to \mathbb{F}^k \cup \{\bot\}$ takes as input a codeword $\boldsymbol{c}$ and proceeds as follows:
  1. Compute $\Lambda_t(\boldsymbol{c})$ to obtain a vector $\boldsymbol{v}' \in \mathbb{F}^n$.
  2. Decode $\boldsymbol{v}'$ using the decoding algorithm $\mathcal{D}$ for the underlying code $\mathcal{C}$. If $\mathcal{D}$ fails, output $\bot$. Otherwise output $\boldsymbol{m} = \mathcal{C}^{-1}(\mathcal{D}(\boldsymbol{v}'))$.

Fig. 1. Coding Scheme $\mathcal{C}_t$

Remark 1. It is possible to see the entire encoding procedure $\mathsf{Enc}_t^{\mathcal{C}}$ as a LSSS for $N = tn$ players: let $\boldsymbol{C} \in \mathbf{Mat}_{n \times k}$ be the transpose of a generator matrix for the code $\mathcal{C}$ and let $\boldsymbol{c}_j$ be its jth row, then the vector $\mathsf{Enc}_t^{\mathcal{C}}(\boldsymbol{m})$ can be seen as a share vector of $\boldsymbol{m} \in \mathbb{F}^k$ in the LSSS defined by the pair $(k, \boldsymbol{M}_t^{\mathcal{C}})$, where $m = k + (t-1)n$ and $\boldsymbol{M}_t^{\mathcal{C}}$ is a $N \times m$ matrix with rows given by $\boldsymbol{m}_i = \boldsymbol{e}_{m,i+k-\lfloor i/t \rfloor}$ for $i \in [nt] \setminus \{t, 2t, \ldots, nt\}$ and $\boldsymbol{m}_{jt} = (\boldsymbol{c}_j, \boldsymbol{0}_{(t-1)n}) - \sum_{i=1}^{t-1} \boldsymbol{m}_{(j-1)t+i}$ for $j \in [n]$.

The set of tn players can be divided in n groups of t players each: define $T_j = \{P_{(j-1)t+1}, \ldots, P_{jt}\}$ for all $j \in [n]$. Thus we can rephrase the encoding procedure $\mathsf{Enc}_t^{\mathcal{C}}$ for a vector $\boldsymbol{m} \in \mathbb{F}^k$ as: first compute the codeword $\boldsymbol{v} = \mathcal{C}(\boldsymbol{m})$ and then, for all $j \in [n]$, share the component $\boldsymbol{v}[j]$ between the players in T_j using the additive LSSS for t players (see Example 1). From the $(t-1)$-privacy property of the additive LSSS, it follows that any subset of players $A \subseteq \{P_1, \ldots, P_n\}$ such that $|A \cap T_j| \le t-1$ for all $j \in [n]$ is unqualified for the scheme $(k, \boldsymbol{M}_t^{\mathcal{C}})$. Instead, if $B \subseteq \{P_1, \ldots, P_n\}$ satisfies $B \cap T_j = T_j$ for at least $n - (d-1)$ indices j, then it is a qualified set for $(k, \boldsymbol{M}_t^{\mathcal{C}})$. Indeed, the players in B can compute at least $n - (d-1)$ components of the codeword $\boldsymbol{v}$ and then they can apply an erasure correction algorithm for $\mathcal{C}$ and recover $\boldsymbol{m}$. In particular if $|B| \ge nt - (d-1)$, then B is qualified.

4   Basic Construction

In this section we present our basic commitment scheme. We will work in the $\mathcal{F}_{\mathrm{OT}}^{t-1,t}$-hybrid model ($t$ being a fixed integer greater or equal than 2) and we will phrase our protocol in terms of a Setup and an Online phase. This decoupling is motivated by the fact that the Setup phase can be run at any time and independently of the inputs of the parties. Once the Setup phase is completed, polynomially many commitments can be executed in the Online phase, when the inputs are known. Moreover, the Setup phase is also completely independent of the number of commitments executed in the Online phase. Finally our scheme is based on a $[n, k, d]$ linear error correcting code $\mathcal{C}$ over $\mathbb{F}$ used in the encoding procedure $\mathsf{Enc}_t^{\mathcal{C}}$ defined in Figure 1 (we consider $\tau = \lfloor \frac{d-1}{2} \rfloor$ the security parameter).

A commitment to a message $\boldsymbol{m} \in \mathbb{F}^k$ will be obtained by sending to the receiver P_r a subset of components (*watch-list*) of the vector $\boldsymbol{w} = \mathsf{Enc}_t^{\mathcal{C}}(\boldsymbol{m})$ computed by the sender P_s. The watch-list has to be chosen in such a way that the components of $\boldsymbol{w}$ contained in it give no information on the message $\boldsymbol{m}$ (hiding property). To open the commitment, the sender P_s has to send to the receiver both $\boldsymbol{m}$ and the randomness used in the procedure $\mathsf{Enc}_t^{\mathcal{C}}$, so that the receiver can compute by itself $\boldsymbol{w}$ and check if it is consistent with the components it already knows from the watch-list. If we design the protocol in such a way that the sender doesn't know which components the receiver will check, then, since P_s can not change the message it committed to without changing a substantial amount of entries, P_r will see a mismatch and catch the cheating opening with high probability (binding property).

The watch-list mechanism is created in the Setup phase. The idea is that the sender and the receiver run n $(t-1)$-out of t OTs on n groups of tn seeds for a PRG, in such a way that for each group the verifier will know only $(t-1)$ of the seeds chosen by the sender. The expanded strings produced by the PRG are used to form a matrix Y. After that, in the Online phase, for each new commitment, the sender choses a new column y^η in Y and use it as one-time pad for sending to P_r the encoding $\mathrm{Enc}_t^{\mathcal{C}}(m)$. This will allow the receiver P_s to view $(t-1)n$ entries of the encodings without the sender knowing which these entries are. Furthermore, in this way we can allow many commitments while using the OT-functionality only once. For every new commitment, the sender and receiver can obtain new one-time pads for the watch-list by simply expanding the PRG seeds into a larger pseudorandom string up to a polynomially bounded length.

Statistical binding property: if the sender wants to open two different messages m and m' for the same commitment (η, c), then it has to produce randomness consistent with two vectors w and w' such that $\mathcal{C}(m) = \Lambda_t(w)$ and $\mathcal{C}(m') = \Lambda_t(w')$. Since the code has minimal distance d and $d \geq 2\tau+1$, at least one of the two different codewords $\Lambda_t(w)$ and $\Lambda_t(w')$ is at distance strictly greater than τ from $\Lambda_t(c-y^\eta)$ (Hamming distance). Assume w. l. o. g. that $\mathrm{d}_{\mathrm{Ham}}(\Lambda_t(w), \Lambda_t(c-y^\eta)) \geq \tau+1$, then in $w - c + y^\eta$ there are at least $\tau+1$ groups of consecutive entries in which at least one entry is not zero. Since the receiver checks $t-1$ entries chosen at random in each group, the probability that he doesn't see any mismatch is at most $\left(\frac{1}{t}\right)^{\tau+1}$.

Computational hiding property: from the security of the PRG G, we can claim that the receiver knows only $t-1$ entries in each group of consecutive entries of $w^\eta = \mathrm{Enc}_t^{\mathcal{C}}(m)$. That is, P_r knows only $t-1$ shares of each component of the codeword $\mathcal{C}(m)$. Thus, the hiding property follows from the $(t-1)$-privacy property of the additive secret-sharing scheme for t players used to share each component of the codeword $\mathcal{C}(m)$.

The protocol Π_{COM} UC-realizes the ideal functionality $\mathcal{F}_{\mathrm{COM}}$ in the $\mathcal{F}_{\mathrm{OT}}^{t-1,t}$-hybrid model, as stated in the following two propositions. See the full version [CDD+14] for the proofs .

Proposition 1 (Statistical Binding Property). *Let $G : \{0,1\}^{l'} \to \{0,1\}^l$ be a pseudorandom generator and $\mathcal{C} : \mathbb{F}^k \to \mathbb{F}^n$ be a $[n, k, d]$ error correction code over $\mathbb{F}$. For every static active adversary $\mathcal{A}$ corrupting only P_s in the $\mathcal{F}_{\mathrm{OT}}^{t-1,t}$-hybrid execution of Π_{COM} and for every environment[1] $\mathcal{Z}$, there exists a simulator $\mathcal{S}$ such that:*

$$\mathrm{IDEAL}_{\mathcal{F}_{\mathrm{COM}}, \mathcal{S}, \mathcal{Z}} \approx \mathrm{HYBRID}_{\Pi_{\mathrm{COM}}, \mathcal{A}, \mathcal{Z}}^{\mathcal{F}_{\mathrm{OT}}^{t-1,t}}$$

where the security parameter is $\tau = \left\lfloor \frac{d-1}{2} \right\rfloor$.

---

[1] Note that in the proof of Proposition 1 the requirement for the environment to be polynomial-time is not necessary. Indeed the proof holds for any environment that interacts with each system only a polynomial number of times.

Protocol Π_{COM} in the $\mathcal{F}_{\text{OT}}^{t-1,t}$-hybrid model

Let $G : \{0,1\}^{l'} \to \{0,1\}^{l}$ be a pseudorandom generator, $\mathcal{C} : \mathbb{F}^k \to \mathbb{F}^n$ be a linear error correction code over $\mathbb{F}$ and $t \geq 2$ a fixed integer. The procedure $\text{Enc}_t^{\mathcal{C}}$ is defined in Figure 1.

A sender P_s and receiver P_r interact between themselves and with $\mathcal{F}_{\text{OT}}^{t-1,t}$ as follows:

OT-Setup phase:

For $i = 1, t+1, 2t+1, \ldots, (n-1)t+1$:

1. P_s samples t strings $\boldsymbol{x}_i, \boldsymbol{x}_{i+1}, \ldots, \boldsymbol{x}_{i+t-1} \leftarrow \{0,1\}^{l'}$ and sends (sender, $sid, ssid, (\boldsymbol{x}_i, \ldots, \boldsymbol{x}_{i+t-1})$) to $\mathcal{F}_{\text{OT}}^{t-1,t}$.

2. P_r samples $\{c_1^i, \ldots, c_{t-1}^i\} \leftarrow \{0, 1, \ldots, t-1\}$ and sends (receiver, $sid, ssid, c_1^i, \ldots, c_{t-1}^i$) to $\mathcal{F}_{\text{OT}}^{t-1,t}$.

3. P_r receives (received, $sid, ssid, \boldsymbol{x}_{i+c_1^i}, \ldots, \boldsymbol{x}_{i+c_{t-1}^i}$) from $\mathcal{F}_{\text{OT}}^{t-1,t}$.

Let W (watch-list) be the set of indices $W = \{i + c_1^i, \ldots, i + c_{t-1}^i \mid i = 1, t+1, 2t+1, \ldots, (n-1)t+1\}$ and let $\boldsymbol{Y} \in \text{Mat}_{tn \times l}$ be the $tn \times l$ matrix with rows $\boldsymbol{y}_j$'s consisting of the row vectors $G(\boldsymbol{x}_j)$'s for $j = 1, \ldots, tn$. Denote by $\boldsymbol{y}^j$ the j'th column of $\boldsymbol{Y}$. P_s knows the entire matrix $\boldsymbol{Y}$, P_r knows the watch-list W and only $(t-1)n$ rows of $\boldsymbol{Y}$, but in a structured way: for each groups of t rows $\boldsymbol{y}_{jt+1}, \ldots, \boldsymbol{y}_{(j+1)t}$ it holds exactly $t-1$ of those[a].

Commit phase:

1. Upon input (commit, $sid, ssid, P_s, P_r, \boldsymbol{m}$) for $\boldsymbol{m} \in \mathbb{F}^k$, P_s samples $\boldsymbol{v}_1, \ldots, \boldsymbol{v}_{t-1} \leftarrow \mathbb{F}^n$ and computes $\boldsymbol{w} = \text{Enc}_t^{\mathcal{C}}(\boldsymbol{m}; \boldsymbol{v}_1, \ldots, \boldsymbol{v}_{t-1})$. Then P_s chooses an unused column $\boldsymbol{y}^n$ from the matrix $\boldsymbol{Y}$ defined in the Setup phase, computes $\boldsymbol{c} = \boldsymbol{w} + \boldsymbol{y}^n$ and sends $(sid, ssid, \eta, \boldsymbol{c})$ to P_r.

2. P_r stores $(sid, ssid, \eta, \boldsymbol{c})$ and outputs (receipt, $sid, ssid, P_s, P_r$).

Open phase:

1. Upon input (reveal, $sid, ssid, P_s, P_r$), P_s sends $(sid, ssid, \boldsymbol{m}, \boldsymbol{v}_1, \ldots, \boldsymbol{v}_{t-1})$ to P_r.

2. P_r receives $(sid, ssid, \boldsymbol{m}, \boldsymbol{v}_1, \ldots, \boldsymbol{v}_{t-1})$, computes $\boldsymbol{w} = \text{Enc}_t^{\mathcal{C}}(\boldsymbol{m}; \boldsymbol{v}_1, \ldots, \boldsymbol{v}_{t-1})$ and checks if $\boldsymbol{w}[i] + \boldsymbol{y}^n[i] = \boldsymbol{c}[i]$ for all $i \in W$. If this check fails P_r rejects the opening and halts. Otherwise P_r outputs (reveal, $sid, ssid, P_s, P_r, \boldsymbol{m}$).

---

[a] We remark that the parties do not need to hold the entire matrices at any one point in time, but can generate it on demand using an appropriate pseudorandom generator.

Fig. 2. Protocol Π_{COM}

Proposition 2 (Computational Hiding Property). *Let* $G : \{0,1\}^{l'} \to \{0,1\}^{l}$ *be a pseudorandom generator and* $\mathcal{C} : \mathbb{F}^k \to \mathbb{F}^n$ *be a* $[n,k,d]$ *error correction code over* $\mathbb{F}$. *For every static active adversary* $\mathcal{A}$ *corrupting only* P_r *in the* $\mathcal{F}_{OT}^{t-1,t}$-*hybrid model execution of* $\mathbf{\Pi}_{COM}$ *and for every environment* $\mathcal{Z}$, *there exists a simulator* $\mathcal{S}$ *such that:*

$$\mathsf{IDEAL}_{\mathcal{F}_{COM},\mathcal{S},\mathcal{Z}} \approx \mathsf{HYBRID}_{\mathbf{\Pi}_{COM},\mathcal{A},\mathcal{Z}}^{\mathcal{F}_{OT}^{t-1,t}}$$

where the security parameter is $\tau = \lfloor \frac{d-1}{2} \rfloor$.

5   Additive Homomorphic Property

Notice that in the protocol $\mathbf{\Pi}_{COM}$ a commitment (i, c) may be accepted in the Open phase by an honest receiver even if $\Lambda_t(w^i)$ is not a codeword, but it is near enough to a codeword. More precisely, if a cheating sender computes w^i in such a way that $\Lambda_t(w^i) = \mathcal{C}(m) + e$ for some error vector e with Hamming weight equal to e, then an honest receiver will accept the commitment (i, c) for the message m with probability equal to $\left(\frac{1}{t}\right)^e$.

Because of this, a cheating sender can setup an attack where with non negligible probability the sum of two commitments can be opened to a message that is different to the sum of the messages contained in the individual commitments. Given the vectors m, m' and $\tilde{m}$ where $\tilde{m} \neq m + m'$, P_s can compute the vectors e, e' and $\tilde{e}$ such that $e + e' + \tilde{e} = \mathcal{C}(m+m') - \mathcal{C}(\tilde{m})$ and the Hamming weight of each of them is less or equal than τ (note that this is possible to achieve as long as $d \leq 3\tau$, which is not disallowed by our assumption $d \geq 2\tau + 1$). In the Commit phase the corrupted P_s defines $w = \Sigma_t(\mathcal{C}(m) - e)$ and $w' = \Sigma_t(\mathcal{C}(m') - e')$ and sends (α, c) and (β, c'), where $c = w + y^\alpha$ and $c' = w' + y^\beta$. Recall that Σ_t is the outer additive code in our encoding. From the above argument, in the Open phase, an honest receiver will accept (α, c) or (β, c') as commitment for m or for m' respectively, with probability strictly greater than $\left(\frac{1}{t}\right)^{\tau+1}$ in both cases. Furthermore with the same probability, P_s can also open the sum $c + c'$ to $\tilde{m}$ because by construction $w + w' = \Sigma_t(\mathcal{C}(\tilde{m}) + \tilde{e})$.

While we could prevent the attack above by imposing the stronger condition $d \geq 3\tau + 1$, it is easy to see that the same problem would still apply to the additions of at least $\lceil \frac{d}{\tau} \rceil - 1$ commitments.

To deal with this problem, we need to assure that for any vector w computed by the sender in the Commit phase, it holds that $\Lambda_t(w)$ is an actual codeword. Since a correct vector w can be seen as a share-vector in the LSSS given by $(k, M_t^{\mathcal{C}})$ (Remark 1), a standard way to achieve this guaranty is to convert $(k, M_t^{\mathcal{C}})$ into a *verifiable secret-sharing scheme* (VSS). The latter is a secret-sharing scheme for which, together with the standard privacy property for unqualified sets of players, a stronger reconstruction property holds for the qualified sets. Indeed, in a VSS, even when the dealer is corrupted, any qualified set of honest players can determine a secret that is consistent with the share held by any honest player in the scheme. In order to obtain the additive homomorphic property for our commitment protocol, the basic idea we will use in Section 5.2 consists in forcing the sender to compute the vector w using a verifiable version of the encoding procedure $\mathsf{Enc}_t^{\mathcal{C}}$. In this way the receiver can verify that w has been properly constructed (i.e. $\Lambda_t(w)$ is a codeword) with overwhelming probability.

5.1 Packed Verifiable Secret-Sharing Scheme

In this section we recall the packed verifiable secret-sharing protocol described in [DDGN14]. We refer to the latter for the proof of the following lemmas. The protocol can be based on any linear secret-sharing scheme (k, M) for N players as defined in Section 2 and it secret-shares k vectors $s_1, \ldots, s_k \in \mathbb{F}^k$ in each its execution (the LSSS is over the field $\mathbb{F}$). In the following, F will be a $m \times m$ matrix with entries in $\mathbb{F}$ (m is the number of columns in M) and f^b will be its the b-th column. For any index $i = 1, \ldots, N$ define the column vector $h^i = F \cdot m_i^\top$ and the row vector $g_i = m_i \cdot F$ (where m_i is the i-th row in M). It is then clear that $m_j \cdot h^i = g_j \cdot m_i^\top$ for all $i, j \in [N]$. The VSS protocol is shown in Figure 3.

Protocol Π_{VSS} (M)

1. Let $s_1, \ldots, s_k \in \mathbb{F}^k$ be the secrets to be shared. The dealer chooses a random $m \times m$ matrix F with entries in $\mathbb{F}$, subject[a] to $\pi_k(f^i) = s_i^\top$, for any $i = 1, \ldots, k$.
2. For any $i = 1, \ldots, N$, the dealer computes h^i and g_i and sends them to P_i
3. Each player P_j sends $g_j \cdot m_i^\top$ to P_i, for $i = 1, \ldots, N$.
4. Each P_i checks, for $j = 1, \ldots, N$, that $m_j \cdot h^i$ equals the value received from P_j. He broadcasts (accept, $sid, ssid,$) if all checks are satisfied, otherwise he broadcasts (reject, $sid, ssid,$).
5. If all players said (accept, $sid, ssid,$), then each P_j stores $g_j[i]$ as his share of s_i, for $i = 1, \ldots, k$. Otherwise the protocol aborts.

---

[a] Recall that we use π_k to denote the projection that outputs the first k coordinates of a vector

Fig. 3. Packed Verifiable Secret-Sharing Scheme

For a column vector $v \in \mathbb{F}^m$, we will say that v *shares* $s \in \mathbb{F}^k$, if $\pi_k(v) = s$ and each honest player P_j holds $m_j \cdot v$. It is clear the the scheme Π_{VSS} is complete, i.e. if the dealer is honest, then all honest players accept and the column vector f^i shares s_i, for any $i = 1, \ldots, k$. Moreover, the scheme has the following reconstruction property:

Lemma 1. *Let B be a qualified subset of b honest players and assume that the protocol Π_{VSS} doesn't abort. Then, for all $i = 1, \ldots, k$, the vector $\tilde{f}^i$ (defined by $\tilde{f}^i = \sum_{j=1}^{b} r_{B,i}[j] h^j$) shares $\pi_k(\tilde{f}^i)$. The vectors $r_{B,i}$ are the reconstruction vectors defined in Section 2.3.*

Lemma 1 assures that if the protocol Π_{VSS} doesn't abort, then, even when the dealer is corrupted, for all $i = 1, \ldots, k$ the info held by a qualified set of honest players at the end of the protocol determine the secret $s_i = \pi_k(\tilde{f}^i)^\top$ and the randomness $\tilde{f}^i$ used by the dealer to share it in such a way that $(M \cdot \tilde{f}^i)[j] = m_j \cdot \tilde{f}^i = g_j[i]$ for any j with P_j honest.

Finally, since Π_{VSS} shares k secrets in one execution, the privacy property can be stated in an extended form which also guarantees that making public any linear combination of the shared secrets doesn't reveal extra info on the individual secrets.

Lemma 2. *If the dealer in Π_{VSS} is honest, then for any unqualified set of players A and for any $\lambda_1, \ldots, \lambda_\ell \in \mathbb{F}$, the distribution of $\{F \cdot M_A^\top, M_A \cdot F, \sum_{j=1}^\ell \lambda_j s^j\}$ is independent of the secrets held by the dealer.*

5.2   Homomorphic Commitment Scheme

In this section we present our additively homomorphic commitment scheme. The protocol is designed in the $\mathcal{F}_{OT}^{t-1,t}$-hybrid model using preprocessing and it will be based on the instantiation of the Π_{VSS} protocol in which the underlying LSSS is the one that is equivalent to our encoding procedure $\mathsf{Enc}_t^\mathcal{C}$. The result is a commitment scheme that can be seen as a concrete exemplification of the homomorphic commitment scheme described in [DDGN14]. Note that in this section, for technical reasons, the fixed integer t has to be strictly greater than 2.

Given the $[n, k, d]$ linear error-correcting code $\mathcal{C}$, we have already noted in Remark 1 that computing the vector $w = \mathsf{Enc}_t^\mathcal{C}(m; v_1, \ldots, v_{t-1})$ is equivalent to computing the share-vector for m in the LSSS defined by $(k, M_t^\mathcal{C})$ for $N = tn$ players. In particular $w = M_t^\mathcal{C} \cdot f$ where the vector f is given by $f = (m, f_1, \ldots, f_n)^\top$ with $f_j = (v_1[j], \ldots, v_{t-1}[j])$ for any $j \in [n]$.

The protocol Π_{HCOM} is presented in Figure 4. In the Setup phase, firstly the same watch-list mechanism of Π_{COM} is created and after the sender runs Π_{VSS} on some random messages $r_1, \ldots, r_k$ computing the vectors h^i, g_i for all $i = 1, \ldots, N$. In particular P_s computes $\mathsf{Enc}_t^\mathcal{C}(r_i) = (g_1[i], \ldots, g_N[i])^\top$. Thanks to the watch-list mechanism, the receiver sees all the vectors h^i, g_i such that i is in the watch-list set W and therefore it can check the relation $m_j \cdot h^i = g_j \cdot m_i^\top$ for all i, j in W. If all these checks are satisfied, then it follows from the strong reconstruction property of the VSS, that the vectors $\mathsf{Enc}_t^\mathcal{C}(r_i)$ have been properly constructed (i.e. $\Lambda_t(\mathsf{Enc}_t^\mathcal{C}(r_i))$ is a codeword) with overwhelming probability. Nevertheless, since the set of players $\{P_i \mid i \in W\}$ is unqualified for the LSSS $(k, M_t^\mathcal{C})$, the receiver has no info about the vectors $r_1, \ldots, r_k$.

In the Online phase, to commit to $m \in \mathbb{F}^k$, the sender takes an unused r_η and sends $c = m + r_\eta$ to the sender. The commitment is represented by the pair (η, c). To open it, the sender reveals m and the randomness used to compute $w = \mathsf{Enc}_t^\mathcal{C}(r_\eta)$, thus the receiver can check if the entries he already knows of the encoding of r_η match the ones of w.

As in the basic protocol, the hiding property follows easily from the privacy of the VSS scheme and the security of the PRG. The binding property, again, follows from the fact that in order to change r_i in r_i' the sender has to change a large amount of entries in $\mathsf{Enc}_t^{\mathcal{C}}(r_i)$ without knowing which entries the receiver checks. Finally, in this protocol we can implement additions: given a commitment (α, c_1) to m_1 and a commitment (β, c_2) to m_2, both the parties can just compute $c_3 = c_1 + c_2$ and store $((\alpha, \beta), c_3)$ as new commitment. To open c_3 to $m_1 + m_2$ the senders sends to P_r the vector $m_1 + m_2$ and the sum of the randomness used in $\mathsf{Enc}_t^{\mathcal{C}}(r_\alpha)$ an in $\mathsf{Enc}_t^{\mathcal{C}}(r_\beta)$. While the receiver will check the received randomness as in an usual Open phase but considering the sum of the encodings of r_α and r_β.

Note that now a commitment will be represented by (η, c), where η can also be a tuple of indices instead of just one index in $[k] = \{1, \ldots, k\}$. Indeed, if c is the commitment obtained by the sum of ℓ standard commitments (i.e. commitments created in the Commit phase), then $\eta \in [k]^\ell$. For this reason, in order to implement the Addition command in the description of the protocol, we will use the following notation: if $\alpha \in [k]^i$ and $\beta \in [k]^j$, then $\gamma = \alpha \parallel \beta = (\alpha, \beta) \in [k]^{i+j}$.

The protocol Π_{HCOM} UC-realizes the ideal functionality $\mathcal{F}_{\mathrm{HCOM}}$ in the $\mathcal{F}_{\mathrm{OT}}^{t-1,t}$-hybrid model, as stated in the following two propositions. See the full version [CDD+14] for the proofs .

Proposition 3 (Statistical Binding Property). *Let $G : \{0,1\}^{l'} \to \{0,1\}^{2m}$ be a pseudorandom generator and $\mathcal{C} : \mathbb{F}^k \to \mathbb{F}^n$ be a $[n,k,d]$ error correction code over $\mathbb{F}$. For every static active adversary $\mathcal{A}$ corrupting only P_s in the $\mathcal{F}_{\mathrm{OT}}^{t-1,t}$-hybrid world execution of Π_{HCOM} and for every environment $\mathcal{Z}$, there exists a simulator $\mathcal{S}$ such that:*

$$\mathrm{IDEAL}_{\mathcal{F}_{\mathrm{HCOM}}, \mathcal{S}, \mathcal{Z}} \approx \mathrm{HYBRID}_{\Pi_{\mathrm{HCOM}}, \mathcal{A}, \mathcal{Z}}^{\mathcal{F}_{\mathrm{OT}}^{t-1,t}}$$

where the security parameter is $\tau = \lfloor \frac{d-1}{2} \rfloor$.

Also in the protocol Π_{HCOM} it is possible to implement polynomial many commitments, after having run the OT-Setup phase only once. Indeed, after that the watch-list W has been settled, the sender can always sample new random vectors $r_1^*, \ldots, r_k^* \leftarrow \mathbb{F}^k$ and, together with the receiver, repeat the execution of the Pre-commitment phase on this new input. We have already recalled in Section 4 that it is possible to expand the PRG output in order to have new one-time keys to use in the each execution of the Pre-commitment phase. After that, P_s and P_r can continue the protocol following the instructions in Π_{HCOM}. Moreover, this doesn't create any restriction about the Addition command: we can allow the sum of commitments that use one-time keys coming from different Pre-commitment phases.

Proposition 4 (Computational Hiding Property). *Let $G : \{0,1\}^{l'} \to \{0,1\}^{2m}$ be a pseudorandom generator and $\mathcal{C} : \mathbb{F}^k \to \mathbb{F}^n$ be a $[n,k,d]$ error correction code over $\mathbb{F}$. For every static active adversary $\mathcal{A}$ corrupting only P_r*

Protocol Π_{HCOM} in the $\mathcal{F}_{\text{OT}}^{t-1,t}$-hybrid model

Let $G : \{0,1\}^{l'} \to \{0,1\}^{2m}$ be a pseudorandom generator, $\mathcal{C} : \mathbb{F}^k \to \mathbb{F}^n$ be a $[n,k,d]$ code over $\mathbb{F}$ and $t \geq 3$ a fixed integer. We recall that $N = tn$, $m = k + (t-1)n$ and the matrix $M_t^{\mathcal{C}}$, whose i-th row is called m_i, is defined in Remark 1.

A sender P_s and receiver P_r interact between themselves and with $\mathcal{F}_{\text{OT}}^{t-1,t}$ as follows:

Setup phase:

 OT-Setup:

  For $i = 1, t+1, 2t+1, \ldots, (n-1)t+1$:

   1. P_s samples t strings $\boldsymbol{x}_i, \boldsymbol{x}_{i+1}, \ldots, \boldsymbol{x}_{i+t-1} \leftarrow \{0,1\}^{l'}$ and sends (sender, $sid, ssid, (\boldsymbol{x}_i, \ldots, \boldsymbol{x}_{i+t-1})$) to $\mathcal{F}_{\text{OT}}^{t-1,t}$.

   2. P_r samples $\{c_1^i, \ldots, c_{t-1}^i\} \leftarrow \{0, 1, \ldots, t-1\}$ and sends (receiver, $sid, ssid, c_1^i, \ldots, c_{t-1}^i$) to $\mathcal{F}_{\text{OT}}^{t-1,t}$.

   3. P_r receives (received, $sid, ssid, \boldsymbol{x}_{i+c_1^i}, \ldots, \boldsymbol{x}_{i+c_{t-1}^i}$) from $\mathcal{F}_{\text{OT}}^{t-1,t}$.

  Let $\boldsymbol{Y} \in \text{Mat}_{N \times 2m}$ be the $N \times 2m$ matrix with rows $\boldsymbol{y}_j$'s consisting of the row vectors $G(\boldsymbol{x}_j)$'s for $j = 1, \ldots, N$ and $W = \{i + c_1^i, \ldots, i + c_{t-1}^i \mid i = 1, t+1, 2t+1, \ldots, (n-1)t+1\}$.

 Pre-commitment:

  1. Upon receiving (received, $sid, ssid$) from $\mathcal{F}_{\text{OT}}^{t-1,t}$, P_s samples $\boldsymbol{r}_1, \ldots, \boldsymbol{r}_k \leftarrow \mathbb{F}^k$ and runs $\Pi_{\text{VSS}} (M_t^{\mathcal{C}})$ using $\boldsymbol{r}_1, \ldots, \boldsymbol{r}_k$ as input and constructing the row vectors $\boldsymbol{w}_i = (\boldsymbol{g}_i, (\boldsymbol{h}^i)^\top) \in \mathbb{F}^{2m}$ for $i = 1, \ldots, N$. Let $\boldsymbol{W} \in \text{Mat}_{N \times 2m}$ be the matrix consisting of the rows $\boldsymbol{w}_i$.

  2. P_s computes $\boldsymbol{A} = \boldsymbol{W} + \boldsymbol{Y}$ and sends $(sid, ssid, \boldsymbol{A})$ to P_r. Denote with $\boldsymbol{a}_i$ the i-th row of $\boldsymbol{A}$.

  3. P_r computes $(\boldsymbol{g}_i, (\boldsymbol{h}^i)^\top) = \boldsymbol{a}_i - \boldsymbol{y}_i$ for all $i \in W$ and checks if $\boldsymbol{m}_j \cdot \boldsymbol{h}^i = \boldsymbol{g}_j \cdot \boldsymbol{m}_i^\top$ for all different indices $i, j \in W$. If all the checks are satisfied, then P_r accepts the Setup phase, otherwise it halts.

Commit phase:

 1. Upon input (commit, $sid, ssid, P_s, P_r, \boldsymbol{m}$) for $\boldsymbol{m} \in \mathbb{F}^k$, P_s chooses an unused $\boldsymbol{r}_\eta$ from the Setup phase, computes $\boldsymbol{c} = \boldsymbol{m} + \boldsymbol{r}_\eta$ and sends $(sid, ssid, \eta, \boldsymbol{c})$ to P_r.

 2. P_r stores $(sid, ssid, \eta, \boldsymbol{c})$ and outputs (receipt, $sid, ssid, P_s, P_r$).

Addition:

 If the tuples $(sid, ssid_1, \alpha, \boldsymbol{c}_1)$, $(sid, ssid_2, \beta, \boldsymbol{c}_2)$ were previously sent by P_s and recorded by P_r, then:

 1. Upon input (add, $sid, ssid_1, ssid_2, ssid_3, P_s, P_r$), both the players P_s and P_r define and store $(sid, ssid_3, \gamma, \boldsymbol{c}_3)$ where $\gamma = \alpha \parallel \beta$ and $\boldsymbol{c}_3 = \boldsymbol{c}_1 + \boldsymbol{c}_2$.

Open phase:

 If $(sid, ssid, \delta, \boldsymbol{c}')$ was stored and $\delta = (\delta_1, \ldots, \delta_\ell) \in [k]^\ell$, then:

 1. Upon input (reveal, $sid, ssid, P_s, P_r$) to reveal message $\boldsymbol{m}'$, P_s sends $(sid, ssid, \boldsymbol{m}', \boldsymbol{v}_1, \ldots, \boldsymbol{v}_{t-1})$ to P_r, where $\boldsymbol{v}_i = \sum_{j=1}^{\ell} \boldsymbol{v}_i^{\delta_j}$ for all $i = 1, \ldots, t-1$ and the vector[a] $\text{Enc}_t^{\mathcal{C}}(\boldsymbol{r}_{\delta_j}; \boldsymbol{v}_1^{\delta_j}, \ldots, \boldsymbol{v}_{t-1}^{\delta_j})$ is the column number δ_j in the matrix $\boldsymbol{W}$ (for all $j = 1, \ldots, \ell$).

 2. P_r receives $(sid, ssid, \boldsymbol{m}', \boldsymbol{v}_1, \ldots, \boldsymbol{v}_{t-1})$ and computes $\boldsymbol{w} = \text{Enc}_t^{\mathcal{C}}(\boldsymbol{c}' - \boldsymbol{m}'; \boldsymbol{v}_1, \ldots, \boldsymbol{v}_{t-1})$. Then, P_r checks if $\boldsymbol{w}[j] = \sum_{i=1}^{\ell} \boldsymbol{g}_j[\delta_i]$ for all the entries $j \in W$. If this check fails P_r rejects the commitment and halts. Otherwise P_r outputs (reveal, $sid, ssid, P_s, P_r, \boldsymbol{m}'$).

---

[a] Since the LSSS defined by $(k, M_t^{\mathcal{C}})$ is equivalent to the encoding procedure $\text{Enc}_t^{\mathcal{C}}$, P_s already knows the vectors $\{\boldsymbol{v}_i^{\delta_j}\}_i$ used to encode $\boldsymbol{r}_{\delta_j}$ from the Pre-commitment phase

Fig. 4. Protocol Π_{HCOM}

in the $\mathcal{F}_{\mathrm{OT}}^{t-1,t}$-hybrid world execution of Π_{HCOM} and for every environment $\mathcal{Z}$, there exists a simulator $\mathcal{S}$ such that:

$$\mathsf{IDEAL}_{\mathcal{F}_{\mathrm{HCOM}},\mathcal{S},\mathcal{Z}} \approx \mathsf{HYBRID}_{\Pi_{\mathrm{HCOM}},\mathcal{A},\mathcal{Z}}^{\mathcal{F}_{\mathrm{OT}}^{t-1,t}}$$

where the security parameter is $\tau = \left\lfloor \frac{d-1}{2} \right\rfloor$.

6   Complexity and Concrete Efficiency

In this section we discuss the computational and communication complexities of the commitment schemes proposed in Sections 4 and 5. We also estimate concrete parameters and compare the efficiency of our schemes with previous works.

6.1   Complexity

The commitment scheme presented by Damgård *et al.* in [DDGN14] suffered from a quadratic computational overhead in order to achieve optimal communication overhead. This issue stems from the fact that their scheme requires an underlying LSSS that operates over constant size fields [CDP12] whose sharing operations consist in matrix multiplications. Our homomorphic scheme circumvents that by constructing the VSS scheme from a linear error correcting code with linear-time encoding where one can compute shares by computing encodings.

The core component of both commitment schemes is the coding scheme $\mathsf{Enc}_t^{\mathcal{C}}$. This construction can be seen both as an error correcting code (ECC) and a linear secret secret sharing scheme for a specific access structure. $\mathsf{Enc}_t^{\mathcal{C}}$ can be built from *any* linear error correcting code, differently from previous results, which require codes whose dual codes have high minimum distance in order to construct LSSS. This fundamental difference in construction allows us to obtain a coding scheme $\mathsf{Enc}_t^{\mathcal{C}}$ (and consequently a LSSS) that runs in linear time on the input length from any linear-time encodable error correcting code. There exist constructions of linear-time encodable codes with constant rate and good (i.e., linear in the codeword length) minimum distance, see [GI01, GI02, GI03, GI05, Spi96]. However, these may even be more sophisticated than what we need since all we require about the minimum distance is that it is at least $2\tau + 1$, where τ is the security parameter.

The encoding and decoding procedures of $\mathsf{Enc}_t^{\mathcal{C}}$ inherit the complexity of the underlying code. Notice that in our constructions we only utilize the encoding procedure of $\mathsf{Enc}_t^{\mathcal{C}}$, since sharing and verifying share consistency in the VSS scheme of Figure 3 can be seen as encoding. Hence, our constructions can even take advantage of recent advances in linear-time encodable codes [DI14].

Combining a linear-time encoding procedure $\mathsf{Enc}_t^{\mathcal{C}}$ with a PRG where we pay only a constant number of elementary bit operations per output bit (see, *e.g.*,

[VZ12]), we obtain UC-secure commitments with optimal computational complexity. Notice that the setup phase (where OTs are needed) is only run once, allowing for an arbitrary number of posterior commitments. Thus, the cost of this phase is amortized over the number of commitments. Communication complexity is also linear in the message length if C has constant rate.

6.2   Concrete Parameters and Efficiency

Even though our schemes can achieve optimal asymptotic computational and communication complexities, we are also interested in obtaining highly efficient concrete instantiations. As an example, we estimate parameters for a concrete instantiation of our schemes with message length $k = 256$ bits and statistical security parameter $\tau = 60$. We refer the reader to the full version [CDD+14] for a generic evaluation of the commitment schemes' performance as a function of the underlying error correcting code parameters and remarks on their suitability for efficiently preprocessing commitments.

Bulding Blocks: The basic building blocks of our commitment scheme are the coding scheme $\mathsf{Enc}_t^{\mathcal{C}}$, a PRG and a UC-secure OT protocol. We select the following constructions of these building blocks for our concrete instances:

- **OT:** The UC-secure protocol presented in [PVW08]. This protocol is round optimal and requires communicating 6 group elements and computing 11 exponentiations per transfer.
- **PRG:** AES in counter mode, using the IV as a PRG seed. AES implementations are readily available in modern hardware (*e.g.* Intel's AES-NI) making the cost of this PRG negligible.
- $\mathsf{Enc}_t^{\mathcal{C}}$: For the basic scheme of Figure 2 we will need a $\mathsf{Enc}_2^{\mathcal{C}}$ coding scheme, while for the additively homomorphic scheme of Figure 4 we need a $\mathsf{Enc}_3^{\mathcal{C}}$ coding scheme. Both schemes are constructed using a binary $[796, 256, \geq 121]$ BCH code (see, *e.g.*, [MS78]) [2] as $\mathcal{C}$ according to the generic construction of Section 3. This code has parameters $k = 256$, $n = 796$ and $d \geq 121$, which corresponds to $\tau = 60$. We obtain $\mathsf{Enc}_2^{\mathcal{C}} : \mathbb{F}^{256} \to \mathbb{F}^{1592}$ and $\mathsf{Enc}_3^{\mathcal{C}} : \mathbb{F}^{256} \to \mathbb{F}^{2388}$. Even though this code doesn't have linear encoding complexity, it was chosen because it is readily available in the Linux Kernel and it achieves good concrete performance.

Evaluating Efficiency: Previous efficiency comparisons between UC-secure commitment schemes have been based on the number of exponentiations required by each scheme. This choice of comparison parameters is justified by the fact

---

[2] More precisely, the $[796, 256, \geq 121]$ code is actually obtained by shortening a BCH-code with parameters $[1023, 483, \geq 121]$. This code was in turn selected by first fixing the message size $k = 256$, the statistical security parameter $\tau = 60$ and the minimum distance $d \geq 2\tau + 1 \geq 121$, then using MAGMA to compute concrete code parameters that fit these constraints.

that this is usually the most costly operation that dominates the concrete execution time of such schemes. However, apart from the setup phase involving OTs, our protocols require no exponentiations at all. After the setup phase of our protocols, the most expensive operation is the encoding procedure of the $\mathsf{Enc}_t^{\mathcal{C}}$ coding scheme (the other operation required is addition).

We compare the efficiency of our schemes with the most efficient previous works [BCPV13, Lin11] by estimating the execution time of the encoding procedure of the BCH code and comparing that to the execution time of exponentiations on the same platform. While the encoding scheme of the ECC and the PRG are used proportionally to the number of commitments one wishes to make and open, the OT protocol is only used for a fixed number of times during the setup phase. Hence, it is interesting to estimate the concrete efficiency of the setup phase separately from the other steps of the protocols, since the cost of running the OT protocol is amortized over the number of commitments.

The concrete computational, round and communication complexities for our schemes when instantiated using the previously described building blocks are presented in Table 1. In this case we consider message length $k = 256$ and statistical security parameter $\tau = 60$, using the $[796, 256, \geq 121]$ BCH code as the building block for $\mathsf{Enc}_2^{\mathcal{C}}$ and $\mathsf{Enc}_3^{\mathcal{C}}$.

Table 1. Concrete efficiency with message length $k = 256$ bits, statistical security parameter $\tau = 60$ and 128-bit computational security (for the schemes of [BCPV13, Lin11]). Exp. and Enc. stand for exponentiations and encodings, respectively.

Scheme	Communication Complexity (in bits)			Round Complexity		Computational Complexity		
	Commit	Open	Total	Commit	Open	Commit	Open	Total
[BCPV13] (Fig. 6)	1024	2048	3072	1	5	10 Exp.	12 Exp.	22 Exp.
[Lin11] (Protocol 2)	1024	2560	3584	1	3	5 Exp.	$18\frac{1}{3}$ Exp.	$23\frac{1}{3}$ Exp.
Fig. 4 (homomorphic, $t = 3$)	34733	1848	36580	1	1	27 Enc.	1 Enc.	28 Enc.
Fig. 2 (basic, $t = 2$)	1592	1052	2644	1	1	1 Enc.	1 Enc.	2 Enc.

The execution time of an elliptic curve "exponentiations" over a field of size 256 bits offering 128-bit security is evaluated through an implementation in SCAPI 2.3 [EFLL12] using an underlying curve implementation provided by OpenSSL 1.1.0. The execution time of the encoding procedure of the $[796, 256, \geq 121]$ BCH code is evaluated using the implementation present in the Linux kernel. The platform used for estimating the running time of these operations is based on a Intel(R) Core(TM) i5-2400 CPU at 3.10 GHz with 4 GB of RAM running a Linux Kernel version 3.13.0.

Our experiments showed that the elliptic curve "exponentiations" take an average of 375 μs while the encodings take an average of 0.75 μs on the same platform. Hence, in this scenario, computing one encoding is on average 500 times faster than computing one exponentiation on the same platform. These data show that our basic commitment scheme is 5500 times more computationally efficient than the scheme of [BCPV13], also achieving 14% lower communication complexity. On the other hand, our additively homomorphic commitment scheme is 392 times faster than the scheme of [BCPV13], though its communication complexity is 12 times higher.

The Random Oracle Model [BR93] has historically been used to construct cryptographic schemes with very high efficiency. Surprisingly, our scheme achieves amortised concrete efficiency comparable to previous universally composable schemes based on the ROM [HM04, DSW08] even though it is constructed in the plain model. The average execution time of a SHA-256 hash function in our evaluation platform is of $0.63\mu s$ for the fastest implementation (BouncyCastle) available on SCAPI 2.3, while the OpenSSL implementation runs in $0.835\mu s$. The protocol introduced in [HM04] requires four evaluations of the ROM, which translates into a total execution time 1.68 times higher than of our basic scheme if SHA-256 is used to instantiate the ROM.

Implementing the setup phase required by our basic scheme in Figure 2 requires $n = 796$ executions of a 1-out-of-2 OT, yielding a cost of 8756 exponentiations. With the above timings and considering the OT protocol of [PVW08], the computational complexity of this scheme is lower when at least 398 commitments are computed, and gets increasingly better as the number of commitments increases. However, 4776 of these exponentiations can be precomputed independently of the messages since it is enough for the receiver to get random messages, lowering the online cost to 3980 exponentiations (*i.e.* the cost of 180 commitments. The additively homomorphic scheme in Figure 4 requires $n = 796$ executions of a 2-out-of-3 OT, yielding a higher cost in terms of exponentiations in the setup phase.

References

[BCPV13] Blazy, O., Chevalier, C., Pointcheval, D., Vergnaud, D.: Analysis and improvement of Lindell's UC-secure commitment schemes. In: Jacobson, M., Locasto, M., Mohassel, P., Safavi-Naini, R. (eds.) ACNS 2013. LNCS, vol. 7954, pp. 534–551. Springer, Heidelberg (2013)

[BCR86] Brassard, G., Crepeau, C., Robert, J.-M.: Information theoretic reductions among disclosure problems. In: 27th Annual Symposium on Foundations of Computer Science 1986, pp. 168–173 (October 1986)

[BR93] Bellare, M., Rogaway, P.: Random oracles are practical: A paradigm for designing efficient protocols. In: Proceedings of the 1st ACM Conference on Computer and Communications Security, CCS 1993, pp. 62–73. ACM, New York (1993)

[Can01] Canetti, R.: Universally composable security: A new paradigm for cryptographic protocols. In: FOCS [DBL01], pp. 136–145

[CDD+14] Cascudo, I., Damgård, I., David, B., Giacomelli, I., Buus Nielsen, J.B., Trifiletti, R.: Additively homomorphic UC commitments with optimal amortized overhead. Cryptology ePrint Archive, Report 2014/829 (2014), Full version of PKC 2015 paper

[CDP12] Cramer, R., Damgård, I., Pastro, V.: On the amortized complexity of zero knowledge protocols for multiplicative relations. In: Smith, A. (ed.) ICITS 2012. LNCS, vol. 7412, pp. 62–79. Springer, Heidelberg (2012)

[CF01]   Canetti, R., Fischlin, M.: Universally composable commitments. In: Kilian, J. (ed.) CRYPTO 2001. LNCS, vol. 2139, pp. 19–40. Springer, Heidelberg (2001)

[CLOS02]   Canetti, R., Lindell, Y., Ostrovsky, R., Sahai, A.: Universally composable two-party and multi-party secure computation. In: STOC, pp. 494–503 (2002)

[DBL01]   42nd Annual Symposium on Foundations of Computer Science, FOCS 2001, October 14–17, Las Vegas, Nevada, USA. IEEE Computer Society (2001)

[DDGN14]   Damgård, I., David, B., Giacomelli, I., Nielsen, J.B.: Compact VSS and efficient homomorphic UC commitments. In: Sarkar, P., Iwata, T. (eds.) ASIACRYPT 2014, Part II. LNCS, vol. 8874, pp. 213–232. Springer, Heidelberg (2014)

[DG03]   Damgård, I., Groth, J.: Non-interactive and reusable non-malleable commitment schemes. In: Larmore and Goemans [LG03], pp. 426–437

[DI14]   Druk, E., Ishai, Y.: Linear-time encodable codes meeting the Gilbert-Varshamov bound and their cryptographic applications. In: Naor, M. (ed.) Innovations in Theoretical Computer Science, ITCS 2014, Princeton, NJ, USA, January 12–14, pp. 169–182. ACM (2014)

[DNO10]   Damgård, I., Nielsen, J.B., Orlandi, C.: On the necessary and sufficient assumptions for UC computation. In: Micciancio, D. (ed.) TCC 2010. LNCS, vol. 5978, pp. 109–127. Springer, Heidelberg (2010)

[DSW08]   Dodis, Y., Shoup, V., Walfish, S.: Efficient constructions of composable commitments and zero-knowledge proofs. In: Wagner, D. (ed.) CRYPTO 2008. LNCS, vol. 5157, pp. 515–535. Springer, Heidelberg (2008)

[EFLL12]   Ejgenberg, Y., Farbstein, M., Levy, M., Lindell, Y.: Scapi: The secure computation application programming interface. Cryptology ePrint Archive, Report 2012/629 (2012). http://eprint.iacr.org/

[GI01]   Guruswam, V., Indyk, P.: Expander-based constructions of efficiently decodable codes. In: 42nd Annual Symposium on Foundations of Computer Science, FOCS 2001, Las Vegas, Nevada, USA, October 14–17 [DBL01], pp. 658–667 (2001)

[GI02]   Guruswami, V., Indyk, P.: Near-optimal linear-time codes for unique decoding and new list-decodable codes over smaller alphabets. In: Reif, J.H. (ed.) Proceedings on 34th Annual ACM Symposium on Theory of Computing, Montréal, Québec, Canada, May 19–21, pp. 812–821. ACM (2002)

[GI03]   Guruswami, V., Indyk, P.: Linear time encodable and list decodable codes. In: Larmore and Goemans [LG03], pp. 126–135

[GI05]   Guruswami, V., Indyk, P.: Linear-time encodable/decodable codes with near-optimal rate. IEEE Transactions on Information Theory 51(10), 3393–3400 (2005)

[GIKW14]   Garay, J.A., Ishai, Y., Kumaresan, R., Wee, H.: On the complexity of UC commitments. In: Nguyen, P.Q., Oswald, E. (eds.) EUROCRYPT 2014. LNCS, vol. 8441, pp. 677–694. Springer, Heidelberg (2014)

[HM04]   Hofheinz, D., Müller-Quade, J.: Universally composable commitments using random oracles. In: Naor, M. (ed.) TCC 2004. LNCS, vol. 2951, pp. 58–76. Springer, Heidelberg (2004)

[IPS09]   Ishai, Y., Prabhakaran, M., Sahai, A.: Secure arithmetic computation with no honest majority. In: Reingold, O. (ed.) TCC 2009. LNCS, vol. 5444, pp. 294–314. Springer, Heidelberg (2009)

[LG03]   Larmore, L.L., Goemans, M.X. (eds.) Proceedings of the 35th Annual ACM Symposium on Theory of Computing, San Diego, CA, USA, June 9–11. ACM (2003)

[Lin11] Lindell, Y.: Highly-efficient universally-composable commitments based on the DDH assumption. In: Paterson, K.G. (ed.) EUROCRYPT 2011. LNCS, vol. 6632, pp. 446–466. Springer, Heidelberg (2011)

[MS78]   MacWilliams, F.J., Sloane, N.J.A.: The Theory of Error-Correcting Codes. 2nd edn. North-Holland Publishing Company (1978)

[Nao91] Naor, M.: Bit commitment using pseudorandomness. J. Cryptology $4(2)$, 151–158 (1991)

[NP99]   Naor, M., Pinkas, B.: Oblivious transfer with adaptive queries. In: Wiener, M. (ed.) CRYPTO 1999. LNCS, vol. 1666, pp. 573–590. Springer, Heidelberg (1999)

[PVW08] Peikert, C., Vaikuntanathan, V., Waters, B.: A framework for efficient and composable oblivious transfer. In: Wagner, D. (ed.) CRYPTO 2008. LNCS, vol. 5157, pp. 554–571. Springer, Heidelberg (2008)

[Spi96] Spielman, D.A.: Linear-time encodable and decodable error-correcting codes. IEEE Transactions on Information Theory $42(6)$, 1723–1731 (1996)

[VZ12]   Vadhan, S., Zheng, C.J.: Characterizing pseudoentropy and simplifying pseudorandom generator constructions. In: Proceedings of the 44th Symposium on Theory of Computing, pp. 817–836. ACM (2012)

Interactive Message-Locked Encryption
and Secure Deduplication

Mihir Bellare$^{(\boxtimes)}$ and Sriram Keelveedhi

Department of Computer Science and Engineering,
University of California San Diego, San Diego, USA
mihir@eng.ucsd.edu, sriramkr@cs.ucsd.edu

Abstract. This paper considers the problem of secure storage of out-sourced data in a way that permits deduplication. We are for the first time able to provide privacy for messages that are both correlated and dependent on the public system parameters. The new ingredient that makes this possible is interaction. We extend the message-locked encryption (MLE) primitive of prior work to interactive message-locked encryption (iMLE) where upload and download are protocols. Our scheme, providing security for messages that are not only correlated but allowed to depend on the public system parameters, is in the standard model. We explain that interaction is not an extra assumption in practice because full, existing deduplication systems are already interactive.

1 Introduction

THE SECURE DEDUPLICATION PROBLEM. Cloud storage providers such as Google, Dropbox and NetApp [31,41,51] derive significant cost savings from what is called *deduplication*. This means that if Alice and Bob upload the same data m, the service provider stores only one copy that is returned to Alice and Bob upon download.

Enter security, namely the desire of clients to keep their data private from the server. Certainly, Alice and Bob can conventionally encrypt their data under their passwords and upload the ciphertext rather than the plaintext. But then, even if they start from the same data m, they will end up with different cipher-texts C_A, C_B, foiling deduplication. The corresponding cost increase for the server would ultimately be passed to the clients in higher storage fees. It is thus in the interest of the parties to cooperate towards storage that is secure but deduplicatable.

Douceur et al. [30] provided the first solution, called convergent encryption (CE). The client encrypts its plaintext m with a *deterministic* symmetric encryption scheme under a k that is itself derived as a deterministic hash of the plaintext m. If Alice and Bob start with the same m, they will arrive at the same ciphertext, and thus deduplication is possible. Despite lacking an analysis until recently [12], CE has long been used in research and commercial systems [2,4,5,18,26,27,29,35,39,46,47,52,54], an indication of practitioners' interest in secure deduplication.

© International Association for Cryptologic Research 2015
J. Katz (Ed.): PKC 2015, LNCS 9020, pp. 516–538, 2015.
DOI: 10.1007/978-3-662-46447-2_23

Scheme(s)	Type	Messages		STD/ROM
		Correlated	Param. dep.	
CE, HCE1, HCE2, RCE [12]	MLE	Yes	No	ROM
XtDPKE, XtESPKE, ... [12]	MLE	Yes	No	STD
BHK [10]	MLE	Yes	No	STD
ABMRS [1]	MLE	No	Yes	RO
FCHECK	iMLE	**Yes**	**Yes**	**STD**

Fig. 1. Features of prior schemes (first four rows) and our scheme (last row). We achieve security for the first time for messages that are *both* correlated *and* parameter dependent. Our scheme is in the standard model. The advance is made possible by exploiting interaction.

MLE. Bellare, Keelveedhi and Ristenpart (BKR) [12] initiated a theoretical treatment of secure deduplication aimed in particular at answering questions like, what security does CE provide and what can one prove about it? To this end they defined a primitive they called message-locked encryption (MLE). An MLE scheme specifies algorithms $\mathsf{K}, \mathsf{E}, \mathsf{D}, \mathsf{T}$. To encrypt m, let $k \leftarrow_\$ \mathsf{K}(p, m)$, where p is a system-wide public parameter, and return ciphertext $c \leftarrow_\$ \mathsf{E}(k, m)$. Decryption $m \leftarrow \mathsf{D}(k', c)$ recovers m as long as $k' \leftarrow_\$ \mathsf{K}(p, m)$ is any key derived from m. Tags, produced via $t \leftarrow \mathsf{T}(c)$, are a way to test whether the plaintexts underlying two ciphertexts are the same or not, all encryptions of m having the same tag but it being hard to find differing plaintexts with matching tags.

Any MLE scheme enables deduplication. Alice, having m_A, computes and retains a key $k_A \leftarrow_\$ \mathsf{K}(p, m_A)$ and uploads $c_A \leftarrow_\$ \mathsf{E}(k, m_A)$. The server stores c_A. Now Bob, having m_B, computes and retains a key $k_B \leftarrow_\$ \mathsf{K}(p, m_B)$ and uploads $c_B \leftarrow_\$ \mathsf{E}(k, m_B)$. If the tags of c_A and c_B match, which means $m_A = m_B$, then the server deduplicates, storing only c_A and returning it to both Alice and Bob upon a download request. Both can decrypt to recover the common plaintext. CE is a particular MLE scheme in which key generation is done by hashing the plaintext.

MLE SECURITY. BKR [12] noted that MLE can only provide security for unpredictable data. (In particular, it cannot provide semantic security.) Within this range, two data dimensions emerge:

1. <u>Correlation</u>: Security holds even when messages being encrypted, although individually unpredictable, are related to each other.

2. <u>Parameter-dependence</u>: Security holds for messages that depend on the public parameters.

These dimensions are orthogonal, and the best would be security for correlated, parameter-dependent messages. This has not been achieved. What we have is schemes for correlated but parameter-independent messages [10, 12] and for non-correlated but parameter-dependent messages [1]. This past work is summarized in Fig. 1 and we now discuss it in a little more detail.

PRIOR SCHEMES. The definition of BKR [12], following [6], was security for correlated but parameter-independent messages. For this notion they proved security of CE in the ROM, gave new, secure ROM schemes, and made partial progress towards the challenging task of security without ROs. An efficient scheme in the standard model, also for correlated but parameter-independent messages, was provided in [10] assuming UCE-secure hash functions. (Specifically, against statistically unpredictable sources.)

Abadi, Boneh, Mironov, Raghunathan and Segev (ABMRS) [1] initiated treatment of security for parameter dependent messages, which they termed lock-dependent security. Achieving this is challenging. They gave a ROM solution that uses NIZK proofs to provide proofs of consistency. But to achieve security for parameter-dependent messages they were forced to sacrifice security for correlated messages. Their result assumes messages being encrypted are independently distributed.

QUESTIONS AND GOALS. The question we pose and address in this paper is, is it possible to achieve the best of both worlds, meaning security for messages that are both correlated *and* parameter dependent? This is important in practice. As indicated above, schemes for secure deduplication are currently deployed and in use in many systems [2,4,5,18,26,27,29,35,39,46,47,52,54]. In usage, messages are very likely to be correlated. For example, suppose Alice has uploaded a ciphertext c encrypting a paper m she is writing. She edits m to m', and uploads the new version. The two plaintexts m, m' could be closely related, differing only in a few places. Also, even if messages of honest users are unlikely to depend on system parameters, attackers are not so constrained. Lack of security for parameter-dependent messages could lead to breaches. This is reflected for example in the BEAST attack on CBC in SSL/TLS [32]. We note that the question of achieving security for messages that are both correlated and parameter dependent is open both in the ROM and in the standard model.

CONTRIBUTIONS IN BRIEF. We answer the above questions by providing a deduplication scheme secure for messages that are both correlated and parameter dependent. Additionally, our scheme is standard-model, not ROM. The key new ingredient is interaction. In our solutions, upload and download are interactive protocols between the client and server. To specify and analyze these protocols, we define a new primitive, interactive MLE or iMLE. We provide a syntax and definitions of security, then specify and prove correct our protocols.

iMLE turns out to be interesting in its own right and yields some other benefits. We are able to provide the first secure deduplication scheme that permits incremental updates. This means that if a client's message changes only a little, for example due to an edit to a file, then, rather than create and upload an entirely new ciphertext, she can update the existing one with communication cost proportional only to the distance between the new and old plaintexts. This is beneficial because communication is a significant fraction of the operating expenditure in outsourced storage services. For example, transferring one giga-byte to the server costs as much storing one gigabyte for a month or longer in popular storage services [3,40,49]. In particular, backup systems, an important use case for deduplication, are likely to benefit, as the operations here are incremental by nature. Incremental cryptography was introduced in [8,9] and further studied in [14,22,34,50].

INTERACTION? One might question the introduction of interaction. Isn't a non-interactive solution preferable? Our answer is that we don't "introduce" interaction. It is already present. Upload and download in real systems is inherently and currently interactive, even in the absence of security. MLE is a cryptographic core, not a full deduplication system. If MLE is used for secure deduplication, the uploads and downloads will be interactive, even though MLE is not, due to extra flows that the full system requires. Interaction being already present, it is natural to exploit it for security. In doing so, we are taking advantage of an existing resource rather than introducing an entirely new one.

MLE considered a single client. But in a full deduplication system, there are multiple clients concurrently executing uploads and downloads. Our iMLE model captures this. iMLE is thus going further towards providing security of the full system rather than just a cryptographic core. We know from experience that systems can fail in practice even when a "proven-secure" scheme is used if the security model does not encompass the full range of attacker capabilities or security goals of the implementation. Modeling that penetrates deeper into the system, as with iMLE, increases assurance in practice.

We view iMLE as a natural extension of MLE. The latter abstracted out an elegant primitive at the heart of the secure deduplication problem that could be studied in isolation. We study the full deduplication system, leveraging MLE towards full solutions with added security features.

DUPLICATE FAKING. In a duplicate faking attack, the adversary concocts and uploads a perverse ciphertext c^* with the following property. When honest Alice uploads an encryption c of her message m, the server's test (wrongly) indicates that the plaintexts underling c^*, c are the same, so it discards c, returning c^* to Alice upon a download request. But when Alice decrypts c^*, she does not get back her original plaintext.

Beyond privacy, BKR [12] defined an integrity requirement for MLE called tag consistency whose presence provides security against duplicate faking attacks. The important tag consistency property is possessed by the prior MLE schemes of Fig. 1 and also by our new iMLE schemes.

Deterministic schemes provide tag consistency quite easily and naturally. But ABMRS [1] indicate that security for parameter-dependent messages requires randomization. Tag consistency now becomes challenging to achieve. Indeed, providing it accounts for the use of NIZKs and the corresponding cost and complexity of the ABMRS scheme [1].

In the interactive setting, we capture the requirement underlying tag consistency by a recovery condition that is part of our soundness definition and requirement. Soundness in particular precludes duplicate faking attacks in the interactive setting. Our scheme provides soundness, in addition to privacy for messages that are both correlated and parameter dependent. Our FCHECK solution uses composable point function obfuscation [17] and FHE [19–21, 28, 36, 38, 55].

CLOSER LOOK. We look in a little more detail at the main definitional and scheme contributions of our work.

Public parameters for an iMLE scheme are created by an Init algorithm. Subsequently, a client can register (Reg), upload (Put) and download (Get). Incremental schemes have an additional update (Upd). All these are interactive protocols between client and server. For soundness, we ask that deduplication happens as expected and that clients can recover their uploaded files even in the presence of an attacker which knows all the files being uploaded and also read the server's storage at any moment. The latter condition protects against duplicate-faking attacks. Our security condition is modeled on that of BKR [12] and requires privacy for correlated but individually unpredictable messages that may depend on the public parameters.

Our FCHECK construction, described and analyzed in Section 4, achieves soundness as well as privacy for messages that are both correlated and parameter dependent, all in the standard model, meaning without recourse to random oracles. The construction builds on a new primitive we call MLE-Without-Comparison (MLEWC). As the name indicates, MLEWC schemes are similar to MLE schemes in syntax and functionality, except that they do not support comparison between ciphertexts. We show that MLEWC can be realized in the standard model, starting from point function obfuscation [17] or, alternatively, UCE-secure hash function families [10]. However, comparison is essential to enable deduplication. To enable comparison, FCHECK employs an interactive protocol using a fully homomorphic encryption (FHE) scheme [19–21, 28, 36, 38, 55], transforming the MLEWC scheme into an iMLE scheme.

We then move on to the problem of incremental updates. Supporting incremental updates over MLE schemes turns out to be challenging: deterministic MLE schemes cannot support incremental updates, as we show in the full version [11], while randomized MLE schemes seem to need complex machinery such as NIZK proofs of consistency [1] to support incremental updates while retaining the same level of security as deterministic schemes, which makes them unfit for practical usage. We show how interaction can be exploited to solve this problem. We describe an efficient ROM scheme IRCE that supports incremental updates. The scheme, in its simplest form, works like the randomized convergent encryption (RCE) scheme [12], where the message is encrypted with a random key using a blockcipher in counter (CTR) mode, and the random key is encrypted with a key derived by hashing the message. We show that this indirection enables incremental updates. However, RCE does not support strong tag consistency and hence cannot offer strong security against duplicate faking attacks. We overcome this in IRCE by including a simple response from the server as part of the upload process. We remark that IRCE is based off a core MLE (non-interactive) scheme permitting incremental updates, interaction being used only for tag consistency.

Run(1^λ, P, inp)

$n \leftarrow 1; i \leftarrow 1; \text{M} \leftarrow \epsilon; \mathbf{a}[1,1] \leftarrow \text{inp}[1]; \mathbf{a}[2,1] \leftarrow \text{inp}[2]$
While $\text{T}[n] = \text{False}$
  $(\mathbf{a}[n, i+1], \text{M}, \text{T}[n]) \leftarrow_{\$} \text{P}[n,i](1^\lambda, \mathbf{a}[n,i], \text{M})$
  If $n = 2$ then $n \leftarrow 1; i \leftarrow i+1$ else $n \leftarrow 2$
Ret $\text{last}(\mathbf{a}[1]), \text{last}(\mathbf{a}[2])$

Msgs(1^λ, P, inp, r)

$n \leftarrow 1; i \leftarrow 1; j \leftarrow 1; \mathbf{a}[1,1] \leftarrow \text{inp}[1]; \mathbf{a}[2,1] \leftarrow \text{inp}[2]; \text{M} \leftarrow \epsilon$
While $\text{T}[n] = \text{False}$
  $(\mathbf{a}[n, i+1], \text{M}, \text{T}[n]) \leftarrow_{\$} \text{P}[n,i](1^\lambda, \mathbf{a}[n,i], \text{M}; r[n,i]); \quad \mathbf{M}[j] \leftarrow \text{M}; j \leftarrow j+1$
  If $n = 2$ then $n \leftarrow 1; i \leftarrow i+1$ else $n \leftarrow 2$
Ret $\mathbf{M}$

Fig. 2. Top: Running a 2-player protocol P. **Bottom:** The Msgs procedure returns the messages exchanged during the protocol when invoked with specified inputs and coins.

2 Preliminaries

We let $\lambda \in \mathbb{N}$ and 1^λ denote the security parameter and its unary representation. The empty string is denoted by ϵ. We let $|S|$ denote the size of a finite set S and let $s \leftarrow_{\$} S$ denote sampling an element from S at random and assigning it to s. If $a, b \in \mathbb{N}$ and $a < b$, then $[a]$ denotes the set $\{1, \ldots, a\}$ and $[a, b]$ denotes the set $\{a, \ldots, b\}$. For a tuple $\mathbf{x}$, we let $|\mathbf{x}|$ denote the number of components in $\mathbf{x}$, and $\mathbf{x}[i]$ denote the i-th component, and $\text{last}(\mathbf{x}) = \mathbf{x}[|\mathbf{x}|]$, and $\mathbf{x}[i, j] = \mathbf{x}[i] \ldots \mathbf{x}[j]$ for $1 \leq i \leq j \leq |\mathbf{x}|$. A binary string s is identified with a tuple over $\{0, 1\}$. The guessing probability of a random variable X, denoted by $\mathbf{GP}(X)$, is defined as $\mathbf{GP}(X) = \max_x \Pr[X = x]$. The conditional guessing probability $\mathbf{GP}(X \mid Y)$ of a random variable X given a random variable Y are defined via $\mathbf{GP}(X \mid Y) = \sum_y \Pr[Y = y] \cdot \max_x \Pr[X = x \mid Y = y]$.

The Hamming distance between $s_1, s_2 \in \{0,1\}^\ell$ is given by $\text{HAMM}(s_1, s_2) = \sum_{i=1}^\ell (s_1[i] \oplus s_2[i])$. We let $\text{patch}_{\text{HAMM}}(s_1, \delta)$ be the string s such that $s[i] = s_1[i]$ if $i \notin \delta$ and $s[i] = \neg s_1[i]$ if $i \in \delta$ and $\text{diff}_{\text{HAMM}}(s_1, s_2) = \{i : s_1[i] \neq s_2[i]\}$.

Algorithms are randomized and run in polynomial time (denoted by PT) unless otherwise indicated. We let $y \leftarrow A(a_1, \ldots; r)$ denote running algorithm A on $a_1, \ldots$ with coins r and assigning the output to y, and let $y \leftarrow_{\$} A(a_1, \ldots)$ denote the same operation with random coins. We let $[A(a_1, \ldots)]$ denote the set of all y that have non-zero probability of being output by A on inputs $a_1, \ldots$. Adversaries are either algorithms or tuples of algorithms. A negligible function f approaches zero faster than the polynomial reciprocal; for every polynomial p, there exists $n_p \in \mathbb{N}$ such that $f(n) \leq 1/p(n)$ for all $n \geq n_p$.

We use the code-based game playing framework of [16] along with extensions of [53] and [12] when specifying security notions and proofs.

A two player q-round protocol P is represented through a $2 \times q$-tuple $(\text{P}[i, j])_{i \in [2], j \in [q]}$ of algorithms where $\text{P}[i, j]$ represents the action of the i-th player invoked for the j-th time. We let $\text{P}[1]$ denote the player who initiates the protocol, and P[2] denote the other player. Each algorithm is invoked with 1^λ, an input **a**, and a message $M \in \{0,1\}^*$, and returns a 3-tuple consisting of an output **a**′, an outgoing message $M' \in \{0,1\}^*$, and a boolean T to indicate termination. The Run algorithm (Fig. 2) captures the execution of P, and Msgs (Fig. 2) returns the messages exchanged in an instance of P, when invoked with specified inputs and coins.

ADVERSARIAL MODEL. A secure deduplication system (built from an iMLE scheme) will operate in a setting with a server and several clients. Some clients will be controlled by an attacker, while others will be legitimate, belonging to honest users and following the protocol specifications. A resourceful attacker, apart from controlling clients, could gain access to server storage, and interfere with communications. Our adversarial model captures an iMLE scheme running in the presence of an attacker with such capabilities.

We now walk through an abstract game G, and explain how this is achieved. The games in the rest of the paper, for soundness, security, and other properties of iMLE largely follow this structure. The game G sets up and controls a server instance. The adversary A is invoked with access to a set of procedures. Usually, the objective of the game involves A violating some property guaranteed to legitimate clients like L, such as ability to recover stored files, or privacy of data.

The MSG procedure can send arbitrary messages to the server and can be used to create multiple clients, and run multiple instances of protocols, which could deviate from specifications.

The INIT and STEP procedures control a single legitimate client L. The INIT procedure starts protocol instances on behalf of L, using inputs of A's choice. The STEP procedure advances a protocol instance by running the next algorithm. Together, these procedures let A run several legitimate and corrupted protocol instances concurrently.

The STATE procedure returns the server's state, which includes stored ciphertexts, public parameters, etc.. In some games, it also returns the state and parameters of L. STATE provides only read access to the server's storage. This restriction is necessary. If A is allowed to modify the storage of the server, then it can always tamper with the data stored by the clients, making secure deduplication impossible.

We assume that A can read, delay and drop messages between the server and legitimate clients. However, A cannot tamper with message contents, reorder messages within a protocol, or redirect messages from one protocol instance to another. This assumption helps us simplify the protocol descriptions and proofs. Standard, efficient techniques can be used to transform the protocols from this setting to be secure in the presence of an attacker that can tamper and reorder messages [7].

3   Interactive Message-Locked Encryption

DEFINITION. An interactive message-locked encryption scheme iMLE consists of an initialization algorithm Init and three protocols Reg, Put, Get. Initialization

$\text{MAIN}(1^\lambda)$ // $\text{REC}^A_{\text{iMLE}}(1^\lambda)$	$\text{STEP}(j)$ // Advance by one step.
win ← False; σ_S ←$ $\text{Init}(1^\lambda)$	$\text{P} \leftarrow \mathbf{PS}[j]$; $n \leftarrow \text{N}[j]$; $i \leftarrow \mathbf{rd}[j]$
$\text{A}^{\text{REG,INIT,STEP,MSG,STATE}}(1^\lambda)$; Ret win	If $\text{T}[j, n]$ then return ⊥
	If $n = 2$ then inp ← σ_S else inp ← $\mathbf{a}[j, i]$
<u>REG</u> // Set up the legitimate client L.	$(\text{outp}, \text{M}[j], \text{T}[j, n]) \leftarrow\!\!\$\ \text{P}[n, i](1^\lambda, \text{inp}, \text{M}[j])$
$(\sigma_C, \sigma_S) \leftarrow\!\!\$\ \text{Run}(\text{Reg}, \epsilon, \sigma_S)$	If $n = 2$ then
	$\quad \sigma_S \leftarrow \text{outp}$; $\text{N}[j] \leftarrow 1$; $\mathbf{rd}[j] \leftarrow \mathbf{rd}[j] + 1$
$\text{INIT}(\text{P}, \text{inp})$ // Start a protocol with L.	Else $\mathbf{a}[j, i + 1] \leftarrow \text{outp}$; $\text{N}[j] \leftarrow 2$
If $\text{P} \notin \{\text{Put}, \text{Get}\}$ then ret ⊥	If $\text{T}[j, 1] \wedge \text{T}[j, 2]$ then $\text{WINCHECK}(j)$
$\text{p} \leftarrow \text{p} + 1$; $j \leftarrow \text{p}$; $\mathbf{PS}[j] = \text{P}$	Ret $\text{M}[j]$
$\mathbf{a}[j, 1] \leftarrow \text{inp}$; $\text{N}[j] \leftarrow 1$; $\text{M}[j] \leftarrow \epsilon$; Ret j	
	$\text{WINCHECK}(j)$ // Check if A has won.
	If $\mathbf{PS}[j] = \text{Put}$ then
$\text{MSG}(\text{P}, i, \text{M})$ // Send message to server.	$\quad (\sigma_C, m) \leftarrow \mathbf{a}[j, 1]$
If $\text{P} \notin \{\text{Reg}, \text{Put}, \text{Get}, \text{Upd}\}$ then ret ⊥	$\quad f \leftarrow \text{last}(\mathbf{a}[j])$; $\text{T}[f] \leftarrow m$
$(\sigma_S, \text{M}, \text{N}, \text{T}) \leftarrow\!\!\$\ \text{P}[2, i](1^\lambda, \sigma_S, \text{M})$; Ret M	If $\mathbf{PS}[j] = \text{Get}$ then
	$\quad (\sigma_C, f) \leftarrow \mathbf{a}[j, 1]$; $m' \leftarrow \text{last}(\mathbf{a}[j])$
	win ← win $\vee$ $(m' \neq T[f])$

Fig. 3. The REC game. The STATE procedure returns σ_S, σ_C.

Init sets up server-side state: $\sigma_S \leftarrow\!\!\$\ \text{Init}(1^\lambda)$. Each protocol P consists of two players - a client P[1] (meaning that the client always initiates), and a server P[2]. All server-side algorithms P[2, ·] take server-side state σ_S as input, and produce an updated state σ'_S as output. The Reg protocol registers new users; here, Reg[1] takes no input and returns client parameters $\sigma_C \in \{0, 1\}^*$. The Put protocol stores files on the server; here, Put[1] takes plaintext $m \in \{0, 1\}^*$ and σ_C as inputs, and outputs an identifier $f \in \{0, 1\}^*$. The Get protocol retrieves files from the server; here, Get[1] takes identifier f and σ_C as inputs, and outputs plaintext $m \in \{0, 1\}^*$.

SOUNDNESS. We require two conditions. First is deduplication, meaning that if a client puts a ciphertext of a file already on the server, then the storage should not grow by the size of the file. A small increase towards book-keeping information, that is independent of the size of the file, is permissible. More precisely, there exists a bound $\ell : \mathbb{N} \rightarrow \mathbb{N}$ such that for all server-side states $\sigma_S \in \{0, 1\}^*$, for all valid client parameters (derived through Reg with fresh coins) σ_C, σ'_C, for all $m \in \{0, 1\}^*$, the expected increase in size of σ''_S over σ'_S when $(f', \sigma'_S) \leftarrow\!\!\$\ \text{Run}(\text{Put}, (\sigma_C, m), \sigma_S)$ and $(f', \sigma''_S) \leftarrow\!\!\$\ \text{Run}(\text{Put}, (\sigma'_C, m), \sigma'_S)$ is bounded by $\ell(\lambda)$.

The second condition is correct recovery of files: if a legitimate client puts a file on the server, it should be able to get the file later. We formalize this requirement by the REC game of Fig. 3, played with an adversary A, which gets access to procedures REG, INIT, STEP, MSG, STATE. We provide an overview of these procedures here.

The REG procedure sets up a legitimate client L by running $\mathsf{Run}(1^\lambda, \mathsf{Reg}, (\epsilon, \sigma_S))$. The INIT procedure lets A run protocols on behalf of L. It takes input inp and P, where P has to be one of Put, Get, and inp should be the a valid input for $\mathsf{P}[1,1]$. A new instance of P is set up, and A is returned $j \in \mathbb{N}$, an index to the instance. The STEP procedure takes input j, advances the instance by one algorithm unless the current instance has terminated. The outgoing message is returned to A. The inputs and outputs of the protocol steps are all stored in an array $\mathbf{a}$. The STATE procedure returns σ_S, σ_C.

If an instance j has terminated, then STEP runs WINCHECK, which maintains a table T. If j is an instance of Put, then m and identifier f are recovered from $\mathbf{a}[j]$ and $T[f]$ gets m. If j is an instance of Get, then WINCHECK obtains f and the recovered plaintext m', and checks if $T[f] = m'$. If this fails, either because $T[f]$ is some value different from m', or is undefined, then WINCHECK sets the win flag, which is the condition for A to win the game. We associate advantage $\mathsf{Adv}^{\mathsf{rec}}_{\mathsf{iMLE},\mathsf{A}}(\lambda) = \Pr[\mathsf{REC}^{\mathsf{A}}_{\mathsf{iMLE}}(1^\lambda)]$ with iMLE and A. For recovery correctness, we require that the advantage should be negligible for all PT A.

SECURITY. The primary security requirement for iMLE schemes is privacy of unpredictable data. Unpredictability (plaintexts drawn from a distribution with negligible guessing probability) is a prerequisite for privacy in MLE schemes [12], as without unpredictability, a simple brute-force attack can recover the contents of a ciphertext by generating keys from all candidate plaintexts and checking if decrypting the ciphertext with the key leads back to the candidate plaintext. A similar argument extends unpredictability as a requirement to secure deduplication schemes as well. We formalize unpredictability as follows.

A source S is an algorithm that on input 1^λ and a string $d \in \{0,1\}^*$ returns a pair of tuples $(\mathbf{m}_0, \mathbf{m}_1)$. There exist $m : \mathbb{N} \to \mathbb{N}$ and $\ell : \mathbb{N} \times \mathbb{N} \to \mathbb{N}$ such that $|\mathbf{m}_0| = |\mathbf{m}_1| = m(\lambda)$, and $|\mathbf{m}_0[i]| = |\mathbf{m}_1[i]| = \ell(\lambda, i)$ for all $i \in [m(\lambda)]$. All components of $\mathbf{m}_0$ and $\mathbf{m}_1$ are unique. The guessing probability $\mathbf{GP}_\mathsf{S}(\lambda)$ of S is defined as $\max_{i,b,d}(\mathbf{GP}(\mathbf{m}_b[i]))$ when $(\mathbf{m}_0, \mathbf{m}_1) \leftarrow_\$ \mathsf{S}(1^\lambda, d)$. We say that S is unpredictable if $\mathbf{GP}_\mathsf{S}(\cdot)$ is negligible. We say that S is a single source if it only outputs one tuple, but satisfies the other conditions. We say that S is an auxiliary source if it outputs a string $z \in \{0,1\}^*$ along with $\mathbf{m}_0, \mathbf{m}_1$ and if it holds that guessing probability conditioned on z is negligible.

The PRIV game of Fig. 4, associated with iMLE, a source S and an adversary A, captures privacy for unpredictable messages independent of the public parameters of the system. As with REC, the game starts by running $\sigma_S \leftarrow_\$ \mathsf{Init}(1^\lambda)$ to set up the server-side state. The game then runs S to get $(\mathbf{m}_0, \mathbf{m}_1)$, picks a random bit b, and uses $\mathbf{m}_b$ as messages to be put on the server. Then, A is invoked with access to REG, PUT, STEP, MSG and STATE. The REG, STATE, and MSG oracles behave in the same way as in REC. The STEP oracle here is similar to that of REC, except that it does not invoke WINCHECK. Adversary A can initialize an instance of Put with a plaintext $\mathbf{m}_b[i]$ by calling $\mathrm{PUT}(i)$.

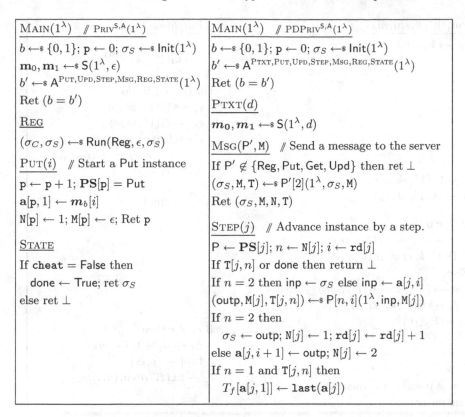

$\text{MAIN}(1^\lambda)$ // $\text{PRIV}^{S,A}(1^\lambda)$	$\text{MAIN}(1^\lambda)$ // $\text{PDPRIV}^{S,A}(1^\lambda)$
$b \leftarrow\!\!\$ \{0,1\};\ p \leftarrow 0;\ \sigma_S \leftarrow\!\!\$ \text{Init}(1^\lambda)$	$b \leftarrow\!\!\$ \{0,1\};\ p \leftarrow 0;\ \sigma_S \leftarrow\!\!\$ \text{Init}(1^\lambda)$
$m_0, m_1 \leftarrow\!\!\$ S(1^\lambda, \epsilon)$	$b' \leftarrow\!\!\$ A^{\text{PTXT,PUT,UPD,STEP,MSG,REG,STATE}}(1^\lambda)$
$b' \leftarrow\!\!\$ A^{\text{PUT,UPD,STEP,MSG,REG,STATE}}(1^\lambda)$	Ret $(b = b')$
Ret $(b = b')$	$\underline{\text{PTXT}(d)}$
$\underline{\text{REG}}$	$m_0, m_1 \leftarrow\!\!\$ S(1^\lambda, d)$
$(\sigma_C, \sigma_S) \leftarrow\!\!\$ \text{Run}(\text{Reg}, \epsilon, \sigma_S)$	$\underline{\text{MSG}(P', M)}$ // Send a message to the server
$\underline{\text{PUT}(i)}$ // Start a Put instance	If $P' \notin \{\text{Reg, Put, Get, Upd}\}$ then ret $\perp$
$p \leftarrow p + 1;\ \mathbf{PS}[p] = \text{Put}$	$(\sigma_S, M, T) \leftarrow\!\!\$ P'[2](1^\lambda, \sigma_S, M)$
$\mathbf{a}[p, 1] \leftarrow m_b[i]$	Ret (σ_S, M, N, T)
$N[p] \leftarrow 1;\ M[p] \leftarrow \epsilon;$ Ret p	$\underline{\text{STEP}(j)}$ // Advance instance by a step.
	$P \leftarrow \mathbf{PS}[j];\ n \leftarrow N[j];\ i \leftarrow \mathbf{rd}[j]$
$\underline{\text{STATE}}$	If $T[j, n]$ or done then return $\perp$
If **cheat** = False then	If $n = 2$ then inp $\leftarrow \sigma_S$ else inp $\leftarrow \mathbf{a}[j, i]$
done $\leftarrow$ True; ret σ_S	$(\text{outp}, M[j], T[j, n]) \leftarrow\!\!\$ P[n, i](1^\lambda, \text{inp}, M[j])$
else ret $\perp$	If $n = 2$ then
	$\qquad \sigma_S \leftarrow \text{outp};\ N[j] \leftarrow 1;\ \mathbf{rd}[j] \leftarrow \mathbf{rd}[j] + 1$
	else $\mathbf{a}[j, i + 1] \leftarrow \text{outp};\ N[j] \leftarrow 2$
	If $n = 1$ and $T[j, n]$ then
	$\qquad T_f[\mathbf{a}[j, 1]] \leftarrow \texttt{last}(\mathbf{a}[j])$

Fig. 4. The PRIV and PDPRIV security games. Apart from MAIN, the games share the same code for all procedures. The PDPRIV game has an additional PTXT procedure.

We associate advantage $\text{Adv}^{\text{priv}}_{\text{iMLE},S,A}(\lambda) = 2\Pr[\text{PRIV}^{S,A}_{\text{iMLE}}(1^\lambda)] - 1$ with a iMLE a source S and an adversary A. We require that the advantage should be negligible for all PT A for all unpredictable PT S.

The PDPRIV game of Fig. 4 extends PRIV-security to messages depending on the public parameters of the system, a notion termed lock-dependent security in [1]. Here, we term this parameter-dependent security. In this game, the adversary A gets access to a PTXT procedure, which runs $S(1^\lambda, \sigma_S)$ to get m_0, m_1. The other procedures follow PRIV. A simpler approach is to run S with σ_S when the game starts (i.e. in main) as in PRIV. However, this leads to trivial constructions where Init is a dummy procedure, and the system parameters are generated when the first client registers. This is avoided in PDPRIV by letting A decide, through PTXT, when S is to be run. We associate advantage $\text{Adv}^{\text{ldpriv}}_{\text{iMLE},S,A}(\lambda) = 2\Pr[\text{PDPRIV}^{S,A}_{\text{iMLE}}(1^\lambda)] - 1$ with a scheme iMLE a source S and an adversary A. We require that advantage should be negligible for all PT A for all unpredictable PT S.

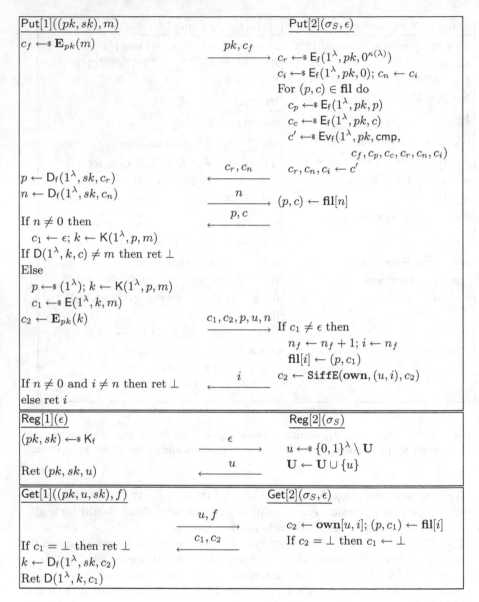

Fig. 5. The FCHECK scheme over $\mathsf{FHE} = (\mathsf{K_f}, \mathsf{E_f}, \mathsf{D_f}, \mathsf{Ev_f})$ and $\mathsf{MLEWC} = (, \mathsf{E}, \mathsf{K}, \mathsf{D})$

4 The FCHECK Scheme

In this section, we describe the the FCHECK construction, which achieves soundness as well as security for messages that are both correlated and parameter-dependent, all in the standard model. As we noted in the introduction, prior to our work, achieving parameter-dependent correlated input security was open

$\text{MAIN}(1^\lambda) \quad /\!/ \text{ WPRIV}^{S,A}(1^\lambda)$
$(\mathbf{m}_0, \mathbf{m}_1, z) \leftarrow\!\!\!\$\ S(1^\lambda, \epsilon);\ b \leftarrow\!\!\!\$\ \{0,1\}$
For $i \in [|\mathbf{m}_b|]$ do
$\quad \mathbf{p}[i] \leftarrow\!\!\!\$\ (1^\lambda);\ \mathbf{k}[i] \leftarrow\!\!\!\$\ K(1^\lambda, \mathbf{p}[i], \mathbf{m}_b[i])$
$\quad \mathbf{c}[i] \leftarrow\!\!\!\$\ E(1^\lambda, \mathbf{k}[i], \mathbf{m}_b[i])$
$b' \leftarrow\!\!\!\$\ A_2(1^\lambda, \mathbf{p}, \mathbf{c}, z);\ \text{Ret}\ (b = b')$

$\text{MAIN}(1^\lambda) \quad /\!/ \text{ CDIPFO}^{S,A}_{OS}(1^\lambda)$
$(\mathbf{p}, z) \leftarrow\!\!\!\$\ S(1^\lambda);\ b \leftarrow\!\!\!\$\ \{0,1\}$
For $i \in [|\mathbf{p}|]$ do
$\quad$ If $b = 1$ then
$\qquad (\alpha, \beta) \leftarrow \mathbf{p}[i];\ \mathsf{F}[i] \leftarrow\!\!\!\$\ \text{Obf}(1^\lambda, (\alpha, \beta))$
$\quad$ Else
$\qquad (\alpha', \beta') \leftarrow \mathbf{p}[i]\ ;\ \alpha \leftarrow\!\!\!\$\ \{0,1\}^{|\alpha'|};\ \beta \leftarrow\!\!\!\$\ \{0,1\}^{|\beta'|}$
$\qquad \mathsf{F}[i] \leftarrow\!\!\!\$\ \text{Obf}(1^\lambda, (\alpha, \beta))$
$b' \leftarrow\!\!\!\$\ A(1^\lambda, \mathsf{F}[i], z);\ \text{Ret}\ (b = b')$

Fig. 6. The WPRIV game on the left, and the and CDIPFO game on the right

even in the random oracle model. We are able to exploit interactivity as a new ingredient to design a scheme that achieves security for parameter-dependent correlated messages.

Our approach starts by going after a new, seemingly weak primitive, one we call MLE-Without-Comparison (MLEWC). As the name indicates, MLEWC schemes are similar to MLE schemes in syntax and functionality, except that they do not support comparison between ciphertexts. We show that MLEWC can be realized in the standard model, starting from point function obfuscation [17] or, alternatively, UCE-secure hash function families [10]. However, comparison is essential to enable deduplication. To enable comparison, FCHECK employs an interactive protocol using a fully homomorphic encryption (FHE) scheme [19–21,28,36,38,55], transforming the MLEWC scheme into an iMLE scheme. We view FCHECK as a theoretical construction, and not an immediately practical iMLE scheme.

MLE WITHOUT COMPARISON (MLEWC). A scheme $\mathsf{MLEWC} = (, \mathsf{E}, \mathsf{K}, \mathsf{D})$ consists of four algorithms. Parameters are generated via $p \leftarrow\!\!\!\$\ (1^\lambda)$. Keys are generated via $k \leftarrow\!\!\!\$\ K(1^\lambda, p, m)$, where $m \in \{0,1\}^{\mu(\lambda)}$ is the plaintext. Encryption E takes p, k, m and returns a ciphertext $c \leftarrow\!\!\!\$\ E(1^\lambda, k, m)$. Decryption D takes input k, c and returns $m \leftarrow D(1^\lambda, k, c)$, or $\bot$. Correctness requires that $D(1^\lambda, k, c) = m$ for all $k \in [K(1^\lambda, p, m)]$, for all $c \in [E(1^\lambda, k, m)]$, for all $p \in [(1^\lambda)]$, for all $m \in \{0,1\}^{\kappa(\lambda)}$ for all $\lambda \in \mathbb{N}$.

The WPRIV game with MLEWC, an auxiliary source S and an adversary A is described in Fig. 6. The game runs S to get two vectors $\mathbf{m}_0, \mathbf{m}_1$, and forms $\mathbf{c}$ by encrypting one of the two vectors, using a fresh parameter for each component, or by picking random strings. A should guess which the case is. We associate advantage $\mathsf{Adv}^{\mathsf{wpriv}}_{\mathsf{MLEWC},\mathsf{S},\mathsf{A}}(\lambda) = 2\Pr[\mathsf{WPRIV}^{\mathsf{A},\mathsf{S}}_{\mathsf{MLEWC}}(1^\lambda)] - 1$. For MLEWC to be WPRIV-secure, advantage should be negligible for all PT adversaries A for all unpredictable PT auxiliary sources S. Note that unlike PRIV, here, a fresh parameter is picked for each encryption, and although we will end up using WPRIV-secure schemes to build parameter-dependent iMLE, in the WPRIV game, the source S is not provided the parameters.

FULLY HOMOMORPHIC ENCRYPTION (FHE) [36]. An FHE scheme $\mathsf{FHE} = (\mathsf{K_f}, \mathsf{E_f}, \mathsf{D_f}, \mathsf{Ev_f})$ is a 4-tuple of algorithms. Key generation $\mathsf{K_f}(1^\lambda)$ returns (pk, sk), encryption $\mathsf{E_f}(1^\lambda,)$ takes pk, plaintext $m \in \mathbf{M}(\lambda)$, and returns ciphertext c, and decryption returns $m' \leftarrow \mathsf{D_f}(1^\lambda, sk, c)$ on input sk and ciphertext c, where $m = \bot$ indicates an error. The set of valid ciphertexts is denoted by $\mathbf{C}(\lambda) = \{c : \mathsf{D_f}(1^\lambda, sk, c) \neq \bot, (pk, sk) \in [\mathsf{K_f}(1^\lambda)]\}$. Decryption correctness requires that $\mathsf{D_f}(1^\lambda, sk, \mathsf{E_f}(1^\lambda, pk, m)) = m$ for all $(pk, sk) \in [\mathsf{K_f}(1^\lambda)]$, for all $m \in \mathbf{M}(\lambda)$ for all $\lambda \in \mathbb{N}$.

Let $\langle . \rangle$ denote an encoding which maps boolean circuits f to strings denoted by $\langle f \rangle$ such that there exists PT Eval which satisfies $\mathsf{Eval}(\langle f \rangle, x) = f(x)$ for every valid input $x \in \{0, 1\}^n$, where n is the input length of f. Evaluation $\mathsf{Ev_f}$ takes input a public key pk, a circuit encoding $\langle f \rangle$ and a tuple of ciphertexts $\mathbf{c}$ such that $|\mathbf{c}|$ is the input length of f and returns $c' \leftarrow_{\$} \mathsf{Ev_f}(1^\lambda, pk, \langle f \rangle, \mathbf{c})$. Evaluation correctness requires that for random keys, on all functions and all inputs, $\mathsf{Ev_f}$ must compute the correct output when run on random coins, except with negligible error.

THE FCHECK SCHEME. Let $\mathsf{FHE} = (\mathsf{K_f}, \mathsf{E_f}, \mathsf{D_f}, \mathsf{Ev_f})$ be an FHE scheme, and let $\mathsf{MLEWC} = (, \mathsf{E}, \mathsf{K}, \mathsf{D})$ be a MLEWC scheme where K is deterministic. The $\mathsf{FCHECK}[\mathsf{FHE}, \mathsf{MLEWC}]$ iMLE scheme is described in Fig. 5. The Init algorithm is omitted: it lets $\mathbf{U} \leftarrow \emptyset$, and lets **fil** and **own** be empty tables.

In FCHECK, clients encrypt their plaintexts with MLEWC to be stored on the server, but pick a fresh parameter each time. The server's storage consists of a list of ciphertext-parameter pairs $\mathbf{c}[i], \mathbf{p}[i]$. When a client wants to put m, for each such $\mathbf{c}[i], \mathbf{p}[i]$, the server should generate a key $\mathbf{k}[i] \leftarrow \mathsf{K}(1^\lambda, \mathbf{p}[i], m)$ and check if $\mathsf{D}(1^\lambda, \mathbf{k}[i], \mathbf{c}[i]) = m$.

A match means that a duplicate ciphertext already exists on the server, while no match means that m is a fresh plaintext. The search for a match should be carried without the server learning m and is hence done over FHE ciphertexts of the components. The client sends pk and $c_f \leftarrow_{\$} \mathsf{E_f}(1^\lambda, pk, m)$ and the server encrypts each $\mathbf{c}[i], \mathbf{p}[i]$ to get c_c and c_p and runs $\mathsf{Ev_f}$ on the cmp circuit described below with these values.

$\underline{\mathsf{cmp}(m, p, c, r, n, i)}$

If $\mathsf{D}(1^\lambda, \mathsf{K}(1^\lambda, p, m), c) = m$ and $r = 0^{\kappa(\lambda)}$ then return $p, i + 1, i + 1$
Else return $r, n, i + 1$

The client is provided the encryptions of r and n in the end. If $n = 0$, no match was found, and the client picks $p \leftarrow_{\$} (1^\lambda)$, computes $c \leftarrow \mathsf{E}(1^\lambda, \mathsf{K}(1^\lambda, p, m), m)$, and sends p, c to be stored on the server. Otherwise, n refers to the index of the match, and serves as the tag, and r refers to the parameter in the match.

Now the client computes $k \leftarrow \mathsf{K}(1^\lambda, r, m)$, encrypts it under its private key, and stores the result on the server. The Reg and Get protocols proceed in a simple manner, and are described in Fig. 5. It can be checked that FCHECK performs deduplication as expected, and we show this formally in the full version.

$\mathsf{E}(1^\lambda, k_\mathsf{H}, k, m)$	$\mathsf{D}(1^\lambda, k_\mathsf{H}, k, c_0, \ldots c_n)$
$c_0 \leftarrow\!\!{\$}\ \mathsf{Obf}(1^\lambda, k, 0))$	If $\mathsf{Eval}(1^\lambda, c_0, k) = \perp$ then ret $\perp$
For $i \in [\lvert m \rvert]$ do	For $i \in [n]$ do
$\quad c_i \leftarrow\!\!{\$}\ \mathsf{Obf}(1^\lambda, k \lVert \langle i, \ell \rangle \lVert m[i], 0)$	$\quad$ If $\mathsf{Eval}(1^\lambda, c_i, k \lVert \langle i, \ell \rangle \lVert 0) = 1$ then
Ret $c_0, \ldots c_{\lvert m \rvert}$	$\qquad m_i \leftarrow 0$
	$\quad$ else $m_i \leftarrow 1$
	Ret $m_1 \lVert \ldots \lVert m_n$

Fig. 7. The HtO MLEWC scheme, with a CR hash HF and a point obfuscation scheme OS. Here, parameters are generated via (1^λ) which runs $\mathsf{K_h}(1^\lambda)$ and returns the output, while message-derived keys are generated by letting $\mathsf{K}(1^\lambda, k_\mathsf{H}, m)$ return $k \leftarrow \mathsf{H}(1^\lambda, k_\mathsf{H}, m)$.

Theorem 1. *If* MLEWC *is a correct* MLEWC *scheme then* FCHECK[MLEWC, FHE] *is* REC-*secure.*

Proof Sketch. Observe that that whenever a client puts m, and a match is found in Put[2, 1], the client asks for the p, c pair corresponding to the index with the match, and checks by itself that this pair is a valid ciphertext for m. This, combined with the immutability of **fil** and **own** leads to perfect recovery correctness.

Theorem 2. *If* MLEWC *is* WPRIV-*secure and* FHE *is* CPA-*secure, then* FCHECK[MLEWC, FHE] *is* PDPRIV-*secure.*

Proof Sketch. We replace the c_2 components with encryptions of random strings, and use the CPA security of FHE to justify this. Now, only the **p, c** pairs of the plaintexts reside on the server, and hence we can hope to show that if there exists an adversary A that can guess the challenge bit from only the **p, c** values, then such an A can be used to build another adversary B which breaks WPRIV security of MLEWC.

But this cannot be accomplished right away. When A asks the game to run Put with some $\mathbf{m}_b[i]$, then B cannot simulate Put[2, 1] which looks through **p, c** for a match for $\mathbf{m}_b[i]$ without knowing $\mathbf{m}_b[i]$. The proof first gets rid of the search step in Put[2, 1] and then builds B. We argue that the search step can be avoided. The adversary A, with no knowledge of the messages that the unpredictable source S produced, would have been able to use MSG to put a ciphertext for a $\mathbf{m}_b[i]$ only with negligible probability.

CONSTRUCTING MLEWC SCHEMES. To get an iMLE scheme via FCHECK, we still need to construct a MLEWC scheme. The lack of comparison means that MLEWC schemes should be easier to construct compared to MLE schemes, but constructions must still overcome two technical challenges: encrypting messages with keys derived from the messages themselves, and dealing with correlated messages. We explore two approaches to overcoming these two challenges. The first utilizes a special kind of point-function obfuscation scheme, and the second uses a UCE-secure [10] hash function. This construction, which we describe in the full version. is straightforward. We start with a hash function family, $\mathsf{HF} = (\mathsf{K_h}, \mathsf{H})$. Parameter generation picks a hash key k_H. Given m, the key is generated as $k \leftarrow \mathsf{H}(1^\lambda, k_\mathsf{H}, m, 1^\lambda)$, and ciphertext as $c \leftarrow \mathsf{H}(1^\lambda, k_\mathsf{H}, k, 1^{|m|}) \oplus m$. Decryption, on input k, c removes the mask to recover m.

We now elaborate on the first approach, which builds a MLEWC scheme from a composable distributional indistinguishable point-function obfuscation scheme (CDIPFO) [17]. To give a high level idea for why CDIPFOs are useful, we note that point-function obfuscation is connected to encryption secure when keys and messages are related [25]. Moreover, CDIPFOs, due to their composability, remain secure even when obfuscations of several correlated points are provided and thus enable overcoming the two challenges described above.

Let $\alpha, \beta \in \{0,1\}^*$. We let $\phi_{\alpha,\beta} : \{0,1\}^* \to \{\beta, \perp\}$ denote the function that on input $\gamma \in \{0,1\}^*$ returns β if $\gamma = \alpha$, and $\perp$ otherwise. We call α the special input, and β the special output. A point function obfuscator $\mathsf{OS} = (\mathsf{Obf}, \mathsf{Eval})$ is a pair of algorithms. Obfuscation takes (α, β) and outputs $\mathsf{F} \leftarrow_\$ \mathsf{Obf}(1^\lambda, (\alpha, \beta))$, while Eval takes F, and a point γ and returns $y \leftarrow_\$ \mathsf{Eval}(1^\lambda, \mathsf{F}, \gamma)$. Correctness requires that $\mathsf{Eval}(1^\lambda, \mathsf{Obf}(1^\lambda, \alpha, \beta), \alpha) = \beta$ for all $\alpha, \beta \in \{0,1\}^*$, for all $\lambda \in \mathbb{N}$.

A PF source S outputs a tuple of point pairs $\mathbf{p}$, along with auxiliary information z. There exist $m : \mathbb{N} \to \mathbb{N}$ and $\ell : \mathbb{N} \times \mathbb{N} \to \mathbb{N}$ such that $|\mathbf{p}| = m(\lambda)$, and $|\mathbf{p}[i,0]| = \ell(\lambda, 0)$ and $|\mathbf{p}[i,1]| = \ell(\lambda, 1)$ for all $i \in [m(\lambda)]$. Guessing probability $\mathbf{GP_S}(\lambda)$ is defined as $\max_i(\mathbf{GP}(\mathbf{p}[i,0]|z))$ when $(\mathbf{p}, z) \leftarrow_\$ \mathsf{S}(1^\lambda)$. We say that S is unpredictable if $\mathbf{GP_S}(\cdot)$ is negligible.

Distributional indistinguishability for point function obfuscators is captured by the CDIPFO game (Fig. 6) associated with OS, an PF source S, and an adversary A. At a high level, the game either provides OS-obfuscations of point functions from S, or from a uniform distribution, and to win, the adversary A should guess which the case is. We associate advantage $\mathsf{Adv}^{\mathsf{cdipfo}}_{\mathsf{OS},\mathsf{S},\mathsf{A}}(\lambda) = 2 \Pr[\mathrm{CDIPFO}^{\mathsf{A},\mathsf{S}}_{\mathsf{OS}}(1^\lambda)] - 1$ with OS, S and A and say that OS is CDIPFO-secure if advantage is negligible for all PT A for all unpredictable PT S. Bitansky and Canetti show that CDIPFOs can be built in the standard model, from the t-Strong Vector Decision Diffie Hellman assumption [17].

Let $\mathsf{HF} = (\mathsf{K_h}, \mathsf{H})$ denote a family of CR hash functions. The Hash-then-Obfuscate transform $\mathsf{HtO}[\mathsf{HF}, \mathsf{OS}] = (, \mathsf{E}, \mathsf{K}, \mathsf{D})$ associates an MLEWC scheme with HF and OS as in Fig. 7, restricting the message space to ℓ-bit strings. At a high level, a key is generated by hashing the plaintext m with HF, and m is obfuscated bit-by-bit, with the hash as the special input. Decryption, given the hash, can recover m from the obfuscations. Correctness follows from the correctness of OS, and the following theorem shows WPRIV-security.

Theorem 3. *If* HF *is* CR-secure, *and* OS *is* CDIPFO-secure, *then* HtO[HF, OS] *is* WPRIV-secure.

The proof of the theorem and some remarks on HtO appear in the full version.

5 Incremental Updates

In this section, we define iMLE with incremental updates, and provide a construction which achieves this goal. Building MLE schemes which can support incremental updates turns out to be challenging. On the one hand, it is easy to show that deterministic MLE schemes cannot support incremental updates. We elaborate on this in full version. On the other hand, randomized MLE schemes seem to need complex machinery such as NIZK proofs of consistency [1] to support incremental updates while retaining the same level of security as deterministic schemes, which makes them unfit for practical usage. We show how interaction can be exploited to achieve incremental updates in a practical manner, by building an efficient ROM iMLE scheme IRCE that supports incremental updates. We fix Hamming distance as the metric. In the full version, we define incremental updates w.r.t edit distance, and extend IRCE to work in this setting.

An interactive message-locked encryption scheme iMLE with updates supports an additional protocol Upd along with the usual three protocols Reg, Put, and Get. The Upd protocol updates a ciphertext of a file m_1 stored on the server to a ciphertext of an updated file m_2. Here, Upd[1] (i.e. the client-side algorithm) takes inputs f, σ_C, and two plaintexts m_1, m_2, and outputs a new identifier $f_2 \in \{0,1\}^*$.

Now, the REC game (Fig. 3) which asks for correct recovery of files also imposes conditions on update, namely that if a legitimate client puts a file on the server, it should be able to get the file later along with updates made to the file. This is captured by letting the adversary pick Upd as the protocol in the INIT procedure. The WINCHECK procedure, which checks if the adversary has won, is now invoked at successful runs of Upd additionally. It infers the value of f used in the update protocol as well as the updated plaintext m_2 and sets $T[f] \leftarrow m_2$, thus letting the adversary to win if a get at f does not return m_2.

We say that a scheme iMLE has incremental updates if the communication cost of updating a ciphertext for m_1 stored on the server to a ciphertext for m_2 is a linear function of $\mathrm{HAMM}(m_1, m_2)$ and $\log |m_2|$. More formally, there exists a linear function $u : \mathbb{N} \times \mathbb{N} \rightarrow \mathbb{N}$ such that for all client parameters σ_C, for all server-side states $\sigma_S \in \{0,1\}^*$, for all plaintexts $m_1, m_2 \in \{0,1\}^*$ such that $|m_1| = |m_2|$, for all coins r_1, r_2, for all $f \in \{0,1\}^*$, if $(m_1, \sigma_S') \leftarrow \mathrm{Run}(\mathrm{Get}, (\sigma_C, f), \sigma_S; r_1)$, and $(f', \sigma_S'') \leftarrow \mathrm{Run}(\mathrm{Upd}, (\sigma_C, m_1, m_2), \sigma_S; r_2)$, and $f' \neq \perp$, then $|\mathrm{Msgs}(\mathrm{Upd}, (\sigma_C, m_1, m_2), \sigma_S; r_2)| \leq \mathrm{HAMM}(m_1, m_2) u(\log |m_1|, \lambda)$.

PRELIMINARIES. A deterministic symmetric encryption (D-SE) scheme SE = (E, D) is a pair of algorithms, where encryption returns $c \leftarrow E(1^\lambda, k, m)$ on input plaintext $m \in \{0,1\}^*$ and key $k \in \{0,1\}^{\kappa(\lambda)}$, and decryption returns $m \leftarrow D(1^\lambda, k, c)$. Correctness requires $D(1^\lambda, k, E(1^\lambda, k, m)) = m$ for all plaintexts

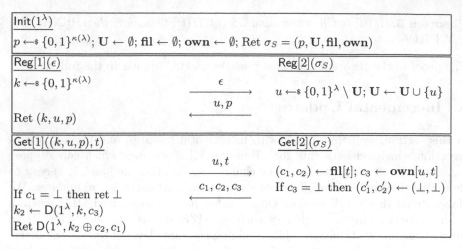

Fig. 8. The Init algorithm, and Reg and Get protocols of the IRCE iMLE scheme

$m \in \{0,1\}^*$ for all keys $k \in \{0,1\}^{\kappa(\lambda)}$ for all $\lambda \in \mathbb{N}$. We say that SE supports incremental updates w.r.t Hamming distance if there exists an algorithm U such that $U(1^\lambda, E(1^\lambda, k, m_1), \text{diff}(m_1, m_2)) = E(1^\lambda, k, m_2)$ for all plaintexts $m_1, m_2 \in \{0,1\}^*$ for all keys $k \in \{0,1\}^{\kappa(\lambda)}$ for all $\lambda \in \mathbb{N}$.

Key-recovery security is defined through game $\text{KR}_{\text{SE}}^{\text{A}}(1^\lambda)$ which lets adversary A query an oracle ENC with a plaintext m then picks $k \leftarrow_{\$} \{0,1\}^{\kappa(\lambda)}$ and returns $E(1^\lambda, k, m)$; A wins if it can guess k.

The CPA security game $\text{CPA}_{\text{SE}}^{\text{A}}(1^\lambda)$, picks $b \leftarrow_{\$} \{0,1\}$ and $k \leftarrow_{\$} \kappa(\lambda)$, runs A with access to ENC, and responds to queries m by returning $c \leftarrow E(k, m)$ if $b = 1$ and returning a random $|c|$-bit string if $b = 0$. To win, the adversary should guess b. We define advantages $\text{Adv}_{\text{SE,A}}^{\text{kr}}(\lambda) = \Pr[\text{KR}_{\text{SE}}^{\text{A}}(1^\lambda)]$ and $\text{Adv}_{\text{SE,A}}^{\text{cpa}}(\lambda) = 2 \cdot \Pr[\text{CPA}_{\text{SE}}^{\text{A}}(1^\lambda)] - 1$ and say that SE is KR-secure (resp. CPA-secure) if $\text{Adv}_{\text{SE,A}}^{\text{kr}}(\cdot)$ (resp. $\text{Adv}_{\text{SE,A}}^{\text{cpa}}(\cdot)$) is negligible for all PT A. The CTR mode of operation over a blockcipher, with a fixed IV is an example of a D-SE scheme with incremental updates, and KR and CPA security.

A hash function H with $\kappa(\lambda)$-bit keys is a PT algorithm that takes $p \in \{0,1\}^{\kappa(\lambda)}$ and a plaintext m returns hash $h \leftarrow H(p, m)$. Collision resistance is defined through game $\text{CR}_{\text{H}}^{\text{A}}(1^\lambda)$, which picks $p \leftarrow_{\$} \{0,1\}^{\kappa(\lambda)}$, runs adversary $A(1^\lambda, p)$ to get m_0, m_1, and returns True if $m_0 \neq m_1$ and $H(p, m_1) = H(p, m_2)$. We say that H is collision resistant if $\text{Adv}_{\text{H,A}}^{\text{cr}}(\lambda) = \Pr[\text{CR}_{\text{H}}^{\text{A}}(1^\lambda)]$ is negligible for all PT A.

A table T is immutable if each entry $T[t]$ can be assigned only one value after initialization. Immutable tables supports the Set-iff-empty, or SiffE operation, which takes inputs a table T, an index f, and a value m. If $T[f] = \bot$ then $T[f] \leftarrow m$ and m is returned; otherwise $T[f]$ is returned.

THE IRCE SCHEME. Let H denote a hash function with $\kappa(\lambda)$-bit keys and $\kappa(\lambda)$-bit outputs, and let $\mathsf{SE} = (\mathsf{E}, \mathsf{D})$ denote a D-SE scheme with $\kappa(\lambda)$-bit keys, where ciphertexts have same lengths as plaintexts and incremental updates are supported through an algorithm U. The IMLE scheme IRCE[SE, H] is described in figures 8 and 9. We call the construction IRCE, expanding to interactive randomized convergent encryption. since it resembles the randomized convergent encryption (RCE) scheme of [12].

To describe how IRCE works, let us consider a IMLE scheme built around RCE. In RCE, to put m on the server, the client encrypts m with a random key ℓ to get c_1, and then encrypts ℓ with $k_m = \mathsf{H}(p, m)$ to get c_2, where p is a system-wide public parameter. Then, k_m is hashed once more to get the tag $t = \mathsf{H}(p, k_m)$. The client sends t, c_1, c_2 and the server stores c_1, c_2 in a table **fil** at index t. If another client starts with m, it will end up with the same t, although it will derive a different c_1', c_2', as ℓ is picked at random. However, when this client sends t, c_1', c_2', the server knows that **fil**$[t]$ is not empty, meaning a duplicate exists, and hence will drop c_1', c_2', thereby achieving deduplication. The second client should be able to recover m by sending t to the server, receiving c_1, c_2, recovering ℓ from c_2 and decrypting c_1. However, the problem with RCE is that, when the first client sends t, c_1, c_2, the server has no way of checking whether c_1, c_2 is a proper ciphertext of m, or a corrupted one. Thus, the second client, in spite of storing a ciphertext of m on the server might not be able to recover m — this violates our soundness requirement. We will now fix this issue with interaction.

The Put protocol in IRCE differs in that, if the server finds that **fil**$[t] \neq \perp$ then it responds with h, c_2', where $(c_1', c_2') \leftarrow$ **fil**$[t]$ and $h \leftarrow \mathsf{H}(p, c_1')$. Now, the client can check that $\mathsf{H}(p, \mathsf{E}(1^\lambda, c_2' \oplus k_m, m)) = h$ which means that whenever deduplication happens, the client can check the validity of the duplicate ciphertext, which in turn guarantees soundness. The Put protocol is specified in Fig. 9, and is a bit more involved than our sketch here. Specifically, the clients are assigned unique identifiers which are provided during Put. The message-derived key k_m is also encrypted to get c_3 (under per-client keys) and stored on the server, in a separate table **own**, which enables checking that a client starting a get protocol with an identifier did put the file earlier. If the client is the first to put a ciphertext with tag t, then the server still returns $\mathsf{H}(p, c_1), c_2, c_3$ so that external adversaries cannot learn if deduplication occurred. We note that in Fig. 9, the **fil** and **own** tables are immutable, and this will help in arguing soundness of the scheme.

The Init algorithm (Fig. 8) sets up the **fil** and **own** tables, and additional server-side state, and picks a key p for H, which becomes the public-parameter of the system. The Reg protocol (Fig. 9) sets up a new client by creating a unique client identifier u, and providing the client p. The client also picks a secret key k without the involvement of the server. The Get protocol (Fig. 9) recovers a plaintext from the identifier, which in the case of IRCE is the tag.

IRCE supports incremental updates, as described in Fig. 9. If the client wants to update m to m_2, it does not have to resend all of c_1, c_2, c_3. Instead, it can use the same key ℓ and incrementally update c_1, and compute new values for c_2

$\mathsf{Put}[1]((k,u,p),m)$	$\mathsf{Put}[2](\sigma_S)$
$\ell \leftarrow\!\!\$ \ \{0,1\}^{\kappa(\lambda)}; \ c_1 \leftarrow \mathsf{E}(1^\lambda, \ell, m)$	
$k_m \leftarrow \mathsf{H}(p,m); \ c_2 \leftarrow k_m \oplus \ell; \ c_3 \leftarrow$	
$\mathsf{E}(1^\lambda, k, k_m)$	
$t \leftarrow \mathsf{H}(p, k_m)$	

$$\xrightarrow{\quad u, c_1, c_2, c_3, t \quad} \quad (c_1, c_2) \leftarrow \mathsf{SiffE}(\mathbf{fil}, t, c_1, c_2)$$
$$h \leftarrow \mathsf{H}(p, c_1)$$
$$\xleftarrow{\quad h, c_2', c_3' \quad} \quad c_3 \leftarrow \mathsf{SiffE}(\mathbf{own}, (u,t), c_3)$$

If $c_3 \neq c_3'$ then ret $\perp$	
$\ell' \leftarrow c_2' \oplus k_m$	
$c_1'' \leftarrow \mathsf{E}(1^\lambda, \ell', m)$	
$h' \leftarrow \mathsf{H}(p, c_1'')$	
If $h = h'$ then ret t Else ret $\perp$	

$\mathsf{Upd}[1]((k,u,p), t, m_1, m_2)$	$\mathsf{Upd}[2](\sigma_S)$
$k_1 \leftarrow \mathsf{H}(p, m_1); \ k_2 \leftarrow \mathsf{H}(p, m_2)$	
$\delta \leftarrow \mathsf{diff}(m_1, m_2); \ t_2 \leftarrow \mathsf{H}(p, k_2)$	
$c_d \leftarrow k_1 \oplus k_2; \ t_1 \leftarrow \mathsf{H}(p, k_1)$	
$c_3 \leftarrow \mathsf{E}(1^\lambda, k, k_2)$	

$$\xrightarrow{\quad u, t_1, t_2, c_3, c_d, \delta \quad}$$

If $\mathbf{own}[u, t_1] \neq \perp$ then
$\quad c_3 \leftarrow \mathsf{SiffE}(\mathbf{own}, (u,t), c_3)$
$\quad c_1, c_2 \leftarrow \mathbf{fil}[t_1]$
$\quad c_1' \leftarrow \mathsf{patch}(c_1, \delta)$
$\quad c_2' \leftarrow c_2 \oplus c_d$
$\quad (c_1', c_2') \leftarrow \mathsf{SiffE}(\mathbf{fil}, t_2, c_1', c_2')$
Else $(c_1', c_2') \leftarrow (\perp, \perp)$
$h \leftarrow \mathsf{H}(p, c_1')$

$$\xleftarrow{\quad h, c_2', c_3' \quad}$$

If $c_3 \neq c_3'$ then ret $\perp$	
$c_1'' \leftarrow \mathsf{E}(1^\lambda, c_2' \oplus k_2, m_2); \ h' \leftarrow \mathsf{H}(p, c_1'')$	
If $h = h'$ then ret t_2; Else ret $\perp$	

Fig. 9. The Put and Upd protocols of the IRCE iMLE scheme. The **fil** and **own** tables are immutable, and support the set-iff-empty operation (SiffE) explained in text.

and c_3, along with the new tag t_2. If the server finds that $\mathbf{fil}[t_2]$ is not empty, the same check as in Put is performed.

It is easy to see that IRCE performs deduplication, and supports incremental updates. In the full version, we formally state and prove the deduplication and incremental updates properties. We also provide a proof of the following theorem which shows that IRCE is REC-secure (which, along with deduplication, establishes soundness).

Theorem 4. *If* H *is collision resistant and* SE *is a correct D-SE scheme, then* IRCE[H, SE] *is* REC-*secure.*

Proof Sketch. To win the REC game, the adversary A must put a plaintext m on the server, possibly update it to some m', complete a Get instance with the identifier for m or m' and show that the result is incorrect.

The proof uses the immutability of **fil** and **own** to argue that the ciphertext stored in the server could not have changed between the failed Get instance and the last time the plaintext was put/updated. However, Put and Upd both ensure that the hash of the ciphertext stored on the server matches with the hash of a correctly formed ciphertext for the plaintext being put/updated. Consequently, whenever A breaks REC-security, it is in effect finding a pair of colliding inputs, namely the hash inputs involved in the comparison. A CR adversary B can be built which has the same advantage as the REC-advantage of A.

The following theorem (the proof of which appears in the full version) shows that IRCE is PRIV-secure in the ROM, assuming that SE is secure. Let $IRCE_{RO}$ denote the ROM analogue of IRCE, formed by modelling H as a random oracle.

Theorem 5. *If* SE *is* CPA-*secure and* KR-*secure, then* $IRCE_{RO}[SE]$ *is* PRIV-*secure.*

Proof Sketch. In PRIV, the source S outputs $\mathbf{m}_0, \mathbf{m}_1$, the game picks $b \leftarrow_\$ \{0,1\}$ and adversary A can put and update components of $\mathbf{m}_b$, and finally gets to learn the server-side state. To win, A should guess b.

First, the c_3 components are changed to encrypt random strings instead of message-derived keys $\mathbf{k}_m[i]$; CPA security of SE makes this change indistinguishable by A. The proof then moves to a game where RO responses are no longer consistent with the keys and tags being generated. For instance, if S or A queries the RO at $p\|\mathbf{m}_b[i]$, it gets a response different from $\mathbf{k}_m[i]$. The remainder of the proof involves two steps. First, we show that once we stop maintaining RO consistency, the adversary gets no information about the ℓ values used to encrypt the messages, and hence guessing b means breaking either the CPA security or key recovery security of SE. Second, we argue that neither S nor A can detect that RO responses are inconsistent. This is because S does not know p, a prefix to the key and tag generation queries. An A that detects the inconsistency will break the CPA security of SE.

Acknowledgments. We thank the PKC 2015 reviewers for their valuable comments. Bellare was supported in part by NSF grants CNS-1228890 and CNS-1116800. Work done while Keelveedhi was at UCSD, supported in part by NSF grants CNS-1228890 and CNS-1116800.

References

1. Abadi, M., Boneh, D., Mironov, I., Raghunathan, A., Segev, G.: Message-locked encryption for lock-dependent messages. In: Canetti, R., Garay, J.A. (eds.) CRYPTO 2013, Part I. LNCS, vol. 8042, pp. 374–391. Springer, Heidelberg (2013)
2. Adya, A., Bolosky, W., Castro, M., Cermak, G., Chaiken, R., Douceur, J., Howell, J., Lorch, J., Theimer, M., Wattenhofer, R.: Farsite: Federated, available, and reliable storage for an incompletely trusted environment. ACM SIGOPS Operating Systems Review **36**(SI), 1–14 (2002)

3. Amazon: S3. http://aws.amazon.com/s3/pricing/
4. Anderson, P., Zhang, L.: Fast and secure laptop backups with encrypted de-duplication. In: Proc. of USENIX LISA (2010)
5. Batten, C., Barr, K., Saraf, A., Trepetin, S.: pStore: A secure peer-to-peer backup system. Unpublished report, MIT Laboratory for Computer Science (2001)
6. Bellare, M., Boldyreva, A., O'Neill, A.: Deterministic and efficiently searchable encryption. In: Menezes, A. (ed.) CRYPTO 2007. LNCS, vol. 4622, pp. 535–552. Springer, Heidelberg (2007)
7. Bellare, M., Canetti, R., Krawczyk, H.: A modular approach to the design and analysis of authentication and key exchange protocols (extended abstract). In: 30th ACM STOC, pp. 419–428. ACM Press, May 1998
8. Bellare, M., Goldreich, O., Goldwasser, S.: Incremental cryptography: the case of hashing and signing. In: Desmedt, Y.G. (ed.) CRYPTO 1994. LNCS, vol. 839, pp. 216–233. Springer, Heidelberg (1994)
9. Bellare, M., Goldreich, O., Goldwasser, S.: Incremental cryptography and application to virus protection. In: 27th ACM STOC, pp. 45–56. ACM Press, May June 1995
10. Bellare, M., Hoang, V.T., Keelveedhi, S.: Instantiating random oracles via uces. Cryptology ePrint Archive, Report 2013/424 (2013). Preliminary version in Crypto 2013
11. Bellare, M., Keelveedhi, S.: Interactive message-locked encryption and secure dedu-plication. Cryptology ePrint Archive (2015). Preliminary version in PKC 2015
12. Bellare, M., Keelveedhi, S., Ristenpart, T.: Message-locked encryption and secure deduplication. In: Johansson, T., Nguyen, P.Q. (eds.) EUROCRYPT 2013. LNCS, vol. 7881, pp. 296–312. Springer, Heidelberg (2013)
13. Bellare, M., Kohno, T.: A theoretical treatment of related-key attacks: RKA-PRPs, RKA-PRFs, and applications. In: Biham, E. (ed.) EUROCRYPT 2003. LNCS, vol. 2656, pp. 491–506. Springer, Heidelberg (2003)
14. Bellare, M., Micciancio, D.: A new paradigm for collision-free hashing: incremen-tality at reduced cost. In: Fumy, W. (ed.) EUROCRYPT 1997. LNCS, vol. 1233, pp. 163–192. Springer, Heidelberg (1997)
15. Bellare, M., Rogaway, P.: Entity authentication and key distribution. In: Stinson, D.R. (ed.) CRYPTO 1993. LNCS, vol. 773, pp. 232–249. Springer, Heidelberg (1994)
16. Bellare, M., Rogaway, P.: The security of triple encryption and a framework for code-based game-playing proofs. In: Vaudenay, S. (ed.) EUROCRYPT 2006. LNCS, vol. 4004, pp. 409–426. Springer, Heidelberg (2006)
17. Bitansky, N., Canetti, R.: On strong simulation and composable point obfusca-tion. In: Rabin, T. (ed.) CRYPTO 2010. LNCS, vol. 6223, pp. 520–537. Springer, Heidelberg (2010)
18. Bitcasa: Bitcasa inifinite storage.
http://blog.bitcasa.com/tag/patented-de-duplication/
19. Brakerski, Z.: Fully homomorphic encryption without modulus switching from clas-sical GapSVP. In: Safavi-Naini, R., Canetti, R. (eds.) CRYPTO 2012. LNCS, vol. 7417, pp. 868–886. Springer, Heidelberg (2012)
20. Brakerski, Z., Vaikuntanathan, V.: Efficient fully homomorphic encryption from (standard) LWE. In: Ostrovsky, R. (ed.) 52nd FOCS, pp. 97–106. IEEE Computer Society Press, October 2011
21. Brakerski, Z., Vaikuntanathan, V.: Fully homomorphic encryption from ring-lwe and security for key dependent messages. In: Rogaway, P. (ed.) CRYPTO 2011. LNCS, vol. 6841, pp. 505–524. Springer, Heidelberg (2011)

22. Buonanno, E., Katz, J., Yung, M.: Incremental unforgeable encryption. In: Matsui, M. (ed.) FSE 2001. LNCS, vol. 2355, pp. 109–124. Springer, Heidelberg (2002)
23. Canetti, R.: Universally composable security: A new paradigm for cryptographic protocols. In: 42nd FOCS, pp. 136–145. IEEE Computer Society Press, October 2001
24. Canetti, R., Dakdouk, R.R.: Obfuscating point functions with multibit output. In: Smart, N.P. (ed.) EUROCRYPT 2008. LNCS, vol. 4965, pp. 489–508. Springer, Heidelberg (2008)
25. Canetti, R., Kalai, Y.T., Varia, M., Wichs, D.: On symmetric encryption and point obfuscation. In: Micciancio, D. (ed.) TCC 2010. LNCS, vol. 5978, pp. 52–71. Springer, Heidelberg (2010)
26. Ciphertite: Ciphertite data backup. https://www.cyphertite.com/faq.php
27. Cooley, J., Taylor, C., Peacock, A.: ABS: the apportioned backup system. MIT Laboratory for Computer Science (2004)
28. Coron, J.-S., Mandal, A., Naccache, D., Tibouchi, M.: Fully homomorphic encryption over the integers with shorter public keys. In: Rogaway, P. (ed.) CRYPTO 2011. LNCS, vol. 6841, pp. 487–504. Springer, Heidelberg (2011)
29. Cox, L.P., Murray, C.D., Noble, B.D.: Pastiche: making backup cheap and easy. SIGOPS Oper. Syst. Rev. **36**, 285–298 (2002)
30. Douceur, J., Adya, A., Bolosky, W., Simon, D., Theimer, M.: Reclaiming space from duplicate files in a serverless distributed file system. In: Proceedings. 22nd International Conference on Distributed Computing Systems, pp. 617–624. IEEE (2002)
31. Dropbox: Deduplication in Dropbox. https://forums.dropbox.com/topic.php?id=36365
32. Duong, T., Rizzo, J.: Here come the ninjas. Unpublished manuscript (2011)
33. Dutch, M.: Understanding data deduplication ratios. In: SNIA Data Management Forum (2008)
34. Fischlin, M.: Incremental cryptography and memory checkers. In: Fumy, W. (ed.) EUROCRYPT 1997. LNCS, vol. 1233, pp. 393–408. Springer, Heidelberg (1997)
35. Flud: The Flud backup system. http://flud.org/wiki/Architecture
36. Gentry, C.: Fully homomorphic encryption using ideal lattices. In: Mitzenmacher, M. (ed.) 41st ACM STOC, pp. 169–178. ACM Press, May June 2009
37. Gentry, C., Halevi, S.: Implementing gentry's fully-homomorphic encryption scheme. In: Paterson, K.G. (ed.) EUROCRYPT 2011. LNCS, vol. 6632, pp. 129–148. Springer, Heidelberg (2011)
38. Gentry, C., Halevi, S., Smart, N.P.: Fully homomorphic encryption with polylog overhead. In: Pointcheval, D., Johansson, T. (eds.) EUROCRYPT 2012. LNCS, vol. 7237, pp. 465–482. Springer, Heidelberg (2012)
39. GNUnet: GNUnet, a framework for secure peer-to-peer networking. https://gnunet.org/
40. Google: Blob store. https://developers.google.com/appengine/docs/pricing
41. Google: Google Drive. http://drive.google.com
42. Goyal, V., O'Neill, A., Rao, V.: Correlated-input secure hash functions. In: Ishai, Y. (ed.) TCC 2011. LNCS, vol. 6597, pp. 182–200. Springer, Heidelberg (2011)
43. Halevi, S., Harnik, D., Pinkas, B., Shulman-Peleg, A.: Proofs of ownership in remote storage systems. In: Proceedings of the 18th ACM Conference on Computer and Communications Security, pp. 491–500. ACM (2011)
44. Harnik, D., Pinkas, B., Shulman-Peleg, A.: Side channels in cloud services: Deduplication in cloud storage. IEEE Security & Privacy **8**(6), 40–47 (2010)

45. Katz, J., Vaikuntanathan, V.: Round-optimal password-based authenticated key exchange. In: Ishai, Y. (ed.) TCC 2011. LNCS, vol. 6597, pp. 293–310. Springer, Heidelberg (2011)
46. Killijian, M., Courtès, L., Powell, D., et al.: A survey of cooperative backup mechanisms (2006)
47. Marques, L., Costa, C.: Secure deduplication on mobile devices. In: Proceedings of the 2011 Workshop on Open Source and Design of Communication, pp. 19–26. ACM (2011)
48. Meister, D., Brinkmann, A.: Multi-level comparison of data deduplication in a backup scenario. In: Proceedings of SYSTOR 2009: The Israeli Experimental Systems Conference, p. 8. ACM (2009)
49. Microsoft: Windows Azure. http://www.windowsazure.com/en-us/pricing/details/storage/
50. Mironov, I., Pandey, O., Reingold, O., Segev, G.: Incremental deterministic public-key encryption. In: Pointcheval, D., Johansson, T. (eds.) EUROCRYPT 2012. LNCS, vol. 7237, pp. 628–644. Springer, Heidelberg (2012)
51. NetApp: NetApp. http://www.netapp.com/us/products/platform-os/dedupe.aspx
52. Rahumed, A., Chen, H., Tang, Y., Lee, P., Lui, J.: A secure cloud backup system with assured deletion and version control. In: 2011 40th International Conference on Parallel Processing Workshops (ICPPW), pp. 160–167. IEEE (2011)
53. Ristenpart, T., Shacham, H., Shrimpton, T.: Careful with composition: limitations of the indifferentiability framework. In: Paterson, K.G. (ed.) EUROCRYPT 2011. LNCS, vol. 6632, pp. 487–506. Springer, Heidelberg (2011)
54. Storer, M., Greenan, K., Long, D., Miller, E.: Secure data deduplication. In: Proceedings of the 4th ACM International Workshop on Storage Security and Survivability, pp. 1–10. ACM (2008)
55. van Dijk, M., Gentry, C., Halevi, S., Vaikuntanathan, V.: Fully homomorphic encryption over the integers. In: Gilbert, H. (ed.) EUROCRYPT 2010. LNCS, vol. 6110, pp. 24–43. Springer, Heidelberg (2010)

Faster ECC over $\mathbb{F}_{2^{521}-1}$

Robert Granger[1]([✉]) and Michael Scott[2]

[1] Laboratory for Cryptologic Algorithms, School of Computer and Communication Sciences, École polytechnique fédérale de Lausanne, 1015 Lausanne, Switzerland
robbiegranger@gmail.com
[2] CertiVox Labs, Dublin, Ireland
mike.scott@certivox.com

Abstract. In this paper we present a new multiplication algorithm for residues modulo the Mersenne prime $2^{521} - 1$. Using this approach, on an Intel Haswell Core i7-4770, constant-time variable-base scalar multiplication on NIST's (and SECG's) curve P-521 requires 1,108,000 cycles, while on the recently proposed Edwards curve E-521 it requires just 943,000 cycles. As a comparison, on the same architecture openSSL's ECDH speed test for curve P-521 requires 1,319,000 cycles. Furthermore, our code was written entirely in C and so is robust across different platforms. The basic observation behind these speedups is that the form of the modulus allows one to multiply residues with as few word-by-word multiplications as is needed for squaring, while incurring very little overhead from extra additions, in contrast to the usual Karatsuba methods.

Keywords: Elliptic curve cryptography · Performance · P-521 · E-521 · Edwards curves · Generalised repunit primes · Crandall numbers · Karatsuba

1 Introduction

Nearly all research on elliptic curve cryptography (ECC) focuses on improving efficiency, the bedrock of which is efficient field arithmetic. Amongst prime fields the multiply-then-reduce paradigm suggests that arithmetic modulo the Mersenne primes $M_k = 2^k - 1$ should be optimal, since modular reduction can be effected by a single modular addition, as is well known. Within this paradigm, research on fast modular multiplication has naturally tended to focus on reducing the cost of the reduction step. This rationale led Solinas in 1999 to introduce *Generalised Mersenne Numbers* (GMNs), five of which feature in the NIST (FIPS 186-2) [17] and SECG [18] standards for use in ECC, ranging in size from 192 to 521 bits, all with fast modular reduction. Solinas' reduction method regards both the output of an integer by integer residue multiplication and the modulus as polynomials in a base $t = 2^w$, with w the word size of the underlying architecture. Reducing the former polynomial modulo the latter then gives an algebraic modular reduction that requires only a few modular additions and/or subtractions and possibly a few final subtractions of the modulus.

© International Association for Cryptologic Research 2015
J. Katz (Ed.): PKC 2015, LNCS 9020, pp. 539–553, 2015.
DOI: 10.1007/978-3-662-46447-2_24

However, more recent approaches to modular multiplication at bitlengths relevant to ECC do not adhere to the multiply-then-reduce paradigm. In particular, Chung and Hasan [10] proposed a slight modification of Solinas' method, viewing it as a two stage process, with residues also regarded as polynomials in base t. For generic residue coefficients, the product of two residues modulo the modulus polynomial is precomputed. Then in the first stage these coefficient expressions are evaluated on the input coefficients; in the second stage the resulting coefficients are renormalised by expanding them in base t and performing the required carries. This small shift in perspective somewhat interleaves the multiplication and reduction steps, and allows one to use a smaller base than before. Using a smaller base is useful since it firstly allows more primes to be represented, and secondly it means that the coefficient evaluations need not overflow beyond double precision on the underlying architecture. The latter property has been applied numerous times [2,3,6,9,11,12,16,19] and is now standard.

Another example of when it is advantageous to allow the form of the modulus to influence how one multiplies residues is for the Mersenne numbers M_k, for $k \to \infty$. In particular, modular multiplication can be carried out using a cyclic convolution effected by an irrational-base discrete weighted transform (IBDWT) [16, §6], whereas for integer multiplication a linear convolution is required, as each multiplicand must be padded with k zeros before a cyclic convolution of length $2k$ can be performed. Hence multiplication modulo a Mersenne number is asymptotically approximately twice as fast as integer multiplication.

Unfortunately, Fast Fourier Transform techniques are not effective at ECC bitlengths and hence can not be applied to M_{521}. However, using a more natural alternative generalisation of the Mersenne numbers than Solinas proposed – already known in the literature as *Generalised Repunit Primes* (GRPs) – Granger and Moss described a modular multiplication algorithm that is surprisingly fast, being about three times faster than Montgomery multiplication for primes of around 600 bits, on a 2.2GHz Intel Core 2 Duo [19]. GRPs are those of the form $\sum_{i=0}^{p-1} t^i$ for prime p and integer $t > 1$. Although they have many attractive features, the only example in the standards is M_{521} with $t = 2$, but in this case t is too small to take advantage of these features.

In this paper we show that one can use an analogue of the multiplication technique of [19] to speed up multiplication modulo M_{521}. For demonstration purposes this operation – as well as constant-time variable-base scalar multiplication – has been implemented in C on a 3.4GHz Intel Haswell Core i7-4770, which has yielded interesting speedups. In particular, on NIST's (and SECG's) curve P-521 this requires 1,108,000 cycles, while on the recently proposed Edwards curve E-521 it requires just 943,000 cycles. As a comparison, on the same architecture openSSL's ECDH speed test for curve P-521 requires 1,319,000 cycles. We note that the Edwards curve E-521 is a particularly attractive target for implementors; according to the safecurves website [5] this curve has been proposed independently three times, by Bernstein-Lange, Hamburg, and Aranha *et al.* [1]. It addresses all of the recent concerns regarding the security of NIST curves (as well as others), having been generated in a deterministic pseudorandom manner while being twist-secure, complete and permitting point representations which are indistinguishable from uniform random strings [4].

Although not described as such, the technique of [19] which forms the basis of our multiplication speedup can be viewed as a 'twisted' version of Karatsuba's trick [21], albeit one in which the form of the modulus lends itself very favourably. Its effectiveness therefore runs counter to conventional wisdom which posits that Karatsuba-like techniques are not efficient at bitlengths relevant to ECC (at least on 64-bit architectures), due to the high number of extra additions required. A recent proposal by Bernstein, Chuengsatiansup and Lange also uses a variation of Karatsuba for fast multiplication modulo $2^{414} - 17$ [3], with efficiencies being extracted at a much lower level than we use in the present paper; indeed *two* Karatsuba levels are used, as well as a clever method to reduce inputs to the required multiplications, rather than outputs (cf. [3, Section 4.6]). Their implementation on the 32-bit ARM Cortex-A8 also exploits vectorisation to great effect. While not directly comparable to Bernstein *et al.*'s implementation, one advantage of our implementation is that it is written entirely in C; it therefore has robust performance characteristics across a range of 64 bit platforms. Having said that, we naturally expect that further optimisations are possible, both on the demonstration and similar architectures, and especially on ARM processors, due to their higher multiplication-to-addition cost ratio. We therefore encourage others to explore these possibilities; our software is freely downloadable, see Section 4.3.

To a lesser extent, our same basic observation may be applied to so-called Crandall numbers, i.e., those of the form $2^k - c$ for c usually much smaller than the word size of the underlying architecture, and we provide two examples of how this may be done.

The sequel is organised as follows. In Section 2 we explain our basic observation, while in Section 3 we show how it may be applied to M_{521}, giving squaring and inversion routines as well. In Section 4 we provide details of the target curves and our implementation results, while in Section 5 we describe how our basic observation may be applied to Crandall numbers. We conclude in Section 6.

2   The Basic Observation

The best way to describe our basic observation is via an example. For an integer t let the modulus be $t^9 - 1$ and let the base t expansion of residues x and y be $\sum_{i=0}^{8} x_i t^i$ and $\sum_{i=0}^{8} y_i t^i$ respectively. For convenience, we also denote x by $\overline{\mathbf{x}} = [x_0, \ldots, x_8]$ and y by $\overline{\mathbf{y}} = [y_0, \ldots, y_8]$.

The multiplication of $\overline{\mathbf{x}}$ and $\overline{\mathbf{y}}$ mod $t^9 - 1$ is just their cyclic convolution; in particular, if $\overline{\mathbf{z}} \equiv \overline{\mathbf{x}}\,\overline{\mathbf{y}} \pmod{t^9 - 1}$ then $\overline{\mathbf{z}} = [z_0, \ldots, z_8] =$

$$[x_0y_0 + x_1y_8 + x_2y_7 + x_3y_6 + x_4y_5 + x_5y_4 + x_6y_3 + x_7y_2 + x_8y_1,$$
$$x_0y_1 + x_1y_0 + x_2y_8 + x_3y_7 + x_4y_6 + x_5y_5 + x_6y_4 + x_7y_3 + x_8y_2,$$
$$x_0y_2 + x_1y_1 + x_2y_0 + x_3y_8 + x_4y_7 + x_5y_6 + x_6y_5 + x_7y_4 + x_8y_3,$$
$$x_0y_3 + x_1y_2 + x_2y_1 + x_3y_0 + x_4y_8 + x_5y_7 + x_6y_6 + x_7y_5 + x_8y_4,$$

$$x_0y_4 + x_1y_3 + x_2y_2 + x_3y_1 + x_4y_0 + x_5y_8 + x_6y_7 + x_7y_6 + x_8y_5, \qquad (2.1)$$
$$x_0y_5 + x_1y_4 + x_2y_3 + x_3y_2 + x_4y_1 + x_5y_0 + x_6y_8 + x_7y_7 + x_8y_6,$$
$$x_0y_6 + x_1y_5 + x_2y_4 + x_3y_3 + x_4y_2 + x_5y_1 + x_6y_0 + x_7y_8 + x_8y_7,$$
$$x_0y_7 + x_1y_6 + x_2y_5 + x_3y_4 + x_4y_3 + x_5y_2 + x_6y_1 + x_7y_0 + x_8y_8,$$
$$x_0y_8 + x_1y_7 + x_2y_6 + x_3y_5 + x_4y_4 + x_5y_3 + x_6y_2 + x_7y_1 + x_8y_0].$$

The coefficients in this expression are about twice the size of t; we assume that t is selected in such a way that there is no overflow beyond double the initial precision of the coefficients. The arithmetic cost of a direct evaluation of each coefficient is then nine coefficient multiplications and eight double length additions, which we count as (and denote by) $9M + 16A$. This gives a total cost of $81M + 144A$.

For bitlengths relevant to ECC it is not beneficial to use asymptotically efficient FFT-based (cyclic) convolutions, as suggested in [14] and as are used for the Lucas-Lehmer primality test for Mersenne numbers, see [15, 16]. However, one can exploit some of the symmetry of (2.1) as follows. Let $s = \sum_{i=0}^{8} x_i y_i$. Then $\bar{z}$ may also be expressed as

$$
\begin{aligned}
[\, & s - (x_1 - x_8)(y_1 - y_8) - (x_2 - x_7)(y_2 - y_7) - (x_3 - x_6)(y_3 - y_6) - (x_4 - x_5)(y_4 - y_5), \\
& s - (x_1 - x_0)(y_1 - y_0) - (x_2 - x_8)(y_2 - y_8) - (x_3 - x_7)(y_3 - y_7) - (x_4 - x_6)(y_4 - y_6), \\
& s - (x_5 - x_6)(y_5 - y_6) - (x_2 - x_0)(y_2 - y_0) - (x_3 - x_8)(y_3 - y_8) - (x_4 - x_7)(y_4 - y_7), \\
& s - (x_5 - x_7)(y_5 - y_7) - (x_2 - x_1)(y_2 - y_1) - (x_3 - x_0)(y_3 - y_0) - (x_4 - x_8)(y_4 - y_8), \\
& s - (x_5 - x_8)(y_5 - y_8) - (x_6 - x_7)(y_6 - y_7) - (x_3 - x_1)(y_3 - y_1) - (x_4 - x_0)(y_4 - y_0), \qquad (2.2) \\
& s - (x_5 - x_0)(y_5 - y_0) - (x_6 - x_8)(y_6 - y_8) - (x_3 - x_2)(y_3 - y_2) - (x_4 - x_1)(y_4 - y_1), \\
& s - (x_5 - x_1)(y_5 - y_1) - (x_6 - x_0)(y_6 - y_0) - (x_7 - x_8)(y_7 - y_8) - (x_4 - x_2)(y_4 - y_2), \\
& s - (x_5 - x_2)(y_5 - y_2) - (x_6 - x_1)(y_6 - y_1) - (x_7 - x_0)(y_7 - y_0) - (x_4 - x_3)(y_4 - y_3), \\
& s - (x_5 - x_3)(y_5 - y_3) - (x_6 - x_2)(y_6 - y_2) - (x_7 - x_1)(y_7 - y_1) - (x_8 - x_0)(y_8 - y_0)].
\end{aligned}
$$

The cost of computing s is $9M + 16A$. The subsequent cost of each coefficient evaluation is $4M + 16A$, since each term costs two single length additions and one double length addition, and there are four terms. Hence the total cost is now $45M + 160A$, giving a saving of $36M$ at the cost of $16A$. This new expression for $\bar{z}$ is of course very reminiscent of Karatsuba's method [21]. Indeed, it only (repeatedly) uses the identity $x_i y_j + x_j y_i = x_i y_i + x_j y_j - (x_i - x_j)(y_i - y_j)$, which is a slight twist of the more common version $x_i y_j + x_j y_i = (x_i + x_j)(y_i + y_j) - x_i y_i - x_j y_j$. Using the 'twisted' version means that precisely the same s term appears in each coefficient, thus saving several additions.

In general, for the modulus $t^n - 1$, evaluating the cyclic convolution using the schoolbook method costs $n^2 M + 2n(n-1)A$, whereas using our basic observation it costs $\frac{1}{2}n(n+1)M + 2(n^2 - 1)A$. This is the same number of multiplications required for squaring with the schoolbook method; this is because the same symmetry is being exploited, however for squaring one can simply express $x_i x_j + x_j x_i$ as $2x_i x_j$. One thus saves nearly half the number of multiplications while incurring very little overhead from extra additions. Hence even at small bitlengths for which the schoolbook method for integer multiplication is faster than Karatsuba techniques, one expects this method to give a speedup for multiplication modulo

$t^n - 1$. A related result which applies in the context of integer multiplication can be found in [23].

Note that if one instead uses the modulus $p = \sum_{i=0}^{n-1} t^i$ then s need not even be computed, since the first term of the i-th coefficient contributes st^i, which altogether gives $s \sum_{i=0}^{n-1} t^i \equiv 0 \pmod{p}$. This was the rationale behind the proposal of Granger and Moss to use GRPs for ECC [19].

3   Application to $M_{521} = 2^{521} - 1$

In this section we show how our basic observation may be applied to the Mersenne prime $M_{521} = 2^{521} - 1$. For the interested reader, we point out that Crandall and Pomerance used this prime to demonstrate Crandall's asymptotically fast algorithm for multiplication modulo Mersenne numbers which uses an IBDWT [13, Alg. 9.5.19]. This algorithm provides a method to obtain integer coefficients when mimicking an irrational-base expansion of residues and of course exploits the cyclic convolution far more cleverly than we do here, but it is not efficient for such small bitlengths.

In order to use the basic observation, first observe that one should not set $t = 2$ and $n = 521$, as this would involve far too much redundancy and too many multiplications. On a 64-bit architecture residues mod p require $\lceil 521/64 \rceil = 9$ words, so what one would like to do is set $n = 9$ and use the irrational base $t = 2^{521/9}$ while using integer coefficients only, either à la Crandall or à la Bernstein's method for performing arithmetic modulo $2^{255} - 19$ [2], which uses the irrational base $2^{25.5}$. It turns out that for our prime of interest, the analogue of Bernstein's method is nothing but operand scaling [24,25]. Since this is easier to explain, we do so here.

Observe that $521 \equiv 8 \pmod{9}$. Hence one can work modulo $2p = t^9 - 2$ instead of p, with $t = 2^{58}$. This representation was used by Langley in OpenSSL 1.0.0e in September 2011, which greatly improved efficiency relative to the base 2^{64} approach[1]. The multiplication formulae are now slightly different; if $\bar{z} \equiv \bar{x}\,\bar{y}$ $\pmod{t^9 - 2}$ then $\bar{z} = [z_0, \ldots, z_8] =$

$$
\begin{aligned}
[&x_0y_0+2x_1y_8+2x_2y_7+2x_3y_6+2x_4y_5+2x_5y_4+2x_6y_3+2x_7y_2+2x_8y_1, \\
&x_0y_1+ \ x_1y_0+2x_2y_8+2x_3y_7+2x_4y_6+2x_5y_5+2x_6y_4+2x_7y_3+2x_8y_2, \\
&x_0y_2+ \ x_1y_1+ \ x_2y_0+2x_3y_8+2x_4y_7+2x_5y_6+2x_6y_5+2x_7y_4+2x_8y_3, \\
&x_0y_3+ \ x_1y_2+ \ x_2y_1+ \ x_3y_0+2x_4y_8+2x_5y_7+2x_6y_6+2x_7y_5+2x_8y_4, \\
&x_0y_4+ \ x_1y_3+ \ x_2y_2+ \ x_3y_1+ \ x_4y_0+2x_5y_8+2x_6y_7+2x_7y_6+2x_8y_5, \\
&x_0y_5+ \ x_1y_4+ \ x_2y_3+ \ x_3y_2+ \ x_4y_1+ \ x_5y_0+2x_6y_8+2x_7y_7+2x_8y_6, \\
&x_0y_6+ \ x_1y_5+ \ x_2y_4+ \ x_3y_3+ \ x_4y_2+ \ x_5y_1+ \ x_6y_0+2x_7y_8+2x_8y_7, \\
&x_0y_7+ \ x_1y_6+ \ x_2y_5+ \ x_3y_4+ \ x_4y_3+ \ x_5y_2+ \ x_6y_1+ \ x_7y_0+2x_8y_8, \\
&x_0y_8+ \ x_1y_7+ \ x_2y_6+ \ x_3y_5+ \ x_4y_4+ \ x_5y_3+ \ x_6y_2+ \ x_7y_1+ \ x_8y_0].
\end{aligned}
\tag{3.1}
$$

---

[1] We independently implemented our multiplication for curve P-521 using this representation in the summer of 2011, but have decided to publish only now due to the recent interest in alternative elliptic curves over M_{521}.

Algorithm 1. MUL

INPUT: $\overline{\mathbf{x}} = [x_0, \ldots, x_8], \overline{\mathbf{y}} = [y_0, \ldots, y_8] \in [-2^{59}, 2^{59} - 1] \times [0, 2^{58} - 1]^8$
OUTPUT: $\overline{\mathbf{z}} \in [-2^{59}, 2^{59} - 1] \times [0, 2^{58} - 1]^8$ where $\overline{\mathbf{z}} \equiv \overline{\mathbf{x}} \cdot \overline{\mathbf{y}} \pmod{t^9 - 2}$

1. $t_0 \leftarrow x_0 y_0 + x_1 y_1 + x_2 y_2 + x_3 y_3 + x_4 y_4$
2. $t_5 \leftarrow x_5 y_5, \ t_6 \leftarrow x_6 y_6, \ t_7 \leftarrow x_7 y_7, \ t_8 \leftarrow x_8 y_8$
3. $t_1 \leftarrow t_5 + t_6 + t_7 + t_8$
4. $t_2 \leftarrow t_0 + t_1 - (x_0 - x_8)(y_0 - y_8) - (x_1 - x_7)(y_1 - y_7)$
     $\qquad - (x_2 - x_6)(y_2 - y_6) - (x_3 - x_5)(y_3 - y_5)$
5. $t_0 \leftarrow t_0 + 4t_1$
6. $t_1 \leftarrow t_2 \bmod t$
7. $t_3 \leftarrow t_0 - (x_4 - 2x_5)(y_4 - 2y_5) - (x_3 - 2x_6)(y_3 - 2y_6)$
     $\qquad - (x_2 - 2x_7)(y_2 - 2y_7) - (x_1 - 2x_8)(y_1 - 2y_8) + 2(t_2 >> 58)$
8. $z_0 \leftarrow t_3 \bmod t$
9. $t_0 \leftarrow t_0 - 2t_5$
10. $t_2 \leftarrow t_0 - (x_0 - x_1)(y_0 - y_1) - (x_4 - 2x_6)(y_4 - 2y_6)$
     $\qquad - (x_2 - 2x_8)(y_2 - 2y_8) - (x_3 - 2x_7)(y_3 - 2y_7) + (t_3 >> 58)$
11. $z_1 \leftarrow t_2 \bmod t$
12. $t_0 \leftarrow t_0 - t_5$
13. $t_3 \leftarrow t_0 - (x_0 - x_2)(y_0 - y_2) - (x_5 - 2x_6)(y_5 - 2y_6)$
     $\qquad - (x_3 - 2x_8)(y_3 - 2y_8) - (x_4 - 2x_7)(y_4 - 2y_7) + (t_2 >> 58)$
14. $z_2 \leftarrow t_3 \bmod t$
15. $t_0 \leftarrow t_0 - 2t_6$
16. $t_2 \leftarrow t_0 - (x_0 - x_3)(y_0 - y_3) - (x_1 - x_2)(y_1 - y_2)$
     $\qquad - (x_4 - 2x_8)(y_4 - 2y_8) - (x_5 - 2x_7)(y_5 - 2y_7) + (t_3 >> 58)$
17. $z_3 \leftarrow t_2 \bmod t$
18. $t_0 \leftarrow t_0 - t_6$
19. $t_3 \leftarrow t_0 - (x_0 - x_4)(y_0 - y_4) - (x_1 - x_3)(y_1 - y_3)$
     $\qquad - (x_5 - 2x_8)(y_5 - 2y_8) - (x_6 - 2x_7)(y_6 - 2y_7) + (t_2 >> 58)$
20. $z_4 \leftarrow t_3 \bmod t$
21. $t_0 \leftarrow t_0 - 2t_7$
22. $t_2 \leftarrow t_0 - (x_0 - x_5)(y_0 - y_5) - (x_1 - x_4)(y_1 - y_4)$
     $\qquad - (x_2 - x_3)(y_2 - y_3) - (x_6 - 2x_8)(y_6 - 2y_8) + (t_3 >> 58)$
23. $z_5 \leftarrow t_2 \bmod t$
24. $t_0 \leftarrow t_0 - t_7$
25. $t_3 \leftarrow t_0 - (x_0 - x_6)(y_0 - y_6) - (x_1 - x_5)(y_1 - y_5)$
     $\qquad - (x_2 - x_4)(y_2 - y_4) - (x_7 - 2x_8)(y_7 - 2y_8) + (t_2 >> 58)$
26. $z_6 \leftarrow t_3 \bmod t$
27. $t_0 \leftarrow t_0 - 2t_8$
28. $t_2 \leftarrow t_0 - (x_0 - x_7)(y_0 - y_7) - (x_1 - x_6)(y_1 - y_6)$
     $\qquad - (x_2 - x_5)(y_2 - y_5) - (x_3 - x_4)(y_3 - y_4) + (t_3 >> 58)$
29. $z_7 \leftarrow t_2 \bmod t$
30. $t_3 \leftarrow t_1 + (t_2 >> 58)$
31. $z_8 \leftarrow t_3 \bmod t$
32. $z_0 \leftarrow z_0 + 2(t_3 >> 58)$
33. Return $\overline{\mathbf{z}}$

Algorithm 2. SQR

INPUT: $\overline{\mathbf{x}} = [x_0, \ldots, x_8] \in [-2^{59}, 2^{59} - 1] \times [0, 2^{58} - 1]^8$
OUTPUT: $\overline{\mathbf{z}} \in [-2^{59}, 2^{59} - 1] \times [0, 2^{58} - 1]^8$ where $\overline{\mathbf{z}} \equiv \overline{\mathbf{x}}^2 \pmod{t^9 - 2}$

1. $t_1 = 2(x_0 x_8 + x_1 x_7 + x_2 x_6 + x_3 x_5) + x_4^2$
2. $t_0 = t_1 \bmod t$
3. $t_2 = 4(x_1 x_8 + x_2 x_7 + x_3 x_6 + x_4 x_5) + x_0^2 + 2(t_1 >> 58)$
4. $z_0 = t_2 \bmod t$
5. $t_1 = 4(x_2 x_8 + x_3 x_7 + x_4 x_6) + 2(x_0 x_1 + x_5^2) + (t_2 >> 58)$
6. $z_1 = t_1 \bmod t$
7. $t_2 = 4(x_3 x_8 + x_4 x_7 + x_5 x_6) + 2 x_0 x_2 + x_1^2 + (t_1 >> 58)$
8. $z_2 = t_2 \bmod t$
9. $t_1 = 4(x_4 x_8 + x_5 x_7) + 2(x_0 x_3 + x_1 x_2 + x_6^2) + (t_2 >> 58)$
10. $z_3 = t_1 \bmod t$
11. $t_2 = 4(x_5 x_8 + x_6 x_7) + 2(x_0 x_4 + x_1 x_3) + x_2^2 + (t_1 >> 58)$
12. $z_4 = t_2 \bmod t$
13. $t_1 = 4 x_6 x_8 + 2(x_0 x_5 + x_1 x_4 + x_2 x_3 + x_7^2) + (t_2 >> 58)$
14. $z_5 = t_1 \bmod t$
15. $t_2 = 4 x_7 x_8 + 2(x_0 x_6 + x_1 x_5 + x_2 x_4) + x_3^2 + (t_1 >> 58)$
16. $z_6 = t_2 \bmod t$
17. $t_1 = 2(x_0 x_7 + x_1 x_6 + x_2 x_5 + x_3 x_4 + x_8^2) + (t_2 >> 58)$
18. $z_7 = t_1 \bmod t$
19. $t_2 = t_0 + (t_1 >> 58)$
20. $z_8 = t_2 \bmod t$
21. $z_0 = z_0 + 2(t_2 >> 58)$
22. Return $\overline{\mathbf{z}}$

There are several possible approaches to applying the basic observation to (3.1), all of which incur a slight overhead relative to (2.2) due to the presence of the factors of 2. For the target architecture, the most efficient one we found is presented in Algorithm 1, which computes and reduces each component of $\overline{\mathbf{z}}$ sequentially. We first detail how we represent residues.

Residue Representation: It is a simple matter to represent a mod p residue x in the form $\overline{\mathbf{x}} = [x_0, \ldots, x_8]$ by taking the base $t = 2^{58}$ expansion. Since we wish to allow negative coefficients, we use signed integers. Due to our choice of reduction method, we stipulate that the first component x_0 in our *reduced format* is in $[-2^{59}, 2^{59} - 1]$ while the remaining components are in $[0, 2^{58} - 1]$, although these bounds are not enforced except for the output coordinates of point addition and doubling.

Multiplication and Squaring: Algorithms 1 and 2 detail pseudocode for our multiplication and squaring routines respectively. Observe that in both algorithms the wrap-around from z_8 to z_0 is computed twice. This is to ensure that there is at most one bit of overflow beyond 58 bits for z_0. One could instead rotate the order in which terms are computed so that the term that is computed twice is $(t_i \gg 58)$ rather than $2(t_i \gg 58)$, which would save one shift operation. However, we chose to keep the components $z_1, \ldots, z_8 \geq 0$ with only z_0 possibly being negative, since this allows one to check whether a given residue is zero or one without mapping back to the integer residue representation.

Addition, subtraction, inversion and multiplication by small constants:
Addition and subtraction are performed component-wise and need not be reduced if the result is used as input to a multiplication or squaring. Constant-time inversion is performed by powering by $M_{521} - 2 = 2^{521} - 3$. Let x be the element to be inverted and denote $x^{2^n - 1}$ by α_n, so $\alpha_1 = x$. Then the inverse of x can be computed at a cost of $520S + 13M$, as follows:

$$\alpha_2 \leftarrow \alpha_1^2 \cdot \alpha_1$$
$$\alpha_3 \leftarrow \alpha_2^2 \cdot \alpha_1$$
$$\alpha_6 \leftarrow \alpha_3^{2^3} \cdot \alpha_3$$
$$\alpha_7 \leftarrow \alpha_6^2 \cdot \alpha_1$$
$$\alpha_8 \leftarrow \alpha_7^2 \cdot \alpha_1$$
$$\alpha_{16} \leftarrow \alpha_8^{2^8} \cdot \alpha_8$$
$$\alpha_{32} \leftarrow \alpha_{16}^{2^{16}} \cdot \alpha_{16}$$
$$\alpha_{64} \leftarrow \alpha_{32}^{2^{32}} \cdot \alpha_{32}$$
$$\alpha_{128} \leftarrow \alpha_{64}^{2^{64}} \cdot \alpha_{64}$$
$$\alpha_{256} \leftarrow \alpha_{128}^{2^{128}} \cdot \alpha_{128}$$
$$\alpha_{512} \leftarrow \alpha_{256}^{2^{256}} \cdot \alpha_{256}$$
$$\alpha_{519} \leftarrow \alpha_{512}^{2^7} \cdot \alpha_7$$
$$x^{2^{521}-3} \leftarrow \alpha_{519}^{2^2} \cdot \alpha_1$$

This inversion technique is an analogue of the one used by Bernstein for curve25519 [2]; it may be possible to reduce the number of multiplications slightly, however this would only have a marginal impact on the efficiency. One could alternatively use Bos' technique [7], but since inversion is required only once during a point multiplication we did not explore this option on the present architecture.

Multiplication by small constants (such as by d for Edwards curves, see Section 4.2) are computed per component and are reduced in-place. We also employ a *short coefficient reduction* (SCR) routine which takes as input a residue $\overline{x} = [x_0, \ldots, x_8] \in [-2^{63}, 2^{63} - 1] \times [-2^{62}, 2^{62} - 1]^8$ and outputs one in reduced form. For both multiplication by small constants and SCR, the wrap-around from z_8 to z_0 is computed twice, as with multiplication and squaring.

4   Curves and Implementation Results

In this section we detail our target curves and implementation results for constant-time variable-base scalar multiplication.

4.1   NIST Curve P-521

The Weierstrass form NIST curve P-521 as standardised in [17,18] has the form $y^2 = x^3 - 3x + b$, with

$b = 1093849038073734274511112390766805569936207598951683748994586394495953116150735$
$0160137087375737596232485921322967063133094384525315910129121423274884784985984,$

and group order

$r_P = 6864797660130609714981900799081393217269435300143305409394463459185543183397655$
$3942450577463332171975329639963713633211138647686124403803403728088927 07005449.$

Using Jacobian projective coordinates, for $P_1 = (X_1, Y_1, Z_1)$ the point $2P_1 = (X_3, Y_3, Z_3)$ is computed as follows:

$$R_0 = Z_1^2, \quad R_1 = Y_1^2, \quad R_2 = X_1 \cdot R_1, \quad R_3 = 3(X_1 + R_0)(X_1 - R_0),$$
$$X_3 = R_3^2 - 8R_2, \quad Z_3 = (Y_1 + Z_1)^2 - R_0 - R_1, \quad Y_3 = R_3 \cdot (4R_2 - X_3) - 8R_1^2.$$

For a point $P_2 = (X_2, Y_2, 1)$ written in affine form which is not equal to P_1, let $P_3 = (X_3, Y_3, Z_3) = P_1 + P_2$. Then P_3 is computed as follows:

$$R_0 = Z_1^2, \quad R_1 = X_2 \cdot R_0, \quad R_2 = Y_2 \cdot Z_1 \cdot R_0, \quad R_3 = R_1 - X_1, \quad R_4 = R_3^2$$
$$R_5 = 4R_4, \quad R_6 = R_3 \cdot R_5, \quad R_7 = 2(R_2 - Y_1), \quad R_8 = X_1 \cdot R_5$$
$$X_3 = R_7^2 - R_6 - 2R_8, \quad Y_3 = R_7(R_8 - X_3) - 2Y_1 R_6, \quad Z_3 = (Z_1 + R_3)^2 - R_0 - R_4.$$

For efficiency we fused several of the required arithmetic operations. As these are standard techniques we do not detail them here, but they may be found in our freely downloadable software.

In order to achieve constant-time variable-base point multiplication, we used Algorithm 1 of [8] with fixed windows of width 5. Cache safety comes at a significant cost; the whole pre-computed table must be processed in order to silently (in the side-channel sense) extract the correct entry without indicating via cache activity which element has been accessed. This militates against larger tables, and also against point representations with multiple coordinates. The method we used is closely related to that described by Käsper [22].

Note that since the cost of inversion is about $365M$ (as may be deduced from Table 1 and the formula $I = 520S + 13M$), one should not convert all the precomputed points to affine coordinates as this only saves 5M per addition, which is unlikely to outweigh the cost of doing so. One method of precomputation which uses Chudnovsky coordinates is detailed in Algorithm 4 of [8]; we instead use Jacobian projective coordinates as above. For a scalar in $[0, \ldots, 2^{521} - 1]$, in terms of multiplications and squarings only, the cost for a constant-time variable-base scalar multiplication is: $168M + 80S$ for precomputation, plus $2704M + 3120S$ for the windowing plus $16M + 521S$ for the final map to affine coordinates, giving a total cost of $2888M + 3721S$.

4.2   Edwards Curve E-521

The Edwards curve E-521 is defined by $x^2 + y^2 = 1 - 376014x^2y^2$ and has group order $4r_E$ where

$$r_E = 1716199415032652428745475199770483043173588250358263523486158647963857958494413$$
$$675475876651663657849636693659065234142604319282948702542317993421293670108523.$$

Point addition, doubling and constant-time point multiplication proceed using exactly the same coordinate systems and formulae described in [3] for curve41417, the only differences being that we use fixed windows of width 4 rather than 5 and multipliers of bitlength 519 rather than 414. We therefore do not reproduce these here and refer the reader to Section 3 and Appendix A of [3] for the relevant details.

For a scalar in $[0, \ldots, 2^{519} - 1]$, the cost for a constant-time variable-base scalar multiplication is: $39M + 15S$ for precomputation, plus $2730M + 2080S$ for the windowing plus $15M + 520S$ for the final map to affine coordinates, giving a total cost of $2784M + 2615S$.

4.3   Timings

We implemented multiplication and squaring as per Algorithms 1 and 2, as well as constant-time variable-base scalar multiplication for curves P-521 and E-521[2], as per Sections 4.1 and 4.2. Our results are detailed in Table 1.

Table 1. Cycle counts for openSSL version 1.0.2-beta2, P-521 and E-521 variable-base scalar multiplication on a 3.4GHz Intel Haswell Core i7-4770 and compiled with gcc 4.7 on Ubuntu 12.04. The counts are given to the nearest thousand and were obtained by taking the minimum over 10^3 data points, where each data point was the average of 10^4 point multiplications. Cycle counts for multiplication and squaring modulo M_{521} are also included and were the minimum of 10^6 such operations.

openSSL	P-521	E-521	M	S
1,319,000	1,108,000	943,000	155	105

Regarding comparisons with previous benchmarks, there are two obvious candidates. For curve P-521, one can test Langley's openSSL implementation (which first featured in version 1.0.0e) using the command openssl speed ecdh. On the same architecture, version 1.0.2-beta2 reports 2578.1 operations per second, which implies a count of approximately 1,319,000 cycles per scalar multiplication. We timed the actual M, S, DBL and ADD functions using several different compilers and options, and found the code to be rather fragile, in that nearly all of them reported a two-fold or more slow down relative to our cycle

---

[2] For our code see indigo.ie/~mscott/ws521.cpp and indigo.ie/~mscott/ed521.cpp respectively.

counts of $155, 105, 1175$ and 1728 for the above operations respectively. However, using gcc 4.7 we obtained cycle counts of $173, 112, 1312$ and 2010 respectively. For a scalar multiplication this implies that our code requires about 88% to 90% of the time required by Langley's in the worst case and less than 50% in the best case.

For E-521, the closest benchmark in the literature is due to Bos *et al.* [8], which reports a cycle count of $1,552,000$ for a constant-time variable-base scalar multiplication on the twisted Edwards curve **ed-521-mers**: $-x^2 + y^2 = 1 + dx^2 y^2$ with $-1/(d+1) = 550440$, on a 3.4GHz Intel Core i7-2600 Sandy Bridge processor (albeit with Intel's Turbo Boost and Hyper-threading disabled). This curve form allows a saving of $1M$ per point addition relative to ordinary Edwards curves, but one can not apply an $\mathbb{F}_p$-isomorphism from E-521 to a curve of this form since -1 is not a square modulo M_{521}. However, one possibility for improving our cycle count would be to map to the 4-isogenous curve with equation $-x^2 + y^2 = 1 - 376015x^2 y^2$, as proposed by Hamburg [20], which then allows $1M$ per point addition to be saved. Our implementation therefore requires only about 60% of the time required by that of Bos *et al.* Apart from the exploitation of our basic observation, much of this difference in performance can be explained by the use of base 2^{58} arithmetic, rather than base 2^{64}. Of course, our basic observation would naturally speed up operations on the two curves **ed-521-mers** and **w-521-mers** in [8] as well.

5 Application to Crandall Numbers

Let the modulus be $t^n - c$ and let residues x and y be represented in base t as $\sum_{i=0}^{n-1} x_i t^i$ and $\sum_{i=0}^{n-1} y_i t^i$ respectively. The multiplication of x and y modulo $t^n - c$ is $z = \sum_{i=0}^{n-1} z_i t^i$ where

$$z_i = \sum_{j=0}^{n-1} d(i,j)\, x_{\langle i-j\rangle}\, y_{\langle j\rangle},$$

where the subscripts of the coefficients of $x_{\langle i-j\rangle}$ and $y_{\langle j\rangle}$ are taken modulo n and

$$d(i,j) = \begin{cases} 1 & \text{if } \langle i-j\rangle + \langle j\rangle < n \\ c & \text{otherwise.} \end{cases} \tag{5.1}$$

In particular, by symmetry (or by (5.1)) the terms $x_{\langle i-j\rangle}\, y_{\langle j\rangle}$ and $x_{\langle j\rangle}\, y_{\langle i-j\rangle}$ occurring in the expression for z_i both have the same $d(i,j)$. If $d(i,j) = 1$ then the expression $x_{\langle i-j\rangle}\, y_{\langle j\rangle} + x_{\langle j\rangle}\, y_{\langle i-j\rangle}$ may be rewritten just as before as

$$x_{\langle i-j\rangle}\, y_{\langle i-j\rangle} + x_{\langle j\rangle}\, y_{\langle j\rangle} - (x_{\langle i-j\rangle} - x_{\langle j\rangle})(y_{\langle i-j\rangle} - y_{\langle j\rangle}).$$

Similarly, the expression $c\,(x_{\langle i-j\rangle}\, y_{\langle j\rangle} + x_{\langle j\rangle}\, y_{\langle i-j\rangle})$ may of course be rewritten as

$$c\,(x_{\langle i-j\rangle}\, y_{\langle i-j\rangle} + x_{\langle j\rangle}\, y_{\langle j\rangle} - (x_{\langle i-j\rangle} - x_{\langle j\rangle})(y_{\langle i-j\rangle} - y_{\langle j\rangle})),$$

or even as

$$x_{\langle i-j\rangle}\, y_{\langle i-j\rangle} + c^2\, x_{\langle j\rangle}\, y_{\langle j\rangle} - (x_{\langle i-j\rangle} - c\, x_{\langle j\rangle})\,(y_{\langle i-j\rangle} - c\, y_{\langle j\rangle}),$$

as was used in Algorithm 1 for M_{521}. Therefore, by precomputing the terms $x_i y_i$ for $i = 0, \ldots, n-1$, the paired terms in the expression for each z_i may be computed as the products above, which again nearly halves the total number of coefficient multiplications required, at the expense of a few additions and multiplications by c.

5.1   Two Examples

In order to use the above observations, it will often be necessary to first multiply a given Crandall number $p = 2^k - c$ by 2^i so that $k+i$ is a multiple of a suitable n, such that all coefficient arithmetic does not overflow beyond double precision. In this case the base $t = 2^{(k+i)/n}$ is a power of two and coefficient renormalisation – which ensures I/O stabilty – can be effected via simple operations (including shifts) only. This will be clear from the following two examples.

5.2   Application to $p = 2^{221} - 3$

This prime was proposed in [1]. For use on a 64-bit architecture we choose $t = 2^{56}$ and use the scaled modulus $8p = t^4 - 24$. The multiplication algorithm is as follows.

Algorithm 3. MUL2213

INPUT: $\overline{x} = [x_0, \ldots, x_3], \overline{y} = [y_0, \ldots, y_3] \in [-2^{57}, 2^{57} - 1] \times [0, 2^{56} - 1]^3$
OUTPUT: $\overline{z} \in [-2^{57}, 2^{57} - 1] \times [0, 2^{56} - 1]^3$ where $\overline{z} \equiv \overline{x} \cdot \overline{y} \pmod{t^4 - 24}$

1. $a_0 \leftarrow x_0 y_0, \ a_1 \leftarrow x_1 y_1, \ a_2 \leftarrow x_2 y_2, \ a_3 \leftarrow x_3 y_3, \ b_2 \leftarrow a_3 + a_2, \ b_1 \leftarrow b_2 + a_1, \ b_0 \leftarrow b_1 + a_0$
2. $t_0 \leftarrow b_0 - (x_0 - x_3)(y_0 - y_3) - (x_1 - x_2)(y_1 - y_2)$
3. $z_3 \leftarrow t_0 \bmod t$
4. $t_1 \leftarrow a_0 + 24(b_1 - (x_1 - x_3)(y_1 - y_3) + (t_0 >> 56))$
5. $z_0 \leftarrow t_1 \bmod t$
6. $a_0 \leftarrow a_0 + a_1$
7. $t_0 \leftarrow a_0 - (x_0 - x_1)(y_0 - y_1) + 24(b_3 - (x_2 - x_3)(y_2 - y_3)) + (t_1 >> 56)$
8. $z_1 \leftarrow t_0 \bmod t$
9. $t_1 \leftarrow a_0 + a_2 + 24a_3 - (x_0 - x_2)(y_0 - y_2) + (t_0 >> 56)$
10. $z_2 \leftarrow t_1 \bmod t$
11. $t_0 \leftarrow z_3 + (t_1 >> 56)$
12. $z_3 \leftarrow t_0 \bmod t$
13. $z_0 \leftarrow z_0 + 24(t_0 >> 56)$
14. Return $\overline{z}$

Note that as with Algorithm 1 we compute the wrap around from the highest coefficient to the lowest twice, in order to maintain I/O stability for the chosen reduced format for residues.

5.3   Application to $p = 2^{255} - 19$

This prime was proposed in [2] and later developed with base $t = 2^{51}$ arithmetic [6], which we use here. We hence use the modulus $p = t^5 - 19$. The multiplication algorithm is as follows.

Algorithm 4. MUL25519

INPUT: $\bar{\mathbf{x}} = [x_0, \ldots, x_4], \bar{\mathbf{y}} = [y_0, \ldots, y_4] \in [-2^{52}, 2^{52} - 1] \times [0, 2^{51} - 1]^4$

OUTPUT: $\bar{\mathbf{z}} \in [-2^{52}, 2^{52} - 1] \times [0, 2^{51} - 1]^4$ where $\bar{\mathbf{z}} \equiv \bar{\mathbf{x}} \cdot \bar{\mathbf{y}} \pmod{t^5 - 19}$

1. $a_0 \leftarrow x_0 y_0, \; a_1 \leftarrow x_1 y_1, \; a_2 \leftarrow x_2 y_2, \; a_3 \leftarrow x_3 y_3, \; a_4 \leftarrow x_4 y_4$
   $b_3 \leftarrow a_4 + a_3, \; b_2 \leftarrow a_3 + a_2, \; b_1 \leftarrow b_2 + a_1, \; b_0 \leftarrow b_1 + a_0$
2. $t_0 \leftarrow b_0 - (x_0 - x_4)(y_0 - y_4) - (x_1 - x_3)(y_1 - y_3)$
3. $z_4 \leftarrow t_0 \bmod t$
4. $t_1 \leftarrow a_0 + 19(b_1 - (x_1 - x_4)(y_1 - y_4) - (x_2 - x_3)(y_2 - y_3) + (t_0 >> 51))$
5. $z_0 \leftarrow t_1 \bmod t$
6. $a_0 \leftarrow a_0 + a_1$
7. $t_0 \leftarrow a_0 - (x_0 - x_1)(y_0 - y_1) + 19(b_2 - (x_2 - x_4)(y_2 - y_4)) + (t_1 >> 51)$
8. $z_1 \leftarrow t_0 \bmod t$
9. $a_0 \leftarrow a_0 + a_2$
10. $t_1 \leftarrow a_0 - (x_0 - x_2)(y_0 - y_2) + 19(b_3 - (x_3 - x_4)(y_3 - y_4)) + (t_0 >> 51)$
11. $z_2 \leftarrow t_1 \bmod t$
12. $t_0 \leftarrow a_0 + a_3 - (x_0 - x_3)(y_0 - y_3) - (x_1 - x_2)(y_1 - x_2) + 19a_4 + (t_1 >> 51)$
13. $z_3 \leftarrow t_0 \bmod t$
14. $t_1 \leftarrow z_4 + (t_0 >> 51)$
15. $z_4 \leftarrow t_1 \bmod t$
16. $z_0 \leftarrow z_0 + 19(t_1 >> 51)$
17. Return $\bar{\mathbf{z}}$

Note that the multiplications by 24 in Algorithm 3 and by 19 in Algorithm 4 are generally on double precision integers, so are sometimes more costly than the usual evaluation of coefficients in which one can sometimes achieve a saving by first multiplying one the inputs to a multiplication by c. Since there are also more additions required than for Algorithm 1's analogue of the basic observation, these formulae may only be interesting when optimised, or when implemented on ARM processors, for instance. As our focus is primarily on M_{521}, P-521 and E-521, we leave such options as open research.

6   Conclusion

We have proposed a very simple way to improve multiplication efficiency over the prime field $\mathbb{F}_{2^{521}-1}$, which requires as few word-by-word multiplications as is needed for squaring, while incurring very little overhead from extra additions. With optimised code our timings may be reduced even further, with potentially interesting results on ARM processors, for which the multiplication-to-addition cost ratio is higher than on the Haswell and for which there are numerous similar methods to represent and multiply residues using 32 bit words. It remains to be seen whether the same basic observation improves the efficiency of multiplication modulo Crandall numbers as well.

Acknowledgments. We thank Dan Bernstein for answering our questions regarding his irrational base modular multiplication method.

References

1. Aranha, D.F., Barreto, P.S.L.M., Pereira, G.C.C.F., Ricardini, J.: A note on high-security general-purpose elliptic curves (2013). http://eprint.iacr.org/2013/647
2. Bernstein, D.J.: Curve25519: new diffie-hellman speed records. In: Yung, M., Dodis, Y., Kiayias, A., Malkin, T. (eds.) PKC 2006. LNCS, vol. 3958, pp. 207–228. Springer, Heidelberg (2006)
3. Bernstein, D.J., Chuengsatiansup, C., Lange, T.: Curve41417: Karatsuba revisited. Cryptology ePrint Archive, Report 2014/526 (2014). http://eprint.iacr.org/
4. Bernstein, D.J., Hamburg, M., Krasnova, A., Lange, T.: Elligator: elliptic-curve points indistinguishable from uniform random strings. In: 2013 ACM SIGSAC Conference on Computer and Communications Security, CCS2013, pp. 967–980. Berlin, Germany, 4–8 November 2013
5. Bernstein, D.J., Lange, T.: Safecurves: choosing safe curves for elliptic-curve cryptography (2014). http://safecurves.cr.yp.to. Accessed 11 September 2014
6. Bernstein, D.J., Duif, N., Lange, T., Schwabe, P., Yang, B.-Y.: High-speed high-security signatures. Journal of Cryptographic Engineering 2(2), 77–89 (2012)
7. Bos, J.W.: Constant time modular inversion. Journal of Cryptographic Engineering, 1–7 (2014)
8. Bos, J.W., Costello, C., Longa, P., Naehrig, M.: Selecting elliptic curves for cryptography: an efficiency and security analysis. Cryptology ePrint Archive, Report 2014/130 (2014). http://eprint.iacr.org/
9. Bos, J.W., Kleinjung, T., Lenstra, A.K., Montgomery, P.L.: Efficient simd arithmetic modulo a mersenne number. In: Proceedings of the 2011 IEEE 20th Symposium on Computer Arithmetic, ARITH 2011, pp. 213–221. IEEE Computer Society, Washington, DC, USA (2011)
10. Chung, J., Hasan, A.: More generalized mersenne numbers. In: Matsui, M., Zuccherato, R.J. (eds.) SAC. LNCS, vol. 3006, pp. 335–347. Springer, Heidelberg (2004)
11. Chung, J., Hasan, M.A.: Montgomery reduction algorithm for modular multiplication using low-weight polynomial form integers. In: ARITH 18, pp. 230–239 (2007)
12. Chung, J., Hasan, M.A.: Low-weight polynomial form integers for efficient modular multiplication. IEEE Transactions on Computers 56(1), 44–57 (Jan 2007)
13. Crandall, R., Pomerance, C.B.: Prime Numbers: A Computational Perspective. Lecture notes in statistics. Springer, Heidelberg (2006)
14. Crandall, R.E.: Method and apparatus for public key exchange in a cryptographic system. US Patent 5,159,632, 27 October 1992
15. Crandall, R.E.: Topics in Advanced Scientific Computation. Electronic Library of Science. Springer-Telos, Heidelberg (1996)
16. Crandall, R., Fagin, B.: Discrete weighted transforms and large-integer arithmetic. Math. Comput. 62(205), 305–324 (1994)
17. US Department of Commerce/N.I.S.T. 2000. Federal Information Processing Standards Publication 186–2. Fips 186–2. digital signature standard
18. Standards for Efficient Cryptography Group. Recommended elliptic curve domain parameters (2000). www.secg.org/collateral/sec2.pdf
19. Granger, R., Moss, A.: Generalised Mersenne numbers revisited. Math. Comp. 82(284), 2389–2420 (2013)
20. Hamburg, M.: Twisting edwards curves with isogenies. http://eprint.iacr.org/2014/027

21. Karatsuba, A., Ofman, Y.: Multiplication of Multidigit Numbers on Automata. Soviet Physics Doklady **7**, 595–596 (January 1963)
22. Käsper, E.: Fast elliptic curve cryptography in openSSL. In: Danezis, G., Dietrich, S., Sako, K. (eds.) FC 2011 Workshops 2011. LNCS, vol. 7126, pp. 27–39. Springer, Heidelberg (2012)
23. Khachatrian, G.H., Kuregian, M.K., Ispiryan, K.R., Massey, J.L.: Fast multiplication of integers for public-key applications. In: Vaudenay, S., Youssef, A.M. (eds.) SAC 2001. LNCS, vol. 2259, p. 245. Springer, Heidelberg (2001)
24. Öztürk, E., Sunar, B., Savaş, E.: Low-power elliptic curve cryptography using scaled modular arithmetic. In: Joye, M., Quisquater, J.-J. (eds.) CHES 2004. LNCS, vol. 3156, pp. 92–106. Springer, Heidelberg (2004)
25. Walter, C.D.: Faster modular multiplication by operand scaling. In: Feigenbaum, J. (ed.) CRYPTO 1991. LNCS, vol. 576, pp. 313–323. Springer, Heidelberg (1992)

Cryptography with Imperfect Keys

Continuous Non-malleable Key Derivation and Its Application to Related-Key Security

Baodong Qin[1,2], Shengli Liu[1]($\boxtimes$), Tsz Hon Yuen[3], Robert H. Deng[4], and Kefei Chen[5]

[1] Department of Computer Science and Engineering,
Shanghai Jiao Tong University, Shanghai 200240, China
{qinbaodong,slliu}@sjtu.edu.cn
[2] Southwest University of Science and Technology, Mianyang 621010, China
[3] Huawei, Singapore
Yuen.Tsz.Hon@huawei.com
[4] School of Information Systems, Singapore Management University, Singapore 178902, Singapore
robertdeng@smu.edu.sg
[5] School of Science, Hangzhou Normal University, Hangzhou 310036, China
kfchen@sjtu.edu.cn

Abstract. Related-Key Attacks (RKAs) allow an adversary to observe the outcomes of a cryptographic primitive under not only its original secret key e.g., s, but also a sequence of modified keys $\phi(s)$, where ϕ is specified by the adversary from a class Φ of so-called Related-Key Derivation (RKD) functions. This paper extends the notion of non-malleable Key Derivation Functions (nm-KDFs), introduced by Faust et al. (EUROCRYPT'14), to *continuous* nm-KDFs. Continuous nm-KDFs have the ability to protect against any a-priori *unbounded* number of RKA queries, instead of just a single time tampering attack as in the definition of nm-KDFs. Informally, our continuous non-malleability captures the scenario where the adversary can tamper with the original secret key repeatedly and adaptively. We present a novel construction of continuous nm-KDF for any polynomials of bounded degree over a finite field. Essentially, our result can be extended to richer RKD function classes possessing properties of *high output entropy and input-output collision resistance*. The technical tool employed in the construction is the one-time lossy filter (Qin et al. ASIACRYPT'13) which can be efficiently obtained under standard assumptions, e.g., DDH and DCR. We propose a framework for constructing Φ-RKA-secure IBE, PKE and signature schemes, using a continuous nm-KDF for the same Φ-class of RKD functions. Applying our construction of continuous nm-KDF to this framework, we obtain the first RKA-secure IBE, PKE and signature schemes for a class of polynomial RKD functions of bounded degree under *standard* assumptions. While previous constructions for the same class of RKD functions all rely on non-standard assumptions, e.g., d-extended DBDH assumption.

Keywords: Related-key attacks · Non-malleable key derivation · One-time lossy filter

© International Association for Cryptologic Research 2015
J. Katz (Ed.): PKC 2015, LNCS 9020, pp. 557–578, 2015.
DOI: 10.1007/978-3-662-46447-2_25

1   Introduction

Traditionally, cryptographic security notions assume that an adversary can only observe the input/output behavior of the system and thus has only "black-box" access to the system. In a real life, however, it may be far from this case. Recent research [8] has shown that an adversary may learn some information about the secret key/internal state through physical side channels (e.g., timing [21] and power consumption [22]) and/or influence the way that the secret key/internal state is used via physical access to a hardware device (e.g., heating it or cutting wires to inject faults [7,8]). These two types of attacks are usually distinguished as "leakage" and "tampering" attacks respectively. In this paper, we consider how to design algorithms enabling devices resilient to tampering attacks when the devices are "leakage-proof" but not "tamper-proof". Specifically, we focus on tampering attacks on the key stored in a cryptographic hardware device. The key might be a signing key of a certificate authority or a decryption key of an encryption cryptosystem. Such tampering attacks are firstly formalized by Bellare and Kohno [5], as Related-Key Attacks (RKAs) in the context of pseudorandom functions/permutations.

MODEL OF RKA SECURITY. Following [4], we view a system as a composition of algorithms (code), public parameters, public keys (if any) and secret keys. Among these components, public parameters are system-wide, meaning that they are generated beforehand and independent of users and hence their public/secret keys. In an implementation, these parameters are part of the algorithm code and stored in a tamper-proof hardware device. Hence, only the public and secret keys are subject to RKAs.

Suppose that $\mathcal{CS}_{\text{PP}}(s, x)$ is a cryptographic system parameterized by a public parameter PP. It admits a secret key s and a message x as input. For example, if $\mathcal{CS}$ has a decryption functionality, then s is a decryption key and x is a ciphertext. The RKA security model for $\mathcal{CS}$ is formalized by a class Φ of admissible key transformations (also named Related-Key Deriving (RKD) functions). An RKA adversary has the ability to repeatedly and adaptively choose x and a (tampering) function $\phi \in \Phi$, and then observe the outcome of $\mathcal{CS}_{\text{PP}}(\phi(s), x)$ under this modified key $\phi(s)$. If the system is still secure, we say $\mathcal{CS}$ is Φ-RKA secure. Unless stated otherwise, in this paper, the RKA-security model allows an adversary to ask for a-priori unbounded number of RKD queries.

1.1   Motivation

It is not an easy task to design a provably secure scheme under RKAs for an especially large non-trivial class of RKD functions. To date, there are few constructions of RKA-secure primitives. The state-of-the-art RKA-security protects against a-priori unbounded number of queries for polynomials of bounded degree. However, all of them rely on non-standard assumptions, e.g., the d-extended DBDH (decisional bilinear Diffie-Hellman) assumption in the RKA-secure IBE [6] (and the degree of RKD polynomials is limited to d). There are generic approaches that use non-malleable codes [15, 17] and non-malleable key derivation functions [17] to protect against tampering attacks even for function class richer than the polynomial one. However, both of them only consider *single time* tampering attack, *not* capturing the scenario of related-key attacks in which the adversary can continuously tamper with the original secret key. Indeed, as far as we know, no formal result shows how to achieve RKA security using these two primitives. Recently, Faust et al. [16] proposed an extension of the standard non-malleable codes, namely *continuous* non-malleable codes which cover the case that allows multiple tampering queries. However, this model relies on self-destruct mechanism, in which tampering queries must be terminated if an invalid code is detected (i.e., the decoding returns $\perp$). Moreover, their continuous non-malleable codes are realized in the split-state model [14] where an encoding is divided into two parts and the tampering must be applied to the two parts independently.

A natural question is whether we can define a stronger security model (than that of [16]) for continuous non-malleable codes or KDFs that can be used to achieve RKA security? Furthermore, can we achieve such continuous non-malleability for larger class of RKD functions under *standard* assumptions? In this paper, we provide affirmative answers to the two questions in the setting of key derivation functions.

1.2 Continuous Non-malleable KDFs

Usually, a key derivation function KDF is equipped with another two probabilistic polynomial-time (PPT) algorithms: KDF.Sys and KDF.Sample. The former takes as input a security parameter 1^κ and outputs a system parameter PP; the later takes as input PP, and outputs a derivation key s and a public key π. The key derivation function KDF is implicitly indexed by the system parameter PP and takes as input (s, π) to derive a key $r = \mathsf{KDF}_\pi(s)$ in polynomial-time. At a high level, we can always view (s, π) together as a derivation key. Since π is publicly accessible, any efficient adversary can tamper with π at its will. For this reason, we only explicitly specify the class Φ of tampering functions over the secret key space in this paper. We omit π if the derivation function does not take the public key as input, for example in [17]. The standard security notion for KDFs requires that the derived key r is indistinguishable from a random key if the adversary only knows the system parameter and the public key. Recently, Faust et al. [17] introduced the notion of non-malleable KDFs which, roughly speaking, guarantees that r is still random even if the adversary obtains another value $\mathsf{KDF}(s')$ as long as $s' \neq s$.

As shown previously, the standard non-malleability cannot protect against tampering attacks in some stateless settings where the adversary can continue to tamper with the original keys. To overcome this drawback, we introduce a new notion, namely continuous non-malleable KDFs, as a natural extension of the standard non-malleability. The continuous non-malleability for function class Φ is defined by the following two experiments: $\mathsf{Real}_{\mathsf{KDF}}(\Phi, \kappa)$ and $\mathsf{Sim}_{\mathsf{KDF}}(\Phi, \kappa)$, in which the derivation key function involves the public key π as an auxiliary input.

1. The challenger generates PP and samples (s, π). In experiment $\mathsf{Real}_{\mathsf{KDF}}$, the challenger computes $r^* = \mathsf{KDF}_\pi(s)$, while in experiment $\mathsf{Sim}_{\mathsf{KDF}}$, the challenger samples r^* uniformly at random from its range.
2. The adversary $\mathcal{A}$ is given (PP, π) and the challenge key r^*.
3. $\mathcal{A}$ can repeatedly and adaptively query the following oracle with (ϕ, π') for any polynomially many times:

$$\text{If } (\phi(s), \pi') = (s, \pi), \text{ return same}^*; \text{ else, return } \mathsf{KDF}_{\pi'}(\phi(s)),$$

where $\phi \in \Phi$, and π' is chosen by $\mathcal{A}$ at its will.

The continuous non-malleability requires that any PPT adversary has negligible advantage in distinguishing the above two experiments.

Though the adversary may tamper with s and π in a different (not necessarily independent) way, we stress that this is not a tampering attack as defined in the split-state model [14,17]. The reason is that π is a public key, any tampered result of π is provided by the adversary *at its will*, instead of being computed by the challenger. As shown in [18], it is impossible to prevent against continuous tampering attacks without any further assumption. Indeed, the continuous non-malleability achieved in the work of Faust et al. [16] limits to self-destruct and split-state model. Our new model above removes these two restrictions, hence is stronger. We will show in Section 4.1 that key derivation functions are still achievable in our new stronger security model, as long as we give a proper restriction (see Definition 1) on the tampering function classes.

Note that in our security model, we consider not only a continuously tampering adversary, but also an adaptive adversary which is allowed to access the tampering oracle after seeing the challenge derived key r^*. It might be of independent interest to consider a non-adaptive tampering adversary, which is only allowed to access the tampering oracle *before* receiving r^*.

1.3   Our Contributions

We summarize our contributions in the following and then detail the techniques that are used in our construction of continuous non-malleable KDF.

- Introduce the notion of *continuous* non-malleable Key Derivation Function (cnm-KDF) for an a-priori class of RKD functions Φ. Informally, we say a key derivation function KDF is continuously non-malleable with respect to Φ, namely Φ-cnm-KDF, if the output of KDF is still pseudo-random even if a PPT adversary tampers with its original key repeatedly and adaptively with function $\phi \in \Phi$.
- Provide a simple construction of continuous non-malleable KDF for the $\Phi_{\mathbb{F}}^{\mathsf{poly}(d)}$-class of polynomial functions of bounded degree d over finite field $\mathbb{F}$. The construction exploits the functionality of one-time lossy filter (introduced by Qin et al. [24]) and some basic properties of polynomial functions over finite field.

- We also generalize the polynomial function class $\Phi_{\mathbb{F}}^{\mathsf{poly}(d)}$ to a larger function class, namely *High Output Entropy and Input-Output Collision Resistance (HOE&IOCR)*, which we denote by $\Phi_{\mathsf{iocr}}^{\mathsf{hoe}}$. Function class $\Phi_{\mathsf{iocr}}^{\mathsf{hoe}}$ possesses similar properties as polynomial functions. We show that our result works well even in such a richer RKD function class $\Phi_{\mathsf{iocr}}^{\mathsf{hoe}}$ ($\Phi_{\mathsf{iocr}}^{\mathsf{hoe}} \supseteq \Phi_{\mathbb{F}}^{\mathsf{poly}(d)}$).
- The state-of-the-art One-Time Lossy Filters (OT-LFs) [24,25] suggest that OT-LFs can be instantiated from standard assumptions including the Decisional Diffie-Hellman (DDH) assumption and the Decisional Composite Residuosity (DCR) assumption. This leads to instantiations of $\Phi_{\mathbb{F}}^{\mathsf{poly}(d)}$-cnm-KDF (w.r.t. $\Phi_{\mathsf{iocr}}^{\mathsf{hoe}}$-cnm-KDF) based on standard assumptions.

- Propose a simple framework which transforms a traditional (non-RKA secure) IBE to a Φ-RKA-secure IBE with the help of Φ-cnm-KDF.
  - The available standard-assumption-based IBEs and $\Phi_{\mathbb{F}}^{\mathsf{poly}(d)}$-cnm-KDF suggests the first instantiations of $\Phi_{\mathbb{F}}^{\mathsf{poly}(d)}$-RKA-secure IBE from standard assumption.
  - Applying the transformation from Φ-RKA-secure IBE to PKE and signature schemes [4,6], we immediately obtain $\Phi_{\mathbb{F}}^{\mathsf{poly}(d)}$-RKA-secure CCA-PKE and signature schemes under standard assumptions.

A CLOSER LOOK AT OUR TECHNIQUES. Our construction of continuous non-malleable KDF employs three cryptographic primitives: one-time lossy filter [24], pairwise independent hash function and one-time signature. A one-time lossy filter $\mathsf{LF}_t(\cdot)$ is a family of (one-way) functions parameterized by a tag t. The tag t can be either injective corresponding to an injective function, or lossy corresponding to a lossy function. One-time lossy filter has the following properties: (1) Injective and lossy tags are computationally indistinguishable; (2) There is a trapdoor to efficiently sample a lossy tag. However, without this trapdoor, it is hard to find a *non-injective* [1] tag even given one lossy tag. Recall that a family of pairwise independent hash functions $\mathcal{H}$ is an average-case strong extractor as long as its input has sufficiently large average min-entropy [13]. In our construction, we simply use h to derive the key $r = h(s)$, where $h \leftarrow_R \mathcal{H}$ and s is a random derivation key. Associated with the derivation key s is a public key computed by $\pi = t\|\mathsf{LF}_t(s)$, where t is a random LF (injective) [2] tag. At a high level, π provides a knowledge proof of s so that an adversary who can compute a correct proof π' that corresponds to $\phi(s)$ must already know $\phi(s)$. To guarantee such property, in the proof, the tag t is moving from injective to lossy making π reveal only constant amount of information of s. Suppose that s is modified to $\phi(s)$ and π to any value $\pi' = t'\|y'$. If $t' \neq t$, t' will be an injective tag with overwhelming probability and hence $\mathsf{LF}_{t'}(\cdot)$ is injective. So, if $\phi(s)$ has high residual min-entropy, the adversary should have negligible probability to correctly guess the value $\mathsf{LF}_{t'}(\phi(s))$. A challenging problem is that the adversary may reuse the lossy tag t, i.e., $t' = t$. To solve this problem, we apply a one-time signature

---

[1] In some case, a tag may be neither injective nor lossy.

[2] With overwhelming probability, a random tag is injective.

scheme to π, guaranteeing that if t is reused, then $\pi' = \pi$ with overwhelming probability. Recall that a lossy tag is indistinguishable from an injective tag, and hence with overwhelming probability if $\pi' = \pi$, then $\phi(s) = s$. So, such case occurs unless $(\phi(s), \pi') = (s, \pi)$. Now, it only leaves us to discuss the entropy of $\phi(s)$ and the probability of $\phi(s) = s$. A simple property (for detail, see Lemma 3) is that for any non-constant polynomial, $\phi(s)$ has nearly the same entropy as s and if ϕ is not the identity function, then $\phi(s)$ equals s with negligible probability, as long as s has sufficiently large entropy. This concludes that except trivial queries (including the case $(\phi, \pi') = (\mathrm{id}, \pi)$ and the case ϕ is constant), it is hard to generate a valid proof π' for $\phi(s)$.

1.4   Related Work and Remarks

So far, there are not many RKA-secure primitives available and the main constructions are limited to PRFs [1,3], symmetric encryption [2,6,19], IBE [6], signature [6], and public-key encryption [6,23,28]. In particular, Bellare et al. [4] presented an almost complete understanding of the relations among these RKA-primitives. For example, RKA-secure PRFs can make any non-RKA secure primitive constructed from PRFs to be secure against RKAs. However, almost all of the realizations are secure only against simple and *claw-free*[3] RKD functions e.g., linear functions [2,23,28]. It may become more challenging to immunize a cryptographic primitive against non-linear and non-claw-free functions, e.g., affine and polynomial functions. One inherent reason is that a simulator, without the secret key s, is hard to detect dangerous queries such that $\phi(s) = s$ if ϕ is non-claw-free. To overcome this issue, all these methods [1,6,19] rely on non-standard assumptions, e.g., the d-extended DBDH (decisional bilinear Diffie-Hellman) assumption used in [6], from which the simulator is able to compute $\phi(s)$ (in the exponent) for any polynomial ϕ of bounded degree d.

Another approach that may be used to achieve RKA-security in a general way is the tamper-resilient codes, including algebraic manipulation detection codes [11] and (continuous) non-malleable codes [15–17]. The secret key stored on the device is now the encoded version of the original key using such a code. These codes considered very practical tampering functions. However, as we mentioned before, their security models have some limitations, e.g., one-time tampering query or split-state model, which are inherent obstacles for capturing the scenario of RKAs security. Recently, Damgård et al.[12] showed that tamper-resilience (even combined with leakage-resilience) can be achieved for arbitrary key relations by restricting the number of adversary's tampering queries.

CONCURRENT WORK. Jafargholi and Wichs [20] considered the same security level of continuous non-malleability and showed that continuous non-malleable codes are achievable if the tampering functions are polynomials or have few fixed points and high entropy (like the properties of HOE&IOCR functions). In contrast to ours, their results are constructed in the information-theoretic

---

[3] A class of RKD functions is called *claw-free*, if for any distinct RKD functions $\phi \neq \phi'$ and all $s \in S$, $\phi(s) \neq \phi'(s)$.

setting. However, the parameter in their construction [16, Corollary 5.6] depends on the number of tampering queries and the size of tampering function class. For efficient codes, the degree of polynomials must be set to some polynomial $d = d(\kappa)$. Additionally, they initiated a general study of continuous non-malleable codes and defined four variants of continuous non-malleability depending on (1) whether a tampering is persistent or non-persistent, meaning that any successive tampering function is applied to the former modified codeword or always applied to the original codeword, (2) whether we can self-destruct or not, meaning that we can stop the experiment if a codeword is invalid or the adversary can continue to tamper. Clearly, non-persistent tampering and no self-destruct require stronger model and is just the model considered in this paper.

ORGANIZATION. We present our RKD function class in Section 3. We present the notion of continuous non-malleable KDF and its construction in Section 4. An application of continuous non-malleable KDF to the RKA-secure IBE is given in Section 5.

2 Preliminary

NOTATIONS. Throughout the paper, $\mathbb{N}$ is the set of natural numbers and $\kappa \in \mathbb{N}$ is the security parameter. If S is a finite set, then $s \leftarrow_R S$ denotes the operation of picking an element s from S uniformly at random. If X is a random variable over S, then we write $x \leftarrow X$ to denote the process of sampling a value $x \in S$ according to the distribution X. We call a function negl negligible in κ, if for every positive polynomial $\mathsf{poly}(\cdot)$ there exists an N such that for all $\kappa > N$, $\mathsf{negl}(\kappa) < 1/\mathsf{poly}(\kappa)$. We say that an event E happens with overwhelming probability, if it happens with probability $1 - \mathsf{negl}(\kappa)$. "PPT" stands for probabilistic polynomial-time. An algorithm A is PPT if it, on input x, computes $A(x)$ using randomness and its running time is bounded by $\mathsf{poly}(\kappa)$.

AVERAGE MIN-ENTROPY. The statistical distance between two random variables X and Y over a finite set Ω is $\Delta(X, Y) = \frac{1}{2}\sum_{\omega \in \Omega} |\Pr[X = \omega] - \Pr[Y = \omega]|$. We say that two variables are ϵ-close if their statistical distance is at most ϵ. The min-entropy of a random variable X is $H_\infty(X) = -\log(\max_x \Pr[X = x])$. Dodis et al. [13] formalized the notion of average min-entropy that captures the unpredictability of X conditioned on a random variable Y. Formally, it is defined as $\tilde{H}_\infty(X|Y) = -\log(E_{y \leftarrow Y}[2^{-H_\infty(X|Y=y)}])$.

We recall the following useful properties of average min-entropy from [13].

Lemma 1 ([13]). *Let X, Y and Z be random variables. Then*

1. *If Y has at most 2^r possible values and Z is any random variable, then $\tilde{H}_\infty(X|(Y, Z)) \geq \tilde{H}_\infty(X|Z) - r$.*
2. *For any $\delta > 0$, the conditional entropy $H_\infty(X|Y = y)$ is at least $\tilde{H}_\infty(X|Y) - \log(1/\delta)$ with probability at least $1 - \delta$ over the choice of y.*

AVERAGE-CASE EXTRACTORS [13]. A function $\mathsf{Ext} : \{0,1\}^n \times \mathcal{H} \to \{0,1\}^m$ is an efficient average-case (n, ν, m, ϵ)-strong extractor, if for all pairs of random variables (X, Z) such that $X \in \{0,1\}^n$ and $\tilde{H}_\infty(X|Z) \geq \nu$, we have $\Delta((Z, h, \mathsf{Ext}(X, h)), (Z, h, U_m)) \leq \epsilon$, where h is uniform over $\mathcal{H}$ and U_m is uniform over $\{0,1\}^m$.

Lemma 2 ([13]). *Let $\mathcal{H}$ be a family of pairwise independent hash functions from $\{0,1\}^n$ to $\{0,1\}^m$. If $X \in \{0,1\}^n$, $\tilde{H}_\infty(X|Z) \geq \nu$ and $m \leq \nu - 2\log 1/\epsilon$, then $\Delta((Z, h, h(X)), (Z, h, U_m)) \leq \epsilon$, where $h \leftarrow_R \mathcal{H}$ and U_m is uniform over $\{0,1\}^m$. In other words, the above family of pairwise independent hash functions can be used as an efficient average-case (n, ν, m, ϵ)-strong extractor.*

ONE-TIME LOSSY FILTER. We adopt the notion of one-time lossy filter from [24]. An $(\mathcal{X}, \ell_{\mathsf{LF}})$-OT-LF LF consists of three PPT algorithms: (1) $\mathsf{LF.Gen}(1^\kappa)$, on input 1^κ, outputs an evaluation key ek_{LF} and a trapdoor td_{LF}. The evaluation key defines a tag space $\mathcal{T} = \{0,1\}^* \times \mathcal{T}_c$ that contains two disjoint subsets, the subset of lossy tags $\mathcal{T}_{loss} \subseteq \mathcal{T}$ and that of injective tags $\mathcal{T}_{inj} \subseteq \mathcal{T}$. A tag $t \in \mathcal{T}$ consists of an auxiliary tag $t_a \in \{0,1\}^*$ and a core tag $t_c \in \mathcal{T}_c$. The trapdoor td_{LF} allows to efficiently sample a lossy tag. (2) $\mathsf{LF.Eval}(ek_{\mathsf{LF}}, t, X)$, on input a tag t and a preimage $X \in \mathcal{X}$, computes $\mathsf{LF}_{ek_{\mathsf{LF}}, t}(X) \in \mathcal{Y}$. (3) $\mathsf{LF.LTag}(td_{\mathsf{LF}}, t_a)$, on input an auxiliary tag t_a, computes a core tag t_c such that $t = (t_a, t_c)$ is lossy.

Besides the above functionalities, LF should satisfy the following properties:

Lossiness. If t is injective, so is the function $\mathsf{LF}_{ek_{\mathsf{LF}}, t}(\cdot)$. If t is lossy, then $\mathsf{LF}_{ek_{\mathsf{LF}}, t}(X)$ has at most $2^{\ell_{\mathsf{LF}}}$ possible values.

Indistinguishability. For any PPT adversary $\mathcal{A}$, it is hard to distinguish a lossy tag from a random tag, i.e., the following advantage is negligible in κ,

$$\mathsf{Adv}^{ind}_{\mathsf{LF}, \mathcal{A}}(\kappa) := |\Pr[\mathcal{A}(ek_{\mathsf{LF}}, (t_a, t_c)) = 1] - \Pr[\mathcal{A}(ek_{\mathsf{LF}}, (t_a, t'_c)) = 1]|,$$

where $(ek_{\mathsf{LF}}, td_{\mathsf{LF}}) \leftarrow \mathsf{LF.Gen}(1^\kappa)$, $t_a \leftarrow \mathcal{A}(ek_{\mathsf{LF}})$, $t_c \leftarrow \mathsf{LF.LTag}(td_{\mathsf{LF}}, t_a)$ and $t'_c \leftarrow_R \mathcal{T}_c$.

Evasiveness. For any PPT adversary $\mathcal{A}$, it is hard to generate a non-injective tag even given a lossy tag, i.e., the following advantage is negligible in κ,

$$\mathsf{Adv}^{eva}_{\mathsf{LF}, \mathcal{A}}(\kappa) := \Pr\left[\begin{array}{c} (t'_a, t'_c) \neq (t_a, t_c) \wedge \\ (t'_a, t'_c) \in \mathcal{T} \setminus \mathcal{T}_{inj} \end{array} : \begin{array}{l} (ek_{\mathsf{LF}}, td_{\mathsf{LF}}) \leftarrow \mathsf{LF.Gen}(1^\kappa) \\ t_a \leftarrow \mathcal{A}(ek_{\mathsf{LF}}) \\ t_c \leftarrow \mathsf{LF.LTag}(td_{\mathsf{LF}}, t_a) \\ (t'_a, t'_c) \leftarrow \mathcal{A}(ek_{\mathsf{LF}}, (t_a, t_c)) \end{array} \right].$$

ONE-TIME SIGNATURE. A one-time signature scheme OTS consists of four (probabilistic) polynomial-time algorithms: (1) $\mathsf{OTS.Sys}(1^\kappa)$, on input 1^κ, outputs a public parameter PP; (2) $\mathsf{OTS.Gen}(\mathrm{PP})$, on input PP, outputs a verification/signing key pair $(vk, sigk)$; (3) $\mathsf{OTS.Sig}(sigk, m)$, on input a message m, outputs a signature σ; (4) $\mathsf{OTS.Vrf}(vk, m, \sigma)$, on input a message/signature pair (m, σ), outputs 1 if σ is indeed a signature of m or 0 otherwise. We say that OTS is strongly secure against chosen-message attacks, if for any stateful PPT adversary $\mathcal{A}$, the following advantage is negligible in κ,

$$\mathsf{Adv}^{\mathsf{cma}}_{\mathsf{OTS},\mathcal{A}}(\kappa) := \Pr\left[\begin{array}{l} (m',\sigma') \neq (m,\sigma) \wedge \\ \mathsf{OTS.Vrf}(vk,m',\sigma') = 1 \end{array} : \begin{array}{l} \mathsf{PP} \leftarrow \mathsf{OTS.Sys}(1^{\kappa}) \\ (vk, sigk) \leftarrow \mathsf{OTS.Gen}(\mathsf{PP}) \\ m \leftarrow \mathcal{A}(\mathsf{PP}, vk) \\ \sigma \leftarrow \mathsf{OTS.Sig}(sigk, m) \\ (m',\sigma') \leftarrow \mathcal{A}(\sigma) \end{array}\right].$$

3 Properties of RKD Functions over Finite Fields

A class Φ of Related-Key Derivation (RKD) functions over $\mathcal{S}$ is a set of functions, all with the same domain and range $\mathcal{S}$. Suppose that $\mathbb{F}$ is a finite field such that $|\mathbb{F}| \geq 2^n$ for some positive integer n. Let $d \geq 0$ be any fixed integer. Define $\Phi_{\mathbb{F}}^{\mathsf{poly}(d)}$ to be the set of all polynomial functions over $\mathbb{F}$ with degree bounded by d. Clearly, $\Phi_{\mathbb{F}}^{\mathsf{poly}(d)}$ includes the identity function $f = \mathsf{id}$ (i.e., $f(x) = x$) and all the constant functions (denoted by $\mathsf{cf} = \{f_c : \mathbb{F} \to c\}_{c \in \mathbb{F}}$). We introduce the following simple lemma.

Lemma 3. *Let $\mathbb{F}$ and $\Phi_{\mathbb{F}}^{\mathsf{poly}(d)}$ be defined as above. Let X be any random variable over $\mathbb{F}$ such that $H_\infty(X) \geq n$. For any $f \in \Phi_{\mathbb{F}}^{\mathsf{poly}(d)} \setminus \mathsf{cf}$, then $H_\infty(f(X)) \geq n - \log d$ and for any $f \in \Phi_{\mathbb{F}}^{\mathsf{poly}(d)} \setminus \{\mathsf{id}\}$ then $\Pr[f(X) = X] \leq \frac{d}{2^n}$.*

Proof. For any polynomial $f \in \Phi_{\mathbb{F}}^{\mathsf{poly}(d)}$, let B_f denote the set of all solutions x over $\mathbb{F}$ such that $f(x) = 0$. Clearly, if f is not identically zero, then $|B_f|$ is bounded by d. For any fixed value $a \in \mathbb{F}$, if f is not a constant function, then $f'(x) = f(x) - a$ is not identically zero. This shows that $f'(x) = 0$ has at most d solutions x, i.e., $|B_{f'}| \leq d$. Then,

$$\Pr_{x \leftarrow X}[f(x) = a] = \Pr_{x \leftarrow X}[x \in B_{f'}] \leq \frac{d}{2^{H_\infty(X)}} \leq \frac{d}{2^n}.$$

Hence, $H_\infty(f(X)) = -\log(\max_{a \in \mathbb{F}} \Pr[f(X) = a]) \geq n - \log d$.

Similar to the above analysis, if f is not identity function, then $f''(x) = f(x) - x$ is not identically zero. Hence $f''(x) = 0$ has at most d solutions over $\mathbb{F}$, i.e., $|B_{f''}| \leq d$. Then

$$\begin{aligned} \Pr[f(X) = X] &= \sum_{a \in \mathbb{F}} \Pr[f(X) = a \wedge X = a] \\ &= \sum_{a \in B_{f''}} \Pr[f(X) = a \wedge X = a] + \sum_{a \in \mathbb{F} \setminus B_{f''}} \Pr[f(X) = a \wedge X = a] \\ &= \Pr_{x \leftarrow X}[x \in B_{f''}] + 0 \\ &\leq \frac{d}{2^{H_\infty(X)}} \leq \frac{d}{2^n}. \end{aligned}$$

This completes the proof of Lemma 3. $\square$

Remark 1. In our main result (see Theorem 1), we restrict the RKD function class to polynomials as the proof needs the properties stated in Lemma 3. In fact, we can extend it to any RKD function class that has similar properties as polynomials. We call such function class *High Output Entropy and Input-Output Collision Resistant (HOE&IOCR)* function class, which is formally defined in Definition 1.

Definition 1 (HOE&IOCR RKD function class). *Let S be a set with super-polynomial size in the security parameter κ. The RKD function class Φ_{iocr}^{hoe} : $S \to S$ is called the class of* High Output Entropy and Input-Output Collision Resistance *(HOE&IOCR) as long as it satisfies the following properties.*

- *(High Output Entropy) When S is chosen uniformly at random from S, for each $\phi \in \Phi_{iocr}^{hoe} \setminus$ cf, the entropy $H_\infty(\phi(S))$ is sufficiently large, i.e., $2^{-H_\infty(\phi(S))}$ is negligible in κ;*
- *(Input-Output Collision Resistance) For each $\phi \in \Phi_{iocr}^{hoe} \setminus \{id\}$, the probability $\Pr[\phi(S) = S]$ is negligible in κ.*

Clearly, $\Phi_{\mathbb{F}}^{poly(d)} \subseteq \Phi_{iocr}^{hoe}$, and $\Phi_{\mathbb{F}}^{poly(d)}$ satisfies $S = \mathbb{F}$, $H_\infty(S) \geq n$, $H_\infty(\phi(S)) \geq n - d$ and $\Pr[\phi(S) = S] \leq \frac{d}{2^n}$.

4 Continuous Non-malleable Key Derivation

A key derivation function consists of three (PPT) algorithms: (1) The public parameter generation algorithm KDF.Sys(1^κ), on input 1^κ, outputs a system parameter PP, which defines the derivation key space S and the derived key space $\{0,1\}^m$. (2) KDF.Sample(PP), on input PP, samples a random derivation key $s \in S$ and computes a public key, denoted by π. (3) The deterministic algorithm KDF$_\pi(s)$, on input (s, π), outputs a derived key r or the special symbol $\perp$, indicating that π is an invalid proof of s. The standard security notion of KDF guarantees that r is (computationally or information theoretically) indistinguishable from a uniform over $\{0,1\}^m$ even given the public parameter PP and the proof π.

The notion of non-malleable key derivation [17] was firstly introduced by Faust et al. at Eurocrypt 2014. Intuitively, a function KDF is a non-malleable key derivation function if KDF(s) [4] is statistically close to uniform even given the output of KDF applied to a related input s' as long as $s' \neq s$. The non-malleability for a key derivation function aims to capture the scenario of one-time tampering attack for tampering function family with all circuits of bounded size. In this section, we extend it to the notion of continuous non-malleability (see Fig. 1) for an a-priori class Φ of RKD functions, making it possible to protect against multiple-time tampering attacks on a fixed secret key (i.e., RKAs).

Definition 2 (Continuous non-malleable KDFs). *Let Φ be a class of RKD functions over the same domain and range S. We say that (KDF.Sys, KDF.Sample, KDF) is a (Φ, ϵ)-continuous non-malleable key derivation function if for any **stateful** PPT adversary $\mathcal{A}$,*

$$|\Pr[\mathcal{A}(\mathsf{Real}_{\mathsf{KDF}}(\Phi, \kappa)) = 1] - \Pr[\mathcal{A}(\mathsf{Sim}_{\mathsf{KDF}}(\Phi, \kappa)) = 1]| \leq \epsilon.$$

The experiments $\mathsf{Real}_{\mathsf{KDF}}(\Phi, \kappa)$ and $\mathsf{Sim}_{\mathsf{KDF}}(\Phi, \kappa)$ are defined in Fig. 1 (Suppose that $\mathcal{A}$ makes at most $Q(\kappa)$ queries).

---

[4] In [17], the key derivation is defined in the information theoretic setting, not taking π as an auxiliary input, i.e., π is empty.

Experiment $\mathsf{Real}_{\mathsf{KDF}}(\varPhi, \kappa)$:	Experiment $\mathsf{Sim}_{\mathsf{KDF}}(\varPhi, \kappa)$:
$\quad$ PP $\leftarrow$ KDF.Sys(1^κ)	$\quad$ PP $\leftarrow$ KDF.Sys(1^κ)
$\quad s\|\pi \leftarrow$ KDF.Sample(PP) $\quad // \ s \in \mathcal{S}$	$\quad s\|\pi \leftarrow$ KDF.Sample(PP) $\quad // s \in \mathcal{S}$
$\quad r = \mathsf{KDF}_\pi(s)$	$\quad r \leftarrow_R \{0,1\}^m$
$\quad$ For $i = 1$ to $Q(\kappa)$	$\quad$ For $i = 1$ to $Q(\kappa)$
$\quad\quad (\phi, \pi') \leftarrow \mathcal{A}(\text{PP}, r, \pi) \quad // \ \phi \in \varPhi$	$\quad\quad (\phi, \pi') \leftarrow \mathcal{A}(\text{PP}, r, \pi) \quad // \ \phi \in \varPhi$
$\quad\quad$ If $\phi(s)\|\pi' = s\|\pi$	$\quad\quad$ If $\phi(s)\|\pi' = s\|\pi$
$\quad\quad\quad$ return same*.	$\quad\quad\quad$ return same*.
$\quad$ Else	$\quad$ Else
$\quad\quad$ return $\mathsf{KDF}_{\pi'}(\phi(s))$.	$\quad\quad$ return $\mathsf{KDF}_{\pi'}(\phi(s))$.

Fig. 1. Experiments for continuous non-malleable KDFs

4.1 The Construction

In this subsection, we construct a continuous non-malleable key derivation function with respect to $\varPhi_{\mathbb{F}}^{\mathsf{poly}(d)}$ from one-time lossy filter.

Let (LF.Gen, LF.Eval, LF.LTag) be a collection of one-time lossy filters with domain $\mathcal{S}$ (such that $\mathcal{S} \subseteq \mathbb{F}$), range $\mathcal{Y}$, residual leakage ℓ_{LF} and tag space $\mathcal{T} = \{0,1\}^* \times \mathcal{T}_c$. Let $\mathcal{H}$ be a family of pairwise independent hash functions from domain $\mathcal{S}$ to range $\{0,1\}^m$. Let (OTS.Sys, OTS.Gen, OTS.Sig, OTS.Vrf) be a strongly secure one-time signature with verification key space $\mathcal{K}_{\mathsf{OTS}}$ and signature space Σ. Define $\Pi := \mathcal{T} \times \mathcal{Y} \times \Sigma$. The construction is given in Fig. 2.

Theorem 1. *The KDF given in Fig. 2 is $(\varPhi_{\mathbb{F}}^{\mathsf{poly}(d)}, \epsilon)$-continuously non-malleable. Concretely, for any $\delta > 0$ and any PPT adversary $\mathcal{A}$ that makes at most $Q(\kappa)$ queries and breaks the continuous non-malleability with advantage ϵ, there exist adversaries $\mathcal{B}, \mathcal{B}'$ and $\mathcal{B}''$ of roughly the same time complexity as $\mathcal{A}$, such that*

$$\epsilon \leq 2\Big(\mathsf{Adv}_{\mathsf{OTS}, \mathcal{B}}^{\mathsf{cma}}(\kappa) + \mathsf{Adv}_{\mathsf{LF}, \mathcal{B}'}^{\mathsf{ind}}(\kappa) + Q(\kappa) \cdot \mathsf{Adv}_{\mathsf{LF}, \mathcal{B}''}^{\mathsf{eva}}(\kappa) +$$
$$Q(\kappa) \cdot \Big(\delta + \frac{d \cdot 2^{m + \ell_{\mathsf{LF}} + \log 1/\delta}}{|\mathcal{S}| - Q(\kappa) + 1} \Big) + \epsilon_{\mathcal{H}} \Big),$$

where $\mathcal{S}$ and ℓ_{LF} respectively are the domain and residual leakage of the one-time lossy filter, m is the output length of the pairwise independent hash, d is the maximum degree of RKD functions and $\log |\mathcal{S}| \geq \max\{\ell_{\mathsf{LF}} + m + 2\log 1/\epsilon_{\mathcal{H}}, \ell_{\mathsf{LF}} + m + \log 1/\delta\}$. Taking into account that ϵ should be negligible in the security parameter κ, we may choose negligible δ and $\epsilon_{\mathcal{H}}$, and choose a OT-LF with sufficiently large domain $\mathcal{S}$ such that $\log |\mathcal{S}| = \ell_{\mathsf{LF}} + m + \omega(\log \kappa)$. Moreover, the degree of RKD functions can be made to 2^κ as long as $\log |\mathcal{S}| = \ell_{\mathsf{LF}} + m + \omega(\log \kappa) + \kappa$.

Proof. We prove it through a sequence of games played between a simulator Sim and a fixed PPT adversary $\mathcal{A}$. The initial game (i.e., Game$_0$) is the experiment $\mathsf{Real}_{\mathsf{KDF}}(\varPhi_{\mathbb{F}}^{\mathsf{poly}(d)}, \kappa)$ and the final game is the experiment $\mathsf{Sim}_{\mathsf{KDF}}(\varPhi_{\mathbb{F}}^{\mathsf{poly}(d)}, \kappa)$ as defined in Fig. 1. Denote by S_i the output of $\mathcal{A}$ in Game$_i$.

- KDF.Sys(1^κ): It runs $(ek_{\mathsf{LF}}, td_{\mathsf{LF}}) \leftarrow \mathsf{LF.Gen}(1^\kappa)$ and $\mathrm{PP_{OTS}} \leftarrow \mathsf{OTS.Sys}(1^\kappa)$, chooses $h \leftarrow_R \mathcal{H}$, and returns $\mathrm{PP_{KDF}} := (ek_{\mathsf{LF}}, \mathrm{PP_{OTS}}, h)$.
- KDF.Sample($\mathrm{PP_{KDF}}$): It runs $(vk, sigk) \leftarrow \mathsf{OTS.Gen}(\mathrm{PP_{OTS}})$, chooses $s \leftarrow_R \mathcal{S}$ and $t_c \leftarrow_R \mathcal{T}_c$, and computes

$$y = \mathsf{LF}_{ek_{\mathsf{LF}}, (vk,t_c)}(s) \text{ and } \sigma = \mathsf{OTS.Sig}(sigk, t_c\|y).$$

Let $\pi := t\|y\|\sigma$ and $t := (vk, t_c)$. Finally, it returns $s\|\pi$.
- KDF$_\pi(s)$: It parses π as $t\|y\|\sigma$ and t as (vk, t_c). If the following two equations

$$\mathsf{LF}_{ek_{\mathsf{LF}}, (vk,t_c)}(s) = y \tag{1}$$

$$\mathsf{OTS.Vrf}(vk, t_c\|y, \sigma) = 1 \tag{2}$$

hold simultaneously, it returns $r = h(s)$; else it returns $\perp$.

Fig. 2. Continuous non-malleable KDF w.r.t. RKD functions $\Phi_{\mathbb{F}}^{\mathrm{poly}(d)}$

Game$_0$ (**The real experiment**): This is the real experiment $\mathsf{Real}_{\mathsf{KDF}}(\Phi_{\mathbb{F}}^{\mathrm{poly}(d)}, \kappa)$ as defined in Fig. 1. For simplicity, we denote by $\mathrm{PP_{KDF}} = (ek_{\mathsf{LF}}, \mathrm{PP_{OTS}}, h)$ the challenge public parameters and denote by $s\|\pi$ the challenge sample, where $\pi = t\|y\|\sigma$, $t = (vk, t_c)$ and vk is the corresponding OTS verification key (with respect to the signing key $sigk$). We write (ϕ, π') as $\mathcal{A}$'s queries, where $\pi' = t'\|y'\|\sigma'$ and $t' = (vk', t_c')$. Then,

$$\Pr[\mathcal{A}(\mathsf{Real}_{\mathsf{KDF}}(\Phi_{\mathbb{F}}^{\mathrm{poly}(d)}, \kappa)) = 1] = \Pr[S_0 = 1].$$

Game$_1$ (**Handling trivial queries without the KDF key**): This game is the same as Game$_0$, except that the simulator uses the new rule R1 to answer some trivial queries as given in Fig. 3. Specifically, for these trivial queries, the simulator never uses the real derivation key s to compute the value of KDF$_{\pi'}(\phi(s))$. Note that, in both Game$_0$ and Game$_1$, LF works in injective mode with overwhelming probability. Recall that $y = \mathsf{LF}_{ek_{\mathsf{LF}}, (vk,t_c)}(s)$. So, for a query (ϕ_c, π'), it satisfies $\phi_c(s)\|\pi' = s\|\pi$ if and only if $\pi' = \pi$ and $\mathsf{LF}_{ek_{\mathsf{LF}}, (vk,t_c)}(c) = y$. Hence, with overwhelming probability, these modifications are just conceptual and

$$\Pr[S_1 = 1] = \Pr[S_0 = 1].$$

Game$_2$ (**Eliminating OTS key reuse**): This game is the same as Game$_1$, except for a modification to the verification oracle as stated in Fig. 3. Let E_{OTS} denote the event that $\mathcal{A}$ submits a query $(\phi, \pi' = (vk', t_c')\|y'\|\sigma')$ such that $vk' = vk$, $(t_c'\|y', \sigma') \neq (t_c\|y, \sigma)$ but $\mathsf{OTS.Vrf}(vk, t_c'\|y', \sigma') = 1$. Clearly, Game$_2$ is identical to Game$_1$ unless the event E_{OTS} occurs. We briefly show that if the adversary makes the event E_{OTS} occur, then an efficient algorithm $\mathcal{B}$ can be constructed to break the strong security of OTS using $\mathcal{A}$ as a subroutine.

Given an OTS challenge instance $(\mathrm{PP_{OTS}}, vk)$, $\mathcal{B}$ runs $(ek_{\mathsf{LF}}, td_{\mathsf{LF}}) \leftarrow \mathsf{LF.Gen}(1^\kappa)$, chooses $h \leftarrow_R \mathcal{H}$, and sets $\mathrm{PP_{KDF}} := (ek_{\mathsf{LF}}, \mathrm{PP_{OTS}}, h)$. Then $\mathcal{B}$ samples

Games:	Key derivation rules :	r:	t_c:
Game$_0$	R0: If $\phi(s)\|\pi' = s\|\pi$, return same*, else if Eq. (1) and Eq. (2) hold, return $\mathsf{KDF}_{\pi'}(\phi(s))$, else return $\perp$.	$r = h(s)$	$t_c \leftarrow_R \mathcal{T}_c$
Game$_1$	**R1**: If $(\phi, \pi') = (\mathrm{id}, \pi)$, return same*. If $\phi = \phi_c$, $\pi' = \pi$ and $\mathsf{LF}_{ek_{\mathsf{LF}},(vk,t_c)}(c) = y$, return same*. If $\phi = \phi_c$ but $\pi' \neq \pi$ or $\mathsf{LF}_{ek_{\mathsf{LF}},(vk,t_c)}(c) \neq y$, return $\mathsf{KDF}_{\pi'}(c)$. R0: As in Game$_0$.	$r = h(s)$	$t_c \leftarrow_R \mathcal{T}_c$
Game$_2$	R1: As in Game$_1$. **R2**: If $vk' = vk$, but $(t_c'\|y', \sigma') \neq (t_c\|y, \sigma)$, return $\perp$. R0: As in Game$_1$.	$r = h(s)$	$t_c \leftarrow_R \mathcal{T}_c$
Game$_3$	R1: As in Game$_2$. R2: As in Game$_2$. **R3**: If $\pi' = \pi$, but $\phi(s) \neq s$, return $\perp$. R0: As in Game$_2$.	$r = h(s)$	$t_c \leftarrow_R \mathcal{T}_c$
Game$_4$	The same as in Game$_3$.	$r = h(s)$	$t_c \leftarrow \mathsf{LF.LTag}(td_{\mathsf{LF}}, vk)$
Game$_5$	R1: As in Game$_4$. R2: As in Game$_4$. *R3*: Replaced by **R0'**. *R0*: Replaced by **R0'**. **R0'**: Return $\perp$.	$r = h(s)$	$t_c \leftarrow \mathsf{LF.LTag}(td_{\mathsf{LF}}, vk)$
Game$_6$	As in Game$_5$.	$r \leftarrow_R \{0,1\}^m$	$t_c \leftarrow \mathsf{LF.LTag}(td_{\mathsf{LF}}, vk)$
Game$_7$	As in Game$_0$.	$r \leftarrow_R \{0,1\}^m$	$t_c \leftarrow_R \mathcal{T}_c$

Fig. 3. Changes in each game

s, t_c and computes $y = \mathsf{LF}_{ek_{\mathsf{LF}},(vk,t_c)}(s)$ by itself. Also, $\mathcal{B}$ generates σ by querying OTS signing oracle once with $t_c\|y$. Since $\mathcal{B}$ knows s, it can answer all the decryption queries (ϕ, π') from $\mathcal{A}$ (recall that decryption does not need the knowledge of the challenge OTS signing key $sigk$). So, $\mathcal{B}$ perfectly simulates the real experiment defined in Game$_1$ for $\mathcal{A}$. If $\mathcal{A}$ submits a query (ϕ, π') making the event E_{OTS} occur, $\mathcal{B}$ returns $(t_c'\|y', \sigma')$ (Note that, $\mathcal{B}$ can check whether the event E_{OTS} occurs or not). From the above observation, we have

$$|\Pr[S_2 = 1] - \Pr[S_1 = 1]| \leq \mathsf{Adv}_{\mathsf{OTS}, \mathcal{B}}^{\mathrm{cma}}(\kappa).$$

Game$_3$ (**Answering a trivial query with the KDF key**): If the adversary submits a query (ϕ, π') such that $\pi' = \pi$ (i.e., $vk' = vk$ and $(t_c'\|y', \sigma') = (t_c\|y, \sigma)$), the simulator first checks whether $\phi(s) = s$. If not, it returns $\perp$ and halts immediately. Otherwise, the simulator handles it as in Game$_2$. Recall that, with overwhelming probability, a randomly chosen LF tag (vk, t_c) is injective. So, if $\phi(s) \neq s$, then $\mathsf{LF}_{ek_{\mathsf{LF}},(vk,t_c)}(\phi(s)) \neq y$. This implies that such queries will also be rejected under the rules of Game$_2$. Hence, with overwhelming probability

$$\Pr[S_3 = 1] = \Pr[S_2 = 1].$$

Game$_4$ **(From injective to lossy LF tag):** Instead of picking $t_c \in \mathcal{T}_c$ uniformly at random, the simulator computes $t_c := \mathsf{LF.LTag}(td_{\mathsf{LF}}, vk)$.

We show that the difference between Game$_3$ and Game$_4$ can be reduced to the indistinguishability of the underlying OT-LF. Given a challenge LF evaluation key ek_{LF}, a PPT algorithm $\mathcal{B}'$ chooses h and PP$_{\mathsf{OTS}}$, samples s and $(vk, sigk)$ by itself. Then, it queries its injective-lossy tag oracle with query $t_a = vk$. $\mathcal{B}'$ will receive a challenge core tag part t_c. It computes $y = \mathsf{LF}_{ek_{\mathsf{LF}},(vk,t_c)}(s)$ and $\sigma = \mathsf{OTS.Sig}(sigk, t_c\|y)$, and sets $\pi = (vk, t_c)\|y\|\sigma$. It sends PP$_{\mathsf{KDF}} = (ek_{\mathsf{LF}}, \mathsf{PP}_{\mathsf{OTS}}, h)$ together with π to $\mathcal{A}$. Since $\mathcal{B}'$ knows the KDF key s, it can answer all the queries issued by $\mathcal{A}$. Finally, $\mathcal{B}'$ outputs whatever $\mathcal{A}$ outputs. Clearly, if t_c is sampled from $\mathcal{T}_c$ uniformly at random, then $\mathcal{B}'$ simulates Game$_3$ perfectly. If t_c is computed by $\mathsf{LF.LTag}(ek_{\mathsf{LF}}, t_a)$, then $\mathcal{B}'$ perfectly simulates Game$_4$. Hence,

$$|\Pr[S_4 = 1] - \Pr[S_3 = 1]| \leq \mathsf{Adv}^{\mathrm{ind}}_{\mathsf{LF}, \mathcal{B}'}(\kappa)$$

for some adversary $\mathcal{B}'$ attacking on the indistinguishability of OT-LF.

Game$_5$ **(Answering all queries without the KDF key):** In this game, the simulator replaces the rules in step R3 and R0 (relying on the KDF key) with R0' (without relying on the KDF key) as stated in Fig. 3. Note that, the new rule directly rejects all queries except those trivial queries which have already be answered by rule R1. Denote by F the event that $\mathcal{A}$ submits a query (ϕ, π') such that the simulator returns the special symbol $\bot$ in Game$_5$, but not in Game$_4$. Also, let E_{ninj} denote the event that among all the queries (ϕ, π'), there exists some non-injective LF tag such that $(vk', t'_c) \neq (vk, t_c)$. Recall that, for the same query (ϕ, π'), if the simulator responds to $\mathcal{A}$ a result not being the special symbol $\bot$ in Game$_5$, then the simulator must return the same result as in Game$_4$. So, unless event F occurs, the two games are identical from the adversary's point of view. By the difference lemma [26, Lemma 1], it follows that $|\Pr[S_5 = 1] - \Pr[S_4 = 1]| \leq \Pr[F]$.

We show the upper bound of the probability $\Pr[F]$ by the following observation

$$\Pr[F] = \Pr[F \wedge E_{\mathrm{ninj}}] + \Pr[F \wedge \overline{E_{\mathrm{ninj}}}] \leq \Pr[E_{\mathrm{ninj}}] + \Pr[F | \overline{E_{\mathrm{ninj}}}]$$

where all probabilities are taken over the randomness used in the experiment in Game$_4$. The following two lemmas show that both the probabilities $\Pr[E_{\mathrm{ninj}}]$ and $\Pr[F | \overline{E_{\mathrm{ninj}}}]$ are negligible in κ. We postpone to prove them after the main proof.

Lemma 4. *Suppose that $\mathcal{A}$ makes at most $Q(\kappa)$ queries. Then*

$$\Pr[E_{\mathrm{ninj}}] \leq Q(\kappa) \cdot \mathsf{Adv}^{\mathrm{eva}}_{\mathsf{LF}, \mathcal{B}''}(\kappa)$$

for some suitable adversary $\mathcal{B}''$ attacking on the evasiveness of OT-LF.

Lemma 5. *Suppose that $\mathcal{A}$ makes at most $Q(\kappa)$ queries. For any $\delta > 0$, we have*

$$\Pr[F | \overline{E_{\mathrm{ninj}}}] \leq Q(\kappa) \cdot \left(\delta + \frac{d \cdot 2^{m + \ell_{\mathsf{LF}} + \log 1/\delta}}{|\mathcal{S}| - Q(\kappa) + 1} \right).$$

Game$_6$ (**Replacing $h(s)$ by a random string**): This game is the same as Game$_5$, except that the simulator samples a random string $r \leftarrow_R \{0,1\}^m$ instead of computing $r = h(s)$. Recall that in both Game$_5$ and Game$_6$, except r, the simulator never uses the KDF derivation key s to answer $\mathcal{A}$'s queries. So, the adversary does not learn any more information on s through the key derivation oracle $\mathsf{KDF}_{\pi'}(\phi(s))$. Observe that from the adversary's point of view, only the value y may reveal information on s and all other values are independent of s (e.g., $\mathsf{PP_{KDF}}$ and (vk, t_c)) or are just functions of y (e.g., σ). It holds by the lossiness property of the OT-LF and by Lemma 1 that

$$\widetilde{H}_\infty(s|(\mathsf{PP_{KDF}}, \pi)) \geq \widetilde{H}_\infty(s|\mathsf{PP_{KDF}}) - \ell_{\mathsf{LF}} = \log|\mathcal{S}| - \ell_{\mathsf{LF}}.$$

Since $\log|\mathcal{S}| - \ell_{\mathsf{LF}} - 2\log(1/\epsilon_{\mathcal{H}}) \geq m$, by Lemma 2, we have that $h(s)$ is $\epsilon_{\mathcal{H}}$-close to uniform over $\{0,1\}^m$ from $\mathcal{A}$'s point of view. Hence,

$$|\Pr[S_6 = 1] - \Pr[S_5 = 1]| \leq \epsilon_{\mathcal{H}}.$$

Game$_7$ (**Reversing to answer all queries with the KDF key**): This game is the same as in Game 6, except that the simulator samples $\mathsf{PP_{KDF}}$ and $s||\pi$, and answers queries (ϕ, π') as in Game$_0$. Note that, in this game, r is still sampled as in Game$_6$. Through defining a sequence of reverse games from Game$_6$ to Game$_0$, we can prove that

$$|\Pr[S_7 = 1] - \Pr[S_6 = 1]| \leq |\Pr[S_6 = 1] - \Pr[S_0 = 1]|.$$

Observe that, Game$_7$ is just the simulated experiment $\mathsf{Sim_{KDF}}(\Phi_{\mathbb{F}}^{\mathsf{poly}(d)}, \kappa)$ and hence

$$\Pr[\mathcal{A}(\mathsf{Sim_{KDF}}(\Phi_{\mathbb{F}}^{\mathsf{poly}(d)}, \kappa)) = 1] = \Pr[S_7 = 1].$$

Taking all together, Theorem 1 follows. $\square$

Now, we prove Lemma 4 and Lemma 5.

Proof (Proof of Lemma 4). Given a challenge LF evaluation key ek_{LF}, $\mathcal{B}''$ simulates $\mathcal{A}$'s environment in Game$_4$ as follows. It first picks $\mathsf{PP_{OTS}} \leftarrow \mathsf{OTS.Sys}(1^\kappa)$, $h \leftarrow_R \mathcal{H}$ and $s \leftarrow_R \mathcal{S}$. It then samples a OTS key pair $(vk, sigk) \leftarrow \mathsf{OTS.Gen}(\mathsf{PP_{OTS}})$. After that, $\mathcal{B}''$ queries $\mathsf{LF.LTag}(ek_{\mathsf{LF}}, \cdot)$ with vk to obtain the challenge core tag part i.e., $t_c = \mathsf{LF.LTag}(td_{\mathsf{LF}}, vk)$. Next, $\mathcal{B}''$ computes $y = \mathsf{LF}_{ek_{\mathsf{LF}}, (vk, t_c)}(s)$ and $\sigma = \mathsf{OTS.Sig}(sigk, t_c||y)$. $\mathcal{B}''$ sends $\mathsf{PP_{KDF}} = (ek_{\mathsf{LF}}, \mathsf{PP_{OTS}}, h)$ and $\pi = (vk, t_c)||y||\sigma$ to the adversary $\mathcal{A}$. Since $\mathcal{B}''$ knows the KDF key s, he can answer all the queries as in Game$_4$. Let $T = \{(vk', t_c')\}$ be the set of tags extracted from $\mathcal{A}$'s queries (ϕ, π') such that $(vk', t_c') \neq (vk, t_c)$. Finally, $\mathcal{B}''$ chooses a tag (vk', t_c') from T uniformly at random as his output. If E_{ninj} occurs, with probability at least $1/Q(\kappa)$, $\mathcal{B}''$ outputs a fresh non-injective tag. Hence, $\Pr[E_{\mathsf{ninj}}] \leq Q(\kappa) \cdot \mathsf{Adv}_{\mathsf{LF}, \mathcal{B}''}^{\mathsf{eva}}(\kappa)$. $\square$

Proof (Proof of Lemma 5). Let (ϕ, π') be the first query that does not satisfy the key derivation rules of R1 and R2 in Game$_4$ and event E_{ninj} does not happen.

We call such query invalid query. Recall that an invalid query is always rejected (output $\perp$) in Game_5. We show that it is not rejected in Game_4 with a negligible probability. Clearly, if $(t'_c||y', \sigma')$ is an invalid signature, then (ϕ, π') will be rejected in both Game_4 and Game_5. We consider three cases:

- Case 0: $\pi' = \pi$ and $\phi(s) \neq s$.
- Case 1: $\pi' = \pi$, $\phi \neq \mathsf{id}$, but $\phi(s) = s$.
- Case 2: $vk' \neq vk$ and $\phi \notin \mathsf{cf}$.

Note that, for any query (ϕ, π'), it always satisfies the key derivation rules defined in either R1 or R2, except for the above three cases. Recall that, in the first case, both Game_4 and Game_5 outputs $\perp$. Hence, only the Case 1 and Case 2 may cause the difference between Game_4 and Game_5. Next, we show that the last two cases will be rejected in Game_4 with overwhelming probability.

Observe that in Game_4, only values r and y may contain information on the KDF derivation key s. The other values are independent of s (e.g., $\mathsf{PP_{KDF}}$ and vk) or just functions of y (e.g., σ). Denote by V the adversary's view in Game_4. From Lemma 1 and the fact that r and y have at most 2^m and $2^{\ell_{\mathsf{LF}}}$ possible values respectively, we have

$$\tilde{H}_\infty(s|V) = \tilde{H}_\infty(s|(\mathsf{PP_{KDF}}, r||\pi)) \geq \tilde{H}_\infty(s|\mathsf{PP_{KDF}}) - m - \ell_{\mathsf{LF}}.$$

Recall that s is independent of $\mathsf{PP_{KDF}}$. So, the average min-entropy of s conditioned on the adversary's point of view is at least $\log|\mathcal{S}| - m - \ell_{\mathsf{LF}}$. According to Lemma 1, for any $\delta > 0$, with probability at least $1 - \delta$,

$$H_\infty(s|V = v) \geq \tilde{H}_\infty(s|V) - \log 1/\delta \geq \log|\mathcal{S}| - m - \ell_{\mathsf{LF}} - \log 1/\delta$$

over the choice of $V = v$.

According to Lemma 3, for any $\phi \neq \mathsf{id}$, we have

$$\Pr[\phi(s) = s] \leq \frac{d}{2^{H_\infty(s|V=v)}}.$$

So, in Case 1, with probability at least $1 - \delta$,

$$\Pr[\phi(s) = s] \leq \frac{d \cdot 2^{m + \ell_{\mathsf{LF}} + \log 1/\delta}}{|\mathcal{S}|}.$$

Again, according to Lemma 3, for any $\phi \notin \mathsf{cf}$

$$H_\infty(\phi(s)|V = v) \geq H_\infty(s|V = v) - \log d \geq \log|\mathcal{S}| - m - \ell_{\mathsf{LF}} - \log 1/\delta - \log d$$

with probability at least $1 - \delta$.

Recall that event E_{ninj} does not happen, so (vk', t'_c) is an injective tag, which means that $\mathsf{LF}_{ek_{\mathsf{LF}}, (vk', t'_c)}(\cdot)$ is injective. As a result, the adversary can correctly guess the value $\mathsf{LF}_{ek_{\mathsf{LF}}, (vk', t'_c)}(\phi(s))$ with probability at most $\delta + d \cdot 2^{m + \ell_{\mathsf{LF}} + \log 1/\delta}/|\mathcal{S}|$. Therefore, the first invalid query passes the key derivation rules in Game_4 with probability at most $\delta + d \cdot 2^{m + \ell_{\mathsf{LF}} + \log 1/\delta}/|\mathcal{S}|$.

An almost identical argument holds for all subsequent invalid queries. The only difference is that the adversary can rule out one more value s from each rejection of invalid query. So, R3 or R0 accepts the i-th invalid query with probability at most $\delta + d \cdot 2^{m+\ell_{\mathsf{LF}}+\log 1/\delta}/(|\mathcal{S}| - i + 1)$. Since $\mathcal{A}$ makes at most $Q(\kappa)$ queries, the event $F|\overline{E_{\mathsf{ninj}}}$ occurs with probability at most

$$Q(\kappa) \cdot \left(\delta + \frac{d \cdot 2^{m+\ell_{\mathsf{LF}}+\log 1/\delta}}{|\mathcal{S}| - Q(\kappa) + 1} \right).$$

This finishes the proof of Lemma 5. $\qquad\qquad\qquad\qquad\qquad\qquad\qquad\qquad\square$

4.2 Instantiations

According to [24,25], OT-LFs can be constructed from standard assumptions including the DDH assumption and the DCR assumption. This results in instantiations of $\Phi_{\mathbb{F}}^{\mathsf{poly}(d)}$-cnm-KDF (w.r.t. $\Phi_{\mathsf{iocr}}^{\mathsf{hoe}}$-cnm-KDF) based on these standard assumptions.

5 Application to RKA-secure IBE

An identity-based encryption scheme IBE consists of five (PPT) algorithms: (1) IBE.Sys(1^κ), on input 1^κ, outputs a system parameter PP, which defines an identity space $\mathcal{ID}$. (2) IBE.Gen(PP), on input PP, outputs a master public key mpk and a master secret key msk. (3) IBE.Ext(msk, id), on input msk and an identity $id \in \mathcal{ID}$, outputs a decryption key dk_{id}. (4) IBE.Enc(mpk, id, M), on input a message M, outputs a ciphertext C encrypted under mpk and identity id. (5) The deterministic algorithm IBE.Dec(dk_{id}, C), on input decryption key dk_{id} and ciphertext C, outputs a message M. Correctness requires that for all public parameter PP $\leftarrow$ IBE.Sys(1^κ), all master public/secret key pair (mpk, msk) $\leftarrow$ IBE.Gen(PP), all identity id and message M, it always has IBE.Dec(dk_{id}, IBE.Enc(mpk, id, M)) $= M$.

RKA-SECURE IBE. We recall the Φ-RKA security of IBE schemes from [4]. In the context of IBE, an RKA adversary is allowed to access a decryption key generation oracle: $\mathcal{O}_{msk}^{\Phi}(\cdot, \cdot)$, on input $(\phi, id) \in \Phi \times \mathcal{ID}$, it returns IBE.Ext($\phi(msk)$, id). Besides this, the oracle initializes an empty set $I := \emptyset$ and $id^* = \perp$. For an RKA query (ϕ, id), if $\phi(msk) = msk$ [5], it adds id to the set $I := I \cup \{id\}$, and if id equals the challenge identity id^*, it returns $\perp$ directly. An IBE scheme is Φ-RKA secure, if for any PPT adversary $\mathcal{A}$, the following advantage

$$\mathsf{Adv}_{\mathsf{IBE}, \mathcal{A}}^{\mathsf{rka}}(\kappa) := \left| \Pr \left[b' = b : \begin{array}{l} \mathrm{PP} \leftarrow \mathsf{IBE.Sys}(1^\kappa) \\ (mpk, msk) \leftarrow \mathsf{IBE.Gen}(\mathrm{PP}) \\ (M_0, M_1, id^*, St) \leftarrow \mathcal{A}^{\mathcal{O}_{msk}^{\Phi}(\cdot, \cdot)}(\mathrm{PP}, mpk) \\ b \leftarrow_R \{0, 1\}, C \leftarrow \mathsf{IBE.Enc}(mpk, id^*, M_b) \\ b' \leftarrow \mathcal{A}^{\mathcal{O}_{msk}^{\Phi}(\cdot, \cdot)}(St, C) \end{array} \right] - \frac{1}{2} \right|$$

---

[5] If msk contains some public information, for example in our construction $msk = (s, \pi)$ where π is completely given to an adversary, we define $\phi(msk) = (\phi(s), \pi')$ and π' is implicitly defined in the adversary's query (ϕ, id).

is negligible in κ, where M_0 and M_1 are two equal length messages. Clearly, if Φ only contains the identity function id, then the above definition is just the traditional CPA-security of IBE schemes [9].

Suppose that IBE.Gen(PP) utilizes an m-bit random string as the internal coin for generating mpk and msk. We write r explicitly in the key generation algorithm, i.e., IBE.Gen(PP; r) $= (mpk, msk)$ (a deterministic algorithm w.r.t. input (PP, r)).

The IBE Construction. Starting from a $(\Phi, \epsilon_{\mathsf{KDF}})$-continuous non-malleable KDF (KDF.Sys, KDF.Sample, KDF) and a CPA-secure IBE scheme (IBE.Sys, IBE.Gen, IBE.Ext, IBE.Enc, IBE.Dec), we construct a new IBE scheme ($\overline{\mathsf{IBE}}$.Sys, $\overline{\mathsf{IBE}}$.Gen, $\overline{\mathsf{IBE}}$.Ext, $\overline{\mathsf{IBE}}$.Enc, $\overline{\mathsf{IBE}}$.Dec) as follows:

- $\overline{\mathsf{IBE}}$.Sys(1^κ): It runs $\mathrm{PP}_{\mathsf{KDF}} \leftarrow$ KDF.Sys(1^κ) and $\mathrm{PP}_{\mathsf{IBE}} \leftarrow$ IBE.Sys(1^κ), and returns $\mathrm{PP}_{\overline{\mathsf{IBE}}} = (\mathrm{PP}_{\mathsf{KDF}}, \mathrm{PP}_{\mathsf{IBE}})$.
- $\overline{\mathsf{IBE}}$.Gen($\mathrm{PP}_{\overline{\mathsf{IBE}}}$): It samples $s\|\pi \leftarrow$ KDF.Sample($\mathrm{PP}_{\mathsf{KDF}}$) and computes $r = $ KDF$_\pi(s)$. Then, it computes $(mpk, msk) = $ IBE.Gen($\mathrm{PP}_{\mathsf{IBE}}; r$) and returns master public key $\overline{mpk} = (mpk, \pi)$ and secret key $\overline{msk} = (s, \pi)$.
- $\overline{\mathsf{IBE}}$.Ext($\overline{msk}, id$): For $\overline{msk} = (s, \pi)$, it computes $r = $ KDF$_\pi(s)$. If r is the special symbol $\bot$, it returns $\bot$ and halts. Otherwise, it computes $(mpk, msk) = $ IBE.Gen($\mathrm{PP}_{\mathsf{IBE}}; r$) and returns $\overline{dk}_{id} = $ IBE.Ext(msk, id).
- $\overline{\mathsf{IBE}}$.Enc($\overline{mpk}, id, M$): It first parses $\overline{mpk}$ as (mpk, π) and then returns $\overline{C} = $ IBE.Enc(mpk, id, M).
- $\overline{\mathsf{IBE}}$.Dec($\overline{dk}_{id}, \overline{C}$): It returns IBE.Dec($\overline{dk}_{id}, \overline{C}$).

Theorem 2. *If* KDF *is* $(\Phi, \epsilon_{\mathsf{KDF}})$-*continuously non-malleable and* IBE *is CPA-secure, then the above construction is a* Φ-*RKA secure IBE scheme. Concretely, for any PPT adversary* $\mathcal{A}$, *there exist KDF distinguisher* $\mathcal{D}$ *and adversary* $\mathcal{B}$ *of roughly the same complexity as* $\mathcal{A}$ *such that*

$$\mathsf{Adv}^{\mathrm{rka}}_{\mathsf{IBE}, \mathcal{A}}(\kappa) \leq \epsilon_{\mathsf{KDF}} + \mathsf{Adv}^{\mathrm{cpa}}_{\mathsf{IBE}, \mathcal{B}}(\kappa).$$

Proof. We prove it through two games: Game_0 and Game_1. The former is just the original experiment of RKA-security and the later is slightly different from the former in which the internal coin r is replaced by a uniform random string. We depict the difference between these two games in Fig. 4. In addition, we define an auxiliary game Game_0', which is the same as Game_0 except that the key extraction oracle works as in Game_1. Observe that, in the case of $\phi(s)\|\pi' = s\|\pi$, the random coin r' computed via KDF$_{\pi'}(\phi(s))$ is always equal to r, the random coin involved in the challenge master key generation algorithm. Hence, this modification is just conceptional and we can view Game_0 as Game_0' in the following proof.

Denote by S_0 and S_1 the event that $\mathcal{A}$ successfully guesses the random coin b in Game_0 and Game_1 respectively. We show shortly that

$$|\Pr[S_0] - \Pr[S_1]| \leq \epsilon_{\mathsf{KDF}} \tag{3}$$

$$|\Pr[S_1] - 1/2| \leq \mathsf{Adv}^{\mathrm{cpa}}_{\mathsf{IBE}, \mathcal{B}}(\kappa). \tag{4}$$

Clearly,

$$\mathsf{Adv}^{\mathrm{rka}}_{\mathsf{IBE}, \mathcal{A}}(\kappa) = |\Pr[S_0] - 1/2|.$$

	In Game$_0$:	In Game$_1$:
Master	$s\|\|\pi \leftarrow$ KDF.Sample(PP$_{\text{KDF}}$)	$s\|\|\pi \leftarrow$ KDF.Sample(PP$_{\text{KDF}}$)
public	$r =$ KDF$_\pi(s)$	$r \leftarrow_R \{0,1\}^m$
key	$(mpk, msk) =$ IBE.Gen(PP$_{\text{IBE}}; r$)	$(mpk, msk) =$ IBE.Gen(PP$_{\text{IBE}}; r$)
	Return $\overline{mpk} = (mpk, \pi)$.	Return $\overline{mpk} = (mpk, \pi)$.
Dec.	If $\phi(s)\|\|\pi' = s\|\|\pi$, set $I := I \cup \{id\}$.	If $\phi(s)\|\|\pi' = s\|\|\pi$, set $I := I \cup \{id\}$ and
key		return $\boxed{\text{IBE.Ext}(msk, id)}$.
oracle		Else compute
	$r' =$ KDF$_{\pi'}(\phi(s))$	$r' =$ KDF$_{\pi'}(\phi(s))$
Input:	If $r' =\bot$, return $\bot$. Else, compute	If $r' =\bot$, return $\bot$. Else, compute
(ϕ, id)	$(mpk', msk') =$ IBE.Gen(PP$_{\text{IBE}}; r'$)	$(mpk', msk') =$ IBE.Gen(PP$_{\text{IBE}}; r'$)
	Return $\overline{dk}_{id} \leftarrow$ IBE.Ext(msk', id).	Return $\overline{dk}_{id} \leftarrow$ IBE.Ext(msk', id).

Fig. 4. Differences between Game$_0$ and Game$_1$

This completes the proof of Theorem 2. $\square$

Proof (Proof of Eq. (3)). Given (PP$_{\text{KDF}}, r, \pi$) where r either equals KDF$_\pi(s)$ or a uniform random string, the simulator chooses PP$_{\text{IBE}}$ and computes $(mpk, msk) =$ IBE.Gen(PP$_{\text{IBE}}; r$). It sends $\overline{mpk} = (mpk, \pi)$ to the adversary and keeps the secret key msk. The simulator answers $\mathcal{A}$'s decryption key queries (ϕ, id) as follows: It sends (ϕ, π') to the KDF oracle and obtains the value r'. If $r' =$ same*, the simulator returns IBE.Ext(msk, id) to $\mathcal{A}$ and updates $I := I \cup \{id\}$. If $r' =\bot$, the simulator returns $\bot$. Otherwise, the simulator computes $(mpk', msk') =$ IBE.Gen(PP$_{\text{IBE}}; r'$) and returns IBE.Ext(msk', id) to $\mathcal{A}$. After the phase of decryption key queries, $\mathcal{A}$ submits two equal-length messages (M_0, M_1) and a challenge identity id^*. The simulator picks $b \leftarrow_R \{0,1\}$ and returns $\overline{C} =$ IBE.Enc(mpk, id^*, M_b) to $\mathcal{A}$. Finally, the simulator outputs what $\mathcal{A}$ outputs. Recall that, the symbol same* implies $\phi(s)\|\|\pi' = s\|\|\pi$. So, if $r =$ KDF$_\pi(s)$, the simulator perfectly simulates Game$_0$. While if r is a uniform string, the simulator simulates Game$_1$. This completes the proof of Eq. (3). $\square$

Proof (Proof of Eq. (4)). Given an IBE challenge instance (PP$_{\text{IBE}}, mpk$), the simulator samples PP$_{\text{KDF}} \leftarrow$ KDF.Sys(1^κ) and sets PP$_{\overline{\text{IBE}}} =$ (PP$_{\text{KDF}}$, PP$_{\text{IBE}}$). It also samples $s\|\|\pi \leftarrow$ KDF.Sample(PP$_{\text{KDF}}$) and sets $\overline{mpk} = (mpk, \pi)$. Then it sends (PP$_{\overline{\text{IBE}}}, \overline{mpk}$) to $\mathcal{A}$. To answer $\mathcal{A}$'s decryption key queries (ϕ, id), the simulator first checks whether $\phi(s)\|\|\pi' = s\|\|\pi$. If so, it submits id to its own decryption key generation oracle and forwards the result to $\mathcal{A}$. Since the simulator knows s and it can handle the case $\phi(s)\|\|\pi' \neq s\|\|\pi$ as in Game$_1$. When $\mathcal{A}$ queries the challenge ciphertext, the simulator forwards (M_0, M_1, id^*) to its own encryption oracle to obtain a challenge ciphertext C. The simulator forwards C to the adversary. Finally, the simulator outputs what $\mathcal{A}$ outputs. Clearly, the simulator perfectly simulates $\mathcal{A}$'s environment in Game$_1$. If $\mathcal{A}$ succeeds, so does the simulator. This completes the proof of Eq. (4). $\square$

From [27], we have a CPA-secure IBE scheme under the standard DBDH assumption. Subsection 4.2 suggests that $\Phi_{\mathbb{F}}^{\text{poly}(d)}$-continuously non-malleable

KDFs can be constructed from the DDH and DCR assumptions. Consequently, our IBE construction above immediately results in the first IBE that is RKA-secure for class $\Phi_{\mathbb{F}}^{\mathsf{poly}(d)}$, i.e., the sets of all polynomial functions of bounded degree, under the standard DBDH assumption, and the security follows from Theorem 1 and Theorem 2. We stress that the degree of our RKD polynomial functions is not limited to polynomial size in κ and we can always enlarge the polynomial function class $\Phi_{\mathbb{F}}^{\mathsf{poly}(d)}$ to class $\Phi_{\mathsf{iocr}}^{\mathsf{hoe}}$ whose functions has high output entropy and input-output collision resistance, as defined in Definition 1. As a result, the $\Phi_{\mathbb{F}}^{\mathsf{poly}(d)}$-RKA security of IBE can be extended to $\Phi_{\mathsf{iocr}}^{\mathsf{hoe}}$, with $\Phi_{\mathsf{iocr}}^{\mathsf{hoe}} \supseteq \Phi_{\mathbb{F}}^{\mathsf{poly}(d)}$.

EXTENSIONS TO PKE AND SIGNATURE. Bellare et al. [6] showed that the CHK [10] IBE-to-CCA-PKE transform and the Naor IBE-to-Sig transform both preserve Φ-RKA security. Thus, we readily obtain $\Phi_{\mathbb{F}}^{\mathsf{poly}(d)}$ (also extended to $\Phi_{\mathsf{iocr}}^{\mathsf{hoe}}$)-RKA-secure CCA-PKE and signature schemes under standard assumptions.

On the other hand, the continuous non-malleable KDFs can also be directly used to transform a cryptographic primitive to a RKA secure version in a modular way, as long as the key generation algorithm of the primitive takes uniform random coins r to generate (secret/public) keys. The transformation with the help of cnm-KDF is as follows. First, sample a random derivation key s together with the public key π such that $\mathsf{KDF}_\pi(s) = r$; Then, store s in the cryptographic hardware device. In addition, we append the proof π of s to the public key of the system. When using r, we retrieve it via computing $\mathsf{KDF}_\pi(s)$. By the property of continuous non-malleability, if s is modified to $\phi(s) \neq s$ and π to π', then $r' = \mathsf{KDF}_{\pi'}(\phi(s))$ is either the rejection symbol $\bot$ or a value independent of r. Finally, the Φ-RKA security is reduced to the original security of the primitive.

Acknowledgments. Baodong Qin and Shengli Liu were supported by the National Natural Science Foundation of China (Grant No. 61170229 and 61373 153), the Specialized Research Fund for the Doctoral Program of Higher Education (Grant No. 20110073110016), and the Scientific innovation projects of Shanghai Education Committee (Grant No. 12ZZ021). Kefei Chen was supported by the National Natural Science Foundation of China (Grant No. 61133014). The authors would also like to thank anonymous reviewers for very useful comments and suggestions on a preliminary version of this paper. Special thanks go to the reviewer who pointed out that our result holds for the extended RKD function class defined in Definition 1.

References

1. Abdalla, M., Benhamouda, F., Passelègue, A., Paterson, K.G.: Related-key security for pseudorandom functions beyond the linear barrier. In: Garay, J.A., Gennaro, R. (eds.) CRYPTO 2014, Part I. LNCS, vol. 8616, pp. 77–94. Springer, Heidelberg (2014)
2. Rosini, M.D.: Applications. In: Rosini, M.D. (ed.) Macroscopic Models for Vehicular Flows and Crowd Dynamics: Theory and Applications. UCS, vol. 12, pp. 217–226. Springer, Heidelberg (2013)

3. Bellare, M., Cash, D.: Pseudorandom functions and permutations provably secure against related-key attacks. In: Rabin, T. (ed.) Crypto 2010. LNCS, vol. 6223, pp. 666–684. Springer, Heidelberg (2010)
4. Bellare, M., Cash, D., Miller, R.: Cryptography secure against related-key attacks and tampering. In: Lee, D.H., Wang, X. (eds.) ASIACRYPT 2011. LNCS, vol. 7073, pp. 486–503. Springer, Heidelberg (2011)
5. Bellare, M., Kohno, T.: A theoretical treatment of related-key attacks: RKA-PRPs, RKA-PRFs, and applications. In: Biham, E. (ed.) EUROCRYPT 2003. LNCS, vol. 2656, pp. 491–506. Springer, Heidelberg (2003)
6. Bellare, M., Paterson, K.G., Thomson, S.: RKA security beyond the linear barrier: IBE, encryption and signatures. In: Wang, X., Sako, K. (eds.) ASIACRYPT 2012. LNCS, vol. 7658, pp. 331–348. Springer, Heidelberg (2012)
7. Biham, E., Shamir, A.: Differential fault analysis of secret key cryptosystems. In: Kaliski Jr, B.S. (ed.) CRYPTO 1997. LNCS, vol. 1294, pp. 513–525. Springer, Heidelberg (1997)
8. Boneh, D., DeMillo, R.A., Lipton, R.J.: On the importance of checking cryptographic protocols for faults. In: Fumy, W. (ed.) EUROCRYPT 1997. LNCS, vol. 1233, pp. 37–51. Springer, Heidelberg (1997)
9. Boneh, D., Franklin, M.: Identity-based encryption from the weil pairing. In: Kilian, J. (ed.) CRYPTO 2001. LNCS, vol. 2139, p. 213. Springer, Heidelberg (2001)
10. Canetti, R., Halevi, S., Katz, J.: Chosen-ciphertext security from identity-based encryption. In: Cachin, C., Camenisch, J.L. (eds.) EUROCRYPT 2004. LNCS, vol. 3027, pp. 207–222. Springer, Heidelberg (2004)
11. Cramer, R., Dodis, Y., Fehr, S., Padró, C., Wichs, D.: Detection of algebraic manipulation with applications to robust secret sharing and fuzzy extractors. In: Smart, N.P. (ed.) EUROCRYPT 2008. LNCS, vol. 4965, pp. 471–488. Springer, Heidelberg (2008)
12. Damgård, I., Faust, S., Mukherjee, P., Venturi, D.: Bounded tamper resilience: how to go beyond the algebraic barrier. In: Sako, K., Sarkar, P. (eds.) ASIACRYPT 2013, Part II. LNCS, vol. 8270, pp. 140–160. Springer, Heidelberg (2013)
13. Dodis, Y., Ostrovsky, R., Reyzin, L., Smith, A.: Fuzzy extractors: how to generate strong keys from biometrics and other noisy data. SIAM J. Comput. **38**(1), 97–139 (2008)
14. Dziembowski, S., Pietrzak, K.: Leakage-resilient cryptography. In: FOCS 2008, pp. 293–302. IEEE Computer Society (2008)
15. Dziembowski, S., Pietrzak, K., Wichs, D.: Non-malleable codes. In: Yao, A.C. (ed.) Innovations in Computer Science - ICS 2010, pp. 434–452. Tsinghua University Press (2010)
16. Faust, S., Mukherjee, P., Nielsen, J.B., Venturi, D.: Continuous non-malleable codes. In: Lindell, Y. (ed.) TCC 2014. LNCS, vol. 8349, pp. 465–488. Springer, Heidelberg (2014)
17. Faust, S., Mukherjee, P., Venturi, D., Wichs, D.: Efficient non-malleable codes and key-derivation for poly-size tampering circuits. In: Nguyen, P.Q., Oswald, E. (eds.) EUROCRYPT 2014. LNCS, vol. 8441, pp. 111–128. Springer, Heidelberg (2014)
18. Gennaro, R., Lysyanskaya, A., Malkin, T., Micali, S., Rabin, T.: Algorithmic tamper-proof (ATP) security: theoretical foundations for security against hardware tampering. In: Naor, M. (ed.) TCC 2004. LNCS, vol. 2951, pp. 258–277. Springer, Heidelberg (2004)
19. Goyal, V., O'Neill, A., Rao, V.: Correlated-input secure hash functions. In: Ishai, Y. (ed.) TCC 2011. LNCS, vol. 6597, pp. 182–200. Springer, Heidelberg (2011)

20. Jafargholi, Z., Wichs, D.: Tamper detection and continuous non-malleable codes. Cryptology ePrint Archive, Report 2014/956 (2014)
21. Kocher, P.C.: Timing attacks on implementations of Diffie-Hellman, RSA, DSS, and other systems. In: Koblitz, N. (ed.) CRYPTO 1996. LNCS, vol. 1109, pp. 104–113. Springer, Heidelberg (1996)
22. Kocher, P.C., Jaffe, J., Jun, B.: Differential power analysis. In: Wiener, M. (ed.) CRYPTO 1999. LNCS, vol. 1666, p. 388. Springer, Heidelberg (1999)
23. Lu, X., Li, B., Jia, D.: Related-key security for hybrid encryption. In: Chow, S.S.M., Camenisch, J., Hui, L.C.K., Yiu, S.M. (eds.) ISC 2014. LNCS, vol. 8783, pp. 19–32. Springer, Heidelberg (2014)
24. Qin, B., Liu, S.: Leakage-resilient chosen-ciphertext secure public-key encryption from hash proof system and one-time lossy filter. In: Sako, K., Sarkar, P. (eds.) ASIACRYPT 2013, Part II. LNCS, vol. 8270, pp. 381–400. Springer, Heidelberg (2013)
25. Qin, B., Liu, S.: Leakage-flexible CCA-secure public-key encryption: simple construction and free of pairing. In: Krawczyk, H. (ed.) PKC 2014. LNCS, vol. 8383, pp. 19–36. Springer, Heidelberg (2014)
26. Shoup, V.: Sequences of games: a tool for taming complexity in security proofs. IACR Cryptology ePrint Archive 2004, 332 (2004). http://eprint.iacr.org/2004/332
27. Waters, B.: Efficient identity-based encryption without random oracles. In: Cramer, R. (ed.) EUROCRYPT 2005. LNCS, vol. 3494, pp. 114–127. Springer, Heidelberg (2005)
28. Wee, H.: Public key encryption against related key attacks. In: Fischlin, M., Buchmann, J., Manulis, M. (eds.) PKC 2012. LNCS, vol. 7293, pp. 262–279. Springer, Heidelberg (2012)

A Tamper and Leakage Resilient von Neumann Architecture

Sebastian Faust[1]($\boxtimes$), Pratyay Mukherjee[2],
Jesper Buus Nielsen[2], and Daniele Venturi[3]

[1] Security and Cryptography Laboratory, EPFL, Lausanne, Switzerland
sebastian.faust@gmail.com
[2] Department of Computer Science, Aarhus University, Aarhus, Denmark
[3] Department of Computer Science, Sapienza University of Rome, Rome, Italy

Abstract. We present a *universal framework* for tamper and leakage resilient computation on a random access machine (RAM). The RAM has one CPU that accesses a storage, which we call the disk. The disk is subject to leakage and tampering. So is the bus connecting the CPU to the disk. We assume that the CPU is leakage and tamper-free. For a fixed value of the security parameter, the CPU has *constant size*. Therefore the code of the program to be executed is stored on the disk, i.e., we consider a von Neumann architecture. The most prominent consequence of this is that the code of the program executed will be subject to tampering.

We construct a compiler for this architecture which transforms any keyed primitive into a RAM program where the key is encoded and stored on the disk along with the program to evaluate the primitive on that key. Our compiler only assumes the existence of a so-called continuous non-malleable code, and it only needs black-box access to such a code. No further (cryptographic) assumptions are needed. This in particular means that given an information theoretic code, the overall construction is information theoretic secure.

Although it is required that the CPU is tamper and leakage proof, its design is independent of the actual primitive being computed and its internal storage is non-persistent, i.e., all secret registers are reset between invocations. Hence, our result can be interpreted as reducing the problem of shielding arbitrary complex computations to protecting a single, simple yet universal component.

1 Introduction

Can cryptographic schemes achieve their security goals when run on non-trusted machines? This fascinating question has recently resulted in a large body of work

---

S. Faust and P. Mukherjee—Received funding from the Marie Curie IEF/FP7 project GAPS, grant number: 626467.

J.B. Nielsen—Partially supported by Danish Council for Independent Research via DFF Starting Grant 10-081612. Partially supported by the European Research Commission Starting Grant 279447.

J. Katz (Ed.): PKC 2015, LNCS 9020, pp. 579–603, 2015.
DOI: 10.1007/978-3-662-46447-2_26

that weakens the traditional assumption of fully trusted computation and gives the adversary partial control over the implementation. Such partial control can either be *passive* where the adversary obtains information about the internal computation, or *active* where the adversary is allowed to change the secret state and/or the computation of the scheme.

One general solution to the above question is given by the appealing notion of leakage and tamper resilient compilers introduced in the pioneering works of Ishai, Prabhakaran, Sahai and Wagner [23,24]. A compiler takes as input a description of some arbitrary cryptographic functionality $\mathcal{G}_K$ and outputs a transformed functionality $\mathcal{G}'_{K'}$ which has the same input/output behavior as $\mathcal{G}_K$ but additionally remains secure in a non-trusted environment. For instance, $\mathcal{G}'_{K'}$ may be secure when the adversary is able to obtain a bounded amount of leakage from the execution of $\mathcal{G}'_{K'}$, or when he can change the secret state K' in some adversarial way. Formally, security is typically modeled by a simulation-based notion. That is, whatever the adversary can learn by interacting with $\mathcal{G}'_{K'}$ in the non-trusted environment, he can also achieve by interacting with the original $\mathcal{G}_K$ when implemented on a fully trusted device.

Tamper resilient compilers. Two different lines of work investigate methods for tamper resilient compilers. The first approach designs so-called tamper resilient circuits [10,11,20,23,26]. That is, given a functionality $\mathcal{G}_K$ that, e.g., computes the AES with key K, the compiler outputs a transformed functionality $\mathcal{G}'_{K'}$ that achieves simulation-based security even if the adversary can tamper with up to a constant fraction of the wires independently. While these works allow the adversary to tamper with the entire circuitry, they typically make very strong assumptions on the type of tampering. In particular, it is assumed that each bit of the computation is tampered with independently (so-called set/reset and toggle attacks). Also, it is not allowed to re-wire the circuit.

The second approach is based on the notion of non-malleable codes [16]. Informally, a code is non-malleable w.r.t. a set of tampering functions if the message contained in a codeword modified via a function in the family is either the original message, or a completely "unrelated" value. A compiler based on non-malleable codes stores the secret key in an encoded form and the compiled functionality decodes the state each time the functionality wants to access the key. As long as the adversary can only apply tampering functions from the family supported by the code, the non-malleability property guarantees that the (possibly tampered) decoded value is not related to the original key. While non-malleable codes exist for rich families that go far beyond the bit-tampering adversary discussed above (see, e.g., [1,2,6–9,15–17,19,27]), the existing compilers based on non-malleable codes only protect the secret key against tampering attacks. In particular, the assumption is that the entire circuitry that evaluates the functionality is implemented on a fully trusted environment and cannot be tampered with.

In this work we show how to *significantly* weaken the assumption of tamper-proof computation. Our solution is also based on non-malleable codes and hence can achieve strong protection against rich families of tampering functions, but simultaneously significantly reduces the assumption on tamper proof circuitry used by the traditional approach described above. In particular, the tamper-proof circuitry we use (the so-called CPU) is a *small* and *universal* component, whose size and functionality is *independent* of the functionality that we want to protect. Notice that this is in contrast to the approach described above, which requires a specifically tailored tamper-proof hardware for each functionality that we intend to protect. Our solution is hence in spirit of earlier works (e.g., [20]) and reduces the problem of protecting arbitrary complicated computation to shielding a single, simple component.

One important feature of our construction is to allow tampering with the program code. In our model the program consists of code built from several instructions such that each instruction is executed by the tamper-proof CPU sequentially. Notice that tampering with the program (and hence with the functionality) is allowed as the code is written on the tamperable disk. Hence, the adversary may attempt to overwrite the code with a malicious program that, e.g., just outputs the secret key. In our construction we prevent this type of attack by again making sure that any change of the code will enforce in tampering with the secret key, which itself is protected by a non-malleable code.

We notice that while our construction works generically for any non-malleable code that satisfies certain composability properties (as explained in more detail below), we will focus in the following exposition mainly on non-malleable codes in the split-state setting. In this well-known setting (c.f. [1,7,15,17,27]) the code-word consists of two parts and the adversary is allowed to tamper independently with them in an arbitrary way.

1.1 Our Model

We put forward a generic model of a tamper and leakage resilient von Neumann random access architecture (alternatively called RAM architecture). To use the established terminology of leakage and tamper resilient compilers, we phrase the model in terms of computing keyed functionalities $\mathcal{G}_K(\cdot)$. However, the model capture arbitrary poly-time computation which keeps a secret state that is initially K.

RAM schemes. We will use a *RAM scheme* to denote a RAM architecture **R** and a compiler **C** for **R**. The RAM **R** has a disk D and a tamper/leakage-proof CPU that is connected with the disk through buses. The RAM compiler **C** takes as input the description of a functionality $\mathcal{G}$ and a key K and outputs an initial encoding of the disk. Inputs to the program are given by writing it on the disk, and outputs are received by reading a special section of the disk. The program runs in *activations*. An activation denotes the time period of evaluating $\mathcal{G}_K(\cdot)$ on some input x. An activation involves several *steps* of the CPU. In each step, the CPU loads a constant number of words from the disk (this might include reading part of the input), executes one computation on the loaded data, and writes the result back to the disk (this might include writing part of the output). We stress that our CPU has no persistent internal (secret) storages, i.e., all secret registers are reset between steps. The CPU contains the following public untamperable components (i) a program counter pc, (ii) an activation counter ac and (iii) a self-destruct bit B. The activation counter ac is incremented after each activation, and the program counter pc specifies, during each activation, at which position of the public disk the CPU shall read the next instruction. The value B is a special self-destruct bit that is initially set to 0, and can once be flipped by the CPU. Whenever B is set to 1, the RAM goes into a special "self-destruct" mode where it is assumed to forever output the all-zero string.

Security. We define security of a RAM scheme via the real-ideal simulation paradigm. In the real world the compiler **C** is run in order to produce the initial contents of the disk. As in previous works on tamper and leakage resilient compilers the pre-processing in the setup is assumed to be tamper and leakage proof and is executed once at the initialization of the system. Think of it as the setup running on a separate, possibly more secure machine. In the online phase, the adversary can specify between steps of the CPU a tampering function Tamper($\cdot$) that modifies the disk: $D \leftarrow$ Tamper(D). It can also specify a leakage function Leak and will then be given Leak(D). Furthermore, the adversary can ask the RAM to perform the next step in the computation (for the current activation), by running the CPU on the (possibly modified) disk. When requesting the next step it also specifies a leakage function Leak$_{Bs}$ and is given back Leak$_{Bs}$(Bs), where Bs contains the values that were loaded or stored by the CPU.

Clearly, no computation is secure in the presence of arbitrary leakage and tampering. We therefore introduce a notion of *adversary class* to restrict the tampering and leakage queries that the adversary can submit. We compare the real execution to a mental experiment featuring a simulator having only black-box access to the original functionality $\mathcal{G}_K(\cdot)$. We call this an *ideal execution*. A RAM scheme is **A**-secure if for all efficient adversaries from **A** there exists an efficient simulator such that for all functionalities $\mathcal{G}$ the output distributions of a real and an ideal execution are computationally close.

We also introduce a notion of secure emulation. An emulator takes as input a RAM scheme (think of a RAM scheme for an idealised highly secure RAM) and outputs another RAM scheme (think of a RAM scheme for more real-world-like highly insecure RAM). We define the notion of security of an emulator such that if one is given a secure RAM scheme for the idealised RAM and applies a secure emulator, then one gets a secure RAM scheme for the less secure architecture. This allows to do modular proofs.

1.2   Motivation and Challenges of our Model

On RAM computation vs. circuits. The reasons why we want to lift the study of leakage and tamper resilience to the RAM setting are motivated by practice. It is well known that computing a function using a circuit instead of a RAM can yield a quadratic blow-up in complexity. Even worse, in a setting as ours, where the data (the encoding of K) is already laid out, the complexity can suffer an exponential blow-up, if a given activation only reads a small part of the key.

Furthermore, it seems a simpler task in practice to produce a lot of tamper proof copies of a small universal piece of hardware than to produce different tamper proof circuits for different desired functionalities.

On the trusted CPU assumption. As non-malleable codes typically do not have any homomorphic properties that enable computation,[1] we assume a tamper and leakage-proof CPU that carries out decoding. The CPU is the only part of the computation that is completely trusted. Notice that while its inputs and outputs may be subject to leakage and tampering attacks, its computation does not leak and its execution is carried out un-tampered. Our CPU is small and independent of the functionality to protect: it merely reads a constant number of encodings from disk, decodes them, executes some instruction (that can be as simple as a NAND operation) and writes the encoded result back to the disk. Notice that in contrast to earlier work on tamper resilient compilers based on non-malleable codes [16,17,27], we allow tampering with intermediate values produced by the program code, and in fact even with the program code itself. Our result hence can be interpreted as a much more granular model of computation than [16,17,27].

One may object that given such a powerful tamper-proof component a solution for tamper and leakage resilience is simple. Let us take a look at an adversary that can apply powerful tampering functions to the state of the disk between executions of the CPU. To this end, observe that the notion of non-malleable codes only guarantees that one cannot change the encoded value to some related value. Nothing, however hinders the adversary to just overwrite an encoding with a valid encoding of some fixed (known) value. Notice that such an attack may not only make it impossible to achieve simulation-based security, but moreover can completely break the scheme.[2] The adversary can also copy valid encodings from some place of the computation to different portions. For instance, he may attempt to copy the encoding of the secret key directly to the output of the program. Our transformation prevents these and other attacks by tying together all encodings with the secret key and the description of the compiled functionality. Hence, any attempt to change any intermediate encoding will destroy the functionality, including the key.

In summary, we show how to reduce the problem of protecting arbitrary computation against continuous leakage and tampering attacks in the split-state model, to shielding a *simple* and *universal* component. We notice that while our work minimizes the trusted hardware assumption made in non-malleable code based compilers, our trusted CPU is significantly more complex than tamper-proof hardware that has been used in works on tamper resilient circuits (cf. Section 1.4 for more details on this).

On the counters. In our model the CPU has public untamperable counters. The reason is that in order to tolerate leakage from the buses (connecting the CPU

---

[1] In fact, a homomorphism would in many cases contradict the non-malleability property of the code.

[2] Consider a contrived program that outputs the secret key if a certain status bit is set to 0, but otherwise behaves normally.

and the disk), we must make sure that the state of the CPU changes after each step. Otherwise, one may execute the following "reset-and-leak attack". The tampering functions can reset the disk to previous states an *unbounded* number of times, and without the counters, the CPU is also always in the same state at the start of an execution, so it would read the same values repeatedly. Notice that, as we allow leakage from the buses, each time the CPU loads a value it leaks through the bus. So, loading any value repeatedly an unbounded number of times implies that all the values on the disk could eventually be leaked at some point. We also stress that we pick a public value for this purpose and not a secret register as we want to minimize the assumption on the hardware—and of course secret un-tamperable memory is a much stronger assumption than public un-tamperable memory.

Moreover, assuming only counters makes our model a *strict generalization* of the circuit model: we can make an equivalent circuit where each gate can be thought of as one invocation of the CPU. Each gate will be identical to the CPU, except that it has the appropriate counters hard-coded into it. Assuming secret registers would not make such a transformation to circuitry possible.

On the self-destruct bit. In addition to the counter we use a *tamper-proof* "self-destruct" bit in our construction. Firstly, such bit is used to serve the same purpose as in the tamper-resilient compiler of [17]: it acts as a flag indicating that tampering has been detected for the first time and, if the execution does not stop at this point, the adversary can continue to learn information on the codeword (eventually recovering the whole codeword) which should, of course, be prevented.[3] Moreover, one may notice that without having a self-destruct bit, it is impossible to tolerate leakage from the buses. Consider, again, the "reset-and-leak attack" described above. The untamperable program counter enables the CPU to detect that a "reset" has taken place (i.e., values read from the disk do not match its internal state). However, at this point it is too late: the values were already on the buses, and hence subject to leakage. In this case the self-destruct bit allows the CPU to stop execution the first time such tampering is detected.

We also stress that having one bit, which is in fact "one-time writable", is optimal. Moreover, this seems as a reasonable hardware assumption: one can think of the CPU having a fuse that it can blow once (and check if it was ever blown).

On minimizing hardware assumptions. We emphasize that the main goal of this work is to study feasibility to securely execute *any* computation in the presence of very strong leakage and tampering attacks (in particular we consider *arbitrary* continuous leakage from buses and *arbitrary* tampering in the split-state model). We show that indeed this can be achieved by a simple, universal, constant-size

---

[3] For example, the tampering function can make the codeword "valid" or "invalid" depending on the first bit of the codeword, and hence learn the first bit based on the outcome.

CPU that is fully trusted. The CPU does not keep any secret state, and only has a short public un-tamperable memory that keeps the program counter (of size logarithmic in the security parameter) and the self-destruct bit. We notice that one can develop easier solutions if the CPU can keep a large, mutable, secret state between executions. In this case the CPU could encrypt the disk and authenticate it using, e.g., a Merkle tree. Of course, keeping a secret state between executions of the CPU is a much stronger hardware assumption.

1.3   Our Techniques

We construct our RAM scheme in two steps. We first formulate a hybrid model, which is a wishful RAM architecture where there is no leakage from the disk, no leakage from the bus and where the only allowed tampering is of the following types: (i) the adversary might copy a word from one position of the disk to another position on the disk (without looking at the value), and (ii) he might overwrite a position on the disk with a word of an arbitrary choice. As a first step we show how to compile securely to this hybrid platform. We then show how to use a non-malleable code to emulate this platform. Below we first describe the compiler, and then the emulator.

The compiler. We construct a RAM scheme for the hybrid architecture described above. We need to mitigate the fact that the adversary can overwrite values and copy them around. At setup, a secret label L is sampled uniformly at random and stored in the first position of the secret disk. Then, each value on the disk is "augmented" with the following information: (i) The position j at which the value was meant to be stored; (ii) The secret label L; and (iii) The values (a, p) of the activation counter $\texttt{ac}$ and the program counter $\texttt{pc}$ when the value was written on disk. Intuitively, adding the secret label (which is unknown to the adversary) prevents the adversary from replacing values from different positions of the secret disk with values that do not have the right label (notice that this label is long enough such that it cannot be guessed by the adversary). This ensures that all the values containing the label are either from the pre-processing or computed and stored by the CPU. Hence, they are in a way "authenticated" by the computation and not introduced by the adversary. On the other hand, the position j prevents the adversary from copying the corresponding value to a location different from j, as the CPU will check that j matches the position from which the value was read.

Note that the adversary can still replace a value at location j with an older value that was stored at location j before, essentially with the goal of resetting the scheme to a previous valid state. By checking the values a and p with the current values of the activation and program counters of the CPU, the CPU can detect such resetting attacks and self-destruct if necessary. Our analysis (see Section 6) shows that the probability that an adversary manages to replace some value on the secret disk (putting the correct label) without generating a self-destruct, is exponentially small in the security parameter. The use of the label to prevent moving and resetting values along with the structure of the compiled program makes our hybrid compiler so-called c-bounded, as required by the emulator (see below).

Notice that this compiler uses no cryptography, so it is information-theoretic secure. Hence, if we can emulate the hybrid architecture with information-theoretic security, the overall security will be information theoretic!

The emulator. The basic idea of the emulator is simple. Given a RAM scheme for the hybrid model and a non-malleable code, each value of the disk is encoded using the code. The CPU will then decode the values after loading them, compute as the CPU of the hybrid scheme and then encode the results and put them back on disk. Intuitively, a non-malleable code has the property that if a codeword is changed it either becomes invalid or an encoding of an unrelated value (known by the adversary). Since codewords can of course be copied around without modifying them, it seems intuitive that the above emulator should work if the RAM only allows leakage and tampering that the code is designed to tolerate. We can in fact take this as an informal definition and say that a given non-malleable code *fits* a given RAM architecture (given by the CPU and the adversary class) if for all hybrid schemes the natural emulator sketched above securely emulates the hybrid scheme. With this definition, we tautologically get that if there is a non-malleable code fitting a given RAM architecture, then there is also a secure RAM scheme for that architecture, namely apply the natural emulator to our secure compiler from above.

We exemplify our approach by showing that the split-state continuous non-malleable code (CNMC) from [17] fits a split-state RAM, where the disk is split into two disks and the adversary is allowed arbitrary independent tampering of each disk. In contrast to traditional non-malleable codes, *continuous* non-malleability guarantees that the code remains secure under continuous attacks without assuming erasures. The natural emulator uses many encodings, so the construction requires also some form of composability of non-malleable codes, where we allow the tampering function to depend on multiple encodings together. We can show by a generic reduction that composability is preserved for any continuous non-malleable split-state code.[4]

We remark that the code construction of [17] is in the common reference string (CRS) model, meaning that at setup a public string crs is generated and made available to all parties. Importantly, the security of the code requires that the adversary is not allowed to modify crs. Similarly, when one uses the code of [17] within our framework, the CRS is assumed to be un-tamperable and chosen by a trusted party; for instance, it can be chosen at production time and be hard-coded into the CPU of the RAM. However, the CRS can be public, and in particular the tampering and leakage from the disks can fully depend on it. Also the CRS is generated once and for all, so it perfectly matches our assumption of

---

[4] In [8] Coretti *et al.* show that the information theoretic construction of [16] in the bit-wise tampering (and no leakage) model is continuously non-malleable, so in that setting our compiler would be information theoretic, albeit only protecting against a weaker adversary class.

having a universal component (the CPU) that can be used to protect arbitrary computation. The assumption of having a public un-tamperable CRS is not new; see, e.g., [25,27] for further discussion.

Bounding RAM scheme. We show by a reduction to the composable CNMC that there exists a hybrid simulator, attacking the hybrid scheme and having limited tamper access (only copy and replace), that produces a distribution that is indistinguishable from the execution of the emulated RAM scheme in the real world. For this reduction to work, it is important that the hybrid scheme being emulated has a property called *c*-boundedness. Informally, this notion says that each value on the secret disk is touched at most *c* times, for a constant *c*. Without this property, the emulator would touch the corresponding codeword an unbounded number of times, and continuous leakage from the buses would reveal the entire code. Our compiler is constructed to have this property. Notice that it is in particular difficult to achieve *c*-bounded schemes in the presence of tampering, as the hybrid adversary may several times move a given value to the next position on the secret disk read by the CPU.

1.4 Other Related Work

Many recent works have studied the security of specific cryptographic schemes (e.g., public key encryption, signatures or pseudorandom functions) against tampering attacks [3–5,13,25,30]). While these works often consider a stronger tampering model and make less assumptions about tamper-proof hardware, they do not work for arbitrary functionalities.

Leakage and tamper-proof circuits. A large body of work studies the security of Boolean circuits against leakage attacks [14,21,22,24,28,29]. While most works on leakage resilient circuit compilers require leakage-proof hardware, the breakthrough work of Goldwasser and Rothblum [22] shows how to completely eliminate leak-proof hardware for leakage in the split-state setting. It is an interesting open question, if one can use the compiler of [22] to implement our CPU and allow leakage also from its execution. We emphasize that most of the work on leakage resilient circuit compilers does not consider tampering attacks.

The concept of tamper resilient circuits has been introduced by Ishai, Prabhakaran, Sahai and Wagner [23] and further studied in [10,11,20,23,26]. On the upside such compilers require simpler tamper-proof hardware,[5] but study a weaker tampering model. Concretely, they assume that an adversary can tamper with individual wires (or constant size gates [26]) independently. That is, the adversary can set the bit carried on a wire to 1, set it to 0 or toggle its value. Moreover, it is assumed that in each execution at least a constant fraction

---

[5] To the best of our knowledge each of these compilers requires a tamper-proof gate that operates on at least *k* inputs where *k* is the security parameter. Asymptotically, this is also the case for our CPU, while clearly from a practical perspective our tamper-proof hardware is significantly more complex.

of the wires is not tampered at all.[6] Our model considers a much richer family of tampering attacks. In particular, we allow the adversary to *arbitrarily* tamper with the entire content of the two disks, as long as the tampering is done independently. In fact, our model even allows the adversary to tamper with the functionality as the program code is read from the disk. Translating this to a circuit model would essentially allow the adversary to "re-wire" the circuit.

Finally, we notice that our RAM model can be thought of, in fact, as a generalization of the circuit model where the RAM program can be, e.g., a Boolean circuit and the CPU evaluates NAND gates on encodings.

Concurrent and independent work. A concurrent and independent paper [12] gives a related result on protecting RAM schemes against memory leakage and tampering. The main difference with the setting considered in this paper is that their model does not cover "reset attacks", i.e., the tampering functions are not allowed to keep a backup storage where previous codewords are stored and continuously tampered. This is enforced in their construction by assuming perfect erasures.

Technically the solutions are very different. Instead of encoding each element on the disk via a non-malleable code, the scheme of [12] encodes only the registers of the CPU to virtually equip it with secret registers, and then uses disk encryption to secure the disk; this can be phrased as using a non-malleable code with local properties. Finally, the scheme of [12] incorporates directly an ORAM, whereas we propose to view this as a separate step. First applying an ORAM and then our compiler will yield a scheme with the same asymptotic complexity of the one in [12]. However, as long as non-malleable codes are less efficient in practice than symmetric encryption, the scheme of [12] appears more practical. On the other hand, if we base our construction on an information theoretically secure code, the whole construction has unconditionally security. The solution in [12] is inherently computational.

2   Preliminaries

2.1   Notation

For $n \in \mathbb{N}$, we write $[n] := \{1, \ldots, n\}$. Given a set $\mathcal{X}$, we write $x \leftarrow \mathcal{X}$ to denote that element x is sampled uniformly from $\mathcal{X}$. If A is an algorithm, $y \leftarrow \mathsf{A}(x)$ denotes an execution of A with input x and output y; if A is randomized, then y is a random variable.

Let $k \in \mathbb{N}$ be a security parameter. We use $negl(k)$ to denote a negligible function on k. Given two random variables X_1 and X_2, we write $X_1 \approx_c X_2$ to denote that X_1 and X_2 are computationally indistinguishable meaning that for all PPT algorithms $\mathcal{A}$ we have that $\Pr[\mathcal{A}(X_1) = 1] - \Pr[\mathcal{A}(X_2) = 1] \leq negl(k)$.

---

[6] In [20,23] it is allowed that faults are persistent so at some point the entire circuitry may be subject to tampering.

2.2 Continuous Non-malleable Codes

In this paper we consider non-malleable codes in the split-state setting and omit to mention it explicitly for the rest of the paper. A split-state encoding scheme $\mathcal{C} = (\text{Init}, \text{Encode}, \text{Decode})$, is a triple of algorithms specified as follows: (1) Init, takes as input the security parameter and outputs a public common reference string $\text{crs} \leftarrow \text{Init}(1^k)$; (2) Encode, takes as input a string $x \in \{0,1\}^\ell$, for some fixed integer ℓ, and the public parameters, and outputs a codeword $c = (c_0, c_1) \leftarrow \text{Encode}(\text{crs}, x)$ where $c \in \{0,1\}^{2n}$; (3) Decode, takes as input a codeword $c \in \{0,1\}^{2n}$ and the public parameters, and outputs a value $x = \text{Decode}(\text{crs}, c)$ where $x \in \{0,1\}^\ell \cup \{\bot\}$. We require that $\text{Decode}(\text{crs}, \text{Encode}(\text{crs}, x)) = x$ for all $x \in \{0,1\}^\ell$ and for all $\text{crs} \leftarrow \text{Init}(1^k)$. Moreover, for any two inputs x_0, x_1 ($|x_0| = |x_1|$) and any efficient function $\mathsf{T}_0, \mathsf{T}_1$ the probability that the adversary guesses the bit b in the following game is negligible: (i) sample $b \leftarrow \{0,1\}$ and compute $(c_0, c_1) \leftarrow \text{Encode}(\text{crs}, x_b)$, and (ii) the adversary obtains $\text{Decode}^*(\mathsf{T}_0(c_0), \mathsf{T}_1(c_1))$, where Decode^* is as Decode except that it returns a special symbol same^* if $(\mathsf{T}_0(c_0), \mathsf{T}_1(c_1)) = (c_0, c_1)$.

The above one-shot game has been extended to the continuous setting in [17], where the adversary may tamper continuously with the encoding. In contrast to the above game, the adversary here obtains access to a tampering oracle $\mathcal{O}^q_{\text{cnm}}((c_0, c_1), \cdot)$, where (c_0, c_1) is an encoding of either x_0 or x_1. The oracle can be queried up to q times with input functions $\mathsf{T}_0, \mathsf{T}_1 : \{0,1\}^n \rightarrow \{0,1\}^n$ and returns either same^* (in case $(\mathsf{T}_0(c_0), \mathsf{T}_1(c_1)) = (c_0, c_1)$), or $\bot$ (in case $\text{Decode}(\text{crs}, (\mathsf{T}_0(c_0), \mathsf{T}_1(c_1))) = \bot$), or $(\mathsf{T}_0(c_0), \mathsf{T}_1(c_1))$ in all other cases. The only additional restriction is that whenever $\bot$ is returned the oracle answers all further queries with $\bot$ (a.k.a. "self-destruct"). Furthermore, in the construction of [17] the adversary has access to leakage oracles $\mathcal{O}^{\text{lb}_{\text{code}}}(c_0, \cdot)$, $\mathcal{O}^{\text{lb}_{\text{code}}}(c_1, \cdot)$, that can be queried to retrieve up to lb_{code} bits of information on each half of the target encoding. The access to the leakage oracles will be useful in our setting to obtain continuous leakage resilience on the buses. We refer the reader to the full version of this paper [18] for a precise definition of continuous non-malleable leakage resilient (CNMLR) codes.

Composability. We also introduce a notion of *adaptive composability* for CNMLR codes, where the adversary can specify two vectors of messages $\mathbf{x}_0 = (x_0^1, \ldots, x_0^m)$ and $\mathbf{x}_1 = (x_1^1, \ldots, x_1^m)$ (such that $|x_0^i| = |x_1^i|$) and the oracle $\mathcal{O}^q_{\text{cnm}}(\mathbf{c}, \cdot)$ is parametrized by a vector of encodings $\mathbf{c} = (\mathbf{c}_0, \mathbf{c}_1) = ((c_0^1, \ldots, c_0^m), (c_1^1, \ldots, c_1^m))$ corresponding to either $\mathbf{x}_0$ or $\mathbf{x}_1$ (depending on the secret bit b above). The tampering functions now have a type $\mathsf{T}_0, \mathsf{T}_1 : (\{0,1\}^n)^m \rightarrow \{0,1\}^n$, and the oracle returns (same^*, i) in case $c' = (c_0^i, c_1^i)$ for some $i \in [m]$. The leakage oracles are also parametrized by $\mathbf{c}_0$ and $\mathbf{c}_1$ and the adversary can leak up to lb_{code} bits from each codeword.

Roughly a CNMLR code is adaptively m-composable if no PPT adversary can guess the value of b with noticeable advantage, even in case the messages in the two vectors $\mathbf{x}_0, \mathbf{x}_1$ are not fixed at the beginning of the game, but instead can be chosen adaptively when the game proceeds. A formal definition, together with a proof of the following theorem can be found in the full version.

Theorem 1. *Let* $\mathcal{C} = (\mathsf{Init}, \mathsf{Encode}, \mathsf{Decode})$ *be a* $(\mathsf{lb}_{\mathsf{code}}, q)$-*CNMLR code. Then* $\mathcal{C}$ *is also adaptively m-composable for any polynomial* $m = poly(k)$.

3   A Generic Leakage and Tamper Resilient RAM

In this section we describe our model of a generic random access machine (RAM) architecture with a leakage and tamper resilient CPU and with memory and buses, which are subject to leakage. Our RAM architecture is meant to implement some keyed functionality $\mathcal{G}_{\mathsf{K}}$, e.g., an AES running with key K taking as input messages and producing the corresponding ciphertexts, but the model also applies to more general computations. The RAM has one tamperable and leaky disk D, and one CPU, which has a size independent of the function to be computed. We interchangeably denote the memory used by the CPU by "disk", "storage" and "memory"; this might physically be any kind of storage that the CPU can access. We assume there is a leak-free and tamper-free pre-processing phase, which outputs an encoding of the functionality $\mathcal{G}_{\mathsf{K}}$. One can think of this as a separate phase where a compiler is run, possibly on a different, more secure machine.

The initial encoding consists of data and instructions, which we store on the disk. The input and output of the function (that can be chosen by the user of the RAM) is stored in some specific locations on the disk (say, right after the program). We allow the exact location of the input and output parameters to be *program specific*, but assume that access to the disk allows to efficiently determine the input and output (in case the disk was not tampered). In the online phase, the CPU loads an instruction and data from the disk (as specified by the instruction). Reading from the disk might involve reading part of the input. Then it computes and stores back the intermediate results on the disk, and processes the next instruction. The next instruction is found on the disk at the location given by a program counter pc, which is incremented by one in each invocation of the CPU and which is reset when the CPU raises a flag $\mathsf{T} = 1$. Writing to the disk could involve writing part of the output. The adversary is allowed to tamper and to leak from the disk between each two invocations of the CPU; furthermore the adversary is allowed to leak from the bus carrying the information between the CPU and the disk. In the following, we give a formal presentation of our model.

Specification of RAM. We use parameters $w, \tau, d, k \in \mathbb{N}$ below, where w is the word length, τ is length of an instruction type, d specifies the number of arguments of an instruction, and k is the security parameter. We require $w \geq \tau + 2kd$. We let the *disk* D be of length 2^k. This is just a convenient convention to avoid specifying a fixed polynomial-size disk. A poly-time program will access only polynomially many positions in the disk and all positions not yet written are by convention 0^w, so a disk D can at any time be represented by a poly-sized data structure. When we pass disks around in the below description, we mean that we pass such a poly-sized representation. We index a disk with $i \in [2^k]$. We also index the disk with bit-strings $i \in \{0,1\}^*$, by considering them binary numbers and then taking the result $\mathrm{mod} 2^k$. An (τ, d)-bounded *instruction* $\mathcal{I}$ is defined as a quadruple $(\mathsf{Y}, \mathsf{I}, \mathsf{O}, \mathsf{Aux})$ where, $\mathsf{Y} \in \{0,1\}^\tau$, $\mathsf{I}, \mathsf{O} \in [2^k]^d$ and $\mathsf{Aux} \in \{0,1\}^{w-(\tau+2kd)}$. One may think of Y as the type of operation (e.g., a NAND operation) that is computed by the instruction. The d-tuples I, O define the position on the disk where to read the inputs and where to write the outputs of the instruction. The string Aux is just auxiliary information used to pad to the right length. When we do not write it explicitly we assume it is all-0.

Formally, a RAM $\mathbf{R}$ is specified by $\mathbf{R} = (w, \tau, d, \mathsf{Init}, \mathsf{Random}, \mathsf{Compute})$ and consists of:

1. A disk $D \in (\{0,1\}^w)^{2^k}$.
2. Init: An algorithm that takes as input the security parameter 1^k, and returns a public common reference string $\mathtt{crs} \leftarrow \mathsf{Init}(1^k)$ (to be hard-coded into the CPU).
3. CPU: A procedure which is formally written as pseudo-code in Fig. 1. The CPU is connected to the disk by a bus Bs, which is used to load and store data. It has $2d+1$ internal temporary registers: $d+1$ input registers $(\mathsf{R}_0, \mathsf{R}_1, \ldots, \mathsf{R}_d)$ and d output registers $(\mathsf{O}_1, \ldots, \mathsf{O}_d)$; each register can store w bits. CPU has the public parameters $\mathtt{crs}$ hard-coded, and takes as inputs data sent through the bus, a strictly increasing activation[7] counter $\mathtt{ac}$, and a program counter $\mathtt{pc}$ which is strictly increasing within one activation and reset between activations. The CPU runs in three steps: (i) d loads, (ii) 1 computation and (iii) d stores. In the computation step CPU calls Random and $\mathsf{Compute}$ to generate fresh randomness and evaluate the instruction.
   (a) Random: This algorithm is used to sample randomness r.
   (b) $\mathsf{Compute}$: This algorithm will evaluate one particular instruction. To this end, it takes data from the temporary registers $(\mathsf{R}_0, \ldots, \mathsf{R}_d)$, the counters $\mathtt{ac}, \mathtt{pc}$ and the randomness $r \leftarrow \mathsf{Random}$ as input and outputs the data to be stored into the output registers $(\mathsf{O}_1, \ldots, \mathsf{O}_d)$, the self-destruct indicator bit B which indicates if CPU needs to stop execution, and the completion indicator bit T which indicates the completion of the current activation. CPU outputs the possibly updated disk D, the self-destruct indicator (B) and the completion indicator (T). Notice that the CPU does not need to take B and T as input as these bits are only written.

Running the RAM involves iteratively executing the CPU. In between executions of the CPU we increment $\mathtt{pc}$. When the CPU returns $\mathsf{T} = 1$ we reset $\mathtt{pc} = 0$ and increment the activation counter $\mathtt{ac}$. When the CPU returns $\mathsf{B} = 1$, the CPU self-destructs. After this no more execution of the CPU takes place.

---

[7] We call the time in which the RAM computes the output $\mathcal{G}_\mathsf{K}(x)$ for single x one activation, and the time in which the procedure CPU is run once, one execution.

Input: $(\mathsf{crs}, D, \mathsf{pc}, \mathsf{ac}, \mathsf{Leak_{Bs}})$
  // Loading...
Parse $D[\mathsf{pc}]$ as an instruction $(\mathsf{Y}, \mathsf{I}, \mathsf{O}, \mathsf{Aux})$
Load $R_0 \leftarrow (\mathsf{Y}, \mathsf{I}, \mathsf{O}, \mathsf{Aux})$
Initialize the bus $\mathsf{Bs} = (\mathsf{pc}, R_0)$
for $j = 1 \to d$ **do**
  Let $\mathsf{loc}_j = \mathsf{I}[j]$ // Load input from disk at position $\mathsf{I}[j]$
  Load $R_j \leftarrow D[\mathsf{loc}_j]$
  Set $\mathsf{Bs} \leftarrow (\mathsf{Bs}, \mathsf{loc}_j, R_j)$ // Write data from disk to bus
end for
  // Computing...
Sample $r \leftarrow \mathsf{Random}$
Compute $((\mathsf{O}_1, \ldots, \mathsf{O}_d), \mathsf{B}, \mathsf{T}) \leftarrow \mathsf{Compute}(\mathsf{crs}, (R_0, R_1, \ldots, R_d), r, \mathsf{pc}, \mathsf{ac})$
  // Storing...
for $j = 1 \to d$ **do**
  Let $\mathsf{loc}_j = \mathsf{O}[j]$
  Store $D[\mathsf{loc}_j] \leftarrow \mathsf{O}_j$ // Store output on disk at position loc_j
  Set $\mathsf{Bs} \leftarrow (\mathsf{Bs}, \mathsf{loc}_j, \mathsf{O}_j)$
end for
Let $\lambda_{\mathsf{Bs}} = \mathsf{Leak_{Bs}}(\mathsf{Bs})$ // Compute leakage from the bus
Output: $(D, \mathsf{B}, \mathsf{T}, \lambda_{\mathsf{Bs}})$

Fig. 1. Algorithm CPU

Input and output to the program will be specified via the user/adversary reading and writing the disk. We therefore need a section of the disk that can be read and written at will. We call this the *public section*. We will model this by given the adversary full read/write access to $D_{\mathsf{pub}} = D[0, 2^{k-1} - 1]$ and limited access to $D_{\mathsf{sec}} = D[2^{k-1}, 2^k - 1]$. We call D_{pub} the public disk and we call D_{sec} the secret disk. Note that $D = D_{\mathsf{pub}} \| D_{\mathsf{sec}}$. Also note that the CPU is taking instructions from the public disk; this means that protecting the access pattern of the program has to be done explicitly.

RAM schemes. Informally, a RAM compiler $\mathbf{C}$ takes as input the description of a functionality $\mathcal{G}$ with secret key K, and outputs an encoding of the functionality itself, to be executed on a RAM $\mathbf{R}$. Formally, a *RAM compiler* $\mathbf{C}$ for $\mathbf{R}$ is a PPT algorithm which takes a keyed-function description $\mathcal{G}$ and a key $\mathsf{K} \in \{0,1\}^*$ as input, and outputs an encoding of the form $((\ell_P, I, \ell_I, O, \ell_O, \mathcal{X}, \mathcal{Y}), \omega)$, called the *program*. Here $\omega = (\omega_{\mathsf{pub}}, \omega_{\mathsf{sec}})$ such that $\omega_{\mathsf{pub}}, \omega_{\mathsf{sec}} \in (\{0,1\}^w)^\ell$ for $\ell \leq 2^{k-1}$. When we say that we *store* ω on the disk we mean that we pad both of $\omega_{\mathsf{pub}}, \omega_{\mathsf{sec}}$ with 0s until they have length 2^{k-1}, giving values $\omega'_{\mathsf{pub}}, \omega'_{\mathsf{sec}}$ and then we assign $\omega'_{\mathsf{pub}} \| \omega'_{\mathsf{sec}}$ to D. We write ℓ_P for the program length, $I \geq \ell_P$ for the position where the input will be put on the disk, ℓ_I for the length of the input, $O \geq I + \ell_I$ for the position where the output is put on the disk, and ℓ_O for the length of the output such that $O + \ell_O \leq 2^{k-1}$. We think of the positions 0 to $\ell_P - 1$ as consisting of instructions, but make no formal requirement. The mappings $\mathcal{X}, \mathcal{Y}$ are used to parse the inputs (resp., the outputs) of the RAM as a certain number of words of length w (resp., as a value in the range of $\mathcal{G}_K$).

We introduce a class $\mathbb{G}$ of functionalities $\mathcal{G}$ that a compiler is supposed to be secure for (e.g., all poly-time functionalities) and a class $\mathbb{P}$ of programs that a compiler is supposed to compile to (e.g., all poly-time programs). We use $\mathbf{C} : \mathbb{G} \to \mathbb{P}$ to denote that on input $\mathcal{G} \in \mathbb{G}$, the compiler $\mathbf{C}$ outputs a program in $\mathbb{P}$.

We define a *RAM scheme* RS as the ordered pair $(\mathbf{C}, \mathbf{R})$ such that $\mathbf{R}$ is a RAM and $\mathbf{C}$ a compiler for $\mathbf{R}$. The correctness of a RAM scheme is formalized via a game where we compare the execution of the RAM with the output of the original functionality $\mathcal{G}_K$, upon an arbitrary sequence of inputs $(x_1, \ldots, x_N)$. Below we define what it means for a RAM scheme RS $= (\mathbf{C}, \mathbf{R})$ to be correct. Informally, the definition says that for any tuple of inputs $(x_1, \ldots, x_N)$ the execution of the RAM $\mathbf{R}$ and the evaluation of the function $\mathcal{G}_K$ have identical output distributions except with negligible probability. This is formalized below.

Definition 1 (Correctness of a RAM Scheme). *We say a RAM scheme* RS *is correct (for function class $\mathbb{G}$ and program class $\mathbb{P}$) if* RS.$\mathbf{C} : \mathbb{G} \to \mathbb{P}$, *and for any function $\mathcal{G} \in \mathbb{G}$, any key $K \in \{0,1\}^*$, and any vector of inputs $(x_1, \ldots, x_N)$ it holds that $\Pr[\mathrm{GAME}_{\mathrm{hon}}^{\mathrm{Real}}(x_1, \ldots, x_N) = 0] \leq negl(k)$, where the experiment $\mathrm{GAME}_{\mathrm{hon}}^{\mathrm{Real}}(x_1, \ldots, x_N)$ is defined as follows:*

- *Sample* crs $\leftarrow \mathbf{R}.\mathsf{Init}(1^k)$.
- *Run the compiler $\mathbf{C}$ on* crs, $(\mathcal{G}, K)$ *to generate the encoding $((I, \ell_I, O, \ell_O, \mathcal{X}, \mathcal{Y}), \omega) \leftarrow \mathbf{C}(\mathrm{crs}, (\mathcal{G}, K))$, and store it into the disk of $\mathbf{R}$ as in $D \leftarrow \omega$.*
- *For $i = 1 \to N$ proceed as follows. Encode the input $(x_{i,0}, \ldots, x_{i,\ell_I-1}) \leftarrow \mathcal{X}(x_i)$, store it on the disk $D[I + j] \leftarrow x_{i,j}$ (for $0 \leq j < \ell_I$) and run the following activation loop:*
  1. *Let* ac $\leftarrow i$ *and* pc $\leftarrow 0$.
  2. *Run* CPU *and update the disk $(D, \mathsf{B}, \mathsf{T}) \leftarrow \mathsf{CPU}(\mathrm{crs}, D, \mathrm{pc}, \mathrm{ac})$.[8]*
  3. *If* $\mathsf{B} = 1$ *return 0 and halt.*
  4. *If* $\mathsf{T} = 0$, *then increment the program counter* pc $\leftarrow$ pc $+ 1$ *and go to Step 2. If* $\mathsf{T} = 1$, *let $y_i \leftarrow \mathcal{Y}(D[O], \ldots, D[O + \ell_O - 1])$. If $y_i \neq \mathcal{G}_K(x_i)$, then return 0 and halt.*
- *Return 1.*

Security. We now proceed to define security of a RAM scheme, using the real-ideal paradigm. In the following we let k denote the security parameter. Consider a RAM scheme RS $= (\mathbf{C}, \mathbf{R})$. First we run $\mathbf{C}$, which takes the description of $\mathcal{G}$ and a key K as inputs and generates an encoding of the form $((I, \ell_I, O, \ell_O, \mathcal{X}, \mathcal{Y}), \omega)$. Then we store ω on the disk D and we advance to the online phase where the adversary $\mathcal{A}$ can run $\mathbf{R}$ on inputs of his choice. Formally, he is allowed to arbitrarily read from and write to D_{pub} and therefore also $D[I], \ldots, D[I + \ell_I - 1]$ and $D[O], \ldots, D[O + \ell_O - 1]$. Moreover, $\mathcal{A}$ can tamper with the secret disk D

---

[8] When we do not specify a leakage function, we assume that it is the constant function outputting the empty string, and we ignore the leakage in the output vector.

1. Initialization: Sample $crs \leftarrow R.Init(1^k)$. Sample the key K according to the distribution needed by the primitive. Initialize the activation counter $ac \leftarrow 0$, the program counter $pc \leftarrow 0$, the self-destruct bit $B \leftarrow 0$, and the activation indicator $T \leftarrow 0$.
2. Pre-processing: Sample an encoding by running the compiler $(P, \omega_{pub}, \omega_{sec}) \leftarrow C(crs, (\mathcal{G}, K))$, where $P = (I, \ell_I, O, \ell_O, \mathcal{X}, \mathcal{Y})$. Store the encoding $\omega = (\omega_{pub}, \omega_{sec})$ into the disk D. Give (crs, P, ω_{pub}) to $\mathcal{A}$.
3. Online: Get command CMD from $\mathcal{A}$ and act as follows according to the command-type.
   (a) If CMD $= (STOP, O_{real})$ then return O_{real} and halt.
   (b) If CMD $= (LEAK, Leak)$, compute $\lambda \leftarrow Leak(D)$ and give λ to $\mathcal{A}$.
   (c) If CMD $= (TAMPER, Tamper)$ then modify D using the tampering function: $D \leftarrow Tamper(D)$.
   (d) If CMD $= (EXEC, Leak, D')$ and $B = 0$ then proceed as follows:
      i. Update the public disk $D_{pub} \leftarrow D'$.
      ii. Run CPU and update the disk: $(D, B, T, \lambda_{Bs}) \leftarrow CPU(crs, D, pc, ac, Leak)$.
      iii. Give $(T, \lambda_{Bs}, D_{pub})$ to $\mathcal{A}$.
      iv. Check the completion of current activation: If $T = 1$ then start a new activation by incrementing the activation counter: $ac \leftarrow ac + 1$ and re-initializing the program counter: $pc \leftarrow 0$.
      v. Increment the program counter: $pc \leftarrow pc + 1$ and go to Step 3.

Fig. 2. Real Execution $REAL_{RS, \mathcal{A}, \mathcal{G}}(k)$

between each execution of the CPU. He specifies a function Tamper and the effect is that the disk is changes to $D \leftarrow Tamper(D)$. The adversary can also leak from the disk between executions. He specifies a function Leak and he is given $Leak(D)$. The adversary also decides when the CPU is invoked, and it gets to specify a leakage function $Leak_{Bs}$ for each invocation obtaining λ_{Bs} as defined in Fig.1. Besides the leakage from the bus, the procedure CPU is leakage and tamper proof.

We introduce the notion of an *adversary class*. This is just a subset **A** of all adversaries. As an example, **A** might be the set of $\mathcal{A}$ which leak at most 42 bits in total from the disk and which does the tampering in a split-state manner (more about this in the following).

We write $REAL_{RS, \mathcal{A}, \mathcal{G}}(k)$ for the output distribution in the real execution and we let $REAL_{RS, \mathcal{A}, \mathcal{G}} = \{REAL_{RS, \mathcal{A}, \mathcal{G}}(k)\}_{k \in \mathbb{N}}$. For a formal description see Fig. 2. A few remarks to the description are in order.

– **Adaptivity.** We stress that by writing the disk, the adversary is allowed to query the RAM on adaptively chosen inputs. Also note that the adversary can always hard-wire known values into a tampering command (e.g., values that were already leaked from the disk), and specify a tampering function that changes the content of the disk depending on the hard-wired values.

- **Tampering within executions.** Notice that the adversary is not allowed to tamper between two executions of the CPU. This is without loss of generality, as later we will allow the adversary to know the exact sequence of locations to be read by the CPU and hence, equivalently, the adversary can just load some location, tamper and then execute before loading the next location. This is possible because our RAMs do not allow indirection as in loading e.g. $D[D[127]]$.
- **On the CRS.** In case no common reference string is required by the RAM scheme, we simply assume that **R.Init** outputs the empty string. In such a case we sometimes avoid to write crs as input of **C**, CPU and Compute.

In the ideal execution, the ideal functionality for evaluating $\mathcal{G}$ interacts with the ideal adversary called the *simulator* $\mathcal{S}$ as follows. First sample a key K and repeat the following until a value is returned: Get a command from $\mathcal{S}$ and act differently according to the command-type.

- If CMD = (STOP, O_{ideal}), then return O_{ideal} and halt.
- If CMD = (EVAL, x), give $\mathcal{G}_K(x)$ to $\mathcal{S}$.

We write $\text{IDEAL}_{\mathcal{S},\mathcal{G}}(k)$ for the output distribution in the ideal execution and we let $\text{IDEAL}_{\mathcal{S},\mathcal{G}} = \{\text{IDEAL}_{\mathcal{S},\mathcal{G}}(k)\}_{k\in\mathbb{N}}$.

Definition 2 (Security of a RAM Scheme). *We say a RAM scheme* RS *is* **A**-*secure (for function class* $\mathbb{G}$ *and program class* $\mathbb{P}$) *if* $\text{RS.C} : \mathbb{G} \to \mathbb{P}$ *and if for any function* $\mathcal{G} \in \mathbb{G}$ *and any* $\mathcal{A} \in \mathbf{A}$ *there exists a PPT simulator* $\mathcal{S}$ *such that* $\text{REAL}_{\text{RS},\mathcal{A},\mathcal{G}} \approx_c \text{IDEAL}_{\mathcal{S},\mathcal{G}}$.

We introduce a notion of emulation, which facilitates designing compilers for less secure RAMs via compilers for more secure RAMs. We call a set $\mathbb{S}$ of RAM schemes a class if there exists $\mathbb{G}$ and $\mathbb{P}$ such that for all $\text{RS} \in \mathbb{S}$ it holds that $\text{RS.C} : \mathbb{G} \to \mathbb{P}$. We write $\mathbb{S} : \mathbb{G} \to \mathbb{P}$. An emulator is a poly-time function $\mathcal{E} : \mathbb{S}_1 \to \mathbb{S}_2$, where $\mathbb{S}_1$ and $\mathbb{S}_2$ are RAM scheme classes $\mathbb{S}_1 : \mathbb{G} \to \mathbb{P}_1$ and $\mathbb{S}_2 : \mathbb{G} \to \mathbb{P}_2$. I.e., given a RAM scheme $\text{RS}_1 \in \mathbb{S}_1$ for some function class $\mathbb{G}$, the emulator outputs another RAM scheme $\text{RS}_2 \in \mathbb{S}_2$ for the same function class.

Definition 3 (Secure Emulation). *Let* $\mathbb{S}_1 : \mathbb{G} \to \mathbb{P}_1$ *and* $\mathbb{S}_2 : \mathbb{G} \to \mathbb{P}_2$ *be RAM scheme classes and let* $\mathcal{E} : \mathbb{S}_1 \to \mathbb{S}_2$ *be an emulator. We say that* $\mathcal{E}$ *is* $(\mathbf{A}_1, \mathbf{A}_2)$-*secure if for all* $\text{RS}_1 \in \mathbb{S}_1$ *and* $\text{RS}_2 = \mathcal{E}(\text{RS}_1)$ *and* $\mathcal{G} \in \mathbb{G}$ *and all* $\mathcal{A}_2 \in \mathbf{A}_2$ *there exists a* $\mathcal{A}_1 \in \mathbf{A}_1$ *such that* $\text{REAL}_{\text{RS}_1,\mathcal{A}_1,\mathcal{G}} \approx_c \text{REAL}_{\text{RS}_2,\mathcal{A}_2,\mathcal{G}}$.

The following theorem is immediate.

Theorem 2. *Let* $\mathcal{E} : \mathbb{S}_1 \to \mathbb{S}_2$ *be an emulator. If* $\mathcal{E}$ *is* $(\mathbf{A}_1, \mathbf{A}_2)$-*secure and* $\text{RS}_1 \in \mathbb{S}_1$ *is* $\mathbf{A}_1$-*secure, then* $\text{RS}_2 = \mathcal{E}(\text{RS}_1)$ *is* $\mathbf{A}_2$-*secure.*

4   Main Theorem

Our main result is a secure RAM scheme for the so-called split-state model, which we review below. This particular model can be cast as a special cases of our generic RAM model. We use ^{sp} to denote the components of the split-state model, i.e., $RS^{sp} = (C^{sp}, R^{sp})$ and the adversary class is called $\mathbf{A}^{sp}$.

In the split-state model we consider the secret disk D_{sec} split into two parts D_1 and D_2, and we require that leakage and tampering is done independently on the two parts. I.e., each position $D_{sec}[i]$ on the secret disk is split into two parts $D_1[i]$ and $D_2[i]$ of equal length such that $D_{sec}[i] = D_1[i] \| D_2[i]$. We let $D_1 = (D_1[2^{k-1}], \ldots, D_1[2^k - 1])$ and $D_2 = (D_2[2^{k-1}], \ldots, D_2[2^k - 1])$. The set $\mathbf{A}^{sp}$ consists of all poly-time algorithms which never violate the following restrictions.

Tampering. We require that a tampering function is of the form $\mathsf{Tamper}^{sp} = (\mathsf{Tamper}_1^{sp}, \mathsf{Tamper}_2^{sp})$ and we let $\mathsf{Tamper}^{sp}(D_{pub} \| D_{sec}) = D_{pub} \| (\mathsf{Tamper}_1^{sp}(D_1), \mathsf{Tamper}_2^{sp}(D_2))$. Beside being split like this, there is no restriction on the tampering, i.e., each part of the secret disk can be arbitrarily tampered.

Disk Leakage. We also require that a disk leakage function is of the form $\mathsf{Leak}^{sp} = (\mathsf{Leak}_1^{sp}, \mathsf{Leak}_2^{sp})$ and we let $\mathsf{Leak}^{sp}(D_{pub} \| D_{sec}) = (\mathsf{Leak}_1^{sp}(D_1), \mathsf{Leak}_2^{sp}(D_2))$. Beside being split like this, we introduce a leakage bound lb_{disk} and we require that the sum of the length of the leakage returned by all the leakage functions Leak_i^{sp} is less than lb_{disk}.

Bus Leakage. We require that a bus leakage function is of the form $\mathsf{Leak}^{sp} = (\mathsf{Leak}_1^{sp}, \mathsf{Leak}_2^{sp})$. For a bus $(i_0, D[i_0], i_1, D[i_1], \ldots, i_{1+2d}, D[i_{1+2d}])$ we let $B = (D[i_1], \ldots, D[i_{1+2d}])$ and we split B into two parts B_1 and B_2 by splitting each word, as done for the disk; the returned leakage is then $(i_0, i_1, i_2, \ldots, i_{1+2d}, \mathsf{Leak}_1^{sp}(B_1), \mathsf{Leak}_2^{sp}(B_2))$. Beside being split like this, we introduce a leakage bound lb_{bus} and we require that the length of the leakage returned by each function Leak_i^{sp} is less than lb_{bus}.

Note that by definition of the bus leakage, the CPU always leaks the program counter and the memory positions that are being read. Besides this it gives independent, bounded leakage on the parts of the words read up from the disk. Since the leakage and tamper classes for a split-state RAM are fully specified by lb_{disk} and lb_{bus} we will denote the adversary class for a split-state RAM simply by $\mathbf{A}^{sp} = (\mathsf{lb}_{disk}, \mathsf{lb}_{bus})$. Let $\mathbb{S}^{sp}$ denote the class of split-state RAM schemes. We are now ready to state our main theorem.

Theorem 3 (Main Theorem). *Let $\mathcal{C}$ be a (lb_{code}, q)-CNMLR code. There exists an efficient RAM scheme $RS \in \mathbb{S}^{sp}$ and a constant $c = O(1)$ such that RS is $(\mathsf{lb}_{disk}, \mathsf{lb}_{bus})$-secure whenever $\mathsf{lb}_{disk} + (c+1)\mathsf{lb}_{bus} \leq \mathsf{lb}_{code}$.*

The proof of the above theorem follows in two steps. We first define an intermediate model, which we call the hybrid model, where the adversary is only allowed a very limited form of leakage and tampering. For this model, we give a hybrid-to-split-state emulator (cf. Theorem 4 in Section 5). Then, we exhibit a RAM scheme that is secure in the hybrid model (cf. Theorem 5 in Section 6). Putting the above two things together with Theorem 2 concludes the proof of Theorem 3.

5   Hybrid-to-Split-State Emulator

We introduce an intermediate security model where the adversary is given only limited tampering/leakage capabilities. We call this model the *hybrid model*, and a RAM that is secure in this model is called a hybrid RAM; as for the split-state model, also the hybrid model can be cast as a special case of our generic RAM model. We use ^{hb} to denote the components of the hybrid model, i.e., $RS^{hb} = (C^{hb}, R^{hb})$ and we call the adversary class A^{hb}.

5.1   The Hybrid Model

In the hybrid model the secret disk is not split. However, the tampering is very restricted: we only allow the adversary to copy values within the secret disk and to overwrite a location of the secret disk with a known value. In addition very little leakage is allowed. The adversary class A^{hb} consists of all poly-time Turing machines never violating the following restrictions.

Tampering. We require that each tampering function is a command of one of the following forms.
- If Tamper = (COPY, (j, j')) for $j, j' \geq 2^{k-1}$, then update $D[j'] \leftarrow D[j]$.
- If Tamper = (REPLACE, (j, val)) for $j \geq 2^{k-1}$ then update $D[j] \leftarrow \text{val}$.

Disk Leakage. There is no other disk leakage from the secret disk, i.e., the adversary is not allowed any disk leakage queries.

Bus Leakage. There is only one allowed bus leakage function, say $\text{Leak}^{hb} = L$, so this is by definition the leakage query used on each execution of the CPU. On this leakage query the adversary is given $(i_0, i_1, i_2, \ldots, i_{1+2d})$.

Note that by definition of the bus leakage, the CPU always leaks the program counter and the memory positions that are being read. Besides this it is given no leakage. Since the leakage and tamper classes for a hybrid RAM are implicitly specified, we will denote the adversary class for a hybrid RAM simply by A^{hb}.

Bounded-access schemes. We later want to compile programs for the hybrid model into more realistic models by encoding the positions in the disk using a code. Because of leakage from the bus, this only works if each value is not read up too many times. We therefore need a notion of a program for the hybrid model being c-bounding, meaning that such a program reads each value at most c times, even when the program is under attack by $\mathcal{A} \in A^{hb}$. To define this notion we use two vectors $Q, C \in \mathbb{N}^{2^k}$. If the value stored in $D[j]$ is necessarily known by the adversary, then $Q[j] = \bot$. Otherwise, $Q[j]$ will be an identifier for the possibly secret value stored in $D[j]$, and for an identifier $id = Q[j]$ the value $C[id]$ counts how many times the secret value with identifier id was accessed by the CPU. Initially $Q[j] = \bot$ for all j and $C[j] = 0$ for all j. After the initial encoding ω is stored, we set $Q[2^{k-1} + j] = j$ for $j = 0, \ldots, |\omega_{\text{sec}}| - 1$. Then let $\text{ns} \leftarrow |\omega_{\text{sec}}|$. We use this counter to remember the identifier for the next secret. During execution, when the adversary executes (COPY, (j, j')), then let

$Q[j'] = Q[j]$. When the adversary executes $(\mathtt{REPLACE}, (j, \mathsf{val}))$, then let $Q[j] = \bot$. When the CPU executes, reading positions $i_0, i_1, \ldots, i_d$ and writing positions $j_1, \ldots, j_d$ then proceed as follows. For $p = 0, \ldots, d$, if $Q[i_p] \neq \bot$, let $C[Q[i_p]] \leftarrow C[Q[i_p]] + 1$. Then proceed as follows. If $Q[i_0] = Q[i_1] = \cdots = Q[i_d] = \bot$, then let $Q[j_1] = \cdots = Q[j_d] = \bot$. Otherwise, let $(Q[j_1], \ldots, Q[j_d]) = (\mathsf{ns}, \ldots, \mathsf{ns} + d - 1)$ and let $\mathsf{ns} \leftarrow \mathsf{ns} + d$. Then for each $j_i < 2^{k-1}$, set $Q[j_i] \leftarrow \bot$.

We say that a hybrid RAM scheme RS is c-bounding if it holds for all $\mathcal{G} \in$ RS.C.$\mathbb{G}$ that if RS.C($\mathcal{G}$) is executed on RS.R under attack by $\mathcal{A} \in \mathbf{A}^{\mathsf{hb}}$ and the above vectors are computed during the attack, then it never happens that $C[j] > c$ for any j. Let $\mathbb{G}$ denote the class of poly-time functionalities. We use $\mathbb{S}_c^{\mathsf{hb}} : \mathbb{G} \rightarrow \mathbb{P}_c^{\mathsf{hb}}$ to denote the class of hybrid RAM schemes which are c-bounding.

Theorem 4. *Let $\mathcal{C}$ be a $(\mathsf{lb}_{\mathsf{code}}, q)$-CNMLR code. Let $\mathbf{A}^{\mathsf{sp}} = (\mathsf{lb}_{\mathsf{disk}}, \mathsf{lb}_{\mathsf{bus}})$ be a split-state adversary class such that $\mathsf{lb}_{\mathsf{disk}} + (c + 1) \cdot \mathsf{lb}_{\mathsf{bus}} \leq \mathsf{lb}_{\mathsf{code}}$. Then there exists an $(\mathbf{A}^{\mathsf{hb}}, \mathbf{A}^{\mathsf{sp}})$-secure emulator $\mathcal{E} : \mathbb{S}_c^{\mathsf{hb}} \rightarrow \mathbb{S}^{\mathsf{sp}}$.*

5.2   The Emulator

The proof of Theorem 4 can be found in the full version [18]; here we provide only a high-level overview. The goal of the emulator $\mathcal{E}$ is to transform a hybrid RAM scheme $\mathsf{RS}^{\mathsf{hb}} = (\mathbf{C}^{\mathsf{hb}}, \mathbf{R}^{\mathsf{hb}}) \in \mathbb{S}_c^{\mathsf{hb}}$ into a split-state RAM scheme $\mathcal{E}(\mathsf{RS}^{\mathsf{hb}}) = \mathsf{RS}^{\mathsf{sp}} = (\mathbf{C}^{\mathsf{sp}}, \mathbf{R}^{\mathsf{sp}})$. In particular, the emulator needs to specify transformations for the components of $\mathsf{RS}^{\mathsf{hb}}$. This includes the contents of the disk as well as the way instructions are stored and processed by the CPU. Below, we give an overview of the construction of the emulator.

We emulate a program as follows $\mathcal{E}(\ell_P, I, \ell_I, O, \ell_O, \mathcal{X}, \mathcal{Y}, \omega^{\mathsf{hb}}) = (\ell_P, I, \ell_I, O, \ell_O, \mathcal{X}, \mathcal{Y}, \omega^{\mathsf{sp}})$, where we simply let $\omega_{\mathsf{pub}}^{\mathsf{sp}}$ be $\omega_{\mathsf{pub}}^{\mathsf{hb}}$. Then for each $j \in [0, |\omega_{\mathsf{sec}}^{\mathsf{hb}}|]$, let $\omega_{\mathsf{sec}}^{\mathsf{sp}}[j] = (\omega_{\mathsf{sec},1}^{\mathsf{sp}}[j], \omega_{\mathsf{sec},2}^{\mathsf{sp}}[j])$ be an encoding of $\omega_{\mathsf{sec}}^{\mathsf{hb}}[j]$ (computed using a CNMLR code, see Section 2). The CPU $\mathsf{Compute}^{\mathsf{sp}}$ runs as follows. It reads up the same instruction $D^{\mathsf{hb}}[\mathsf{pc}]$ that $\mathsf{Compute}^{\mathsf{hb}}$ would. Then for each additional position $D^{\mathsf{hb}}[i]$ read up, if $i < 2^{k-1}$ it lets $v_i = D^{\mathsf{hb}}[i]$ and if $i \geq 2^{k-1}$ it lets $(v_{1,i}, v_{2,i}) = D^{\mathsf{hb}}[i]$ and decodes $(v_{1,i}, v_{2,i})$ to v_i. If any decoding fails, then $\mathsf{Compute}^{\mathsf{sp}}$ self-destructs. Otherwise it runs $\mathsf{Compute}^{\mathsf{hb}}$ on the v_j values. Finally, it encodes all values v_j to be stored on $D_{\mathsf{sec}}^{\mathsf{sp}}$ and writes them back to disk. Then values v_j to be stored on $D_{\mathsf{pub}}^{\mathsf{sp}}$ are stored in "plaintext" as v_j.

Security of emulation. To argue security of emulation, we need to show that for all adversaries $\mathcal{A} \in \mathbf{A}^{\mathsf{sp}}$ there exists a simulator $\mathcal{B} \in \mathbf{A}^{\mathsf{hb}}$ able to fake $\mathcal{A}$'s view in a real execution with $\mathsf{RS}^{\mathsf{sp}}$ given only its limited leakage/tampering capabilities (via $\mathtt{REPLACE}$ and $\mathtt{COPY}$ commands). The simulator $\mathcal{B}$ runs $\mathcal{A}$ as a sub-routine, and works in two phases: the pre-processing and the online phase. Initially, in the pre-processing $\mathcal{B}$ samples crs and creates encodings of 0 for all the values on the secret disk using the CNMLR code, and puts dummy encodings $(v_1, v_2) \leftarrow \mathsf{Encode}(\mathsf{crs}, 0)$ on the corresponding simulated virtual disks. For the positions on the public disk, the simulator can put the correct values, which is possible as it can read $\omega_{\mathsf{pub}}^{\mathsf{hb}}$ from $D_{\mathsf{pub}}^{\mathsf{hb}}$ and $\omega_{\mathsf{pub}}^{\mathsf{hb}} = \omega_{\mathsf{pub}}^{\mathsf{sp}}$. Depending on the queries in the online phase $\mathcal{B}$ will update these virtual disks in the following. TAMPER queries are simulated easily by applying the corresponding tamper functions to the current state of the virtual disks D_1 and D_2. Notice that also the leakage from the disks and the buses will essentially be done using the contents of the virtual disks. Hence, the main challenge of the simulation is how to keep these virtual disks consistent with what the adversary expects to see from an EXEC query. This is done by a rather involved case analysis and we only give the main idea here.

We distinguish the case when all the values on the disk that are used by the CPU to evaluate the current instruction are *public* (corresponding to the case $Q[j_1] = \cdots = Q[j_d] = \perp$ in the definition of c-bounded) and the case where some are *secret*. The first case may happen if the adversary $\mathcal{A}$ replaces the contents of the secret disks with some encoding of his choice by tampering. Notice that in this case the simulation is rather easy as $\mathcal{B}$ "knows" all the values and can simulate the execution of the CPU (including the outputs and the new contents of the disks). If, on the other hand, some values that are used by the CPU in the current execution are secret, then $\mathcal{B}$'s only chance to simulate $\mathcal{A}$ is to run $\mathsf{CPU}^{\mathsf{hb}}$ in the hybrid game. The difficulty is to keep the state of the secret hybrid disk D^{hb} consistent with the contents of the virtual disks D_1, D_2 maintained by $\mathcal{A}$. This is achieved by careful book-keeping and requires $\mathcal{B}$ to make use of his REPLACE and COPY commands to the single secret disk D^{hb}. The simulator $\mathcal{B}$ manages this book-keeping by using two records: (i) the vector S that stores dummy encodings (v_1, v_2) corresponding to values unknown to $\mathcal{B}$ (either generated during the pre-processing, or resulting from an evaluation of $\mathsf{CPU}^{\mathsf{hb}}$ on partially secret inputs); (ii) the backup storage $\mathcal{BP}$ that $\mathcal{B}$ maintains on the hybrid disk D^{hb} that stores a copy of all values that are unknown to the adversary (essentially, the values on $\mathcal{BP}$ correspond to the values that the dummy encodings in S where supposed to encode). Then the simulator can always copy the corresponding secret value to the position on D^{hb}, which corresponds to the value that *should* have been inside the encoding on the same position on the two virtual disks. The trick is that each secret value, i.e., a value that would have an identifier in the definition of c-boundedness, has an associated dummy encoding generated by the simulator and a corresponding value on $D^{\mathsf{hb}}_{\mathsf{pub}}$. The simulator uses the book-keeping to keep these values "lined up". All other encodings were not generated by the simulator, and can therefore be decoded to values independent of the values in the dummy encodings. These therefore correspond to public values. A reduction to continuous non-malleability then allows to replace the 0's in the dummy encoding by the correct values on D^{hb}.

6   The Hybrid Scheme

In this section we describe an $O(1)$-bounding, RAM scheme $\mathsf{RS}^{\mathsf{hb}} = (\mathbf{C}^{\mathsf{hb}}, \mathbf{R}^{\mathsf{hb}})$ that is secure in the hybrid model. Recall that a hybrid schemes $\mathsf{RS}^{\mathsf{hb}}$ consists of a hybrid RAM $\mathbf{R}^{\mathsf{hb}}$ and a hybrid compiler $\mathbf{C}^{\mathsf{hb}}$ which takes a functionality $\mathcal{G}$ with secret key K and outputs an encoding of the form $(P, \omega^{\mathsf{hb}})$ to be executed on $\mathbf{R}^{hb}$. The RAM $\mathbf{R}^{hb}$ consists of a CPU CPU^{hb}, which is specified by two functions Random^{hb} and $\mathsf{Compute}^{hb}$. Below, we present an outline of our hybrid RAM scheme RS^{hb} and refer the reader to the full version [18] for the details.

Overview. We assume $\mathcal{G}$ is described by a "regular program" (i.e., a sequence of instructions) for computing $\mathcal{G}_K$ in a "regular" RAM (i.e., a RAM with a disk and a CPU without any security). This regular program essentially "encodes" the original functionality in a format that is compatible with the underlying RAM; for example the key is parsed as a sequence of words that are written in the corresponding locations of the disk. The RAM needs to be neither tamper nor leakage resilient, and the "regularity" essentially comes from the fact that it emulates $\mathcal{G}_K$ correctly and has no pathological behaviour, like overwriting the key during an activation. We also need that it reads each value $O(1)$ times. It is easy to see that one can always translate the functionality into such a regular program, generically, using, e.g., a bounded fan-out circuit layed out as a RAM program. We refer the reader to the full version for the complete specifications.

Let $\mathbb{G}$ be the class of poly-time keyed functions $\mathcal{G}$. (each described a regular program as outlined above). We show the following theorem.

Theorem 5. *There exists an $\mathbf{A}^{hb}$-secure RAM scheme $\mathsf{RS}^{hb} = (\mathbf{C}^{hb}, \mathbf{R}^{hb})$ for function class $\mathbb{G}$ and program class $\mathbb{P}_c^{hb}$ for $c = O(1)$.*

The hybrid scheme. Our hybrid compiler $\mathbf{C}^{hb}$ takes as input $\mathcal{G} \in \mathbb{G}$ and is supposed to produce a *compiled* program (during the pre-processing phase) to be run by the hybrid RAM $\mathbf{R}^{hb}$ (during the on-line phase). The compiled program is placed on the disk from which CPU^{hb} reads in sequence. Our CPU $\mathsf{CPU}^{hb} = (\mathsf{Compute}^{hb}, \mathsf{Random}^{hb})$ will be deterministic, and hence Random^{hb} just outputs the empty string at each invocation. This means that we only have to specify the compiler $\mathbf{C}^{hb}$ and the function $\mathsf{Compute}^{hb}$ for a complete specification of RS^{hb}.

Recall that the adversary in a hybrid execution is only allowed a limited form of tampering, by which he can copy values within the secret disk and replace some value with a known one. The main idea will be to store the regular program (and all intermediary values) in the disk; each value will be stored in a special "augmented" form. The augmentation includes: (a) A secret label L (sampled once and for all at setup, and thus unknown to the adversary); (b) The position j at which the value is stored; (c) The current values (a, p) of the activation and program counters $(\mathtt{ac}, \mathtt{pc})$ when the value was written. Intuitively, the secret label ensures that the adversary cannot use the "replace" command as that would require to guess the value of the label. On the other hand the position j will allow the CPU to check that it loaded a value from the right position, preventing the adversary to use the "copy" command to move values created by the CPU (or at setup) to another location. Finally, the pair (a, p) prevents the adversary from swapping values sharing the same L and the same j (i.e., trying to reset the CPU by forcing it the CPU to re-use a previously encoded value).

Whenever algorithm $\mathsf{Compute}^{hb}$ of the CPU loads some instruction, it uses the above augmented encodings to check that it is loading the right instruction, that the correct location was read, that the label matches, and that the counters are consistent; if any of the above fails, it self-destructs. Otherwise, it runs the specific instruction of the emulated regular program, and writes the resulting value to the disk (in the augmented form). A detailed description can be found in the full version of this paper.

Analysis. Next, we turn to a high-level overview of the security proof (the actual proof can be found in the full version). Our goal is to prove that the above RAM scheme is secure in the hybrid model, namely for all adversaries $\mathcal{B} \in \mathbf{A}^{hb}$ attacking the RAM scheme in a real execution, there exists a simulator $\mathcal{S}$ faking the view of $\mathcal{B}$ only given black-box access to the original functionality $\mathcal{G}_K$.

As a first step, we prove that the probability by which the adversary succeeds in using a "replace" command to write some value on the disk with the correct secret label, and having the CPU read this value without provoking a self-destruct, is essentially equal to the probability of guessing the secret label (which is exponentially small). This means we can assume that all the values put on the disk using a "replace" command do not contain the secret label. In each execution our CPU CPU^{hb} will check that all loaded values contain the same label, and will write back values where the augmentation contains this label. It then follows that all values containing the secret label in the augmentation were written by the pre-processing or by CPU^{hb}, and it also follows that all values not having the secret label in the augmentation are known by the adversary: they were put on disk using a REPLACE command or computed by CPU^{hb} on values known by the adversary. We then argue that CPU^{hb} (by design) will never write two values $V \neq V'$ sharing the same augmentation (j, L, a, p). This is because the augmentation includes the strictly increasing pair (a, p), and we also prove that CPU^{hb} can predict what (a, p) should be for all loaded values in all executions. It follows from an inductive argument that all values containing the secret label in the augmentation are correct. Hence all values on the disk are either correct secret values or incorrect values known by the adversary. So, when CPU^{hb} writes a result to the disk, it is either an allowed output or a value already known by the adversary. From the above intuition, it is straight-forward, although rather tedious, to derive a simulator.

References

1. Aggarwal, D., Dodis, Y., Lovett, S.: Non-malleable codes from additive combinatorics. IACR Cryptology ePrint Archive 2013:201 (2013)
2. Agrawal, S., Gupta, D., Maji, H.K., Pandey, O., Prabhakaran, M.: Explicit non-malleable codes resistant to permutations and perturbations. IACR Cryptology ePrint Archive 2014:316 (2014)
3. Bellare, Mihir, Cash, David: Pseudorandom functions and permutations provably secure against related-key attacks. In: Rabin, Tal (ed.) CRYPTO 2010. LNCS, vol. 6223, pp. 666–684. Springer, Heidelberg (2010)
4. Bellare, M., Kohno, T.: A theoretical treatment of related-key attacks: RKA-PRPs, RKA-PRFs, and applications. In: EUROCRYPT, pp. 491–506 (2003)

5. Bellare, Mihir, Paterson, Kenneth G., Thomson, Susan: RKA security beyond the linear barrier: IBE, encryption and signatures. In: Wang, Xiaoyun, Sako, Kazue (eds.) ASIACRYPT 2012. LNCS, vol. 7658, pp. 331–348. Springer, Heidelberg (2012)
6. Cheraghchi, M., Guruswami, V.: Capacity of non-malleable codes. In: ICS, pp. 155–168 (2014)
7. Cheraghchi, Mahdi, Guruswami, Venkatesan: Non-malleable coding against bit-wise and split-state tampering. In: Lindell, Yehuda (ed.) TCC 2014. LNCS, vol. 8349, pp. 440–464. Springer, Heidelberg (2014)
8. Coretti, S., Maurer, U., Tackmann, B., Venturi, D.: From single-bit to multi-bit public-key encryption via non-malleable codes. In: TCC (2015, To appear)
9. Coretti, S., Dodis, Y., Tackmann, B., Venturi, D.: Self-destruct non-malleability. IACR Cryptology ePrint Archive 2014:866 (2014)
10. Dachman-Soled, Dana, Kalai, Yael Tauman: Securing circuits against constant-rate tampering. In: Safavi-Naini, Reihaneh, Canetti, Ran (eds.) CRYPTO 2012. LNCS, vol. 7417, pp. 533–551. Springer, Heidelberg (2012)
11. Dachman-Soled, Dana, Kalai, Yael Tauman: Securing circuits and protocols against 1/poly(k) tampering rate. In: Lindell, Yehuda (ed.) TCC 2014. LNCS, vol. 8349, pp. 540–565. Springer, Heidelberg (2014)
12. Dachman-Soled, D., Liu, F.-H., Shi, E., Zhou, H.-S.: Locally decodable and updat-able non-malleable codes and their applications. In: TCC (2015, To appear)
13. Damgård, Ivan, Faust, Sebastian, Mukherjee, Pratyay, Venturi, Daniele: Bounded tamper resilience: how to go beyond the algebraic barrier. In: Sako, Kazue, Sarkar, Palash (eds.) ASIACRYPT 2013, Part II. LNCS, vol. 8270, pp. 140–160. Springer, Heidelberg (2013)
14. Dziembowski, Stefan, Faust, Sebastian: Leakage-resilient circuits without compu-tational assumptions. In: Cramer, Ronald (ed.) TCC 2012. LNCS, vol. 7194, pp. 230–247. Springer, Heidelberg (2012)
15. Dziembowski, Stefan, Kazana, Tomasz, Obremski, Maciej: Non-malleable codes from two-source extractors. In: Canetti, Ran, Garay, Juan A. (eds.) CRYPTO 2013, Part II. LNCS, vol. 8043, pp. 239–257. Springer, Heidelberg (2013)
16. Dziembowski, S., Pietrzak, K., Wichs, D.: Non-malleable codes. In: ICS, pp. 434–452 (2010)
17. Faust, Sebastian, Mukherjee, Pratyay, Nielsen, Jesper Buus, Venturi, Daniele: Con-tinuous non-malleable codes. In: Lindell, Yehuda (ed.) TCC 2014. LNCS, vol. 8349, pp. 465–488. Springer, Heidelberg (2014)
18. Faust, S., Mukherjee, P., Nielsen, J.B., Venturi, D.: A tamper and leakage resilient von Neumann architecture. Cryptology ePrint Archive, Report 2014/338 (2014). http://eprint.iacr.org/
19. Faust, Sebastian, Mukherjee, Pratyay, Venturi, Daniele, Wichs, Daniel: Effi-cient non-malleable codes and key-derivation for poly-size tampering circuits. In: Nguyen, Phong Q., Oswald, Elisabeth (eds.) EUROCRYPT 2014. LNCS, vol. 8441, pp. 111–128. Springer, Heidelberg (2014)
20. Faust, Sebastian, Pietrzak, Krzysztof, Venturi, Daniele: Tamper-proof circuits: how to trade leakage for tamper-resilience. In: Aceto, Luca, Henzinger, Monika, Sgall, Jiří (eds.) ICALP 2011, Part I. LNCS, vol. 6755, pp. 391–402. Springer, Heidelberg (2011)
21. Faust, Sebastian, Rabin, Tal, Reyzin, Leonid, Tromer, Eran, Vaikuntanathan, Vinod: Protecting Circuits from Leakage: the Computationally-Bounded and Noisy Cases. In: Gilbert, Henri (ed.) EUROCRYPT 2010. LNCS, vol. 6110, pp. 135–156. Springer, Heidelberg (2010)

22. Goldwasser, S., Rothblum, G.N.:. How to compute in the presence of leakage. In: FOCS, pp. 31–40 (2012)
23. Ishai, Yuval, Prabhakaran, Manoj, Sahai, Amit, Wagner, David: Private circuits II: keeping secrets in tamperable circuits. In: Vaudenay, Serge (ed.) EUROCRYPT 2006. LNCS, vol. 4004, pp. 308–327. Springer, Heidelberg (2006)
24. Ishai, Yuval, Sahai, Amit, Wagner, David: Private circuits: securing hardware against probing attacks. In: Boneh, Dan (ed.) CRYPTO 2003. LNCS, vol. 2729, pp. 463–481. Springer, Heidelberg (2003)
25. Kalai, Yael Tauman, Kanukurthi, Bhavana, Sahai, Amit: Cryptography with tamperable and leaky memory. In: Rogaway, Phillip (ed.) CRYPTO 2011. LNCS, vol. 6841, pp. 373–390. Springer, Heidelberg (2011)
26. Kiayias, Aggelos, Tselekounis, Yiannis: Tamper resilient circuits: the adversary at the gates. In: Sako, Kazue, Sarkar, Palash (eds.) ASIACRYPT 2013, Part II. LNCS, vol. 8270, pp. 161–180. Springer, Heidelberg (2013)
27. Liu, Feng-Hao, Lysyanskaya, Anna: Tamper and leakage resilience in the split-state model. In: Safavi-Naini, Reihaneh, Canetti, Ran (eds.) CRYPTO 2012. LNCS, vol. 7417, pp. 517–532. Springer, Heidelberg (2012)
28. Miles, E., Viola, E.: Shielding circuits with groups. In: STOC, pp. 251–260 (2013)
29. Prouff, Emmanuel, Rivain, Matthieu: Masking against side-channel attacks: a formal security proof. In: Johansson, Thomas, Nguyen, Phong Q. (eds.) EUROCRYPT 2013. LNCS, vol. 7881, pp. 142–159. Springer, Heidelberg (2013)
30. Wee, H.: Public key encryption against related key attacks. In: Public Key Cryptography, pp. 262–279 (2012)

Low Noise LPN: KDM Secure Public Key Encryption and Sample Amplification

Nico Döttling[⊠]

Department of Computer Science, Aarhus University, Aarhus, Denmark
nico.doettling@cs.au.dk

Abstract. Cryptographic schemes based on the Learning Parity with Noise (LPN) problem have several very desirable aspects: Low computational overhead, simple implementation and conjectured post-quantum hardness. Choosing the LPN noise parameter sufficiently low allows for public key cryptography. In this work, we construct the first standard model public key encryption scheme with key dependent message security based solely on the low noise LPN problem. Additionally, we establish a new connection between LPN with a bounded number of samples and LPN with an unbounded number of samples. In essence, we show that if LPN with a small error and a small number of samples is hard, then LPN with a slightly larger error and an unbounded number of samples is also hard. The key technical ingredient to establish both results is a variant of the LPN problem called the extended LPN problem.

Keywords: Low noise LPN · Key dependent message security · LPN hardness reduction

1 Introduction

The LPN Problem The learning parity with noise (LPN) problem asks to find a secret binary vector $\mathbf{s} \in \mathbb{F}_2^n$ given noisy linear samples of the form $(\mathbf{a}, \langle \mathbf{a}, \mathbf{s} \rangle + e) \in \mathbb{F}_2^n \times \mathbb{F}_2$ where $\mathbf{a}$ is chosen uniformly at random and e is an additive noise term that occurs with probability ρ. Due to its simplicity and binary arithmetic, the LPN problem has become a central hub in secret key cryptography [13, 27,28,30,33]. These applications use the *high noise* LPN problem where the noise rate $\rho < 1/2$ is a constant. In the *low noise* LPN problem, the noise rate ρ tends asymptotically to 0. Alekhnovich [6] provided a construction of a public key encryption scheme based on LPN for noise rates $\rho = O(1/\sqrt{n})$.

Supported by European Research Commission Starting Grant no. 279447.

N. Döttling—The authors acknowledge support from the Danish National Research Foundation and The National Science Foundation of China (under the grant 61061130540) for the Sino-Danish Center for the Theory of Interactive Computation, within which part of this work was performed; and also from the CFEM research center (supported by the Danish Strategic Research Council) within which part of this work was performed.

J. Katz (Ed.): PKC 2015, LNCS 9020, pp. 604–626, 2015.
DOI: 10.1007/978-3-662-46447-2_27

Recently, more complex cryptographic primitives have been constructed from low noise LPN such as chosen ciphertext secure public key encryption [22,31] and composable oblivious transfer [18]. In the original formulation of the LPN problem, the search algorithm/adversary may demand an unbounded number of samples whereas the bounded samples version (e.g. used in [6,22,31]) only provides an a priori bounded number of samples to the search algorithm. So far, it was unknown whether the hardness of LPN with a bounded number of samples implies the hardness of LPN with an unbounded number of samples, even if a modest increase in the noise rate is tolerated.

Key Dependent Message Security. A public key encryption scheme is called key dependent message (KDM) secure, if encryptions of the secret key, or more generally encryptions of functions of several secret keys are indistinguishable of encryptions of (say) the all-zero message. We will exclusively consider KDM-CPA security in this work, i.e. KDM adversaries do not have access to a decryption oracle. While for most natural cryptographic tasks standard notions of security are sufficient, the notion of KDM security is relevant for contexts such as computational soundness [2,12] or when hard-disks are encrypted that store the corresponding secret key (as mentioned in [15]). It has been shown that standard IND-CPA (or even IND-CCA) security does not imply KDM security [1,16], i.e. there exist public key encryption schemes with IND-CPA security relative to some standard assumption which are provably not KDM secure. Standard model KDM secure public key public key cryptosystems were constructed from a variety of assumptions, starting with the construction of Boneh et al [15]. Applebaum et al. [10] provided both a circular secure public key encryption scheme from the LWE assumption and a circular secure *private key* encryption scheme from the (high noise) LPN problem. The latter scheme was later shown to fulfill the stronger notion of related-key KDM security by Applebaum [9]. In [8], Applebaum provided a construction of a KDM secure PKE for arbitrary (bounded size) circuits from any KDM secure PKE for affine functions. Constructing a KDM secure public key encryption scheme from low noise LPN has remained an open problem so far.

1.1 Extended LPN

The central tool we use in our constructions is a version of the LPN problem called *extended decisional LPN problem*, or eDLPN in short. The eDLPN problem can be seen as a special case for $q = 2$ of the extended LWE problem introduced O'Neill, Peikert and Waters [35] and proven hard under standard LWE by Alperin-Sheriff and Peikert [7]. The binary version we use in this work was first discussed by Kiltz, Masny and Pietrzak [31].

In the eDLPN problem, the adversary's goal is to distinguish $(\mathbf{A}, \mathbf{RA}, \mathbf{e}, \mathbf{Re})$ from $(\mathbf{A}, \mathbf{U}, \mathbf{e}, \mathbf{Re})$, where $\mathbf{A}$ is a randomly chosen matrix, $\mathbf{R}$ is a randomly chosen low weight matrix, $\mathbf{U}$ is a randomly chosen matrix and $\mathbf{e}$ follows some distribution χ. This is similar to the dual formulation of the decisional LPN problem, where the adversary has to distinguish $(\mathbf{A}, \mathbf{RA})$ from $(\mathbf{A}, \mathbf{U})$. However, in the extended decisional LPN problem, the adversary obtains an extra advice $\mathbf{Re}$ about a secret matrix $\mathbf{R}$, where the vector $\mathbf{e}$ can have any distribution. Kiltz, Masny and Pietrzak [31] observed that in the LPN case, this advice can be extremely useful to enable reductions to simulate faithfully. In particular, the eDLPN problem can effectively be used as a computational substitute for the (generalized) leftover hash lemma [19,29] or gaussian regularity lemmata for lattices [26].

In the full version [21], we provide a generalization of the extended LPN problem we call leaky LPN (ℓ-LPN), which may be of independent interest. In the ℓ-LPN problem, the advice given to the adversary can be described by an arbitrary adversarially chosen leakage function γ from a family $\mathcal{L}$ and is not limited to linear functions as in the extended LPN problem. Clearly, the hardness of the extended LPN problem follows immediately from the hardness of the leaky LPN problem when instantiating the leakage functions with linear functions. If the functions in $\mathcal{L}$ output short strings, say strings of at most logarithmic length, then the hardness of the ℓ-LPN *search* problem follows immediately from the standard LPN problem, since all possible leakage values can be efficiently enumerated (or guessed). The situation is slightly different for decisional problems. In general, decisional problems become easy if even a single bit of arbitrary leakage is allowed. However, we only allow the leakage to depend on $\mathbf{R}$ and in particular not on $\mathbf{A}$. We show that a sample preserving search to decision reduction of Applebaum et al. [11] is in fact *leakage preserving*. We can thus base the hardness of the decisional problem ℓ-DLPN on ℓ-LPN, and therefore on LPN given that the functions in $\mathcal{L}$ only provide short advice.

1.2   KDM Secure Public Key Encryption

We will now provide an overview of our construction of a KDM secure public key encryption scheme from LPN. The construction is inspired by the public key encryption scheme of Applebaum et al. [10], which however lives in the LWE realm. The basic idea, as in [10], is to make encryptions of the secret key syntactically similar to the public key. More specifically, public keys in our scheme will be of the form $(\mathbf{A}, \mathbf{y} = \mathbf{As} + \mathbf{e})$ where $\mathbf{s}$ is the secret key. It follows immediately from the decisional LPN problem that the public key is pseudorandom. Encryption takes a message $\mathfrak{m}$ and computes

$$\mathbf{C}_1 = \mathbf{RA}$$
$$\mathbf{c}_2 = \mathbf{Ry} + \mathbf{Gm},$$

where the matrix $\mathbf{R}$ is chosen from a low weight distribution and $\mathbf{G}$ is the generator matrix of a good, efficiently decodable binary linear code. We remark that while this scheme bears strong resemblances with (and is inspired by) the LWE based scheme of [10], it is rather incomparable to the (high noise) LPN based private key encryption schemes of [9,10] or previous low-noise LPN public key encryption schemes [6,22,31]. Notice that standard IND-CPA security of this scheme follows directly from the fact that $\mathbf{y}$ is pseudorandom and thus also

$(\mathbf{RA}, \mathbf{Ry})$ is pseudorandom given the public key $(\mathbf{A}, \mathbf{y})$, by using the dual formulation of the decisional LPN problem (i.e. $(\mathbf{A}', \mathbf{RA}') \approx_c (\mathbf{A}', \mathbf{U})$). To decrypt a ciphertext $\mathbf{c} = (\mathbf{C}_1, \mathbf{c}_2)$, we basically compute

$$\mathbf{z} = \mathbf{c}_2 - \mathbf{C}_1 \mathbf{s}$$

and recover $\mathfrak{m}$ from $\mathbf{z}$ by using the efficient decoding algorithm for the code generated by $\mathbf{G}$. Correctness of the scheme follows from the fact that

$$\begin{aligned} \mathbf{z} &= \mathbf{c}_2 - \mathbf{C}_1 \mathbf{s} \\ &= \mathbf{Ry} + \mathbf{Gm} - \mathbf{RAs} \\ &= \mathbf{R}(\mathbf{As} + \mathbf{e}) + \mathbf{Gm} - \mathbf{RAs} \\ &= \mathbf{Gm} + \mathbf{Re}. \end{aligned}$$

Since we have chosen $\mathbf{R}$ and $\mathbf{e}$ from low noise distributions, the term $\mathbf{Re}$ has low weight with high probability. Thus it follows that a decoder of the code generated by $\mathbf{G}$ will be able to recover $\mathfrak{m}$ from $\mathbf{z}$. We will briefly sketch how to establish 1-circular security of this scheme, where the adversary gets a single encryption of the secret key (or an encryption of 0). For the full proof of KDM security for affine functions, refer to Section 3. An encryption of the secret key has the form $(\mathbf{RA}, \mathbf{Ry} + \mathbf{Gs})$. Figure 1 provides the game transform for this security reduction.

	Game	public key	challenge ciphertext	remark
1.	Real	$(\mathbf{A}, \mathbf{y} = \mathbf{As} + \mathbf{e})$	$(\mathbf{RA}, \mathbf{Ry} + \mathbf{Gs})$	
2.	Real	$(\mathbf{A}, \mathbf{As} + \mathbf{e})$	$(\mathbf{RA}, \mathbf{R}(\mathbf{As} + \mathbf{e}) + \mathbf{Gs})$	identical
3.	Real	$(\mathbf{A}, \mathbf{As} + \mathbf{e})$	$(\mathbf{RA}, (\mathbf{RA} + \mathbf{G})\mathbf{s} + \mathbf{Re})$	identical
4.	$\mathbf{H}_1$	$(\mathbf{A}, \mathbf{As} + \mathbf{e})$	$(\mathbf{U}, (\mathbf{U} + \mathbf{G})\mathbf{s} + \mathbf{Re})$	eDLPN
5.	$\mathbf{H}_1$	$(\mathbf{A}, \mathbf{As} + \mathbf{e})$	$(\mathbf{U}' - \mathbf{G}, \mathbf{U}'\mathbf{s} + \mathbf{Re})$	identical
6.	$\mathbf{H}_2$	$(\mathbf{A}, \mathbf{As} + \mathbf{e})$	$(\mathbf{RA} - \mathbf{G}, \mathbf{RAs} + \mathbf{Re})$	eDLPN
7.	$\mathbf{H}_2$	$(\mathbf{A}, \mathbf{As} + \mathbf{e})$	$(\mathbf{RA} - \mathbf{G}, \mathbf{R}(\mathbf{As} + \mathbf{e}))$	identical
8.	$\mathbf{H}_3$	$(\mathbf{A}, \mathbf{u})$	$(\mathbf{RA} - \mathbf{G}, \mathbf{Ru})$	DLPN
9.	$\mathbf{H}_3$	$(\mathbf{A}, \mathbf{u})$	$(\mathbf{U} - \mathbf{G}, \mathbf{u}')$	DDLPN
10.	$\mathbf{H}_3$	$(\mathbf{A}, \mathbf{u})$	$(\mathbf{U}, \mathbf{u}')$	identical

Fig. 1. The Game Transform for KDM-CPA security

The first three steps shown in Figure 1 do not change the real experiment but basically rewrite the challenge ciphertext. From step 3 to step 4 we replace the matrix $\mathbf{RA}$ by a uniformly random matrix $\mathbf{U}$. Since we also need the additional term $\mathbf{Re}$ to provide the correct distribution to the adversary, we will use the extended decisional LPN problem to show that these two experiments are computationally indistinguishable. In particular, we use $\mathbf{A}$ and $\mathbf{e}$ provided by the eDLPN problem to construct a public key, while we use $\mathbf{RA}$ and the advice $\mathbf{Re}$ to construct the encryption of the secret key. Then, we replace $\mathbf{RA}$ by a random matrix $\mathbf{U}$, which yields an indistinguishable experiment by the hardness of eDLPN. Step 4 to 5 is another bridging step which does not change the experiment. Since $\mathbf{U}$ is distributed uniformly random, so is the matrix $\mathbf{U}' = \mathbf{U} + \mathbf{G}$. Thus, instead of choosing $\mathbf{U}$ uniformly at random we can choose $\mathbf{U}'$ uniformly at random and set $\mathbf{U} = \mathbf{U}' - \mathbf{G}$. From step 5 to step 6 we replace the matrix $\mathbf{U}'$ by $\mathbf{RA}$. Again, we have to use the extended decisional LPN problem as we need the extra advice $\mathbf{Re}$. It now becomes clear that we have used steps 3 to 6 to *pull* the matrix $\mathbf{G}$ from the second component of the challenge ciphertext to its first component, i.e. we have transformed $(\mathbf{RA}, (\mathbf{RA} + \mathbf{G})\mathbf{s} + \mathbf{Re})$ into $(\mathbf{RA} - \mathbf{G}, \mathbf{RAs} + \mathbf{Re})$. Step 6 to step 7 is another basic bridging step. From step 7 to step 8 we replace the second component $\mathbf{As} + \mathbf{e}$ of the public key by a randomly chosen $\mathbf{u}$, indistinguishability follows from the standard decisional LPN problem. From step 8 to step 9 we replace $(\mathbf{A}, \mathbf{RA}, \mathbf{u}, \mathbf{Ru})$ by $(\mathbf{A}, \mathbf{U}, \mathbf{u}, \mathbf{u}')$ for uniformly random $\mathbf{U}$ and $\mathbf{u}'$, indistinguishability follows from the dual formulation of the decisional LPN problem. Finally, from step 9 to step 10, we replace $\mathbf{U} - \mathbf{G}$ by $\mathbf{U}$. We can do this since the uniform distribution $\mathbf{U}$ is invariant under an additive shift by a constant matrix $\mathbf{G}$. Thus, in the last experiment the challenge ciphertext is just uniformly random, which concludes this outline.

1.3 Unbounded Samples LPN from Bounded Samples LPN

In the following we will distinguish between bounded and unbounded samples LPN. We will denote search LPN with a secret of length n, m samples and noise rate ρ by $\mathsf{LPN}(n, m, \rho)$ and decisional LPN with a secret of length n, unbounded samples and noise rate ρ' by $\mathsf{DLPN}(n, \rho')$. Our second contribution is a hardness reduction which bases the hardness of $\mathsf{DLPN}(n, \rho')$ on $\mathsf{LPN}(n, 2n, \rho)$. More specifically, we show that if $\mathsf{LPN}(n, 2n, \rho)$ is hard, then $\mathsf{DLPN}(n, \rho')$ is also hard, where

$$\rho' = \frac{1}{2} - \frac{1}{2}(1 - 2\rho)^{\lfloor \rho 2n \rfloor} \leq 2\rho^2 n.$$

For the Learning With Errors (LWE) problem, there exists a statistical *random self reduction* [10,26]. The idea of this reduction is to use $m \approx n \log(q)$ *seed samples* to generate arbitrarily many fresh samples. The noise rate in the new samples increases only slightly. Specifically, if $(\mathbf{A}, \mathbf{y} = \mathbf{As} + \mathbf{z})$ is such a given set of *seed samples*, then one can generate new samples by drawing $\mathbf{e} \in \mathbb{Z}_q^m$ from a discrete gaussian [5,34] and setting $\mathbf{a}' = \mathbf{A}^\top \mathbf{e}$ and $y' = \mathbf{e}^\top \mathbf{y}$. Now it holds

$$y' = \mathbf{e}^\top \mathbf{y} = \mathbf{e}^\top \mathbf{As} + \mathbf{e}^\top \mathbf{z} = \mathbf{a}'^\top \mathbf{s} + \langle \mathbf{e}, \mathbf{z} \rangle.$$

The pair $(\mathbf{a}', y' + e')$, where e' is a gaussian smoothing term, is a proper LWE sample, as $\mathbf{a}' = \mathbf{e}^\top \mathbf{A}$ can be shown to be statistically close to uniform *and* $\langle \mathbf{e}, \mathbf{z} \rangle$ follows an independent discrete gaussian distribution even conditioned on $\mathbf{a}' = \mathbf{e}^\top \mathbf{A}$ [1].

---

[1] This can be established via a Lemma due to Regev [37] or its refinement due to Peikert [36], which show that the distribution of $\mathbf{e}$ remains discrete gaussian even conditioned on $\mathbf{e}^\top \mathbf{A}$, though the variance of the distribution decreases.

Such an approach, however, cannot be directly transferred to the LPN setting. For the vector $\mathbf{a}' = \mathbf{A}^\top \mathbf{e}$ to be statistically close to uniform, $\mathbf{e}$ must have min-entropy $\approx n$, and thus high weight. But this in turn means that $\langle \mathbf{e}, \mathbf{z} \rangle$ will only have a negligibly small bias. We remark that such a high noise sample amplification was used Lyubashevsky [32] to cryptanalize LPN in sub-exponential time, but this technique does not seem to be applicable in the context of an *efficient* (i.e. PPT) hardness reduction, especially when the number of samples is at most polynomial.

Therefore, in our reduction we will replace the statistical tools in the above reduction by a computational technique based on the eDLPN problem. Again, we start with a given amount of $m = 2n$ seed samples and generate new samples from these. While we cannot hope that the samples we generate in this way have the proper distribution (in the statistical sense), we will be able to show that the distribution generated in this way is computationally indistinguishable from the real LPN distribution. More specifically, let $(\mathbf{A}, \mathbf{y})$ be the LPN seed samples. We will compute new samples by choosing a random low weight $\mathbf{r}$ and setting $\mathbf{a} = \mathbf{A}^\top \mathbf{r}$ and $y' = \mathbf{r}^\top \mathbf{y} = \langle \mathbf{r}, \mathbf{y} \rangle$. Now, assume first that $\mathbf{y} = \mathbf{As} + \mathbf{e}$. Then it holds that

$$y' = \mathbf{r}^\top \mathbf{As} + \langle \mathbf{r}, \mathbf{e} \rangle = \langle \mathbf{a}, \mathbf{s} \rangle + \langle \mathbf{r}, \mathbf{e} \rangle.$$

While $(\mathbf{a}, y')$ syntactically looks like an LPN sample, it is statistically far away from a correctly distributed sample. There are two issues. First, $\mathbf{a} = \mathbf{r}^\top \mathbf{A}$ is not distributed uniformly. Second, the noise term $\langle \mathbf{r}, \mathbf{e} \rangle$ is correlated with $\mathbf{a}$. The first issue *alone* could be resolved by assuming the hardness of the DLPN. To deal with both issues simultaneously, we will resort to the eDLPN problem, which allows us to present a noise term $\langle \mathbf{r}, \mathbf{e} \rangle$ with the right distribution. More specifically, the eDLPN problem allows us to replace $\mathbf{a} = \mathbf{r}^\top \mathbf{A}$ by a uniformly random $\mathbf{a}$ but also provides us with an *advice* $(\mathbf{e}, \langle \mathbf{r}, \mathbf{e} \rangle)$ that allows us to simulate the noise term $\langle \mathbf{r}, \mathbf{e} \rangle$ correctly. On the other hand, if $\mathbf{y}$ was chosen uniformly at random, then the pseudorandomness of $(\mathbf{a}, y') = (\mathbf{r}^\top \mathbf{A}, \mathbf{r}^\top \mathbf{y})$ follows easily from the dual formulation of the LPN problem DLPN. Since we can base the hardness of all auxiliary problems on $\mathsf{LPN}(n, 2n, \rho)$, it follows that $\mathsf{DLPN}(n, \rho')$ is at least as hard as $\mathsf{LPN}(n, 2n, \rho)$. This concludes this outline.

2 Preliminaries

In the following, let λ always denote the security parameter. We call a machine PPT if it runs in probabilistic (expected) polynomial time. For a search problem P and an adversary/search algorithm $\mathcal{A}$ let $\mathsf{Adv_P}(\mathcal{A})$ denote the probability of $\mathcal{A}$ finding a solution of a random instance of P. For a decisional problem D which consists in distinguishing two distributions X and Y and a distinguishing algorithm $\mathcal{D}$ define $\mathsf{Adv_D}(\mathcal{D}) = |\Pr[\mathcal{D}(X) = 1] - \Pr[\mathcal{D}(Y) = 1]|$. When we don't write it explicitly, we will implicitly assume that search algorithms and distinguishers get 1^λ as an additional input. We will denote the Hamming weight of a vector $\mathbf{x} \in \mathbb{F}_2^n$ by $\|\mathbf{x}\|_0 = |\{i : x_i \neq 0\}|$. For a matrix $\mathbf{M} \in \mathbb{F}_2^{m \times n}$, we define the Hamming weight of $\mathbf{M}$ by $\|\mathbf{M}\|_0 = \max_i \|\mathbf{m}_i\|_0$ where the $\mathbf{m}_i$ are the column vectors of $\mathbf{M}$. It follows easily for all $\mathbf{M} \in \mathbb{F}_2^{m \times n}$ and $\mathbf{x} \in \mathbb{F}_2^n$ that $\|\mathbf{Mx}\|_0 \leq \|\mathbf{M}\|_0 \cdot \|\mathbf{x}\|_0$. We need asymptotically good, efficiently decodable binary linear codes for the construction of our KDM secure public key encryption scheme. A binary linear $[k, n]$ code C is a n dimensional subspace of $\mathbb{F}_2^k$. We call $\mathbf{G} \in \mathbb{F}_2^{k \times n}$ a generator matrix of C if every $\mathbf{c} \in C$ can be written as $\mathbf{c} = \mathbf{Gx}$ for some $\mathbf{x} \in \mathbb{F}_2^n$. We assume codes C come with efficient encoding and decoding procedures C.Encode and C.Decode, where C.Encode($\mathbf{x}$) $= \mathbf{G} \cdot \mathbf{x}$ for some generator matrix $\mathbf{G}$ of C. An error correcting code can efficiently correct an α fraction of errors, if for every $\mathbf{e} \in \mathbb{F}_2^k$ with $\|\mathbf{e}\|_0 \leq \alpha k$, it holds that C.Decode(C.Encode($\mathbf{x}$) $+ \mathbf{e}$) $= \mathbf{x}$. There exists a large corpus of literature of linear codes that can efficiently correct a constant fraction of errors, for instance concatenated codes [25] or expander codes [38,39].

2.1 Learning Parity with Noise

We will denote the Bernoulli distribution with parameter $\rho \in [0, 1/2]$ on $\mathbb{F}_2^m$ by $\mathsf{Ber}(m, \rho)$. For an $\mathbf{e} \leftarrow_\$ \mathsf{Ber}(m, \rho)$, each component e_i of $\mathbf{e}$ independently takes the value 1 with probability ρ and 0 with probability $1 - \rho$. We write $\mathsf{Ber}(\rho) := \mathsf{Ber}(1, \rho)$. We will distinguish between LPN with a bounded and an unbounded number of samples.

Definition 1 (Learning Parity with Noise). *Let χ be an error distribution on $\mathbb{F}_2^m$ and $\rho = \rho(\lambda) \in [0, 1/2]$. Let $\mathbf{A} \leftarrow_\$ \mathbb{F}_2^{m \times n}$ be chosen uniformly at random, let $\mathbf{s} \leftarrow_\$ \mathbb{F}_2^n$ be chosen uniformly at random and let $\mathbf{e} \leftarrow_\$ \chi$.*

1. *In the bounded samples search problem $\mathsf{LPN}(n, m, \chi)$, the goal is to find $\mathbf{s}$, given $(\mathbf{A}, \mathbf{As} + \mathbf{e})$.*
2. *In the unbounded samples search problem $\mathsf{LPN}(n, \rho)$, the goal is to find $\mathbf{s}$, given an oracle that outputs an arbitrary number of samples of the form $(\mathbf{a}, \langle \mathbf{a}, \mathbf{s} \rangle + e)$, where $\mathbf{a} \leftarrow_\$ \mathbb{F}_2^n$ and $e \leftarrow_\$ \mathsf{Ber}(\rho)$.*
3. *In the bounded samples decisional problem $\mathsf{DLPN}(n, m, \chi)$, the goal is to distinguish the distributions $(\mathbf{A}, \mathbf{As} + \mathbf{e})$ and $(\mathbf{A}, \mathbf{u})$, where $\mathbf{u} \leftarrow_\$ \mathbb{F}_2^m$ is chosen uniformly at random.*
4. *In the unbounded samples decisional problem $\mathsf{DLPN}(n, \rho)$, the goal is to distinguish two oracles, namely one that outputs samples of the form $(\mathbf{a}, \langle \mathbf{a}, \mathbf{s} \rangle + e)$ (where $\mathbf{a} \leftarrow_\$ \mathbb{F}_2^n$ and $e \leftarrow_\$ \mathsf{Ber}(\rho)$) from one that outputs samples of the form $(\mathbf{a}, u)$ (where $\mathbf{a} \leftarrow_\$ \mathbb{F}_2^n$ and $u \leftarrow_\$ \mathbb{F}_2$).*

For bounded samples LPN with errors $\mathbf{e}$ from the Bernoulli distribution $\mathsf{Ber}(m, \rho)$ we will write $\mathsf{LPN}(n, m, \rho)$ for $\mathsf{LPN}(n, m, \mathsf{Ber}(m, \rho))$ and also $\mathsf{DLPN}(n, m, \rho)$ for $\mathsf{DLPN}(n, m, \mathsf{Ber}(m, \rho))$. By a standard argument, one can show that if $\mathbf{e} \in \mathbb{F}_2^m$ is distributed according to $\mathsf{Ber}(m, \rho)$ and $\mathbf{z} \in \mathbb{F}_2^m$ is an arbitrary vector of weight $\lfloor \rho m \rfloor$, then $\langle \mathbf{z}, \mathbf{e} \rangle$ is distributed according to $\mathsf{Ber}(\rho')$, where $\rho' = \frac{1}{2} - \frac{1}{2}(1 - 2\rho)^{\lfloor \rho m \rfloor} \leq \rho^2 m$. Following Alekhnovich [6], we will choose the noise parameter ρ of the form $O(1/\sqrt{n})$ and $n, m = \Omega(\lambda^2)$ to be able to use low weight vectors as trapdoors and have 2^λ (conjectured) security for $\mathsf{LPN}(n, m, \rho)$.

A series of works have established relations between search and decisional LPN problems [11,13,30]. The hardness reduction of Applebaum et al. [11] is sample preserving, i.e. it shows that the hardness of $\mathsf{DLPN}(n, m, \chi)$ follows directly from the hardness of $\mathsf{LPN}(n, m, \chi)$, for any error distribution χ.

Lemma 1 (Applebaum et al. [11]). *Let χ be an error distribution on $\mathbb{F}_2^m$ and assume that $\mathsf{LPN}(n, m, \chi)$ is hard. Then $\mathsf{DLPN}(n, m, \chi)$ is also hard. More specifically, assume there exists a PPT adversary $\mathcal{A}$ that distinguishes $\mathsf{DLPN}(n, m, \chi)$ with advantage ϵ. Then there exists a PPT adversary $\mathcal{A}'$ that breaks $\mathsf{LPN}(n, m, \chi)$ with advantage $\epsilon^2/8$.*

Let $\mathsf{S}(m, \rho)$ denote the distribution on $\mathbb{F}_2^m$ which outputs uniformly random vectors in $\mathbb{F}_2^m$ of weight $\lfloor \rho m \rfloor$, i.e. $\mathsf{S}(m, \rho)$ is the uniform distribution on the set $M = \{ \mathbf{x} \in \mathbb{F}_2^m \mid \|\mathbf{x}\|_0 = \lfloor \rho m \rfloor \}$. It is easy to see that if $\mathsf{LPN}(n, m, \rho)$ is hard, then $\mathsf{LPN}(n, m, \mathsf{S}(m, \rho))$ is also hard.

Corollary 1. *Let $\mathcal{A}$ be a PPT adversary that breaks $\mathsf{LPN}(n, m, \mathsf{S}(m, \rho))$ with advantage ϵ. Then there exists a PPT adversary $\mathcal{A}'$ that breaks $\mathsf{LPN}(n, m, \rho)$ with advantage $\frac{(1-o(1))\epsilon}{\sqrt{2\pi m \rho(1-\rho)}}$. Moreover, if there exists a PPT distinguisher $\mathcal{D}$ that distinguishes $\mathsf{DLPN}(n, m, \mathsf{S}(m, \rho))$ with advantage ϵ, then there exists a PPT adversary $\mathcal{A}'$ that breaks $\mathsf{LPN}(n, m, \rho)$ with advantage $\frac{(1-o(1))\epsilon^2}{8 \cdot \sqrt{2\pi m \rho(1-\rho)}}$.*

For a proof of Corollary 1, refer to the full version [21]. As a convenient reformulation of the LPN problem, we define the decisional dual LPN problem.

Definition 2. *Let $\mathbf{A} \leftarrow_\$ \mathbb{F}_2^{m \times n}$, $\mathbf{R} \leftarrow_\$ \mathsf{Ber}(k \times m, \rho)$, $\mathbf{a} \leftarrow_\$ \mathbb{F}_2^m$, $\mathbf{U} \leftarrow_\$ \mathbb{F}_2^{k \times n}$ and $\mathbf{u} \leftarrow_\$ \mathbb{F}_2^k$. The goal of the $\mathsf{DDLPN}(n, m, k, \rho)$ problem is to distinguish the distributions $(\mathbf{A}, \mathbf{RA}, \mathbf{a}, \mathbf{Ra})$ and $(\mathbf{A}, \mathbf{U}, \mathbf{a}, \mathbf{u})$.*

The hardness of $\mathsf{DDLPN}(n, m, k, \rho)$ follows from $\mathsf{DLPN}(n, m, \rho)$ (see e.g. [10] or [22]) using the fact that for a randomly chosen matrix $\mathbf{A}$ we can also sample a random $\mathbf{H}$ such that it holds $\mathbf{H} \cdot \mathbf{A} = 0$ and $\mathbf{H}$ is uniformly random (not given $\mathbf{A}$).

Lemma 2. *Let $m \geq 2n$. Assume there exists a PPT distinguisher $\mathcal{D}$ that distinguishes the problem $\mathsf{DDLPN}(n, m, k, \rho)$ with advantage ϵ. Then there exists a PPT adversary $\mathcal{A}$ that breaks $\mathsf{LPN}(n, m, \rho)$ with advantage $\frac{\epsilon^2}{8k^2}$.*

Following Kiltz et al. [31] and Alperin-Sheriff and Peikert [7], we provide a definition of the extended LPN problem. We only define the extended LPN problem for Bernoulli error distributions.

Definition 3. *Let χ be any distribution on $\mathbb{F}_2^m$. Let $\mathbf{A} \leftarrow_\$ \mathbb{F}_2^{m \times n}$, $\mathbf{R} \leftarrow_\$ \mathsf{Ber}(k \times m, \rho)$, $\mathbf{U} \leftarrow_\$ \mathbb{F}_2^{k \times n}$ and $\mathbf{e} \leftarrow_\$ \chi$. The goal of the $\mathsf{eDLPN}(n, m, k, \rho, \chi)$ problem is to distinguish the distributions $(\mathbf{A}, \mathbf{RA}, \mathbf{e}, \mathbf{Re})$ and $(\mathbf{A}, \mathbf{U}, \mathbf{e}, \mathbf{Re})$.*

The hardness of $\mathsf{eDLPN}(n, m, k, \rho, \chi)$ can be established from $\mathsf{LPN}(n, m, \rho)$.

Lemma 3. *Let $m \geq 2n$. Then for any distribution χ on $\mathbb{F}_2^m$ and any $k = \text{poly}(\lambda)$ it holds that if there exists a PPT distinguisher $\mathcal{D}$ that distinguishes* $\text{eDLPN}(n, m, k, \rho, \chi)$ *with advantage ϵ, then there exists a PPT adversary $\mathcal{A}$ that breaks* $\text{LPN}(n, m, \rho)$ *with advantage $\frac{\epsilon^2}{8k^2}$.*

For a proof of Lemma 3 we refer the reader either to [7] or the full version of this paper [21].

2.2   Key Dependent Message Secure Public Key Encryption

Syntactically, a public key encryption scheme PKE consists of three PPT algorithms PKE.KeyGen, PKE.Enc and PKE.Dec, such that PKE.KeyGen generates a pair (pk, sk) of public and secret keys, PKE.Enc takes a public key pk and a plaintext $\mathfrak{m}$ and outputs a ciphertext $\mathfrak{c}$ and PKE.Dec takes a secret key sk and a ciphertext $\mathfrak{c}$ and outputs a plaintext $\mathfrak{m}$. We say that PKE is correct, if it holds for all plaintexts $\mathfrak{m}$ (of size corresponding to λ) that if $(pk, sk) \leftarrow \text{PKE.KeyGen}(1^\lambda)$, then

$$\text{PKE.Dec}(sk, \text{PKE.Enc}(pk, \mathfrak{m})) = \mathfrak{m},$$

except with negligible probability over the randomness used by PKE.KeyGen, PKE.Enc and PKE.Dec. The security notion we consider in this work is key dependent message security under chosen plaintext attacks. In the security experiment corresponding to this notion, the adversary gets a list of public keys $\{pk_i\}$ and access to an oracle that computes encryptions of functions of the secret keys. We call such dependencies *key cycles*, even though the functional relationships the adversary obtains can be more complex than key cycles.

Definition 4. *We say a public key encryption-scheme PKE is ciphertext indistinguishable under key dependent message chosen plaintext attacks (KDM-CPA) for cycles of length l with respect to a class $\mathcal{F}$ of functions mapping l secret keys to a plaintext, if every PPT-adversary $\mathcal{A}$ has success-probability at most negligibly better than $1/2$ in the experiment* $\text{KDM} - \text{CPA}_{\mathcal{F},l}$, *i.e.* $\Pr[\text{KDM} - \text{CPA}_{\mathcal{F},l}(\mathcal{A}) = 1] \leq \frac{1}{2} + \text{negl}(\lambda).$

Experiment $\text{KDM} - \text{CPA}_{\mathcal{F},l}$	$\mathcal{O}_{\text{KDM}}(f, j)$
For $i = 1, \ldots, l$	If $b = 0$
$\quad (pk_i, sk_i) \leftarrow \text{PKE.KeyGen}(1^\lambda)$	$\quad f \leftarrow \mathbf{0}$
$b \leftarrow_\$ \{0, 1\}$	$\mathfrak{c} \leftarrow \text{PKE.Enc}(pk_j, f(\{sk_i\}))$
$b' \leftarrow \mathcal{A}^{\mathcal{O}_{\text{KDM}}(\cdot, \cdot)}(\{pk_i\}, 1^\lambda)$	Return $\mathfrak{c}$
Return 1 iff $b = b'$.	

Remark 1. We implicitly assume that sanity checks are performed by the oracle, i.e. it only accepts KDM queries with $f \in \mathcal{F}$ and $j \in \{1, \ldots, l\}$. Moreover, we assume that the KDM oracle may have access to all local variables of the experiment KDM-CPA, in particular the pk_i and sk_i and the bit b.

Applebaum [8] provides a general transfomation which transforms any public key encryption scheme with KDM security against *affine functions* into a public key encryption scheme with KDM security against arbitrary functions with circuits of *bounded size*. Thus, it is sufficient to construct a public key encryption scheme with KDM security against affine functions to obtain a scheme with security against the more general class of functions.

3 KDM Secure Public Key Encryption from Low Noise LPN

In this section we will provide a public key encryption scheme with KDM security for affine functions based on the hardness of the low noise LPN problem.

Construction 1. *Let $n, m, k = \mathsf{poly}(\lambda)$ be positive integers with $m > k > n$. Let C be binary linear code of length k and dimension n and efficient encoding and decoding procedures $\mathsf{C.Encode}$ and $\mathsf{C.Decode}$. The public key encrypion scheme $\mathsf{PKE} = (\mathsf{PKE.KeyGen}, \mathsf{PKE.Enc}, \mathsf{PKE.Dec})$ is given by the following algorithms. The message space of PKE is $\mathbb{F}_2^n$.*

$\mathsf{PKE.KeyGen}(1^\lambda)$:	$\mathsf{PKE.Enc}(pk, \mathsf{m})$:	$\mathsf{PKE.Dec}(sk, \mathfrak{c})$:
$\mathbf{A} \leftarrow_\$ \mathbb{F}_2^{m \times n}$	Parse $pk = (\mathbf{A}, \mathbf{b})$	Parse $\mathfrak{c} = (\mathbf{C}_1, \mathbf{c}_2)$ and $sk = \mathbf{s}$
$\mathbf{s} \leftarrow_\$ \mathbb{F}_2^n$	$\mathbf{R} \leftarrow_\$ \mathsf{Ber}(k \times m, \rho)$	$\mathbf{z} \leftarrow \mathbf{c}_2 - \mathbf{C}_1 \mathbf{s}$
$\mathbf{e} \leftarrow_\$ \mathsf{Ber}(m, \rho)$	$\mathbf{C}_1 \leftarrow \mathbf{R} \cdot \mathbf{A}$	$\mathsf{m} \leftarrow \mathsf{C.Decode}(\mathbf{z})$
$\mathbf{y} \leftarrow \mathbf{As} + \mathbf{e}$	$\mathbf{c}_2 \leftarrow \mathbf{R} \cdot \mathbf{y} + \mathsf{C.Encode}(\mathsf{m})$	Return m
$pk \leftarrow (\mathbf{A}, \mathbf{y})$	$\mathfrak{c} \leftarrow (\mathbf{C}_1, \mathbf{c}_2)$	
$sk \leftarrow \mathbf{s}$	Return $\mathfrak{c}$	
Return (pk, sk)		

3.1 Correctness

We will first show that the scheme PKE is correct.

Lemma 4. *Assume that $\mathsf{C.Decode}$ can efficiently decode from $\rho' = 4\rho^2 km$ errors. Then the scheme PKE is correct.*

The condition of Lemma 4 can be met by choosing $m, k = \Omega(n)$ and $\rho = O(1/\sqrt{n})$. Thus, to obtain conjectured 2^λ-hardness for LPN, we can take usual parameter choices of $m, n, k = \Theta(\lambda^2)$ and $\rho = \Theta(1/\lambda)$ (as in [6, 22, 31]).

Proof. Assume that $\mathfrak{c} = (\mathbf{C}_1, \mathbf{c}_2)$ is a ciphertext generated by PKE.Enc. Consider the term $\mathbf{z}$ computed during decryption. It holds that

$$\begin{aligned}
\mathbf{z} &= \mathbf{c}_2 - \mathbf{C}_1 \mathbf{s} \\
&= \mathbf{R}\mathbf{y} + \mathsf{C.Encode}(\mathfrak{m}) - \mathbf{R}\mathbf{A}\mathbf{s} \\
&= \mathsf{C.Encode}(\mathfrak{m}) + \mathbf{R}(\mathbf{A}\mathbf{s} + \mathbf{e}) - \mathbf{R}\mathbf{A}\mathbf{s} \\
&= \mathsf{C.Encode}(\mathfrak{m}) + \mathbf{R}\mathbf{e}
\end{aligned}$$

By a Chernoff bound, it holds that $\|\mathbf{e}\| \leq 2\rho m$, except with negligible probability $e^{-\frac{1}{3}\rho m}$. Also by a Chernoff bound and a union bound, it holds that $\|\mathbf{R}\|_0 \leq 2\rho k$, except with negligible probability $m \cdot e^{-\frac{1}{3}\rho k}$. Therefore,

$$\|\mathbf{R}\mathbf{e}\|_0 \leq \|\mathbf{R}\|_0 \cdot \|\mathbf{e}\|_0 \leq 4\rho^2 km,$$

except with negligible probability over the choice of $\mathbf{e}$ and $\mathbf{R}$. Consequently, C.Decode will be able to decode $\mathfrak{m}$ from $\mathbf{z}$.

3.2   KDM-CPA Security

We will now prove KDM-CPA security of PKE.

Theorem 1. *Let λ be a security parameter and $n, m, k, l = \mathsf{poly}(\lambda)$ with $m \geq 2n$ and $l \geq 1$. Let $\rho = \rho(\lambda) \in [0, 1/2]$. Let $\mathcal{F} = \{f : (\mathbb{F}_2^n)^l \to \mathbb{F}_2^n\}$ be a family of affine functions. If $\mathsf{eDLPN}(n, m, k, \rho, \mathsf{Ber}(m, \rho))$, $\mathsf{DLPN}(n, l \cdot m, \rho)$ and $\mathsf{DDLPN}(n, m, k, \rho)$ are hard, then the scheme PKE is $\mathsf{KDM} - \mathsf{CPA}_{\mathcal{F},l}$ secure. More precisely, assume that $\mathcal{A}$ is a PPT adversary that breaks the $\mathsf{KDM} - \mathsf{CPA}_{\mathcal{F},l}$ security of PKE with advantage $\mathsf{Adv}_{\mathsf{KDM-CPA}}(\mathcal{A})$ and queries its KDM oracle at most $q = \mathsf{poly}(\lambda)$ times. Then there exist PPT distinguishers $\mathcal{D}_1$ and $\mathcal{D}_2$ against the problem $\mathsf{eDLPN}(n, m, k, \rho, \mathsf{Ber}(m, \rho))$, $\mathcal{D}_3$ against $\mathsf{DLPN}(n, l \cdot m, \rho)$ and $\mathcal{D}_4$ against $\mathsf{DDLPN}(n, m, k, \rho)$ such that*

$$\begin{aligned}
\mathsf{Adv}_{\mathsf{KDM-CPA}}(\mathcal{A}) \leq{} & lq \cdot \mathsf{Adv}_{\mathsf{eDLPN}}(\mathcal{D}_1) + lq \cdot \mathsf{Adv}_{\mathsf{eDLPN}}(\mathcal{D}_2) \\
& + \mathsf{Adv}_{\mathsf{DLPN}}(\mathcal{D}_3) + lq \cdot \mathsf{Adv}_{\mathsf{DDLPN}}(\mathcal{D}_4).
\end{aligned}$$

Corollary 2. *Let n, m, k, l, ρ and $\mathcal{F}$ be as in Theorem 1. If $\mathsf{LPN}(n, l \cdot m, \rho)$ is hard, then PKE is $\mathsf{KDM} - \mathsf{CPA}_{\mathcal{F},l}$ secure. More precisely, assume that $\mathcal{A}$ is a PPT adversary that breaks the $\mathsf{KDM} - \mathsf{CPA}_{\mathcal{F},l}$ of PKE with advantage ϵ and queries its KDM oracle at most $q = \mathsf{poly}(\lambda)$ times. Then there exists a PPT adversary $\mathcal{A}^*$ that solves $\mathsf{LPN}(n, l \cdot m, \rho)$ with advantage $\frac{\epsilon^2}{128k^2l^2q^2}$.*

The qualitative statement of Corollary 2 follows directly from Theorem 1 and Lemmas 1, 2 and 3. For the quantitative statement refer to the full version of this paper [21]. We will now provide a sketch for the proof of Theorem 1. See the full version [21] for the complete proof.

Proof (Proof Sketch for Theorem 1). Let $\mathcal{A}$ be a KDM-CPA adversary against PKE. Consider the following sequence of hybrid games. For notational convenience we assume that the oracles have access to all local variables of the games (without explicitly specifying so). We will first provide an overview of game 1 - 8 on the next pages.

Game 1
For $i = 1, \ldots, l$
   $\mathbf{A}_i \leftarrow_\$ \mathbb{F}_2^{m \times n}$
   $\mathbf{s}_i \leftarrow_\$ \mathbb{F}_2^n$, $\mathbf{e}_i \leftarrow_\$ \mathsf{Ber}(m, \rho)$
   $\mathbf{y} \leftarrow \mathbf{A}_i \mathbf{s}_i + \mathbf{e}_i$
   $pk_i \leftarrow (\mathbf{A}_i, \mathbf{y}_i)$, $sk \leftarrow \mathbf{s}_i$
$b \leftarrow_\$ \{0, 1\}$
$b' \leftarrow \mathcal{A}^{\mathcal{O}_{\mathsf{KDM}}(\cdot, \cdot)}(\{pk_i\}, 1^\lambda)$
Return 1 iff $b = b'$

$\mathcal{O}_{\mathsf{KDM}}(f, j)$
   If $b = 0$
      $f \leftarrow 0$
   $\mathbf{R} \leftarrow_\$ \mathsf{Ber}(k \times m, \rho)$
   $\mathbf{C}_1 \leftarrow \mathbf{R} \cdot \mathbf{A}_j$
   $\mathbf{c}_2 \leftarrow \mathbf{R} \cdot \mathbf{y}_j + \mathsf{C.Encode}(f(\{sk_i\}))$
   $\mathfrak{c} \leftarrow (\mathbf{C}_1, \mathbf{c}_2)$
   Return $\mathfrak{c}$

Game 2
$\mathbf{s} \leftarrow \mathbb{F}_2^n$
For $i = 1, \ldots, l$
   $\mathbf{A}_i \leftarrow_\$ \mathbb{F}_2^{m \times n}$, $\mathbf{e}_i \leftarrow_\$ \mathsf{Ber}(m, \rho)$
   $\mathbf{y}_i' \leftarrow \mathbf{A}_i \mathbf{s} + \mathbf{e}_i$
   $\mathbf{s}_i' \leftarrow_\$ \mathbb{F}_2^n$
   $\mathbf{s}_i \leftarrow \mathbf{s} + \mathbf{s}_i'$, $\mathbf{y}_i \leftarrow \mathbf{y}_i' + \mathbf{A}_i \mathbf{s}_i'$
   $pk_i \leftarrow (\mathbf{A}_i, \mathbf{y}_i)$, $sk \leftarrow \mathbf{s}_i$
$b \leftarrow_\$ \{0, 1\}$
$b' \leftarrow \mathcal{A}^{\mathcal{O}_{\mathsf{KDM}}(\cdot, \cdot)}(\{pk_i\}, 1^\lambda)$
Return 1 iff $b = b'$

$\mathcal{O}_{\mathsf{KDM}}(f, j)$
   If $b = 0$
      $f \leftarrow 0$
   Compute $\mathbf{T}_f$, $\mathbf{t}_f$ s.t. $f(\{sk_i\}) = \mathbf{T}_f \mathbf{s} + \mathbf{t}_f$,
      using that $sk_i = \mathbf{s} + \mathbf{s}_i'$
   $\mathbf{R} \leftarrow_\$ \mathsf{Ber}(k \times m, \rho)$
   $\mathbf{C}_1 \leftarrow \mathbf{R} \cdot \mathbf{A}_j$
   $\mathbf{c}_2 \leftarrow \mathbf{R} \cdot \mathbf{y}_j + \mathbf{G} \cdot (\mathbf{T}_f \mathbf{s} + \mathbf{t}_f)$
   $\mathfrak{c} \leftarrow (\mathbf{C}_1, \mathbf{c}_2)$
   Return $\mathfrak{c}$

Game 3
$\mathbf{s} \leftarrow \mathbb{F}_2^n$
For $i = 1, \ldots, l$
   $\mathbf{A}_i \leftarrow_\$ \mathbb{F}_2^{m \times n}$, $\mathbf{e}_i \leftarrow_\$ \mathsf{Ber}(m, \rho)$
   $\mathbf{y}_i' \leftarrow \mathbf{A}_i \mathbf{s} + \mathbf{e}_i$
   $\mathbf{s}_i' \leftarrow_\$ \mathbb{F}_2^n$
   $\mathbf{s}_i \leftarrow \mathbf{s} + \mathbf{s}_i'$, $\mathbf{y}_i \leftarrow \mathbf{y}_i' + \mathbf{A}_i \mathbf{s}_i'$
   $pk_i \leftarrow (\mathbf{A}_i, \mathbf{y}_i)$, $sk \leftarrow \mathbf{s}_i$
$b \leftarrow_\$ \{0, 1\}$
$b' \leftarrow \mathcal{A}^{\mathcal{O}_{\mathsf{KDM}}(\cdot, \cdot)}(\{pk_i\}, 1^\lambda)$
Return 1 iff $b = b'$.

$\mathcal{O}_{\mathsf{KDM}}(f, j)$
   If $b = 0$
      $f \leftarrow 0$
   Compute $\mathbf{T}_f$, $\mathbf{t}_f$ s.t. $f(\{sk_i\}) = \mathbf{T}_f \mathbf{s} + \mathbf{t}_f$,
      using that $sk_i = \mathbf{s} + \mathbf{s}_i'$
   $\mathbf{R} \leftarrow_\$ \mathsf{Ber}(k \times m, \rho)$
   $\mathbf{C}_1 \leftarrow \mathbf{R} \cdot \mathbf{A}_j$
   $\mathbf{c}_2 \leftarrow (\mathbf{C}_1 + \mathbf{G}\mathbf{T}_f) \cdot \mathbf{s} + \mathbf{R}\mathbf{e}_j + \mathbf{G}\mathbf{t}_f + \mathbf{C}_1 \mathbf{s}_i'$
   $\mathfrak{c} \leftarrow (\mathbf{C}_1, \mathbf{c}_2)$
   Return $\mathfrak{c}$

Game 4
$\mathbf{s} \leftarrow \mathbb{F}_2^n$
For $i = 1, \ldots, l$
   $\mathbf{A}_i \leftarrow_\$ \mathbb{F}_2^{m \times n}$, $\mathbf{e}_i \leftarrow_\$ \mathsf{Ber}(m, \rho)$
   $\mathbf{y}_i' \leftarrow \mathbf{A}_i \mathbf{s} + \mathbf{e}_i$
   $\mathbf{s}_i' \leftarrow_\$ \mathbb{F}_2^n$
   $\mathbf{s}_i \leftarrow \mathbf{s} + \mathbf{s}_i'$, $\mathbf{y}_i \leftarrow \mathbf{y}_i' + \mathbf{A}_i \mathbf{s}_i'$
   $pk_i \leftarrow (\mathbf{A}_i, \mathbf{y}_i)$, $sk \leftarrow \mathbf{s}_i$
$b \leftarrow_\$ \{0, 1\}$
$b' \leftarrow \mathcal{A}^{\mathcal{O}_{\mathsf{KDM}}(\cdot, \cdot)}(\{pk_i\}, 1^\lambda)$
Return 1 iff $b = b'$.

$\mathcal{O}_{\mathsf{KDM}}(f, j)$
   If $b = 0$
      $f \leftarrow 0$
   Compute $\mathbf{T}_f$, $\mathbf{t}_f$ s.t. $f(\{sk_i\}) = \mathbf{T}_f \mathbf{s} + \mathbf{t}_f$,
      using that $sk_i = \mathbf{s} + \mathbf{s}_i'$
   $\mathbf{R} \leftarrow_\$ \mathsf{Ber}(k \times m, \rho)$
   $\mathbf{U} \leftarrow_\$ \mathbb{F}_2^{k \times n}$
   $\mathbf{C}_1 \leftarrow \mathbf{U}$
   $\mathbf{c}_2 \leftarrow (\mathbf{C}_1 + \mathbf{G}\mathbf{T}_f) \cdot \mathbf{s} + \mathbf{R}\mathbf{e}_j + \mathbf{G}\mathbf{t}_f + \mathbf{C}_1 \mathbf{s}_j'$
   $\mathfrak{c} \leftarrow (\mathbf{C}_1, \mathbf{c}_2)$
   Return $\mathfrak{c}$

Game 5

$\mathbf{s} \leftarrow \mathbb{F}_2^n$

For $i = 1, \dots, l$

$\quad \mathbf{A}_i \leftarrow_\$ \mathbb{F}_2^{m \times n}, \mathbf{e}_i \leftarrow_\$ \mathsf{Ber}(m, \rho)$

$\quad \mathbf{y}_i' \leftarrow \mathbf{A}_i \mathbf{s} + \mathbf{e}_i$

$\quad \mathbf{s}_i' \leftarrow_\$ \mathbb{F}_2^n$

$\quad \mathbf{s}_i \leftarrow \mathbf{s} + \mathbf{s}_i', \mathbf{y}_i \leftarrow \mathbf{y}_i' + \mathbf{A}_i \mathbf{s}_i'$

$\quad pk_i \leftarrow (\mathbf{A}_i, \mathbf{y}_i), sk \leftarrow \mathbf{s}_i$

$b \leftarrow_\$ \{0, 1\}$

$b' \leftarrow \mathcal{A}^{\mathcal{O}_{\mathsf{KDM}}(\cdot, \cdot)}(\{pk_i\}, 1^\lambda)$

Return 1 iff $b = b'$.

$\mathcal{O}_{\mathsf{KDM}}(f, j)$

If $b = 0$

$\quad f \leftarrow \mathbf{0}$

Compute $\mathbf{T}_f, \mathbf{t}_f$ s.t. $f(\{sk_i\}) = \mathbf{T}_f \mathbf{s} + \mathbf{t}_f$,

$\quad$ using that $sk_i = \mathbf{s} + \mathbf{s}_i'$

$\mathbf{R} \leftarrow_\$ \mathsf{Ber}(k \times m, \rho)$

$\mathbf{U} \leftarrow_\$ \mathbb{F}_2^{k \times n}$

$\mathbf{C}_1 \leftarrow \mathbf{U} - \mathbf{G} \mathbf{T}_f$

$\mathbf{c}_2 \leftarrow \mathbf{U} \mathbf{s} + \mathbf{R} \mathbf{e}_j + \mathbf{G} \mathbf{t}_f + \mathbf{C}_1 \mathbf{s}_j'$

$\mathbf{c} \leftarrow (\mathbf{C}_1, \mathbf{c}_2)$

Return $\mathbf{c}$

Game 6

$\mathbf{s} \leftarrow \mathbb{F}_2^n$

For $i = 1, \dots, l$

$\quad \mathbf{A}_i \leftarrow_\$ \mathbb{F}_2^{m \times n}, \mathbf{e}_i \leftarrow_\$ \mathsf{Ber}(m, \rho)$

$\quad \mathbf{y}_i' \leftarrow \mathbf{A}_i \mathbf{s} + \mathbf{e}_i$

$\quad \mathbf{s}_i' \leftarrow_\$ \mathbb{F}_2^n$

$\quad \mathbf{s}_i \leftarrow \mathbf{s} + \mathbf{s}_i', \mathbf{y}_i \leftarrow \mathbf{y}_i' + \mathbf{A}_i \mathbf{s}_i'$

$\quad pk_i \leftarrow (\mathbf{A}_i, \mathbf{y}_i), sk \leftarrow \mathbf{s}_i$

$b \leftarrow_\$ \{0, 1\}$

$b' \leftarrow \mathcal{A}^{\mathcal{O}_{\mathsf{KDM}}(\cdot, \cdot)}(\{pk_i\}, 1^\lambda)$

Return 1 iff $b = b'$.

$\mathcal{O}_{\mathsf{KDM}}(f, j)$

If $b = 0$

$\quad f \leftarrow \mathbf{0}$

Compute $\mathbf{T}_f, \mathbf{t}_f$ s.t. $f(\{sk_i\}) = \mathbf{T}_f \mathbf{s} + \mathbf{t}_f$,

$\quad$ using that $sk_i = \mathbf{s} + \mathbf{s}_i'$

$\mathbf{R} \leftarrow_\$ \mathsf{Ber}(k \times m, \rho)$

$\mathbf{C}_1 \leftarrow \mathbf{R} \mathbf{A}_j - \mathbf{G} \mathbf{T}_f$

$\mathbf{c}_2 \leftarrow \mathbf{R} \mathbf{A}_j \mathbf{s} + \mathbf{R} \mathbf{e}_j + \mathbf{G} \mathbf{t}_f + \mathbf{C}_1 \mathbf{s}_j'$

$\mathbf{c} \leftarrow (\mathbf{C}_1, \mathbf{c}_2)$

Return $\mathbf{c}$

Game 7

For $i = 1, \dots, l$

$\quad \mathbf{A}_i \leftarrow_\$ \mathbb{F}_2^{m \times n}$

$\quad \mathbf{y}_i' \leftarrow_\$ \mathbb{F}_2^m$

$\quad \mathbf{s}_i' \leftarrow_\$ \mathbb{F}_2^n$

$\quad \mathbf{y}_i \leftarrow \mathbf{y}_i' + \mathbf{A}_i \mathbf{s}_i'$

$\quad pk_i \leftarrow (\mathbf{A}_i, \mathbf{y}_i)$

$b \leftarrow_\$ \{0, 1\}$

$b' \leftarrow \mathcal{A}^{\mathcal{O}_{\mathsf{KDM}}(\cdot, \cdot)}(\{pk_i\}, 1^\lambda)$

Return 1 iff $b = b'$.

$\mathcal{O}_{\mathsf{KDM}}(f, j)$

If $b = 0$

$\quad f \leftarrow \mathbf{0}$

Compute $\mathbf{T}_f, \mathbf{t}_f$ s.t. $f(\{sk_i\}) = \mathbf{T}_f \mathbf{s} + \mathbf{t}_f$,

$\quad$ using that $sk_i = \mathbf{s} + \mathbf{s}_i'$

$\mathbf{R} \leftarrow_\$ \mathsf{Ber}(k \times m, \rho)$

$\mathbf{C}_1 \leftarrow \mathbf{R} \mathbf{A}_j - \mathbf{G} \mathbf{T}_f$

$\mathbf{c}_2 \leftarrow \mathbf{R} \mathbf{y}_j' + \mathbf{G} \mathbf{t}_f + \mathbf{C}_1 \mathbf{s}_j'$

$\mathbf{c} \leftarrow (\mathbf{C}_1, \mathbf{c}_2)$

Return $\mathbf{c}$

Game 8

For $i = 1, \dots, l$

$\quad \mathbf{A}_i \leftarrow_\$ \mathbb{F}_2^{m \times n}$

$\quad \mathbf{y}_i' \leftarrow_\$ \mathbb{F}_2^m$

$\quad \mathbf{s}_i' \leftarrow_\$ \mathbb{F}_2^n$

$\quad \mathbf{y}_i \leftarrow \mathbf{y}_i' + \mathbf{A}_i \mathbf{s}_i'$

$\quad pk_i \leftarrow (\mathbf{A}_i, \mathbf{y}_i)$

$b \leftarrow_\$ \{0, 1\}$

$b' \leftarrow \mathcal{A}^{\mathcal{O}_{\mathsf{KDM}}(\cdot, \cdot)}(\{pk_i\}, 1^\lambda)$

Return 1 iff $b = b'$.

$\mathcal{O}_{\mathsf{KDM}}(f, j)$

$\mathbf{U} \leftarrow_\$ \mathbb{F}_2^{k \times n}$

$\mathbf{u} \leftarrow_\$ \mathbb{F}_2^k$

$\mathbf{C}_1 \leftarrow \mathbf{U}$

$\mathbf{c}_2 \leftarrow \mathbf{u}$

$\mathbf{c} \leftarrow (\mathbf{C}_1, \mathbf{c}_2)$

Return $\mathbf{c}$

- **Game 1** is identical to the KDM-CPA experiment, we only replace the algorithms PKE.KeyGen and PKE.Enc with their instantiations according to PKE.
- In **game 2**, we change the experiment in three ways. First, the public and secret keys are computed from a *master secret* $\mathbf{s}$. More specifically, we first choose $\mathbf{s} \leftarrow_\$ \mathbb{F}_2^n$ uniformly at random and then compute $\mathbf{y}'_i \leftarrow \mathbf{A}_i \mathbf{s} + \mathbf{e}_i$ for each index i. We obtain the public and secret keys by rerandomizing $\mathbf{s}$ and $\mathbf{y}'_i$ correlated way. Specifically, we set $\mathbf{s}_i = \mathbf{s} + \mathbf{s}'_i$ and $\mathbf{y}_i = \mathbf{y}'_i + \mathbf{A}_i \mathbf{s}'_i$ for a uniformly random and independent $\mathbf{s}'_i$. Since $\mathbf{s}_i$ is uniformly random and independent of $\mathbf{s}$ and further

$$\mathbf{y}_i = \mathbf{y}'_i + \mathbf{A}_i \mathbf{s}'_i = \mathbf{A}_i \mathbf{s}_i + \mathbf{e}_i,$$

we have that the (pk_i, sk_i) are identically distributed to game 1. Thus, this modification to the experiment did not introduce any statistical difference. Secondly, we write C.Encode$(\cdot)$ using the generator matrix $\mathbf{G}$ of C, which is also merely a syntactical change.

The third modification consists in changing the way the functions f the encryption oracle is queried with are evaluated. Since each f is restricted to be an affine function, we can write it as

$$f(\{sk_i\}) = \sum_{i=1}^{l} \mathbf{T}_i \mathbf{s}_i + \mathbf{t}.$$

for $\mathbf{T}_1, \ldots, \mathbf{T}_l \in \mathbb{F}_2^{n \times n}$ and $\mathbf{t} \in \mathbb{F}_2^n$. Using that $\mathbf{s}_i = \mathbf{s} + \mathbf{s}'_i$ we can write

$$f(\{sk_i\}) = \sum_{i=1}^{l} \mathbf{T}_i(\mathbf{s} + \mathbf{s}'_i) + \mathbf{t}$$

$$= \left(\sum_{i=1}^{l} \mathbf{T}_i \right) \mathbf{s} + \sum_{i=1}^{l} \mathbf{T}_i \mathbf{s}'_i + \mathbf{t}.$$

Therefore, setting $\mathbf{T}_f = \sum_{i=1}^{l} \mathbf{T}_i$ and $\mathbf{t}_f = \sum_{i=1}^{l} \mathbf{T}_i \mathbf{s}'_i + \mathbf{t}$ we can write $f(\{sk_i\}) = \mathbf{T}_f \mathbf{s} + \mathbf{t}_f$. Thus, also the third modification does not introduce any statistical difference.
- In **game 3** we change the way $\mathbf{c}_2$ is computed. However, plugging in $\mathbf{y}_j = \mathbf{A}_j \mathbf{s}_j + \mathbf{e}_j = \mathbf{A}_j(\mathbf{s} + \mathbf{s}'_j) + \mathbf{e}_j$ and rearranging terms yields

$$\begin{aligned}
\mathbf{c}_2 &= \mathbf{R} \cdot \mathbf{y}_j + \mathbf{G} \cdot (\mathbf{T}_f \mathbf{s} + \mathbf{t}_f) \\
&= \mathbf{R} \cdot (\mathbf{A}_j(\mathbf{s} + \mathbf{s}'_j) + \mathbf{e}_j) + \mathbf{G} \cdot (\mathbf{T}_f \mathbf{s} + \mathbf{t}_f) \\
&= (\mathbf{R}\mathbf{A} + \mathbf{G}\mathbf{T}_f)\mathbf{s} + \mathbf{R}\mathbf{e}_j + \mathbf{G}\mathbf{t}_f + \mathbf{R}\mathbf{A}\mathbf{s}'_j \\
&= (\mathbf{C}_1 + \mathbf{G}\mathbf{T}_f)\mathbf{s} + \mathbf{R}\mathbf{e}_j + \mathbf{G}\mathbf{t}_f + \mathbf{C}_1 \mathbf{s}'_j.
\end{aligned}$$

- In **game 4**, at every call to $\mathcal{O}_{\mathsf{KDM}}$ the value $\mathbf{C}_1$ is chosen uniformly at random instead of computed by $\mathbf{C}_1 \leftarrow \mathbf{R}\mathbf{A}_j$. We can show that game 3 and game 4 are computationally indistinguishable, given that the problem eDLPN$(n, m, k, \rho, \mathsf{Ber}(m, \rho))$ is hard. The reduction loses a factor if lq.

- In **game 5** we compute $\mathbf{C}_1$ by $\mathbf{C}_1 \leftarrow \mathbf{U} - \mathbf{GT}_f$. Since $\mathbf{U}$ is chosen independently and uniformly at random, **game 4** and **game 5** are identically distributed from the view of $\mathcal{A}$.
- In **game 6** we replace $\mathbf{U}$ again by $\mathbf{RA}_j$. We can show that game 5 and game 6 are computationally indistinguishable provided that the problem $\mathsf{eDLPN}(n, m, k, \rho, \mathsf{Ber}(m, \rho))$ is hard. The reduction loses a factor if lq.
- In **game 7** we choose the $\mathbf{y}'_i$ uniformly at random instead of by $\mathbf{y}'_i \leftarrow \mathbf{A}_i \mathbf{s} + \mathbf{e}_i$. We can show that game 6 and game 7 are computationally indistinguishable, given that $\mathsf{DLPN}(n, l \cdot m, \rho)$ is hard. This reduction is tight.
- In **game 8** the values $\mathbf{C}_1$ and $\mathbf{c}_2$ are chosen uniformly at random. Therefore the output of $\mathcal{O}_{\mathsf{KDM}}$ is independent of the challenge bit b and consequently $\mathcal{A}$'s advantage in game 8 is 0. We can show that game 7 and game 8 are computationally indistinguishable given that $\mathsf{DDLPN}(n, m, k, \rho)$ is hard. This reduction loses a factor of lq.

4   LPN Sample Amplification

In this Section, we will show that the hardness of LPN with a bounded number of samples implies the hardness of LPN with an unbounded number of samples, if one is willing to accept an increase in the amount of noise. Recall that $\mathsf{S}(2n, \rho)$ is the uniform distribution on vectors of weight $\lfloor \rho 2n \rfloor$ in $\mathbb{F}_2^n$.

Theorem 2. *Let λ be a security parameter, $n = \mathsf{poly}(\lambda)$ be a positive integer and $\rho = \rho(\lambda) \in [0, 1/2]$. Let*

$$\rho' \geq \frac{1}{2}(1 - (1 - 2\rho)^{\lfloor \rho 2n \rfloor}).$$

If $\mathsf{eDLPN}(n, 2n, 1, \rho, \mathsf{S}(2n, \rho))$, $\mathsf{DLPN}(n, 2n, \mathsf{S}(2n, \rho))$ and $\mathsf{DDLPN}(n, 2n, 1, \rho)$ are hard, then it holds that $\mathsf{DLPN}(n, \rho')$ is also hard. Precisely, if $\mathcal{D}$ is a PPT distinguisher against $\mathsf{DLPN}(n, \rho')$ that makes at most q queries to its LPN oracle, then there exist PPT distinguishers $\mathcal{D}_1$ against $\mathsf{eDLPN}(n, 2n, 1, \rho, \mathsf{S}(2n, \rho))$, $\mathcal{D}_2$ against $\mathsf{DLPN}(n, 2n, \mathsf{S}(2n, \rho))$ and $\mathcal{D}_3$ against $\mathsf{DDLPN}(n, 2n, 1, \rho)$ such that

$$\mathsf{Adv}_{\mathsf{DLPN}}(\mathcal{D}) \leq q \cdot \mathsf{Adv}_{\mathsf{eDLPN}}(\mathcal{D}_1) + \mathsf{Adv}_{\mathsf{DLPN}}(\mathcal{D}_2) + q \cdot \mathsf{Adv}_{\mathsf{DDLPN}}(\mathcal{D}_3).$$

Corollary 3. *Let n, ρ and ρ' be as in Theorem 2. If $\mathsf{LPN}(n, 2n, \rho)$ is hard, then $\mathsf{DLPN}(n, \rho')$ is also hard. More precisely, if $\mathcal{D}$ is a PPT distinguisher which distinguishes $\mathsf{DLPN}(n, \rho')$ with advantage ϵ and makes at most q queries to its LPN oracle, then there exists a PPT adversary $\mathcal{A}^*$ which breaks $\mathsf{LPN}(n, 2n, \rho)$ with advantage*

$$\mathsf{Adv}_{\mathsf{LPN}}(\mathcal{A}^*) \geq \frac{\epsilon^2}{72q^2}.$$

The qualitative statement of Corollary 3 follows immediately from Theorem 2 and Lemmas 1, 2 and 3. For the quantitative part we refer to the full version of this paper [21].

Corollary 3 can be seen as a trade-off between noise and extra samples. We tolerate that the amount of noise required gets squared, while in turn we get an arbitrary polynomial amount of samples.

Proof (Proof of Theorem 2). We will prove the theorem for the minimal ρ', i.e. $\rho' = \frac{1}{2}(1 - (1 - 2\rho)^{\lfloor \rho 2n \rfloor})$. Let $\mathcal{D}$ be a PPT distinguisher against $\mathsf{DLPN}(n, \rho')$. We will provide a series of hybrid experiments $\mathsf{Exp}_1, \mathsf{Exp}_2, \mathsf{Exp}_3, \mathsf{Exp}_4$ and show that from the view of $\mathcal{D}$ any two of experiments the are indistinguishable. We will provide the experiments by defining the sample oracles $\mathcal{O}$ the distinguisher $\mathcal{D}$ gets access to.

Experiment Exp_1	**Experiment** Exp_2	**Experiment** Exp_3	**Experiment** Exp_4
Initialization:	Initialization:	Initialization:	Initialization:
$\mathbf{s} \leftarrow_\$ \mathbb{F}_2^n$	$\mathbf{A} \leftarrow_\$ \mathbb{F}_2^{2n \times n}$	$\mathbf{A} \leftarrow_\$ \mathbb{F}_2^{2n \times n}$	-
Oracle $\mathcal{O}_{\mathsf{Exp}_1}()$	$\mathbf{s} \leftarrow_\$ \mathbb{F}_2^n$	$\mathbf{r} \leftarrow_\$ \mathbb{F}_2^{2n}$	Oracle $\mathcal{O}_{\mathsf{Exp}_4}()$
$\quad \mathbf{a} \leftarrow_\$ \mathbb{F}_2^n$	$\mathbf{z} \leftarrow_\$ S(2n, \rho)$	Oracle $\mathcal{O}_{\mathsf{Exp}_3}()$	$\quad \mathbf{a} \leftarrow_\$ \mathbb{F}_2^n$
$\quad e \leftarrow_\$ \mathsf{Ber}(\rho')$	$\mathbf{r} \leftarrow \mathbf{As} + \mathbf{z}$	$\quad \mathbf{e} \leftarrow_\$ \mathsf{Ber}(2n, \rho)$	$\quad y \leftarrow_\$ \mathbb{F}_2$
$\quad y \leftarrow \langle \mathbf{a}, \mathbf{s} \rangle + e$	Oracle $\mathcal{O}_{\mathsf{Exp}_2}()$	$\quad \mathbf{a} \leftarrow \mathbf{e}^\top \mathbf{A}$	$\quad$ Return $(\mathbf{a}, y)$
$\quad$ Return $(\mathbf{a}, y)$	$\quad \mathbf{e} \leftarrow_\$ \mathsf{Ber}(2n, \rho)$	$\quad y \leftarrow \langle \mathbf{e}, \mathbf{r} \rangle$	
	$\quad \mathbf{a} \leftarrow \mathbf{e}^\top \mathbf{A}$	$\quad$ Return $(\mathbf{a}, y)$	
	$\quad y \leftarrow \langle \mathbf{e}, \mathbf{r} \rangle$		
	$\quad$ Return $(\mathbf{a}, y)$		

Clearly, experiment Exp_1 provides samples from the LPN distribution while experiment Exp_4 provides uniformly random samples. Thus, we need to establish that from the view of $\mathcal{D}$ the experiments Exp_1 and Exp_4 are indistinguishable. We will start with the indistinguishability of Exp_1 and Exp_2. Assume that $\mathcal{D}$ distinguishes with advantage ϵ_1 between Exp_1 and Exp_2, i.e.

$$| \Pr[\mathsf{Exp}_1(\mathcal{D}) = 1] - \Pr[\mathsf{Exp}_2(\mathcal{D}) = 1]| = \epsilon_1.$$

Assume further that $q = \mathsf{poly}(\lambda)$ is an upper bound on the number of samples $\mathcal{D}$ queries. We will construct a PPT distinguisher $\mathcal{D}_1$ that distinguishes the problem $\mathsf{eDLPN}(n, 2n, 1, \rho, S(2n, \rho))$ with advantage $\geq \epsilon_1/q$. The distinguisher $\mathcal{D}_1$ is given on the left side of Figure 2.

Notice that $\mathcal{D}_1$ answers the first $i^* - 1$ oracle queries of $\mathcal{D}$ exactly like Exp_1, while it answers the last $q - i^*$ queries like Exp_2. In the i^*-th query however, $\mathcal{D}_1$ embeds its own challenge. Moreover, notice that $\mathcal{D}_1$ is efficient as $\mathcal{D}$ is efficient. To analyze the distinguishing advantage of $\mathcal{D}_1$, we will define a sequence of hybrid experiments $\mathsf{H}_0, \ldots, \mathsf{H}_q$. H_i is crafted to answer the first i queries like Exp_1, while it answers the last $q - i$ queries like Exp_2. Experiment H_i is given on the right side of Figure 2.

Distinguisher $\mathcal{D}_1$	Oracle $\mathcal{O}_{\mathcal{D}_1}()$	**Experiment** H_i	Oracle $\mathcal{O}_{\mathsf{H}_i}()$
Input: $(\mathbf{A}, \mathbf{c}, \mathbf{z}, t)$	If $cnt < i^*$	Initialization:	If $cnt \leq i$
$i^* \leftarrow_\$ \{1, \ldots, q\}$	$\mathbf{a} \leftarrow_\$ \mathbb{F}_2^n$	$\mathbf{A} \leftarrow_\$ \mathbb{F}_2^{2n \times n}$	$\mathbf{a} \leftarrow_\$ \mathbb{F}_2^n$
$\mathbf{s} \leftarrow_\$ \mathbb{F}_2^n$	$e \leftarrow_\$ \mathsf{Ber}(\rho')$	$\mathbf{s} \leftarrow_\$ \mathbb{F}_2^n$	$e \leftarrow_\$ \mathsf{Ber}(\rho')$
$\mathbf{r} = \mathbf{As} + \mathbf{z}$	$y \leftarrow \langle \mathbf{a}, \mathbf{s} \rangle + e$	$\mathbf{z} \leftarrow_\$ \mathsf{S}_{2n}(\lfloor \rho 2n \rfloor)$	$y \leftarrow \langle \mathbf{a}, \mathbf{s} \rangle + e$
$cnt = 1$	If $cnt = i^*$	$\mathbf{r} \leftarrow \mathbf{As} + \mathbf{z}$	If $cnt > i$
$b \leftarrow \mathcal{D}^{\mathcal{O}_{\mathcal{D}_1}}()$	$\mathbf{a} \leftarrow \mathbf{c}^\top$	$cnt \leftarrow 1$	$e \leftarrow_\$ \mathsf{Ber}(2n, \rho)$
return b	$y \leftarrow \langle \mathbf{c}, \mathbf{s} \rangle + t$		$\mathbf{a} \leftarrow (\mathbf{e}^\top \mathbf{A})^\top$
	If $cnt > i^*$		$y \leftarrow \langle \mathbf{e}, \mathbf{r} \rangle$
	$e \leftarrow_\$ \mathsf{Ber}(2n, \rho)$		$cnt \leftarrow cnt + 1$
	$\mathbf{a} \leftarrow (\mathbf{e}^\top \mathbf{A})^\top$		Return $(\mathbf{a}, y)$
	$y \leftarrow \langle \mathbf{e}, \mathbf{r} \rangle$		
	$cnt \leftarrow cnt + 1$		
	Return $(\mathbf{a}, y)$		

Fig. 2. The distinguisher $\mathcal{D}_1$ and the hybrid experiments H_i

We are now ready to analyze the distinguishing advantage of $\mathcal{D}_1$. First assume that $\mathcal{D}_1$'s input is of the form $(\mathbf{A}, \mathbf{e}^\top \mathbf{A}, \mathbf{z}, \mathbf{e}^\top \mathbf{z} = \langle \mathbf{z}, \mathbf{e} \rangle)$. Observe that since $\mathbf{z}$ has weight $\lfloor \rho m \rfloor$ and $\mathbf{e}$ is distributed according to $\mathsf{Ber}(m, \rho)$ it holds that $\langle \mathbf{z}, \mathbf{e} \rangle$ is distributed according to $\mathsf{Ber}(\rho')$. Fix the random choice $i^* = i$. Then the sample oracle $\mathcal{O}_{\mathcal{D}_1}()$ implemented by $\mathcal{D}_1$ behaves identical to the sample oracle of H_{i-1}. Consequently, it holds that

$$\Pr[\mathcal{D}_1(\mathbf{A}, \mathbf{e}^\top \mathbf{A}, \mathbf{z}, \mathbf{e}^\top \mathbf{z}) = 1 | i^* = i] = \Pr[\mathsf{H}_{i-1}(\mathcal{D}) = 1]$$

and thus, as i^* is uniformly chosen from $\{1, \ldots, q\}$

$$\Pr[\mathcal{D}_1(\mathbf{A}, \mathbf{e}^\top \mathbf{A}, \mathbf{z}, \mathbf{e}^\top \mathbf{z}) = 1] = \sum_{i=1}^{q} \frac{1}{q} \cdot \Pr[\mathcal{D}_1(\mathbf{A}, \mathbf{e}^\top \mathbf{A}, \mathbf{z}, \mathbf{e}^\top \mathbf{z}) = 1 | i^* = i]$$

$$= \sum_{i=1}^{q} \frac{1}{q} \cdot \Pr[\mathsf{H}_{i-1}(\mathcal{D}) = 1].$$

Next assume that $\mathcal{D}_1$'s input is of the form $(\mathbf{A}, \mathbf{u}, \mathbf{z}, \mathbf{e}^\top \mathbf{z})$. Again, fix the random choice of i^* to $i^* = i$. Then the sample oracle $\mathcal{O}_{\mathcal{D}_1}()$ implemented by $\mathcal{D}_1$ behaves identical to the sample oracle of H_i, as $\langle \mathbf{z}, \mathbf{e} \rangle$ is distributed according to $\mathsf{Ber}(\rho')$. Consequently,

$$\Pr[\mathcal{D}_1(\mathbf{A}, \mathbf{u}, \mathbf{z}, \mathbf{e}^\top \mathbf{z}) = 1 | i^* = i] = \Pr[\mathsf{H}_i(\mathcal{D}) = 1]$$

and thus

$$\Pr[\mathcal{D}_1(\mathbf{A}, \mathbf{u}, \mathbf{z}, \mathbf{e}^\top \mathbf{z}) = 1] = \sum_{i=1}^{q} \frac{1}{q} \cdot \Pr[\mathcal{D}_1(\mathbf{A}, \mathbf{u}, \mathbf{z}, \mathbf{e}^\top \mathbf{z}) = 1 | i^* = i]$$

$$= \sum_{i=1}^{q} \frac{1}{q} \cdot \Pr[\mathsf{H}_i(\mathcal{D}) = 1].$$

Together, this yields

$$\mathsf{Adv}_{\mathsf{eDLPN}}(\mathcal{D}_1) = |\Pr[\mathcal{D}_1(\mathbf{A}, \mathbf{e}^\top \mathbf{A}, \mathbf{z}, \mathbf{e}^\top \mathbf{z}) = 1] - \Pr[\mathcal{D}_1(\mathbf{A}, \mathbf{u}, \mathbf{z}, \mathbf{e}^\top \mathbf{z}) = 1]|$$

$$= \left| \sum_{i=1}^{q} \frac{1}{q} \cdot \Pr[\mathsf{H}_{i-1}(\mathcal{D}) = 1] - \sum_{i=1}^{q} \frac{1}{q} \cdot \Pr[\mathsf{H}_i(\mathcal{D}) = 1] \right|$$

$$= \frac{1}{q} |\Pr[\mathsf{H}_0(\mathcal{D}) = 1] - \Pr[\mathsf{H}_k(\mathcal{D}) = 1]|$$

$$= \frac{1}{q} |\Pr[\mathsf{Exp}_2(\mathcal{D}) = 1] - \Pr[\mathsf{Exp}_1(\mathcal{D}) = 1]|$$

$$\geq \epsilon_1/q.$$

Thus, $\mathcal{D}_1$ distinguishes $\mathsf{eDLPN}(n, 2n, 1, \rho, \mathsf{S}(2n, \rho))$ with advantage ϵ_1/q.

Next, we turn to the indistinguishability of Exp_2 and Exp_3. Assume towards contradiction that $\mathcal{D}$ distinguishes between Exp_2 and Exp_3 with advantage ϵ_2, i.e.

$$|\Pr[\mathsf{Exp}_2(\mathcal{D}) = 1] - \Pr[\mathsf{Exp}_3(\mathcal{D}) = 1]| = \epsilon_2.$$

We will construct a PPT distinguisher $\mathcal{D}_2$ against $\mathsf{DLPN}(n, 2n, \mathsf{S}(2n, \rho))$. $\mathcal{D}_2$ is given as follows.

Distinguisher $\mathcal{D}_2$	Sample Oracle $\mathcal{O}_{\mathcal{D}_2}()$
Input: $(\mathbf{A}, \mathbf{r})$	$\mathbf{e} \leftarrow_\$ \mathsf{Ber}(2n, \rho)$
$b \leftarrow \mathcal{D}^{\mathcal{O}_{\mathcal{D}_2}}()$	$\mathbf{a} \leftarrow \mathbf{e}^\top \mathbf{A}$
return b	$y \leftarrow \langle \mathbf{e}, \mathbf{r} \rangle$
	Return $(\mathbf{a}, y)$

The distinguisher $\mathcal{D}_2$ is efficient, as $\mathcal{D}$ is efficient. First, assume that $\mathcal{D}_2$'s input is of the form $(\mathbf{A}, \mathbf{A}\mathbf{s} + \mathbf{z})$, where $\mathbf{s}$ is chosen uniformly from $\mathbb{F}_2^n$ and $\mathbf{z}$ is chosen from $\mathsf{S}(2n, \rho)$. Then clearly the sample oracle $\mathcal{O}_{\mathcal{D}_2}$ behaves just as in Exp_2. On the other hand, if $\mathcal{D}_2$'s input is of the form $(\mathbf{A}, \mathbf{u})$ with $\mathbf{u}$ chosen uniformly random from $\mathbb{F}_2^{2n}$, then the sample $\mathcal{O}_{\mathcal{D}_2}$ simulated by $\mathcal{D}_2$ behaves like the sample oracle in Exp_3. Consequently, it holds that

$$\mathsf{Adv}_{\mathsf{DLPN}}(\mathcal{D}_2) = |\Pr[\mathcal{D}_2(\mathbf{A}, \mathbf{A}\mathbf{s} + \mathbf{z}) = 1] - \Pr[\mathcal{D}_2(\mathbf{A}, \mathbf{u}) = 1]|$$

$$= |\Pr[\mathsf{Exp}_2(\mathcal{D}) = 1] - \Pr[\mathsf{Exp}_3(\mathcal{D}) = 1]|$$

$$= \epsilon_2.$$

Thus, the distinguishing advantage of $\mathcal{D}_2$ against $\mathsf{DLPN}(n, 2n, \mathsf{S}(2n, \rho))$ is ϵ_2.

We will finally turn to showing that from the view of $\mathcal{D}$, Exp_3 and Exp_4 are indistinguishable. Assume towards contradiction that $\mathcal{D}$ distinguishes between Exp_3 and Exp_4 with advantage ϵ_3, i.e.

$$| \Pr[\mathsf{Exp}_3(\mathcal{D}) = 1] - \Pr[\mathsf{Exp}_4(\mathcal{D}) = 1]| = \epsilon_3.$$

Assume further $\mathcal{D}$ makes at most $q = \mathsf{poly}(\lambda)$ queries to its sample oracle. We will construct a PPT distinguisher $\mathcal{D}_3$ that distinguishes $\mathsf{DDLPN}(n, 2n, 1, \rho)$ with advantage ϵ_3/q. The distinguisher $\mathcal{D}_3$ is given on the left side of Figure 3.

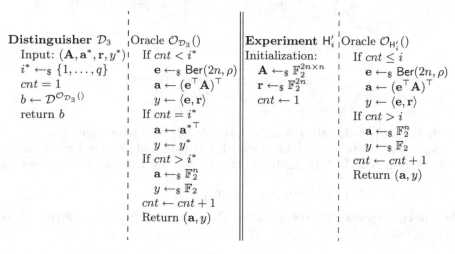

Fig. 3. The distinguisher $\mathcal{D}_3$ and the hybrid experiments H'_i

It is clear that $\mathcal{D}_3$ is efficient, once $\mathcal{D}$ is efficient. Again, to analyze the distinguishing advantage of $\mathcal{D}_3$, we will define a sequence of hybrid experiments $\mathsf{H}'_0, \ldots, \mathsf{H}'_q$. H'_i is crafted to answer the first i queries like Exp_3, while it answers the last $q - i$ queries like Exp_4. Hybrid H'_i is given on the right side of Figure 3. First assume that $\mathcal{D}_3$'s input is of the form $(\mathbf{A}, \mathbf{e}^\top \mathbf{A}, \mathbf{r}, \mathbf{e}^\top \mathbf{r})$. Then it holds that

$$\mathbf{a}^* = (\mathbf{e}^\top \mathbf{A})^\top$$
$$y^* = \mathbf{e}^\top \mathbf{r} = \langle \mathbf{e}, \mathbf{r} \rangle$$

Now fix a random choice $i^* = i$. Then $\mathcal{O}_{\mathcal{D}_3}()$ in $\mathcal{D}_3$'s simulation behaves identically to the sample oracle in H'_i. Thus it holds that

$$\Pr[\mathcal{D}_3(\mathbf{A}, \mathbf{e}^\top \mathbf{A}, \mathbf{r}, \mathbf{e}^\top \mathbf{r}) = 1 | i^* = i] = \Pr[\mathsf{H}'_i(\mathcal{D}) = 1],$$

and consequently

$$\Pr[\mathcal{D}_3(\mathbf{A}, \mathbf{e}^\top \mathbf{A}, \mathbf{r}, \mathbf{e}^\top \mathbf{r}) = 1] = \sum_{i=1}^{q} \frac{1}{q} \Pr[\mathcal{D}_3(\mathbf{A}, \mathbf{e}^\top \mathbf{A}, \mathbf{r}, \mathbf{e}^\top \mathbf{r}) = 1 | i^* = i]$$

$$= \sum_{i=1}^{q} \frac{1}{q} \Pr[\mathsf{H}_i'(\mathcal{D}) = 1].$$

Now suppose that $\mathcal{D}_3$'s input is of the form $(\mathbf{A}, \mathbf{u}, \mathbf{r}, u')$, where $\mathbf{u}^\top \leftarrow_\$ \mathbb{F}_2^n$ and $u' \leftarrow_\$ \mathbb{F}_2$ are chosen uniformly at random. Then it holds that $\mathbf{a}^* = \mathbf{u}$ and $y^* = u'$. Again, fix a random choice $i^* = i$. Then $\mathcal{O}_{\mathcal{D}_3}()$ in $\mathcal{D}_3$'s simulation behaves identically to the sample oracle in H_{i-1}'. Thus it holds that

$$\Pr[\mathcal{D}_3(\mathbf{A}, \mathbf{u}, \mathbf{r}, u') = 1 | i^* = i] = \Pr[\mathsf{H}_{i-1}'(\mathcal{D}) = 1],$$

and consequently

$$\Pr[\mathcal{D}_3(\mathbf{A}, \mathbf{u}, \mathbf{r}, u') = 1] = \sum_{i=1}^{q} \frac{1}{q} \Pr[\mathcal{D}_3(\mathbf{A}, \mathbf{u}, \mathbf{r}, u') = 1 | i^* = i]$$

$$= \sum_{i=1}^{q} \frac{1}{q} \Pr[\mathsf{H}_{i-1}'(\mathcal{D}) = 1].$$

Putting all together, we get

$$\mathsf{Adv}_{\mathsf{DDLPN}}(\mathcal{D}_3) = |\Pr[\mathcal{D}_3(\mathbf{A}, \mathbf{e}^\top \mathbf{A}, \mathbf{r}, \mathbf{e}^\top \mathbf{r}) = 1] - \Pr[\mathcal{D}_3(\mathbf{A}, \mathbf{u}, \mathbf{r}, u') = 1]|$$

$$= \left| \sum_{i=1}^{q} \frac{1}{q} \cdot \Pr[\mathsf{H}_i'(\mathcal{D}) = 1] - \sum_{i=1}^{q} \frac{1}{q} \cdot \Pr[\mathsf{H}_{i-1}'(\mathcal{D}) = 1] \right|$$

$$= \frac{1}{q} |\Pr[\mathsf{H}_k'(\mathcal{D}) = 1] - \Pr[\mathsf{H}_0'(\mathcal{D}) = 1]|$$

$$= \frac{1}{q} |\Pr[\mathsf{Exp}_3(\mathcal{D}) = 1] - \Pr[\mathsf{Exp}_4(\mathcal{D}) = 1]|$$

$$\geq \epsilon_3/q.$$

Thus, $\mathcal{D}_3$ distinguishes $\mathsf{DDLPN}(n, 2n, 1, \rho)$ with advantage ϵ_3/q.

We will now turn to the quantitative statement of the theorem. By the triangle inequality it holds that

$$\mathsf{Adv}_{\mathsf{DLPN}}(\mathcal{D}) \leq \epsilon_1 + \epsilon_2 + \epsilon_3$$

$$\leq q \cdot \mathsf{Adv}_{\mathsf{eDLPN}}(\mathcal{D}_1) + \mathsf{Adv}_{\mathsf{DLPN}}(\mathcal{D}_2) + q \cdot \mathsf{Adv}_{\mathsf{DDLPN}}(\mathcal{D}_3).$$

This concludes the proof.

5   Conclusion

In this work we have constructed the first public key encryption scheme with KDM-CPA security for affine functions from the low-noise LPN assumption. Moreover, we have provided a novel connection between LPN with a bounded number of samples and LPN with an unbounded number of samples. Both results have analogues in the LWE realm (the KDM-CPA secure scheme of Applebaum et al. [10] and the LWE random self-reduction of Gentry et al. [26]). Both our results follow the same blueprint as their LWE counterparts. However, while in the LWE realm powerful statistical tools such as gaussian regularity [26] and the leftover-hash lemma [19,29] are available, no comparable statistical techniques are available in the LPN realm. Instead, our approach, following Kiltz et al. [31] was to substitute these techniques with computational counterparts based on LPN. Specifically the extended LPN problem turned out to be very useful in filling this gap. A natural future direction in this line of work would be to try to lift further results from the LWE/SIS realm into the LPN realm, such as identity based encryption [3,4,7,17] or efficient and compact signature schemes [14,23,24].

Acknowledgments. I would like to thank the anonymous reviewers of PKC 2015 for their useful feedback. I would further like to thank Daniel Masny for explaining to me the subtleties in the construction of [31] involving the eDLPN problem. Finally, I would like to thank Chris Peikert for pointing me to LWE random self-reductions some time ago. The LPN sample amplification part of this work appeared in my PhD thesis [20], but has not been published in any other peer reviewed publication.

References

1. Acar, T., Belenkiy, M., Bellare, M., Cash, D.: Cryptographic agility and its relation to circular encryption. In: Gilbert, H. (ed.) EUROCRYPT 2010. LNCS, vol. 6110, pp. 403–422. Springer, Heidelberg (2010)
2. Adão, P., Bana, G., Herzog, J.C., Scedrov, A.: Soundness of formal encryption in the presence of key-cycles. In: di Vimercati, S.C., Syverson, P.F., Gollmann, D. (eds.) ESORICS 2005. LNCS, vol. 3679, pp. 374–396. Springer, Heidelberg (2005)
3. Agrawal, S., Boneh, D., Boyen, X.: Efficient lattice (H)IBE in the standard model. In: Gilbert, H. (ed.) EUROCRYPT 2010. LNCS, vol. 6110, pp. 553–572. Springer, Heidelberg (2010)
4. Agrawal, S., Boneh, D., Boyen, X.: Lattice basis delegation in fixed dimension and shorter-ciphertext hierarchical IBE. In: Rabin, T. (ed.) CRYPTO 2010. LNCS, vol. 6223, pp. 98–115. Springer, Heidelberg (2010)
5. Aharonov, D., Regev, O.: A lattice problem in quantum NP. In: Proceedings of 44th Symposium on Foundations of Computer Science (FOCS 2003), pp. 210–219, Cambridge, MA, USA, 11–14 October 2003
6. Alekhnovich, M.: More on average case vs approximation complexity. In: Proceedings 44th Symposium on Foundations of Computer Science (FOCS 2003), pp. 298–307, Cambridge, MA, USA, 11–14 October 2003

7. Alperin-Sheriff, J., Peikert, C.: Circular and KDM security for identity-based encryption. In: Fischlin, M., Buchmann, J., Manulis, M. (eds.) Public Key Cryptography PKC 2012. LNCS. Springer, Heidelberg (2012)
8. Applebaum, B.: Key-dependent message security: generic amplification and completeness. In: Paterson, K.G. (ed.) EUROCRYPT 2011. LNCS, vol. 6632, pp. 527–546. Springer, Heidelberg (2011)
9. Applebaum, B.: Garbling XOR gates "For Free" in the standard model. In: Sahai, A. (ed.) TCC 2013. LNCS, vol. 7785, pp. 162–181. Springer, Heidelberg (2013)
10. Applebaum, B., Cash, D., Peikert, C., Sahai, A.: Fast cryptographic primitives and circular-secure encryption based on hard learning problems. In: Halevi, S. (ed.) CRYPTO 2009. LNCS, vol. 5677, pp. 595–618. Springer, Heidelberg (2009)
11. Applebaum, B., Ishai, Y., Kushilevitz, E.: Cryptography with constant input locality. In: Menezes, A. (ed.) CRYPTO 2007. LNCS, vol. 4622, pp. 92–110. Springer, Heidelberg (2007)
12. Black, J., Rogaway, P., Shrimpton, T.: Encryption-scheme security in the presence of key-dependent messages. In: Nyberg, K., Heys, H. (eds.) Selected Areas in Cryptography. LNCS. Springer, Heidelberg (2002)
13. Blum, A., Furst, M.L., Kearns, M., Lipton, R.J.: Cryptographic primitives based on hard learning problems. In: Stinson, D.R. (ed.) CRYPTO 1993. LNCS, vol. 773, pp. 278–291. Springer, Heidelberg (1994)
14. Böhl, F., Hofheinz, D., Jager, T., Koch, J., Seo, J.H., Striecks, C.: Practical signatures from standard assumptions. In: Johansson, T., Nguyen, P.Q. (eds.) EUROCRYPT 2013. LNCS, vol. 7881, pp. 461–485. Springer, Heidelberg (2013)
15. Boneh, D., Halevi, S., Hamburg, M., Ostrovsky, R.: Circular-secure encryption from decision diffie-hellman. In: Wagner, D. (ed.) CRYPTO 2008. LNCS, vol. 5157, pp. 108–125. Springer, Heidelberg (2008)
16. Cash, D., Green, M., Hohenberger, S.: New definitions and separations for circular security. In: Fischlin, M., Buchmann, J., Manulis, M. (eds.) Public Key Cryptography PKC 2012. LNCS. Springer, Heidelberg (2012)
17. Cash, D., Hofheinz, D., Kiltz, E., Peikert, C.: Bonsai Trees, or how to delegate a lattice basis. In: Gilbert, H. (ed.) EUROCRYPT 2010. LNCS, vol. 6110, pp. 523–552. Springer, Heidelberg (2010)
18. David, B., Dowsley, R., Nascimento, A.C.A.: Universally composable oblivious transfer based on a variant of LPN. In: Gritzalis, D., Kiayias, A., Askoxylakis, I. (eds.) CANS 2014. LNCS, vol. 8813, pp. 143–158. Springer, Heidelberg (2014)
19. Dodis, Y., Reyzin, L., Smith, A.: Fuzzy extractors: how to generate strong keys from biometrics and other noisy data. In: Cachin, C., Camenisch, J.L. (eds.) EUROCRYPT 2004. LNCS, vol. 3027, pp. 523–540. Springer, Heidelberg (2004)
20. Döttling, N.: Cryptography based on the hardness of decoding. Ph.D. thesis, Karlsruhe Institute of Technology, May 2014. http://nbn-resolving.org/urn:nbn:de:swb: 90-411105
21. Döttling, N.: Low noise lpn: Kdm secure public key encryption and sample amplification. Cryptology ePrint Archive, Report 2015/013 (2015). http://eprint.iacr. org/
22. Döttling, N., Müller-Quade, J., Nascimento, A.C.A.: IND-CCA secure cryptography based on a variant of the LPN problem. In: Wang, X., Sako, K. (eds.) ASIACRYPT 2012. LNCS, vol. 7658, pp. 485–503. Springer, Heidelberg (2012)
23. Ducas, L., Durmus, A., Lepoint, T., Lyubashevsky, V.: Lattice signatures and bimodal Gaussians. In: Canetti, R., Garay, J.A. (eds.) CRYPTO 2013, Part I. LNCS, vol. 8042, pp. 40–56. Springer, Heidelberg (2013)

24. Ducas, L., Micciancio, D.: Improved short lattice signatures in the standard model. In: Garay, J.A., Gennaro, R. (eds.) CRYPTO 2014, Part I. LNCS, vol. 8616, pp. 335–352. Springer, Heidelberg (2014)

25. Forney, G.D.: Generalized minimum distance decoding. IEEE Transactions on Information Theory **12**(2), 125–131 (1966)

26. Gentry, C., Peikert, C., Vaikuntanathan, V.: Trapdoors for hard lattices and new cryptographic constructions. In: Proceedings of the 40th Annual ACM Symposium on Theory of Computing, Victoria, British Columbia, pp. 197–206, Canada, 17–20 May (2008)

27. Heyse, S., Kiltz, E., Lyubashevsky, V., Paar, C., Pietrzak, K.: Lapin: an efficient authentication protocol based on ring-LPN. In: Canteaut, A. (ed.) FSE 2012. LNCS, vol. 7549, pp. 346–365. Springer, Heidelberg (2012)

28. Hopper, N.J., Blum, M.: Secure human identification protocols. In: Boyd, C. (ed.) ASIACRYPT 2001. LNCS, vol. 2248, p. 52. Springer, Heidelberg (2001)

29. Impagliazzo, R., Levin, L.A., Luby, M.: Pseudo-random generation from one-way functions (extended abstracts). In: Proceedings of the 21st Annual ACM Symposium on Theory of Computing, pp. 12–24, Seattle, Washigton, USA, 14–17 May (1989)

30. Katz, J., Shin, J.S., Smith, A.: Parallel and concurrent security of the HB and hb$^+$ protocols. J. Cryptology **23**(3), 402–421 (2010)

31. Kiltz, E., Masny, D., Pietrzak, K.: Simple chosen-ciphertext security from low-noise lpn. In: Public Key Cryptography, pp. 1–18 (2014)

32. Lyubashevsky, V.: The parity problem in the presence of noise, decoding random linear codes, and the subset sum problem. In: Chekuri, C., Jansen, K., Rolim, J.D.P., Trevisan, L. (eds.) APPROX 2005 and RANDOM 2005. LNCS, vol. 3624, pp. 378–389. Springer, Heidelberg (2005)

33. Lyubashevsky, V., Masny, D.: Man-in-the-middle secure authentication schemes from LPN and weak PRFs. In: Canetti, R., Garay, J.A. (eds.) CRYPTO 2013, Part II. LNCS, vol. 8043, pp. 308–325. Springer, Heidelberg (2013)

34. Micciancio, D., Regev, O.: Worst-case to average-case reductions based on gaussian measures. In: Proceedings of 45th Symposium on Foundations of Computer Science (FOCS 2004), pp. 372–381, Rome, Italy, 17–19 October (2004)

35. O'Neill, A., Peikert, C., Waters, B.: Bi-deniable public-key encryption. In: Rogaway, P. (ed.) CRYPTO 2011. LNCS, vol. 6841, pp. 525–542. Springer, Heidelberg (2011)

36. Peikert, C.: An efficient and parallel gaussian sampler for lattices. In: Rabin, T. (ed.) CRYPTO 2010. LNCS, vol. 6223, pp. 80–97. Springer, Heidelberg (2010)

37. Regev, O.: On lattices, learning with errors, random linear codes, and cryptography. In: Proceedings of the 37th Annual ACM Symposium on Theory of Computing, pp. 84–93, Baltimore, MD, USA, 22–24 May (2005)

38. Sipser, M., Spielman, D.A.: Expander codes. In: 35th Annual Symposium on Foundations of Computer Science, pp. 566–576, Santa Fe, New Mexico, USA, 20–22 November (1994)

39. Spielman, D.A.: Linear-time encodable and decodable error-correcting codes. In: Proceedings of the Twenty-Seventh Annual ACM Symposium on Theory of Computing, pp. 388–397, Las Vegas, Nevada, USA, 29 May–1 June (1995)

Interactive Proofs

Adaptive Proofs of Knowledge
in the Random Oracle Model

David Bernhard[1](✉), Marc Fischlin[2], and Bogdan Warinschi[1]

[1] University of Bristol, Bristol, UK
{bernhard,bogdan}@compsci.bristol.ac.uk
[2] Technische Universität Darmstadt, Darmstadt, Germany
marc.fischlin@cryptoplexity.de

Abstract. We formalise the notion of adaptive proofs of knowledge in the random oracle model, where the extractor has to recover witnesses for multiple, possibly adaptively chosen statements and proofs. We also discuss extensions to simulation soundness, as typically required for the "encrypt-then-prove" construction of strongly secure encryption from IND-CPA schemes. Utilizing our model we show three results:

(1) Simulation-sound adaptive proofs exist.
(2) The "encrypt-then-prove" construction with a simulation-sound adaptive proof yields CCA security. This appears to be a "folklore" result but which has never been proven in the random oracle model. As a corollary, we obtain a new class of CCA-secure encryption schemes.
(3) We show that the Fiat-Shamir transformed Schnorr protocol is *not* adaptively secure and discuss the implications of this limitation.

Our result not only separates adaptive proofs from proofs of knowledge, but also gives a strong hint why Signed ElGamal as the most prominent encrypt-then-prove example has not been proven CCA-secure without making further assumptions.

1 Introduction

Proofs of knowledge [5,22,31,50] are a generic tool to ensure correct operation in many cryptographic constructions, including voting protocols, e-cash systems, or group signatures. More generally, they can turn passively secure multi-party protocols into actively secure ones. The value of proofs of knowledge in security arguments is that whenever a participant makes a proof of knowledge on some statement as part of a protocol, one can "hop" into an alternate, virtual world in which the participant outputs the witness along with the statement. This approach of pretending that each proof makes its witness available in a security argument relies on the extractor that exists by definition of a proof of knowledge: when a participant outputs a proof, we "freeze" the protocol, and invoke the extractor to get the witness. This extraction is usually carried out by rewinding

© International Association for Cryptologic Research 2015
J. Katz (Ed.): PKC 2015, LNCS 9020, pp. 629–649, 2015.
DOI: 10.1007/978-3-662-46447-2_28

the party and branching into another protocol execution. Then we resume the protocol with the witness now being available.

The problem with the "freeze-extract-resume" approach is that its implementation can easily become expensive. Each extraction and its rewinding can double the running time of a reduction such that, if a participant makes a badly nested "chain" of n proofs, a naive approach ends up with an exponential running time of 2^n to get all the witnesses. This is certainly true for interactive proofs of knowledge, but also in the case of non-interactive proofs of knowledge in the random oracle model. Such random-oracle based proofs are paramount if efficiency is vital, especially in the form of Fiat-Shamir transformed Sigma protocols a.k.a. "Schnorr-type" proofs. In this context the rewinding problem was first mentioned explicitly by Shoup and Gennaro [47].

Shoup and Gennaro [47] required nested proofs in the random oracle model for the construction of CCA secure public-key encryption from IND-CPA secure encryption via the encrypt-then-prove approach (e.g., for signed ElGamal). The idea behind this approach, gradually refined in a sequence of works [13,17,36, 38,43,52], is to attach to each ciphertext a proof of knowledge of the message. Intuitively, if one has to know the message to create a ciphertext, a decryption oracle should be redundant, so encrypt-then-prove should lift CPA security to CCA security. Unfortunately, there is no general proof of this intuition which also covers the setting with random oracles. Currently, the best result for signed ElGamal, without making additional "knowledge type" assumptions as in [43, 51], is that the scheme is non-malleable (NM-CPA) [12].

ADAPTIVE PROOFS OF KNOWLEDGE. Our notion and formalisation of *adaptive* proofs of knowledge allows to capture the case of having to extract from multiple proofs, possibly chosen adaptively by a malicious prover. We focus on the case of non-interactive proofs in the random oracle. As a first step, we will cast the (single-round) proof of knowledge property as a game between a prover (or attacker) and an extractor. The prover wins the game if it makes a statement and a valid proof but such that the extractor cannot find a witness. The extractor wins the game if it can return a witness (or if the prover does not produce a valid proof). A proof scheme is a proof of knowledge if there is an extractor that wins against any prover with overwhelming probability.

For extending our simple game to the adaptive case, the prover can now produce many statement/witness pairs in rounds and the scheme is an adaptive proof if the extractor can find all witnesses (for a prover who makes a polynomially bounded number of queries). The game is adaptive because the extractor must return each found witness to the prover before the prover makes her next query.

In addition to adaptive proofs, we define *simulation-sound* adaptive proofs of knowledge. These proofs are obtained by the exact same change that extends proofs of knowledge to simulation-sound proofs of knowledge: in addition to producing statements and proofs of her own, the prover can simultaneously ask the zero-knowledge simulator for proofs on valid statements of her choice.

Of course, the prover cannot ask the extractor to extract a witness from a simulated proof.

OUR RESULTS. After we provide a formalisation of adaptive proofs we can argue about instantiations and applications. We provide three main results in this regard:

(1.) *Simulation-sound adaptive proofs exist.* We discuss that the construction of straight-line proofs of knowledge by Fischlin [26] satisifies our notion. Fischlin's transformation is an alternative to the common Fiat-Shamir transformation and allows any Sigma protocol with unique responses to be turned into a non-interactive proof.

(2.) *Adaptive simulation-sound proofs yield CCA security.* We propose that adaptive proofs are to proof schemes what CCA security is to encryption schemes. Only an adaptive proof gives you a formal guarantee that the intuition behind proofs of knowledge still works when they are used over multiple rounds of a protocol.

We prove that the encrypt-then-prove construction using an IND-CPA encryption scheme and a simulation sound adaptive proof yields CCA security. Our proof is to our knowledge the first proof of CCA security that considers a potentially rewinding reduction in an adaptive case. While our proof follows the same high-level direction as proofs of existing CCA schemes (using the reduction to answer decryption queries), the need to handle rewinding without causing an exponential blow-up makes for a complicated argument. We develop a new proof technique called coin splitting to deal with some of the problems that arise.

(3.) *Fiat-Shamir-Schnorr is not adaptively secure.* We prove that the most common and efficient construction of proofs of knowledge via the Fiat-Shamir transformation [25] is not adaptively secure. Our proof constructs a prover who makes a "chain" of n Fiat-Shamir-Schnorr statement/proof pairs, following the ideas of Shoup and Gennaro [47]. We then show that any extractor that wins the adaptive proof game against this prover either reduces to breaking the one-more discrete logarithm problem or launches $\Omega(2^n)$ copies of the prover. The key technical tools in the proof are the meta-reduction paradigm and a technique which we term coin splitting.

Coin splitting allows us to perform a kind of hybrid argument on attackers which have rewinding black-box access to several copies of the same algorithm. We can change these copies individually as long as we can argue that the attacker does not notice the difference. Coin splitting is a technique to show that some changes which we make to individual copies are indeed indistinguishable to an attacker who cannot break a more basic security assumption. The idea of this technique originates in papers on resettable zero-knowledge [14].

RELATED WORK. We recall some related work here and discuss that so far no previous work has given a profound answer to the issue of adaptive simulation-sound proofs of knowledge in the random oracle model. A longer discussion can be found in the full version of our paper. The notion of simulation-soundness of zero-knowledge proofs has been introduced for proofs of membership by Sahai

[41], showing that the Naor-Yung paradigm [36] yields CCA secure encryptions in the common reference string model. In the context of proofs of knowledge, De Santis and Persiano [19] already augmented ciphertexts by proofs in the common reference string model to aim at CCA security, albeit their argument seems to miss simulation-soundness as an important ingredient. This property has been considered in works by Groth [33], Chase and Lysanskaya [15], and by Dodis et al. [20], but once more in the common reference string model only. The first formal definitions of simulation-sound proofs of knowledge in the random oracle model were concurrently given by Bernhard et al. [12] and Faust et al. [21]; both works show that proofs derived via Fiat-Shamir transform meet this notion. Both formulations, however, consider an extractor that needs only to extract from non-adaptively chosen proofs, and in case of [21] only once (for security of their signature construction). In conclusion, our work here fills in a gap allowing to argue about important properties of adaptivity and simulation-soundness of proofs of knowledge in the random oracle model.

2   Zero-Knowledge Proofs

In this section we discuss zero-knowledge proofs of knowledge and simulation soundness in the random oracle model (ROM). Our central idea for zero-knowledge and its extension of simulation soundness is a game between two players, a malicious prover $\hat{\mathcal{P}}$ and an extractor $\mathcal{K}$. The prover's aim is to produce a statement and a proof that verifies such that the extractor cannot extract a witness from this proof. The extractor's goal is to extract a witness from the proof that the prover provides.

We use a code-based game-playing model à la Bellare and Rogaway [9] to define adaptive proofs of knowledge. The game mediates between all involved players, e.g., between the adversarial prover and the extractor and possibly also the simulator in case of simulation soundness. The game starts by running the initialisation algorithm which ends by specifying to which player it wishes to transfer control to first. Executions are token-based: at any time, either the game or one of the players is running ("holding the token") and a call from one participant to another yields control. All game variables are global and persist between calls so the game may maintain state between calls. The game eventually declares the winner among the prover and the extractor.

To ensure termination, we assume strict polynomial-time provers and extractors (in the size of implicit parameters such as the size of the groups over which the proofs are constructed). Our notions could also be achieved by having the game "time out" if one player does not reply in a bounded number of time steps, though this would require a more involved model of concurrency. The important property is in any case that all players in the game must, on receiving an input, eventually produce an output. In particular, a prover cannot prevent a "perfect" extractor from winning a game by entering an infinite loop instead of producing a proof.

2.1   Proof Schemes

Below we give the common definition for proof schemes for NP relations R. For Fiat-Shamir proof schemes we occasionally also need to parametrise over the underlying number-theoretic group $\mathbb{G}(\lambda)$ in a straightforward way, but we omit this for sake of representational simplicity.

Definition 1. *A non-interactive proof scheme for a relation R over groups consists of two algorithms $(\mathcal{P}, \mathcal{V})$ over groups. $\mathcal{P}$ may be randomised, $\mathcal{V}$ must be deterministic. For any pair $(x, w) \in R$, if $\pi \leftarrow \mathcal{P}(x, w)$ then $\mathcal{V}(x, \pi)$ must output "true".*

The elements of the relation R are called statement and witness. $\mathcal{P}$ is called the prover and its outputs π are called proofs. $\mathcal{V}$ is called the verifier and a statement/proof pair on which $\mathcal{V}$ outputs "true" is called a valid proof. In the random oracle model, both $\mathcal{P}$ and $\mathcal{V}$ may call the random oracle but the relation R' itself must be independent of any oracles. The last condition in the definition of proof schemes is called correctness and says that proofs produced by the genuine prover are valid. In the random oracle model, the prover and verifier in the definition of the correctness property have access to the same random oracle, i.e. the oracle answers consistently for both algorithms.

Our definitions of properties for proof schemes are centered around a game with multiple interfaces to which various parties such as provers, extractors or simulators may connect. We give our games as collections of algorithms where each algorithm has both a name and a description of the interface to which it applies. A `return` statement in an algorithm terminates the algorithm and outputs the return value on the same interface that called the algorithm. Where an algorithm should terminate and send a value on a different interface, we use the keyword `send` instead. The keyword `halt` in the code of a game terminates not just an algorithm but the entire game — when this occurs, the game will announce a winner.

2.2   Zero-Knowledge

A proof scheme is called zero-knowledge if there is an algorithm $\mathcal{S}$, called the simulator, which is able to produce proofs indistinguishable from genuine ones after seeing only the statement but no witness. Informally, $\pi \leftarrow \mathcal{P}(x, w)$ and $\pi' \leftarrow \mathcal{S}(x)$ should be indistinguishable for any pair $(x, w) \in R$.

In the (programmable) random oracle model we define zero-knowledge in such a way that the simulator is responsible for the random oracle (if present). Formally, we treat the prover $\mathcal{P}$ as an interactive algorithm that may issue oracle queries and get responses, and that eventually outputs a proof. A simulator is a stateful interactive algorithm $\mathcal{S}$ that can respond to two kinds of queries: a `prove` query which takes a value x as input and should produce a proof π as output, and a `ro` query which takes an arbitrary $x \in \Sigma^*$ as input and returns a $y \in \Sigma^*$. A simulator does not have access to a random oracle, but simulates its own random oracle towards its "clients". A proof scheme is zero-knowledge in the random oracle model if the following two games are indistinguishable:

- The first game internally runs a random oracle RO . On input a pair (x, w), if $R(x, w)$ does not hold then the game returns $\perp$ and halts. If the relation holds, the game runs $\pi \leftarrow \mathcal{P}(x, w)$ and returns π. The prover $\mathcal{P}$ uses the game's random oracle. The adversary may then query the game's random oracle (which $\mathcal{P}$ used) directly, as often as she wants.
- The second game does not run a random oracle. On input a pair (x, w), again if $R(x, w)$ does not hold the game returns $\perp$ and halts. Otherwise, the game runs $\pi \leftarrow \mathcal{S}(x)$ and returns π to the adversary. The adversary may then issue random oracle queries which the game delegates to the simulator's random oracle.

We specify this property using pseudocode in Figure 1. We use the following notation: An oracle is a stateful process which other processes can access via a well-defined set of queries. If $\mathcal{O}$ is an oracle and q is one if its supported queries then we write $\mathcal{O}.\mathsf{q}(x)$ to denote the invocation of this query with parameter x. We write $x \leftarrow_{\$} S$ for selecting x uniformly at random from the set S and $y \leftarrow_{\$} \mathcal{A}^{O_1,\ldots,O_n}(x)$ for calling the (potentially randomised) algorithm $\mathcal{A}$ on input x to get output y. The superscripts denote the oracles that $\mathcal{A}$ can use while it is running. Sometimes, we will allow these oracles to call each other directly (for example if several oracles need access to a random oracle) and to issue a command halt that halts the entire execution.

To maintain random oracle queries in later definitions we write [ ] for the empty list and $L :: l$ to concatenate element l to list L. When L is a list of pairs, we define $L(x)$ to be y such that (x, y) is the first element in L of the form $(x, \cdot)$. If no such element exists then $L(x)$ is defined to be $\perp$.

In Figure 1 we give the games G_1 and G_2 and the methods that the adversary can call. Since it will be helpful later on to give each kind of query a name, we call the adversary's initial query with parameters (x, w) a prove query. Similarly, we call the two operations that a simulator $\mathcal{S}$ admits prove and ro queries.

At the moment, our code may seem like an unnecessarily complicated way of stating a simple property. This level of formalism will become necessary when we move on to adaptive proofs however.

Definition 2. *A proof scheme $(\mathcal{P}, \mathcal{V})$ is zero knowledge in the random oracle model for a relation R if there exists a simulator $\mathcal{S}$ satisfying the following condition. For any security parameter λ let $\delta(\lambda)$ be the distinguishing advantage of any efficient adversary between the games G_1 and G_2 of Figure 1 and for relation R and simulator $\mathcal{S}$. Then $\delta(\lambda)$ is negligible as a function of λ.*

2.3 Proofs of Knowledge

A proof scheme is a proof of knowledge if there is an extractor $\mathcal{K}$ such that for any prover $\widehat{\mathcal{P}}$ which can make a statement/proof pair that verifies, $\mathcal{K}$ can deliver an associated witness. Formalising this statement requires that we not only take care of random oracles but also the extractor's ability to "fork" the prover.

We first consider the non-rewinding case as a warm-up. A prover $\widehat{\mathcal{P}}$ is a randomized interactive algorithm that may make random oracle queries and

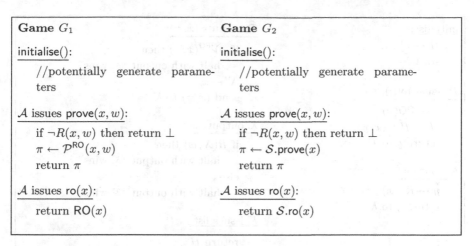

Fig. 1. Games for zero-knowledge (ZK) in the random oracle model. A scheme $(\mathcal{P}, \mathcal{V})$ is ZK if the two games G_1 and G_2 are indistinguishable. The adversary $\mathcal{A}$ may issue prove once and ro any number of times. RO is a random oracle.

eventually outputs a pair (x, π). A non-rewinding extractor $\mathcal{K}$ is an algorithm that takes a pair (x, π) as input, may make random oracle queries and eventually outputs a value w. We consider the game G that runs a random oracle RO internally and connects a prover and an extractor as in Figure 2. A proof scheme is an R-proof of knowledge if there is an extractor $\mathcal{K}$ such that for every prover $\widehat{\mathcal{P}}$, the game mediating between the two algorithms outputs "$\mathcal{K}$ wins" with overwhelming probability.

The game as in Figure 2, in which both the prover $\widehat{\mathcal{P}}$ and the extractor $\mathcal{K}$ can access a random oracle and where the extractor is supposed to find a witness for a valid proof produced by the prover, is actually too demanding to be useful: It basically says that anyone is able to extract a witness from the proof. To derive some sensible notion we give the extractor some advantage and allow it to inspect the random oracle queries made by the prover. That is, the extractor $\mathcal{K}$ can make an extra query list in response to which the game G returns the list H. This gives us a notion of straight-line proofs in the random oracle model which is actually sufficient for capturing the approach used by Fischlin [26].

Definition 3. *A proof scheme $(\mathcal{P}, \mathcal{V})$ is a straight-line proof of knowledge in the ROM w.r.t. a relation R if there is an extractor $\mathcal{K}$ such that for any prover $\widehat{\mathcal{P}}$, the game in Figure 2 augmented with a list query that allows $\mathcal{K}$ to see the list H returns "$\mathcal{K}$ wins" with overwhelming probability.*

The above definition is less general than the one first proposed by Bellare and Goldreich [5]. There the authors relate the extractor's success probability to that of the prover (in producing a valid proof), whereas our definition lets the extractor win by default if the prover does not make a proof. However, our notion generalises more easily to the adaptive setting where the probability of

initialise:
  $H \leftarrow [\,]$
  start $\widehat{\mathcal{P}}$
	$\widehat{\mathcal{P}}$ outputs (x, π):
	  if $\neg \mathcal{V}^{\mathrm{RO}}(x, \pi)$ then
	    halt with output "$\mathcal{K}$ wins"
	  $X \leftarrow x$
	  send (x, π) to $\mathcal{K}$

$\widehat{\mathcal{P}}$ issues $\mathsf{ro}(x)$:
  $y \leftarrow \mathrm{RO}(x)$
  $H \leftarrow H :: (x, y)$
  return y to $\widehat{\mathcal{P}}$
	$\mathcal{K}$ outputs w:
	  if $R(X, w)$ then
	    halt with output "$\mathcal{K}$ wins"
	  else
	    halt with output "$\widehat{\mathcal{P}}$ wins"

$\mathcal{K}$ issues $\mathsf{ro}(x)$:
  $y \leftarrow \mathrm{RO}(x)$
  return y to $\mathcal{K}$
	$\mathcal{K}$ issues list :
	  return H

Fig. 2. The game G defining proofs of knowledge in the random oracle model. Capital-X is part of the game's internal state that persists between calls (so that the extractor's witness is verified against the same statement that the prover provided earlier).

the prover making a valid proof is no longer well-defined, since it also depends on the extractor's response to earlier proofs.

2.4   Rewinding Extractors

The next standard notion that we formalise in our game-based model is that of a rewinding extractor in the ROM, running the prover multiple times. We model the extractor's rewinding ability by giving the extractor access to further copies of the prover, initialised with the same random string as the main incarnation of the prover's algorithm which connects to the proof of knowledge game. We call these further copies "rewound copies". Although all copies of the prover share the same random string, this string is not available to the extractor directly. This prevents the extractor from just simulating the prover on its own and reading off any witness used to make a proof.

The rewound copies of the prover connect to the extractor directly as sketched in Figure 3. In particular, the extractor is responsible for answering the random oracle queries for the rewound copies and can use this ability to "fork" them at any point. In order to apply the forking strategy to proofs made by the main prover, the extractor may make use of the list H that records all random oracle queries and answers for the main execution.

The game itself is the same as for non-rewound provers. For example, for the prover in Schnorr's protocol, one extraction strategy is to start a rewound copy of the prover and run it up until the point that it asks the oracle query which the main prover used to make its proof. Then, the extractor gives the rewound copy a different answer to the oracle query and hopes to obtain a new proof with the same commitment, in order to extract via special soundness. If the main prover made other oracle queries before the "target" one, then the extractor looks these up in the list H and gives the rewound copy the same answers when it makes the relevant queries.

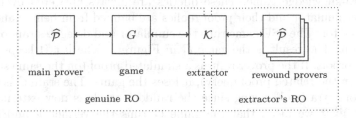

Fig. 3. Extending the straight-line proof of knowledge game to the rewinding case

Definition 4. *A proof scheme is a rewinding proof of knowledge in the ROM if it satisfies the conditions of Definition 3 (proof of knowledge) for an extractor K that has black box access to further copies of the main prover with the same random string.*

2.5 Simulation Soundness and Extractability

Simulation soundness is a property of some zero-knowledge proofs, where even after seeing a simulated proof you cannot construct a new proof of a false statement. Simulation soundness was introduced by Sahai [41] for proofs of statements; unlike proofs of knowledge these do not require an extractor. Sahai used simulation soundness to show that the Naor-Yung "double encryption" transformation can be used to obtain CCA secure encryption. Naor-Yung is not an encrypt-then-prove construction. The latter use only a single encryption but require a proof of knowledge; their security arguments make use of the extractor.

In fact, encrypt-then-prove requires a proof scheme for which one can apply both the zero-knowledge simulator and the proof-of-knowledge extractor in the same security argument. The formal property that models this is called simulation-sound extractability (SSE) [33]. Specifically, the extractor must still work even if the simulator has been invoked, as long as one does not try to extract from a simulated proof. Simulation soundness is often challenging to achieve outside the random oracle model. The proof scheme of Groth and Sahai [50] for example, even in the instantiations that are proofs of knowledge, operates with a setup parameter that can be constructed in two ways: either one can simulate proofs or one can extract, but not both simultaneously. In the random oracle model simulation soundness is typically easier to achieve, e.g., it comes almost for free with Schnorr-type proofs. However, it takes some care to formalise this property as the simulator works under the condition that it controls the random oracle. Hence, the extractor must now succeed w.r.t. the simulator's random oracle in this case.

We model simulation-sound extractability by taking the game for proofs of knowledge and giving the prover the extra ability to ask prove queries just like in the zero-knowledge game. These queries are always answered by the zero-knowledge simulator and their proof replies are banned from being handed over to the extractor. The SSE game runs the simulator and delegates random oracle queries to it. The result is the game G in Figure 4. The list Π keeps track of simulated proofs. If the prover returns a simulated proof (on the same statement as it used in the related proof query), it loses the game. The state C is required for a bit of extra bookkeeping since the random oracle is now external to the game. By $\mathcal{V}^{S.\text{ro}}$ we mean that the game G runs the verifier $\mathcal{V}$ and uses the simulator's random oracle to answer any oracle queries made by the verifier. In other words, in the SSE game even the notion of a valid proof depends on the simulator. Unlike the prover $\widehat{\mathcal{P}}$ which is one of the players in our game, the simulator S is assumed to always produce valid proofs by the zero-knowledge property. The extractor's list query returns both the random oracle queries and the proof queries made by the main prover so far — this allows the extractor to make a rewound copy of the prover run in identical executions as in the main copy.

In addition to the main game G, we define an auxiliary game $\widehat{G}$ that sits between the extractor $\mathcal{K}$ and its rewound provers (there is one copy of $\widehat{G}$ for each rewound prover). The task of $\widehat{G}$ is to "sanitize" prove queries made by rewound provers. When a rewound prover makes such a query, the extractor must play the role of the simulator — after all, the extractor is already simulating the rewound prover's random oracle. (The extractor may run a copy of the simulator S internally.) However, provers make prove queries containing both a statement x and a witness w whereas the simulator only ever gets to see x. The auxiliary game $\widehat{G}$ strips the witness from these proof queries. Otherwise, $\widehat{G}$ acts as a channel between $\mathcal{K}$ and a rewound copy of $\widehat{\mathcal{P}}$. This is slightly tedious to write in our notation; we make the convention that $\widehat{G}$ prefixes a string to every message from $\widehat{\mathcal{P}}$ to $\mathcal{K}$ to indicate whether the value is meant to be a random oracle, extraction or proof query. Messages (responses) flowing in the other direction can always be passed on unchanged — the prover will hopefully remember what its last query was when it gets a response.

Definition 5. *A proof scheme* $(\mathcal{P}, \mathcal{V})$ *is simulation sound in the ROM for a relation R if it satisfies the following conditions. An s-prover is an algorithm $\widehat{\mathcal{P}}$ that can ask random oracle and proof queries and eventually outputs an extraction query containing a statement/proof pair.*

- *The proof scheme is zero-knowledge w.r.t. R for a simulator S and a proof of knowledge w.r.t. R for an extractor $\mathcal{K}$.*
- *For every s-prover $\widehat{\mathcal{P}}$, if we connect $\mathcal{K}$ to $\widehat{\mathcal{P}}$ through the game G of Figure 4 and give $\mathcal{K}$ access to further rewound copies of the prover (with the same*

initialise:
    $H \leftarrow [\,]$; $\Pi \leftarrow [\,]$
    start $\widehat{\mathcal{P}}$
	$\widehat{\mathcal{P}}$ outputs (x, π):
	    if $\neg\mathcal{V}^{\mathcal{S}.\text{ro}}(x, \pi)$ or $(x, \pi) \in \Pi$ then
	        halt with output "$\mathcal{K}$ wins"
	    $X \leftarrow x$

$\widehat{\mathcal{P}}$ issues $\text{ro}(x)$:
    $C \leftarrow$ "prover"; $I \leftarrow x$
    send x to $\mathcal{S}.\text{ro}$
	send (x, π) to $\mathcal{K}$
	$\mathcal{K}$ outputs w:
	    if $R(X, w)$ then

$\mathcal{K}$ issues $\text{ro}(x)$:
    $C \leftarrow$ "extractor"
    send x to $\mathcal{S}.\text{ro}$
	halt with output "$\mathcal{K}$ wins"
	    else
	        halt with output "$\widehat{\mathcal{P}}$ wins"

$\mathcal{S}.\text{ro}$ returns a value y:
    if $C =$ "prover" then
        $H \leftarrow H :: (I, y)$
        send y to $\widehat{\mathcal{P}}$
    else
        send y to $\mathcal{K}$
	$\widehat{\mathcal{P}}$ issues $\text{prove}(x, w)$:
	    if $\neg R(x, w)$ then
	        halt with output "$\mathcal{K}$ wins"
	    $X' \leftarrow x$
	    send x to $\mathcal{S}.\text{prove}$

$\mathcal{K}$ calls list:
    return (H, Π)
	$\mathcal{S}.\text{prove}$ returns π:
	    $\Pi \leftarrow \Pi :: (X', \pi)$
	    send π to $\widehat{\mathcal{P}}$

Fig. 4. The game G defining SSE in the random oracle model.

random string) through the auxiliary game $\widehat{G}$ of Figure 5 then with overwhelming probability the game G returns "$\mathcal{K}$ wins".

3 Adaptive Proofs of Knowledge

Given our game-centric view of proofs of knowledge we can extend the approach to adaptive proofs of knowledge. An adaptive proof is simply a proof scheme where the extractor can still win if the prover is given multiple turns to make proofs. The adaptive part is that the game hands the extractor's witness in each turn back to the prover before the prover must take her next turn. Should a prover be able to produce a proof for which she does not know the witness, she could then use the extractor's ability to find a witness to help make her next proof. The intuition is essentially the same for the cases with and without simulation soundness. We first introduce adaptive proofs formally without simulation soundness using so-called n-proofs, where n is a parameter describing the number of rounds the prover plays. In a later step we add simulation soundness.

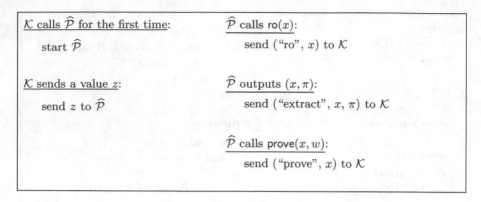

Fig. 5. The auxiliary game $\widehat{G}$ for SSE. It acts mostly as a channel between $\mathcal{K}$ and a rewound prover $\widehat{P}$ except that it strips witnesses from proof queries. We use the convention that $\widehat{G}$ indicates to $\mathcal{K}$ whether a value is for a random oracle, extraction or proof query by prefixing a string.

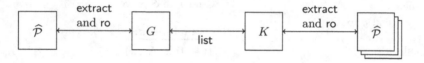

Fig. 6. The adaptive proof game and the queries that the various algorithms can exchange

3.1   Adaptive Proofs and n-Proofs

Let $(\mathcal{P}, \mathcal{V})$ be a proof scheme for a relation R. An adaptive prover $\widehat{P}$ in the ROM is a component that can make two kinds of queries, repeatedly and in any order. The first are random oracle queries; these are self-explanatory. The second are extraction queries which take a statement and a proof as parameters. The response to an extraction query is a witness. (Correctness conditions will be enforced by the game, not the prover.) Adaptive provers may also halt. For example, a non-adaptive prover can be seen as an adaptive prover that halts after its first extraction query.

An adaptive extractor $\mathcal{K}$ is a component that can make list and random oracle queries and receive and process extraction queries from an adaptive prover. In addition, an extractor may have black-box access to further rewinding copies of the adaptive prover (with the same random string) and answer all of their queries.

The n-proof game takes a parameter n as input and connects an adaptive prover and extractor. It runs up to n rounds in which the prover may make a statement and proof and the extractor must return a witness. The extractor wins if it can deliver all n witnesses or if the prover halts earlier than this, or fails to make a valid proof. The extractor loses if it does not supply a valid witness to one of the first n extraction queries.

---

initialise(n):

    $H \leftarrow [\,]$
    $K \leftarrow 0$
    start $\widehat{\mathcal{P}}$

$\widehat{\mathcal{P}}$ issues ro(x):

    $y \leftarrow \mathsf{RO}(x)$
    $H \leftarrow H :: (x, y)$
    return y to $\widehat{\mathcal{P}}$

$\mathcal{K}$ issues ro(x):

    $y \leftarrow \mathsf{RO}(x)$
    return y to $\mathcal{K}$

$\mathcal{K}$ issues list :

    return H to $\mathcal{K}$

$\widehat{\mathcal{P}}$ halts: halt with output "$\mathcal{K}$ wins"

$\widehat{\mathcal{P}}$ issues extract(x, π):

    if $\neg \mathcal{V}^{\mathsf{RO}}(x, \pi)$ then
        halt with output "$\mathcal{K}$ wins"
    $X \leftarrow x$
    send (x, π) to $\mathcal{K}$

$\mathcal{K}$ outputs w:

    if $\neg R(X, w)$ then
        halt with output "$\widehat{\mathcal{P}}$ wins"
    $K \leftarrow K + 1$
    if $K = n$ then
        halt with output "$\mathcal{K}$ wins"
    else
        send w to $\widehat{\mathcal{P}}$

Fig. 7. The game G for adaptive proofs with parameter n

Definition 6. *A proof scheme is an n-proof in the ROM for a relation R if there exists an extractor $\mathcal{K}$ such that for every adaptive prover $\widehat{\mathcal{P}}$ the game G of Figure 7 when connected to $\widehat{\mathcal{P}}$ and $\mathcal{K}$ returns "$\mathcal{K}$ wins" with overwhelming probability.*

If $\mathcal{K}$ also has access to further copies of $\widehat{\mathcal{P}}$ with the same random string then we call the proof scheme a rewinding n-proof, otherwise we call it a straight line n-proof.

If for every polynomial $p(x)$ there is an extractor $\mathcal{K}_{p(x)}$ making a particular scheme a $p(n)$-proof, we say that the scheme is an adaptive proof.

3.2   Simulation-Sound Adaptive Proofs

Adding simulation soundness to adaptive proofs works the same way as for non-adaptive proofs. Adaptive s-provers may make random oracle, proof and extraction queries (the simulation sound n-proof game only limits the number of extraction queries, not proof queries). We give the new algorithms in Figure 8. Random oracle calls from the main prover go to the simulator; simulated proofs are logged and provided on request to the extractor (via a list query) and are banned from extraction queries. The rewinding copies of the prover are connected to the extractor through the same games $\widehat{G}$ as in the non-adaptive case: extraction queries and witnesses found by the extractor are simply passed back and forth. Only the witnesses in prove queries are stripped out.

---

initialise(n):

    $H \leftarrow [\,]$; $\Pi \leftarrow [\,]$
    $K \leftarrow 0$
    start $\widehat{\mathcal{P}}$

$\widehat{\mathcal{P}}$ issues ro(x):

    $C \leftarrow$ "prover"; $I \leftarrow x$
    send x to $\mathcal{S}$.ro

$\mathcal{K}$ issues ro(x):

    $C \leftarrow$ "extractor"
    send x to $\mathcal{S}$.ro

$\mathcal{S}$.ro returns a value y:

    if $C =$ "prover" then
        $H \leftarrow H :: (I, y)$
        send y to $\widehat{\mathcal{P}}$
    else
        send y to $\mathcal{K}$

$\mathcal{K}$ issues list:

    return (H, Π)

$\widehat{\mathcal{P}}$ halts:

    halt with output "$\mathcal{K}$ wins"

$\widehat{\mathcal{P}}$ issues extract(x, π):

    if $\neg \mathcal{V}^{\mathcal{S}.\mathsf{ro}}(x, \pi)$ or $(x, \pi) \in \Pi$ then
        halt with output "$\mathcal{K}$ wins"
    $X \leftarrow x$
    send (x, π) to $\mathcal{K}$

$\mathcal{K}$ outputs w:

    if $\neg R(X, w)$ then
        halt with output "$\widehat{\mathcal{P}}$ wins"
    $K \leftarrow K + 1$
    if $K = n$ then
        halt with output "$\mathcal{K}$ wins"
    else
        send w to $\widehat{\mathcal{P}}$

$\widehat{\mathcal{P}}$ issues prove(x, w):

    if $\neg R(x, w)$ then
        halt with output "$\mathcal{K}$ wins"
    $X' \leftarrow x$
    send x to $\mathcal{S}$.prove

$\mathcal{S}$.prove returns π:

    $\Pi \leftarrow \Pi :: (X', \pi)$
    send π to $\widehat{\mathcal{P}}$

Fig. 8. Simulation sound n-proofs in the random oracle model

Consider a proof scheme $(\mathcal{P}, \mathcal{V})$ that is zero-knowledge for a relation R with simulator $\mathcal{S}$. The simulation sound n-proof experiment for this scheme, an adaptive s-prover $\widehat{\mathcal{P}}$ and an extractor $\mathcal{K}$ is the following experiment. Connect the prover $\widehat{\mathcal{P}}$, the simulator $\mathcal{S}$ and the extractor $\mathcal{K}$ to the game G of Figure 8. Let $\mathcal{K}$ have black box access to further copies of $\widehat{\mathcal{P}}$ mediated by $\widehat{G}$ as in Figure 5 that forwards all messages in both directions except that it strips witnesses from proof queries.

Definition 7. *Let $(\mathcal{P}, \mathcal{V})$ be a proof scheme for a relation R that is zero-knowledge with simulator $\mathcal{S}$. The scheme is a simulation sound n-proof if there*

is an extractor $\mathcal{K}$ such that for any adaptive s-prover $\widehat{\mathcal{P}}$, the simulation sound n-proof experiment returns "$\mathcal{K}$ wins" with overwhelming probability. If the extractor works for all polynomially bounded n, we call the scheme an adaptive simulation sound proof.

4   Overview of Our Results

In this section we briefly discuss our main results. Since the proofs of our theorems are long and contain many technical/formal details that are not particularly enlightening, we have chosen to give only an overview of our results here.

4.1   Adaptive Proofs Exist

First, we establish that simulation-sound adaptive proofs in the random oracle model exist. An existing construction due to Fischlin [26] is adaptively secure. Fischlin gives a transformation of Sigma protocols to non-interactive proof schemes as an alternative to the more common Fiat-Shamir transformation.

The following theorem shows that Fischlin proofs are adaptively secure.

Theorem 1. *A Fischlin-transformed Sigma protocol with special soundness is a simulation-sound adaptive proof in the random oracle model.*

4.2   Encrypt-Then-Prove

Our main positive result is that the encrypt-then-prove transformation does what it is intuitively supposed to do — boost IND-CPA to CCA — if the proof scheme is a simulation-sound adaptive proof. To define the transformation we first clarify a point about NP languages. In the introduction, we said that encrypt-then-prove uses a proof of the "randomness and message" used to encrypt. This is not precise enough for a formal definition. This informal statement would give us a proof over a relation $R_1 : \{(c, (m, r)) \mid c = \mathsf{Encrypt}(pk, m; r)\}$ where statements are ciphertexts and witnesses are message/randomness pairs. However, Signed ElGamal (which we will define soon) uses a Schnorr proof which is a proof of knowledge of a discrete logarithm, namely the randomness in an ElGamal ciphertext. This would suggest a relation $R_2 : \{(c, r) \mid c = \mathsf{Encrypt}(pk, m; r)\}$. Of course, the point of the proof is that the message can be computed from a ciphertext and its randomness, but that is not the same thing as the formal definition of the proof's NP relation. In addition, since the NP relation and proof depends on the public key as an extra parameter, when we define the transformation formally we are actually working with a parametrised family of relations. Further, the encrypt-then-prove transformation still works if one adds extra features to the proof. For example, the Helios voting scheme for example uses encrypt-then-prove ciphertexts that additionally prove that the encrypted message is a valid vote.

We address all these problems with an abstract definition of compatibility between encryption and proof schemes; any schemes that meet this definition can be used in the encrypt-then-prove transformation. Our definition also means that we will not have a concrete NP relation to work with in our main theorem. Instead, compatibility says that the NP relation can be anything that supports the two features we need: from a witness you can compute a message and from the list of all inputs used to form a ciphertext, you can derive a witness.

Definition 8. *An encryption scheme* $\mathfrak{E} = (\mathsf{KeyGen}, \mathsf{Encrypt}, \mathsf{Decrypt})$ *and a proof scheme* $\mathfrak{P} = (\mathcal{P}, \mathcal{V})$ *for relation* R *are compatible if there are efficient algorithms* M *and* W *such that:*

1. *For any tuple* (pk, c, w) *of public key, ciphertext and witness such that* $R((pk, c), w)$ *holds, the value* $m := \mathsf{M}(pk, c, w)$ *is the message such that* c *is an encryption of* m *under public key* pk.
2. *For any tuple* (pk, c, m, r) *of public key, ciphertext, message and random string, the value* $w := \mathsf{W}(pk, c, m, r)$ *is a witness for which* $R((pk, c), w)$ *holds.*

Definition 9. *Let* $\mathfrak{E}$ *and* $\mathfrak{P}$ *be compatible encryption and proof schemes (for a relation* R *and algorithms* M, W. *The encrypt-then-prove transformation of* $\mathfrak{E}$ *and* $\mathfrak{P}$ *is the encryption scheme in Figure 9 where* RS *is the space of random strings for* $\mathfrak{E}.\mathsf{Encrypt}$.

KeyGen():	Encrypt(pk, m):	Decrypt(sk, c):
$(pk, sk) \leftarrow \mathfrak{E}.\mathsf{KeyGen}()$	$r \leftarrow_\$ RS$	parse c as (e, π)
return (pk, sk)	$c \quad\quad\quad\leftarrow$	if $\mathfrak{P}.\mathcal{V}((pk, e), \pi) = 0$
	$\mathfrak{E}.\mathsf{Encrypt}(pk, m; r)$	then
	$w \leftarrow \mathsf{W}(pk, c, m, r)$	return $\bot$
	$\pi \leftarrow \mathfrak{P}.\mathcal{P}((pk, c), w)$	$m \leftarrow \mathfrak{E}.\mathsf{Decrypt}(sk, e)$
	return (c, π)	return m

Fig. 9. The encrypt-then-prove transformation of compatible $\mathfrak{E}$ and $\mathfrak{P}$. RS is the space of random strings used by the original encryption algorithm.

Signed ElGamal. As an example, we present the Signed ElGamal scheme. Signed ElGamal is ElGamal encryption with a Fiat-Shamir-Schnorr proof. It operates over a cyclic group $\mathbb{G}$ of prime order q with a generator G. To generate keys, pick a random $sk \leftarrow_\$ \mathbb{F}_q$ and set your public key to $pk \leftarrow G^{sk}$. To encrypt a message $m \in \mathbb{G}$, pick a random $r \leftarrow_\$ \mathbb{F}_q$ and create an ElGamal ciphertext $e \leftarrow (G^r, pk^r \cdot m)$. Then pick another random value $a \leftarrow_\$ \mathbb{F}_q$ and create the Schnorr commitment $A \leftarrow G^a$, challenge $c \leftarrow \mathcal{H}(pk, e, A)$ and response $s \leftarrow a + c \cdot r \pmod q$. The ciphertext is (e, A, s). To decrypt a ciphertext (e, A, s) with secret key sk, parse e as a pair (u, v) and check that $G^s = A + \mathcal{H}(pk, e, A) \cdot u$

(mod q). If this fails, the ciphertext is invalid. If it succeeds, the decryption is $m \leftarrow v/u^{sk}$. The relation R for Signed ElGamal is $R((pk, (u, v)), r) :\Leftrightarrow u = G^r$. Here (u, v) is an ElGamal ciphertext and $(pk, (u, v))$ is a statement consisting of a public key/ciphertext pair. The maps to make the encryption scheme and proof compatible are $\mathsf{M}(pk, (u, v), w) := v/pk^w$ and $\mathsf{W}(pk, (u, v), m, r) := r$.

4.3   Simulation-Sound Adaptive Proofs Yield CCA

Our main positive result expresses the intuition behind encrypt-then-prove.

Theorem 2. *Let $\mathfrak{E}$ be an IND-CPA secure encryption scheme and let $\mathfrak{P}$ be a compatible simulation-sound adaptive proof scheme in the random oracle model. Then the encrypt-then-prove transformation of these schemes is a CCA secure encryption scheme in the random oracle model.*

As a corollary we immediately obtain a new CCA secure encryption scheme.

Corollary 1. *The encrypt-then-prove transformation of ElGamal using Fischlin-Schnorr proofs is CCA secure.*

The final step of the proof follows the basic intuition behind all encrypt-then-prove constructions. We reduce CCA security to IND-CPA security. Our reduction sends the two challenge messages to the IND-CPA game for the basic scheme, gets a ciphertext back and simulates a proof on it to create the challenge ciphertext of the encrypt-then-prove construction. When the CCA attacker makes a decryption query with an encrypt-then-prove ciphertext, the reduction invokes the extractor using the IND-CPA ciphertext component as the statement and the proof component as the proof. The witness contains the encrypted message which the reduction returns to the attacker. Since we are simulating and extracting in the same reduction, we require simulation sound extractability.

Unfortunately, this idea does not explain how the reduction is supposed to deal with the extractor requesting a further copy of the attacker. Worse still, the "prover" that we are simulating towards the extractor is a combination of the attacker and the IND-CPA challenger. We definitely cannot clone or rewind our challenger. To our knowledge, our proof is the first proof of a CCA construction that involves rewinding.

After an intial step in which we simulate all proofs on challenge ciphertexts, most of the proof is an argument how and why a single reduction can provide the extractor with a consistent simulation of multiple copies of the same algorithm. We call this technique coin splitting. It works on two principles. (1.) Keep track of which copies are "clones" of other copies. If a copy C is getting the exact same queries that another copy D has already answered, let C simply replay D's answers. (2.) Make sure that all cases not handled by the last point involve fresh, independent randomness. Then the reduction can simply draw fresh random values from one source to simulate all copies.

Coin splitting lets us use our one IND-CPA challenge for the extractor's main prover and simulate our own challenges for the rewinding provers. To the extractor, all this will look just like fresh randomness each time.

4.4   Fiat-Shamir-Schnorr Is Not Adaptively Secure

Our third result is negative. It separates proofs of knowledge from adaptive proofs and shows that Fiat-Shamir Schnorr is an example that separates the two notions.

Theorem 3. *The Fiat-Shamir-Schnorr (FSS) proof scheme is not adaptively secure under the one-more discrete logarithm assumption. Specifically, for any n there is a prover $\widehat{P}$ who makes a sequence of n FSS proofs. For any extractor $\mathcal{K}$ who can win the adaptive proof experiment against $\widehat{P}$, either $\mathcal{K}$ calls at least 2^n rewinding copies of $\widehat{P}$ or there is a reduction that solves the one-more discrete logarithm problem in the underlying group with a comparable success rate to $\mathcal{K}$.*

The prover in question follows the same ideas as Shoup and Gennaro's CCA attacker [47]. While the cited work gave the attacker as an example why the "obvious" proof fails, it did not show any inherent limitation of the Fiat-Shamir technique; it did not show that this limitation cannot be overcome by using a different proof technique. Our paper is the first to give a proof that Fiat-Shamir transformed sigma protocols have an unavoidable limitation.

Acknowledgments. We thank the current and earlier reviewers of this paper for their helpful comments. This work has been supported in part by the European Union under the Seventh Framework Programme (FP7/2007-2013), grant agreement 609611 (PRACTICE) and the ERC Advanced Grant ERC-2010-AdG-267188-CRIPTO. Marc Fischlin is supported by the Heisenberg grant Fi 940/3-2 of the German Research Foundation (DFG).

References

1. Abe, M.: Combining Encryption and Proof of Knowledge in the Random Oracle Model. The Computer Journal **47**(1), 58–70 (2004)
2. Abdalla, M., Bellare, M., Rogaway, P.: The oracle diffie-Hellman assumptions and an analysis of DHIES. In: Naccache, D. (ed.) CT-RSA 2001. LNCS, vol. 2020, p. 143. Springer, Heidelberg (2001)
3. Adida, B.: Helios: web-based open-audit voting. In: 17th USENIX security symposium, pp. 335–348. Helios website (2008). http://heliosvoting.org paper: http://www.usenix.org/events/sec08/tech/full_papers/adida/adida.pdf
4. Bagherzandi, A., Cheaon, J.H., Jarecki, S.: Multisignatures secure under the discrete logarithm assumption and a generalized forking lemma. In: CCS 2008, pp. 449–458. ACM press (2008)
5. Bellare, M., Goldreich, O.: On defining proofs of knowledge. In: Brickell, E.F. (ed.) CRYPTO 1992. LNCS, vol. 740, pp. 390–420. Springer, Heidelberg (1993)
6. Bellare, M., Goldreich, O.: On probabilistic versus deterministic provers in the definition of proofs of knowledge. In: Goldreich, O. (ed.) Studies in Complexity and Cryptography. LNCS, vol. 6650, pp. 114–123. Springer, Heidelberg (2011)
7. Bellare, M., Namprempre, C., Pointcheval, D., Semanko, M.: The One-More-RSA-Inversion Problems and the Security of Chaum's Blind Signature Scheme. J. Cryptology **16**(3), 185–215 (2003). Springer

8. Bellare, M., Neven, G.: Multi-signatures in the plain public-key model and a general forking lemma. In: Proceedings of ACM Conference on Computer and Communications Security, pp. 390–399 (2006)
9. Bellare, M., Rogaway, P.: Random oracles are practical: a paradigm for designing efficient protocols. In: ACM Conference on Computer and Communications Security, pp. 62–73. ACM (1993)
10. Bellare, M., Rogaway, P.: The security of triple encryption and a framework for code-based game-playing proofs. In: Vaudenay, S. (ed.) EUROCRYPT 2006. LNCS, vol. 4004, pp. 409–426. Springer, Heidelberg (2006). Full version of 27 November 2008 (Draft 3.0) at eprint.iacr.org/2004/331
11. Bellare, M., Sahai, A.: Non-malleable encryption: equivalence between two notions, and an indistinguishability-based characterization. In: Wiener, M. (ed.) CRYPTO 1999. LNCS, vol. 1666, pp. 519–536. Springer, Heidelberg (1999)
12. Bernhard, D., Pereira, O., Warinschi, B.: How not to prove yourself: pitfalls of the Fiat-Shamir Heuristic and applications to Helios. In: Wang, X., Sako, K. (eds.) ASIACRYPT 2012. LNCS, vol. 7658, pp. 626–643. Springer, Heidelberg (2012)
13. Blum, M., Feldman, P., Micali, S.: Non-interactive zero-knowledge and its applications. In: Proceedings of the twentieth annual ACM symposium on theory of computing (STOC 1990), pp. 103–112 (1988)
14. Canetti, R., Goldreich, O., Goldwasser, S., Micali, S.: Resettable zero-knowledge. In: STOC, pp. 235–244. ACM Press (2000)
15. Chase, M., Lysyanskaya, A.: On signatures of knowledge. In: Dwork, C. (ed.) CRYPTO 2006. LNCS, vol. 4117, pp. 78–96. Springer, Heidelberg (2006)
16. Cramer, R., Shoup, V.: A practical public key cryptosystem provably secure against adaptive chosen ciphertext attack. In: Krawczyk, H. (ed.) CRYPTO 1998. LNCS, vol. 1462, p. 13. Springer, Heidelberg (1998)
17. Damgård, I.B.: Towards practical public key systems secure against chosen ciphertext attacks. In: Feigenbaum, J. (ed.) CRYPTO 1991. LNCS, vol. 576, pp. 445–456. Springer, Heidelberg (1992)
18. De Santis, A., Di Crescenzo, G., Ostrovsky, R., Persiano, G., Sahai, A.: Robust non-interactive zero knowledge. In: Kilian, J. (ed.) CRYPTO 2001. LNCS, vol. 2139, p. 566. Springer, Heidelberg (2001)
19. De Santis, A., Persiano, G.: Zero-knowledge proofs of knowledge without interaction (extended abstract). In: FOCS, pp. 427–436 (1992)
20. Dodis, Y., Haralambiev, K., López-Alt, A., Wichs, D.: Efficient public-key cryptography in the presence of key leakage. In: Abe, M. (ed.) ASIACRYPT 2010. LNCS, vol. 6477, pp. 613–631. Springer, Heidelberg (2010)
21. Faust, S., Kohlweiss, M., Marson, G.A., Venturi, D.: On the non-malleability of the Fiat-Shamir transform. In: Galbraith, S., Nandi, M. (eds.) INDOCRYPT 2012. LNCS, vol. 7668. Springer, Heidelberg (2012)
22. Feige, U., Fiat, A., Shamir, A.: Zero-knowledge proofs of identity. Journal of Cryptology 1(2), 77–94 (1988)
23. Feige, U., Lapidot, D., Shamir, A.: Multiple non-interactive zero knowledge proofs based on a single random string (extended abstract). In: FOCS, pp. 308–317 (1990)
24. Feige, U., Shamir, A.: Zero knowledge proofs of knowledge in two rounds. In: Brassard, G. (ed.) CRYPTO 1989. LNCS, vol. 435, pp. 526–544. Springer, Heidelberg (1990)
25. Fiat, A., Shamir, A.: How to prove yourself: practical solutions to identification and signature problems. In: Odlyzko, A.M. (ed.) CRYPTO 1986. LNCS, vol. 263, pp. 186–194. Springer, Heidelberg (1987)

26. Fischlin, M.: Communication-efficient non-interactive proofs of knowledge with online extractors. In: Shoup, V. (ed.) CRYPTO 2005. LNCS, vol. 3621, pp. 152–168. Springer, Heidelberg (2005)

27. Fouque, P.-A., Pointcheval, D.: Threshold cryptosystems secure against chosen-ciphertext attacks. In: Boyd, C. (ed.) ASIACRYPT 2001. LNCS, vol. 2248, p. 351. Springer, Heidelberg (2001)

28. Fujisaki, E., Okamoto, T.: Secure Integration of Asymmetric and Symmetric Encryption Schemes. J. Cryptology 26(1), 80–101 (2013)

29. Garay, J.A., MacKenzie, P.D., Yang, K.: Strengthening Zero-Knowledge Protocols Using Signatures. J. Cryptology 19(2), 169–209 (2006). Springer

30. Garg, S., Bhaskar, R., Lokam, S.V.: Improved bounds on security reductions for discrete log based signatures. In: Wagner, D. (ed.) CRYPTO 2008. LNCS, vol. 5157, pp. 93–107. Springer, Heidelberg (2008)

31. Goldwasser, S., Micali, S., Rackoff, C.: The Knowledge Complexity of Interactive Proof Systems. SIAM J. Comput. 18(1), 186–208 (1989)

32. Goldreich, O., Ostrovsky, R.: Software Protection and Simulation on Oblivious RAMs. J. ACM 43(3), 431–473 (1996)

33. Groth, J.: Simulation-sound NIZK proofs for a practical language and constant size group signatures. In: Lai, X., Chen, K. (eds.) ASIACRYPT 2006. LNCS, vol. 4284, pp. 444–459. Springer, Heidelberg (2006)

34. Kiltz, E., Malone-Lee, J.: A General Construction of IND-CCA2 Secure Public Key Encryption. IMA Int. Conf. 152–166 (2003)

35. Lindell, Y.: A Simpler Construction of CCA2-Secure Public-KeyEncryption under General Assumptions. J. Cryptology 19(3), 359–377 (2006). Springer

36. Naor, M., Yung, M.: Public-key cryptosystems provably secure against chosen ciphertext attacks. In: Proceedings of the twenty-second annual ACM symposium on theory of computing (STOC 1990), pp. 42–437 (1990)

37. Pointcheval, D., Stern, J.: Security Arguments for Digital Signatures and Blind Signatures. J. Cryptolog 13(3), 361–396 (2000). Springer

38. Rackoff, C., Simon, D.R.: Non-interactive zero-knowledge proof of knowledge and chosen ciphertext attack. In: Feigenbaum, J. (ed.) CRYPTO 1991. LNCS, vol. 576, pp. 433–444. Springer, Heidelberg (1992)

39. Sahai, A.: Non-malleable non-interactive zero knowledge and adaptive chosen-ciphertext security. In: Proceedings of the 40th annual symposium on foundations of computer science (FOCS 1999), pp. 543–553 (1999)

40. Schnorr, C.P.: Efficient signature generation for smart cards. Journal of cryptology 4, 161–174 (1991). Springer

41. Schnorr, C.-P., Jakobsson, M.: Security of signed elgamal encryption. In: Okamoto, T. (ed.) ASIACRYPT 2000. LNCS, vol. 1976, p. 73. Springer, Heidelberg (2000)

42. Seurin, Y.: On the exact security of schnorr-type signatures in the random oracle model. In: Pointcheval, D., Johansson, T. (eds.) EUROCRYPT 2012. LNCS, vol. 7237, pp. 554–571. Springer, Heidelberg (2012)

43. Seurin, Y., Treger, J.: A robust and plaintext-aware variant of signed elgamal encryption. In: Dawson, E. (ed.) CT-RSA 2013. LNCS, vol. 7779, pp. 68–83. Springer, Heidelberg (2013)

44. Shoup, V.: A Proposal for an ISO Standard for Public Key Encryption. Version 2.1 (2001). www.shoup.net

45. Shoup, V., Gennaro, R.: Securing threshold cryptosystems against chosen cipher-text attack. In: Nyberg, K. (ed.) EUROCRYPT 1998. LNCS, vol. 1403, pp. 1–16. Springer, Heidelberg (1998)

46. Shoup, V., Gennaro, R.: Securing Threshold Cryptosystems against Chosen Ciphertext Attack. J. Cryptology 15(2), 75–96 (2002). Springer
47. Tompa, M., Woll, H.: Random self-reducibility and zero knowledge interactive proofs of possession of information. In: FOCS, pp. 472–482 (1987)
48. Tsiounis, Y., Yung, M.: On the security of elgamal based encryption. In: Imai, H., Zheng, Y. (eds.) PKC 1998. LNCS, vol. 1431, p. 117. Springer, Heidelberg (1998)
49. Wee, H.: Zero knowledge in the random oracle model, revisited. In: Matsui, M. (ed.) ASIACRYPT 2009. LNCS, vol. 5912, pp. 417–434. Springer, Heidelberg (2009)
50. Groth, J., Sahai, A.: Efficient non-interactive proof systems for bilinear groups. In: Smart, N.P. (ed.) EUROCRYPT 2008. LNCS, vol. 4965, pp. 415–432. Springer, Heidelberg (2008)
51. Wikström, D.: Simplified submission of inputs to protocols. In: Ostrovsky, R., De Prisco, R., Visconti, I. (eds.) SCN 2008. LNCS, vol. 5229, pp. 293–308. Springer, Heidelberg (2008)
52. Zheng, Y., Seberry, J.: Practical approaches to attaining security against adaptively chosen ciphertext attacks. In: Brickell, E.F. (ed.) CRYPTO 1992. LNCS, vol. 740. Springer, Heidelberg (1992)

Making Sigma-Protocols Non-interactive Without Random Oracles

Pyrros Chaidos$^{(\boxtimes)}$ and Jens Groth

University College London, London, UK
{pyrros.chaidos.10,j.groth}@ucl.ac.uk

Abstract. Damgård, Fazio and Nicolosi (TCC 2006) gave a transformation of Sigma-protocols, 3-move honest verifier zero-knowledge proofs, into efficient non-interactive zero-knowledge arguments for a designated verifier. Their transformation uses additively homomorphic encryption to encrypt the verifier's challenge, which the prover uses to compute an encrypted answer. The transformation does not rely on the random oracle model but proving soundness requires a complexity leveraging assumption.

We propose an alternative instantiation of their transformation and show that it achieves culpable soundness without complexity leveraging. This improves upon an earlier result by Ventre and Visconti (Africacrypt 2009), who used a different construction which achieved *weak* culpable soundness.

We demonstrate how our construction can be used to prove validity of encrypted votes in a referendum. This yields a voting system with homomorphic tallying that does not rely on the Fiat-Shamir heuristic.

Keywords: Sigma-protocols · Non-interactive zero-knowledge designated verifier argument · DFN transformation · Culpable soundness · Voting

1 Introduction

Cryptographic applications often require a party to demonstrate that a statement is true without revealing any additional details. For example, a voter may wish to prove that an encrypted message contains a vote for a valid candidate without disclosing the actual candidate. This can be done using *zero-knowledge* proofs [17] that enable a prover to demonstrate to a verifier that a statement x belongs to a language L in NP defined by a relation R without giving the verifier any information about the witness w such that $(x, w) \in R$.

Pyrros Chaidos—This author was supported by an EPSRC scholarship (EP/G037264/1 – Security Science DTC).

Jens Groth—This research was supported by the European Research Council under the European Union's Seventh Framework Programme (FP/2007-2013) / ERC Grant Agreement n. 307937.

J. Katz (Ed.): PKC 2015, LNCS 9020, pp. 650–670, 2015.
DOI: 10.1007/978-3-662-46447-2_29

Σ-protocols are particular types of 3-move honest verifier zero-knowledge proofs that can be highly efficient. However, in many applications it is preferable for a protocol to be non-interactive [5] with the prover preparing a proof with no need for direct input from the verifier. The Fiat-Shamir transformation [13] produces a non-interactive version of a Σ-protocol by substituting the verifier's challenge with the output of a hash function on the prover's statement and messages. The transformation can be proven secure in the random oracle model [3]. However, the random oracle model is regarded with some skepticism since there exist pathological protocols that can be proven secure in the random oracle model but fail in any real-world instantiation [6,16].

Damgård, Fazio and Nicolosi (DFN) [11] introduced an alternative transformation. The DFN transformation works in the Registered Key Model (RKM) [2] where a verifier registers a public key and transforms a Σ-protocol with linear answer into a non-interactive zero-knowledge argument that can be verified by this specific verifier [23]. The transformation works by having the verifier encrypt his challenge under an additively homomorphic encryption scheme and relies on the Σ-protocol having an answer that can be computed using linear algebra and the homomorphic property of the encryption scheme to enable the prover to complete an encrypted version of the answer in the Σ-protocol. Their construction is secure for a logarithmic number of proofs but soundness rests on a complexity leveraging assumption.

Ventre and Visconti [28] give an alternative proof of soundness for a construction based on a two ciphertext variation of the DFN transformation in the style of Naor and Yung [25]. They replace the complexity leveraging assumption by introducing a modification of culpable soundness[1] [21] that they call *weak culpable soundness*. Standard culpable soundness restricts adversaries to being "aware" of the falsehood of the statement they are proving. Weak culpable soundness furthermore requires that the adversary is also aware of the fact that she has succeeded in producing a convincing proof of a false statement, by producing a second auxiliary proof to that effect.

In the DFN setting using weak culpable soundness would require the adversary to prove statements containing ciphertexts addressed to the designated verifier. It would be challenging to provide such an adversary with enough power to perform the required proofs without having knowledge of the verifier's secret decryption key. We instead opt to construct the underlying protocol with the property that forged proofs reveal the challenge. This is enough to contradict the semantic security of the encryption scheme used for the designated verifier proof if a false proof is ever produced.

1.1   Our Contribution

We give an instantiation of the DFN transformation that achieves standard culpable soundness without complexity leveraging. The transformation relies on an

---

[1] Culpable soundness was also called co-soundness in an earlier version of [21].

IND-CPA secure additively homomorphic encryption scheme and is quite efficient. The tranformation can be applied to Σ-protocols that have linear answers and unique identifiable challenges (Sect. 2.2).

We can use our resulting non-interactive zero-knowledge designated verifier arguments to efficiently prove statements about encrypted plaintexts. In particular, we can prove that a ciphertext contains either 0 or 1 without disclosing the plaintext. This can in turn be used to prove that a set of ciphertexts encrypt a witness for the satisfiability of a circuit. For the appropriate Σ-protocols to be in place, we require the encryption scheme to be additively homomorphic modulo a prime and satisfy a few other requirements (Sect. 2.1). We use Okamoto-Uchiyama encryption [26] as an example.

We proceed to give an example application of our non-interactive zero-knowledge arguments to provide publicly verifiable arguments in the context of electronic voting. In voting systems such as Helios [1] voters submit their votes encrypted under a homomorphic encryption scheme accompanied with non-interactive arguments (typically using the Fiat-Shamir transformation) that the encrypted votes are in fact valid. Ciphertexts with convincing arguments are aggregated homomorphically to produce an encrypted tally which is then decrypted to produce the result. By releasing the designated verifier keys to the public (similar to [29]), once vote submission has concluded, we can use our non-interactive designated verifier arguments in place of the usual non-interactive zero-knowledge arguments with minimal changes to the design.

1.2 Related Work

Since the introduction of non-interactive zero-knowledge proofs by Blum, Feldman and Micali [5] much effort has been spent on reducing their size [10,15, 19,24]. The introduction of pairing-based techniques [18,21,22] has led to practically efficient non-interactive zero-knowledge proofs that can be used in the context of pairing-based cryptography.

The Fiat-Shamir heuristic can be used to make a Σ-protocol non-interactive. This can lead to highly efficient non-interactive zero-knowledge proofs but relies on the random oracle model when proving security. Recently pairing-based succinct non-interactive zero-knowledge arguments [14,20,27] have become very compact even for large scale statements, however, they rely on knowledge extractor assumptions over bilinear groups.

The above research yields non-interactive zero-knowledge proofs that are publicly verifiable. However, there are many settings where it suffices to have non-interactive zero-knowledge arguments intended for a designated verifier. Cramer and Shoup used universal hash proofs to build a highly efficient chosen ciphertext attack secure public-key encryption scheme [8,9]. Non-interactive proofs for a designated verifier for all languages in NP can be found in [2] in the key registration model where parties register keys.

The most closely related works are the DFN transformation by Damgård, Fazio and Nicolosi [11] and the work by Ventre and Visconti [28] that we have already discussed.

2   Preliminaries

We write $y = A(x; r)$ when the algorithm A on input x and randomness r, outputs y. We write $y \leftarrow A(x)$ for the process of picking randomness r at random and setting $y = A(x; r)$. We also write $y \leftarrow S$ for sampling y uniformly at random from the set S.

All algorithms get as input a security parameter n written in unary as 1^n. Sometimes we do not explicitly write this input to the algorithms but we will always assume it is implicitly available to the algorithms. The intuition is that the higher the security parameter, the more secure the cryptographic system.

Given two functions $f, g : \mathbb{N} \to [0, 1]$ we write $f(n) \approx g(n)$ when $|f(n) - g(n)| = O(n^{-c})$ for every constant $c > 0$. We say that f is *negligible* if $f(n) \approx 0$ and that f is *overwhelming* if $f(n) \approx 1$.

An NP-relation is a binary relation R consisting of pairs (x, w) that can be decided in polynomial time in the length of x. We call x the statement and w the witness. The relation R gives rise to a language $L_R = \{x \mid \exists w : (x, w) \in R\}$ of statements in R. To incorporate the security parameter into the relations, we will without loss of generality assume all statements are of a form such that n can be easily derived (all statements in this paper could be reformulated to be of the form $x = (1^n, x')$ although for notational convenience we will not do this) and all statements and witnesses are of size polynomial in n. We define R_n as the relation R restricted to statements corresponding to n.

2.1   Additively Homomorphic Encryption

A public key encryption scheme is a triple of probabilistic polynomial time algorithms $(\mathcal{K}, \mathcal{E}, \mathcal{D})$. The key generation function $\mathcal{K}$ given a security parameter returns a public encryption key ek and a private decryption key dk. The encryption algorithm $\mathcal{E}$ given an encryption key ek and a message m returns a ciphertext $c \leftarrow \mathcal{E}_{ek}(m)$. The deterministic decryption algorithm $\mathcal{D}$ given a decryption key dk and a ciphertext c returns a message m or a special symbol $\perp$ if the ciphertext is invalid.

The public encryption key ek defines a message space $\mathcal{M}_{ek}$ of possible plaintexts, a randomness space $\mathcal{R}_{ek}$ and a ciphertext space $\mathcal{C}_{ek}$. In this paper we will make use of an encryption scheme where the message space is $\mathbb{Z}_p$ for some large integer p, which is explicitly or implicitly defined by the public key, and with size $|p| = \ell_p(n)$ for a publicly known polynomial ℓ_p. We say that $(\mathcal{K}, \mathcal{E}, \mathcal{D})$ is *additively homomorphic* if the randomness and ciphertext spaces are finite groups as well (written additively and multiplicatively respectively) and for all possible keys ek and plaintexts $m_1, m_2 \in \mathcal{M}_{ek}$ and $r_1, r_2 \in \mathcal{R}_{ek}$ we have

$$\mathcal{E}_{ek}(m_1; r_1) \cdot \mathcal{E}_{ek}(m_2; r_2) = \mathcal{E}_{ek}(m_1 + m_2; r_1 + r_2).$$

We say that an additively homomorphic scheme $(\mathcal{K}, \mathcal{E}, \mathcal{D})$ is a *strongly additively homomorphic scheme* if it satisfies the four additional properties described below:

Prime order message space: The message space is $\mathbb{Z}_p$ for some *prime p*.

Decryption homomorphic[2]: Membership of the ciphertext space can be efficiently tested and the decryption algorithm on all elements in $\mathcal{C}_{ek}$ returns a plaintext in $\mathcal{M}_{ek}$ (i.e., decryption does not fail). Furthermore, decryptions respect the additively homomorphic operation, i.e., for all possible key pairs (ek, dk) and $c_1, c_2 \in \mathcal{C}_{ek}$ we have

$$\mathcal{D}_{dk}(c_1) + \mathcal{D}_{dk}(c_2) = \mathcal{D}_{dk}(c_1 \cdot c_2).$$

Extended randomness: $R_{ek} = \mathbb{Z}_N$ for some integer N but the encryption function accepts randomness in $\mathbb{Z}$ and for all $m \in \mathcal{M}_{ek}$ and $r \in \mathbb{Z}$

$$\mathcal{E}(m; r) = \mathcal{E}(m; r \bmod N).$$

Verifiable keys: There exists an efficient test VerifyKey($1^n, ek, dk$) that given a public key ek and decryption key dk (or without loss of generality the randomness used in the key generation) returns 1 if and only if (ek, dk) is a valid key pair using security parameter n.

For notational convenience, we let c^z be the vector $(c^{z_1}, \ldots, c^{z_n})$ given a ciphertext c and a vector of integers $z = (z_1, \ldots, z_n)$. Given a vector w we also define $c \leftarrow \mathcal{E}_{ek}(w)$ as the vector of ciphertexts given by $(\mathcal{E}_{ek}(w_1), \ldots, \mathcal{E}_{ek}(w_n))$.

Definition 1 (IND-CPA security). *We say that $(\mathcal{K}, \mathcal{E}, \mathcal{D})$ is indistinguishable under chosen plaintext attack (IND-CPA secure) if for all probabilistic polynomial time stateful adversaries $\mathcal{A}$*

$$\Pr\left[(ek, dk) \leftarrow \mathcal{K}(1^n); (m_0, m_1) \leftarrow \mathcal{A}(ek); b \leftarrow \{0, 1\}; c \leftarrow \mathcal{E}_{ek}(m_b) : \mathcal{A}(c) = b\right] \approx \frac{1}{2},$$

where $\mathcal{A}$ outputs $m_0, m_1 \in \mathcal{M}_{ek}$.

Okamoto-Uchiyama Encryption [26]. The Okamoto-Uchiyama [26] cryptosystem is strongly additively homomorphic with a message space $\mathbb{Z}_p$ for a prime p that is implicitly defined by the public key.

$\mathcal{K}(1^n)$: Pick two different $\ell_p(n)$-bit primes p, q and let $N = p^2 \cdot q$. Then choose a random g in $\mathbb{Z}_N^*$ such that $g \bmod p^2$ has order $p(p - 1)$ in $\mathbb{Z}_{p^2}^*$. The public key is $ek = (N, g)$ and the secret decryption key is $dk = (ek, p)$.

$\mathcal{E}_{ek}(m)$: Given $m \in \mathbb{Z}_p$ return $\mathcal{E}_{ek}(m; r) = g^{m+rN} \bmod N$, where $r \leftarrow \mathbb{Z}_N$.

$\mathcal{D}_{dk}(c)$: Return $m = \frac{L(c^{p-1} \bmod p^2)}{L(g^{p-1} \bmod p^2)} \bmod p$, where $L(x) = \frac{x-1}{p}$.

For a given public key $ek = (N, g)$ the randomness space is $\mathbb{Z}_N$ and the ciphertext space is $\mathbb{Z}_N^*$. Even though the message space is defined as $\mathbb{Z}_p$, in practice we cannot disclose p but as long as the encrypting party picks messages

---

[2] This property is trivial for cryptosystems where the entire cipherspace consists of valid encryptions but in the general case it must be stated explicitly.

$m \in \{0,1\}^{\ell_p(n)-1}$ we are guaranteed that they fall within the message space and will decrypt correctly.

Direct calculation confirms that Okamoto-Uchiyama encryption is decryption homomorphic and that it is easy to extend the randomness space to $R_{ek} = \mathbb{Z}$. The keys are verifiable in the sense that given the decryption key, i.e., the factorization of N, it is easy to check that the keys are a valid output of the key generation algorithm and that the encryption scheme satisfies all the required properties.

2.2 Σ-Protocols with Linear Answers and Unique Identifiable Challenges

A Σ-protocol for an NP-relation R is a 3-move protocol that enables a prover to demonstrate to a verifier that a statement x satisfies $x \in L_R$, i.e. that there exists w such that $(x, w) \in R$ without disclosing anything else, in particular not disclosing the value of w that the prover has in mind. A typical run of a Σ-proocol is illustrated in Fig. 1.

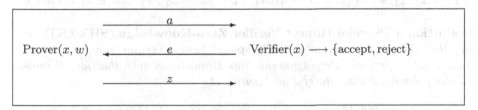

Fig. 1. Σ-protocol with statement x and witness w

A Σ-protocol is *public-coin*, which means that the challenge e chosen by the verifier is picked uniformly at random without the verifier storing any private information about it. We will consider protocols where e is picked as a random n-bit string, where n is the security parameter.

We will restrict ourselves to Σ-protocols with a *linear answer over the integers*. By this we mean without loss of generality that we can consider a prover that generates the initial message a and two integer vectors z_1 and z_2. The answer to a challenge $e \in \{0,1\}^n$ can then be computed as the integer vector $z = ez_1 + z_2$. We will assume that all the integers in z_1, z_2, z are non-negative and that there is a known polynomial upper bound $\ell_z(n)$ on the bit-size of the integers.

We can now describe a Σ-protocol for an NP-relation R with linear answer as a pair $(\mathcal{P}_\Sigma, \mathcal{V}_\Sigma)$, where $\mathcal{P}_\Sigma, \mathcal{V}_\Sigma$ are probabilistic polynomial time algorithms. The Σ-protocol runs as follows:

$(a, z_1, z_2) \leftarrow \mathcal{P}_\Sigma(x, w)$: The prover given a statement and witness pair $(x, w) \in R_n$ generates an initial message a and a state z_1, z_2.

$e \leftarrow \{0,1\}^n$: An n-bit challenge is chosen uniformly at random.

$z \leftarrow ez_1 + z_2$: An answer to the challenge e can be computed as $z = ez_1 + z_2$.

$\{0,1\} \leftarrow \mathcal{V}_\Sigma(x, a, e, z)$: The verifier given a statement x and a protocol transcript (a, e, z) returns 1 if accepting and 0 if rejecting. The verifier will always reject if any inputs are malformed, for instance if $e \notin \{0,1\}^n$ or z contains an entry $z_i \notin \{0,1\}^{\ell_z(n)}$.

A Σ-protocol is required to operate correctly when used by honest participants (*completeness*), to prevent dishonest provers from convincing verifiers that false statements hold (*soundness*), and not to leak information about w (*zero-knowledge*). Formally, we require that a Σ-protocol $(\mathcal{P}_\Sigma, \mathcal{V}_\Sigma)$ for an NP-relation R with linear answer should be complete and special honest verifier zero-knowledge as defined below. With respect to soundness, we will for our purposes be interested in a special class of Σ-protocols that have unique identifiable challenges.

Definition 2 (Completeness). *We say $(\mathcal{P}_\Sigma, \mathcal{V}_\Sigma)$ is perfectly complete if for all $n \in \mathbb{N}$ and $(x, w) \in R_n$*

$$\Pr\left[(a, z_1, z_2) \leftarrow \mathcal{P}_\Sigma(x, w); e \leftarrow \{0,1\}^n; z = ez_1 + z_2 : \mathcal{V}_\Sigma(x, a, e, z) = 1\right] = 1.$$

Definition 3 (Special Honest Verifier Zero-Knowledge (SHVZK)). *We say that $(\mathcal{P}_\Sigma, \mathcal{V}_\Sigma)$ is computationally special honest verifier zero-knowledge if there exists a probabilistic polynomial time simulator S such that for all probabilistic polynomial time stateful adversaries $\mathcal{A}$*

$$\Pr\left[\begin{array}{l}(x, w) \leftarrow \mathcal{A}(1^n); (a, z_1, z_2) \leftarrow \mathcal{P}_\Sigma(x, w); e \leftarrow \{0,1\}^n; z \leftarrow ez_1 + z_2 : \\ (x, w) \in R_n \text{ and } \mathcal{A}(a, e, z) = 1\end{array}\right]$$

$$\approx \Pr\left[\begin{array}{l}(x, w) \leftarrow \mathcal{A}(1^n); e \leftarrow \{0,1\}^n; (a, z) \leftarrow S(x, e) : \\ (x, w) \in R_n \text{ and } \mathcal{A}(a, e, z) = 1\end{array}\right]$$

If this holds also for unbounded adversaries $\mathcal{A}$, we say $(\mathcal{P}_\Sigma, \mathcal{V}_\Sigma)$ is statistically special honest verifier zero-knowledge.

Traditionally, Σ-protocols are required to have *special soundness*, which says that if the prover, after having created the initial message a, can answer two different challenges e and e' then it is possible to compute a witness w for the statement x being proved such that $(x, w) \in R$.

We do not need the witness to be extractable in this paper and will therefore relax the soundness definition to just saying that on a false statement there is at most a single unique challenge the prover can answer after having created the initial message a.

However, we will require that under certain circumstances this unique answerable challenge should be identifiable, i.e., if the prover "knows" the statement is false in a certain way then she can actually compute the unique challenge e she will be able to answer if she can answer any challenge at all. We define this by adapting the notion of culpable soundness from [21]. We say that the unique challenge is identifiable using an NP-relation R_{guilt}, which only contains false statements, if when the prover produces a statement x and a witness w_{guilt} of being guilty of cheating such that $(x, w_{\text{guilt}}) \in R_{\text{guilt}}$, then it is possible to efficiently compute a unique challenge where the verifier may possibly accept. The relation R_{guilt} will typically include all false statements that have a special form, depending on the specifics.

Definition 4 (Soundness with unique identifiable challenge). *We say $(\mathcal{P}_\Sigma, \mathcal{V}_\Sigma)$ has a unique identifiable challenge using NP-relation R_{guilt} if there is a polynomial time algorithm E that takes as input the statement, witness and initial message and returns the unique challenge e that can be answered. Formally, we require that for all $n, x, w_{\text{guilt}}, a, e, z$ where $(x, w_{\text{guilt}}) \in R_{\text{guilt},n}$ and $\mathcal{V}_\Sigma(x, a, e, z) = 1$ that $e = E(x, w_{\text{guilt}}, a)$.*

A frequently asked question is why would the adversary want to provide a witness for cheating. The answer is that there are many natural scenarios where the real adversary is only a part of a larger system that contains the guilt witness. It may well be that the system would never provide a guilt witness in a normal execution but even when that is the case the notion can still be useful in security proofs: by framing a "standard" adversary within such a system we are able to explicitly use privileged information held by honest parties in security reductions. In Sect. 4 we give voting as a concrete example of how culpable soundness can be used to prevent cheating by voters. Voters prove that they have encrypted valid votes using the election system's public key. The guilt witness is the decryption key, which the voting system will never make public since it would reveal all the votes. However, if a cheating voter exists, it is enough to point out that the guilt witness will exist in the possession of the electoral authorities. To satisfy the definition we may consider a new adversary which consists of the cheating voter's behaviour, with the decryption key added to the output in a post-processing step. Culpable soundness then guarantees the voter cannot cheat and submit an invalid vote.

We note that the extractor E only requires the guilt witness and the initial message from the prover. This will be critical in the next section where the protocol is made non-interactive via the DFN transformation and the prover's answer will be encrypted. In general, we cannot require that a cheating prover knows the contents of that ciphertext since it might have been assembled in a way that differs from the protocol.

Σ-protocol for Additively Homomorphic Encryption of 0 or 1. Consider a strongly additively homomorphic encryption scheme $(\mathcal{G}, \mathcal{E}, \mathcal{D})$ with message space $\mathbb{Z}_p$ for a prime p defined by the encryption key. We will now give a Σ-protocol for proving that a ciphertext encrypts 0 or 1 using randomness $r \in \{0,1\}^{\ell_r(n)}$ bounded by a polynomial $\ell_r(n)$.

Let

$$R = \left\{ \big((ek, c), (m, r)\big) : m \in \{0,1\} \text{ and } r \in \{0,1\}^{\ell_r(n)} \text{ and } c = \mathcal{E}_{ek}(m; r) \right\},$$

$$\boxed{\begin{array}{ll}
\text{Prover}((ek,c),(m,r)) & \text{Verifier}(ek,c) \\[4pt]
m_a \leftarrow \{1\}\|\{0,1\}^{2n} & \text{Accept if and only if} \\
r_a \leftarrow \{0,1\}^{\ell_r(n)+2n}; a \leftarrow \mathcal{E}_{ek}(m_a;r_a) & a,b,c \in \mathcal{C}_{ek}, f \in \{0,1\}^{2n+2} \\
r_b \leftarrow \{0,1\}^{\ell_r(n)+3n}; b \leftarrow \mathcal{E}_{ek}(-mm_a;r_b) & z_a \in \{0,1\}^{\ell_r(n)+2n+1} \\
 & z_b \in \{0,1\}^{\ell_r(n)+3n+1} \\
f := em + m_a, z_a := er + r_a & c^e a = \mathcal{E}_{ek}(f;z_a) \\
z_b := (f-e)r + r_b & c^{f-e}b = \mathcal{E}_{ek}(0;z_b)
\end{array}}$$

With arrows: $\xrightarrow{\quad a,b \quad}$, $\xleftarrow{\ e \leftarrow \{0,1\}^n\ }$, $\xrightarrow{\ f, z_a, z_b\ }$

Fig. 2. Σ-protocol for encryption of 0 or 1

$$R_{\text{guilt}} = \left\{ \left((ek,c),dk\right) : c \in \mathcal{C}_{ek} \text{ and } \mathcal{D}_{dk}(c) \notin \{0,1\} \text{ and } \text{VerifyKey}(1^n,ek,dk)=1 \right\}.$$

Theorem 1. *Fig. 2 describes a Σ-protocol for R with linear answer and unique identifiable challenge using R_{guilt} assuming $(\mathcal{G},\mathcal{E},\mathcal{D})$ is a strongly additively homomorphic encryption scheme with message space $\mathbb{Z}_p$ of sufficiently large size such that $\ell_p(n) > n$.*

Proof. The algorithms are probabilistic polynomial time. The protocol has linear answer with a polynomial upper bound of $\ell_z(n) = \ell_r(n) + 3n + 1$ on the bit-lengths of the integers in the answer. Direct verification shows that the protocol is perfectly complete.

The protocol is statistical SHVZK. The simulator given challenge $e \in \{0,1\}^n$ picks $f \leftarrow \{1\}\|\{0,1\}^{2n}$, $z_a \leftarrow \{0,1\}^{\ell_r(n)+2n}$ and $z_b \leftarrow \{0,1\}^{\ell_r(n)+3n}$. It then computes $a = c^{-e}\mathcal{E}_{ek}(f;z_a)$ and $b = c^{e-f}\mathcal{E}_{ek}(0;z_b)$ and returns the simulated proof (a,b,f,z_a,z_b). Observe that the simulated f, z_a, z_b are statistically close to those of a real proof. To see the simulation is statistically indistinguishable from a real proof with challenge e all that remains to be seen is that given f, z_a, z_b, the initial message containing a, b is fixed by the verification equations in both real and simulated proofs.

Finally, let us show that the protocol has unique identifiable challenges using R_{guilt}. A witness in R_{guilt} gives us the decryption key for the encryption scheme. We can verify the correctness of the decryption key and decrypt c to get m and also decrypt a, b to get plaintexts m_a and m_b. In a succesful argument, the value f must be $f = em + m_a \bmod p$ since otherwise the first verification equation would fail. The second verification equation gives us $(f-e)m + m_b = 0 \bmod p$, which means $e(m-1)m + m_a m + m_b = 0 \bmod p$. If $m \notin \{0,1\}$ we have that $(m-1)m \neq 0 \bmod p$ and therefore the equation uniquely determines $e \bmod p$. With $p > 2^n$ this identifies at a unique challenge $e \in \{0,1\}^n$ that the prover may be able to answer or shows that no answerable challenge exists.   □

2.3   Non-interactive Designated Verifier Zero-Knowledge Arguments

It is often desirable to operate in a single step, avoiding the interaction needed to execute a Σ-protocol. The prover still wishes to demonstrate to the verifier the truth of a statement $x \in L_R$ for an NP-relation R without disclosing any other information about her witness w.

In a non-interactive designated verifier zero-knowledge argument system, we imagine the verifier sets up a public key pk for the proof together with a secret verification key vk that can be used to verify the arguments. The system therefore consists of three probabilistic polynomial time algorithms $(\mathcal{G}, \mathcal{P}, \mathcal{V})$.

$(pk, vk) \leftarrow \mathcal{G}(1^n)$: The key generation algorithm, given the security parameter as input, generates a public key pk and a secret verification key vk.

$\pi \leftarrow \mathcal{P}(pk, x, w)$: Given a public key pk and $(x, w) \in R_n$, the prover algorithm generates an argument π.

$\{0, 1\} \leftarrow \mathcal{V}(vk, x, \pi)$: Given a secret verification key vk, a statement x and an argument π, the verification algorithm returns 1 if accepting the argument and 0 for rejection of the argument.

$(\mathcal{G}, \mathcal{P}, \mathcal{V})$ is said to be a non-interactive designated verifier zero-knowledge argument system for R with culpable soundness with respect to R_{guilt} if it is complete, culpably sound and zero-knowledge as defined below.

Definition 5 (Completeness). $(\mathcal{G}, \mathcal{P}, \mathcal{V})$ *is perfectly complete if for all* $n \in \mathbb{N}$ *and all* $(x, w) \in R_n$

$$\Pr\left[(pk, vk) \leftarrow \mathcal{G}(1^n); \pi \leftarrow \mathcal{P}(pk, x, w) : \mathcal{V}(vk, x, \pi) = 1\right] = 1.$$

Intuitively, the argument is zero-knowledge if it does not leak information about the witness. The arguments we construct will be zero-knowledge assuming the keys are honestly generated. We define this notion through the existence of a simulator that can simulate arguments given the verifier's secret verification key. In our constructions we will get zero-knowledge even if the adversary knows the secret verification key, a strong type of zero-knowledge called composable zero-knowledge in [18] due to it making composition of zero-knowledge proofs easier.

Definition 6 (Composable zero-knowledge). $(\mathcal{G}, \mathcal{P}, \mathcal{V})$ *is computationally composable zero-knowledge if for all probabilistic polynomial time stateful adversaries* $\mathcal{A}$

$$\Pr\left[(pk, vk) \leftarrow \mathcal{G}(1^n); (x, w) \leftarrow \mathcal{A}(pk, vk); \pi \leftarrow \mathcal{P}(pk, x, w) : (x, w) \in R_n \text{ and } \mathcal{A}(\pi) = 1\right]$$
$$\approx \Pr\left[(pk, vk) \leftarrow \mathcal{G}(1^n); (x, w) \leftarrow \mathcal{A}(pk, vk); \pi \leftarrow \mathcal{S}(vk, x) : (x, w) \in R_n \text{ and } \mathcal{A}(\pi) = 1\right].$$

If the above holds also for unbounded stateful adversaries $\mathcal{A}$ *then we say the argument is statistically composable zero-knowledge.*

Culpable soundness [21] is a relaxation of soundness that restricts the prover in the following way: First, we only consider false statements in a subset L_{guilt} of $\bar{L}_R$ characterised by a relation R_{guilt}. Second, we require a successful cheating prover to also output a guilt witness w_{guilt} along with his false statement x such that $(x, w_{\mathrm{guilt}}) \in R_{\mathrm{guilt}}$. Intuitively this definition captures the notion of a malicious prover being aware of the falsehood of the statement for which she is creating a fake proof.

Definition 7 (Adaptive culpable soundness). *We say* $(\mathcal{G}, \mathcal{P}, \mathcal{V})$ *is culpably sound with respect to the relation* R_{guilt} *if for all probabilistic polynomial time* $\mathcal{A}$

$$\Pr\left[(pk, vk) \leftarrow \mathcal{G}(1^n); (x, \pi, w_{\text{guilt}}) \leftarrow \mathcal{A}(pk) : (x, w_{\text{guilt}}) \in R_{\text{guilt}, n} \text{ and } \mathcal{V}(vk, x, \pi) = 1\right] \approx 0.$$

The above definition does not directly cover the adversary, $\mathcal{A}$ having access to a verification oracle $\mathcal{V}(vk, \cdot, \cdot)$. However it is straightforward to handle cases where the adversary has access to a logarithmic number of queries (as in [11]), since that can be simulated by guessing the responses with inverse polynomial probability.

3 Transformation

We will now use the DFN transformation on a Σ-protocol with linear answer over the integers and unique identifiable challenges to get a non-interactive designated verifier argument. The verifier uses an additively homomorphic encryption scheme $(\mathcal{K}, \mathcal{E}, \mathcal{D})$ to encrypt a random challenge e. Since the Σ-protocol has linear answer, the prover can now use the homomorphic property of the encryption scheme to compute an encryption of the answer z in the Σ-protocol, which is sent together with the initial message a. The verifier decrypts the ciphertext from the prover to get z and checks whether (a, e, z) is a valid proof. The full non-interactive designated verifier argument is described in Fig. 3.

$\mathcal{G}(1^n)$	$\mathcal{P}(pk, x, w)$	$\mathcal{V}(vk, x, \pi)$
$(ek, dk) \leftarrow \mathcal{K}(1^n)$	$(a, z_1, z_2) \leftarrow \mathcal{P}_\Sigma(x, w)$	Parse $\pi = (a, c_z)$
$e \leftarrow \{0, 1\}^n$	$c_z \leftarrow c^{z_1} \mathcal{E}_{ek}(z_2)$	$z \leftarrow \mathcal{D}_{dk}(c_z)$
$c \leftarrow \mathcal{E}_{ek}(e)$	Return $\pi := (a, c_z)$	Return $\mathcal{V}_\Sigma(x, a, e, z)$
$pk := (ek, c)$		
$vk := (dk, e)$		
Return (pk, vk)		

Fig. 3. Non-interactive designated verifier argument

Theorem 2. $(\mathcal{G}, \mathcal{P}, \mathcal{V})$ *specified in Fig. 3 is a non-interactive designated verifier argument for* R *with culpable soundness for* R_{guilt} *if* $(\mathcal{P}_\Sigma, \mathcal{V}_\Sigma)$ *is a* Σ-protocol for R *with linear answer over the integers and soundness with unique identifiable challenge using* R_{guilt} *and if* $(\mathcal{K}, \mathcal{E}, \mathcal{D})$ *is an additively homomorphic, IND-CPA secure public key encryption scheme where* $\mathbb{Z}_p$ *is of sufficiently large size to include the answers, i.e.,* $\ell_p(n) > \ell_z(n)$.

Proof. Since $(\mathcal{P}_\Sigma, \mathcal{V}_\Sigma)$ and $(\mathcal{K}, \mathcal{E}, \mathcal{D})$ are probabilistic polynomial time algorithms so are $(\mathcal{G}, \mathcal{P}, \mathcal{V})$. Perfect completeness follows from the additive homomorphicity of the encryption scheme and that $0 \leq z_i < 2^{\ell_z(n)} < p$ for all entries z_i in z combined with the perfect completeness of $(\mathcal{P}_\Sigma, \mathcal{V}_\Sigma)$.

Next, we will prove that the construction is zero-knowledge. The simulator knows the secret verification key $vk = (dk, e)$. It starts by running the SHVZK simulator for the Σ-protocol to get a simulated proof (a, e, z) for the statement x. It then generates $c_z \leftarrow \mathcal{E}_{ek}(z)$ and returns the simulated argument $\pi := (a, c_z)$.

To see a that simulated argument is indistinguishable from a real argument consider a hybrid simulator that does get the witness as input. This hybrid simulator proceeds by following the Σ-protocol to get an argument (a, e, z) and then encrypts z to get c_z. Since the encryption scheme is also homomorphic with respect to the randomness used for encryption, the hybrid arguments generated this way and real arguments are perfectly indistinguishable. Furthermore, since the Σ-protocol is SHVZK, hybrid arguments and simulated arguments are computationally indistinguishable. Furthermore, if the Σ-protocol has statistical SHVZK then the hybrid arguments and simulated arguments are statistically indistinguishable.

Finally, we will prove that the construction has adaptive culpable soundness with respect to R_{guilt}. Plugging our construction into the probability defining culpable soundness with a probabilistic polynomial time adversary $\mathcal{A}$ we get

$$\Pr\left[\begin{array}{l} (ek, dk) \leftarrow \mathcal{G}(1^n); e \leftarrow \{0,1\}^n; c \leftarrow \mathcal{E}_{ek}(e) \\ (x, (a, c_z), w_{\text{guilt}}) \leftarrow \mathcal{A}(ek, c); z \leftarrow \mathcal{D}_{dk}(c_z) \end{array} : \begin{array}{l} (x, w_{\text{guilt}}) \in R_{\text{guilt}} \\ \mathcal{V}_\Sigma(x, a, e, z) = 1 \end{array} \right].$$

By the unique identifiable challenge property of the Σ-protocol this probability is at most the chance that e is the unique answerable challenge:

$$\Pr\left[\begin{array}{l} (ek, dk) \leftarrow \mathcal{G}(1^n); e \leftarrow \{0,1\}^n; c \leftarrow \mathcal{E}_{ek}(e) \\ (x, (a, c_z), w_{\text{guilt}}) \leftarrow \mathcal{A}(ek, c); z \leftarrow \mathcal{D}_{dk}(c_z) \end{array} : \begin{array}{l} (x, w_{\text{guilt}}) \in R_{\text{guilt}} \\ e = E(x, w_{\text{guilt}}, a) \end{array} \right].$$

By the IND-CPA security of the encryption scheme, this probability is at most negligibly larger than the same expression with c encrypting a random challenge e'

$$\Pr\left[\begin{array}{l} (ek, dk) \leftarrow \mathcal{G}(1^n); e, e' \leftarrow \{0,1\}^n; c \leftarrow \mathcal{E}_{ek}(e') \\ (x, (a, c_z), w_{\text{guilt}}) \leftarrow \mathcal{A}(ek, c); z \leftarrow \mathcal{D}_{dk}(c_z) \end{array} : \begin{array}{l} (x, w_{\text{guilt}}) \in R_{\text{guilt}} \\ e = E(x, w_{\text{guilt}}, a) \end{array} \right].$$

Since e is chosen uniformly random this latter probability is at most 2^{-n}, which is negligible. $\qquad\square$

3.1 Non-interactive Designated Verifier Arguments for Statements about Ciphertexts

In Sect. 2.2 we gave a Σ-protocol for proving a ciphertext having either 0 or 1 as plaintext. Using the DFN transformation, this leads to a non-interactive designated verifier argument with culpable soundness for a ciphertext encrypting 0 or 1, i.e., for the relation

$$R = \left\{ ((ek, c), (m, r)) : m \in \{0, 1\} \text{ and } r \in \{0, 1\}^{\ell_r(n)} \text{ and } c = \mathcal{E}_{ek}(m; r) \right\}$$

with culpable soundness using

$$R_{\text{guilt}} = \left\{ ((ek, c), dk) : c \in \mathcal{C}_{ek} \text{ and } \mathcal{D}_{dk}(c) \notin \{0, 1\} \text{ and } \text{VerifyKey}(1^n, ek, dk) = 1 \right\}.$$

This designated verifier argument works for ciphertexts produced by all strongly additively homomorphic encryption schemes that have message space $\mathbb{Z}_p$ for $p > 2^n$ such as for instance the Okamoto-Uchiyama [26] encryption scheme from Sect. 2.1. A second instance of the same strongly additively homomorphic encryption scheme but with larger message space can also be used for the DFN transformation. However, in the interest of more efficient implementations, it might be desirable to use a different encryption scheme for the DFN transformation. Specifically, DFN does not require the message space to be of prime order or the scheme to be *strongly* additively homomorphic, giving us the option of using an encryption scheme better suited for encrypting long messages such as Damgård-Jurik [12].

It is fairly simple to adapt standard Σ-protocols for other languages expressing properties about ciphertexts. In particular, in addition to the argument for encryption of 0 or 1 it is possible to construct non-interactive designated verifier arguments for the following relations:

Plaintext is 0: We can prove that a ciphertext c encrypts 0, i.e., give a non-interactive designated verifier argument for the relation

$$R^0 = \left\{ ((ek, c), r) : r \in \{0, 1\}^{\ell_r(n)} \text{ and } c = \mathcal{E}_{ek}(0; r) \right\}.$$

Equivalence of plaintexts: Given two ciphertexts c and c', we can give a non-interactive designated verifier argument for them having the same plaintext by proving that c/c' is an encryption of 0 using the above designated verifier argument.

Multiplicative relationship: Given a triple of ciphertexts c_0, c_1 and c_2, we can prove that the plaintexts m_0, m_1 and m_2 satisfy $m_0 = m_1 m_2 \bmod p$. More precisely, we can construct a designated verifier argument for the relation

$$R^M = \left\{ \begin{array}{c} ((ek, c_0, c_1, c_2), (m_1, m_2, r_0, r_1, r_2)) : m_1, m_2 \in \mathbb{Z}_p, r_0, r_1, r_2 \in \{0, 1\}^{\ell_r(n)} \\ c_0 = \mathcal{E}_{ek}(m_1 m_2; r_0) \text{ and } c_1 = \mathcal{E}_{ek}(m_1; r_1) \text{ and } c_2 = \mathcal{E}_{ek}(m_2; r_2) \end{array} \right\}.$$

In all cases, the corresponding guilt witness w_{guilt} consists of the decryption key, which can be used to decrypt the ciphertexts in the statement.

Circuit Satisfiability. We will now show that given a circuit consisting of NAND-gates and encryptions of the wires it is possible to prove that the plaintexts correspond to a satisfying assignment. A circuit C with $k + 1$ wires and s gates can be described as $\{(j_1, j_2, j_3)\}_{j=1}^{s}$, which means that the wires should satisfy $w_{j_3} = \neg(w_{j_1} \wedge w_{j_2})$. We let the output wire be $w_0 = 1$ and the corresponding ciphertext be $c_0 = \mathcal{E}_{ek}(1; 0)$ encrypted with randomness $r_0 = 0$. We consider the relations:

$$R^C = \left\{ \begin{array}{c} ((C, ek, c_1, \ldots, c_k), (w_1, r_1, \ldots, w_k, r_k)) \mid \forall j = 1, \ldots, s : w_{j_3} = \neg(w_{j_1} \wedge w_{j_2}) \\ \forall i = 1, \ldots, k : w_i \in \{0, 1\} \wedge r_i \in \{0, 1\}^{\ell_r(n)-2} \wedge c_i = \mathcal{E}_{ek}(w_i; r_i) \end{array} \right\},$$

$$R_{\text{guilt}}^C = \left\{ \begin{array}{c} ((C, ek, c_1, \ldots, c_k), dk) \mid \text{VerifyKey}(1^n, ek, dk) = 1 \text{ and } \forall i = 1, \ldots k : c_i \in \mathcal{C}_{ek} \\ \exists i \in \{1, \ldots, k\} : w_i = \mathcal{D}_{dk}(c_i) \notin \{0, 1\} \text{ or } \exists j \in \{1, \ldots, s\} : w_{j_3} \neq \neg(w_{j_1} \wedge w_{j_2}) \end{array} \right\}.$$

The strategy in the designated verifier argument for R^C is to first prove that each ciphertext contains a wire value $w_i \in \{0, 1\}$. Next, the prover proves for each NAND-gate (j_1, j_2, j_3) that $w_{j_3} = \neg(w_{j_1} \wedge w_{j_2})$. Following [21] we have for $w_{j_1}, w_{j_2}, w_{j_3} \in \{0, 1\}$

$$w_{j_3} = \neg(w_{j_1} \wedge w_{j_2}) \quad \text{if and only if} \quad w_{j_1} + w_{j_2} + 2w_{j_3} - 2 \in \{0, 1\}.$$

Using the homomorphic properties of the encryption scheme, we will therefore for each NAND-gate show $c_{j_1} c_{j_2} c_{j_3}^2 \mathcal{E}_{ek}(-2; 0)$ contains 0 or 1. The full construction can be found in Fig. 4

$\mathcal{P}^C(pk, (C, ek, c_1, \dots, c_k), (w_1, r_1, \dots, w_k, r_k))$	$\mathcal{V}^C(vk, (C, ek, c_1, \dots, c_k), \pi)$
$w_0 = 1, r_0 = 0, c_0 = \mathcal{E}_{ek}(w_0; r_0)$	$w_0 = 1, r_0 = 0, c_0 = \mathcal{E}_{ek}(w_0; r_0)$
For $i = 1, \dots, k$	Parse $C = \{(j_1, j_2, j_3)\}_{j=1}^s$
$\quad \pi_i \leftarrow \mathcal{P}(pk, c_i, (w_i, r_i))$	For $j = 1, \dots, s$
Parse $C = \{(j_1, j_2, j_3)\}_{j=1}^s$	$\quad c_j' = c_{j_1} c_{j_2} c_{j_3}^2 \mathcal{E}_{ek}(-2; 0)$
For $j = 1, \dots, s$	Parse $\pi = (\pi_1, \dots, \pi_k, \pi_1', \dots, \pi_s')$
$\quad c_j' = c_{j_1} c_{j_2} c_{j_3}^2 \mathcal{E}_{ek}(-2; 0)$	Accept if and only if
$\quad m_j' = w_{j_1} + w_{j_2} + 2w_{j_3} - 2$	For $i = 1, \dots, k$
$\quad r_j' = r_{j_1} + r_{j_2} + 2r_{j_3}$	$\quad \mathcal{V}(vk, c_i, \pi_i) = 1$
$\quad \pi_j' \leftarrow \mathcal{P}(pk, c_j', (m_j', r_j'))$	For $j = 1, \dots, s$
Return $\pi = (\pi_1, \dots, \pi_k, \pi_1', \dots, \pi_s')$	$\quad \mathcal{V}(vk, c_j', \pi_j') = 1$

Fig. 4. Non-interactive designated verifier argument $(\mathcal{G}^C, \mathcal{P}^C, \mathcal{V}^C)$ for encryption of satisfying assignment of wires in a circuit using $\mathcal{G}^C = \mathcal{G}$ where $(\mathcal{G}, \mathcal{P}, \mathcal{V})$ is a designated verifier argument for encryption of 0 or 1

Theorem 3. $(\mathcal{G}^C, \mathcal{P}^C, \mathcal{V}^C)$ *given in Fig. 4 is a non-interactive designated verifier argument for* R^C *with culpable soundness using* R_{guilt}^C *if* $(\mathcal{G}, \mathcal{P}, \mathcal{V})$ *is a non-interactive designated verifier argument for encryption of 0 or 1 using* R_{guilt} *from Sect. 2.2.*

Proof. Perfect completeness follows from the homomorphic properties of the encryption scheme and the perfect completeness of $(\mathcal{G}, \mathcal{P}, \mathcal{V})$.

We will now prove composable zero-knowledge. The simulator $\mathcal{S}^C(vk, (C, ek, c_1, \dots, c_k))$ runs like the prover except it simulates the proofs $\pi_1, \dots, \pi_k, \pi_1', \dots, \pi_s'$ as $\pi_i \leftarrow \mathcal{S}(vk, (ek, c_i))$ and $\pi_j' \leftarrow \mathcal{S}(vk, c_j')$. A straightforward hybrid argument shows that this is indistinguishable from a real proof.[3]

Finally, we will prove that the argument is culpably sound. By the culpable soundness of $(\mathcal{G}, \mathcal{P}, \mathcal{V})$ when we are given dk by the adversary, the proofs

---

[3] We remark that here the usefulness of *composable* zero-knowledge comes into play since the hybrid arguments are indistinguishable even to an adversary with access to the verification key vk, which allows the hybrid argument to go through.

$\pi_1, \ldots, \pi_k$ guarantee each ciphertext contains 0 or 1. The homomorphic property of the encryption scheme combined with the culpable soundness of the proofs $\pi_1', \ldots, \pi_s'$ then shows that the plaintexts respect the NAND-gates. Since the output is $w_0 = 1$ this means the circuit is satisfied by the encrypted values. $\square$

4 Applications in Voting with Homomorphic Tallying

We will use a basic referendum voting scheme as an illustration of how to use non-interactive zero-knowledge designated verifier arguments with culpable soundness. We use a modification of the framework by Bernhard et al. [4] which generalises the Helios voting system. Such schemes operate by having eligible voters post their votes on a bulletin board encrypted with an additively homomorphic encryption scheme. The election result can then be produced by a single decryption operation on the homomorphic sum of the individual votes. Zero-knowledge protocols ensure that the various participating parties remain honest.

4.1 Voting Schemes

We assume a bulletin board BB holds all messages posted by the various participants in the election, and that it behaves honestly for the entirety of the election. During the submission of ballots, it operates in an append-only mode *without* disclosing its contents. After voting has concluded, the bulletin board reveals the ballots it contains and checks their validity. The checks use only public information and as such are reproducible by any party; the bulletin board performs them for convenience. Finally, we assume that the history of the bulletin board is publicly accessible as well as the current state.

Our use of a *delayed* bulletin board is a departure from usual practice and is aimed at preventing attacks based on malleability. The additional trust placed on the board by this requirement may be mitigated by having the bulletin board immediately display commitments to ballots or eliminated by augmenting the ballot encryption to be submission secure [29]. We also note that Cortier et al. [7] develop techniques to guard against misbehaving boards.

In the interest of simplicity, we restrict the options in the referendum to $\{0, 1\}$ without giving the option of casting an abstention ballot. The election is run by two trustees, $\mathcal{T}_D$ and $\mathcal{T}_V$, tasked with holding the decryption and verification keys for the election. We will for simplicity consider them to be trusted parties but they could be implemented using threshold cryptography.

Definition 8 (Voting Scheme). *A voting scheme Π consists of five probabilistic polynomial time algorithms:* **Setup**, **Vote**, **SubmitBallot**, **CheckBoard**, **Tally**, *which operate as follows:*

Setup. *The setup algorithm takes as input a security parameter 1^n. It produces secret information SEC, public information PUB and verification information AUG. It also initialises the bulletin board BB and sets it to be hidden. PUB is assumed to be public knowledge after* **Setup** *has run.*

Vote. *Vote accepts a vote* $m \in \{0, 1\}$ *and outputs a ballot B encoding m.*

SubmitBallot. *SubmitBallot(B, BB) takes as input a ballot B and the current state of the bulletin board BB and outputs either* $(0, BB)$ *if it rejects B or* $(1, BB \overset{+}{\leftarrow} B)$ *if it accepts it.*

CheckBoard. *CheckBoard(BB, AUG) makes BB visible, and then checks all ballots on BB, replacing with* $\perp$ *any ballots that do not pass the verification tests. After checking, the verification information of valid ballots can be removed from the board.*

Tally. *Tally (BB, SEC) takes as input a verified bulletin board BB and the secret information SEC and outputs the election result.*

For correctness we require that the ballots of honest voters are counted correctly, and that ballots cast by malicious voters cannot influence the election more than an honest one (i.e casting q malicious ballots can only add q votes and subtract none).

$\mathbf{Exp}_{\Pi,\mathcal{A}}^{COR}(n)$	$\mathbf{VoteOracle}(v)$
$(PUB, SEC, AUG) \leftarrow \mathbf{Setup}(1^n)$	$B \leftarrow \mathbf{Vote}(v)$
$(vsum, q) \leftarrow (0, 0)$	$(r, BB) \leftarrow \mathbf{SubmitBallot}(B, BB)$
$\mathcal{A}^{\mathbf{VoteOracle}(\cdot), \mathbf{BallotOracle}(\cdot)}(PUB)$	if $r = accept : vsum \leftarrow (vsum + v)$
$BB \leftarrow \mathbf{CheckBoard}(BB, AUG)$	Return (r, B)
$result \leftarrow \mathbf{Tally}(BB, SEC)$	
Return $(result, vsum, q)$	$\mathbf{BallotOracle}(B)$
	$(r, BB) \leftarrow \mathbf{SubmitBallot}(B, BB)$
	$q \leftarrow q + 1$
	Return r

Fig. 5. The referendum correctness experiment, and the oracles provided to the adversary

Definition 9 (Correctness). *We say that a referendum voting scheme* Π *is correct if for all efficient adversaries* $\mathcal{A}$:

$$\Pr\left[(result, vsum, q) \leftarrow \mathbf{Exp}_{\Pi,\mathcal{A}}^{COR}(n) : vsum \leq result \leq q + vsum\right] \approx 1$$

Definition 10 (Ballot Privacy). *We say that a voting scheme* Π *satisfies ballot privacy if for all efficient stateful interactive adversaries* $\mathcal{A}$:

$$\Pr\left[\mathbf{Exp}_{\Pi,\mathcal{A}}^{BP}(n) = 1\right] \approx \frac{1}{2}$$

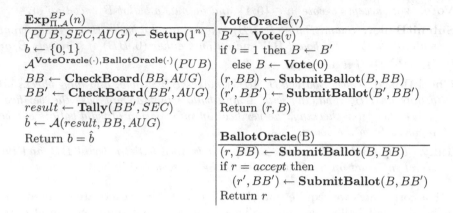

Fig. 6. The Ballot Privacy experiment, and the oracles provided to the adversary

4.2 A Referendum Voting Scheme

We will now describe a voting scheme Π^{REF} for a yes-no referendum, based on an additively homomorphic encryption scheme such as $(\mathcal{K}, \mathcal{E}, \mathcal{D})$ and with a non-interactive designated verifier argument system $(\mathcal{G}, \mathcal{P}, \mathcal{V})$ for a plaintext being 0 or 1 such as the one given in Fig. 3.

For simplicity, we omit correctness proofs for keys having been generated correctly but point out that since the setup involves a limited number of parties we could assume the use of online zero-knowledge protocols using standard techniques. We also assume that the bulletin board behaves honestly. We now give descriptions of the Voting Protocol Algorithms:

Setup. The setup algorithm takes as input a security parameter 1^n. The decryption trustee $\mathcal{T}_D$ runs $K(1^n)$ to produce (ek, dk) and the verification trustee then runs $\mathcal{G}(1^n)$ to obtain (pk, vk). Let, $PUB = (ek, pk)$, $AUG = vk$ and $SEC = dk$. The procedure also initialises the bulletin board BB to be hidden, and publishes PUB.

Vote(m). Pick $r \leftarrow \{0,1\}^{\ell_r(n)}$ and return (c, π), where $c = \mathcal{E}_{ek}(m; r)$ and $\pi \leftarrow \mathcal{P}(pk, (ek, c, r))$.

SubmitBallot(B,BB). Return $(accept, BB \overset{+}{\leftarrow} B)$.

CheckBoard(BB,AUG). The bulletin board BB becomes visible. $\mathcal{T}_V$ publishes AUG. For every ballot $B = (c, \pi)$ in BB we check whether $c \in \mathcal{C}_{ek}$ and $\mathcal{V}(vk, (ek, c), \pi) = 1$. If not, they will be omitted from the tally.

Tally(BB,SEC). The decryption trustee publishes $result = \mathcal{D}_{dk}(\prod_{i=1}^{k} c_i)$, where $c_1, \ldots, c_k$ are the encrypted votes that passed the validity check.

Theorem 4. *The referendum scheme Π^{REF} defined above is correct.*

Proof. Let $\mathcal{A}$ be an adversary against $\mathbf{Exp}_{\Pi,\mathcal{A}}^{COR}(n)$ that causes *result* to be out of bounds with non-negligible probability. We construct a simulator $\mathcal{B}$ that contradicts the adaptive culpable soundness of $(\mathcal{G}, \mathcal{P}, \mathcal{V})$. $\mathcal{B}$ will simulate the correctness experiment for $\mathcal{A}$ while acting as the adversary for the adaptive culpable soundness experiment. $\mathcal{B}$ operates by running the correctness experiment normally with the difference that it does not generate (pk, vk) but instead obtains pk from the adaptive culpable soundness experiment.

Because $(\mathcal{K}, \mathcal{E}, \mathcal{D})$ is correct and additively homomorphic, *result* being out of bounds implies one of the submitted ballots $B = (c, \pi)$ is such that c encrypts a value other than 0 or 1 while at the same time $\mathcal{V}(vk, (ek, c), \pi) = 1$. Choosing one of the q ballots at random, $\mathcal{B}$ outputs $(x, \pi, w_{\mathrm{guilt}})$ to the experiment, where $x = (c, pk)$ and $w_{\mathrm{guilt}} = dk$. Since q is polynomial in n this gives $\mathcal{B}$ a non-negligible probability of winning the experiment. □

Theorem 5. *The scheme* Π^{REF} *satisfies ballot privacy.*

Proof. We will prove that $\mathcal{A}$ can not do better than guess the value of b in the ballot privacy experiment via a series of hybrid games. We exploit the fact that the $(\mathcal{G}, \mathcal{P}, \mathcal{V})$ argument system achieves statistical zero-knowledge, the fact that $(\mathcal{K}, \mathcal{E}, \mathcal{D})$ is IND-CPA secure as well as the delay on the bulletin board. We also take advantage of the fact that in a referendum the number of possible results is linear in the number of votes.

We will focus on the **VoteOracle** calls that the adversary makes, as that is where the experiment diverges depending on b. Let q_v, q_b be upper bounds on the number of **VoteOracle** and **BallotOracle** queries made by $\mathcal{A}$ for a particular security parameter n. Let $q_\Sigma = q_v + q_b$ be the total number of queries.

We define as $\mathbf{Exp}^2$ the experiment $\mathbf{Exp}_{\Pi^{REF},\mathcal{A}}^{BP}$ where all **VoteOracle** calls produce a ballot with a simulated proof π instead of a real one. We also define a series of hybrid games H_i^1 for $i \in \{0, q_v\}$ in which the first i **VoteOracle** calls produce a ballot with a simulated proof π instead of a real one. Via a straightforward hybrid argument, if $\mathcal{A}$ can distinguish between $\mathbf{Exp}^2 = H_{q_v}^1$ and $\mathbf{Exp}_{\Pi^{REF},\mathcal{A}}^{BP} = H_0^1$ with a non-negligible probability there must be a value of i such that he can distinguish H_i^1 and H_{i+1}^1. This contradicts the honest verifier zero knowledge property of $(\mathcal{G}, \mathcal{P}, \mathcal{V})$, since for all i, H_i^1 and H_{i+1}^1 differ (at most) only in a single proof transcript. Thus $\mathcal{A}$ wins $\mathbf{Exp}^2$ with probability negligibly close to $\mathbf{Exp}_{\Pi^{REF},\mathcal{A}}^{BP}$.

We also define a series of hybrid games H_i^2 for $i \in \{0, q_v\}$ as $\mathbf{Exp}^2$ in which the first i **VoteOracle** calls operate as if $b = 1$ and the rest as if $b = 0$. If $\mathcal{A}$ can win $\mathbf{Exp}^2$ with non-negligible probability, he can distinguish between H_0^2 and $H_{q_v}^2$ and thus there must be a value of i such that $\mathcal{A}$ can distinguish H_i^2 and H_{i+1}^2.

Let the variable RES be the sum of the votes contained in ballots with correct proofs which appear in the bulletin board BB' before **CheckBoard** is called. We note that RES only takes values in $\{0, \ldots, q_\Sigma\}$.

Let $p(n)$ be a polynomial such that $\mathcal{A}$ can distinguish between H_i^2 and H_{i+1}^2 with probability at least $\frac{1}{2} + \frac{1}{p(n)}$ for an infinite number of $n \in \mathbb{N}$. We will construct an adversary $\mathcal{B}$ that can obtain non-negligible advantage against the IND-CPA security of $(\mathcal{K}, \mathcal{E}, \mathcal{D})$ by simulating an election against $\mathcal{A}$. Initially $\mathcal{B}$ obtains a public key ek from the IND-CPA experiment and completes the setup as normal, obtaining (pk, vk) from $\mathcal{G}$. $\mathcal{B}$ proceeds by following Π^{REF} with the following difference: the first i **VoteOracle** calls operate as if $b = 1$. The next **VoteOracle** (which we can assume w.l.o.g to be $v^* = 1$) is answered as if it was successful, but $\mathcal{B}$ does not update BB. Afterwards, before **CheckBoard** is called, the experiment is suspended and the state st of $\mathcal{A}$ is saved along with the bulletin boards and keys as $\sigma = (ek, (pk, vk), st, BB, BB')$. $\mathcal{B}$ does not know the value of RES, but knows that it takes values in $\{0, \ldots, q_\Sigma\}$.

Let $\mathbf{Exp}^3(\sigma, v, r)$, where $\sigma = (ek, (pk, vk), st, BB, BB')$ be the following experiment: Produce B^* as a fresh ballot (with simulated proof) containing v, add B^* to BB, restore the adversary's state to st and resume the voting protocol starting at **CheckBoard**. The **Tally** query is answered with r. The result of the experiment is $v == \hat{b}$ where $\hat{b}$ is $\mathcal{A}$'s reply.

We note when $r = RES$, $\mathbf{Exp}^3(\sigma, v, r)$ produces the same output as H_i^2 or H_{i+1}^2 depending only on v. We call a saved state σ "good" if $\mathcal{A}$ has a non-negligible advantage in distinguishing $\mathbf{Exp}^3(\sigma, 0, RES)$ from $\mathbf{Exp}^3(\sigma, 1, RES)$, where RES is determined uniquely by BB'. Because $\mathcal{A}$ can distinguish between H_i^2 and H_{i+1}^2, a state created by $\mathcal{B}$ must be "good" with non-negligible probability.

$\mathcal{B}$ repeats the following $n \cdot p(n)$ times: run $\mathbf{Exp}^3(\sigma, v, r)$ for all combinations of $v \in \{0, 1\}$ and $r \in \{0, \ldots, q_\Sigma\}$.

Afterwards, $\mathcal{B}$ can determine the value of r for which $\mathcal{A}$ has best distinguished between $v = 0$ and 1. We note that because the true value of RES is included in the iterations, if σ is a "good" state, there is a value of r for which $\mathcal{A}$ achieves at least $\frac{1}{p(n)}$ advantage in distinguishing v, and after $n \cdot p(n)$ experiments Chernoff-bounds show that $\mathcal{B}$ has a good estimate of $\mathcal{A}$'s advantage for each value of r.

After determining the optimal value of r, $\mathcal{B}$ will send $(0, 1)$ to the IND-CPA experiment and obtain a challenge ciphertext $\hat{c}$. $\mathcal{B}$ produces a simulated proof $\hat{\pi}$ for c, adds $\hat{B}$ to the saved board and resumes the experiment a final time. $\mathcal{B}$ finally forwards the reply of A to the IND-CPA experiment.

Because $\mathcal{B}$ will proceed without restarting with non-negligible probability, it runs in expected polynomial time. Because with overwhelming probability $\mathcal{B}$ proceeds only when σ is a "good" state, the advantage in distinguishing whether c contains 0 or 1 is non-negligible. □

References

1. Adida, B.: Helios: web-based open-audit voting. In: Security Symposium, SS 2008, pp. 335–348. USENIX Association (2008)
2. Barak, B., Canetti, R., Nielsen, J.B., Pass, R.: Universally composable protocols with relaxed set-up assumptions. In: Foundations of Computer Science, FOCS 2004, pp. 186–195. IEEE (2004)

3. Bellare, M., Rogaway, P.: Random oracles are practical: a paradigm for designing efficient protocols. In: Computer and Communications Security, pp. 62–73. ACM (1993)
4. Bernhard, D., Cortier, V., Pereira, O., Smyth, B., Warinschi, B.: Adapting helios for provable ballot privacy. In: Atluri, V., Diaz, C. (eds.) ESORICS 2011. LNCS, vol. 6879, pp. 335–354. Springer, Heidelberg (2011)
5. Blum, M., Feldman, P., Micali, S.: Non-interactive zero-knowledge and its applications. In: Theory of Computing, STOC 1988, pp. 103–112. ACM (1988)
6. Canetti, R., Goldreich, O., Halevi, S.: The random oracle methodology, revisited. Journal of the ACM (JACM) **51**(4), 557–594 (2004)
7. Cortier, V., Galindo, D., Glondu, S., Izabachène, M.: Distributed ElGamal á la Pedersen: application to Helios. In: Privacy in the Electronic Society, WPES 2013, pp. 131–142. ACM (2013)
8. Cramer, R., Shoup, V.: A practical public-key encryption schemes secure against adaptive chosen ciphertext attack. In: Krawczyk, H. (ed.) CRYPTO '98. LNCS, vol. 1462. Springer, Heidelberg (1998)
9. Cramer, R., Shoup, V.: Universal hash proofs and a paradigm for adaptive chosen ciphertext secure public-key encryption. In: Knudsen, L.R. (ed.) EUROCRYPT 2002. LNCS, vol. 2332, p. 45. Springer, Heidelberg (2002)
10. Damgård, I.B.: Non-interactive circuit based proofs and non-interactive perfect zero-knowledge with preprocessing. In: Rueppel, R.A. (ed.) EUROCRYPT 1992. LNCS, vol. 658, pp. 341–355. Springer, Heidelberg (1993)
11. Damgård, I.B., Fazio, N., Nicolosi, A.: Non-interactive zero-knowledge from homomorphic encryption. In: Halevi, S., Rabin, T. (eds.) TCC 2006. LNCS, vol. 3876, pp. 41–59. Springer, Heidelberg (2006)
12. Damgård, I., Jurik, M., Nielsen, J.B.: A generalization of Paillier's public-key system with applications to electronic voting. International Journal of Information Security **9**(6), 371–385 (2010)
13. Fiat, A., Shamir, A.: How to prove yourself: practical solutions to identification and signature problems. In: Odlyzko, A.M. (ed.) CRYPTO 1986. LNCS, vol. 263, pp. 186–194. Springer, Heidelberg (1987)
14. Gennaro, R., Gentry, C., Parno, B., Raykova, M.: Quadratic span programs and succinct NIZKs without PCPs. In: Johansson, T., Nguyen, P.Q. (eds.) EUROCRYPT 2013. LNCS, vol. 7881, pp. 626–645. Springer, Heidelberg (2013)
15. Gentry, C., Groth, J., Ishai, Y., Peikert, C., Sahai, A., Smith, A.: Using fully homomorphic hybrid encryption to minimize non-interative zero-knowledge proofs. Journal of Cryptology, 1–24 (2014)
16. Goldwasser, S., Kalai, Y.T.: On the (in)security of the Fiat-Shamir paradigm. In: Foundations of Computer Science, FOCS 2003, pp. 102–113. IEEE (2003)
17. Goldwasser, S., Micali, S., Rackoff, C.: The knowledge complexity of interactive proof systems. SIAM Journal on computing **18**(1), 186–208 (1989)
18. Groth, J.: Simulation-sound NIZK proofs for a practical language and constant size group signatures. In: Lai, X., Chen, K. (eds.) ASIACRYPT 2006. LNCS, vol. 4284, pp. 444–459. Springer, Heidelberg (2006)
19. Groth, J.: Short non-interactive zero-knowledge proofs. In: Abe, M. (ed.) ASIACRYPT 2010. LNCS, vol. 6477, pp. 341–358. Springer, Heidelberg (2010)
20. Groth, J.: Short pairing-based non-interactive zero-knowledge arguments. In: Abe, M. (ed.) ASIACRYPT 2010. LNCS, vol. 6477, pp. 321–340. Springer, Heidelberg (2010)
21. Groth, J., Ostrovsky, R., Sahai, A.: New techniques for noninteractive zero-knowledge. Journal of the ACM **59**(3), 11:1–11:35 (2012)

22. Groth, J., Sahai, A.: Efficient noninteractive proof systems for bilinear groups. SIAM Journal on Computing **41**(5), 1193–1232 (2012)
23. Jakobsson, M., Sako, K., Impagliazzo, R.: Designated verifier proofs and their applications. In: Maurer, U.M. (ed.) EUROCRYPT 1996. LNCS, vol. 1070, pp. 143–154. Springer, Heidelberg (1996)
24. Kilian, J., Petrank, E.: An efficient noninteractive zero-knowledge proof system for NP with general assumptions. Journal of Cryptology **11**(1), 1–27 (1998)
25. Naor, M., Yung, M.: Public-key cryptosystems provably secure against chosen ciphertext attacks. In: Theory of Computing, STOC 2013, pp. 427–437. ACM (1990)
26. Okamoto, T., Uchiyama, S.: A new public-key cryptosystem as secure as factoring. In: Nyberg, K. (ed.) EUROCRYPT 1998. LNCS, vol. 1403, pp. 308–318. Springer, Heidelberg (1998)
27. Parno, B., Howell, J., Gentry, C., Raykova, M.: Pinocchio: nearly practical verifiable computation. In: Security and Privacy, pp. 238–252. IEEE (2013)
28. Ventre, C., Visconti, I.: Co-sound zero-knowledge with public keys. In: Preneel, B. (ed.) AFRICACRYPT 2009. LNCS, vol. 5580, pp. 287–304. Springer, Heidelberg (2009)
29. Wikström, D.: Simplified submission of inputs to protocols. In: Ostrovsky, R., De Prisco, R., Visconti, I. (eds.) SCN 2008. LNCS, vol. 5229, pp. 293–308. Springer, Heidelberg (2008)

Lattice-Based Cryptography

Bootstrapping BGV Ciphertexts with a Wider Choice of p and q

Emmanuela Orsini[✉], Joop van de Pol, and Nigel P. Smart

Department of Computer Science, University of Bristol, Bristol, UK
{Emmanuela.Orsini,Joop.VandePol}@bristol.ac.uk, nigel@cs.bris.ac.uk

Abstract. We describe a method to bootstrap a packed BGV cipher-text which does not depend (as much) on any special properties of the plaintext and ciphertext moduli. Prior "efficient" methods such as that of Gentry et al. (PKC 2012) required a ciphertext modulus q which was close to a power of the plaintext modulus p. This enables our method to be applied in a larger number of situations. Also unlike previous methods our depth grows only as $O(\log p + \log \log q)$ as opposed to the $\log q$ of previous methods. Our basic bootstrapping technique makes use of a representation of the group $\mathbb{Z}_q^+$ over the finite field $\mathbb{F}_p$ (either based on polynomials or elliptic curves), followed by polynomial interpolation of the reduction mod p map over the coefficients of the algebraic group.

This technique is then extended to the full BGV packed ciphertext space, using a method whose depth depends only logarithmically on the number of packed elements. This method may be of interest as an alternative to the method of Alperin-Sheriff and Peikert (CRYPTO 2013). To aid efficiency we utilize the ring/field switching technique of Gentry et al. (SCN 2012, JCS 2013).

1 Introduction

Since the invention of Fully Homomorphic Encryption (FHE) by Gentry in 2009 [14,15], one of the main open questions in the field has been how to "bootstrap" a Somewhat Homomorphic Encryption (SHE) scheme into a FHE scheme. Recall an SHE scheme is one which can evaluate circuits of a limited multiplicative depth, whereas an FHE scheme is one which can evaluate circuits of arbitrary depth. Gentry's bootstrapping technique is the only known way of obtaining unbounded FHE.

The ciphertexts of all known SHE schemes include some noise to ensure security, and unfortunately this noise grows as more and more homomorphic operations are performed, until it is so large that the ciphertext will no longer decrypt correctly. In a nutshell, bootstrapping "refreshes" a ciphertext that can not support any further homomorphic operation by homomorphically decrypting it, and obtaining in this way a new encryption of the some plaintext, but with smaller noise. This is possible if the underlying SHE scheme has enough homomorphic capacity to evaluate its own decryption algorithm. Bootstrapping is computationally very expensive and it represents the main bottleneck in FHE constructions.

© International Association for Cryptologic Research 2015
J. Katz (Ed.): PKC 2015, LNCS 9020, pp. 673–698, 2015.
DOI: 10.1007/978-3-662-46447-2_30

Several SHE schemes, with different bootstrapping procedures, have been proposed in the past few years [1,2,4,6–8,10,14,15,18,19,32]. The most efficient are ones which allow SIMD style operations, by packing a number of plaintext elements into independent "slots" in the plaintext space. The most studied of such "SIMD friendly" schemes being the BGV scheme [5] based on the Ring-LWE Problem [25].

Prior Work on Bootstrapping. In *almost all* the SHE schemes supporting bootstrapping, decryption is performed by evaluating some linear function D, dependent on the ciphertext c, on the secret key $\mathfrak{st}$ modulo some integer q, and then reducing the result modulo some prime p, i.e. $\mathsf{dec}(c, \mathfrak{st}) = ((D_C(\mathfrak{st}) \bmod q) \bmod p)$. Given an encryption of the secret key, bootstrapping consists in evaluating the above decryption formula homomorphically. One can divide the bootstrapping of all efficient currently known SHE schemes into three distinct sub-problems.

1. The first problem is to homomorphically evaluate the reduction $(\bmod\ p)$-map on the group $\mathbb{Z}_q^+$ (see Fig. 1), where for the domain one takes representatives centered around zero. To do this the group $\mathbb{Z}_q^+$ is first mapped to a set $\mathbb{G}$ in which one can perform operations native to the homomorphic cryptosystem. In other words we first need to specify a *representation*, $\mathsf{rep} : \mathbb{Z}_q^+ \longrightarrow \mathbb{G}$, which takes an integer in the range $(-q/2, \ldots, q/2]$ and maps it to the set $\mathbb{G}$. The group operation on $\mathbb{Z}_q^+$ needs to induce a group operation on $\mathbb{G}$ which can be evaluated homomorphically by the underlying SHE scheme. Then we describe the induced map $\mathsf{red} : \mathbb{G} \longrightarrow \mathbb{Z}_p$ as a algebraic operation, which can hence be evaluated homomorphically.
2. The second problem is to encode the secret key in a way that one can publicly, using a function $\mathsf{dec\text{-}eval}$ (decryption evaluation), create a set of ciphertexts which encrypt the required input to the function red.
3. And thirdly one needs a method to extend this to packed ciphertexts.

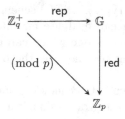

Fig. 1.

To solidify ideas we now expand on these problems in the context of the BGV scheme [5]. Recall for BGV we have a set of $L+1$ moduli, corresponding to the levels of the scheme, $q_0 < q_1 < \ldots < q_L$, and a (global) ring R, which is often the ring of integers of a cyclotomic number field. We let p denote the (prime) plaintext modulus, i.e. the plaintexts will be elements in R_p (the localisation of R at the prime p), and to ease notation we set $q = q_0$. The secret key $\mathfrak{st}$ is a small element in R. A "fresh" ciphertext encrypting $\mu' \in R_p$ is an element $\mathfrak{ct}' = (c_0', c_1')$ in $R_{q_L}^2$ such that

$$(c_0' + \mathfrak{st} \cdot c_1' \pmod{q_L}) \pmod{p} = \mu'.$$

After the evaluation of L levels of multiplication one obtains a ciphertext $\mathfrak{ct} = (c_0, c_1)$ in R_q^2, encrypting a plaintext μ, such that

$$(c_0 + \mathfrak{st} \cdot c_1 \pmod{q}) \pmod{p} = \mu.$$

At this point to perform further calculations one needs to bootstrap, or recrypt, the ciphertext to one of a higher level.

Assume for the moment that each plaintext only encodes a single element of $\mathbb{Z}_p$, i.e. each plaintext is a constant polynomial in polynomial basis for R_p. To perform bootstrapping we need to place a "hint" in the public key $\mathfrak{pt}$ (usually an encryption of $\mathfrak{st}$ at level L), which allows the following operations. Firstly, we can evaluate homomorphically a function dec-eval which takes $\mathfrak{ct}$ and the "hint", and outputs a representation of the $\mathbb{Z}_q$ element corresponding to the constant term of the element $c_0 + \mathfrak{st} \cdot c_1 \pmod{q}$. This representation is an encryption of an element in $\mathbb{G}$, i.e. dec-eval also evaluates the rep map as well as the decryption map. Then we apply, homomorphically, the function red to this representation to obtain a fresh encryption of the plaintext. Since to homomorphically evaluate red we need the input to red to be defined over the plaintext space, this means the representation of $\mathbb{Z}_q$ must be *defined over* $\mathbb{F}_p$. One is then left with the task of extending such a procedure to packed ciphertexts.

In the original bootstrapping technique of Gentry [15], implemented in [16], the function dec-eval is obtained from a process of bit-decomposition. Thus the representation $\mathbb{G}$ of $\mathbb{Z}_q$ is the bit-representation of an integer in the range $(-q/2, \ldots, q/2]$, i.e. we use a representation defined over $\mathbb{F}_2$. The function to evaluate red is then the circuit which performs reduction modulo p. The extension of this technique to packed ciphertexts, in the context of the Smart–Vercauteren SIMD optimisations [29] of Gentry's SHE scheme, was given in [30]. Due to the use of bit-decomposition techniques this method is mainly suited to the case of $p = 2$, although one can extend it to other primes by applying a p-adic decomposition and then using an arithmetic circuit to evaluate the reduction modulo p map.

In [18] the authors present a bootstrapping technique, primarily targeted at the BGV scheme, which does away with the need for evaluating the "standard" circuit for the reduction modulo p map. This is done by choosing q close to a power of p, i.e. one selects $q = p^t \pm a$ for some t and a small value of a, typically $a \in \{-1, 1\}$. The paper [18] expands on this idea for the case of $p = 2$, but the authors mention it can be clearly extended to arbitrary p. The advantage is that the mapping red can now be expressed as algebraic formulae; in fact formulae of multiplicative depth $\log_2 q$. The operation dec-eval obtains the required representation for $\mathbb{Z}_q$ by mapping it into $\mathbb{Z}_{p^{t+1}}$. The resulting technique requires the extension of the modulus of the plaintext ring to p^{t+1} (for which all the required properties of R_p carry over, assuming that p does not ramify). The extension to packed ciphertexts is performed using an elaborate homomorphic evaluation of the Fourier Transform.

To enable the faster evaluation of this Fourier Transform step from [18], a method for ring/field switching is presented in [17]. The technique of ring/field switching also enables general improvements in efficiency as ciphertext noise grows. This enables the ring R to be changed to a sub-ring S (both for the ciphertext and plaintext spaces). In [1] this use of field switching is combined with the red map from [18] to obtain an asymptotically efficient bootstrapping method for BGV style SHE schemes; although the resulting technique does not fully map to our blueprint, as $q = p^v$ for some value of v. In [28] this method is implemented, with surprisingly efficient runtimes, for the case of plaintext space $\mathbb{F}_2$; i.e. $p = 2$ and no plaintext SIMD-packing is supported.

In another line of work, the authors of [2] and [8] present a bootstrapping technique for the GSW [21] homomorphic encryption scheme. The GSW scheme is one based on matrices, and this property is exploited in [2] by taking a matrix representation of $\mathbb{Z}_q$ and then expressing the map red via a very simple algebraic relationship on the associated matrices. In particular the authors represent elements of $\mathbb{Z}_q$ by matrices (of some large dimension) over $\mathbb{F}_p$.

Thus we see *almost all* bootstrapping techniques require us to come up with a representation $\mathbb{G}$ of $\mathbb{Z}_q$ for which there is an algebraic method over $\mathbb{F}_p$ to evaluate the induced mapping, red, from the said representation of $\mathbb{Z}_q$, to $\mathbb{Z}_p$. Since SHE schemes usually homomorphically have add and multiply operations as their basic homomorphic operations, this implies we are looking for representations of $\mathbb{Z}_q^+$ as a subgroup of an algebraic group over $\mathbb{F}_p$.

Our Contribution. We return to consider the Ring-LWE based BGV scheme, and we present a new bootstrapping technique with small depth growth, compared with previous methods, and which supports a larger choice of p and q. Instead of concentrating on the case of plaintext moduli p such that a power of p is close to q, we look at a much larger class of plaintext moduli. Recall the most efficient prior technique, based on [1] and [18], requires a method whose multiplicative depth is $O(\log q)$, and for which q is close to a power of p. As p increases the ability to select a suitable modulus q which is both close to a power of p, is of the correct size for most efficient implementation (i.e. the smallest needed to ensure security), and has other properties related to efficiency (i.e. the ring R_q has a double-CRT representation as in [20]) diminishes.

To allow a wider selection for p we utilize two "new" (for bootstrapping) representations of the ring $\mathbb{Z}_q$, in much the same way as [2] used an $\mathbb{F}_p$-matrix representation (a.k.a. a linear algebraic group) of $\mathbb{Z}_q^+$. The first one, used for much of this paper for ease of presentation, is based on a polynomial representation for $\mathbb{Z}_q^+$ over $\mathbb{F}_p$, the second one (which is less efficient but allows a greater freedom in selecting q) is based on a representation via elliptic curves. The evaluation of the mapping red using these representations can then be done in expected multiplicative depth $O(\log p + \log \log q)$, i.e. a much shallower circuit than used in prior works, using polynomial interpolation of the red map over the coefficients of the algebraic group.

To ensure this method works, and is efficient, we do not have completely free reign in selecting q for the first polynomial representation. Whilst [18] required $q = p^t \pm a$, for a small value of a, we instead will require that q divides

$$\mathsf{lcm}\left(p^{k_1} - 1, \ldots, p^{k_t} - 1\right),$$

for some pairwise co-prime values k_i. Even with this restriction, the freedom on selecting q is much greater than for the method in [18], especially for large values of p. In the second representation, described in Section 7, we simply need to find elliptic curves over $\mathbb{F}_{p^{k_i}}$ whose group order is divisible by e_i where $\prod e_i = q$. For the elliptic curve based version we do not need pairwise co-prime values of k_i. Indeed on setting $t = 1$ we simply need one curve $E(\mathbb{F}_{p^{k_1}})$ whose group order is divisible by q, which is highly likely to exist, since $p \ll q$, by the near uniform distribution of elliptic curve group orders in the Hasse interval.

Note also that, in the polynomial representation, one does not have complete freedom on selecting the k_i values. If we let $E = \sum k_i$ and $M = \frac{1}{2}\sum k_i \cdot (k_i + 1)$ then the depth of the circuit (which is approximately $\log_2 \log_2 q - \log_2 \log_2 E$) to evaluate red will decrease as E grows, but the number of multiplications required, which is a monotonically increasing function of M, will increase. Note, we can asymptotically make $M = O(\sum k_i \cdot \log k_i)$ using FFT techniques, or $M = O(\sum k_i^{1.58})$ using Karatsuba based techniques, but in practice the k_i will be too small to make such optimization fruitful. For the elliptic curve based version we replace the above E by $E + 1$ and we replace M by a constant multiple of M. However, the depth required by our elliptic curve based version increases.

Our method permits to bootstrap a certain number of packed ciphertexts in parallel, using a form of p-adic decomposition and a matrix representation of the ciphertext ring, combined with ring switching. The resulting depth depends only logarithmically on the number of packed ciphertexts.

Overview and Paper Organization. Here we give a brief overview of the paper. In Section 2 and 3 we recall the basic algebraic background required for our construction, and the BGV SHE scheme from [5], respectively. Typically, the main technical difficult in bootstrapping is to homomorphically evaluate in a efficient way the $(\bmod\ p)$-map on the group $\mathbb{Z}_q^+$. In Section 4 we describe a simple way to evaluate the $(\bmod\ p)$-map using a polynomial representation of the group $\mathbb{G}$ in Fig. 1. In Section 5 we prepare to bootstrap packed ciphertexts and we show how to homomorphically evaluate a product of powers of SIMD vectors. In particular we calculate the depth and the number of multiplications required to compute this operation. Finally, in Section 6 we show how to bootstrap BGV ciphertexts. We use a matrix representation of the product of two elements in a ring and a single ring switching step in such a way that we can bootstrap a number, say C, of packed ciphertexts in one step. We describe the homomorphic evaluation of the decryption equation using the SIMD evaluation of the maps red and rep. Using the calculation of Section 5, we can compute the depth and the number of multiplications necessary to bootstrap C packed ciphertexts in parallel. In Section 7 we give a different instantiation of our method using elliptic curves.

2   Preliminaries

Throughout this work vectors are written using bold lower-case letters, whereas bold upper-case letters are used for matrices. We denote by $M_{a \times b}(K)$ the set of $a \times b$ dimensional matrices with entries in K. For an integer modulus q, we let $\mathbb{Z}_q = \mathbb{Z}/q\mathbb{Z}$ denote the quotient ring of integers modulo q, and $\mathbb{Z}_q^+$ its additive group. This notation naturally extends to the localisation R_q of a ring R at q.

2.1   Algebraic Background

Let m be a positive integer we define the mth cyclotomic field to be the field $\mathbb{K} = \mathbb{Q}[X]/\Phi_m(X)$, where $\Phi_m(X)$ is the mth cyclotomic polynomial. $\Phi_m(X)$ is a monic irreducible polynomial over the rational, and $\mathbb{K}$ is a field extension of degree $N = \phi(m)$ over $\mathbb{Q}$ since $\Phi_m(X)$ has degree N. Let ζ_m be an abstract primitive mth roots of unity, we have that $\mathbb{K} \cong \mathbb{Q}(\zeta_m)$ by identifying ζ_m with X. In the same way, let us denote by R the mth cyclotomic ring $\mathbb{Z}[\zeta_m] \cong \mathbb{Z}[X]/\Phi_m(X)$, with "power basis" $\{1, \zeta_m, \ldots, \zeta_m^{N-1}\}$. The complex embeddings of $\mathbb{K}$ are $\sigma_i : \mathbb{K} \to \mathbb{C}$, defined by $\sigma_i(X) = \zeta_m^i$, $i \in \mathbb{Z}_m^*$. In particular $\mathbb{K}$ is Galois over $\mathbb{Q}$ and $\mathrm{Gal}(\mathbb{Q}(\zeta_m)/\mathbb{Q}) \cong \mathbb{Z}_m^*$. As a consequence we can define the $\mathbb{Q}$-linear (field) trace $\mathrm{Tr}_{\mathbb{K}/\mathbb{Q}} : \mathbb{K} \to \mathbb{Q}$ as the sum of the embeddings σ_i, i.e. $\mathrm{Tr}_{\mathbb{K}/\mathbb{Q}}(a) = \sum_{i \in \mathbb{Z}_m^*} \sigma_i(a) \in \mathbb{Q}$. Concretely, these embeddings map ζ_m into each of its conjugates, and they are the only field homomorphisms from $\mathbb{K}$ to $\mathbb{C}$ that fix every element of $\mathbb{Q}$. The *canonical embedding* $\sigma : \mathbb{K} \to \mathbb{C}^N$ is the concatenation of all the complex embeddings, i.e. $\sigma(a) = (\sigma_i(a))_{i \in \mathbb{Z}_m^*}$, $a \in \mathbb{K}$.

Looking ahead, we will use the ring R and its localisation R_q, for some modulus q. Given a polynomial $a \in R$, we denote by $\|\mathbf{a}\|_\infty = \max_{0 \le j \le N-1} |a_j|$ the standard l_∞-norm. All estimates of noise are taken with respect to the *canonical embedding norm* $\|a\|_\infty^{\mathsf{can}} = \|\sigma(a)\|_\infty$, $a \in R$. When considering short elements in R_q, we define short in terms of the following quantity:

$$|a|_q^{\mathsf{can}} = \min\{\|a'\|_\infty^{\mathsf{can}} : a' \in R \text{ and } a' \equiv a \mod q\}.$$

To map from norms in the canonical embedding to norms on the coefficients of the polynomial defining the elements of R, we have $\|\mathbf{a}\|_\infty \le c_m \cdot \|a\|_\infty^{\mathsf{can}}$, where c_m is the *ring constant*. For more details about c_m see [13]. Note, if the dual basis techniques of [26] are used, then one can remove the dependence on c_m. However, for ease of exposition we shall use only polynomial basis in this work.

Let m' be a positive integer such that $m'|m$. As before we define $\mathbb{K}' \cong \mathbb{Q}(\zeta_{m'})$ and $S \cong \mathbb{Z}[\zeta_{m'}]$, such that $\mathbb{K}'$ has degree $n = \phi(m')$ over $\mathbb{Q}$ and $\mathrm{Gal}(\mathbb{K}'/\mathbb{Q}) \cong$

$\mathbb{Z}_{m'}^*$. It is trivial to show that $\mathbb{K}$ and R are a field and a ring extension of $\mathbb{K}'$ and R', respectively, both of dimension N/n. In particular we can see S as a subring of R via the ring embedding that maps $\zeta_{m'} \mapsto \zeta_m^{m/m'}$.

It is a standard fact that if $\mathbb{Q} \subseteq \mathbb{K}' \subseteq \mathbb{K}$ is a tower of number field, then $\mathrm{Tr}_{\mathbb{K}/\mathbb{Q}}(a) = \mathrm{Tr}_{\mathbb{K}'/\mathbb{Q}}(\mathrm{Tr}_{\mathbb{K}/\mathbb{K}'}(a))$, and that all the $\mathbb{K}'$-linear maps $L : \mathbb{K} \to \mathbb{K}'$ are exactly the maps of the form $\mathrm{Tr}_{\mathbb{K}/\mathbb{K}'}(r \cdot a)$, for some $r \in \mathbb{K}$.

2.2 Plaintext Slots

Let p be a prime integer, coprime to m, and R_p the localisation of R at p. The polynomial $\Phi_m(X)$ factors modulo p into $\ell^{(R)}$ irreducible factors, i.e. $\Phi_m(X) \equiv \prod_{i=1}^{\ell^{(R)}} F_i(X) \pmod{p}$. Each $F_i(X)$ has degree $d^{(R)} = \phi(m)/\ell^{(R)}$, where $d^{(R)}$ is the multiplicative order of p in $\mathbb{Z}_m^*$. Looking ahead, each of these $\ell^{(R)}$ factors corresponds to a "plaintext slot", i.e.

$$R_p \cong \mathbb{Z}_p[X]/F_1(X) \times \cdots \times \mathbb{Z}_p[X]/F_{\ell^{(R)}}(X) \cong (\mathbb{F}_{p^{d^{(R)}}})^{\ell^{(R)}}.$$

More precisely, we have $\ell^{(R)}$ isomorphisms $\psi_i : \mathbb{Z}_p[X]/F_i(X) \to \mathbb{F}_{p^{d^{(R)}}}$, $i = 1, \ldots, \ell^{(R)}$, that allow to represent $\ell^{(R)}$ plaintext elements of $\mathbb{F}_{p^{(d)}}$ as a single element in R_p. By the Chinese Remainder Theorem, addition and multiplication correspond to SIMD operations on the slots and this allows to process $\ell^{(R)}$ input values at once.

2.3 Ring Switching

As mentioned in the introduction, our technique uses a method for ring/field switching from [17] so as to aid efficiency. We use two different cyclotomic rings R and S such that $S \subseteq R$. This procedure permits to transform a ciphertext $\mathfrak{ct} \in (R_q)^2$ corresponding to a plaintext $\mu \in R_p$ with respect to a secret key $\mathfrak{sk} \in R$, into a ciphertext $\mathfrak{ct}' \in (S_q)^2$ corresponding to a plaintext $\mu' \in S_p$ with respect to a secret key $\mathfrak{sk}' \in S$. The security of this method relies on the hardness of the ring-LWE problem in S ([25]). At a high level the ring switching consists of three steps. Given an input ciphertext $\mathfrak{ct} \in (R_q)^2$:

- First, it switches the secret key; it uses the "classical" key-switching ([6],[5]), getting a ciphertext $\bar{\mathfrak{ct}} \in (R_q)^2$, still encrypting $\mu \in R_p$, but with respect to a secret key $\mathfrak{sk}' \in S$.
- Second, it multiplies $\bar{\mathfrak{ct}}$ by a fixed element $r \in R$, which is determined by a S-linear function $L : R_p \to S_p$ corresponding to the induced projection function $P : (\mathbb{F}_{p^{d^{(R)}}})^{\ell^{(R)}} \to (\mathbb{F}_{p^{d^{(S)}}})^{\ell^{(S)}}$ (see [17] for details).
- Finally, it applies to $\bar{\mathfrak{ct}}$ the trace function $\mathrm{Tr}_{R/S} : R \to S$. In such a way the output of the ring-switching is a ciphertext $\mathfrak{ct} \in S$ with respect to the secret key $\mathfrak{sk}'$ and encrypting the plaintext $\mu' = L(\mu)$.

We conclude this section noting that, while big-ring ciphertexts correspond to $\ell^{(R)}$ plaintext slots, small-ring ciphertexts only correspond to $\ell^{(S)} \leq \ell^{(R)}$

plaintext slots. The input ciphertexts to our bootstrapping procedure are defined over $(S_q)^2$, and so are of degree n and contain $\ell^{(S)}$ slots. We take $\ell^{(R)}/n$ of these ciphertexts and use the dec-eval map to encode the coefficients of the plaintext polynomials in the slots of a single big-ring ciphertext. Eventually, via ring switching and polynomial interpolation, we return to $\ell^{(R)}/n$ ciphertexts which have been bootstrapped and are at level one (or more). These fresh ciphertexts may be defined over the big ring or the small ring (depending when ring switching occurs). However, our parameter estimates imply that ring switching is best performed at the lowest level possible, and so our bootstrapped ciphertexts will be in the big ring. We could encode all of the slots of the bootstrapped ciphertexts in a big-ring single ciphertext, or not, depending on the application, since slot manipulation is a linear operation.

3   The BGV Somewhat Homomorphic Encryption Scheme

In this section we outline what we need about the BGV SHE scheme [5]. As anticipated in Section 2, we present the scheme with the option of utilizing two rings, and hence at some point we will make use of the ring/field switching procedure from [17]. We first define two rings $R = \mathbb{Z}[X]/F(X)$ and $S = \mathbb{Z}[X]/f(X)$, where $F(X)$ (resp. $f(x)$) is an irreducible polynomial over Z of degree N (resp. n). In practice both $F(X)$ and $f(X)$ will likely be cyclotomic polynomials. We assume that n divides N, and so here is an embedding $\iota : S \longrightarrow R$ which maps elements in S to their appropriate equivalent in R. The map ι can be expressed as a linear mapping on the coefficients of the polynomial representation of the elements in S, to the coefficients of the polynomial representation of the elements in R. In this way we can consider S to be a subring of R.

Let R_q (resp. S_q) denote the localisation of R (resp S) at q, i.e. $\mathbb{Z}_q[X]/F(X)$ (resp. $\mathbb{Z}_q[X]/f(X)$), which can be constructed for any positive integer q. Let p be a prime number, which does not ramify in either R or S. Since the rings are Galois, the ring R_p (resp. S_p) splits into $\ell^{(R)}$ (resp. $\ell^{(S)}$) "slots"; with each slot being a finite field extension of $\mathbb{F}_p$ of degree $d^{(R)} = N/\ell^{(R)}$ (resp. $d^{(S)} = n/\ell^{(S)}$). We make the assumption that n divides $\ell^{(R)}$. This is not strictly necessary but it ensures that we can perform bootstrapping of a single ciphertext with the smallest amount of memory. In fact our method will support the bootstrapping of $\ell^{(R)}/n$ ciphertexts in parallel.

There will be two secret keys for our scheme; depending on whether the ciphertexts/plaintexts are associated with the ring R or the ring S. We denote these secret keys by $\mathfrak{sk}^{(R)}$ and $\mathfrak{sk}^{(S)}$, which are "small" elements in the ring R (resp. S). The modulus $q = q_0 = p_0$ will denote the smallest modulus in the set of BGV levels. Fresh ciphertexts are defined for the modulus $Q = q_L = \prod_{i=0}^{L} p_i$ and live in the ring R_Q^2 (thus at some point we not only perform modulus switching but also ring switching). We assume L_1 levels are associated with the big ring R and L_2 levels are associated with the small ring S, hence $L_1 + L_2 = L$ (level zero is clearly associated with the small ring S, but we do not count it in the number of levels in L_2). Thus we encrypt at level L; perform standard homomorphic operations down to level zero, with a single field switch at level $L_2 + 1$. For ease of analysis we assume no multiplications are performed at level $L_2 + 1$. This means that we can evaluate a depth $L - 1$ circuit.

A ciphertext at level $i > L_2$, encrypting a message $\mu \in R_p$, is a pair $\mathsf{ct} = (c_0, c_1) \in R_{q_i}^2$, where $q_i = \prod_{j=0}^{i} p_j$, such that

$$\left(c_0 + \mathfrak{s}\mathfrak{k}^{(R)} \cdot c_1 \pmod{q_i}\right) \pmod{p} = \mu.$$

We let $\mathsf{Enc}_{\mathsf{p}\mathfrak{k}}(\mu)$ denote the encryption of a message $\mu \in R_p$, this produces a ciphertext at level L. A similar definition holds for ciphertexts at level $i < L_2$, for messages in S_p and secret keys/ciphertexts elements in S_{q_i}. When performing a ring switching operation between levels $L_2 + 1$ and L_2, the $\ell^{(R)}$ plaintext slots, associated with the input ciphertext at level $L_2 + 1$, become associated with $\ell^{(R)}/\ell^{(S)}$ distinct ciphertexts at level L_2.

We want to "bootstrap" a set of BGV ciphertexts. Each of these ciphertexts is a pair $\mathsf{ct}_j = (c_0^{(j)}, c_1^{(j)}) \in S_q^2$, for $j = 1, \ldots, \ell^{(R)}/n$, such that

$$\left(c_0^{(j)} + \mathfrak{s}\mathfrak{k}^{(S)} \cdot c_1^{(j)} \pmod{q}\right) \pmod{p} = \mu_j, \text{ for } j = 1, \ldots, \ell^{(R)}/n.$$

4   Evaluating the Map red ∘ rep : $\mathbb{Z}_q^+ \longrightarrow \mathbb{F}_p$ (Simple Version)

As explained in the introduction at the heart of most bootstrapping procedures is a method to evaluate the induced mapping red∘rep : $\mathbb{Z}_q^+ \longrightarrow \mathbb{F}_p$. In this section we present our simpler technique for doing this based on polynomials over $\mathbb{F}_p$, in Section 7 we present a more general (and complicated in terms of depth) technique based on elliptic curves. The key, in this and in all techniques, is to find a representation $\mathbb{G}$ for $\mathbb{Z}_q^+$ for which the reduction modulo p map can be evaluated algebraically over $\mathbb{F}_p$. This means that the representation of $\mathbb{Z}_q$ must defined over $\mathbb{F}_p$. Prior work has looked at the bit-representation (when $p = 2$), the p-adic representation and a matrix representation; we use a polynomial representation.

We select a coprime factorization $q = \prod_{i=1}^{t} e_i$ (with the e_i not necessarily prime, but pairwise coprime), such that e_i divides $p^{k_i} - 1$ for some k_i. Since $\mathbb{F}_{p^{k_i}}^*$ is cyclic we know that $\mathbb{F}_{p^{k_i}}^*$ has a subgroup of order e_i. We fix a polynomial representation of $\mathbb{F}_{p^{k_i}}$, i.e. an irreducible polynomial $f_i(x)$ of degree k_i such that $\mathbb{F}_{p^{k_i}} = \mathbb{F}_p[x]/f_i(x)$. Let $g_i \in \mathbb{F}_{p^{k_i}}$ denote a fixed element of order e_i in $\mathbb{F}_{p^{k_i}}$.

By the Chinese Remainder Theorem we therefore have a group embedding

$$\mathsf{rep} : \begin{cases} \mathbb{Z}_q^+ \longrightarrow \mathbb{G} = \prod_{i=1}^{t} \mathbb{F}_{p^{k_i}}^* \\ a \longmapsto (g_1^{a_1}, \ldots, g_t^{a_t}) \end{cases} \tag{1}$$

where $a_i = a \pmod{e_i}$. Without loss of generality we can assume that the k_i are also coprime, by modifying the decomposition of q into coprime e_is. Given this group representation of $\mathbb{Z}_q^+$ in $\mathbb{G}$, addition in $\mathbb{Z}_q^+$ translates into multiplication in $\mathbb{G}$. With one addition in $\mathbb{Z}_q^+$ translating into $M = \frac{1}{2} \sum_{i=1}^{t} k_i \cdot (k_i + 1)$ multiplications in $\mathbb{F}_p$ (and a comparable number of additions; assuming school book multiplication is used). Each element in the image of rep requires $E = \sum_{i=1}^{t} k_i$ elements in $\mathbb{F}_p$ to represent it.

There will be a map red : $\mathbb{G} \to \mathbb{F}_p$, such that red $\circ$ rep is the reduction modulo p map; and red can be defined by *algebraically* from the coefficient representation of $\mathbb{G}$ to $\mathbb{F}_p$. Here algebraically refers to algebraic operations over $\mathbb{F}_p$. An arbitrary algebraic expression on E variables of degree d will contain $^{d+E}C_d$ terms. Thus, by interpolating, we expect the degree d of the map red to be the smallest d such that $^{d+E}C_d > q$, which means we expect we expect $d \approx E \cdot (2^{\log(q)/E} - 1)$. Thus the larger E is, the smaller d will be. This interpolating function needs to be created once and for all for any given set of parameters, thus we ignore the cost in generating it in our analysis.

The algebraic circuit which implements the map red can hence be described as a circuit of depth $\lceil \log_2 d \rceil$ which requires $D(E, d) = {}^{E+d}C_d - (E + 1)$ multiplications (corresponding to the number of distinct monomials in E variables of degree between two and d). In particular, by approximating $E \approx \log_2(q)/\log_2(p)$, we obtain that the circuit implementing the map red has depth $\lceil \log_2 d \rceil = \log_2(p - 1) + \log_2(\log_2(q)) - \log_2(\log_2(p)))$.

We pause to note the following. By selecting a large finite field it would appear at first glance that one can reduce our degree d even further. This however comes at the cost of having more terms, i.e. a larger value of E. This in turn increases the overall complexity of the method (i.e. the number of multiplications needed) but not the depth.

5   A Product of Powers of SIMD Vectors

Before proceeding with our method to turn the above methodology for reduction modulo p into a bootstrapping method for our set of BGV ciphertexts, we first examine how to homomorphically compute the following function

$$\mathbf{v} \cdot \prod_{k=0}^{\lambda} \mathbf{v}_k^{\mathbf{M}_k},$$

where each $\mathbf{v}$ and $\mathbf{v}_k$, $k = 0, \ldots, \lambda$, represents a set of E ciphertexts, each of which encode (in a SIMD manner) $\ell^{(R)}$ elements in $\mathbb{F}_p$. The multiplication of two such sets of E ciphertexts is done with respect to the multiplication operation in $\mathbb{G}$, and thus requires M homomorphic multiplications (this is for our simple variation of red, for the variant based on elliptic curve the number of ciphertexts and the complexity of the group operation in $\mathbb{G}$ increase a little). The values $\mathbf{M}_k$ are matrices in $M_{\ell^{(R)} \times \ell^{(R)}}(\mathbb{F}_p)$. By the notation $\mathbf{u} = \mathbf{v}^{\mathbf{M}}$, where $\mathbf{M} = (m_{i,j})$, we mean the vector with components

$$u_i = \prod_{j=1}^{\ell^{(R)}} v_j^{m_{i,j}}, \quad i \in \{1, \ldots, \ell^{(R)}\}.$$

Notice that each u_i and v_j is a vector of E elements in $\mathbb{F}_p$ representing a single element in $\mathbb{G}$. In what follows we divide this operation into three sub-procedures and compute the number of multiplications, and the depth required, to evaluate the function.

5.1 SIMD Raising of an Encrypted Vector to the Power of a Public Vector

The first step is to take a vector $\mathbf{v}$ which is the SIMD encryption of E sets of $\ell^{(R)}$ elements in $\mathbb{F}_p$, i.e. it represents $\ell^{(R)}$ elements in $\mathbb{G}$. We then raise $\mathbf{v}$ to the power of some public vector $\mathbf{c} = (c_1, \ldots, c_{\ell^{(R)}})$, i.e. we want to compute

$$\mathbf{x} = \mathbf{v}^{\mathbf{c}}.$$

In particular $\mathbf{v}$ actually consists of E vectors each with $\ell^{(R)}$ components in their slots. We write

$$\mathbf{v} = (\mathbf{v}_{1,0}, \ldots, \mathbf{v}_{1,k_1-1}, \ldots, \mathbf{v}_{t,0}, \ldots, \mathbf{v}_{t,k_t-1}).$$

Note, multiplying such a vector by another vector of the same form requires M homomorphic multiplications and depth 1. We first write

$$\mathbf{c} = \mathbf{c}_0 + 2 \cdot \mathbf{c}_1 + \ldots + 2^{\lceil \log_2 p \rceil} \cdot \mathbf{c}_{\lceil \log_2 p \rceil},$$

where $\mathbf{c}_i \in \{0,1\}^{\ell^{(R)}}$. We let $\mathbf{c}_i^*$ denote the bitwise complement of $\mathbf{c}_i$. Thus to compute $\mathbf{x} = \mathbf{v}^{\mathbf{c}}$ we use the following three steps:

Step 1: Compute $\mathbf{v}^{2^i}$ for $i = 1, \ldots, \lceil \log_2 p \rceil$, by which we mean every element in $\mathbf{v}$ is raised to the power 2^i. This requires $\lceil \log_2 p \rceil \cdot M$ homomorphic multiplications and depth $\lceil \log_2 p \rceil$.

Step 2: For $i \in \{0, \ldots, \lceil \log_2 p \rceil\}$, $j \in \{1, \ldots, t\}$ and $k = \{0, \ldots, k_t-1\}$ compute,

$$\mathbf{w}_{j,k}^{(i)} = \begin{cases} \mathsf{Enc}_{\mathsf{p\ell}}(\mathbf{c}_i) \cdot \mathbf{v}_{j,k}^{2^i} & k \neq 0, \\ \\ \mathsf{Enc}_{\mathsf{p\ell}}(\mathbf{c}_i) \cdot \mathbf{v}_{j,k}^{2^i} + \mathsf{Enc}_{\mathsf{p\ell}}(\mathbf{c}_i^*) & k = 0. \end{cases}$$

Where $\mathsf{Enc}_{\mathsf{p\ell}}(\mathbf{c}_i)$ means encrypt the vector $\mathbf{c}_i$ so that the jth component of $\mathbf{c}_i$ is mapped to the jth plaintext slot of the ciphertext. The above procedure selects the values which we want to include in the final product. This involves a homomorphic multiplication by a constant in $\{0,1\}$ and the homomorphic addition of a constant in $\{0,1\}$ for each entry, and so is essentially fast (and moderately bad on the noise, so we will ignore this and call it depth $1/2$).

Step 3: We now compute **x** as

$$\mathbf{x} = \prod_{i=0}^{\lceil \log_2 p \rceil} \mathbf{w}^{(i)},$$

where we think of $\mathbf{w}^{(i)}$ as a vector of E SIMD encryptions. This step (assuming a balanced multiplication tree) requires depth $\lceil \log_2 \lceil \log_2 p \rceil \rceil$ and $M \cdot \lceil \log_2 p \rceil$ multiplications.

Executing all three steps above therefore requires a depth of $\frac{1}{2} + \lceil \log_2 p \rceil + \lceil \log_2 \lceil \log_2 p \rceil \rceil$, and $2 \cdot M \cdot \lceil \log_2 p \rceil$ multiplications.

5.2   Computing $\mathbf{u} = \mathbf{v}^M$

Given the previous subsection, we can now evaluate $u_i = \prod_{j=1}^{\ell^{(R)}} v_j^{m_{i,j}}, i = 1, \ldots,$ $\ell^{(R)}$, where **v** is a SIMD vector consisting of E vectors encoding $\ell^{(R)}$ elements, as is the output **u**. For this we use a trick for systolic matrix-vector multiplication in [22], but converted into multiplicative notation.

We write the matrix **M** as $\ell^{(R)}$ SIMD vectors $\mathbf{d}_i$, for $i = 1, \ldots, \ell^{(R)}$, so that $\mathbf{d}_{i,j} = m_{j,(j+i-1) \pmod{\ell^{(R)}}}$ for $j = 1, \ldots, \ell^{(R)}$. We let $\mathbf{v} \lll i$ denote the SIMD vector **v** rotated left i positions (with wrap around). Since **v** actually consists of E SIMD vectors this can be performed using time proportional to E multiplications, but with no addition to the overall depth (it is an expensive in terms of time, but cheap in terms of noise. See the operations in Table 1 of [22]).

Step 1: First compute, for $i = 1, \ldots, \ell^{(R)}$,

$$\mathbf{x}_i = (\mathbf{v} \lll (i-1))^{\mathbf{d}_i}$$

using the method previously described in Subsection 5.1. This requires a depth of $\frac{1}{2} + \lceil \log_2 p \rceil + \lceil \log_2 \lceil \log_2 p \rceil \rceil$, and essentially $\ell^{(R)} \cdot (E + 2 \cdot M \cdot \lceil \log_2 p \rceil)$ multiplications.

Step 2: All we need now do is compute

$$\mathbf{u} = \prod_{i=1}^{\ell^{(R)}} \mathbf{x}_i.$$

This requires (assuming a balanced multiplication tree) a depth of $\lceil \log_2 \ell^{(R)} \rceil$ and $\ell^{(R)}$ multiplications in $\mathbb{G}$.

Thus far, for the operations in Subsection 5.1 and this subsection we have used a total depth of $\frac{1}{2} + \lceil \log_2 \ell^{(R)} \rceil + \lceil \log_2 p \rceil + \lceil \log_2 \lceil \log_2 p \rceil \rceil$ and a cost of $\ell^{(R)} \cdot (M + E + 2 \cdot M \cdot \lceil \log_2 p \rceil)$ multiplications.

5.3   Computing $\mathbf{v} \cdot \prod_{k=0}^{\lambda} \mathbf{v}_k^{M_k}$

To evaluate our required output we need to execute the above steps λ times, in order to obtain the elements which we then multiply together. Thus in total we have a depth of

$$\frac{1}{2} + \lceil \log_2 \ell^{(R)} \rceil + \lceil \log_2 p \rceil + \lceil \log_2 \lceil \log_2 p \rceil \rceil + \lceil \log_2 \lambda \rceil$$

and a cost of

$$\lambda \cdot \left(M + \ell^{(R)} \cdot (M + E + 2 \cdot M \cdot \lceil \log_2 p \rceil) \right)$$

multiplications.

6   Bootstrapping a Set of Ciphertexts

To perform our bootstrapping operation we introduce another representation, this time more standard. This is the matrix representation of the ring S_q. Since S_q can be considered a vector space over $\mathbb{Z}_q$ by the usual polynomial embedding, we can associate an element a to its coefficient vector $\mathbf{a}$. We can also associate an element b to a $n \times n$ matrix $\mathbf{M}_b$ over $\mathbb{Z}_q$ such that the vector

$$\mathbf{c} = \mathbf{M}_b \cdot \mathbf{a}$$

is the coefficient vector of c where $c = a \cdot b$. This representation, which associates an element in S_q to a matrix, is called the matrix representation.

Recall we want to bootstrap $\ell^{(R)}/n$ ciphertexts in one go. We also recall the maps red and rep from Section 4 and define $\tau = \mathsf{red} \circ \mathsf{rep}$ to be the reduction modulo p map on $\mathbb{Z}_q^+$. To do this we can first extend rep and τ to the whole of S_q^+ by linearity, with images in $\mathbb{G}^n$ and $\mathbb{F}_p^n$ respectively. Similarly, we can extend rep and τ to $S_q^{\ell^{(R)}/n}$ to obtain maps $\overline{\mathsf{rep}} : (S_q^+)^{\ell^{(R)}/n} \longrightarrow \mathbb{G}^{\ell^{(R)}}$ and $\overline{\tau} : (S_q^+)^{\ell^{(R)}/n} \longrightarrow \mathbb{F}_p^{\ell^{(R)}}$, as in Section 4. Again this induces a map $\overline{\mathsf{red}}$, which is just the SIMD evaluation of red on the image of $\overline{\mathsf{rep}}$ in $\mathbb{G}^{\ell^{(R)}}$. We let $\overline{\mathsf{rep}}_{j,i}$ denote the restriction of $\overline{\mathsf{rep}}$ to the $(i-1)$th coefficient of the j-th S_q component, for $1 \leq i \leq n$ and $1 \leq j \leq \ell^{(R)}/n$.

We can then rewrite the decryption equation of our $\ell^{(R)}/n$ ciphertexts as

$$\left(\left(c_0^{(j)} + \mathfrak{s}\mathfrak{k}^{(S)} \cdot c_1^{(j)} \pmod{q} \right) \pmod{p} \right)_{j=1}^{\ell^{(R)}/n}$$

$$= \overline{\mathsf{red}} \left(\overline{\mathsf{rep}} \left(c_0^{(1)} + \mathfrak{s}\mathfrak{k}^{(S)} \cdot c_1^{(1)}, \dots \right. \right.$$

$$\left. \left. \dots, c_0^{(\ell^{(R)}/n)} + \mathfrak{s}\mathfrak{k}^{(S)} \cdot c_1^{(\ell^{(R)}/n)} \right) \right)$$

$$= \overline{\mathsf{red}} \left(\overline{\mathsf{rep}} \left(\mathbf{x} \right) \right),$$

where $\mathbf{x}$ is the vector consisting of S_q elements $c_0^{(j)} + \mathfrak{s}\mathfrak{k}^{(S)} \cdot c_1^{(j)}$, for $j = 1, \dots, \ell^{(R)}/n$. Thus, if we can compute $\overline{\mathsf{rep}}(\mathbf{x})$, then to perform the bootstrap we need only evaluate (in $\ell^{(R)}$-fold SIMD fashion) the arithmetic circuit of multiplicative depth $\lceil \log_2 d \rceil$ representing $\overline{\mathrm{red}}$. Since we have enough slots, $\ell^{(R)}$, in the large plain text ring, we are able to do this homomorphically on fully packed ciphertexts. The total number of monomials in the arithmetic circuit (i.e. the multiplications we would need to evaluate $\overline{\mathrm{red}}$) being $D(E, d)$.

6.1   Homomorphically Evaluating $\overline{\mathrm{rep}}(\mathbf{x})$

We wish to homomorphically evaluate $\overline{\mathrm{rep}}(\mathbf{x})$ such that the output is a set of E ciphertexts and if we took the $i + (j-1) \cdot \ell^{(R)}/n$th slot of each plaintext we would obtain the E values which represent $\overline{\mathrm{rep}}_{j,i}(\mathbf{x})$. Let $\lambda = \lceil \log q / \log p \rceil$. We add to the public key of the SHE scheme the encryption of $\overline{\mathrm{rep}}(p^k \cdot \mathfrak{st}^{(S)}, \ldots, p^k \cdot \mathfrak{st}^{(S)})$ for $k = 0, \ldots, \lambda$ (where each component is copied $\ell^{(R)}/n$ times). For a given k this is a set of E ciphertexts, such that if we took the $i + (j-1) \cdot \ell^{(R)}/n$th slot of each plaintext we would obtain the E values which represent $\overline{\mathrm{rep}}_{j,i}(p^k \cdot \mathfrak{st}^{(S)})$. Let the resulting vector of ciphertexts be denoted $\mathfrak{ct}_k$, for $k = 1, \ldots, \lambda$, where $\mathfrak{ct}_k$ is a vector of length E.

Let $\mathbf{M}_{c_1^{(j)}}$ be the matrix representation of the second ciphertext component $c_1^{(j)}$ of the j-th ciphertext that we want to bootstrap. We write

$$\mathbf{M}_{c_1^{(j)}} = \sum_{k=0}^{\lambda} p^k \cdot \mathbf{M}_1^{(j,k)}$$

where $\mathbf{M}_1^{(j,k)}$ is a matrix with coefficients in $\{0, \ldots, p-1\}$. We then have that

$$c_0^{(j)} + \mathfrak{st}^{(S)} \cdot c_1^{(j)} = c_0^{(j)} + \sum_{k=0}^{\lambda} \left(p^k \cdot \mathbf{M}_1^{(j,k)} \cdot \underline{\mathfrak{st}}^{(S)} \right)$$

$$= c_0^{(j)} + \sum_{k=0}^{\lambda} \left(\mathbf{M}_1^{(j,k)} \cdot (p^k \cdot \underline{\mathfrak{st}}^{(S)}) \right),$$

where $\underline{\mathfrak{st}}^{(S)}$ is the vector of coefficients of the secret key $\mathfrak{st}^{(S)}$.

We let $\mathbf{M}_1^{(k)} = \bigoplus_{j=1}^{\ell^{(R)}/n} \mathbf{M}_1^{(j,k)} = \mathbf{diag}(\mathbf{M}_1^{(1,k)}, \ldots, \mathbf{M}_1^{(\ell^{(R)}/n,k)})$. We now apply $\overline{\mathrm{rep}}$ to both sides, which means we need to compute homomorphically the ciphertext which represents

$$\overline{\mathrm{rep}}\left(c_0^{(1)}, \ldots, c_0^{(\ell^{(R)}/n)}\right) \cdot \prod_{k=0}^{\lambda} \overline{\mathrm{rep}}\left(p^k \cdot \underline{\mathfrak{st}}^{(S)}, \ldots, p^k \cdot \underline{\mathfrak{st}}^{(S)}\right)^{\mathbf{M}_1^{(k)}}.$$

We are thus in the situation described in Section 5. Thus the homomorphic evaluation of $\overline{\mathrm{rep}}(\mathbf{x})$ requires a depth of

$$\frac{1}{2} + \lceil \log_2 \ell^{(R)} \rceil + \lceil \log_2 p \rceil + \lceil \log_2 \lceil \log_2 p \rceil \rceil + \lceil \log_2 \lambda \rceil$$

and

$$\lambda \cdot \left(M + \ell^{(R)} \cdot (M + E + 2 \cdot M \cdot \lceil \log_2 p \rceil) \right)$$

multiplications.

6.2   Repacking

At this point in the bootstrapping procedure (assuming for simplicity that a ring switch has not occured) we have a single ciphertext $\mathfrak{ct}$ whose $\ell^{(R)}$ slots encode the coefficients (over the small ring) of the $\ell^{(R)}/n$ ciphertexts that we are bootstrapping. Our task is now to extract these coefficients to produce a ciphertext (or set of ciphertexts) which encode the same data. Effectively this is the task of performing $\ell^{(R)}/n$ inverse Fourier transforms (a.k.a interpolations) over S in parallel, and then encoding the result as elements in R via the embedding $\iota : S \longrightarrow R$.

There are a multitude of ways of doing this step (bar performing directly an inverse FFT algorithm), for example the general method of Alperin-Sheriff and Peikert [1] could be applied. This makes the observation that the FFT to a vector of Fourier coefficients $\mathbf{x}$ is essentially applying a linear operation, and hence we can compute it by taking the trace of a value $\alpha \cdot \mathbf{x}$ for some fixed constant α.

We select a more naive, and simplistic approach. Suppose $\mathbf{x}$ is the vector which is encoded by the input ciphertext. We first homomorphically compute

$$\mathbf{b}_1, \ldots, \mathbf{b}_{\ell^{(R)}} = \mathsf{replicate}(\mathbf{x}).$$

Where $\mathsf{replicate}(\mathbf{x})$ is the Full Replication algorithm from [22]. This produces $\ell^{(R)}$ ciphertexts, the ith of which encodes the constant polynomial over R_p equal to the i slot in $\mathbf{x}$. In [22] this is explained for the case where $\ell^{(R)} = N$, but the method clearly works when $\ell^{(R)} < N$. The method requires time $O(\ell^{(R)})$ and depth $O(\log \log \ell^{(R)})$.

Given the output $\mathbf{b}_1, \ldots, \mathbf{b}_{\ell^{(R)}}$, which encode the coefficients of the $\ell^{(R)}/n$ original plaintext vectors, we can now apply ι (which recall is a linear map) to obtain *any* linear function of the underlying plaintexts. For example we could produce $\ell^{(R)}/n$ ciphertexts each of which encodes one of the original plaintexts, or indeed a single ciphertext which encodes all of them.

So putting all of the sub-procedures for bootstrapping together, we find that we can bootstrap $\ell^{(R)}/n$ ciphertexts in parallel using a procedure of depth of

$$\lceil \log_2 d \rceil + \frac{1}{2} + \lceil \log_2 \ell^{(R)} \rceil + \lceil \log_2 p \rceil + \lceil \log_2 \lceil \log_2 p \rceil \rceil + \lceil \log_2 \lambda \rceil + O(\log_2 \log_2 \ell^{(R)})$$

and a cost of

$$D(E, d) + \lambda \cdot \left(M + \ell^{(R)} \cdot (M + E + 2 \cdot M \cdot \lceil \log_2 p \rceil) \right) + O(\ell^{(R)})$$

multiplications, where $d \approx (\log_2 q) \cdot (p - 1)/(\log_2 p)$, $E = \sum_{i=1}^{t} k_i$ and $M = \frac{1}{2} \cdot \sum_{i=1}^{t} k_i \cdot (k_i + 1)$.

7   Elliptic Curves Based Variant

We now extend our algorithm from representations in finite fields to representations in elliptic curve groups. Recall we need to embed $\mathbb{Z}_q^+$ into a group defined over $\mathbb{F}_p$ whose operations can be expressed in terms of the functionality of the homomorphic encryption scheme. This means that the range of the representation should be an algebraic group. We have already seen linear algebraic groups (a.k.a. matrix representations) used in this context in work of Alperin-Sherriff and Peikert, thus as it is natural (to anyone who has studied algebraic groups) to consider algebraic varieties. The finite field case discussed in the previous sections corresponds to the genus zero case, thus the next natural extension would be to examine the genus one case (a.k.a. elliptic curves).

The reason for doing this is the value of q from Table 2 compared to the estimated values from Table 1 are far from optimal. This is because we have few possible group orders of $\mathbb{F}_{p^{k_i}}^*$. The standard trick in this context (used for example in the ECM factorization method, the ECPP primality prover, or even indeed in all of elliptic curve cryptography) is to replace the multiplicative group of a finite field by an elliptic curve group.

Just as before we select a coprime factorization $q = \prod_{i=1}^{t} e_i$ (with the e_i not necessarily prime, but pairwise coprime). But now we require that e_i divides the order of an elliptic curve E_i defined over p^{k_i}. Since the group orders of elliptic curves are distributed roughly uniformly within the Hasse interval it is highly likely that there are such elliptic curves. Determining such curves may however be a hard problem for a fixed value of q; a problem which arose previously in cryptography in [3]. However, since we have some freedom in selecting q in our scheme we can select q and the E_i simultaneously, and hence finding the elliptic curves will not be a problem.

Again, we fix a polynomial representation of $\mathbb{F}_{p^{k_i}}$, i.e. an irreducible polynomial $f_i(x)$ of degree k_i such that $\mathbb{F}_{p^{k_i}} = \mathbb{F}_p[x]/f_i(x)$, and now we let $G_i \in E_i(\mathbb{F}_{p^{k_i}})$ denote a fixed point on the elliptic curve of order e_i. We now can translate our method into this new setting. For example (1) translates to

$$\mathsf{rep} : \begin{cases} \mathbb{Z}_q^+ \longrightarrow \mathbb{G} = \prod_{i=1}^{t} E_i(\mathbb{F}_{p^{k_i}}) \\ a \longmapsto ([a_1]G_1, \ldots, [a_t]G_t) \end{cases} \tag{2}$$

where $a_i = a \pmod{e_i}$.

Homomorphic calculations in $\mathbb{G}$ are then performed using Jacobian Projective coordinates. This means that general point addition can be performed with multiplicative depth five and $M' = 16 \cdot M$ homomorphic multiplications. Our method then proceeds as before, except we replace homomorphic multiplication in $\mathbb{F}_{p^{k_i}}^*$ with Jacobian projective point addition in $E_i(\mathbb{F}_{p^{k_i}})$.

The computation of red is then performed as follows. We first homomorphically map the projective points in $\mathbb{G}$ into an affine point. Each such conversion, in component i, requires an $\mathbb{F}_{p^{k_i}}$-field inversion and three $\mathbb{F}_{p^{k_i}}$-field multiplications. If we let DInv_i (resp. MInv_i) denote the depth (resp. number of multiplications in $\mathbb{F}_p$) of the circuit to invert in the field $\mathbb{F}_{p^{k_i}}$. This implies that the conversion of a set of projective points in $\mathbb{G}$ to a set of affine points requires depth $3 + \max_{i=1}^{t} \mathsf{DInv}_i$ and $4 \cdot M + \sum_{i=1}^{t} \mathsf{MInv}_i$ homomorphic multiplications over $\mathbb{F}_p$.

Given this final conversion to affine form, we have effectively $E' = E + t$, as opposed to E, variables defining the elements in $\mathbb{G}$. The extra t variables coming from the y-coordinate; it is clear we only need to store t such variables as opposed to E such variables as each x coordinate corresponds to at most two y-coordinates and hence a naive form of homomorphic point compression can be applied.

This means the map red (after the conversion to affine coordinates so as to reduce the multiplicative complexity of the interpolated polynomial) can be expressed as a degree d' map; where we expect d' to be the smallest d' such that $^{E'+d'}C_{d'} > q$, which means we expect $d' \approx E' \cdot (2^{\log(q)/\log(E')} - 1)$. This means, as before, that the resulting depth will be $\lceil \log_2 d' \rceil$ and the number of multiplications will be $D(E', d')$.

So putting all of the sub-procedures for bootstrapping together, we find that we can use the elliptic curve variant of our bootstrapping method to bootstrap $\ell^{(R)}/n$ ciphertexts in parallel using a procedure of depth of

$$\lceil \log_2 d' \rceil + 5 \cdot \left(\frac{1}{2} + \lceil \log_2 \ell^{(R)} \rceil + \cdot \lceil \log_2 p \rceil + \cdot \lceil \log_2 \lceil \log_2 p \rceil \rceil + \lceil \log_2 \lambda \rceil \right)$$

$$+ 3 + \max_{i=1}^{t} \mathsf{DInv}_i + O(\log_2 \log_2 \ell^{(R)})$$

and

$$D(E', d') + \lambda \cdot \left(M' + \ell^{(R)} \cdot (M' + 3 \cdot E + 2 \cdot M' \cdot \lceil \log_2 p \rceil) \right)$$

$$+ 4 \cdot M + \sum_{i=1}^{t} \mathsf{MInv}_i + O(\ell^{(R)})$$

multiplications, where $d' \approx \log q / \log E'$, $E' = \sum_{i=1}^{t}(k_i + 1)$, $M = \sum_{i=1}^{t} k_i \cdot (k_i + 1)/2$ and $M' = 16 \cdot M$. Note the $3 \cdot E$ term comes from needing to rotate the three projective coordinates.

However, the ability to use arbitrary q comes at a penalty; the depth required has dramatically increased due to the elliptic curve group operations. For example if we consider a prime p of size roughly 2^{16} and $k = 2$, then we need about 200 levels, as opposed to 56 with the finite field variant. This then strongly influences the required value of N, pushing it up from around $85,000$ to $220,000$. Thus in practice the elliptic curve variant is unlikely to be viable.

A Parameter Calculation

In [20] a concrete set of parameters for the BGV SHE scheme was given for the case of binary message spaces, and arbitrary L. In [12] this was adapted to the case of message space R_p for 2-power cyclotomic rings, but only for the schemes which could support one level of multiplication gates (i.e. for $L = 1$). In [11] these two approaches were combined, for arbitrary L and p, and the analysis was (slightly) modified to remove the need for a modulus switching upon encryption. In this section we modify again the analysis of [11] to present an analysis which includes a step of field switching from [17]. We assume in this section that the reader is familiar with the analysis and algorithms from [11,17,20].

Our analysis will make extensive use of the following fact: If $a \in R$ be chosen from a distribution such that the coefficients are distributed with mean zero and standard deviation σ, then if ζ_m is a primitive mth root of unity, we can use $6 \cdot \sigma$ to bound $a(\zeta_m)$ and hence the canonical embedding norm of a. If we have two elements with variances σ_1^2 and σ_2^2, then we can bound the canonical norm of their product with $16 \cdot \sigma_1 \cdot \sigma_2$.

Ensuring We Can Evaluate the Required Depth: Recall we have two rings R and S of degree N and n respectively. The ring S is a subring of R and hence n divides N. We require a chain of moduli $q_0 < q_1 \ldots < q_L$ corresponding to each level of the scheme. We assume (for sake of simplicity) that $q_i/q_{i-1} = p_i$ are primes. Thus $q_L = q_0 \cdot \prod_{i=1}^{i=L} p_i$. Also note, that as in [11], we apply a SHE.LowerLevel (a.k.a. modulus switch) algorithm *before* a multiplication operation. This often leads to lower noise values in practice (which a practical instantiation can make use of). In addition it eliminates the need to perform a modulus switch after encryption, which happened in [20].

We utilize the following constants described in [12], which are worked out for the case of message space defined modulo p (the constants in [12] make use of an additional parameter, arising from the key generation procedure. In our case we can take this constant equal to one). In the following h is the Hamming weight of the secret keys $\mathfrak{sk}^{(R)}$ and $\mathfrak{sk}^{(S)}$.

$$B_{\text{Clean}} = N \cdot p/2 + p \cdot \sigma \cdot \left(\frac{16 \cdot N}{\sqrt{2}} + 6 \cdot \sqrt{N} + 16 \cdot \sqrt{h \cdot N} \right)$$

$$B_{\text{Scale}}^{(R)} = p \cdot \sqrt{3 \cdot N} \cdot \left(1 + \frac{8}{3} \cdot \sqrt{h} \right)$$

$$B_{\text{Scale}}^{(S)} = p \cdot \sqrt{3 \cdot n} \cdot \left(1 + \frac{8}{3} \cdot \sqrt{h} \right)$$

$$B_{\text{Ks}}^{(R)} = p \cdot \sigma \cdot N \cdot \left(1.49 \cdot \sqrt{h \cdot N} + 2.11 \cdot h + 5.54 \cdot \sqrt{h} + 1.96\sqrt{N} + 4.62 \right)$$

$$B_{\text{Ks}}^{(S)} = p \cdot \sigma \cdot n \cdot \left(1.49 \cdot \sqrt{h \cdot n} + 2.11 \cdot h + 5.54 \cdot \sqrt{h} + 1.96\sqrt{n} + 4.62 \right)$$

As in [20] we define a small "wiggle room" ξ which we set to be equal to eight; this is set to enable a number of additions to be performed without needing to individually account for them in our analysis. These constants arise in the following way:

- A freshly encrypted ciphertext at level L has noise bounded by B_{Clean}.
- In the worst case, when applying SHE.LowerLevel to a (big ring) ciphertext at level $\mathfrak{l} > L_2 + 1$ with noise bounded by B' one obtains a new ciphertext at level $\mathfrak{l} - 1$ with noise bounded by

$$\frac{B'}{p_{\mathfrak{l}}} + B_{\mathsf{Scale}}^{(R)}.$$

- In the worst case, when applying SHE.LowerLevel to a (small ring) ciphertext at level $\mathfrak{l} \leq L_2 + 1$ with noise bounded by B' one obtains a new ciphertext at level $\mathfrak{l} - 1$ with noise bounded by

$$\frac{B'}{p_{\mathfrak{l}}} + B_{\mathsf{Scale}}^{(S)}.$$

- When applying the tensor product multiplication operation to (big ring) ciphertexts of a given level $\mathfrak{l} > L_2 + 1$ of noise B_1 and B_2 one obtains a new ciphertext with noise given by

$$B_1 \cdot B_2 + \frac{B_{\mathsf{Ks}}^{(R)} \cdot q_{\mathfrak{l}}}{P_R} + B_{\mathsf{Scale}}^{(R)},$$

where P_R is a value to be determined later.
- When applying the tensor product multiplication operation to (small ring) ciphertexts of a given level $\mathfrak{l} \leq L_2$ of noise B_1 and B_2 one obtains a new ciphertext with noise given by

$$B_1 \cdot B_2 + \frac{B_{\mathsf{Ks}}^{(S)} \cdot q_{\mathfrak{l}}}{P_S} + B_{\mathsf{Scale}}^{(S)},$$

where again P_S is a value to be determined later.

A general evaluation procedure begins with a freshly encrypted ciphertext at level L with noise B_{Clean}. When entering the first multiplication operation we first apply a SHE.LowerLevel operation to reduce the noise to a universal bounds. $B^{(R)}$, whose value will be determined later. We therefore require

$$\frac{\xi \cdot B_{\mathsf{Clean}}}{p_L} + B_{\mathsf{Scale}}^{(R)} \leq B^{(R)},$$

i.e.

$$p_L \geq \frac{8 \cdot B_{\mathsf{Clean}}}{B^{(R)} - B_{\mathsf{Scale}}^{(R)}}. \tag{3}$$

We now turn to dealing with the SHE.LowerLevel operations which occurs before a multiplication gate at level $\mathfrak{l} \in \{1, \ldots, L-1\} \setminus \{L_2 + 1\}$. In what follows we assume $\mathfrak{l} > L_2 + 1$, to obtain the equations for $\mathfrak{l} \leq L_2$ one simply replaces the R-constants by their equivalent S-constants. We perform a worst case analysis and assume that the input ciphertexts are at level $\mathfrak{l}$. We can then assume that the input to the tensoring operation in the previous multiplication gate (just after the previous SHE.LowerLevel) was bounded by $B^{(R)}$, and so the output noise from the previous multiplication gate for each input ciphertext is bounded by $(B^{(R)})^2 + B_{\mathsf{Ks}}^{(R)} \cdot q_{\mathfrak{l}} / P_R + B_{\mathsf{Scale}}^{(R)}$. This means the noise on entering the SHE.LowerLevel operation is bounded by ξ times this value, and so to maintain our invariant we require

$$\frac{\xi \cdot (B^{(R)})^2 + \xi \cdot B_{\mathsf{Scale}}^{(R)}}{p_{\mathfrak{l}}} + \frac{\xi \cdot B_{\mathsf{Ks}}^{(R)} \cdot q_{\mathfrak{l}}}{P_R \cdot p_{\mathfrak{l}}} + B_{\mathsf{Scale}}^{(R)} \leq B^{(R)}.$$

Rearranging this into a quadratic equation in $B^{(R)}$ we have

$$\frac{\xi}{p_{\mathfrak{l}}} \cdot (B^{(R)})^2 - B^{(R)} + \left(\frac{\xi \cdot B_{\mathsf{Scale}}^{(R)}}{p_{\mathfrak{l}}} + \frac{\xi \cdot B_{\mathsf{Ks}}^{(R)} \cdot q_{\mathfrak{l}-1}}{P_R} + B_{\mathsf{Scale}}^{(R)} \right) \leq 0.$$

We denote the constant term in this equation by $R_{\mathfrak{l}-1}$. We now assume that all primes $p_{\mathfrak{l}}$ are of roughly the same size (for the ring R), and noting the we need to only satisfy the inequality for the largest modulus $\mathfrak{l} = L - 1$ (resp. $\mathfrak{l} = L_2$ for the ring S). We now fix R_{L-2} by trying to ensure that R_{L-2} is close to $B_{\mathsf{Scale}}^{(R)} \cdot (1 + \xi/p_{L-1}) \approx B_{\mathsf{Scale}}^{(R)}$, so we set $R_{L-2} = (1 - 2^{-3}) \cdot B_{\mathsf{Scale}}^{(R)} \cdot (1 + \xi/p_{L-1})$, and obtain

$$P_R \approx 8 \cdot \frac{\xi \cdot B_{\mathsf{Ks}}^{(R)} \cdot q_{L-2}}{B_{\mathsf{Scale}}^{(R)}}, \tag{4}$$

since $B_{\mathsf{Scale}}^{(R)} \cdot (1 + \xi/p_{L-1}) \approx B_{\mathsf{Scale}}^{(R)}$. Similarly for the small ring we find

$$P_S \approx 8 \cdot \frac{\xi \cdot B_{\mathsf{Ks}}^{(S)} \cdot q_{L_2-1}}{B_{\mathsf{Scale}}^{(S)}}, \tag{5}$$

To ensure we have a solution we require $1 - 4 \cdot \xi \cdot R_{L-2}/p_{L-1} \geq 0$, (resp. $1 - 4 \cdot \xi \cdot R_{L_2-1}/p_{L_2} \geq 0$) which implies we should take, for $i = 2, \ldots, L - 1$,

$$p_i \approx \begin{cases} 4 \cdot \xi \cdot R_{L-2} \approx 32 \cdot B_{\mathsf{Scale}}^{(R)} = p_R & \text{For } i = L_2 + 2, \ldots, L - 1, \\ 4 \cdot \xi \cdot R_{L_2-1} \approx 32 \cdot B_{\mathsf{Scale}}^{(S)} = p_S & \text{For } i = 1, \ldots, L_2. \end{cases} \tag{6}$$

We now examine what happens at level $L_2 + 1$ when we perform a ring switch operation. Following Lemma 3.2 of [17] we know the noise increases by a factor of $(p/2) \cdot \sqrt{N/n}$. The noise output from the previous multiplication gate is bounded by $(B^{(R)})^2 + B_{\mathsf{Ks}}^{(R)} \cdot q_{L_2+2}/P_R + B_{\mathsf{Scale}}^{(R)}$. Note that

$$\frac{B_{Ks}^{(R)} \cdot q_{L_2+2}}{P_R} \approx \frac{B_{Ks}^{(R)} \cdot q_{L_2+2} \cdot B_{Scale}^{(R)}}{8 \cdot \xi \cdot B_{Ks}^{(R)} \cdot q_{L-2}}$$

$$\approx \frac{B_{Scale}^{(R)}}{8 \cdot \xi \cdot p_R^{L_1-4}}$$

Thus the we know that the noise after the ring switch operation is bounded by

$$B_{RingSwitch} = \frac{p}{2} \cdot \sqrt{N/n} \cdot \left((B^{(R)})^2 + \frac{B_{Scale}^{(R)}}{8 \cdot \xi \cdot p_R^{L_1-4}} + B_{Scale}^{(R)} \right).$$

We now modulus switch down to level L_2, and obtain a ciphertext (over the ring S) with noise bounded by

$$\frac{B_{RingSwitch}}{p_{L_2+1}} + B_{Scale}^{(S)}.$$

We would like this to be less than the universal bound $B^{(S)}$, which implies

$$p_{L_2+1} \geq \frac{B_{RingSwitch}}{B^{(S)} - B_{Scale}^{(S)}}. \tag{7}$$

We now need to estimate the size of p_0. Due to the above choices the ciphertext to which we apply the bootstrapping has norm bound by $B^{(S)}$. This means that we require

$$q_0 = p_0 \geq 2 \cdot B^{(S)} \cdot c_{m'}, \tag{8}$$

to ensure a valid decryption/bootstrapping procedure. Recall $c_{m'}$ is the ring constant for the polynomial ring S and it depends only on m' (see [13] for details).

Ensuring We Have Security: The works before [23,31], such as Lindner and Peikert [24], did not include the rank of the lattice into account when estimating the cost of the attacker. The reason is that the lattice rank appears to be only a second order term in the cost of the attack. However, for applications such as FHE, the dimension is usually very big, e.g. 2^{16}, and lattice algorithms are often polynomial in the rank. Therefore, even as a second order term it can contribute significantly to the cost of the attack. The largest modulus used in our big ring (resp. small ring) key switching matrices, i.e. the largest modulus used in an LWE instance, is given by $Q_{L-1} = P_R \cdot q_{L-1}$ (resp. $Q_{L_2} = P_S \cdot q_{L_2}$).

We recall the approach of [23,31] here. First, fix some security level as measured in enumeration nodes, e.g. 2^{128}. Now, use estimates by Chen and Nguyen [9] are used to determine the cost of running BKZ 2.0 for various block sizes β. Combining this with the security level gives an upper bound on the rounds an attacker can perform, depending on β. Then, for various lattice dimensions r, the BKZ 2.0 simulator by Chen and Nguyen is used to determine the quality of the vector as measured by the root-Hermite factor $\delta(\beta, r) = (\|\mathbf{b}\|/\text{vol}(L)^{1/r})^{1/r}$. Now, the best possible root-Hermite factor achievable by the attacker is given by $\delta(r) = \min_\beta \delta(\beta, r)$

In LWE, the relevant parameters for the security are the ring dimension n (resp. N), the modulus $Q = Q_{L_2}$ (resp. $Q = Q_{L-1}$) and the standard deviation σ. Note that in most scenarios, an adversary can choose how many LWE samples he uses in his attack. This number r is equal to the rank of the lattice. The distinguishing attack against LWE uses a short vector in the dual SIS lattice to distinguish the LWE distribution from the uniform distribution. More precisely, an adversary can distinguish between these two distributions with distinguishing advantage ε if the shortest vector he can obtain (in terms of its root-Hermite factor) satisfies

$$\delta(r)^r \cdot Q^{n/r-1} \cdot \sigma < \sqrt{-\log(\varepsilon)/\pi}.$$

It follows that in order for our system to be secure against the previously described adversary, we need that

$$\log_2(Q) \leq \min_{r>n} \frac{r^2 \cdot \log_2(\delta(r)) + r \cdot \log_2(\sigma/\alpha)}{r - n}, \tag{9}$$

where $\alpha = \sqrt{-\log(\varepsilon)/\pi}$. See also[23, 24, 27] for more information. For every n we can now compute an upper bound on $\log_2(q)$ by iterating the right hand side of (9) over m and selecting the minimum.

Putting it All Together. As in [12, 20], we set $\sigma = 3.2$, $B^{(R)} = 2 \cdot B^{(R)}_{\text{Scale}}$ and $B^{(S)} = 2 \cdot B^{(S)}_{\text{Scale}}$. From our equations (3), (4), (5), (6), (7), and (8) we obtain equations for p_i for $i = 0, \ldots, L$, P_R and P_S in terms of n, N, L, h and the security level κ.

B Example Parameters

In Appendix 7 we present a calculation of suitable parameters for our scheme, and the resulting complexity of the polynomial representation of red, here we work out a concrete set of parameters for various plaintext moduli p.

We target $\kappa = 128$-bits of security, and set the Hamming weight h of the secret key $\mathfrak{st}$ to be 64 as in [12, 20]. On input N and n the to the formulae in Appendix 7 we obtain an upper bounds on $\log(Q_{L-1})$ and $\log(Q_{L_2})$. We now use equations (3)-(8) from the Appendix for different values of the plaintext modulus p to obtain a lower bound on $\log(Q_{L-1})$ and $\log(Q_{L_2})$. Then, we increase N and n until the lower bound on Q_{L-1} and Q_{L_2} from the functionality is below the upper bound from the security analysis. In this way we obtain lower bounds for N and n.

In Table 1 we consider four different values of p; for simplicity we also set $t = 1$ in (1), i.e. $\mathbb{G} = \mathbb{F}^*_{p^k}$, for a suitable choice of k. After finding approximate values for N, n and q we can then search for exact values of N, n and q. More precisely, we are looking for cyclotomic rings R and S such that the degree

Table 1. Lower bounds on N and n

p	κ	$c = \ell^{(R)}/n$	$n \approx$	$N \approx$	$q \approx$
2	128	1	860	23100	11637
		2		24100	
$\approx 2^8$	128	1	1040	51800	1635087
		2		53100	
		3, 4,		56000	
		$[5, \ldots, 10]$		57600	
$\approx 2^{16}$	128	1	1300	96000	467989106
		2, 3		98500	
		$[4, \ldots, 10]$		103000	
$\approx 2^{32}$	128	1	1750	181000	$3.558467651 \cdot 10^{13}$
		2		183000	
		$[3, \ldots, 10]$		185000	

Table 2. A concrete set of cyclotomic rings with an estimation of the number of multiplications and the depth required to perform our bootstrapping step

p	m	$N = \phi(m)$	m'	$n = \phi(m')$	$c_{m'}$	$\ell^{(R)}/n$	k	L	# Mults	q
2	31775	24000	1271	1200	3.93	1	16	23	$\approx 8.3 \cdot 10^6$	65535
	32767	27000	1057	900	2.69	2	15	23	$\approx 1.02 \cdot 10^7$	32767
$2^8 + 1$	62419	51840	1687	1440	2.72	1	3	40	$\approx 4.6 \cdot 10^6$	4243648
	91149	58080	1321	1320	1.28	1	3	39	$\approx 2.3 \cdot 10^6$	2121824
	137384	63360	1321	1320	1.28	4	3	41	$\approx 3.5 \cdot 10^6$	2121824
$2^{16} + 1$	113993	100800	2651	2400	2.9	1	2	56	$\approx 1.5 \cdot 10^9$	2147549184
	160977	102608	2333	2332	1.28	2	2	58	$\approx 6.3 \cdot 10^8$	715849728
	272200	108800	1361	1360	1.28	4	2	57	$\approx 4.8 \cdot 10^8$	536887296
$2^{32} + 15$	198203	183040	2227	2080	3.6	1	2	79	$\approx 1.1 \cdot 10^{14}$	414161297767368
	202051	199872	2083	2082	1.28	4	2	79	$\approx 3.9 \cdot 10^{13}$	50637664608480
	352317	190512	2649	1764	1.81	6	2	82	$\approx 5.1 \cdot 10^{14}$	50637664608480

$N = \phi(m)$ of $F(X) = \Phi_m(X)$ and $n = \phi(m')$ of $f(x) = \Phi_{m'}(X)$ are larger than the bounds above and n divides both N and $\ell^{(R)}$ (the number of plaintext slots associated with R). In addition we require that q divides $p^k - 1$. See Table 2 for some values.

Notice that the value of q is strongly influenced by the ring constant $c_{m'}$. In Table 1 we set $c_{m'} = 1.28$ (i.e. we assume the best case of m' being prime), whereas in Table 2 we compute the actual value of the ring constant for each cyclotomic ring we consider. For example for $p = 2$, in Table 1 we obtain an approximate value $q \approx 11637$, but in Table 2 we need a larger value due to the additional condition that q divides $p^k - 1$, and the ring constant, which is bigger than 1.27 for $m' = 1271$ and $m' = 1057$.

Acknowledgments. This work has been supported in part by ERC Advanced Grant ERC-2010-AdG-267188-CRIPTO, by EPSRC via grant EP/I03126X, by the European Commission under the H2020 project HEAT and by the Defense Advanced Research

Projects Agency (DARPA) and the Air Force Research Laboratory (AFRL) under agreement number FA8750-11-2-0079.[1]

References

1. Alperin-Sheriff, J., Peikert, C.: Practical bootstrapping in quasilinear time. In: Canetti, R., Garay, J.A. (eds.) CRYPTO 2013, Part I. LNCS, vol. 8042, pp. 1–20. Springer, Heidelberg (2013)
2. Alperin-Sheriff, J., Peikert, C.: Faster bootstrapping with polynomial error. In: Garay, J.A., Gennaro, R. (eds.) CRYPTO 2014, Part I. LNCS, vol. 8616, pp. 297–314. Springer, Heidelberg (2014)
3. Boneh, D., Lipton, R.J.: Algorithms for black-box fields and their application to cryptography (extended abstract). In: Koblitz, N. (ed.) CRYPTO 1996. LNCS, vol. 1109, pp. 283–297. Springer, Heidelberg (1996)
4. Brakerski, Z.: Fully homomorphic encryption without modulus switching from classical GapSVP. In: Safavi-Naini, R., Canetti, R. (eds.) CRYPTO 2012. LNCS, vol. 7417, pp. 868–886. Springer, Heidelberg (2012)
5. Brakerski, Z., Gentry, C., Vaikuntanathan, V.: (Leveled) fully homomorphic encryption without bootstrapping. In: ITCS, pp. 309–325. ACM (2012)
6. Brakerski, Z., Vaikuntanathan, V.: Efficient fully homomorphic encryption from (standard) LWE. In: FOCS, pp. 97–106. IEEE (2011)
7. Brakerski, Z., Vaikuntanathan, V.: Fully homomorphic encryption from ring-LWE and security for key dependent messages. In: Rogaway, P. (ed.) CRYPTO 2011. LNCS, vol. 6841, pp. 505–524. Springer, Heidelberg (2011)
8. Brakerski, Z., Vaikuntanathan, V.: Lattice-based FHE as secure as PKE. In: ITCS, pp. 1–12 (2014)
9. Chen, Y., Nguyen, P.Q.: BKZ 2.0: better lattice security estimates. In: Lee, D.H., Wang, X. (eds.) ASIACRYPT 2011. LNCS, vol. 7073, pp. 1–20. Springer, Heidelberg (2011)
10. Cheon, J.H., Coron, J.-S., Kim, J., Lee, M.S., Lepoint, T., Tibouchi, M., Yun, A.: Batch fully homomorphic encryption over the integers. In: Johansson, T., Nguyen, P.Q. (eds.) EUROCRYPT 2013. LNCS, vol. 7881, pp. 315–335. Springer, Heidelberg (2013)
11. Choudhury, A., Loftus, J., Orsini, E., Patra, A., Smart, N.P.: Between a rock and a hard place: interpolating between MPC and FHE. In: Sako, K., Sarkar, P. (eds.) ASIACRYPT 2013, Part II. LNCS, vol. 8270, pp. 221–240. Springer, Heidelberg (2013)
12. Damgård, I., Keller, M., Larraia, E., Pastro, V., Scholl, P., Smart, N.P.: Practical covertly secure MPC for dishonest majority – or: breaking the SPDZ limits. In: Crampton, J., Jajodia, S., Mayes, K. (eds.) ESORICS 2013. LNCS, vol. 8134, pp. 1–18. Springer, Heidelberg (2013)

---

[1] The US Government is authorized to reproduce and distribute reprints for Government purposes notwithstanding any copyright notation thereon. The views and conclusions contained herein are those of the authors and should not be interpreted as necessarily representing the official policies or endorsements, either expressed or implied, of Defense Advanced Research Projects Agency (DARPA) or the U.S. Government.

13. Damgård, I., Pastro, V., Smart, N., Zakarias, S.: Multiparty computation from somewhat homomorphic encryption. In: Safavi-Naini, R., Canetti, R. (eds.) CRYPTO 2012. LNCS, vol. 7417, pp. 643–662. Springer, Heidelberg (2012)
14. Gentry, C.: A fully homomorphic encryption scheme. PhD thesis, Stanford University (2009). crypto.stanford.edu/craig
15. Gentry, C.: Fully homomorphic encryption using ideal lattices. In: STOC, pp. 169–178. ACM (2009)
16. Gentry, C., Halevi, S.: Implementing gentry's fully-homomorphic encryption scheme. In: Paterson, K.G. (ed.) EUROCRYPT 2011. LNCS, vol. 6632, pp. 129–148. Springer, Heidelberg (2011)
17. Gentry, C., Halevi, S., Peikert, C., Smart, N.P.: Field switching in BGV-style homomorphic encryption. Journal of Computer Security 21(5), 663–684 (2013)
18. Gentry, C., Halevi, S., Smart, N.P.: Better bootstrapping in fully homomorphic encryption. In: Fischlin, M., Buchmann, J., Manulis, M. (eds.) PKC 2012. LNCS, vol. 7293, pp. 1–16. Springer, Heidelberg (2012)
19. Gentry, C., Halevi, S., Smart, N.P.: Fully homomorphic encryption with polylog overhead. In: Pointcheval, D., Johansson, T. (eds.) EUROCRYPT 2012. LNCS, vol. 7237, pp. 465–482. Springer, Heidelberg (2012)
20. Gentry, C., Halevi, S., Smart, N.P.: Homomorphic evaluation of the AES circuit. In: Safavi-Naini, R., Canetti, R. (eds.) CRYPTO 2012. LNCS, vol. 7417, pp. 850–867. Springer, Heidelberg (2012)
21. Gentry, C., Sahai, A., Waters, B.: Homomorphic encryption from learning with errors: conceptually-simpler, asymptotically-faster, attribute-based. In: Canetti, R., Garay, J.A. (eds.) CRYPTO 2013, Part I. LNCS, vol. 8042, pp. 75–92. Springer, Heidelberg (2013)
22. Halevi, S., Shoup, V.: Algorithms in HElib. Cryptology ePrint Archive, Report 2014/106 (2014)
23. Lepoint, T., Naehrig, M.: A comparison of the homomorphic encryption schemes FV and YASHE. In: Pointcheval, D., Vergnaud, D. (eds.) AFRICACRYPT. LNCS, vol. 8469, pp. 318–335. Springer, Heidelberg (2014)
24. Lindner, R., Peikert, C.: Better key sizes (and attacks) for LWE-based encryption. In: Kiayias, A. (ed.) CT-RSA 2011. LNCS, vol. 6558, pp. 319–339. Springer, Heidelberg (2011)
25. Lyubashevsky, V., Peikert, C., Regev, O.: On ideal lattices and learning with errors over rings. In: Gilbert, H. (ed.) EUROCRYPT 2010. LNCS, vol. 6110, pp. 1–23. Springer, Heidelberg (2010)
26. Lyubashevsky, V., Peikert, C., Regev, O.: A toolkit for ring-LWE cryptography. In: Johansson, T., Nguyen, P.Q. (eds.) EUROCRYPT 2013. LNCS, vol. 7881, pp. 35–54. Springer, Heidelberg (2013)
27. Micciancio, D., Regev, O.: Lattice-based cryptography. In: Post-Quantum Cryptography, pp. 147–191. Springer (2009)
28. Rohloff, K., Cousins, D.B.: A scalable implementation of fully homomorphic encryption built on NTRU. In: Böhme, R., Brenner, M., Moore, T., Smith, M. (eds.) FC 2014 Workshops. LNCS, vol. 8438, pp. 221–234. Springer, Heidelberg (2014)
29. Smart, N.P., Vercauteren, F.: Fully homomorphic encryption with relatively small key and ciphertext sizes. In: Nguyen, P.Q., Pointcheval, D. (eds.) PKC 2010. LNCS, vol. 6056, pp. 420–443. Springer, Heidelberg (2010)

30. Smart, N.P., Vercauteren, F.: Fully homomorphic SIMD operations. Designs, Codes and Cryptography **71**, 57–81 (2014)
31. van de Pol, J., Smart, N.P.: Estimating key sizes for high dimensional lattice-based systems. In: Stam, M. (ed.) IMACC 2013. LNCS, vol. 8308, pp. 290–303. Springer, Heidelberg (2013)
32. van Dijk, M., Gentry, C., Halevi, S., Vaikuntanathan, V.: Fully homomorphic encryption over the integers. In: Gilbert, H. (ed.) EUROCRYPT 2010. LNCS, vol. 6110, pp. 24–43. Springer, Heidelberg (2010)

Packing Messages and Optimizing Bootstrapping in GSW-FHE

Ryo Hiromasa[1]($\boxtimes$), Masayuki Abe[2], and Tatsuaki Okamoto[2]

[1] Kyoto University, Kyoto, Japan
hiromasa@ai.soc.i.kyoto-u.ac.jp
[2] NTT Secure Platform Laboratories, Tokyo, Japan
{abe.masayuki,hiromasa}@lab.ntt.co.jp

Abstract. We construct the first fully homomorphic encryption (FHE) scheme that encrypts *matrices* and supports homomorphic *matrix* addition and multiplication. This is a natural extension of packed FHE and thus supports more complicated homomorphic operations. We optimize the bootstrapping procedure of Alperin-Sheriff and Peikert (CRYPTO 2014) by applying our scheme. Our optimization decreases the lattice approximation factor from $\tilde{O}(n^3)$ to $\tilde{O}(n^{2.5})$. By taking a lattice dimension as a larger polynomial in a security parameter, we can also obtain the same approximation factor as the best known one of standard lattice-based public-key encryption *without* successive dimension-modulus reduction, which was essential for achieving the best factor in prior works on bootstrapping of standard lattice-based FHE.

1   Introduction

Fully homomorphic encryption (FHE) allows us to evaluate any function over encrypted data by only using public information. This can be used, for example, to outsource computations to remote servers without compromising privacy. Since the breakthrough work by Gentry [12,13], many different varieties of FHE have been proposed[5–8,11,17,18]. To date, the fastest (and simplest) FHE based on the *standard* lattice assumption is the one by Gentry, Sahai, and Waters [17]. (hereafter, referred to as GSW-FHE). However, it is required to take heavy cost for evaluating a large number of ciphertexts. The way to deal with this issue is to *pack* multiple messages into one ciphertext.

Packing messages allows us to apply *single-instruction-multiple data* (SIMD) homomorphic operations to all encrypted messages. In the case where a remote server stores encrypted data and we want to retrieve certain data from this server, we first apply the equality function to every encrypted data. If the stored data have been packed into one ciphertext, we can do that by only one homomorphic evaluation of the equality function. Smart and Vercautren [25], for the first time, showed that applying the Chinese reminder theorem (CRT) to number fields partitions the message space of the Gentry's FHE [12,13] scheme into a vector of *plaintext slots*. On the standard lattice-based FHE schemes, Brakerski, Gentry, and Halevi [4] used the method of [22], which described a way to construct packed Regev's encryption [23], to pack messages in the FHE variants [5–7] of [23]. In this paper,

© International Association for Cryptologic Research 2015
J. Katz (Ed.): PKC 2015, LNCS 9020, pp. 699–715, 2015.
DOI: 10.1007/978-3-662-46447-2_31

we construct a matrix variant of [17] (whose security is also based on the standard lattice assumption) to implement SIMD homomorphic operations, and describe how to bring out the potential of our scheme: specifically optimizing *bootstrapping*.

The bootstrapping technique [12,13] is currently the only way to go from limited amount of homomorphism to unlimited amount of homomorphism. The limited nature is caused by noise terms included in ciphertexts of all known FHE, which are needed to ensure security. Since homomorphic operations increases the noise level and the noise prevents us from correctly decrypting ciphertexts if the level increases too high, it is required to consider methods that reduce the noise. The bootstrapping technique is the one of such a methods, and achieved by homomorphically evaluating the decryption circuit of FHE.

There have recently been the significant progresses [1,9] in improving the bootstrapping procedure on standard lattice-based FHE. Their progresses stem from the observation that noise terms in ciphertexts of GSW-FHE grow *asymmetrically*: for a parameter n (the dimension in the underlying lattice assumption), the noise of multiplication between two ciphertexts with noise size e_1 and e_2 grows to $e_1 + \text{poly}(n) \cdot e_2$. For example, if we want to multiply ℓ ciphertexts with the same noise size in *sequence*, the noise in the result increases by a factor of $\ell \cdot \text{poly}(n)$, which is in contrast to the noise blowup factor for all known FHE, $\text{poly}(n)^{\log \ell}$. To suppress the growth in noise from the bootstrapping procedure, the two recent developments [1,9] tried to *sequentialize* the decryption circuit.

Brakerski and Vaikuntanathan [9] transformed the decryption circuit of [17] to a branching program by using the Barrington's theorem [2], and homomorphically evaluated the program. Since the Barrington's theorem can convert the decryption circuit to a polynomial length branching program, evaluating the program increases the noise by a factor of $\text{poly}(n)$. This procedure, however, has a significant drawback: the Barrington's theorem generates a branching program of *large* polynomial length. The scheme [9] also used a kind of *dimension leveraging* technique and successive dimension-modulus reduction to obtain the best approximation factor that is the same as standard lattice-based (plain) PKE.

Unlike most previous works, Alperin-Sheriff and Peikert [1] viewed the decryption as an arithmetic circuit. The decryption of all known standard lattice-based FHE consists of the inner product and rounding: for a ciphertext vector c and secret key vector s, the decryption algorithm computes $\lfloor \langle c, s \rangle \rceil_2 \in \{0, 1\}$ (where $\lfloor \cdot \rceil_2$ is the rounding function introduced later). The authors observed that the inner product in the decryption can be expressed as a subset sum of the secret key elements. The subset sum can be computed only in the additive group, and the additive group is isomorphic to a group of cyclic permutations. The authors rewrote the inner product to the sequence of compositions of the cyclic permutations. Since this does not use the Barrington's theorem, the bootstrapping procedure of [1] can refresh ciphertexts faster and keep the noise growth in a *smaller* polynomial than that of [9], but the underlying security assumption was slightly stronger than that of [9] [1]. In addition, the procedure of [1] was not fully

---

[1] By using successive dimension-modulus reduction, [1] can also obtain the same approximation factor as that of [9].

sequentialized, that is, there is a little room for sequentializing the decryption: the rounding.

1.1   Our Results

In this paper, we construct the first FHE scheme that encrypts matrices and supports homomorphic matrix operations. This is a natural extension of packed FHE and supports more complicated homomorphic operations. Using this scheme, we fully sequentialize and thus optimize the bootstrapping procedure of [1]. The result of the optimization is described in the following:

Theorem 1. *Our optimized bootstrapping scheme can be secure assuming the hardness of approximating the standard lattice problem to within the factor* $\tilde{O}(n^{1.5}\lambda)$ *on any n dimensional lattices.*

For 2^λ hardness, we need to take $n = \Omega(\lambda)$. Asymptotically minimal selection of $n = \tilde{O}(\lambda)$ leads to the approximation factor $\tilde{O}(n^{2.5})$ for the underlying worst-case lattice assumption, which is smaller than $\tilde{O}(n^3)$, the factor of [1]. Using a kind of dimension leveraging technique: selecting a larger dimension $n = \lambda^{1/\epsilon}$ for $\epsilon \in (0,1)$, we can also obtain the best known approximation factor, $\tilde{O}(n^{1.5+\epsilon})$, *without* successive dimension-modulus reduction, which was essential for achieving the best factor in the prior works on bootstrapping of standard lattice-based FHE.

1.2   Our Techniques

Matrix GSW-FHE. The starting point of our scheme is the GSW-FHE scheme. In that scheme, a ciphertext of a plaintext $m \in \{0,1\}$ is a matrix $C \in \mathbb{Z}_q^{(n+1)\times N}$ such that $sC = m \cdot sG + e$ for a secret key vector $s \in \mathbb{Z}_q^{n+1}$, small noise vector $e \in \mathbb{Z}^N$, and fixed matrix $G \in \mathbb{Z}_q^{(n+1)\times N}$. A simple extension of the plaintext space from bits to binary vectors cannot yield plaintext-slot-wise addition and multiplication. Instead, we use matrices to store binary vectors in their diagonal entries. Actually, our construction even supports homomorphic matrix addition and multiplication that are richer than homomorphic plaintext-slot-wise operations.

Let $S \in \mathbb{Z}_q^{r\times(n+r)}$ be a secret key matrix, $B \in \mathbb{Z}_q^{n\times m}$ be a Learning with Errors (LWE) matrix such that $SB \approx 0$, and $G \in \mathbb{Z}^{(n+r)\times N}$ be a fixed matrix. To encrypt a square integer matrix $M \in \{0,1\}^{r\times r}$, the ciphertext $C \in \mathbb{Z}^{(n+r)\times N}$ must be of the form $BR + XG$ for a matrix $X \in \mathbb{Z}^{(n+r)\times(n+r)}$ such that $SX = MS$, and small random matrix $R \in \mathbb{Z}^{m\times N}$. The ciphertext C satisfies $SC = E + MSG$ for a small noise matrix $E \in \mathbb{Z}^{r\times N}$. Homomorphic matrix addition is just matrix addition. For example, given two ciphertexts C_1 and C_2, it holds that

$$S(C_1 + C_2) = (E_1 + E_2) + (M_1 + M_2)SG.$$

Homomorphic matrix multiplication corresponds to a simple preimage sampling and matrix multiplication. For a matrix $C \in \mathbb{Z}_q^{(n+r) \times N}$, let $G^{-1}(C)$ be the function that outputs a matrix $X' \in \mathbb{Z}_q^{N \times N}$ such that $GX' \equiv C \pmod{q}$. If we let $X'_2 \xleftarrow{R} G^{-1}(C_2)$, then it holds that

$$SC_1 X'_2 = (E_1 + M_1 SG) X'_2$$
$$= E_1 X'_2 + M_1 E_2 + M_1 M_2 SG.$$

Now, the problem is how to construct a matrix X such that $SX = MS$. By construction, S includes an identity matrix: $S = [I \parallel S']$ for a matrix $S' \in \mathbb{Z}_q^{r \times n}$. The idea is to make X have MS in its top rows and 0 below. This X clearly satisfies the condition, but cannot publicly be computed without knowing the secret key. We translate the resulting symmetric scheme to the asymmetric one by using the method similar to [3,24]. In particular, let $M_{(i,j)} \in \{0,1\}^{r \times r}$ $(i, j = 1, \ldots, r)$ be the matrix with 1 in the (i,j)-th entry and 0 in the others. We first publish symmetric encryptions of $M_{(i,j)}$ for all $i, j \in [r]$. A ciphertext for a plaintext matrix M is publicly computed by summing up all encryptions of $M_{(i,j)}$ such that the (i,j)-th entry of M is equal to 1, and using B to randomize the sum. Since the public key includes the ciphertexts that encrypt partial information of the secret key, security of our scheme cannot directly be proven from the LWE assumption. The way to deal with this problem is to introduce a circular security assumption.

Optimizing Bootstrapping of [1]. For a dimension d and modulus q, let $c \in \{0,1\}^d$ be the $\ell - 1$-th column of a binary GSW-FHE ciphertext under the secret key $s \in \mathbb{Z}_q^d$. Since the decryption algorithm of GSW-FHE computes $\lfloor \langle c, s \rangle \rceil_2$ ($\lfloor \cdot \rceil_2$ is the rounding function that outputs 1 if the input is close to $q/4$ and 0 otherwise), and $\langle c, s \rangle = \sum_{i=1}^{d} c_i s_i = \sum_{i \in [d]: c_i = 1} s_i$, the decryption can be viewed as a subset sum of $\{s_i\}_{i \in [d]}$. To bootstrap ciphertexts, we only have to be able to compute additions in $\mathbb{Z}_q$ homomorphically. The additive group $\mathbb{Z}_q^+$ is isomorphic to a group of cyclic permutations, where $x \in \mathbb{Z}_q^+$ corresponds to a cyclic permutation that can be represented by an indicator vector with 1 in the x-th position. The permutation matrix can be obtained from the cyclic rotation of the indicator vector. The addition in $\mathbb{Z}_q^+$ leads to the composition of the permutations (i.e., the multiplication of the corresponding permutation matrices), and the rounding function $\lfloor \cdot \rceil_2 : \mathbb{Z}_q \to \{0,1\}$ can be computed by summing the entries of the indicator vector corresponding to those values in $\mathbb{Z}_q$.

The bootstrapping procedure of [1] consists of two parts that compute an inner product and a rounding operation. The rounding checks equalities and computes summation. The matrix GSW-FHE scheme allows us to rewrite the bootstrapping procedure except for the summation as a *sequence* of homomorphic matrix multiplications, while the procedure of [1] computes only the inner product part as a sequence. Intuitively, our optimization use the matrix GSW-FHE scheme to *sequentialize* the bootstrapping procedure of [1]. The asymmetric noise growth property is more effective in estimating how much noise the procedure yields.

The inner product can be computed by compositions of cyclic permutations. The bootstrapping procedure of [1] represents elements in $\mathbb{Z}_q$ as cyclic permutations, and evaluates their compositions by the naive matrix multiplication algorithm on the ciphertexts that encrypt every elements in the permutation matrices. Instead of that, our bootstrapping procedure uses homomorphic matrix multiplication to directly evaluate the compositions. The rounding part tests for every value close to $q/4$ whether the output of the inner product part encrypts the permutation corresponding to the value, and sums their results (that are 0 or 1). Our procedure also use homomorphic matrix multiplication to realize the equality test. The result of the inner product is represented as an indicator vector, and encrypted component-wise in a SIMD encryption. The inner product equals to x if and only if its indicator vector has 1 in the x-th position. The homomorphic equality test between the inner product and x is computed by homomorphically permuting x-th slot to the first slot in the SIMD ciphertext. The result of the test is encrypted in the first slot. From the above, the bootstrapping procedure except for the summation can be represented as a sequence of $\tilde{O}(\lambda)$ homomorphic multiplications for a security parameter λ.

1.3 Related Work

Multilinear maps[10,14,15] are extensions of bilinear maps, and built from variants of FHE. The new multilinear maps construction of Gentry, Gorbunov, and Halevi [15] also starts from GSW-FHE. Recall that in GSW-FHE, a ciphertext of $m \in \{0,1\}$ is a matrix $C \in \mathbb{Z}_q^{(n+1) \times N}$ such that $sC = m \cdot sG + e$ for a secret key vector $s \in \mathbb{Z}_q^{(n+1)}$ and small noise vector $e \in \mathbb{Z}^N$. That is, valid ciphertexts of GSW-FHE have the secret key as the *approximate eigenvector* and the message as the eigenvalue. The multilinear maps construction of [15] replaced the approximate eigenvector with the *approximate eigenspace* by increasing the dimension. In the construction, an encoding of $M \in \mathbb{Z}^{r \times r}$ is a matrix $C \in \mathbb{Z}_q^{N \times N}$ such that $SC = E + MS$ for a random matrix $S \in \mathbb{Z}_q^{r \times N}$ and small noise matrix $E \in \mathbb{Z}^{r \times N}$. The approximate eigenspace is the matrix S. To obtain the encoding C, the construction samples a preimage of $MS + E$ for the function $f_S(x) = Sx \bmod q$. In our scheme, a ciphertext $C \in \mathbb{Z}_q^{N \times N}$ of $M \in \mathbb{Z}^{r \times r}$ is a preimage of

$$BR + \begin{pmatrix} MS \\ 0 \end{pmatrix} G$$

for the function f_G. Since the ciphertext C satisfies $(SG)C = M(SG) + E$ for a small noise matrix $E \in \mathbb{Z}^{r \times N}$, the matrix SG can be seen as the approximate eigenspace.

1.4 Organization

In Section 2, we describe some preliminaries on the LWE assumption and subgaussian random variables. In Section 3, we present how to construct a matrix variant of [17]. In Section 4, we show that our scheme improves the bootstrapping procedure of [1].

2   Preliminaries

We denote the set of natural numbers by $\mathbb{N}$, the set of integers by $\mathbb{Z}$, the set of rational numbers by $\mathbb{Q}$, and the set of real numbers by $\mathbb{R}$. Let $\mathbb{G}$ be some group and $\mathcal{P}$ be some probability distribution, then we use $a \xleftarrow{U} \mathbb{G}$ to denote that a is chosen from $\mathbb{G}$ uniformly at random, and use $b \xleftarrow{R} \mathcal{P}$ to denote that b is chosen along $\mathcal{P}$. We take all logarithms to base 2, unless otherwise noted.

We assume that vectors are in column form and are written by using bold lower-case letters, e.g., $\boldsymbol{x}$, and the i-th element of a vector is denoted by x_i. We denote the ℓ_∞ norm (the maximum norm) of the vector $\boldsymbol{x}$ by $\|\boldsymbol{x}\|_\infty$, and the ℓ_2 norm (the Euclidean norm) of $\boldsymbol{x}$ by $\|\boldsymbol{x}\|_2$. The inner product between two vectors is denoted by $\langle \boldsymbol{x}, \boldsymbol{y} \rangle$. Matrices are written by using bold capital letters, e.g., $\boldsymbol{X}$, and the i-th column vector of a matrix is denoted by $\boldsymbol{x}_i$. For a matrix $\boldsymbol{X} \in \mathbb{R}^{m \times n}$, we define the ℓ_∞ and ℓ_2 norms of $\boldsymbol{X}$ as $\|\boldsymbol{X}\|_\infty := \max_{i \in [n]}\{\|\boldsymbol{x}_i\|_\infty\}$ and $\|\boldsymbol{X}\|_2 := \max_{i \in [n]}\{\|\boldsymbol{x}_i\|_2\}$, respectively. For a matrix $\boldsymbol{X} \in \mathbb{R}^{m \times n}$, the notation $\boldsymbol{X}^T \in \mathbb{R}^{n \times m}$ denotes the transpose of $\boldsymbol{X}$. For matrices $\boldsymbol{A} \in \mathbb{R}^{m \times n_1}$ and $\boldsymbol{B} \in \mathbb{R}^{m \times n_2}$, $[\boldsymbol{A} \parallel \boldsymbol{B}] \in \mathbb{R}^{m \times (n_1+n_2)}$ denotes the concatenation of $\boldsymbol{A}$ with $\boldsymbol{B}$. When we refer to the $n \times n$ identity matrix, we denote it by $\boldsymbol{I}_n$.

2.1   Learning with Errors

The *learning with errors (LWE) assumption* was first introduced by Regev [23].

Definition 1 (DLWE). *For a security parameter λ, let $n := n(\lambda)$ be an integer dimension, let $q := q(\lambda) \geq 2$ be an integer modulus, and let $\chi := \chi(\lambda)$ be an error distribution over $\mathbb{Z}$. $\mathsf{DLWE}_{n,q,\chi}$ is the problem to distinguish the following two distributions: In the first distribution, a tuple $(\boldsymbol{a}_i, b_i)$ is sampled from uniform over $\mathbb{Z}_q^n \times \mathbb{Z}_q$; In the second distribution, $\boldsymbol{s} \xleftarrow{U} \mathbb{Z}_q^n$ and then a tuple $(\boldsymbol{a}_i, b_i)$ is sampled by sampling $\boldsymbol{a}_i \xleftarrow{U} \mathbb{Z}_q^n$, $e_i \xleftarrow{R} \chi$, and setting $b_i := \langle \boldsymbol{a}_i, \boldsymbol{s} \rangle + e_i \bmod q$. The $\mathsf{DLWE}_{n,q,\chi}$ assumption is that $\mathsf{DLWE}_{n,q,\chi}$ is infeasible.*

Recall that GapSVP_γ is the promise problem to distinguish between the case in which the lattice has a vector shorter than $r \in \mathbb{Q}$, and the case in which all the lattice vectors are greater that $\gamma \cdot r$. SIVP_γ is the problem to find the set of short linearly independent vectors in a lattice. $\mathsf{DLWE}_{n,q,\chi}$ has reductions to the standard lattice assumptions as follows. These reductions take χ to be a discrete Gaussian distribution $D_{\mathbb{Z},\alpha q}$ (that is centered around 0 and has parameter αq for some $\alpha < 1$), which is statistically indistinguishable from a B-bounded distribution (i.e., $\mathbb{E}[X] = 0$ and $|X| \leq B$) for an appropriate B.

Corollary 1 ([19–21,23]). *Let $q := q(n) \in \mathbb{N}$ be a power of primes $q := p^r$ or a product of distinct prime numbers $q := \prod_i q_i$ ($q_i := \mathrm{poly}(n)$ for all i), and let $\alpha \geq \sqrt{n}/q$. If there exists an efficient algorithm that solves (average-case) $\mathsf{DLWE}_{n,q,D_{\mathbb{Z},\alpha q}}$,*

- *there exists an efficient quantum algorithm that can solve $\mathsf{GapSVP}_{\tilde{O}(n/\alpha)}$ and $\mathsf{SIVP}_{\tilde{O}(n/\alpha)}$ in the worst-case for any n-dimensional lattices.*

- if in addition we have $q \geq \tilde{O}(2^{n/2})$, there exists an efficient classical algorithm that can solve $\mathsf{GapSVP}_{\tilde{O}(n/\alpha)}$ in the worst-case for any n-dimensional lattices.

2.2 Subgaussian

A real random variable X is subgaussian with parameter s if for all $t \in \mathbb{R}$, its (scaled) moment generating function holds $\mathbb{E}[\exp(2\pi t X)] \leq \exp(\pi s^2 t^2)$. Any B-bounded (centered) random variable X is subgaussian with parameter $B \cdot \sqrt{2\pi}$. Subgaussian random variables have the following two properties that can be easily obtained from the definition of subgaussian random variables:

- Homogeneity: If the subgaussian random variable X has parameter s, then cX is subgaussian with parameter cs.
- Pythagorean additivity: For two subgaussian random variables X_1 and X_2 (that is independent from X_1) with parameter s_1 and s_2, respectively, $X_1 + X_2$ is subgaussian with parameter $\sqrt{s_1^2 + s_2^2}$.

The above can be extended to vectors. A real random vector $\boldsymbol{x}$ is subgaussian with parameter s if for all real unit vectors $\boldsymbol{u}$, their marginal $\langle \boldsymbol{u}, \boldsymbol{x} \rangle$ is subgaussian with parameter s. It is clear from the definition that the concatenation of subgaussian variables or vectors, each of which has a parameter s and is independent of the prior one, is also subgaussian with parameter s. The homogeneity and Pythagorean additivity also hold from linearity of vectors. It is known that the euclidean norm of the subgaussian random vector has the following upper bound.

Lemma 1 ([26]). *Let $\boldsymbol{x} \in \mathbb{R}^n$ be a random vector that has independent subgaussian coordinates with parameter s. Then there exists a universal constant C such that $\Pr[\|\boldsymbol{x}\|_2 > C \cdot s\sqrt{n}] \leq 2^{-\Omega(n)}$.*

To suppress the growth in noise, Gentry et al. [17] made use of a procedure that decomposes a vector in binary representation. Alperin-Sheriff and Peikert [1] observed that instead of the decomposition procedure, using the following algorithm $\boldsymbol{G}^{-1}$ that samples a subgaussian random vector allows us to re-randomize errors in ciphertexts and tightly analyze the noise growth in [17]. Lemma 2 can be extended to matrices in the obvious way. Let $\boldsymbol{g}^T := (1, 2, 2^2, \dots, 2^{\lceil \log q \rceil - 1})$ and $\boldsymbol{G} := \boldsymbol{g}^T \otimes \boldsymbol{I}_n$.

Lemma 2 ([1], which is adapted from [20]). *There is a randomized, efficiently computable function $\boldsymbol{G}^{-1} : \mathbb{Z}_q^n \rightarrow \mathbb{Z}^{n \cdot \lceil \log q \rceil}$ such that for any $\boldsymbol{a} \in \mathbb{Z}_q^n$, $\boldsymbol{x} \xleftarrow{R} \boldsymbol{G}^{-1}(\boldsymbol{a})$ is subgaussian with parameter $O(1)$ and $\boldsymbol{a} = [\boldsymbol{G}\boldsymbol{x}]_q$.*

2.3 Homomorphic Encryption, Circular Security, and Bootstrapping

Here we describe the syntax of homomorphic encryption scheme to introduce a definition of circular security and the Gentry's bootstrapping theorem. Let $\mathcal{M}$ and $\mathcal{C}$ be the message and ciphertext space. A homomorphic encryption scheme consists of four algorithms, $\{\mathsf{KeyGen}, \mathsf{Enc}, \mathsf{Dec}, \mathsf{Eval}\}$.

- KeyGen(1^λ): output a public encryption key pk, a secret decryption key sk, and a public evaluation key evk.
- Enc$_{\mathsf{pk}}(m)$: using a public key pk, encrypt a plaintext $m \in \mathcal{M}$ into a ciphertext $c \in \mathcal{C}$.
- Dec$_{\mathsf{sk}}(c)$: using a secret key sk, recover the message encrypted in the ciphertext c.
- Eval$_{\mathsf{evk}}(f, c_1, \ldots, c_\ell)$: using the evaluation key evk, output a ciphertext $c_f \in \mathcal{C}$ that is obtained by applying the function $f : \mathcal{M}^\ell \to \mathcal{M}$ to $c_1, \ldots, c_\ell$.

To prove the security of our construction, we introduce a special kind of circular security for a homomorphic encryption scheme.

Definition 2 (Circular security). *Let $\mathcal{K}$ be the key space defined by a security parameter λ. Let f be a function from $\mathcal{K}$ to $\mathcal{C}$. A homomorphic encryption scheme HE = {KeyGen, Enc, Dec, Eval} is circular secure with respect to f if for all probabilistic polynomial-time adversary $\mathcal{A}$, the advantage of $\mathcal{A}$ in the following game is negligible in λ:*

1. *A challenger computes* $(\mathsf{pk}, \mathsf{sk}, \mathsf{evk}) \xleftarrow{R} \mathsf{KeyGen}(1^\lambda)$, *and chooses a bit* $b \xleftarrow{U} \{0, 1\}$.
2. *Let* $f_+ : \mathcal{M} \times \mathcal{M} \to \mathcal{M}$ *be a function that computes* $f_+(x, y) := x + y \in \mathcal{M}$. *The challenger computes a challenge ciphertext c^* as follows and sends it to $\mathcal{A}$.*

$$c^* := \begin{cases} \mathsf{Eval}_{\mathsf{evk}}(f_+, \mathsf{Enc}_{\mathsf{pk}}(0), f(\mathsf{sk})) & \text{if } b = 0, \\ \mathsf{Enc}_{\mathsf{pk}}(0) \in \mathcal{C} & \text{otherwise.} \end{cases}$$

3. *$\mathcal{A}$ outputs a guess $b' \in \{0, 1\}$.*

The advantage of $\mathcal{A}$ is $\Pr[b = b'] - 1/2$.

In LWE-based FHE schemes, $\mathsf{Eval}_{\mathsf{evk}}(f_+, \mathsf{Enc}_{\mathsf{pk}}(0), f(\mathsf{sk}))$ can be seen as a kind of ciphertexts that encrypt $f(\mathsf{sk})$. This is why we call the above security notion circular security.

Gentry's bootstrapping theorem states the way to go from limited homomorphism to unlimited homomorphism. This relates to augmented decryption circuits.

Definition 3 (Augmented decryption circuit). *Let* (sk, pk, evk) *be a tuple of keys generated appropriately, and $\mathcal{C}$ be the set of decryptable ciphertexts. Then the set of augmented decryption functions* $\{f_{c_1, c_2}\}_{c_1, c_2 \in \mathcal{C}}$ *is defined by*

$$f_{c_1, c_2}(x) = \overline{\mathsf{Dec}_x(c_1) \wedge \mathsf{Dec}_x(c_1)}.$$

That is, the function uses its input as the secret key, decrypts c_1 and c_2, and returns the NAND of the results.

Theorem 2 (Bootstrapping theorem [12,13]). *A scheme that can evaluate the family of the augmented decryption circuits can be transformed into a "leveled" FHE scheme (in which KeyGen takes as additional input 1^L and we can only evaluate depth L circuits) with the same decryption circuit, ciphertext space, and public key.*

In addition, if the above scheme is weak circular secure (remains secure against an adversary that can obtain encryptions of the bits of the secret key), it can be "pure" FHE scheme (in which the number of homomorphic evaluations is unlimited).

3   Matrix GSW-FHE

We translate [17] to be able to encrypt a *matrix* and homomorphically compute *matrix* addition and multiplication. This is a natural extension of packed FHE schemes. In Section 3.1, we present our matrix FHE scheme. In Section 3.2, we discuss the relationship between our scheme and packed FHE schemes.

3.1   Construction

Let λ be the security parameter. Our scheme is parameterized by an integer lattice dimension n, an integer modulus q, and a distribution χ over $\mathbb{Z}$ that is assumed to be subgaussian , all of which depends on λ. We let $\ell := \lceil \log q \rceil$, $m := O((n + r) \log q)$, and $N := (n + r) \cdot \ell$. Let r be the number of bits to be encrypted, which defines the message space $\{0, 1\}^{r \times r}$. The ciphertext space is $\mathbb{Z}_q^{(n+r) \times N}$. Our scheme uses the rounding function $\lfloor \cdot \rceil_2$ that for any $x \in \mathbb{Z}_q$, $\lfloor x \rceil_2$ outputs 1 if x is close to $q/4$, and 0 otherwise. Recall that $\boldsymbol{g}^T = (1, 2, \ldots, 2^{\ell-1})$ and $\boldsymbol{G} = \boldsymbol{g}^T \otimes \boldsymbol{I}_{n+r}$.

- KeyGen($1^\lambda, r$): Set the parameters n, q, m, ℓ, N, and χ as described above. Sample a uniformly random matrix $\boldsymbol{A} \xleftarrow{U} \mathbb{Z}_q^{n \times m}$, secret key matrix $\boldsymbol{S}' \xleftarrow{R} \chi^{r \times n}$, and noise matrix $\boldsymbol{E} \xleftarrow{R} \chi^{r \times m}$. Let $\boldsymbol{S} := [\boldsymbol{I}_r \parallel -\boldsymbol{S}'] \in \mathbb{Z}_q^{r \times (n+r)}$. We denote by $\boldsymbol{s}_i^T$ the i-th row of $\boldsymbol{S}$. Set

$$\boldsymbol{B} := \begin{pmatrix} \boldsymbol{S}'\boldsymbol{A} + \boldsymbol{E} \\ \boldsymbol{A} \end{pmatrix} \in \mathbb{Z}_q^{(n+r) \times m}.$$

Let $\boldsymbol{M}_{(i,j)} \in \{0,1\}^{r \times r}$ $(i, j = 1, \ldots, r)$ be the matrix with 1 in the (i, j)-th position and 0 in the others. For all $i, j = 1, \ldots, r$, first sample $\boldsymbol{R}_{(i,j)} \xleftarrow{U} \{0,1\}^{m \times N}$, and set

$$\boldsymbol{P}_{(i,j)} := \boldsymbol{B}\boldsymbol{R}_{(i,j)} + \begin{pmatrix} \boldsymbol{M}_{(i,j)}\boldsymbol{S} \\ \boldsymbol{0} \end{pmatrix} \boldsymbol{G} \in \mathbb{Z}_q^{(n+r) \times N}.$$

Output $\mathsf{pk} := (\{\boldsymbol{P}_{(i,j)}\}_{i,j \in [r]}, \boldsymbol{B})$ and $\mathsf{sk} := \boldsymbol{S}$.
- SecEnc$_{\mathsf{sk}}(\boldsymbol{M} \in \{0,1\}^{r \times r})$: Sample a random matrices $\boldsymbol{A}' \xleftarrow{U} \mathbb{Z}_q^{n \times N}$ and $\boldsymbol{E} \xleftarrow{R} \chi^{r \times N}$, parse $\boldsymbol{S} = [\boldsymbol{I}_r \parallel -\boldsymbol{S}']$, and output the ciphertext

$$\boldsymbol{C} := \left[\begin{pmatrix} \boldsymbol{S}'\boldsymbol{A}' + \boldsymbol{E} \\ \boldsymbol{A}' \end{pmatrix} + \begin{pmatrix} \boldsymbol{M}\boldsymbol{S} \\ \boldsymbol{0} \end{pmatrix} \boldsymbol{G} \right]_q \in \mathbb{Z}_q^{(n+r) \times N}.$$

– $\mathsf{PubEnc_{pk}}(M \in \{0,1\}^{r \times r})$: Sample a random matrix $R \xleftarrow{U} \{0,1\}^{m \times N}$, and output the ciphertext

$$C := BR + \sum_{i,j \in [r]: M[i,j]=1} P_{(i,j)} \in \mathbb{Z}_q^{(n+r) \times N},$$

where $M[i,j]$ is the (i,j)-th element of M.

– $\mathsf{Dec_{sk}}(C)$: Output the matrix $M = (\lfloor \langle s_i, c_{j\ell-1} \rangle \rceil_2)_{i,j \in [r]} \in \{0,1\}^{r \times r}$.

– $C_1 \oplus C_2$: Output $C_{add} := C_1 + C_2 \in \mathbb{Z}_q^{(n+r) \times N}$ as the result of homomorphic addition between the input ciphertexts.

– $C_1 \odot C_2$: Output $C_{mult} := C_1 G^{-1}(C_2) \in \mathbb{Z}_q^{(n+r) \times N}$ as the result of homomorphic multiplication between the input ciphertexts.

Definition 4. *We say that a ciphertext C encrypts a plaintext matrix M with noise matrix E if C is an encryption of M and $E = SC - MSG \pmod{q}$.*

The following lemma states the correctness of our asymmetric encryption. Similar to this, the correctness of our symmetric encryption can be proven immediately.

Lemma 3. *If a ciphertext C encrypts a plaintext matrix $M \in \{0,1\}^{r \times r}$ with noise matrix E such that $\|E\|_\infty < q/8$, then $\mathsf{Dec_{sk}}(C) = M$.*

Proof. We have

$$SC = S \left(BR + \sum_{i,j \in [r]: M[i,j]=1} BR_{(i,j)} + \begin{pmatrix} MS \\ 0 \end{pmatrix} G \right)$$
$$= ER + \sum_{i,j \in [r]: M[i,j]=1} ER_{(i,j)} + MSG$$
$$= ER + \sum_{i,j \in [r]: M[i,j]=1} ER_{(i,j)} + [M(g^T \otimes I_r) \| -MS'(g^T \otimes I_n)]$$

Because of $\|E(R + \sum_{i,j \in [r]: M[i,j]=1} R_{(i,j)})\|_\infty < q/8$ and $2^{\ell-2} \in [q/4, q/2)$, for all $i,j = 1, \ldots, r$, $\langle s_i, c_{j\ell-1} \rangle \approx q/4$ if $m_{i,j} = 1$, and $\langle s_i, c_{j\ell-1} \rangle \approx 0$ otherwise.

Security of SecEnc directly holds from $\mathsf{DLWE}_{n,q,\chi}$. For a matrix $M \in \{0,1\}^{r \times r}$, let f_M be a function from $\mathbb{Z}_q^{r \times (n+r)}$ to $\mathbb{Z}_q^{(n+r) \times N}$ such that for a matrix $S \in \mathbb{Z}_q^{r \times (n+r)}$,

$$f_M(S) = \begin{pmatrix} MS \\ 0 \end{pmatrix} G \in \mathbb{Z}_q^{(n+r) \times N}.$$

The security of PubEnc directly holds by $\mathsf{DLWE}_{n,q,\chi}$ and assuming our scheme circular secure with respect to $f_{M_{(i,j)}}$.

Lemma 4. *Let $B, M_{(i,j)}, R_{(i,j)}, P_{(i,j)}$ $(i,j = 1, \ldots, r)$ be the matrices generated in KeyGen, and R be the matrix generated in PubEnc. For every $i,j = 1, \ldots, r$, if our scheme is circular secure with respect to $f_{M_{(i,j)}}$ and $\mathsf{DLWE}_{n,q,\chi}$ holds, then the joint distribution $(B, BR_{(i,j)}, P_{(i,j)}, BR)$ is computationally indistinguishable from uniform over $\mathbb{Z}_q^{(n+r) \times m} \times \mathbb{Z}_q^{(n+r) \times N} \times \mathbb{Z}_q^{(n+r) \times N} \times \mathbb{Z}_q^{(n+r) \times N}$.*

We need to estimate the noise growth by the evaluation of homomorphic matrix addition and multiplication. Similar to [1], we employ the properties of subgaussian random variables for tight analysis. We collect the results of the estimation in the following lemma.

Lemma 5. *Let $S \in \mathbb{Z}^{r \times (n+r)}$ be a secret key matrix. Let $C_1 \in \mathbb{Z}_q^{(n+r) \times N}$ and $C_2 \in \mathbb{Z}_q^{(n+r) \times N}$ be ciphertexts that encrypt $M_1 \in \{0,1\}^{r \times r}$ and $M_2 \in \{0,1\}^{r \times r}$ with noise matrices $E_1 \in \mathbb{Z}^{r \times N}$ and $E_2 \in \mathbb{Z}^{r \times N}$, respectively. Let $e_{1,i}^T \in \mathbb{Z}^{1 \times N}$ ($i = 1, \ldots, r$) be the i-th row vector of E_1. Let $C_{add} := C_1 \oplus C_2$ and $C_{mult} \overset{R}{\leftarrow} C_1 \odot C_2$. Then, we have*

$$SC_{add} = E_{add} + (M_1 + M_2)SG \in \mathbb{Z}_q^{r \times N},$$

$$SC_{mult} = E_{mult} + (M_1 M_2)SG \in \mathbb{Z}_q^{r \times N},$$

where $E_{add} := E_1 + E_2$ and $E_{mult} := E + M_1 E_2$. In particular, E has in the i-th row the independent subgaussian entries with parameter $O(\|e_{1,i}\|_2)$.

Proof. We can immediately prove the statements for C_{add}. For C_{mult}, we have

$$\begin{aligned}
SC_{mult} &= SC_1 G^{-1}(C_2) \\
&= (E_1 + M_1 SG) G^{-1}(C_2) \\
&= E_1 G^{-1}(C_2) + M_1 E_2 + M_1 M_2 SG.
\end{aligned}$$

From the subgaussian properties and Lemma 2, we can see that the i-th row entries of $E := E_1 G^{-1}(C_2)$ are independent subgaussian with parameter $O(\|e_{1,i}\|_2)$.

Similar to the original GSW scheme, our scheme also has the asymmetric noise growth property, and thereby computing a polynomial length chain of homomorphic multiplications incurs the noise growth by a multiplicative polynomial factor. For ease of analyzing our optimized bootstrapping procedure described in the next section, we set the following corollary immediately proven from Lemma 5 and the properties of subgaussian random variables. This corollary includes the fixed ciphertext $G \in \mathbb{Z}^{(n+r) \times N}$ of the message I_r with noise 0. This makes the noise in the output ciphertext subgaussian and independent from the noise in the input ciphertexts.

Corollary 2. *For $i = 1, \ldots, k$, let $C_i \in \mathbb{Z}^{(n+r) \times N}$ be a ciphertext that encrypts a message matrix $M_i \in \{0,1\}^{r \times r}$ such that for a matrix $E \in \mathbb{Z}^{r \times N}$, $\|(M_i E)^T\|_2 \le \|E^T\|_2$ with noise matrix $E_i \in \mathbb{Z}^{r \times N}$. Let*

$$C \overset{R}{\leftarrow} \bigodot_{i=1}^{k} C_i \odot G = C_1 \odot (C_2 \odot (\cdots (C_{k-1} \odot (C_k \odot G))) \cdots).$$

For $i = 1, \ldots, k$, let e_i^T be a row vector of E_i whose norm is equal to $\|E_i^T\|_2$, and $e^T := [e_1^T \| e_2^T \| \cdots \| e_k^T] \in \mathbb{Z}^{1 \times kN}$. Then the noise matrix of C has in every row the independent subgaussian entries with parameter $O(\|e\|_2)$.

Proof. The ciphertext C encrypts the message $\prod_{i=1}^{k} M_i$ with noise $E_1 X_1 + \sum_{i=2}^{k} (\prod_{j=1}^{i-1} M_j) E_i X_i$, where X_i is the matrix used in the evaluation of each $\odot$. By Lemma 5, the elements of $E_1 X_1$ in every row are independent and subgaussian with parameter $O(\|e_1\|_2)$. Since we have $\|(M_i E)^T\|_2 \leq \|E^T\|_2$, $(\prod_{j=1}^{i-1} M_j) E_i X_i$ has in its every row the independent subgaussian entries with parameter $O(\|e_i\|_2)$. By the Pythagorean additivity of subgaussian random variables, $E_1 X_1 + \sum_{i=2}^{k} (\prod_{j=1}^{i-1} M_j) E_i X_i$ has in every row the independent subgaussian entries with parameter $O(\|e\|_2)$.

3.2   Relation to Packed FHE

The matrix GSW-FHE above is a natural extension of packed FHE. Plaintext slots in packed FHE correspond to diagonal entries of plaintext matrices in the matrix GSW-FHE scheme. It is easy to see that we can correctly compute homomorphic slot-wise addition and multiplication. In applications of packed FHE such as in [16], we may want to permute plaintext slots. This can be achieved by multiplying the encryptions of a permutation and its inverse from left and right. Security and correctness of the following algorithms clearly holds from Lemmas 4 and 5.

- SwitchKeyGen(S, σ): Given a secret key matrix $S \in \mathbb{Z}_q^{r \times (n+r)}$ and a permutation σ, let $\Sigma \in \{0,1\}^{r \times r}$ be a matrix corresponding to σ, and generate

$$W_\sigma \xleftarrow{R} \mathsf{SecEnc}_S(\Sigma),$$
$$W_{\sigma^{-1}} \xleftarrow{R} \mathsf{SecEnc}_S(\Sigma^T).$$

  Output the switch key $\mathsf{ssk}_\sigma := (W_\sigma, W_{\sigma^{-1}})$.
- SlotSwitch$_{\mathsf{ssk}_\sigma}(C)$: Take as input a switch key ssk_σ and a ciphertext C, output

$$C_\sigma \xleftarrow{R} W_\sigma \odot (C \odot (W_{\sigma^{-1}} \odot G)),$$

  where $G \in \mathbb{Z}^{(n+r) \times N}$ is the fixed encryption of I_r with noise zero.

One nice feature of our plaintext-slot switching is that it does not suffer from the inconvenience of the security as in [4]: we do not have to use a larger modulus than the matrix GSW-FHE scheme. Brakerski et al. [4] made use of a larger modulus $Q = 2^\ell q$ to suppress noise growth when switching decryption keys, so the security of the plaintext-slot switching in [4] must have related to Q. The larger modulus leads the larger modulus-to-noise ratio. To obtain the same security level as the SIMD scheme of [4], it was required to select a larger dimension. As opposed to this, our plaintext-slot switching can use the same modulus as the matrix GSW-FHE scheme.

4   Optimizing Bootstrapping

We describe how to optimize the bootstrapping procedure of [1] by using our scheme. In Section 4.1, we present the optimized bootstrapping procedure outlined in Section 1.2, whose correctness and security are discussed in Section 4.2.

4.1   Optimized Procedure

Let Q be the modulus of the ciphertext to be refreshed. Using the dimension-modulus reduction technique [7,9], we can publicly switch the modulus and the dimension to the arbitrary and possibly smaller ones $q, d = \tilde{O}(\lambda)$. Here, q has the form $q := \prod_{i=1}^{t} r_i$, where r_i are small and powers of distinct primes (and hence pairwise coprime). The following lemma allows us to choose a sufficiently large q that the correctness of the dimension-modulus reduction holds by letting it be the product of all maximal prime powers r_i bounded by $O(\log \lambda)$, and then there exists $t = O(\log \lambda / \log \log \lambda)$.

Lemma 6 ([1]). *For all $x \geq 7$, the product of all maximal prime powers $r_i \leq x$ is at least $\exp(3x/4)$.*

By CRT, $\mathbb{Z}_q^+$ is isomorphic to the direct product $\mathbb{Z}_{r_1}^+ \times \cdots \times \mathbb{Z}_{r_t}^+$. For all $i \in [t]$, $x \in \mathbb{Z}_{r_i}^+$ corresponds to a cyclic permutation that can be represented by a indicator vector with 1 in the x-th position. Let $\phi_i : \mathbb{Z}_q \to \{0,1\}^r$ be the isomorphism of an element in $\mathbb{Z}_q$ into the cyclic permutation that corresponds to an element in $\mathbb{Z}_{r_i}$, where $r := \max_i \{r_i\}$.

Our optimized bootstrapping procedure consists of two algorithms, BootKeyGen and Bootstrap. The procedure can be used to refresh ciphertexts of all known standard LWE-based FHE. We achieve the input ciphertext $c \in \{0,1\}^d$ for Bootstrap from the dimension-modulus reduction and bit-decomposition of the ciphertext to be bootstrapped, and let $s \in \mathbb{Z}_q^d$ be a secret key that corresponds to c. This pre-processing is the same as that in [1], so see for further details.

- BootKeyGen(sk, s): given a secret key sk for our scheme and the secret key $s \in \mathbb{Z}_q^d$ for ciphertexts to be refreshed, output a bootstrapping key. For every $i \in [t]$ and $j \in [d]$, let $\pi_{\phi_i(s_j)}$ be the permutation corresponding to $\phi_i(s_j)$, and compute

$$\tau_{i,j} \xleftarrow{R} \mathsf{SecEnc_{sk}}(\mathrm{diag}(\phi_i(s_j))),$$

$$\mathsf{ssk}_{i,j} \xleftarrow{R} \mathsf{SwitchKeyGen}(\mathsf{sk}, \pi_{\phi_i(s_j)}),$$

  where for a vector $x \in \mathbb{Z}^r$, $\mathrm{diag}(x) \in \mathbb{Z}^{r \times r}$ is the square integer matrix that has x in its diagonal entries and 0 in the others. In addition, we generate hints to check the equality on packed indicator vectors. For every $i \in [t]$, and $x \in \mathbb{Z}_q$ such that $\lfloor x \rfloor_2 = 1$ [2], generate

$$\mathsf{ssk}_{\phi_i(x)} \xleftarrow{R} \mathsf{SwitchKeyGen}(\mathsf{sk}, \pi_{\phi_i(x)}),$$

  where $\pi_{\phi_i(x)}$ is the cyclic permutation that maps the ($x \bmod r_i$)-th row to the first row in the matrix. To mask the first plaintext slot, generate an encryption of $(1, 0, \ldots, 0)$:

$$\boldsymbol{P}_{(1,0,\ldots,0)} \xleftarrow{R} \mathsf{SecEnc_{sk}}(\mathrm{diag}((1, 0, \ldots, 0))).$$

---

[2] Obviously, our procedure can work on not only the rounding function $\lfloor \cdot \rceil_2$ but also some arbitrary functions $f : \mathbb{Z}_q \to \{0,1\}$.

Output the bootstrapping key

$$\mathsf{bk} := \{(\tau_{i,j}, \mathsf{ssk}_{i,j}, \boldsymbol{P}_{(1,0,\ldots,0)}, \mathsf{ssk}_{\phi_i(x)})\}_{i\in[t], j\in[d], x\in\mathbb{Z}_q : \lfloor x\rfloor_2 = 1}.$$

– Bootstrap$_{\mathsf{bk}}(\boldsymbol{c})$: Given a bootstrapping key bk and a ciphertext $\boldsymbol{c} \in \mathbb{Z}_q^d$, output the refreshed ciphertext $\boldsymbol{C}^*$. The decryption of all FHE based on the standard LWE computes $\lfloor\langle\boldsymbol{c}, \boldsymbol{s}\rangle\rfloor_2$. The algorithm Bootstrap consists of two phases that evaluate the inner product and rounding.

    Inner Product: For every $i \in [t]$, homomorphically compute an encryption of $\phi_i(\langle\boldsymbol{c}, \boldsymbol{s}\rangle)$. Let $h := \min\{j \in [d] : c_j = 1\}$. For $i = 1,\ldots,t$, set $\boldsymbol{C}_i^* := \tau_{i,h}$, and iteratively compute

$$\boldsymbol{C}_i^* \xleftarrow{R} \mathsf{SlotSwitch}_{\mathsf{ssk}_{i,j}}(\boldsymbol{C}_i^*)$$

for $j = h+1,\ldots,d$ such that $c_j = 1$.

    Rounding: For each $x \in \mathbb{Z}_q$ such that $\lfloor x\rfloor_2 = 1$, homomorphically check the equality between x and $\langle\boldsymbol{c}, \boldsymbol{s}\rangle$, and sum their results. The refreshed ciphertext is comuted as:

$$\boldsymbol{C}^* \xleftarrow{R} \bigoplus_{x\in\mathbb{Z}_q \,:\, \lfloor x\rfloor_2 = 1} \left(\bigodot_{i\in[t]} \left(\mathsf{SlotSwitch}_{\mathsf{ssk}_{\phi_i(x)}}(\boldsymbol{C}_i^*) \right) \odot \boldsymbol{P}_{(1,0,\ldots,0)} \right). \quad (1)$$

The post-processing is almost the same as that in [1] except for the way to extract a matrix ciphertext. When finishing the bootstrapping procedure, we have a ciphertext $\boldsymbol{C}^*$ that encrypts in the first slot the same plaintext as the ciphertext $\boldsymbol{c}$. A vector ciphertext like [5,6,8] can be obtained to just take the $\ell - 1$-th column vector of $\boldsymbol{C}^*$, and a matrix ciphertext like [17] can be obtained by removing from the second row to the r-th row and from the $l+1$-th column to rl-th column, and aggregating the remainders. We can utilize the key-switching procedure [5,8] for switching from s_1 back to the original secret key $\boldsymbol{s}$. This requires us to assume circular security.

Our bootstrapping procedure is more time- and space- efficient than that of [1]. The procedure [1] encrypts every elements of the permutation matrices corresponding to the secret key elements, and homomorphically evaluates naive matrix multiplications to obtain encryptions of compositions of permutations. In our procedure, a permutation is encrypted in one ciphertext, and a composition is computed by two homomorphic multiplications. This makes our procedure time-efficient by roughly a $O(\log^2 \lambda)$ factor, and space-efficient by a $O(\log \lambda)$ factor.

4.2   Correctness and Security

From the security of our scheme, it is easy to see that our bootstrapping procedure can be secure by assuming the circular security and DLWE. Correctness holds as the following lemma.

Lemma 7. *Let* sk *be the secret key for our scheme. Let* c *and* s *be a ciphertext and secret key described in our bootstrapping procedure. Then, for* bk$\xleftarrow{R}$BootKeyGen(sk, s), *the refreshed ciphertext* $C^* \xleftarrow{R}$Bootstrap$_{\text{bk}}(c)$ *encrypts* $\lfloor \langle s, c \rangle \rceil_2 \in \{0, 1\}$ *in the first slot.*

Proof. From Lemma 5 and group homomorphism of ϕ_i, C_i^* encrypts $\phi_i([\langle s, c \rangle]_q)$. Since $\mathbb{Z}_q$ is isomorphic to $\mathbb{Z}_{r_1} \times \cdots \times \mathbb{Z}_{r_t}$ by CRT, $\bigodot_{i \in [t]}(\text{SlotSwitch}_{\text{ssk}_{\phi_i(x)}}(C_i^*)) \odot P_{(1,0,\dots,0)}$ encrypts 1 in the first slot if and only if $x = \langle s, c \rangle$ mod q. Finally, C^* encrypts 1 if and only if $\lfloor \langle s, c \rangle \rceil_2 = 1$.

Here, we let s be the Gaussian parameter. Recall that n is the LWE dimension, r is the number of encrypted bits, $\ell = \lceil \log Q \rceil$, $N = (n + r) \cdot \ell$, $t = O(\log \lambda / \log \log \lambda)$, $d = \tilde{O}(\lambda)$ and $q = \tilde{O}(\lambda)$. We estimate the noise growth by our optimized bootstrapping procedure.

Lemma 8. *For any ciphertext* $c \in \{0, 1\}^d$ *described in our bootstrapping procedure, the noise in the refreshed ciphertext* $C^* \xleftarrow{R}$Bootstrap$_{\text{bk}}(c)$ *has independent subgaussian entries with parameter* $O(s\sqrt{n\ell dtq})$, *except with probability* $2^{-\Omega((n+r)\ell dt)}$ *over the random choice of* bk *and* Bootstrap.

Proof. Since the parenthesized part before the additions in Eq. (1) can be broken down into a sequence of $O(dt)$ homomorphic multiplications, Corollary 2 and Lemma 1 tell us that the term has subgaussian noise with parameter $O(s\sqrt{Ndt})$, except with probability $2^{-\Omega(Ndt)}$. From the Pythagorean additivity of subgaussian random variables and $N = (n + r) \cdot \ell$, the noise in C^* are subgaussian with parameter $O(s\sqrt{(n+r)\ell dtq})$, and so $O(s\sqrt{n\ell dtq})$ by the fact $n > r$.

From the above lemma, we can see that our procedure refreshes ciphertexts with error growth by the $O(\sqrt{n\ell dtq})$ factor. Our scheme can evaluate its augmented decryption circuit by choosing a larger modulus than the final noise, and thus be pure FHE by the Gentry's bootstrapping theorem (Theorem 2) and the circular security assumption.

Theorem 3. *Our optimized bootstrapping scheme can be correct and secure assuming*

- *the quantum worst-case hardness of approximating* GapSVP$_{\tilde{O}(n^{1.5}\lambda)}$ *and* SIVP$_{\tilde{O}(n^{1.5}\lambda)}$,
- *or the classical worst-case hardness of approximating* GapSVP$_{\tilde{O}(n^2\lambda)}$

on any n dimensional lattice.

Proof. By Lemma 1, to rely on the quantum worst-case hardness, we choose $s = \Theta(\sqrt{n})$. From Lemma 8, for correctness we only have to select $Q = \tilde{\Omega}(n\lambda \log Q)$, which satisfies $Q = \tilde{O}(n\lambda)$. Since the LWE inverse error rate is $1/\alpha = Q/s = \tilde{O}(\sqrt{n}\lambda)$, the security of our bootstrapping scheme is reduced to GapSVP$_{\tilde{O}(n^{1.5}\lambda)}$ and SIVP$_{\tilde{O}(n^{1.5}\lambda)}$.

In the case of reducing to the classical hardness of the lattice problem, since $1/\alpha = \tilde{\Omega}(\lambda\sqrt{n\log Q})$ and we must take $Q \approx 2^{n/2}$, the LWE inverse error rate satisfies $1/\alpha = \tilde{\Omega}(\lambda \cdot n)$. Therefore, the security of our optimized bootstrapping scheme is reduced to the classical hardness of GapSVP$_{\tilde{O}(n^2\lambda)}$.

Since all known algorithms that approximate GapSVP and SIVP on any n dimensional lattices to within a poly(n)-factor run in time $2^{\Omega(n)}$, the 2^λ hardness requires us to choose $n = \Theta(\lambda)$. This makes the problems to which the security is reduced in the quantum case have the approximation factor $\tilde{O}(n^{2.5})$, which is smaller than $\tilde{O}(n^3)$, the one of [1]'s bootstrapping scheme. In the classical case, the LWE inverse error rate is $1/\alpha = \tilde{\Omega}(n^2)$ and hence our approximation factor is $\tilde{O}(n^3)$. Furthermore, by selecting a larger dimension $n = \lambda^{1/\epsilon}$ for $\epsilon > 0$ (so at the cost of efficiency), the approximation factor can be $\tilde{O}(n^{1.5+\epsilon})$, which is comparable to the one of [9] and so the best known factor of standard lattice-based PKE. Consequently, our optimized bootstrapping scheme can be as secure as any other standard lattice-based PKE *without* successive dimension-modulus reduction, which is essential in all the known bootstrapping procedures [1,9] provided recently.

Acknowledgments. We thank anonymous PKC reviewers for their helpful comments.

References

1. Alperin-Sheriff, J., Peikert, C.: Faster bootstrapping with polynomial error. In: Garay, J.A., Gennaro, R. (eds.) CRYPTO 2014, Part I. LNCS, vol. 8616, pp. 297–314. Springer, Heidelberg (2014)
2. Barrington, D.A.M.: Bounded-Width polynomial-size branching programs recognize exactly those languages in NC^1. In: STOC, pp. 1–5 (1986)
3. Barak, B.: Cryptography course - Lecture Notes, COS 433. Princeton University, Computer Science Department (2010). http://www.cs.princeton.edu/courses/archive/spring10/cos433
4. Brakerski, Z., Gentry, C., Halevi, S.: Packed ciphertexts in LWE-based homomorphic encryption. In: Kurosawa, K., Hanaoka, G. (eds.) PKC 2013. LNCS, vol. 7778, pp. 1–13. Springer, Heidelberg (2013)
5. Brakerski, Z., Gentry, C., Vaikuntanathan, V.: (leveled) fully homomorphic encryption without bootstrapping. In: ITCS, pp. 309–325 (2012)
6. Brakerski, Z.: Fully homomorphic encryption without modulus switching from classical GapSVP. In: Safavi-Naini, R., Canetti, R. (eds.) CRYPTO 2012. LNCS, vol. 7417, pp. 868–886. Springer, Heidelberg (2012)
7. Brakerski, Z., Vaikuntanathan, V.: Efficient fully homomorphic encryption from (standard) LWE. In: FOCS, pp. 97–106 (2011)
8. Brakerski, Z., Vaikuntanathan, V.: Fully homomorphic encryption from Ring-LWE and security for key dependent messages. In: Rogaway, P. (ed.) CRYPTO 2011. LNCS, vol. 6841, pp. 505–524. Springer, Heidelberg (2011)
9. Brakerski, Z., Vaikuntanathan, V.: Lattice-based FHE as secure as PKE. In: ITCS, pp. 1–12 (2014)
10. Coron, J.-S., Lepoint, T., Tibouchi, M.: Practical multilinear maps over the integers. In: Canetti, R., Garay, J.A. (eds.) CRYPTO 2013, Part I. LNCS, vol. 8042, pp. 476–493. Springer, Heidelberg (2013)
11. van Dijk, M., Gentry, C., Halevi, S., Vaikuntanathan, V.: Fully Homomorphic Encryption over the Integers. In: Gilbert, H. (ed.) EUROCRYPT 2010. LNCS, vol. 6110, pp. 24–43. Springer, Heidelberg (2010)

12. Gentry, C.: A Fully Homomorphic Encryption Scheme. PhD thesis, Stanford University (2009). http://crypto.stanford.edu/craig
13. Gentry, C.: Fully homomorphic encryption using ideal lattices. In: STOC, pp. 169–178 (2009)
14. Garg, S., Gentry, C., Halevi, S.: Candidate multilinear maps from ideal lattices. In: Johansson, T., Nguyen, P.Q. (eds.) EUROCRYPT 2013. LNCS, vol. 7881, pp. 1–17. Springer, Heidelberg (2013)
15. Gentry, C., Gorbunov, S., Halevi, S.: Graph-Induced Multilinear Maps from Lattices. IACR Cryptology ePrint Archive **2014**, 645 (2014)
16. Gentry, C., Halevi, S., Smart, N.P.: Better bootstrapping in fully homomorphic encryption. In: Fischlin, M., Buchmann, J., Manulis, M. (eds.) PKC 2012. LNCS, vol. 7293, pp. 1–16. Springer, Heidelberg (2012)
17. Gentry, C., Sahai, A., Waters, B.: Homomorphic encryption from learning with errors: conceptually-simpler, asymptotically-faster, attribute-based. In: Canetti, R., Garay, J.A. (eds.) CRYPTO 2013, Part I. LNCS, vol. 8042, pp. 75–92. Springer, Heidelberg (2013)
18. López-Alt, A., Tromer, E., Vaikuntanathan, V.: On-the-fly multiparty computation on the cloud via multikey fully homomorphic encryption. In: STOC, pp. 1219–1234 (2012)
19. Micciancio, D., Mol, P.: Pseudorandom knapsacks and the sample complexity of LWE search-to-decision reductions. In: Rogaway, P. (ed.) CRYPTO 2011. LNCS, vol. 6841, pp. 465–484. Springer, Heidelberg (2011)
20. Micciancio, D., Peikert, C.: Trapdoors for lattices: simpler, tighter, faster, smaller. In: Pointcheval, D., Johansson, T. (eds.) EUROCRYPT 2012. LNCS, vol. 7237, pp. 700–718. Springer, Heidelberg (2012)
21. Peikert, C.: Public-key cryptosystems from the worst-case shortest vector problem. In: STOC, pp. 333–342 (2009)
22. Peikert, C., Vaikuntanathan, V., Waters, B.: A framework for efficient and composable oblivious transfer. In: Wagner, D. (ed.) CRYPTO 2008. LNCS, vol. 5157, pp. 554–571. Springer, Heidelberg (2008)
23. Regev, O.: On lattices, learning with errors, random linear codes, and cryptography. In: STOC, pp. 84–93 (2005)
24. Rothblum, R.: Homomorphic encryption: from private-key to public-key. In: Ishai, Y. (ed.) TCC 2011. LNCS, vol. 6597, pp. 219–234. Springer, Heidelberg (2011)
25. Smart, N.P., Vercauteren, F.: Fully homomorphic encryption with relatively small key and ciphertext sizes. In: Nguyen, P.Q., Pointcheval, D. (eds.) PKC 2010. LNCS, vol. 6056, pp. 420–443. Springer, Heidelberg (2010)
26. Vershynin, R.: Introduction to the non-asymptotic analysis of random matrices. In: Eldar, Y.C., Kutyniok, G. (eds.) Compressed Sensing, Theory and Applications, ch. 5, pp. 210–268. Cambridge University Press (2012). http://www-personal.umich.edu/romanv/papers/non-asymptotic-rmt-plain.pdf

Simple Lattice Trapdoor Sampling from a Broad Class of Distributions

Vadim Lyubashevsky[1]([⊠]) and Daniel Wichs[2]

[1] Inria/ENS, Paris, France
vadim.lyubashevsky@inria.fr
[2] Northeastern University, Boston, USA
wichs@ccs.neu.edu

Abstract. At the center of many lattice-based constructions is an algorithm that samples a short vector $\mathbf{s}$, satisfying $[\mathbf{A}|\mathbf{AR}-\mathbf{HG}]\mathbf{s} = \mathbf{t} \bmod q$ where $\mathbf{A}, \mathbf{AR}, \mathbf{H}, \mathbf{G}$ are public matrices and $\mathbf{R}$ is a trapdoor. Although the algorithm crucially relies on the knowledge of the trapdoor $\mathbf{R}$ to perform this sampling efficiently, the distribution it outputs should be independent of $\mathbf{R}$ given the public values. We present a new, simple algorithm for performing this task. The main novelty of our sampler is that the distribution of $\mathbf{s}$ does not need to be Gaussian, whereas all previous works crucially used the properties of the Gaussian distribution to produce such an $\mathbf{s}$. The advantage of using a non-Gaussian distribution is that we are able to avoid the high-precision arithmetic that is inherent in Gaussian sampling over arbitrary lattices. So while the norm of our output vector $\mathbf{s}$ is on the order of $\sqrt{n}$ to n - times larger (the representation length, though, is only a constant factor larger) than in the samplers of Gentry, Peikert, Vaikuntanathan (STOC 2008) and Micciancio, Peikert (EUROCRYPT 2012), the sampling itself can be done very efficiently. This provides a useful time/output trade-off for devices with constrained computing power. In addition, we believe that the conceptual simplicity and generality of our algorithm may lead to it finding other applications.

1 Introduction

At the core of many lattice-based cryptosystems is the many-to-one one-way function $f_{\mathbf{A}}(\mathbf{s}) = \mathbf{As} \bmod q$, where $\mathbf{A} \in \mathbb{Z}_q^{m \times n}$ is a random (short & fat) matrix and $\mathbf{s} \in \mathbb{Z}_q^m$ is a "short" vector. The works of [Ajt96, Ajt99] showed that this function is one-way under a worst-case lattice assumption, and moreover, that there is a way to sample a random $\mathbf{A}$ along with a trapdoor that allows one to invert the function $f_{\mathbf{A}}$. However, since the function $f_{\mathbf{A}}$ is many-to-one, the choice of which pre-image we sample might depend on which trapdoor for $\mathbf{A}$ we use. Not leaking information about the trapdoor, which is used as a secret key in cryptographic schemes, is essential for security – both "provable" and actual. Some early lattice schemes, such as GGH [GGH97] and NTRU [HHGP03]

V. Lyubashevsky—Partially supported by the French ANR-13-JS02-0003 "CLE" Project

D. Wichs—Supported by NSF grants 1347350, 1314722, 1413964.

© International Association for Cryptologic Research 2015
J. Katz (Ed.): PKC 2015, LNCS 9020, pp. 716–730, 2015.
DOI: 10.1007/978-3-662-46447-2_32

signatures, did not have security proofs, and it was subsequently shown that obtaining a small amount of signature samples was enough to completely recover the secret key [NR09].

The first algorithm which was able to sample pre-images of $f_{\mathbf{A}}$ without leaking any information about the trapdoor was devised in the breakthrough work of Gentry, Peikert, and Vaikuntanathan [GPV08]. It was able to output such a pre-image $\mathbf{s}$ according to a discrete Gaussian distribution using a short basis of the lattice $\mathcal{L}_q^{\perp}(\mathbf{A}) := \{\mathbf{v} \in \mathbb{Z}^m : \mathbf{A}\mathbf{v} = \mathbf{0} \bmod q\}$ as a trapdoor. Following the intuition of the two-sided sampler of Agrawal, Boneh, and Boyen [ABB10], Micciancio and Peikert introduced a sampling procedure that did not explicitly require a short basis of the underlying lattice [MP12]. In particular, instead of sampling a uniformly random matrix, they sampled a statistically close matrix $\mathbf{A}' = [\mathbf{A}|\mathbf{A}\mathbf{R} - \mathbf{H}\mathbf{G}]$, where $\mathbf{A}$ is a uniformly random (short & fat) matrix over $\mathbb{Z}_q$, $\mathbf{R}$ is a matrix with small coefficients, $\mathbf{H}$ is any matrix invertible over $\mathbb{Z}_q$, and $\mathbf{G}$ is a special (publicly-known) matrix that allows one to easily compute a small vector $\mathbf{x}$ satisfying $\mathbf{G}\mathbf{x} = \mathbf{t} \bmod q$ for any $\mathbf{t} \in \mathbb{Z}_q^n$. We think of $\mathbf{A}, \mathbf{A}\mathbf{R}, \mathbf{G}, \mathbf{H}$ as publicly known and think of $\mathbf{R}$ as a secret trapdoor. They showed how to sample a short pre-image $\mathbf{s} = (\mathbf{s}_1, \mathbf{s}_2)$ given some target $\mathbf{t}$ so as to satisfy:

$$f_{\mathbf{A}'}(\mathbf{s}) = \mathbf{A}'\mathbf{s} = [\mathbf{A}|\mathbf{A}\mathbf{R} - \mathbf{H}\mathbf{G}]\mathbf{s} = \mathbf{A}\mathbf{s}_1 + (\mathbf{A}\mathbf{R} - \mathbf{H}\mathbf{G})\mathbf{s}_2 = \mathbf{t} \bmod q. \quad (1)$$

Furthermore, they ensure that the distribution of $\mathbf{s}$ does not depend on the trapdoor $\mathbf{R}$.

The intuition for how the Micciancio-Peikert sampler produces short vectors while hiding the exact value of $\mathbf{R}$ is as follows. If we define $\mathbf{A}' = [\mathbf{A}|\mathbf{A}\mathbf{R} - \mathbf{H}\mathbf{G}]$ and $\mathbf{R}' = \begin{bmatrix} \mathbf{R} \\ -\mathbf{I} \end{bmatrix}$, then $\mathbf{A}'\mathbf{R}' = \mathbf{H}\mathbf{G}$. To sample an $\mathbf{s}$ such that $\mathbf{A}'\mathbf{s} = \mathbf{t} \bmod q$, one first samples a vector $\mathbf{w}$ from a particular distribution, then samples a discrete Gaussian vector $\mathbf{z}$ satisfying $\mathbf{G}\mathbf{z} = \mathbf{H}^{-1}(\mathbf{t} - \mathbf{A}'\mathbf{w}) \bmod q$, and finally outputs $\mathbf{s} = \mathbf{w} + \mathbf{R}'\mathbf{z}$. One can check that $\mathbf{A}'\mathbf{s} = \mathbf{A}'\mathbf{w} + \mathbf{A}'\mathbf{R}'\mathbf{z} = \mathbf{t} - \mathbf{H}\mathbf{G}\mathbf{z} = \mathbf{t} \bmod q$. The main part of [MP12] consisted of proving that the distribution of $\mathbf{s}$ is independent of $\mathbf{R}$. If $\mathbf{z}$ is a discrete Gaussian with a large-enough standard deviation, then the distribution of $\mathbf{R}'\mathbf{z}$ is also a discrete Gaussian with covariance matrix approximately $\mathbf{R}'\mathbf{R}'^T$. Then, if the distribution of $\mathbf{w}$ was also a discrete Gaussian with covariance matrix $s^2\mathbf{I} - \mathbf{R}'\mathbf{R}'^T$, the covariance matrix of the distribution of $\mathbf{s} = \mathbf{w} + \mathbf{R}'\mathbf{z}$ is very close to the sum of the covariance matrices [Pei10], which is $s^2\mathbf{I}$, and is therefore independent of $\mathbf{R}$.[1]

Both the GPV and the Micciancio-Peikert samplers strongly rely on the Gaussian nature of the output distribution. The GPV algorithm samples vectors along the Gram-Schmidt decomposition of the trapdoor, which ends up being Gaussian due to the rotational invariance of the Gaussian distribution. Similarly, the Micciancio-Peikert sampler crucially relies on the convolution theorem for

---

[1] The matrix $\mathbf{H}$ does not in any way help in the inversion procedure. It is present only because it is very useful in constructions of various schemes such as CCA-secure encryption, digital signatures, and identity-based encryption schemes (we refer the reader to [MP12] for more details).

Gaussian distributions, which is also an implicit consequence of the rotational invariance.

1.1   Our Result

Our main result is another sampler (which is very much inspired by the works of [ABB10] and [MP12]) that outputs an $\mathbf{s}$ satisfying Equation (1) that does not inherently rely on the special properties of any distribution. For example, it is able to output an $\mathbf{s} = (\mathbf{s}_1, \mathbf{s}_2)$ where both $\mathbf{s}_1$ and $\mathbf{s}_2$ come from (different) uniform distributions, or the distribution of $\mathbf{s}_2$ could be uniform while $\mathbf{s}_1$ is a discrete Gaussian. The algorithm is also conceptually very simple. To sample an $\mathbf{s}$, we rewrite $\mathbf{As}_1 + (\mathbf{AR} - \mathbf{HG})\mathbf{s}_2 = \mathbf{t} \bmod q$ as $\mathbf{Gs}_2 = \mathbf{H}^{-1}(\mathbf{A}(\mathbf{s}_1 + \mathbf{Rs}_2) - \mathbf{t}) \bmod q$. We first pick the variable $\mathbf{y}$ corresponding to $\mathbf{s}_1 + \mathbf{Rs}_2$ according to some distribution P_y. Once this $\mathbf{y}$ is fixed, the value of $\mathbf{s}_2$ is deterministically determined via the equation $\mathbf{Gs}_2 = \mathbf{H}^{-1}(\mathbf{Ay} - \mathbf{t}) \bmod q$ according to some rule – for example, if $\mathbf{G}$ is the "powers-of-2" matrix (see (4) in Section 3.2), then $\mathbf{s}_2$ is just a concatenation of the binary decompositions of each coefficient of $\mathbf{H}^{-1}(\mathbf{Ay} - \mathbf{t}) \bmod q$.[2] Once $\mathbf{s}_2$ is chosen, the value of $\mathbf{s}_1$ is uniquely determined to be $\mathbf{s}_1 = \mathbf{y} - \mathbf{Rs}_2$. At this point, outputting $\mathbf{s} = (\mathbf{s}_1, \mathbf{s}_2)$ would leak $\mathbf{R}$, and we need to use rejection sampling to break the dependency. The idea is similar to that in [Lyu09, Lyu12], except that in our case $\mathbf{y}$ and $\mathbf{s}_2$ are dependent on each other (in particular, the only entropy in the whole algorithm is in $\mathbf{y}$ and in the coins that are eventually used for the rejection sampling) and one needs a more careful argument to show that the distribution of $(\mathbf{s}_1, \mathbf{s}_2)$ can have a distribution that is independent of $\mathbf{R}$.

The main advantage of our sampler lies in its conceptual simplicity and the generality of its output distribution. A hidden cost of discrete Gaussian sampling over arbitrary lattices is that it requires the storage of, and computation with, vectors of real numbers (for example, the Gram-Schmidt orthogonalization in [GPV08] or the square root of the covariance matrix in [Pei10, MP12]) with precision of at least the security parameter. This could pose a serious implementation obstacle on devices in which storage space and/or computational power are at a premium.[3] Using our new sampling algorithm, on the other hand, we can choose the distributions for $\mathbf{s}_1$ and $\mathbf{s}_2$ to be uniform, and then one only needs to perform uniform sampling over $\mathbb{Z}_q$ and the rejection sampling part of the algorithm simply involves checking whether all the coefficients are in a particular interval (see the first example in Section 3.2). If a little more processing power or storage capacity is available, we can change the distribution of $\mathbf{s}_1$ to a discrete Gaussian over $\mathbb{Z}^m$, which will make the outputs slightly shorter but will require some additional resources for doing discrete Gaussian sampling over

---

[2] One could choose $\mathbf{s}_2$ according to some (non-deterministic) distribution instead, but we do not at present see any reason to do so.

[3] It should be pointed out that the signature schemes of [Pei10, MP12] can do a lot of the necessary high-precision computations "offline" before receiving the message to be signed. In such an "online/offline" model, this can save on the computation time during the online phase, but the storage space still remains an issue.

$\mathbb{Z}^m$ (cf. [DDLL13, DG14, PDG14]) and for the rejection sampling step (see the second example in Section 3.1).

The main disadvantage of our sampler is that the norm of the produced vector $\mathbf{s}_1$, and therefore the norm of the entire vector $\mathbf{s} = (\mathbf{s}_1, \mathbf{s}_2)$ of our algorithm, is larger by at least a $\sqrt{n}$ factor than of the ones produced by the samplers of [GPV08, MP12] (see the examples in Section 3.2). In practice, having the norms of the outputs be larger by a factor of $O(\sqrt{n})$ results in the bit-length of the output $\mathbf{s}$ to increase by a factor of 2 or 3 (e.g. compare [GLP12] to [DDLL13]). Therefore we believe that our sampler provides a time vs. size trade-off that is most useful in instances where Gaussian sampling over arbitrary lattices is either not possible or prohibitively expensive.

2   Preliminaries

Let X, Y be distributions or random variables with support S. We define their *statistical distance* by $\mathsf{SD}(X, Y) = \frac{1}{2} \sum_{s \in S} |\Pr[X = s] - \Pr[Y = s]|$. We write $X \approx_\varepsilon Y$ and say that X and Y are ε-statistically close to denote that $\mathsf{SD}(X, Y) \le \varepsilon$. For a random variable X, we define the min-entropy of X as $H_\infty(X) := -\log(\max_x \Pr[X = x])$.

Lemma 2.1 (Leftover Hash Lemma). *[HILL99, NZ96] Let $\mathcal{H} = \{h : D \to R\}$ be a universal hash function family, meaning that for all $x \ne y \in D$ we have $\Pr_{h \leftarrow \mathcal{H}}[h(x) = h(y)] \le 1/|R|$. Let X be any random variable with support D and min-entropy $H_\infty(X) \ge \log(|R|) + 2\log(1/\varepsilon)$. Then $(h, h(x))$ is ε-statistically close to (h, r) where $h \xleftarrow{\$} \mathcal{H}, x \xleftarrow{\$} X$ and $r \xleftarrow{\$} R$.*

In particular, for a prime q, setting $D = \mathbb{Z}_q^m$, $R = \mathbb{Z}_q^n$ and $\mathcal{H} = \{h_\mathbf{A}(\mathbf{x}) := \mathbf{A}\mathbf{x} \mid \mathbf{A} \in \mathbb{Z}_q^{n \times m}\}$, for any distribution $\mathbf{x}$ over $\mathbb{Z}_q^m$ having entropy $H_\infty(\mathbf{x}) \ge n\log(q) + 2\log(1/\varepsilon)$ we have $(\mathbf{A}, \mathbf{A}\mathbf{x})$ is ε-statistically close to $(\mathbf{A}, \mathbf{r})$ where $\mathbf{A} \xleftarrow{\$} \mathbb{Z}_q^{n \times m}$ and $\mathbf{r} \xleftarrow{\$} \mathbb{Z}_q^n$.

Lemma 2.2. *[Lyu12, Lemma 4.7]*

Let f, g be probability distributions with the property that

$$\exists M \in \mathbb{R}^+ \text{ such that, } \Pr_{z \xleftarrow{\$} f}[Mg(z) \ge f(z)] \ge 1 - \varepsilon$$

then the distribution of the output of the following algorithm $\mathcal{A}$:

1: $z \xleftarrow{\$} g$

2: output z with probability $\min\left(\frac{f(z)}{Mg(z)}, 1\right)$

is within statistical distance ε/M of the distribution of the following algorithm $\mathcal{F}$:

1: $z \xleftarrow{\$} f$

2: output z with probability $1/M$

Moreover, the probability that $\mathcal{A}$ outputs something is at least $(1 - \varepsilon)/M$.

Ideal Distribution

   1: Generate $\mathbf{s}_2 \xleftarrow{\$} P_2$
   2: Generate $\mathbf{s}_1 \xleftarrow{\$} P_1 | \mathbf{A}\mathbf{s}_1 = \mathbf{t} + (\mathbf{HG} - \mathbf{AR})\mathbf{s}_2 \bmod q$
   3: Output $\mathbf{s} = (\mathbf{s}_1, \mathbf{s}_2)$

Real Distribution

   1: Generate $\mathbf{y} \xleftarrow{\$} P_y$
   2: Compute $\mathbf{s}_2 \leftarrow \mathbf{G}^{-1} \left(\mathbf{H}^{-1}(\mathbf{Ay} - \mathbf{t}) \bmod q \right)$
   3: Compute $\mathbf{s}_1 \leftarrow \mathbf{y} - \mathbf{R}\mathbf{s}_2$
   4: Output $\mathbf{s} = (\mathbf{s}_1, \mathbf{s}_2)$ with probability $\frac{P_1(\mathbf{s}_1)}{M \cdot P_y(\mathbf{s}_1 + \mathbf{R}\mathbf{s}_2)}$
   5: If nothing was output, GOTO 1.

Fig. 1. Ideal and Real Distributions

3   The Sampling Algorithm

Given matrices $\mathbf{A} \in \mathbb{Z}_q^{n \times m}$, $\mathbf{R} \in \mathbb{Z}_q^{m \times l}$, $\mathbf{G} \in \mathbb{Z}_q^{n \times l}$, $\mathbf{H} \in \mathbb{Z}_q^{n \times n}$ and a target $\mathbf{t} \in \mathbb{Z}_q^n$, we would like to output a short vector $\mathbf{s} = (\mathbf{s}_1, \mathbf{s}_2)$ that satisfies

$$[\mathbf{A} | \mathbf{AR} - \mathbf{HG}]\mathbf{s} = \mathbf{A}\mathbf{s}_1 + (\mathbf{AR} - \mathbf{HG})\mathbf{s}_2 = \mathbf{t} \bmod q \tag{2}$$

and furthermore, the distribution of $\mathbf{s}$ is independent of $\mathbf{R}$ given the "public" values $\mathbf{A}, \mathbf{AR}, \mathbf{H}, \mathbf{G}$. In other words, if we think of $\mathbf{R}$ as a trapdoor needed to perform the sampling, we want to ensure that the sample $\mathbf{s}$ should not reveal anything about the trapdoor $\mathbf{R}$.

We present a general framework for performing such sampling with many different choices on the distribution of $\mathbf{s}_1, \mathbf{s}_2$. The framework is defined in terms of three component distributions that we call P_1, P_2 and P_y. Using these three distributions, we compare between an efficiently sampleable distribution which uses $\mathbf{R}$ and which we call the "real distribution", and an "ideal distribution" which is not efficiently sampleable but does not use $\mathbf{R}$. We present the ideal and real distributions in Figure 1. The ideal distribution directly samples $\mathbf{s}_2$ from the desired distribution P_2, and then samples $\mathbf{s}_1$ from some distribution P_1 conditioned on the fact that Equation (2) should be satisfied. Clearly, since $\mathbf{R}$ is never used in the sampling procedure of the ideal distribution, it does not depend on $\mathbf{R}$, but only on the publicly-available information.

The real distribution that our sampling algorithm samples from, first generates a $\mathbf{y}$ from an intermediate distribution P_y. This $\mathbf{y}$ will now deterministically determine both $\mathbf{s}_2$ and $\mathbf{s}_1$. To compute $\mathbf{s}_2$, we first compute $\mathbf{H}^{-1}(\mathbf{Ay} - \mathbf{t}) \bmod q \in \mathbb{Z}_q^n$, and then find an $\mathbf{s}_2$ in the support of P_2 such that $\mathbf{G}\mathbf{s}_2 = \mathbf{H}^{-1}(\mathbf{Ay} - \mathbf{t}) \bmod q$. By our choice of $\mathbf{G}$, this value of $\mathbf{s}_2$ will be unique and easily computable, and we denote it by $\mathbf{s}_2 = \mathbf{G}^{-1}(\mathbf{H}^{-1}(\mathbf{A}\mathbf{y}-\mathbf{t}) \bmod q)$.[4] We then compute $\mathbf{s}_1$ as $\mathbf{y}-\mathbf{R}\mathbf{s}_2$. At this point, the distribution of $(\mathbf{s}_1, \mathbf{s}_2)$ is not as in the ideal distribution. To correct the discrepancy, we use rejection sampling, and output $(\mathbf{s}_1, \mathbf{s}_2)$ with probability $\frac{P_1(\mathbf{s}_1)}{M \cdot P_y(\mathbf{s}_1+\mathbf{R}\mathbf{s}_2)}$ where M is some positive real (if this fraction is greater than 1, we define the probability to be 1).

In Section 3.1, we state the relationships between the matrices and the distributions that are required for our sampling algorithm to produce a distribution statistically close to the ideal distribution. Then in Section 3.2, we give two illustrative examples of instantiations over general lattices and polynomial rings.

3.1 Requirements and Security Proof

Theorem 3.1. *Consider matrices* $\mathbf{A} \in \mathbb{Z}_q^{n \times m}$, $\mathbf{R} \in \mathbb{Z}_q^{m \times l}$, $\mathbf{G} \in \mathbb{Z}_q^{n \times l}$, *and* $\mathbf{H} \in \mathbb{Z}_q^{n \times n}$, *and distributions* P_1, P_2, P_y *over* $\mathbb{Z}^m$, $\mathbb{Z}^l$, *and* $\mathbb{Z}^m$ *respectively, such that the following four conditions are satisfied:*

1. *For the two distributions* $\mathbf{s} \overset{\$}{\leftarrow} P_1$ *and* $\mathbf{s} \overset{\$}{\leftarrow} P_y$, *the statistical distance between* $\mathbf{A}\mathbf{s} \bmod q$ *and the uniform distribution over* $\mathbb{Z}_q^n$ *is at most* $2^{-(n \log q + \lambda)}$.
2. $\mathbf{H}$ *is invertible modulo* q.
3. *The function* $\mathbf{G}$ *mapping the support of* P_2 *to* $\mathbb{Z}_q^n$, *defined by* $\mathbf{G}(\mathbf{s}) = \mathbf{G}\mathbf{s}$, *is 1-to-1 and onto and is efficiently invertible via a function* $\mathbf{G}^{-1}$. *Furthermore,* P_2 *is uniformly random over its support.*
4. $\Pr_{(\mathbf{x}_1,\mathbf{x}_2) \overset{\$}{\leftarrow} IdealDistribution} \left[\frac{P_1(\mathbf{x}_1)}{P_y(\mathbf{x}_1+\mathbf{R}\mathbf{x}_2)} \leq M \right] \geq 1 - 2^{-\lambda}$ *for some positive* $M \geq 1$.

then the outputs of the ideal distribution and the real distribution are ε-*close for* $\varepsilon = \lambda \cdot (2M + 1) \cdot 2^{-\lambda}$, *whenever* $\lambda > 4$. *Furthermore, the expected number of iterations of the sampling algorithm is* $\approx M$.

Proof. We first describe an intermediate distribution, which we will call the *hybrid distribution* defined as follows.

Hybrid Distribution without Rejection:
    Generate $\mathbf{s}_2 \overset{\$}{\leftarrow} P_2$
    Generate $\mathbf{y} \overset{\$}{\leftarrow} P_y | (\mathbf{A}\mathbf{y} = \mathbf{t} + \mathbf{H}\mathbf{G}\mathbf{s}_2 \bmod q)$
    Compute $\mathbf{s}_1 \leftarrow \mathbf{y} - \mathbf{R}\mathbf{s}_2$
    Output $\mathbf{s} = (\mathbf{s}_1, \mathbf{s}_2)$

We also define a "Hybrid Distribution with Rejection" which first samples $(\mathbf{s}_1, \mathbf{s}_2)$ from the above-described Hybrid Distribution and then outputs it with probability $\frac{P_1(\mathbf{s}_1)}{M \cdot P_y(\mathbf{s}_1+\mathbf{R}\mathbf{s}_2)}$, else tries again.

---

[4] This is an abuse of notation since $\mathbf{G}^{-1}$ is not a matrix but rather a deterministic function satisfying $\mathbf{G} \cdot \mathbf{G}^{-1}(\mathbf{z}) = \mathbf{z}$.

Lemma 3.2. *Let f be the probability density function of the Ideal Distribution and g be the probability density function of the Hybrid Distribution (without rejection). Then*

$$\frac{f(\mathbf{x}_1, \mathbf{x}_2)}{g(\mathbf{x}_1, \mathbf{x}_2)} = \frac{P_1(\mathbf{x}_1)}{P_y(\mathbf{x}_1 + \mathbf{R}\mathbf{x}_2)}(1 + \delta) \text{ for some } \delta : -2 \cdot 2^{-\lambda} \leq \delta \leq 3 \cdot 2^{-\lambda}$$

In particular, for $\lambda > 4$, this means that the Ideal Distribution is $\lambda(M+1)2^{-\lambda}$ close to the Hybrid Distribution with Rejection.

Proof.

$$\frac{f(\mathbf{x}_1, \mathbf{x}_2)}{g(\mathbf{x}_1, \mathbf{x}_2)} = \frac{\Pr_{\mathbf{s}_2 \overset{\$}{\leftarrow} P_2}[\mathbf{s}_2 = \mathbf{x}_2] \cdot \Pr_{\mathbf{s}_1 \overset{\$}{\leftarrow} P_1}[\mathbf{s}_1 = \mathbf{x}_1 | \mathbf{A}\mathbf{s}_1 = \mathbf{t} + (\mathbf{H}\mathbf{G} - \mathbf{A}\mathbf{R})\mathbf{x}_2 \bmod q]}{\Pr_{\mathbf{s}_2 \overset{\$}{\leftarrow} P_2}[\mathbf{s}_2 = \mathbf{x}_2] \cdot \Pr_{\mathbf{y} \overset{\$}{\leftarrow} P_y}[\mathbf{y} = \mathbf{x}_1 + \mathbf{R}\mathbf{x}_2 | \mathbf{A}\mathbf{y} = \mathbf{t} + \mathbf{H}\mathbf{G}\mathbf{x}_2 \bmod q]}$$

$$= \frac{\Pr_{\mathbf{s}_1 \overset{\$}{\leftarrow} P_1}[\mathbf{s}_1 = \mathbf{x}_1] \cdot \Pr_{\mathbf{y} \overset{\$}{\leftarrow} P_y}[\mathbf{A}\mathbf{y} = \mathbf{t} + \mathbf{H}\mathbf{G}\mathbf{x}_2 \bmod q]}{\Pr_{\mathbf{y} \overset{\$}{\leftarrow} P_y}[\mathbf{y} = \mathbf{x}_1 + \mathbf{R}\mathbf{x}_2] \cdot \Pr_{\mathbf{s}_1 \overset{\$}{\leftarrow} P_1}[\mathbf{A}\mathbf{s}_1 = \mathbf{t} + (\mathbf{H}\mathbf{G} - \mathbf{A}\mathbf{R})\mathbf{x}_2 \bmod q]}$$

$$= \frac{P_1(\mathbf{x}_1)}{P_y(\mathbf{x}_1 + \mathbf{R}\mathbf{x}_2)} \cdot \frac{\Pr_{\mathbf{y} \overset{\$}{\leftarrow} P_y}[\mathbf{A}\mathbf{y} = \mathbf{t} + \mathbf{H}\mathbf{G}\mathbf{x}_2 \bmod q]}{\Pr_{\mathbf{s}_1 \overset{\$}{\leftarrow} P_1}[\mathbf{A}\mathbf{s}_1 = \mathbf{t} + (\mathbf{H}\mathbf{G} - \mathbf{A}\mathbf{R})\mathbf{x}_2 \bmod q]}$$

$$= \frac{P_1(\mathbf{x}_1)}{P_y(\mathbf{x}_1 + \mathbf{R}\mathbf{x}_2)} \cdot \frac{q^{-n} + \delta_1}{q^{-n} + \delta_y} \quad \text{where } -q^{-n}2^{-\lambda} \leq \delta_1, \delta_y \leq q^{-n}2^{-\lambda}$$

$$\tag{3}$$

$$= \frac{P_1(\mathbf{x}_1)}{P_y(\mathbf{x}_1 + \mathbf{R}\mathbf{x}_2)}(1 + \delta) \text{ where } -2 \cdot 2^{-\lambda} \leq \delta \leq 3 \cdot 2^{-\lambda}$$

Line 3 follows from the requirement of Theorem 3.1 that the distributions of $\mathbf{A}\mathbf{y} \bmod q$ and $\mathbf{A}\mathbf{s}_1 \bmod q$ are $q^{-n}2^{-\lambda}$-close to uniformly random over $\mathbb{Z}_q^n$ when $\mathbf{y} \overset{\$}{\leftarrow} P_y$ and $\mathbf{s}_1 \overset{\$}{\leftarrow} P_1$. This proves the first part of the lemma.

For the second part of the lemma, we define one more hybrid distribution, that we call the "Hybrid Distribution with Ideal Rejection". It is the same as the "Hybrid Distribution with Rejection", but we set the rejection probability to $\gamma_{ideal} = \min\left(\frac{f(\mathbf{s}_1, \mathbf{s}_2)}{M(1+\delta^+)g(\mathbf{s}_1, \mathbf{s}_2)}, 1\right)$ for $\delta^+ = 3 \cdot 2^{-\lambda}$. This is instead of the rejection probability $\gamma_{real} = \min\left(\frac{P_1(\mathbf{s}_1)}{MP_y(\mathbf{s}_1 + \mathbf{R}\mathbf{s}_2)}, 1\right)$ used in the original "Hybrid Distribution with Rejection" (in real life, we don't know γ_{ideal} exactly, and therefore are forced to use γ_{real} as an approximation). Note that by the first part of the lemma, $\gamma_{ideal} = \min\left(\frac{(1+\delta)P_1(\mathbf{s}_1)}{M(1+\delta^+)P_y(\mathbf{s}_1 + \mathbf{R}\mathbf{s}_2)}, 1\right)$ for some $\delta \in [-2 \cdot 2^{-\lambda}, \delta^+]$ and therefore $|\gamma_{real} - \gamma_{ideal}| \leq 5(2^{-\lambda})$. Furthermore, in the "Hybrid Distribution with Ideal Rejection", the rejection sampling step only occurs at most λM times with probability $1 - \left(1 - \frac{1}{(1+\delta^+)M}\right)^{\lambda M} \geq 1 - 2^{-\lambda}$. Therefore, the statistical distance between the "Hybrid Distribution with Rejection" and the "Hybrid Distribution with Ideal Rejection" is at most $\lambda M \cdot 2^{-\lambda}$.

Next, we show that the "Hybrid Distribution with Ideal Rejection" is $\lambda \cdot 2^{-\lambda}$-statistically close to the ideal distribution. This relies on the rejection sampling lemma (Lemma 2.2). We note that by requirement (4) of the theorem: we have for $\delta^+ = 3 \cdot 2^{-\lambda}$:

$$\Pr_{(\mathbf{s}_1, \mathbf{s}_2) \xleftarrow{\$} f} [M(1 + \delta^+) g(\mathbf{s}_1, \mathbf{s}_2) \geq f(\mathbf{s}_1, \mathbf{s}_2)] = \Pr_{(\mathbf{s}_1, \mathbf{s}_2) \xleftarrow{\$} f} \left[\frac{f(\mathbf{s}_1, \mathbf{s}_2)}{g(\mathbf{s}_1, \mathbf{s}_2)} \leq M(1 + \delta^+) \right]$$

$$\geq \Pr_{(\mathbf{s}_1, \mathbf{s}_2) \xleftarrow{\$} f} \left[\frac{P_1(\mathbf{s}_1)}{P_y(\mathbf{s}_1 + \mathbf{R}\mathbf{s}_2)} \leq M \right]$$

$$\geq 1 - 2^{-\lambda}$$

Therefore, by the "rejection sampling lemma" (Lemma 2.2), each iteration of the "Hybrid Distribution with Ideal Rejection" outputs something which is $2^{-\lambda}/M$ statistically close to outputting a sample from the ideal distribution with probability $\frac{1}{M(1+\delta^+)}$. Furthermore, the rejection sampling step only occurs at most λM times with probability $1 - \left(1 - \frac{1}{(1+\delta^+)M}\right)^{\lambda M} \geq 1 - 2^{-\lambda}$. Therefore, the statistical distance between the "Hybrid Distribution with Ideal Rejection" and the "Ideal Distribution" is at most $\lambda \cdot 2^{-\lambda}$.

Combining the above, the statistical distance between the "Hybrid Distribution with Rejection" and the "Ideal Distribution" is at most $\lambda M \cdot 2^{-\lambda} + \lambda \cdot 2^{-\lambda} = \lambda(M + 1)2^{-\lambda}$ as claimed.   □

Now we introduce another distribution that we call the "Real Distribution without Rejection" which matches the real distribution without the rejection sampling step:

Real Distribution without Rejection:
  Generate $\mathbf{y} \xleftarrow{\$} P_y$
  Compute $\mathbf{s}_2 \leftarrow \mathbf{G}^{-1} \left(\mathbf{H}^{-1}(\mathbf{A}\mathbf{y} - \mathbf{t}) \bmod q \right)$
  Compute $\mathbf{s}_1 \leftarrow \mathbf{y} - \mathbf{R}\mathbf{s}_2$.
  Output $(\mathbf{s}_1, \mathbf{s}_2)$.

Lemma 3.3. *The statistical distance between the "Real Distribution without Rejection" and the "Hybrid Distribution without Rejection" is at most $2^{-\lambda}$. In particular, this also means that the statistical distance between the "Real Distribution with Rejection" and the "Hybrid Distribution with Rejection" is at most $\lambda M \cdot 2^{-\lambda}$.*

Proof. Let us define a randomized function $f(\mathbf{u})$ which gets as input $\mathbf{u} \in \mathbb{Z}_q^n$ and does the following:

Sample: $\mathbf{s}_2 \stackrel{\$}{\leftarrow} P_2 | \mathbf{t} + \mathbf{HGs}_2 = \mathbf{u} \bmod q$.
Sample: $\mathbf{y} \stackrel{\$}{\leftarrow} P_y | \mathbf{Ay} = \mathbf{u} \bmod q$.
Compute: $\mathbf{s}_1 \leftarrow \mathbf{y} - \mathbf{Rs}_2$.
Output: $(\mathbf{s}_1, \mathbf{s}_2)$.

It is easy to see that, when $\mathbf{u} \stackrel{\$}{\leftarrow} \mathbb{Z}_q^n$, then $f(\mathbf{u})$ is equivalent to the "Hybrid Distribution". This is because the distribution of $\mathbf{t} + \mathbf{HGs}_2 \bmod q$ for $\mathbf{s}_2 \leftarrow P_2$ is indeed uniformly random (due to requirements (2) and (3) of Theorem 3.1).

On the other hand, if we instead sample $\mathbf{u}$ by choosing $\mathbf{y}' \stackrel{\$}{\leftarrow} P_y$ and setting $\mathbf{u} := \mathbf{Ay}' \bmod q$ then $f(\mathbf{u})$ is equivalent to the "Real Distribution without Rejection".

Therefore, the statistical distance between the hybrid and real distributions without rejection sampling is the statistical distance between $\mathbf{Ay}' \bmod q$: $\mathbf{y}' \stackrel{\$}{\leftarrow} P_y$ and the uniform distribution over $\mathbb{Z}_q^n$. By definition, this is at most $2^{-(n \log q + \lambda)} \leq 2^{-\lambda}$.

The distributions with rejection sampling just depend on at most λM copies of the corresponding distributions without rejection sampling with overwhelming probability $1 - 2^{-\lambda}$ (using the same argument as in the previous lemma) and therefore we can use the hybrid argument to argue that the statistical distance between them is at most $\lambda M \cdot 2^{-\lambda}$.   □

Combining the above lemmas, proves the theorem.   □

3.2   Two examples

We will now give two examples of matrices and distributions that satisfy the requirements of Theorem 3.1. Even though the examples are specific in the choices of parameters, we believe that they illustrate the techniques needed to apply our algorithm in other scenarios.

In both examples, we will let q be some prime[5], set $m = l = n\lceil \log q \rceil$, and define $\mathbf{G}$ as the matrix

$$\mathbf{G} = \begin{bmatrix} 1\,2\,4 \ldots 2^{\lceil \log q \rceil} & & & \\ & 1\,2\,4 \ldots 2^{\lceil \log q \rceil} & & \\ & & \ldots & \\ & & & 1\,2\,4 \ldots 2^{\lceil \log q \rceil} \end{bmatrix} \quad (4)$$

Notice that with this $\mathbf{G}$, for every element $\mathbf{t} \in \mathbb{Z}^n$ with coefficients between 0 and $q - 1$ there is a unique vector $\mathbf{s}_2 \in \{0,1\}^m$ such that $\mathbf{Gs}_2 = \mathbf{t}$ (without reduction modulo q). We denote this vector by $\mathbf{s}_2 = \mathbf{G}^{-1}(\mathbf{t})$, but note that this

---

[5] The requirement that q is prime only comes from the use of the leftover hash-lemma, and it can be relaxed. For example, it suffices that the smallest prime divisor of q is at least as large as $2\|\mathbf{s}\|_\infty$. Alternatively, if q is a product of primes and $\mathbf{s}$ has high entropy modulo each of the primes, then we can use the leftover-hash lemma for each prime divisor separately. For simplicity, we only mention these relaxations in passing and concentrate on the case when q is prime in what follows.

is an abuse of notation as the matrix $\mathbf{G}$ is not actually an invertible matrix. The distribution P_2 in our examples will simply be the distribution of $\mathbf{s}_2 = \mathbf{G}^{-1}(\mathbf{t})$ for a uniformly random $\mathbf{t} \in \mathbb{Z}^n$ having coefficients between 0 and $q - 1$. Such a choice of $\mathbf{G}$ and P_2 satisfy requirement (3) of the theorem.

We will choose our matrix $\mathbf{A}$ at random from $\mathbb{Z}_q^{n \times m}$ and the distributions P_1, P_y to have min-entropy at least $3n \log q + 4\lambda$.[6] This ensures that, by the Leftover Hash Lemma (Lemma 2.1), the statistical distance between $(\mathbf{A}, \mathbf{A} \cdot \mathbf{s} \bmod q)$ and $(\mathbf{A}, \mathbf{r})$ where $\mathbf{s} \xleftarrow{\$} P_1$ (resp. P_y) and $\mathbf{r} \xleftarrow{\$} \mathbb{Z}_q^n$, is bounded by $2^{-(n \log q + 2\lambda)}$. Let's say that a fixed matrix $\mathbf{A}$ is "good for P_1" (resp. "good for P_y") if the statistical distance between $\mathbf{As}$ and $\mathbf{r}$ is at most $\varepsilon = 2^{-n \log q + \lambda}$ when $\mathbf{s} \xleftarrow{\$} P_1$ (resp. $\mathbf{s} \xleftarrow{\$} P_y$). Then, by Markov's inequality, the probability that a random $\mathbf{A}$ is good for P_1 (resp. good for P_y) is at least $1 - 2^{-\lambda}$. Let's say that $\mathbf{A}$ is "good" if it is good for both P_1 and P_y. By the union bound, a random $\mathbf{A}$ is good with probability at least $1 - 2 \cdot 2^{-\lambda}$. Therefore if the distributions P_1, P_y have min-entropy at least $3n \log q + 4\lambda$, requirement (1) of the theorem is satisfied with probability at least $1 - 2 \cdot 2^{-\lambda}$.

In both examples, we will take the matrix $\mathbf{R}$ to be uniformly random from $\{-1, 0, 1\}^{m \times m}$. The important property we will need from $\mathbf{R}$ is that the norm of $\mathbf{Rs}_2$ is not too large.

By the Chernoff bound, we obtain that for any $\mathbf{s}_2 \in \{0, 1\}^m$, there exists a $k_\infty = \Theta\left(\sqrt{\lambda m}\right)$ such that

$$\Pr_{\mathbf{R} \xleftarrow{\$} \{-1,0,1\}^{m \times m}} [\|\mathbf{Rs}_2\|_\infty \leq k_\infty] \geq 1 - 2^{-2\lambda}. \tag{5}$$

For the distribution P_2 over $\{0, 1\}^m$, we say that a fixed matrix $\mathbf{R}$ is ℓ_∞-good if $\Pr_{\mathbf{s}_2 \xleftarrow{\$} P_2}[\|\mathbf{Rs}_2\|_\infty > k_\infty] \leq 2^{-\lambda}$. By the above equation we have

$$\Pr_{\mathbf{s}_2 \xleftarrow{\$} P_2, \mathbf{R} \xleftarrow{\$} \{-1,0,1\}^{m \times m}} [\|\mathbf{Rs}_2\|_\infty > k_\infty] \leq 2^{-2\lambda}$$

and therefore by Markov inequality, a random $\mathbf{R}$ is ℓ_∞-good with probability $1 - 2^{-\lambda}$.

We can also establish a bound on the ℓ_2 norm of $\mathbf{Rs}_2$. By [Ver10, Theorem 5.39], for all $\mathbf{s}_2 \in \{0, 1\}^m$, there exists a $k_2 = \Theta(m + \sqrt{\lambda m}) = \Theta(m)$ such that

$$\Pr_{\mathbf{R} \xleftarrow{\$} \{-1,0,1\}^{m \times m}} [\|\mathbf{Rs}_2\| \leq k_2] \geq 1 - 2^{-2\lambda}. \tag{6}$$

For the distribution P_2 over $\{0, 1\}^m$, we say that a fixed matrix $\mathbf{R}$ is ℓ_2-good if $\Pr_{\mathbf{s}_2 \xleftarrow{\$} P_2}[\|\mathbf{Rs}_2\| > k_2] \leq 2^{-\lambda}$. By the same reasoning as above, a random $\mathbf{R}$ is ℓ_2-good with probability $1 - 2^{-\lambda}$.

---

[6] This entropy lower bound is not really a restriction on the distributions P_1 and P_y. The distributions that we will need to pick to satisfy property (4) of the theorem will easily meet this bound.

We now proceed to show how to pick the distributions P_1 and P_y to satisfy the requirement (4) of the theorem. We will assume that the randomly-chosen $\mathbf{A}$ and $\mathbf{R}$ are good for these distributions (as defined above), which happens with overwhelming probability $1 - 4 \cdot 2^{-\lambda}$. In our first example, both P_1 and P_y will be uniform distributions in some cube. The advantage of such distributions is that they are particularly easy to sample. Our second example will have both of these distributions be discrete Gaussians over $\mathbb{Z}^m$. The advantage of using discrete Gaussians rather than the uniform distribution is that the norm of $\mathbf{s}_1$ will end up being smaller. The disadvantage is that sampling the discrete Gaussian distribution over $\mathbb{Z}^m$ is a more involved procedure than sampling the uniform distribution over $\mathbb{Z}_q$. Still, sampling a discrete Gaussian over $\mathbb{Z}^m$ is more efficient and requires less precision than sampling such a distribution over an arbitrary lattice.

Example for P_1 and P_y Being Uniform in an m-dimensional Integer Cube. We define the distribution P_1 (respectively P_y) to be the uniform distribution over all vectors $\mathbf{x} \in \mathbb{Z}^m$ such that $\|\mathbf{x}\|_\infty \leq mk_\infty$ (respectively $\|\mathbf{x}\|_\infty \leq mk_\infty + k_\infty$). And we set the constant

$$M = \left(\frac{2mk_\infty + 2k_\infty + 1}{2mk_\infty + 1} \right)^m \approx e. \tag{7}$$

We will now show that the above choices satisfy the necessary requirements of Theorem 3.1. First, we will lower-bound the entropies of P_1 and P_y.

$$H_\infty(P_y) > H_\infty(P_1) = -\log\left(\frac{1}{(2mk_\infty + 1)^m} \right)$$
$$> m \log m > n \log n \log q > 3n \log q + 4\lambda,$$

and so the first requirement of the theorem is satisfied.

We will conclude by showing that requirement (4) of the theorem is also satisfied. First, it's easy to see that for any $\mathbf{x}_1$ output by the ideal distribution, $P_1(\mathbf{x}_1) = \frac{1}{(2mk_\infty+1)^m}$. Additionally, for any $\mathbf{x}_1$ in the support of P_1, if $\|\mathbf{R}\mathbf{x}_2\|_\infty \leq k_\infty$, then $\mathbf{x}_1 + \mathbf{R}\mathbf{x}_2$ is in the support of P_2, and so $P_y(\mathbf{x}_1 + \mathbf{R}\mathbf{x}_2) = \frac{1}{(2mk_\infty+2k_\infty+1)^m}$. Therefore if $\|\mathbf{R}\mathbf{x}_2\|_\infty \leq k_\infty$, we have

$$\frac{P_1(\mathbf{x}_1)}{P_y(\mathbf{x}_1 + \mathbf{R}\mathbf{x}_2)} = \left(\frac{2mk_\infty + 2k_\infty + 1}{2mk_\infty + 1} \right)^m < \left(1 + \frac{1}{m} \right)^m < e, \tag{8}$$

and so if we let f be the ideal distribution, then

$$\Pr_{(\mathbf{x}_1, \mathbf{x}_2) \xleftarrow{\$} f} \left[\frac{P_1(\mathbf{x}_1)}{P_y(\mathbf{x}_1 + \mathbf{R}\mathbf{x}_2)} \leq M \right] \geq \Pr_{(\mathbf{x}_1, \mathbf{x}_2) \xleftarrow{\$} f} [\|\mathbf{R}\mathbf{x}_2\|_\infty \leq k_\infty] \geq 1 - 2^{-\lambda},$$

where the last inequality follows by our choice of k_∞.

Note that since $\mathbf{s}_1$ is chosen to have coordinates of size $mk_\infty = \Theta(m^{1.5}\sqrt{\lambda})$, we have $\|\mathbf{s}\| \approx \|\mathbf{s}_1\| = \Theta(m^2\sqrt{\lambda})$. We also point out that the rejection sampling part of our sampler in Figure 1 is actually very simple and one does not in fact need to compute any probability distributions or even the value of M in equation (7) – simply looking at the infinity norm of $\mathbf{s}_1$ is enough. If $\mathbf{s}_1$ (in line 3) is outside the support of P_1 (i.e. $\|\mathbf{s}_1\|_\infty > mk_\infty$), then $P_1(\mathbf{s}_1) = 0$ and we always reject. On the other hand, if $\|\mathbf{s}_1\|_\infty \le mk_\infty$, then $\frac{P_1(\mathbf{x}_1)}{MP_y(\mathbf{x}_1+\mathbf{R}\mathbf{x}_2)} = 1$ (by (7) and (8)), and we always accept.

Example for P_1 and P_y Being Discrete Gaussians Over $\mathbb{Z}^m$. The discrete Gaussian distribution with standard deviation σ over $\mathbb{Z}^m$ is defined as

$$D_\sigma^m(\mathbf{x}) = \frac{e^{-\|\mathbf{x}\|^2/2\sigma^2}}{\sum\limits_{\mathbf{v}\in\mathbb{Z}^m} e^{-\|\mathbf{v}\|^2/2\sigma^2}}.$$

In this example, we will define both P_1 and P_y to be distributions D_σ^m for $\sigma = 2k_2\sqrt{\lambda}$, and we set the constant $M = e^{1+1/8\lambda}$. We will first lower-bound the min-entropy of P_1. Notice that the heaviest element of the distribution is $\mathbf{0}$, and from the proof of [Lyu12, Lemma 4.4], we have $\sum\limits_{\mathbf{v}\in\mathbb{Z}^m} e^{-\|\mathbf{v}\|^2/2\sigma^2} > (\sqrt{2\pi}\sigma - 1)^m$. Thus,

$$H_\infty(P_1) = -\log\left(D_\sigma^m(\mathbf{0})\right) = -\log\left(\frac{1}{\sum\limits_{\mathbf{v}\in\mathbb{Z}^m} e^{-\|\mathbf{v}\|^2/2\sigma^2}}\right) > m\log\sigma > 3n\log q + 4\lambda.$$

We will now move on to prove that requirement (4) of Theorem 3.1 is also satisfied. First, we write

$$\frac{P_1(\mathbf{x}_1)}{P_y(\mathbf{x}_1 + \mathbf{R}\mathbf{x}_2)} = \frac{e^{-\|\mathbf{x}_1\|^2/2\sigma^2}}{e^{-\|\mathbf{x}_1+\mathbf{R}\mathbf{x}_2\|^2/2\sigma^2}} = e^{(2\langle\mathbf{x}_1,\mathbf{R}\mathbf{x}_2\rangle + \|\mathbf{R}\mathbf{x}_2\|^2)/2\sigma^2} \le e^{\frac{\langle\mathbf{x}_1,\mathbf{R}\mathbf{x}_2\rangle}{\sigma^2}+1/8\lambda},$$

where the last inequality follows from our assumption that the random $\mathbf{R}$ satisfies the condition in Equation (6).

We now would like to upper-bound the above quantity when $\mathbf{x}_1, \mathbf{x}_2$ are distributed according to the ideal distribution. If we let $\mathbf{t}' = \mathbf{t} + (\mathbf{HG} - \mathbf{AR})\mathbf{x}_2$, then the probability that the absolute value of the dot product $\langle\mathbf{x}_1,\mathbf{R}\mathbf{x}_2\rangle$ is less than some arbitrary positive real r is

$$\Pr_{\mathbf{x}_1 \xleftarrow{\$} P_1}\left[|\langle\mathbf{x}_1,\mathbf{R}\mathbf{x}_2\rangle| \le r \,|\, \mathbf{A}\mathbf{x}_1 = \mathbf{t}'\right]$$

$$= \frac{\Pr\limits_{\mathbf{x}_1 \xleftarrow{\$} P_1}\left[\mathbf{A}\mathbf{x}_1 = \mathbf{t}' \,|\, |\langle\mathbf{x}_1,\mathbf{R}\mathbf{x}_2\rangle| \le r\right] \cdot \Pr\limits_{\mathbf{x}_1 \xleftarrow{\$} P_1}\left[|\langle\mathbf{x}_1,\mathbf{R}\mathbf{x}_2\rangle| \le r\right]}{\Pr\limits_{\mathbf{x}_1 \xleftarrow{\$} P_1}\left[\mathbf{A}\mathbf{x}_1 = \mathbf{t}'\right]}$$

By [Lyu12, Lemma 4.3], we have that for $r = 2k_2\sigma\sqrt{\lambda}$,

$$\Pr_{\mathbf{x}_1 \xleftarrow{\$} P_1} [|\langle \mathbf{x}_1, \mathbf{R}\mathbf{x}_2 \rangle| \leq r] > 1 - 2^{-\lambda}.$$

Furthermore,

$$
\begin{aligned}
H_\infty(P_1 \mid |\langle \mathbf{x}_1, \mathbf{R}\mathbf{x}_2 \rangle| \leq r) &\geq H_\infty(P_1) - \log(1 - 2^{-\lambda}) \\
&> H_\infty(P_1) - 1 \\
&> m \log \sigma \\
&> 3n \log q + 4\lambda,
\end{aligned}
$$

which allows us to apply the Leftover Hash Lemma (Lemma 2.1) to conclude that

$$\Pr_{\mathbf{x}_1 \xleftarrow{\$} P_1} [|\langle \mathbf{x}_1, \mathbf{R}\mathbf{x}_2 \rangle| \leq r | \mathbf{A}\mathbf{x}_1 = \mathbf{t}'] \geq \frac{q^{-n} - \delta_1}{q^{-n} + \delta_1} \cdot (1 - 2^{-\lambda}) \geq (1 - \delta)(1 - 2^{-\lambda})$$

where $\delta_1 \leq q^{-n} 2^{-\lambda}$ and $\delta < 3 \cdot 2^{-\lambda}$. If we let f be the ideal distribution, then putting everything together, we obtain that

$$
\begin{aligned}
\Pr_{(\mathbf{x}_1, \mathbf{x}_2) \xleftarrow{\$} f} &\left[\frac{P_1(\mathbf{x}_1)}{P_y(\mathbf{x}_1 + \mathbf{R}\mathbf{x}_2)} \leq e^{1 + 1/8\lambda} \right] \\
&\geq \Pr_{(\mathbf{x}_1, \mathbf{x}_2) \xleftarrow{\$} f} \left[\frac{2\langle \mathbf{x}_1, \mathbf{R}\mathbf{x}_2 \rangle + \|\mathbf{R}\mathbf{x}_2\|^2}{2\sigma^2} \leq 1 + 1/8\lambda \right] \\
&= \Pr_{\mathbf{x}_1 \xleftarrow{\$} P_1} [|\langle \mathbf{x}_1, \mathbf{R}\mathbf{x}_2 \rangle| \leq 2k_2\sigma\sqrt{\lambda} | \mathbf{A}\mathbf{x}_1 = \mathbf{t}'] \\
&\geq (1 - 3 \cdot 2^{-\lambda}) \cdot (1 - \lambda) > 1 - 4 \cdot 2^{-\lambda}.
\end{aligned}
$$

Since $\mathbf{s}_1$ is chosen from D_σ^m for $\sigma = 2k\sqrt{\lambda} = \Theta(m\sqrt{\lambda})$, the norm of $\mathbf{s}_1$ is tightly concentrated around $\Theta(m^{1.5}\sqrt{\lambda})$ [Ban93]. Therefore choosing the distribution P_1 to be a discrete Gaussian rather than uniform (as in the previous example), allowed us to keep the distribution P_2 of $\mathbf{s}_2$ exactly the same, while reducing the expected length of the vector $\mathbf{s}_1$.

Sampling over polynomial rings. Just like the sampler of [MP12], ours also naturally extends to sampling vectors over polynomial rings $R = \mathbb{Z}[x]/(f(x))$, where $f(x)$ is a monic polynomial with integer coefficients. This allows the sampler to be used in constructions of more efficient lattice primitives based on the hardness of Ring-SIS [PR06,LM06] and Ring-LWE [LPR13a].

For sampling over polynomial rings, one can keep all the notation exactly the same, simply taking care that all additions and multiplications that were done over the rings $\mathbb{Z}$ and $\mathbb{Z}_q$ are now done over the rings $\mathbb{Z}[x]/(f(x))$ and $\mathbb{Z}_q[x]/(f(x))$. The only thing to be careful about is the application of the leftover hash lemma for satisfying part (1) of Theorem 3.1. If the ring is a field (i.e. $f(x)$ is irreducible over $\mathbb{Z}_q$), then everything is very simple because the function mapping $\mathbf{s}$ to $\mathbf{As}$ is still universal. If, on the other hand, $f(x)$ does split, then the function becomes an *almost* universal hash function whose universality may degrade with the number of terms into which $f(x)$ splits. In particular, if $f(x)$ splits into many terms, then it may in fact be impossible to reach the necessary statistical distance for satisfying condition (1), and one will instead need to use different distributions and leftover hash lemmas, (cf. [Mic07, Theorem 4.2], [SS11, Theorem 2], [LPR13b, Theorem 7.4]).

References

[ABB10] Agrawal, S., Boneh, D., Boyen, X.: Efficient lattice (H)IBE in the standard model. In: Gilbert, H. (ed.) EUROCRYPT 2010. LNCS, vol. 6110, pp. 553–572. Springer, Heidelberg (2010)

[Ajt96] Ajtai, M.: Generating hard instances of lattice problems (extended abstract). In: STOC, pp. 99–108 (1996)

[Ajt99] Ajtai, M.: Generating hard instances of the short basis problem. In: Wiedermann, J., Van Emde Boas, P., Nielsen, M. (eds.) ICALP 1999. LNCS, vol. 1644, p. 1. Springer, Heidelberg (1999)

[Ban93] Banaszczyk, W.: New bounds in some transference theorems in the geometry of numbers. Mathematische Annalen **296**, 625–635 (1993)

[DDLL13] Ducas, L., Durmus, A., Lepoint, T., Lyubashevsky, V.: Lattice Signatures and bimodal gaussians. In: Canetti, R., Garay, J.A. (eds.) CRYPTO 2013, Part I. LNCS, vol. 8042, pp. 40–56. Springer, Heidelberg (2013)

[DG14] Dwarakanath, N.C., Galbraith, S.D.: Sampling from discrete gaussians for lattice-based cryptography on a constrained device. Appl. Algebra Eng. Commun. Comput. **25**(3), 159–180 (2014)

[GGH97] Goldreich, O., Goldwasser, S., Halevi, S.: Public-Key cryptosystems from lattice reduction problems. In: Kaliski Jr., B.S. (ed.) CRYPTO 1997. LNCS, vol. 1294, pp. 112–131. Springer, Heidelberg (1997)

[GLP12] Güneysu, T., Lyubashevsky, V., Pöppelmann, T.: Practical lattice-based cryptography: a signature scheme for embedded systems. In: Prouff, E., Schaumont, P. (eds.) CHES 2012. LNCS, vol. 7428, pp. 530–547. Springer, Heidelberg (2012)

[GPV08] Gentry, C., Peikert, C., Vaikuntanathan, V.: Trapdoors for hard lattices and new cryptographic constructions. In: STOC, pp. 197–206 (2008)

[HHGP03] Hoffstein, J., Howgrave-Graham, N., Pipher, J., Silverman, J.H., Whyte, W.: NTRUSIGN: digital signatures using the NTRU lattice. In: Joye, M. (ed.) CT-RSA 2003. LNCS, vol. 2612, pp. 122–140. Springer, Heidelberg (2003)

[HILL99] Håstad, J., Impagliazzo, R., Levin, L.A., Luby, M.: A pseudorandom generator from any one-way function. SIAM J. Comput. **28**(4), 1364–1396 (1999)

[LM06] Lyubashevsky, V., Micciancio, D.: Generalized compact knapsacks are collision resistant. In: Bugliesi, M., Preneel, B., Sassone, V., Wegener, I. (eds.) ICALP 2006, Part II. LNCS, vol. 4052, pp. 144–155. Springer, Heidelberg (2006)

[LPR13a] Lyubashevsky, V., Peikert, C., Regev, O.: On ideal lattices and learning with errors over rings. J. ACM **60**(6), 43 (2013). Preliminary version appeared in EUROCRYPT 2010

[LPR13b] Lyubashevsky, V., Peikert, C., Regev, O.: A toolkit for Ring-LWE cryptography. In: Johansson, T., Nguyen, P.Q. (eds.) EUROCRYPT 2013. LNCS, vol. 7881, pp. 35–54. Springer, Heidelberg (2013)

[Lyu09] Lyubashevsky, V.: Fiat-Shamir with aborts: applications to lattice and factoring-based signatures. In: Matsui, M. (ed.) ASIACRYPT 2009. LNCS, vol. 5912, pp. 598–616. Springer, Heidelberg (2009)

[Lyu12] Lyubashevsky, V.: Lattice signatures without trapdoors. In: Pointcheval, D., Johansson, T. (eds.) EUROCRYPT 2012. LNCS, vol. 7237, pp. 738–755. Springer, Heidelberg (2012)

[Mic07] Micciancio, D.: Generalized compact knapsacks, cyclic lattices, and efficient one-way functions. Computational Complexity 16(4), 365–411 (2007)

[MP12] Micciancio, D., Peikert, C.: Trapdoors for lattices: simpler, tighter, faster, smaller. In: Pointcheval, D., Johansson, T. (eds.) EUROCRYPT 2012. LNCS, vol. 7237, pp. 700–718. Springer, Heidelberg (2012)

[NR09] Nguyen, P.Q., Regev, O.: Learning a parallelepiped: Cryptanalysis of GGH and NTRU signatures. J. Cryptology 22(2), 139–160 (2009)

[NZ96] Nisan, N., Zuckerman, D.: Randomness is linear in space. J. Comput. Syst. Sci. 52(1), 43–52 (1996)

[PDG14] Pöppelmann, T., Ducas, L., Güneysu, T.: Enhanced lattice-based signatures on reconfigurable hardware. In: Batina, L., Robshaw, M. (eds.) CHES 2014. LNCS, vol. 8731, pp. 353–370. Springer, Heidelberg (2014)

[Pei10] Peikert, C.: An efficient and parallel gaussian sampler for lattices. In: Rabin, T. (ed.) CRYPTO 2010. LNCS, vol. 6223, pp. 80–97. Springer, Heidelberg (2010)

[PR06] Peikert, C., Rosen, A.: Efficient collision-resistant hashing from worst-case assumptions on cyclic lattices. In: Halevi, S., Rabin, T. (eds.) TCC 2006. LNCS, vol. 3876, pp. 145–166. Springer, Heidelberg (2006)

[SS11] Stehlé, D., Steinfeld, R.: Making NTRU as secure as worst-case problems over ideal lattices. In: Paterson, K.G. (ed.) EUROCRYPT 2011. LNCS, vol. 6632, pp. 27–47. Springer, Heidelberg (2011)

[Ver10] Vershynin, R.: Introduction to the non-asymptotic analysis of random matrices. CoRR, abs/1011.3027 (2010)

Identity-Based, Predicate, and Functional Encryption

Simple Functional Encryption Schemes
for Inner Products

Michel Abdalla[✉], Florian Bourse, Angelo De Caro,
and David Pointcheval

ENS, CNRS, INRIA, and PSL,
45 Rue d'Ulm, 75230 Paris Cedex 05, France
{michel.abdalla,florian.bourse,angelo.decaro,
david.pointcheval}@ens.fr

Abstract. Functional encryption is a new paradigm in public-key encryption that allows users to finely control the amount of information that is revealed by a ciphertext to a given receiver. Recent papers have focused their attention on constructing schemes for general functionalities at expense of efficiency. Our goal, in this paper, is to construct functional encryption schemes for less general functionalities which are still expressive enough for practical scenarios. We propose a functional encryption scheme for the *inner-product* functionality, meaning that decrypting an encrypted vector $\mathbf{x}$ with a key for a vector $\mathbf{y}$ will reveal only $\langle \mathbf{x}, \mathbf{y} \rangle$ and nothing else, whose security is based on the DDH assumption. Despite the simplicity of this functionality, it is still useful in many contexts like descriptive statistics. In addition, we generalize our approach and present a generic scheme that can be instantiated, in addition, under the LWE assumption and offers various trade-offs in terms of expressiveness and efficiency.

Keywords: Functional Encryption · Inner-Product · Generic Constructions

1 Introduction

Functional Encryption. Whereas, in traditional public-key encryption, decryption is an all-or-nothing affair (i.e., a receiver is either able to recover the entire message using its key, or nothing), in *functional encryption* (FE), it is possible to finely control the amount of information that is revealed by a ciphertext to a given receiver. For example, decrypting an encrypted data set with a key for computing the mean will reveal only the mean computed over the data set and nothing else. Somewhat more precisely, in a functional encryption scheme for functionality F, each secret key (generated by a master authority having a *master secret key*) is associated with value k in some *key space* K; Anyone can encrypt via the public parameters; When a ciphertext Ct_x that encrypts x, in some *message space* X, is decrypted using a secret key Sk_k for value k, the result is $F(k, x)$. A notable subclass of functional encryption is

© International Association for Cryptologic Research 2015
J. Katz (Ed.): PKC 2015, LNCS 9020, pp. 733–751, 2015.
DOI: 10.1007/978-3-662-46447-2_33

that of *predicate encryption* (PE) which are defined for functionalities whose message space X consists of two subspaces I and M called respectively *index space* and *payload space*. In this case, the functionality F is defined in terms of a predicate $P : K \times I \rightarrow \{0, 1\}$ as follows: $F(k, (\mathsf{ind}; \mathsf{m})) = \mathsf{m}$ if $P(k, \mathsf{ind}) = 1$, and $\perp$ otherwise, where $k \in K$, $\mathsf{ind} \in I$ and $\mathsf{m} \in M$. Those schemes are also called *predicate encryption with private-index*. Examples of those schemes are Anonymous Identity-Based Encryption (AIBE) [BF01, Gen06], Hidden Vector Encryption [BW07] and Orthogonality [KSW08, LOS+10, OT12], among the others. On the other hand, when the index ind is easily readable from the ciphertext those schemes are called *predicate encryption with public-index* (PIPE). Examples of PIPE schemes are Identity-Based Encryption (IBE) [Sha84, BF01, Coc01], Attribute-Based Encryption (ABE) [SW05, GPSW06], Functional Encryption for Regular Languages [Wat12].

The standard notion of security for functional encryption is that of *indistinguishability-based security* (IND). Informally, it requires that an adversary cannot tell apart which of two messages x_0, x_1 has been encrypted having oracle access to the key generation algorithm under the constraint that, for each k for which the adversary has seen a secret key, it holds that $F(k, x_0) = F(k, x_1)$. This models the idea that an individual's messages are still secure even if an arbitrary number of other users of the system collude against that user. Boneh, Sahai, and Waters [BSW11] and O'Neill [O'N10] showed that the IND definition is weak in the sense that a trivially insecure scheme implementing a certain functionality can be proved IND-secure anyway. The authors, then, initiate the study of *simulation-based* (SIM) notions of security for FE, which asks that the "view" of the adversary can be simulated by simulator given neither ciphertexts nor keys but only the corresponding outputs of the functionality on the underlying plaintexts, and shows that SIM-security is not always achievable.

In a recent series of outstanding results, [GGH+13, BCP14, Wat14, GGHZ14] proposed IND-secure FE schemes for general circuits whose security is based either on indistinguishable obfuscation and its variants or polynomial hardness of simple assumptions on multilinear maps. Those schemes are far from being practical and this led us to investigate the possibility of having functional encryption schemes for *functionalities of practical interest* which are still expressive enough for practical scenarios. In doing so, we seek for schemes that offer *simplicity*, in terms of understanding of how the schemes work, and *adaptability* in terms of the possibility of choosing the instantiations and the parameters that better fit the constraints and needs of a specific scenario the user is interested in.

This Work. In this paper, we focus on the *inner-product* functionality, which has several practical applications. For example, in descriptive statistics, the discipline of quantitatively describing the main features of a collection of information, the *weighted mean* is a useful tool. Here are a few examples:

Slugging average in baseball. A batter's slugging average, also called slugging percentage, is computed by: $\mathsf{SLG} = (1 * \mathsf{SI} + 2 * \mathsf{DO} + 3 * \mathsf{TR} + 4 * \mathsf{HR})/\mathsf{AB}$, where SLG is the slugging percentage, SI is the number of singles, DO the

number of doubles, TR the number of triples, HR the number of home runs, and AB is total number of at-bats. Here, each single has a *weight* of 1, each double has a *weight* of 2, etc. The average counts home runs four times as important as singles, and so on. An at-bat without a hit has a *weight* of zero.
Course grades. A teacher might say that the *test average* is 60% of the grade, *quiz average* is 30% of the grade, and a *project* is 10% of the grade. Suppose Alice got 90 and 78 on the tests; 100, 100 and 85 on the quizzes; and an 81 on the project. Then, Alice's test average is $(90 + 78)/2 = 84$, quiz average is $(100 + 100 + 85)/3 = 95$, and her course grade would then be: $.60 \cdot 84 + .30 \cdot 95 + .10 \cdot 81 = 87$.

Our goal then is to design a simple and efficient functional encryption scheme for inner products that can be used, for instance, to compute a weighted mean and to protect the privacy of Alice's grades, in the example involving course grades. In fact, we can imagine that Alice's grades, represented as a vector $\mathbf{x} = (x_1, \ldots, x_\ell)$ in some finite field, says $\mathbb{Z}_p$ for prime p, are encrypted in a ciphertext $\mathsf{Ct}_\mathbf{x}$ and the teacher has a secret key $\mathsf{Sk}_\mathbf{y}$ for the vector of weights $\mathbf{y} = (y_1, \ldots, y_\ell)$. Then Alice's course grade can be computed as the *inner-product* of $\mathbf{x}$ and $\mathbf{y}$, written as $\langle \mathbf{x}, \mathbf{y} \rangle = \sum_{i \in [\ell]} x_i \cdot y_i$. We would like to stress here that, unlike the inner-product predicate schemes in [KSW08, LOS+10, OT12], our goal is to output the actual value of the inner product.

A very simple scheme can be constructed to compute the above functionality whose security can be based on the DDH assumption. Informally, it is like this:

$$mpk = \left(\mathbb{G}, (h_i = g^{s_i})_{i \in [\ell]} \right)$$
$$\mathsf{Ct}_\mathbf{x} = \left(\mathsf{ct}_0 = g^r, (\mathsf{ct}_i = h_i^r \cdot g^{x_i})_{i \in [\ell]} \right)$$
$$\mathsf{Sk}_\mathbf{y} = \langle \mathbf{s}, \mathbf{y} \rangle = \sum_{i \in [\ell]} s_i \cdot y_i,$$

where $msk = \mathbf{s} = (s_1, \ldots, s_\ell)$ is the master secret key used to generate secret keys $\mathsf{Sk}_\mathbf{y}$. Then, decryption is done by computing the discrete log of $(\prod_{i \in [\ell]} \mathsf{ct}_i^{y_i})/\mathsf{ct}_0^{\mathsf{Sk}_\mathbf{y}}$. Please refer to Section 3 for more details.

Despite its simplicity, this DDH-based scheme can be proved secure, in a selective security model[1], against any adversary that issues an unbounded, but polynomially related to the security parameter, number of secret key queries. The adversary will not learn anything more than what it is implied by the linear combination of their keys.

An astute reader could now ask what happens if an adversary possesses secret keys $\mathsf{Sk}_{\mathbf{y}_i}$, for $i \in [q]$, such that the $\mathbf{y}_i$'s form a basis for $\mathbb{Z}_p^\ell$. Clearly, this adversary can then recover completely $\mathbf{x}$ from the ciphertext and wins the security game. But notice that this has nothing to do with the specific implementation of the functionality, it is something inherent to the functionality itself. This happens also for other functionalities: Consider the case of the *circuit* functionality, where

---

[1] In the selective model, the adversary is asked to commit to its challenge before seeing the public parameters.

secret keys correspond to Boolean circuits over ℓ Boolean variables and one-bit output, and ciphertexts to vectors in $\{0,1\}^\ell$. Then, an adversary having secret keys for circuits C_i, where C_i extract the i-th bit of the input, can recover completely the input from a ciphertext no matter how the scheme, supporting this circuit functionality, is implemented. This subtle aspect will appear in the security proof, if the adversary asks such a set of secret keys then the simulator will not be able to answer all those queries. Notice that this is reasonable, because it is like requiring security when the adversary possesses the master secret key.

One drawback of the above scheme is that restrictions must be put in place in order to guarantee that the final computed value has small magnitude and the discrete log can be computed efficiently. To overcome this limitation, let us first describe some interesting characteristics of the above scheme. To start, please notice that a ciphertext for a vector $\mathbf{x}$ consists of ElGamal ciphertexts [ElG84] $(g^r, (h_i^r \cdot g^{x_i})_i)$ under public keys $h_i = g^{s_i}$, sharing the same randomness r. Then, a secret key for a vector $\mathbf{y}$ consists of a linear combination of the underlying ElGamal secrets s_i. Now notice that, by the ElGamal scheme's homomorphic properties, it holds that

$$\prod_{i \in [\ell]} \mathsf{ct}_i^{y_i} = \prod_{i \in [\ell]} h_i^{r \cdot y_i} \cdot g^{x_i \cdot y_i} = h^r \cdot g^{\langle \mathbf{x}, \mathbf{y} \rangle}$$

where h is an ElGamal public key corresponding to secret key $\langle \mathbf{s}, \mathbf{y} \rangle$. The above observations point out that, by possibly combining public-key encryption schemes secure under randomness reuse [BBS03], and having specific syntactical, non-security-related, properties, we can generalize the above construction with the aim of (1) having a scheme whose security can be based on different assumptions and that can provide different trade-offs in terms of efficiency and expressiveness, (2) have a generic proof of security that reduces security to that of the underlying public-key encryption scheme. We present our generalization in Section 4.

Related Work. One of the first example of investigation on reductions between various primitives has been given by [Rot11] who shows a simple reduction between any semantically secure private-key encryption scheme which possesses a simple homomorphic, namely that the product of two ciphertexts Ct_1 and Ct_2, encrypting plaintexts m_1 and m_2, yields a new ciphertext $\mathsf{Ct} = \mathsf{Ct}_1 \cdot \mathsf{Ct}_2$ which decrypts to $\mathsf{m}_1 + \mathsf{m}_2 \mod 2$. Goldwasser *et al.* [GLW12] investigated the construction of PIPE schemes for specific predicates. In particular, they show how public-key encryption schemes which possess a linear homomorphic property over their keys as well as hash proof system features with certain algebraic structure can be used to construct an efficient identity-based encryption (IBE) scheme that is secure against bounded collusions (BC-IBE). This weaker security notion restricts the adversary to issue only a bounded number of secret keys during the security game. In more details, they rely on a public-key encryption scheme whose secret keys and public keys are elements of respective groups (with possibly different operations, which we denote by $+$ and $\cdot$), and there exists an homomorphism μ such that $\mu(\mathsf{sk}_0 + \mathsf{sk}_1) = \mu(\mathsf{sk}_0) \cdot \mu(\mathsf{sk}_1)$, where $\mu(\mathsf{sk}_0)$ and $\mu(\mathsf{sk}_1)$ are valid public keys for which sk_0 and sk_1 yield correct decryption, respectively. Then, to obtain a BC-IBE, the construction by Goldwasser *et al.* generates multiple public-key/secret-key pairs $(\mathsf{pk}_1, \mathsf{sk}_1), \ldots, (\mathsf{pk}_\ell, \mathsf{sk}_\ell)$, letting the public-parameters and the master secret key of the scheme be $\mathsf{params} = (\mathsf{pk}_1, \ldots, \mathsf{pk}_\ell)$ and $msk = (\mathsf{sk}_1, \ldots, \mathsf{sk}_\ell)$, respectively. Then, an efficient map ϕ associates every identity ID with a vector $[id_1, \ldots, id_\ell]$, and a message m is encrypted for an identity ID as the ciphertext $\mathsf{Ct} = \mathsf{Encrypt}(\mathsf{pk_{ID}}, m)$, where $\mathsf{pk_{ID}} = \prod_{i=1}^n \mathsf{pk}_i^{\mathsf{ID}_i}$. Then, μ guarantees that Ct can be decrypted using $\mathsf{sk_{ID}} = \sum_{i=1}^n \mathsf{ID}_i \cdot \mathsf{sk}_i$, since by the homomorphism it holds that $\mathsf{pk_{ID}} = \mu(\mathsf{sk_{ID}})$. The map ϕ is subject to a combinatorial requirement that disallows computing $\mathsf{sk_{ID}}$ given $\mathsf{sk_{ID'}}$ for t different $\mathsf{ID'} \neq \mathsf{ID}$. Later, Tessaro and Wilson [TW14] presented generic constructions of BC-IBE which rely on encryption schemes that solely satisfy the standard security notion of semantic security in addition to some syntactical, non-security-related, properties. We will use Tessaro and Wilson to present a generalization of our results.

As already mentioned, in a recent series of outstanding results, [GGH+13, BCP14, Wat14, GGHZ14] proposed IND-secure FE scheme for general circuits whose security is based either on indistinguishable obfuscation and its variants or polynomial hardness of simple assumptions on multilinear maps. Clearly, those schemes can be used to implement the inner-product functionality, but this would defeat our main goal which is to construct somewhat efficient functional encryption schemes for less general functionalities which are still expressive enough for practical scenarios.

In another line of research, Katz, Sahai, and Waters [KSW08] proposed a functional encryption scheme for a functionality called *orthogonality* (in the literature it is also know as inner-product encryption), meaning that decrypting an encrypted vector $\mathbf{x}$ with a key for a vector $\mathbf{y}$ will reveal only if $\langle \mathbf{x}, \mathbf{y} \rangle$ is equals to zero (meaning that the two vectors are orthogonal) or not, and nothing else. This functionality is of little help in our case because what we need is for the decryptor to be able to recover the value $\langle \mathbf{x}, \mathbf{y} \rangle$.

Parameter Sizes For Our Constructions. In Table 1, we present the size of the parameters and ciphertexts for our concrete construction. Each column refers to an instantiation of our general scheme and is indexed by its underlying assumption. Each row describes the size of an element of the scheme. The master public key size does not include public parameters that can be re-used such that $(g, \mathbf{A})$. Message space is the number of different messages that can be decrypted using this instantiation. The DDH instantiation can give short ciphertexts and keys using elliptic curves, but requires the computation of a discrete logarithm in the decryption, which makes it usable for small message space only. LWE enables short ciphertexts and keys together with a message space that is independent of the security parameter, which allows shorter ciphertexts for a smaller message space.

Table 1. Parameter Sizes. Here, ℓ is the length of the vectors encrypted in the ciphertexts and encoded in the secret keys. In DDH, p is the size of a group element. In LWE, q is the size of a group element, p is the order of the message space, and k is the size of a message in base r.

	DDH	LWE
mpk	$\ell \log p$	$(k+1)m\ell \log q$
msk	$\ell \log p$	$(k+1)n\ell \log q$
$\mathsf{Ct_x}$	$(\ell+1)\log p$	$(n+(k+1)\ell)\log q$
$\mathsf{Sk_y}$	$\log p$	$n \log q$
message space	bounded by computation	$\ell r^{2(k+1)}$
$\lvert\{\langle \mathbf{x}, \mathbf{y}\rangle\}\rvert$	of discrete logarithms	computations $\bmod p$

2   Basic Tools

In this section, we recall some of the definitions and basic tools that will be used in the remaining sections, such as the syntax of code-based games, functional encryption and the assumptions.

2.1   Notation and Conventions

Let $\mathbb{N}$ denote the set of natural numbers. If $n \in \mathbb{N}$, then $\{0,1\}^n$ denotes the set of n-bit strings, and $\{0,1\}^*$ is the set of all bit strings. The empty string is denoted ε. More generally, if S is a set, then S^n is the set of n-tuples of elements of S, $S^{\leq n}$ is the set of tuples of length at most n. If x is a string then $|x|$ denotes its length, and if S is a set then $|S|$ denotes its size. If S is finite, then $x \xleftarrow{R} S$ denotes the assignment to x of an element chosen uniformly at random from S. If $\mathcal{A}$ is an algorithm, then $y \leftarrow \mathcal{A}(x)$ denotes the assignment to y of the output of $\mathcal{A}$ on input x, and if $\mathcal{A}$ is randomized, then $y \xleftarrow{R} \mathcal{A}(x)$ denotes that the output of an execution of $\mathcal{A}(x)$ with fresh coins is assigned to y. Unless otherwise indicated, an algorithm may be randomized. "PT" stands for polynomial time and "PTA" for polynomial-time algorithm or adversary. We denote by $\lambda \in \mathbb{N}$ the security parameter. A function $\nu : \mathbb{N} \to [0,1]$ is said to be *negligible* if for every $c \in \mathbb{N}$ there exists a $\lambda_c \in \mathbb{N}$ such that $\nu(\lambda) \leq \lambda^{-c}$ for all $\lambda > \lambda_c$, and it is said to be *overwhelming* if the function $|1 - \nu(\lambda)|$ is negligible.

Let $\mathbf{e}_i$ be the vector with all 0 but one 1 in the i-th position.

Code-Based Games. We use the code-based game-playing [BR06] to define the security notions. In such games, there exist procedures for initialization (**initialize**) and finalization (**Finalize**) and procedures to respond to adversary oracle queries. A game G is executed with an adversary $\mathcal{A}$ as follows. First, **initialize** executes and its outputs are the inputs to $\mathcal{A}$. Then $\mathcal{A}$ executes, its oracle queries being answered by the corresponding procedures of G. When $\mathcal{A}$ terminates, its output becomes the input to the **Finalize** procedure. The output of the latter, denoted G($\mathcal{A}$), is called the output of the game, and "G($\mathcal{A}$) = y" denotes the event that the output takes a value y. Boolean flags are assumed initialized to false. Games G_i, G_j are *identical until* bad if their code differs only in statements that follow the setting of bad to true.

2.2 Public-Key Encryption

Definition 1 (Public-Key Encryption Scheme). *A public-key encryption (PKE) scheme $\mathcal{E}$ is a tuple $\mathcal{E} = (\mathsf{Setup}, \mathsf{Encrypt}, \mathsf{Decrypt})$ of 3 algorithms:*

1. $\mathsf{Setup}(1^\lambda)$ *outputs public and secret keys* $(\mathsf{pk}, \mathsf{sk})$ *for security parameter* λ;

2. $\mathsf{Encrypt}(\mathsf{pk}, m)$, *on input public key* pk *and message m in the allowed message space, outputs ciphertext* Ct;

3. $\mathsf{Decrypt}(\mathsf{sk}, \mathsf{Ct})$ *on input secret key* sk *and ciphertext* Ct, *outputs messages* m'.

In addition we make the following correctness requirement: for all $(\mathsf{pk}, \mathsf{sk}) \leftarrow \mathsf{Setup}(1^\lambda)$, *all messages m and ciphertexts* $\mathsf{Ct} \leftarrow \mathsf{Encrypt}(\mathsf{pk}, m)$, *we have that* $\mathsf{Decrypt}(\mathsf{sk}, \mathsf{Ct}) = m$ *except with negligible probability.*

We often also allow public-key encryption schemes to additionally depend on explicit public parameters params (randomly generated in an initial phase and shared across multiple instances of the PKE scheme) on which all of Setup, Encrypt, and Decrypt are allowed to depend. Examples include the description of a group $\mathbb{G}$ with its generator g. We will often omit them in the descriptions of generic constructions from PKE schemes.

Indistinguishability-Based Security. We define *security against chosen-plaintext attacks* (IND-CPA *security*, for short) for a PKE scheme $\mathcal{E} = (\mathsf{Setup}, \mathsf{Encrypt}, \mathsf{Decrypt})$ via the security game depicted on Figure 1. Then, we say that $\mathcal{E}$ is secure against chosen-plaintext attacks (IND-CPA secure, for short) if

$$\left| \Pr[\mathsf{Exp}_{\mathcal{E},\lambda}^{\mathrm{ind\text{-}cpa\text{-}0}}(\mathcal{A}) = 1] - \Pr[\mathsf{Exp}_{\mathcal{E},\lambda}^{\mathrm{ind\text{-}cpa\text{-}1}}(\mathcal{A}) = 1] \right| = \mathsf{negl}(\lambda).$$

We also define *selective security against chosen-plaintext attacks* (s-IND-CPA *security*, for short) when the challenge messages m_0^* and m_1^* have to be chosen before hand. Actually, in this case, the procedures **initialize** and **LR** can be merged into an **initialize** procedure that outputs both the public key pk and the challenge ciphertext Ct^*.

2.3 Functional Encryption

Following Boneh *et al.* [BSW11], we start by defining the notion of functionality and then that of functional encryption scheme $\mathcal{FE}$ for functionality F.

Definition 2 (Functionality). *A functionality F defined over (K, X) is a function $F : K \times X \to \Sigma \cup \{\bot\}$ where K is the key space, X is the message space and Σ is the output space and $\bot$ is a special string not contained in Σ. Notice that the functionality is undefined for when either the key is not in the key space or the message is not in the message space.*

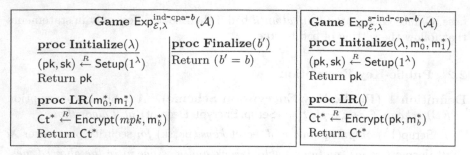

Fig. 1. Games $\mathrm{Exp}_{\mathcal{E},\lambda}^{\mathrm{ind\text{-}cpa\text{-}}b}(\mathcal{A})$ and $\mathrm{Exp}_{\mathcal{E},\lambda}^{\mathrm{s\text{-}ind\text{-}cpa\text{-}}b}(\mathcal{A})$ define IND-CPA and s-IND-CPA security (respectively) of $\mathcal{E}$. The procedure **Finalize** is common to both games, which differ in their **initialize** and **LR** procedures.

Definition 3 (Functional Encryption Scheme). *A functional encryption (FE) scheme $\mathcal{FE}$ for functionality F is a tuple $\mathcal{FE} = (\mathsf{Setup}, \mathsf{KeyDer}, \mathsf{Encrypt}, \mathsf{Decrypt})$ of 4 algorithms:*

1. *$\mathsf{Setup}(1^\lambda)$ outputs public and master secret keys (mpk, msk) for security parameter λ;*
2. *$\mathsf{KeyDer}(msk, k)$, on input a master secret key msk and key $k \in K$ outputs secret key sk_k;*
3. *$\mathsf{Encrypt}(mpk, x)$, on input public key mpk and message $x \in X$ outputs ciphertext Ct;*
4. *$\mathsf{Decrypt}(mpk, \mathsf{Ct}, \mathsf{sk}_k)$ outputs $y \in \Sigma \cup \{\bot\}$.*

We make the following correctness requirement: for all $(mpk, msk) \leftarrow \mathsf{Setup}(1^\lambda)$, all $k \in K$ and $m \in M$, for $\mathsf{sk}_k \leftarrow \mathsf{KeyDer}(msk, k)$ and $\mathsf{Ct} \leftarrow \mathsf{Encrypt}(mpk, m)$, we have that $\mathsf{Decrypt}(mpk, \mathsf{Ct}, \mathsf{sk}_k) = F(k, m)$ whenever $F(k, m) \neq \bot^2$, except with negligible probability.

Indistinguishability-Based Security. For a functional encryption scheme $\mathcal{FE} = (\mathsf{Setup}, \mathsf{KeyDer}, \mathsf{Encrypt}, \mathsf{Decrypt})$ for functionality F, defined over (K, X), we define *security against chosen-plaintext attacks* (IND-CPA *security*, for short) via the security game depicted on Figure 2. Then, we say that $\mathcal{FE}$ is secure against chosen-plaintext attacks (IND-CPA secure, for short) if

$$\left| \Pr[\mathrm{Exp}_{\mathcal{FE},\lambda}^{\mathrm{ind\text{-}cpa\text{-}}0}(\mathcal{A}) = 1] - \Pr[\mathrm{Exp}_{\mathcal{FE},\lambda}^{\mathrm{ind\text{-}cpa\text{-}}1}(\mathcal{A}) = 1] \right| = \mathsf{negl}(\lambda).$$

We also define *selective security against chosen-plaintext attacks* (s-IND-CPA *security*, for short) when the challenge messages m_0^* and m_1^* have to be chosen before hand.

Inner-Product Functionality. In this paper we are mainly interested in the *inner-product functionality* over $\mathbb{Z}_p$ (IP, for short) defined in the following way. It is a family of functionalities with key space K_ℓ and message space X_ℓ both

---

[2] See [BO12, ABN10] for a discussion about this condition.

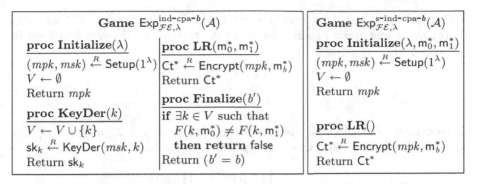

Game $\mathrm{Exp}_{\mathcal{FE},\lambda}^{\mathrm{ind\text{-}cpa}\text{-}b}(\mathcal{A})$		Game $\mathrm{Exp}_{\mathcal{FE},\lambda}^{\mathrm{s\text{-}ind\text{-}cpa}\text{-}b}(\mathcal{A})$
proc Initialize(λ)	**proc LR**$(\mathsf{m}_0^*, \mathsf{m}_1^*)$	**proc Initialize**$(\lambda, \mathsf{m}_0^*, \mathsf{m}_1^*)$
$(mpk, msk) \xleftarrow{R} \mathsf{Setup}(1^\lambda)$	$\mathsf{Ct}^* \xleftarrow{R} \mathsf{Encrypt}(mpk, \mathsf{m}_b^*)$	$(mpk, msk) \xleftarrow{R} \mathsf{Setup}(1^\lambda)$
$V \leftarrow \emptyset$	Return Ct^*	$V \leftarrow \emptyset$
Return mpk		Return mpk
	proc Finalize(b')	
proc KeyDer(k)	**if** $\exists k \in V$ such that	**proc LR**$()$
$V \leftarrow V \cup \{k\}$	$F(k, \mathsf{m}_0^*) \neq F(k, \mathsf{m}_1^*)$	$\mathsf{Ct}^* \xleftarrow{R} \mathsf{Encrypt}(mpk, \mathsf{m}_b^*)$
$\mathsf{sk}_k \xleftarrow{R} \mathsf{KeyDer}(msk, k)$	**then return** false	Return Ct^*
Return sk_k	Return $(b' = b)$	

Fig. 2. Games $\mathrm{Exp}_{\mathcal{FE},\lambda}^{\mathrm{ind\text{-}cpa}\text{-}b}(\mathcal{A})$ and $\mathrm{Exp}_{\mathcal{FE},\lambda}^{\mathrm{s\text{-}ind\text{-}cpa}\text{-}b}(\mathcal{A})$ define IND-CPA and s-IND-CPA security (respectively) of $\mathcal{FE}$. The procedures **KeyDer** and **Finalize** are common to both games, which differ in their **initialize** and **LR** procedures.

consisting of vectors in $\mathbb{Z}_p$ of length ℓ: for any $k \in K_\ell, x \in X_\ell$ the functionality $\mathsf{IP}_\ell(k, x) = \langle k, x \rangle \mod p$. When it is clear from the context we remove the reference to the length ℓ.

3   Inner-Product from DDH

In this section, we present our first functional encryption scheme for the inner-product functionality whose security can be based on the plain DDH assumption.

The Decisional Diffie-Hellman assumption. Let $\mathsf{GroupGen}$ be a probabilistic polynomial-time algorithm that takes as input a security parameter 1^λ, and outputs a triplet $(\mathbb{G}, p, g)$ where $\mathbb{G}$ is a group of order p that is generated by $g \in \mathbb{G}$, and p is an λ-bit prime number. Then, the *Decisional Diffie-Hellman (DDH) assumption* states that the tuples (g, g^a, g^b, g^{ab}) and (g, g^a, g^b, g^c) are computationally indistinguishable, where $(\mathbb{G}, p, g) \leftarrow \mathsf{GroupGen}(1^\lambda)$, and $a, b, c \in \mathbb{Z}_p$ are chosen independently and uniformly at random.

Construction 1 (DDH-IP Scheme). *We define our functional encryption scheme for the inner-product functionality* $\mathsf{IP} = (\mathsf{Setup}, \mathsf{KeyDer}, \mathsf{Encrypt}, \mathsf{Decrypt})$ *as follows:*

- $\mathsf{Setup}(1^\lambda, 1^\ell)$ *samples* $(\mathbb{G}, p, g) \leftarrow \mathsf{GroupGen}(1^\lambda)$ *and* $\mathbf{s} = (s_1, \ldots, s_\ell) \leftarrow \mathbb{Z}_p^\ell$, *and sets* $mpk = (h_i = g^{s_i})_{i \in [\ell]}$ *and* $msk = \mathbf{s}$. *The algorithm returns the pair* (mpk, msk);
- $\mathsf{Encrypt}(mpk, \mathbf{x})$ *on input master public key* mpk *and message* $\mathbf{x} = (x_1, \ldots, x_\ell) \in \mathbb{Z}_p^\ell$, *chooses a random* $r \leftarrow \mathbb{Z}_p$ *and computes* $\mathsf{ct}_0 = g^r$ *and, for each* $i \in [\ell]$, $\mathsf{ct}_i = h_i^r \cdot g^{x_i}$. *Then the algorithm returns the ciphertext* $\mathsf{Ct} = (\mathsf{ct}_0, (\mathsf{ct}_i)_{i \in [\ell]})$;
- $\mathsf{KeyDer}(msk, \mathbf{y})$ *on input master secret key* msk *and vector* $\mathbf{y} = (y_1, \ldots, y_\ell) \in \mathbb{Z}_p^\ell$, *computes and outputs secret key* $\mathsf{sk}_\mathbf{y} = \langle \mathbf{y}, \mathbf{s} \rangle$;

- Decrypt(mpk, Ct, $sk_\mathbf{y}$) *on input master public key mpk, ciphertext* Ct $= (ct_0,$ $(ct_i)_{i\in[\ell]})$ *and secret key* $Sk_\mathbf{y}$ *for vector* $\mathbf{y}$, *returns the discrete logarithm in basis g of*

$$\prod_{i\in[\ell]} ct_i^{y_i}/ct_0^{sk_\mathbf{y}}.$$

Correctness. For all $(mpk, msk) \leftarrow \mathsf{Setup}(1^\lambda, 1^\ell)$, all $\mathbf{y} \in \mathbb{Z}_p^\ell$ and $\mathbf{x} \in \mathbb{Z}_p^\ell$, for $sk_\mathbf{y} \leftarrow \mathsf{KeyDer}(msk, \mathbf{y})$ and Ct $\leftarrow \mathsf{Encrypt}(mpk, \mathbf{x})$, we have that

$$\mathsf{Decrypt}(mpk, \mathsf{Ct}, \mathsf{sk}) = \frac{\prod_{i\in[\ell]} ct_i^{y_i}}{ct_0^{sk_\mathbf{y}}} = \frac{\prod_{i\in[\ell]} (g^{s_i r + x_i})^{y_i}}{g^{r(\sum_{i\in[\ell]} y_i s_i)}}$$

$$= g^{\sum_{i\in[\ell]} y_i s_i r + \sum_{i\in[\ell]} y_i x_i - r(\sum_{i\in[\ell]} y_i s_i)}$$

$$= g^{\sum_{i\in[\ell]} y_i x_i} = g^{\langle \mathbf{x},\mathbf{y} \rangle}.$$

The above scheme limits the expressiveness of the functionality that can be computed because in order to recover the final inner-product value a discrete logarithm computation must take place. In the next section, in order to overcome this limitation and to generalize to other settings we will present a generic scheme whose security can be based on the semantic security of the underlying public-key encryption scheme under randomness reuse. Before moving to the generic scheme and its proof of security, we sketch below the proof of security for the above IP scheme to offer to the reader useful intuitions that will be reused in the proof of security of our generic functional encryption scheme for the inner-product functionality.

Theorem 1. *Under the DDH assumption, the above IP scheme is* s-IND-CPA.

Proof Sketch. For the sake of contradiction, suppose that there exists an adversary $\mathcal{A}$ that breaks s-IND-CPA security of our IP scheme with non-negligible advantage. Then, we construct a simulator $\mathcal{B}$ that given in input an instance of the DDH assumption, (g, g^a, g^b, g^c) where c is either ab or uniformly random, breaks it by using $\mathcal{A}$.

If the challenge messages $\mathbf{x}_0$ and $\mathbf{x}_1$ are different, there exists a vector in the message space for which the key shouldn't be known by the adversary ($\mathbf{x}_1 - \mathbf{x}_0$ is one of them).

To generate the master public key, $\mathcal{B}$ first generates secret keys for a basis $(\mathbf{z}_i)$ of $(\mathbf{x}_1 - \mathbf{x}_0)^\perp$. Setting implicitly a as secret key for $\mathbf{x}_1 - \mathbf{x}_0$, $\mathcal{B}$ generates the master public key using g^a. Actually, once group elements are generated for the basis $(\mathbf{y}_i)$ completed with $(\mathbf{x}_1 - \mathbf{x}_0)$, one can find the public key, for the canonical basis.

To generate the challenge ciphertext, $\mathcal{B}$ chooses a random bit μ and using g^b and g^c, generates a ciphertext for message $\mathbf{x}_\mu$.

Finally, notice that by the constraints of the s-IND-CPA security game, $\mathcal{A}$ is allowed to ask only secret keys for vectors in the vector sub-space generated by the z_i's, and thus orthogonal to $x_1 - x_0$. For those vectors, $\mathcal{B}$ will be able to generate the corresponding secret keys.

Now, if $c = ab$, then the challenge ciphertext is a well-distributed ciphertext of the message x_μ. On the other hand, if c is random, the challenge ciphertext encrypts message $ux_0 + (1 - u)x_1$ where u is uniformly distributed and in this case μ is information theoretically hidden: for all $\mathsf{sk_y}$ asked, since y is orthogonal to $x_1 - x_0$, and thus $\langle x_0, y \rangle = \langle x_1, y \rangle$, while the ciphertexts decrypt to the inner products

$$
\begin{aligned}
\langle ux_0 + (1 - u)x_1, y \rangle &= u\langle x_0, y \rangle + (1 - u)\langle x_1, y \rangle \\
&= u\langle x_\mu, y \rangle + (1 - u)\langle x_\mu, y \rangle \\
&= \langle x_\mu, y \rangle \ .
\end{aligned}
$$

4 A Generic Inner-Product Encryption Scheme

In this section, we present a generic functional encryption scheme for the inner-product functionality based on any public-key encryption scheme that possesses some specific properties. The security of this scheme can be then based solely on the semantic security of the underlying public-key encryption scheme.

We start with a public-key scheme $\mathcal{E} = (\mathsf{Setup}, \mathsf{Encrypt}, \mathsf{Decrypt})$ whose secret keys are elements of a group $(G, +, 0_G)$, public keys are elements of group $(H, \cdot, 1_H)$, and messages are elements of $\mathbb{Z}_q$ for some q.

In addition, we rely on three other special properties of the cryptosystem. First, we require that it remains secure when we reuse randomness for encrypting under different keys [BBS03]. Then, we require some homomorphic operation, on the keys and on the ciphertexts. More specifically:

Randomness Reuse. We require the ciphertexts to consist of two parts $\mathsf{ct_0}$ and $\mathsf{ct_1}$. The first part $\mathsf{ct_0}$ corresponds to some *commitment* $\mathsf{C}(r)$ of the randomness r used for the encryption. The second part $\mathsf{ct_1}$ is the *encryption* $\mathsf{E}(\mathsf{pk}, x; r)$ in a group $(I, \cdot, 1_I)$ of the message x under public key pk and randomness r.

Then, we say that a PKE has *randomness reuse* (RR, for short) if $\mathsf{E}(\mathsf{pk}, x; r)$ is *efficiently computed* given the triple (x, pk, r), or the triple $(x, \mathsf{sk}, \mathsf{C}(r))$ where sk is a secret key corresponding to pk. (In [BBS03], this property is also called *reproducibility* and guarantees that it is secure to reuse randomness when encrypting under several independent public keys. The idea of randomness reuse was first considered by [Kur02]);

Linear Key Homomorphism. We say that a PKE has *linear key homomorphism* (LKH, for short) if for any two secret keys $\mathsf{sk_1}, \mathsf{sk_2} \in G$ and any $y_1, y_2 \in \mathbb{Z}_q$, the component-wise G-linear combination formed by $y_1\mathsf{sk_1} + y_2\mathsf{sk_2}$ can be computed efficiently only using public parameters, the secret keys $\mathsf{sk_1}$ and $\mathsf{sk_2}$ and the coefficients y_1 and y_2. And this combination $y_1\mathsf{sk_1} + y_2\mathsf{sk_2}$ also functions as a secret key, with a corresponding public key that can be computed efficiently from y_1, y_2 and the public keys pk_1 and pk_2 of sk_1 and sk_2 respectively, fixing the same public parameters, for example $\mathsf{pk}_1^{y_1} \cdot \mathsf{pk}_2^{y_2}$.

Linear Ciphertext Homomorphism Under Shared Randomness.   We say that a PKE has *linear ciphertext homomorphism under shared randomness* (LCH, for short) if $\mathsf{E}(\mathsf{pk}_1\mathsf{pk}_2, x_1 + x_2; r)$ can be efficiently computed from $\mathsf{E}(\mathsf{pk}_1, x_1; r)$, $\mathsf{E}(\mathsf{pk}_2, x_2; r)$ and $\mathsf{C}(r)$, for example $\mathsf{E}(\mathsf{pk}_1\mathsf{pk}_2, x_1 + x_2; r) = \mathsf{E}(\mathsf{pk}_1, x_1; r) \cdot \mathsf{E}(\mathsf{pk}_2, x_2; r)$. (It doesn't actually have to be $\mathsf{pk}_1\mathsf{pk}_2$ but a public key corresponding to $\mathsf{sk}_1 + \mathsf{sk}_2$ if sk_1 and sk_2 are secret keys corresponding to pk_1 and pk_2).

4.1   Construction

Construction 2 (PKE-IP Scheme). *Let* $\mathcal{E} = (\mathsf{Setup}, \mathsf{Encrypt}, \mathsf{Decrypt})$ *be a PKE scheme with the properties defined above, we define our* functional encryption *scheme for the inner-product functionality* $\mathsf{IP} = (\mathsf{Setup}, \mathsf{KeyDer}, \mathsf{Encrypt}, \mathsf{Decrypt})$ *as follows.*

- $\mathsf{Setup}(1^\lambda, 1^\ell)$ *calls* $\mathcal{E}$*'s key generation algorithm to generate* ℓ *independent* $(\mathsf{sk}_1, \mathsf{pk}_1), \ldots, (\mathsf{sk}_\ell, \mathsf{pk}_\ell)$ *pairs, sharing the same public parameters* params. *Then, the algorithm returns* $mpk = (\mathsf{params}, \mathsf{pk}_1, \ldots, \mathsf{pk}_\ell)$ *and* $msk = (\mathsf{sk}_1, \ldots, \mathsf{sk}_\ell)$.
- $\mathsf{KeyDer}(msk, \mathbf{y})$ *on input master secret key* msk *and a vector* $\mathbf{y} = (y_1, \ldots, y_\ell) \in \mathbb{Z}_q^\ell$, *computes* $\mathsf{sk}_\mathbf{y}$ *as an* G*-linear combination of* $(\mathsf{sk}_1, \ldots, \mathsf{sk}_n)$ *with coefficients* $(y_1, \ldots, y_\ell)$, *namely* $\mathsf{sk}_\mathbf{y} = \sum_{i \in [\ell]} y_i \cdot \mathsf{sk}_i$.
- $\mathsf{Encrypt}(mpk, \mathbf{x})$ *on input master public key* mpk *and message* $\mathbf{x} = (x_1, \ldots, x_\ell) \in \mathbb{Z}_q^\ell$, *chooses shared randomness* r *in the randomness space of* $\mathcal{E}$, *and computes* $\mathsf{ct}_0 = \mathcal{E}.\mathsf{C}(r)$ *and* $\mathsf{ct}_i = \mathcal{E}.\mathsf{E}(\mathsf{pk}_i, x_i; r)$. *Then the algorithm returns the ciphertext* $\mathsf{Ct} = (\mathsf{ct}_0, (\mathsf{ct}_i)_{i \in [\ell]})$.
- $\mathsf{Decrypt}(mpk, \mathsf{Ct}, \mathsf{sk}_\mathbf{y})$ *on input master public key* mpk, *ciphertext* $\mathsf{Ct} = (\mathsf{ct}_0, (\mathsf{ct}_i)_{i \in [\ell]})$, *and secret key* $\mathsf{Sk}_\mathbf{y}$ *for vector* $\mathbf{y} = (y_1, \ldots, y_\ell)$, *returns the output of* $\mathcal{E}.\mathsf{Decrypt}(\mathsf{Sk}_\mathbf{y}, (\mathsf{ct}_0, \prod_{i \in [\ell]} \mathsf{ct}_i^{y_i}))$.

Correctness. For all $(mpk, msk) \leftarrow \mathsf{Setup}(1^\lambda, 1^\ell)$, all $\mathbf{y} \in \mathbb{Z}_q^\ell$ and $\mathbf{x} \in \mathbb{Z}_q^\ell$, for $\mathsf{sk}_\mathbf{y} \leftarrow \mathsf{KeyDer}(msk, \mathbf{y})$ and $\mathsf{Ct} \leftarrow \mathsf{Encrypt}(mpk, \mathbf{x})$, we have that

$$\mathsf{Decrypt}(mpk, \mathsf{Ct}, \mathsf{sk}_\mathbf{y}) = \mathcal{E}.\mathsf{Decrypt}(\mathsf{Sk}_\mathbf{y}, (\mathsf{ct}_0, \prod_{i \in [\ell]} \mathsf{ct}_i^{y_i}))$$

$$= \mathcal{E}.\mathsf{Decrypt}(\mathsf{Sk}_\mathbf{y}, (\mathsf{ct}_0, \prod_{i \in [\ell]} \mathcal{E}.\mathsf{E}(\mathsf{pk}_i, x_i; r)^{y_i}))$$

$$= \mathcal{E}.\mathsf{Decrypt}(\mathsf{Sk}_\mathbf{y}, (\mathsf{ct}_0, \mathcal{E}.\mathsf{Encrypt}(\prod_{i \in [\ell]} \mathsf{pk}_i^{y_i}, \sum_{i \in [\ell]} y_i x_i; r)))$$

$$= \sum_{i \in [\ell]} y_i x_i \ .$$

by the LCH property. Finally, note that the decryption is allowed because $(\mathsf{Sk_y}, \prod_{i \in [\ell]} \mathsf{pk}_i^{y_i})$ is a valid key pair, due to the LKH property.

4.2 Proof of Security

In this section, we prove the following theorem:

Theorem 2. *If the underlying PKE $\mathcal{E}$ is s-IND-CPA, even under randomness-reuse, and satisfies the LKH and LCH properties, then the IP scheme of Section 4.1 is s-IND-CPA.*

Proof. his proof follows the intuition provided in the proof sketch of Theorem 1. To prove the security of our scheme we will show that the s-IND-CPA game is indistinguishable from a game where the challenge ciphertext encrypts a random combination of the challenge messages whose coefficients sum up to one. Thus, the challenge ciphertext decrypts to the expected values and information theoretically hides the challenge bit.

More specifically, given an adversary $\mathcal{A}$ that breaks the s-IND-CPA security of our IP scheme with non-negligible probability ε, we construct an adversary $\mathcal{B}$ that breaks the s-IND-CPA security of the underlying PKE scheme $\mathcal{E}$ with comparable probability.

$\mathcal{B}$ starts by picking a random element a in the full message space of the underlying PKE $\mathcal{E}$, and sends challenge messages 0 and a to the challenger $\mathcal{C}$ of PKE security game. $\mathcal{C}$ answers by sending an encryption $\mathsf{Ct} = (\mathsf{ct}_0, \mathsf{ct}_1)$ of either 0 or a and public key pk.

$\mathcal{B}$ then invokes $\mathcal{A}$ on input the security parameter and gets two different challenge messages in output, namely $(\mathbf{x}_i = (x_{i,1}, \ldots, x_{i,\ell}))_{i \in \{0,1\}}$ both in $\mathbb{Z}_q^\ell$.

Recall that, by the constraints of security game, the adversary can only issue secret key queries for vectors $\mathbf{y}$ such that $\langle \mathbf{x}_0, \mathbf{y} \rangle = \langle \mathbf{x}_1, \mathbf{y} \rangle$. Thus, we have that $\langle \mathbf{y}, \mathbf{x}_1 - \mathbf{x}_0 \rangle = 0$ meaning that $\mathbf{y}$ is in the vector space defined by $(\mathbf{x}_1 - \mathbf{x}_0)^\perp$.

Then, $\mathcal{B}$ generates the view for $\mathcal{A}$ in the following way:

Public Key. To generate master public key mpk, $\mathcal{B}$ does the following. First, $\mathcal{B}$ finds a basis $(\mathbf{z}_1, \mathbf{z}_2, \ldots, \mathbf{z}_{\ell-1})$ of $(\mathbf{x}_1 - \mathbf{x}_0)^\perp$. Then we can write the canonical vectors in this basis: for $i \in [\ell], j \in [\ell - 1]$, there exist $\lambda_{i,j} \in \mathbb{Z}_q$ and $\alpha_i \in \mathbb{Z}_q$ such that:

$$\mathbf{e}_i = \alpha_i(\mathbf{x}_1 - \mathbf{x}_0) + \sum_{j \in [\ell-1]} \lambda_{i,j} \mathbf{z}_j. \tag{1}$$

Then, for $j \in [\ell - 1]$, $\mathcal{B}$ sets $(\mathsf{pk}_{\mathbf{z}_j}, \mathsf{sk}_{\mathbf{z}_j}) = \mathcal{E}.\mathsf{Setup}(1^\lambda)$, and for $i \in [\ell]$,

$$\gamma_i = \prod_{j \in [\ell-1]} \mathsf{pk}_{\mathbf{z}_j}^{\lambda_{i,j}} \quad \text{and} \quad \mathsf{pk}_i = \mathsf{pk}^{\alpha_i} \gamma_i.$$

Eventually, $\mathcal{B}$ invokes $\mathcal{A}$ on input $mpk = (\mathsf{pk}_i)_{i \in [\ell]}$.

Notice that, $\mathcal{B}$ is implicitly setting $\mathsf{sk}_i = \alpha_i \mathsf{sk} + \sum_{j \in [\ell-1]} \lambda_{i,j} \mathsf{sk}_{\mathbf{z}_j}$ because of the LKH property, where sk is the secret key corresponding to pk, which is unknown to $\mathcal{B}$.

Challenge Ciphertext. $\mathcal{B}$ computes the challenge ciphertext Ct^* as follows. $\mathcal{B}$ randomly picks $b \overset{R}{\leftarrow} \{0,1\}$, computes $\mathcal{E}.\mathsf{E}(\gamma_i, 0; r)$ from ct_0 and $\sum_{j \in [\ell-1]} \lambda_{i,j} \mathsf{sk}_{\mathbf{z}_j}$ and $\mathcal{E}.\mathsf{E}(1_H, x_{b,i}; r)$ from secret key 0_G and ct_0, by randomness reuse. $\mathcal{B}$ then sets

$$\mathsf{ct}_0^* = \mathsf{ct}_0 \quad \text{and} \quad (\mathsf{ct}_i^* = \mathsf{ct}_1^{\alpha_i} \cdot \mathcal{E}.\mathsf{E}(\gamma_i, 0; r) \cdot \mathcal{E}.\mathsf{E}(1_H, x_{b,i}; r))_{i \in [\ell]} \ ,$$

Then the algorithm returns the challenge ciphertext $\mathsf{Ct}^* = (\mathsf{ct}_0^*, (\mathsf{ct}_i^*)_{i \in [\ell]})$.

Secret Keys. To generate a secret key for vector $\mathbf{y}$, $\mathcal{B}$ computes $\mathsf{sk}_{\mathbf{y}}$ as

$$\mathsf{sk}_{\mathbf{y}} = \sum_{j \in [\ell-1]} \left(\sum_{i \in [\ell]} y_i \lambda_{i,j} \right) \mathsf{sk}_{\mathbf{z}_j}$$

At the end of the simulation, if $\mathcal{A}$ correctly guesses b, then $\mathcal{B}$ returns 0 ($\mathcal{B}$ guesses that $\mathcal{C}$ encrypted 0), else $\mathcal{B}$ returns 1 ($\mathcal{B}$ guesses that $\mathcal{C}$ encrypted a). This concludes the description of adversary $\mathcal{B}$.

It remains to verify that $\mathcal{B}$ correctly simulates $\mathcal{A}$'s environment.

First see that the master public key is well distributed, because we are just applying a change of basis to a well distributed master public key. Now it holds that $\alpha_i = \frac{x_{1,i} - x_{0,i}}{\|\mathbf{x}_1 - \mathbf{x}_0\|^2}$ because

$$x_{1,i} - x_{0,i} = \langle \mathbf{x}_1 - \mathbf{x}_0, \mathbf{e}_i \rangle$$

$$= \alpha_i \|\mathbf{x}_1 - \mathbf{x}_0\|^2 + \sum_{j \in [\ell-1]} \lambda_{i,j} \langle \mathbf{x}_1 - \mathbf{x}_0, \mathbf{z}_j \rangle$$

$$= \alpha_i \|\mathbf{x}_1 - \mathbf{x}_0\|^2 .$$

Now recall that a vector $\mathbf{y}$ satisfying the security game constraints is such that $\langle \mathbf{y}, \mathbf{x}_0 \rangle = \langle \mathbf{y}, \mathbf{x}_1 \rangle$, so

$$\sum_{i \in [\ell]} y_i \alpha_i = \sum_{i \in [\ell]} y_i \frac{x_{1,i} - x_{0,i}}{\|\mathbf{x}_1 - \mathbf{x}_0\|^2} = 0$$

which in turn implies that a secret key $\mathsf{sk}_{\mathbf{y}}$ for the vector $\mathbf{y}$ is distributed as

$$\mathsf{sk}_{\mathbf{y}} = \sum_{i \in [\ell]} y_i \mathsf{sk}_i = \sum_{i \in [\ell]} y_i \alpha_i \mathsf{sk} + \sum_{i \in [\ell]} \sum_{j \in [\ell-1]} y_i \lambda_{i,j} \mathsf{sk}_{\mathbf{z}_j}$$

$$= \sum_{j \in [\ell-1]} \left(\sum_{i \in [\ell]} y_i \lambda_{i,j} \right) \mathsf{sk}_{\mathbf{z}_j}$$

On the other hand, if $\mathcal{A}$ asks for a secret key for some vector $\mathbf{y} \notin (\mathbf{x}_1 - \mathbf{x}_0)^{\perp}$, $\mathcal{B}$ would need to know sk in order to generate a correct secret key for $\mathbf{y}$.

Now, we have to analyze the following two cases, depending on which message was encrypted by $\mathcal{C}$ in the challenge ciphertext:

1. $\mathcal{C}$ encrypted 0. Then, the challenge ciphertext Ct^* for message $\mathbf{x}_b$ is distributed as

$$\mathsf{ct}_0^* = \mathsf{ct}_0$$

and

$$\begin{aligned}
\mathsf{ct}_i^* &= \mathcal{E}.\mathsf{E}(\mathsf{pk}, 0; r)^{\alpha_i} \cdot \mathcal{E}.\mathsf{E}(\gamma_i, 0; r) \cdot \mathcal{E}.\mathsf{E}(1_H, x_{b,i}; r) \\
&= \mathcal{E}.\mathsf{E}(\mathsf{pk}_i, x_{b,i}; r) \;,
\end{aligned}$$

thanks to the LCH property, and then as in the real game.

Thus, in this case, $\mathcal{B}$ generates a view identical to that $\mathcal{A}$ would see in the real game. Hence, the advantage of $\mathcal{B}$ in this game is ε, the same advantage as $\mathcal{A}$ against s-IND-CPA of IP when 0 has been encrypted.

2. $\mathcal{C}$ encrypted a. First, in Equation 1, we have $\alpha_i = (x_{1,i} - x_{0,i})/\|\mathbf{x}_1 - \mathbf{x}_0\|^2$. Let us analyze the distribution of the challenge ciphertext in this case. We have $\mathsf{ct}_0^* = \mathsf{ct}_0$ and

$$\begin{aligned}
\mathsf{ct}_i^* &= \mathcal{E}.\mathsf{E}(\mathsf{pk}, a; r)^{\alpha_i} \cdot \mathcal{E}.\mathsf{E}(\gamma_i, 0; r) \cdot \mathcal{E}.\mathsf{E}(1_H, x_{b,i}; r) \\
&= \mathcal{E}.\mathsf{E}(\mathsf{pk}_i, x_{b,i} + \alpha_i a; r) \\
&= \mathcal{E}.\mathsf{E}(\mathsf{pk}_i, \hat{x}_i; r),
\end{aligned}$$

thanks to the LCH property, where $\hat{x}_i$ is defined as follows:

$$\begin{aligned}
\hat{x}_i = x_{b,i} + \alpha_i a &= \frac{a}{\|\mathbf{x}_1 - \mathbf{x}_0\|^2}(x_{1,i} - x_{0,i}) + x_{b,i} \\
&= \frac{a}{\|\mathbf{x}_1 - \mathbf{x}_0\|^2}(x_{1,i} - x_{0,i}) + x_{0,i} + b(x_{1,i} - x_{0,i}).
\end{aligned}$$

Let us set $u = a/\|\mathbf{x}_1 - \mathbf{x}_0\|^2 + b$, which is a random value in the full message space of $\mathcal{E}$, given that a is random in the same space, then $\hat{x}_i = u x_{1,i} + (1 - u)x_{0,i}$. Then, the challenge ciphertext is a valid ciphertext for the message $\hat{\mathbf{x}} = u\mathbf{x}_1 + (1 - u)\mathbf{x}_0$, which is a random linear combination of the vectors $\mathbf{x}_0$ and $\mathbf{x}_1$ whose coefficients sum up to one, as expected. Notice that b is information theoretically hidden because the distribution of u is independent from b. Hence, the advantage of $\mathcal{B}$ in this game is 0, when a random non-zero a has been encrypted.

Eventually, this shows that ε is bounded by the best advantage one can get against s-IND-CPA of $\mathcal{E}$. Hence, taking the maximal values, the best advantage one can get against s-IND-CPA of IP is bounded by the best advantage one can get against s-IND-CPA of $\mathcal{E}$.

5   Instantiations

5.1   Instantiation from DDH

The scheme of Section 3 can be obtained by plugging into our generalization the ElGamal encryption scheme [ElG85] which supports the properties that we require. Namely:

RR, LKH and LCH properties. The secret key space of this PKE is the group $(\mathbb{Z}_p, +, 0)$, and the public key space is the group $(\mathbb{G}, \times, 1)$. It is easy to see that $\mathsf{pk}_1^a \mathsf{pk}_2$ is the public key corresponding to the secret key $a\mathsf{sk}_1 + \mathsf{sk}_2$, and that

$$\mathsf{ct}_1 \cdot \mathsf{ct}_1' = \mathsf{pk}^r g^m \cdot \mathsf{pk}'^r g^{m'} = (\mathsf{pk} \cdot \mathsf{pk}')^r \cdot g^{m+m'}.$$

For RR, see that $\mathsf{ct}_0^{\mathsf{sk}} = \mathsf{pk}^r$.

5.2   Instantiation from LWE

The LWE Assumption. The learning with errors (LWE) problem was introduced by Regev [Reg05]. Let n, q be integer parameters. For any noise distribution χ on $\mathbb{Z}_q$, and vector $\mathbf{s} \in \mathbb{Z}_q^n$, the oracle $\mathsf{LWE}_{q,n,\chi}(\mathbf{s})$ samples a fresh random n-dimensional vector $\mathbf{a} \leftarrow \mathbb{Z}_q^n$, as well as noise $e \leftarrow \chi$, and returns $(\mathbf{a}, \langle \mathbf{a}, \mathbf{s} \rangle + e)$. The LWE assumption with noise χ states that for every PPT distinguisher $\mathcal{D}$,

$$\Pr[\mathbf{s} \leftarrow \mathbb{Z}_q^n \; : \; \mathcal{D}^{\mathsf{LWE}_{q,n,\chi}(\mathbf{s})} = 1] - \Pr[\mathbf{s} \leftarrow \mathbb{Z}_q^n \; : \; \mathcal{D}^{\mathsf{LWE}_{q,n,U}(\mathbf{s})} = 1] = \mathsf{negl}(n),$$

where U is the uniform distribution on $\mathbb{Z}_q$.

In other words, in addition to $\mathbf{a}$, the oracle $\mathsf{LWE}_{q,n,U}(\mathbf{s})$ simply returns uniform random samples, independent of $\mathbf{s}$. In general, the error distribution χ is chosen to be a discrete Gaussian on $\mathbb{Z}_q$.

Let $n \in \mathbb{Z}^+$ be a security parameter. Let $q = q(n)$, $m = m(n)$, and $1 < p < q$ be positive integers. Let $\alpha = \alpha(n)$ be positive real Gaussian parameters. Let $r = r(n) \geq 2$ be an integer and define $k = k(n) := \lfloor \log_r q \rfloor$.

Construction 3 (LWE-PKE Scheme). *We define our public-key encryption scheme $\mathcal{E} = (\mathsf{Setup}, \mathsf{Encrypt}, \mathsf{Decrypt})$ as follows.*

- $\mathsf{Setup}(1^n)$ *samples* $\mathbf{A} \leftarrow \mathbb{Z}_q^{m \times n}$. *Then, for* $\gamma = 0, \dots, k$, *samples* $\mathbf{s}_\gamma \leftarrow \mathbb{Z}_q^n$ *and computes* $\mathbf{b}_\gamma = \mathbf{A}\mathbf{s}_\gamma + \mathbf{e}_\gamma \in \mathbb{Z}_q^m$, *where* $\mathbf{e}_\gamma \leftarrow \chi^m$. *Then, the algorithm sets* $\mathsf{pk} = (\mathbf{A}, (\mathbf{b}_\gamma)_\gamma)$ *and* $\mathsf{sk} = (\mathbf{s}_\gamma)_\gamma$, *and returns the pair* $(\mathsf{pk}, \mathsf{sk})$.
- $\mathsf{Encrypt}(\mathsf{pk}, x)$ *on input public key* pk, *and message* $x \in \mathbb{Z}_p$, *chooses random* $\mathbf{r} \leftarrow \{0, 1\}^m$ *and computes*

$$\mathsf{ct}_0 = \mathbf{A}^\top \mathbf{r} \in \mathbb{Z}_q^n$$

and, for $\gamma = 0, \dots, k$,

$$\mathsf{ct}_\gamma = \langle \mathbf{r}, \mathbf{b}_\gamma \rangle + \left\lfloor \frac{q}{p} \right\rfloor r^\gamma x_\gamma \in \mathbb{Z}_q,$$

where $\sum_\gamma x_\gamma r^\gamma = x$. *Then the algorithm returns the ciphertext* $\mathsf{Ct} = (\mathsf{ct}_0, (\mathsf{ct}_\gamma)_\gamma)$.
- $\mathsf{Decrypt}(\mathsf{pk}, \mathsf{Ct}, \mathsf{sk})$ *on input public key* pk, *ciphertext* $\mathsf{Ct} = (\mathsf{ct}_0, (\mathsf{ct}_\gamma))$ *and secret key* sk, *returns the evaluation*

$$y = \left\lfloor \frac{p}{q} \cdot \left(\sum \mathsf{ct}_\gamma - \langle \mathsf{ct}_0, \mathsf{sk} \rangle \right) \right\rceil .$$

Semantic security. Notice that the above scheme is the Regev scheme where the message is r-decomposed to ensure that the error doesn't grow too much. Then, the proof of the semantic security of this encryption scheme can be found in [Reg05]. Essentially, the proof relies on two key properties:

- $\mathbf{A}^\top \mathbf{r} \in \mathbb{Z}_q^n$ is computationally indistinguishable from a random vector;
- Distinguishing a $\mathbf{As}_\gamma + \mathbf{e}_\gamma$ from a random vector is breaking the LWE assumption.

RR, LKH and LCH properties. The secret key space of this PKE is the group $((\mathbb{Z}_q^n)^{k+1}, +, \mathbf{0})$, and the public key space is the group $((\mathbb{Z}_q^m)^{k+1}, +, \mathbf{0})$. It is easy to see that $a\mathsf{pk}_1 + \mathsf{pk}_2$ corresponds to the secret key $a\mathsf{sk}_1 + \mathsf{sk}_2$, and that

$$\mathsf{ct}_\gamma + \mathsf{ct}'_\gamma = \langle \mathbf{r}, \mathbf{b}_\gamma \rangle + \left\lfloor \frac{q}{p} \right\rfloor r^\gamma x_\gamma + \langle \mathbf{r}, \mathbf{b}'_\gamma \rangle + \left\lfloor \frac{q}{p} \right\rfloor r^\gamma x'_\gamma$$

$$= \langle \mathbf{r}, \mathbf{b}_\gamma + \mathbf{b}'_\gamma \rangle + \left\lfloor \frac{q}{p} \right\rfloor r^\gamma (x_\gamma + x'_\gamma).$$

For RR, see that $\langle \mathbf{A}^\top \mathbf{r}, \mathbf{s} \rangle = \langle \mathbf{r}, \mathbf{As} \rangle$.

Acknowledgments. We thank the anonymous reviewers for their fruitful comments and for pointing out an issue with an instantiation based on Paillier's encryption scheme.

This work was supported in part by the European Research Council under the European Community's Seventh Framework Programme (FP7/2007-2013 Grant Agreement no. 339563 – CryptoCloud), by the French ANR-14-CE28-0003 Project EnBiD, and by the Chaire France Telecom.

References

[ABN10] Abdalla, M., Bellare, M., Neven, G.: Robust Encryption. In: Micciancio, D. (ed.) TCC 2010. LNCS, vol. 5978, pp. 480–497. Springer, Heidelberg (2010)

[BBS03] Bellare, M., Boldyreva, A., Staddon, J.: Randomness re-use in multi-recipient encryption schemeas. In: Desmedt, Y., (ed.) PKC 2003. LNCS, vol. 2567. pp. 85–99. Springer, Heidlburg (2003)

[BCP14] Boyle, E., Chung, K.-M., Pass, R.: On Extractability Obfuscation. In: Lindell, Y. (ed.) TCC 2014. LNCS, vol. 8349, pp. 52–73. Springer, Heidelberg (2014)

[BF01] Boneh, D., Franklin, M.: Identity-Based Encryption from the Weil Pairing. In: Kilian, J. (ed.) CRYPTO 2001. LNCS, vol. 2139, pp. 213–229. Springer, Heidelberg (2001)

[BO12] Bellare, M., O'Neill, A.: Semantically-secure functional encryption: Possibility results, impossibility results and the quest for a general definition. Cryptology ePrint Archive, Report 2012/515 (2012). http://eprint.iacr.org/2012/515

[BR06] Bellare, M., Rogaway, P.: The Security of Triple Encryption and a Framework for Code-Based Game-Playing Proofs. In: Vaudenay, S. (ed.) EUROCRYPT 2006. LNCS, vol. 4004, pp. 409–426. Springer, Heidelberg (2006)

[BSW11] Boneh, D., Sahai, A., Waters, B.: Functional Encryption: Definitions and Challenges. In: Ishai, Y. (ed.) TCC 2011. LNCS, vol. 6597, pp. 253–273. Springer, Heidelberg (2011)

[BW07] Boneh, D., Waters, B.: Conjunctive, Subset, and Range Queries on Encrypted Data. In: Vadhan, S.P. (ed.) TCC 2007. LNCS, vol. 4392, pp. 535–554. Springer, Heidelberg (2007)

[Coc01] Cocks, C.: An Identity Based Encryption Scheme Based on Quadratic Residues. In: Honary, B. (ed.) Cryptography and Coding 2001. LNCS, vol. 2260, pp. 360–363. Springer, Heidelberg (2001)

[ElG84] El Gamal, T.: A Public Key Cryptosystem and a Signature Scheme Based on Discrete Logarithms. In: Blakely, G.R., Chaum, D. (eds.) CRYPTO 1984. LNCS, vol. 196, pp. 10–18. Springer, Heidelberg (1985)

[ElG85] ElGamal, T.: A public key cryptosystem and a signature scheme based on discrete logarithms. IEEE Transactions on Information Theory 31, 469–472 (1985)

[Gen06] Gentry, C.: Practical Identity-Based Encryption Without Random Oracles. In: Vaudenay, S. (ed.) EUROCRYPT 2006. LNCS, vol. 4004, pp. 445–464. Springer, Heidelberg (2006)

[GGH+13] Garg, S., Gentry, C., Halevi, S., Raykova, M., Sahai, A., Waters, B.: Candidate indistinguishability obfuscation and functional encryption for all circuits. Cryptology ePrint Archive, Report 2013/451 (2013). http://eprint.iacr.org/2013/451

[GGHZ14] Garg, S., Gentry, C., Halevi, S., Zhandry, M.: Fully secure attribute based encryption from multilinear maps. Cryptology ePrint Archive, Report 2014/622 (2014). http://eprint.iacr.org/2014/622

[GLW12] Goldwasser, S., Lewko, A., Wilson, D.A.: Bounded-Collusion IBE from Key Homomorphism. In: Cramer, R. (ed.) TCC 2012. LNCS, vol. 7194, pp. 564–581. Springer, Heidelberg (2012)

[GPSW06] Goyal, V., Pandey, O., Sahai, A., Waters, B.: Attribute-based encryption for fine-grained access control of encrypted data. In Juels, A., Wright, R.N., De Capitani di Vimercati, S. (eds) ACM CCS 2006, pp. 89–98. ACM Press (October / November 2006). Available as Cryptology ePrint Archive Report 2006/309

[KSW08] Katz, J., Sahai, A., Waters, B.: Predicate Encryption Supporting Disjunctions, Polynomial Equations, and Inner Products. In: Smart, N.P. (ed.) EUROCRYPT 2008. LNCS, vol. 4965, pp. 146–162. Springer, Heidelberg (2008)

[Kur02] Kurosawa, K.: Multi-recipient Public-Key Encryption with Shortened Ciphertext. In: Naccache, D., Paillier, P. (eds.) PKC 2002. LNCS, vol. 2274, pp. 48–63. Springer, Heidelberg (2002)

[LOS+10] Lewko, A., Okamoto, T., Sahai, A., Takashima, K., Waters, B.: Fully Secure Functional Encryption: Attribute-Based Encryption and (Hierarchical) Inner Product Encryption. In: Gilbert, H. (ed.) EUROCRYPT 2010. LNCS, vol. 6110, pp. 62–91. Springer, Heidelberg (2010)

[O'N10] O'Neill, A.: Definitional issues in functional encryption. Cryptology ePrint Archive, Report 2010/556 (2010). http://eprint.iacr.org/2010/556

[OT12] Okamoto, T., Takashima, K.: Adaptively Attribute-Hiding (Hierarchical) Inner Product Encryption. In: Pointcheval, D., Johansson, T. (eds.) EUROCRYPT 2012. LNCS, vol. 7237, pp. 591–608. Springer, Heidelberg (2012)

[Reg05] Regev, O.: On lattices, learning with errors, random linear codes, and cryptography. In: Gabow, H.N., Fagin, R. (eds) 37th ACM STOC, pp. 84–93. ACM Press (May 2005)

[Rot11] Rothblum, R.: Homomorphic Encryption: From Private-Key to Public-Key. In: Ishai, Y. (ed.) TCC 2011. LNCS, vol. 6597, pp. 219–234. Springer, Heidelberg (2011)

[Sha84] Shamir, A.: Identity-Based Cryptosystems and Signature Schemes. In: Blakely, G.R., Chaum, D. (eds.) CRYPTO 1984. LNCS, vol. 196, pp. 47–53. Springer, Heidelberg (1985)

[SW05] Sahai, A., Waters, B.: Fuzzy Identity-Based Encryption. In: Cramer, R. (ed.) EUROCRYPT 2005. LNCS, vol. 3494, pp. 457–473. Springer, Heidelberg (2005)

[TW14] Tessaro, S., Wilson, D.A.: Bounded-Collusion Identity-Based Encryption from Semantically-Secure Public-Key Encryption: Generic Constructions with Short Ciphertexts. In: Krawczyk, H. (ed.) PKC 2014. LNCS, vol. 8383, pp. 257–274. Springer, Heidelberg (2014)

[Wat12] Waters, B.: Functional Encryption for Regular Languages. In: Safavi-Naini, R., Canetti, R. (eds.) CRYPTO 2012. LNCS, vol. 7417, pp. 218–235. Springer, Heidelberg (2012)

[Wat14] Waters, B.: A punctured programming approach to adaptively secure functional encryption. Cryptology ePrint Archive, Report 2014/588 (2014). http://eprint.iacr.org/2014/588

Predicate Encryption for Multi-dimensional Range Queries from Lattices

Romain Gay[✉], Pierrick Méaux, and Hoeteck Wee

ENS, Paris, France
{rgay,meaux,wee}@di.ens.fr

Abstract. We construct a lattice-based predicate encryption scheme for multi-dimensional range and multi-dimensional subset queries. Our scheme is selectively secure and weakly attribute-hiding, and its security is based on the standard learning with errors (LWE) assumption. Multi-dimensional range and subset queries capture many interesting applications pertaining to searching on encrypted data. To the best of our knowledge, these are the first lattice-based predicate encryption schemes for functionalities beyond IBE and inner product.

1 Introduction

Predicate encryption [8,17,20] is a new paradigm for public-key encryption that supports search queries on encrypted data. In predicate encryption, ciphertexts are associated with descriptive values x in addition to a plaintext, secret keys are associated with a query predicate f, and a secret key decrypts the ciphertext to recover the plaintext if and only if $f(x) = 1$. The security requirement for predicate encryption enforces privacy of x and the plaintext even amidst multiple search queries, namely an adversary holding secret keys for different query predicates learns nothing about x and the plaintext if none of them is individually authorized to decrypt the ciphertext.

Multi-dimensional Range Queries. Following [8,20], we focus on predicate encryption for multi-dimensional range queries, as captured by the following examples:

- For network intrusion detection on logfiles, we would encrypt network flows labeled with a set of attributes from the network header, such as the source and destination addresses, port numbers, time-stamp, and protocol numbers. We could then issue auditors with restricted secret keys that can only decrypt the network flows that fall within a particular range of IP addresses and some specific time period.

R. Gay— Supported in part by ANR-14-CE28-0003 (Project EnBiD).
P. Méaux— INRIA and ENS. Supported in part by ANR-13-JS02-0003 (Project CLE).
H. Wee— ENS and CNRS. Supported in part by ANR-14-CE28-0003 (Project EnBiD), NSF Award CNS-1445424, ERC Project CryptoCloud (FP7/2007-2013 Grant Agreement no. 339563), the Alexander von Humboldt Foundation and a Google Faculty Research Award.

© International Association for Cryptologic Research 2015
J. Katz (Ed.): PKC 2015, LNCS 9020, pp. 752–776, 2015.
DOI: 10.1007/978-3-662-46447-2_34

- For credit card fraud investigation, we would encrypt credit card transactions labeled with a set of attributes such as time, costs and zipcodes. We could then issue investigators with restricted secret keys that decrypt transactions over $1,000 which took place in the last month and originated from a particular range of zipcodes.
- For online dating, we would encrypt personal profiles labeled with dating preferences pertaining to age, height, weight and salary. Secret keys are associated with specific attributes and can only decrypt profiles for which the attributes match the dating preferences.

More generally, in multi-dimensional range queries, we are given a point $(z_1, \ldots, z_D) \in [T]^D$ and interval ranges $[x_1, y_1], \ldots, [x_D, y_D] \subseteq [T]$ and we want to know if $(x_1 \leq z_1 \leq y_1) \wedge \cdots \wedge (x_D \leq z_D \leq y_D)$. We also consider more general multi-dimensional subset queries where we are given subset $S_1, \ldots, S_D \subseteq [T]$ and we want to know if $(z_1 \in S_1) \wedge \cdots \wedge (z_D \in S_D)$. Note that in the first two examples, the search queries are associated with the keys, whereas in the third example, the search queries are associated with the ciphertext. We will refer to encryption schemes for the former as "key-policy" schemes, and schemes for the latter as "ciphertext-policy" schemes. In all of these examples, it is important that unauthorized parties do not learn the contents of the ciphertexts, nor of the meta-data associated with the ciphertexts, such as the network header or dating preferences. On the other hand, it is often okay to leak the meta-data to authorized parties. We stress that privacy of the meta-data is an additional security requirement provided by predicate encryption but not attribute-based encryption [14,15].

Prior Works. The first constructions of predicate encryption for multi-dimensional range queries were given in the works of Boneh and Waters [8] and Shi, et. al [20]; all of these constructions rely on bilinear groups and achieve parameters that are linear in the number of dimensions D. The latter work also presents a generic "brute force" construction based on any anonymous IBE, where the parameters grow exponentially in D.

1.1 Our Contributions

In this work, we construct a lattice-based predicate encryption scheme for multi-dimensional range queries, whose security is based on the standard learning with errors (LWE) assumption. Our scheme is selectively secure and weakly attribute-hiding, that is, we only guarantee privacy of the ciphertext attribute against collusions that are not authorized to decrypt the challenge ciphertext. The scheme is best suited for applications where the range T is very large but the number of dimensions D is a small constant, as is the case for the three applications outlined earlier and also the scenario considered in [20]. In addition, we extend our techniques to multi-dimensional subset queries, where we obtain improved efficiency over prior schemes [8]. We summarize our schemes in Table 1 and 2.

Our Approach. At a high level, our approach follows that of Shi et al. [20], who showed how to boost an anonymous IBE scheme into a predicate encryption scheme for multi-dimensional range queries. We show how to carry out a similar transformation over lattices, starting from the LWE-based anonymous IBE schemes in [1,4,9]. We highlight the main novelties in this work:

- First, we present a more modular and conceptually simpler approach for handling multi-dimensional range queries. We construct our scheme for the simpler AND-OR-EQ predicate (conjunction of disjunction of equalities), and present a combinatorial reduction from multi-dimensional range queries to this predicate. The simpler AND-OR-EQ predicate is symmetric, which immediately yields both key-policy and ciphertext-policy schemes for multi-dimensional range queries. We can only prove security for our lattice-based AND-OR-EQ predicate encryption under an "at most one" promise, which necessitates a more delicate reduction from multi-dimensional range queries to AND-OR-EQ where we decompose range queries into disjoint sub-intervals. Indeed, the same technical issue arises in the previous pairing-based schemes.

- To handle the inner disjunction of equality like $(X = a) \vee (X = b)$ for the key-policy AND-OR-EQ predicate where X is associated with the ciphertext and (a, b) with the key, our new ciphertext is an anonymous IBE ciphertext for the identity X, and the key comprises two IBE keys for a and b; decryption works by trying all possible IBE keys. Following [20], we will pad the plaintext with zeroes, so that we know which of the decryptions corresponds to the correct plaintext. To handle the outer conjunction, we rely on secret sharing, as with prior lattice-based fuzzy IBE [3].

- Correctness for the inner disjunction requires more care than that in the bilinear groups. Roughly speaking, we need to show that decrypting an IBE ciphertext for identity a with a key for identity $b \neq a$ yields a random-looking value. The straight-forward argument that relies on IBE security yields computational correctness. To achieve statistical correctness in the lattice-based setting, we rely on a simple but seemingly novel analysis of the output of lattice-based trapdoor sampling algorithms (c.f. Lemma 13).

- The intuition for security for the inner disjunction is as follows: if X is different from a and b, then both X and the plaintext remain hidden via security of the underlying IBE. On the other hand, if X is equal to one of a, b, then the decryptor does learn the exact value of X, which means that we cannot hope to achieve strong attribute-hiding using these techniques. To establish the weak attribute-hiding for the general AND-OR-EQ, we rely on techniques from lattice-based inner product encryption [4].

To the best of our knowledge, this is the first lattice-based predicate encryption scheme for functionalities beyond IBE and inner product [1,4,9,21], and we hope that it would inspire further research into lattice-based predicate encryption. We defer a more detailed overview of our construction to Section 4.

Table 1. Summary of existing predicate encryption schemes for multi-dimensional range queries: given a point $(z_1, \ldots, z_D) \in [T]^D$ and interval ranges $[x_1, y_1]$, $\ldots, [x_D, y_D] \subseteq [T]$, we want to know if $(x_1 \leq z_1 \leq y_1) \wedge \cdots \wedge (x_D \leq z_D \leq y_D)$. Here, D denotes the number of dimensions and T the number of points in each dimension. We omit the $\mathrm{poly}(n)$ multiplicative overhead, where n is the security parameter.

Reference	Size			Time		Attribute
	Public key	Ciphertext	Secret key	Encryption	Decryption	hiding
[8] (KP)	$O(D \cdot T)$	$O(D \cdot T)$	$O(D)$	$O(D \cdot T)$	$O(D)$	fully
[20] (KP, CP)	$O(D \log T)$	$O(D \log T)$	$O(D \log T)$	$O(D \log T)$	$O((\log T)^D)$	weakly
this paper (KP, CP)	$O(D \log T)$	$O(D \log T)$	$O(D \log T)$	$O(D \log T)$	$O((\log T)^D)$	weakly

Table 2. Summary of existing predicate encryption schemes for multi-dimensional subset queries: given a point $(z_1, \ldots, z_D) \in [T]^D$ and subsets $S_1, \ldots, S_D \subseteq [T]$, we want to know if $(z_1 \in S_1) \wedge \cdots \wedge (z_D \in S_D)$. Here, D denotes the number of dimension and T the size of the sets. We omit the $\mathrm{poly}(n)$ multiplicative overhead, where n is the security parameter. (KP) stands for key-policy and (CP) stands for ciphertext-policy.

Reference	Size			Time		Attribute
	Public key	Ciphertext	Secret key	Encryption	Decryption	hiding
[8]	$O(D \cdot T)$	$O(D \cdot T)$	$O(D \cdot T)$	$O(D \cdot T)$	$O(D \cdot T)$	fully
this paper (KP)	$O(D)$	$O(D)$	$O(D \cdot T)$	$O(D)$	$O(T^D)$	weakly
this paper (CP)	$O(D \cdot T)$	$O(D \cdot T)$	$O(D)$	$O(D \cdot T)$	$O(D)$	weakly

Organization. The rest of the paper is organized as follows. We recall the relevant background on lattices and the security model of predicate encryption in Section 2. We introduce the so-called AND-OR-EQ predicate, and show how to reduce multi-dimensional subset queries and multi-dimensional range queries to AND-OR-EQ in Section 3. We give our lattice-based predicate encryption scheme for AND-OR-EQ in Section 4, and we show that it gives an efficient construction for multi-dimensional range queries. Finally, we show in Section 5 how to improve the construction of Section 4 in order to obtain an efficient scheme for multi-dimensional subset queries.

2   Preliminaries

Notations. We denote by $s \leftarrow_R S$ the fact that s is picked uniformly at random from a finite set S or from a distribution. By PPT, we denote a probabilistic polynomial-time algorithm. Throughout this paper, we use 1^n as the security parameter. For every vector $\mathbf{u} \in \mathbb{Z}_q^n$, we write $\mathbf{u} = (u_1, \ldots, u_n)$, and for any matrix $\mathbf{M} \in \mathbb{Z}_q^{n \times m}$, we write $M_{i,j}$ the (i, j) entry of $\mathbf{M}$. For any $x \in \mathbb{R}$, we denote by $\lfloor x \rfloor$ the largest integer less than or equal to x. For any $z \in [0, 1]$, we denote by $\lfloor z \rceil$ the closest integer to z.

Randomness Extraction. We use the following variant of the left-over hash lemma [11,16] from [1]:

Lemma 1 ([1], Lemma 13). *Let* $m > (n + 1) \log q + \omega(\log n)$, $q > 2$ *be a prime number,* $\mathbf{R} \leftarrow_R \{-1, 1\}^{m \times \ell} \mod q$, *where* $\ell = \ell(n)$ *is polynomial in* n. *Let* $\mathbf{A} \leftarrow_R \mathbb{Z}_q^{n \times m}, \mathbf{B} \leftarrow_R \mathbb{Z}_q^{n \times \ell}$; *For all vectors* $\mathbf{u} \in \mathbb{Z}^m$ *the distribution* $(\mathbf{A}, \mathbf{AR}, \mathbf{u}^\top \mathbf{R})$ *is statistically close from the distribution* $(\mathbf{A}, \mathbf{B}, \mathbf{u}^\top \mathbf{R})$.

LWE Assumption. The decisional Learning With Error problem (dLWE) was introduced by Regev [19],

Definition 1 (dLWE). *For an integer* $q = q(n) \geq 2$, *an adversary* $\mathcal{A}$ *and an error distribution* $\chi = \chi(n)$ *over* $\mathbb{Z}_q$, *we define the following advantage function:*

$$\mathsf{Adv}_{\mathcal{A}}^{\mathsf{dLWE}_{n,m,q,\chi}} := |\Pr[\mathcal{A}(\mathbf{A}, \mathbf{z}_0) = 1] - \Pr[\mathcal{A}(\mathbf{A}, \mathbf{z}_1) = 1]|$$

where

$$\mathbf{A} \leftarrow_R \mathbb{Z}_q^{n \times m}, \mathbf{s} \leftarrow_R \mathbb{Z}_q^n, \mathbf{e} \leftarrow_R \chi^m, \mathbf{z}_0 := \mathbf{s}^\top \mathbf{A} + \mathbf{e}^\top \quad and \quad \mathbf{z}_1 \leftarrow_R \mathbb{Z}_q^m$$

The $\mathsf{dLWE}_{n,m,q,\chi}$ *assumption asserts that for all* PPT *adversaries* $\mathcal{A}$, *the advantage* $\mathsf{Adv}_{\mathcal{A}}^{\mathsf{dLWE}_{n,m,q,\chi}}$ *is a negligible function in* n.

Throughout the paper, we denote by $\chi_{\max} < q$ the bound on the noise distribution χ.

2.1   Lattice Preliminaries

Lattices. For any matrix $\mathbf{A} \in \mathbb{Z}_q^{n \times m}$ and any vector $\mathbf{p} \in \mathbb{Z}_q^n$, we define the orthogonal q-ary lattice of $\mathbf{A}$: $\Lambda_q^\perp(\mathbf{A}) := \{\mathbf{u} \in \mathbb{Z}^m : \mathbf{Au} = \mathbf{0} \mod q\}$ and the shifted lattice: $\Lambda_q^{\mathbf{p}}(\mathbf{A}) := \{\mathbf{u} \in \mathbb{Z}^m : \mathbf{Au} = \mathbf{p} \mod q\}$. Similarly, for any matrix $\mathbf{P} \in \mathbb{Z}_q^{n \times \ell}$, we define: $\Lambda_q^{\mathbf{P}}(\mathbf{A}) := \{\mathbf{U} \in \mathbb{Z}^{m \times \ell} : \mathbf{AU} = \mathbf{P} \mod q\}$.

Matrix Norms. For any vector $\mathbf{x}$, we denote by $\|\mathbf{x}\|$ its ℓ_2 norm. For any matrix $\mathbf{R} \in \mathbb{Z}_q^{n \times \ell}$ we define the three following norms:

1. $\|\mathbf{R}\|$ denotes the maximum of the ℓ_2 norm over the columns of $\mathbf{R}$.
2. $\|\mathbf{R}\|_{\mathrm{GS}}$ denotes the Gram-Schmidt norm of $\mathbf{R}$ (see [7] for further details).
3. $\|\mathbf{R}\|_2$ denotes the operator norm of $\mathbf{R}$ defined as $\|\mathbf{R}\|_2 = \sup_{\|\mathbf{x}\|=1} \|\mathbf{Rx}\|$.

Note that for any matrix $\mathbf{S} \in \mathbb{Z}_q^{\ell \times m}$, and any vector $\mathbf{e} \in \mathbb{Z}_q^n$, we have $\|\mathbf{R} \cdot \mathbf{S}\| \leq \|\mathbf{R}\|_2 \cdot \|\mathbf{S}\|$, and $\|\mathbf{e}^\top \mathbf{F}\|_\infty \leq \|\mathbf{e}\| \cdot \|\mathbf{F}\|$.

Gaussian Distributions. For any positive parameter $\sigma \in \mathbb{R}_{>0}$, let $\rho_\sigma(\mathbf{x}) := \exp(-\pi\|\mathbf{x}\|^2/\sigma^2)$ be the Gaussian function on $\mathbb{R}^n$ of center $\mathbf{0}$ and parameter σ. For any $n \in \mathbb{N}$ and any subset D of $\mathbb{Z}^n$, we define $\rho_\sigma(D) := \sum_{\mathbf{x} \in D} \rho_\sigma(\mathbf{x})$ the discrete integral of ρ_σ over D, and $\mathcal{D}_{D,\sigma}$ the discrete Gaussian distribution over D of parameter σ. That is, for all $\mathbf{y} \in D$, we have $\mathcal{D}_{D,\sigma}(\mathbf{y}) := \frac{\rho_\sigma(\mathbf{y})}{\rho_\sigma(D)}$.

Lemma 2 ([7], Lemma 2.5). *Let $n, m, \ell, q > 0$ be integers and $\sigma > 0$ be a Gaussian parameter. For all $\mathbf{A} \in \mathbb{Z}_q^{n \times m}$, $\mathbf{P} \in \mathbb{Z}_q^{n \times \ell}$, $\mathbf{U} \leftarrow_{\mathrm{R}} \mathcal{D}_{\Lambda_q^{\mathbf{P}}(\mathbf{A}),\sigma}$ and $\mathbf{R} \leftarrow_{\mathrm{R}} \{-1,1\}^{m \times m}$, with overwhelming probability in m,*

$$\|\mathbf{U}\| \leq \sigma\sqrt{m} \ , \ \|\mathbf{R}\|_2 \leq 20\sqrt{m}$$

Trapdoor Generators. The following lemmas state properties of algorithms for generating short basis of lattices.

Lemma 3 ([5,6,18]). *Let $n, m, q > 0$ be integers with q prime and $m = \Theta(n \log q)$. There is a PPT algorithm TrapGen defined as follows:*

TrapGen($1^n, 1^m, q$):
Inputs: *a security parameter n, an integer m such that $m = \Theta(n \log q)$, and a prime modulus q.*
Outputs: *a matrix $\mathbf{A} \in \mathbb{Z}_q^{n \times m}$ and a basis $\mathbf{T_A} \in \mathbb{Z}_q^{m \times m}$ for $\Lambda_q^\perp(\mathbf{A})$ such that the distribution of $\mathbf{A}$ is $\mathrm{negl}(n)$-close to uniform and $\|\mathbf{T_A}\|_{\mathrm{GS}} = O(\sqrt{n \log q})$, with all but negligible probability in n.*

Lemma 4 ([18]). *Let $n, m, q > 0$ be integers with q prime and $m = \Theta(n \log q)$. There is a full-rank matrix $\mathbf{G}$ such that the lattice $\Lambda_q^\perp(\mathbf{G})$ has a publicly known basis $\mathbf{T_G} \in \mathbb{Z}^{m \times m}$ with $\|\mathbf{T_G}\|_{\mathrm{GS}} \leq \sqrt{5}$.*

Lemma 5 ([13], Lemmas 5.1 and 5.2)

- Let $m \geq 2n \log q$. With all but $\mathrm{negl}(n)$ probability, $\mathbf{A} \leftarrow_{\mathrm{R}} \mathbb{Z}_q^{n \times m}$ is full rank (i.e. the subset-sums of the columns of $\mathbf{A}$ generate $\mathbb{Z}_q^n$).
- Assume $\mathbf{A} \in \mathbb{Z}_q^{n \times m}$ is full-rank and $\sigma = \omega(\sqrt{\log n})$. Then, the following distributions are statistically close:

$$\{(\mathbf{u}, \mathbf{Au}) : \mathbf{u} \leftarrow_{\mathrm{R}} \mathcal{D}_{\mathbb{Z}^m,\sigma}\} \quad \text{and} \quad \{(\mathbf{u}, \mathbf{p}) : \mathbf{p} \leftarrow_{\mathrm{R}} \mathbb{Z}_q^n, \mathbf{u} \leftarrow_{\mathrm{R}} \mathcal{D}_{\Lambda_q^{\mathbf{P}}(\mathbf{A}),\sigma}\}$$

2.2 Sampling Algorithms

Given a matrix $\mathbf{F} := [\mathbf{A}\|\mathbf{B}]$ and a matrix $\mathbf{P}$, we would like to sample random low-norm matrices $\mathbf{U}$ such that $\mathbf{FU} = \mathbf{P}$. Specifically, we want to sample $\mathbf{U}$ from the distribution $\mathcal{D}_{\Lambda_q^{\mathbf{P}}(\mathbf{F}),\sigma}$. The following lemma tells us we could do so given either (1) a low-norm basis $\mathbf{T_A}$ of $\Lambda_q^\perp(\mathbf{A})$ using RightSample, or (2) a low-norm matrix $\mathbf{R}$ and an invertible matrix $\mathbf{H}$ such that $\mathbf{B} = \mathbf{HG} + \mathbf{AR}$ using LeftSample. We will use (1) in the actual scheme, and (2) in the security proof.

Lemma 6 ([2,9,13,18] and [7], Lemma 2.8)
There exist PPT *algorithms* RightSample *and* LeftSample *such that:*

RightSample$(\mathbf{A}, \mathbf{T_A}, \mathbf{B}, \mathbf{P}, \sigma)$:
Inputs: *full-rank matrices* $\mathbf{A}, \mathbf{B} \in \mathbb{Z}_q^{n \times m}$, *a basis* $\mathbf{T_A}$ *of* $\Lambda_q^{\perp}(\mathbf{A})$, *a matrix* $\mathbf{P} \in \mathbb{Z}_q^{n \times (\ell+n)}$ *and a Gaussian parameter* $\sigma = O(\|\mathbf{T_A}\|_{\mathrm{GS}})$.
Output: *a matrix* $\mathbf{U} \in \mathbb{Z}_q^{2m \times (\ell+n)}$ *whose distribution is statistically close to* $\mathcal{D}_{\Lambda_q^{\mathbf{P}}[\mathbf{A}\|\mathbf{B}], \sigma \cdot \omega(\sqrt{\log m})}$.

Remark 1. We can sample a short matrix $\mathbf{U} = \begin{pmatrix} \mathbf{U}_1 \\ \mathbf{U}_2 \end{pmatrix} \in \mathbb{Z}_q^{2m \times (\ell+k)}$ in the same

way that [2]. That is, we first sample the bottom part $\mathbf{U}_2 \in \mathbb{Z}_q^{m \times (\ell+k)}$ from $\mathcal{D}_{\mathbb{Z}_q^{m \times (\ell+k)}, \sigma \cdot \omega(\sqrt{\log n})}$ and then, we sample the top part $\mathbf{U}_1 \in \mathbb{Z}_q^{m \times (\ell+k)}$ from a distribution statistically close to $\mathcal{D}_{\Lambda_q^{\mathbf{P}-\mathbf{B}\mathbf{U}_2}(\mathbf{A}), \sigma \cdot \omega(\sqrt{\log m})}$, using $\mathbf{T_A}$.

LeftSample$(\mathbf{A}, \mathbf{R}, \mathbf{G}, \mathbf{H}, \mathbf{P}, \sigma)$:
Inputs: *a full-rank matrix* $\mathbf{A} \in \mathbb{Z}_q^{n \times m}$, *a matrix* $\mathbf{R} \in \mathbb{Z}_q^{m \times m}$, *a full-rank matrix* $\mathbf{G} \in \mathbb{Z}_q^{n \times m}$ *as defined in Lemma 4, an invertible matrix* $\mathbf{H} \in \mathbb{Z}_q^{n \times n}$, *a matrix* $\mathbf{P} \in \mathbb{Z}_q^{n \times (\ell+n)}$ *and a Gaussian parameter* $\sigma = O(\|\mathbf{R}\|_2)$.
Output: *a matrix* $\mathbf{U} \in \mathbb{Z}_q^{2m \times (\ell+n)}$ *whose distribution is statistically close to* $\mathcal{D}_{\Lambda_q^{\mathbf{P}}[\mathbf{A}\|\mathbf{H}\mathbf{G}+\mathbf{A}\mathbf{R}], \sigma \cdot \omega(\sqrt{\log m})}$.

2.3   Predicate Encryption

A predicate encryption scheme for a predicate $\mathsf{P}(\cdot, \cdot)$ consists of four algorithms (Setup, Enc, KeyGen, Dec):

Setup$(1^n, \mathcal{X}, \mathcal{Y}, \mathcal{M}) \rightarrow (\mathsf{mpk}, \mathsf{msk})$. The setup algorithm gets as input the security parameter n, the attribute universe $\mathcal{X}$, the predicate universe $\mathcal{Y}$, and the message space $\mathcal{M}$.

Enc$(\mathsf{mpk}, x, m) \rightarrow \mathsf{ct}$. The encryption algorithm gets as input mpk, an attribute $x \in \mathcal{X}$ and a message $m \in \mathcal{M}$. It outputs a ciphertext ct.

KeyGen$(\mathsf{mpk}, \mathsf{msk}, y) \rightarrow \mathsf{sk}_y$. The key generation algorithm gets as input msk and a value $y \in \mathcal{Y}$. It outputs a secret key sk_y. Note that y is public given sk_y.

Dec$(\mathsf{mpk}, \mathsf{sk}_y, \mathsf{ct}) \rightarrow m$. The decryption algorithm gets as input sk_y and a ciphertext ct. It outputs a message m.

Correctness. We require that for all $(x, y) \in \mathcal{X} \times \mathcal{Y}$ such that $\mathsf{P}(x, y) = 1$ and all $m \in \mathcal{M}$,

$$\Pr[\mathsf{ct} \leftarrow \mathsf{Enc}(\mathsf{mpk}, x, m); \mathsf{Dec}(\mathsf{sk}_y, \mathsf{ct}) = m)] = 1 - \mathrm{negl}(n),$$

where the probability is taken over $(\mathsf{mpk}, \mathsf{msk}) \leftarrow \mathsf{Setup}(1^n, \mathcal{X}, \mathcal{Y}, \mathcal{M})$ and the coins of Enc.

Security Model. For a stateful adversary $\mathcal{A}$, we define the advantage function

$$
\mathsf{Adv}_{\mathcal{A}}^{\mathrm{PE}}(n) := \Pr \left[\beta = \beta' :
\begin{array}{l}
(x_0^*, x_1^*) \leftarrow \mathcal{A}(1^\lambda); \\[4pt]
\beta \leftarrow_{\mathrm{R}} \{0,1\}; \\[4pt]
(\mathsf{mpk}, \mathsf{msk}) \leftarrow \mathsf{Setup}(1^n, \mathcal{X}, \mathcal{Y}, \mathcal{M}); \\[4pt]
(m_0, m_1) \leftarrow \mathcal{A}^{\mathsf{KeyGen}(\mathsf{msk}, \cdot)}(\mathsf{mpk}); \\[4pt]
\mathsf{ct} \leftarrow \mathsf{Enc}(\mathsf{mpk}, x_\beta, m_\beta); \\[4pt]
\beta' \leftarrow \mathcal{A}^{\mathsf{KeyGen}(\mathsf{msk}, \cdot)}(\mathsf{ct})
\end{array}
\right] - \frac{1}{2}
$$

with the restriction that all queries y that $\mathcal{A}$ makes to $\mathsf{KeyGen}(\mathsf{msk}, \cdot)$ satisfies $\mathsf{P}(x_0^*, y) = \mathsf{P}(x_1^*, y) = 0$ (that is, sk_y does not decrypt ct). A predicate encryption scheme is *selectively secure and weakly attribute-hiding*[1] if for all PPT adversaries $\mathcal{A}$, the advantage $\mathsf{Adv}_{\mathcal{A}}^{\mathrm{PE}}(n)$ is a negligible function in n.

3 Reductions Amongst Predicates

3.1 AND-OR-EQ Predicate

In this section we state our general predicate, and exhibit the reductions from multi-dimensional subset queries and multi-dimensional range queries to the latter. This general predicate is symmetric (c.f. Lemma 11), which will allow us to obtain both ciphertext-policy and key-policy predicate encryption schemes in Section 4.

Disjunction of Equality Queries. Here, $\mathsf{P}_{\mathrm{OR\text{-}EQ}} : \mathbb{Z}_q^\ell \times \mathbb{Z}_q^\ell \to \{0,1\}$, and

$$
\mathsf{P}_{\mathrm{OR\text{-}EQ}}(\mathbf{x}, \mathbf{y}) = 1 \text{ iff } \bigvee_{i=1}^{\ell} (x_i = y_i).
$$

We generalize the previous predicate to a multi-dimensional setting as follows $\mathsf{P}_{\mathrm{AND\text{-}OR\text{-}EQ}} : \mathbb{Z}_q^{D \times \ell} \times \mathbb{Z}_q^{D \times \ell} \to \{0,1\}$, and:

$$
\mathsf{P}_{\mathrm{AND\text{-}OR\text{-}EQ}}(\mathbf{X}, \mathbf{Y}) = 1 \text{ iff } \bigwedge_{i=1}^{D} \bigvee_{j=1}^{\ell} (X_{i,j} = Y_{i,j})
$$

We impose a so-called "at most one" promise on the input domains of the predicate for our predicate encryption scheme in Section 4. This technical property is required for our lattice-based instantiations (see Remark 3 in Section 4) and also implicitly used in prior pairing-based ones. We define

---

[1] In an adaptively secure scheme, the adversary specifies (x_0^*, x_1^*) after seeing mpk and making key queries. In a fully attribute-hiding scheme, the adversary is allowed key queries y for which $\mathsf{P}(x_0^*, y) = \mathsf{P}(x_1^*, y) = 1$, in which case the challenge messages m_0, m_1 must be equal.

the predicate $P_{\text{AT MOST ONE}} : \mathbb{Z}_q^\ell \times \mathbb{Z}_q^\ell \to \{0,1\}$ and its multi-dimensional variant $P_{\text{AND AT MOST ONE}} : \mathbb{Z}_q^{D \times \ell} \times \mathbb{Z}_q^{D \times \ell} \to \{0,1\}$ by:

$$P_{\text{AT MOST ONE}}(\mathbf{x}, \mathbf{y}) = 1 \text{ iff there exists at most one } j \in [\ell], x_j = y_j$$

$$P_{\text{AND AT MOST ONE}}(\mathbf{X}, \mathbf{Y}) = 1 \text{ iff } \forall i \in [D], \text{ there exists at most one } j \in [\ell] \text{ s.t. } X_{i,j} = Y_{i,j}$$

We require that the input domains $\mathcal{X}, \mathcal{Y} \subseteq \mathbb{Z}_q^{D \times \ell}$ for $P_{\text{AND-OR-EQ}}$ satisfy the "at most one" promise, namely for all $\mathbf{X} \in \mathcal{X}, \mathbf{Y} \in \mathcal{Y}$,

$$P_{\text{AND AT MOST ONE}}(\mathbf{X}, \mathbf{Y}) = 1$$

Indeed, the promise is satisfied by all of our reductions in this section.

3.2 Multi-dimensional Subset Queries

Predicate (ciphertext-policy). Here, $P_{\text{CP-SUBSET}} : \{0,1\}^{D \times T} \times [T]^D \to \{0,1\}$ and

$$P_{\text{CP-SUBSET}}(\mathbf{W}, \mathbf{z}) = 1 \text{ iff } \bigwedge_{i=1}^{D} W_{i,z_i} = 1$$

For each dimension $i \in [D]$, the i'th row of $\mathbf{W}$ is the characteristic vector of a subset of $[T]$.

Reducing $P_{\text{cp-subset}}$ to $P_{\text{and-or-eq}}$. We map $(\mathbf{W}, \mathbf{z}) \in \{0,1\}^{D \times T} \times [T]^D$ to $(\widetilde{\mathbf{W}}, \widetilde{\mathbf{Z}}) \in \mathbb{Z}_q^{D \times T} \times \mathbb{Z}_q^{D \times T}$ where

- $\widetilde{\mathbf{W}}$ is the matrix $\mathbf{W}$ where zeros are replaced by -1, that is, for all $(i,j) \in [D] \times [T]$, $\widetilde{W}_{i,j} = 1$ if $W_{i,j} = 1$, and $\widetilde{W}_{i,j} = -1$ otherwise. (We need this modification in order to satisfy the "at most one" promise.)
- $\widetilde{\mathbf{Z}} \in \mathbb{Z}_q^{D \times T}$ denotes the matrix whose i'th row is $\mathbf{e}_{z_i} \in \mathbb{Z}_q^{1 \times T}$, where $(\mathbf{e}_1, \ldots, \mathbf{e}_T)$ denotes the standard basis of $\mathbb{Z}^{1 \times T}$.
  For instance, we map $((0,1,1), 2)$ to $((-1,1,1), (0,1,0))$.

We can check that the following lemma holds:

Lemma 7 ($P_{\text{cp-subset}}$ to $P_{\text{and-or-eq}}$) *Let* $(\mathbf{W}, \mathbf{z}) \in \{0,1\}^{D \times T} \times [T]^D$, *and* $(\widetilde{\mathbf{W}}, \widetilde{\mathbf{Z}}) \in \mathbb{Z}_q^{D \times T} \times \mathbb{Z}_q^{D \times T}$ *defined as above.*

- $P_{\text{CP-SUBSET}}(\mathbf{W}, \mathbf{z}) = 1$ *iff* $P_{\text{AND-OR-EQ}}(\widetilde{\mathbf{W}}, \widetilde{\mathbf{Z}}) = 1$
- $P_{\text{AND AT MOST ONE}}(\widetilde{\mathbf{W}}, \widetilde{\mathbf{Z}}) = 1$

3.3 Multi-dimensional Range Queries

Predicate (key-policy). Here, $P_{\text{KP-RANGE}} : [T]^D \times \mathcal{I}(T)^D \to \{0,1\}$ and $P_{\text{KP-RANGE}}(\mathbf{z}, \mathbf{I}) = 1$ iff $\bigwedge_{j=1}^{D} (z_j \in I_j)$, where $\mathcal{I}(T)$ denotes the set of all intervals of $[T]$.

We show how to reduce $P_{\text{KP-RANGE}}$ to $P_{\text{AND-OR-EQ}}$, which involves rewriting points and intervals as vectors.

Writing Points and Intervals as Vectors. For simplicity, we write t for $\lceil \log T \rceil$. In order to realize the "at most one" promise, we need to decompose intervals into disjoint sub-intervals where each sub-interval contains all the points with some fixed prefix, e.g. $[010, 110]$ can be written as $[010, 011] \cup [100, 101] \cup [110, 110]$. Indeed, any interval in $[T]$ can be partitioned into at most $2t$ disjoint sub-intervals with this property [10, Lemma 10.10].[2] In addition, we can ensure that there are exactly $2t$ sub-intervals by padding with empty intervals ε (using empty intervals ensures that no point ever lies in more than one of these $2t$ sub-intervals).

Lemma 8 (interval to vector [10]). *There is an efficient* PPT *algorithm* IntVec *that on input* $I \subseteq [T]$ *outputs* $(w_1, w_2, \ldots, w_{2t}) \in \left(\{0,1\}^* \cup \{\varepsilon\} \right)^{2t}$, *where* $t := \lceil \log T \rceil$, *with the following properties:*
  - *for each* $i = 1, \ldots, t$, *we have* $w_{2i-1}, w_{2i} \in \{0,1\}^i \cup \{\varepsilon\}$;
  - *for all* $z \in [T]$, *we have* $z \in I$ *iff one of* $w_1, \ldots, w_{2t}$ *is a prefix of* z;
  - *for all* $z \in [T]$, *at most one of* $w_1, \ldots, w_{2t}$ *is a prefix of* z.

Here, ε *is not a prefix of any string.*

For instance, $\mathsf{IntVec}([010, 110]) = (\varepsilon, \varepsilon, 01, 10, 110, \varepsilon)$.

Remark 2 (Hashing bit strings into $\mathbb{Z}_q$). *We map* $\{0,1\}^t \cup \{\varepsilon\}$ *where* $t := \lceil \log T \rceil$ *into* $\mathbb{Z}_q$ *in the straight-forward way, which requires that* $q \geq T + 1$. *We can handle also larger* T *by using matrices over* $\mathbb{Z}_q$ *à la [1, Section 5].*

Now we give the description of algorithm PtVec, used to map points to vectors.

PtVec: On input $z \in [T]$, output $(v_1, \ldots, v_{2t}) \in \mathbb{Z}_q^{2t}$, where $v_{2i-1} = v_{2i} :=$ i-bit prefix of z, $i = 1, \ldots, t$.
For instance, $\mathsf{PtVec}(011) = (0, 0, 01, 01, 011, 011)$.

Lemma 9. *For any point* $z \in [T]$ *and any interval* $I \subseteq [T]$,
  - $z \in I$ *iff* $\mathsf{P}_{\text{OR-EQ}}(\mathsf{PtVec}(z), \mathsf{IntVec}(I)) = 1$
  - $\mathsf{P}_{\text{AT MOST ONE}}(\mathsf{PtVec}(z), \mathsf{IntVec}(I)) = 1$.

Lemma 9 follows readily from Lemma 8.

Reducing $\mathsf{P}_{\text{kp-range}}$ to $\mathsf{P}_{\text{and-or-eq}}$. We map $(\mathbf{z}, \mathbf{I})$ to $(\mathsf{PtVec}^D(\mathbf{z}), \mathsf{IntVec}^D(\mathbf{I}))$ where
  - $\mathsf{PtVec}^D(\mathbf{z}) \in \mathbb{Z}_q^{D \times 2t}$ denotes the matrix whose i'th row is $\mathsf{PtVec}(z_i)$
  - $\mathsf{IntVec}^D(\mathbf{I}) \in \mathbb{Z}_q^{D \times 2t}$ denotes the matrix whose j'th row is $\mathsf{IntVec}(I_j)$

Lemma 10 ($\mathsf{P}_{\text{kp-range}}$ to $\mathsf{P}_{\text{and-or-eq}}$). *For all* $\mathbf{z} \in [T]^D$ *and* $\mathbf{I} \subseteq (\mathcal{I}[T])^D$,
  - $\mathsf{P}_{\text{KP-RANGE}}(\mathbf{z}, \mathbf{I}) = 1$ *iff* $\mathsf{P}_{\text{AND-OR-EQ}}(\mathsf{PtVec}^D(\mathbf{z}), \mathsf{IntVec}^D(\mathbf{I})) = 1$
  - $\mathsf{P}_{\text{AND AT MOST ONE}}(\mathsf{PtVec}^D(\mathbf{z}), \mathsf{IntVec}^D(\mathbf{I})) = 1$

Lemma 10 follows readily from Lemma 9, applied to each dimension $i \in [D]$.

---

[2] See http://en.wikipedia.org/wiki/Segment_tree for a visualization.

Predicate (ciphertext-policy). Here, $\mathsf{P}_{\text{CP-RANGE}} : \mathcal{I}(T)^D \times [T]^D \to \{0,1\}$ and

$$\mathsf{P}_{\text{CP-RANGE}}(\mathbf{I}, \mathbf{z}) = 1 \text{ iff } \bigwedge_{j=1}^{D} (z_j \in I_j)$$

The predicates $\mathsf{P}_{\text{OR-EQ}}$ and $\mathsf{P}_{\text{AT MOST ONE}}$ are symmetric:

Lemma 11 (Symmetry of $\mathsf{P}_{\text{or-eq}}$ and $\mathsf{P}_{\text{at most one}}$). *For all* $\mathbf{x}, \mathbf{y} \in \mathbb{Z}_q^\ell$, *we have:*

- $\mathsf{P}_{\text{OR-EQ}}(\mathbf{x}, \mathbf{y}) = 1 \iff \mathsf{P}_{\text{OR-EQ}}(\mathbf{y}, \mathbf{x}) = 1$
- $\mathsf{P}_{\text{AT MOST ONE}}(\mathbf{x}, \mathbf{y}) = 1 \iff \mathsf{P}_{\text{AT MOST ONE}}(\mathbf{y}, \mathbf{x}) = 1$

Thanks to this symmetry, we can reduce $\mathsf{P}_{\text{CP-RANGE}}$ to $\mathsf{P}_{\text{AND-OR-EQ}}$ in the same way we did for $\mathsf{P}_{\text{KP-RANGE}}$.

Reducing $\mathsf{P}_{\text{cp-range}}$ to $\mathsf{P}_{\text{and-or-eq}}$. Following the previous reduction, we map $(\mathbf{I}, \mathbf{z})$ to $(\mathsf{IntVec}^D(\mathbf{I}), \mathsf{PtVec}^D(\mathbf{z}))$.

Lemma 12 ($\mathsf{P}_{\text{cp-range}}$ to $\mathsf{P}_{\text{and-or-eq}}$). *For all* $\boldsymbol{I} \subseteq (\mathcal{I}[T])^D$ *and* $\mathbf{z} \in [T]^D$,

- $\mathsf{P}_{\text{CP-RANGE}}(\boldsymbol{I}, \mathbf{z}) = 1$ *iff* $\mathsf{P}_{\text{AND-OR-EQ}}(\mathsf{IntVec}^D(\boldsymbol{I}), \mathsf{PtVec}^D(\mathbf{z})) = 1$
- $\mathsf{P}_{\text{AND AT MOST ONE}}(\mathsf{IntVec}^D(\boldsymbol{I}), \mathsf{PtVec}^D(\mathbf{z})) = 1$.

Lemma 12 follows from Lemma 10 and Lemma 11.

4   Predicate Encryption for AND-OR-EQ

Here we describe our predicate encryption scheme for the AND-OR-EQ predicate defined in Section 3.1, selectively secure and lattice-based. Recall that $\mathsf{P}_{\text{AND-OR-EQ}} : \mathbb{Z}_q^{D \times \ell} \times \mathbb{Z}_q^{D \times \ell} \to \{0,1\}$, and

$$\mathsf{P}_{\text{AND-OR-EQ}}(\mathbf{X}, \mathbf{Y}) = 1 \text{ iff } \bigwedge_{i=1}^{D} \bigvee_{j=1}^{\ell} (X_{i,j} = Y_{i,j})$$

The security of our scheme relies on the fact the ciphertext attributes and secret key predicates come from a restricted domain $\mathcal{X}, \mathcal{Y} \subseteq \mathbb{Z}_q^{D \times \ell}$ satisfying the "at most one" promise, namely for all $\mathbf{X} \in \mathcal{X}, \mathbf{Y} \in \mathcal{Y}$,

$$\mathsf{P}_{\text{AND AT MOST ONE}}(\mathbf{X}, \mathbf{Y}) = 1$$

Indeed, the promise is satisfied by all of our reductions in Section 3.1.

Overview. We begin with the special case $D = 1$. Given an attribute matrix $\mathbf{x} \in \mathbb{Z}_q^{1 \times \ell}$, the ciphertext is an LWE sample corresponding to a matrix of the form

$$[\mathbf{A}\|\mathbf{A}_1 + x_1\mathbf{G}\|\cdots\|\mathbf{A}_\ell + x_\ell\mathbf{G}]$$

where $\mathbf{A}$, the $\mathbf{A}_i$'s and $\mathbf{G}$ are publicly known matrices, and the message is masked using an LWE sample corresponding to a public matrix $\mathbf{P}$. The secret key corresponding to $\mathbf{y} \in \mathbb{Z}_q^{1\times\ell}$ is a collection of ℓ short matrices $\mathbf{U}_1,\ldots,\mathbf{U}_\ell$ such that for all $j \in [\ell]$,

$$[\mathbf{A}\|\mathbf{A}_j + y_j\mathbf{G}]\mathbf{U}_j = \mathbf{P}$$

To understand how decryption works, let us first suppose that there exists a unique j such that $x_j = y_j$ and that the decryptor knows j; then, the decryptor can use $\mathbf{U}_j$ to recover the plaintext. However, since the decryptor does not know $\mathbf{x}$, he will try to decrypt the ciphertext using each of $\mathbf{U}_1,\ldots,\mathbf{U}_\ell$. We will also need to pad the plaintext with redundant zeros so that the decryptor can identify the correct plaintext.

To establish security with respect to some selective challenge $\mathbf{x}^*$, we will need to simulate secret keys for all $\mathbf{y}$ such that $x_j^* \neq y_j$ for all $j \in [\ell]$. We can then simulate $\mathbf{U}_j$ using an "all-but-one" simulation (while puncturing at x_j^*) exactly as in prior IBE schemes in [1]. In order to establish weak attribute-hiding, we adopt a similar strategy to that for inner product encryption in [4]: roughly speaking, we will show that the challenge ciphertext is computational indistinguishable from an encryption of a random plaintext message under a random attribute $\mathbf{x}$.

Higher Dimensions. Given an attribute matrix $\mathbf{X} \in \mathbb{Z}_q^{D\times\ell}$, the ciphertext is an LWE sample corresponding to a matrix of the form

$$[\mathbf{A}\|\mathbf{A}_{1,1} + X_{1,1}\mathbf{G}\|\cdots\|\mathbf{A}_{1,\ell} + X_{1,\ell}\mathbf{G}\|\mathbf{A}_{2,1} + X_{2,1}\mathbf{G}\|\cdots\|\mathbf{A}_{D,\ell} + X_{D,\ell}\mathbf{G}]$$

The secret key corresponding to $\mathbf{Y} \in \mathbb{Z}_q^{D\times\ell}$ is a collection of $D \cdot \ell$ short matrices $\mathbf{U}_{1,1},\ldots,\mathbf{U}_{D,\ell}$ such that for $i \in [D]$, $j \in [\ell]$:

$$[\mathbf{A}\|\mathbf{A}_{i,j} + Y_{i,j}\mathbf{G}]\mathbf{U}_{i,j} = \mathbf{P}_i$$

where $\mathbf{P}_1,\ldots,\mathbf{P}_D$ is an additive secret-sharing of $\mathbf{P}$.

For correctness, observe that if there exist indices $(j_1,\ldots,j_D) \in [\ell]^D$ such that for all $i \in [D]$ $X_{i,j_i} = Y_{i,j_i}$ then the decryptor can use $\mathbf{U}_{1,j_1},\cdots,\mathbf{U}_{D,j_D}$ to recover the plaintext. As with the case $D = 1$, the decryptor will need to enumerate over all $(j_1,\ldots,j_D) \in [\ell]^D$.

To simulate secret keys for $\mathbf{Y}$ with respect to some selective challenge $\mathbf{X}^*$, we first fix i^* such that $X_{i^*,j}^* \neq Y_{i^*,j}$ for all $j \in [\ell]$. Without loss of generality, suppose $i^* = 1$, that is, for all $j \in [\ell]$, $X_{1,j}^* \neq Y_{1,j}$.

Using the "at most one" promise on $\mathbf{X}$ and $\mathbf{Y}$, we know that for all $i \geq 2$, we have $X_{i,j}^* = Y_{i,j}$ for at most one $j \in [\ell]$, which we call j_i. That is, there exists a vector of indices $(j_2,\ldots,j_D) \in [\ell]^{D-1}$ such that for all $i \geq 2$ and all $j \neq j_i$, we have $X_{i,j}^* \neq Y_{i,j}$. We then proceed as follows:

- Sample random short matrices $\mathbf{U}_{2,j_2},\ldots,\mathbf{U}_{D,j_D}$, which in turn determines the shares $\mathbf{P}_2,\ldots,\mathbf{P}_D$.

- Use an all-but-one simulation strategy to sample the short matrices $\mathbf{U}_{i,j}$, for all $i \geq 2$, and $j \neq j_i$.
- Define $\mathbf{P}_1 := \mathbf{P} - \sum_{i=2}^{D} \mathbf{P}_i$ and use an all-but-one simulation strategy to sample the remaining short matrices in the secret key.

Note that the construction relies crucially on the "at most one" promise on $\mathbf{X}$ and $\mathbf{Y}$. In fact, the scheme given in Section 4.1 is insecure if this promise is not fulfilled, that is, there is a PPT adversary that wins the game defined in Section 2.3 with non negligible advantage. The attack goes as follows. Suppose that the adversary holds a secret key for $\mathbf{Y} \in \mathbb{Z}_q^{D \times \ell}$ such that $\mathsf{P}_{\text{AND-OR-EQ}}(\mathbf{X}, \mathbf{Y}) = 0$ and $\mathsf{P}_{\text{AND AT MOST ONE}}(\mathbf{X}, \mathbf{Y}) = 0$. Since $\mathsf{P}_{\text{AND AT MOST ONE}}(\mathbf{X}, \mathbf{Y}) = 0$, for some dimension $i \in [D]$, there are at least two indices $j_1, j_2 \in [\ell]$ such that $X_{i,j_1} = Y_{i,j_1}$ and $X_{i,j_2} = Y_{i,j_2}$, and therefore, both short matrices $\mathbf{U}_{i,j_1}$ and $\mathbf{U}_{i,j_2}$ allow to recover the same LWE sample corresponding to the matrix $\mathbf{P}_i$, up to some error. When $X_{i,j_2} \neq Y_{i,j_2}$ however, $\mathbf{U}_{i,j_2}$ with the corresponding (i, j_2) component of the ciphertext only gives a uniformly random vector. Therefore, the fact that $\mathbf{U}_{i,j_1}$ and $\mathbf{U}_{i,j_2}$ both decrypts to (almost) the same LWE sample tells the adversary that $X_{i,j_1} = Y_{i,j_1}$ and $X_{i,j_2} = Y_{i,j_2}$ with high probability, contradicting the fact that the scheme is weakly attribute hiding. This induces an attack whose running time is polynomial in the security parameter.

4.1 Construction

Let $n \in \mathbb{N}$ be the security parameter. Let the attribute space $\mathcal{X}$ and predicate space $\mathcal{Y}$ be subsets of $\mathbb{Z}_q^{D \times \ell}$ satisfying the "at most one" promise. Let $q = q(n)$, $m = m(n, \ell, D)$ and $\chi_{\max} = \chi_{\max}(n, q, \ell, D)$ be positive integers. Let $\sigma = \sigma(n, q, \ell, D)$ be a Gaussian parameter.

Setup$(1^n, \mathcal{X}, \mathcal{Y}, \mathcal{M})$: On inputs the security parameter n, $\mathcal{X} \subseteq \mathbb{Z}_q^{D \times \ell}$, $\mathcal{Y} \subseteq \mathbb{Z}_q^{D \times \ell}$ and $\mathcal{M} := \{0, 1\}^k$, do:

- Pick $(\mathbf{A}, \mathbf{T_A}) \leftarrow \mathsf{TrapGen}(1^n, 1^m, q)$.
- For all $i \in [D]$ and all $j \in [\ell]$, pick $\mathbf{A}_{i,j} \leftarrow_{\text{R}} \mathbb{Z}_q^{n \times m}$.
- Pick $\mathbf{P} \leftarrow_{\text{R}} \mathbb{Z}_q^{n \times (k+n)}$.
- Compute $(\mathbf{G}, \mathbf{T_G})$ as defined in Lemma 4.
- Output $\mathsf{mpk} := (\mathbf{P}, \mathbf{A}, \mathbf{A}_{1,1}, \ldots, \mathbf{A}_{D,\ell}, \mathbf{G}, \mathbf{T_G})$ and $\mathsf{msk} := \mathbf{T_A}$

Enc$(\mathsf{mpk}, \mathbf{X}, \mathbf{b})$: On input mpk, $\mathbf{X} \in \mathcal{X}$ and $\mathbf{b} \in \{0, 1\}^k$, do:

- Pick $\mathbf{s} \leftarrow_{\text{R}} \mathbb{Z}_q^n$, $\mathbf{e} \leftarrow_{\text{R}} \chi^m$, and compute $\mathbf{c}_0 := \mathbf{s}^\top \mathbf{A} + \mathbf{e}^\top$.
- For all $i \in [D]$ and all $j \in [\ell]$, do:
  - Pick $\mathbf{R}_{i,j} \leftarrow \{-1, 1\}^{m \times m}$.
  - Compute $\mathbf{c}_{i,j} := \mathbf{s}^\top (\mathbf{A}_{i,j} + X_{i,j} \mathbf{G}) + \mathbf{e}^\top \mathbf{R}_{i,j}$.
- Set $\mathbf{b}' := (\mathbf{b}, 0, \ldots, 0) \in \{0, 1\}^{k+n}$, pick $\mathbf{e}' \leftarrow_{\text{R}} \chi^{k+n}$, and compute $\mathbf{c}_f := \mathbf{s}^\top \mathbf{P} + \mathbf{e}'^\top + \mathbf{b}'^\top \cdot \lfloor q/2 \rfloor$.
- Output $\mathsf{ct} := (\mathbf{c}_0, \mathbf{c}_{1,1}, \ldots, \mathbf{c}_{D,\ell}, \mathbf{c}_f)$

KeyGen$(\mathsf{mpk}, \mathsf{msk}, \mathbf{Y})$: On input the public parameters mpk, the master secret key msk, and a predicate matrix $\mathbf{Y} \in \mathcal{Y}$, do:

- Secret share $\mathbf{P}$ as $\{\mathbf{P}_i, i \in [D]\}$, such that $\sum_{i=1}^{D} \mathbf{P}_i = \mathbf{P}$.
- For all $i \in [D]$ and all $j \in [\ell]$:
  Sample a short matrix $\mathbf{U}_{i,j} \in \mathbb{Z}_q^{2m \times (k+n)}$ such that $[\mathbf{A} \| \mathbf{A}_{i,j} + Y_{i,j}\mathbf{G}]\mathbf{U}_{i,j} = \mathbf{P}_i$ using
  RightSample$(\mathbf{A}, \mathbf{T_A}, \mathbf{A}_{i,j} + Y_{i,j}\mathbf{G}, \mathbf{P}_i, \sigma)$ with $\sigma = O(\sqrt{n \log q})$.
- output the secret key $\mathsf{sk}_\mathbf{Y} = (\mathbf{U}_{1,1}, \ldots, \mathbf{U}_{D,\ell})$

Dec(mpk, $\mathsf{sk}_\mathbf{Y}$, ct): On input the public parameters mpk, a secret key $\mathsf{sk}_\mathbf{Y} = (\mathbf{U}_{1,1}, \ldots, \mathbf{U}_{D,\ell})$ for a predicate matrix $\mathbf{Y}$, and a ciphertext ct $= (\mathbf{c}_0, \mathbf{c}_{1,1}, \ldots, \mathbf{c}_{D,\ell}, \mathbf{c}_f)$, do:

- For all $(j_1, \ldots, j_D) \in [\ell]^D$, compute $\mathbf{d} := \mathbf{c}_f - \sum_{i=1}^{D} [\mathbf{c}_0 \| \mathbf{c}_{i,j_i}]\mathbf{U}_{i,j_i} \mod q$.

- If $\left\lfloor \frac{\mathbf{d}}{q/2} \right\rceil \in \{0,1\}^k \times 0^n$, then output the first k bits of $\left\lfloor \frac{\mathbf{d}}{q/2} \right\rceil$. For any $z \in [0,1]$, we denote by $\lfloor z \rceil$ the closest integer to z.
- Otherwise, abort.

Running Time. The running times are:

- $O(D \cdot \ell \cdot \text{poly}(n))$ for encryption;
- $O(D \cdot \ell \cdot \text{poly}(n))$ for key generation;
- $O(\ell^D \cdot \text{poly}(n))$ for decryption.

The above numbers take into account matrix multiplications and additions. When done naively, the above Dec algorithm takes $O(D \cdot \ell^D \cdot \text{poly}(n))$ time. However, if one saves the intermediate results $[\mathbf{c}_0 \| \mathbf{c}_{i,j}]\mathbf{U}_{i,j}$ for all $(i,j) \in [D] \times [\ell]$, one can do it in $O(\ell^D \cdot \text{poly}(n))$ time.

4.2 Correctness

Lemma 13. *Suppose that* $\chi_{\max}$ *is such that*

$$\chi_{\max} \leq q/4 \cdot \left(1 + D \cdot (1 + 20\sqrt{m}) \cdot s \cdot 2m\right)^{-1}$$

where $s = \sigma \cdot \omega(\sqrt{\log n})$. *Let* $(\mathbf{X}, \mathbf{Y}) \in \mathcal{X} \times \mathcal{Y}$ *such that* $\mathsf{P}_{\text{AND-OR-EQ}}(\mathbf{X}, \mathbf{Y}) = 1$.
Let $\mathsf{sk}_\mathbf{Y} = (\mathbf{U}_{1,1}, \ldots, \mathbf{U}_{D,\ell}) \leftarrow \mathsf{KeyGen}(mpk, msk, \mathbf{Y})$
and ct $= (\mathbf{c}_0, \ldots, \mathbf{c}_f) \leftarrow \mathsf{Enc}(mpk, \mathbf{X}, \mathbf{b})$
With overwhelming probability in n, *Dec does not abort and outputs* $\mathbf{b}$.

Proof. Recall that Dec computes $\mathbf{d}$ for all $(j_1, \ldots, j_D) \in [\ell]^D$. We consider two cases:

Case 1: $\forall i, X_{i,j_i} = Y_{i,j_i}$. We show that with overwhelming probability in n, $\left\lfloor \frac{\mathbf{d}}{q/2} \right\rceil = (\mathbf{b}, 0, \ldots, 0) := \mathbf{b}'$.
For all $i \in [D]$,

$$[\mathbf{A} \| \mathbf{A}_{i,j_i} + X_{i,j_i}\mathbf{G}]\mathbf{U}_{i,j_i} = \mathbf{P}_i \text{ thus } \sum_{i=1}^{D}[\mathbf{A} \| \mathbf{A}_{i,j_i} + X_{i,j_i}\mathbf{G}]\mathbf{U}_{i,j_i} = \mathbf{P}$$

This implies

$$\sum_{i=1}^{D}[\mathbf{c}_0\|\mathbf{c}_{i,j_i}]\mathbf{U}_{i,j_i} \approx \sum_{i=1}^{D}\mathbf{s}^\top[\mathbf{A}\|\mathbf{A}_{i,j_i}+X_{i,j_i}\mathbf{G}]\mathbf{U}_{i,j_i} = \mathbf{s}^\top\mathbf{P} \approx \mathbf{c}_f - \mathbf{b}'^\top\cdot\lfloor q/2\rfloor$$

and thus $\mathbf{d} \approx \mathbf{b}'\cdot\lfloor q/2\rfloor$. To obtain $\left\lceil\frac{\mathbf{d}}{q/2}\right\rceil = \mathbf{b}'$, it suffices to bound the error term and show that

$$\left\|\mathbf{e}'^\top - \sum_{i=1}^{D}(\mathbf{e}^\top\|\mathbf{e}^\top\mathbf{R}_{i,j_i})\mathbf{U}_{i,j_i}\right\|_\infty < q/4.$$

We know that $\|\mathbf{e}'^\top\|_\infty \le \chi_{\max}$. In addition, for all $i \in [D]$,

$$\left\|(\mathbf{e}^\top\|\mathbf{e}^\top\mathbf{R}_{i,j_i})\mathbf{U}_{i,j_i}\right\|_\infty \le \left\|(\mathbf{e}^\top\|\mathbf{e}^\top\mathbf{R}_{i,j_i})\right\|\cdot\left\|\mathbf{U}_{i,j_i}\right\| \le \left(\|\mathbf{e}\|+\|\mathbf{R}_{i,j_i}\|_2\cdot\|\mathbf{e}\|\right)\cdot\left\|\mathbf{U}_{i,j_i}\right\|$$

By Lemma 6, $\|\mathbf{U}_{i,j_i}\| \le \sigma\cdot\omega(\sqrt{\log n})\cdot\sqrt{2m}$ and by Lemma 2, $\|\mathbf{R}_{i,j_i}\|_2 \le 20\sqrt{m}$. Combining these bounds, we obtain

$$\left\|\mathbf{e}'^\top - \sum_{i=1}^{D}(\mathbf{e}^\top\|\mathbf{e}^\top\mathbf{R}_{i,j_i})\mathbf{U}_{i,j_i}\right\|_\infty \le \chi_{\max}(1+D(1+20\sqrt{m})\cdot\sigma\cdot\omega(\sqrt{\log m})\sqrt{2m})$$

We will set the parameters in Section 4.4 so that the quantity on the right is bounded by $q/4$.

Case 2: $\exists i^*, X_{i^*,j_{i^*}} \ne Y_{i^*,j_{i^*}}$. We show that the computed value $\mathbf{d}$ has a distribution which is statistically close to uniform, and therefore the probability that the last n bits of $\left\lceil\frac{\mathbf{d}}{q/2}\right\rceil$ are all 0 is negligible in n.

By an analogous calculation to that in Case 1, we have:

$$\sum_{i=1}^{D}[\mathbf{A}\|\mathbf{A}_{i,j_i}+X_{i,j_i}\mathbf{G}]\mathbf{U}_{i,j_i} = \mathbf{P} + \sum_{i=1}^{D}[\mathbf{0}\|(X_{i,j_i}-Y_{i,j_i})\mathbf{G}]\mathbf{U}_{i,j_i}$$

We know that there exists some $i^* \in [D]$ such that $X_{i^*,j_{i^*}} \ne Y_{i^*,j_{i^*}}$, and we focus on

$$\left[\mathbf{0}^\top\|\mathbf{s}^\top(X_{i^*,j_{i^*}}-Y_{i^*,j_{i^*}})\mathbf{G}\right]\mathbf{U}_{i^*,j_{i^*}}$$

By Remark 1, we know that the bottom part $\mathbf{U}_2 \in \mathbb{Z}_q^{m\times(k+n)}$ of $\mathbf{U}_{i^*,j_{i^*}}$ is sampled from $\mathcal{D}_{\mathbb{Z}_q^m,\sigma\cdot\omega(\sqrt{\log n})}$. Therefore, since $X_{i^*,j_{i^*}} - Y_{i^*,j_{i^*}} \ne 0$ and $\mathbf{G}$ is a full-rank matrix, by Lemma 5, we know that the distribution of $\mathbf{G}\mathbf{U}_2$ is indistinguishable from uniform over $\mathbb{Z}_q^{n\times(k+n)}$ and then, the entire sum is indistinguishable from uniform over $\mathbb{Z}_q^{k+n}$. Therefore,

$$\mathbf{d} = \mathbf{c}_f - \sum_{i=1}^{D}[\mathbf{c}_0\|\mathbf{c}_{i,j_i}]\mathbf{U}_{i,j_i} \mod q$$

is indistinguishable from uniform over $\mathbb{Z}_q^{k+n}$, and the probability that the last n bits of $\left\lceil\frac{\mathbf{d}}{q/2}\right\rceil$ are all 0 is negligible in n.

4.3   Proof of Security

Lemma 14. *For any adversary $\mathcal{A}$ on the predicate encryption scheme, there exists an adversary $\mathcal{B}$ on the LWE assumption whose running time is roughly the same as that of $\mathcal{A}$ and such that*

$$\mathsf{Adv}_{\mathcal{A}}^{\mathsf{PE}}(n) \leq \mathsf{Adv}_{\mathcal{B}}^{\mathsf{dLWE}_{n,m+n+k,q,\chi}} + \mathsf{negl}(n)$$

The proof follows via a series of games, analogous to those in [4]. We first define several auxiliary algorithms for generating the simulated ciphertexts and secret keys, upon which we can describe the games.

Auxiliary Algorithms. We introduce the following auxiliary algorithms:

$\widetilde{\mathsf{Setup}}(1^n, \mathcal{X}, \mathcal{Y}, \mathcal{M}, \mathbf{A}, \mathbf{P}, \mathbf{X}^*)$: on a security parameter n, an attribute space $\mathcal{X} \subseteq \mathbb{Z}_q^{D \times \ell}$, a predicate space $\mathcal{Y} \subseteq \mathbb{Z}_q^{D \times \ell}$ satisfying the "at most one promise", a message space $\mathcal{M} := \{0,1\}^k$, a matrix $\mathbf{A} \in \mathbb{Z}_q^{n \times m}$, a matrix $\mathbf{P} \in \mathbb{Z}_q^{n \times (k+n)}$ and the challenge attribute matrix $\mathbf{X}^*$, do:

- Compute $(\mathbf{G}, \mathbf{T_G})$ as defined in Lemma 4.
- For all $i \in [D]$ and all $j \in [\ell]$, pick $\mathbf{R}_{i,j} \leftarrow \{-1,1\}^{m \times m}$ and set $\mathbf{A}_{i,j} := \mathbf{AR}_{i,j} - X_{i,j}^* \mathbf{G}$.
- Output $\mathsf{mpk} := (\mathbf{P}, \mathbf{A}, \mathbf{A}_{1,1}, \ldots, \mathbf{A}_{D,\ell}, \mathbf{G}, \mathbf{T_G})$ and
  $\widetilde{\mathsf{msk}} := (\mathbf{X}^*, \mathbf{R}_{1,1}, \cdots, \mathbf{R}_{D,\ell}, \mathbf{T_A})$

$\widetilde{\mathsf{Enc}}(\mathsf{mpk}, \mathbf{b}; \widetilde{\mathsf{msk}}, \mathbf{d}_0, \mathbf{d}_f)$: On input the public parameters mpk, a message $\mathbf{b} \in \{0,1\}^k$, the master secret key $\widetilde{\mathsf{msk}}$, and the extra inputs $\mathbf{d}_0 \in \mathbb{Z}_q^m$, $\mathbf{d}_f \in \mathbb{Z}_q^{k+n}$ do:

- Set $\mathbf{c}_0 := \mathbf{d}_0^{\mathsf{T}}$,
- For all $i \in [D]$ and all $j \in [\ell]$, compute $\mathbf{c}_{i,j} := \mathbf{d}_0^{\mathsf{T}} \mathbf{R}_{i,j}$,
- Compute $\mathbf{b}' := (\mathbf{b}, 0, \ldots, 0) \in \{0,1\}^{k+n}$, and set $\mathbf{c}_f := \mathbf{d}_f^{\mathsf{T}} + \mathbf{b}'^{\mathsf{T}} \lfloor q/2 \rfloor$.
- Output $(\mathbf{c}_0, \ldots, \mathbf{c}_f)$.

$\widetilde{\mathsf{KeyGen}}(\mathsf{mpk}, \widetilde{\mathsf{msk}}, \mathbf{Y}, \mathbf{X}^*)$: On input the public parameters mpk, the master secret key $\widetilde{\mathsf{msk}}$, a predicate matrix $\mathbf{Y}$ and the challenge attribute matrix $\mathbf{X}^*$ do:

- If $\mathsf{P}(\mathbf{X}^*, \mathbf{Y}) = 1$, abort.
- Otherwise, since $\mathsf{P}(\mathbf{X}^*, \mathbf{Y}) = 0$, there must exist a $i^* \in [D]$ such that for all $j \in [\ell]$, $X_{i^*,j}^* \neq Y_{i^*,j}$. By the "at most one" property, for all $i \in [D]$, there is at most one $j_i \in [\ell]$ such that $X_{i,j_i}^* = Y_{i,j_i}$.
  We proceed in three steps :
  1. First, for all $i \in [D] \setminus \{i^*\}$ we sample: $\mathbf{U}_{i,j_i} \leftarrow_{\mathsf{R}} \mathcal{D}_{\mathbb{Z}_q^{2m \times (k+n)}, \sigma \cdot \omega(\sqrt{\log n})}$ with $\sigma = O(\sqrt{n \log q})$ and set

$$\mathbf{P}_i := \left[\mathbf{A} \| \mathbf{AR}_{i,j_i}\right] \mathbf{U}_{i,j_i} \in \mathbb{Z}_q^{n \times (k+n)}$$

2. Next, we set $\mathbf{P}_{i^*}$ to be: $\mathbf{P}_{i^*} := \mathbf{P} - \sum_{i \neq i^*} \mathbf{P}_i$

3. We sample the remaining matrices as follows:

$$\mathbf{U}_{i,j} \leftarrow \mathsf{LeftSample}(\mathbf{A}, \mathbf{R}_{i,j}, \mathbf{G}, Y_{i,j} - X_{i,j}^*, \mathbf{P}_i, \sigma).$$

This is possible because $Y_{i,j} - X_{i,j}^* \neq 0$, whenever $i = i^*$ or whenever $j \neq j_i$.

- Output $(\mathbf{U}_{1,1}, \ldots, \mathbf{U}_{D,\ell})$.

Game Sequence. We present a series of games. We write Adv_{xxx} to denote the advantage of $\mathcal{A}$ in Game_{xxx}.

- Game_0: is the real security game, as defined in Section 2.3.
- Game_1: same as Game_0, except that the challenger runs

$$\widetilde{\mathsf{Setup}}(1^n, \mathcal{X}, \mathcal{Y}, \mathcal{M}; \mathbf{A}, \mathbf{P}, \mathbf{X}_\beta^*) \quad \text{and} \quad \widetilde{\mathsf{Enc}}(\mathsf{mpk}, \mathbf{b}_\beta; \widetilde{\mathsf{msk}}, \mathbf{s}^\top \mathbf{A} + \mathbf{e}^\top, \mathbf{s}^\top \mathbf{P} + \mathbf{e}'^\top)$$

with $(\mathbf{A}, \mathbf{T}_\mathbf{A}) \leftarrow_\mathrm{R} \mathsf{TrapGen}(1^n, 1^m), \mathbf{P} \leftarrow_\mathrm{R} \mathbb{Z}_q^{n \times (k+n)}, \mathbf{s} \leftarrow_\mathrm{R} \mathbb{Z}_q^n, \mathbf{e} \leftarrow_\mathrm{R} \chi^m$, and $\mathbf{e}' \leftarrow_\mathrm{R} \chi^{k+n}$.

- Game_2: same as Game_1 except that the challenger runs $\widetilde{\mathsf{KeyGen}}$.
- Game_3: same as Game_2 except that the challenger runs

$$\widetilde{\mathsf{Enc}}(\mathsf{mpk}, \mathbf{b}_\beta; \widetilde{\mathsf{msk}}, \mathbf{d}_0, \mathbf{d}_f)$$

where $\mathbf{d}_0 \leftarrow_\mathrm{R} \mathbb{Z}_q^m$ and $\mathbf{d}_f \leftarrow_\mathrm{R} \mathbb{Z}_q^{k+n}$.

- Game_4: is the same as Game_3 except that the challenger runs KeyGen.

We show in the following lemmas that each pair of games (Game_i, Game_{i+1}) are either statistically indistinguishable or computationally indistinguishable under the decision-LWE assumption. Finally, we show in Lemma 19 that no information is leaked about β is the last game Game_4.

Lemma 15 (Game_0 to Game_1). *For all $m > (n+1)\log q + \omega(\log n)$, we have* $|\mathsf{Adv}_0 - \mathsf{Adv}_1| = \mathrm{negl}(n)$.

Proof. From Game_0 to Game_1, we switch from $\mathsf{Setup}, \mathsf{Enc}$ to $\widetilde{\mathsf{Setup}}, \widetilde{\mathsf{Enc}}$.

Note that the only difference between Game_0 and Game_1 is that for all $i \in [D]$ and $j \in [\ell]$, the matrix $\mathbf{A}_{i,j}$ is set to be $\mathbf{A}_{i,j} \leftarrow_\mathrm{R} \mathbb{Z}_q^{n \times m}$ in Game_0, whereas it is set to be $\mathbf{A}_{i,j} := \mathbf{A}\mathbf{R}_{i,j} - X_{i,j}^* \mathbf{G}$ in Game_1, where $\mathbf{R}_{i,j} \leftarrow_\mathrm{R} \{-1, 1\}^{m \times m}$. The matrix $\mathbf{A}_{i,j}$ only appears in the mpk and in the component $\mathbf{c}_{i,j} = \mathbf{s}^\top(\mathbf{A}_{i,j} + X_{i,j}^* \mathbf{G}) + \mathbf{e}^\top \mathbf{R}_{i,j}$ of the ciphertext.

Therefore it suffices to show that the distribution of $(\mathbf{A}, \mathbf{e}, \mathbf{A}_{i,j}, \mathbf{e}^\top \mathbf{R}_{i,j})$ in Game_0 and Game_1 are statistically close, that is,

$$(\mathbf{A}, \mathbf{e}, \mathbf{A}_{i,j}, \mathbf{e}^\top \mathbf{R}_{i,j}) \approx_s (\mathbf{A}, \mathbf{e}, \mathbf{A}\mathbf{R}_{i,j} - X_{i,j}^* \mathbf{G}, \mathbf{e}^\top \mathbf{R}_{i,j})$$

where $\mathbf{A}_{i,j} \leftarrow_R \mathbb{Z}_q^{n \times m}$, $\mathbf{R}_{i,j} \leftarrow_R \{-1,1\}^{m \times m}$, and $\mathbf{e} \leftarrow_R \chi^m$. Observe that

$$
\begin{aligned}
&(\mathbf{A}, \mathbf{e}, \mathbf{A}_{i,j}, \mathbf{e}^\top \mathbf{R}_{i,j}) \\
&\equiv (\mathbf{A}, \mathbf{e}, \mathbf{A}_{i,j} - X_{i,j}^* \mathbf{G}, \mathbf{e}^\top \mathbf{R}_{i,j}) && \text{since } \mathbf{A}_{i,j} \leftarrow_R \mathbb{Z}_q^{n \times m} \\
&\approx_s (\mathbf{A}, \mathbf{e}, \mathbf{A}\mathbf{R}_{i,j} - X_{i,j}^* \mathbf{G}, \mathbf{e}^\top \mathbf{R}_{i,j}) && \text{by Lemma 1}
\end{aligned}
$$

Lemma 16 (Game$_1$ to Game$_2$). $|\mathsf{Adv}_1 - \mathsf{Adv}_2| = \mathrm{negl}(n)$.

Proof. From Game$_1$ to Game$_2$, we switch from KeyGen to $\widetilde{\mathsf{KeyGen}}$. Therefore, it suffices to show that for any predicate $\mathbf{Y}$ such that $\mathsf{P}(\mathbf{X}^*, \mathbf{Y}) = 0$, the following distributions are statistically close:

$$
\mathsf{KeyGen}(\mathsf{mpk}, \mathsf{msk}, \mathbf{Y}) \approx_s \widetilde{\mathsf{KeyGen}}(\mathsf{mpk}, \widetilde{\mathsf{msk}}, \mathbf{Y}, \mathbf{X}^*)
$$

We write: $\mathbf{F}_{i,j} := (\mathbf{A} \| \mathbf{A}_{i,j} + Y_{i,j}\mathbf{G}) = (\mathbf{A} \| \mathbf{A}\mathbf{R}_{i,j} + (Y_{i,j} - X_{i,j}^*)\mathbf{G}) \in \mathbb{Z}_q^{n \times 2m}$. Since $\mathsf{P}(\mathbf{X}^*, \mathbf{Y}) = 0$, we know that there must exist a $i^* \in [D]$ such that $Y_{i^*,j} \neq X_{i^*,j}^*$ for all $j \in [\ell]$. Because $\mathsf{P}_{\text{AND AT MOST ONE}}(\mathbf{X}^*, \mathbf{Y}) = 1$, we know that for all $i \in [D]$, there is at most one $j_i \in [\ell]$ such that $Y_{i,j_i} = X_{i,j_i}^*$. We proceed in three steps:

1. First, we argue that the joint distribution $\{\mathbf{P}_i, \mathbf{U}_{i,j_i} : i \in [D], i \neq i^*\}$ is statistically close in KeyGen and in $\widetilde{\mathsf{KeyGen}}$. This follows readily from Lemma 5.

2. Next, we argue that the joint distribution $\{\mathbf{P}_i : i \in [D]\}$ is statistically close in KeyGen and in $\widetilde{\mathsf{KeyGen}}$. This follows readily from secret sharing.

3. Finally, fix $\mathbf{P}_1, \ldots, \mathbf{P}_D$. We argue that the distribution of the remaining matrices is statistically close in KeyGen and in $\widetilde{\mathsf{KeyGen}}$. This follows from Lemma 6, which tells us that the output $\mathbf{U}_{i,j}$ of both RightSample in KeyGen and LeftSample in $\widetilde{\mathsf{KeyGen}}$, are statistically close to $\mathcal{D}_{\Lambda_q^{\mathbf{P}_i}(\mathbf{F}_{i,j}), \sigma \cdot \omega(\sqrt{\log n})}$.

   We can sample these $\mathbf{U}_{i,j}$ in $\widetilde{\mathsf{KeyGen}}$ applying LeftSample because $Y_{i,j} - X_{i,j}^* \neq 0$ whenever $i = i^*$ or whenever $j \neq j_i$.

Remark 3. Note that the "at most one" promise is crucial here, because when $Y_{i,j} - X_{i,j}^* = 0$, we cannot use LeftSample to sample a short matrix $\mathbf{U}_{i,j}$ such that $(\mathbf{A} \| \mathbf{A}\mathbf{R}_{i,j} + (Y_{i,j} - X_{i,j}^*)\mathbf{G}) \mathbf{U}_{i,j} = \mathbf{P}_i$. If there exists "at most one" $j_i \in [\ell]$ such that $Y_{i,j_i} - X_{i,j_i}^* = 0$, we can sample a short matrix $\mathbf{U}_{i,j_i}$ from some discrete Gaussian distribution, and set $\mathbf{P}_i$ to be $\mathbf{P}_i := (\mathbf{A} \| \mathbf{A}\mathbf{R}_{i,j} + 0 \cdot \mathbf{G}) \mathbf{U}_{i,j}$. Lemma 5 ensures that both $\mathbf{U}_{i,j}$ and $\mathbf{P}_i$ are correctly distributed. However, if there exist at least 2 indices j_i and $j_i' \in [\ell]$ such that $Y_{i,j_i} - X_{i,j_i}^* = Y_{i,j_i'} - X_{i,j_i'}^* = 0$, then there is more than one matrix that we cannot sample using LeftSample, and the previous technique does not work anymore.

Lemma 17 (Game$_2$ to Game$_3$). *There exists an adversary $\mathcal{B}$ whose running time is roughly the same as that of $\mathcal{A}$ and such that*

$$
|\mathsf{Adv}_2 - \mathsf{Adv}_3| \leq \mathsf{Adv}_{\mathcal{B}}^{\mathsf{dLWE}_{n,m+k+n,q,\chi}}
$$

Note that only difference between Game_2 and Game_3 is that we switch the distribution of the inputs $(\mathbf{d}_0, \mathbf{d}_{D+1})$ to $\widetilde{\mathsf{Enc}}$ from LWE instances to random ones.

Proof. On input an LWE challenge

$$(\mathbf{A}, \mathbf{P}, \mathbf{d}_0, \mathbf{d}_{D+1})$$

where $\mathbf{A} \leftarrow_R \mathbb{Z}_q^{n \times m}$ and $\mathbf{P} \leftarrow_R \mathbb{Z}_q^{n \times (k+n)}$ and $(\mathbf{d}_0, \mathbf{d}_{D+1})$ is either $(\mathbf{s}^\top \mathbf{A} + \mathbf{e}^\top, \mathbf{s}^\top \mathbf{P} + \mathbf{e}'^\top)$ or random, $\mathcal{B}$ simulates $\mathcal{A}$ and proceeds as follows:

- runs $\widetilde{\mathsf{Setup}}(1^n, \mathcal{X}, \mathcal{Y}, \mathcal{M}; \mathbf{A}, \mathbf{P}, \mathbf{X}_\beta^*)$ as in Game_2;
- answers $\mathcal{A}$'s private key queries by using $\widetilde{\mathsf{KeyGen}}$ as in Game_2;
- runs $\widetilde{\mathsf{Enc}}(\mathsf{mpk}, \mathbf{b}_\beta; \widetilde{\mathsf{msk}}, \mathbf{d}_0, \mathbf{d}_{D+1})$ to generate the challenge ciphertext;
- Finally, $\mathcal{A}$ guesses if it is interacting with a Game_2 or a Game_3 challenger. $\mathcal{B}$ outputs $\mathcal{A}$'s guess as the answer to the LWE challenge it is trying to solve.

When the LWE challenge is pseudorandom as in Definition 1, the adversary's view is as in Game_2. When the LWE challenge is random the adversary's view is as in Game_3. Therefore, $\mathcal{B}$'s advantage in solving LWE is the same as $\mathcal{A}$'s advantage in distinguishing Game_2 and Game_3.

Lemma 18 (Game_3 to Game_4). $|\mathsf{Adv}_3 - \mathsf{Adv}_4| = \mathrm{negl}(n)$

Proof. The differences between Game_3 and Game_4 are:
- In Game_3, $\mathbf{A} \leftarrow_R \mathbb{Z}_q^{n \times m}$, and $\mathbf{T_A} := \bot$, whereas in Game_4, $(\mathbf{A}, \mathbf{T_A}) \leftarrow_R \mathsf{TrapGen}(1^n, 1^m)$.
- In Game_3, the challenger answers the adversary's secret key using the $\widetilde{\mathsf{KeyGen}}$ algorithm, whereas he answers using the KeyGen algorithm in Game_4.

The proof is the same as the one of Lemma 16, by symmetry of the games.

Lemma 19 (Game_4).   *We have* $|\mathsf{Adv}_4 - 1/2| = \mathrm{negl}(n)$

Proof. In Game_4, both the challenge ciphertext and the secret keys are independent of β. Moreover, by Lemma 1, we know that for all $i \in [D]$, for all $j \in [\ell]$ the two following distributions are statistically close

$$(\mathbf{A}, \mathbf{A}_{i,j}) \approx_s (\mathbf{A}, \mathbf{A}\mathbf{R}_{i,j} - X_{i,j}^* \mathbf{G})$$

where $\mathbf{A}_{i,j} \leftarrow_R \mathbb{Z}_q^{n \times m}$, $\mathbf{R}_{i,j} \leftarrow_R \{-1, 1\}^{m \times m}$, and $\mathbf{e} \leftarrow_R \chi^m$. Thus, the mpk does not leak any information on $\mathbf{X}_\beta^*$. Therefore, we get $|\mathsf{Adv}_4 - 1/2| = \mathrm{negl}(n)$.

4.4 Parameter Selection

- By Lemma 1, we need $m > (n+1) \log q + \omega(\log n)$
- By Lemma 3, and Lemma 4, we require $m = \Theta(n \log q)$
- By Lemma 5, we need $m \geq 2n \log q$

- By Lemma 6, we need $\sigma = O(\|\mathbf{T_A}\|_{GS})$ and $\sigma = O(\|\mathbf{T_G}\|_{GS} \cdot (1 + \|\mathbf{R}\|_2))$ where $\|\mathbf{T_A}\|_{GS} = O(\sqrt{n \log q})$ and $\|\mathbf{R}\|_2 \leq 20\sqrt{m}$ with overwhelming probability in n, according to Lemma 3 and Lemma 5, respectively.
- For correctness of decryption, we require $\chi_{\max} \leq \frac{q}{4} \left(1 + D(1 + 20\sqrt{m}) \cdot s \cdot 2m\right)^{-1}$, where $s = \sigma \cdot \omega(\sqrt{\log n})$.

Consequently we take $m = \Theta(n \log q)$, $\sigma = O(\sqrt{n \log q})$ and $\chi_{\max} = O\left(\frac{q}{D(n \log q)^{3/2} s}\right)$ where $s = \sigma \cdot \omega(\sqrt{\log n})$.

4.5 Putting Everything Together for Multi-dimensional Range Queries

When D denotes the number of dimensions and T the number of points in each, combining the preceding scheme with the reduction in Section 3.3, we get a scheme for $\mathsf{P}_{\text{CP-RANGE}}$ and $\mathsf{P}_{\text{KP-RANGE}}$ with ciphertexts and secret keys of sizes $O(D \log T)$ and running times $O(D \cdot \log T \cdot \mathrm{poly}(n))$ for encryption and key generation, $O((\log T)^D \cdot \mathrm{poly}(n))$ for decryption.

5 Shorter Ciphertexts and Secret Keys for Multi-dimensional Subset Queries

The predicate encryption scheme for $\mathsf{P}_{\text{AND-OR-EQ}}$ exhibited in Section 4 together with the reductions presented in Section 3 lead to efficient predicate encryption schemes for multi-dimensional subset queries.

Indeed, when D denotes the dimension and T denotes the size of the sets, we obtain a predicate encryption scheme for $\mathsf{P}_{\text{KP-SUBSET}}$ and $\mathsf{P}_{\text{CP-SUBSET}}$ with ciphertexts and secret keys of size $O(D \cdot T)$.

However, in this section we show how we can improve the size of the secret keys and ciphertexts in order to obtain:

- ciphertexts of size $O(D)$ for $\mathsf{P}_{\text{KP-SUBSET}}$
- secret keys of size $O(D)$ for $\mathsf{P}_{\text{CP-SUBSET}}$

5.1 Multi-dimensional Subset Queries, Ciphertext Policy

We can obtain a predicate encryption scheme for $\mathsf{P}_{\text{CP-SUBSET}}$ using the reduction to $\mathsf{P}_{\text{AND-OR-EQ}}$ defined in section 3.2, with secret keys of size $O(D \cdot T)$. We reduce the size of the secret keys size down to $O(D)$ using the fact that in each dimension, only one of the T matrices in the secret key is needed to decrypt.

On the one hand, for each dimension i, the reduction maps a point $z \in [T]$ into the vector $\mathbf{e}_z$. Therefore, for all $j \neq z$ the KeyGen algorithm generates a short matrix $\mathbf{U}_{i,j}$ which is a preimage of some target for the matrix $\left[\mathbf{A} \| \mathbf{A}_{i,j} + 0 \cdot \mathbf{G}\right]$.

On the other hand, a characteristic vector $\mathbf{w} \in \{0,1\}^T$, is mapped into a $-1, 1$ vector. Thus, for all j, the (i,j)'th component of the ciphertext is an LWE sample corresponding to the matrix $\left[\mathbf{A}_{i,j} + *\mathbf{G}\right], * \in \{-1, 1\}$.

Consequently, the matrices $\mathbf{U}_{i,j}$ for $j \neq z$ do not yield any useful information to decrypt the ciphertext. Therefore, we can remove them, and still satisfies correctness. Moreover, it is clear that removing parts of the secret key will not affect the security. Removing these matrices, we obtain a scheme whose secret keys have size $O(D)$, and whose decryption algorithm runs in time $O(D \cdot \mathrm{poly}(n))$ (instead of $O(T^D \cdot \mathrm{poly}(n))$).

Construction. Let $n \in \mathbb{N}$ be the security parameter and T, D positive integers. Let $q = q(n, T, D)$, $m = m(n, T, D)$ and $\chi_{\max} = \chi_{\max}(n, T, D)$ be positive integers, and $\sigma = \sigma(n, T, D)$ be a Gaussian parameter.

Setup($1^n, \mathcal{X}, \mathcal{Y}, \mathcal{M}$): on a security parameter n, an attribute space $\mathcal{X} := \{0, 1\}^{D \times T}$, a predicate space $\mathcal{Y} := \mathbb{Z}_q^D$, and a message space $\mathcal{M} := \{0, 1\}^k$, do:

- Pick $(\mathbf{A}, \mathbf{T_A}) \leftarrow \mathsf{TrapGen}(1^n, 1^m, q)$.
- Pick $\mathbf{A}_{1,1}, \ldots, \mathbf{A}_{D,T} \leftarrow_{\mathrm{R}} \mathbb{Z}_q^{n \times m}$.
- Pick $\mathbf{P} \leftarrow_{\mathrm{R}} \mathbb{Z}_q^{n \times (k+n)}$.
- Compute $(\mathbf{G}, \mathbf{T_G})$ as defined in Lemma 4.
- Output: $\mathsf{mpk} := (\mathbf{P}, \mathbf{A}, \mathbf{A}_{1,1}, \ldots, \mathbf{A}_{D,T}, \mathbf{G}, \mathbf{T_G})$ and $\mathsf{msk} := \mathbf{T_A}$

Enc($\mathsf{mpk}, \mathbf{X}, \mathbf{b}$): On input the public parameters mpk, an predicate matrix $\mathbf{X} \in \mathcal{X}$, and a message $\mathbf{b} \in \{0, 1\}^k$, do:

- Pick $\mathbf{s} \leftarrow_{\mathrm{R}} \mathbb{Z}_q^n$, $\mathbf{e} \leftarrow_{\mathrm{R}} \chi^m$, and compute $\mathbf{c}_0 := \mathbf{s}^\top \mathbf{A} + \mathbf{e}^\top$.
- for all $i \in [D]$ and all $j \in [T]$, do:
  - Pick $\mathbf{R}_{i,j} \leftarrow \{-1, 1\}^{n \times m}$.
  - Compute $\mathbf{c}_{i,j} := \mathbf{s}^\top \left(\mathbf{A}_{i,j} + X_{i,j} \mathbf{G} \right) + \mathbf{e}^\top \mathbf{R}_{i,j}$.
- Set $\mathbf{b}' := (\mathbf{b}, 0, \ldots, 0) \in \{0, 1\}^{k+n}$, pick an $\mathbf{e}' \leftarrow_{\mathrm{R}} \chi^{k+n}$, and compute $\mathbf{c}_f := \mathbf{s}^\top \mathbf{P} + \mathbf{e}'^\top + \mathbf{b}'^\top \cdot \lfloor q/2 \rfloor$.
- Output: $\mathsf{ct} := (\mathbf{c}_0, \mathbf{c}_{1,1}, \ldots, \mathbf{c}_{D,T}, \mathbf{c}_f)$

KeyGen($\mathsf{mpk}, \mathsf{msk}, \mathbf{y}$): On input the public parameters mpk, the master secret key msk, and an attribute vector $\mathbf{y} \in \mathcal{Y}$, do:

- Secret share $\mathbf{P}$ as $\{\mathbf{P}_i, i \in [D]\}$, such that $\sum_{i=1}^{D} \mathbf{P}_i = \mathbf{P}$.
- For all $i \in [D]$:
  Sample a short matrix $\mathbf{U}_i \in \mathbb{Z}_q^{2m \times (k+n)}$ such that $[\mathbf{A} \| \mathbf{A}_{i,y_i} + \mathbf{G}] \mathbf{U}_i = \mathbf{P}_i$ using $\mathsf{RightSample}(\mathbf{A}, \mathbf{T_A}, \mathbf{A}_{i,y_i} + \mathbf{G}, \mathbf{P}_i, \sigma)$ with $\sigma = O(\sqrt{n \log q})$.
- Output the secret key $\mathsf{sk}_\mathbf{Y} = (\mathbf{U}_1, \ldots, \mathbf{U}_D)$.

Dec($\mathsf{mpk}, \mathsf{sk}_\mathbf{y}, \mathsf{ct}$): On input the public parameters mpk, a secret key $\mathsf{sk}_\mathbf{y} = (\mathbf{U}_1, \ldots, \mathbf{U}_D)$ for an attribute vector $\mathbf{y}$, and a ciphertext $\mathsf{ct} = (\mathbf{c}_0, \mathbf{c}_{1,1}, \ldots, \mathbf{c}_{D,T}, \mathbf{c}_f)$, do:

- Compute $\mathbf{d} := \mathbf{c}_f - \sum_{i=1}^{D} [\mathbf{c}_0 \| \mathbf{c}_{i,y_i}] \mathbf{U}_i \mod q$.
- Output the first k bits of $\lfloor \frac{\mathbf{d}}{q/2} \rceil$. For any $z \in [0, 1]$, we denote by $\lfloor z \rceil$ the closest integer of z.

Correctness and Security. Correctness and security proofs follow readily from those of $P_{\text{AND-OR-EQ}}$ in Section 4.

5.2   Multi-dimensional Subset Queries, Key-Policy

The following scheme is similar (however simpler) to the one presented in Section 4 for $P_{\text{AND-OR-EQ}}$.

Overview. We begin with the special case $D = 1$. Given an attribute vector $x \in [T]^D$, the ciphertext is an LWE sample corresponding to the matrix $[\mathbf{A}\|\mathbf{A}_1 + x\mathbf{G}]$ and the message is masked using an LWE sample corresponding to a public matrix $\mathbf{P}$. The secret key corresponding to $\mathbf{Y} \in \{0,1\}^T$ is a collection of T short matrices $\mathbf{U}_1, \ldots, \mathbf{U}_T$ such that:

$$[\mathbf{A}\|\mathbf{A}_1 + j\mathbf{G}]\mathbf{U}_j = \mathbf{P} \quad \text{if } \mathbf{Y}_j = 1$$
$$\mathbf{U}_j = \perp \quad \text{if } \mathbf{Y}_j = 0$$

For correctness, observe that if $\mathbf{Y}_x = 1$, then the decryptor can use $\mathbf{U}_x$ to recover the plaintext. However, since the decryptor does not know x, he will try to decrypt the ciphertext using each of $\mathbf{U}_1, \ldots, \mathbf{U}_T$. We will need to pad the plaintext with redundant zeroes so that the decryptor can identify the correct plaintext.

To establish security with respect to some selective challenge x^*, we will need to simulate the secret keys for all $\mathbf{Y}$ such that $\mathbf{Y}_{x^*} = 0$. Observe that for all $j = 1, \ldots, T$,

$$\mathbf{Y}_j = 1 \Longrightarrow j \neq x^*$$

We can then simulate $\mathbf{U}_j$ using an "all-but-one" simulation (while puncturing at x^*) exactly as in prior IBE schemes in [1]. In order to establish weak attribute-hiding, we adopt a similar strategy to that for inner product encryption in [4].

Higher Dimensions. Given an attribute vector $\mathbf{x} \in [T]^D$, the ciphertext is an LWE sample corresponding to the matrix $[\mathbf{A}\|\mathbf{A}_1 + x_1\mathbf{G}\|\cdots\|\mathbf{A}_D + x_D\mathbf{G}]$.

The secret key corresponding to $\mathbf{Y} \in \{0,1\}^{D \times T}$ is a collection of $D \cdot T$ short matrices $\mathbf{U}_{1,1}, \ldots, \mathbf{U}_{D,T}$ such that for $j = 1, \ldots, T, i = 1, \ldots, D$:

$$[\mathbf{A}\|\mathbf{A}_i + j\mathbf{G}]\mathbf{U}_{i,j} = \mathbf{P}_i \quad \text{if } \mathbf{Y}_{i,j} = 1$$
$$\mathbf{U}_{i,j} = \perp \quad \text{if } \mathbf{Y}_{i,j} = 0$$

where $\mathbf{P}_1, \ldots, \mathbf{P}_D$ is an additive secret-sharing of $\mathbf{P}$.

For correctness, observe that if $\mathbf{Y}_{1,x_1} = \mathbf{Y}_{2,x_2} = \ldots = \mathbf{Y}_{D,x_D} = 1$, then the decryptor can use $\mathbf{U}_{1,x_1}, \cdots, \mathbf{U}_{D,x_D}$ to recover the plaintext. As with the case $D = 1$, the decryptor will need to enumerate over all $\mathbf{x}' \in [T]^D$.

To simulate secret keys for $\mathbf{Y}$ with respect to some selective challenge $\mathbf{x}^*$, first we fix i^* such that $\mathbf{Y}_{k, x_{i^*}^*} = 0$. Without loss of generality, suppose $i^* = 1$, that is, $\mathbf{Y}_{1, x_1^*} = 0$. We then proceed as follows:

- Sample random short matrices $\mathbf{U}_{2,x_2^*}, \ldots, \mathbf{U}_{D,x_D^*}$, which in turn determines the shares $\mathbf{P}_2, \ldots, \mathbf{P}_D$.
- Define $\mathbf{P}_1 := \mathbf{P} - \sum_{i=2}^{D} \mathbf{P}_i$ and use an all-but-one simulation strategy to sample the remaining short matrices in the secret key.

Construction. Let $n \in \mathbb{N}$ be the security parameter and T, D be positive integers. Let $q = q(n)$, $m = m(n, T, D)$ and $\chi_{\max} = \chi_{\max}(n, q, T, D)$ be positive integers, and $\sigma = \sigma(n, q, T, D)$ be a Gaussian parameter.

Setup$(1^n, \mathcal{X}, \mathcal{Y}, \mathcal{M})$: on n, $\mathcal{X} := \mathbb{Z}_q^D$, $\mathcal{Y} := \{0,1\}^{D \times T}$ and $\mathcal{M} := \{0,1\}^k$, do:

- Pick $(\mathbf{A}, \mathbf{T_A}) \leftarrow \mathsf{TrapGen}(1^n, 1^m, q)$.
- Pick $\mathbf{A}_1, \ldots, \mathbf{A}_D \leftarrow_{\mathrm{R}} \mathbb{Z}_q^{n \times m}$.
- Pick $\mathbf{P} \leftarrow_{\mathrm{R}} \mathbb{Z}_q^{n \times (k+n)}$.
- Compute $(\mathbf{G}, \mathbf{T_G})$ as defined in Lemma 4.
- Output: $\mathsf{mpk} := (\mathbf{P}, \mathbf{A}, \mathbf{A}_1, \ldots, \mathbf{A}_D, \mathbf{G}, \mathbf{T_G})$ and $\mathsf{msk} := \mathbf{T_A}$

Enc$(\mathsf{mpk}, \mathbf{x}, \mathbf{b})$: On input mpk, $\mathbf{x} \in \mathcal{X}$ and $\mathbf{b} \in \{0,1\}^k$:

- Pick $\mathbf{s} \leftarrow_{\mathrm{R}} \mathbb{Z}_q^n$, $\mathbf{e} \leftarrow_{\mathrm{R}} \chi^m$, and compute $\mathbf{c}_0 := \mathbf{s}^{\mathsf{T}} \mathbf{A} + \mathbf{e}^{\mathsf{T}}$.
- For all $i \in [D]$:
  - Pick $\mathbf{R}_i \leftarrow \{-1, 1\}^{m \times m}$.
  - Compute $\mathbf{c}_i := \mathbf{s}^{\mathsf{T}} (\mathbf{A}_i + x_i \mathbf{G}) + \mathbf{e}^{\mathsf{T}} \mathbf{R}_i$.
- Set $\mathbf{b}' := (\mathbf{b}, 0, \ldots, 0) \in \{0,1\}^{k+n}$, pick $\mathbf{e}' \leftarrow_{\mathrm{R}} \chi^{k+n}$, and compute $\mathbf{c}_f := \mathbf{s}^{\mathsf{T}} \mathbf{P} + \mathbf{e}'^{\mathsf{T}} + \mathbf{b}'^{\mathsf{T}} \cdot \lfloor q/2 \rfloor$.
- Output: $\mathsf{ct} := (\mathbf{c}_0, \mathbf{c}_1, \ldots, \mathbf{c}_D, \mathbf{c}_f)$

KeyGen$(\mathsf{mpk}, \mathsf{msk}, \mathbf{Y})$: On input mpk, msk, and $\mathbf{Y} \in \mathcal{Y}$, do:

- Secret share $\mathbf{P}$ as $\{\mathbf{P}_i, i \in [D]\}$, such that $\sum_{i=1}^{D} \mathbf{P}_i = \mathbf{P}$.
- For all $i \in [D]$ and $j \in [T]$:
  - If $Y_{i,j} = 1$ then sample a short matrix $\mathbf{U}_{i,j} \in \mathbb{Z}_q^{2m \times (k+n)}$ such that

$$[\mathbf{A} \| \mathbf{A}_i + j\mathbf{G}] \mathbf{U}_{i,j} = \mathbf{P}_i$$

  using $\mathsf{RightSample}(\mathbf{A}, \mathbf{T_A}, \mathbf{A}_i + j\mathbf{G}, \mathbf{P}_i, \sigma)$ with $\sigma = O(\sqrt{n \log q})$.
  - Otherwise set $\mathbf{U}_{i,j} := \perp$.
- Output the secret key $\mathsf{sk}_{\mathbf{Y}} = (\mathbf{U}_{1,1}, \ldots, \mathbf{U}_{D,T})$.

Dec$(\mathsf{mpk}, \mathsf{sk}_{\mathbf{Y}}, \mathsf{ct})$: On input the public parameters mpk, a secret key $\mathsf{sk}_{\mathbf{Y}} = (\mathbf{U}_{1,1}, \ldots, \mathbf{U}_{D,T})$ for a predicate matrix $\mathbf{Y}$, and a ciphertext $\mathsf{ct} = (\mathbf{c}_0, \mathbf{c}_1, \ldots, \mathbf{c}_D, \mathbf{c}_f)$, do:

- For all $\mathbf{x}' = (x_1', \ldots, x_D') \in [T]^D$, compute $\mathbf{d}_{\mathbf{x}'} := \mathbf{c}_f - \sum_{i=1}^{D} [\mathbf{c}_0 \| \mathbf{c}_i] \mathbf{U}_{i, x_i'}$ mod q.

- If $\left\lfloor \frac{d_{x'}}{q/2} \right\rceil \in \{0,1\}^k \times 0^n$ for exactly one vector $x' \in [T]^D$, then output the first k bits of $\left\lfloor \frac{d_{x'}}{q/2} \right\rceil$. For any $z \in [0,1]$, we denote by $\lfloor z \rceil$ the closest integer of z.
- Otherwise, abort.

We defer the proofs of correctness and security to the full version [12].

References

1. Agrawal, S., Boneh, D., Boyen, X.: Efficient Lattice (H)IBE in the Standard Model. In: Gilbert, H. (ed.) EUROCRYPT 2010. LNCS, vol. 6110, pp. 553–572. Springer, Heidelberg (2010)
2. Agrawal, S., Boneh, D., Boyen, X.: Lattice Basis Delegation in Fixed Dimension and Shorter-Ciphertext Hierarchical IBE. In: Rabin, T. (ed.) CRYPTO 2010. LNCS, vol. 6223, pp. 98–115. Springer, Heidelberg (2010)
3. Agrawal, S., Boyen, X., Vaikuntanathan, V., Voulgaris, P., Wee, H.: Functional Encryption for Threshold Functions (or, Fuzzy IBE) from Lattices. In: Public Key Cryptography, pp. 280–297 (2012)
4. Agrawal, S., Freeman, D.M., Vaikuntanathan, V.: Functional Encryption for Inner Product Predicates from Learning with Errors. In: Lee, D.H., Wang, X. (eds.) ASIACRYPT 2011. LNCS, vol. 7073, pp. 21–40. Springer, Heidelberg (2011)
5. Ajtai, M.: Generating Hard Instances of Lattice Problems (Extended Abstract). In: STOC, pp. 99–108 (1996)
6. Alwen, J., Peikert, C.: Generating Shorter Bases for Hard Random Lattices. In: STACS, pp. 75–86 (2009)
7. Boneh, D., Gentry, C., Gorbunov, S., Halevi, S., Nikolaenko, V., Segev, G., Vaikuntanathan, V., Vinayagamurthy, D.: Fully Key-Homomorphic Encryption, Arithmetic Circuit ABE and Compact Garbled Circuits. In: Nguyen, P.Q., Oswald, E. (eds.) EUROCRYPT 2014. LNCS, vol. 8441, pp. 533–556. Springer, Heidelberg (2014)
8. Boneh, D., Waters, B.: Conjunctive, Subset, and Range Queries on Encrypted Data. In: Vadhan, S.P. (ed.) TCC 2007. LNCS, vol. 4392, pp. 535–554. Springer, Heidelberg (2007)
9. Cash, D., Hofheinz, D., Kiltz, E., Peikert, C.: Bonsai Trees, or How to Delegate a Lattice Basis. In: Gilbert, H. (ed.) EUROCRYPT 2010. LNCS, vol. 6110, pp. 523–552. Springer, Heidelberg (2010)
10. De Berg, M., Van Kreveld, M., Overmars, M., Schwarzkopf, O.: Computational Geometry. Springer, Heidelberg (2000)
11. Dodis, Y., Ostrovsky, R., Reyzin, L., Smith, A.: Fuzzy Extractors: How to Generate Strong Keys from Biometrics and Other Noisy Data. SIAM J. Comput. 38(1), 97–139 (2008)
12. Gay, R., Méaux, P., Wee, H.: Predicate Encryption for Multi-Dimensional Range Queries from Lattices. Cryptology ePrint Archive, Report 2014/965 (2014), http://eprint.iacr.org/
13. Gentry, C., Peikert, C., Vaikuntanathan, V.: Trapdoors for hard lattices and new cryptographic constructions. In: STOC, pp. 197–206 (2008)
14. Gorbunov, S., Vaikuntanathan, V., Wee, H.: Attribute-based encryption for circuits. In: STOC, pp. 545–554 (2013), also, Cryptology ePrint Archive, Report 2013/337

15. Goyal, V., Pandey, O., Sahai, A., Waters, B.: Attribute-based encryption for fine-grained access control of encrypted data. In: ACM Conference on Computer and Communications Security, pp. 89–98 (2006)
16. Impagliazzo, R., Levin, L.A., Luby, M.: Pseudo-random generation from one-way functions. In: STOC 1989 Proceedings of the Twenty-First Annual ACM Symposium on Theory of Computing, pp. 12–24. ACM, New York (1989)
17. Katz, J., Sahai, A., Waters, B.: Predicate Encryption Supporting Disjunctions, Polynomial Equations, and Inner Products. In: Smart, N.P. (ed.) EUROCRYPT 2008. LNCS, vol. 4965, pp. 146–162. Springer, Heidelberg (2008)
18. Micciancio, D., Peikert, C.: Trapdoors for Lattices: Simpler, Tighter, Faster, Smaller. In: Pointcheval, D., Johansson, T. (eds.) EUROCRYPT 2012. LNCS, vol. 7237, pp. 700–718. Springer, Heidelberg (2012)
19. Regev, O.: On lattices, learning with errors, random linear codes, and cryptography. In: STOC. pp. 84–93 (2005)
20. Shi, E., Bethencourt, J., Chan, H.T.H., Song, D.X., Perrig, A.: Multi-Dimensional Range Query over Encrypted Data. In: IEEE Symposium on Security and Privacy, pp. 350–364 (2007)
21. Xagawa, K.: Improved (Hierarchical) Inner-Product Encryption from Lattices. In: Public Key Cryptography, pp. 235–252 (2013)

On the Practical Security of Inner Product Functional Encryption

Shashank Agrawal[1]([✉]), Shweta Agrawal[2], Saikrishna Badrinarayanan[3], Abishek Kumarasubramanian[4], Manoj Prabhakaran[1], and Amit Sahai[3]

[1] University of Illinois Urbana-Champaign, Champaign, USA
{sagrawl2,mmp}@illinois.edu
[2] Indian Institute of Technology Delhi, New Delhi, India
shweta@cse.iitd.ac.in
[3] University of California Los Angeles, Los Angeles, USA
{saikrishna,sahai}@cs.ucla.edu
[4] Google, California, USA
abishekk@cs.ucla.edu

Abstract. Functional Encryption (FE) is an exciting new paradigm that extends the notion of public key encryption. In this work we explore the security of Inner Product Functional Encryption schemes with the goal of achieving the highest security against practically feasible attacks. While there has been substantial research effort in defining meaningful security models for FE, known definitions run into one of the following difficulties – if general and strong, the definition can be shown impossible to achieve, whereas achievable definitions necessarily restrict the usage scenarios in which FE schemes can be deployed.

We argue that it is extremely hard to control the nature of usage scenarios that may arise in practice. Any cryptographic scheme may be deployed in an arbitrarily complex environment and it is vital to have meaningful security guarantees for general scenarios. Hence, in this work, we examine whether it is possible to analyze the security of FE in a wider variety of usage scenarios, but with respect to a meaningful class of adversarial attacks known to be possible in practice. Note that known impossibilities necessitate that we must either restrict the usage scenarios (as done in previous works), or the class of attacks (this work). We study real world loss-of-secrecy attacks against Functional Encryption

S. Agrawal, M. Prabhakaran—Research supported in part by NSF grant 1228856.
S. Badrinarayanan—Part of the work was done while the author was at University of Illinois Urbana-Champaign, supported by S. N. Bose scholarship.
A. Sahai—Research supported in part from a DARPA/ONR PROCEED award, NSF Frontier Award 1413955, NSF grants 1228984, 1136174, 1118096, and 1065276, a Xerox Faculty Research Award, a Google Faculty Research Award, an equipment grant from Intel, and an Okawa Foundation Research Grant. This material is based upon work supported by the Defense Advanced Research Projects Agency through the U.S. Office of Naval Research under Contract N00014-11- 1-0389. The views expressed are those of the author and do not reflect the official policy or position of the Department of Defense, the National Science Foundation, or the U.S. Government.

© International Association for Cryptologic Research 2015
J. Katz (Ed.): PKC 2015, LNCS 9020, pp. 777–798, 2015.
DOI: 10.1007/978-3-662-46447-2_35

for Inner Product predicates constructed over elliptic curve groups. Our main contributions are as follows:

- We capture a large variety of possible usage scenarios that may arise in practice by providing a *stronger*, more general, intuitive framework that supports *function privacy* in addition to data privacy, and a separate *encryption key* in addition to public key and master secret key. These generalizations allow our framework to capture program obfuscation as a special case of functional encryption, and allows for a separation between users that encrypt data, access data and produce secret keys.

- We note that the landscape of attacks over pairing-friendly elliptic curves have been the subject of extensive research and there now exist constructions of pairing-friendly elliptic curves where the complexity of all known non-generic attacks is (far) greater than the complexity of generic attacks. Thus, by appropriate choice of the underlying elliptic curve, we can capture all known practically feasible attacks on secrecy by restricting our attention to generic attacks.

- We construct a new inner product FE scheme using prime order groups and show it secure under our new, hitherto strongest known framework in the generic group model, thus ruling out all generic attacks in arbitrarily complex real world environments. Since our construction is over prime order groups, we rule out factoring attacks that typically force higher security parameters. Our concrete-analysis proofs provide guidance on the size of elliptic curve groups that are needed for explicit complexity bounds on the attacker.

Keywords: Functional Encryption · Practical security · Pairing based cryptography · Inner-product encryption · Generic attacks · Simulation based security

1 Introduction

Functional Encryption [44,45] (FE) is an exciting new paradigm that generalizes public key encryption. In functional encryption, each decryption key corresponds to a specific function. When the holder of a decryption key for the function f gets an encryption of a message m, the only thing his key allows him to learn is $f(m)$, but nothing more.

Classic results in the area focused on constructing FE for restricted classes of functions – point functions or identity based encryption (IBE) [12,17,21, 46] [3,4,20,29] threshold functions [45], membership checking [16], boolean formulas [11,35,39], inner product functions [5,36,39] and more recently, even regular languages [49]. Recent constructions of FE support general functions: Gorbunov et al. [34] and Garg et al. [27] provided the first constructions for an important subclass of FE called "public index FE" (also known as "attribute based encryption") for all circuits, Goldwasser et al. [32] constructed succinct simulation-secure single-key FE scheme for all circuits. In a breakthrough result, Garg et al. [26] constructed indistinguishability-secure multi-key FE schemes for all circuits. Goldwasser et al. and Ananth et al. [7,31] constructed FE for Turing machines. Recently, Functional Encryption has even been generalized to multi-input functional encryption [30].

Alongside ever-more-sophisticated constructions, there has been significant work in defining the right security model for FE. Boneh, Sahai and Waters [15] and O'Neill [43] proposed definitional frameworks to study Functional Encryption in its general form. These works discussed the subtleties involved in defining a security model for FE that captures meaningful real world security. Since then there has been considerable research focus on understanding what security means for FE and whether it can be achieved [6,9,10,15,19,43]. The strongest, most intuitive notions of security turned out to be impossible to realize theoretically, while weaker notions restricted the usage scenarios in which FE schemes could be deployed (more on this below).

Security of Functional Encryption in practice. In this work we explore the security of Functional Encryption schemes from a practical standpoint, with the goal of trying to achieve maximum security against all practically feasible attacks. While there has been considerable progress in defining meaningful security models for FE, existing definitions do not capture a number of real world usage scenarios that will likely arise in practice. However, it is essential to understand how Functional Encryption systems behave in complex real world environments, since this is inevitable in the future of FE. Towards this end, we examine security features that we believe are desirable in practice, and discuss whether these can be achieved.

- *Can we hide the function?* Consider the application of keyword searching on encrypted data, where the keywords being searched for are sensitive and must remain hidden. This scenario is well motivated in practice; for example the FBI might recruit untrusted server farms to perform searches on confidential encrypted data, but desire not to reveal the words being searched. Can FE schemes achieve this?
- *Can we limit what the adversary learns to* only *the function's output?* Intuitively, a functional encryption scheme should only reveal to a decryptor the function output, and nothing more. For example, if the function has some computational hiding properties, can we guarantee that the FE scheme does not leak any additional information beyond the function output?
- *Can an adversary break FE schemes where it can ask for keys after receiving ciphertexts?* In real world applications, it is very likely that an adversary can receive authorized decryption keys even after it obtains the ciphertext that it is trying to break. For example, in searchable encryption, the decryption key corresponding to a search would only be given out after the encrypted database is publicly available. Similarly in Identity Based Encryption, a user may receive an email encrypted with his identity before he obtains the corresponding secret key. Can one guarantee that an attacker who obtains an arbitrary interleaving of ciphertexts and keys, can learn nothing beyond the legitimate function values?

None of the existing security definitions for FE [6,9,10,15,43] provide comprehensive guarantees against all the above usage scenarios. Below, we discuss why this is the case, and examine alternate approaches to providing meaningful security guarantees against a wide range of practical attacks, in all the above scenarios.

Recap of security definitions. Before we discuss our approach, it will be useful to recap existing definitions of security and discuss their restrictions. Known definitions of security for FE may be divided into two broad classes: Indistinguishability (IND) based or Simulation (SIM) based. Indistinguishability based security stipulates that it is infeasible to distinguish encryptions of any two messages, without getting a secret key that decrypts the ciphertexts to distinct values; simulation-based security stipulates that there exists an efficient simulator that can simulate the view of the adversary, given only the function evaluated on messages and keys. Both of these notions can be further classified as follows: [43] described the divide between *adaptive* (AD) versus *non-adaptive* (NA) which captures whether the adversary's queries to the key derivation oracle may or may not depend on the challenge ciphertext; and [33] described the divide between *one* versus *many*, which depends on whether the adversary receives a single or multiple challenge ciphertexts. Thus, existing definitions of security belong to the class $\{1, \mathsf{many}\} \times \{\mathsf{NA}, \mathsf{AD}\} \times \{\mathsf{IND}, \mathsf{SIM}\}$.

Standard model woes. Unfortunately, none of the above definitions capture security in all the usage scenarios discussed above. For example, Boneh et al. and O'Neill [15,43] showed that IND based definitions do not capture scenarios where it is required that the user learn *only* the output of the FE function, for eg., when the function hides something computationally. To get around this, [15,43] proposed SIM based definitions that study FE in the "ideal world-real world" paradigm. However, the world of SIM security for FE has been plagued with impossibilities of efficient simulation. Moreover, even the strongest known SIM based definitions (many-AD-SIM) do not capture function hiding. Even disregarding function hiding, [15] showed that many-AD-SIM is impossible even for very simple functionalities. A weakening of AD-SIM, namely NA-SIM [43] does not capture scenarios where users may obtain keys *after* obtaining new third-party-generated ciphertexts. Despite this severe restriction on usage, NA-SIM was also shown to be impossible [6], seemingly ruling out security for even those usage scenarios that *are* captured.

Does this mean nothing can be said about real world security of FE in scenarios not captured by definitions or ruled out by impossibilities for simulation? Given that strong, intuitive definitions capturing real world scenarios are unachievable, are practitioners doomed to make do with the restricted usage scenarios offered by IND based security?

There seem to be two complementary directions forward. The first is to seek notions of security "in-between" IND and SIM that are achievable, thus providing guarantees for a restricted (but larger than IND) class of usage scenarios against all efficient attackers. Indeed, there is already research effort pursuing this agenda [2,6,9]. However, it is extremely hard (if not impossible) to control the nature of usage scenarios that arise in practice. A second direction is to examine whether it is possible to address as many usage scenarios as we can, but restrict ourselves to analyzing security only against classes of attacks that are known to be practically feasible. This is the approach we take in this work.

In this work we study the practical security of Functional Encryption for Inner Product predicates, which is the state of the art for general FE [5,36,39]. However, we believe that the ideas developed in this work will be applicable to all FE schemes that are built from pairings on elliptic curves, which captures the majority of known FE constructions [11,12,17,35,36,39,45,49].

Real world attacks on elliptic curve based FE. The impossibilities exhibited by [6,15] work by arguing that there exist scenarios which preclude existence of a simulator by information theoretic arguments. However, non-existence of a simulator does not imply real world attacks in the sense of distinguishing between ciphertexts or recovering any useful information about the message or the key. Arguably, attacks that cause actual loss of secrecy are the attacks that we care about in practice, and this is the class of attacks we consider in this work.

For pairing friendly elliptic curves that are used for FE constructions, there has been extensive research effort studying practically feasible attacks. Attacks can be of two kinds: those that respect the algebraic structure of the underlying groups, which are called *generic* attacks, and those that do not, or *non-generic* attacks. Generic attacks are described as algorithms that act oblivious of particular group representations. Due to its importance and wide applicability, much research effort has been focused on studying the complexity of generic and non-generic attacks on pairing-friendly elliptic curves. By now, there is a long line of work [8,22–24] focused on constructing pairing friendly elliptic curves where the complexity of all known non-generic attacks is extremely high. If such elliptic curves are used to build cryptographic schemes, there is strong heuristic evidence that the only successful practically feasible attacks will be generic in nature. We stress that we will work with elliptic curve groups of prime order, and so factoring-based attacks will not be relevant.

A well known mathematical model to study generic attacks is the *Generic Group Model* (GGM) [40,48]. In the GGM, all algorithms obtain access to elements of the group via random "handles" (of sufficient length) and remain unaware of their actual representations. The GGM has a strong track record of usefulness; indeed, even notable critics of provable security, Koblitz and Menezes, despite their criticisms, admit that the generic group model has been unreasonably successful at resisting attack [37].

Our Results. We investigate the security of inner product FE in the generic group model under a new strong framework for security, that captures *all* the usage scenarios discussed above simultaneously. This rules out a large class of attacks – namely arbitrary generic attacks – against the scheme deployed in an arbitrary usage environment. We construct a new inner product FE scheme based on prime order elliptic curve groups. Our results may be summarized as follows.

- *Capturing arbitrary usage scenarios:* We begin by providing a strong, simple and intuitive framework for security which captures all usage scenarios discussed above. Our framework captures function hiding in addition to data hiding; thus it guarantees that CT_x and SK_f reveal no information about *either* x or f beyond what is revealed by $f(x)$. Generalized this way, our framework can be seen to subsume program obfuscation. We also introduce the idea of having a separate encryption key in the context of Functional Encryption. This setting lies between public and symmetric key functional encryption, in that while the encryption key is not publicly known to all users, it is also not the same as the master secret key used for generating secret keys for users in the system. This allows for a division between the people that create encryptions and the people that issue secret keys. We believe this setting is well motivated in the real world, since it is often the case that there is a hierarchy that separates the people that create encrypted data and people that access it. A real-world example would be an FBI encrypted database where police officers can be granted access to parts of the database, but only FBI personnel can add to the database.
- *Resisting generic attacks:* We show that our inner product FE scheme is secure under our strong framework in the Generic Group Model, resolving the problem left open by [15] and [9]. We obtain *unconditional statistical security* for our scheme under our framework in the GGM. Our positive results also translate to the setting of obfuscation, achieving obfuscation for hyperplane membership secure against generic attacks.
- *Concrete security analysis:* Our security analysis is concrete, and as a result we can show exactly what parameters are needed to (provably) achieve security against attackers with different computational resources. For example, we show that with a pairing-friendly elliptic curve group whose order is a 222-bit prime, an attacker who is restricted to 2^{80} generic computations, breaks our scheme with at most 2^{-60} probability of success. Additional security calculations are provided in Table 1.

Table 1. The table entries contain the bit length of security parameter to achieve the corresponding level of security

Adversary Runtime	Success Probability	Required Prime Group Order (bit-length)
2^{80}	2^{-60}	222 bits
2^{80}	2^{-80}	242 bits
2^{100}	2^{-80}	282 bits
2^{128}	2^{-80}	338 bits
2^{128}	2^{-128}	386 bits

Our perspective. By showing that our strong security framework is realizable against all generic attacks, we are providing strong evidence of real-world security even when the generic model is instantiated in a heuristic manner – in our case with a suitably chosen pairing-friendly elliptic curve group. Much care and study is required for how, what, and when security is preserved in such instantiations – indeed this is a very active and important area of research in our community for the Random Oracle Model. We believe that guarantees obtained by such analysis are extremely useful in practice. For example, consider the example of an IBE used in practice, say in a large organization [1]. Suppose the public parameters are published, and some user creates and publishes $2n$ encryptions for users who have yet to obtain their secret keys. Now, if n out of $2n$ users are chosen in some arbitrary, ciphertext-dependent way, and these users obtain their keys, are the remaining n encryptions secure? Simulation based definitions are the only definitions we know that capture security of the IBE in such scenarios, but it was shown by [15] that there cannot exist a simulator for many-AD-SIM security of IBE. On the positive side, [15] also showed that IBE does satisfy many-AD-SIM in the Random Oracle Model. We believe that this is evidence that IBEs indeed provide *practical security* in scenarios such as the above, *even despite* the impossibility of simulation in this scenario.

We do caution that care needs to be exercised in understanding the requirements of any application of FE, and there may be applications for which our guarantees of security against generic attacks do not suffice. Intuitively these are applications where the main threat is not leaking secret information but in *not* being able to actually *simulate* some view. The only example of such a security property that we know of is *deniability*, where only the existence of a simulator would give plausible deniability to a participant. We stress that our analysis of generic attacks should not be taken to imply any kind of deniability.

Function privacy and obfuscation. The question of function privacy (or key hiding) was considered by Shen et al. [47], in the symmetric key setting and more recently by Boneh et al. [13,14] in the public key setting under IND based definitions. [47] provide a construction of FE for inner product predicates in the standard model, under the IND based notion of security, using composite order groups and assuming hardness of factoring (even when viewed in the GGM). Our result, on the other hand, is unconditionally statistically secure in the generic group model, under a strong simulation based definition of security, using prime order groups. Our construction for inner product FE is inspired by the scheme of [36] and the works of [25,28,38,39,42]. It implies a program obfuscator for hyperplane membership in the generic group model – for details see Appendix D, a candidate for which was also given by [18] under a strong variant of the DDH assumption.

Our Techniques. Prior to our work, the only techniques to achieve positive results for many-AD-SIM security of FE were in the programmable ROM, for the anonymous IBE and public-index functionalities, based on techniques to build non-committing encryption in the ROM [15]. We develop new and entirely different techniques to achieve positive results for inner product FE in the GGM under a definition stronger than many-AD-SIM.

As an illustrative example, consider the scenario where the adversary has the encryption key. In this setting, the adversary may encrypt any vector of his choice, and run the decrypt operation with the secret key he is given and the messages he encrypted to learn relations between them. The simulator needs to learn what vectors the adversary is encrypting so as to query the function oracle and program the requisite relations to hold. However, this strategy is complicated by the fact that the adversary need not generate ciphertexts honestly and attempt to decrypt them honestly; instead he can carry out an arbitrarily obfuscated sequence of group operations, which may implicitly be encrypting and decrypting values. Our proof handles this issue by deploying a novel algebraic message extraction technique – the simulator keeps track of all algebraic relations that the adversary is developing, and is able to test if the algebraic relation depends on some property of an unknown vector v corresponding to a decryption key. We prove by algebraic means that if this happens, the adversary *can only* be checking whether v is orthogonal to some other vector u. No other algebraic relations about v can be checked by the adversary because of the randomization present in our inner product FE scheme, except with negligible probability. Furthermore, in this case we prove that the vector u can only be either a vector corresponding to some challenge (honestly generated by the system, not the adversary) ciphertext, or a vector u that the simulator can fully extract from the adversary's algebraic queries.

The generic group model allows us to bypass impossibility because the adversary is forced to perform computations via the generic group oracle which the simulator can control. At a high level, the simulator keeps track of the queries requested by the adversary, uses these queries to learn what the adversary is doing, and carefully programming the oracle to maintain the requisite relations between group elements to behave like the real world in the view of the adversary. For further technical details, please see the proof in Section 5.

2   Preliminaries

In Appendix A, we define some standard notation that is used throughout the paper. We emphasize that all our groups are multiplicative, and any additive notation refers to computations in the exponent.

2.1   Functional Encryption

A functional encryption scheme $\mathcal{FE}$ consists of four algorithms defined as follows.

- Setup(1^κ) is a probabilistic polynomial time (p.p.t.) algorithm that takes as input the unary representation of the security parameter and outputs the public parameters, encryption key and master secret key (PP, EK, MSK). Implicit in the public parameters PP are the security parameter and a function class $\mathcal{F}_{PP} = \{f : \mathcal{X}_{PP} \to \mathcal{Y}_{PP}\}$.
- KeyGen(PP, MSK, f) is a p.p.t. algorithm that takes as input the public parameters PP, the master secret key MSK and a function $f \in \mathcal{F}_{PP}$ and outputs a corresponding secret key SK_f.

- Encrypt(PP, EK, x) is a p.p.t. algorithm that takes as input the public parameters PP, the encryption key EK and an input message $x \in X_{PP}$ and outputs a ciphertext CT_x.
- Decrypt(PP, SK$_f$, CT$_x$) is a deterministic algorithm that takes as input the public parameters PP, the secret key SK$_f$ and a ciphertext CT$_x$ and outputs $f(x)$.

Definition 1 (Correctness). *A functional encryption scheme $\mathcal{FE}$ is correct if for all* (PP, MSK, EK) *generated by* Setup(1^κ), *all* $f \in \mathcal{F}_{PP}$ *and* $x \in X_{PP}$,

$$\Pr[\mathsf{Decrypt}(\mathsf{KeyGen}(\mathsf{PP}, \mathsf{MSK}, f), \mathsf{Encrypt}(\mathsf{PP}, \mathsf{EK}, x)) \neq f(x)]$$

is a negligible function of κ, where the probability is taken over the coins of KeyGen *and* Encrypt.

Remark 1. A functional encryption scheme $\mathcal{FE}$ may permit some *intentional leakage of information*. In this case, the secret SK$_f$ or the ciphertext CT$_x$ may leak some legitimate information about the function f or the message x respectively. A common example of this type of information is the length of the message $|x|$ that is leaked in any public key encryption scheme. This is captured by [15] via the "empty" key, by [6] by giving this information to the simulator directly and by [9] by restricting to adversaries who do not trivially break the system by issuing challenges that differ in such leakage. We use the approach of [6] and pass on any intentionally leaked information directly to the simulator.

2.2   Generic Group (GG) Model Overview

The generic group model [40,48] provides a method by which to study the security of algorithms that act oblivious of particular group representations. All algorithms obtain access to elements of the group via random "handles" (of sufficient length) and remain unaware of their actual representations. In our work we will require two groups $\mathcal{G}, \mathcal{G}_T$ (called the source and target group respectively) where $\mathcal{G}$ is equipped with a bilinear map $e : \mathcal{G} \times \mathcal{G} \to \mathcal{G}_T$. Algorithms with generic access to these may request group multiplications and inverses on either group, as well as pairings between elements in the source group.

Given group elements in $\mathcal{G}, \mathcal{G}_T$ an adversary will only be able to perform group exponentiations, multiplications, pairings and equality comparisons. Given this restricted way in which an adversary is allowed to access the groups $\mathcal{G}, \mathcal{G}_T$, he is only able to compute certain relations between elements which we call Admissible Relations, as defined below.

Definition 2 (Admissible Relations). *Consider a group $\mathcal{G}$ of order p, which supports a bilinear map $e : \mathcal{G} \times \mathcal{G} \to \mathcal{G}_T$. Let g and g_T be the generators of $\mathcal{G}$ and $\mathcal{G}_T$ respectively. Let $\{A_i\}_{i=1}^{\ell}$, $\{B_i\}_{i=1}^{m}$ be sets of formal variables taking values from $\mathbb{Z}_p$, representing the exponents of g and g_T respectively. Then we define admissible relations over the set $\{A_i\} \cup \{B_i\}$ to be all relations of the form $\sum_k \gamma_k A_k \overset{?}{=} 0$ or $\sum_k \gamma_k B_k + \sum_{i,j} \gamma_{i,j} A_i A_j \overset{?}{=} 0$ where $\gamma_k, \gamma_{i,j} \in \mathbb{Z}_p$.*

Admissible relations capture the only relations an adversary can learn given only generic access to elements in the source and target group, described in the exponent for ease of exposition. Thus, exponentiation of a group element becomes multiplication in the exponent (eg. $(g^{A_k})^{\gamma_k}$ becomes $g^{\gamma_k A_k}$), multiplication of two elements in the same group becomes addition in the exponent ($\prod_k (g^{A_k})^{\gamma_k}$ becomes $g^{\sum_k \gamma_k A_k}$) and pairing between source group elements becomes multiplication in the target group exponent ($e(g^{A_i}, g^{A_j})$ becomes $g_T^{A_i A_j}$).

We will also need the Schwartz Zippel lemma.

Theorem 1 (Schwartz Zippel Lemma). *Let g_1, g_2 be any two different ℓ-variate polynomials with coefficients in field $\mathbb{Z}_p$. Let the degree of the polynomial $g_1 - g_2$ be t. Then,*

$$\Pr_{\{X_i\}_{i=1}^{\ell} \xleftarrow{\$} \mathbb{Z}_p} [g_1(X_1, \ldots, X_\ell) = g_2(X_1, \ldots, X_\ell)] \le \frac{t}{p}$$

3 Wishful Security for Functional Encryption

In this section, we present the dream version security definition for Functional Encryption, which captures data hiding as well as function hiding in the strongest, most intuitive way via the ideal world-real world paradigm. This definition extends and generalizes the definition of [9,15] to support function hiding in addition to data hiding (subsuming obfuscation), and encryption key in addition to public key. In the spirit of multiparty computation, this framework guarantees privacy for inputs of honest parties, whether messages or functions.

We fix the functionality of the system to be $\mathcal{F}_\kappa = \{f : \mathcal{X}_\kappa \to \mathcal{Y}_\kappa\}$. We will refer to $x \in \mathcal{X}$ as "message" and $f \in \mathcal{F}$ as "function" or "key". Our framework consists of an external environment Env who acts as an interactive distinguisher attempting to distinguish the real and ideal worlds, potentially in an adversarial manner.

Ideal-World. The ideal-world in a functional encryption system consists of the functional encryption oracle $\mathcal{O}$, the ideal world adversary (or simulator) $\mathcal{S}$, and an environment Env which is used to model all the parties external to the adversary. The adversary $\mathcal{S}$ and the environment Env are modeled as interactive p.p.t Turing machines.

Throughout the interaction, $\mathcal{O}$ maintains a two-dimensional table $\mathcal{T}$ with rows indexed by messages $x_1, \ldots x_{\text{rows}}$ and columns indexed by functions $f_1, \ldots, f_{\text{cols}}$, and the entry corresponding to row x_i and column f_j is $f_j(x_i)$. At a given time, the table contains all the message-key pairs seen in the interactions with $\mathcal{O}$ until then. $\mathcal{O}$ is initialized with a description of the functionality[1]. The environment Env interacts arbitrarily with the adversary $\mathcal{S}$. The interaction between the players is described below:

---

[1] For eg., for the inner product functionality, $\mathcal{O}$ needs to be provided the dimension of the vectors.

- **External ciphertexts and keys:**
    - **Ciphertexts:** Env may send $\mathcal{O}$ ciphertext commands $(\mathsf{CT}, \boldsymbol{x})$ upon which $\mathcal{O}$ creates a new row corresponding to $\boldsymbol{x}$, populates all the newly formed entries $f_1(\boldsymbol{x}), \ldots, f_{\mathsf{cols}}(\boldsymbol{x})$ and returns the newly populated table entires to $\mathcal{S}$.
    - **Keys:** Env may send $\mathcal{O}$ secret key commands (SK, f) upon which $\mathcal{O}$ creates a new column corresponding to f, populates all the newly formed entries $f(\boldsymbol{x}_1), \ldots, f(\boldsymbol{x}_{\mathsf{rows}})$ and returns the newly populated table entries to $\mathcal{S}$.
- **Switch to public key mode:** Upon receiving a command $(\mathsf{PK}\ \mathsf{mode})$ from Env, $\mathcal{O}$ forwards this message to $\mathcal{S}$. From this point on, $\mathcal{S}$ may query $\mathcal{O}$ for the function value corresponding to any message $\boldsymbol{x} \in \mathcal{X}$ of its choice, and any key in the system. Upon receiving command $(\boldsymbol{x}, \mathsf{keys})$, $\mathcal{O}$ updates $\mathcal{T}$ as follows: it adds a new row corresponding to $\boldsymbol{x}$, computes all the table entries for this row, and returns the newly populated row entries to $\mathcal{S}$.

At any point in time we allow $\mathcal{S}$ to obtain any intentionally leaked information (as defined in Remark 1) about all the messages and keys present in $\mathcal{T}$ from $\mathcal{O}$. Note that $\mathcal{S}$ may add any message or key of its choice to the system at any point in time through the adversarial environment Env with which it interacts arbitrarily. Hence, we omit modeling this option in our ideal world. We define $\mathsf{VIEW}_{\mathsf{IDEAL}}(1^\kappa)$ to be the view of Env in the ideal world.

Real-World. The real-world consists of an adversary $\mathcal{A}$, a system administrator Sys and external environment Env, which encompasses all external key holders and encryptors. The adversary $\mathcal{A}$ interacts with other players in the game through Sys. The environment Env may interact arbitrarily with $\mathcal{A}$. Sys obtains $(\mathsf{PP}, \mathsf{EK}, \mathsf{MSK}) \leftarrow \mathsf{Setup}(1^\kappa)$. PP is provided to Env and $\mathcal{A}$. The interaction between the players can be described as follows:

- **External ciphertexts and keys:**
    - **Ciphertexts:** Env may send Sys encryption commands of the form $(\mathsf{CT}, \boldsymbol{x})$ upon which, Sys obtains $\mathsf{CT}_{\boldsymbol{x}} = \mathsf{Encrypt}(\mathsf{EK}, \boldsymbol{x})$ sends $\mathsf{CT}_{\boldsymbol{x}}$ to $\mathcal{A}$.
    - **Keys:** Env may send Sys secret key commands of the form (SK, f) upon which, Sys obtains $\mathsf{SK}_f = \mathsf{KeyGen}(\mathsf{MSK}, f)$ and returns SK_f to $\mathcal{A}$.
- **Switch to public key mode:** Upon receiving a command $(\mathsf{PK}\ \mathsf{mode})$ from Env, Sys sends EK to $\mathcal{A}$.

We define $\mathsf{VIEW}_{\mathsf{REAL}}(1^\kappa)$ to be the view of Env in the real world.

We say that a functional encryption scheme is *strongly simulation secure* in this framework, if for every real world adversary $\mathcal{A}$, there exists a simulator $\mathcal{S}$ such that for every environment Env:

$$\{\mathsf{VIEW}_{\mathsf{IDEAL}}(1^\kappa)\}_{\kappa \in \mathbb{N}} \overset{c}{\approx} \{\mathsf{VIEW}_{\mathsf{REAL}}(1^\kappa)\}_{\kappa \in \mathbb{N}}$$

While simulation based security has been shown impossible to achieve even for data privacy alone, we will show that the stronger definition presented above can be achieved against a large class of real world attacks, namely generic attacks. We believe that this provides evidence that FE schemes enjoy far greater security in practice.

4 Functional Encryption for Inner Products over Prime Order Groups

We present a new functional encryption scheme for inner products in the encryption key setting from prime order bilinear groups. Our scheme starts from the composite order scheme for inner product FE presented in [36]. It then applies a series of transformations, as developed in [25,28,38,41,42], to convert it to a scheme over prime order groups. We will show our scheme to be be fully simulation secure in the generic group model. To begin with, we define some notation that will be useful to us.

Notation for Linear Algebra over groups. When working over the prime order group $\mathcal{G}$, we will find it convenient to consider tuples of group elements. Let $\boldsymbol{v} = (v_1, \cdots, v_d) \in \mathbb{Z}_p^d$ for some $d \in \mathbb{Z}^+$ and $g \in \mathcal{G}$. Then we define $g^{\boldsymbol{v}} := (g^{v_1}, \ldots, g^{v_d})$. For ease of notation, we will refer to $(g^{v_1}, \ldots, g^{v_d})$ by $(v_1, \ldots, v_d)$. This notation allows us to do scalar multiplication and vector addition over tuples of group elements as:

$$(g^{\boldsymbol{v}})^a = g^{(a\boldsymbol{v})} \text{ and } g^{\boldsymbol{v}} \cdot g^{\boldsymbol{w}} = g^{(\boldsymbol{v}+\boldsymbol{w})}.$$

Finally we define a new function, $\boldsymbol{e}$, which deals with pairings two d-tuples of elements $\boldsymbol{v}, \boldsymbol{w}$ as:

$$\boldsymbol{e}(g^{\boldsymbol{v}}, g^{\boldsymbol{w}}) := \prod_{i=1}^{d} e(g^{v_i}, g^{w_i}) = e(g, g)^{\boldsymbol{v} \cdot \boldsymbol{w}},$$

where the vector dot product $\boldsymbol{v} \cdot \boldsymbol{w}$ in the last term is taken modulo p. Here g is assumed to be some fixed generator of $\mathcal{G}$.

Dual Pairing Vector Spaces. We will employ the concept of dual pairing vector spaces from [38,41,42]. For a fixed dimension d, let $\mathbb{B} = (\boldsymbol{b}_1, \ldots, \boldsymbol{b}_d)$ and $\mathbb{B}^* = (\boldsymbol{b}_1^*, \ldots, \boldsymbol{b}_d^*)$ be two random bases (represented as column vectors) for the vector space $\mathbb{Z}_p^d$. Furthermore, they are chosen so that

$$\begin{pmatrix} \boldsymbol{b}_1^T \\ \vdots \\ \boldsymbol{b}_d^T \end{pmatrix} \cdot \begin{pmatrix} \boldsymbol{b}_1^* \cdots \boldsymbol{b}_d^* \end{pmatrix} = \psi \cdot \mathbf{I}_{d \times d}, \tag{1}$$

where $\mathbf{I}_{d \times d}$ is the identity matrix and $\psi \xleftarrow{\$} \mathbb{Z}_p$. Lewko [38] describes a standard procedure which allows one to pick such bases.

We use the notation $(\mathbb{B}, \mathbb{B}^*) \leftarrow \mathsf{Dual}(\mathbb{Z}_p^3)$ in the rest of this work to describe the selection of such basis vectors for $d = 3$. Furthermore, we overload vector notation (the usage will be clear from context) by associating with a three tuple of formal polynomials (a_1, a_2, a_3), the vector of formal polynomials $a_1 \boldsymbol{b}_1 + a_2 \boldsymbol{b}_2 + a_3 \boldsymbol{b}_3$, and with the tuple $(a_1, a_2, a_3)^*$, the vector $a_1 \boldsymbol{b}_1^* + a_2 \boldsymbol{b}_2^* + a_3 \boldsymbol{b}_3^*$.

Construction. The functionality $\mathcal{F} : \mathbb{Z}_p^n \times \mathbb{Z}_p^n \to \{0, 1\}$ is described as $\mathcal{F}(\boldsymbol{x}, \boldsymbol{v}) = 1$ if $\langle \boldsymbol{x} \cdot \boldsymbol{v} \rangle = 0 \mod p$, and 0 otherwise. Let GroupGen be a group generation algorithm which takes as input a security parameter κ and outputs the description of a bilinear group of order p, where p is a κ-bit prime. In the description of the scheme and in the proof, we will "work in the exponent" for ease of notation as described at the beginning of this section.

The four algorithms Setup, KeyGen, Encrypt and Decrypt are defined as follows.

- Setup(1^κ): Let $(p, \mathcal{G}, \mathcal{G}_T, e) \leftarrow \mathsf{GroupGen}(1^\kappa)$. Let $n \in \mathbb{Z}, n > 1$ be the dimension of the message space. Pick $(\mathbb{B}, \mathbb{B}^*) \leftarrow \mathsf{Dual}(\mathbb{Z}_p^3)$ and let $P, Q, R, R_0,$
$H_1, R_1, H_2, R_2, \ldots, H_n, R_n \xleftarrow{\$} \mathbb{Z}_p$. Set

$$\mathsf{PP} = (p, \mathcal{G}, \mathcal{G}_T, e),$$

$$\mathsf{EK} = \left(P \cdot \boldsymbol{b}_1, Q \cdot \boldsymbol{b}_2 + R_0 \cdot \boldsymbol{b}_3, R \cdot \boldsymbol{b}_3, \{H_i \cdot \boldsymbol{b}_1 + R_i \cdot \boldsymbol{b}_3\}_{i=1}^{i=n} \right),$$

$$\mathsf{MSK} = \left(P, Q, \{H_i\}_{i=1}^{i=n}, \boldsymbol{b}_1, \boldsymbol{b}_2, \boldsymbol{b}_3, \boldsymbol{b}_1^*, \boldsymbol{b}_2^*, \boldsymbol{b}_3^* \right).$$

- Encrypt($\mathsf{EK}, \boldsymbol{x}$): Let $\boldsymbol{x} = (x_1, \ldots, x_n)$, $x_i \in \mathbb{Z}_p$. Let $s, \alpha, r_1, \ldots, r_n \xleftarrow{\$} \mathbb{Z}_p$ and construct $\mathsf{CT}_{\boldsymbol{x}} = (C_0, C_1, \ldots, C_n)$ as

$$C_0 = s \cdot P \cdot \boldsymbol{b}_1,$$

and for $i \in [1, n]$,

$$C_i = s \cdot (H_i \cdot \boldsymbol{b}_1 + R_i \cdot \boldsymbol{b}_3) + \alpha \cdot x_i \cdot (Q \cdot \boldsymbol{b}_2 + R_0 \cdot \boldsymbol{b}_3) + r_i \cdot R \cdot \boldsymbol{b}_3.$$

- KeyGen($\mathsf{MSK}, \boldsymbol{v}$): Let $\boldsymbol{v} = (v_1, \ldots, v_n), v_i \in \mathbb{Z}_p$. Let $\delta_1, \ldots, \delta_n, \zeta, T \xleftarrow{\$} \mathbb{Z}_p$ and construct $\mathsf{SK}_{\boldsymbol{v}} = (K_0, K_1, \ldots, K_n)$ as

$$K_0 = \left(-\sum_{i=1}^{n} H_i \cdot \delta_i \right) \cdot \boldsymbol{b}_1^* + T \cdot \boldsymbol{b}_3^*,$$

and for $i \in [1, n]$,

$$K_i = \delta_i \cdot P \cdot \boldsymbol{b}_1^* + Q \cdot \zeta \cdot v_i \cdot \boldsymbol{b}_2^*.$$

- Decrypt($\mathsf{SK}_{\boldsymbol{v}}, \mathsf{CT}_{\boldsymbol{x}}$): Compute $b = e(C_0, K_0) \cdot \prod_{i=1}^{i=n} e(C_i, K_i)$ and output 1 if $b = e(g, g)^0$ and 0 otherwise.

Intentionally leaked information as defined in Remark 1 for the above scheme is n, the dimension of the message and key space. Correctness of the scheme relies on the cancellation properties between the vectors in $\mathbb{B}$ and $\mathbb{B}^*$ as described in Eqn 1. We provide proof of correctness in Appendix B.

5   Proof of Security

We will now provide a proof that the scheme presented in Section 4 is fully simulation secure in the generic group model as per the framework presented in Section 3. We begin by describing the construction of our simulator.

5.1   Simulator Construction

Intuition. Broadly speaking, our simulator will run the adversary and provide secret keys and ciphertexts to him, as well as simulate the GG oracle. Our simulator maintains a table where it associates each group handle that it issues to the adversary with a formal polynomial. Through its interaction with the generic group oracle (played by $\mathcal{S}$), $\mathcal{A}$ may learn relations between the group handles that it obtains. Note that since we are in the GG model, $\mathcal{A}$ will only be able to learn admissible relations (Definition 2). Whatever dependencies $\mathcal{A}$ learns, $\mathcal{S}$ programs these using its table. To do this, it keeps track of what $\mathcal{A}$ is doing via its requests to the GG oracle, extracts necessary information from $\mathcal{A}$ cleverly where required and sets up these (formal polynomial) relations, thus ensuring that the real and ideal world views are indistinguishable. This is tricky in the public key mode, where the adversary may encrypt messages of its choice (using potentially bad randomness) and attempt to learn relations with existing keys using arbitrary generic group operations. In this case, the simulator needs to be able to extract the message from the adversary, obtain the relevant function values from the oracle, and program the dependencies into the generic group.

Formal Construction. Formally, the simulator $\mathcal{S}$ is specified as follows:

- **Initialization:** $\mathcal{S}$ constructs a table called *simulation table* to simulate the GG oracle $(p, \mathcal{G}, \mathcal{G}_T, e)$. A simulation table consists of two parts one each for the source group $\mathcal{G}$ and the target group $\mathcal{G}_T$ respectively. Each part is a list that contains two columns labelled formal polynomial and group handle respectively. Group handles are strings from $\{0,1\}^{2\kappa}$. A formal polynomial is a multivariate polynomial defined over $\mathbb{Z}_p$. We assume that there is a canonical ordering amongst the variables used to create the formal polynomial entries and thus each polynomial may be represented by a unique canonical representation.
- **Setup:** Upon receiving the dimension n of message and key space from $\mathcal{O}$, $\mathcal{S}$ executes the setup algorithm of the scheme as follows. He generates new group handles corresponding to the identity elements of $\mathcal{G}$ and $\mathcal{G}_T$. He picks 18 new formal variables that represent the bases $(\mathbb{B}, \mathbb{B}^*) \leftarrow \mathsf{Dual}(\mathbb{Z}_p^3)$, as well as a new formal variable ψ. Next, $\mathcal{S}$ picks new formal variables $P, Q, R, R_0, \{H_i, R_i\}_{i=1}^{i=n}$. He sets up the encryption key and master secret key by generating new group handles to represent the formal polynomials: $\mathsf{EK} = \{(P, 0, 0), (0, 0, R), (0, Q, R_0), \{(H_i, 0, R_i)\}_{i=1}^{n}\}$ and $\mathsf{MSK} = \{P, Q, \{H_i\}_{i=1}^{i=n}, \boldsymbol{b}_1, \boldsymbol{b}_2, \boldsymbol{b}_3, \boldsymbol{b}_1^*, \boldsymbol{b}_2^*, \boldsymbol{b}_3^*\}$. He stores these associations in the simulation table.

- **Running the adversary:** $\mathcal{S}$ runs the adversary $\mathcal{A}(1^\kappa)$ and gives it the public parameters $\mathsf{PP} = (p, \mathcal{G}, \mathcal{G}_T, e)$. This amounts to $\mathcal{S}$ providing the adversary with oracle access to $\mathcal{G}, \mathcal{G}_T, e$ and sending him p.
- **Request for Public Key:** When $\mathcal{S}$ receives the command PK mode from $\mathcal{O}$, he sends the group handles of EK to $\mathcal{A}$.
- **External Ciphertexts and Keys:** At any time, $\mathcal{S}$ may receive a message of the form MsgIdx_x, $f_1(x), \ldots, f_{\mathsf{cols}}(x)$ from $\mathcal{O}$. In response:
  - $\mathcal{S}$ follows the outline of the Encrypt algorithm in the following way. He picks new formal variables $s, \alpha, \{x_i\}_{i=1}^n, \{r_i\}_{i=1}^n$ (all indexed by the particular index MsgIdx_x, dropped here for notational convenience). He then constructs the formal polynomials associated with the following 3-tuples:

$$C = \left\{ C_0 = (sP,\ 0,\ 0), \left\{ C_i = (sH_i,\ \alpha x_i Q,\ sR_i + \alpha x_i R_0 + r_i R) \right\}_{i=1}^n \right\},$$

    and adds each formal polynomial thus generated in C to the simulation table along with a new group handle.
  - $\mathcal{S}$ then programs the generic group to incorporate the function values $f_1(x), \ldots, f_{\mathsf{cols}}(x)$ that were received. To do this, $\mathcal{S}$ retrieves the formal polynomials associated with all the keys in the table $\{K^j = (K_0^j, K_1^j, \ldots, K_n^j)\}_{j \in [\mathsf{cols}]}$. Then, for each j, he computes the formal polynomials associated with the decrypt operation between C and K^j, i.e., $b = e(C_0, K_0^j) \cdot \prod_{i=1}^{i=n} e(C_i, K_i^j)$. If $f_j(x) = 0$, he sets the resultant expression to correspond to the group handle for the identity element in the target group. Else, he generates a new group handle and stores the resultant expression to correspond to it.
  - $\mathcal{S}$ then sends the group handles corresponding to C to $\mathcal{A}$.

  He acts analogously in the case of a KeyIdx_j, $f_j(x_1), \ldots, f_j(x_{\mathsf{rows}})$ message by following the KeyGen algorithm to generate formal polynomials corresponding to a new key and programming the decrypt expressions to correspond to the received function values.
- **Generic Group Operations:** At any stage, $\mathcal{A}$ may request generic group operations from $\mathcal{S}$ by providing the corresponding group handle(s) and specifying the requested operation, such as pairing, identity, inverse or group operation. In response, $\mathcal{S}$ looks up its simulation table for the formal polynomial(s) corresponding to the specified group handle(s), computes the operation between the formal polynomials, simplifies the resultant expression and does a reverse lookup in the table to find a group handle corresponding to the resultant polynomial. If it finds it, $\mathcal{S}$ will return this group handle to $\mathcal{A}$, otherwise it randomly generates a new group handle, stores it in the simulation table against the resultant formal polynomial, and returns this to $\mathcal{A}$. For more details, we refer the reader to Appendix C.

Tracking admissible relations learnt by $\mathcal{A}$: If $\mathcal{A}$ requests generic group operations to compute a polynomial involving a term $\psi Q^2 \mathsf{expr}$ where expr is an expression containing a term of the form $\sum_{i=1}^n c_i v_i$ for some constant $c_i \in \mathbb{Z}_p$, then $\mathcal{S}$ considers this as a function evaluation by $\mathcal{A}$ on message that he encrypted himself. He extracts the message $x = (c_1, \ldots, c_n)$. $\mathcal{S}$ then sends the message (x, keys) to $\mathcal{O}$. Upon receiving $\mathsf{MsgIdx}_x, f_1(x), \ldots, f_{\mathsf{cols}}(x)$ from $\mathcal{O}$, $\mathcal{S}$ computes the decrypt expressions for the extracted message with all the keys and programs the linear relations in the generic group oracle as in the previous step.

In the full version of the paper we show that the real and ideal worlds are indistinguishable to Env. Formally, we prove the following theorem:

Theorem 2. *For all p.p.t. adversaries $\mathcal{A}$, the simulator $\mathcal{S}$ constructed in Section 5.1 is such that for all Env with auxiliary input z, $\{\mathsf{VIEW}_{\mathsf{IDEAL}}(1^\kappa, z)\}_{\kappa \in \mathbb{Z}^+, z \in \{0,1\}^*} \approx \{\mathsf{VIEW}_{\mathsf{REAL}}(1^\kappa, z)\}_{\kappa \in \mathbb{Z}^+, z \in \{0,1\}^*}$ in the generic group model.*

5.2   Concrete Parameters

From the proof of Theorem 2, we observe that the only case for distinguishability between real and ideal worlds is the hybrid where we move from Generic Group elements to polynomials in formal variables.

Thus, we have that if the adversary receives q group elements in total from the groups $\mathbb{G}$ and $\mathbb{G}_T$, then the probability that he would be able to distinguish between the real and ideal worlds is

$$q \frac{(q-1)}{2} \frac{t}{p}$$

where t is the maximum degree of any formal variable polynomial that could be constructed in our cryptosystem. It is a maximum of 3 for each element in the source group for our FE scheme and thus $t = 6$ considering possible pairings. p is the order of the group.

5.3   Practical Considerations

We observe that every pairing in our scheme is between some element of the ciphertext and an element of the key. Thus suppose $\mathbb{G}_1, \mathbb{G}_2, \mathbb{G}_T, e : \mathbb{G}_1 \times \mathbb{G}_2 \to \mathbb{G}_T$ be a set of groups with an asymmetric bilinear map. Then it is easy to see that our scheme extends to this setting by choosing the ciphertext elements from $\mathbb{G}_1$ and the key elements from $\mathbb{G}_2$. Furthermore, our security proof also extends to this setting, as a generic group adversary is now further restricted in the set of queries he could make. This allows for a scheme in the faster setting of asymmetric bilinear maps.

We also note that our scheme is shown to be secure against generic attacks and that non-generic attacks do exist in all known bilinear groups. However, a long list of previous research focuses on constructing elliptic curves where the complexity of any non-generic attack is worse than generic attacks [8,12,22–24] making our work relevant and meaningful. These constructions are practical as well. Hence we believe that FE constructions over suitably chosen elliptic curve groups have the potential of being practically secure.

A   Notation

We say that a function $f : \mathbb{Z}^+ \to \mathbb{R}^+$ is negligible if $f(\lambda) \in \lambda^{-\omega(1)}$. For two distributions $\mathcal{D}_1$ and $\mathcal{D}_2$ over some set Ω we define the statistical distance $\text{SD}(\mathcal{D}_1, \mathcal{D}_2)$ as

$$\text{SD}(\mathcal{D}_1, \mathcal{D}_2) := \frac{1}{2} \sum_{x \in \Omega} \left| \Pr_{\mathcal{D}_1}[x] - \Pr_{\mathcal{D}_2}[x] \right|$$

We say that two distribution ensembles $\mathcal{D}_1(\lambda)$ and $\mathcal{D}_2(\lambda)$ are statistically close or statistically indistinguishable if $\text{SD}(\mathcal{D}_1(\lambda), \mathcal{D}_2(\lambda))$ is a negligible function of λ.

We say that two distribution ensembles $\mathcal{D}_1(\lambda), \mathcal{D}_2(\lambda)$ are computationally indistinguishable, denoted by $\overset{c}{\approx}$, if for all probabilistic polynomial time turing machines $\mathcal{A}$,

$$\left| \Pr[\mathcal{A}(1^\lambda, \mathcal{D}_1(\lambda)) = 1] - \Pr[\mathcal{A}(1^\lambda, \mathcal{D}_2(\lambda)) = 1] \right|$$

is a negligible function of λ.

We use $a \overset{\$}{\leftarrow} S$ to denote that a is chosen uniformly at random from the set S.

B   Correctness of Inner Product Scheme

For any SK_v and CT_x, the pairing evaluations in the decryption part of our scheme proceed as follows. Terms that are marked $(\times)$ are ones that we do not care about.

$$e(C_0, K_0) = e\left((sP \cdot \boldsymbol{b}_1), \left((-\sum_{i=1}^{n} H_i \cdot \delta_i) \cdot \boldsymbol{b}_1^* + T \cdot \boldsymbol{b}_3^* \right) \right)$$

$$= (-sP \sum_{i=1}^{n} H_i \delta_i) \cdot (\boldsymbol{b}_1^T \cdot \boldsymbol{b}_1^*) + (\times)(\boldsymbol{b}_1^T \cdot \boldsymbol{b}_3^*)$$

$$= \psi(-sP \sum_{i=1}^{n} H_i \delta_i) \text{ (by Equation 1)}$$

$$e(C_i, K_i) = e\left((s(H_i \cdot \boldsymbol{b}_1 + R_i \cdot \boldsymbol{b}_3) + \alpha \cdot x_i \cdot (Q \cdot \boldsymbol{b}_2 + R_0 \cdot \boldsymbol{b}_3) + r_i \cdot \boldsymbol{b}_3), \right.$$
$$\left. (\delta_i \cdot P \cdot \boldsymbol{b}_1^* + Q \cdot \zeta \cdot v_i \cdot \boldsymbol{b}_2^*) \right)$$

$$= (sH_i\delta_iP)\boldsymbol{b}_1^T\boldsymbol{b}_1^* + (\alpha x_i Q \cdot Q\zeta v_i)\boldsymbol{b}_2^T\boldsymbol{b}_2^* + (\times)(\boldsymbol{b}_1^T \cdot \boldsymbol{b}_2^* + \boldsymbol{b}_2^T \cdot \boldsymbol{b}_1^* + $$
$$\boldsymbol{b}_3^T \cdot \boldsymbol{b}_1^* + \boldsymbol{b}_3^T \cdot \boldsymbol{b}_2^*)$$

$$= \psi(sH_i\delta_iP + \alpha\zeta Q^2 x_i v_i) \text{ (by Equation 1)}$$

Thus, $e(C_0, K) \cdot \prod_{i=1}^{i=n} e(C_i, K_i)$

$$= \psi(-sP \sum_{i=1}^{n} H_i\delta_i) + \sum_{i=1}^{n} \left(\psi(sH_i\delta_iP + \alpha\zeta Q^2 x_i v_i) \right)$$

$$= \psi Q^2 \alpha \zeta (\sum_{i=1}^{n} x_i v_i)$$

When $\sum_{i=1}^{n} x_i v_i$ is 0 mod p, the final answer is always the identity element of the target group and when it is not, the answer evaluates to a random element in the target group (as $\psi, Q, \alpha, \zeta \xleftarrow{\$} \mathbb{Z}_p$).

C   Generic Group Operations

Whenever $\mathcal{A}$ requests the GG oracle for group operations corresponding $\mathcal{G}, \mathcal{G}_T$ or the pairing operation e, $\mathcal{S}$ does the following:

1. **Request for Identity:** When $\mathcal{A}$ requests for the identity element of the group $\mathcal{G}$, $\mathcal{S}$ looks up the simulation table for the formal polynomial 0 in the part that corresponds to $\mathcal{G}$ and returns the group handle corresponding to it to the adversary. He acts analogously with request for the identity of $\mathcal{G}_T$.

2. **Request for Inverses:** When $\mathcal{A}$ requests the inverse of a group handle h in $\mathcal{G}$, $\mathcal{S}$ looks up the formal polynomial associated with h from the simulation table, denoted by $\hat{h}$. He computes the polynomial $(-1)\hat{h}$ and looks for it in the simulation table. If he finds an associated group handle, he returns it to $\mathcal{A}$. If not, he generates a new group handle and adds the association between $(-1)\hat{h}$ and the generated handle to the first part of the table. He returns the newly generated handle to $\mathcal{A}$. He acts analogously for requests involving handles in $\mathcal{G}_T$.

3. **Request for group operation:** When $\mathcal{A}$ requests a group operation on two group elements $h, \ell \in \mathcal{G}$, $\mathcal{S}$ looks them both up in the simulation table and obtains their corresponding formal polynomials $\hat{h}$ and $\hat{\ell}$. He computes the formal polynomial $\hat{q} = \hat{h} + \hat{\ell}$. $\mathcal{S}$ then does a look up in the simulation table for the polynomial $\hat{q}$ and if it finds an associated group handle, returns it to $\mathcal{A}$. If it doesn't find a group handle corresponding to $\hat{q}$, it generates a new group handle and adds this association to the first part of the simulation table and returns the newly generated handle to $\mathcal{A}$. He acts analogously for requests involving handles in $\mathcal{G}_T$.

4. **Request for Pairing operation:** When $\mathcal{A}$ requests a pairing operation on two group elements $h, \ell \in \mathcal{G}$, $\mathcal{S}$ looks them both up in the simulation table and obtains their corresponding formal polynomials $\hat{h}$ and $\hat{\ell}$. He computes the formal polynomial $\hat{q} = \hat{h} \times \hat{\ell}$, where $\times$ denotes polynomial multiplication. $\mathcal{S}$ then does a look up in the simulation table for the polynomial $\hat{q}$ and if it finds an associated group handle, returns it to $\mathcal{A}$. If it doesn't find a group handle corresponding to $\hat{q}$, it generates a new group handle and adds this association to the second part of the simulation table and returns the newly generated handle to $\mathcal{A}$.

D   Obfuscation Scheme

In this section we present an obfuscation scheme for hyperplane membership. We begin by providing a definition for obfuscation schemes from [18].

D.1 Formal Definition of Obfuscation

Let $\mathcal{C} = \{C_\kappa\}_{\kappa \in \mathbb{Z}^+}$ be a family of polynomial-size circuits, where C_κ denotes all circuits of input length κ. A p.p.t. algorithm $\mathcal{O}$ is an obfuscator for the family $\mathcal{C}$ if the following three conditions are met.

- **Approximate functionality**: There exists a negligible function ϵ such that for every κ, every circuit $C \in C_\kappa$ and every x in the input space of C, $Pr[\mathcal{O}(C)(x) = C(x)] > 1-\epsilon(\kappa)$, where the probability is over the randomness of $\mathcal{O}$. If this probability always equals 1, then we say that $\mathcal{O}$ has exact functionality.
- **Polynomial slowdown**: There exists a polynomial q such that for every κ, every circuit $C \in C_\kappa$, and every possible sequence of coin tosses for $\mathcal{O}$, the circuit $\mathcal{O}(C)$ runs in time at most $q(|C|)$.
- **Virtual black-box**: For every p.p.t. adversary A and polynomial δ, there exists a p.p.t. simulator S such that for all sufficiently large κ, and for all $C \in C_\kappa$,

$$\left| \Pr[A(\mathcal{O}(C)) = 1] - \Pr[S^C(1^\kappa) = 1] \right| < \frac{1}{\delta(\kappa)},$$

where the first probability is taken over the coin tosses of A and $\mathcal{O}$, and the second probability is taken over the coin tosses of S.

D.2 Construction

Hyperplane membership testing amounts to computing inner-product over a vector space [18], for which we constructed a functional encryption scheme in Section 4. The circuit family for hyperplane membership, though, is defined in a slightly different way because the circuits have the description of a hyperplane hardwired in them, which is just a vector. More formally, let p be a κ-bit prime and n a positive integer $(n > 1)$. For a vector $v \in \mathbb{Z}_p^n$, let F_v be a circuit which on input $x \in \mathbb{Z}_p^n$ outputs 1 if $\langle x \cdot v \rangle = 0 \mod p$, and 0 otherwise. We provide an obfuscator $\mathcal{O}$ for the function family $\mathcal{F}_{p,n} = \{F_v \mid v \in \mathbb{Z}_p^n\}$, basing it directly on the functional encryption scheme from Section 4.

- Run $\mathsf{Setup}(1^\kappa)$ to obtain $(\mathsf{PP}, \mathsf{MSK}, \mathsf{EK})$. Publish these values as public parameters.
- **Obfuscator $\mathcal{O}$**: On input $v \in \mathcal{F}_{p,n}$, execute $\mathsf{KeyGen}(\mathsf{MSK}, v)$ to get SK_v. Output a circuit with EK and SK_v hardwired. On input x, this circuit first computes $\mathsf{CT}_x \leftarrow \mathsf{Encrypt}(\mathsf{EK}, x)$, then outputs $\mathsf{Decrypt}(\mathsf{SK}_v, \mathsf{CT}_x)$.

D.3 Proof of Security

We informally mention the reason why construction from D.2 is a valid obfuscation scheme.

- **Approximate functionality**: The scheme $\mathcal{O}$ achieves exact functionality from the exact correctness of the underlying FE scheme.

- **Polynomial slowdown**: The scheme achieves polynomial slowdown because of the polynomial runtime of Encrypt and Decrypt algorithms of the underlying FE scheme.
- **Virtual black-box**: The scheme satisfies the virtual black-box property *in the generic group model* from the proof of security of the underlying FE scheme. We defer a formal proof of this last property to the full version.

References

1. Voltage security. http://www.voltage.com/
2. Agrawal, S., Agrawal, S., Prabhakaran, M.: Cryptographic agents: towards a unified theory of computing on encrypted data. In: To appear in Eurocrypt 2015 (2015)
3. Agrawal, S., Boneh, D., Boyen, X.: Efficient lattice (H)IBE in the standard model. In: Gilbert, H. (ed.) EUROCRYPT 2010. LNCS, vol. 6110, pp. 553–572. Springer, Heidelberg (2010)
4. Agrawal, S., Boneh, D., Boyen, X.: Lattice basis delegation in fixed dimension and shorter-ciphertext hierarchical IBE. In: Rabin, T. (ed.) CRYPTO 2010. LNCS, vol. 6223, pp. 98–115. Springer, Heidelberg (2010)
5. Agrawal, S., Freeman, D.M., Vaikuntanathan, V.: Functional encryption for inner product predicates from learning with errors. In: Lee, D.H., Wang, X. (eds.) ASIACRYPT 2011. LNCS, vol. 7073, pp. 21–40. Springer, Heidelberg (2011)
6. Agrawal, S., Gorbunov, S., Vaikuntanathan, V., Wee, H.: Functional encryption: New perspectives and lower bounds. In: Canetti, R., Garay, J.A. (eds.) CRYPTO 2013, Part II. LNCS, vol. 8043, pp. 500–518. Springer, Heidelberg (2013)
7. Ananth, P., Boneh, D., Garg, S., Sahai, A., Zhandry, M.: Differing-inputs obfuscation and applications. Cryptology Eprint Arxiv (2013). http://eprint.iacr.org/2013/689.pdf
8. Aranha, D.F., Fuentes-Castañeda, L., Knapp, E., Menezes, A., Rodríguez-Henríquez, F.: Implementing pairings at the 192-bit security level. In: Abdalla, M., Lange, T. (eds.) Pairing 2012. LNCS, vol. 7708, pp. 177–195. Springer, Heidelberg (2013)
9. Barbosa, M., Farshim, P.: On the semantic security of functional encryption schemes. In: Kurosawa, K., Hanaoka, G. (eds.) PKC 2013. LNCS, vol. 7778, pp. 143–161. Springer, Heidelberg (2013)
10. Bellare, M., O'Neill, A.: Semantically-secure functional encryption: possibility results, impossibility results and the quest for a general definition. In: Abdalla, M., Nita-Rotaru, C., Dahab, R. (eds.) CANS 2013. LNCS, vol. 8257, pp. 218–234. Springer, Heidelberg (2013)
11. Bethencourt, J., Sahai, A., Waters, B.: Ciphertext-policy attribute-based encryption. In: IEEE Symposium on Security and Privacy, pp. 321–334 (2007)
12. Boneh, D., Franklin, M.: Identity-based encryption from the weil pairing. In: Kilian, J. (ed.) CRYPTO 2001. LNCS, vol. 2139, pp. 213–229. Springer, Heidelberg (2001)
13. Boneh, D., Raghunathan, A., Segev, G.: Function-private identity-based encryption: hiding the function in functional encryption. In: Canetti, R., Garay, J.A. (eds.) CRYPTO 2013, Part II. LNCS, vol. 8043, pp. 461–478. Springer, Heidelberg (2013)
14. Boneh, D., Raghunathan, A., Segev, G.: Function-private subspace-membership encryption and Its applications. In: Sako, K., Sarkar, P. (eds.) ASIACRYPT 2013, Part I. LNCS, vol. 8269, pp. 255–275. Springer, Heidelberg (2013)

15. Boneh, D., Sahai, A., Waters, B.: Functional encryption: definitions and challenges. In: Ishai, Y. (ed.) TCC 2011. LNCS, vol. 6597, pp. 253–273. Springer, Heidelberg (2011)

16. Boneh, D., Waters, B.: Conjunctive, subset, and range queries on encrypted data. In: Vadhan, S.P. (ed.) TCC 2007. LNCS, vol. 4392, pp. 535–554. Springer, Heidelberg (2007)

17. Boyen, X., Waters, B.: Anonymous hierarchical identity-based encryption (without random oracles). In: Dwork, C. (ed.) CRYPTO 2006. LNCS, vol. 4117, pp. 290–307. Springer, Heidelberg (2006)

18. Canetti, R., Rothblum, G.N., Varia, M.: Obfuscation of hyperplane membership. In: Micciancio, D. (ed.) TCC 2010. LNCS, vol. 5978, pp. 72–89. Springer, Heidelberg (2010)

19. De Caro, A., Iovino, V., Jain, A., O'Neill, A., Paneth, O., Persiano, G.: On the achievability of simulation-based security for functional encryption. In: Canetti, R., Garay, J.A. (eds.) CRYPTO 2013, Part II. LNCS, vol. 8043, pp. 519–535. Springer, Heidelberg (2013)

20. Cash, D., Hofheinz, D., Kiltz, E., Peikert, C.: Bonsai trees, or how to delegate a lattice basis. In: Gilbert, H. (ed.) EUROCRYPT 2010. LNCS, vol. 6110, pp. 523–552. Springer, Heidelberg (2010)

21. Cocks, C.: An identity based encryption scheme based on quadratic residues. In: Honary, B. (ed.) Cryptography and Coding 2001. LNCS, vol. 2260, pp. 360–363. Springer, Heidelberg (2001)

22. Costello, C.: Particularly friendly members of family trees. IACR Cryptology ePrint Archive, 2012:72 (2012)

23. Freeman, D.: Constructing pairing-friendly elliptic curves with embedding degree 10. In: Hess, F., Pauli, S., Pohst, M. (eds.) ANTS 2006. LNCS, vol. 4076, pp. 452–465. Springer, Heidelberg (2006)

24. Freeman, D., Scott, M., Teske, E.: A taxonomy of pairing-friendly elliptic curves. Journal of Cryptology 23(2), 224–280 (2010)

25. Freeman, D.M.: Converting pairing-based cryptosystems from composite-order groups to prime-order groups. In: Gilbert, H. (ed.) EUROCRYPT 2010. LNCS, vol. 6110, pp. 44–61. Springer, Heidelberg (2010)

26. Garg, S., Gentry, C., Halevi, S., Raykova, M., Sahai, A., Waters, B.: Candidate indistinguishability obfuscation and functional encryption for all circuits. In: FOCS (2013)

27. Garg, S., Gentry, C., Halevi, S., Sahai, A., Waters, B.: Attribute-based encryption for circuits from multilinear maps. In: Canetti, R., Garay, J.A. (eds.) CRYPTO 2013, Part II. LNCS, vol. 8043, pp. 479–499. Springer, Heidelberg (2013)

28. Garg, S., Kumarasubramanian, A., Sahai, A., Waters, B.: Building efficient fully collusion-resilient traitor tracing and revocation schemes. In: ACM Conference on Computer and Communications Security, pp. 121–130 (2010)

29. Gentry, C., Peikert, C., Vaikuntanathan, V.: Trapdoors for hard lattices and new cryptographic constructions. In: STOC, pp. 197–206 (2008)

30. Goldwasser, S., Gordon, S.D., Goyal, V., Jain, A., Katz, J., Liu, F.-H., Sahai, A., Shi, E., Zhou, H.-S.: Multi-input functional encryption. In: Nguyen, P.Q., Oswald, E. (eds.) EUROCRYPT 2014. LNCS, vol. 8441, pp. 578–602. Springer, Heidelberg (2014)

31. Goldwasser, S., Kalai, Y.T., Popa, R.A., Vaikuntanathan, V., Zeldovich, N.: How to run turing machines on encrypted data. In: Canetti, R., Garay, J.A. (eds.) CRYPTO 2013, Part II. LNCS, vol. 8043, pp. 536–553. Springer, Heidelberg (2013)

32. Goldwasser, S., Kalai, Y.T., Popa, R.A., Vaikuntanathan, V., Zeldovich, N.: Reusable garbled circuits and succinct functional encryption. In: STOC, pp. 555–564 (2013)
33. Gorbunov, S., Vaikuntanathan, V., Wee, H.: Functional encryption with bounded collusions from multiparty computation. In: CRYPTO (2012)
34. Gorbunov, S., Vaikuntanathan, V., Wee, H.: Attribute based encryption for circuits. In: STOC (2013)
35. Goyal, V., Pandey, O., Sahai, A., Waters, B.: Attribute-based encryption for fine-grained access control of encrypted data. In: ACM conference on computer and communications security, pp. 89–98 (2006)
36. Katz, J., Sahai, A., Waters, B.: Predicate encryption supporting disjunctions, polynomial equations, and inner products. In: Smart, N.P. (ed.) EUROCRYPT 2008. LNCS, vol. 4965, pp. 146–162. Springer, Heidelberg (2008)
37. Koblitz, N., Menezes, A.: Another look at generic groups. In: Advances in Mathematics of Communications, pp. 13–28 (2006)
38. Lewko, A.: Tools for simulating features of composite order bilinear groups in the prime order setting. In: Pointcheval, D., Johansson, T. (eds.) EUROCRYPT 2012. LNCS, vol. 7237, pp. 318–335. Springer, Heidelberg (2012)
39. Lewko, A., Okamoto, T., Sahai, A., Takashima, K., Waters, B.: Fully secure functional encryption: attribute-based encryption and (hierarchical) inner product encryption. In: Gilbert, H. (ed.) EUROCRYPT 2010. LNCS, vol. 6110, pp. 62–91. Springer, Heidelberg (2010)
40. Nechaev, V.I.: Complexity of a determinate algorithm for the discrete logarithm. Mathematical Notes 55 (1994)
41. Okamoto, T., Takashima, K.: Homomorphic encryption and signatures from vector decomposition. In: Galbraith, S.D., Paterson, K.G. (eds.) Pairing 2008. LNCS, vol. 5209, pp. 57–74. Springer, Heidelberg (2008)
42. Okamoto, T., Takashima, K.: Hierarchical predicate encryption for inner-products. In: Matsui, M. (ed.) ASIACRYPT 2009. LNCS, vol. 5912, pp. 214–231. Springer, Heidelberg (2009)
43. O'Neill, A.: Definitional issues in functional encryption. Cryptology ePrint Archive, Report 2010/556 (2010). http://eprint.iacr.org/
44. Sahai, A., Waters, B.: Functional encryption:beyond public key cryptography. Power Point Presentation (2008). http://userweb.cs.utexas.edu/~bwaters/presentations/files/functional.ppt
45. Sahai, A., Waters, B.: Fuzzy identity-based encryption. In: Cramer, R. (ed.) EUROCRYPT 2005. LNCS, vol. 3494, pp. 457–473. Springer, Heidelberg (2005)
46. Shamir, A.: Identity-based cryptosystems and signature schemes. In: Blakely, G.R., Chaum, D. (eds.) CRYPTO 1984. LNCS, vol. 196, pp. 47–53. Springer, Heidelberg (1985)
47. Shen, E., Shi, E., Waters, B.: Predicate privacy in encryption systems. In: Reingold, O. (ed.) TCC 2009. LNCS, vol. 5444, pp. 457–473. Springer, Heidelberg (2009)
48. Shoup, V.: Lower bounds for discrete logarithms and related problems. In: Fumy, W. (ed.) EUROCRYPT 1997. LNCS, vol. 1233, pp. 256–266. Springer, Heidelberg (1997)
49. Waters, B.: Functional encryption for regular languages. In: Safavi-Naini, R., Canetti, R. (eds.) CRYPTO 2012. LNCS, vol. 7417, pp. 218–235. Springer, Heidelberg (2012)

Identity-Based Encryption with (Almost) Tight Security in the Multi-instance, Multi-ciphertext Setting

Dennis Hofheinz$^{(\boxtimes)}$, Jessica Koch, and Christoph Striecks

KIT, Karlsruhe, Germany
{Dennis.Hofheinz,Jessica.Koch,Christoph.Striecks}@kit.edu

Abstract. We construct an identity-based encryption (IBE) scheme that is tightly secure in a very strong sense. Specifically, we consider a setting with many instances of the scheme and many encryptions per instance. In this setting, we reduce the security of our scheme to a variant of a simple assumption used for a similar purpose by Chen and Wee (Crypto 2013). The security loss of our reduction is $\mathbf{O}(k)$ (where k is the security parameter). Our scheme is the first IBE scheme to achieve this strong flavor of tightness under a simple assumption.

Technically, our scheme is a variation of the IBE scheme by Chen and Wee. However, in order to "lift" their results to the multi-instance, multi-ciphertext case, we need to develop new ideas. In particular, while we build on (and extend) their high-level proof strategy, we deviate significantly in the low-level proof steps.

1 Introduction

Tight Security. For many cryptographic primitives, we currently cannot prove security directly. Hence, we typically *reduce* the security of a given scheme to the hardness of a computational problem, in the sense that every successful attack on the scheme yields a successful problem solver. Now it is both a theoretically and practically interesting question to look at the *loss* of such a reduction. Informally, the loss of a reduction quantifies the difference between the success of a hypothetical attacker on the cryptographic scheme, and the success of the derived problem solver. From a theoretical perspective, for instance, the loss of a reduction can also be viewed as a quantitative measure of (an upper bound for) the "distance" between primitive and assumption. But "tight" (or, "loss-free") reductions are also desirable from a practical perspective: the tighter a reduction, the better are the security guarantees we can give for a specific instance of the scheme. Hence, we can recommend smaller keylengths (which lead to more efficiency) for schemes with tighter security reduction.

However, in most practical usage scenarios, a cryptographic primitive is used multiple times. (For instance, in a typical multi-user encryption scenario,

D. Hofheinz—was supported by DFG grants GZ HO 4534/2-2 and GZ HO 4534/4-1.

J. Koch—was supported by BMBF project "KASTEL".

C. Striecks—was supported by DFG grant GZ HO 4534/2-2.

J. Katz (Ed.): PKC 2015, LNCS 9020, pp. 799–822, 2015.
DOI: 10.1007/978-3-662-46447-2_36

many instances of the encryption scheme are used to produce even more cipher-texts.) Hence, tight security reductions become particularly meaningful when they reduce an attacker on the whole system (with many instances of the cryptographic scheme) to a problem solver. In fact, while for many primitives (such as secret-key [2] or public-key [3] encryption), one-instance security is known to imply multi-instance security, the corresponding security guarantees for concrete schemes may indeed vanish in the number of instances [2].

Existing Tightly Secure Schemes. The loss of security reductions has been considered explicitly by Bellare et al. [2] for the case of encryption schemes. The first "somewhat tight" reductions (whose loss is independent of the number of instances of the scheme, but not of the number of ciphertexts) for public-key encryption (PKE) schemes could be given in [4]. In the following years, more tight (or somewhat tight) reductions for encryption schemes were constructed in the random oracle model [7,10,14], or from "q-type" assumptions [15,16].[1]

However, only recently, the first PKE schemes emerged [1,18,20] whose tight security (in the multi-instance, multi-ciphertext setting) can be proved under simple assumptions in the standard model.[2] Even more recently, *identity-based* encryption (IBE) schemes with "somewhat tight" security (under simple assumptions) have been constructed [6,11]. (This required new techniques, since it is not clear how to extend the techniques of [1,18,20] to the IBE setting.) In this case, "somewhat tight" means that their security reduction loses only a small multiplicative factor, but still considers the standard IBE security experiment [9] with one encryption and one instance of the scheme. Nonetheless, while the IBE schemes from [6,11] are not proved tightly secure in a multi-user, multi-ciphertext setting, these schemes imply tightly secure PKE schemes (even in the multi-user, multi-ciphertext setting) when plugged into the transformations of [9,18,20].[3]

Our Contribution. In this work, we construct the first IBE scheme with an almost tight security reduction in the multi-instance, multi-ciphertext scenario. Our reduction is only almost tight, since it loses a factor of $\mathbf{O}(k)$, where k is the security parameter. However, we stress that this loss is independent of the number of ciphertexts, revealed user secret keys, or instances of the scheme.

---

[1] A "q-type" assumption may depend on the size of the investigated cryptographic system. (That is, larger cryptographic systems may only be secure under a stronger instance of the assumption.) Hence, a tight reduction (even in a multi-instance scenario) to a q-type assumption may not yield security guarantees that are independent of the number of users.

[2] A "simple" assumption is defined through a security game in which an adversary first gets a challenge whose size only depends on the security parameter, and must then output a unique solution without further interaction. Examples of simple assumptions are DLOG, DDH, or RSA, but not Strong Diffie-Hellman [8] or q-ABDHE [15].

[3] More specifically, Boneh and Franklin [9] mention (and attribute this observation to Naor) that every IBE scheme can be viewed as a signature scheme. The signature schemes thus derived from [6,11] are then suitable for the conversions of [18,20], yielding PKE schemes tightly secure in the multi-user, multi-ciphertext setting.

In our security reduction, we rely on a computational assumption in composite-order pairing-friendly groups; this assumption is a variant of an assumption used by Chen and Wee [11] for their IBE scheme, and in particular simple in the above sense. We note that a conversion to the prime-order setting using the techniques from [13,17,19,21] (see also [5]) seems plausible—specifically since Chen and Wee [11] already describe such a conversion for their assumption—, but we leave such a conversion as an open problem.

Our Approach. Our scheme is a variant of the IBE scheme by Chen and Wee [11] (which is almost tightly secure in the one-instance, one-ciphertext setting), and our proof strategy draws heavily from theirs. Hence, to describe our techniques, let us first briefly sketch their strategy.

In a nutshell, Chen and Wee start with a real security game, in which an adversary A receives a master public key mpk of the scheme, as well as access to arbitrarily many user secret keys usk_{id} for adversarially chosen identities id. At some point, A selects a fresh challenge identity id^* and two messages M_0^*, M_1^*, and then receives the encryption $C_{id^*}^* \leftarrow \mathsf{Enc}(mpk, id^*, M_b)$ (under identity id^*) of one of these messages. After potentially querying more user secret keys (for identities $id \neq id^*$), A eventually outputs a guess b^* for b. If $b^* = b$, we say that A wins. Chen and Wee then show security by gradually changing this game (being careful not to significantly decrease A's success), until A trivially cannot win (except by guessing).

As a first preparatory change, Chen and Wee use the user secret key usk_{id^*} to construct the challenge ciphertext $C_{id^*}^*$. (This way, the encryption random coins for $C_{id^*}^*$ do not have to be known to the security game.) Additionally $C_{id^*}^*$ is now of a special, "pseudo-normal" form that will later enable a gradual randomization of the encrypted message. The core of the proof then consists of a number of hybrid steps, in which the distribution of all generated user secret keys (including the user secret key usk_{id^*} used to generate $C_{id^*}^*$) is modified. Concretely, in the i-th hybrid game, each used usk_{id} contains an additional "blinding term" of the form $R(id|_i)$, where $id|_i$ is the i-bit prefix of id, and R is a truly random function. Eventually, each user secret key usk_{id} will be fully randomized by a truly random value $R(id)$. In particular, at this point, the key usk_{id^*} used to prepare $C_{id^*}^*$ is blinded by a fresh random value $R(id^*)$. By the special "pseudo-normal" form of $C_{id^*}^*$, this means that the corresponding encrypted message is also blinded, and A's view is finally independent of the challenge bit b.

We keep this high-level proof structure, extending it of course to multiple ciphertexts and multiple instances of the scheme. However, as we will explain below, the way Chen and Wee gradually introduce the blinding terms $R(id|_i)$ does not immediately extend to many ciphertexts or instances; hence, we need to deviate from their proof strategy here.

The Problem. Specifically, Chen and Wee move from the $(i-1)$-th to the i-th hybrid through a single reduction as follows: first, they guess the i-th bit id_i^* of the challenge identity id^*. Then, they set up things such that

(a) all user secret keys for identities id with $id_i = id_i^*$ (i.e., that coincide in the i-th bit with id^*) behave as in the previous hybrid (i.e., carry a blinding term $R(id|_{i-1})$),

(b) all user secret keys for identities id with $id_i = 1 - id_i^*$ carry a blinding term of $R(id|_{i-1}) \cdot R'(id|_{i-1}))$. Depending on the input of the reduction, we have either that $R' = 1$ (such that the overall blinding term is $R(id|_{i-1})$), or that R' is an independently random function. (In particular, all usk_{id} with $id_i = 1 - id_i^*$ contain an embedded computational challenge R'.)

Depending on whether or not $R' = 1$, this setup simulates the $(i-1)$-th or the i-th hybrid. However, we remark that the setup of Chen and Wee only allows to generate "pseudo-normal" challenge ciphertexts $C_{id^*}^*$ for identities id^* with the initially guessed i-th bit id_i^*. (Intuitively, any pseudo-normal ciphertext for an identity id with $id_i = 1 - id_i^*$ would "react with" an additional blinding term $R'(id|_{i-1})$ in usk_{id}, allowing to trivially solve the computational challenge.)

Hence, in their i-th game hop, only challenge ciphertexts for identities with the same i-th bit can be generated. Thus, their approach cannot in any obvious way be extended to multiple challenge ciphertexts for different identities. (For similar reasons, a generalization to multiple instances of the scheme fails.)

Our Solution. In order to move from the $(i-1)$-th to the i-th hybrid, we thus follow a different strategy that involves three reductions. The main technical ingredient in our case is the ability to distribute the blinding terms $R(id|_i)$ in user secret keys into two different "compartments" (i.e., subgroups) of the composite-order group we are working in. (In particular, a term $R(id|_i)$ in one compartment can be changed independently of terms in the other compartment.)

More specifically, recall that in the $(i-1)$-th hybrid, all user secret keys carry an additional $R(id|_{i-1})$ blinding term, and all challenge ciphertexts are pseudo-normal (in the sense that they "react with" the blinding terms in user secret keys). In our first step, we move all blinding terms $R(id|_{i-1})$ in the usk_{id} into the two compartments, depending on the i-th bit of id. (That is, if $id_i = 0$, then the corresponding blinding term $R(id|_{i-1})$ goes into the first compartment, and if $id_i = 1$, then it goes into the second.)

In our second step, we can now treat the embedded blinding terms for $id_i = 0$ and $id_i = 1$ separately. In particular, since these cases are now "decoupled" by being in different compartments, we can completely re-randomize the underlying random function R in exactly one of those compartments. (This does not lead to trivial distinctions of the computational challenge since we do not introduce *new* blinding terms that would "react with" pseudo-normal ciphertexts and thus become easily detectable. Instead, we simply *decouple* existing blinding terms in different subgroups.) Note however that since now different random functions, say, $\widehat{R}$ and $\widetilde{R}$, determine the blinding terms used for identities with $id_i = 0$ and $id_i = 1$, we essentially obtain blinding terms that depend on the first i (and not only $i-1$) bits of id.

Finally, we revert the first change and move all blinding terms in the usk_{id} into one compartment. In summary, this series of three moves has thus created blinding terms that depend on the first i bits of id. Thus, we have moved to the i-th hybrid. If we follow the high-level strategy of Chen and Wee again, this yields a sequence of $\mathbf{O}(k)$ reductions that show the security of our IBE scheme. (From a conceptual perspective, it might also be interesting to note that none of our reductions needs to *guess*, e.g., an identity bit.)

Outline of the Paper. After introducing some preliminary definitions in Section 2, we explain the necessary algebraic structure (mentioned in the "compartment discussion" above) of "extended nested dual system groups" (ENDSGs) in Section 3. (This structure extends a similar structure of Chen and Wee [11].) In Section 4, we present our IBE scheme from ENDSGs, and in Section 5, we show how to instantiate ENDSGs in composite-order pairing-friendly groups.

2   Preliminaries

Notation. For $n \in \mathbb{N}$, let $[n] := \{1, \ldots, n\}$, and let $k \in \mathbb{N}$ be the security parameter. For a finite set $\mathcal{S}$, we denote by $s \leftarrow \mathcal{S}$ the process of sampling s uniformly from $\mathcal{S}$. For an algorithm A, let $y \leftarrow A(k, x)$ be the process of running A on input k, x with access to uniformly random coins and assigning the result to y. (We may omit to mention the k-input explicitly and assume that all algorithms take k as input.) To make the random coins r explicit, we write $A(k, x; r)$. We say an algorithm A is probabilistic polynomial time (PPT) if the running time of A is polynomial in k. A function $f : \mathbb{N} \to \mathbb{R}$ is negligible if it vanishes faster than the inverse of any polynomial (i.e., if $\forall c \exists k_0 \forall k \geq k_0 : |f(k)| \leq 1/k^c$). Further, we write vectors in bold font, e.g., $\mathbf{v} = (v_1, \ldots, v_n)$ for a vectors of length $n \in \mathbb{N}$ and with components $v_1, \ldots, v_n$. (We may also write $\mathbf{v} = (v_i)_{i \in [n]}$ or even $\mathbf{v} = (v_i)_i$ in this case.) In the following, we use a *component-wise* multiplication of vectors, i.e., $\mathbf{v} \cdot \mathbf{v}' = (v_1, \ldots, v_n) \cdot (v'_1, \ldots, v'_n) = (v_1 \cdot v'_1, \ldots, v_n \cdot v'_n)$. Further, we write $\mathbf{v}^j := (v_1^j, \ldots, v_n^j)$, for $j \in \mathbb{N}$, and $\mathbf{v}_{-i} := (v_1, \ldots, v_{i-1}, v_{i+1}, \ldots, v_n)$, for $i \in [n]$, and $s^{\mathbf{v}} := (s^{v_1}, \ldots, s^{v_n})$. For two random variables X, Y, we denote with $\mathsf{SD}(X \, ; \, Y)$ is the statistical distance of X and Y.

Identity-Based Encryption. An identity-based encryption (IBE) scheme IBE with identity space $\mathcal{ID}$ and message space $\mathcal{M}$ consists of the five PPT algorithms $\mathsf{Par}, \mathsf{Gen}, \mathsf{Ext}, \mathsf{Enc}, \mathsf{Dec}$. Parameter sampling $\mathsf{Par}(k)$, on input a security parameter k, outputs public parameters pp and secret parameters sp. Key generation $\mathsf{Gen}(pp, sp)$, on input pp and sp, outputs a master public key mpk and a master secret key msk. User secret key extraction $\mathsf{Ext}(msk, id)$, given msk and an identity $id \in \mathcal{ID}$, outputs a user secret key usk_{id} associated with id. Encryption $\mathsf{Enc}(mpk, id, M)$, given mpk, an identity $id \in \mathcal{ID}$, and a message $M \in \mathcal{M}$, outputs an id-associated ciphertext C_{id}. Decryption $\mathsf{Dec}(usk_{id}, C_{id})$, given usk_{id} for an identity id, and ciphertext C_{id}, outputs $M \in \mathcal{M} \cup \{\bot\}$. For correctness, we require that for any $k \in \mathbb{N}$, for all $(pp, sp) \leftarrow \mathsf{Par}(k)$, for all $(mpk, msk) \leftarrow \mathsf{Gen}(pp, sp)$, for all $id \in \mathcal{ID}$, for all $usk_{id} \leftarrow \mathsf{Ext}(msk, id)$, for all $M \in \mathcal{M}$, and for all $C_{id} \leftarrow \mathsf{Enc}(mpk, id, M)$, Dec satisfies $\mathsf{Dec}(usk_{id}, C_{id}) = M$. For security, we define multi-instance, multi-ciphertext IBE security, dubbed (μ, q)-IBE-IND-CPA security, for $(\mu, q) \in \mathbb{N}^2$, as follows.

$$
\boxed{
\begin{array}{l}
\textbf{Experiment } \mathsf{Exp}_{\mathsf{IBE},A}^{(\mu,q)\text{-ibe-ind-cpa}}(k) \\[4pt]
(pp, sp) \leftarrow \mathsf{Par}(k) \\[2pt]
(mpk_j, msk_j)_{j \in [\mu]} \leftarrow (\mathsf{Gen}(pp, sp))^{\mu} \\[2pt]
b \leftarrow \{0,1\} \\[2pt]
b^* \leftarrow A^{(\mathsf{Ext}(msk_j, \cdot), \mathsf{Enc}'(mpk_j, \cdot, b, \cdot, \cdot))_{j \in [\mu]}}(pp, (mpk_j)_{j \in [\mu]}) \\[2pt]
\text{if } A \text{ is valid and } b = b^* \text{ then return } 1 \text{ else return } 0
\end{array}
}
$$

Fig. 1. The (μ, q)-IBE-IND-CPA security experiment

(Weak) (μ, q)-IBE-IND-CPA Security. An IBE scheme IBE defined as above is (μ, q)-IBE-IND-CPA-secure if and only if any PPT adversary A succeeds in the following experiment only with probability at most negligibly larger than $1/2$. Let $\mathsf{Enc}'(mpk, id, b, M_0, M_1)$ be a PPT auxiliary encryption oracle that, given a master public key mpk, a challenge identity $id \in \mathcal{ID}$, a bit $b \in \{0,1\}$, and two messages $M_0, M_1 \in \mathcal{M}$, outputs a challenge ciphertext $C_{id} \leftarrow \mathsf{Enc}(mpk, id, M_b)$. First, A gets honestly generated public parameter pp and master public keys $(mpk_1, \dots, mpk_\mu)$. During the experiment, A may adaptively query $\mathsf{Ext}(msk_j, \cdot)$-oracles and $\mathsf{Enc}'(mpk_j, \cdot, b, \cdot, \cdot)$-oracles, for corresponding mpk_j, msk_j and a (uniform) bit $b \leftarrow \{0,1\}$, for all $j \in [\mu]$. Eventually, A outputs a guess b^*. We say that A is valid if and only if A never queries an $\mathsf{Ext}(msk_j, \cdot)$ oracle on an identity id for which it has already queried the corresponding $\mathsf{Enc}'(mpk_j, \cdot, b, \cdot, \cdot)$ oracle (and vice versa); each message pair A selected as input to Enc' contained only equal-length messages; and A has only queried its Enc'-oracles at most q times per j-instance. We say that A succeeds if and only if A is valid and $b = b^*$. Concretely, the previous described experiment is given in Figure 1 and denoted $\mathsf{Exp}_{\mathsf{IBE},A}^{(\mu,q)\text{-ibe-ind-cpa}}$. Further, we define the advantage function for any PPT A as $\mathsf{Adv}_{\mathsf{IBE},A}^{(\mu,q)\text{-ibe-ind-cpa}}(k) := |\Pr\left[\mathsf{Exp}_{\mathsf{IBE},A}^{(\mu,q)\text{-ibe-ind-cpa}}(k) = 1\right] - 1/2|$.

Furthermore, we call IBE *weakly* (μ, q)-IBE-IND-CPA secure if and only if $\mathsf{Adv}_{\mathsf{IBE},A}^{(\mu,q)\text{-ibe-ind-cpa}}$ is negligible for all *weak* PPT adversaries A. Here, A is weak if it never requests challenge ciphertexts for the same scheme instance and identity twice (i.e., if it never queries any $\mathsf{Enc}'(mpk_j, \cdot, b, \cdot, \cdot)$ oracle twice with the same identity id).

Finally, we remark that the one-instance, one-ciphertext notion $(1,1)$-IBE-IND-CPA is the standard notion of IBE security considered in, e.g., [6,9,11].

Pairings. Let G, H, G_T be cyclic groups of order N. A *pairing* $e : G \times H \to G_T$ is a map that is *bilinear* (i.e., for all $g, g' \in G$ and $h, h' \in H$, we have $e(g \cdot g', h) = e(g, h) \cdot e(g', h)$ and $e(g, h \cdot h') = e(g, h) \cdot e(g, h')$), *non-degenerate* (i.e., for generators $g \in G, h \in H$, we have that $e(g, h) \in G_T$ is a generator), and *efficiently computable*.

3   Extended Nested Dual System Groups

(Nested) Dual System Groups. Nested dual system groups (NDSG) [11] can be seen as a variant of dual system groups (DSG) [12] which itself are based on the dual system framework introduced by Waters [21]. NDSGs were recently defined by Chen and Wee and enabled to prove the first IBE (almost) tightly and fully secure under simple assumptions. In the following, based on NDSGs, we construct a new notion we call extended nested dual system groups.

A Variant of Nested Dual System Groups. We introduce a variant of Chen and Wee's nested dual system groups (NDSG) [11], dubbed extended NDSG (ENDSG). (Mainly, we re-use and extend the notions from [11].) Further, let $G(k, n')$ be a group generator that, given integers k and n', generates the tuple $(G, H, G_T, N, (g_{p_1}, \ldots, g_{p_{n'}}), (h_{p_1}, \ldots, h_{p_{n'}}), g, h, e)$, for a pairing $e : G \times H \to G_T$, for composite-order groups G, H, G_T, all of known group order $N = p_1 \cdots p_{n'}$, for k-bit primes $(p_i)_i$. Further, g and h are generators of G and H, and $(g_{p_i})_i$ and $(h_{p_i})_i$ are generators of the (proper) subgroups $G_{p_i} \subset G$ and $H_{p_i} \subset H$ of order $|G_{p_i}| = |H_{p_i}| = p_i$, respectively. In this setting, an ENDSG ENDSG consists of algorithms SampP, SampG, SampH, $\widehat{\mathsf{SampG}}$, $\widetilde{\mathsf{SampG}}$:

Parameter sampling. $\mathsf{SampP}(k, n)$, given security parameter k and parameter $n \in \mathbb{N}$, samples $(G, H, G_T, N, (g_{p_1}, \ldots, g_{p_{n'}}), (h_{p_1}, \ldots, h_{p_{n'}}), g, h, e) \leftarrow G(k, n')$, for an integer n' determined by SampP, and outputs public parameters $pp = (G, H, G_T, N, g, h, e, m, n, pars)$ and secret parameters $sp = (\widehat{h}, \widetilde{h}, \widehat{pars}, \widetilde{pars})$, where $m : H \to G_T$ is a linear map, $\widehat{h}, \widetilde{h}$ are nontrivial H-elements, and $pars, \widehat{pars}, \widetilde{pars}$ may contain arbitrary additional information used by SampG, SampH, and $\widehat{\mathsf{SampG}}$ and $\widetilde{\mathsf{SampG}}$.

G-group sampling. $\mathsf{SampG}(pp)$, given pp, outputs $\mathbf{g} = (g_0, \ldots, g_n) \in G^{n+1}$.
H-group sampling. $\mathsf{SampH}(pp)$, given pp, outputs $\mathbf{h} = (h_0, \ldots, h_n) \in H^{n+1}$.
Semi-functional G-group sampling 1. $\widehat{\mathsf{SampG}}(pp, sp)$, given pp and sp, outputs $\widehat{\mathbf{g}} = (\widehat{g}_0, \ldots, \widehat{g}_n) \in G^{n+1}$.
Semi-functional G-group sampling 2. $\widetilde{\mathsf{SampG}}(pp, sp)$, given pp and sp, outputs $\widetilde{\mathbf{g}} = (\widetilde{g}_0, \ldots, \widetilde{g}_n) \in G^{n+1}$.

Correctness of ENDSG. For correctness, for all $k \in \mathbb{N}$, for all integers $n = n(k) > 1$, for all pp, where pp is the first ouput of $\mathsf{SampP}(k, n)$, we require:

Associativity. For all $(g_0, \ldots, g_n) \leftarrow \mathsf{SampG}(pp)$ and for all $(h_0, \ldots, h_n) \leftarrow \mathsf{SampH}(pp)$, we have $e(g_0, h_i) = e(g_i, h_0)$, for all i.
Projective. For all $s \leftarrow \mathbb{Z}_N^*$, for all g_0 which is the first output of $\mathsf{SampG}(pp; s)$, for all $h \in H$, we have $m(h)^s = e(g_0, h)$.

Security of ENDSG. For security, for all $k \in \mathbb{N}$, for all integers $n = n(k) > 1$, for all $(pp, sp) \leftarrow \mathsf{SampP}(k, n)$, we require:

Orthogonality. For m specified in pp, for $\widehat{h}, \widetilde{h}$ specified in sp, we have $m(\widehat{h}) = m(\widetilde{h}) = 1$. For $g_0, \widehat{g}_0,$ and $\widetilde{g}_0$ that are the first outputs of $\mathsf{SampG}(pp)$, $\widehat{\mathsf{SampG}}(pp, sp)$, and $\widetilde{\mathsf{SampG}}(pp, sp)$, respectively, we have that $e(g_0, \widehat{h}) = 1$, $e(g_0, \widetilde{h}) = 1$, $e(\widehat{g}_0, \widetilde{h}) = 1$, and $e(\widetilde{g}_0, \widehat{h}) = 1$.

G- and H-subgroups. The outputs of SampG, $\widehat{\text{SampG}}$, and $\widetilde{\text{SampG}}$ are distributed uniformly over the generators of different nontrivial subgroups of G^{n+1} (that only depend on pp) of coprime order, respectively, while the output of SampH is uniformly distributed over the generators of a nontrivial subgroup of H^{n+1} (that only depends on pp).

Non-degeneracy. For $\widehat{h}$ specified in sp and for $\widehat{g}_0$ which is the first output of $\widehat{\text{SampG}}(pp, sp)$, it holds that $e(\widehat{g}_0, \widehat{h})$ is uniformly distributed over the generators of a nontrivial subgroup of G_T (that only depends on pp). Similarly, $e(\widetilde{g}_0, \widetilde{h})$ is uniformly distributed over the generators of a nontrivial subgroup of G_T (that only depends on pp), where $\widetilde{h}$ is specified in sp and $\widetilde{g}_0$ is the first output of $\widetilde{\text{SampG}}(pp, sp)$.

Left-subgroup indistinguishability 1 (LS1). For any PPT adversary D, we have that the function

$$\text{Adv}^{\text{ls1}}_{\text{ENDSG},G,D}(k, n) := |\Pr[D(pp, \mathbf{g}) = 1] - \Pr[D(pp, \mathbf{g}\widehat{\mathbf{g}}) = 1]|$$

is negligible in k, where $\mathbf{g} \leftarrow \text{SampG}(pp)$, $\widehat{\mathbf{g}} \leftarrow \widehat{\text{SampG}}(pp, sp)$.

Left-subgroup indistinguishability 2 (LS2). For any PPT adversary D, we have that the function

$$\text{Adv}^{\text{ls2}}_{\text{ENDSG},G,D}(k, n) := \left|\Pr\left[D(pp, \widehat{h}\widetilde{h}, \mathbf{g}'\widehat{\mathbf{g}}', \mathbf{g}\widehat{\mathbf{g}}) = 1\right]\right.$$
$$\left. - \Pr\left[D(pp, \widehat{h}\widetilde{h}, \mathbf{g}'\widehat{\mathbf{g}}', \mathbf{g}\widetilde{\mathbf{g}}) = 1\right]\right|$$

is negligible in k, where $\mathbf{g}, \mathbf{g}' \leftarrow \text{SampG}(pp)$, $\widehat{\mathbf{g}}, \widehat{\mathbf{g}}' \leftarrow \widehat{\text{SampG}}(pp, sp)$, $\widetilde{\mathbf{g}} \leftarrow \widetilde{\text{SampG}}(pp, sp)$, for $\widehat{h}$ and $\widetilde{h}$ specified in sp.

Nested-hiding indistinguishability (NH). For any PPT adversary D, for all integers $q' = q'(k)$, the function

$$\text{Adv}^{\text{nh}}_{\text{ENDSG},G,D}(k, n, q') :=$$
$$\max_{i \in [\lfloor \frac{n}{2} \rfloor]} \left(\left|\Pr\left[D(pp, \widehat{h}, \widetilde{h}, \widehat{\mathbf{g}}_{-(2i-1)}, \widetilde{\mathbf{g}}_{-2i}, (\mathbf{h}_1, \ldots, \mathbf{h}_{q'})) = 1\right]\right.\right.$$
$$\left.\left. - \Pr\left[D(pp, \widehat{h}, \widetilde{h}, \widehat{\mathbf{g}}_{-(2i-1)}, \widetilde{\mathbf{g}}_{-2i}, (\mathbf{h}'_1, \ldots, \mathbf{h}'_{q'})) = 1\right]\right|\right),$$

is negligible in k, where $\widehat{\mathbf{g}} \leftarrow \widehat{\text{SampG}}(pp, sp)$, $\widetilde{\mathbf{g}} \leftarrow \widetilde{\text{SampG}}(pp, sp)$, and

$$\mathbf{h}_{i'} := (h_{i',0}, \ldots, h_{i',n}) \leftarrow \text{SampH}(pp),$$

$$\mathbf{h}'_{i'} := (h_{i',0}, \ldots, h_{i',2i-1} \cdot (\widehat{h})^{\widehat{\gamma}_{i'}}, h_{i',2i} \cdot (\widetilde{h})^{\widetilde{\gamma}_{i'}}, \ldots, h_{i',n}),$$

for $\widehat{h}, \widetilde{h}$ specified in sp, for $\widehat{\gamma}_{i'}, \widetilde{\gamma}_{i'} \leftarrow \mathbb{Z}^*_{\text{ord}(H)}$, and for all $i' \in [q']$.

(Informal) Comparison of NDSGs and ENDSGs. Loosely speaking, in contrast to the NDSGs from [11], ENDSGs have a second semi-functional G-group sampling algorithm $\widetilde{\text{SampG}}$ as well as a second nontrivial H-element in sp (i.e., $\widetilde{h}$). Further, we omit the SampGT-algorithm. Concerning the ENDSG properties, we extend the NDSG properties and assumptions appropriately and introduce one additional assumption (i.e., LS2).

4   An (Almost) Tightly (μ, q)-IBE-IND-CPA-Secure IBE

A Variant of the IBE of Chen and Wee [11]. We are now ready to present our variant of Chen and Wee's IBE scheme [11]. We use an ENDSG $\mathsf{ENDSG} = (\mathsf{SampP}, \mathsf{SampG}, \mathsf{SampH}, \widehat{\mathsf{SampG}}, \widetilde{\mathsf{SampG}})$ from Section 3 as a basic building block. Besides, for groups G_T (defined below), let $\mathcal{UH}$ be a family of universal hash functions $\mathsf{H} : G_T \to \{0,1\}^k$ such that for any nontrivial subgroup $G_T' \subset G_T$, and for $\mathsf{H} \leftarrow \mathcal{UH}$, $X \leftarrow G_T'$, and $U \leftarrow \{0,1\}^k$, we have $\mathsf{SD}\left((\mathsf{H}, \mathsf{H}(X)) ; (\mathsf{H}, U)\right) = \mathbf{O}(2^{-k})$. Let $\mathsf{IBE} = (\mathsf{Par}, \mathsf{Gen}, \mathsf{Ext}, \mathsf{Enc}, \mathsf{Dec})$ with identity space $\mathcal{ID} = \{0,1\}^n$ and message space $\mathcal{M} = \{0,1\}^k$ be defined as follows:

Parameter Generation. $\mathsf{Par}(k,n)$ samples $(pp', sp') \leftarrow \mathsf{SampP}(k, 2n)$, with $pp' = (G, H, G_T, N, g, h, e, m, 2n, pars)$ and $sp' = (\widehat{h}, \widetilde{h}, \widehat{pars}, \widetilde{pars})$, and $\mathsf{H} \leftarrow \mathcal{UH}$, and then outputs the public and secret parameters (pp, sp), where $pp = (G, H, G_T, N, g, h, e, m, 2n, \mathsf{H}, pars)$ and $sp = sp'$.

Key Generation. $\mathsf{Gen}(pp, sp)$ samples $msk \leftarrow H$, and outputs a master public key $mpk := (pp, m(msk))$ and a master secret key msk.

Secret-Key Extraction. $\mathsf{Ext}(msk, id)$, given $msk \in H$ and an identity $id = (id_1 \ldots id_n) \in \mathcal{ID}$, samples $(h_0, \ldots, h_{2n}) \leftarrow \mathsf{SampH}(pp)$ and outputs a user secret key

$$usk_{id} := (h_0, msk \cdot \prod_{i=1}^{n} h_{2i-id_i}).$$

Encryption. $\mathsf{Enc}(mpk, id, M)$, given $mpk = (pp, m(msk))$, an identity $id = (id_1 \ldots id_n) \in \mathcal{ID}$, and a message $M \in \mathcal{M}$, computes $(g_0, \ldots, g_{2n}) := \mathsf{SampG}(pp; s)$, for $s \leftarrow \mathbb{Z}_N^*$, and $g_T := m(msk)^s \; (= e(g_0, msk))$, and outputs a ciphertext

$$C_{id} := (g_0, \prod_{i=1}^{n} g_{2i-id_i}, \mathsf{H}(g_T) \oplus M).$$

Decryption. $\mathsf{Dec}(usk_{id}, C_{id'})$, given a user secret key $usk_{id} =: (K_0, K_1)$ and a ciphertext $C_{id'} =: (C_0, C_1, C_2)$, outputs

$$M := \mathsf{H}\left(\frac{e(C_0, K_1)}{e(C_1, K_0)}\right) \oplus C_2.$$

Correctness of IBE. We have

$$\mathsf{H}\left(\frac{e(C_0, K_1)}{e(C_1, K_0)}\right) \oplus C_2 = \mathsf{H}\left(\frac{e(g_0, msk \cdot \prod_{i=1}^{n} h_{2i-id_i})}{e(\prod_{i=1}^{n} g_{2i-id_i'}, h_0)}\right) \oplus \mathsf{H}(g_T) \oplus M$$

$$\overset{(*)}{=} \mathsf{H}(g_T) \oplus \mathsf{H}(g_T) \oplus M,$$

for $id = id'$. $(*)$ holds due to ENDSG's associativity and projective properties.

(μ, q)-**IBE-IND-CPA Security of IBE.** We base our high-level proof strategy on the IBE-IND-CPA proof strategy of Chen and Wee [11], but deviate on the low level. First, we define auxiliary encryption $\overline{\mathsf{Enc}}$ and auxiliary secret-key extraction $\overline{\mathsf{Ext}}$, random functions $\widehat{\mathsf{R}}_{j,i}$ and $\widetilde{\mathsf{R}}_{j,i}$, pseudo-normal ciphertexts, semi-functional type-$(\cdot, i)$ ciphertexts, and semi-functional type-i user secret keys as in [11]:

Auxiliary Secret-Key Extraction. $\overline{\mathsf{Ext}}(pp, msk, id; \mathbf{h})$, given pp, master secret key msk, an identity $id = id_1 \ldots id_n \in \mathcal{ID}$, and $\mathbf{h} = (h_0, \ldots, h_{2n}) \in (H)^{2n+1}$, outputs a user secret key

$$usk_{id} := (h_0, msk \cdot \prod_{i=1}^{n} h_{2i-id_i}).$$

Auxiliary Encryption Function. $\overline{\mathsf{Enc}}(pp, id, M; msk, \mathbf{g})$, given parameter pp, identity $id = id_1 \ldots id_n \in \mathcal{ID}$, message $M \in \mathcal{M}$, master secret key msk, and $\mathbf{g} = (g_0, \ldots, g_{2n}) \in (G)^{2n+1}$, outputs a ciphertext

$$C_{id} := (g_0, \prod_{i=1}^{n} g_{2i-id_i}, \mathsf{H}(e(g_0, msk)) \oplus M).$$

Random Function Families. Let $id|_i := id_1 \ldots id_i$ be the i-bit prefix of an identity id, and let $\mathcal{ID}|_i := \{0,1\}^i$. For an instance j and $i \in [n] \cup \{0\}$, consider functions $\widehat{\mathsf{R}}_{j,i} : \mathcal{ID}|_i \to H$, $id|_i \mapsto (\widehat{h})^{\widehat{\gamma}_{j,i}(id|_i)}$ and $\widetilde{\mathsf{R}}_{j,i} : \mathcal{ID}|_i \to H$, $id|_i \mapsto (\widetilde{h})^{\widetilde{\gamma}_{j,i}(id|_i)}$,, where $\widehat{\gamma}_{j,i} : \mathcal{ID}|_i \to \mathbb{Z}^*_{\mathsf{ord}(H)}, id|_i \mapsto \widehat{\gamma}_{j,id|_i}$ and $\widetilde{\gamma}_{j,i} : \mathcal{ID}|_i \to \mathbb{Z}^*_{\mathsf{ord}(H)}, id|_i \mapsto \widetilde{\gamma}_{j,id|_i}$ are independently and truly random.

Pseudo-normal Ciphertexts. Pseudo-normal ciphertexts are generated as

$$C_{id} := \overline{\mathsf{Enc}}(pp, id, M; msk, \mathbf{g}\widehat{\mathbf{g}})$$
$$= (g_0\widehat{g}_0, \prod_{i=1}^{n} g_{2i-id_i}\widehat{g}_{2i-id_i}, \mathsf{H}(e(g_0\widehat{g}_0, msk)) \oplus M),$$

for uniform $\mathbf{g} = (g_0, \ldots, g_{2n}) \leftarrow \mathsf{SampG}(pp)$ and $\widehat{\mathbf{g}} = (\widehat{g}_0, \ldots, \widehat{g}_{2n}) \leftarrow \widehat{\mathsf{SampG}}(pp, sp)$. (Hence, pseudo-normal ciphertexts have semi-functional G-components sampled from $\widehat{\mathsf{SampG}}$.)

Semi-functional type-$(\wedge, i)$ and type-$(\sim, i)$ Ciphertexts. Let $\widehat{\mathsf{R}}_{j,i}$ and $\widetilde{\mathsf{R}}_{j,i}$ be random functions as defined above. Semi-functional ciphertexts of type $(\wedge, i)$ are generated as

$$\widehat{C}_{id} := \overline{\mathsf{Enc}}(pp, id, M; msk \cdot \widehat{\mathsf{R}}_{j,i}(id|_i) \cdot \widetilde{\mathsf{R}}_{j,i}(id|_i), \mathbf{g}\widehat{\mathbf{g}})$$
$$\overset{(1)}{=} (g_0\widehat{g}_0, \prod_{i=1}^{n} g_{2i-id_i}\widehat{g}_{2i-id_i}, \mathsf{H}(e(g_0\widehat{g}_0, msk \cdot \widehat{\mathsf{R}}_{j,i}(id|_i))) \oplus M)$$

while semi-functional ciphertexts of type $(\sim, i)$ are generated as

$$\widetilde{C}_{id} := \overline{\mathsf{Enc}}(pp, id, M; msk \cdot \widehat{\mathsf{R}}_{j,i}(id|_i) \cdot \widetilde{\mathsf{R}}_{j,i}(id|_i), \mathbf{g}\widetilde{\mathbf{g}})$$
$$\overset{(2)}{=} (g_0\widetilde{g}_0, \prod_{i=1}^{n} g_{2i-id_i}\widetilde{g}_{2i-id_i}, \mathsf{H}(e(g_0\widetilde{g}_0, msk \cdot \widetilde{\mathsf{R}}_{j,i}(id|_i))) \oplus M),$$

where $\mathbf{g} = (g_0, \ldots, g_{2n}) \leftarrow \mathsf{SampG}(pp)$, $\widehat{\mathbf{g}} = (\widehat{g}_0, \ldots, \widehat{g}_{2n}) \leftarrow \widehat{\mathsf{SampG}}(pp)$, and $\widetilde{\mathbf{g}} = (\widetilde{g}_0, \ldots, \widetilde{g}_{2n}) \leftarrow \widetilde{\mathsf{SampG}}(pp)$, while (1) and (2) hold due to ENDSG's properties.

Semi-functional type-i User Secret Keys. Let $\widehat{\mathsf{R}}_{j,i}$ and $\widetilde{\mathsf{R}}_{j,i}$ be defined as above. For $\mathbf{h} = (h_0, \ldots, h_{2n}) \leftarrow \mathsf{SampH}(pp)$, semi-functional type-$i$ user secret keys are generated as

$$uskid := \overline{\mathsf{Ext}}(pp, msk \cdot \widehat{\mathsf{R}}_{j,i}(id|_i) \cdot \widetilde{\mathsf{R}}_{j,i}(id|_i), id; \mathbf{h})$$

$$= (h_0, msk \cdot \widehat{\mathsf{R}}_{j,i}(id|_i) \cdot \widetilde{\mathsf{R}}_{j,i}(id|_i) \cdot \prod_{i=1}^{n} h_{2i-id_i}).$$

Theorem 1. *If ENDSG is a correct and secure ENDSG, then IBE defined as above is weakly (μ, q)-IBE-IND-CPA-secure. Concretely, for any weak PPT adversary A with at most $q' = q'(k)$ extraction queries per instance and running time t in the (μ, q)-IBE-IND-CPA security experiment with IBE, there are distinguishers D_1 on LS1, D_2 on LS2, and D_3 on NH with running times $t'_1 \approx t'_2 \approx t'_3 \approx t + \mathbf{O}(\mu q q' n k^c)$, respectively, some constant $c \in \mathbb{N}$, with*

$$\mathsf{Adv}_{\mathsf{IBE},A}^{(\mu,q)\text{-ibe-ind-cpa}}(k, n) \leq \mathsf{Adv}_{\mathsf{ENDSG},\mathsf{G},D_1}^{\mathsf{ls1}}(k, 2n) + 2n \cdot \mathsf{Adv}_{\mathsf{ENDSG},\mathsf{G},D_2}^{\mathsf{ls2}}(k, 2n)$$

$$+ n \cdot \mathsf{Adv}_{\mathsf{ENDSG},\mathsf{G},D_3}^{\mathsf{nh}}(k, 2n, q') + \mu q \cdot \mathbf{O}(2^{-k}), \qquad (1)$$

for group generator G defined as above.

Proof. We show the (μ, q)-IBE-IND-CPA security of IBE for any weak PPT adversary A in a sequence of games where we successively change the games until we arrive at a game where A has only negligible advantage (i.e., success probability of $1/2$) in the sense of (μ, q)-IBE-IND-CPA. Let $S_{A,j}$ be the event that A succeeds in Game j. We give an overview how the challenge ciphertexts and user secret keys are generated in Table 1.

Game 0. Game 0 is the (μ, q)-IBE-IND-CPA experiment as defined above.

Game 1. Game 1 is defined as Game 0 apart from the fact that all challenge ciphertexts are pseudo-normal.

Game 2.i.0. Game 2.i.0 is defined as Game 1 except that all user secret keys are semi-functional of type $(i - 1)$ and all challenge ciphertexts are semi-functional of type-$(\wedge, i - 1)$, for all $i \in [n]$.

Game 2.i.1. Game 2.i.1 is defined as Game 2.i.0 except that if and only if the i-th bit of a challenge identity is 1, then the corresponding challenge ciphertext is semi-functional of type $(\sim, i - 1)$. (Otherwise, if and only if the i-th bit of a challenge identity is 0, then the corresponding challenge ciphertext is semi-functional of type $(\wedge, i - 1)$, for all j.)

Game 2.i.2. Game 2.i.2 is defined as Game 2.i.1 except that the challenge ciphertexts are semi-functional of type $(\cdot, i)$ (where $\cdot$ can be $\wedge$ or $\sim$ as defined in Game 2.i.1, i.e., depending on the i-th challenge identity bit) and the user secret keys are semi-functional of type i.

Table 1. Instance-j challenge ciphertexts for challenge identity $id^*_{j,i'}$, for $\mathbf{g} \leftarrow$ SampG(pp), for $\widehat{\mathbf{g}} \leftarrow \widehat{\text{SampG}}(pp, sp)$, for $\widetilde{\mathbf{g}} \leftarrow \widetilde{\text{SampG}}(pp, sp)$, for $R_{j,i'} \leftarrow \{0,1\}^k$, and for instance-$j$ user secret keys for identity id, for $\mathbf{h} \leftarrow$ SampH(pp), for all $(j, i', i) \in [\mu] \times [q] \times [n]$. The differences between games are given by underlining.

	Challenge ciphertexts for $id^*_{j,i'}$
Game 0	Enc($mpk_j, id^*_{j,i'}, M^*_{j,i',b}$)
Game 1	$\overline{\text{Enc}}$($pp, id^*_{j,i'}, M^*_{j,i',b}; msk_j, \mathbf{g}\widehat{\mathbf{g}}$)
Game 2.i.0	$\overline{\text{Enc}}$($pp, id^*_{j,i'}, M^*_{j,i',b}; msk_j \cdot \widehat{R}_{j,i-1}(id^*_{j,i'}|_{i-1}), \mathbf{g}\widehat{\mathbf{g}}$)
Game 2.i.1	if $id^*_{j,i',i} = 0:\ \overline{\text{Enc}}$($pp, id^*_{j,i'}, M^*_{j,i',b}; msk_j \cdot \widehat{R}_{j,i-1}(id^*_{j,i'}|_{i-1}), \mathbf{g}\widehat{\mathbf{g}}$)
	if $id^*_{j,i',i} = 1:\ \overline{\text{Enc}}$($pp, id^*_{j,i'}, M^*_{j,i',b}; msk_j \cdot \widetilde{R}_{j,i-1}(id^*_{j,i'}|_{i-1}), \mathbf{g}\widetilde{\mathbf{g}}$)
Game 2.i.2	if $id^*_{j,i',i} = 0:\ \overline{\text{Enc}}$($pp, id^*_{j,i'}, M^*_{j,i',b}; msk_j \cdot \widehat{R}_{j,i}(id^*_{j,i'}|_i), \mathbf{g}\widehat{\mathbf{g}}$)
	if $id^*_{j,i',i} = 1:\ \overline{\text{Enc}}$($pp, id^*_{j,i'}, M^*_{j,i',b}; msk_j \cdot \widetilde{R}_{j,i}(id^*_{j,i'}|_i), \mathbf{g}\widetilde{\mathbf{g}}$)
Game 3	$\overline{\text{Enc}}$($pp, id^*_{j,i'}, M^*_{j,i',b}; msk_j \cdot \widehat{R}_{j,n}(id^*_{j,i'}), \mathbf{g}\widehat{\mathbf{g}}$)
Game 4	$\overline{\text{Enc}}$($pp, id^*_{j,i'}, R_{j,i'}; msk_j \cdot \widehat{R}_{j,n}(id^*_{j,i'}), \mathbf{g}\widehat{\mathbf{g}}$)
	User secret keys for id
Game 0	Ext(msk_j, id)
Game 1	$\overline{\text{Ext}}$($pp, msk_j, id; \mathbf{h}$)
Game 2.i.0	$\overline{\text{Ext}}$($pp, msk_j \cdot \widehat{R}_{j,i-1}(id|_{i-1}) \cdot \widetilde{R}_{j,i-1}(id|_{i-1}), id; \mathbf{h}$)
Game 2.i.1	$\overline{\text{Ext}}$($pp, msk_j \cdot \widehat{R}_{j,i-1}(id|_{i-1}) \cdot \widetilde{R}_{j,i-1}(id|_{i-1}), id; \mathbf{h}$)
Game 2.i.2	$\overline{\text{Ext}}$($pp, msk_j \cdot \widehat{R}_{j,i}(id|_i) \cdot \widetilde{R}_{j,i}(id|_i), id; \mathbf{h}$)
Game 3	$\overline{\text{Ext}}$($pp, msk_j \cdot \widehat{R}_{j,n}(id) \cdot \widetilde{R}_{j,n}(id), id; \mathbf{h}$)
Game 4	$\overline{\text{Ext}}$($pp, msk_j \cdot \widehat{R}_{j,n}(id) \cdot \widetilde{R}_{j,n}(id), id; \mathbf{h}$)

Game 3. Game 3 is defined as Game 2.n.0 except that the challenge ciphertexts are semi-functional of type $(\wedge, n)$ and the user secret keys are semi-functional of type n.

Game 4. Game 4 is defined as Game 3 except that the challenge ciphertext messages are uniform k-length bitstrings, for all $(j, i') \in [\mu] \times [q]$.

Lemma 1 (Game 0 to Game 1). *Let* G *be a group generator as defined above. If the* G- *and* H-*subgroups property and* LS1 *of* ENDSG *hold, Game 0 and Game 1 are computationally indistinguishable. Concretely, for any PPT adversary A with at most $q' = q'(k)$ extraction queries in each instance and running time t in the (μ, q)-IBE-IND-CPA security experiment with* IBE *there is an distinguisher D on* LS1 *with running time $t' \approx t + \mathbf{O}(\mu q q' n k^c)$, for integer $n = n(k)$ and some constant $c \in \mathbb{N}$, such that*

$$|\Pr[S_{A,0}] - \Pr[S_{A,1}]| \leq \text{Adv}^{\text{ls1}}_{\text{ENDSG},\text{G},D}(k, 2n). \tag{2}$$

Proof. In Game 0, all challenge ciphertexts are normal in the sense of IBE while in Game 1, all challenge ciphertexts are pseudo-normal. In the following, we give a description and its analysis of a LS1 distinguisher that uses any efficient IBE-attacker in the (μ, q)-IBE-IND-CPA sense.

Description. The challenge input is provided as $(pp, \mathbf{T})$, where $\mathbf{T}$ is either $\mathbf{g}$ or $\mathbf{g}\widehat{\mathbf{g}}$, for $pp = (G, H, G_T, N, e, m, 2n, \mathsf{H}, pars)$, $\mathbf{g} \leftarrow \mathsf{SampG}(pp)$, and $\widehat{\mathbf{g}} \leftarrow \widehat{\mathsf{SampG}}(pp, sp)$. First, D samples $(msk_j)_j \leftarrow (H)^\mu$, sets $mpk_j := (pp, m(msk_j))$, for all j, and sends $(mpk_j)_j$ to A. During the experiment, D answers instance-j secret key extraction queries to oracle $\mathsf{Ext}(msk_j, \cdot)$, for $id \in \mathcal{ID}$, with

$$\overline{\mathsf{Ext}}(pp, msk_j, id; \mathsf{SampH}(pp)),$$

for all j. (We assume that A queries at most $q' = q'(k)$ user secret keys per instance.) Then, D fixes a bit $b \leftarrow \{0, 1\}$. A may adaptively query its Enc'-oracle; for A-chosen instance-j challenge identities $(id^*_{j,i})_i$ and equal-length messages $(M^*_{j,i,0}, M^*_{j,i,1})_i$, for all $i \in [q]$. D returns

$$\overline{\mathsf{Enc}}(pp, id^*_{j,i}, M^*_{j,i,b}; msk_j, \mathbf{T}^{s_{j,i}})$$

to A, for $s_{j,i} \leftarrow \mathbb{Z}^*_N$, for all (j, i). (We assume that A queries at most q challenge ciphertexts per instance.) Eventually, A outputs a guess b'. D outputs 1 if $b' = b$ and A is valid in the sense of (μ, q)-IBE-IND-CPA, else outputs 0.

Analysis. The provided master public keys and the A-requested user secret keys yield the correct distribution and are consistent in the sense of Game 0 and Game 1. Due to ENDSG's G- and H-subgroups property, we have that $\mathbf{T}$ is uniformly distributed over the generators of a nontrivial subgroup of G^{2n+1}. Hence, $\mathbf{T}^s$, for $s \leftarrow \mathbb{Z}^*_N$, is distributed uniformly over the generators of a nontrivial subgroup of G^{2n+1} and, thus, all challenge ciphertexts yield the correct distribution in the sense of Game 0 and Game 1. If $\mathbf{T} = \mathbf{g}$, then the challenge ciphertexts are distributed identically as in Game 0. Otherwise, i.e., if $\mathbf{T} = \mathbf{g}\widehat{\mathbf{g}}$, then the challenge ciphertexts are distributed identically as in Game 1. Hence, (2) follows.

Lemma 2 (Game 1 to Game 2.1.0). *If the orthogonality property of* ENDSG *holds, the output distributions of Game 1 and Game 2.1.0 are the same. Concretely, for any PPT adversary A in the (μ, q)-IBE-IND-CPA security experiment with* IBE *defined as above it holds that*

$$\Pr[S_{A,1}] = \Pr[S_{A,2.1.0}]. \tag{3}$$

Proof. In this bridging step, we argue that each instance-j master secret key msk_j, with $msk_j \leftarrow H$, generated as in Game 1 and the (implicit) instance-j master secret keys msk'_j, with $msk'_j := msk''_j \cdot \widehat{\mathsf{R}}_{j,0}(\varepsilon) \cdot \widetilde{\mathsf{R}}_{j,0}(\varepsilon)$, for $msk''_j \leftarrow H$ and $\widehat{\mathsf{R}}_{j,0}, \widetilde{\mathsf{R}}_{j,0}$ defined as above, generated as in Game 2.1.0, are identically distributed, for all j. Note that the master public keys for A contain $(m(msk_j))_j$; but since $((m(msk'_j))_j = (m(msk''_j))_j$, which is due to the orthogonality property of ENDSG, no $\widehat{\mathsf{R}}_{j,0}$-information and no $\widetilde{\mathsf{R}}_{j,0}$-information is given out in the master public keys. Further, since $(msk_j)_j$ and $(msk''_j)_j$ are identically distributed, it follows that (3) holds.

Lemma 3 (Game 2.i.0 to Game 2.i.1). *Let* G *be a group generator as defined above. If the* G- *and* H-*subgroups property and LS2 of* ENDSG *hold, Game 2.i.0 and Game 2.i.1 are computationally indistinguishable. Concretely, for any PPT adversary* A *with at most* $q' = q'(k)$ *extraction queries in each instance and running time* t *in the* (μ, q)-*IBE-IND-CPA security experiment with* IBE *defined as above, there is a distinguisher* D *on LS2 with running time* $t' \approx t + \mathbf{O}(\mu q q' n k^c)$, *for integer* $n = n(k)$ *and some constant* $c \in \mathbb{N}$, *such that*

$$|\Pr[S_{2.i.0}] - \Pr[S_{2.i.1}]| \leq \mathsf{Adv}^{\mathsf{ls2}}_{\mathsf{ENDSG},\mathsf{G},D}(k, 2n), \tag{4}$$

for all $i \in [n]$.

Proof. In Game 2.i.0, we have semi-functional type-$(\wedge, i-1)$ challenge ciphertexts while in Game 2.i.1, challenge ciphertexts are semi-functional of type $(\sim, i-1)$ if and only if the i-th challenge identity bit is 1.

Description. The challenge input is provided as $(pp, \widehat{h}\widetilde{h}, \mathbf{g}'\widehat{\mathbf{g}}', \mathbf{T})$, where $\mathbf{T}$ is either $\mathbf{g}\widehat{\mathbf{g}}$ or $\mathbf{g}\widetilde{\mathbf{g}}$, for pp as before, for $\widehat{h}, \widetilde{h}$ specified in sp, for $\mathbf{g}, \mathbf{g}' \leftarrow \mathsf{SampG}(pp)$, $\widehat{\mathbf{g}}, \widehat{\mathbf{g}}' \leftarrow \widehat{\mathsf{SampG}}(pp, sp)$, and $\widetilde{\mathbf{g}} \leftarrow \widetilde{\mathsf{SampG}}(pp, sp)$. First, D samples $(msk_j)_j \leftarrow (H)^\mu$, sets $mpk_j := (pp, m(msk_j))$, for all j, for m specified in pp, and sends $(mpk_j)_j$ to A. Further, D defines a truly random function $\mathsf{R} : [\mu] \times \{0,1\}^{i-1} \to \langle \widehat{h}\widetilde{h} \rangle$. During the experiment, D answers instance-j secret key extraction queries to oracle $\mathsf{Ext}(msk_j, \cdot)$ as

$$\overline{\mathsf{Ext}}(pp, msk_j \cdot \mathsf{R}(j, id|_{i-1}), id; \mathsf{SampH}(pp)),$$

for $id \in \mathcal{ID}$ and all j. (Again, we assume that A queries at most $q' = q'(k)$ user secret keys per instance and we set $id|_0 = \{0,1\}^0 =: \varepsilon$.) A may adaptively query its Enc'-oracle; for A-chosen instance-j challenge identity $id^*_{j,i'} = id^*_{j,i',1} \ldots, id^*_{j,i',n} \in \mathcal{ID}$ and equal-length messages $(M^*_{j,i',0}, M^*_{j,i',1})_{i'}$, for all $i' \in [q]$. D returns

$$\overline{\mathsf{Enc}}(pp, id^*_{j,i'}, M^*_{j,i',b}; msk_j \cdot \mathsf{R}(j, id^*_{j,i'}|_{i-1}), (\mathbf{g}'\widehat{\mathbf{g}}')^{s_{j,i'}}) \quad \text{if } id^*_{j,i',i} = 0,$$

$$\overline{\mathsf{Enc}}(pp, id^*_{j,i'}, M^*_{j,i',b}; msk_j \cdot \mathsf{R}(j, id^*_{j,i'}|_{i-1}), \mathbf{T}^{s_{j,i'}}) \quad \text{if } id^*_{j,i,i'} = 1,$$

to A, for (fixed) $b \leftarrow \{0,1\}$, for $s_{j,i'} \leftarrow \mathbb{Z}^*_N$, for all (j, i'). Eventually, A outputs a guess b'. D outputs 1 if $b' = b$ and A is valid in the sense of (μ, q)-IBE-IND-CPA, else outputs 0.

Analysis. The master public keys yield the correct distribution as well as the requested user secret keys (which is due to ENDSG's G- and H-subgroups property). For challenge ciphertexts, note that $\mathbf{g}'\widehat{\mathbf{g}}'$ and $\mathbf{T}$ are uniformly distributed over the generators of their respective nontrivial subgroup of G^{2n+1} and, hence, $(\mathbf{g}'\widehat{\mathbf{g}}')^s$ and $\mathbf{T}^s$, for $s \leftarrow \mathbb{Z}^*_N$, are distributed uniformly over the generators of their respective nontrivial G^{2n+1}-subgroup as well. If $\mathbf{T} = \mathbf{g}\widehat{\mathbf{g}}$, then the challenge ciphertexts are distributed identically as in Game 2.i.0. Otherwise, if $\mathbf{T} = \mathbf{g}\widetilde{\mathbf{g}}$, then the challenge ciphertexts are distributed identically as in Game 2.i.1 (where, in both cases, ENDSG's orthogonality and non-degeneracy properties hold; thus, $\widehat{h}$ and $\widetilde{h}$ must contain coprime nontrivial elements and the challenge ciphertexts yield the correct distribution). Hence, (4) follows.

Lemma 4 (Game 2.i.1 to Game 2.i.2). *Let* G *be a group generator as defined above. If the* G*- and* H*-subgroups property and NH of* ENDSG *hold, Game 2.i.1 and Game 2.i.2 are computationally indistinguishable. Concretely, for any PPT adversary* A *with at most* $q' = q'(k)$ *extraction queries in each instance and running time* t *in the* (μ, q)-*IBE-IND-CPA security experiment with* IBE *defined as above there is a distinguisher* D *on NH with running time* $t' \approx t + O(\mu q q' n k^c)$, *for integer* $n = n(k)$ *and some constant* $c \in \mathbb{N}$, *such that*

$$| \Pr[S_{2.i.1}] - \Pr[S_{2.i.2}] | \leq \mathsf{Adv}^{\mathsf{nh}}_{\mathsf{ENDSG,G},D}(k, 2n, q'), \qquad (5)$$

for all $i \in [n]$.

Proof. In Game 2.i.1, the challenge ciphertexts are semi-functional of type $(\wedge, i-1)$ if the i-th bit of the challenge identity is 0 and semi-functional of type $(\sim, i-1)$ if the i-th bit of the challenge identity is 1, while in Game 2.i.1, all challenge ciphertexts are of type $(\cdot, i)$.

Description. The challenge input is $(pp, \widehat{h}, \widetilde{h}, \widehat{\mathbf{g}}_{-(2i-1)}, \widetilde{\mathbf{g}}_{-2i}, (\mathbf{T}_1, \ldots, \mathbf{T}_{q'}))$, where $\mathbf{T}_{i'}$ equals either

$$(h_{i',0}, \ldots, h_{i',n}) \quad \text{or} \quad (h_{i',0}, \ldots, h_{i',2i-1} \cdot (\widehat{h})^{\widehat{\gamma}_{j,i'}}, h_{i',2i} \cdot (\widetilde{h})^{\widetilde{\gamma}_{j,i'}}, \ldots, h_{i',n}),$$

for pp as before, $\widehat{h}, \widetilde{h}$ as in sp, for $\widehat{\mathbf{g}} \leftarrow \widehat{\mathsf{SampG}}(pp, sp)$, for $\widetilde{\mathbf{g}} \leftarrow \widetilde{\mathsf{SampG}}(pp, sp)$, for $(h_{i',0}, \ldots, h_{i',n}) \leftarrow \mathsf{SampH}(pp)$, for uniform $\widehat{\gamma}_{j,i'}, \widetilde{\gamma}_{j,i'} \in \mathbb{Z}^*_{\mathsf{ord}(H)}$. D samples $(msk_j)_j \leftarrow (H)^\mu$, sets $mpk_j := (pp, m(msk_j))$, for all j, for m specified in pp, and sends $(mpk_j)_j$ to A. Further, D defines random functions $\widehat{\mathsf{R}}_{j,i-1}, \widetilde{\mathsf{R}}_{j,i-1}$ as above. In addition, for identity $id = id_1 \ldots id_n \in \mathcal{ID}$, we define

$$\widehat{\mathsf{R}}_{j,i}(id|_i) := \widehat{\mathsf{R}}_{j,i-1}(id|_{i-1}) \text{ and (implicitly) } \widetilde{\mathsf{R}}_{j,i}(id|_i) := \widetilde{\mathsf{R}}_{j,i-1}(id|_{i-1}) \cdot (\widetilde{h})^{\widetilde{\gamma}_{j,i'}}$$

if $id_i = 0$ and

$$\widetilde{\mathsf{R}}_{j,i}(id|_i) := \widetilde{\mathsf{R}}_{j,i-1}(id|_{i-1}) \text{ and (implicitly) } \widehat{\mathsf{R}}_{j,i}(id|_i) := \widehat{\mathsf{R}}_{j,i-1}(id|_{i-1}) \cdot (\widehat{h})^{\widehat{\gamma}_{j,i'}}$$

if $id_i = 1$. During the experiment, D returns the i_j-th instance-j secret-key-extraction query to oracle $\mathsf{Ext}(msk_j, \cdot)$ for an identity id, with prefix $id|_i$ not an prefix of an already queried identity, as

$$\overline{\mathsf{Ext}}(pp, msk_j \cdot \widehat{\mathsf{R}}_{j,i}(id|_i) \cdot \widetilde{\mathsf{R}}_{j,i-1}(id|_{i-1}), id; \mathbf{T}_{i'}) \quad \text{if } id_i = 0,$$

$$\overline{\mathsf{Ext}}(pp, msk_j \cdot \widehat{\mathsf{R}}_{j,i-1}(id|_{i-1}) \cdot \widetilde{\mathsf{R}}_{j,i}(id|_i), id; \mathbf{T}_{i'}) \quad \text{if } id_i = 1.$$

(We assume that A queries at most $q' = q'(k)$ user secret keys per instance.) For an identity prefixes $id|_i$ that is an prefix of an already queried identity, let $i'' \in [q']$ be the index of that query. In that case, D returns

$$\overline{\mathsf{Ext}}(pp, msk_j \cdot \widehat{\mathsf{R}}_{j,i}(id|_i) \cdot \widetilde{\mathsf{R}}_{j,i-1}(id|_{i-1}), id; \mathbf{T}_{i''} \cdot \mathsf{SampH}(pp)) \quad \text{if } id_i = 0,$$

$$\overline{\mathsf{Ext}}(pp, msk_j \cdot \widehat{\mathsf{R}}_{j,i-1}(id|_{i-1}) \cdot \widetilde{\mathsf{R}}_{j,i}(id|_i), id; \mathbf{T}_{i''} \cdot \mathsf{SampH}(pp)) \quad \text{if } id_i = 1,$$

for all i''. (Note that we use SampH to re-randomize the H^{2n+1}-subgroup elements of $\mathbf{T}_{i''}$.) Further, A may adaptively query its Enc'-oracle; for A-chosen instance-j challenge identity $id^*_{j,i'''} = id^*_{j,i'''},1 \ldots, id^*_{j,i'''},n$ and equal-length messages $(M^*_{j,i''',0}, M^*_{j,i''',1})_{i'''}$, for all i'''. D returns

$$\overline{\mathsf{Enc}}(pp, id^*_{j,i'''}, M^*_{j,i''',b}; msk_j \cdot \widehat{\mathsf{R}}_{j,i}(id^*_{j,i'''}|i), (\mathbf{g}_{-(2i-1)}\widehat{\mathbf{g}}_{-(2i-1)})^{s_{j,i'''}}) \text{ if } id^*_{j,i''',i} = 0,$$

$$\overline{\mathsf{Enc}}(pp, id^*_{j,i'''}, M^*_{j,i''',b}; msk_j \cdot \widetilde{\mathsf{R}}_{j,i}(id^*_{j,i'''}|i), (\mathbf{g}_{-2i}\widetilde{\mathbf{g}}_{-2i})^{s_{j,i'''}}) \text{ if } id^*_{j,i''',i} = 1,$$

to A, for $s_{j,i'''} \leftarrow \mathbb{Z}^*_N$, for $\mathbf{g} \leftarrow \mathsf{SampG}(pp)$, for fixed $b \leftarrow \{0,1\}$, for all (j, i'''). (Note that a modified $\overline{\mathsf{Enc}}$-input is provided which has only $4n + 2$ elements instead of $4n + 4$ elements. Nevertheless, the removed elements are not needed to generate a valid ciphertext since it is consistent with $id^*_{j,i'''}$; thus, we assume that the algorithm works as defined above.) Eventually, A outputs a guess b'. D outputs 1 if $b' = b$ and A is valid in the sense of (μ, q)-IBE-IND-CPA, else outputs 0.

Analysis. Note that the provided master public keys yield the correct distribution; for the A-requested user secret keys note that, since $\widehat{h}$ and $\widetilde{h}$ have nontrivial H-elements of coprime order (again, this is due to the orthogonality and non-degeneracy properties), the random functions $\widehat{\mathsf{R}}_{j,i-1}, \widehat{\mathsf{R}}_{j,i}$ and $\widetilde{\mathsf{R}}_{j,i-1}, \widetilde{\mathsf{R}}_{j,i}$ yield the correct distributions in the sense of Game $2.i.1$ and Game $2.i.2$, respectively. Due to the G- and H-subgroups property of ENDSG, $\mathbf{g}_{-(2i-1)}$ and $\widehat{\mathbf{g}}_{-(2i-1)}$ as well as $\mathbf{g}_{-2i}$ and $\widetilde{\mathbf{g}}_{-2i}$ are uniformly distributed over the generators of their respective nontrivial subgroups of G^{2n} and, thus, $(\mathbf{g}_{-(2i-1)}\widehat{\mathbf{g}}_{-(2i-1)})^s$ and $(\mathbf{g}_{-2i}\widetilde{\mathbf{g}}_{-2i})^s$, for $s \leftarrow \mathbb{Z}^*_N$, are distributed uniformly over the generators of their respective nontrivial subgroup of G^{2n}. Further, if $id^*_{j,i''',i} = 0$, then it holds that $\widehat{\mathsf{R}}_{j,i}(id^*_{j,i'''}|i) = \widehat{\mathsf{R}}_{j,i}(id^*_{j,i'''}|i-1)$ and all required semi-functional components $\widehat{\mathbf{g}}_{-(2i-1)}$ to create the challenge ciphertexts are given. Analogously, if $id^*_{j,i''',i} = 1$, then we have $\widetilde{\mathsf{R}}_{j,i}(id^*_{j,i'''}|i) = \widetilde{\mathsf{R}}_{j,i-1}(id^*_{j,i'''}|i-1)$ and all necessary semi-functional components $\widetilde{\mathbf{g}}_{-2i}$ are provided as needed. (Thus, the challenge ciphertexts and user secret keys yield the correct distribution.) If $\mathbf{T}_{i'} = (h_{i',0}, \ldots, h_{i',n})$, for all i', then the user secret keys are distributed identically as in Game $2.i.1$. If $\mathbf{T}_{i'} = (h_{i',0}, \ldots, h_{i',2i-1} \cdot (\widehat{h})^{\widehat{\gamma}_{j,i'}}, h_{i',2i} \cdot (\widetilde{h})^{\widetilde{\gamma}_{j,i'}}, \ldots, h_{i',n})$, for all i', then the user secret keys are distributed identically as in Game $2.i.2$. Thus, (5) follows.

Lemma 5 (Game 2.i-1.2 to Game 2.i.0). *Let G be a group generator as defined above. If the G- and H-subgroups property and LS2 of ENDSG hold, Game $2.i$-1.1 and Game $2.i.0$ are computationally indistinguishable. Concretely, for any PPT adversary A with at most $q' = q'(k)$ extraction queries in each instance and running time t in the (μ, q)-IBE-IND-CPA security experiment with IBE, defined as above, there is a distinguisher D with running time $t' \approx t + \mathbf{O}(\mu q q' n k^c)$, for integer $n = n(k)$ and some constant $c \in \mathbb{N}$, such that*

$$|\Pr[S_{2.i-1.2}] - \Pr[S_{2.i.0}]| \leq \mathsf{Adv}^{\mathsf{ls2}}_{\mathsf{ENDSG},\mathsf{G},D}(k, 2n), \tag{6}$$

for all $i \in [n] \setminus \{1\}$.

Proof. The proof is essentially the proof of Lemma 3 except that the challenge ciphertexts and user secret keys depend on the $(i-1)$-th instead of the i-th challenge identity bit.

Lemma 6 (Game 2.n.2 to Game 3). *Let* G *be a group generator as defined above. If the G- and H-subgroups property and LS2 of ENDSG hold, Game 2.n.2 and Game 3 are computationally indistinguishable. Concretely, for any PPT adversary A with at most $q' = q'(k)$ extraction queries in each instance and running time t in the (μ, q)-IBE-IND-CPA security experiment with IBE defined as above there is a distinguisher D with running time $t' \approx t + \mathbf{O}(\mu q q' n k^c)$, for integer $n = n(k)$ and some constant $c \in \mathbb{N}$, such that*

$$|\Pr[S_{A,2.n.2}] - \Pr[S_{A,3}]| \leq \mathsf{Adv}^{\mathsf{ls2}}_{\mathsf{ENDSG},G,D}(k, 2n). \tag{7}$$

Proof. It is easy to see that Game 3 and a potential Game 2.n+1.0 would be identical. Thus, we can reassemble the proof of Lemma 5 with $i := n + 1$ and (7) directly follows.

Lemma 7 (Game 3 to Game 4). *Then Game 3 and Game 4 are statistically indistinguishable. Concretely, for any PPT adversary A on the (μ, q)-IBE-IND-CPA security of IBE defined as above it holds that*

$$|\Pr[S_{A,3}] - \Pr[S_{A,4}]| \leq \mu q \cdot \mathbf{O}(2^{-k}). \tag{8}$$

Proof. In Game 4, we replace each challenge message $M_{j,i',b}$, for challenge bit $b \in \{0,1\}$, with a (fresh) uniformly random k-length bitstring $R_{j,i'} \leftarrow \{0,1\}^k$. We argue with ENDSG's non-degeneracy property and the universality of H for this change. Concretely, for instance-j Game-3 challenge ciphertexts

$$\overline{\mathsf{Enc}}(pp, id^*_{j,i'}, M^*_{j,i',b}; msk_j \cdot \widehat{\mathsf{R}}_{j,n}(id^*_{j,i'}), (\mathbf{g}\widehat{\mathbf{g}})^{s_{j,i'}})$$

$$= ((g_0\widehat{g}_0)^{s_{j,i'}}, (\prod_{i=1}^{n} g_{2i-id^*_{j,i',i}}\widehat{g}_{2i-id^*_{j,i',i}})^{s_{j,i'}}, \mathsf{H}(e((g_0\widehat{g}_0)^{s_{j,i'}}, msk_j \cdot \widehat{\mathsf{R}}_{j,n}(id^*_{j,i'})))$$

$$\oplus M^*_{j,i',b}),$$

for $\mathbf{g} \leftarrow \mathsf{SampG}(pp)$, for $\widehat{\mathbf{g}} \leftarrow \widehat{\mathsf{SampG}}(pp, sp)$, for $s_{j,i'} \leftarrow \mathbb{Z}^*_N$, for all $i' \in [q]$, note that $e((\widehat{g}_0)^{s_{j,i'}}, \widehat{\mathsf{R}}_{j,n}(id^*_{j,i'})) = e((\widehat{g}_0)^{s_{j,i'}}, \widehat{h})^{\widehat{\gamma}_{j,i'}}$, for uniform $\widehat{\gamma}_{j,i'} \in \mathbb{Z}^*_{\mathsf{ord}(H)}$, is uniformly distributed in a subgroup $G'_T \subset G_T$ due to the non-degeneracy property of ENDSG. Furthermore, since A is a *weak* adversary, all the $\widehat{\mathsf{R}}{j}, n$ are for different preimages and thus independently random. Hence, since H is a (randomly chosen) universal hash function, we have that $\varepsilon := \mathsf{SD}((\mathsf{H}, \mathsf{H}(X)); (\mathsf{H}, U)) = \mathbf{O}(2^{-k})$, for $X \leftarrow G'_T$ and $U \leftarrow \{0,1\}^k$. A union bound yields (8).

Lemma 8 (Game 4). *For any PPT adversary A in the (μ, q)-IBE-IND-CPA security experiment with IBE defined as above it holds that*

$$\Pr[S_{A,4}] = 1/2. \tag{9}$$

Proof. In Game 4, for (uniform) challenge bit $b \in \{0, 1\}$, we provide the adversary A with challenge ciphertexts that include only a uniform k-length bitstring instead of a A-chosen b-dependent messages, for each instance and challenge. Hence, b is completely hidden from A and (9) follows.

Taking (2), (3), (4), (5), (6), (7), (8), and (9) together, shows (1).

From Weak to Full (μ, q)-IBE-IND-CPA Security. The analysis above shows only weak security: we must assume that the adversary A never asks for encryptions under the same challenge identity and for the same scheme instance twice. We do not know how to remove this restriction assuming only the abstract properties of ENDSGs. However, at the cost of one tight additional reduction to (a slight variant of) the Bilinear Decisional Diffie-Hellman (BDDH) assumption, we can show full (μ, q)-IBE-IND-CPA security.

Concretely, in Game 3, challenge ciphertexts for A are prepared using (the hash value of) $e(\widehat{g}_0^s, \widehat{h}^\gamma)$ as a mask to hide the plaintext behind. Here, $\widehat{g}_0^s$ and $\widehat{h}$ are public (as part of the ciphertext, resp. public parameters), s is a fresh exponent chosen randomly for each encryption, and γ is a random exponent that however only depends on the scheme instance and identity. (Thus, γ will be reused for different encryptions under the same identity). Hence, if we show that many tuples $(\widehat{g}^{s_i}, e(\widehat{g}_0^{s_i}, \widehat{h}^\gamma))$ (for different s_i but the same γ) are computationally indistinguishable from random tuples, we obtain that even multiple encryptions under the same identity hide the plaintexts, and we obtain full security.

Of course, the corresponding reduction should be tight, in the sense that it should not degrade in the number of tuples, or in the number of considered γ. In the full version, we show such a reduction to the BDDH assumption (in suitable subgroups of G). (In a nutshell, we set up $e(\widehat{g}_0^s, \widehat{h}^\gamma) = e(g, g)^{abc}$ for a generator g and random exponents a, b, c with $\widehat{g}_0^s = g^a$ and $\widehat{h}^\gamma = g^{bc}$. The BDDH assumption now states that $e(g, g)^{abc}$ looks random even given g, g^a, g^b, g^c. Furthermore, by the random self-reducibility of BDDH, the corresponding reduction is tight.)

5   Instantiations of ENDSGs in Composite-Order Groups

Assumptions in Groups with Composite Order. We slightly modify two (known) dual system assumptions (i.e., see DS1, DS3 below, and [11]) and define one (new) dual system assumption (see DS2 below). Let $\mathsf{G}(k, 4)$ be a composite-order group generator that outputs the following group parameters $(G, H = G, G_T, N, e, g, g_{p_1}, g_{p_2}, g_{p_3}, g_{p_4})$ with the composite-order groups G, G_T, each of order $N = p_1 \cdots p_4$, for pairwise-distinct k-bit primes $(p_i)_i$. Further, g_{p_i} is a generator of the subgroup $G_{p_i} \subset G$ of order p_i, and g is a generator of G. More generally, we write $G_q \subseteq G$ for the unique subgroups of order q. The assumptions in groups with composite order are as follows:

Dual System Assumption 1 (DS1). For any PPT adversary D, the function

$$\mathsf{Adv}_{\mathsf{G}, D}^{\mathsf{ds1}}(k) := |\Pr\left[D(pars, g'_{p_1}) = 1\right] - \Pr\left[D(pars, g'_{p_1 p_2}) = 1\right]|$$

is negligible in k, for $(G, G_T, N, e, g, (g_{p_i})_i) \leftarrow \mathsf{G}(k, 4)$,

$$pars := (G, G_T, N, e, g, g_{p_1}, g_{p_3}, g_{p_4}), \text{ and } g'_{p_1} \overset{g}{\leftarrow} G_{p_1}, \; g'_{p_1 p_2} \overset{g}{\leftarrow} G_{p_1 p_2}.$$

Dual System Assumption 2 (DS2). For any PPT adversary D, the function

$$\mathsf{Adv}^{\mathsf{ds2}}_{\mathsf{G},D}(k) := |\Pr\left[D(pars, g'_{p_1 p_2}) = 1\right] - \Pr\left[D(pars, g'_{p_1 p_3}) = 1\right]|$$

is negligible in k, for $(G, G_T, N, e, g, (g_{p_i})_i) \leftarrow \mathsf{G}(k, 4)$,

$$pars := (G, G_T, N, e, g, g_{p_1}, g_{p_4}, g_{p_1 p_2}, g_{p_2 p_3}),$$

$$g_{p_1 p_2} \overset{g}{\leftarrow} G_{p_1 p_2}, \; g_{p_2 p_3} \overset{g}{\leftarrow} G_{p_2 p_3}, \text{ and } g'_{p_1 p_2} \overset{g}{\leftarrow} G_{p_1 p_2}, \; g'_{p_1 p_3} \overset{g}{\leftarrow} G_{p_1 p_3}.$$

Dual System Assumption 3 (DS3). For any PPT adversary D, the function

$$\mathsf{Adv}^{\mathsf{ds3}}_{\mathsf{G},D}(k) := |\Pr\left[D(pars, g^{xy}_{p_2}, g^{xy}_{p_3}) = 1\right] - \Pr\left[D(pars, g^{xy+\gamma'}_{p_2}, g^{xy+\gamma'}_{p_3}) = 1\right]|$$

is negligible in k, for $(G, G_T, N, e, g, (g_{p_i})_i) \leftarrow \mathsf{G}(k, 4)$,

$$pars := (G, G_T, N, e, g, g_{p_1}, g_{p_2}, g_{p_3}, g_{p_4}, g^x_{p_2}\widehat{X}_4, g^y_{p_2}\widehat{Y}_4, g^x_{p_3}\widetilde{X}_4, g^y_{p_3}\widetilde{Y}_4),$$

$$\widehat{X}_4, \widetilde{X}_4, \widehat{Y}_4, \widetilde{Y}_4 \overset{g}{\leftarrow} G_{p_4}, \; x, y, \leftarrow \mathbb{Z}^*_N, \text{ and } \gamma' \leftarrow \mathbb{Z}^*_N.$$

ENDSGs in Groups with Composite Order. Let $\mathsf{G}(k, 4)$ be as defined above. For simplicity, we write $g_i := g_{p_i}$ and $g_{ij} := g_{p_i p_j}$, for all $(i, j) \in [4] \times [4]$. We instantiate ENDSGs $\mathsf{ENDSG}_{\mathsf{co}} = (\mathsf{SampP}, \mathsf{SampG}, \mathsf{SampH}, \widehat{\mathsf{SampG}}, \widetilde{\mathsf{SampG}})$ in composite-order groups as follows:

Parameter Sampling. $\mathsf{SampP}(k, n)$, given k and n, samples $(G, H, G_T, (p_i)_i, e, g, h, (g_i)_i) \leftarrow \mathsf{G}(k, 4)$ and outputs $pp := (G, H, G_T, N, g, e, m, n, pars, \mathsf{H})$ and $sp := (\widehat{h}, \widetilde{h}, \widehat{pars}, \widetilde{pars})$, for
- $m : H \to G_T, h' \mapsto e(g_1, h')$,
- $pars := (g_1, g_4, g^{\mathbf{w}}_1, h, h^{\mathbf{w}} \cdot \mathbf{R}_4)$, for $\mathbf{w} \leftarrow (\mathbb{Z}^*_N)^n, \mathbf{R}_4 \overset{g}{\leftarrow} (G_{p_4})^n$,
- $\widehat{h} \overset{g}{\leftarrow} G_{p_2 p_4}, \widetilde{h} \overset{g}{\leftarrow} G_{p_3 p_4}$,
- $\widehat{pars} := (g_2, g^{\mathbf{w}}_2), \widetilde{pars} := (g_3, g^{\mathbf{w}}_3)$.

G-Group Sampling. $\mathsf{SampG}(pp)$ samples $s \leftarrow \mathbb{Z}^*_N$ and outputs $(g^s_1, g^{s \cdot \mathbf{w}}_1)$.

H-Group Sampling. $\mathsf{SampH}(pp)$ samples $r \leftarrow \mathbb{Z}^*_N$ and outputs $(h^r, h^{r \cdot \mathbf{w}} \cdot \mathbf{R}'_4)$, for $\mathbf{R}'_4 \overset{g}{\leftarrow} (G_{p_4})^n$.

Semi-functional G-group Sampling 1. $\widehat{\mathsf{SampG}}(pp, sp)$ samples $s \leftarrow \mathbb{Z}^*_N$ and outputs $(g^s_2, g^{s \cdot \mathbf{w}}_2)$.

Semi-functional G-group Sampling 2. $\widetilde{\mathsf{SampG}}(pp, sp)$ samples $s \leftarrow \mathbb{Z}^*_N$ and outputs $(g^s_3, g^{s \cdot \mathbf{w}}_3)$.

Correctness of $\mathsf{ENDSG}_{\mathsf{co}}$. For all $k, n \in \mathbb{N}$ and group parameters $(G, H, G_T, N, e, g, h, (g_i)_i) \leftarrow \mathsf{G}(k, 4)$, we have:

Associativity. For all $s, r \leftarrow \mathbb{Z}_N^*$, for all $(g_1^s, g_1^{s \cdot \mathbf{w}}) \leftarrow \mathsf{SampG}(pp; s)$, for all $(h^r, h^{r \cdot \mathbf{w}} \cdot \mathbf{R}'_4) \leftarrow \mathsf{SampH}(pp; r)$, for $\mathbf{R}'_4 = (R'_i)_i \in (G_{p_4})^n$, it holds that

$$e(g_1^s, h^{r \cdot w_i} \cdot R'_i) = e(g_1^s, h^{r \cdot w_i}) = e(g_1^{s \cdot w_i}, h^r)$$

for all $i \in [n]$, and for $\mathbf{w} = (w_1, \ldots, w_n) \in (\mathbb{Z}_N^*)^n$.

Projective. For all $s \leftarrow \mathbb{Z}_N^*$, for all $h' \in H$, it holds that $m(h')^s = e(g_1, h')^s = e(g_1^s, h')$. (Note that g_1^s is the first output of $\mathsf{SampG}(pp; s)$.)

Security of ENDSG_{co}. Let G be a composite-order group generator as defined above, for all $k, n, \in \mathbb{N}$, for all $(pp, sp) \leftarrow \mathsf{SampP}(k, n)$, we have:

Orthogonality. For $\widehat{h}, \widetilde{h}$ specified in sp, we have

$$m(\widehat{h}) = e(g_1, \widehat{h}) = e((g^{p_2 p_3 p_4})^{\gamma_{g_1}}, (g^{p_1 p_3})^{\gamma_{\widehat{h}}}) = 1$$

and

$$m(\widetilde{h}) = e(g_1, \widetilde{h}) = e((g^{p_2 p_3 p_4})^{\gamma_{g_1}}, (g^{p_1 p_2})^{\gamma_{\widetilde{h}}}) = 1$$

for suitable exponents $\gamma_{g_1}, \gamma_{\widehat{h}}, \gamma_{\widetilde{h}} \in \mathbb{Z}_N^*$. Further, for $g_1^s, g_2^{s'}$, and $g_3^{s''}$ that are the first outputs of $\mathsf{SampG}(pp; s)$, $\widehat{\mathsf{SampG}}(pp, sp; s')$, and $\widetilde{\mathsf{SampG}}(pp, sp; s'')$, for $s, s', s'' \leftarrow \mathbb{Z}_N^*$, we have $e(g_1^s, \widehat{h}) = e(g_1^s, \widetilde{h}) = e(g_2^{s'}, \widetilde{h}) = e(g_3^{s''}, \widehat{h}) = 1$.

G- and H-subgroups. Since g_1, g_2, and g_3 are generators of subgroups G_{p_1}, G_{p_2}, and G_{p_3} of coprime order, the outputs of SampG, $\widehat{\mathsf{SampG}}$, and $\widetilde{\mathsf{SampG}}$ are uniform over the generators, which generates nontrivial subgroups of G of coprime order. Since h is a generator of H and $\mathbf{R}'_4$ is uniform over the generators of $(G_{p_4})^n$, the output of SampH is uniformly distributed over the generators of H.

Non-degeneracy. For the first output g_2^s of $\widehat{\mathsf{SampG}}(pp, sp; s)$ (with uniform $s \in \mathbb{Z}_N^*$), and for $\widehat{h} \in G_{p_2 p_3}$ as specified in sp, it holds that $e(g_2^s, \widehat{h}) = e(g_2, \widehat{h})^s$ is uniformly distributed over the generators of the subgroup generated by $e(g_2, \widehat{h})$. Similarly, for the first output g_3^s of $\widetilde{\mathsf{SampG}}(pp, sp; s)$, it holds that $e(g_3^s, \widetilde{h}) = e(g_3, \widetilde{h})^s$ is distributed uniformly over the generators of the subgroup generated by $e(g_3, \widetilde{h})$.

Left-Subgroup Indistinguishability 1. We prove the following lemma

Lemma 9 (DS1 to LS1). *For any PPT adversary D with running time t on LS1 of ENDSG_{co} as defined above there is a distinguisher D' on DS1 with running time $t' \approx t$ such that*

$$\mathsf{Adv}^{ls1}_{\mathsf{ENDSG}_{co}, \mathsf{G}, D}(k, n) = \mathsf{Adv}^{ds1}_{\mathsf{G}, D'}(k), \tag{10}$$

for G as defined above. Hence, LS1 holds under DS1.

Proof. **Description.** The challenge input to D' is provided as $(pars, \mathbf{T})$, where $\mathbf{T}$ is either $g'_1 \leftarrow G_{p_1}$ or $g'_{12} \leftarrow G_{p_1 p_2}$, for $pars = (G, G_T, N, e, g, g_1, g_3, g_4)$. First, D' sets the public parameter as $pp := (G, H := G, G_T, N, g, e, m,$

$n, pars')$, for $m : h' \mapsto e(g_1, h')$, $pars' := (g_1, g_4, g_1^{\mathbf{w}}, h := g, h^{\mathbf{w}})$, for $\mathbf{w} \leftarrow (\mathbb{Z}_N^*)^n$, and for some integer n determined by D'. Then, D' sends $(pp, \mathbf{T}, \mathbf{T}^{\mathbf{w}})$ to D. Finally, D outputs a value which D' forwards to its own challenger.

Analysis. Note that pp is distributed as defined in LS1. If $\mathbf{T} = g_1'$, then $(g_1', (g_1')^{\mathbf{w}})$ is distributed as the output of $\mathsf{SampG}(pp)$ as needed and, hence, $\Pr[D'(pars, g_1') = 1] = \Pr[D(pp, (g_1', (g_1')^{\mathbf{w}})) = 1]$ follows. Otherwise, if $\mathbf{T} = g_{12}'$, then $(g_{12}', (g_{12}')^{\mathbf{w}})$ is distributed as $\mathsf{SampG}(pp) \cdot \widehat{\mathsf{SampG}}(pp, sp)$, for suitable sp, as desired and, hence, we have that $\Pr[D'(pars, g_{12}') = 1] = \Pr[D(pp, (g_{12}', (g_{12}')^{\mathbf{w}})) = 1]$. As a consequence, (10) follows.

Left-subgroup indistinguishability 2. We prove the following lemma

Lemma 10 (DS2 to LS2). *For any PPT adversary D with running time t on LS2 of ENDSG_{co} defined as above there is a distinguisher D' on DS2 with running time $t' \approx t$ such that*

$$\mathsf{Adv}^{\mathsf{ls2}}_{\mathsf{ENDSG}_{co}, \mathsf{G}, D}(k, n) = \mathsf{Adv}^{\mathsf{ds2}}_{\mathsf{G}, D'}(k), \tag{11}$$

for G as defined above. Hence, LS2 holds under DS2.

Proof. **Description.** The challenge input to D' is provided as $(pars, \mathbf{T})$, where $\mathbf{T}$ is either $g_{12}' \leftarrow G_{p_1 p_2}$ or $g_{13}' \leftarrow G_{p_1 p_3}$, for $pars = (G, G_T, N, e, g, g_1, g_4, g_{12}, g_{23})$. First, D' defines the public parameter as $pp := (G, H := G, G_T, N, g, e, m, n, pars')$, for $m : h' \mapsto e(g_1, h')$, $pars' := (g_1, g_4, g_1^{\mathbf{w}}, h := g, h^{\mathbf{w}})$, for $\mathbf{w} \leftarrow (\mathbb{Z}_N^*)^n$, and for some integer n determined by D'. Then, D' sends $(pp, g_{23} g_4^\gamma, g_{12}, \mathbf{T}, \mathbf{T}^{\mathbf{w}})$, for $\gamma \leftarrow \mathbb{Z}_N^*$, to D. Eventually, D outputs a value which is forwarded by D' to its own challenger.

Analysis. Note that pp is distributed as defined in LS2. If $\mathbf{T} = g_{12}'$, then $(g_{12}', (g_{12}')^{\mathbf{w}})$ is distributed as $\mathsf{SampG}(pp) \cdot \widehat{\mathsf{SampG}}(pp, sp)$, for suitable sp, as needed and, hence, we have that $\Pr[D'(pars, g_{12}') = 1] = \Pr[D(pp, g_{23} g_4^\gamma, g_{12}, (g_{12}', (g_{12}')^{\mathbf{w}})) = 1]$ follows. Otherwise, if $\mathbf{T} = g_{13}'$, then $(g_{13}', (g_{13}')^{\mathbf{w}})$ is distributed as $\mathsf{SampG}(pp) \cdot \widehat{\mathsf{SampG}}(pp, sp)$, for suitable sp, as desired and, hence, $\Pr[D'(pars, g_{13}') = 1] = \Pr[D(pp, g_{23} g_4^\gamma, g_{12}, (g_{13}', (g_{13}')^{\mathbf{w}})) = 1]$ holds. As a consequence, (11) follows.

Nested-hiding indistinguishability. We prove the following lemma

Lemma 11 (DS3 to NH). *For any PPT adversary D with running time t on NH of ENDSG_{co} there is a distinguisher D' on DS3 with running time $t' \approx t$ such that*

$$\mathsf{Adv}^{\mathsf{nh}}_{\mathsf{ENDSG}_{co}, \mathsf{G}, D}(k) \le \mathsf{Adv}^{\mathsf{ds3}}_{\mathsf{G}, D'}(k), \tag{12}$$

for G as defined above. Hence, NH holds under DS3.

Proof. The proof follows the same strategy as shown in Chen and Wee's work [11] except that we have to integrate two coprime-order semi-functional generators $\widehat{h}$ and $\widetilde{h}$ instead of just one as in [11].

Description. The challenge input to D' is provided as $(pars, \mathbf{T})$, where $\mathbf{T} := (\widehat{\mathbf{T}}, \widetilde{\mathbf{T}})$ is either (g_2^{xy}, g_3^{xy}) or $(g_2^{xy+\gamma'}, g_3^{xy+\gamma'})$, for

$$pars =: (G, G_T, N, e, g_1, g_2, g_3, g_4, g_2^x \widehat{X}_4, g_2^y \widehat{Y}_4, g_3^x \widetilde{X}_4, g_3^y \widetilde{Y}_4),$$

for $\widehat{X}_4, \widehat{Y}_4, \widetilde{X}_4, \widetilde{Y}_4 \stackrel{g}{\leftarrow} G_{p_4}$, $x, y \leftarrow \mathbb{Z}_N^*$, and for $\gamma' \leftarrow \mathbb{Z}_N^*$. Furthermore, D' receives an auxiliary input $i \in [\lfloor \frac{n}{2} \rfloor]$, for some integer $n \in \mathbb{N}$ determined by D'. First, D' samples $r, \hat{r}, \tilde{r}, \hat{s}, \tilde{s} \leftarrow \mathbb{Z}_N^*$, $\mathbf{R}'_4 \stackrel{g}{\leftarrow} (G_{p_4})^n$, $\mathbf{w}' \leftarrow (\mathbb{Z}_N^*)^n$, and sets

$$h := (g_1 g_2 g_3 g_4)^r, \qquad \widehat{h} := (g_2 g_4)^{\hat{r}}, \qquad \widetilde{h} := (g_3 g_4)^{\tilde{r}},$$

$$\widehat{\mathbf{g}}_{-(2i-1)} := (g_2^{\hat{s}}, g_2^{\hat{s}\mathbf{w}'})_{-(2i-1)}, \qquad \widetilde{\mathbf{g}}_{-2i} := (g_3^{\tilde{s}}, g_3^{\tilde{s}\mathbf{w}'})_{-(2i)},$$

where h, $\widehat{h}$, and $\widetilde{h}$ are generators of G, $G_{p_2 p_4}$, and $G_{p_3 p_4}$. Then, D' defines public parameter as

$$pp := (G, H := G, G_T, N, g, e, n, m, pars'),$$

for $m : h' \mapsto e(g_1, h')$ and

$$pars' := (g_1, g_4, g_1^{\mathbf{w}'}, h, h^{\mathbf{w}'} (g_2^y \widehat{Y}_4)^{r \mathbf{e}_{2i-1}} (g_3^y \widetilde{Y}_4)^{r \mathbf{e}_{2i}} \mathbf{R}'_4)$$
$$= (g_1, g_4, g_1^{\mathbf{w}}, h, h^{\mathbf{w}} \mathbf{R}_4),$$

where $\mathbf{e}_j$ is the j-th unit vector of length n and, implicitly, we have

$$\mathbf{w} = \begin{cases} \mathbf{w}' \mod p_1 p_4 \\ \mathbf{w}' + y \cdot \mathbf{e}_{2i-1} \mod p_2 \quad \text{and} \quad \mathbf{R}_4 = \mathbf{R}'_4 + \widehat{Y}_4^r \cdot \mathbf{e}_{2i-1} + \widetilde{Y}_4^r \cdot \mathbf{e}_{2i}. \\ \mathbf{w}' + y \cdot \mathbf{e}_{2i} \mod p_3 \end{cases}$$

Now, by running the algorithm from [12, Lemma 6] on input $(1^{q'}, (g_2, g_4, g_2^x \widehat{X}_4, g_2^y \widehat{Y}_4, \widehat{\mathbf{T}}))$ and on input $(1^{q'}, (g_3, g_4, g_3^x \widetilde{X}_4, g_3^y \widetilde{Y}_4, \widetilde{\mathbf{T}}))$, D' generates tuples

$$(g_2^{\hat{r}_j} \widehat{X}_{4,j}, \widehat{\mathbf{T}}_j)_{j=1}^{q'} \quad \text{and} \quad (g_3^{\tilde{r}_j} \widetilde{X}_{4,j}, \widetilde{\mathbf{T}}_j)_{j=1}^{q'},$$

respectively, where

$$\widehat{\mathbf{T}}_j = \begin{cases} g_2^{\hat{r}_j y} \cdot \widehat{Y}_{4,j}, & \text{if } \widehat{\mathbf{T}} = g_2^{xy} \\ g_2^{\hat{r}_j y} \cdot \widehat{Y}_{4,j} \cdot g_2^{\hat{\gamma}'_j}, & \text{if } \widehat{\mathbf{T}} = g_2^{xy+\gamma'} \end{cases}$$

and

$$\widetilde{\mathbf{T}}_j = \begin{cases} g_3^{\tilde{r}_j y} \cdot \widetilde{Y}_{4,j}, & \text{if } \widetilde{\mathbf{T}} = g_3^{xy} \\ g_3^{\tilde{r}_j y} \cdot \widetilde{Y}_{4,j} \cdot g_3^{\tilde{\gamma}'_j}, & \text{if } \widetilde{\mathbf{T}} = g_3^{xy+\gamma'}. \end{cases}$$

Further, D' samples $r'_j \leftarrow \mathbb{Z}_N^*$, $\mathbf{X}'_{4,j} \stackrel{g}{\leftarrow} (G_{p_4})^n$, for all $j \in [q']$, and sends

$$(pp, \widehat{h}, \widetilde{h}, \widehat{\mathbf{g}}_{2i-1}, \widetilde{\mathbf{g}}_{2i}, (\mathbf{T}_1, \ldots, \mathbf{T}_{q'}))$$

to D, where

$$
\mathbf{T}_j = (h^{r'_j} \cdot g_2^{\hat{r}_j} \widehat{X}_{4,j} \cdot g_3^{\tilde{r}_j} \widetilde{X}_{4,j}, (h^{r'_j} \cdot g_2^{\hat{r}_j} \widehat{X}_{4,j} \cdot g_3^{\tilde{r}_j} \widetilde{X}_{4,j})^{\mathbf{w}'} \cdot
$$
$$
((g_2^y \widehat{Y}_4)^{r'_j r} \widehat{\mathbf{T}}_j)^{\mathbf{e}_{2i-1}} \cdot ((g_3^y \widetilde{Y}_4)^{r'_j r} \widetilde{\mathbf{T}}_j)^{\mathbf{e}_{2i}} \mathbf{X}'_{4,j})
$$

$$
= \begin{cases} (h^{r_j}, h^{r_j \cdot \mathbf{w}} \cdot \mathbf{X}_{4,j}) & \text{if } \widehat{\mathbf{T}}_j = g_2^{\hat{r}_j y} \cdot \widehat{Y}_{4,j} \\ & \text{and } \widetilde{\mathbf{T}}_j = g_3^{\tilde{r}_j y} \cdot \widetilde{Y}_{4,j} \\ (h^{r_j}, h^{r_j \cdot \mathbf{w}} \cdot g_2^{\hat{\gamma}_j \mathbf{e}_{2i-1}} \cdot g_3^{\tilde{\gamma}_j \mathbf{e}_{2i}} \cdot \mathbf{X}_{4,j}) & \text{if } \widehat{\mathbf{T}}_j = g_2^{\hat{r}_j y} \cdot \widehat{Y}_{4,j} \cdot g_2^{\hat{\gamma}_j} \\ & \text{and } \widetilde{\mathbf{T}}_j = g_3^{\tilde{r}_j y} \cdot \widetilde{Y}_{4,j} \cdot g_3^{\tilde{\gamma}_j} \end{cases}
$$

for $h^{r_j} := h^{r'_j} \cdot g_2^{\hat{r}_j} \widehat{X}_{4,j} \cdot g_3^{\tilde{r}_j} \widetilde{X}_{4,j}$ and $\mathbf{X}_{4,j} := \mathbf{X}'_{4,j} + \widehat{Y}_4^{r'_j r} \mathbf{e}_{2i-1} + \widetilde{Y}_4^{r'_j r} \mathbf{e}_{2i}$ implicitly and $\mathbf{w}$ as above.

Analysis. Note that pp is distributed as defined in NH. If $\mathbf{T} = (g_2^{xy}, g_3^{xy})$, then $\widehat{\mathbf{T}}_j = g_2^{\hat{r}_j y} \cdot \widehat{Y}_{4,j}$ and $\widetilde{\mathbf{T}}_j = g_3^{\tilde{r}_j y} \cdot \widetilde{Y}_{4,j}$, for all $j \in [q']$, and, thus, $(\mathbf{T}_1, \ldots, \mathbf{T}_{q'})$ is distributed as $(\mathbf{h}_1, \ldots, \mathbf{h}_{q'})$, for suitable sp, as needed. Otherwise, if $\mathbf{T} = (g_2^{xy+\gamma'}, g_3^{xy+\gamma'})$, then $\widehat{\mathbf{T}}_j = g_2^{\hat{r}_j y} \cdot \widehat{Y}_{4,j} \cdot g_2^{\hat{\gamma}_j}$ and $\widetilde{\mathbf{T}}_j = g_3^{\tilde{r}_j y} \cdot \widetilde{Y}_{4,j} \cdot g_3^{\tilde{\gamma}_j}$ for all $j \in [q']$, and, thus, $(\mathbf{T}_1, \ldots, \mathbf{T}_{q'})$ is distributed as $(\mathbf{h}'_1, \ldots, \mathbf{h}'_{q'})$, for suitable sp, since $(\tilde{h}, g_2^{\hat{\gamma}_j} \cdot \widehat{Y}_{4,j})$ and $(\tilde{h}, g_3^{\tilde{\gamma}_j} \cdot \widetilde{Y}_{4,j})$ are identically distributed as $(\tilde{h}, (\tilde{h})^{\hat{\gamma}_j} \cdot \widehat{Y}_{4,j})$ and $(\tilde{h}, (\tilde{h})^{\tilde{\gamma}_j} \cdot \widetilde{Y}_{4,j})$, respectively, for $\hat{\gamma}_j, \tilde{\gamma}_j \leftarrow \mathbb{Z}_N^*, \widehat{Y}_{4,j}, \widetilde{Y}_{4,j} \xleftarrow{g} G_{p_4}$, for all $j \in [q']$.

Acknowledgments. We thank the anonymous reviewers for helpful remarks.

References

1. Abe, M., David, B., Kohlweiss, M., Nishimaki, R., Ohkubo, M.: Tagged one-time signatures: tight security and optimal tag size. In: Kurosawa, K., Hanaoka, G. (eds.) PKC 2013. LNCS, vol. 7778, pp. 312–331. Springer, Heidelberg (2013)
2. Bellare, M., Desai, A., Jokipii, E., Rogaway, P.: A concrete security treatment of symmetric encryption. In: 38th FOCS, pp. 394–403. IEEE Computer Society Press (October 1997)
3. Bellare, M., Desai, A., Pointcheval, D., Rogaway, P.: Relations among notions of security for public-key encryption schemes. In: Krawczyk, H. (ed.) CRYPTO 1998. LNCS, vol. 1462, pp. 26–45. Springer, Heidelberg (1998)
4. Bellare, M., Boldyreva, A., Micali, S.: Public-key encryption in a multi-user setting: security proofs and improvements. In: Preneel, B. (ed.) EUROCRYPT 2000. LNCS, vol. 1807, pp. 259–274. Springer, Heidelberg (2000)
5. Bellare, M., Waters, B., Yilek, S.: Identity-based encryption secure against selective opening attack. In: Ishai, Y. (ed.) TCC 2011. LNCS, vol. 6597, pp. 235–252. Springer, Heidelberg (2011)
6. Blazy, O., Kiltz, E., Pan, J.: (Hierarchical) identity-based encryption from affine message authentication. In: Garay, J.A., Gennaro, R. (eds.) CRYPTO 2014, Part I. LNCS, vol. 8616, pp. 408–425. Springer, Heidelberg (2014)
7. Boldyreva, A.: Strengthening security of RSA-OAEP. In: Fischlin, M. (ed.) CT-RSA 2009. LNCS, vol. 5473, pp. 399–413. Springer, Heidelberg (2009)

8. Boneh, D., Boyen, X.: Short signatures without random oracles. In: Cachin, C., Camenisch, J.L. (eds.) EUROCRYPT 2004. LNCS, vol. 3027, pp. 56–73. Springer, Heidelberg (2004)

9. Boneh, D., Franklin, M.: Identity-based encryption from the weil pairing. In: Kilian, J. (ed.) CRYPTO 2001. LNCS, vol. 2139, pp. 213–229. Springer, Heidelberg (2001)

10. Cash, D.M., Kiltz, E., Shoup, V.: The twin diffie-hellman problem and applications. In: Smart, N.P. (ed.) EUROCRYPT 2008. LNCS, vol. 4965, pp. 127–145. Springer, Heidelberg (2008)

11. Chen, J., Wee, H.: Fully, (almost) tightly secure IBE and dual system groups. In: Canetti, R., Garay, J.A. (eds.) CRYPTO 2013, Part II. LNCS, vol. 8043, pp. 435–460. Springer, Heidelberg (2013)

12. Chen, J., Wee, H.: Dual system groups and its applications – compact hibe and more. Cryptology ePrint Archive, Report 2014/265 (2014). http://eprint.iacr.org/

13. Freeman, D.M.: Converting pairing-based cryptosystems from composite-order groups to prime-order groups. In: Gilbert, H. (ed.) EUROCRYPT 2010. LNCS, vol. 6110, pp. 44–61. Springer, Heidelberg (2010)

14. Galindo, D., Martín, S., Morillo, P., Villar, J.L.: Easy verifiable primitives and practical public key cryptosystems. In: Boyd, C., Mao, W. (eds.) ISC 2003. LNCS, vol. 2851, pp. 69–83. Springer, Heidelberg (2003)

15. Gentry, C.: Practical identity-based encryption without random oracles. In: Vaudenay, S. (ed.) EUROCRYPT 2006. LNCS, vol. 4004, pp. 445–464. Springer, Heidelberg (2006)

16. Gentry, C., Halevi, S.: Hierarchical identity based encryption with polynomially many levels. In: Reingold, O. (ed.) TCC 2009. LNCS, vol. 5444, pp. 437–456. Springer, Heidelberg (2009)

17. Groth, J., Sahai, A.: Efficient non-interactive proof systems for bilinear groups. In: Smart, N.P. (ed.) EUROCRYPT 2008. LNCS, vol. 4965, pp. 415–432. Springer, Heidelberg (2008)

18. Hofheinz, D., Jager, T.: Tightly secure signatures and public-key encryption. In: Safavi-Naini, R., Canetti, R. (eds.) CRYPTO 2012. LNCS, vol. 7417, pp. 590–607. Springer, Heidelberg (2012)

19. Lewko, A.: Tools for simulating features of composite order bilinear groups in the prime order setting. In: Pointcheval, D., Johansson, T. (eds.) EUROCRYPT 2012. LNCS, vol. 7237, pp. 318–335. Springer, Heidelberg (2012)

20. Libert, B., Joye, M., Yung, M., Peters, T.: Concise multi-challenge CCA-secure encryption and signatures with almost tight security. In: Sarkar, P., Iwata, T. (eds.) ASIACRYPT 2014, Part II. LNCS, vol. 8874, pp. 1–21. Springer, Heidelberg (2014)

21. Waters, B.: Dual system encryption: realizing fully secure IBE and HIBE under Simple assumptions. In: Halevi, S. (ed.) CRYPTO 2009. LNCS, vol. 5677, pp. 619–636. Springer, Heidelberg (2009)

22. Waters, B.: Efficient identity-based encryption without random oracles. In: Cramer, R. (ed.) EUROCRYPT 2005. LNCS, vol. 3494, pp. 114–127. Springer, Heidelberg (2005)

Author Index

Printed in the United States
By Bookmasters

Printed in the United States
By Bookmasters